WORLD
CIVILIZATIONS

W·W·NORTON & COMPANY · NEW YORK · LONDON

EDWARD MCNALL BURNS

PHILIP LEE RALPH

ROBERT E. LERNER

STANDISH MEACHAM

WORLD CIVILIZATIONS

Their History and Their Culture

SIXTH EDITION

To our students

W. W. Norton & Company, Inc. 500 Fifth Avenue, New York, N.Y.
10110
W. W. Norton & Company Ltd. 37 Great Russell Street, London
WC1B 3NU

ISBN 0-393-95077-8

2 3 4 5 6 7 8 9 0

CONTENTS

Part Two THE WORLD IN THE CLASSICAL ERA

Part Three   THE WORLD IN THE MIDDLE AGES

Part Four　THE EARLY MODERN WORLD

Part Six THE WEST AT THE WORLD'S
CENTER

Part Seven   THE EMERGENCE OF WORLD
             CIVILIZATIONS

MAPS

ILLUSTRATIONS IN COLOR

(Illustrations appear facing or following the pages indicated)

ILLUSTRATIONS IN THE TEXT

PREFACE

Edward McNall Burns observed in an earlier preface:

"The time has long since passed when modern man could think of the world as consisting of Europe and the United States. Western culture is, of course, primarily a product of European origins. But it has never been that exclusively. Its original foundations were in Southwestern Asia and North Africa. These were supplemented by influences seeping in from India and eventually from China. From India and the Far East the West derived its knowledge of the zero, the compass, gunpowder, silk, cotton, and probably a large number of religious and philosophical concepts. Especially in recent times the East has increased in importance. The exhaustion of Europe by two World Wars, the revolt of the colored races against Caucasian domination, and the struggle for the world between the Communist powers and the United States have made every part of the earth of vital importance to every other. If peace is indivisible, so are prosperity, justice, and freedom; so, in fact, is civilization itself.

"The purpose of this work is to present a compact survey of man's struggle for civilization from early times to the present. No major area or country of the globe has been omitted. Europe, the Commonwealth of Nations, the Middle East, Southeast Asia, Africa, India, China, Japan, and North, Central, and South America have all received appropriate emphasis. Obviously, the history of none of them could be covered in full detail. The authors believe, however, that a broad view of the world as a whole is necessary to understand the basic problems of any of its parts. This thesis acquires additional validity as the nations increase in interdependence. Perspective in history becomes more and more urgent as the momentous problems of our own generation press for solution. If there is any basic philosophical interpretation underlying the narrative, it is the conviction that most of human progress thus far has resulted from the growth of intelligence and respect for the rights of man, and that therein lies the chief hope for a better world in the future."

As its title indicates, this work is not exclusively or even primarily a political history. Political events are recognized as important, but they are not the whole substance of history. In the main, the facts of political history are subordinated to the development of institutions and ideas or are presented as the groundwork of cultural, social, and economic movements. The authors consider the effects of the Industrial Revolutions to be no less important than the Napoleonic Wars. They believe it is of greater value to understand the significance of Buddha, Confucius, Newton, Darwin, and Einstein than it is to be able to name the kings of France. In accordance with this broader conception of history, more space has been given to the teachings of John Locke, Karl Marx, and John Stuart Mill, of Mahatma Gandhi, Mao Tse-tung, and Julius Nyerere than to the military exploits of Gustavus Adolphus or the Duke of Wellington.

The first edition of *World Civilizations* was published in 1955, the second in 1958, the third in 1964, the fourth in 1969, and the fifth in 1974. Each edition has included the whole of Edward McNall Burns' *Western Civilizations,* except for sections on the non-Western world, which are more fully covered in this work. The sixth edition of *World Civilizations* incorporates Burns' *Western Civilizations* as revised for its ninth edition by Robert E. Lerner of Northwestern University and Standish Meacham of the University of Texas at Austin. The qualities that have made the Burns text a leader during the past thirty years have been preserved, while at the same time Professors Lerner and Meacham, utilizing the results of recent scholarship, have sharpened the focus on areas of greatest concern for today's students. The authors' considerable reorganization of the chapters dealing with the Western world has enabled them to give fuller treatment to the Middle Ages and to the nineteenth century, to living conditions during the successive stages of Western development, and to the status of women and minority groups.

In addition to the extensive changes in the chapters on Western history, those devoted to the non-Western and third world have been thoroughly revised. They contain much new material, designed not merely to supply up-to-date information on the course of events but also to take account of new interpretations and to provide a clearer perspective on the character, competing forces, and problems of the troubled era into which contemporary societies have been propelled. In accord with this objective, more space has been allotted to Latin America and to the Middle East than in the previous edition. This edition, like its immediate predecessor, benefits substantially from the contribution of Professor Richard Hull of New York University, who has revised, updated, and expanded the sections on Africa in Chapters 12, 17, 23, 32, and 38. His narrative provides a compact and enlightening account of the peoples and the major civilizations of the African continent and of their present state. For all chapters, the accompanying reading lists have been revised.

The sixth edition of *World Civilizations* has been redesigned for easier reading and to accommodate literally hundreds of new illustrations from Western and non-Western archives. Virtually 50 percent of the 950 illustrations are new to this edition. The text was the first to include color illustrations and continues to include far more color plates than any other book in the field. Most of the 65 maps are either new or thoroughly amended. The new edition is published in both a one-volume and a two-volume format. Available for use with either is a new Teacher's Manual and a thoroughly revised Study Guide, which, as its most distinctive feature, includes numerous extracts from original sources.

In preparing this revision the authors have profited from the assistance and counsel of many individuals whose services no words of appreciation can adequately measure. The list would include not only various specialists but also teachers and students who have used the text in their courses. The authors owe a debt of gratitude to demanding but kindly editors who have worked with them over the years. For this edition, as for the preceding one, Robert E. Kehoe of W. W. Norton & Company has been an indispensable adviser and co-worker. The authors are continually indebted to their wives for often unacknowledged assistance and, even more, for their forbearance, patience, and understanding.

Philip Lee Ralph

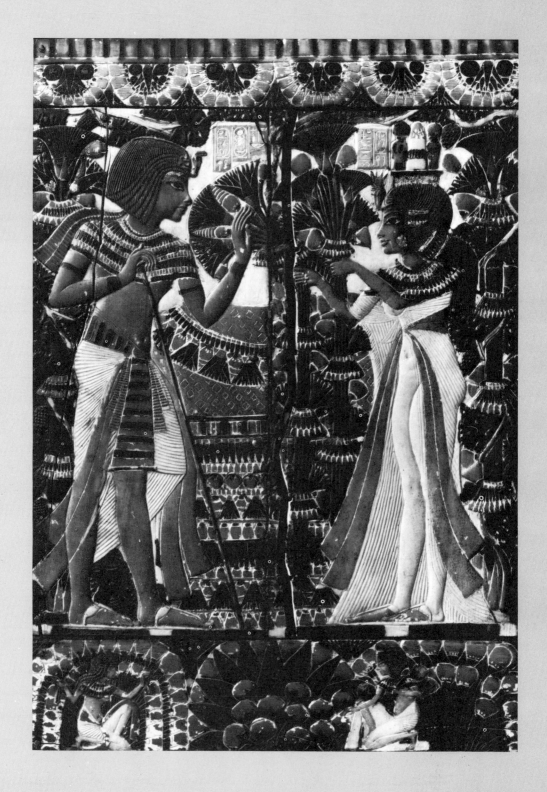

Part One

THE DAWN OF HISTORY

No one knows the place of origin of the human species. There is evidence, however, that it may have been south-central Africa or possibly central or south-central Asia. Here climatic conditions were such as to favor the evolution of a variety of human types from primate ancestors. From their place or places of origin members of the human species wandered to southeastern and eastern Asia, northern Africa, Europe, and eventually, to America. For hundreds of centuries they remained primitive, leading a life which was at first barely more advanced than that of the higher animals. About 3500 B.C., a few of them, enjoying special advantages of location and climate, slowly developed superior civilizations. These civilizations, which attained knowledge of writing and considerable advancement in the arts and sciences and in social organization, began in that part of the world known as the Near East. This region extends from modern-day Iran to the Mediterranean Sea and to the farther bank of the Nile. Here flourished, at different periods between 3000 and 300 B.C., the mighty empires of the Egyptians, the Babylonians, the Assyrians, the Chaldeans, and the Persians, together with the smaller states of such peoples as the Hittites, the Phoenicians, and the Hebrews. The only other very early civilization existed in India in the area of the Indus valley from about 2500 to 1500 B.C. The earliest signs of civilization in China date from about 1800 B.C., and the earliest civilizations in Europe—on the island of Crete and mainland Greece—similarly date from around that time.

The Earliest Development of Humanity

	CULTURE PERIOD	TYPE OF HUMAN	CHARACTERISTIC ACHIEVEMENTS
2 million years ago	Earlier Paleolithic (Early Old Stone Age)	*Homo habilis*	Walking erect; use of objects taken from nature as tools; hunting
500,000 years ago		Java Man; Peking Man	Larger brains: greater intelligence
50,000 years ago		Neanderthal Man: first *Homo sapiens*	Speech; ability to think in the abstract; earliest tool-making
20,000 years ago	Later Paleolithic (Late Old Stone Age)	Cro-Magnon Man	Variety of tools and weapons made from stone and bone; cooked food; cave-painting
12,000 years ago	Mezolithic (Middle Stone Age)	Modern physical types	More settled living conditions; earliest transition from food-gathering to food-raising
7,000 years ago	Neolithic (New Stone Age)		Agriculture; domestication of animals; pottery; earliest village life; origin of states
5,500 years ago	Bronze Age		Earliest civilizations in Egypt and Mesopotamia; writing; bronze metallurgy; developed political, social, and economic institutions

Chapter 1

THE EARLIEST BEGINNINGS

As we turn to the past itself . . . we might well begin with a pious tribute
to our nameless [preliterate] ancestors, who by inconceivably arduous
and ingenious effort succeeded in establishing a human race. They made
the crucial discoveries and inventions, such as the tool, the seed, and the
domesticated animal; their development of agriculture, the "neolithic revolution" that introduced a settled economy, was perhaps the greatest
stride forward that man has ever taken. They created the marvelous instrument of language, which enabled man to discover his humanity, and
eventually to disguise it. They laid the foundations of civilization: its economic, political, and social life, and its artistic, ethical, and religious traditions. Indeed, our "savage" ancestors are still very near to us, and not
merely in our capacity for savagery.

— Herbert J. Muller, *The Uses of the Past*

1. THE NATURE OF HISTORY

Catherine Morland, the heroine of Jane Austen's novel *North-
anger Abbey,* complained that history "tells me nothing that
does not either vex or weary me. The quarrels of popes and
kings, with wars or pestilences in every page; the men all so good for
nothing, and hardly any women at all, it is very tiresome." Although
Jane Austen's heroine said this around 1800, she might have lodged
the same complaint until quite recently, for until deep into the twentieth century most historians considered history to be little more than
"past politics"—and a dry chronicle of past politics at that. The content of history was restricted primarily to battles and treaties, the personalities and politics of statesmen, the laws and decrees of rulers. But
important as such data are, they by no means constitute the whole
substance of history. Especially within the last few decades historians
have come to recognize that history comprises a record of past human
activities in every sphere—not just political developments, but also
social, economic, and intellectual ones. Women as well as men, the
ruled as well as the rulers, the poor as well as the rich, are part of his-

*History more than battles
and treaties*

tory. So too are the social and economic institutions that men and women have created and that in turn have shaped their lives: family and social class; manorialism and city life; capitalism and industrialism. Ideas and attitudes too, not just of intellectuals but also of men and women whose lives may have been virtually untouched by "great books," are all part of the historian's concern. And, most important, history includes an inquiry into the causes of events and patterns of human organization and ideas—a search for the forces that impelled humanity toward its great undertakings, and the reasons for its successes and failures.

New historical methods

As historians have extended the compass of their work, they have also equipped themselves with new methods and tools, the better to practice their craft. No longer do historians merely pore over the same old chronicles and documents to ask whether Charles the Fat was at Ingelheim or Lustnau on July 1, 887. To introduce the evidence of statistics they learn the methods of the computer scientist. To interpret the effect of a rise in the cost of living, they study economics. To deduce marriage patterns or evaluate the effect upon an entire population of wars and plagues, they master the skills of the demographer. To explore the phenomena of cave-dwelling or modern urbanization, they become archeologists, studying fossil remains, fragments of pots, or modern city landscapes. To understand the motives of the men and women who have made history, they draw on the insights of social psychologists and cultural anthropologists. To illuminate the lives of the poor and of those who have left few written records, they look for other cultural remains—folk songs, for example, and the traditions embodied in oral history.

Necessity for studying past on its own terms

Perhaps the most important lesson historians have learned is that they must no longer condescend to the past, no longer assume that their civilization is worthier than those that have come before. History is primarily the study of change over time, but that does not mean that it is a tale of uninterrupted progress from past to present or that all change was ordained to produce our own modern world. Those who write history and those who study it must look to see how one event led to another and how the entire past is prologue to the present, but they must also appreciate the past on its own terms, examining it, so far as possible, through the eyes and with the minds of those who lived it.

2. HISTORY AND PREHISTORY

The so-called prehistoric era

It is the custom among many historians to distinguish between historic and prehistoric periods in the evolution of human society. By the former they mean history based upon written records. By the latter they mean the record of human achievement before the invention of writing. But this distinction is not altogether satisfactory. It suggests that human accomplishments before they were recorded in characters or symbols representing words or concepts were not important. Nothing could be farther from the truth. The foundations, at least, of many of the great accomplishments of modern technology, and even of social and political systems, were laid before human beings could write a word. It is preferable, therefore, that the whole period of human life on earth be regarded as historic, and that the era before the invention of writing be designated by a term such as "preliterate." The records of preliterate societies are, of course, not books and documents, but tools, weapons, fossils, utensils, carvings, paintings, and fragments of jewelry and ornamentation. These, commonly known as "artifacts," are often almost as valuable as the written word in providing knowledge of a people's deeds and modes of living.

The entire span of human history can be divided roughly into two periods, the Age of Stone and the Age of Metals. The former is roughly coterminous with the Preliterate Age, or the period before the invention of writing. The latter coincides roughly with the period of history based upon written records. The Preliterate Age covered all but the smallest fraction of humanity's existence and did not come to an end until about 3500 B.C., although some Stone Age cultures persisted after that time and a few tribes still exist in remote areas. The Age of Metals practically coincides with the history of civilized nations. The Age of Stone is subdivided into the Paleolithic, or Old Stone Age, and the Neolithic, or New Stone Age. Each takes its name from the type of stone tools and weapons characteristically manufactured during the period. Thus during the greater part of the Paleolithic Age implements were commonly made by chipping pieces off a large stone or flint and using the core that remained as a hand ax or "fist hatchet." Toward the end of the period the chips themselves were used as knives or spearheads, and the core thrown away. The Neolithic Age witnessed the supplanting of chipped stone tools by implements made by grinding and polishing stone.

Fist Hatchet

3. THE CULTURE OF THE EARLIER
PALEOLITHIC PEOPLES

The Paleolithic period can be dated from roughly 2,000,000 B.C. to 10,000 B.C. It is commonly divided into two stages, an earlier and a later one. The earlier Paleolithic period was vastly the longer of the two, covering about 99 percent of the entire Old Stone Age. During this time at least four species of humanlike creatures inhabited the earth. Momentous discoveries pertaining to the earliest of these have been made very recently by scientific teams working in East Africa. In 1961, the anthropologist Jonathan Leakey uncovered in Tanzania parts

Homo habilis

The Skull (left) *of a Young Woman of the Species Homo habilis,* believed to have lived in Tanzania, East Africa, about 1,750,000 years ago. On the right is the skull of a present-day African. Though *Homo habilis* was smaller than a pygmy, the brain casing was shaped like that of modern humans.

Java Man

of a skull that was about 1.8 million years old, far older than any humanlike skull previously known. (Chemical tests such as the carbon-14 method or the potassium-argon method are used in determining the age of the geological strata in which bones are found and sometimes the age of the bones themselves.) Then, in 1972, a team led by Jonathan's brother Richard discovered in Kenya a similar and nearly complete skull that was more than 2 million years old. The species which left behind these remains has been named *Homo habilis,* or "man having ability." *Homo habilis* may be counted as a true ancestor of modern man because he walked erect, possessed a brain that was larger than that of any apes, and was intelligent enough to use tools. Of course, his tools were extremely primitive. For the most part they consisted of objects taken from nature: bones of animals, limbs from trees, and chunks of stone, perhaps broken or crudely chipped. But they allowed *Homo habilis* to survive in times of food shortage as a hunter rather than as a food gatherer or forager. It must not be thought that reliance on hunting led these earliest ancestors to kill each other. Quite to the contrary, their survival depended upon cooperation. Most likely only after the development of agriculture and herding—more than a million years later—did humans start warring with each other for the possession of territory. The cooperation necessary in hunting made *Homo habilis* the first truly social creature and led toward the use of language. *Homo habilis* was, therefore, clearly in the vanguard of the human race.

Two subsequent inhabitants of the earlier Paleolithic period were Java man and Peking man. Java man was long thought to be the oldest of humanlike creatures, but it is now generally agreed that the date of his origin was about 500,000 B.C. His skeletal remains were found on the island of Java in 1891. The remains of Peking man were found in China, about twenty-five miles southwest of Peking between 1926 and 1930. Since the latter date, fragments of no fewer than thirty-two skeletons of the Peking type have been located, making possible a complete reconstruction of at least the head of this ancient species. Anthropologists generally agree that Peking man and Java man are of approximately the same antiquity, and that both probably descended from the same ancestral type.

During the last 25,000 years of the earlier Paleolithic period a fourth species of ancient man made an appearance. He was Neanderthal man, famous as an early caveman. Although first discovered a few years earlier at Gibraltar, Neanderthal man is named after a find of skeletal fragments in 1856 in the valley of the Neander, near Düsseldorf, in northwestern Germany. Since then numerous other discoveries have been made, in some cases complete skeletons, in such widely separated regions as Belgium, Spain, Italy, Yugoslavia, Russia, and Israel. So closely did Neanderthal man resemble modern man that he is classified as a member of the same species, *Homo sapiens*. The resemblance, however, was by no means perfect. Neanderthalers, on the average, were only about five feet, four inches in height. They had receding chins and heavy eyebrow ridges. Although their foreheads sloped back and their brain cases were low-vaulted, their average cranial capacity was slightly greater than that of modern Caucasians. What this may have signified with respect to their intelligence cannot be determined.

The knowledge we possess of the culture of earlier Paleolithic peoples is scanty. The skills they achieved and the learning they acquired must have been pitiful in quantity even when compared with the accomplishments of modern primitive groups. Yet Neanderthal man and his successors were not mere apes, forgetting in a moment the chance triumphs they had made. They undoubtedly had the capacity for speech, which enabled them to communicate with their fellows and to pass on what they had learned to succeeding generations. The Neanderthalers had some ability to think in the abstract, as evidenced by their burial of their dead with objects intended for use in an afterlife. They also progressed beyond *Homo habilis* by fashioning their own tools instead of just using the ones they found. They discovered that stones could be chipped in such a way as to give them cutting edges. Thus were developed spearheads, borers, and much superior knives and scrapers. Indications have been found also of a degree of advancement in nonmaterial culture. In the entrances to caves where Neanderthalers lived, or at least took refuge, evidence has been discovered of flint-working floors and stone hearths where huge fires ap-

Neanderthal Man

Peking Man

Accomplishments of earlier Paleolithic peoples

Cro-Magnon Man

Later Paleolithic Fishhook

pear to have been made. These would suggest the origins of cooperative group life and possibly the crude beginnings of social institutions.

4. LATER PALEOLITHIC CULTURE

About 30,000 B.C. the culture of the Old Stone Age passed to the later Paleolithic stage. This period lasted for only about two hundred centuries, or from 30,000 to 10,000 B.C. A new and superior type of human being dominated the earth in this time. Biologically these peoples were closely related to modern humans. Their foremost predecessors, Neanderthal men, had ceased to exist as a distinct variety. What became of the Neanderthalers is not known.

The name used to designate the prevailing breed of later Paleolithic humans is Cro-Magnon, from the Cro-Magnon cave in southern France where some of the most typical remains were discovered. These people lived by hunting reindeer, bison, and mammoths, which freely roamed through southern Europe and Asia because the climate, dominated by glaciers, was very cold. The Cro-Magnon people were tall, broad-shouldered, and walked erect, the males averaging over six feet. They had high foreheads, well-developed chins, and a cranial capacity about equal to the modern average. The heavy eyebrows so typical of earlier species were absent. Whether Cro-Magnon men left any survivors is a debatable question. They do not seem to have been exterminated but appear to have been driven into mountainous regions and to have been ultimately absorbed into other breeds.

Later Paleolithic culture was markedly more advanced than that which had gone before. Not only were tools and implements better made, they existed in greater variety. They were not fashioned merely from flakes of stone and an occasional shaft of bone; other materials were used in abundance, particularly reindeer horn and ivory. Examples of the more complicated tools included the fishhook, the harpoon, the dart-thrower, and, at the very end, the bow and arrow. That later Paleolithic people wore clothing is indicated by the fact that they invented the needle (made out of bone). They did not know how to weave cloth, but animal skins sewn together proved a satisfactory substitute. It is certain that they cooked their food, for enormous hearths, evidently used for roasting meat, have been discovered. In the vicinity of one at Solutré, in southern France, was a mass of charred bones, estimated to contain the remains of a hundred thousand large animals. Although Cro-Magnon people built no houses, except a few simple huts in regions where natural shelters did not abound, their life was not wholly nomadic. Evidence found in caves that served as homes indicate that they must have been used, seasonally at least, for years at a time.

With respect to nonmaterial elements there are also indications that later Paleolithic culture represented a marked advancement. Group life was now more highly organized than ever before. The profusion of charred bones at Solutré and elsewhere probably indicates cooperative enterprise in the hunt and sharing of the results in community feasts. The amazing workmanship displayed in tools and weapons and highly developed techniques in the arts could scarcely have been achieved without some division of labor. It appears certain, therefore, that later Paleolithic communities included professional artists and skilled craftsmen. In order to acquire such talents, certain members of the communities must have gone through long periods of training and given all their time to the practice of their specialties.

Substantial proof exists that the Cro-Magnons had highly developed notions of a world with supernatural aspects. They bestowed more care upon the bodies of the dead than did the Neanderthalers, painting the corpses, folding the arms over the heart, and depositing pendants, necklaces, and richly carved weapons in the graves. The Cro-Magnons also formulated an elaborate system of sympathetic magic designed to increase their food supply. Sympathetic magic is based upon the principle that imitating a desired result will bring about that result. Applying this principle, Cro-Magnon people

Sympathetic magic

Later Paleolithic Engraving and Sculpture. The two objects at the top and upper right are dart-throwers. At the lower right is the famous Venus of Willendorf.

The Venus of Laussel

painted murals on the walls of their caves depicting, for example, the capture of reindeer in the hunt. At other times they fashioned clay models of the bison or mammoth and mutilated them with dart thrusts. The purpose of such representation was probably to facilitate the results portrayed and thereby to increase the hunter's success and make easier the struggle for existence. Possibly incantations or ceremonies accompanied the making of these pictures or images, and it is likely that the work of producing them was carried on while the actual hunt was in progress.

In fact, the supreme achievement of the Cro-Magnon people was their art—an achievement so original and resplendent that it ought to be counted among the Seven Wonders of the World. Nothing else illustrates so well the great gulf between their culture and that of their predecessors. Later Paleolithic art included nearly every branch that the material culture of the time made possible. Sculpture, painting, and carving were all represented. The ceramic arts and architecture were lacking; pottery had not yet been invented; and the only buildings erected were of simple design. The Cro-Magnon art par excellence was cave painting. On cave walls were exhibited the greatest number and variety of their talents—their discrimination in the use of color, their meticulous attention to detail, their capacity for the employment of scale in depicting a group, and above all, their genius for imitating natural detail. Especially noteworthy was their skill in representing movement. Almost all of the murals depict animals running, leaping, chewing their cud, or facing the hunter at bay. Ingenious devices were often employed to give the impression of motion. Chief among them was the drawing or painting of additional outlines to indicate the areas in which the legs or the head of the animal had moved. The scheme was so shrewdly executed that no appearance whatever of artificiality resulted.

Cave painting throws a flood of light on many problems relating to primitive mentality and folkways. To a certain extent it was undoubtedly an expression of a true aesthetic sense. Cro-Magnon people did obviously take some delight in a graceful line or symmetrical pattern or brilliant color. The fact that they painted and tattooed their bodies and wore ornaments gives evidence of this. But their chief works of art can scarcely have been produced for the sake of creating beautiful objects. Such a possibility must be excluded for several reasons. To begin with, the best of the paintings and drawings are usually to be found on the walls and ceilings of the darkest and most inaccessible parts of the caves. The gallery of paintings at Niaux, for instance, is more than half a mile from the entrance of the cave. No one could see the artists' creations except in the imperfect light of torches or primitive lamps, which must have smoked and sputtered badly, for the only illuminating fluid available was animal fat. Furthermore, there is evidence that Cro-Magnon people were largely indifferent to their

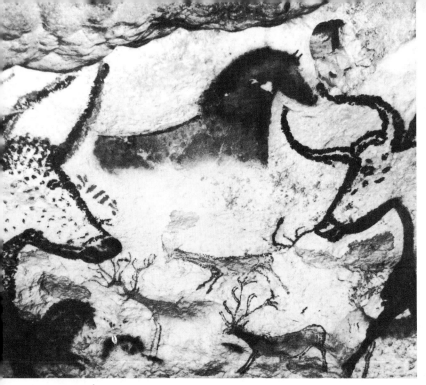

Cave Drawings at Lascaux, France. On the left are characteristic examples of the realism of Cro-Magnon art. On the right, a view of the entrance to the caves.

murals after they were finished. Numerous examples have been found of paintings or drawings superimposed upon earlier ones of the same or of different types. Evidently the important thing was not the finished work itself, but the act of making it.

The real purpose of nearly all of later Paleolithic art was apparently not to delight the senses but to increase the supply of animals useful for food. The artist was not an aesthete but a magician, and art was a form of magic designed to promote the hunter's success. In this purpose lay its chief significance and the foundation of most of its special qualities. It suggests, for example, the real reason why game animals were almost the exclusive subjects of the great murals and why plant life and inanimate objects were seldom represented. It aids us in understanding the Cro-Magnons' neglect of finished paintings and the predominant interest in the process of making them. The placing of the art in the most inaccessible part of the cave is further proof of a religious motivation on the part of the artist—the art then becomes secreted in a sacred place.

Art an aid in the struggle for existence

Later Paleolithic culture ended around 10,000 B.C. because of a disappearance of the food supply. As the last glacier retreated farther and farther north, the climate of southern Europe became too warm for the reindeer, and they gradually migrated to the shores of the Baltic.

The end of later Paleolithic culture

The mammoth, whether for the same or for different reasons, became extinct. Cro-Magnon peoples probably followed the reindeer northward, but any later cultural achievements remain unknown to us.

5. NEOLITHIC CULTURE

From roughly 10,000 B.C. to roughly 5000 B.C., varying very much according to location, ensued the Mesolithic, or Middle Stone Age. This was a transitional period in which peoples became more sedentary and found new sources of food, such as shellfish and edible grasses, now that most of the world was freed from ice. The Mesolithic stage was succeeded by the Neolithic, or New Stone Age. This name is applied because stone weapons and tools were now generally made by grinding and polishing instead of by chipping or fracturing as in the preceding periods. The bearers of Neolithic culture were new varieties of modern peoples who poured into Africa and southern Europe from western Asia. Since no evidence exists of their later extermination or wholesale migration, they must be regarded as the immediate ancestors of most of the peoples now living in Europe.

It is impossible to fix exact dates for the Neolithic period because different peoples passed through the Neolithic stage of development at different rates in different areas. Exciting recent archeological discoveries on the west bank of the Jordan River give evidence of Neolithic settlements in their earliest forms around 7500 B.C. Fully developed Neolithic culture existed in Mesopotamia and Egypt by 5000 B.C., but the culture was not well established in Europe until about 3000 B.C. There is also variation in the dates of its ending. It was superseded in Mesopotamia and Egypt by the first literate civilizations around 3500 B.C., but except on the island of Crete it did not come to an end anywhere in Europe before 2000, and in northern Europe much later still. In a few regions of the world it has not terminated yet. The peoples of some islands of the Pacific, the Arctic regions of North America, and the jungles of Brazil are still in the Neolithic culture stage except for a few customs acquired from explorers and missionaries.

In many respects the New Stone Age was the most significant in the history of the world thus far. The level of material progress rose to new heights. Neolithic peoples had a better mastery of their environment than any of their predecessors. They were less likely to perish from a shift in climatic conditions or from the failure of some part of their food supply. This decided advantage was the result primarily of the development of agriculture and the domestication of animals. Whereas all of the peoples who had lived heretofore were mere food-gatherers, Neolithic peoples were *food-producers*. Tilling the soil and keeping flocks and herds provided them with much more dependable food resources and at times even yielded them a surplus. The development of agriculture, one of the most important of all transitions in human history, promoted a settled existence and made possible an increase in population. Such were the elements of a great social and economic revolution whose importance it would be impossible to exaggerate.

The new culture also derives significance from the fact that it was the first to be distributed over the *entire* world. Although some earlier cultures, especially those of the Neanderthalers and Cro-Magnons, were widely dispersed, they were confined chiefly to the accessible mainland areas of the Old World. Neolithic culture penetrated into every habitable area of the earth's surface—from Arctic wastes to the jungles of the tropics. Neolithic peoples apparently made their way from a number of centers of origin to every nook and cranny of both hemispheres. They traveled enormous distances by water as well as by land, and eventually occupied every major island of the oceans, no matter how remote.

The wide diffusion of the Neolithic culture

Migration over long distances was not the only example of Neolithic achievements. Neolithic peoples developed the arts of knitting and weaving. They made the first pottery and knew how to produce fire by friction. They built houses of wood and sun-dried mud. Toward the end of the period they discovered the possibilities of metals, and a few implements of copper and gold were added to their stock. Since nothing was yet known of the arts of smelting and refining, the use of metals was limited to the more malleable ones occasionally found in the pure state in the form of nuggets.

New tools and technical skills

Activities Around a Neolithic Dwelling. This model represents part of a Neolithic village that was located at Troldebjerg, Denmark, about 2700 B.C. Note the hunters, the wood-gatherer, the potter, the weaver, the grain-grinder, and the carver.

Neolithic Flint Sickles

But the real foundations of Neolithic culture were the domestication of animals and the development of agriculture. Without these it is inconceivable that the culture would have attained the complexity it did. More than anything else they made possible a settled mode of existence and the growth of villages and social institutions. The first animal to be domesticated is generally thought to have been the dog, on the assumption that he would be continually hanging around the hunter's camp to pick up bones and scraps of meat. Eventually it would be discovered that he could be put to use in hunting, or possibly in guarding the camp. After achieving success in domesticating the dog, Neolithic peoples would logically turn their attention to other animals, especially those used for food. Before the period ended, at least five species—the cow, the dog, the goat, the sheep, and the pig—had been made to serve their needs.

The exact spot where agriculture originated has never been determined. All we know is that wild grasses which were probably the ancestors of the cereal grains have been found in a number of places. Types of wheat grow wild in the Near East and southern Russia. Wild ancestors of barley have been reported in North Africa, the Near East, and central Asia. Though it is probable that these were the first crops of Neolithic agriculture, they were by no means the only ones. Millet, vegetables, and numerous fruits were also grown. Flax was cultivated in the Eastern Hemisphere for its textile fiber, and in some localities the growing of the poppy for opium had already begun. In the Western Hemisphere maize (Indian corn) was the only cereal, but the American Indians cultivated numerous other crops, including tobacco, beans, squashes, tomatoes, and potatoes.

The most important consequence of Neolithic settled life was the development of lasting institutions. An institution may be defined as a combination of group beliefs and activities organized in a relatively permanent fashion for the purpose of fulfilling some group need. It ordinarily includes a body of customs and traditions, a code of rules and standards, and physical extensions such as buildings, punitive devices, and facilities for communication and indoctrination. Since humans are social beings, some of these elements probably existed from earliest times, but institutions in their fully developed form seem to have been an achievement of the Neolithic Age.

One of the most ancient of human institutions is the family. Sociologists do not agree upon how it should be defined. Historically, however, the family has always meant a more or less permanent unit composed of parents and their offspring, which serves the purposes of care of the young, division of labor, acquisition and transmission of property, and preservation and transmission of beliefs and customs. The family is not now, and never has been, exclusively biological in character. Like most institutions, it has evolved through a long period of changing conventions which have given it a variety of functions and forms. No doubt there were primitive families in Paleolithic times, but we know practically nothing about them and they probably were not very stable. In Neolithic times the family clearly emerges and appears to have been dominated by the male patriarch who had one or more wives depending upon region.

A second institution known earlier but developed in more complex form by Neolithic peoples was religion. On account of its infinite variations, it is hard to define, but perhaps the following would be accepted as an accurate definition of the institution in at least its basic character: "Religion is everywhere an expression in one form or another of a sense of dependence on a power outside ourselves, a power which we may speak of as a spiritual or moral power."[1] Modern anthropologists emphasize the fact that early religion was not so much a matter of belief as a matter of rites. For the most part, the rites came first; the myths, dogmas, and theologies were later rationalizations. Primitive people were universally dependent upon nature—on the regular succession of the seasons, on the rain falling when it should, on the growth of plants and the reproduction of animals. Unless they performed sacrifices and rites these natural phenomena, according to this notion, would not occur. For this reason they developed rainmaking ceremonies in which water was sprinkled on ears of corn to imitate the falling of the rain. The members of a whole village or even a whole tribe would attire themselves in animal skins and mimic the habits and activities of some species they depended upon for food. They apparently had an idea that by imitating the life pattern of the species they were helping to guarantee its continuance.

The nature of primitive religion; rites and ceremonies

Still another of the great institutions to be developed by Neolithic peoples was the state. This may be defined as an organized society occupying a specific territory and possessing an authoritative government independent of external control. The essence of the state is the power to make and administer laws and to preserve social order by punishing people for infractions of those laws. Except in time of crisis the state does not exist in a very large proportion of preliterate societies—a fact which probably indicates that it originated rather late in the Neolithic culture stage.

The state: definition

The major explanation for the development of states in the Neolithic period lies in the development of agriculture. In areas such as the Nile valley, where a large population lived by cultivating intensively a limited area of fertile soil, a high degree of social organization was absolutely essential. Ancient customs would not suffice for the definition of rights and duties in such a society, with its high standard of living, its unequal distribution of wealth, and its wide scope for the clash of personal interests. New measures of social control would become necessary, which could scarcely be achieved in any other way than by set-

Role of agriculture in the origin of states

[1] A. R. Radcliffe-Brown, *Structure and Function in Primitive Society,* p. 157.

ting up a government of sovereign authority and submitting to it; in other words, by establishing a state.

As important as the emergence of agriculture was in the origin of states, it was not the only cause. In some areas where there was no settled agriculture, states evidently were founded as a result of military activities. That is, they emerged for the purposes of conquest, for defense against invasion, or to make possible the expulsion of an invader from the country. The Hebrew monarchy seems to have been a product of the first of these reasons. With the war for the conquest of the Holy Land none too successful, the Hebrew people petitioned their leader Samuel to give them a king, that they might be "like all the nations" with a powerful ruler to keep them in order and to lead them to victory in battle. One has only to observe the effects of modern warfare, both offensive and defensive, in enlarging the powers of government to see how similar influences might have operated to bring the state into existence in the first place.

Other causes

6. FACTORS RESPONSIBLE FOR THE ORIGIN AND GROWTH OF CIVILIZATIONS

Some time around 3500 B.C. the earliest *civilizations* emerged out of Neolithic culture. We may say that civilization is a stage in human historical development when writing is used to a considerable extent; some progress has been made in the arts and sciences; and political, social, and economic institutions have developed sufficiently to conquer at least some of the problems of order, security, and efficiency in a complex society. What causes contributed to the rise of civilizations? What factors account for their growth? Why do some civilizations reach much higher levels of development than others? Inquiry into these questions is one of the chief pursuits of historians and social scientists. Some decide that factors of geography are most important. Others stress economic resources, food supply, contact with older civilizations, and so on. Usually a variety of causes is acknowledged, but one is commonly singled out by historians as deserving special emphasis.

The meaning of civilization

Probably the most popular of the theories accounting for the rise of advanced cultures are those which come under the heading of geography. Prominent among them is the hypothesis of climate. The climatic theory, advocated by such philosophers as Aristotle and Montesquieu, received its most eloquent exposition in the writings of an American geographer, Ellsworth Huntington. Huntington acknowledged the importance of other factors, but he insisted that no nation, ancient or modern, rose to the highest cultural status except under the influence of a climatic stimulus. He described the ideal climate as one in which the mean temperature seldom falls below 38 degrees or rises

Geographic theories: the climatic hypothesis

above 64 degrees Fahrenheit. But temperature is not alone important. Moisture is also essential, and the humidity should average about 75 percent. Finally, the weather must not be uniform: cyclonic storms, or ordinary storms resulting in weather changes from day to day, must have sufficient frequency and intensity to clear the atmosphere every once in a while and produce those sudden variations in temperature which seem to be necessary to exhilarate and revitalize human beings.[2]

Much can be said in favor of the climatic hypothesis. Certainly some parts of the earth's surface, under existing atmospheric conditions, could never give rise to a superior culture. They are either too hot, too humid, too cold, or too dry. Such is the case in regions beyond the Arctic Circle, the larger desert areas, and the rainforests of India, Central America, and Brazil. Evidence is available, moreover, to show that some of these places have not always existed under climate so adverse as that now prevalent. Desolate sections of Asia, Africa, and America contain unmistakable traces of better days in the past. Here and there are the ruins of towns and cities where now the supply of water is totally inadequate, or which are entrapped by growths of dense foliage. Roads traverse deserts which at present are impassable, or come to an end at the mouth of a jungle.

The best-known evidences of the cultural importance of climatic change are those pertaining to the civilization of the Mayas. Mayan civilization flourished in Guatemala, Honduras, and on the peninsula of Yucatan in Mexico from about 400 to 1500 A.D. Numbered among its achievements were the making of paper, the invention of the zero, the perfection of a solar calendar, and the development of a system of writing partly phonetic. Great cities were built; marked progress was made in astronomy; and sculpture and architecture reached advanced levels. At present most of the civilization is in ruins. No doubt many factors conspired to produce its end, including deadly wars between tribes, but climatic change was also probably involved. The remains of most of the great Mayan cities are now surrounded by jungles, where malaria is prevalent and agriculture difficult. That the Mayan civilization or any other could have grown to maturity under present-day conditions is hard to believe.

Related to the climatic hypothesis is the soil-exhaustion theory. A group of modern conservationists has hit upon this theory as the sole explanation of the decay and collapse of the great empires of the past and as a universal threat to the nations of the present and future. At best it is only a partial hypothesis, since it offers no theory of the birth or growth of civilizations. But its proponents seem to think that almost any environment not ruined by humans is capable of nourishing a superior culture. The great deserts and barren areas of the earth, they maintain, are not natural but artificial, created by bad grazing and

[2] Ellsworth Huntington, *Civilization and Climate,* 3d ed., pp. 220–23.

farming practices. Ecologists discover innumerable evidences of waste and neglect that have wrought havoc in such areas as Mesopotamia, Palestine, Greece, Italy, China, and Mexico. The mighty civilizations that once flourished in these countries were ultimately doomed by the fact that their soil would no longer provide sufficient food for the population. As a consequence, the more intelligent and enterprising citizens migrated elsewhere and left others to sink slowly into stagnation and apathy. But the fate that overtook the latter was not of their making alone. The whole nation had been guilty of plundering the forests, mining the soil, and pasturing flocks on the land until the grass was eaten down to the very roots. Among the tragic results were floods alternating with droughts, since there were no longer any forests to regulate the run-off of rain or snow. At the same time, much of the top soil on the close-cropped or excessively cultivated hillsides was blown away or washed into the rivers to be carried eventually down to the sea. The damage done was irreparable, since about three hundred years are required to produce a single inch of topsoil.

A recent hypothesis of the origin of civilizations is the British historian Arnold J. Toynbee's adversity theory. According to this theory, conditions of hardship or adversity are the real causes which have brought superior cultures into existence. Such conditions constitute a *challenge* which not only stimulates humans to try to overcome it but generates additional energy for new achievements. The challenge may take the form of a desert, a jungle area, rugged topography, or a grudging soil. The Hebrews and Arabs were challenged by the first, the Indians of the Andes by the last. The challenge may also take the form of defeat in war or even enslavement. Thus the Carthaginians, as a result of defeat in the First Punic War, were stimulated to conquer a new empire in Spain. In general it is true that the greater the challenge, the greater the achievement; nevertheless, there are limits. The challenge must not be too severe, else it will deal a crushing blow to all who attempt to meet it.

7. WHY THE EARLIEST CIVILIZATIONS BEGAN WHERE THEY DID

Which of the great civilizations of antiquity was the oldest is still a sharply debated question. The judgment of some scholars inclines toward the Egyptian, though a larger body of authority supports the claims of the Tigris-Euphrates valley. These two areas were geographically the most favored sections in the Near East. In both, larger numbers of artifacts of undoubted antiquity have been found than in any other regions. Furthermore, progress in the arts and sciences had reached unparalleled heights in both of these areas as early as 3000 B.C., when most of the rest of the world was backward in the extreme. If the foundations of this progress were really laid elsewhere, it seems strange that they should have disappeared, although of course there is no telling what archeologists may uncover in the future.

Of the several causes responsible for the earliest rise of civilizations in the Nile and Tigris-Euphrates valleys, geographic factors would seem to have been the most important. Both regions had the notable advantage of a limited area of exceedingly fertile soil. Although it extended for a distance of 750 miles, the valley of the Nile was not more than 10 miles wide in some places, and its maximum width was 31 miles. The total area was less than 10,000 square miles, or roughly the equivalent of Maryland. Through countless centuries the river had carved a vast canyon or trench, bounded on either side by cliffs ranging in height from a few hundred to a thousand feet. The floor of the canyon was covered with a rich alluvial deposit, which in places reached a depth in excess of thirty feet. The soil was of such amazing productivity that as many as three crops per year could be raised on the same land. This broad and fertile canyon constituted the arable land of ancient Egypt. Here several million people were concentrated. In Roman times the population of the valley approximated seven million, and probably it was not much smaller in the days of the pharaohs. Beyond the cliffs there was nothing but desert—the Libyan desert on the west and the Arabian on the east.

A limited area of fertile soil in the Nile valley

See color map facing page 96

In the Tigris-Euphrates valley—a part of the region known as the Fertile Crescent—similar conditions prevailed. As in Egypt, the rivers provided excellent facilities for inland transportation and were alive with fish and waterfowl for a plentiful supply of protein. The distance between the Tigris and Euphrates rivers at one point was less than twenty miles, and nowhere in the lower valley did it exceed forty-five miles. Since the surrounding country was desert, the people were kept from scattering over too great an expanse of territory. The result, as in Egypt, was the welding of the inhabitants into a compact society, under conditions that facilitated a ready interchange of ideas and discoveries. As the population increased, the need for agencies of social control became ever more urgent. Numbered among such agencies were government, schools, legal and moral codes, and institutions for the production and distribution of wealth. At the same time conditions of living became more complex and artificial and necessitated the keeping of records of things accomplished and the perfection of new techniques. Among the consequences were the invention of writing, the practice of smelting metals, the performance of mathematical operations, and the development of astronomy and the rudiments of physics. With these achievements the first great ordeal of civilization was passed.

A similar condition in Mesopotamia

Climatic influences also played their part in both regions. The atmosphere of Egypt is dry and invigorating. Even the hottest days produce none of the oppressive discomfort which is often experienced during the summer seasons in more northern countries. The mean temperature in winter varies from 56 degrees Fahrenheit in the Nile

Climatic advantages in Egypt

Delta to 66 degrees in the valley above. The summer mean is 83 degrees and an occasional maximum of 122 is reached, but the nights are always cool and the humidity is extremely low. Except in the Delta, rainfall occurs in negligible quantities, but the deficiency of moisture is counteracted by the annual floods of the Nile from July to October. Also very significant from the historical standpoint is the total absence of malaria in Upper Egypt, while even in the coastal region it is practically unknown. The direction of the prevailing winds is likewise a favorable factor of more than trivial importance. For more than three-quarters of the year the wind comes from the north, blowing in opposition to the force of the Nile current. The effect of this is to simplify immensely the problem of transportation. Upstream traffic, with the propulsion of the wind to counteract the force of the river, presents no greater difficulty than downstream traffic. This factor in ancient times must have been of enormous advantage in promoting communication among a numerous people, some of whom were separated by hundreds of miles.

Climatic influences in Mesopotamia

Climatic conditions in Mesopotamia do not seem to have been quite so favorable as in Egypt. The summer heat is more relentless; the humidity is somewhat higher; and tropical diseases take their toll. Nevertheless, the torrid winds from the Indian Ocean, while enervating to human beings, blow over the valley at just the right season to bring the fruit of the date palm to a full ripeness. More than anything else the excellent yield of dates, the dietary staple of the Near East, encouraged the settlement of large numbers of people in the valley of the two rivers. Finally, the melting of the snows in the mountains of the north produced an annual flooding of the Babylonian plain similar to that in Egypt. The effect was to enrich the soil with moisture and to cover it over with a layer of mud of unusual fertility. At the same time, it should be noted that water conditions in Mesopotamia were less dependable than in Egypt. Floods were sometimes catastrophic, a factor which left its mark on the development of culture.

The importance of scanty rainfall as a spur to initiative

Most significant of all of the geographic influences, however, was the fact that the scanty rainfall in both regions provided a spur to initiative and inventive skill. In spite of the yearly floods of the rivers there was insufficient moisture left in the soil to produce abundant harvests. A few weeks after the waters had receded, the earth was baked to a stony hardness. Irrigation was accordingly necessary if full advantage was to be taken of the richness of the soil. As a result, in both Egypt and Mesopotamia elaborate systems of dams and irrigation canals were constructed as long as five thousand years ago. The mathematical skill, engineering ability, and social cooperation necessary for the development of these projects were available for other uses and so fostered the achievement of civilization.

Which of the two civilizations, the Egyptian or the Mesopotamian, was the older? Until recently most historians appeared to take it for granted that the Egyptian was the older. They based their assumption upon the conclusions of two of the world's most renowned Egyptologists, James H. Breasted and Alexandre Moret. Between the two world wars of the twentieth century, however, facts were unearthed which seemed to prove a substantial Mesopotamian influence in the Nile valley as early as 3500 B.C. This influence was exemplified by the use of cylinder seals, methods of building construction, art motifs, and elements of a system of writing of undoubted Mesopotamian origin. That such achievements could have radiated into Egypt from the Tigris-Euphrates valley at so early a date indicated beyond doubt that the Mesopotamian civilization was one of vast antiquity. It did not necessarily prove, though, that it was older than the Egyptian. For the achievements mentioned were not taken over and copied slavishly. Instead, the Egyptians modified them radically to suit their own culture pattern. On the basis of this evidence, it would seem that the only conclusion which can be safely drawn is that both civilizations were very old, and that to a large extent they developed concurrently. With them both we begin the story of the history of Western civilizations.

Uncertainty as to which civilization was older

SELECTED READINGS

• *Items so designated are available in paperback editions.*
• Ashley Montague, M. F., ed., *Culture and the Evolution of Man*, New York, 1962.
• Boas, Franz, *The Mind of Primitive Man*, New York, 1927. A very influential and thought-provoking older work.
•Childe, V. Gordon, *Man Makes Himself*, London, 1936.
• ———, *What Happened in History?* New York, 1943. Emphasizes materialistic explanations for the emergence of the earliest civilizations. A modern classic.
   Clark, Grahame, *World Prehistory in New Perspective: An Illustrated Third Edition*, New York, 1978. Highly recommended.
   Hawkes, Jacquetta, *Prehistory*, New York, 1965. A thorough, up-to-date introduction.
   Leakey, Richard E., and R. Lewin, *People of the Lake*, New York, 1978. A recent popular account of Leakey's discoveries pertaining to *Homo habilis* and their significance.
   Linton, Ralph, *The Tree of Culture*, New York, 1955.
• Malinowski, B., *Magic, Science and Religion*, New York, 1954. Essays by one of the founders of modern anthropology.
• Piggott, Stuart, *Approach to Archaeology*, New York, 1965. An excellent introduction to the whole field of archeological studies.
• Radcliffe-Brown, A. R., *Structure and Function in Primitive Society*, Glencoe, Ill., 1952.
•Sandars, N. K., *Prehistoric Art in Europe*, Baltimore, 1968.
   Vlahos, Olivia, *Human Beginnings*, New York, 1966. A brisk, informal account of human origins up through the invention of writing and the emergence of civilizations.

	POLITICAL	ECONOMIC
3000 **B.C.**	Old Kingdom in Egypt, c. 3100–c. 2200	Development of irrigation and large-scale farming in Egypt and Mesopotamia, c. 3500–c. 2500
	Supremacy of Sumerian cities in Mesopotamia, c. 2800–c. 2340 Indus Valley civilization, c. 2500–1500 Dominance of Akkadian Empire in Mesopotamia, 2334–c. 2200	
2000 **B.C.**	Sumerian revival, c. 2200–c. 2000 Middle Kingdom in Egypt, 2050–1786 Old Babylonian Empire in Mesopotamia, c. 2000–c. 1550 Height of Minoan civilization under leadership of Knossos and Phaistos, c. 2000–c. 1500 Hyksos conquer Egypt, 1786–1575 Shang Dynasty in China, c. 1766–1027	Extended commerce in Egypt and Crete, c. 2000
	Mycenaean civilization on mainland Greece, c. 1600–c. 1200 Hittite Empire in Asia Minor, c. 1600–c. 1200 The Empire in Egypt, 1575–1087 Kassites overthrow Babylonians, c. 1550	Slavery in Egypt, c. 1575
1500 **B.C.**	Mycenaean dominance on Crete, c. 1500–c. 1400 Destruction of Knossos and end of Minoan civilization, c. 1400 Hebrew occupation of Canaan, c. 1300–c. 1025	Use of iron by Hittites, c. 1500
	Trojan War, c. 1250	
	Mycenaeans succumb to Dorians in Greece, c. 1200–c. 1100 Chou Dynasty in China, 1100–256 Unified Hebrew monarchy under Saul, David, and Solomon, c. 1025–922	
1000 **B.C.**	Height of Phoenician civilization, c. 1000–c. 700 Kingdom of Israel, 922–722 Kingdom of Judah, 922–586 Feudalism in China, 800–250	Mediterranean trade of Phoenicians, c. 1000–c. 700
	Height of Assyrian Empire, c. 750–612 Chaldean Empire, 612–539 Nebuchadnezzar conquers Jerusalem, 586 Persian Empire, 559–330 Height of Lydia under Croesus, c. 550	Invention of coinage by Lydians, c. 625
500 **B.C.**	Persian conquest of Egypt, 525 Darius the Great, height of Persia, 522–486	Royal Road of Persians, c. 500

CULTURAL	RELIGIOUS	
Egyptian hieroglyphic writing, c. 3100	Egyptian sun worship, c. 3000	**3000** B.C.
Sumerian cunieform writing, c. 3000		
Construction of great pyramids in Egypt, c. 2700		
Development of Indus Valley writing, c. 2500	Egyptian belief in personal immortality, c. 2500	
Sumerian legal codes, c. 2100		
Gilgamesh epic, c. 2000		**2000** B.C.
Code of Hammurabi, c. 1790	Ethical religion in Egypt, c. 1800	
Egyptian diagnostic medicine, c. 1700		
Development of ideographic writing in China, c. 1700		
Egyptian temple architecture, c. 1580–c. 1090		
Development of alphabet by Phoenicians, c. 1500		**1500** B.C.
Naturalistic art in Egypt under Ikhnaton, c. 1375	Religious revolution of Ikhnaton, c. 1375	
	Hebrew worship of Yahweh, c. 1000	**1000** B.C.
Realistic sculpture of Assyrians, c. 750	Hebrew prophetic revolution, c. 750–c. 600	
	Astral religion of Chaldeans, c. 600–c. 500	
Deuteronomic code, c. 600	Zoroaster, c. 600	
		500 B.C.
Book of Job, c. 400		

Chapter 2

THE EGYPTIAN CIVILIZATION

Thou makest the Nile in the Nether World,
Thou bringest it as thou desirest,
To preserve alive the people of Egypt.
For thou hast made them for thyself,
Thou lord of them all, who weariest thyself for them;
Thou sun of day, great in glory. . . .

—Hymn to Aton, from reign of the Pharaoh Ikhnaton

Modern crowds that flood museums to view fabled treasures of Egyptian art are still caught by the spell of one of the oldest and most fascinating civilizations in history. Although the Egyptian civilization was not necessarily the oldest in the ancient world, it was certainly of great antiquity; its origins date from about 3500 B.C. We may consider it here first because somewhat more is known about its accomplishments than about those of most other early peoples. It should be borne in mind while reading this chapter, however, that Mesopotamian and, later, other civilizations were developing simultaneously and sometimes influenced Egyptian developments.

Chronological primacy of Egypt and Mesopotamia

The hallmark of Egyptian civilization was the sense of stability offered by the Nile valley. The fact that the Nile flooded regularly year after year gave Egyptians a feeling that nature was predictable and benign. Moreover, the fertility of the soil in the valley provided for great agricultural wealth, and the fact that the valley was surrounded by deserts and the sea meant that Egypt was comparatively free from threats of foreign invasion. For all these reasons Egyptian civilization was both very advanced and remarkably peaceful. The Greek historian Herodotus was undoubtedly correct when he referred to Egypt as "the gift of the Nile."

Favorable conditions for the development of Egyptian civilization

I. POLITICAL HISTORY UNDER THE PHARAOHS

The ancient history of Egypt is usually divided into three periods: the Old Kingdom, the Middle Kingdom, and the Empire. Even before the Old Kingdom some cultural achievements had been attained. The Egyptians had begun their earliest attempts at irrigation and drainage. They had also learned to use copper tools in place of stone ones, thereby benefiting from the advantages that copper outlasted stone and that copper could be easily sharpened or recast when blunted. Above all, they had developed a system of laws based upon customs and had worked out the initial stage of a system of writing.

About 3100 B.C. Egypt was united into a single unit known as the Old Kingdom. From 3100 B.C. to 2200 B.C. six dynasties ruled the country. Each was headed by a line of "pharaohs," from the Egyptian *per-o,* meaning "great house" or "royal house." The pharaoh was considered to be the son of the sun god and was forbidden to marry anyone other than one of his own sisters lest the divine blood be contaminated. Limitation of rule to the members of a single family also meant that there could be fewer claimants to the throne, and hence less chance of revolution. The authority of the pharaoh was limited to the ancient law: he was not above the law but subject to it. No separation of religious and political life existed. The pharaoh's chief subordinates were priests, and he himself was the chief priest.

The government of the Old Kingdom was founded upon a policy of peace and nonaggression. In this respect it was virtually unique among ancient states. The pharaoh had no standing army, nor was there anything that could be called a national militia. Each local area had its own militia, but militias were commanded by civil officials, and when called into active service generally devoted their energies to labor on the public works. In case of a threat of invasion the various local units were assembled at the call of the pharaoh and placed under the command of one of his civil subordinates. At no other time did the head of the government have a military force at his disposal. The Egyptians of the Old Kingdom were content for the most part to work out their own destinies and to let other nations alone. The reasons for this attitude are to be found in the protected position of their country, in their possession of land of inexhaustible fertility, and in the fact that their state was a product of cooperative need instead of being grounded in exploitation.

After roughly a millennium of peace and relative prosperity the Old Kingdom came to an end about 2200 B.C. Several causes were responsible. Governmental revenues became exhausted because the pharaohs invested heavily in such grandiose projects as pyramid-building. These enterprises also placed great burdens upon Egyptian subjects who were pressed into forced labor and helped to impoverish and demoralize them. In the meantime provincial nobles usurped more and

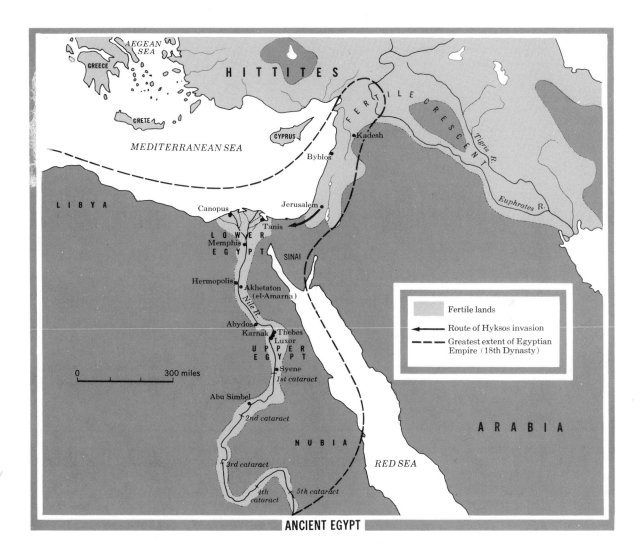

ANCIENT EGYPT

more power until central authority virtually disappeared. The period which followed is called the First Intermediate Age. Anarchy now prevailed. The nobles created their own rival principalities, and political chaos was aggravated by internal brigandage and invasion by desert tribes. The Intermediate Age did not end until the rise of the Eleventh Dynasty which restored centralized rule around 2050 B.C. The next great stage of Egyptian history, known as the Middle Kingdom, ensued.

Throughout most of its life the government of the Middle Kingdom was more socially responsible than that of the Old Kingdom. The Eleventh Dynasty could not withstand the power of the nobles, but the Twelfth, which followed around 1990 and lasted until 1786 B.C., ruled strongly by means of an alliance with a middle class com-

The Middle Kingdom

posed of officials, merchants, artisans, and farmers. This alliance kept the nobility in check and laid the foundations for unprecedented prosperity. During the rule of the Twelfth Dynasty there were advances in social justice and much intellectual achievement. Public works that benefited the whole population, such as extensive drainage and irrigation projects, replaced the building of pyramids, which had no practical use. There was also a democratization of religion which extended to common people a hope for salvation that they had not been granted before. Religion now emphasized proper moral conduct instead of ritual dependent on wealth. For all these reasons the reign of the Twelfth Dynasty is commonly considered to be Egypt's classical or golden age.

The invasion of the Hyksos

Immediately afterwards, however, Egypt entered its Second Intermediate Era. This was another period of internal chaos and foreign invasion which lasted for more than two centuries, or from 1786 to 1575 B.C. The contemporary records are scanty, but they seem to show that the internal disorder was the result of a counterrevolt of the nobles. The pharaohs were again reduced to impotence, and much of the social progress of the Twelfth Dynasty was destroyed. About 1750 the land was invaded by the Hyksos, or "Rulers of Foreign Lands," a mixed horde originating in western Asia. Their military prowess is commonly ascribed to the fact that they possessed horses and war chariots, but their victory was certainly made easier by the dissension among the Egyptians themselves. Their rule had profound effects upon Egyptian history. Not only did they familiarize the Egyptians with new methods of warfare, but by providing them with a common grievance in the face of foreign tyranny they also enabled them to forget their differences and unite in a common cause.

Near the end of the seventeenth century B.C. the rulers of northern Egypt launched a revolt against the Hyksos, a movement which was eventually joined by most of the Egyptians of the south. By 1575 all of the conquerors who had not been killed or enslaved had been driven from the country. The hero of this victory, Ahmose, founder of the Eighteenth Dynasty, now made himself master of Egypt. The regime he established was much more highly consolidated than any that had hitherto existed. In the great resurgence of nationalism which had accompanied the struggle against the Hyksos, local loyalties were reduced, and with it the power of the nobles.

The period which followed the accession of Ahmose is called the period of the Empire. It lasted from 1575 to 1087 B.C., during which time the country was ruled by three dynasties of pharaohs in succession: the Eighteenth, Nineteenth, and Twentieth. No longer was the prevailing state policy pacific and isolationist; a spirit of aggressive imperialism rapidly pervaded the nation. The causes of this change are not far to seek. The military ardor generated by the successful war against the Hyksos whetted an appetite for further victories. A vast

Ramses II (XIXth Dynasty)

military machine had been created to expel the invader, which proved to be too valuable an adjunct to the pharaoh's power to be discarded immediately.

The first steps in the direction of the new policy were taken by the immediate successors of Ahmose in making extensive raids into Palestine and claiming sovereignty over Syria. With one of the most formidable armies of ancient times the new pharaohs speedily annihilated all opposition in Syria and eventually made themselves masters of a vast domain extending from the Euphrates to the farther cataracts of the Nile. But they never succeeded in welding the conquered peoples into loyal subjects, and weakness was the signal for widespread revolt in Syria. Their successors suppressed the uprising and managed to hold the Empire together for some time, but ultimate disaster could not be averted. More territory had been annexed than could be managed successfully. The influx of wealth into Egypt weakened the national fiber by fostering corruption and luxury, and the constant revolts of the vanquished eventually sapped the strength of the state beyond all hope of recovery. By the twelfth century most of the conquered provinces had been permanently lost.

Failures of the Empire

The government of the Empire resembled that of the Old Kingdom, except for the fact that it was more absolute. Military power was now the basis of the pharaoh's rule. A professional army was always available with which to overawe his subjects. Most of the former nobles now became courtiers or members of the royal bureaucracy under the complete domination of the king.

The government of the Empire

The last of the great pharaohs was Ramses III, who ruled from 1182 to 1151 B.C. He was succeeded by a long line of nonentities who inherited his name but not his ability. By the middle of the twelfth century Egypt had fallen prey to numerous ills of invasion and social decadence. Libyans and Nubians were swarming over the country and gradually debasing cultural standards. About the same time the Egyptians themselves appear to have lost their creative talent. To win immortality by magic devices was now the commanding interest of people of every class. The process of decline was hastened also by the growing power of the priests, who finally usurped the royal prerogatives and dictated the pharaoh's decrees.

The last of the pharaohs

From the middle of the tenth century to nearly the end of the eighth a dynasty of Libyans occupied the throne of the pharaohs. The Libyans were followed by a line of Nubians, who came in from the desert regions west of the Upper Nile. Nubia, though flourishing throughout most of its history in the shadow of Egypt, enjoyed a rich civilization as early as 3500 B.C. with cultural traditions of its own. By 2000 B.C. their sophisticated civilization radiated from the city of Kerma, some one thousand miles south of Aswan in what is today the Sudan Republic. Ancient Nubians were noted for their delicate polychrome pottery, far more sophisticated than anything produced else-

The downfall of Egypt

where along the Nile Valley at that time, and their steep-sided pyramids, bearing strong Egyptian influence. By 750 B.C. the black-skinned Nubians had formed a unified kingdom, making it the oldest truly Negro nation. In 670 Egypt was conquered by the Assyrians, who succeeded in maintaining their supremacy for only eight years. After the collapse of Assyrian rule in 662 the Egyptians regained their independence, and a brilliant renaissance of culture ensued. It was doomed to an untimely end, however, for in 525 B.C. the country was conquered by the Persians. The ancient civilization was never again revived.

2. EGYPTIAN RELIGION

The importance of religion in Egypt

Religion played a dominant role in the life of the ancient Egyptians, leaving its impress upon almost everything. The art was an expression of religious symbolism. The literature and philosophy were suffused with religious teachings. The government of the Old Kingdom was to a large extent a theocracy, and even the military pharaohs of the Empire professed to rule in the name of the gods. Material resources in considerable amounts were expended in providing elaborate tombs and in supporting priests.

The early religious evolution

The religion of the ancient Egyptians went through various stages: from simple polytheism to the earliest known expression of monotheism, and then back to polytheism. In the beginning each city or district appears to have had its local deities, who were guardian gods of the locality or personifications of nature powers. The unification of the country under the Old Kingdom resulted not only in a consolidation of territory but in a fusion of divinities as well. All of the guardian deities were merged into the great sun god Re. Under the Middle Kingdom, with the establishment of Theban dynasties in control of the government, this deity was commonly called Amon or Amon-Re from the name of the chief god of Thebes. The gods who personified the vegetative powers of nature were fused into a deity called Osiris, who was also the god of the Nile. Throughout Egyptian history these two great powers who ruled the universe, Amon and Osiris, vied with each other for supremacy. Other deities, as we shall see, were recognized also, but they occupied a distinctly subordinate place.

The solar faith

During the period of the Old Kingdom the solar faith, embodied in the worship of Re, was the dominant system of belief. It served as an official religion whose chief function was to give immortality to the state and to the people collectively. The pharaoh was the living representative of this faith on earth; through his rule the rule of the god was maintained. But Re was not only a guardian deity. He was in addition the god of righteousness, justice, and truth, and the upholder of the moral order of the universe. He offered no spiritual blessings or even material rewards to people as individuals. The solar faith was not a religion for the masses as such, except insofar as their welfare coincided with that of the state.

The cult of Osiris, as we have already observed, began its existence as a nature religion. The god personified the growth of vegetation and the life-giving powers of the Nile. The career of Osiris was wrapped about with an elaborate legend. In the remote past, according to belief, he had been a benevolent ruler, who taught his people agriculture and other practical arts and gave them laws. After a time he was treacherously slain by his wicked brother Set, and his body cut into pieces. His wife Isis, who was also his sister, went in search of the pieces, put them together, and miraculously restored his body to life. The risen god regained his kingdom and continued his beneficent rule for a time, but eventually descended to the nether world to serve as judge of the dead. Horus, his posthumous son, finally grew to manhood and avenged his father's death by killing Set.

The Osiris cult

Originally this legend seems to have been little more than a nature myth. The death and resurrection of Osiris symbolized the recession of the Nile in the autumn and the coming of the flood in the spring. But in time the Osiris legend began to take on a deeper significance. The human qualities of the deities concerned—the paternal solicitude of Osiris for his subjects, the faithful devotion of his wife and son— appealed to the emotions of average Egyptians, who were now able to see their own tribulations and triumphs mirrored in the lives of the gods. More important still, the death and resurrection of Osiris came to be regarded as conveying a promise of personal immortality. As the

Significance of the Osiris legend

Funerary Papyrus. The scene shows the heart of a princess of the XXIst Dynasty being weighed in a balance before the god Osiris. On the other side of the balance are the symbols for life and truth.

god had triumphed over death and the grave, so might also the individual who followed him faithfully inherit everlasting life. Finally, the victory of Horus over Set appeared to foreshadow the ultimate ascendancy of good over evil.

Egyptian ideas of the hereafter

Egyptian ideas of the hereafter attained their full development in the later history of the Middle Kingdom. For this reason elaborate preparations had to be made to prevent the extinction of one's earthly remains. Not only were bodies mummified but wealthy men left munificent endowments to provide their mummies with food and other essentials. As the religion advanced toward maturity, however, a less naive conception of the afterlife was adopted. The dead were now believed to appear before Osiris to be judged according to their deeds on earth.

Rewards and punishments

All of the departed who met the tests included in this system of judgment entered a celestial realm of physical delights and simple pleasures. Here in marshes of lilies and lotus-flowers they would hunt wild geese and quail with never-ending success. Or they might build houses in the midst of orchards with luscious fruits of unfailing yield. They would find lily-lakes on which to sail, pools of sparkling water in which to bathe, and shady groves inhabited by singing birds and every manner of gentle creature. The unfortunate victims whose hearts revealed their vicious lives were utterly destroyed.

The Egyptian religion attained its highest perfection about the end of the Middle Kingdom. By this time the solar faith and the cult of Osiris had been merged in such a way as to preserve the best features of both. The province of Amon as the god of the living, as the champion of good in this world, was accorded almost equal importance with the functions of Osiris as the giver of personal immortality and the judge of the dead. The religion was now quite clearly an ethical one. People repeatedly avowed their desire to do justice because such conduct was pleasing to the great sun god.

Soon after the establishment of the Empire the religion which has just been described underwent a serious debasement. Its ethical significance was largely destroyed, and superstition and magic gained the ascendancy. The chief cause seems to have been that the long and bitter war for the expulsion of the Hyksos fostered the growth of irrational attitudes and correspondingly depreciated the intellect. The result was a marked increase in the power of the priests, who preyed upon the fears of the masses to promote their own advantage. They inaugurated the practice of selling magical charms, which were supposed to have the effect of preventing the heart of the deceased from betraying his or her real character. They also sold formulas which, inscribed on rolls of papyrus and placed in the tomb, were alleged to be effective in facilitating the passage of the dead to the celestial realm. The aggregate of these formulas constituted what is referred to as the Book of the Dead.

Ikhnaton and His Wife Nefertiti Making Offerings to Aton. A stele from the XVIIIth Dynasty. Aton is symbolized as the sun.

Contrary to the general impression, it was not an Egyptian Bible, but merely a collection of mortuary inscriptions.

This degradation of the religion at the hands of the priests into a system of magical practices finally resulted in a great religious upheaval. The leader of this movement was the Pharaoh Amenhotep IV, who began his reign about 1375 B.C. and died or was murdered about fifteen years later. After some fruitless attempts to correct the most flagrant abuses, he resolved to crush the system entirely. He drove the priests from the temples, hacked the names of the traditional deities from the public monuments, and initiated the worship of a new god whom he called "Aton," an ancient designation for the physical sun. He changed his own name from Amenhotep ("Amon rests") to Ikhnaton, which meant "Aton is satisfied." His wife Nefertiti became Nefer-nefru-aton: "Beautiful is the beauty of Aton." In keeping with his desire to begin entirely anew, Ikhnaton built a new capital, El-Amarna, which he dedicated to the worship of the new deity.

More important than these physical changes was the new set of doctrines enunciated by the reforming pharaoh. He taught first of all a religion of qualified monotheism. Aton and Ikhnaton himself were the only gods in existence. Like none of the gods before him, Aton had no human or animal shape but was to be conceived in terms of the life-giving, warming rays of the sun. He was the creator of all, and thus god not merely of Egypt but of the whole universe. Ikhnaton deemed himself to be Aton's heir and co-regent; while the pharaoh and his wife worshiped Aton, others were to worship Ikhnaton as a living deity. Aside from this important qualification Ikhnaton restored the ethical quality of Egyptian religion at its best by insisting that Aton was the author of the moral order of the world and the rewarder of mankind for integrity and purity of heart. He envisaged the new god as the sustainer of all that is of benefit to humanity, and as a heavenly father who watches with benevolent care over all his creatures. Conceptions like these of the unity, righteousness, and benevolence of God were not attained again until the time of the Hebrew prophets some 600 years later.

Despite the energy with which Ikhnaton pursued his religious revolution it was still a failure. The religion of Aton gained little popular following because the masses remained devoted to their old gods. The new religion was too strange for them and was lacking in the greatest attraction of the older faith: the promise of an afterlife. Moreover, the pharaohs who followed Ikhnaton were allied with the priests of Amon and accordingly restored the older modes of worship. Ikhnaton's successor, the pharaoh whom we refer to as "King Tut," changed his name from Tutankh*aton* to Tutankh*amen,* abandoned El-Amarna for the old capital of Thebes, and presided over a return to all the old ways. His own burial was a lavish demonstration of commitment to

Monotheism under Ikhnaton

Tutankhamen or "King Tut." This solid gold coffin weighs 2,500 pounds.

the old rituals and belief in life after death. Thereafter Egyptian religion was characterized by growing faith in ritualism and magic. Priests sold formulas and charms which were supposed to trick the gods into granting salvation: thus even the cult of Osiris lost most of its elevated moral quality.

3. EGYPTIAN INTELLECTUAL ACHIEVEMENTS

The general character of Egyptian philosophy

The philosophy of ancient Egypt was chiefly ethical and political, although traces of broader philosophic conceptions are occasionally to be found. The idea that the universe is controlled by mind or intelligence, for example, is a notion that appeared from time to time in the writings of priests. Other philosophic ideas of the ancient Egyptians included the conception of an eternal universe, the notion of constantly recurring cycles of events, and the doctrine of natural cause and effect. No Egyptian writers could be classified as "pure" philosophers. They were concerned primarily with religion and with questions of individual conduct and social justice.

The earliest ethical philosophy

The earliest examples of Egyptian ethical philosophy were maxims similar to those of the Book of Proverbs in the Old Testament. They went little beyond practical wisdom, but occasionally they enjoined tolerance, moderation, and justice.

The Plea of the Eloquent Peasant

As political philosophers the Egyptians developed a concept of the state as a welfare institution presided over by a benevolent ruler. This concept was embodied especially in the *Plea of the Eloquent Peasant,* written about 2050 B.C. It sets forth the idea of a ruler committed to benevolence and justice for the good of his subjects. He is urged to act as the father of the orphan, the husband of the widow, and the brother of the forsaken. He is supposed to judge impartially and to execute punishment upon whom it is due; and to promote such an order of harmony and prosperity that no one will be deprived of basic human necessities.

Nature of Egyptian science

The branches of science which most absorbed the attention of the Egyptians were astronomy, mathematics, and medicine. All were developed for practical ends—astronomy primarily to compute the time of the Nile floods, mathematics for building purposes, and medicine for healing. The Egyptians were by no means pure scientists. They had little interest in the nature of the universe as such, a fact which probably accounts for their failure to advance very far in the science of astronomy. Nonetheless they did perfect a calendar based on the annual appearance of Sirius, the brightest star in the sky, whose yearly rising invariably preceded the overflowing of the Nile. In addition they worked out a lunar calendar to mark the succession of religious rites.

Mathematics was more highly developed. The Egyptians laid the foundations for arithmetic and geometry. They devised the arithmetical operations of addition, subtraction, and division, but never discovered how to multiply except through a series of additions. They invented the decimal system, but had no symbol for zero. Fractions caused them some difficulty: all those with a numerator greater than one had to be broken down into a series, each with *one* as the numerator, before they could be used in mathematical calculations. The only exception was the fraction two-thirds, which the scribes had learned to use as it stood. The Egyptians also achieved a surprising degree of skill in the mathematics of measurement, computing with accuracy the areas of triangles, rectangles, and hexagons. The ratio of the circumference of a circle to its diameter they calculated to be 3.16, thereby coming very close to the modern calculation of 3.14. They learned how to compute the volume of the pyramid, the cylinder, and the hemisphere.

*Achievements in
mathematics*

The Egyptians also did some remarkable work in medicine. Early medical practice was conservative and profusely corrupted by superstition, but a document dating from about 1700 B.C. reveals a fairly adequate conception of scientific diagnosis and treatment. Egyptian physicians were frequently specialists: some were oculists, others were dentists, surgeons, specialists in diseases of the stomach, and so on. In the course of their work they made many discoveries of lasting value. They recognized the importance of the heart and had some appreciation of the significance of the pulse. They acquired a degree of skill in the treatment of fractures and performed simple operations. Unlike some peoples of later date they ascribed disease to natural causes. They discovered the value of cathartics, noted the curative properties of numerous drugs, and compiled the first *materia medica,* or catalogue of medicines. Many of their remedies were later carried into Europe by the Greeks and are still employed by the peasantry of isolated regions.

Medicine

In other scientific fields the Egyptians contributed less. Although they achieved great building feats, they possessed but the scantiest knowledge of physics. They knew the principle of the inclined plane, which they applied to the building of pyramids, but they were ignorant of the pulley. To their credit, on the other hand, must be assigned considerable progress in metallurgy, the invention of the sundial, and the making of papyrus and glass. With all their deficiencies as pure scientists, they equaled or surpassed in actual accomplishment most of the other peoples of the ancient Near East.

*Other scientific
accomplishments*

The Egyptians developed their first form of writing during the predynastic period. This system, known as the *hieroglyphic,* from the Greek words meaning sacred carving, was originally composed of pictographic signs denoting concrete objects. Gradually, certain of these signs were conventionalized and used to represent abstract concepts. Other characters were introduced to designate separate syllables which could be combined to form words. Finally, twenty-four sym-

The hieroglyphic system

bols, each representing a single consonant sound of the human voice, were added early in the Old Kingdom. Thus the hieroglyphic system of writing had come to include at an early date three separate types of characters, the pictographic, syllabic, and alphabetic.

The ultimate step in this evolution of writing would have been the complete separation of the alphabetic from the nonalphabetic characters and the exclusive use of the former in written communication. But the Egyptians, although they made frequent use of the consonant signs, did not commonly employ them as an independent system of writing. It was left for the Phoenicians to do this some 1,500 years later. Nevertheless, the Egyptians must be credited with the invention of the principle of the alphabet. It was they who first perceived the value of single symbols for the individual sounds of the human voice. The Phoenicians merely copied this principle, based their own system of writing on it, and diffused the idea among neighboring nations. In the final analysis it is therefore true that the Egyptian alphabet was the parent of every other that has ever been used in the Western world.

4. THE MEANING OF EGYPTIAN ART

No single interpretation will suffice to explain the meaning of Egyptian art. In general, it expressed the aspirations of a collectivized national life. It was not art for art's sake, nor did it serve to convey the individual's reactions to the problems of his or her personal world. Yet there were times when the conventions of a communal society were broken down, and the supremacy was accorded to a spontaneous individual art that expressed the beauty of a flower or caught the radiant idealism of a youthful face. Seldom was the Egyptian genius for faithful reproduction of nature entirely suppressed. Even the rigid formalism of official architecture was commonly relieved by touches of naturalism—columns in imitation of palm trunks, lotus-blossom capitals, and occasional statues of pharaohs that were not stylized types but true individual portraits.

See color plates following page 96

In most civilizations where the interests of society are exalted above those of individuals, architecture tends to be the most typical and the most highly developed of the arts. Egypt was no exception. Whether in the Old Kingdom, Middle Kingdom, or Empire it was the problems of building construction that absorbed the talent of the artist. Although sculpture and painting were by no means primitive, they nevertheless had as their primary function the embellishment of temples. Only at times did they rise to the status of independent arts.

The characteristic examples of Old Kingdom architecture were the pyramids, the first of which were built at least as early as 2700 B.C. An amazing amount of labor and skill were expended in their construction. The Greek historian Herodotus estimated that 100,000 workers

The Pyramids of Gizeh with the Sphinx in the Foreground

must have been employed for twenty years to complete the single pyramid of Khufu (or Cheops) at Gizeh. Its height was 481 feet, and the more than 2 million limestone blocks it contains are fitted together with a precision which few modern masons could duplicate. Each of the blocks weighs between 2.5 and 15 tons. They were evidently hewn out of rock cliffs with drills and wedges and then dragged by gangs of workers without the aid of wheeled vehicles (as yet unknown) up earthen ramps and fitted into place.

Several theories have been advanced to explain the building of the pyramids. They may have been intended for the economic purpose of providing employment opportunities. This explanation would assume that the population had increased to overcrowding, and that the resources of agriculture, mining, industry, and commerce were no longer adequate to provide a livelihood for all the people. There may be some validity to this theory, but it is certain that the pyramids had primarily religious significance for those who ordered them built. The pyramids were unquestionably meant to be the tombs of the divine pharaohs: the mightier the pharaoh, the larger his resting place was supposed to be. Since the pharaoh stood for the state the pyramids probably also took on political significance. Not only did they glorify the rulers but they may have helped to enhance the idea that the might of the Egyptian state was indestructible.

During the Middle Kingdom and the Empire, when concern for personal salvation became predominant, the temple displaced the pyr-

Significance of the pyramids

The temples

amid as the leading architectural form. The most noted examples were the great temples at Karnak and Luxor, built during the period of the Empire. Many of their gigantic, richly carved columns still stand as silent witnesses of a splendid architectural talent. Egyptian temples were characterized by massive size. The temple at Karnak, with a length of about 1,300 feet, covered the largest area of any religious edifice ever built. Its central hall alone could contain almost any of the Gothic cathedrals of Europe. The columns used in the temples had stupendous proportions. The largest of them were seventy feet high, with diameters in excess of twenty feet. It has been estimated that the capitals which surmounted them could furnish standing room for a hundred men.

Egyptian sculpture

As already mentioned, Egyptian sculpture and painting served primarily as adjuncts to architecture. The former was heavily laden with conventions that governed its style and meaning. Statues of pharaohs were commonly of colossal size. Those produced during the Empire ranged in height from seventy-five to ninety feet. Some of them were colored to enhance the portrait, and the eyes were frequently inlaid with rock crystal. The figures were nearly always rigid, with the arms folded across the chest or fixed to the sides of the body and with the eyes staring straight ahead. Countenances were generally represented as impassive, utterly devoid of emotional expression. Anatomical distortion was frequently practiced: the natural length of the thighs might be increased, the squareness of the shoulders accentuated, or all of the fingers of the hand made equal in length. A familiar example of nonnaturalistic sculpture was the Sphinx, of which there were thousands in Egypt; the best-known example was the Great Sphinx at Gizeh. This represented the head of a pharaoh on the body of a lion. The purpose was probably to symbolize the notion that the pharaoh possessed the lion's qualities of strength and courage. The figures of

The Temple at Karnak. Most of this building has collapsed or been carried away, but the huge pylons and statues give an idea of the massiveness of Egyptian temples.

sculpture in relief were even less in conformity with nature. The head was presented in profile, with the eye full-face; the torso was shown in the frontal position, while the legs were rendered in profile.

The meaning of Egyptian sculpture is not hard to perceive. The colossal size of the statues of pharaohs was doubtless intended to symbolize their power and the power of the state they represented. It is significant that the size of these statues increased as the empire expanded and the government became more absolute. The conventions of rigidity and impassiveness were meant to express the timelessness and stability of the national life. Here was a nation which, according to the ideal, was not to be torn loose from its moorings by the uncertain mutations of fortune but was to remain fixed and imperturbable. The portraits of its chief men consequently must betray no anxiety, fear, or triumph, but an unvarying calmness throughout the ages. In similar fashion, the anatomical distortion can probably be interpreted as a deliberate attempt to express some national ideal.

An intriguing exception to the mainstream of Egyptian artistic development is the art produced during the reign of Ikhnaton. Because the pharaoh wished to break with all manifestations of the ancient Egyptian religion, including its artistic conventions, he presided over an artistic revolution. The new style he patronized was naturalistic because his new religion reverenced nature as the handiwork of Aton. Accordingly portrait busts of the pharaoh himself and his queen Nefertiti abandoned the earlier grandiloquent impassivity and distortion in favor of more realistic detail. A surviving bust of Nefertiti which reveals her slightly quizzical and haunting femininity is one of the greatest monuments in the history of art. For the same reasons painting under the patronage of Ikhnaton also emerged as a highly expressive art form. Murals of this period display the world of experience above all in terms of movement. They catch the instant action of the wild bull leaping in the swamp, the headlong flight of the frightened stag, and the effortless swimming of ducks in a pond. But just as Ikhnaton's religious reform was not lasting, neither was the more naturalistic art of his reign.

5. SOCIAL AND ECONOMIC LIFE

During the greater part of the history of Egypt the population was divided into five classes: the royal family; the priests; the nobles; the middle class of scribes, merchants, artisans, and wealthy farmers; and the peasants, who comprised by far the bulk of the population. During the Empire a sixth class, the professional soldiers, was added, ranking immediately below the nobles. Thousands of slaves were also captured in this period, and for a time these formed a seventh class. Despised by all, they were forced to labor in the government quarries and on the temple estates. Gradually, however, they were allowed to enlist in the army and even in the personal service of the pharaoh.

Pharaoh Mycerinus and His Queen. Sculpture from the IVth Dynasty, c. 2590 B.C.—an example of the impassive, grandiloquent style.

Nefertiti. The famous portrait bust executed in Ikhnaton's studios at El-Amarna.

Fishing and Fowling: Wall Painting, Thebes, XVIIIth Dynasty. Most of the women appear to belong to the prosperous classes, while the simple garb and insignificant size of the men indicates that they are probably slaves.

The principal classes of Egyptian society

With these developments they ceased to constitute a separate class. The position of the various ranks of society shifted from time to time. In the Old Kingdom the nobles and priests among all of the pharaoh's subjects held the supremacy. During the Middle Kingdom the classes of commoners came into their own. Merchants, artisans, and farmers gained concessions from the government. Particularly impressive is the dominant role played by the merchants and manufacturers in this period. The establishment of the Empire, accompanied as it was by the extension of government functions, resulted in the ascendancy of a new nobility, made up primarily of officials. The priests also gained more power with the growth of magic and ritualism.

The gulf between rich and poor

The gulf that separated the standards of living of the upper and lower classes of Egypt was perhaps even wider than it is today in Europe and America. The wealthy nobles lived in splendid villas that opened into fragrant gardens and shady groves. Their food had all the richness and variety of sundry kinds of meat, poultry, cakes, fruit, wine, and sweets. They ate from vessels of alabaster, gold, and silver, and adorned their persons with expensive fabrics and costly jewels. By contrast, the life of the poor was wretched indeed. The laborers in the towns inhabited congested quarters composed of mud-brick hovels with roofs of thatch. Their only furnishings were stools and boxes and a few crude pottery jars. The peasants on the great estates enjoyed a less crowded but no more abundant life.

Although polygamy was permitted, normally the basic social unit was the monogamous family. Even the pharaoh, who could keep a

Sowing Seed and Working It into the Soil. From a bag which he wears over his left shoulder, the sower casts seed under the feet of cattle yoked to a plow. The plow is here used to harrow the soil. While one laborer guides the cows with a stick, another guides the plow straight and keeps the plowshare in the ground by bearing down on the handles. Sheep are then driven across the field to trample in the seed. From wall paintings at Sheikh Saîd, about 2700 B.C.

harem of secondary wives and concubines, had a chief wife. Concubinage, however, was a socially reputable institution. Yet compared to women in most other ancient societies, Egyptian women were not entirely subordinated to men. Wives were not totally secluded; women could own and inherit property and engage in business. Almost alone among ancient peoples the Egyptians late in their history permitted women to succeed to the throne.

Egyptian women

The Egyptian economic system rested primarily upon an agrarian basis. Agriculture was diversified and highly developed, and the soil yielded excellent crops of wheat, barley, millet, vegetables, fruits, flax, and cotton. Theoretically the land was the property of the pharaoh, but in the earlier periods he granted most of it to his subjects, so that in actual practice it was largely in the possession of individuals.

Agriculture, trade, and industry

Ikhnaton's son, "King Tut," and His Queen. The child-rulers in their garden are portrayed in the more naturalistic style held over from Ikhnaton's reign.

Commerce did not amount to much before 2000 B.C., but after that date it grew rapidly to a position of first-rate importance. A flourishing trade was carried on with the island of Crete, with Phoenicia, Palestine, and Syria. Gold mines in Libya controlled by Egypt were an important source of wealth. The chief articles of export consisted of gold, wheat, linen fabrics, and fine pottery. Imports were confined largely to silver, ivory, and lumber. Of no less significance than commerce was manufacturing. As early as 3000 B.C. large numbers of people were already engaged in industrial pursuits, mostly in separate crafts. In later times factories were established, employing twenty or more persons under one roof, and with some degree of division of labor. The leading industries were quarrying, shipbuilding, and the manufacture of pottery, glass, and textiles.

The development of instruments of business

From an early date the Egyptians made progress in the perfection of instruments of business. They knew the elements of accounting and bookkeeping. Their merchants issued orders and receipts for goods. They invented deeds for property, written contracts, and wills. While they had no system of coinage, they had nevertheless attained a money economy. Rings of copper or gold of definite weight circulated as media of exchange. This Egyptian ring-money is apparently the oldest currency in the history of civilizations. Probably it was not used except for larger transactions. The simple dealings of the peasants and poorer townsfolk doubtless continued on a basis of barter.

Economic collectivism

The Egyptian economic system was always collective. From the very beginning the energies of the people had been drawn into socialized channels. The interests of the individual and the interests of society were conceived as identical. The productive activities of the entire nation revolved around huge state enterprises, and the government remained by far the largest employer of labor. But this collectivism was not all-inclusive; a considerable sphere was left for private initia-

Left: *Making Sun-dried Bricks.* Nile mud (generally mixed with chaff or straw) is being worked with a hoe, carried away in buckets and dumped in a pile. Lying on the ground in a row are three bricks, from the last of which a wooden mold, used in shaping them, is being lifted. An overseer with a stick is seated close by. The finished bricks are carried off by means of a yoke across the shoulders. From a wall-painting at Thebes about 1500 B.C. Right: *Stonecutters Dressing Blocks.* Men with mallets and chisels are dressing down blocks to true surfaces. Below, two of them test the accuracy of the dressed surface. After two edges of the block are determined, a cord is stretched between two pegs to help gauge how much remains to be chiseled away.

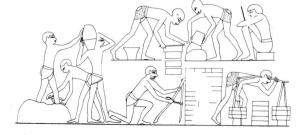
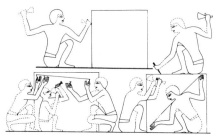

Sculptors at Work. From a tomb of the VIth Dynasty, c. 2300 B.C.

tive. Merchants conducted their own businesses; many of the craftsmen had their own shops; and as time went on, larger and larger numbers of peasants gained the status of independent farmers. The government continued to operate the quarries and mines, to build pyramids and temples, and to farm the royal estates.

The extreme development of state control came with the founding of the Empire. The growth of a military absolutism and the increasing frequency of wars of conquest augmented the need for revenue and for unlimited production of goods. To fulfill this need the government extended its control over economic life. The services of craftsmen were conscripted for the erection of magnificent temples and for the manufacture of implements of war, while foreign trade became a state monopoly. As the Empire staggered toward its downfall, the government absorbed more and more of the economic activities of the people.

The extreme development of state control under the Empire

6. THE EGYPTIAN ACHIEVEMENT

Few civilizations of ancient times surpassed the Egyptian in impressive accomplishments. Important elements of mathematics and science had their beginnings in the Nile valley. The Egyptians also perfected techniques of irrigation, engineering, and the making of pottery and glass. They were one of the first peoples to have any clear conception of art for other than utilitarian purposes, and they originated architectural principles that were destined for extensive use in subsequent ages.

Egyptian contributions: (1) intellectual and artistic

Equally noteworthy were Egyptian religious and ethical ideas. Aside from the Persians, the dwellers on the banks of the Nile were the only peoples of the ancient world to build a national religion around the doctrine of personal immortality and the idea of rewards and punishments after death. Beyond that, Ikhnaton's experiment in the cult of Aton was the first example in history of a religion of universal monotheism. Egyptian ethical prescriptions, moreover, were remarkably advanced in embracing not only the ordinary prohibitions of lying, theft, and murder, but in including exalted ideals of justice, benevolence, and equal rights. Egyptian thought had little direct influence on subsequent formulations because the Egyptian language and writing was hardly understood by others, but all told the Egyptian civilization stands as a remarkable and ever-fascinating monument of human accomplishments at the dawn of recorded time.

7. KUSHITIC CIVILIZATION

Egyptian splendor rested in large measure on vast human and physical resources lying beyond its southern periphery. Successive Egyptian dynasties drew heavily on the area known today as the Sudan Republic for laborers and soldiers as well as for precious stones and exotic woods used in the crafting of jewelry and fine furniture. The contributions of these darker-skinned neighbors are vividly recorded in scenes etched on objets d'art found in the tombs of Egypt's pharaohs.

The origin of the Negroid southerners, long shrouded in mystery, is beginning to come to light through recent archeological discoveries. We are now fairly certain that from at least 2200 B.C. food-producing Neolithic groups from the ecologically-deteriorating southern Sahara were dispersing to more fertile parts of Africa. Some migrated to the Lower Nile where they joined peoples of Mediterranean and Asian stock in laying the foundations of the so-called New Kingdom of Egypt. Others wandered southward to the Upper Nile in a region

Foundation of the
Kingdom of Kush

Egyptian Tomb Art. Egypt's Sundanic neighbors were frequently portrayed in Egyptian art.

later known to the Egyptians as "Kush." By 1500 B.C. these black-complexioned Kushites, showing remarkable cultural affinities to late predynastic Egypt, had established their own kingdom. Indeed, this Kingdom of Kush became the first highly advanced, essentially Negroid, civilization in Africa. Its vigorous inhabitants traded actively with Egypt and borrowed extensively from their culture. Within four centuries, the capital at Napata, just south of the Fourth Cataract, had flowered into a major religious center for the worship of the Egyptian god Amon-Re.

Under their king, Kashta, the Kushites began to take advantage of Egypt's decaying social fabric. In about 750 B.C. Kashta's armies swept into the temple city of Thebes, capital of Upper Egypt. Kashta's son, Piankhy, went on to capture Memphis and to extend Kushitic dominion over Lower Egypt as well. With the entire country in hand, Piankhy assumed the title of pharaoh and established Egypt's Twenty-fifth Dynasty

Kushitic invasion of Egypt

The rule of the Kushites was short-lived. Their genius at governance was no match for the Iron Age Assyrians who burst into Egypt in 670 B.C. The Kushites quickly retreated to their former homelands along the far reaches of the Upper Nile. A new Kushitic power base was established at Meroë, some 120 miles north of modern Khartoum, in the fertile pastures between the river Atbara and the Blue Nile. They may have acquired from the Assyrians the technique of iron-smelting, for Meroë soon became the major iron-working center of ancient Africa and the first black industrial city south of the Sahara.

Meroë: black Africa's first industrial city

The Kushites made an indelible imprint on numerous Mediterranean civilizations. By the fifth century B.C. their likeness appeared on vases, wall murals, and statues from Cyprus in the eastern Mediterranean to ancient Etruria on the Italian peninsula. They were variously depicted as athletes, dancers, court attendants, and warriors. Greek merchants, active in Egyptian markets, called the Kushites "Ethiopians" meaning "men with burnt faces."

Kushitic impact on Mediterranean civilizations

In 322 B.C. Egypt was conquered by Alexander the Great and became a Greek-ruled kingdom. Thenceforth, via Hellenized Egypt, Kushitic exposure to Mediterranean civilizations increased. A brisk trade with the Greeks and Hellenized Egyptians brought prosperity to Kush and enabled its people to develop distinctive architectural and artistic traditions. Unique stone pyramids cast haunting shadows across the Nile at Meroë; and Meroitic pottery, decorated with incised geometric designs, could compare favorably to the finest produced in the ancient world at that time. Kush reached its zenith between 250 B.C. and 200 A.D. By that time Meroitic hieroglyphs had even begun to replace Egyptian as the literary language.

The flowering of Kushitic civilization 250 B.C.–200 A.D.

The Kushitic window on the non-African world opened still further between 13 A.D. and the third century, when Egypt was under Roman rule. After that, Nile valley trade quickly declined and with it Kushitic

The downfall of Kush

Ancient trans-Saharan links

civilization. For centuries, the Nile's treacherous cataracts had shielded Kush from northern invasions and permitted its inhabitants to adopt only those aspects of Egyptian, Greek, and Roman culture they found desirable. But with the Nile valley connection weakened, Kush suffered economically and fell vulnerable to desert infiltrators from the west. This made it rather easy in the mid-fourth century for Meroë to be overrun by the armies of neighboring Axum, a rising kingdom in the southeast.

Tantalizing legends suggest that Meroë's royal family migrated to West Africa where they may have contributed to the evolution of new political and cultural institutions. West Africans were less advanced politically and economically even though their trans-Saharan links with North Africa and the Nile extend far into antiquity. Since at least 130 B.C. West Africans supplied the north with gold, slaves, precious stones, and wild animals for sports arenas. An ancient chariot route extended from the Punic settlements on the North African coast through the oases of the Fezzan to the Chad Basin. The Kushitic refugees may have followed an even more ancient trail connecting the Nile with the Niger river by way of Fezzan.

8. THE CHRISTIAN KINGDOM OF ETHIOPIA

Axumite foundations

Unlike landlocked Kush, Axum to the southeast could profit from a fast moving trade with Ptolemaic Egypt via the Red Sea. Axumite seaports were busy entrepôts for interior goods destined for the Mediterranean world, the Persian Gulf, India, and beyond. Egyptian Greek middlemen provided Axumites a window on the eastern Mediterranean while their Arabian counterparts exposed them to the outlets of the Orient.

The Axumite people

The Axumites as a people were the product of peaceful mingling of African and Semitic Arabians. The latter had been migrating in small bands toward the rugged Ethiopian highlands since 1000 B.C. With intermarriage came cultural enrichment, so superbly reflected in giant religious obelisks, cut with incredible precision from single blocks of stone. Great strides were also made in agricultural productivity through the introduction of the plow and the art of stone terracing and irrigation.

Conversion to Christianity and the rise of monasticism

In the mid-fourth century King Ezana converted to Christianity and declared it the official state religion. Christianity became an effective instrument for the cultural and political unification of the various Axumite chieftaincies into a centralized kingdom called Ethiopia. Monasteries took root in Ethiopia and served as vital centers of learning and cultural transmission. Ethiopian monks translated the Bible into Ge'ez, the indigenous language. In time, the monasteries became economically powerful, as successive emperors endowed them with huge tracts of land. Monasticism as a way of life spread quickly to neighboring Nubian kingdoms, before it had appeared in Christian western Europe.

Ethiopia, centered in mountainous and almost inaccessible highlands, became a natural citadel. In relative seclusion, its inhabitants forged a powerfully stable monarchy and a distinctive Christian culture. Representing one of the world's most stable and enduring civilizations, Ethiopia continued into the twentieth century under essentially the same time-honored institutions and the same royal family.

An enduring kingdom

SELECTED READINGS

• *Items so designated are available in paperback editions.*

Aldred, Cyril, *The Egyptians,* New York, 1963. A short but reliable account covering culture as well as political history.

Bibby, Geoffrey, *Four Thousand Years Ago,* Baltimore, 1961. Egyptian developments from 2000 to 1000 B.C. seen from the perspective of contemporary events elsewhere.

• Breasted, James H., *The Development of Religion and Thought in Ancient Egypt,* New York, 1912. Stimulating, but exaggerated in its claims for the work of Ikhnaton; should be read in conjunction with Wilson.

——, *History of Egypt,* New York, 1912. The standard older work by America's first great Egyptologist. Full of valuable information but now somewhat out of date in its extreme claims for Egyptian originality and influence.

• Childe, V. Gordon, *New Light on the Most Ancient East,* 4th ed., New York, 1957. Covers origins of civilization not just in Egypt but also in Mesopotamia and India.

Cottrell, Leonard, *Life under the Pharaohs,* New York, 1960. Fascinating account of life during the period of the Empire.

Desroches-Noblecourt, C., *Egyptian Wall Paintings,* New York, 1962.

• Edwards, I. E. S., *The Pyramids of Egypt,* Baltimore, 1961. Traces evolution of the form and speculates on the meaning of the pyramids.

Emery, Walter, *Archaic Egypt,* Baltimore, 1961. Controversial account of the earliest period.

• Frankfort, Henri, *Ancient Egyptian Religion: An Interpretation,* New York, 1948. A penetrating, profound study.

• Mertz, B., *Temples, Tombs and Hieroglyphs,* New York, 1965. Intriguing approach by means of archeological discoveries.

Smith, W. S., *Art and Architecture of Ancient Egypt,* Baltimore, 1958.

• Steindorff, G., and K. C. Seele, *When Egypt Ruled the East,* Chicago, 1963. Best account of political history of the Empire.

• Wilson, John H., *The Burden of Egypt,* Chicago, 1951. (Paperback edition under the title, *The Culture of Ancient Egypt.*) In a class by itself as the one book to read on Egypt if the student only wishes to read one book. Scintillating and masterful.

Grayson, A. Kirk, and D. B. Redford, eds., *Papyrus and Tablet,* Englewood Cliffs, N.J., 1973. Sources from both ancient Egypt and Mesopotamia. The best short collection for the beginner.

• Pritchard, James B., *The Ancient Near East: An Anthology of Texts and Pictures,* Princeton, N.J., 1965. Also covers both Egypt and Mesopotamia. An excellent selection.

Chapter 3

THE MESOPOTAMIAN AND PERSIAN CIVILIZATIONS

If a son strike his father, they shall cut off his fingers.
If a man destroy the eye of another man, they shall destroy his eye.
If one break a man's bone, they shall break his bone.
If one destroy the eye of a freeman or break the bone of a freeman, he shall
    pay one mina of silver.
If one destroy the eye of a man's slave or break a bone of a man's slave he
    shall pay one-half his price.

          —The Code of Hammurabi, lines 195–199

T he other of the most ancient civilizations was that which began in the Tigris-Euphrates valley at least as early as 3500 B.C. This civilization was formerly called the Babylonian or Babylonian-Assyrian civilization. It is now known, however, that the civilization was not founded by either the Babylonians or the Assyrians but by an earlier people called the Sumerians. It seems better, therefore, to use the name Mesopotamian to cover the whole civilization, even though Mesopotamia is sometimes applied only to the northern portion of the land between the two rivers.

Origin of the Mesopotamian civilization

The Mesopotamian civilization differed from the Egyptian in many fundamental respects. Because the Tigris and Euphrates rivers—unlike the Nile—flooded irregularly, and sometimes disastrously, the Mesopotamians, unlike the Egyptians, could not take nature for granted. Furthermore the Mesopotamians were not naturally protected, as the Egyptians were, from foreign incursions. In general, therefore, life in the Tigris-Euphrates regions was far more of a struggle. The results of this can be seen in both political and cultural history. The political history of the Mesopotamian area was marked by much sharper interruptions than transpired in Egypt, as the dominance of one people succeeded that of another. Mesopotamian culture too was more warlike and far more gloomy and pessimistic than the Egyptian.

Comparisons with Egypt

Moreover, whereas the native of Egypt believed in immortality and dedicated a large part of his energy to preparing for the life to come, his Mesopotamian counterpart lived in the present and cherished few hopes regarding human fate beyond the grave. Further religious differences were that the Mesopotamians never advanced as far as the Egyptians did toward monotheism and conceived of their divinities more in terms of fear than of love. Finally, Mesopotamian art was fiercer and less personal than the Egyptian.

Similarities

But there were also important similarities between the two. Both civilizations made progress in ethical theory and in concepts of social justice. Both had their evils of slavery and imperialism, of oppressive kings and priests. Both had common problems of irrigation and land boundaries; and, as a result, both made notable progress in the sciences, especially in mathematics. Finally, rivalry among small states led eventually to consolidation and to the growth of mighty empires, especially in the case of Mesopotamia.

1. FROM THE SUMERIAN TO THE PERSIAN CONQUEST

The Sumerians

The pioneers in the development of the Mesopotamian civilization were the people known as Sumerians, who settled in the lower Tigris-Euphrates valley around 3500 B.C. Their exact place of origin is obscure, but it seems likely that they came from the plateau of central Asia. They spoke a language unrelated to any now known, although their culture bore a certain resemblance to the earliest civilization of India. By a process of peaceful interaction they gradually began to guide the natives hitherto living in the lower valley, a mysterious people who were already advancing well beyond the Neolithic cultural stage. From around 2800 to 2340 B.C. a number of independent Sumerian city-states, the most important of which were Ur and Lagash, flourished in Lower Mesopotamia. Then, however, the period of Sumerian predominance was interrupted by a successful invasion from the north of Mesopotamia led by the mighty Sargon of Akkad (c. 2334–2279).[1] The Akkadians were Semites, a large grouping of peoples of the Near East who spoke related languages (the leading Semitic peoples today are Arabs and Jews). Under Sargon's leadership the Akkadians established the first extensive military empire in Mesopotamia, but this declined around 2200 B.C. and was supplanted by a Sumerian revival led by the city of Ur.

See color map following page 96

The period of Sumerian revival did not last long. Around 2000 B.C. the Amorites, another tribe of Semites, advanced from the west, conquered the Sumerian cities, and established a new empire in the Meso-

---

[1]Here, as elsewhere, dates following a ruler's name refer to dates of reign.

potamian region. Since the Amorites made the village of Babylon the capital of their empire they are commonly called the Babylonians, or the Old Babylonians, to distinguish them from the Neo-Babylonians or Chaldeans, who occupied the Tigris-Euphrates valley much later. The rise of the Old Babylonians inaugurated the second important stage of Mesopotamian civilization after the Sumerian stage. Although most of the Sumerian culture survived, Sumerian dominance was now at an end. The Babylonians established an autocratic state and during the reign of their most famous king, Hammurabi (c. 1792–1750 B.C.), extended their dominion north to Assyria. But after his time their empire gradually declined until it was finally overthrown by the Kassites about 1550 B.C.

With the downfall of Old Babylonia a period of retrogression set in which lasted for 600 years. The Kassites were barbarians with no interest in the cultural achievements of their predecessors. Their lone contribution was the introduction of the horse into the Tigris-Euphrates valley. The old culture would have died out entirely had it not been for its partial adoption by another Semitic people who, as early as 3000 B.C., had founded a tiny kingdom on the plateau of Assur some 500 miles up the Tigris River. These people came to be called the Assyrians, and their ultimate rise to power marked the beginning of the third stage in the development of the Mesopotamian civilization. They began to expand about 1300 B.C. and soon afterward made themselves masters of the whole northern valley. In the tenth century they overturned what was left of Kassite power in Babylonia. Their empire reached its height in the eighth and seventh centuries under Sargon II (722–705 B.C.) and Sennacherib (705–681), who built Nineveh, a magnificent new capital on the Tigris. The Assyrian Empire had now come to include nearly all of the Near East, since the Assyrians had conquered, one after another, Syria, Phoenicia, the Kingdom of Israel, and Egypt. Only the little Kingdom of Judah was able to withstand the Assyrian hosts, probably because of an outbreak of pestilence in the ranks of Sennacherib's army, alluded to in the Old Testament (II Kings 19: 35) as a deathly visit by an angel of the Lord.

Brilliant though the successes of the Assyrians were, they did not endure. So rapidly were new territories annexed that the empire soon reached an unmanageable size. The Assyrians' genius for government was far inferior to their appetite for conquest. Subjugated nations chafed under the despotism that had been forced upon them and, as the empire gave signs of cracking from within, determined to regain their freedom. The death blow was delivered by the Chaldeans (pronounced Kaldeans), a nation of Semites who had settled southeast of the valley of the two rivers. Under the leadership of Nabopolassar, who had served the Assyrian emperors in the capacity of a provincial governor, they organized a revolt and finally captured Nineveh in 612 B.C. The most famous of the Chaldeans was Nebuchadnezzar

The rise and fall of the Old Babylonians

The Kassites and the Assyrians

Assyrians Storming an Enemy City

(605–562 B.C.), who conquered Judah and made his capital of Babylon the leading city of the Near East.

In 539 B.C. the empire of the Chaldeans fell, after an existence of less than a century. It was overthrown by Cyrus the Persian, as he himself declared, "without a battle and without fighting." The easy victory appears to have been made possible by assistance from the Jews, who were being held captive in Babylon, and by a conspiracy of the priests of Babylon to deliver the city to Cyrus as an act of vengeance against the Chaldean king, whose policies they did not like. Members of other influential classes appear also to have looked upon the Persians as deliverers.

Although the Persian state incorporated all of the territories that had once been embraced by the Mesopotamian empires, it included many other provinces besides. It was the vehicle, moreover, of a new and different culture. The downfall of Chaldea must therefore be taken as marking the end of Mesopotamian political history.

2. SUMERIAN ORIGINS OF MESOPOTAMIAN CIVILIZATION

More than to any other people, the Mesopotamian civilization owed its character to the Sumerians. Much of what used to be ascribed to the Babylonians and Assyrians is now known to have been developed by the nation that preceded them. The system of writing was of Sumerian origin; likewise the religion, the laws, and a great deal of the science and commercial practice. Only in the evolution of government and military tactics and in the development of the arts was the originating talent of the later conquerors particularly manifest.

Through the greater part of their history the Sumerians lived in a loose confederation of city-states, united only for military purposes. At the head of each was a *patesi,* who combined the functions of chief priest, commander of the army, and superintendent of the irrigation system. Occasionally one of the more ambitious of these rulers would extend his power over a number of cities and assume the title of king, but no true empire was ever created like those of the Akkadians, or subsequent Babylonians, Assyrians, or Chaldeans.

The Sumerian economic pattern was relatively simple and permitted a wider scope for individual enterprise than was generally allowed in Egypt. The land was never the exclusive property of the ruler either in theory or in practice. Neither was trade or industry a monopoly of the government. The temples, however, seem to have fulfilled many of the functions of a collectivist state. They owned a large portion of the land and operated business enterprises. Because the priests alone had the technical knowledge to calculate the coming of the seasons and lay out canals, they controlled the irrigation system. The masses of the

Diorama of a Part of Ur about 2000 B.C. A modern archeologist's conception. Walls are omitted to show interiors at left.

people had little they could call their own. Many of them were serfs, but even those who were technically free were little better off, forced as they were to pay high rents and to labor on public works. Slavery in the strict sense of the word was not an important institution.

Agriculture

Agriculture was the chief economic pursuit of most of the citizens, and the Sumerians were excellent farmers. By virtue of their knowledge of irrigation they produced large crops of cereal grains and subtropical fruits. Since most of the land was divided into large estates held by the rulers, the priests, and the army officers, the average rural citizen was either a tenant farmer or a serf. Commerce was the second most important source of Sumerian wealth. A flourishing trade was established with all of the surrounding areas, revolving around the exchange of metals and timber from the north and west for agricultural products and handicrafted goods from the lower valley. Nearly all of the familiar adjuncts of business were highly developed; bills, receipts, notes, and letters of credit were regularly used.

Sumerian law

The most distinctive achievement of the Sumerians was their system of law. It was the product of a gradual evolution of local usage merging together with ideas absorbed from neighboring Semitic peoples. Only a few fragments of this law have survived in their original form, but the famous Code of Hammurabi, the Babylonian king, is now recognized to have been little more than a revision of the code of the Sumerians. Ultimately this code became the basis of the laws of nearly all of the Semites—Babylonians, Assyrians, Chaldeans, and Hebrews.

The following may be regarded as the essential features of the Sumerian law:

Essential features of Sumerian law

(1) The *lex talionis,* or law of retaliation in kind—"an eye for an eye, a tooth for a tooth, a limb for a limb." This fundamental concept was one that the Sumerians learned from the Semites.

(2) Semiprivate administration of justice. It was incumbent upon the victim or his family to bring the offender to justice. The court served principally as an umpire in the dispute between the plaintiff and defendant, not as an agency of the state to maintain public security, although constables attached to the court might assist in the execution of the sentence.

(3) Inequality before the law. The code divided the population into three classes: patricians or aristocrats; burghers or commoners; serfs and slaves. Penalties were graded according to the rank of the victim, but also in some cases according to the rank of the offender. The killing or maiming of a patrician was a much more serious offense than a similar crime committed against a burgher or a slave. On the other hand, when a patrician was the offender he was punished *more severely* than a person of inferior status would be for the same crime. The origin of this curious rule was probably to be found in considerations of military discipline. Since the patricians were army officers and therefore the chief defenders of the state, they could not be permitted to give vent to their passions or to indulge in riotous conduct.

(4) Inadequate distinction between accidental and intentional homicide. A person responsible for killing another accidentally did not escape penalty, as under modern law, but had to pay a fine to the family of the victim, apparently on the theory that children were the property of their fathers and wives the property of their husbands.

Quite as much as their law, the religion of the Sumerians illuminates their social attitudes and the character of their culture. They did not succeed in developing a very exalted religion; yet it occupied an important place in their lives. To begin with, it was polytheistic and anthropomorphic. They believed in a number of gods and goddesses, each a distinct personality with human attributes. Shamash, the sun god; Enlil, the lord of the rain and wind; and Ishtar, the goddess of the generative powers of nature, were only a few of them. All of these numerous deities were thought to be capable of performing both good and evil.

The Sumerian religion was a religion for this world exclusively; it offered no hope for a blissful, eternal afterlife. The afterlife was a mere temporary existence in a dreary, shadowy place which later came to be called Sheol. Here the ghosts of the dead lingered for a time, perhaps a generation or so, and then disappeared. No one could look forward to resurrection in another world and a joyous external existence as a recompense for the evils of this life; the victory of the grave was complete. In accordance with these beliefs the Sumerians bestowed only limited care upon the bodies of their dead. No mummification was practiced, and no elaborate tombs were built. Corpses were commonly interred beneath the floor of the house without a coffin and with comparatively few articles for the use of the ghost.

There was little spiritual content in Sumerian religion. As we have seen, the gods were not spiritual beings but creatures cast in the

Male Votive Figure, Sumer. This statue of white gypsum colored with bitumen shows the huge staring eyes characteristic of Mesopotamian art.

human mold, with most of the weaknesses and passions of mortals. Nor were the purposes of the religion any more spiritual. It provided no blessings in the form of solace, uplift of the soul, or oneness with God. If it benefited humanity at all, it did so chiefly in the form of material gain—abundant harvests and prosperity in business. The religion did have some ethical content. All the major deities in the Sumerian pantheon were extolled in hymns as lovers of truth, goodness, and justice. The goddess Nanshe, for example, was said "to comfort the orphan, to make disappear the widow, to set up a place of destruction for the mighty." Yet the same deities who personified these noble ideals created such evils as falsehood and strife, and endowed every human being with a sinful nature. "Never," it was said, "has a sinless child been born to its mother."

In the field of intellectual endeavor the Sumerians achieved no small distinction. They produced a system of writing which was destined to be used for a thousand years after the downfall of their nation. This was the celebrated *cuneiform* writing, consisting of wedge-shaped characters (*cuneus* is Latin for wedge) imprinted on clay tablets with a square-tipped reed. At first a pictographic system, it was gradually transformed into an aggregate of syllabic and phonetic signs, some 350 in number. No alphabet was ever developed out of it, but cuneiform nonetheless became the standard medium for commercial transactions throughout most of the Near East (often including Egypt) from about 3000 to about 500 B.C. The Sumerians wrote nothing that could be called philosophy, but they did make some notable beginnings in science. In mathematics, for example, they surpassed the Egyptians in every field except geometry. They discovered the processes of multiplication and division and even the extraction of square and cube root. Their systems of numeration and of weights and measures were duodecimal, with the number sixty as the most common unit. They invented the water clock and the lunar calendar, the latter an inaccurate division of the year into months based upon cycles of the moon. In order to bring it into harmony with the solar year, an extra month had to be added from time to time. The Sumerians were the first known peoples to believe in astrology—the belief that that human fates are determined by the courses of the stars—and this interest led them to pioneer in astronomical observations and predictions of planetary movements. Their medicine was a curious compound of herbalism and magic. The repertory of the physician consisted primarily of charms to exorcise the evil spirits which were believed to be the cause of the disease.

Gudea of Lugash. A black diorite statue of the late Sumerian ruler.

As artists, the Sumerians excelled in metalwork, gem carving, and sculpture. They produced some remarkable specimens of naturalistic art in their weapons, vessels, jewelry, and animal representations, which revealed alike a technical skill and a gift of imagination. Evidently religious conventions had not yet imposed any paralyzing influence, and consequently the artist was still free to follow his own im-

*The Great Ziggurat, or Flat-
topped Temple, at Ur*

See color plates following
page 96

pulses. Architecture, on the other hand, was distinctly inferior,
probably because of the limitations enforced by the scarcity of good
building materials. Since there was no stone in the valley, the architect
had to depend upon sun-dried brick. The characteristic Sumerian edifice, extensively copied by their Semitic successors, was the *ziggurat,* a
terraced tower set on a platform and surmounted by a shrine. Its construction was massive, its lines were monotonous, and little architectural ingenuity was exhibited in it. The royal tombs and private
houses showed more originality. It was in them that the Sumerian inventions of the arch, the vault, and the dome were regularly employed, and the column was used occasionally.

3. OLD BABYLONIAN DEVELOPMENTS

Although the Old Babylonians were an alien nation, they had lived
long enough in close contact with the Sumerians to be influenced
profoundly by them. They had little culture of their own when they
came into the valley, and in general they only appropriated and modified what the Sumerians had already developed. Thus the changes in
Mesopotamian culture during the Old Babylonian period were essentially variations on Sumerian themes.

*The shortcomings of the
Old Babylonians*

First among the alterations which the Old Babylonians made in
their inheritance may be mentioned the political and legal. As military
conquerors holding in subjection numerous vanquished nations, they
found it necessary to establish a consolidated state. Vestiges of the old

system of local autonomy were swept away, and the power of the king of Babylon was made supreme. Kings became gods, or at least claimed divine origin. A system of royal taxation was adopted as well as compulsory military service. The system of law was also changed to conform to the new condition of centralized despotism. The list of crimes against the state was enlarged, and the king's officers assumed a more active role in apprehending and punishing offenders, although it was still impossible for any criminal to be pardoned without the consent of the victim or the victim's family. The severity of penalties was decidedly increased, particularly for crimes involving any suggestion of treason or sedition. Such apparently trivial offenses as "gadding about" and "disorderly conduct at a tavern" were made punishable by death, probably on the assumption that they would be likely to foster disloyal activities. Whereas under the Sumerian law the harboring of fugitive slaves was punishable merely by a fine, the Babylonian law made it a capital crime. According to the Sumerian code, the slave who disputed his master's rights over him was to be sold; the Code of Hammurabi prescribed that he should have his ear cut off. Adultery was also made a capital offense, whereas under the Sumerian law it did not even necessarily result in divorce. In a few particulars the new system of law revealed some improvement. Wives and children sold for debt could not be held in bondage for longer than four years, and a female slave who had borne her master a child could not be sold at all.

The Old Babylonian laws also reflect a more extensive development of business than that which existed in the preceding culture. That an influential merchant class traded for profit and enjoyed a privileged position in society is evidenced by the fact that the commercial provisions of Hammurabi's code were based upon the principle of "Let the buyer beware." The Babylonian rulers did not believe in a regime of free competition, however. Trade and industry were subject to elaborate regulation by the state. There were laws regarding partnership, storage, and agency; laws respecting deeds, wills, and the taking of interest on money; and a host of others. For a deal to be negotiated without a written contract or without witnesses was punishable by death. Agriculture, which was still the occupation of a majority of the citizens, did not escape regulation. The code provided penalties for failure to cultivate a field and for neglect of dikes and canals. Both government ownership and private tenure of land were permitted; but, regardless of the status of the owner, the tenant farmer was required to pay two-thirds of all he produced as rent.

Religion under the Old Babylonians underwent only superficial changes. Deities that had been venerated by the Sumerians were now neglected and new ones exalted in their stead. Above all, a new god, Marduk, was imported to head the Mesopotamian pantheon. He and the other new deities carried no spiritual significance, however, conveying no promise of resurrection from the dead or of personal im-

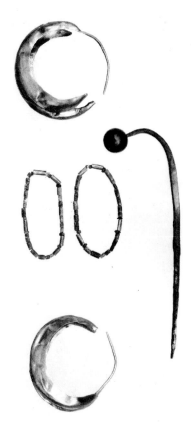

Gold Jewelry from Ur, c. 3500–2800 B.C.

Changes in religion

Panel of Glazed Brick, Babylon, Sixth Century B.C. An ornamental relief on a background of earth brown. The lion is in blue, white, and yellow glazes.

Scenes from the Epic of Gilgamash. A Sumerian inlaid shell panel.

mortality. The Old Babylonians were no more otherworldly in their outlook than the Sumerians. The religions of both peoples were fundamentally materialistic.

Although there was some decline in artistic accomplishments during the period of Babylonian rule, this was by no means true of developments in literature. Building upon legends and myths already evolving under the Sumerians, the Babylonians contributed to world literature one of the greatest epics of all time, the epic of *Gilgamesh.* This long poem, comparable in sweep and power to the Greek *Iliad* and *Odyssey,* is a compilation of stories that were told and re-told over many generations. Its hero, Gilgamesh, is a Mesopotamian king who experiences many adventures. In one he seeks the secret of immortality from an old man and his wife who had been saved when the gods had decided to destroy the world by a flood. Many of the elements of this story are strikingly similar to the Old Testament story of Noah, including the details that the couple had survived the flood by floating in an ark. But the message is rather different, for the Babylonian hero learns only resignation from the old couple: the gods will preserve those that they please and there is nothing mankind can do to understand divine decisions. Gilgamesh does learn from the old pair of a plant that will at least bring back his youth, but after gaining it with great effort from the floor of the sea he leaves it unguarded while asleep, and a snake eats it instead. According to the epic, this is why snakes gain new life every year when they shed their skins. But the human hero is finally forced to recognize that he himself can never transcend old age and death. As the epic states in resigned summary: "When the gods created man, they let death be his share, and life they kept in their own hands."

4. THE METAMORPHOSIS UNDER ASSYRIA

Of all the peoples of the Mesopotamian area after the time of the Sumerians, the Assyrians went through the most completely independent evolution. For several centuries they had lived a comparatively isolated existence on top of their small plateau in the upper valley of the Tigris. Eventually they came under the influence of the Babylonians, but not until after the course of their own history had been partially fixed. As a consequence, the period of Assyrian supremacy (from about 1300 B.C. to 612 B.C.) had a more peculiar character than any other era of Mesopotamian history.

The evolution of Assyrian supremacy

The Assyrians were preeminently a nation of warriors because of the special conditions of their own environment. The limited resources of their original home and the constant danger of attack from hostile nations around them forced the development of warlike habits and imperial ambitions. It is therefore not strange that their hunger for territory should have known no limits. The more they conquered, the more they felt they had to conquer, in order to protect what they had already gained. Every success excited ambition and riveted the chains of militarism more firmly than ever. Disaster was inevitable.

A nation of warriors

The exigencies of war determined the whole character of the Assyrian system. The state was a great military machine. The army commanders were at once the richest and the most powerful class in the country. Not only did they share in the plunder of war, but they were frequently granted huge estates as rewards for victory. At least one of

Features of Assyrian militarism

Assyrian Winged Human-Headed Bull. This relief was found in the palace of King Sargon II (722–705 B.C.). It measures 16 feet wide by 16 feet high and weighs approximately 40 tons.

them, Sargon II, dared to usurp the throne. The military establishment itself represented the last word in preparedness. The standing army greatly exceeded in size that of any other nation of the Near East. New and improved armaments and techniques of fighting gave to the Assyrian soldiers unparalleled advantages. Iron swords, heavy bows, long lances, battering rams, fortresses on wheels, and metal breastplates, shields, and helmets were only a few examples of their superior equipment.

Frightfulness

But swords and spears and engines of war were not their only instruments of combat. As much as anything else the Assyrians depended upon frightfulness as a means of overcoming their enemies. Upon soldiers captured in battle, and sometimes upon noncombatants as well, they inflicted unspeakable cruelties—skinning them alive, impaling them on stakes, cutting off ears, noses, and sex organs, and then exhibiting the mutilated victims in cages for the benefit of cities that had not yet surrendered. Accounts of these cruelties are not taken from atrocity stories circulated by their enemies; they come from the records of the Assyrians themselves. Their chroniclers boasted of them as evidences of valor, and the people believed in them as guaranties of security and power. It is clear why the Assyrians were the most hated of all the nations of antiquity.

The tragedy of Assyrian militarism

Seldom has the decline of an empire been so complete as was that of Assyria. In spite of its magnificent armaments and its wholesale destruction of its foes, Assyria's period of imperial splendor lasted little more than a century. Nation after nation conspired against the Assyrians and finally accomplished their downfall. Their enemies took frightful vengeance. The whole land was so thoroughly sacked and the people so completely enslaved or exterminated that it has been difficult to trace any subsequent Assyrian influence upon history. The power and security which military strength was supposed to provide proved a mockery in the end. If Assyria had been utterly defenseless, its fate could hardly have been worse.

Assyrian economic life

With so complete an absorption in military pursuits, it was inevitable that the Assyrians should have neglected in some measure the arts of peace. Industry and commerce appear to have declined under the regime of the Assyrians; for such pursuits were generally scorned as beneath the dignity of a soldierly people. The minimum of manufacturing and trade which had to be carried on was left quite largely to the Arameans, a people closely related to the Phoenicians and the Hebrews. The Assyrians themselves preferred to derive their living from agriculture. The land system included both public and private holdings. The temples held the largest share of the landed wealth. Although the estates of the crown were likewise extensive, they were constantly being diminished by grants to army officers.

Neither the economic nor the social order was sound. The frequent military campaigns depleted the energies and resources of the nation. In the course of time the army officers became a pampered aristocracy, delegating their duties to their subordinates and devoting themselves to luxurious pleasures. The stabilizing influence of a prosperous and intelligent merchant class was precluded by the rule that only foreigners and slaves could engage in commercial activities. Yet more serious was the treatment accorded to the lower classes, the serfs and the slaves. The former comprised the bulk of the rural population. Some of them cultivated definite portions of their master's estates and retained a part of what they produced for themselves. Others were "empty" men, without even a plot to cultivate and dependent on the need for seasonal labor to provide for their means of subsistence. All were extremely poor and were subject to the additional hardships of labor on public works and compulsory military service. The slaves, who were chiefly an urban working class, were of two different types: the domestic slaves, who performed household duties and sometimes engaged in business for their masters; and the war captives. The former were not numerous and were allowed a great deal of freedom, even to the extent of owning property. The latter suffered much greater miseries. Bound by heavy shackles, they were compelled to labor to the point of exhaustion in building roads, canals, and palaces.

Defects in the economic system

Whether the Assyrians adopted the law of the Old Babylonians has never been settled. Undoubtedly they were influenced by it, but several of the features of Hammurabi's code are entirely absent. Notable among these are the *lex talionis* and the system of gradation of penalties according to the rank of the victim and the offender. Whereas the Babylonians prescribed the most drastic punishments for crimes suggestive of treason or sedition, the Assyrians reserved theirs for such offenses as abortion and homosexuality, probably for the military reason of preventing a decline in the birthrate. Another contrast is the more complete subjection of Assyrian women. Wives were treated as chattels of their husbands, the right of divorce was placed entirely in the hands of the male, a plurality of wives was permitted, and all married women were forbidden to appear in public with their faces unveiled.

Assyrian law

That a military nation like the Assyrians should not have taken first rank in intellectual achievement is easily understandable. The atmosphere of a military campaign is not favorable to reflection or disinterested research. Yet the demands of successful campaigning may lead to a certain accumulation of knowledge, for practical problems have to be solved. Under such circumstances the Assyrians accomplished some measure of scientific progress. They appear to have divided the circle into 360 degrees and to have estimated locations on the surface of the earth in something resembling latitude and longitude. They recognized and named five planets and achieved some success in predicting eclipses. Since the health of armies is important, medicine received considerable attention. More than five hundred drugs, both vegetable and mineral, were catalogued and their uses indicated. Symptoms of various diseases were described and were generally in-

Scientific achievements

terpreted as due to natural causes, although incantations and the prescription of disgusting compounds to drive out demons were still commonly employed as methods of treatment.

The excellence of Assyrian art

In the domain of art the Assyrians surpassed the Old Babylonians and at least equaled the work of the Sumerians, although in different form. Sculpture was the art most highly developed, particularly in the low reliefs. These portrayed dramatic incidents of war and the hunt with the utmost fidelity to nature and a vivid description of movement. The Assyrians delighted in depicting the cool bravery of the hunter in the face of terrific danger, the ferocity of lions at bay, and the death agonies of wounded beasts. Unfortunately this art was limited almost entirely to the two themes of war and sport. Its purpose was to

See color plates following page 96

glorify the exploits of the ruling class. Architecture ranked second to sculpture from the standpoint of artistic excellence. Assyrian palaces and temples were built of stone, obtained from the mountainous areas of the north, instead of the mud brick of former times. Their principal features were the arch and the dome. The column was also used but never very successfully. The chief demerit of this architecture was its hugeness, which the Assyrians appeared to regard as synonymous with beauty.

5. THE CHALDEAN RENASCENCE

The Chaldean or final stage in Mesopotamian civilization

The Mesopotamian civilization entered its final stage with the overthrow of Assyria and the establishment of Chaldean supremacy. This stage is often called the Neo–Babylonian, because Nebuchadnezzar and his followers restored the capital at Babylon and attempted to revive the culture of Hammurabi's time. As might have been expected, their attempt was not wholly successful. The Assyrian metamorphosis had altered that culture in various profound and ineffaceable ways. Besides, the Chaldeans themselves had a history of their own which they could not entirely escape. Nevertheless, they did manage to revive certain of the old institutions and ideals. They restored the ancient law and literature, the essentials of the Old Babylonian form of government, and the economic system of earlier times with its dominance of industry and trade. Farther than this they were unable to go.

It was in religion that the failure of the Chaldean renascence was most conspicuous. Although Marduk was restored to his traditional place at the head of the pantheon, the system of belief was little more than superficially Babylonian. What the Chaldeans really did was to develop an astral religion. The gods were divested of their human qualities and exalted into transcendent, omnipotent beings. They were actually identified with the planets themselves. Though still not entirely aloof from humans, they certainly lost their character as beings who could be cajoled and threatened and coerced by magic. They ruled the universe almost mechanically. While their immediate intentions were sometimes discernible, their ultimate purposes were inscrutable.

The astral religion of the Chaldeans

Two significant results flowed from these conceptions. The first was an even greater attitude of fatalism than before. Since the ways of the gods were past finding out, all that humans could do was to resign themselves to their fate. It behooved them therefore to submit absolutely to the gods, to trust in them implicitly, in the vague hope that the results in the end would be good. Thus arose for the first time in history the concept of piety as submission—a concept which was adopted in several other religions, as we shall see in succeeding chapters. For the Chaldeans it implied no otherwordly significance; one did not resign oneself to calamities in this life in order to be justified in the next. The Chaldeans had no interest in a life to come. Submission might bring certain earthly rewards, but in the main, as they conceived it, it was not a means to an end at all. It was rather the expression of an attitude of despair, of humility in the face of mysteries that could not be fathomed.

The growth of fatalism

The second great result which came from the growth of an astral religion was the development of a stronger spiritual consciousness. This is revealed in the penitential hymns of unknown authors and in the prayers which were ascribed to Nebuchadnezzar and other kings as the spokesmen for the nation. In most of them the gods are addressed as exalted beings who are concerned with justice and righteous conduct on the part of humanity, although the distinction between ceremonial and genuine morality is not always sharply drawn. It has been asserted by one scholar that these hymns could have been used by the Hebrews with little modification except for the substitution of the name of Yahweh for that of the Chaldean god.

The development of a spiritual consciousness

With the gods promoted to so lofty a plane, it was perhaps inevitable that human beings should have been abased. Creatures possessed of mortal bodies could not be compared with the transcendent, pas-

The abasement of human beings

Chaldean morality

Chaldean achievements in astronomy

Other aspects of Chaldean culture

sionless beings who dwelt in the stars and guided the destinies of the earth. Humans were lowly creatures, sunk in iniquity and vileness, and hardly even worthy of approaching the gods. The consciousness of sin already present in the Babylonian and Assyrian religions now reached a stage of almost pathological intensity. In the hymns people are compared to prisoners, bound hand and foot, languishing in darkness. Their transgressions are "seven times seven." Their misery is increased by the fact that their evil nature has prompted them to sin unwittingly. Never before had humans been regarded as so hopelessly depraved, nor had religion been fraught with so gloomy a view of life.

Curiously enough, the pessimism of the Chaldeans does not appear to have affected their morality very much. So far as the evidence reveals, they indulged in no rigors of asceticism. They did not mortify the flesh, nor did they even practice self-denial. Apparently they took it for granted that humans could not avoid sinning, no matter how hard they tried. They seem to have been just as deeply engrossed in the material interests of life and in the pursuit of the pleasures of the senses as any of the earlier nations. Occasional references were made in their prayers and hymns to reverence, kindness, and purity of heart as virtues, and to oppression, slander, and anger as vices, but these were intermingled with ritualistic conceptions of cleanness and uncleanness and with expressions of desire for physical satisfactions. When the Chaldeans prayed, it was not always that their gods would make them good, but more often that they would grant long years, abundant offspring, and luxurious living.

Aside from religion, the Chaldean culture differed from that of the Sumerians, Babylonians, and Assyrians chiefly in regard to scientific achievements. Without doubt the Chaldeans were the most capable scientists in all of Mesopotamian history, although their accomplishments were limited primarily to astronomy. They worked out the most elaborate system for recording the passage of time that had yet been devised, with their invention of the seven-day week and their division of the day into twelve double-hours of 120 minutes each. They kept accurate records of their observation of eclipses and other celestial occurrences for more than 350 years—until long after the downfall of their empire. The motivating force behind Chaldean astronomy was religion. The chief purpose of mapping the heavens and collecting astronomical data was to discover the future the gods had prepared for mankind. Since the planets were gods themselves, that future could best be divined in the movements of the heavenly bodies. Astronomy was therefore primarily astrology.

Sciences other than astronomy continued in a backward state. Medicine showed little advance beyond the stage it had reached under the Assyrians. The same was true of the remaining aspects of Chaldean culture. Art differed only in its greater magnificence. Literature, dominated by the antiquarian spirit, revealed a lack of originality. The writings of the Old Babylonians were extensively copied and reedited, but they were supplemented by little that was new.

6. THE PERSIAN EMPIRE AND ITS HISTORY

Comparatively little is known of the Persians before the sixth century B.C. Up to that time they appear to have led an obscure and peaceful existence on the eastern shore of the Persian Gulf. They were not Semites but spoke an Indo-European language, that is, one of a group that includes Sanskrit (the language of ancient India), Greek, Latin, and most of the modern European tongues. Their homeland afforded only modest advantages. On the east it was hemmed in by high mountains, and its coastline was destitute of harbors. The fertile valleys of the interior, however, were capable of providing a generous subsistence for a limited population. Save for the development of an elaborate religion, the people had made little progress. At the dawn of their history they were not independent but were vassals of the Medes, a kindred people who ruled over a great empire north and east of the Tigris River.

The Persian background

In 559 B.C. a prince by the name of Cyrus became king of a southern Persian tribe. About five years later he made himself ruler of all the Persians, overthrew the domination of the Medes, and then began to conquer neighboring areas. As Cyrus the Great he has gone down in history as one of the most sensational conquerors of all time. Within the short space of twenty years he founded a vast empire, larger than any that had previously existed.

The rise of Cyrus

The first of the conquests of Cyrus was the kingdom of Lydia, which occupied the western half of Asia Minor and was separated from the lands of the Medes by the Halys River, in what is now northern Turkey. Perceiving the ambitions of the Persians, Croesus, the fabulously rich Lydian king, decided to wage a preventive war to preserve his own nation from conquest. According to the Greek historian Herodotus, Croesus consulted the oracle at Delphi as to the advisability of an immediate attack and gained the reply that if he would cross the Halys and assume the offensive he would destroy a great nation. He did, but that nation was his own. His forces were completely overwhelmed, and his prosperous realm was annexed as a province of the Persian state. Seven years later, in 539 B.C., Cyrus took advantage of discontent and conspiracies in the Chaldean Empire to capture the city of Babylon. His victory was an easy one, for he had the assistance of the Jews within the city and of the Chaldean priests, who were dissatisfied with the policies of their king. The conquest of the Chaldean capital made possible the rapid extension of control over the whole empire and thereby added the Fertile Crescent to the domains of Cyrus.

The conquests of Cyrus

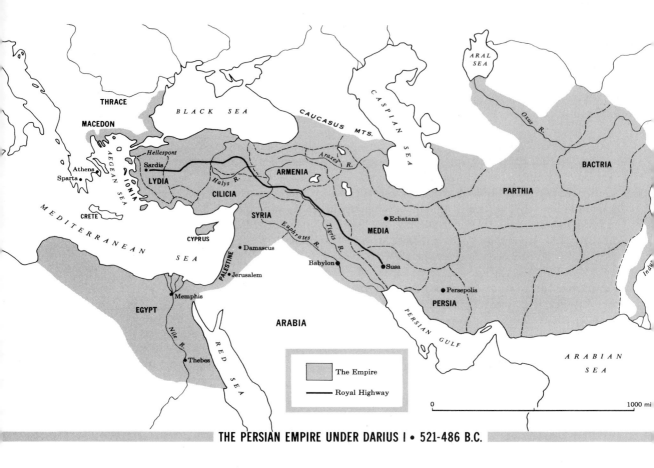

THE PERSIAN EMPIRE UNDER DARIUS I • 521-486 B.C.

The successors of Cyrus

Cyrus the Great died in 529 B.C., as the result of wounds received in a war with barbarian tribes. Soon afterward a succession of troubles overtook the state he had founded. Like so many other empire-builders both before and since, he had devoted too much energy to conquest and not enough to internal development. He was succeeded by his son Cambyses, who conquered Egypt in 525 B.C. During the new king's absence revolt spread throughout his Asiatic possessions. Chaldeans and Medes strove to regain their independence. The chief minister of the realm, abetted by the priests, organized a movement to gain possession of the throne for a pretender who was one of their puppets. Upon learning of conditions at home, Cambyses set out from Egypt with his most dependable troops, but he was murdered on the way. The most serious of the revolts was finally crushed by Darius, a powerful noble, who killed the pretender and seized the throne for himself.

Darius the Great

Darius I, or the Great, as he is often called, ruled the empire from 522 to 486 B.C. The early years of his reign were occupied in suppressing the revolts of subject peoples and in improving the administrative organization of the state. He completed the division of the empire into satrapies, or provinces, and fixed the annual tribute due from each province. He standardized the currency and weights and measures. He repaired and completed a primitive canal from the Nile to the Red Sea. He followed the example of Cyrus in tolerating and protecting the institutions of subject peoples. Not only did he restore ancient temples and foster local cults, but he ordered his satrap of Egypt to codify the Egyptian laws in consultation with the native priests. But in some of his military exploits Darius overreached himself. In order to check the incursions of the Scythians, who lived on the European shore of the Black Sea, he crossed the Hellespont and conquered a large part of the Thracian coast. In addition, he increased the oppression of the Greeks on the shore of Asia Minor, who had fallen under Persian domination with the conquest of Lydia. He collected heavier tribute from them, and forced them to serve in his armies. The immediate result was a revolt of the Greek cities with the assistance of Athens. And when Darius attempted to punish the Athenians for their part in the rebellion, he found that they offered stiff resistance.

Darius the Great died before the war with Athens and allied Greek cities had come to an end. The struggle was prosecuted vigorously but ineffectively by his successor, Xerxes I. By 479 B.C. the Persians had been driven from all of Greece. Though they recovered temporarily possession of the Ionian islands and continued to hold sway as a major power in Asia, their attempt to extend their dominion into Europe was thwarted. The last century and a half of the empire's existence was marked by frequent assassinations, revolts of provincial governors, and barbarian invasions, until finally, in 330 B.C., its independence was annihilated by the armies of Alexander the Great.

*The end of the Persian
Empire*

Although the Persian government had its defects, it was certainly superior to most of the others that had existed in the Near East. The Persian kings did not imitate the terrorism of the Assyrians. They levied tribute upon conquered peoples, but they generally allowed them to keep their own customs, religions, and laws. Indeed, it may be said that the chief significance of the Persian Empire lay in the fact that it resulted in a synthesis of Near-Eastern cultures, including those of Persia itself, Mesopotamia, Asia Minor, the Syria-Palestine coast, and Egypt.

*Significance of the Persian
Empire*

The Persian kings built excellent roads to help hold their empire together. Most famous was the Royal Road, some 1,600 miles in length. It extended from Susa near the Persian Gulf to Sardis near the western coast of Asia Minor. So well kept was this highway that the king's messengers, traveling day and night, could cover its entire length in less than a week. Other roads linked the various provinces with one or another of the four leading Persian cities: Susa, Persepolis, Babylon, and Ecbatana. Although they naturally contributed to ease of trade, the highways were all built primarily to facilitate control over the outlying sections of the empire.

Persian roadways

*The eclectic culture of
Persia*

7. PERSIAN CULTURE

The culture of the Persians, in the narrower sense of intellectual and artistic achievements, was largely derived from that of previous civilizations. Much of it came from Mesopotamia, but a great deal of it from Egypt, and some from Lydia and northern Palestine. Their system of writing was originally the cuneiform, but in time they devised an alphabet of thirty-nine letters, based upon the alphabet of the Arameans who traded within their borders. In science they accomplished nothing, except to adopt with some slight modifications the solar calendar of the Egyptians and to encourage exploration as an aid to commerce. They deserve credit also for diffusing a knowledge of the Lydian coinage throughout many parts of western Asia.

*The eclectic character of
Persian architecture*

It was the architecture of the Persians which gave the most positive expression of the eclectic character of their culture. They copied the raised platform and the terraced building style that had been so common in Babylonia and Assyria. They imitated also the winged bulls, the brilliantly colored glazed bricks, and other decorative motifs of Mesopotamian architecture. But at least two of the leading features of Mesopotamian construction were not used by the Persians at all—the arch and the vault. In place of them they adopted the column and the colonnade from Egypt. Such matters as interior arrangement and the use of palm and lotus designs at the base of columns also point very distinctly toward Egyptian influence. On the other hand, the fluting of the columns and the volutes or scrolls beneath the capitals were not Egyptian but Greek, adopted not from the mainland of Greece itself but from the Ionian cities of Asia Minor. If there was anything unique about Persian architecture, it was the fact that it was purely secular.

The Great Palace of Darius and Xerxes at Persepolis. Persian architecture made use of fluted columns, probably copied from the Greeks, and reliefs resembling those of the Assyrians.

Two Reliefs from the Staircase of the Great Palace at Persepolis

The great Persian structures were not temples but palaces. They served to glorify not gods, but the "King of Kings." The most famous were the magnificent residences of Darius and Xerxes at Persepolis. The latter, built in imitation of the temple at Karnak, had an enormous central audience-hall containing a hundred columns and surrounded by innumerable rooms which served as offices and as quarters for the eunuchs and members of the royal harem.

8. THE ZOROASTRIAN RELIGION

By far the most enduring influence left by the ancient Persians was that of their religion. Their system of faith was of ancient origin. It was already highly developed when they began their conquests. So strong was its appeal, and so ripe were the conditions for its acceptance, that it spread through most of western Asia. Its doctrines turned other religions inside out, displacing beliefs which had been held for ages.

The religion of the Persians

Although the roots of this religion can be traced as far back as the fifteenth century B.C., its real founder was Zoroaster (the Greek form of the Persian name Zarathustra), who appears to have lived shortly before 600 B.C. From him the religion derives its name of Zoroastrianism. Zoroaster was probably the first real theologian in history, the first known person to devise a completely developed system of religious belief. He seems to have conceived it to be his mission to purify the traditional customs of his people—to eradicate polytheism, animal sacrifice, and magic—and to establish their worship on a more spiritual and ethical plane. But in spite of his reforming efforts many of the old superstitions survived and were gradually fused with the new ideals.

The founding of Zoroastrianism

Characteristics of Zoroastrianism: (1) dualism

Zoroastrianism had a character unique among the religions of the world up to that time. It was dualistic—not monistic like the Sumerian and Babylonian religions, in which the same gods were capable of both good and evil; but it did not go as far in the direction of monotheism as did the religion of the Hebrews. According to Zoroaster, two spiritual principles ruled the universe: one, Ahura-Mazda, supremely good and incapable of any wickedness, embodied the principles of light, truth, and righteousness; the other, Ahriman, treacherous and malignant, presided over the forces of darkness and evil. The two were engaged in a desperate struggle for supremacy. Although they were about evenly matched in strength, the god of light would eventually triumph, and the world would be saved from the powers of darkness. On the last great day Ahura-Mazda would overpower Ahriman and cast him down into the abyss. The dead would then be raised from their graves to be judged according to their deserts. The righteous would enter into immediate bliss, while the wicked would be sentenced to the flames of hell. Ultimately, though, all would be saved; for the Persian hell, unlike the Christian, did not last forever.

(2) an ethical religion

The Zoroastrian religion was definitely an ethical one. Although it contained suggestions of predestination, of the election of some from all eternity to be saved, in the main it rested upon the assumption that humans possessed free will, that they were free to sin or not to sin, and that they would be rewarded or punished in the afterlife in accordance with their conduct on earth. Ahura-Mazda commanded that men should be truthful, that they should love and help one another to the best of their power, that they should befriend the poor and practice hospitality. The essence of these broader virtues was perhaps expressed in another of the god's decrees: "Whosoever shall give meat to one of the faithful . . . he shall go to Paradise." The forms of conduct forbidden were sufficiently numerous and varied to cover the whole list of the Seven Cardinal Sins of medieval Christianity and a great many more. Pride, gluttony, sloth, covetousness, wrathfulness, lust, adultery, abortion, slander, and waste were among the more typical. The taking of interest on loans to others of the same faith was described as the "worst of sins," and the accumulation of riches was strongly discountenanced. The restraints which believers were to practice included also a kind of negative Golden Rule: "That nature alone is good which shall not do unto another whatever is not good for its own self."

9. THE MYSTICAL AND OTHERWORLDLY HERITAGE FROM PERSIA

The religion of the Persians as taught by Zoroaster did not long continue in its original state. It was corrupted, first of all, by the persis-

tence of primitive superstitions, of magic and priestcraft. The farther
the religion spread, the more of these relics of barbarism were en-
grafted upon it. As the years passed, additional modification resulted
from the influence of alien faiths, particularly that of the Chaldeans.
The outcome was the growth of a powerful synthesis in which the
dualism of the Persians was combined with the pessimism and fatalism of the Chaldeans.

Out of this synthesis gradually emerged a profusion of cults, alike in
their basic dogmas but according them different emphases. The oldest
of these cults was Mithraism, deriving its name from Mithras, the
chief lieutenant of Ahura-Mazda in the struggle against the powers of
evil. At first only a minor deity in the religion of Zoroastrianism,
Mithras finally won recognition by many of the Persians as the god
most deserving of worship. The reason for this change was probably
the emotional appeal made by the incidents of his career. He was
believed to have lived an earthly existence involving great suffering
and sacrifice. He performed miracles giving bread and wine to man
and ending a drought and also a disastrous flood. Finally, he created
much of the ritual of Zoroastrianism, proclaiming Sunday as the most
sacred day of the week and the twenty-fifth of December as the most
sacred day of the year. Since the sun was the giver of light and the
faithful ally of Mithras, his day was naturally the most sacred. The
twenty-fifth of December also possessed its solar significance: as the
approximate date of the winter solstice it marked the return of the sun
from its long journey south of the Equator. It was in a sense the
"birthday" of the sun, since it connoted the revival of its life-giving
powers for the benefit of humanity.

Mithraism

Exactly when the worship of Mithras became a definite cult is unknown, but it was certainly not later than the fourth century B.C. Its
spread thereafter was rapid. In the last century B.C. it was introduced
into Rome, although it was of little importance in Italy itself until after
100 A.D. It drew its converts especially from the lower classes, from
the ranks of soldiers, foreigners, and slaves. Ultimately it rose to the
status of one of the most popular religions of the empire, the chief
competitor of Christianity and of old Roman paganism itself. After
275, however, its strength rapidly waned. How much influence this
astonishing cult exerted is impossible to say. Its superficial resemblance to Christianity is certainly not hard to perceive, but this does
not mean, of course, that the two were identical, or that one was an
offshoot of the other. Nevertheless, it is probably true that Christianity as the younger of the two rivals borrowed a good many of its
externals from Mithraism, at the same time preserving its own philosophy essentially untouched.

*The spread and influence
of Mithraism*

One of the principal successors of Mithraism in transmitting the
legacy from Persia was Manicheism, founded around 250 A.D. by Mani,
a high-born priest of Ecbatana. Like Zoroaster he conceived it to be
his mission to reform the prevailing religion, but he received scant

Manicheism

sympathy in his own country and had to be content with missionary ventures in India and western China. About 276 A.D. he was condemned and executed by his Persian opponents. Following his death his teachings were carried by his disciples into practically every country of western Asia and finally into Italy about 330 A.D.

Of all the Zoroastrian teachings, the one that made the deepest impression upon the mind of Mani was dualism. But Mani gave to this doctrine a broader interpretation than it had ever received in the earlier religion. He conceived not merely of two deities engaged in a relentless struggle for supremacy, but of a whole universe divided into two kingdoms, each the antithesis of the other. The first was the kingdom of spirit ruled over by a God eternally good. The second was the kingdom of matter under the dominion of Satan. Only "spiritual" substances such as fire, light, and the souls of human beings were created by God. Darkness, sin, desire, and all things bodily and material owed their origin to Satan.

The moral implications of this rigorous dualism were readily apparent. Since everything connected with sensation or desire was the work of Satan, humanity should strive to free itself as completely as possible from enslavement to physical needs. Humans should refrain from all forms of sensual enjoyment, the eating of meat, the drinking of wine, the gratification of sexual desire. Even marriage was prohibited, for this would result in the begetting of more physical bodies to people the kingdom of Satan. In addition, humans should subdue the flesh by prolonged fasting and infliction of pain. Recognizing that this program of austerities would be too difficult for ordinary mortals, Mani divided the human race into the "perfect" and the "hearers." Only the former would be obliged to adhere to the full program as the ideal of what all should hope to attain. To aid humanity in its struggle against the powers of darkness, God had sent prophets and redeemers from time to time to give comfort and inspiration. Noah, Abraham, Zoroaster, Jesus, and Paul were numbered among these divine emissaries; but the last and greatest of them was Mani. Since Mani called himself "the apostle of Jesus Christ," many Manicheans in the West, including the great St. Augustine during his early career, considered themselves to be radical Christians. The faith had many followers in the Roman Empire around 400, but it died out thereafter as a result of persecution.

The third most important cult which developed as an element in the Persian heritage was Gnosticism (from the Greek *gnosis,* meaning knowledge). It had no single founder but evolved out of Persian and Greek religious ideas and came to be fully formed around the first century A.D. It reached the height of its popularity in the latter half of the second century. Although it gained some followers in Italy, its influence was confined primarily to the Near East.

The feature which most sharply distinguished this cult from the others was mysticism. The Gnostics denied that the truths of religion could be discovered by reason or could even be made intelligble. They regarded themselves as the exclusive possessors of a secret spiritual knowledge revealed to them directly by God. This knowledge was alone important as a guide to faith and conduct.

The combined influence of these several Persian-derived religions was enormous. Most of them were launched at a time when political and social conditions were particularly conducive to their spread. The breakup of Alexander the Great's empire about 300 B.C. inaugurated a peculiar period in the history of the ancient world. International barriers were broken down; there was an extensive migration and in-termingling of peoples; and the collapse of the old social order gave rise to profound disillusionment and a vague yearning for individual salvation. People's attentions were centered as never before upon compensations in a life to come. Under such circumstances religions of the kind described were bound to flourish like the green bay tree. Otherwordly and mystical, they offered the very escape that people were seeking from a world of anxiety and confusion.

The combined influence of the several off-shoots of Zoroastrianism

Although not exclusively religious, the heritage left by the Persians contained few elements of a secular nature. Their form of government was adopted by the later Roman monarchs, not in its purely political aspect, but in its character of a divine-right despotism. When such em-perors as Diocletian and Constantine I invoked divine authority as a basis for their absolutism and required their subjects to prostrate themselves in their presence, they were really following patterns laid down by the Persians. At the same time the Romans were impressed by the Persian idea of a world empire. Darius and his successors con-ceived of themselves as the rulers of the whole civilized world, with a mission to reduce it to unity and, under Ahura-Mazda, to govern it justly. For this reason they generally conducted their wars with a minimum of savagery and treated conquered peoples humanely. Their ideal was a kind of prototype of the Roman peace. Traces of Persian influence upon certain Hellenistic philosophies are also discernible; but here again it was essentially religious, for it was confined almost en-tirely to spiritual and mystical theories.

Persian legacy

SELECTED READINGS

• *Items so designated are available in paperback editions.*
• Chiera, Edward, *They Wrote on Clay*, Chicago, 1956. An engrossing account of the discovery and decipherment of cuneiform tablets.
  Contenau, G., *Everyday Life in Babylonia and Assyria*, New York, 1954. Based on archeological evidence and well illustrated.
• Frankfort, H., *The Art and Architecture of the Ancient Orient*, rev. ed., Balti-more, 1971.

————, *The Birth of Civilization in the Near East*, Bloomington, Ind., 1951. Brief but useful.

• ————, et al., *The Intellectual Adventure of Ancient Man*, Chicago, 1946. Essays by leading experts on ancient myths; see that by T. Jakobsen on Mesopotamia.

Frye, R. N., *The Heritage of Persia*, New York, 1963. A fascinating history of Persia from earliest times to the triumph of Islam in the seventh century A.D.

• Ghirshman, R., *Iran*, Baltimore, 1954.

• Hallo, W. W., and W. K. Simpson, *The Ancient Near East: A History*, New York, 1971. An authoritative survey.

• Kramer, S. N., *History Begins at Sumer*, New York, 1959.

• ————, *Sumerian Mythology*, New York, 1961. Develops different point of view about early myth than that found in Frankfort, et al., *Intellectual Adventure*.

• ————, *The Sumerians, Their History, Culture, and Character*, Chicago, 1963. Best general treatment of Sumerian civilization.

Lloyd, Seton, *Foundations in the Dust*, Baltimore, 1955. Describes the development and accomplishments of Mesopotamian archeology.

• Moscati, S., *The Face of the Ancient Orient*, New York, 1962. Deals with Assyrians and Chaldeans.

Neugebauer, Otto, *The Exact Sciences in Antiquity*, Princeton, 1952. Excellent on Mesopotamian mathematical accomplishments.

• Olmstead, A. T., *History of the Persian Empire*, Chicago, 1948. Detailed but somewhat uncritical.

• Oppenheim, A. Leo, *Ancient Mesopotamia*, Chicago, 1964. Concentrates on Babylonian and Assyrian culture.

• Roux, G., *Ancient Iraq*, London, 1964.

Russell, Jeffrey B., *The Devil: Perceptions of Evil from Antiquity to Primitive Christianity*, Ithaca, N.Y., 1977. Particularly strong on the religious revolution accomplished by Zoroaster.

• Saggs, H. W. F., *The Greatness That Was Babylon*, London, 1962.

Widengren, G., *Mani and Manicheism*, London, 1965.

• Woolley, C. L., *The Sumerians*, New York, 1928. A pioneer work, brief and interestingly written.

Zaehner, R. C., *The Dawn and Twilight of Zoroastrianism*, New York, 1961. The standard treatment.

SOURCE MATERIALS

• *Epic of Gilgamesh*, tr. N. Sandars, Baltimore, 1960.

Grayson, A. K., and D. B. Redford, *Papyrus and Tablet*, Englewood Cliffs, N.J., 1973.

Herodotus, *The Persian Wars*, tr. A. de Sélincourt, Baltimore, 1954.

Luckenbill, D. D., *Ancient Records of Assyria and Babylonia*, Chicago, 1926, 2 vols.

Pritchard, James B., *Ancient Near Eastern Texts Relating to the Old Testament*, Princeton, N.J., 1965.

Chapter 4

THE HEBREW CIVILIZATION

I am the Lord thy God, which brought thee out of the land of Egypt from
    the house of bondage.
Thou shalt have none other Gods before me.
Thou shalt not make thee any graven image, or any likeness of any thing
    that is in heaven above, or that is in the earth beneath, or that is in the
    waters beneath the earth . . .
Thou shalt not take the name of the Lord thy God in vain.

                       —Deuteronomy 5: 6–11

Of all the peoples of the ancient Near East, none has been of greater importance to the modern world than the Hebrews. It was the Hebrews, of course, who provided much of the background of the Christian religion—its Commandments, its stories of the Creation and the Flood, its concept of a single, transcendent God as law-giver and judge, and more than two-thirds of its Bible. Hebrew conceptions of morality and political theory have also profoundly influenced modern nations. For these reasons we tend today to think of the Hebrew accomplishment as unique, and there is much truth in that assumption. But although Hebrew culture gradually came to differ greatly from that of neighboring Egypt and Mesopotamia it is necessary to remember that the Hebrews did not develop their culture in a vacuum. No more than any other people were they able to escape the influence of nations around them.

Importance of the Hebrew civilization

1. HEBREW ORIGINS AND RELATIONS WITH OTHER PEOPLES

The origin of the Hebrews is still a puzzling problem. Certainly they did not have any physical characteristics sufficient to distinguish them clearly from their neighbors, and their language belonged to the Near-

Hebrew migrations

The Promised Land

Efforts to conquer the Promised Land

Eastern Semitic family. Most scholars agree that the original home of the Hebrews was the Arabian Desert. The first definite appearance of the founders of the nation of Israel, however, was in northwestern Mesopotamia. Apparently as early as 1800 B.C. a group of Hebrews under the leadership of Abraham had settled there. Later Abraham's grandson Jacob led a migration westward and began the occupation of Palestine. It was from Jacob, subsequently called Israel, that the Israelites derived their name. Sometime after 1600 B.C. certain tribes of Israelites, together with other Hebrews, went down into Egypt to escape the consequences of famine. They appear to have settled in the Nile delta and to have been enslaved by the pharaoh's government. Around 1300–1250 B.C. their descendants found a new leader in the indomitable Moses, who freed them from bondage, led them to the Sinai peninsula, and persuaded them to become worshipers of Yahweh, a god whose name was much later written erroneously as Jehovah. Hitherto Yahweh had been the deity of Hebrew shepherd folk in the general locality of Sinai. Making use of a Yahwist cult as a nucleus, Moses welded the various tribes of his followers into a confederation. It was this confederation which played the dominant role in the occupation of Palestine, or the land of Canaan.

With its scanty rainfall and rugged terrain, Palestine was a barren and inhospitable place. But compared with the arid wastes of Arabia it was a veritable paradise, and it is not surprising that the leaders should have pictured it as a "land flowing with milk and honey." Most of it was already occupied by the Canaanites, another people of Semitic speech who had lived there for centuries. Through contact with the Babylonians, Hittites, and Egyptians they had built up a culture which was no longer primitive. They practiced agriculture and carried on trade. They knew the art of writing, and they had adapted the laws of Hammurabi's code to the needs of their simpler existence. Their religion, which was also derived in large part from Babylonia, was cruel and sensual, including human sacrifice and temple prostitution.

The Hebrew occupation of the land of Canaan was a slow and difficult process. Seldom did the tribes unite in a combined attack, and even when they did, the enemy cities were well enough fortified to resist capture. After several generations of sporadic fighting the Hebrews had succeeded in taking only the limestone hills and a few of the less fertile valleys. In the intervals between wars they mingled freely with the Canaanites and adopted no small amount of their culture. Before they had a chance to complete the conquest, they found themselves confronted by a new and more formidable enemy, the Philistines, who had come into Palestine from Asia Minor and from the islands of the Aegean Sea. Stronger than either the Hebrews or Canaanites, especially because they used iron weapons while the others used bronze, the new invaders rapidly overran the country and forced the Hebrews to surrender much of the territory they had already gained. It is from the Philistines that Palestine derives its name.

2. THE RECORD OF POLITICAL HOPES AND FRUSTRATIONS

The crisis produced by the Philistine conquests served not to discourage the Hebrews but to unite them and to intensify their ardor for battle. Moreover, it led directly to the founding of the Hebrew monarchy about 1025 B.C. Up to this time the nation had been ruled by "judges," who possessed little more than the authority of religious leaders over twelve independent Hebrew tribes. But now with a greater need for organization and discipline, the people demanded a king to rule them and lead them in war. The man selected as the first incumbent of the office was Saul, a member of the tribe of Benjamin, who at first gained considerable success.

The founding of the Hebrew monarchy

But the reign of King Saul ultimately was not a happy one, either for the nation or for the ruler himself. Only a few suggestions of the reasons are given in the Old Testament account. Evidently Saul incurred the displeasure of Samuel, the last of the great judges, who had expected to remain the power behind the throne. Before long there appeared on the scene the ambitious David, who, with the encouragement of Samuel, carried on skillful maneuvers to draw popular support from the king. Waging his own military campaigns, he achieved one bloody triumph after another. By contrast, the armies of Saul met disastrous reverses. Finally the king, being critically wounded, requested his armor-bearer to kill him. When the latter would not, Saul drew his own sword, fell upon it, and died.

The reign of King Saul

David now became king and ruled for forty years. His reign was one of the most glorious periods in Hebrew history. He smote the Philistines hip and thigh and reduced their territory to a narrow strip of coast in the south. He united the twelve tribes into a consolidated state under an absolute monarch, and he began the construction of a magnificent capital at Jerusalem. But strong government, military glory, and material splendor were not unmixed blessings for the people. Their inevitable accompaniments were high taxation and conscription. As a consequence, before David died, rumblings of discontent were plainly to be heard in certain parts of his kingdom.

The mighty David

David was succeeded by his son Solomon, the last of the kings of the united monarchy. As a result of the nationalist aspirations of later times, Solomon has been pictured in Hebrew lore as one of the wisest and most enlightened rulers in all history. The facts of his career furnish little support for such a belief. About all that can be said in his favor is that he was a shrewd diplomat and an active patron of trade. Most of his policies were oppressive, although of course not deliberately so. Ambitious to copy the luxury and magnificence of other Oriental despots, he established a harem of 700 wives and 300 concubines and completed the construction of sumptuous palaces, stables for 4,000 horses, and a costly temple in Jerusalem. Since Palestine was

Solomon aspires to Oriental magnificence

Model of King Solomon's Temple. Significant details are: A, royal gates; B, treasury; C, royal palace; D, people's gate; E, western (wailing) wall; F, priests' quarters; G, courthouse; H, Solomon's porch.

poor in resources, most of the materials for the building projects had to be imported. Gold, silver, bronze, and cedar were brought in in such quantities that the revenues from taxation and from the tolls levied upon trade were insufficient to pay for them. To make up the deficit Solomon ceded twenty towns and resorted to a system of conscripting labor. Every three months 30,000 Hebrews were drafted and sent into Phoenicia to work in the forests and mines of King Hiram of Tyre, from whom the most expensive materials had been purchased.

The secession of the Ten Tribes

Solomon's extravagance and oppression produced acute discontent among his subjects. His death in 922 B.C. was the signal for open revolt. The ten northern tribes, refusing to submit to his son Rehoboam, seceded and set up their own kingdom. Sectional differences played their part also in the disruption of the nation. The northern Hebrews were sophisticated and accustomed to urban living. They benefited from their location at the crossroads of Near-Eastern trade. While this factor increased their prosperity, it also caused them to be steeped in foreign influences. By contrast, the two southern tribes were composed very largely of pastoral and agricultural folk, loyal to the religion of their fathers, and hating the ways of the foreigner. Perhaps these differences alone would have been sufficient in time to break the nation asunder.

Roman Coin Celebrating the Destruction of Jerusalem. This coin, struck about 70 A.D., bears the inscription "IVDAEA CAPTA" (Captive Judea), and shows a female personification of the Jews propping her head in an attitude of dejection.

The northern kingdom came to be known as the Kingdom of Israel, having its capital in Samaria, while the two southern tribes comprised the Kingdom of Judah, which continued to have its capital in Jerusalem. For more than two centuries the two little states maintained their separate existences. But in 722 B.C. the Kingdom of Israel was conquered by the Assyrians. Its inhabitants were scattered throughout the vast empire of their conquerors and were eventually absorbed by the more numerous population around them. They have ever since been referred to as the Ten Lost Tribes of Israel. The Kingdom of Judah managed to survive for more than a hundred years longer, successfully outlasting the Assyrian menace. But in 586 B.C. it was

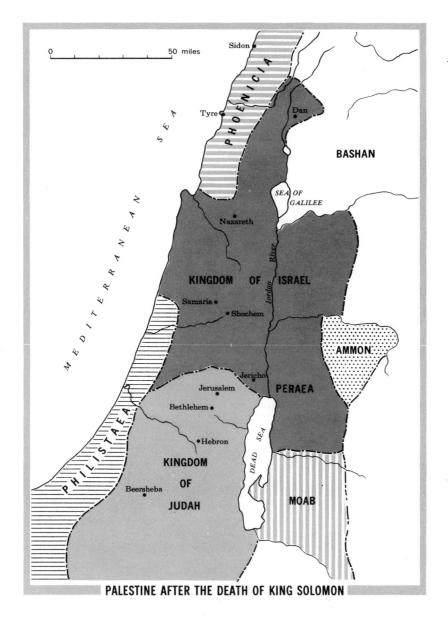

PALESTINE AFTER THE DEATH OF KING SOLOMON

overthrown by the Chaldeans under Nebuchadnezzar. Jerusalem was plundered and burned, and its leading citizens were carried off into captivity in Babylon. When Cyrus the Persian conquered the Chaldeans, he freed the Jews and permitted them to return to their native land. Few were willing to go, and considerable time elapsed before it was possible to rebuild the temple. From 539 to 332 B.C. Palestine was a vassal state of Persia. In 332 B.C. it was conquered by Alexander the Great and after his death was placed under the rule of Egypt. In 63 B.C. it became a Roman protectorate. Its political history as a Jewish commonwealth was ended in 70 A.D. after a desperate revolt which the

Masada. This ancient mountaintop fortress, which towers above the western shore of the Dead Sea in Israel, was the final outpost of the Jews in their war against Roman domination. The fortress, occupied by 1,000 men, women, and children, was besieged by the Roman army for two years before it fell in 73 A.D. Defiant to the end, almost all of the Jewish defenders killed themselves rather than be captured and enslaved by the Romans.

Romans punished by destroying Jerusalem and annexing the country as a province. The inhabitants were gradually diffused through other parts of the Roman Empire.

The Diaspora

The destruction of Jerusalem and annexation of the country by the Romans were the principal factors in the so-called Diaspora, or dispersion of the Jews from Palestine. Even earlier large numbers of them had fled into various parts of the Greco-Roman world on account of difficulties in their homeland. In their new environment they rapidly succumbed to foreign influences, a fact which was of tremendous importance in promoting a fusion of Greek and Oriental ideas. It was a Hellenized Jew, St. Paul, who was mainly responsible for remolding Christianity in accordance with Greek philosophical doctrines.

3. THE HEBREW RELIGIOUS EVOLUTION

Reasons for the varied evolution of Hebrew religion

Few peoples in history have gone through a religious evolution comparable to that of the Hebrews. Its cycle of development ranged all the way from the crudest superstitions to the loftiest spiritual and ethical conceptions. Part of the explanation is doubtless to be found in the peculiar geographic position occupied by the Hebrew people. Located as they were after their conquest of Canaan on the highroad between Egypt and the major civilizations of Asia, they were bound to be affected by an extraordinary variety of influences.

At least four different stages can be distinguished in the growth of the Hebrew religion. The first we can call the pre-Mosaic stage, from the earliest beginnings of the people to approximately 1250 B.C. This stage was characterized at first by animism, the worship of spirits that dwelt in trees, mountains, sacred wells and springs, and even in stones of peculiar shape. Diverse forms of magic were practiced also at this time—necromancy, imitative magic, scapegoat sacrifices, and so on. Numerous relics of these early beliefs and practices are preserved in the Old Testament.

The pre-Mosaic stage

Gradually animism gave way to anthropomorphic gods. How this transition occurred cannot be determined. Perhaps it was related to the fact that Hebrew society had become patriarchal, that is, the father exercised absolute authority over the family and descent was traced through the male line. The gods may have been thought to occupy a similar position in the clan or tribe. Apparently few of the new deities were as yet given names; each was usually referred to merely by the generic name of "El," that is, "God." They were guardian deities of particular places and probably of separate tribes. No *national* worship of Yahweh was known at this time.

Anthropomorphic gods

The second stage, which lasted from the thirteenth century B.C. to the ninth, is frequently designated the stage of national monolatry. The term may be defined as the exclusive worship of one god but without any denial that other gods exist. Due chiefly to the influence of Moses, the Hebrews gradually adopted as their national deity during this period a god whose name appears to have been written "Yhwh." How it was pronounced no one knows, but scholars generally agree that it was probably uttered as if spelled "Yahweh." The meaning is also a mystery. When Moses inquired of Yahweh what he should tell the people when they demanded to know what god had sent him, Yahweh replied: "I AM THAT I AM: and he said, Thus shalt thou say unto the children of Israel, I AM hath sent me unto you" (Exodus 3: 13–14).

The stage of national monolatry

During the time of Moses and for two or three centuries thereafter Yahweh was a somewhat peculiar deity. He was conceived almost exclusively in anthropomorphic terms. He possessed a physical body and the emotional qualities of men. He was capricious on occasions, and somewhat irascible—as capable of evil and wrathful judgments as he was of good. His decrees were often quite arbitrary, and he would punish someone who sinned unwittingly just about as readily as one whose guilt was real. By way of illustration, Yahweh reportedly struck Uzza dead merely because that unfortunate individual placed his hand upon the Ark of the Covenant to steady it while it was being transported to Jerusalem (I Chronicles 13: 9–10). Omnipotence was scarcely an attribute that Yahweh could claim, for his power was limited to the territory occupied by the Hebrews themselves. Nonetheless, some of the most important Hebrew contributions to subsequent Western thought were first formulated during this time. It was during this period that the Hebrews came to believe that God was not part of nature but entirely outside of it, and that humans, while part of na-

Characteristics of Yahweh

ture, became the rulers of nature by divine dispensation. This "transcendent" theology meant that God could gradually be understood in purely intellectual or abstract terms, and that humanity could be regarded as having the potential for altering nature as it pleased.

The supremacy of law and ritual

The religion of this stage was neither primarily ethical nor profoundly spiritual. Yahweh was revered as a supreme law-giver and as the stern upholder of the moral order of the universe. According to the Biblical account, he issued the Ten Commandments to Moses on top of Mount Sinai. Old Testament scholars, however, do not generally accept this tradition. They admit that a primitive set of commandments may have existed in Mosaic times, but they doubt that the Ten Commandments in the form in which they are preserved in the Book of Exodus go back any farther than the seventh century. In any event, it is clear that Moses's God was interested just about as much in sacrifice and in ritualistic observances as he was in good conduct or in purity of heart. Moreover, the religion was not vitally concerned with spiritual matters. It offered nothing but material rewards in this life and none at all in a life to come. Finally, the belief in monolatry was corrupted by certain elements of fetishism, magic, and even grosser superstitions that lingered from more primitive times or that were gradually acquired from neighboring peoples. These varied all the way from serpent worship to bloody sacrifices and fertility orgies.

The stage of the prophetic revolution

The really important work of religious reform was accomplished by the great prophets—Amos, Hosea, Isaiah,[1] and Micah. And their achievements represented the third stage in the development of the Hebrew religion, the stage of the prophetic revolution, which occupied the eighth and seventh centuries B.C. The great prophets were men of broader vision than any of their forerunners. Three basic doctrines made up the substance of their teachings: (1) rudimentary monotheism—Yahweh is the ruler of the universe; He even makes use of nations other than the Hebrews to accomplish His purposes; the gods of other peoples are false gods and should not be worshiped for any reason; (2) Yahweh is a god of righteousness exclusively; He is not really omnipotent, but His power is limited by justice and goodness; the evil in the world comes from humanity not from God; (3) the purposes of religion are chiefly ethical; Yahweh cares nothing for ritual and sacrifice, but that His followers should "seek justice, relieve the oppressed, judge the fatherless, plead for the widow." Or as Micah expressed it: "What doth the Lord require of thee, but to do justly, and to love mercy, and to walk humbly with thy God?" (Micah 6: 8).

These doctrines contained a definite repudiation of nearly every-

---

[1] Most Old Testament authorities consider the Book of Isaiah the work of three authors. They ascribe the first part to Isaiah, the second part from chapters 40 to 55 to Deutero-Isaiah, or the second Isaiah, and the end to someone who wrote after the return to Jerusalem. The second Isaiah was more emphatic than the first in denying the existence of the gods of other peoples.

Remains of an Ancient Synagogue at Capernaum. Capernaum was supposed to have been the scene of many of the miracles attributed to Jesus. Here also he called out Peter, Andrew, and Matthew to be his disciples.

thing that the older religion had stood for. Such, however, was apparently not the intention of the prophets. They conceived it rather as their mission to restore the religion to its ancient purity. The crudities within it they regarded as foreign corruptions. But like many such leaders, they built better than they knew. Their actual accomplishments went so far beyond their original objectives that they amounted to a religious revolution. To a considerable extent this revolution also had its social and political aspects. Wealth had become concentrated in the hands of a few. Thousands of small farmers had lost their freedom and had passed under subjection to rich proprietors. If we can believe the testimony of Amos, bribery was so rife in the law courts that the plaintiff in a suit for debt had merely to give the judge a pair of shoes and the defendant would be handed over as a slave (Amos 2: 6). Overshadowing all was the threat of Assyrian domination. To enable the nation to cope with that threat, the prophets believed that social abuses should be stamped out and the people united under a religion purged of its alien corruptions.

Contrasts with the older religion; political and social aspects

The results of this revolution must not be misinterpreted. It did eradicate some of the most flagrant forms of oppression, and it rooted out permanently most of the barbarities that had crept into the religion from foreign sources. But the Hebrew faith did not yet bear much resemblance to modern orthodox Judaism. It contained little of a spiritual character. Instead of being otherwordly, it was oriented toward this life. Its purposes were social and ethical—to promote a just and harmonious society and to abate man's inhumanity to man—not to confer individual salvation in an afterlife. As yet there was no belief in heaven and hell or in Satan as a powerful opponent of God. The shades of the dead went down into Sheol to linger there for a time in the dust and gloom and then disappear.

The religion not yet otherworldly or mystical

The final significant stage in Hebrew religious evolution was the post-Exilic stage or the period of Persian influence. This period may be considered to have covered the years from 539 to about 300 B.C. Perhaps enough has been said already to indicate the character of the influence from Persia. It will be recalled from the preceding chapter that Zoroastrianism was a dualistic, messianic, otherwordly, and esoteric religion. In the period following the exile in Babylon these ideas gained wide acceptance among the Jews. They adopted a belief in Satan as the Great Adversary and the author of evil. They developed an eschatology (a set of doctrines concerning the end of the world) which included such notions as the coming of a spiritual savior, the resurrection of the dead, and a last judgment. They turned their attention to salvation in an afterworld as more important than enjoyment of this life. Lastly, they embraced the conception of a revealed religion, that is, they regarded the books of their Bible as having been directly inspired by God Himself.

4. HEBREW CULTURE

In certain respects the Hebrew genius was inferior to that of some other great nations of antiquity. In the first place, it revealed no talent for science. Not a single important discovery in any scientific field has ever been traced to the ancient Hebrews. Nor were they particularly adept in appropriating the knowledge of others. They could not build a bridge or a tunnel except of the crudest sort. Whether it was from lack of interest in these things or whether it was because of too deep an absorption in religious affairs is not clear. In the second place, they seem to have been almost entirely devoid of artistic skill. In part because of religious prohibitions concerning "graven images" they had no sculpture, but they also had no architecture or painting worthy of mention. The famous temple at Jerusalem was not a Hebrew building at all but a product of Phoenician skill, for Solomon imported artisans from Tyre to finish the more complicated tasks.

It was rather in law, literature, and philosophy that the Hebrew genius was most perfectly expressed. Although all of these subjects were closely allied with religion, they did have their secular aspects. The finest example of Jewish law was the Deuteronomic Code, which forms the core of the Book of Deuteronomy. Despite claims of its great antiquity, it was probably an outgrowth of the prophetic revolution. It was based in part upon an older Code of the Covenant, which was derived in considerable measure from the laws of the Canaanites and the Old Babylonians. In general, its provisions were more enlightened than those of Hammurabi's code. One of them enjoined liberality to the poor and to the stranger. Another commanded that the Hebrew slave who had served six years should be freed, and insisted that he must not be sent away empty. A third provided that judges and other officers should be chosen by the people and forbade them to accept gifts or to show partiality in any form. A fourth condemned witchcraft, divination, and necromancy. A fifth denounced the punishment of children for the guilt of their fathers and affirmed the principle of individual responsibility for sin. A sixth prohibited the taking of interest on any kind of loan made by one Jew to another. A seventh required that at the end of every seven years there should be a "release" of debts. "Every creditor that lendeth aught unto his neighbour shall release it; he shall not exact it of his neighbour, or of his brother . . . save when there shall be no poor among you" (Deuteronomy 15: 1–4).

The literature of the Hebrews was the best that the ancient Near East produced. Nearly all of it now extant is preserved in the Old Testament and in the books of the Apocrypha (ancient Hebrew works not recognized as scriptural because of doubtful religious authority). Except for a few fragments like the Song of Deborah in Judges 5, it is not really so old as is commonly supposed. Scholars now recognize that the Old Testament was built up mainly through a series of collections and revisions in which the old and new fragments were merged and generally assigned to an ancient author—Moses, for example. But the oldest of these revisions was not prepared any earlier than 850 B.C. The majority of the books of the Old Testament were of even more recent origin, with the exception, of course, of certain of the chronicles. As one would logically expect, the philosophical books were of later authorship. Although the bulk of the Psalms were ascribed to King David, a good many of them actually refer to events of the Babylonian Captivity. It seems certain that the collection as a whole was the work of several centuries. Most recent of all were the books of Ecclesiastes, Esther, and Daniel, composed no earlier than the third century B.C. Likewise, the Apocryphal books did not see the light of day until Hebrew civilization was almost extinct. Some, like Maccabees I and II, relate events of the second century B.C. Others, including the Wisdom of Solomon and the Book of Enoch, were written under the influence of Greco-Oriental philosophy.

Hebrew literature

Not all of the writings of the Hebrews had high literary merit. A considerable number were dull, repetitious chronicles. Nevertheless, many, whether in the form of battle song, prophecy, love lyric, or drama, were rich in rhythm, concrete images, and emotional vigor. Few passages in any language can surpass the scornful indictment of social abuses voiced by the prophet Amos:

*Amos's indictment of
social abuses*

Hear this, O ye that swallow up the needy, even to make the
  poor of the land to fail,
Saying, when will the new moon be gone, that we may sell
  corn?

King David as a Musician. A much later conception of David from the eighth century A.D. shows the Hebrew king playing his lyre and charming animals. According to tradition, David was the author of the Psalms, which he sung to his lyre (also known as a *psaltery*).

And the sabbath that we may set forth wheat,
Making the ephah small, and the shekel great,
And falsifying the balances by deceit?
That we may buy the poor for silver, and the need for a pair
   of shoes;
Yea, and sell the refuse of the wheat?

The Song of Songs

    The most beautiful of Hebrew love lyrics was the Song of Songs, or the Song of Solomon. Its theme was probably derived from an old Canaanite hymn of spring, celebrating the passionate affection of the Shulamith or fertility goddess for her lover, but it had long since lost its original meaning. The following verses are typical of its sensuous beauty:

> I am the rose of Sharon
> and the lily of the valleys.
> As the lily among thorns,
> so is my love among the daughters.
>
> .   .   .   .
>
> My beloved is white and ruddy,
> the chiefest among ten thousand.
> His head is as the most fine gold;
> his locks are bushy and black as a raven:
> His eyes are as the eyes of doves by the rivers of waters,
> washed with milk and fitly set.

His cheeks are as a bed of spices, as sweet flowers;
his lips like lilies, dropping sweet smelling myrrh.
. . . .

How beautiful are thy feet with shoes, O prince's daughter!
The joints of thy thighs are like jewels,
the work of the hands of a cunning workman.

One other of the supreme Hebrew literary achievements was the
Book of Job, written sometime between 500 and 300 B.C. In form the
work is a drama of the tragic struggle between man and fate. Its cen- *The Book of Job*
tral theme is the problem of evil: how it can be that the righteous suffer while the wicked prosper. The story was an old one, adapted very
probably from an Old Babylonian writing of similar content. But the
Hebrews introduced into it a much deeper realization of philosophical
possibilities. The main character, Job, a man of unimpeachable virtue,
is suddenly overtaken by a series of disasters: he is despoiled of his
property, his children are killed, and his body is afflicted with a painful
disease. His attitude at first is one of stoic resignation; the evil must be
accepted along with the good. But as his sufferings increase he is
plunged into despair. He curses the day of his birth and praises death,
where "the wicked cease from troubling and the weary be at rest."

Then follows a lengthy debate between Job and his friends over the
meaning of evil. The latter take the traditional Hebraic view that all
suffering is a punishment for sin, and that those who repent are for- *The problem of evil*
given and strengthened in character. But Job is not satisfied with any
of their arguments. Torn between hope and despair, he strives to
review the problem from every angle. He even considers the possibility that death may not be the end, that there may be some adjustment
of the balance hereafter. But the mood of despair returns, and he
decides that God is an omnipotent demon, destroying without mercy
wherever His caprice or anger directs. Finally, in his anguish he appeals to the Almighty to reveal Himself and make known His ways to
him. God answers him out of the whirlwind with a magnificent exposition of the tremendous works of nature. Convinced of his own insignificance and of the unutterable majesty of God, Job despises himself and repents in dust and ashes. In the end no solution is given of the
problem of individual suffering. No promise is made of recompense
in a life hereafter, nor does God make any effort to refute the hopeless
pessimism of Job. Humans must take comfort in the philosophic reflection that the universe is greater than themselves, and that God in
the pursuit of His sublime purposes cannot really be limited by human
standards of equity and goodness.

As philosophers the Hebrews surpassed every other people before
the Greeks, including the Egyptians. Although they were not brilliant
metaphysicians and constructed no great theories of the universe, they *Hebrew philosophy: early*
did concern themselves with most of the problems relating to human *examples*
life and destiny. Their thought was essentially personal rather than ab-

stract. Probably the earliest of their writings of a distinctly philosophical character were the Book of Proverbs and the Book of Ecclesiasticus. In their final form both were of late composition, but much of the material they contain was doubtless quite ancient. Not all of it was original, for a considerable portion had been taken from Egyptian sources as early as 1000 B.C. The books have as their essential teaching: be temperate, diligent, wise, and honest, and you will surely be rewarded with prosperity, long life, and a good reputation. Only in such isolated passages as the following is any recognition given to higher motives of sympathy or respect for the rights of others: "Whoso mocketh the poor reproacheth his Maker; and he that is glad at calamities shall not be unpunished" (Proverbs 17: 5).

Ecclesiastes

A much more profound and critical philosophy is contained in Ecclesiastes, an Old Testament book, not to be confused with the Ecclesiasticus mentioned above. The author of Ecclesiastes is unknown. In some way it came to be attributed to Solomon, but he certainly did not write it, for it includes doctrines and forms of expression unknown to the Hebrews for hundreds of years after his death. Modern critics date it no earlier than the third century B.C. The basic ideas of its philosophy may be summarized as follows:

(1) Mechanism. The universe is a machine that rolls on forever without evidence of any purpose or goal. Sunrise and sunset, birth and death are but phases of constantly recurring cycles and "there is nothing new under the sun."

(2) Fatalism. Humans are victims of the whims of fate. There is no necessary relation between effort and success. "The race is not to the swift, nor the battle to the strong, neither yet bread to the wise . . . but time and chance happeneth to them all."

(3) Pessimism. "All is vanity and vexation of spirit." Fame, riches, extravagant pleasure are snares and delusions in the end. Although wisdom is better than folly, even it is not a sure key to happiness, for an increase in knowledge brings a keener awareness of suffering.

(4) Moderation. Extremes of asceticism and extremes of indulgence are both to be avoided. "Be not righteous over much . . . be not over much wicked: why shouldest thou die before thy time?"

5. THE MAGNITUDE OF THE HEBREW INFLUENCE

The nature of the Hebrew influence

The influence of the Hebrews, like that of most other Near-Eastern peoples, has been chiefly religious and ethical. While it is true that the Old Testament has served as a source of inspiration for some of the literature and art of medieval and early modern civilizations, this has resulted largely because the Bible was already familiar material as a part of the religious heritage. The same explanation can be applied to the use of the Old Testament as a source of law and political theory by the Calvinists in the sixteenth century, and by many other Christians both before and since.

But these facts do not mean that the Hebrew influence has been slight. On the contrary, the history of nearly every Western civilization during the past two thousand years would have been radically different without the heritage from Israel. For it must be remembered that the Hebrews developed the first sustained monotheism known to mankind and that Hebrew beliefs were among the principal foundations of Christianity. The relationship between the two religions is frequently misunderstood. The movement inaugurated by Jesus of Nazareth is commonly represented as a revolt against Judaism; but such was only partly the case. On the eve of the Christian era the Jewish nation had come to be divided into several different religious parties, including a majority group of Pharisees, and minority groups of Sadducees and Essenes. The Pharisees represented the middle classes and some of the better educated common folk. They believed in the resurrection, in rewards and punishments after death, and in the coming of a political messiah. Intensely nationalistic, they advocated participation in government and faithful observance of the ancient ritual. They regarded all parts of the law as of virtually equal importance, whether they applied to matters of ceremony or to obligations of social ethics. Their concern for the law was so great that they debated such questions as whether one could eat an egg laid on the Sabbath.

Hebrew foundations of Christianity: the beliefs of the Pharisees

Representing altogether different strata of society, the minority parties disagreed with the Pharisees on both religious and political issues. The Sadducees, including the priests and the wealthier classes, were most famous for their denial of the resurrection and of rewards and punishments in an afterlife. Although they favored the temporary acceptance of Roman rule, their attitude toward the ancient law was even more inflexible than that of the Pharisees. The Essenes, who were not even a unified party but consisted of various similar but separate communities, drew their members from the lower classes, practiced asceticism and preached otherworldliness as means of protest against the wealth and power of priests and rulers. They ate and drank only enough to keep themselves alive, held all their goods in common, and looked upon marriage as a necessary evil. Far from being fanatical patriots, they regarded government with indifference and refused to take oaths under any conditions. They emphasized the spiritual aspects of religion rather than the ceremonial, and stressed particularly the immortality of the soul, the coming of a religious messiah, and the early destruction of the world.

The Sadducees and the Essenes

Until recently scholars were dependent for their knowledge of the Essenes almost entirely upon secondary sources. But in 1947 an Arab shepherd unwittingly opened the way to one of the most spectacular discoveries of documentary evidence in world history. Searching for a lost sheep on the western shore of the Dead Sea, he threw a stone that

The Dead Sea scrolls

The Dead Sea Scrolls. Now on display in an underground vault at the Hebrew University in Jerusalem. The oldest extant examples of Hebrew religious literature, they furnish us with evidence of the activities of the Essenes and mystical and other worldly sects about the beginning of the Christian era.

entered a hole in the rocks and made such a peculiar noise that he ran away in fright. He returned, however, with a friend to investigate and discovered a cave in which were stored about fifty cylindrical earthen jars stuffed with writings on leather scrolls. Studied by scholars, the scrolls revealed the existence of a monastic community which flourished from about 130 B.C. to 67 A.D. Its members lived a life of humility and self-denial, holding their goods in common, and devoting their time to prayer and sacraments and to studying and copying Biblical texts. They looked forward confidently to the coming of a messiah, the overthrow of evil, and the establishment of God's kingdom on earth. That they belonged to the same general movement that fostered the growth of the Essenes seems beyond question.

Hebrew influence upon Christianity

All branches of Judaism except the Sadducees strongly influenced the development of Christianity. From Jewish sources Christianity obtained its cosmogony, or theory of the origin of the universe; the Ten Commandments; and a large portion of its theology, including the "transcendent" view of God as outside of nature and humanity as master of nature. Jesus himself, although he condemned the Pharisees for their legalism and hypocrisy, did not repudiate all of their tenets. Instead of abolishing the ancient law, as he is popularly supposed to have done, he demanded its fulfillment, insisting, however, that it should not be made the essential part of religion. In the first flush of enthusiasm at the discovery of the Dead Sea Scrolls it seemed as if Christianity might have been most directly influenced by the Essenes. Scholars now, however, speak less of direct influences than of similarities, for early Christians, like the Essenes, practiced asceticism, regarded government with indifference and the Roman Empire with hostility, held their goods in common, and believed in the imminent end of the world. These parallels do not mean, of course, that Christianity was a mere adaptation of beliefs and practices emanating from Judaism. There was much in it that was unique; but that is a subject which can be discussed more conveniently later on.[2]

The ethical and political influence of the Hebrews has also been substantial. Their moral conceptions have been a leading factor in the development of the negative approach toward ethics which has prevailed for so long in Western countries. For the early Hebrews, "righteousness" consisted primarily in the observance of taboos or prohibitions. "Thou shalt not . . ." is a major theme of many parts of the Old Testament. But a positive morality of charity and social justice made rapid headway during the time of the prophets and has had its great influence as well. With respect to political thought, Hebrew ideals of the sovereignty of law, and regard for the dignity and worth of the individual have been among the major formative influences which have shaped the growth of modern democracy. It is now almost universally recognized that the traditions of Judaism contributed equally with the influence of Christianity and Stoic philosophy in fostering recognition of human rights and in promoting the development of free society.

Ethical and political influence of the Hebrews

SELECTED READINGS

• *Items so designated are available in paperback editions.*

Albright, W. F., *The Archaeology of Palestine,* Baltimore, 1949. The best survey by the master of American archeologists of the Holy Land.

• ———, *From the Stone Age to Christianity,* New York, 1957. Emphasizes the development of Hebrew monotheism.

Baron, Salo W., *A Social and Religious History of the Jews,* 3 vols., New York, 1937. A modern classic.

• Bickermann, E., *From Ezra to the Last of the Maccabees: Foundations of Post-Biblical Judaism,* New York, 1962.

Bright, John, *A History of Israel,* Philadelphia, 1959. A balanced account.

Chase, Mary E., *Life and Language in the Old Testament,* New York, 1955.

De Burgh, W. G., *The Legacy of the Ancient World,* 3rd ed., New York, 1960. Includes a good survey of the influence of Hebrew thought.

Harrison, R. K., *The Dead Sea Scrolls: An Introduction,* New York, 1961. A valuable guide for the beginner.

Hermann, Siegfried, *A History of Israel in Old Testament Times,* London, 1975. Iconoclastic and challenging.

Klausner, Joseph, *The Messianic Idea in Israel,* New York, 1955. By one of the greatest Jewish scholars of our age.

Meek, T. J., *Hebrew Origins,* rev. ed., New York, 1950. Very scholarly and fundamental.

Noth, Martin, *History of Israel,* 2nd ed., New York, 1960. A basic reappraisal.

[2] See Chapter 11.

Oesterley, W. O. E., and T. H. Robinson, *Hebrew Religion, Its Origin and Development,* New York, 1932.

• Orlinsky, H. M., *Ancient Israel,* 2nd ed., Ithaca, N.Y., 1960. The best brief introduction.

• Roth, Cecil, *The Dead Sea Scrolls,* New York, 1965. Contends that the scrolls were not produced by the Essenes but by the Zealots, a warlike sect deeply involved in the rebellion against Rome in 70 A.D.

Rowley, H. H., *Growth of the Old Testament,* New York, 1963. Helpful account of scholarly opinion on circumstances of origin of all the Old Testament books.

Schürer, E., *The History of the Jewish People in the Time of Jesus,* 5 vols., Edinburgh, 1885–91. An older but irreplaceable work.

• Vaux, Roland de, *Ancient Israel: Its Life and Institutions,* New York, 1962. Especially valuable for archeological data.

SOURCE MATERIALS

Baron, Salo W., and J. L. Blau, eds., *Judaism: Post-Biblical and Talmudic Periods,* New York, 1954.

Gaster, T. H., tr., *The Dead Sea Scriptures in English Translation,* New York, 1964.

The *Old Testament* and the *Apocrypha,* many editions.

Pritchard, J. B., ed., *Ancient Near Eastern Texts Relating to the Old Testament,* rev. ed., Princeton, 1965.

Chapter 5

THE HITTITE, MINOAN, MYCENAEAN, AND LESSER CIVILIZATIONS

But for them among these gods will be bled for annual food:
to the god Karnua one steer and one sheep;
to the goddess Kupapa one steer and one sheep;
to the divinity Sarku one sheep;
and a Kutupalis sheep to the male divinities.

> —Hittite sacrifice formula, translated
> from a hieroglyph by
> H. T. Bossert

A few other ancient civilizations require more than passing attention. Chief among them are the Hittite, the Minoan, the Mycenaean, the Phoenician, and the Lydian. The Hittites are important primarily as intermediaries between East and West. They were one of the main connecting links between the civilizations of Egypt, the Tigris-Euphrates valley, and the region of the Aegean Sea. It appears certain also that they were the original discoverers of iron. The Minoan and the Mycenaean civilizations are the oldest ones of Europe. They are significant above all for their remarkable achievements in the arts and as the starting points of Greek history. As for the Phoenicians, no one could overlook the importance of their distribution of a knowledge of the alphabet and a primitive commercial law to the surrounding civilized world. The Lydians have gone down in history as the originators of the first system of coinage.

Importance of these civilizations

1. THE HITTITES

Until about a century ago little was known of the Hittites except their name. They were commonly assumed to have played no role of any

*The discovery of remains
of the Hittite civilization*

significance in the drama of history. The slighting references to them in the Bible give the impression that they were little more than a half-barbarian tribe. But in 1870 some curiously inscribed stones were found at Hama in Syria. This was the beginning of an extensive inquiry which has continued with a few interruptions to the present day. It was not long until scores of other monuments and clay tablets were discovered over most of Asia Minor and through the Near East as far as the Tigris-Euphrates valley. In 1907 some evidences of an ancient city were unearthed near the village of Boghaz-Koy in Turkey. Further excavation eventually revealed the ruins of a great fortified capital which was known as Hattusas or Hittite City. Within its walls were discovered more than 20,000 clay tablets, most of them apparently laws and decrees.

The Hittite Empire

On the basis of these finds and other evidences gradually accumulated, it was soon made clear that the Hittites were once the rulers of a mighty empire covering most of Asia Minor and extending to the upper reaches of the Euphrates. Part of the time it included Syria as well and even portions of Phoenicia and Palestine. The Hittites reached the zenith of their power during the years from 1600 to 1200 B.C. In the last century of this period they waged a long and exhausting war with Egypt, which had much to do with the downfall of both empires. Neither was able to regain its strength. After 1200 B.C. Carchemish on the Euphrates River became for a time the leading Hittite city, but as a commercial center rather than as the capital of a great empire. The days of imperial glory were over. Finally, after 717 B.C., all the remaining Hittite territories were conquered and absorbed by the Assyrians, Lydians, and Phrygians.

*The mystery of the race
and language of the
Hittites*

Where the Hittites came from and what were their relationships to other peoples are problems which still defy a perfect solution. Most modern scholars trace their place of origin to Turkestan and consider them related to the Greeks. Their language was Indo-European. Its secret was unlocked during World War I by the Czech scholar Bedrich Hrozny. Since then thousands of clay tablets making up the laws and official records of the emperors have been deciphered. They reveal a civilization resembling more closely the Old Babylonian than any other.

*The economic life of the
Hittites*

Hardly enough evidence has yet been collected to make possible an accurate appraisal of Hittite civilization. Some modern historians refer to it as if it were on a level with the Mesopotamian or even with the Egyptian civilization. Such may have been the case from the material standpoint, for the Hittites undoubtedly had an extensive knowledge of agriculture and a highly developed economic life in general. They mined great quantities of silver, copper, and lead, which they sold to surrounding nations. They discovered the mining and use of iron and made that material available for the rest of the civilized world. Trade was also one of their principal economic pursuits. In fact, they seem to have depended almost as much upon commercial penetration as upon war for the expansion of their empire.

The literature of the Hittites consisted chiefly of mythology, including adaptations of creation and flood legends from the Old Babylonians. They had nothing that could be described as philosophy, nor is there any evidence of scientific originality outside of the metallurgical arts. They evidently possessed some talent for the perfection of writing, for in addition to a modified cuneiform adapted from Mesopotamia they also developed a hieroglyphic system which was partly phonetic in character.

The intellectual level of Hittite culture

One of the most significant achievements of the Hittites was their system of law. Approximately two hundred separate paragraphs or decrees, covering a great variety of subjects, have been translated. They reflect a society comparatively urbane and sophisticated but subject to minute governmental control. The title to all land was vested in the king or in the governments of the cities. Grants were made to individuals only in return for military service and under the strict requirement that the land be cultivated. Prices were fixed in the laws themselves for an enormous number of commodities—not only for articles of luxury and the products of industry, but even for food and clothing. All wages and fees for services were likewise minutely prescribed, with the pay of women fixed at less than half the rate for men.

Hittite law

On the whole, the Hittite law was more humane than that of the Old Babylonians. Death was the punishment for only eight offenses— such as witchcraft, and theft of property from the palace. Even premeditated murder was punishable only by a fine. Mutilation was not specified as a penalty at all except for arson or theft when committed by a slave. The contrast with the cruelties of Assyrian law was more striking. Not a single example is to be found in the Hittite decrees of such fiendish punishments as flaying, castration, and impalement, which the rulers at Nineveh seemed to think necessary for maintaining their authority.

Humane character of Hittite law

The art of the Hittites was not of outstanding excellence. So far as we know, it included only sculpture and architecture. The former was generally crude, but at the same time it revealed much freshness and vigor. Most of it was in the form of reliefs depicting scenes of war and mythology. Architecture was ponderous and huge. Temples and palaces were squat, unadorned structures with small, two-columned porches and great stone lions guarding the entrance.

The art of the Hittites

Not a great deal is known about the Hittite religion except that it had an elaborate mythology, innumerable deities, and forms of worship of Mesopotamian origin. A sun god was worshiped, along with a host of other deities, some of whom appear to have had no particular function at all. The Hittites seem to have welcomed into the divine company practically all of the gods of the peoples they conquered and even of the nations that bought their wares. The practices of the re-

Hittite religion

Hittite Sculpture. Perhaps the most highly conventionalized sculpture of the ancient world is found in Hittite reliefs.

ligion included divination, sacrifice, purification ceremonies, and the offering of prayers. Nothing can be found in the records to indicate that the religion was in any sense ethical.

The importance of the Hittites

The chief historical importance of the Hittites probably lies in the role which they played as intermediaries between the Tigris-Euphrates valley and the westernmost portions of the Near East. Doubtless in this way certain culture elements from Mesopotamia were transmitted to the Canaanites and to the peoples of the Aegean islands.

2. THE MINOAN AND MYCENAEAN CIVILIZATIONS

Long-forgotten civilizations

By a strange coincidence the discovery of the existence of the Hittite, Minoan, and Mycenaean civilizations was made at just about the same time. Before 1870 scarcely anyone dreamed that great civilizations had flourished on the Aegean islands and on the shores of Asia Minor for hundreds of years prior to the rise of classical Greek civilization. Students of the *Iliad* knew, of course, of the references to a strange people who were supposed to have dwelt in Troy, to have kidnaped the fair Helen, and to have been punished by the Greeks for this act by the siege and destruction of their city. But it was commonly supposed that these accounts were mere figments of a poetical imagination. Today we are certain that Greek history, and thus European history, began over one thousand years before the Golden Age of Athens.

The discoveries by Schliemann and others

The first discovery of a highly developed Aegean culture center was made not by a professional archeologist but by a retired German businessman, Heinrich Schliemann. Fascinated from early youth by the stories of the Homeric epics, he determined to dedicate his life to archeological research as soon as he had sufficient income to enable

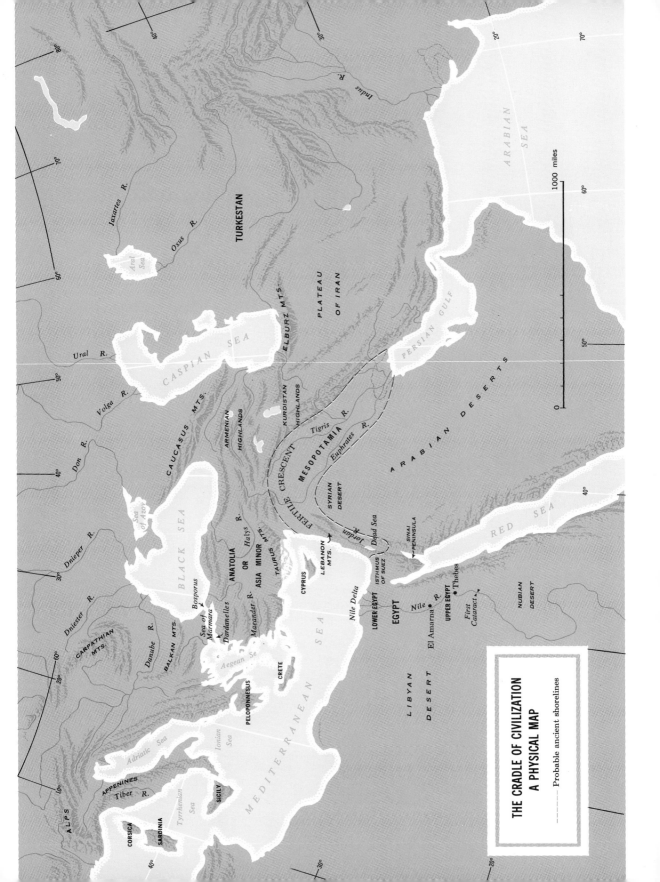

THE CRADLE OF CIVILIZATION
A PHYSICAL MAP

- - - - Probable ancient shorelines

1000 miles

ALPS
APPENINES
Tiber R.
CORSICA
SARDINIA
SICILY
Tyrrhenian Sea
Ionian Sea
Adriatic Sea
MEDITERRANEAN SEA
PELOPONNESUS
CRETE
Aegean Se
Dardanelles
Sea of Marmara
Bosporus
BLACK SEA
Sea of Azov
BALKAN MTS.
CARPATHIAN MTS.
Danube R.
Dniester R.
Dnieper R.
Don R.
Volga R.
Ural R.
CAUCASUS MTS.
CASPIAN SEA
ARMENIAN HIGHLANDS
KURDISTAN HIGHLANDS
ELBURZ MTS.
PLATEAU OF IRAN
TURKESTAN
Aral Sea
Oxus R.
Jaxartes R.
Indus R.
ARABIAN SEA
PERSIAN GULF
Tigris R.
Euphrates R.
MESOPOTAMIA
FERTILE CRESCENT
SYRIAN DESERT
ARABIAN DESERTS
RED SEA
NUBIAN DESERT
First Cataract
Thebes
UPPER EGYPT
El Amarna
Nile R.
EGYPT
LOWER EGYPT
Nile Delta
ISTHMUS OF SUEZ
SINAI PENINSULA
Dead Sea
Jordan R.
LEBANON MTS.
CYPRUS
ANATOLIA OR ASIA MINOR
TAURUS MTS.
Halys R.
Maeander R.
LIBYAN DESERT

Egyptian Pottery Jar, c. 3600 B.C. It was filled with food or water and placed in the tomb to provide for the afterlife. (MMA)

An Egyptian Official and His Son. Painted limestone, c. 2500 B.C.

Gold and Inlay Pendant of Princess Sit Hat-Hor Yunet. Egyptian, Twelfth Dynasty.

Farm Hand Plowing. Egyptian tomb figures, c. 1900 B.C.

Thutmose III as Amon, 1450 B.C. The Pharaoh wears the crown and the beard of the god, and carries a scimitar and the symbol of "life."

Jeweled Headdress of Gold, Carnelian, and Glass. Egyptian, 1475 B.C.

Part of the Egyptian "Book of the Dead." A collection of magic formulas to enable the deceased to gain admission to the realm of Osiris and to enjoy its eternal benefits.

Silversmiths Working on a Stand and a Jar. Egyptian, c. 1450 B.C.

A scribe writing on a papyrus roll. Egyptian, c. 1415 B.C.

Shawabty ("to answer") Figures, c. 1400 B.C. These were put in the tomb to do any degrading work the rich man might be called upon to do in the next world.

Stele or Grave Marker. It shows the deceased being presented to the Sun god on his throne. She is holding her heart in her hand.

Scarab or Beetle-Shaped Charm of a Pharaoh, c. 1395 B.C. The beetle was sacred in ancient Egypt.

Wall painting of an Egyptian house, c. 1400 B.C.

Painted limestone figures, c. 1300 B.C.

Head of Ramses II, 1324–1258 B.C.

Painted Wood Shrine Box for Shawabty Figures. *Ca.* 1200 B.C.

A hieroglyphic character for the idea "Millions of Years," 500–330 B.C.

A carved sandstone capital, c. 370 B.C., representing a bundle of papyrus reeds.

Silver Figurine of a Kneeling Bull Holding a Vessel. Elamite, c. 3000 B.C.

Gold, Silver, Shell, and Lapis Lazuli Statuette of a Ram in a Thicket. Sumerian, 2500 B.C.

Gold and Lapis Lazuli Lyre with Bull's Head. Sumerian, c. 2500 B.C.

Stone Head of Ur-Ningirsu, Son of Gudea of Lagash. Sumerian, c. 2100 B.C.

Gold Plaque with Animals and Stylized Trees in Relief. Persian, VII cent. B.C.

Bronze Bull, Symbol of Strength. Arabian, VI cent. B.C.

Ivory Screen of Four Winged Figures. Assyrian, VIII cent. B.C.

Geometric Horse, VIII cent. B.C. Greek art of this early period was angular, formal, and conventionalized.

Geometric Jar, VIII cent. B.C. Another example of the stylized decorative patterns of early Greek art.

Sphinx, c. 540–530 B.C. Though doubtless of Oriental derivation, Greek sphinxes had a softer and more human aspect than the Oriental.

Statue of an Amazon, one of the fabled tribe of women warriors, V cent. B.C. (Roman copy)

Departure of a Warrior. Gravestone, c. 530 B.C., a period when naturalism was the dominant note of Greek art.

Athena, c. 460 B.C. The young, graceful patron-goddess of Athens is about to send forth an owl as a sign of victory.

Jar, 500–490 B.C. The figures depicted in a fine black glaze on the natural red clay show athletes in the Panathenaic games.

Chorus of Satyrs, c. 420 B.C. The background is black with the figures in red clay. The satyrs, dressed in fleecy white, with flowing tails, are the chorus of a play.

Toilet Box, 465–460 B.C., showing the Judgment of Paris, an early incident in the Trojan War.

Bronze Mirror Case, V cent. B.C. Greek articles of everyday use were commonly finished with the same delicacy and precision as major works of art.

Diadoumenos, after Polykleitos, V cent. B.C. An idealized statue of a Greek athlete tying the "diadem," or band of victory, around his head.

Bracelet Pendant, IV–III cent. B.C. This tiny figure of the god Pan is a masterpiece of detail and expression.

Woman Arranging Her Hair, 400–300 B.C. Sculptors of antiquity took pride in these statuettes of ordinary people in ordinary activities, which were usually made of terra cotta painted soft blue, pink, or yellow.

Head of an Athlete, c. 440–420 B.C. The sculptor aimed to express manly beauty in perfect harmony with physical and intellectual excellence.

Statuette of Hermarchos, III cent. B.C. An example of the realism of Hellenistic sculpture.

Sleeping Eros, 250–150 B.C. Along with a penchant for realism, Hellenistic sculptors were fond of portraying serenity or repose.

Comic Actor, 200–100 B.C. Hellenistic realism often included portrayal of ugly and even deformed individuals.

Unidentified Man, I cent. B.C. The Romans excelled in portraits of sharp individuality.

Augustus, Reigned 31 B.C.–14 A.D. This portrait suggests the contradictory nature of the genius who gave Rome peace after years of strife.

Constantine, Reigned 306–337 A.D. The head is from a statue sixteen feet in height.

Mummy Portrait, II cent. A.D. A Roman woman buried in Egypt.

Mosaic, I cent. A.D. A floor design composed of small pieces of colored marble fitted together to form a picture.

Wall Painting of a Satyr Mask, I cent. B.C. The belief in satyrs, thought to inhabit forests and pastures, was taken over from the Greeks.

Architectural Wall Painting from a Pompeiian Villa. I cent. B.C., suggesting the Greek origin of Roman forms of architecture.

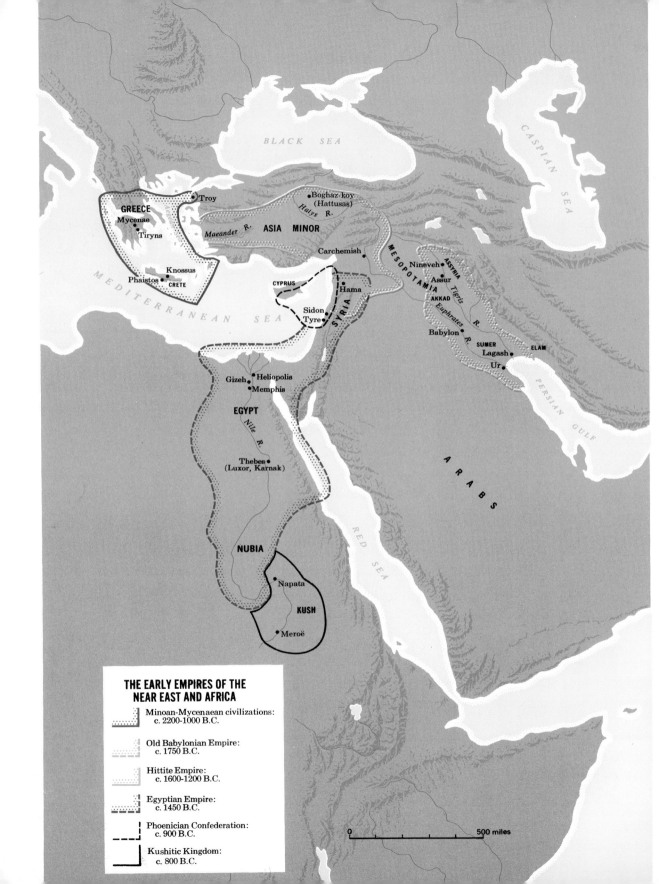

BLACK SEA

CASPIAN SEA

GREECE
• Troy
Mycenae •
Tiryns •

Maeander R. ASIA MINOR

• Boghaz-koy
(Hattusas)

Halys R.

MESOPOTAMIA

Nineveh • ASSYRIA
ASSUR
Assur •

Tigris R.

Carchemish •

Knossos •
Phaistos • CRETE

MEDITERRANEAN SEA

CYPRUS

SYRIA

Hama •

Sidon •
Tyre •

AKKAD

Euphrates R.

Babylon •

SUMER
Lagash •
Ur •

ELAM

PERSIAN GULF

Gizeh • • Heliopolis
• Memphis

EGYPT

Nile R.

Thebes •
(Luxor, Karnak)

A R A B S

RED SEA

NUBIA

• Napata

KUSH

• Meroë

**THE EARLY EMPIRES OF THE
NEAR EAST AND AFRICA**

Minoan-Mycenaean civilizations:
c. 2200-1000 B.C.

Old Babylonian Empire:
c. 1750 B.C.

Hittite Empire:
c. 1600-1200 B.C.

Egyptian Empire:
c. 1450 B.C.

Phoenician Confederation:
c. 900 B.C.

Kushitic Kingdom:
c. 800 B.C.

0   500 miles

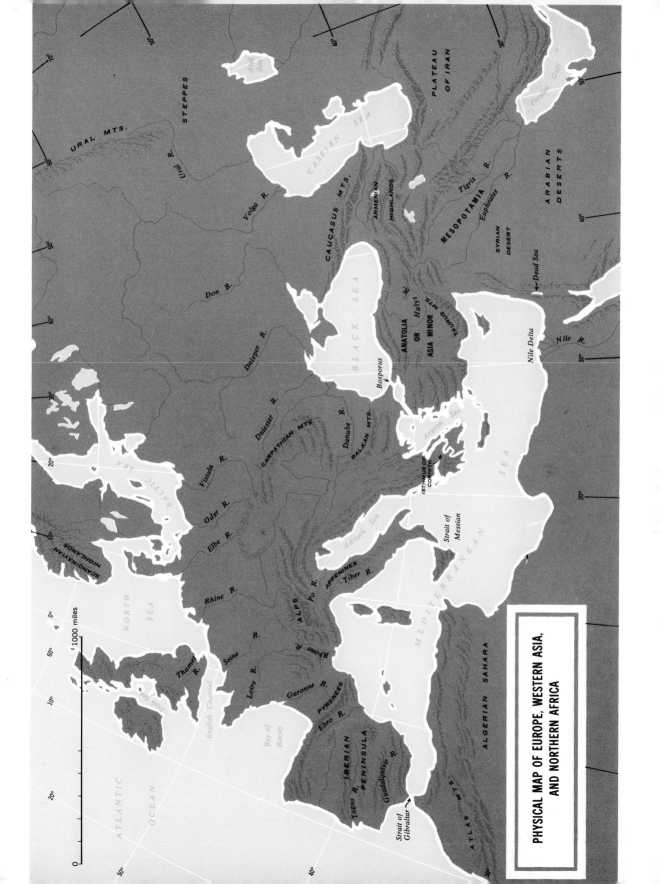

PHYSICAL MAP OF EUROPE, WESTERN ASIA,
AND NORTHERN AFRICA

ATLANTIC OCEAN

NORTH SEA

1000 miles

BALTIC SEA

Thames R.

English Channel

Irish Sea

Seine R.

Loire R.

Garonne R.

Bay of Biscay

PYRENEES

Ebro R.

IBERIAN PENINSULA

Tagus R.

Guadalquivir R.

Strait of Gibraltar

ATLAS MTS.

ALGERIAN SAHARA

SCANDINAVIAN HIGHLANDS

Rhine R.

Elbe R.

Oder R.

Vistula R.

ALPS

Po R.

APPENINES

Rhône R.

Tiber R.

Adriatic Sea

CARPATHIAN MTS.

Dniester R.

Dnieper R.

Danube R.

BALKAN MTS.

Strait of Messian

MEDITERRANEAN SEA

ISTHMUS OF CORINTH

Aegean Sea

Bosporus

BLACK SEA

CAUCASUS MTS.

Don R.

Volga R.

Ural R.

URAL MTS.

STEPPES

Aral Sea

CASPIAN SEA

ARMENIAN HIGHLANDS

ANATOLIA OR ASIA MINOR

Halys

TAURUS MTS.

MESOPOTAMIA

Tigris R.

Euphrates R.

SYRIAN DESERT

Dead Sea

Nile Delta

Nile R.

ARABIAN DESERTS

PLATEAU OF IRAN

Persian Gulf

0°

10°

20°

30°

40°

50°

60°

70°

0

50°

40°

30°

20°

10°

20°

30°

40°

50°

60°

70°

80°

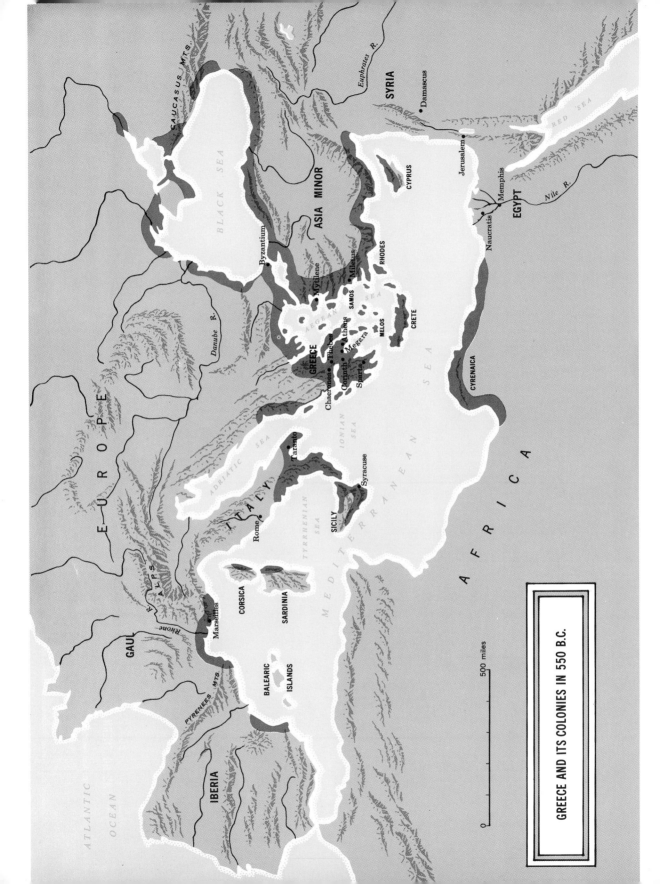

GREECE AND ITS COLONIES IN 550 B.C.

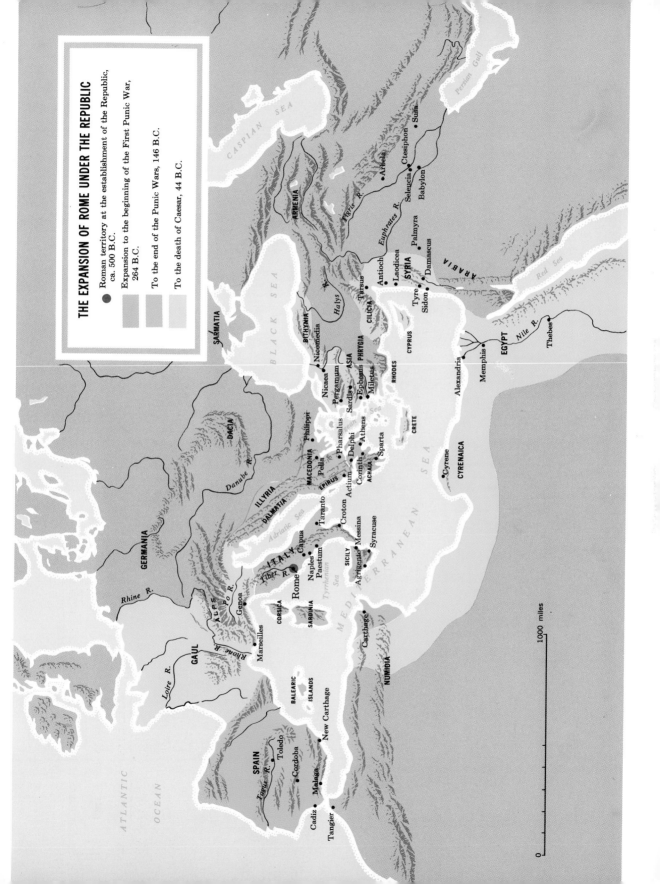

THE EXPANSION OF ROME UNDER THE REPUBLIC

- Roman territory at the establishment of the Republic, ca. 500 B.C.

Expansion to the beginning of the First Punic War, 264 B.C.

To the end of the Punic Wars, 146 B.C.

To the death of Caesar, 44 B.C.

SARMATIA

CASPIAN SEA

ARMENIA

Tigris R.

Arbela

Ctesiphon · Susa

Seleucia · Babylon

Euphrates R.

Palmyra

Antioch

Laodicea

SYRIA

Damascus

ARABIA

Tyre

Sidon

Red Sea

BLACK SEA

BITHYNIA

Nicomedia

Halys R.

Tarsus

CILICIA

Nicaea

Pergamum

PHRYGIA

ASIA

Sardis

Ephesus

Miletus

CYPRUS

RHODES

EGYPT

Nile R.

Thebes

Memphis

Alexandria

Philippi

MACEDONIA

Pella

Pharsalus

Aegean Sea

EPIRUS

Delphi

Athens

Corinth

ACHAIA

Sparta

CRETE

CYRENAICA

Cyrene

MEDITERRANEAN SEA

DACIA

R.

ILLYRIA

DALMATIA

Danube R.

Adriatic Sea

Taranto

Croton

Actium

GERMANIA

Capua

ITALY

Naples

Paestum

Rome

Tiber R.

Po R.

Genoa

ALPS

CORSICA

SARDINIA

Tyrrhenian Sea

Messina

Agrigento

SICILY

Syracuse

Carthage

NUMIDIA

Rhine R.

GAUL

Rhône R.

Marseilles

Loire R.

BALEARIC ISLANDS

New Carthage

SPAIN

Toledo

Tagus R.

Cordoba

Malaga

Cadiz

Tangier

ATLANTIC OCEAN

1000 miles

0

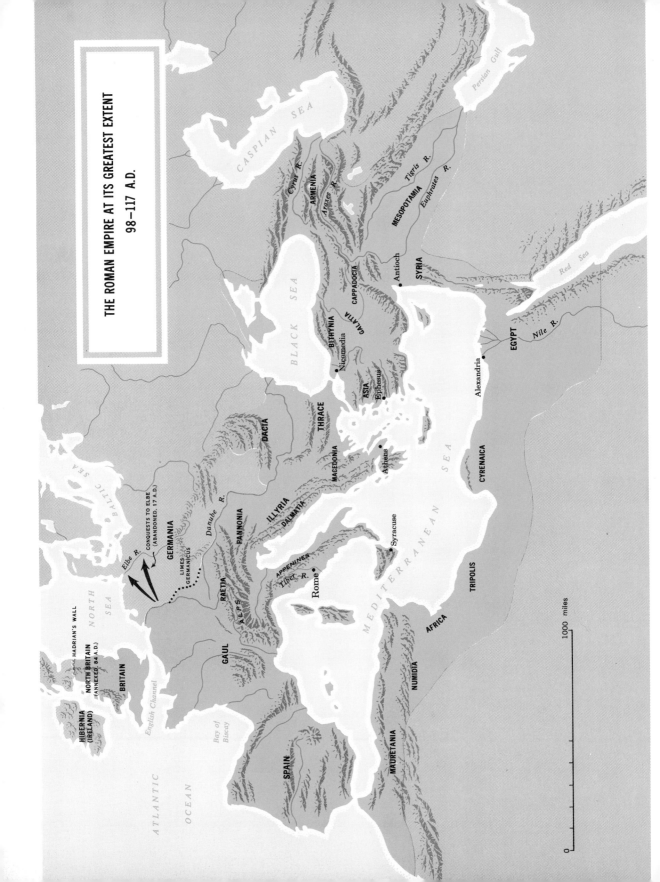

THE ROMAN EMPIRE AT ITS GREATEST EXTENT
98–117 A.D.

ATLANTIC OCEAN

HIBERNIA (IRELAND)

HADRIAN'S WALL

NORTH BRITAIN (ANNEXED 84 A.D.)

BRITAIN

BALTIC SEA

NORTH SEA

English Channel

Bay of Biscay

SPAIN

GAUL

Elbe R.

CONQUESTS TO ELBE (ABANDONED 17 A.D.)

GERMANICUS

GERMANIA

LIMES GERMANICUS

Danube R.

RAETIA

ALPS

APPENNINES

Tiber R.

Rome

PANNONIA

ILLYRIA

DALMATIA

DACIA

MACEDONIA

Athens

Syracuse

MEDITERRANEAN SEA

MAURETANIA

NUMIDIA

AFRICA

TRIPOLIS

CYRENAICA

BLACK SEA

THRACE

ASIA

Ephesus

BITHYNIA

Nicomedia

GALATIA

CAPPADOCIA

CASPIAN SEA

Cyrus R.

ARMENIA

Araxes R.

Tigris R.

Euphrates R.

MESOPOTAMIA

Antioch

SYRIA

Persian Gulf

Red Sea

EGYPT

Nile R.

Alexandria

1000 miles

0

him to do so. Luckily for him and for the world he accumulated a fortune in Russian business ventures and then retired to spend both time and money in the pursuit of his boyhood dreams. In 1870 he began excavating at Troy. Within a few years he had uncovered portions of nine different cities, each built upon the ruins of its predecessor. The second of these cities he identified as the Troy of the *Iliad,* although it has been proved since that Troy was the seventh city. After fulfilling his first great ambition, he started excavations on the mainland of Greece and eventually uncovered two other Aegean cities, Mycenae (pronounced My-sée-nee) and Tiryns. The work of Schliemann was soon followed by that of other investigators, notably the Englishman Sir Arthur Evans, who discovered Knossos, the resplendent capital of the Minoan kings of Crete. Up to the present time more than half of the ancient Aegean sites have been carefully searched, and a wealth of knowledge has been accumulated about various aspects of the culture.

The Minoan and Mycenaean civilizations originated on the island of Crete. (See the map on p. 185 below.) In few other cases in history does the geographic interpretation of culture origins fit so neatly. Crete has a benign and equable climate. While the soil is fertile, it is not of unlimited area; consequently, as the population increased, people were impelled to sharpen their wits and to contrive new means of earning a living. Some emigrated; others took to the sea; but a larger number remained at home and developed articles for export. The latter included wine and olive oil, pottery, gems and seals, knives and daggers, and objects of skilled craftsmanship. The chief imports were foodstuffs and metals. As a result of such trade, prosperity increased and extensive contacts were made with the surrounding civilized world. Added to these factors of a favorable environment were the beauties of nature which abounded almost everywhere, stimulating the development of a marvelous art.

The Minoan civilization, named after the legendary Cretan ruler

*The favorable natural
environment of Crete*

Central Staircase of the Palace at Knossos

Minos, was founded by peoples who emigrated from Asia Minor to
Crete around 3000 B.C. In the millennium thereafter they made the
transition from the Neolithic stage to the age of metals; by 2000 B.C.
they had developed cities and an early form of writing. From then
until about 1500 B.C. their civilization developed under the leadership
of the cities of Knossos and Phaistos. Recently evidence has been
found of the existence of another great city, Kato Zakros, on the east
coast of Crete. Here was a huge palace of 250 rooms, with a swimming pool, parquet floors, and thousands of decorated vases. Only
severe earthquakes, which periodically shook the island, interrupted
the serene existence of the sophisticated Cretans. These quakes caused
much devastation, but after each one the inhabitants of the Cretan cities set about the work of rebuilding and usually managed to construct
even more splendid palaces than the ones which had been destroyed.
So confident were the inhabitants of Knossos that they faced no threat
whatsoever of foreign invasion that they left their magnificent city
without any protective walls.

Ultimately such confidence proved to be mistaken. While Cretan
civilization was flourishing, a related one was emerging on the mainland of Greece. Around 1900 B.C. Indo-European peoples who spoke
the earliest form of Greek invaded the Greek peninsula, and by 1600
B.C. they were beginning to form settled communities. After around
1600 they became greatly influenced in their cultural development by
the neighboring civilization of Minoan Crete, with which they had
been developing trading relations. The civilization that resulted from
the fusion of Greek and Minoan elements is usually called *Mycenaean,*
after Mycenae, the leading city of Greece from about 1600 to 1200 B.C.
It was this civilization that became dominant in the Aegean world
after about 1500 and even gained predominance on the island of Crete
itself.

One of the greatest scholarly accomplishments of recent times has
radically altered our understanding of Cretan and Greek history in the
century between 1500 and 1400. It used to be thought that Greece
throughout that time was still a semibarbarous economic colony of
splendid Crete and that internal changes on Crete between 1500 and
1400 could be attributed to the rise of a "new dynasty." It was known
that numerous specimens of the same linear script (called "Linear B")
could be found on both Crete and the Greek mainland, but it was simply assumed that the script was Cretan in origin and spread from
Crete to Greece. But in 1952 a brilliant young Englishman, Michael
Ventris, who was then only thirty years old (and tragically died in an
automobile accident four years later), succeeded in deciphering Linear
B and demonstrating that it expressed an early form of Greek. Ventris's discovery revolutionized preclassical Greek studies by showing
that the mainlanders dominated Crete in the late Minoan period and
not vice versa.

A Linear B Tablet from Knossos

The new scholarly consensus is that the Mycenaeans supplanted the Minoans as rulers of the Aegean world sometime shortly after 1500 B.C. Around 1500 a great earthquake on Crete probably brought about sufficient weakness to allow the mainlanders to take control of the island. These Mycenaean Greeks helped to rebuild Knossos and presided over roughly a century of continued prosperity and artistic accomplishment on Crete. Around 1400, however, another wave of Greek invaders crossed over to the island, destroyed Knossos entirely, and put a cataclysmic end to the Minoan civilization. Why this invasion was so destructive cannot be known, but it left mainland Greece unrivaled as the center of civilization in the Aegean world for about another 200 years. Around 1250 B.C. the Mycenaeans waged their successful war with the Trojans of western Asia Minor, but their own demise was now in the offing. In the course of the century between 1200 B.C. and 1100 B.C., the Mycenaeans, whose civilization seems to have been decaying from within, succumbed to the Dorians—barbaric northern Greeks who had iron weapons. (Iron weapons may not at first have been much superior to the bronze ones used by the Mycenaeans, but they were far cheaper, thereby allowing many more fighters to wield them.) Because the Dorians were primitive in all but their weaponry their ascendancy initiated a dark age in Greek history which lasted until about 800 B.C.

The end of the Minoan and Mycenaean civilizations

As can be seen from the foregoing account, the Minoan and Mycenaean civilizations were closely interrelated; even the greatest experts have difficulty in determining exactly where one left off and the other began. The problem is complicated by the fact that two forms of writing which predate Linear B and have been found on Crete alone have not yet been deciphered. (Anyone who wishes to become as famous as Schliemann, Evans, or Ventris may take the decipherment of Cretan writing as his or her goal.) Accordingly, discussions of Minoan civilization before about 1500 B.C. rely exclusively on visual and archeological evidence, leaving much to the realm of speculation. Such evidence, however, does suggest that Cretan civilization was one of the freest and most progressive in all of early history.

The Minoan ruler was no bristling warlord like the Assyrian and Persian kings. He does seem to have commanded a large navy, but

Mycenaean Warrior Vase, c. 1250 B.C. Found in the ruins of Mycenae, this vase displays the warlike aspects of Mycenaean culture: the men might be marching off to the Trojan War.

Difficulty of distinguishing between early Minoan and Mycenaean characteristics

A Minoan Vase, c. 1400 B.C. The potter's wheel, probably invented by the Minoans, allowed a greater variety of shapes for vessels and encouraged Minoan artists to employ new styles and methods of decoration.

this was not for war but for the maintenance of trade. In fact, the king was the chief entrepreneur in the country. The workshops located in the environs of his palace turned out great quantities of fine pottery, textiles, and metal goods. Although private enterprise apparently was not prohibited it seems to have been heavily taxed. Nevertheless there were some privately owned workshops especially in smaller towns, and much agriculture was also in private hands.

The Cretan state is probably best described as a bureaucratic monarchy. The ruler of each leading city and its surrounding territory appears to have been absolute, and towards the end of Minoan history (exactly when is hard to say) the ruler of Knossos appears to have taken over the entire island. The absolute Cretan ruler governed by means of a large administrative class. Scribes, who seem to have had a monopoly of learning, kept close accounts of all aspects of economic life. All agricultural production and manufacturing was closely supervised for purposes of gathering or taxing whatever was owed to the king. Foreign trade too seems to have been closely supervised by the state; most likely the large Cretan ships that put into ports as far away as Syria and Egypt were owned or at least heavily taxed by the ruler and carefully watched over by the bureaucratic administration.

Evidences of social equality

Despite such close supervision, the Cretan people of nearly all classes appear to have led fairly prosperous lives. Although there were great social and economic distinctions between the rulers and the ruled, there were apparently few gradations of wealth or status among the common people. If slavery existed at all, it certainly occupied an unimportant place. The dwellings in the poorest quarters of smaller towns such as Gournia were substantially built and commodious, often with as many as six or eight rooms, but we do not know how many families resided in them. Women seem to have enjoyed equality with men. Regardless of class there was no public activity from which they were debarred, and no occupation which they could not enter. In this, the Minoans were the exception in the ancient world. Crete had female bullfighters and even female pugilists. Women of the upper strata devoted much time to fashion and other leisure activities.

The love of sports and games

The natives of Crete delighted in games and sports of every description. Dancing, running matches, and boxing rivaled each other in their attraction for the people. The Cretans were the first to build stone theaters where processions and music entertained large audiences.

The matriarchal nature of Minoan religion

So far as we know, Minoan religion was a medley of strange characteristics. First of all it was apparently matriarchal. The chief deity was not a god but a goddess, who was the ruler of the entire universe—the sea and the sky as well as the earth. Originally no male deity appears to have been worshiped, but later a god was associated with the goddess as her son and consort. Although, like the divine sons in several other religions, he apparently died and rose from the dead, he was

Scenes from the Bull Ring: Minoan Mural, c. 1500 B.C. Evident are the youth, skill, and agility of the Cretan athletes, the center one a male, the other two female. The body and horns of the bull are exaggerated, as are the slenderness of the athletes and their full-face eyes in profile heads. There is probably also some exaggeration in content: modern experts in bull-fighting insist that it is impossible to somersault over the back of a charging bull.

never regarded by the Cretans as of particular importance. In the second place, the Minoan religion was thoroughly monistic. The mother goddess was the source of evil as well as of good, but not in any morbid or terrifying sense. Though she brought the storm and spread destruction in her path, these served for the replenishment of nature. Death itself was interpreted as the prerequisite for life. Whether the religion had any body of ethical precepts is unknown.

Other features of the religion of the Minoans included the worship of animals and birds (the bull, the snake, and the dove); the worship of sacred trees; the veneration of sacred objects which were probably reproductive symbols (the double-axe, the pillar, and the cross); and, in accordance with the matriarchal nature of the belief system, the employment of priestesses instead of priests to administer sacred rites.

Since we cannot yet decipher the early Cretan scripts it is impossible to tell whether the Minoans had any literature or philosophy, although the existence of either seems extremely unlikely because there is none written in Linear B. The problem of scientific achievements is easier to solve, since we have material remains for our guidance. Archeological discoveries on the island of Crete indicate that the ancient inhabitants were gifted inventors and engineers. They built excellent roads of concrete about eleven feet wide. Nearly all the basic principles of modern sanitary engineering were known to the designers of the palace of Knossos, with the result that the royal family of Crete in the seventeenth century B.C. enjoyed comforts and conveniences, such as indoor running water, that were not available to the wealthiest rulers of Western countries in the seventeenth century A.D.

If there was any one achievement of the Minoans that appears more

Minoan Snake Goddess, Sixteenth Century B.C. A statuette made of ivory and gold.

than others to emphasize the vitality and freedom of their culture, it was their art. With the exception of the classical Greek, no other art of the ancient world was quite its equal. Its distinguishing features were delicacy, spontaneity, and naturalism. It served not to glorify the ambitions of an arrogant ruling class or to inculcate the doctrines of a religion, but to express the delight of the individual in the beauty and splendor of the Minoan world. As a result, it was remarkably free from the retarding influence of ancient tradition. It was unique, moreover, in the universality of its application, for it extended not merely to paintings and statues but even to the humblest objects of ordinary use.

Of the major arts, architecture was the least developed. The great palaces were not remarkably beautiful buildings but rambling structures designed primarily for capaciousness and comfort. As more and more functions were absorbed by the state, the palaces were enlarged to accommodate them. New quarters were annexed to those already built or piled on top of them without regard for order or symmetry. The interiors, however, were decorated with beautiful paintings and furnishings. The architecture of Crete may be said to have resembled the modern international style in its subordination of form to utility and in its emphasis upon a pleasing and livable interior as more important than external beauty.

Painting was the supreme Cretan art. Nearly all of it consisted of murals done in fresco, although painted reliefs were occasionally to be found. The murals in the palaces of Crete were by all odds the best that have survived from ancient times. They revealed almost perfectly the remarkable gifts of the Minoan artist—an instinct for the dramatic, a sense of rhythm, a feeling for nature in its most characteristic moods. So sophisticated and elegant was Cretan art that a Frenchman who was unearthing the remains of a fresco at Knossos could not help exclaiming when he saw a painting of a striking woman portrayed with curls, vivid eyes, and sensuous lips: "Mais, c'est la Parisienne!" ("Why, she's just like a woman from Paris!").

"La Parisienne"

Sculpture and the ceramic and gem-carving arts were also developed to a high stage of perfection. The sculpture of the Cretans differed from that of any other people in the ancient Near East. It never relied upon size as a device to convey the idea of power. The Cretans produced no colossi like those of Egypt or reliefs like those of Babylonia depicting a king of gigantic proportions smiting his puny enemies. Instead, they preferred sculpture in miniature. Nearly all of the statues of human beings or of deities that the archeologists have found are smaller than life-size.

Mycenaean civilization appears to have been more warlike and less refined than the Minoan, but the most recent scholarship warns us to beware of exaggerating these differences. As on Crete, so on mainland Greece, the city was the center of civilization—the leading Mycenaean cities being Mycenae itself (according to Homer the home of the leading Greek king Agamemnon), Pylos (according to Homer the home of the wise Nestor), and Tiryns. Each city and its surrounding area was ruled over by a king called a *wanax*, who in many respects ruled like an oriental despot. As on Crete, the Mycenaean state was a bureaucratic monarchy. We know for certain about some of the workings of this monarchy because of the decipherment of numerous Linear B tablets, all of which are records of a highly regulatory bureaucratic apparatus. Linear B tablets from Pylos report the minutest details of the economic lives of the king's subjects: the exact acreage of a given estate; the number of cooking utensils owned by so-and-so; the personal names given to somebody else's two oxen ("Glossy" and "Blackie"). Such detailed inventories show us that the state was highly centralized and that it was as supreme in its control over the economic activities of its citizens as any other in the Near East.

Although the bureaucratic monarchies of Crete and Mycenaean Greece were probably similar, there were still at least a few notable differences between the two related civilizations. One was that the Mycenaeans definitely had a slave system and another was that they did not award equal status to women. Mycenaean society too was geared much more greatly toward warfare. Because Mycenaean cities were frequently at war with one another they were built on hilltops and heavily fortified. In keeping with a somewhat more rugged and barbaric style of life than that which obtained on Crete, Mycenaean kings built themselves ostentatious graves in which they buried their best inlaid bronze daggers and other signs of their power and wealth.

It is also true that Mycenaean art is less elegant than Minoan. Without question the Mycenaeans never equaled the artistic delicacy and grace of their Minoan predecessors. Nevertheless, Mycenaean artwork done in Knossos between 1500 and 1400 B.C., while stiffer and more symmetrical in composition than earlier Minoan work, is by no means wholly different in kind. Moreover, the "Parisian woman" of Minoan Knossos has some very close stylistic relatives in a female procession fresco from about 1300 B.C. found in Mycenaean Tiryns. Nor should it be thought that all the best traits of Mycenaean art can merely be seen as debased borrowings from the Minoans: the superbly executed and exquisite Mycenaean inlaid daggers have no antecedents anywhere on Crete.

The significance of the Minoan and the Mycenaean civilizations should not be estimated primarily in terms of subsequent influences. Minoan culture hardly influenced any peoples other than the Mycenaeans and it was then destroyed more or less without a trace after about 1400 B.C. The Mycenaeans left behind a few more traces, but still not very many. Later Greeks retained some Mycenaean gods and goddesses like Zeus, Hera, Hermes, and Poseidon, but they com-

Detail from a Procession Fresco at Tiryns, c. 1300 B.C. Note the similarity of this Mycenaean female profile to the Minoan "La Parisienne" shown on p. 102.

pletely altered their role in the religious pantheon. It may also be that the later Greeks gained from the Mycenaeans their devotion to athletics and their system of weights and measures, but these connections remain uncertain. Homer definitely remembered the successful Mycenaean siege of Troy, but it is just as important to realize how much Homer forgot: writing in the eighth century B.C. Homer (actually several different writers who have come down to us under that name) entirely forgot the whole pattern of Mycenaean bureacratic monarchy which we know from the Linear B tablets. It may well be that the break between the Mycenaeans and Homer was all for the good. Some historians maintain that the destruction of despotic Mycenae by the Dorians was a necessary prelude to the emergence of the freer and more enlightened later Greek outlook.

*Importance of the Minoan
and Mycenaean
civilizations*

Although the Minoan and Mycenaean civilizations had little subsequent influence, they are still noteworthy for at least four reasons. First of all, they were the earliest civilizations of Europe. Before the Cretan accomplishments all civilizations had existed further east, but afterwards Europe was to witness the development of one highly impressive civilization after another. Secondly, in some respects the Minoans and the Mycenaeans seem to have looked forward to certain later European values and accomplishments even if they did not directly influence them. Minoan and Mycenaean political organization was similar to that of many Asian states but Minoan art in particular seems very different and more characteristic of later European patterns. Unlike most ancient Near-Eastern artists, the Minoan gloried not in portraying the slaughter of armies or the sacking of cities but in picturing flowery landscapes, joyous festivals, thrilling exhibitions of athletic prowess, and similar scenes of a free and peaceful existence. Thirdly, the Minoan civilization, and to a lesser degree also the Mycenaean one, is significant for its worldly and progressive outlook. This is exemplified in the devotion of the Aegean peoples to comfort and opulence, in their love of amusement, zest for life, and courage for experimentation. And finally, the Minoan civilization is particularly remarkable for having flourished so long in peace. If there has never again been as peaceful a civilization as the Minoan then that is a fact we should not celebrate but deplore.

3. THE LYDIANS AND THE PHOENICIANS

The Kingdom of Lydia

After the last remnants of the Hittite Empire fell in the eighth century B.C., one of the successor states in Asia Minor was the Kingdom of Lydia. The Lydians established their rule in what is now the western part of Turkey. They quickly secured control of the Greek cities on the coast of Asia Minor and of the entire plateau west of the Halys River. But their power was short-lived. In 547 B.C. their king, Croesus, fancied he saw a good opportunity to add to his domain the territory of the Medes east of the Halys. The Median king had just been deposed by Cyrus the Great of Persia. Thinking this meant an easy triumph for his own armies, Croesus set out to capture the territory beyond the river. After an indecisive battle with Cyrus, he returned to his own capital (Sardis) for reinforcements. Here Cyrus caught him unprepared in a surprise attack and captured and burned the city. The Lydians never recovered from the blow, and soon afterward all of their territory, including the Greek cities on the coast, passed under the dominion of Cyrus.

The Lydian people and their culture

The Lydians were a people of Indo-European speech, who were probably a mixture of native peoples of Asia Minor with migrant stocks from eastern Europe. Benefiting from the advantages of favorable location and abundance of resources, they enjoyed one of the highest standards of living of ancient times. They were famous for the splendor of their armored chariots and the quantities of gold and articles of luxury possessed by the citizens. The wealth of their kings was legendary, as attested by the simile "rich as Croesus." The chief sources of this prosperity were gold from the streams, wool from the thousands of sheep on the hills, and the profits of the extensive commerce which passed overland from the Tigris-Euphrates valley to the Aegean Sea. But with all their wealth and opportunities for leisure, they succeeded in making only one original contribution to civilization. This was the coinage of money from electrum or "white gold," a natural mixture of gold and silver found in the sands of one of their rivers. Hitherto all systems of money had consisted of weighed rings or bars of metal. The new coins, of varying sizes, were stamped with a definite value more or less arbitrarily given by the ruler who issued them.

The Phoenician cities and confederation

In contrast with the Lydians, who gained their ascendancy as a result of the downfall of the Hittites, were the Phoenicians, who benefited from the break-up of Aegean supremacy. But the Phoenicians were neither conquerors nor the builders of an empire. They exerted their influence through the arts of peace, especially through commerce. During most of their history their political system was a loose confederation of city-states, which frequently bought their security by paying tribute to foreign powers. The territory they occupied was the narrow strip north of Palestine between the Lebanon Mountains and the Mediterranean Sea and the islands off the coast. With good harbors and a central location, it was admirably situated for trade. The great centers of commerce included Tyre and Sidon. Under the leadership of Tyre, Phoenicia reached the zenith of its accomplishments from the tenth to the eighth century B.C. During the sixth century it passed under the domination of the Chaldeans and then of the Persians. In

*An Early Lydian Coin, Probably
Struck During the Reign of
Croesus*

332 B.C. Tyre was destroyed by Alexander the Great after a siege of seven months.

The Phoenicians were a people of Semitic language, closely related to the Canaanites. They displayed very little creative genius, but were remarkable adapters of the achievements of others. They produced no original art worthy of the name, and they made but slight contributions to literature. Their religion, like that of the Canaanites, was characterized by human sacrifice to the god Moloch and by licentious fertility rites. They excelled, however, in specialized manufactures, in geography and navigation. They founded colonies at Carthage and Utica in North Africa, near modern-day Palermo on the island of Sicily, on the Balearic Islands, and at Cadiz and Malaga in Spain. They were renowned throughout the ancient world for their glass and metal industries and for their purple dye obtained from a mollusk in the adjacent seas. They developed the art of navigation to such a stage that they could sail by the stars at night. To less venturesome peoples, the North Star was known for some time as the Phoenicians' star. Phoenician ships and sailors were recruited by all the great powers. The most lasting achievement of the Phoenicians, however, was the completion and diffusion of an alphabet based upon principles discovered by the Egyptians. The Phoenician contribution was the adoption of a system of signs representing the sounds of the human voice, and the elimination of all pictographic and syllabic characters. This alphabet was taken up by the Greeks, who adapted it for their own language.

4. LESSONS FROM THE HISTORY OF THE NEAR-EASTERN STATES

Like most other periods in world history, the period of the states we have studied thus far was an era of contention and strife. Nearly all of the great empires, and the majority of the smaller states as well, devoted their energies most of the time to policies of expansion and aggression. The only notable exceptions were the Minoan and Egyptian, but even the Egyptians, in the later period of their history, yielded to no one in their addiction to imperialism. The causes were largely geographic. Each nation grew accustomed to the pursuit of its own interests in some fertile river valley or on some easily defended plateau. Isolation bred fear of foreigners and an incapacity to think of one's own people as members of a common humanity. The feelings of insecurity that resulted seemed to justify aggressive foreign policies and the annexation of neighboring states to serve as buffers against a hostile world.

It seems possible to trace nearly all of the woes of the Near-Eastern nations to wars of aggression and imperialist greed. Arnold J. Toynbee has shown this in devastating fashion in the case of the Assyrians. He contends that it was no less true of such later peoples as the Spartans, the Carthaginians, the Macedonians, and the Ottoman Turks. Each made militarism and conquest its gods and wrought such destruction upon itself that when it made its last heroic stand against its enemies, it was a mere "corpse in armor." Not death by foreign conquest but national suicide was the fate which befell it.[1] The way of the warrior brought racism, a love of ease and luxury, crime and racketeering, and crushing burdens of taxation. Expansion of empire promoted a fictitious prosperity, at least for the upper classes, and aroused enough envy among poorer nations to make them willing conspirators against a rich neighbor who could easily be portrayed as an oppressor. The use of hungry and discontented allies against powerful rivals is not new in history.

Results of Near-Eastern imperialism

SELECTED READINGS

• *Items so designated are available in paperback editions.*

Alsop, Joseph, *From the Silent Earth: A Report on the Greek Bronze Age,* New York, 1964. An enthusiastic account by a modern political reporter of some of the most exciting recent discoveries and hypotheses. Favors the Mycenaeans in discussions of their relationships to the Minoans.

Blegen, C. W., *Troy and the Trojans,* New York, 1963. The most reliable archeological appraisal.

Ceram, C. W., *The Secret of the Hittites,* New York, 1956. The best popular account.

• Chadwick, John, *The Decipherment of Linear B,* 2nd ed., New York, 1968. Chadwick was a research colleague of Michael Ventris and here gives the most accessible account of Ventris's brilliant work.

• ———, *The Mycenaean World,* New York, 1976.

• Gordon, Cyrus H., *The Ancient Near East,* New York, 1965.

• ———, *The Common Background of Greek and Hebrew Civilizations,* New York, 1965. Very controversial. Gordon believes that Greek culture was in its origins Semitic.

Gurney, O. R., *The Hittites,* Baltimore, 1961. More scholarly than Ceram.

Harden, Donald, *The Phoenicians,* New York, 1962. Best account of the Phoenicians at home and abroad.

Higgins, Reynold, *Minoan and Mycenaean Art,* New York, 1967.

History of the Hellenic World, Vol. I, *Prehistory and Protohistory,* University Park, Pa., 1974.

Hutchinson, R. W., *Prehistoric Crete,* Baltimore, 1962.

Lloyd, Seton, *Early Anatolia,* Baltimore, 1956.

• MacDonald, William A., *Progress into the Past: The Rediscovery of Mycenaean Civilization,* New York, 1967.

[1] D. C. Somervell (ed.), A. J. Toynbee's *A Study of History,* I, 338–43.

Palmer, L. R., *Mycenaeans and Minoans,* New York, 1962. Includes bold statements on many debatable problems of interpretation.

• Pendlebury, J. D. S., *The Archaeology of Crete,* New York, 1939.

• Vermeule, Emily, *Greece in the Bronze Age,* Chicago, 1964. The best book on the subject.

Chapter 6

ANCIENT INDIAN CIVILIZATION

Hinduism does not distinguish ideas of God as true and false, adopting
one particular idea as the standard for the whole human race. It accepts
the obvious fact that mankind seeks its goal of God at various levels and
in various directions, and feels sympathy with every stage of the search.

—S. Radhakrishnan, *The Hindu View of Life*

The subcontinent of India has an area slightly more than half
that of the United States and is inhabited by more than three
times as many people. Not only is India a vast and densely
populated region but it includes many different levels of culture, different religions, languages, and economic conditions, and its history
is extremely complex. Five or six separate families of languages are
represented among its people. The population contains admixtures of
all of the three great races of mankind—black, yellow, and white—in
various combinations and proportions. One of the most ancient peoples, a Negrito strain related to the Pygmies of Africa, has almost
disappeared from India but is still found in the Andaman Islands to
the east. In striking contrast to this type are the fair-skinned Mediter-
raneans of the north and northwest, descendants of the Indo-Aryans
who invaded the country some 3,500 years ago. The most widespread
group in southern India is that known as Dravidian, but because the
term is applied to all whose language belongs to the Dravidian family,
it no longer denotes a single ethnic stock. Another type, perhaps more
ancient than the Dravidians, is called Australoid, because of its relationship with primitive peoples extending over parts of southeastern
Asia and as far east as Australia. The Mongolian element is confined
chiefly to the border region of the north and northeast. Alpine types
are found along the western coast, sometimes with a slight Nordic
admixture (evidenced by gray or blue eyes). Thus the common practice of referring to the natives of India as "colored" or "brown-
skinned" is misleading. Their skins are indeed of various shades, but

The peoples of India

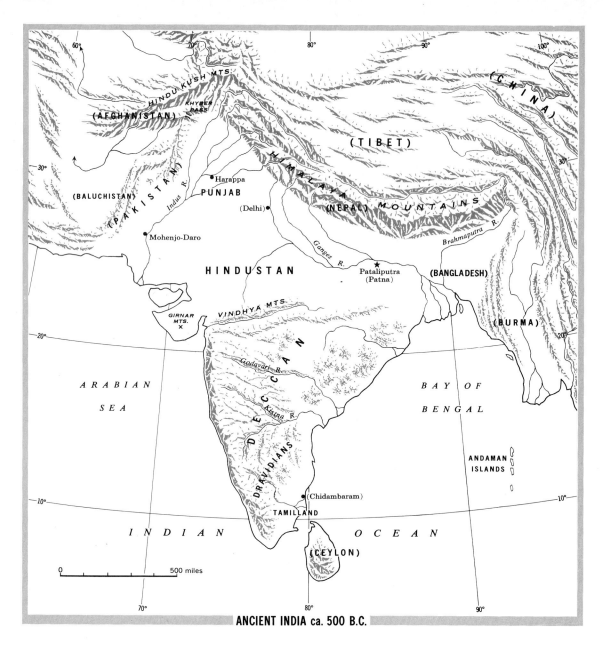

ANCIENT INDIA ca. 500 B.C.

since early times white stocks have been conspicuously present, especially in northern India. Even today some of the most typical examples of the tall variety of the Mediterranean white race can be seen in the Punjab and the northwest frontier. Yet they exist in close proximity to people who reveal Alpine, Australoid, Mongoloid, or Negrito features. Over the course of centuries, and in spite of the inexorable segregation of the caste system in historic times, India has been a human melting pot.

Geographically India falls into two main divisions. The southern triangle or peninsular portion, known as the Deccan, lies entirely within the tropics. The northern or continental half, also triangular in shape, is in the same latitudes as Mexico and the southern United States and has temperatures ranging from tropical heat to the intense cold of the northern mountain peaks. The northern Deccan is semi-mountainous and heavily forested, and shelters some of the primitive hill tribes whose ancestors were crowded into the wilderness by the pressure of expansion from more civilized communities. The greater part of the peninsula, however, is a gently sloping plateau, traversed by rivers, and containing rich agricultural lands. The northern half of India, called Hindustan, is bounded on the north by the lofty Himalayan range and is separated from the Deccan by the low-lying Vindhya Mountains. Most of Hindustan is a level plain comprising an area about as large as France, Germany, and Italy combined, drained by the great river systems of the Indus and the Ganges. The rivers of Hindustan take their rise in the Himalayas or beyond and are fed by snows and glaciers. The Indus and the Brahmaputra each originate in Tibet and flow in opposite directions around the mountain ranges until they turn south into India, bringing with them virgin soil from the highlands which is deposited on the plain. The gently flowing Ganges, less subject to floods than the Indus, is the most beneficent of all. Referred to as "Mother Ganges," it has long been the sacred river of the Hindus. It is no wonder that its central valley, where every inch of soil is productive and no stone even the size of a pebble can be found, is one of the most densely populated spots in the world. The

The Srinagar Valley. Low-lying areas are regularly inundated by the floodwaters of the Jhelum River, a tributary of the Indus River in northwestern India. The floodwaters leave rich soil in their wake.

mouths of the Ganges (in Bengal) are surrounded by forbidding jungle, and a desert separates the lower Indus valley from the Ganges and its tributaries; but the Indo-Gangetic region as a whole is lavishly endowed by nature. Here the most influential centers of Indian civilization have been located.

India a geographic unit

All India enjoys the advantage of the monsoon rains, and the greater part of the country is suitable for cultivation. Moreover, there is no impenetrable barrier between Hindustan and the Deccan and there has always been communication between the two sections. In spite of its size and contrasting terrain, India is a natural geographic unit. That its peoples have been united politically only during relatively brief periods of their history is attributable to many factors, including disturbances from without, but it cannot be ascribed to geographic necessity.

1. THE VEDIC AGE IN INDIA

The earliest civilization of India

Remains of Neolithic and of early metal-age cultures have been discovered both in Hindustan and the Deccan. The first highly advanced civilization began its history as early as 3000 B.C. and reached its peak between 2500 and 2000 B.C. It covered a large area extending 1000 miles through the Indus valley and along the coast of the Arabian Sea both to the east and west of the mouth of the Indus. It was essentially an urban civilization, with a cosmopolitan society and extensive trade with the outside world. Among some 70 metropolitan centers thus far uncovered, the two principal sites are Mohenjo-Daro, about 300 miles from the seacoast, and Harappa, about 400 miles farther up the river.

Excavations at Harappa. These digs have provided the means of reconstructing the urban civilization of the Indus Valley between 3000 B.C. and 2000 B.C. Note the extensive use of brick in the buildings of the period.

Skeletons at Mohenjo-Daro. Although the downfall of this culture is a mystery, barbarian conquest was an important factor.

Both were durably constructed of brick and laid out in accordance with ambitious and intelligent planning. Private houses were solidly built and equipped with bathrooms which drained into sewer pipes running underneath the principal streets and discharging into the river. Evidences of intellectual achievement are scanty, although proofs are available that standards of weight and measurement and a system of writing had been developed. The writing, which has not yet been deciphered, is in the form of pictographic signs on delicately carved stone seals. A group of Scandinavian scholars who are studying it believe that the language of the Indus valley inscriptions can be classified as Proto-Dravidian. Several of the arts reflected a high degree of skill, especially the fabrication of small objects for personal adornment. Some examples of sculpture, also, indicate a talent for grace and naturalness. The religion of this early civilization centered upon the worship of fertility deities, notably a mother goddess. The principal rite was animal sacrifice.

Archeological evidence supports the conclusion that the Indus valley civilization was one of the earliest in the world and that it was comparable in level of achievement to those of contemporary Egypt and Mesopotamia. Whether it was indigenous to India or was introduced by settlers from the west is still a matter of speculation. It long maintained intercourse with other civilized regions, especially Mesopotamia, where Indus-type stone seals and other objects belonging to the period about 2300–2000 B.C. have been discovered. For reasons not entirely clear, the Indus valley civilization decayed and disappeared from the scene of history about 1600 B.C. Probably a major cause was a series of floods and earthquakes which altered the course of the Indus River and inundated densely inhabited cities. Whatever

Bull Seal. Impression of stone seal from Mohenjo-Daro, 2500 B.C., probably used as a signature. The animal figure (of a Brahmani bull or zebu) is assumed to have had religious significance.

Dyers' Troughs or Drains Uncovered at Mohenjo-Daro.

Unicorn Seal. The "unicorn" (perhaps actually the profile of an ox) is the animal most frequently depicted on the Indus civilization seals. The object under the animal's head may represent a brazier or incense holder. The inscription has not been deciphered. This specimen was found in the Deccan, some 600 miles from the Indus Valley.

the causes, the civilization went down to so complete an oblivion that no one was aware of its existence until evidences were unearthed by archeologists about sixty years ago. Shortly before the downfall of the Indus valley cities, India was invaded by seminomadic tribes who were destined to be the founders of a more enduring civilization. These were the so-called Aryans,[1] or Indo-Aryans, who came in by way of Afghanistan through the passes of the Hindu Kush Mountains. For many centuries the Aryan influence was confined to northern India, and here it developed the distinctive Hindu pattern of society, culture, and religion. Though the Aryan (Indo-European) languages never became dominant in the south, they are the most widely spoken group of languages in India today.

For some 1,000 years following the Indo-Aryan invasions the political history of India is largely unknown. There is no reason to assume a wholesale displacement of population. As the invading tribes extended their sway over northern India they intermingled with the inhabitants of the conquered regions. The process of assimilation between conquerors and conquered affected the culture of the invaders to a degree that cannot be clearly determined but which undoubtedly was profound, especially in the development of religion and social structure. The absence of reliable historical records for such a long period of time, among people who achieved a variegated, colorful, and highly intellectual civilization, is extraordinary. The scarcity of historical information is not entirely accidental, although it is partly

[1] "Aryan" was the name by which these invaders identified themselves. The theory of a distinctive Aryan race, expounded from time to time by various propagandists, has been exploded. In current usage the term "Aryan" is properly applied only to a family of related languages (the Indo-European group).

accounted for by the fact that the Indo-Aryans had no system of writing until about 1,000 years after their settlement in India. A more potent cause was the character of their civilization itself and especially of their philosophy, which stressed the importance of timeless qualities and the relative insignificance of temporal events and conditions. When they looked back to the past, they were inclined to give free scope to their imagination and to reckon in terms of vast eras and aeons, symmetrical but fantastic, extending to millions or even billions of years. The failure to produce factual chronicles does not mean that no changes or exciting events occurred. On the contrary, the available evidence suggests the normal amount of conflict, turmoil, and upheaval.

The sources of information for early Indo-Aryan civilization are almost exclusively in literary tradition. The oldest literary monument is the collection of religious poems and hymns called the *Vedas*. No one knows when they were composed. The oldest portions may have originated as early as 3000 B.C., and they were passed on orally without any written aids whatsoever until several centuries after the collection was complete. The *Vedas* reflect the culture of the primitive Aryan communities in the upper Indus valley and the "Middle Land" between the two rivers, or roughly the period from 2000 to 800 B.C., which is accordingly called the Vedic age. The latter portion of the *Vedas*, however, shows that profound changes had taken place during these centuries. The second major literary landmark consists of two long epic poems, the *Ramayana* and the *Mahabharata*. Like the *Vedas*, and in spite of their tremendous bulk, the epics were preserved by memory and oral repetition for many generations, but they reflect a different set of conditions, customs, and beliefs from those most typical of the *Vedas*. The epics reveal that by the close of the Vedic age Indo-Aryan culture had been transformed into a complex and stratified social and religious system. It had become Hinduism.

In the early Vedic period the Indo-Aryan tribes had a simple, largely pastoral economy. They cultivated barley and probably other grains, using a wooden plow drawn by bullocks. They ate the flesh of sheep, goats, and oxen, usually at the time of sacrificing these animals to the gods, but their favorite foods were dairy products—milk, cream, and ghee (melted butter). Cattle were the most prized possessions and served as a medium of exchange. Apparently they were not yet worshiped, nor was their slaughter forbidden. Domesticated animals also included the horse, used to pull the war chariot and also for chariot racing. All the common handicrafts, including metal work, were practiced. Music, both vocal and instrumental—with flutes, drums, cymbals, and stringed lutes or harps—was a popular source of entertainment, as was dancing. Gambling with dice was a national pastime and seems to have come close to being a national obsession.

In its typical features this early Indian society was vigorous and uninhibited, its members delighting in song and dance, in feasting,

Scantiness of the early records

Vedas and epics

Dancing Girl. Bronze statuette of a female dancer, from Mohenjo-Daro, a striking example of the art of the ancient Indus civilization. Bracelets and bangles have retained their popularity among the women of India to the present day.

carousing, and feats of strength. Warfare was frequent, and many stories have been preserved of the incredible powers of strong-armed heroes. The social unit was the patriarchal family, in which woman's position was inferior, although considerably freer than in later Indian society. Women were not permitted to participate in religious sacrifice and only sons could inherit property. Polygamy was permissible, but such later Hindu institutions as the immolation of a widow upon her husband's funeral pyre (suttee) and child marriage were completely unknown.

Political institutions

As might be expected, political and legal institutions were rudimentary among the primitive Aryans. Each tribe had its king (raja), whose chief function was to lead his warriors in battle. Associated with the king in ruling was an assembly. Its composition and duties are not at all clear, but its existence suggests a limitation upon the royal authority. Some of the tribes were organized as aristocratic republics rather than hereditary monarchies, with government resting with the heads of the clans or an elected raja. In the early days the raja's powers could hardly have been awe-inspiring in any case. He had no populous cities from which to extract riches, only country villages; and the villages managed their own internal affairs, paying part of their produce to the raja for "protection." The handling of crime and punishment followed patterns similar to those of many other primitive societies. The injured party or his family was expected to take the initiative in prosecuting an offender. Compensation for injuries was usually a payment in money or commodities to the plaintiff or, in the case of murder, to the victim's family. Theft was the most frequent complaint, especially cattle stealing, even though this crime was looked upon as highly reprehensible. An insolvent debtor—usually one who had gambled too recklessly—might be enslaved to his creditor.

The Vedas *as literature*

The most significant achievement of the Vedic age was the composition of the poetry and prose which give the period its name. Ultimately there were four *Vedas,* each containing a large collection of prayers, chants, or hymns, supplemented by prose commentary. The literal meaning of *Veda* is "knowledge" or "wisdom," and the entire collection was believed to have been imparted to ancient seers by the gods rather than invented by men. The *Vedas* constitute the canonical books of the Indo-Aryan—and of the later Hindu—religion; they were considered divinely inspired and uniquely sacred, as were the Hebrew and Christian Scriptures by the members of those faiths. However, because the early Aryans were illiterate, their sacred books were said to have been "heard" rather than "revealed." The *Vedas* cover an amazing variety and range of subjects. Some portions are litanies intended to be chanted by priests during a sacrifice. Others are catalogues of spells and charms, including alleged remedies for fever and snake bite, love formulas, and recipes for exterminating one's enemies. Still others incorporate customs and folklore or display a profound insight into philosophical or religious truth. Although much of the content of the *Vedas* is repetitious and monotonous, in vividness and imagination the best verses deserve to rank with the *Iliad* of Homer.

The religion of the early Aryans as illustrated in the *Vedas* was a comprehensive polytheism, with little ethical significance. Their gods—*deva,* or "shining ones"—were the forces of nature or personifications of these forces. No images or temples were erected, and worship consisted chiefly in performing sacrifices to the gods. Grain and milk were sacrificed, animal flesh was burned upon the altars (the worshipers themselves eating the flesh), but the choicest offering was *soma,* an alcoholic or psychedelic beverage fermented from the juice of a mountain plant. The gods were looked upon in much the same way as the Olympian deities were regarded by the Greeks. They were conceived as splendid and powerful creatures, with human attributes but immortal as long as they drank the *soma* juice, and, on the whole, benevolent. It was assumed that they would reward men out of gratitude for the homage and gifts presented to them. Gradually, however, the insidious notion took root that if the holy rites were conducted with unfailing accuracy they would compel the god to obedience, whether he was willing or not. It is easy to see how such an interpretation would enhance the prestige and authority of the priests who controlled the wonder-working formulas.

The roster of gods was a large one and tended to increase. While several deities can be identified with those of other Indo-European peoples, they did not have as clear-cut personalities as the Greek or Norse gods. The Indian mind ran toward specialization and abstraction, tending to invent a new god or a new variant of an old god for every conceivable occasion. Dyaus, lord of the bright sky, was equivalent to the Greek Zeus (though less important). Varuna represented the sky or heaven in its capacity to encompass all things and hold the universe together. He was called Asura, a term which suggests close kinship with the supreme Persian deity, Ahura-Mazda. At least five different divinities were identified with the sun. One of them, Mitra, shared a common origin with the Persian Mithras, but this deity did not assume the prominence in India that Mithras attained in Persia and the West. Surya was the sun's golden disk, Pushan embodied its power to assist vegetation and animal growth, and Vishnu personified the swift-moving orb that traverses the sky in three strides.

The most popular deity of all in Vedic times was Indra, whose original significance is uncertain. He was alleged to have benefited mankind by slaying a malignant serpent, the demon of drought, thus releasing the pent-up waters to refresh the earth. Also, it was said, he discovered the light, made a path for the sun, and created lightning. He was chiefly honored as a mighty warrior and god of battle, the slayer of demons and the "black-skinned" enemies of the Aryans. Indra was supposed to be particularly fond of *soma,* which fired his blood for combat, and he was reputed to be able to drink three lakes of this potent fluid at one draft while devouring the flesh of 300 buffaloes. *Soma,* the sacred liquor, was also deified, as was the sacrificial fire, Agni. Agni was conceived both as a god and as the mouth of the gods or as the servant who carried their savory food offerings up to the heavens for them.

Spiritual and ethical elements

Although religion in the Vedic age was hardly spiritual, it contained traces of such a quality. Some hymns to Varuna are remarkable for their devoutness and ethical content. Varuna is described as the great regulator of the universe, who keeps the rivers in their courses and the sun and planets in their proper orbits. He is also pictured as the upholder of rules and ordinances for both gods and men, capable of binding sinners with fetters. To him were addressed prayers for forgiveness of sin. Offenses likely to incur divine wrath included not only infractions of religious taboos but also violations of the moral code, such as adultery, witchcraft, gambling, and drunkenness. However, despite intimations of a belief in life after death, by far the greater emphasis was placed upon the enjoyment of life here and now.

The Brahmanas

Associated with each of the *Vedas* is a prose manual called a *Brahmana* because it was for the instruction and assistance of the Brahmans (priests) who officiated at the sacrifices. While the Vedic hymns are generally unaffected and artless, the *Brahmanas* betray a shrewd calculation on the part of the custodians of the sacred traditions and also illustrate the tendency of such traditions to degenerate into empty mechanical formulas. A modern Indian scholar describes the *Brahmanas* as "an arid desert of puerile speculations on ritual ceremonies," and even as "filthy and repulsive," with a morality "no higher than that of primitive medicine-men."[2] The greed and arrogance of the Brahmans is illustrated by such assertions as that judgment should always be awarded to a Brahman in every dispute with a layman and that murder is not actually murder unless the victim is a Brahman.

The Upanishads

In view of the decadent tendencies evident in the *Brahmanas* it is all the more notable that the concluding portion of Vedic literature is of an elevated philosophical character, giving proof both of intellectual maturity and of ethical and spiritual insight. Evidently, side by side with the naïve popular cults and with the mechanical rituals of priestcraft had grown up a tradition of skepticism and bold speculation, which attempted to delve beneath the surface of sense experience and formulate answers to eternally recurring questions. This concluding portion, called *Vedanta* ("end of the *Vedas*"), comprises the famous *Upanishads,* of which there are some 200. The *Upanishads* (the word means a "sitting down near" or session with a teacher) are treatises or rambling discourses in prose and poetry, dealing with the nature of being, man, and the universe. Their content varies in subject matter

[2] B. K. Ghosh, in *The History and Culture of the Indian People,* Vol. II, *The Vedic Age,* pp. 225, 418.

and in quality of thought, ranging from the trivial and absurd to the sublime. Scholars and philosophers from the Occident as well as from the Orient have long been attracted by the subtle probing, the sweeping imagination, and the idealistic concepts evident in the *Upanishads,* the best of which rival the products of Greek philosophical genius. However, if the end of ancient Greek inquiry was knowledge for its own sake, that of the *Upanishads* was knowledge as the means to power: true wisdom could give its possessor mastery not only of self, but of the entire cosmos. Although part of the *Vedas,* the *Upanishads* largely ignore the popular mythology of the Vedic hymns and also challenge the presumptuousness of Brahmans and their reliance on ritual and ceremony.

While the *Upanishads* do not fall into a single pattern of thought, their most essential philosophical teachings are fairly consistent. The key concepts, which may be described as idealistic, monistic, and pantheistic, are (1) the supreme reality of the World Soul or Absolute Being; (2) the unreality of the material world; (3) transmigration, or the rebirth of individual souls; and (4) the attainment of serenity through escape from the cycle of recurring births by union with Absolute Being. Evil and suffering are explained on the ground that they are incidental to matter and material creatures. But matter is held to be an illusion (*maya*); the only true reality is the soul or spirit. If the soul could manage to disentangle itself from matter (which actually is only an appearance anyway), it would be free from discord and suffering. Not only does life in the flesh entail sorrow and pain, but, according to this philosophy, death fails to provide relief because the soul will be born again into another body. In developing the theory of an endless chain of births, the philosophers of the *Upanishads* insisted that the process was not purely accidental and uncontrollable. They taught that a person's conduct in life determined the type of body and condition which he would experience in his next incarnation. He might go down in the scale—even to the animal or insect level—or he might go up—to the state of a noble, king, or saint. This is the *karma* doctrine, which holds that actions, thoughts, and motives bear fruit. It resembles the Christian teaching "Whatsoever a man soweth, that shall he also reap"—except that the retribution or reward for actions is held over to another earthly existence. However, if it is assumed that all physical existence is unsatisfactory and illusory, obviously there is not much to be gained from moving a few rungs up the ladder of human wretchedness. Hence the *Upanishads* taught that preferable even to the faithful performance of *dharma* (moral uprightness and the conscientious discharge of one's duties) was a deliberate break with the habits and engagements which lead to the renewal of births. Separation from the chain of births could be achieved only by following a standard of conduct higher than that of righteousness in the ordinary sense of the term. Evil action would

Philosophy of the
Upanishads

produce evil fruit or *karma,* and righteous action would produce good *karma;* but still more desirable was conduct which, being "neither black nor white," could lead to the extinction of *karma* altogether. In other words, only when a person acts with complete disinterestedness, detaching himself entirely from the idea of reward for his merit, do the fetters which bind him to the world of sense begin to loosen and ultimately dissolve. When this happens, the liberated soul attains blessedness or *nirvana,*[3] which does not mean either annihilation or entrance into a heaven, but a union with *Brahma,* the undefinable Universal Soul or eternal Absolute Being.

Pessimism and optimism

The philosophy of the *Upanishads* is pessimistic regarding the world and man's present state, because it depreciates everything material and holds that the natural physical life is a burden. However, it is optimistic as to ultimate ends and as to the possibility of human emancipation. It teaches that there is in every man an indestructible fragment of reality. The basic precept is that *atman* (the individual soul) is actually a part of *Brahma* (the Universal Soul or rational principle which pervades the universe); and that although the soul has been separated from its source, it can be reunited with it—not through a miracle, but through the individual's own efforts. Moreover, the state of *nirvana,* while a remote goal for the majority, is declared to be attainable during the mortal existence of a sufficiently dedicated person.

2. THE EPIC AGE: THE EMERGENCE OF HINDUISM

The Indian epics

Long before the *Vedas* were completed, the two Indian epics were in process of development. The epics were not cast into their final form until sometime between 400 B.C. and 200 A.D., but they refer to events of a much earlier date, and the Epic age overlaps with the Vedic. The epics were composed in Sanskrit, a dialect which is derived from but not identical with that of the *Vedas,* and which came to be regarded as the "classical" form of the Indo-Aryan speech, somewhat as Latin is regarded as classical by the Indo-European peoples of Europe. Furthermore, in spite of the lack of precise dividing dates, it is clear that the epics represent a later stage of social and cultural evolution than do the *Vedas.*

Content of the epics

The Indian epics are comparable to the epic poems of the ancient Greeks in that they celebrate the deeds of legendary national heroes, but they are much more encyclopedic and diffuse than the Homeric poems. The *Mahabharata,* the longer of the two Indian epics, is more than seven times the length of the *Iliad* and *Odyssey* combined. While the epics treat of bloody conflicts and amazing exploits, they also

---

[3] Although not appearing in the genuine *Upanishads,* nirvana became the popular term for the concept of liberation from the cycle of rebirths. Its literal meaning is "extinction."

Ravana, Rama, and Lakshmana. An Indian painting of the eighteenth century depicting an incident from the *Ramayana.* Rama, the epic hero, and his brother Lakshmana are fighting against Ravana, the demon king of Ceylon, who carried off Rama's faithful wife Sita.

incorporate quantities of religious lore, and through the centuries they, rather than the *Vedas,* have served as a Bible for the common people. This is partly because the Brahmans imposed restrictions upon the study of the sacred Vedic texts, whereas anyone could listen to a recitation of the epics.

The *Ramayana* has as its central theme the story of Prince Rama, who, with his beautiful wife Sita, was exiled through the jealous intrigue of a wicked stepmother. It relates how Sita was carried off to Ceylon by the demon king of that country and finally recovered by Rama with the help of a monkey general. The narrative is highly artificial as well as fantastic, and easily lends itself to allegorical interpretation. The poem indicates some familiarity with both southern India and Ceylon and provides evidence that Aryan influence, if not extensive conquests, had penetrated into the Deccan. The story was reworked many times in later Indian literature and embellished with symbolism. Rama and Sita came to be idealized as the perfect types of manly courage and feminine purity and devotion, respectively, and Rama was traditionally regarded as an incarnation of the god Vishnu. It is possible that the poem may be, in part, an allegory of the progress of agriculture, in which Rama represents the plow and Sita the furrow. (In the epic, after returning to her husband's kingdom she is swallowed up by the earth.)

The *Mahabharata* is just as enigmatic as the *Ramayana,* though livelier in its story and richer in the variety and scope of its subject matter. "If it is not in the *Mahabharata,* it is not in India," has become a proverb. A narrative core, which gives the poem its name, is the account

The Ramayana

The Mahabharata

of a great battle between two related but feuding families, the Pandavas and the Kauravas, of Bharata descent. The "Great Bharata War" probably commemorates a historic battle fought near the modern city of Delhi about 1400 B.C., but the epic version is a tissue of myth and fable. Some scholars believe that the Pandavas (who on the whole are the heroes of the story) were not really kinsmen of the Kauravas but a different tribe altogether, perhaps of Mongolian race. The five Pandava brothers are described as having one wife in common, an obvious reference to the institution of polyandry, which was foreign to the Aryan communities but which is still practiced by the Tibetans. As a chronicle of battle the poetic version is gory enough but still full of odd contradictions. Acts of ruthlessness and chicanery are recorded along with examples of exaggerated chivalry and scrupulousness. The god Krishna (supposedly one of the incarnations of Vishnu) takes part in the encounter with rare impartiality—serving as charioteer for one of the Pandava princes but sending his own forces to fight on the other side. The battle is described as raging furiously for eighteen days, by which time practically all the antagonists on both sides have been killed. Finally the five royal Pandava brothers, victorious but the sole survivors of their line, renounce the world and, with their wife and dog, set off for the Himalayas in search of Paradise. Some of the contradictions and inconsistencies in the account can be explained by the fact that the poem was several centuries in the making. Ethical sensibilities and the warriors' code of conduct changed considerably during this period until rough-and-ready practices which were once considered normal came to be looked upon with disapproval.

The Bhagavad-Gita

Interpolated in the story of the great war is a philosophical dialogue which contrasts startlingly with the rapid pace and bloody tone of the main narrative. This passage, which like the rest of the *Mahabharata* is of unknown authorship, is called the *Bhagavad-Gita* or "the Lord's Song." In form, it is a discourse between the warrior Arjuna and his charioteer Krishna (who represents the god Vishnu), precipitated by Arjuna's reluctance to begin the slaughter of his relatives when the lines of battle are drawn up. In substance, it is a dramatic and colorful exposition of some of the most fertile ideas of the *Upanishads,* with greater emotional impact because it speaks not in abstractions but in terms of love for a personal god. At the outset of the dialogue Arjuna expresses his aversion to combat, saying flatly that he will not engage in it: "Better I deem it . . . to face them weaponless, and bare my breast to shaft and spear, than answer blow with blow." Krishna assures him that he must fight, not because there is any virtue in it but because as a member of the warrior caste fighting is his duty (*dharma*). Similarly, Arjuna is reminded that both death and birth are only incidents and that the soul is indestructible: "Life is not slain." Soon, however, the conversation proceeds to a penetrating discussion of the value of different types of action, suggestive of Christian arguments over the respective merits of "faith" and "works." Krishna outlines

Cotton Tapestry. Embroidered with colored silks and silver (eighteenth century), it illustrates scenes from the *Mahabharata.*

four levels of conduct or four paths to virtue. At the lowest level are good works, prescribed by reason. Better than works of diligence is knowledge: "The right act is less than the right-thinking mind." Still higher is worship or pure devotion, meditation which is above the bonds of sense and "troubled no longer by the priestly lore." But on the very highest level is placed the renunciation of self. The ideal worshiper, while not neglecting his duty, will play his part "with unyoked soul," "with spirit unattached." He acts "unmoved by passion and unbound by deeds, setting result aside"—that is, with no thought of reward either material or spiritual. Although in the dialogue the warrior is enjoined to fulfill his warlike function—with complete indifference to victory or defeat—the *Bhagavad-Gita* verses have been interpreted by some Hindus, including Mahatma Gandhi, as a text for pacifism.

Aside from their narrative and philosophical interest, the epics reveal that during the 1000 or 1500 years since the settlement of the Indo-Aryans in India extensive changes had taken place among the people, especially in religion and the organization of society. The carefree, boisterous optimism of the early Vedic period was giving way to attitudes of pessimism, discouragement, and resignation; society, instead of being flexible and largely uninhibited, was tending toward a rigid stratification of functions and privileges. The causes of such marked change are not entirely clear. But whatever the reasons, before the close of the Epic age Indian society had assumed many of the characteristics which have distinguished it down to modern times. Together they make up the culture complex which is Hinduism.

Significance of the epics

Popular religion had changed from a simple polytheism to an intricate network of beliefs and rituals with a tremendous hierarchy of gods. The catalogue and ranking of deities and the forms of worship

Shiva. The dance of Shiva portrayed in this eleventh-century bronze is symbolic of the destructive forces in the world.

Three Faces of Shiva. An eighth-century traditional representation of "the Destroyer," with three faces and four arms.

varied from one locality to another and among different strata of the population. With a few exceptions, the more prominent of the early Aryan deities faded into the background as new gods were added to the pantheon with the absorption of local pre-Aryan cults. Eventually the number of divine and semidivine beings accorded recognition ran into the thousands, or possibly millions. Thus, while philosophy was tending toward monotheism, the popular faiths were moving in the opposite direction. Three gods, however, came to be considered as paramount, although without agreement as to their qualities and import. Vishnu, the old solar deity, believed to have had many incarnations, was worshiped under several names. He was still conceived as a benevolent and cheerful god, "the Preserver," representing the creative or formative principle in the universe. Because he was supposed to disapprove of bloodshed, Vishnu received no animal sacrifice but was offered garlands of flowers. Quite different was Shiva, "the Destroyer" (perhaps identical with one of the Indus valley deities), who, in spite of his frightening aspects, has proved to be a more widely favored object of worship than Vishnu. Typically Shiva was pictured as five-faced and four-armed. He was regarded as beneficent in some aspects because destructive force—symbolized by the dance of Shiva—is a necessary agency in the evolution of the world and living forms, but his power could be prostrating. While some devotees of Shiva were ascetics and mystics, among other groups his worship called for bloody sacrifice, and was also associated with a fertility cult employing orgiastic rites. The third and least influential of the major deities was Brahma, a personification of the Absolute Being or World Soul of the philosophers. Representing an abstract principle, Brahma did not seize upon the popular imagination as did Vishnu and Shiva. He was visualized as a tiny figure who could sit on a lotus leaf. This god, however, has stimulated mystic contemplation. The avowed end of the famous *yoga* discipline is to attain a union of the soul with Brahma.

In many respects Hinduism differs from the pattern of religion familiar to Western peoples. It has no creed, no set of dogmas, no single congregation of the faithful, no established church. It assumes that divine truth wears many faces and that the paths to salvation are myriad. Hinduism is actually a social and religious complex, presenting a wide range of variations from region to region and from one social level to another, but given coherence by the authority accorded to the Brahmans or priests. Throughout India the Brahmans established themselves as ministrants of the rites and recipients of reverence and material compensation. They did not enforce any orthodox creed or crusade against heretics, but they insisted successfully that only they could mediate between gods and men. The chief points of emphasis in Hinduism as a social discipline came to be: (1) respect for and support of the Brahmans; (2) noninjury to animal life, especially cattle (although there are many exceptions to this rule); (3) the inferior status of women; and (4) acceptance of the regulations of caste.

The chief distinguishing characteristic of Hindu religious and social life is the institution of caste, the most rigorous and refined instrument of segregation ever invented. Caste is much more complex than the typical division of a nation into social or economic classes, even when these classes are hereditary. Aside from heredity, membership in a caste is not based upon any single principle nor does it follow a logical pattern. The best definition of caste is a simple one: "A group of families internally united by peculiar rules for the observance of ceremonial purity, especially in the matters of diet and marriage." Typically, a person must marry within his or her caste and should not accept food from a member of a lower caste. Caste is the antithesis of democracy. It is a vast hierarchy, exalting the Brahmans at the top and degrading the "untouchables" or outcastes at the bottom of the social pyramid.

According to orthodox Hindu tradition, caste has always existed; it is part of the order of nature. The word used to denote it (*jat*) literally means "species." Historical evidence, however, shows that caste developed gradually over a long period of time. Caste was unknown to the Indo-Aryan society of the early Vedic age, but by the time of the epics it was already regarded as an ancient institution. Thus the system has probably been operating in India for the past 3000 years, and its origins are lost in obscurity. Its starting point, undoubtedly, was the racial pride of the Aryan conquerors, who were determined to prevent contamination by intermarriage with the supposedly inferior "black-skinned" peoples whom they were fighting and reducing to subjection. In this case the distinction was based on color (*varna*); but as time went on various other criteria entered into the drawing of caste lines, including occupations, religious deviation, migrations from one section of India to another, and later invasions by non-Hindu peoples who could not be expelled but who might be prevented from destroying the Hindu system by assigning them a place within it. While the origins of caste are obscure and its causes multiple, the development and final acceptance of the institution was probably influenced by the exertions of the Brahmans in their struggle for a position of dominance over all other groups, a struggle in which they did not scruple to use religious weapons to discomfit their competitors. The keenest rivalry was between the Brahmans and the warrior nobles (including rajas). The nobles had the advantage of being recognized wielders of authority backed by force; but the Brahmans had the advantage of education, mastery of the sacred *Vedas*, and wonder-working powers in the eyes of the people. Socially the Brahmans and nobles were on a par. There are records of Brahman kings and of kings or nobles who became skilled in the *Vedas*. But eventually the Brahmans won recognition for their claim to the highest rank of all, and the nobles were forced to accept classification as the second caste (*kshatriya*). As the price of their pre-eminence, the Brahmans were expected to devote themselves more unreservedly to their religious and educational functions, adopting a modest and mildly ascetic manner of life and leaving political dominion to the *kshatriyas*. However, as tutors and advisers to kings, the Brahmans managed to retain considerable political influence.

The major castes

Once the principle of caste was accepted by the leading groups in society, it was not difficult to impose it upon the others. Originating in northern India, the institution was extended among the Dravidians and other peoples of the Deccan as Aryan influence permeated that region. Many occupational groups or guilds became castes, but division does not always follow vocational lines. Brahmans may, without incurring disapproval, engage in a variety of occupations, including comparatively humble ones. At the same time, members of the higher castes avoid tasks which are considered defiling, such as the disposal of corpses, butchering animals, or preparing hides. It is impossible to enumerate precisely the castes of India because the number is enormous and fluctuates from time to time. Theoretically, there are four great castes with subdivisions: *brahmans* (priests), *kshatriyas* (warriors), *vaisyas* (farmers, herdsmen, and artisans), and *sudras* (laborers, servants, and slaves). Actually, except for the first, these categories have little significance. Probably they once represented the general classes of Aryan society before caste had taken hold, but they are much too broad to define caste as it has existed in historic times. The effective

Dravidian Temple of Nataraja at Chidambaram. The gorgeously sculptured spire is a gem of Dravidian art; the temple is believed to be the oldest in South India.

divisions are more minute. There are some 1,800 subdivisions of Brahmans alone, and the total number of castes and subcastes in India has been reckoned at more than 3,000.

Undeniably caste has had a stultifying effect upon Indian society. The rules of caste observance are arbitrary, tedious, and time-consuming, especially in the everyday matters of social intercourse and eating. The fear of pollution becomes an obsession. Not only are there varying degrees of uncleanness in food (depending on the ingredients and the method of cooking as well as who has prepared it), but absolute prohibitions on certain foods restrict the diet unduly, impairing the health of the population. Whether or not a consequence of caste, the position of women in the patriarchal society of India became degraded as the caste system solidified. A man might in some cases marry beneath his caste; for a woman to do so was considered shameful. Caste duty for a woman lay in absolute obedience to her father and then to her husband. The custom of child marriage was introduced, defended with the argument that it saved a girl from the monstrous crime of falling in love with any other man than her future husband. Although child marriages made it inevitable that there would be a large number of widows, a widow was shamed by the belief that some sin of hers had caused her husband's death. She was forbidden to remarry and could best redeem her reputation by committing suicide in flames on her husband's pyre. The most inhumane feature of caste was the treatment accorded the lowest groups in the scale, especially the "Untouchables," who were considered to be outside the border of even the lowest caste, and therefore hardly human beings at all. In southern India the greatest humiliation of the "Untouchables" took place. Their shadow, it was thought, would pollute a well. They were required to live in segregated quarters and to warn people of their approach by uttering cries.

The fact that the caste system has endured in India for tens of centuries and is still operative (though with important changes) is a testimony to the toughness of social institutions, once they have become established. At the same time it should be pointed out that the role of caste in India was not wholly negative. On the positive side it gave the Indian people a sense of identity when confronted with alien cultures or conquerors. It also offered the individual a feeling of security within his group and fostered various forms of mutual assistance. In spite of intercaste rivalries, the separate castes learned to cooperate with one another, notably in the constitution and administration of local village councils. Eventually caste came to be looked upon as a normal and necessary arrangement, especially as it was hedged about by religious sanctions. Particularly effectual were the twin beliefs: *karma* and the transmigration or rebirth of souls. These concepts, which were given an idealistic interpretation by the philosophers of the *Upanishads,* served in the popular imagination to explain and justify caste. If a person was born into a high caste he was thought to be receiving his reward for meritorious behavior in a previous existence. He had produced good *karma,* which carried him upward on the ladder. Similarly, a member of the despised castes was supposed to have incurred his lot because of misdeeds in a previous incarnation. Unfair as the distinctions of caste seemed to be, they were accepted as a just and precise recognition of the individual's deserts. The person who suffered abuse was told to blame only himself and to strive for perfection within the prescribed limits of his present caste in order that his condition would be improved the next time his soul returned to earth. Since it was possible to go either up or down in the succession of births, patience, diligence, and conformity became supreme virtues. Devotion to duty and the certainty of retribution—*dharma* and *karma*—were the cement which held the caste structure together.

3. REFORM MOVEMENTS: THE RISE OF BUDDHISM

The revolt against Brahmanism

In the sixth century B.C. the stratification of society and the hardening of religious ritual provoked a simmering discontent that found an outlet in several protest movements, led by members of the nobility. Because these protests were directed against the extravagant claims of the Brahmans, they assumed at the outset a heretical or even antireligious form. Most of them proved to be only temporary, but two resulted in philosophical and religious schools of enduring influence— Jainism and Buddhism. There were many parallels between these two movements. They originated in the same section of India, north of the Ganges in eastern Hindustan, and the leader of each was a member of the noble or *kshatriya* caste. Each repudiated the authority of priests and *Vedas,* rejecting all the paraphernalia of religion and replacing it by a system of philosophy. At the same time each was ethical and reformist, attempting to provide moral and personal satisfaction to its adherents. Each drew heavily upon the background of Hindu philosophic tradition and formulated goals which, though original in form, were not alien to the spirit of this tradition. And, ironically, each finally turned into a religion, Jainism taking its place within Hinduism, and Buddhism becoming a separate faith. Although Buddhism carried within itself many elements of Hindu thought, it ultimately obtained its widest following in Asian lands outside India and practically disappeared in the country of its birth. However, Buddhism flourished in India for 1000 years after the life of its founder; it helped to liberalize Hinduism and to keep it from becoming an agency of unlimited exploitation in the hands of the Brahmans. Buddhism also contributed heavily to Indian architecture and sculpture, and the Buddhist sacred texts were the first works committed to writing in India.

Jainism is associated with a figure known as Mahavira ("Great Hero"), who, although probably not its founder, gave it a distinctive form. Mahavira expounded a complex metaphysics which embraced the notion that not only living creatures but almost every object possesses a soul. Employing the familiar concepts of transmigration and *karma,* he held that the soul when attached to matter is in bondage and that it will never be content until freed from and entirely independent of the physical body. The purport of his message was to point out the way to the soul's liberation. Insisting that prayers and worship were of no avail, he prescribed a course of mental and moral discipline, the highest stage of which was withdrawal into a state of meditation with complete denial of the claims of the flesh. The exalting of extreme asceticism remained one of the chief characteristics of Jainism, and particular honor was reserved for the zealot who was able to carry self-denial to the point of starving himself to death, as a number of Jain saints are reputed to have done. Another cardinal emphasis among the Jains (derived from their animistic belief in a multiplicity of souls) is the doctrine of *ahimsa,* or the necessity of refraining from injury to any living creature. This doctrine has led to commendable efforts to prevent cruelty to animals, although it has sometimes been carried to extremes in attempting to protect even pests and vermin. Surrounded by the atmosphere of Hinduism, the Jains relinquished their early antireligious tenets, instituting prayers to various deities, including the deified Mahavira. The Jain sect, which numbers slightly more than a million members, is monastic in organization. The monks are bound by five vows, while the laity, who are considered part of the order although not of the same degree of holiness as the monks, may subscribe to "small vows." Through plying the trade of moneylending the Jains became a wealthy order, in spite of their rigorous asceticism.

Much more significant than Jainism was the contemporary movement destined to be known as Buddhism because its founder, Gautama, was accorded the title of Buddha, "the Enlightened One."

Jain Temples on Girnar Mountain. These temples exhibit the lavish sculpture characteristic of Indian architecture.

Gautama: the founder of Buddhism

Gautama Buddha in the State of Nirvana. A fragment from the Early Khmer period.

Gautama's metaphysics and psychology

Gautama (c. 563–483 B.C.) was the son of the head of a small state located on the slopes of the Himalayas in what is now Nepal. This tribal state, like many others of that time, elected its ruler; hence Gautama, although of noble blood, was not a hereditary prince as later tradition claimed. Little is known about the events of his life, but legends have supplied innumerable details, most of them miraculous. There is factual evidence to support the conclusion that he was one of those rare personalities who deliberately relinquished a safe and comfortable existence in order to devote himself to the quest of higher values and the service of his fellow men. Tradition has it that at the age of twenty-nine he left his sumptuous abode in the middle of the night after a fond glance at his young wife and infant son, cut off his hair, and sent back his jewels and fine clothes to his father. Then came years of wandering and disappointment in which he found no answer to the problem that vexed him—the cause and cure of human suffering. After studying philosophy with the Brahmans he concluded that this was a vain pursuit. Next, it is said, he spent six years practicing an extreme asceticism, until his body had almost wasted away. This course he also abandoned as leading only to despair. The climax of his life came when, discouraged and weary, he sat down under a large Bo tree to meditate. Suddenly he had an overwhelming experience, a revelation or a flash of insight in which he seemed to penetrate the mystery of evil and suffering. Henceforth he was free from doubts, but, instead of retiring to enjoy his state of Enlightenment, he determined to teach others how they might also secure it. For the next forty years until his death at the age of eighty, he wandered through the Ganges valley, relying upon charity for his livelihood and instructing the disciples who gathered about him.

The substance of Gautama Buddha's teachings has been better preserved than the facts of his life. Some scholars consider him the most intellectual of all the founders of the world's great religions. He had no intention of establishing a religion, and his ideas, although conditioned by his Hindu religious background, were not sectarian. His doctrines embodied a philosophy or metaphysics, a psychology, and an ethics, of which the last is most important. The basis of his philosophy was materialism. In direct opposition to the absolute idealism of the *Upanishads* and in contrast to Mahavira's teaching, he held that nothing exists except matter and denied the actuality of the soul. Because matter is in a state of flux, constantly changing its form, he said that all things are impermanent. Hence, there is no Absolute Being or fixed universal principle other than the law of change—growth and decay. Buddha's psychological principles followed logically from his materialist metaphysics. If there is no soul, no permanent entity, there can be no distinct individual personality or being. Not only the soul but the *self* is an illusion, he affirmed. What seems to be an individual personality is only a bundle of attributes (such as sense experience and consciousness) held together temporarily as the spokes of a wheel are fastened around the hub.

Gautama's negative and deflating intellectual doctrines were intended to be encouraging rather than discouraging, as shown in the development of his system of ethics. The source of human anguish is, as he saw it, the individual's attempt to attain the unattainable. Desire or craving is the root of all evil. It can never be satisfied because the desired objects and emotional states are transitory; but the abandonment of desire can bring satisfaction and peace (the state of *nirvana*). The most persistent and futile craving, underlying a multitude of vain desires, is the ego impulse—the struggle to enhance and perpetuate the self. Since, according to Gautama, the self is only an illusion, the egoist is doomed to chase a will-o'-the-wisp. Thus it follows that selflessness is more realistic as well as more satisfying than selfishness. Oddly enough, Gautama, while denying the existence of the soul, retained the doctrine of *karma,* insisting that a person's actions would affect the condition of another person yet unborn—just as an expiring lamp can light the flame of another lamp. The ultimate goal which he projected was, like that of the Vedic philosophers, the complete extinction of *karma* through the cultivation of selflessness, so that the cycle of births, travail, and tragedy would be no more.

In his ethical teachings Gautama's emphasis was positive rather than negative. He proclaimed the ideal of universal love, to be exemplified by service and helpfulness. Rather than a saintly hermit, he was apparently a gifted teacher, with a stock of homely illustrations and parables. He gave sensible advice in regard to domestic and marital relations, occupations, business matters, and so on. As a rule of personal conduct he advocated "the Middle Path," by which he meant the avoidance of extremes—renouncing both indulgence and injurious asceticism, rejecting prayers and ritual and also the idea of escape into a heaven of bliss. Gautama repeatedly declared that dogmas are much less important than behavior and inner attitudes. And he was firmly opposed to forcing ideas upon anyone, believing that discussion and the power of example are the only valid means of establishing truth. Although he was an ethical rather than a social reformer and made no direct attack upon the caste system, caste distinctions were dissolved among his own group of disciples. He admonished his followers to develop their faculties to the full and to exert themselves for the benefit of others. His last words are said to have been, "Work out your emancipation with diligence."

The Buddhist movement in Gautama's lifetime had few of the characteristics of a religion. In the course of a century or two, however, it developed its own rites, mystic symbols, and other supernatural elements. The Buddhists in India gradually became an order of monks and nuns. Candidates for admission to the order were required to undergo a long period of training. After completing the training, the novitiate shaved his head, put on the yellow robes, and took the monastic vows of poverty and chastity. In contrast to Christian monks, he did not take a vow of obedience, because membership was considered a matter of free choice. The monks customarily remained in a monastery during the three months of the rainy season, which Gautama had devoted to instructing his disciples; for the rest of the year they lived as wandering mendicants, dependent upon the alms which they received in their beggars' bowls as they passed from village to village. Lay men or women who accepted the Buddhist teachings and contributed to the support of the monks were considered adherents of the faith and entitled to its benefits.

Buddhist sects: Hinayana *and* Mahayana

Various sects of Buddhism arose as the movement spread. The two principal schools, representing a cleavage which apparently began soon after Gautama's death, are the *Hinayana* ("Lesser Vehicle") and the *Mahayana* ("Great Vehicle"). The term *Hinayana* was at first applied reproachfully, because the members of this group were bent upon their own self-perfection, claiming that it was possible for the diligent individual to attain *nirvana* in three lifetimes. The *Mahayana* school was characterized by the doctrine of the buddha-elect—a person who had won Enlightenment but chose deliberately to remain in the world of sorrow in order to work for the liberation of all mankind. In spite of its noble beginning, however, the *Mahayana* tradition became more corrupted than the *Hinayana* as time went on. The *Hinayana* school of Buddhism is represented in its purest form in Ceylon, where it was established as early as the third century B.C., and it is also the prevailing religion of Burma and Thailand. In these countries, Gautama is still theoretically regarded as a man, but in actual practice he is worshiped as a deity, and offerings of flowers or incense are made to his image. The intellectual vigor and the moral challenge of Gautama's teachings have been greatly obscured, and elements of primitive religions have retained their hold on the people. However, the Buddha's emphasis upon kindliness, patience, and the avoidance of injury to living creatures is still prominent. *Mahayana* Buddhism was eventually developed in many different forms in Nepal, Tibet, and eastern Asia. It came to include the worship not only of Buddha but of his several supposed reincarnations, and it also transformed the concept of *nirvana* into a conventional paradise of bliss.

Intellectual achievements in ancient India

During the period so far discussed, covering more than 1000 years, the physical and external aspects of Indian civilization were still elementary. Writing was unknown until the eighth, or perhaps the seventh, century B.C., and even then it was used only for business purposes. The people lived in villages or small towns rather than cities, architecture was very simple, and political units were small. There was none of the magnificence which characterized ancient Egypt, Mesopotamia, or the extinct Indus valley civilization. To a remarkable degree the achievements of the ancient Indians were in the fields of the imagination and intellect, expressed in song and poetry, in the epics, and in philosophical and religious speculation. Their intellectual achievements also included considerable scientific progress. Medicine was highly developed as early as the Vedic age. Not only were many specific remedies listed, but dissection was practiced and delicate operations were performed. The knowledge of human anatomy was extensive, and a beginning had been made in the study of embryology. Medical science and the surgeon's vocation were held in high respect, until the caste system introduced a fear of pollution through bodily contact with unclean persons. Many fanciful elements, however, were intermingled with medical lore. An appreciable knowledge of astronomy was acquired in spite of its perversion into astrology. The suggestion that the earth revolves on its axis and that the sun only appears to rise and set was put forward in the *Vedas,* apparently without being taken very seriously. The most brilliant scientific attainments were those in mathematics. The ancient Indians were able to handle extremely large numbers in their calculations and knew how to extract square and cube roots. Besides using the decimal system they invented the all-important principle of the zero, which was eventually adopted by the rest of the world. In geometry their progress was not equal to that of the Greeks, but they surpassed the Greeks in the development of algebra.

During the fourth and third centuries B.C., partly in response to stimulation from without, political developments in India led temporarily in the direction of greater efficiency and unification. As a result of the conquests of the Persian king, Darius I, about 500 B.C., the Indus valley had become a province (satrapy) of the Persian Empire, furnishing mercenary soldiers and an annual tribute in gold. After Alexander the Great, the famous Macedonian conqueror, overthrew the Persian Empire, he conducted his troops eastward through the passes of the Hindu Kush Mountains into the upper Indus valley (327–326 B.C.). He spent less than two years in India but traversed most of the Punjab, fought and negotiated with local rajas, and installed Macedonian officials in the region. Although Alexander's invasion provides the first verifiable date in Indian history, it made so little impression upon the Hindus that their contemporary records do not even mention his name. However, the invasion promoted cultural exchange between the Hindus and the Greek-speaking world, and, more immediately, it paved the way for the erection of a powerful state in India.

Conquest of the Indus valley by Alexander the Great

In the revolts and confusion that followed the death of Alexander in 323 B.C., an Indian adventurer named Chandragupta Maurya seized the opportunity to found a dynasty. Chandragupta had profited from observing Greek military tactics and led in the movement to expel the Macedonian officials from India. Then he turned his army against the Magadha kingdom, which was the strongest state in Hindustan at this

The rise of the Maurya Dynasty

time. He defeated and killed the Magadhan king and established himself as ruler with his capital at Pataliputra (now Patna), a magnificent city eight miles long commanding the south bank of the Ganges. When Seleucus (Alexander's successor in Syria and Persia) tried to recover the lost Indian territory, Chandragupta defeated him soundly and forced him to cede Baluchistan and part of Afghanistan. Chandragupta extended his power over most of northern India and founded the first empire in Indian history. Although his dynasty, known as the Maurya, lasted less than a century and a half, its record is a distinguished one.

The reign of Chandragupta

Chandragupta was a much more imposing figure than the rajas of the Vedic age. His government was efficient but very harsh. Social and economic activities were carefully regulated, an elaborate tax system had been devised, and the death penalty was meted out freely, sometimes through the administering of poison. The king kept a large standing army, with divisions of infantry, cavalry, chariots, and elephants. In spite of his far-reaching authority, and his maintenance of secret police or spies, he seems to have lived in dread of assassination and took the precaution to change his sleeping quarters every night. On the credit side was his construction and improvement of public irrigation works and the building of roads. The Royal Road, from the capital to the western frontier, was 1,200 miles long.

King Asoka: Buddhist conqueror

The greatest member of the Maurya Dynasty, and one of the most remarkable rulers in the annals of any civilization, was Chandragupta's grandson, King Asoka, the royal patron of Buddhism, whose beneficent reign lasted some forty years (c. 273–232 B.C.). Merely as a conqueror Asoka could lay claim to fame, because he held under Mauryan rule not only Hindustan and the region northwest of the Indus but most of the Deccan as well, thus bringing the greater part of India into one administration. His conquests, however, were the aspect of his reign that he considered least important. In fact, he fought only one major war—by which he was enabled to gain control of the Deccan—and he felt remorseful ever after for the bloodshed which accompanied this campaign. Attracted to the Buddhist teachings, he at first became a lay adherent and later took the formal vows and joined the order but without relinquishing his position as king. He attempted, rather, to exemplify the precepts of Buddhism in his personal life and to apply them to the administration of the empire. Thus, without being a theocrat or divine-right ruler, he provides an almost unique example of the injection of religious idealism into statecraft.

The benevolent reign of King Asoka

It is impossible to know how completely Asoka's benign purposes were carried out. He was particularly active in establishing rest houses for travelers, in having trees planted, wells dug, and watering places built along the roads for the refreshment of man and beast, and in improving facilities for the treatment of the sick. He sent commission-

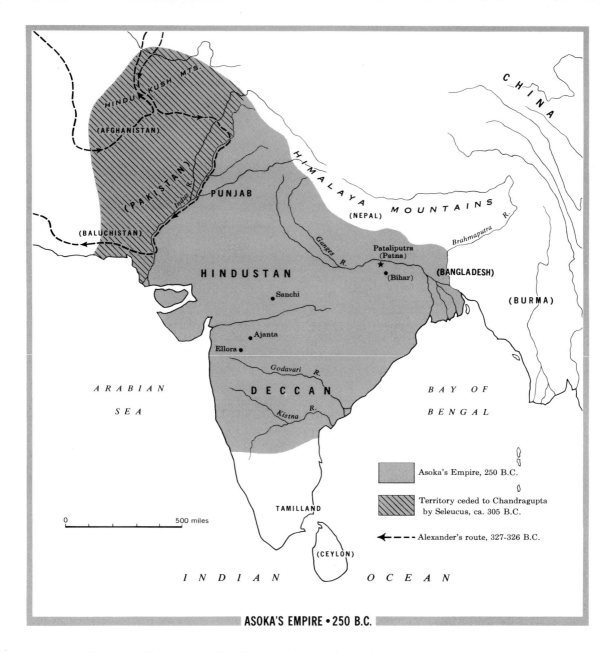

ASOKA'S EMPIRE • 250 B.C.

Map legend:

Asoka's Empire, 250 B.C.

Territory ceded to Chandragupta
by Seleucus, ca. 305 B.C.

Alexander's route, 327-326 B.C.

ers throughout the kingdom to inquire into the needs of the people, teach them religion, and report on their spiritual progress. In deference to the Buddhist injunction against taking life, Asoka gave up hunting (replacing this sport by "pious tours" or pilgrimages) and gradually reduced the meat consumption in the royal household until—according to his announcement—only a vegetable diet was permitted. He reformed the harsh system of punishments which his grandfather had used, but he did not entirely abolish the death penalty. There is no evidence of any trend toward democracy in Asoka's

Asokan Bull Capital. From Rampurva, Bihar (northeastern India), third century B.C. Emperor Asoka erected huge stone pillars and utilized some already standing as impressive memorials to his own authority and to the law of Buddha. The bell-shaped capital shows the influence of contemporary Persian architecture.

government. He adhered to the tradition of autocratic rule, but exercised it with conscience and benevolence. Although he was earnest in his support of Buddhism, Asoka opposed fanaticism. He made religious toleration a state policy and urged that the Brahmans of all the Hindu sects be treated with respect. He stated that he cared less about what his subjects believed than he did about their actions and attitudes. To commemorate his authority he had erected in various parts of his empire gigantic sandstone pillars, each cut from a single block of stone and standing forty or fifty feet high. The capitals of animal figures and the beautifully polished surface of these columns—some of which are still preserved—testify to the engineering and artistic skill of the royal workmen.

Asoka's patronage during his long reign contributed markedly to the growth of the Buddhist religion. He sent missionaries of the faith to Ceylon, Burma, Kashmir, Nepal, and apparently even west to Macedonia, Syria, and Egypt. The king's own son was the missionary to Ceylon. Buddhist monks held a general council in 250 B.C. at Asoka's capital, Pataliputra, where they agreed upon the basic texts that should be regarded as authentic. This "Council of Patna" established the canonical books of Buddhism, especially for the *Hinayana* school. The Buddhist scriptures are the oldest written literature of India—that is, they were the first to be committed to writing. However, although the texts were settled upon in 250 B.C., they were still memorized and transmitted only by word of mouth. Except for the excerpts in Asoka's rock carvings, the texts were not actually written out in full until about 80 B.C. in Ceylon.

Asoka's extraordinary administrative system did not long survive him. His successors seem to have been mediocrities who lacked both his reforming zeal and his organizing ability. In 184 B.C. the last

Laughing Boy. Terracotta head of a laughing male, from Pataliputra (Patna). An example of the realistic sculpture of the Maurya period.

Maurya ruler was assassinated by the army commander, an ambitious Brahman who seated his own family on the throne. The efficiency of Asoka's government was not duplicated until about 500 years after the end of his dynasty.

SELECTED READINGS

• *Items so designated are available in paperback editions.*
• Basham, A. L., *The Wonder That Was India: A Survey of the Culture of the Indian Sub-Continent before the Coming of the Muslims,* New York, 1955. Illustrated.
———, ed., *A Cultural History of India,* New York, 1975.
• Brown, W. N., *The United States and India, Pakistan, Bangladesh,* Cambridge, Mass. 1972. An excellent general introduction.
Cambridge History of India, Supplementary Volume: Wheeler, Mortimer, *The Indus Civilization,* 3d ed., Cambridge, 1968.
Conze, Edward, *Buddhist Thought in India,* London, 1962.
• Coomaraswamy, A. K., *History of Indian and Indonesian Art,* New York, 1927.
Eliot Charles, *Hinduism and Buddhism: An Historical Sketch,* 3 vols., New York, 1954. A standard work.
Fairservis, W. A., Jr., *The Roots of Ancient India: The Archaeology of Early Indian Civilization,* New York, 1971. An interesting and provocative account.
Garratt, G. T., ed., *The Legacy of India,* Oxford, 1937.
Hutton, J. S., *Caste in India,* 3rd ed., Oxford, 1961.
Kabir, Humayun, *The Indian Heritage,* New York, 1955.
Kramrisch, Stella, *The Art of India: Traditions of Indian Sculpture, Painting, and Architecture,* New York, 1954. Admirable photographs, with brief introduction.
Lee, S. E., *A History of Far Eastern Art,* New York, 1965.
Majumdar, R. C., ed., *The History and Culture of the Indian People,* Vol. I, London, 1951; Vol. II, 2d ed., Bombay, 1953.
• Moore, C. A., ed., *The Indian Mind: Essentials of Indian Philosophy and Culture,* Honolulu, 1967.
Moreland, W. H., and A. C. Chatterjee, *A Short History of India,* 4th ed., New York, 1957.
• Piggott, Stuart, *Prehistoric India,* Baltimore, 1950.
• Prabhavananda, Swami, and F. Manchester, *The Upanishads, Breath of the Eternal,* New York, 1957.
Prebish, C. S., ed., *Buddhism: A Modern Perspective,* University Park, Pa., 1975. A useful account.
• Rawlinson, H. G., *India, a Short Cultural History,* rev. ed., New York, 1952. An excellent interpretive study.
———, *A Concise History of the Indian People,* 2d ed., New York, 1950.
Rowland, Benjamin, *The Art and Architecture of India: Buddhist, Hindu, Jain,* Baltimore, 1953. Informative and discriminating.
Smith, V. A., *Asoka,* Oxford, 1920.

Spear, Percival, ed., *The Oxford History of India,* 2d ed., New York, 1979.
- Wheeler, Mortimer, *Civilizations of the Indus Valley and Beyond,* London, 1966.
  ———, *Early India and Pakistan to Ashoka,* New York, 1959.
- Wolpert, Stanley, *A New History of India,* New York, 1977. An admirable survey, informative, and well written.

SOURCE MATERIALS

- Arnold, Edwin, tr., *The Song Celestial—The Bhagavad-Gita,* Boston, 1885.
- de Bary, W. T., ed., *Sources of Indian Tradition,* "Brahmanism"; "Jainism and Buddhism"; "Hinduism," New York, 1958.
- Edgerton, Franklin, *The Beginnings of Indian Philosophy,* Cambridge, Mass., 1965. Carefully selected examples with a valuable introduction.
- ———, tr., *The Bhagavad Gita,* Chicago, 1925. Translation and interpretation.
- Hamilton, C. H., ed., *Buddhism, a Religion of Infinite Compassion,* New York, 1952.

  Lin Yutang, ed., *The Wisdom of China and India,* New York, 1942. Hymns from the *Rigveda,* Selections from the *Upanishads.*
- Mueller, Max, tr., *The Upanishads,* 2 vols.
- Narayan, R. K., *Gods, Demons and Others,* London, 1964. Fine translation of ancient Indian stories.

  The *Ramayana* and the *Mahabharata.*

  Sastri, S. R., tr., *The Bhagavadgita,* New York, 1959. An accurate translation with explanatory and critical comment.

Chapter 7

ANCIENT CHINESE CIVILIZATION

There have been many kings, emperors, and great men in history who enjoyed fame and honor while they lived and came to nothing at their death, while Confucius, who was but a common scholar clad in a plain gown, became the acknowledged Master of scholars for over ten generations. All people in China who discuss the six arts, from the emperors, kings, and princes down, regard the Master as the final authority. He may be called the Supreme Sage.

—*Historical Records* of Ssu-ma Ch'ien (145–c. 85 B.C.)

The beginning of a high civilization in China did not occur until about a thousand years after the flowering of the Indus-valley civilization in India. However, when once established the Far Eastern culture continued—not without changes and interruptions but with its essential features intact—into the twentieth century of our own era. The civilization of China, although it took form much later than that of Egypt, Mesopotamia, or the Indus valley, is one of the oldest in existence. Furthermore, its foundations rest upon a population that has retained its identity to a remarkable degree. Throughout successive cultural epochs, in spite of political upheavals and invasions, the Chinese have remained basically the same people since Neolithic times. In contrast to such regions as the Near East, the Mediterranean basin, and Europe, the area of China yielded a civilization that was both independent in origins and unmatched in durability. This does not mean that the Chinese were isolated from the rest of the world or that they did not benefit from foreign contacts. They did their share of conquering, but the lands they annexed were almost exclusively undeveloped territories. They rarely attempted to impose their will upon conquered peoples by force, but considered it their mission to assimilate them and make them the beneficiaries of their superior ethical system.

Reasons for long survival of Chinese civilization

*Early man in China:
Peking man*

I. THE FORMATIVE STAGE

In our study of preliterate cultures we have learned already that China was the home of one of the earliest human species, the so-called Peking man. His skeletal remains were found between 1926 and 1930 in a cave about 25 miles southwest of Peking. Fossilized fragments of over forty separate individuals were discovered, but, unfortunately, after being stored in a warehouse, most were lost during World War II. Anthropologists estimate that Peking man lived at least 500,000 years ago, and that he was probably a contemporary of Java man, one of the oldest human types. His culture was, of course, extremely primitive, but there is evidence that he used stone and bone tools, had a knowledge of fire, and buried his dead. Archeological research—interrupted by World War II but pursued vigorously since 1949 under the People's Republic—has yielded a wealth of information concerning early man in China. Recent excavations at the site where the bones of Peking man were first discovered have unearthed new specimens of the same human type but belonging to a period some 200,000 years later than that assigned to the first appearance of Peking man. Study of these recent finds reveals significant evolutionary changes in the course of 200 millennia. While the creature's teeth and jaws diminished in size, brain capacity increased by as much as 20 percent, indicating a growth in intelligence as well as changes in dietary habits. Contrary to what was formerly believed, it is now known that much of the area of China was continuously occupied by subhuman or human types throughout the Stone Ages. *Homo sapiens* appeared perhaps as early as 50,000 years ago. A later Paleolithic culture—the remains of which have not yet been fully excavated and classified—is identified with people who apparently were Mongoloid in race.

The Neolithic Age in China can be dated from the sixth millennium

The Loess Highlands of Northern China

B.C. At least two Neolithic cultures have been discovered, one centered in the great highland plain that surrounds the Yellow River valley, the other predominant in the southeast coastal area, including the island of Taiwan. Both were developed by communities of farmers, with millet the chief crop in the north and roots and tubers in the southeast, and each produced a distinctive type of pottery.

Neolithic cultures

There is still disagreement as to where and when Neolithic culture advanced to the level of civilization, characterized by metal working, city living, writing, and effective political organization. One contemporary scholar contends that the cradle of Chinese civilization was the semiarid northern plain. He asserts that, in contrast to the inhabitants of the well-watered Nile and Tigris-Euphrates valleys, the Chinese began as dry-land farmers and may have lacked irrigation facilities until the sixth century B.C. The highlands bordering the middle reaches of the Yellow River are covered with a type of soil known as loess, composed of fine particles of loam and dust borne by northwest winds from the central plateaus of Asia and deposited in the valley and along the northeastern coast. This soil, which from its color has given rise to such geographical names as Yellow River and Yellow Sea, is pliable enough to be easily worked with primitive digging sticks, and also has the advantage of being free from a heavy growth of forest or grasses. In choosing farm sites close to the river or its tributaries but on high ground, the early inhabitants avoided the danger of floods. But they had to depend on plants capable of surviving with a minimum of rainfall. The principal crops of northern China in the Neolithic Age were several varieties of millet, hemp, and the mulberry (for raising silkworms). Rice, too, was grown in the marsh areas of the northern plain, probably introduced from the Yangtze region to the south, where it was indigenous.[1] In view of the wide extent of Neolithic communities in China, however, it is quite possible that an advance behind this cultural level took place in more than one area. At any rate, contacts between regions were sufficient to promote the growth and spread of a homogeneous civilization.

The loess highlands, cradle of Chinese civilization

Archeological finds in China have thrown light not only on preliterate epochs but on the early historical period as well. They have established that the Bronze Age—universally associated with the oldest civilizations—began in China somewhere around 2000 B.C. Excavations of Bronze Age remains in northern China supply concrete evidence concerning the Shang Dynasty, which according to tradition was the second of China's ruling houses (c. 1766–1027 B.C.). Long regarded by scholars as almost purely legendary, the Shang (or Yin) Dynasty has been verified and impressive examples of its workmanship recovered. Precise dates are not yet determined, but the civiliza-

The Bronze Age and the beginning of the Shang Dynasty

---

[1] Ping-ti Ho, "The Loess and the Origin of Chinese Agriculture," *American Historical Review,* October 1969, pp. 1–36.

Shang civilization

The economy: agriculture

Shang housing

Material culture

tion was flourishing by 1400 B.C. A study of objects that have been unearthed and especially the all-important deciphering of inscriptions make it possible to construct a fairly complete picture of this formative period of Chinese history.

Shang culture was based upon that of the Neolithic farming communities. Presumably the dynasty was inaugurated by the conquest of a military chieftain, with no extensive displacement of population. Distinctive aspects of the civilization included the construction of fortified cities, the use of horse-drawn chariots in warfare, a highly developed bronze metallurgy, an elaborate system of writing, and a sharply stratified society composed of an aristocracy, craftsmen, and farmers. The Shang kingdom evidently controlled only a small part of China—the plain surrounding the middle Yellow River valley—but its influence extended over a wide area. The Shang people carried on trade with other regions, including the Yangtze valley to the south, and they had to defend themselves against nomadic tribes from the north and west. The last capital of the dynasty was a city located at the northern tip of Honan Province, about 80 miles north of the Yellow River (the site of modern An-yang).

Though developing in close proximity to the wandering herdsmen of Mongolia, the Chinese were primarily a nation of farmers. Agriculture was the chief source of livelihood of the Shang people, although their tools for cultivating the soil were still quite primitive. Grains were the principal crop; wheat and barley were grown in addition to millet. Hunting and herding contributed to the food supply. Many animals had been domesticated, including not only the dog, pig, goat, sheep, ox, horse, and chicken, but also the water buffalo, monkey, and probably the elephant. Dog flesh as well as pork was a popular item of diet.

The houses the Shang people constructed show an intelligent adaptation to the environment. The Neolithic inhabitants of the region commonly lived in pits hollowed out of the loess. In Shang times rural villagers apparently also occupied pit dwellings, but the city residents built more comfortable houses above ground. For a foundation the firmly packed earth served admirably. Upon the rectangular foundation was erected a gabled-roof structure, with wooden poles holding up the central ridge of the roof and shorter posts supporting each of the two sides at the eaves. Thatching was used for the roof and packed earth for the outside walls of the house. This type of dwelling, which by coincidence is closer in design to the European style of home than to the tents of Mongolia or the mud-brick houses of Egypt and Mesopotamia, has been employed by the Chinese throughout their history.

The specimens of Shang craftsmanship that archeologists have recovered reveal a high degree of skill and versatility. In spite of familiarity with metal, Shang artisans still made many objects of

Bronze Ritual Vessel. Shang Dynasty (1523–1027 B.C.).

stone—knives, axes, and even dishes—as well as of bone, shell, and horn. Bone implements inlaid with turquoise and exquisitely carved pieces of ivory were produced in abundance. Cowrie shells were used for jewelry and probably also served as money. The bow and arrow was the most formidable weapon for the hunt or for combat. Bamboo arrows were feathered and tipped with bronze or bone points. The bow was of the composite or reflex type, formed of two separate arcs of wood held together with horn, and said to be almost twice as powerful as the famous English long bow. Two-horse chariots, of elaborate workmanship and with spoked wheels, were probably the exclusive property of the aristocracy. Armor was made of leather, sometimes reinforced with wooden slats. Evidently the people were fond of music. For musical instruments they employed drums, stones emitting a bell-like tone when struck, and a small pipe of hollow bone with five finger-holes.

The artistry of the Shang people is illustrated most strikingly by their sculpture and engraving. The examples of sculpture thus far discovered are generally of small dimensions. Shang metal work was truly remarkable, especially the superb bronze castings of intricate design. Bronze articles included weapons and chariot and harness fittings, but most impressive were the objects intended for religious and ceremonial functions—tripods, libation bowls, drinking cups, and grotesquely figured masks. The technique employed in their making was superlative. A leading American specialist in early Chinese culture asserts that it was more flawless than the technique employed for bronze sculpture at the height of the Italian Renaissance.

Bronze Tripod Cup. Shang Dynasty. This cup was used in sacrificial ceremonies.

Art of the Shang people

Bronze Ritual Vessel with Removable Top. Shang Dynasty.

Oracle Bone. Dating from 1300 B.C., this artifact records the appearance of a new star. Note the pictographic characters.

As has already been mentioned, this early civilization possessed a system of writing. The writing brush and an ink made of soot had been invented. Writing materials included silk cloth and wood, and it is quite possible that books were compiled from narrow strips of bamboo joined together by a thong. Fortunately, a great many specimens of writing have been preserved inscribed on pieces of animal bone, horn, and tortoise shells and pottery. These served in a process of divination by the king and priests; hence they are referred to as "oracle bones." After a question had been directed to the spirits, a flat piece of split cattle bone or a tortoise shell was heated until it cracked; then the shape of the crack was studied to ascertain the answer from the spirit world. The majority of the oracle bones contain no writing; but in about 10 percent of the cases the question was engraved upon the object after the divination rite had been performed. Although the inscriptions are brief, a careful study of them has thrown light upon many aspects of Shang society and activities.

The Shang writing was not primitive but in an advanced pictographic stage. While the Shang symbols are the earliest examples found in the Far East, they presuppose a long period of evolution from more rudimentary forms. Each character represented an entire word, as it does in the classical Chinese. In some cases, only the shape of the sign has changed. For example, the Shang character for *sun* was round—obviously a picture of the sun—while now it is square. Practically all the principles which the Chinese literary language employs in the process of character formation were already in use. The Shang characters were not only pictographs but sometimes ideographs, in which the meaning was conveyed by combining different symbols or concepts (the sun and moon joined together represent *bright* or *brightness;* the sun rising behind a tree stands for *east*). The phonetic principle was also applied. A character having one meaning might be used to indicate a word of different meaning but pronounced the same way. To avoid confusion, the phonetic symbol was combined with a conceptual symbol in the same character. Not surprisingly, fewer characters were employed in Shang times than later, although it is probable that the list compiled from the oracle bones is only partial. About 3,000 characters have been distinguished in the Shang records; the written language eventually came to include more than fifteen times that number.

Little definite information is available as to the political and social institutions of the Shang period. In addition to military activities, the king probably supervised public works and was important as the chief religious functionary. He was assisted by an educated class of priests, who served as astrologers, performed the divination rites, and supervised the calendar. Because the calendar was a lunar one, it frequently had to be adjusted to bring it into harmony with the solar year. There is some evidence from the oracle bones that the Shang priests had made considerable achievements in mathematics and astronomy. As early as the fourteenth century B.C. they recorded eclipses and perhaps had already conceived the decimal system.

The family was the basic social institution. The king, or a great aristocrat, might have several wives, but monogamy seems to have been the more usual practice even in the royal family, as it almost certainly was among the people generally. Slavery existed and there were gradations in the ranks of society, but there is no evidence of a feudal system during this period.

The family

Ample testimony exists for the religious practices of the Shang people. They worshiped many natural objects and forces—the earth, rivers, the winds, even the directions. To these gods they performed sacrifices in temples. Burnt offerings of animal flesh were common, and a kind of wine or beer made from millet was also considered acceptable. Although the Shang were in some ways highly civilized, there is gruesome evidence that they practiced human sacrifice on a large scale. Apparently the victims were usually captives who had been taken in battle, and sometimes raiding expeditions were sent out for the express purpose of securing a batch of foreign tribesmen to be offered in sacrifice. The principal deity seems to have been a god concerned primarily with rainfall, the crops, and war. His name, Shang Ti, has persisted into later times. There is no evidence that Shang religion was essentially spiritual or ethical; it was directed toward the procuring of human prosperity, as among the Sumerians and Babylonians. The king was not a divinity like the Egyptian pharaoh, but he became an object of worship after his death, and sacrifices were performed to the departed spirits of both kings and queens. The royal tombs were sumptuous affairs. A large pit was excavated, provided with stairways, and a wooden tomb chamber was constructed at the bottom. The royal corpse was surrounded with magnificent furnishings, including figured bronzes and pottery, marble statuary, and richly adorned implements and jewels. After the funeral ceremonies the entire excavation was filled with firmly tamped earth.

Religion of the Shang period

It is noteworthy that the typical Chinese institution of ancestor worship was already in existence, at least in the circle of the court. Ancestral spirits were believed to possess the power of helping or hurting their descendants, and yet they depended upon their living representatives for nourishment in the form of food offerings. It was also customary, even among people of humble circumstance, to bury valuable objects with the deceased. Divination by means of the oracle bones—the practice which bequeathed so many valuable inscriptions—was a by-product of the cult of ancestor worship and the belief in the potency of departed spirits.

Ancestor worship

The Shang society represents the earliest genuine civilization of Eastern Asia for which historical records are available. In addition, it laid the foundation and provided materials for the distinctive Chinese culture pattern, as illustrated by methods of agriculture, handicrafts, artistic and architectural forms, emphasis upon the family as the basic social unit, religious concepts, and a system of writing. About 1027 B.C.[2] the city of Shang was captured and the dynasty overthrown, but the new rulers preserved basic institutions, encouraged cultural progress, and gave their name (Chou) to the longest dynasty in China's history.

2. THE CHOU DYNASTY, THE CLASSICAL AGE OF CHINA (c. 1100–256 B.C.)

While the civilization of the Vedic Age in India was still in its early stages, in the Yellow River valley of China the Shang Dynasty was succeeded by the Chou. However, the advent of a new ruling house brought no such profound change in the character of society as did the Indo-Aryan invasion of India. The Chou people, located west of the Shang frontier, were of the same ethnic stock (possibly with a trace of Turkish or Tibetan influence added) and possessed a culture similar to that of the Shang, with whom they had had considerable contact. The demise of the Shang Dynasty was probably the result of an internal power struggle and bore little resemblance to a barbarian conquest.[3] Cultural developments continued uninterruptedly on foundations already laid and eventually completed the pattern of Chinese civilization for centuries to come.

The new dynasty exerted zealous efforts to convince the people that it was a legitimate succession rather than a usurpation. Its spokesmen advanced the claim that the last Shang ruler had been incompetent and debauched, and that the divine powers had used the Chou as an instrument for his removal. The "Mandate of Heaven," they alleged, had been transferred from the Shang house to the Chou. There is no evidence that the Shang king was guilty of the faults ascribed to him, but the charge, even if a fabrication, shows the desire of the conquerors to fit their authority into accepted conventions rather than to break with the past. And the concept of governmental power as a commission from Heaven rather than an absolute and inalienable right—although possibly invented by the Chou for propaganda purposes—was to become a persistent element in Chinese political history.

The Chou form of government was a monarchy, although not identical with that of the Shang. The early Chou rulers maintained their capital near modern Sian (Shensi province) in the Wei valley, where their power had already been established. In addition to the Shang territory they added other conquests, especially southward in the middle Yangtze valley. The king exercised direct rule over the

[2] The exact date is in dispute among scholars. Estimates range from 1122 to 1018 B.C.
[3] K. C. Chang, *The Archaeology of Ancient China*, 3d ed., p. 383.

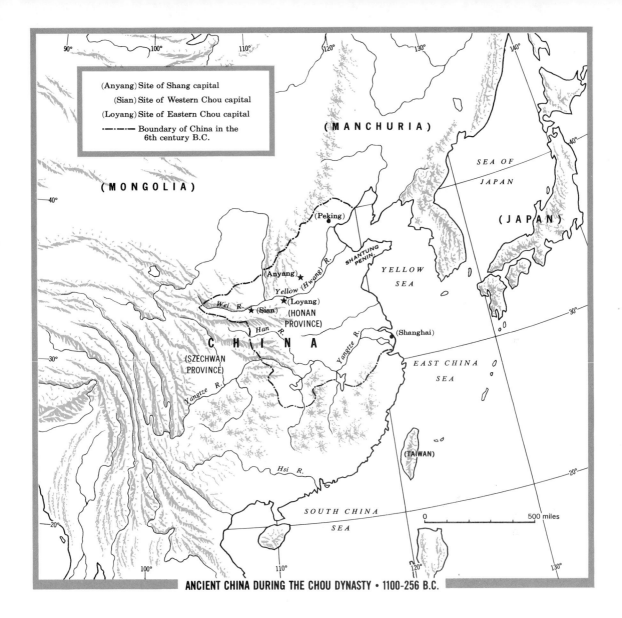

(MONGOLIA)

(MANCHURIA)

SEA OF
JAPAN

(Peking)

(JAPAN)

SHANTUNG
PENIN.

YELLOW
SEA

(Anyang) ★

Yellow (Hwang) R.

Wei R.   ★(Loyang)
    ★ (Sian)   (HONAN
           PROVINCE)

C H I N A

Han

Yangtze R.

(Shanghai)

(SZECHWAN
PROVINCE)

EAST CHINA

SEA

Yangtze R.

(TAIWAN)

Hsi R.

SOUTH CHINA   0   500 miles

SEA

ANCIENT CHINA DURING THE CHOU DYNASTY · 1100-256 B.C.

region surrounding his capital but administered the outlying areas
indirectly, through appoined officials who were given almost complete jurisdiction within their own districts. The Chou administrative
system was roughly similar to that which developed in Europe in the
age of feudalism some 2,000 years later. The district governors, originally members of the royal family or generals of proved competence,
were the king's vassals, but they were also great territorial lords,
exercising wide military and judicial powers, and they gradually
transformed their position from that of appointive official to hereditary ruler. Chou feudalism—like the later European variety—contained elements of danger for the central government, although for

two or three centuries the Chou court was strong enough to remove overly ambitious officials and keep its own authority paramount.

By the eighth century B.C. the vigor of the ruling house had declined to the point where it was no longer able to protect the western frontier effectively against the attacks of barbarians. The fortunes of the dynasty seemed to reach their lowest point in 771 B.C., when a worthless king almost duplicated the villainies that had been unjustifiably attributed to the last of the Shang rulers. King Yu, particularly through his extravagant efforts to amuse his favorite concubine, angered the nobles beyond endurance. When he lit the beacon fires to summon aid in the face of a combined attack by barbarian tribes and one of the outraged nobles, his men refused to answer the summons. King Yu was killed and his palace looted. The dynasty might have been ended then and there, but the nobles of the realm found it expedient to install the king's son as nominal head, keeping in their own hands the actual authority over their respective dominions. This event marks the close of the "Western Chou" period. The royal seat of government was now moved about 100 miles east into safer territory (near the modern city of Honan), and the ensuing period (771–c. 250 B.C.) is known accordingly as the "Eastern Chou."

During the 500 years of the Eastern Chou Dynasty, China suffered from political disunity and internal strife. The king actually ruled over a domain much smaller than that of some of the great hereditary princes. For the kingdom as a whole his powers, while theoretically supreme (he was officially styled "Son of Heaven"), were limited to religious and ceremonial functions and to adjudicating disputes concerning precedence and the rights of succession in the various states. In spite of these conditions, however, it is not quite accurate to describe the Eastern Chou era as an age of feudalism. It is true that hereditary nobles enjoyed social prominence, wealth, and power, and acquired different degrees of rank, roughly equivalent to the European titles of duke, marquis, count, viscount, and baron. They became lords and vassals, held fiefs for which they owed military service, and were supported by the labor of the peasants on their lands. These warrior aristocrats not only raised armies and collected revenues from their dominions but also administered justice. Custom supplied the greater part of law, but severe penalties, including fines, mutilation, and death, were inflicted upon offenders. Nevertheless, a number of factors prevented the complete ascendancy of a feudal regime. In the first place, a large proportion of the nobility failed to acquire estates of their own and remained jealous of the great territorial lords. The lesser aristocracy, generally well educated and frequently unemployed, constituted a sort of middle class that could not fit comfortably into a feudalized society. More important still, towns were growing and trade increasing throughout the Chou period, and the merchants (including part of the aristocracy) attained economic

Ceremonial Bronze Basin. Chou Dynasty (1100–256 B.C.). The inscription on this bronze piece, known as the *San P'an,* records the settlement of a territorial dispute between the feudal states of San and Nieh in Western Shensi Province.

importance. Moreover, rulers of the larger states successfully pushed forward a program of centralization within their own dominions. They introduced regular systems of taxation based upon agriculture. To offset the entrenched position of the nobles they developed their own administrative bureaucracies and staffed them with trained officials, recruited largely from the ranks of the lesser aristocracy. In spite of the disorganized condition of China as a whole, the period provided valuable experience in the art of government which could eventually be drawn upon in the task of reuniting the country.

Although China was divided during the Eastern Chou period into many principalities with shifting boundaries and frequent wars, a few of the larger states held the balance of power, especially four which were located on the outer frontiers to the north, west, and south. Usually one state at a time was recognized as paramount and its ruler, designated as "First Noble," took the lead in organizing the defense of the kingdom as a whole and even in collecting the revenues. The boundaries of Chinese civilization were extended by the aggressive initiative of the rulers of the frontier states. The Shantung peninsula, the seacoast as far south as modern Shanghai and Hangchow, and the rich Yangtze valley were all brought under Chinese jurisdiction. Thus the total area was much larger than the old Shang kingdom and included more than half of the eighteen provinces which have constituted the state of China during the greater portion of its history. The southern part of Manchuria was also occupied, and walls of earth— the first stages of the famous Great Wall of China—were constructed both south and north of the Yellow River for protection against the nomads of Mongolia.

Expansion of the frontiers

Beginning about the middle of the fifth century B.C., internal conditions became extremely chaotic, inaugurating a bloody period

Bronze Ceremonial Vessel. Chou Dynasty.

known as that of "the Warring States." The relatively restrained competition which the feudal principalities had carried on with one another gave way to a struggle for supremacy in which proprieties and recognized codes were disregarded. The rulers of several of the states even assumed the title of "king" (*wang*), previously reserved for the prince of Chou. In the fourth and third centuries B.C. the state of Ch'in, seated in the Wei valley on the western frontier, gained ascendancy over the others. Not only were the Ch'in rulers aggressive, but within their own dominions they had developed the most effectively centralized government in China. After annexing the fertile plain lying south of the Wei valley (in modern Szechwan province), they constructed a splendid irrigation system which has lasted until the present day. Probably the Ch'in people had also mingled with and absorbed some of the barbarian tribesmen, but they were no less Chinese in culture than their rivals. In spite of alliances formed against them by other feudal princes, the Ch'in forces, employing ruthlessness, massacre, and treachery, annexed one region after another. Finally, in 256 B.C., they seized the tiny remaining portion of the royal domain and ended the Chou Dynasty. Within thirty-five years the Ch'in prince had brought all the Chinese territories under his control and, to indicate the extent of his triumph, assumed the imposing title of "First Emperor" (Shih Huang Ti). Although the Ch'in Dynasty hardly outlasted its founder, it did China the valuable service of abolishing the remnants of feudalism. The highly centralized government which the Ch'in emperor established did not prove to be permanent, but the feudal system never reappeared.

During the 800 or 900 years of the Chou Dynasty, in spite of inter-

Ancient Irrigation Canal. Still in use, this is part of one of the oldest and most elaborate irrigation systems in the world.

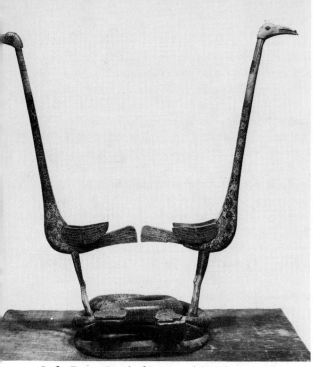

Left: *Drum Stand of Lacquered Wood*. Late Chou Dynasty. Right: *Ceremonial Bronze Tripod*. Late Chou Dynasty, fourth century B.C. This piece is thought to have been part of the Li-Yu treasure.

nal conflicts, cultural progress was almost continuous. The period is regarded as the classical age of Chinese civilization, and its contributions were fundamental to the whole subsequent history of the Far East. As has already been indicated, the culture of the Chou was based upon foundations that had been laid by their predecessors. Handicraft techniques improved under the Chou and the smelting of iron was introduced, although iron did not entirely displace bronze. While the great majority of the population lived in rural villages, there were some large towns and the merchant class assumed importance. Trade was by no means exclusively local. With the introduction of the donkey, and especially the camel (probably not before the third century B.C.), it became possible to develop caravan trade routes across Central Asia for the transportation of grain, salt, silk, and other commodities. Coined copper money came into use before the close of the fifth century B.C. The manufacture of silk, already an old industry, was increased, and the fibers of several domestic plants were also employed in making textiles.

Cultural progress under the Chou

From time immemorial the all-important Chinese enterprise has been farming. It was extended under the Chou by reclamation measures—the building of irrigation canals and reservoirs and the draining of swamps—and also by acquisition of the moist and fertile rice-producing lands of the Yangtze valley. The soybean—valuable not only as a food but for restoring fertility to the soil—was added to the

Agriculture under the Chou

list of crops. The methods of cultivation developed during the Shang and Chou periods have remained essentially unchanged ever since.

The persistence of unvarying techniques over 3,000 years is attributable not to the inability of the Chinese to progress but to the fact that these techniques were admirably adapted to the terrain and to the objectives of Chinese society. While they were primitive in some ways, they embodied a great deal of experience and foresight. China has been said to possess a "vegetable civilization," because its people, while not socially or intellectually stagnant, adapted themselves so completely to the potentialities of their environment. The typical Chinese farming village—with fields of various sizes, often tiny but all carefully tended—appears almost as if it were part of the natural landscape instead of being an effort on man's part to manipulate nature for his own benefit. Although China is a large country, the relative scarcity of arable land made it difficult for food production to keep pace with an expanding population. Much of the country is hilly or mountainous, and the north and west portions are subject to drought which cannot be entirely overcome by irrigation. Consequently, attention was lavished upon every suitable plot that could be found. The bulk of labor was done by hand, with simple tools but in such a way as to produce the greatest possible yield. Wastes which had fertilizing value were collected and returned to the soil, as were ashes and even powdered sun-dried bricks when no longer serviceable for building purposes. Crops were rotated to avoid soil exhaustion, and hillsides were terraced to conserve moisture and prevent erosion.

Although draft animals had been known from early times and the ox-drawn plow was introduced about the sixth century B.C., their use was restricted because of the cheapness and—on small plots—greater efficiency of human labor. Besides, hayfields or grazing lands to provide animal fodder represented a curtailment of the area devoted to producing foodstuffs for human beings. The Chinese have subsisted largely on a vegetable diet, not because they had religious scruples against eating flesh as did the Hindus, but for practical reasons of economy. Instead of raising crops to feed cattle and then eating the cattle, they preferred to consume the crops directly themselves. For meats they chose animals that could be reared inexpensively—chickens, ducks, and especially pigs, which were also useful scavengers, and fish, with which even temporary ponds could be profitably stocked. Chinese methods of agriculture thus were intensive rather than extensive. As compared with modern Western countries, particularly the United States and Canada, the yield was low in proportion to the number of men employed and the hours of labor, but high in terms of acreage. While Chinese farming demanded exacting and arduous toil on the part of the cultivators, it made possible the growth of a large population.

Society during the Chou period had a decidedly aristocratic character. There was a tremendous gulf between the great landowners and the peasants, who comprised the vast majority of the people. But while class lines were rigidly drawn, Chinese society was never stratified by a caste system like that of India. There were only two clearly distinguished classes, the commoners or serfs and the nobles; and as civilization became more complex the nobility included contrasting interests and conditions rather than remaining a solidly united order. Because the numbers of the aristocracy tended to increase, many of them consequently possessed little or no landed property. They were forced to seek administrative employment with a powerful noble, to engage in trade, or even to undertake menial occupations, thereby undermining the fiction of the inherent superiority of the hereditary aristocracy. Unfortunately, very little is known about the condition of the lower classes. Evidently before the close of the Chou period a considerable number of peasants had become landowners. Others, however, were actually slaves, and most of the commoners were serfs, attached to the soil without having legal title to it and compelled to give the lord a large share of the produce.

While the family is always a basic social institution, it has been so to an almost unique degree in China. Here the family was a tightly organized unit, bent upon preserving the welfare of its members against any outside agency, official or unofficial, and was probably the only safeguard of any consequence against the unlimited exploitation of the lower classes. Typically the Chinese family was large because it embraced several generations. When a son married he customarily brought his bride home to live under the paternal roof or in a closely neighboring house. Theoretically the family also included the departed ancestral spirits, thus extending vertically into time as well as horizontally among contemporary relatives. Authority was vested in the father (or grandfather), and the utmost emphasis was placed upon respect for elders, so that even grown men were bound by their parents' wishes. Such a custom led to extreme conservatism and sometimes inflicted hardships upon youth, but it had the advantage of developing qualities of patience, loyalty, and consideration for the helpless aged.

Women became definitely subordinate to men in the patriarchal family and in Chinese society at large, although their position was not utterly intolerable. Allegedly, in early Chou times the young men and maidens of the peasant class were allowed to choose their mates freely after a Spring Festival characterized by complete license. However that may be, among the aristocracy neither men nor women had freedom of choice in marriage unless they defied convention and parental authority. Marriages were arranged by the parents of the respective parties, usually with the assistance of a matchmaker or go-between. After the bride was brought to her husband's home she was considered as on probation for a three-month period, after which if she had

Labor intensive farming

The family as a social institution

Subordination of women

Large Bronze Bell. This bell, with bosses or nipples, decorative panels, and inscriptions, is typical of the Middle Chou style (ninth century B.C.). It was hung from the ring at the base of the shaft and was sounded by striking with a wooden mallet. The bell has a scooped mouth instead of being even at the bottom. (In the picture it is resting on a cushion.)

proved satisfactory she was allowed to participate in the ancestral sacrifice and became an accepted member of the family. In regard to the laxity of conduct permitted and the right of divorce, the woman was also at a disadvantage. Only the husband could have recourse to divorce, and he could obtain it on any one of a number of grounds, including that his wife talked too much. Actually, however, divorces were rare, especially among people of humble circumstance. Undoubtedly the practices of polygamy and concubinage, permitting a man to have more than one consort, added to the hardships and humiliation of women. But these practices were confined to the wealthy classes and were by no means universal among them. In spite of the inferior position of woman in Chinese society, she had definite rights and privileges and on the whole was much better off than in the caste-ridden society of India. It is strange that, in a predominantly agrarian economy such as China's, labor in the fields was not regarded as woman's normal work, although among poor families she often had to assist. The wife's own family did not renounce all interest in her when she left their home for her husband's and might interfere in case she was abused. Children were taught to love and venerate both parents, and as a woman grew older she shared in the honors accorded to age. The domineering position which a grandmother or mother-in-law sometimes assumed became proverbial.

The Chinese family was not only an economic and sociological unit but a religious and political one as well. Some scholars maintain that during the Chou period the servile peasants were not permitted the dignity of having surnames, and that they had no share in the cult of ancestor worship. However, that condition could not endure in view of the tremendous emphasis placed upon family relationships among the dominant classes, in public administration, and in the literature of the age. Throughout the greater part of Chinese history, religion for the ordinary person consisted largely in caring for his family graves and making prayers and offerings to the spirits of his ancestors. As a political unit the family enforced discipline and considered misconduct on the part of one of its members as a collective disgrace. Very commonly the inflicting of punishment for minor offenses was left to the head of a family rather than to a public official. The strong solidarity and sense of collective responsibility of the family had disadvantages as well as advantages. Because the family was answerable for the behavior of its members, one of them might be punished for the misconduct of another if the true offender was not apprehended by the authorities, or a whole family might be wiped out for a crime committed by one person. On the whole, however, the family gave the individual a greater feeling of security and support than has been typical in most societies.

Religion was fundamentally the same as it had been in Shang times. Many deities were worshiped, ranging from local spirits and nature gods with limited powers to such majestic divinities as Earth and

Heaven. The practice of human sacrifice gradually disappeared and came to be strongly condemned, but animals, agricultural produce, and liquor were offered upon the altars. Evidence of a "chariot sacrifice" was uncovered by archeologists north of the Yellow River when they excavated a deep pit about 30 feet square. In this instance seventy-two horses harnessed to twelve chariots, and eight dogs with bells fastened to their necks, had apparently been placed in the pit and buried alive. While worship did not necessarily include prayer, prayers were sometimes written out and burned with the sacrificial offering. A prominent deity from Chou times on was the one called T'ien, translated as "Heaven." Although of separate origin, this divinity was similar to and became practically identical with the earlier Shang Ti. T'ien was not conceived of primarily as a personal god but as representing the supreme spiritual powers collectively, the universal moral law, or an underlying impersonal cosmic force. It was by the "Mandate of Heaven" (*T'ien-ming*) that the king was supposed to rule, and he was referred to as "Son of Heaven," without, however, implying that he was divine. The worship of the earth as an agricultural deity came to be supplemented by the veneration of a specific locality with which the fortunes of the worshipers were associated. Every village had its sacred mound of earth; the lord of large territories had a mound to represent his domain; and the mound of the king was believed to have significance for the whole land of China. The most important rituals took place either at these mounds or in ancestral temples.

Among the Chinese at this time, as among the Hindus, there was no clear-cut religious system, no fixed creed, and no church. In contrast to Hindu society, however, the Chinese priests did not become a sacrosanct class in a position to dominate other groups. The priests, like those of the ancient Greeks, were merely assistants in the ritual. The indispensable religious functionaries were the heads of families, including, of course, the king, whose ancestral spirits were particularly formidable, and who propitiated the great deities of the rivers, earth, and sky. For most of the people religion was either a family affair, consisting of social functions invested with sentiment and emphasizing filial piety, or a matter of state, maintained by the proper authorities to ensure the general welfare. Sacrifices to the greatest gods were ordinarily performed only by the highest officials, to lesser deities by lower officials, and so on down to the ordinary folk who sacrificed to their own ancestors in the form of wooden tablets. They believed that the spirits of these ancestors could bring prosperity to the family and that dire consequences would follow any neglect of the rites. Aside from traditional ceremonies, everyday life was complicated by a medley of folklore and superstition hardly classifiable as religion but exerting a potent influence. This included the belief in witchcraft, in good and evil omens, in divination and spirit messages conveyed through mediums, and in the necessity of avoiding offense to numerous malignant beings. "Hungry ghosts," whose sacrifices had been neglected or cut off through the extinction of a family, were considered especially dangerous. In spite of the strong faith that the soul outlived the body, the notion of rewards and punishments in an afterlife was almost entirely lacking. The worst fate that could happen to a disembodied spirit, it was thought, was for it to be deprived of the nourishment supplied by sacrificial offerings.

By far the most significant contributions of the Chou period were in the fields of literature and philosophy. The Shang system of writing, already highly advanced, was continued with slight modifications. Evidently the Chinese now considered written records as indispensable to the conduct of both public and private affairs. They sometimes recorded important transactions in lengthy inscriptions on bronze vessels, but they more frequently wrote with the brush upon wood or cloth of silk. Books composed of thin strips of bamboo were produced in abundance. Although only a minority of the population was literate, it must have been a large minority and included the feudal nobility as well as the merchants. In contrast to the feudal age of western Europe when writing was confined almost entirely to the clergy, the Chou aristocrats were versed in literature and kept full records of their properties, their dependents, and sometimes of their personal activities. Not only the king but the head of every feudal state maintained archives to preserve the luster of family traditions and to aid in settling disputes with rival princes. The Chinese, even in ancient times, were at the opposite pole from the Hindus in their attitude toward the importance of chronology and the recording of factual events (although this does not mean that Chinese documents were entirely accurate or free from fanciful elements). A young nobleman or prince, in the process of his education, was reminded by his tutors that later generations would study the annals of his administration and that he should, accordingly, choose his actions with care. Princes were regularly given instruction in history "to stimulate them to good conduct and warn them against evil"—apparently with no better results than have attended most modern efforts in this direction.

Of the tremendous output of Chou literature, only a few authentic portions have survived (aside from the imperishable bronze inscriptions). Some of them, however, are from a date earlier than 600 B.C. Probably the most ancient work is the *Book of Changes*. It contains a collection of hexagrams formed of straight and broken lines arranged in different combinations, with accompanying text. The figures, like the earlier Shang oracle bones, were used for divination. Thus the book was originally hardly more than a sorcerer's manual, but it came to be venerated as a work of mystic and occult wisdom.[4] Very differ-

Written records of the Chou period

Literature of the Chou period

---

[4] For a contrary view see H. Wilhelm, *Change: Eight Lectures on the I Ching,* 1960. Wilhelm interprets the classic as an affirmation of man's ability to control his own destiny.

ent is the *Document Classic* (less accurately called *Book of History*), which is a collection of official documents, proclamations, and speeches purporting to be from the early Chou period. The *Book of Etiquette,* dealing with ceremonial behavior, formal occasions, and preparation for adult responsibilities, was intended to assist in the education of the lesser aristocracy. Most interesting of all is the *Book of Poetry,* an anthology of about 300 poems covering a wide range of subjects and moods. Some of the poems are religious, in the nature of prayers or hymns to accompany the rites of sacrifice; others celebrate the exploits of heroes; still others are lyrical in quality, voicing the laments of a discharged official, a soldier's homesickness, delight in the beauties of nature, and the frustration or rapture of young lovers. Neither in quantity nor in profundity do these odes approach the *Vedas* of India, but they are graceful in expression and show vividly the practical down-to-earth temperament of the Chinese and their lively interest in and optimistic attitude toward the business of living—at least among the aristocracy. While the poems on the whole are neither philosophical nor spiritual, a few suggest the reforming fervor of the Hebrew prophets.

In view of the extent and the variety of writing during the Chou period, the literary collections which have survived are rather disappointing. But this deficiency is amply compensated for by achievements in the realm of philosophy, which reached a brilliant climax between the sixth and third centuries B.C. For some unexplained reason—perhaps by mere coincidence—philosophical activity of a high order was carried on at about the same time in three widely separated regions of the ancient world. While the Greeks were inquiring into the nature of the physical universe, and Indian thinkers were pondering the relationship of the soul to Absolute Being, Chinese sages were attempting to discover the basis of human society and the underlying principles of good government. The Chinese thinkers were not much interested in either physical science or metaphysics; the philosophy they propounded was social, political, and ethical. Exhortatory and reformist in tone, it undoubtedly, reflected the influence of the recurrent strife and political disorders of a period when feudal ideas and institutions were becoming increasingly irrelevant but had not yet been clearly repudiated. Against the background of upheaval which marked the late Chou era, philosophers sought to formulate principles for the stabilizing of society and the betterment of the individual. The leaders in this intellectual activity were largely from the lesser aristocracy, a scholarly group, fond of disputation, but also maintaining an interest in the practice of government and sometimes holding administrative posts or coaching pupils who aspired to such posts. It was a time of lively interchange of ideas, and a great variety of opinions was put forward. Out of this intellectual ferment and debate—one of the most productive in the annals of human thought—four main philo-

Philosophy

Confucius in Royal Dress. A traditional representation in bronze.

Confucius as a teacher

sophic schools emerged, the most important being the Confucianist and the Taoist.

Confucius (c. 551–479 B.C.), who has proved to be one of the most influential men in all history, was largely a failure from the standpoint of what he hoped to accomplish. He spent his life advocating reforms that were not adopted; yet he left an indelible stamp upon the thought and political institutions of China and other lands that came under Chinese influence. He was a native of the state of Lu (in modern Shantung province) and was reputed to have been the child of an aged father, a gentleman soldier named K'ung (Confucius is the Latinized form of the name K'ung Fu-tzu, or "Master K'ung"). Probably his family was of the lesser aristocracy, respectable but poor. When he was only about twenty-one he began to teach informally a group of young friends who were attracted by his alert mind and by his precocious knowledge of traditional forms and usages. Although his reputation spread rapidly, little is known concerning the incidents of his career. Possibly as a mature man he held office for a short time under the Duke of Lu. For more than ten years, until old age overtook him, he wandered from state to state, refusing to be employed as a timeserving flatterer but continually hoping that some ruler would give him a chance to apply his ideals and thus set in motion a tide of reform that might sweep the entire country. Although revered by his small band of disciples, some of whom became officeholders, Confucius received no offer of appointment that he could accept in good conscience. Finally he returned to his native country where he died, discouraged, at the age of seventy-two.

Frustrated as a statesman, Confucius made his real contribution as a teacher. The memoranda of his conversations with his disciples (the *Analects*)—which are considered on the whole authentic, even though not written down in the master's lifetime—convey the impression of a lively and untrammeled mind which challenged those with whom it came in contact. Like his contemporary Gautama Buddha, and like his near-contemporary Socrates, Confucius earnestly believed that knowledge was the key to happiness and successful conduct. He also believed that almost anyone was capable of acquiring knowledge, but only through unrelenting effort. He insisted that his student-disciples should think for themselves, saying that if he had demonstrated one corner of a subject it was up to them to work out the other three corners, and constantly pricking their complacency. While no ascetic, he frowned on indulgence and urged his associates to strive continually for improvement. Though he had moments of petulance and harshness, the nobility of his character is unmistakable, and he refused to let his disappointments make him cynical. His regret, he said, was not that he was misunderstood but that he did not understand others sufficiently.

The doctrines of Confucius centered upon the good life and the good community. He respected religious ceremonies as part of established custom, but he refused to speculate on religious or supernatural questions, saying, in substance: "We do not know life; how can we understand death? We do not fully understand our obligations to the living; what can we know of our obligations to the dead?" He was optimistic regarding the material world and regarding human nature, which he thought was essentially good; but he believed that the individual's worth would not be realized unless he was properly guided in the development of his faculties. For this reason he stressed propriety and the observance of ceremonial forms—which he thought were helpful in the acquisition of self-discipline—although he was really more concerned with sincerity and intelligence than with appearances. Impressed as he was by the evils of feudal contention, Confucius advocated the restoration of central authority in the kingdom, combined however, with a logical distribution of power. He visualized the ideal state as a benevolent paternalism, with the ruler not only commanding but also setting an example of conduct for the people to follow. He did not believe in equality and, rather than democracy, advocated an aristocracy of talent and high principles from whom officials would be selected to guide the ruler in his administration. The health of the entire state would depend upon the welfare of each village, and harmony would be achieved by the combined efforts of the common people from below and of the scholar-officials from above.

Confucius' teachings therefore embodied a political philosophy, which regarded the state as a natural institution but modifiable by man, and devoted to promoting the general well-being and the fullest growth of individual personalities. The state existed for man, not man for the state. On the ethical side he emphasized fellow feeling or reciprocity, the cultivation of sympathy and cooperation, which must begin in the family and then extend by degrees into the larger areas of association. He stressed the importance of the five cardinal human relationships which were already traditional among the Chinese: (1) ruler and subject, (2) father and son, (3) elder brother and younger brother, (4) husband and wife, and (5) friend and friend. These could be expanded indefinitely and were not bounded even by Chinese lines. The logic of this train of thought was summarized in the famous saying, "All men are brothers." But Confucius argued that a person must be a worthy member of his own community before he could think in terms of world citizenship. Laying no claim to originality, Confucius urged a return to an ideal order which he attributed to the ancients but which actually had never existed. Unknowingly, he was supplying guiding principles which could be utilized in the future.

Aside from its founder, the ablest exponent of the Confucianist

Mencius and Hsün-tzu

school was Mencius (Meng-tzu), who lived about a century later (c. 373–288 B.C.). Like his master, Mencius affirmed the inherent goodness of human nature and the necessity of exemplary leadership to develop it. He looked upon government primarily as a moral enterprise, and he was more emphatic than Confucius in insisting that the material condition of the people should be improved. He wanted the government to take the initiative in lessening inequalities and in raising the living standards of the common folk. Perhaps because political confusion had increased since Confucius' day, he was outspoken in criticizing contemporary rulers. He taught that only a benevolent government, resting upon the tacit consent of the people, can possess the "Mandate of Heaven," and he defended the people's right to depose a corrupt or despotic sovereign. Hsün-tzu (c. 300–237 B.C.) is usually classified as a Confucianist, although his precepts diverged radically from those of Mencius. While both Confucius and Mencius had started with the assumption that man has a natural propensity for good, Hsün-tzu regarded human nature as basically evil. However, like the earlier Confucianists he believed that man can be improved by proper education and rigorous discipline. He laid great stress upon observance of ritual, formal training in the classics and a strictly hierarchical ordering of society. In spite of his gloomy view of the natural man, he was far from a complete pessimist. He recommended vigorous action by the state to institute reforms and, like Mencius, favored the regulation of economic activities.

The Taoist philosophical school was in many ways the opposite of the Confucianist. Its traditional founder was Lao-tzu ("Old Sage"), a shadowy figure of the sixth century B.C. Little is known about the facts of his life, and some scholars doubt that he was an actual historical person. According to tradition he served as an official at the Chou capital in charge of the archives until, becoming weary of the world, he set out for the western mountains in quest of peace and, at the request of a guard at the mountain pass, set down his words of wisdom in a little book before he disappeared. But the real authorship of the *Tao Teh Ching* (Classic of Nature and Virtue), from which the principles of Taoism are derived, is undetermined, and it may not have been written earlier than the third century B.C. The book is not only brief but enigmatical, paradoxical, and perhaps ironical. With its terse and cryptic style it seems almost like an intentional antidote to the Confucian glorification of scholarship, exhortation, and patient explanation. On the whole the Taoist book exalts nature (sometimes in the sense of impersonal cosmic force, "the Boundless" or Absolute) and deprecates human efforts. Its spirit is romantic, mystical, anti-intellectual. It not only lauds the perfection of nature but idealizes the primitive, suggesting that people would be better off without the arts of civilization, living in blissful ignorance and keeping records by

Lao-tzu and Taoism

means of knotted cords rather than writing. Wealth creates avarice and laws produce criminals, it asserts. It is useless to try to improve society by preachment, ritual, or elaborate regulations; the more virtue is talked about the less it is practiced. "Those who teach don't know anything; those who know don't teach." A person learns more by staying home than by traveling; the wise man sits and meditates instead of bustling about trying to reform the world.

As a political philosophy, Taoism advocates laissez faire. Unlike Confucius, Lao-tzu believed that governmental interference was the source of iniquity and that, if people were left to follow their intuition, they would live in harmony with nature and with one another. Nevertheless, Lao-tzu's ideal was not pure anarchism. Like Confucius he assumed the necessity of a wise and benevolent (although largely passive) ruler, and agreed that the only legitimate purpose of government was to promote human happiness. Perhaps his thought also reflects a rural protest against both the self-important aristocracy and the artificial society of the rapidly growing towns. In Lao-tzu's teachings there are strains of pacifism and the doctrine of nonretaliation for injury ("The virtuous man is for patching up; the vicious man is for fixing guilt"); of the efficacy of love in human relations ("Heaven arms with love those it would not see destroyed"); and of equalitarianism ("It is the way of Heaven to take away from those that have too much and give to those that have not enough"). The Taoist school produced several able thinkers in late Chou times and played a part in the shaping of Chinese philosophical traditions. However, in contrast to Confucianism, the Taoist doctrines were eventually transformed into a religious system, with a priesthood, temples, ritual, and emotional elements. But the Taoism that became one of the prominent religions of China had little connection with the principles expounded in the *Tao Teh Ching*.

A third school of political and ethical philosophy was associated with Mo Ti (or Mo-tzu), whose career is placed in the middle of the fifth century B.C. A man of decided originality, Mo Ti may have been of peasant stock; his sympathies lay with the downtrodden, and he regarded luxury and extravagance with aversion. The distinguishing feature of his thought is that he combined the doctrine of utilitarianism—insisting that everything should be judged by its usefulness—with a sweeping idealism that drew inspiration from religious faith. He condemned elaborate ceremonies dear to Confucianists, including the traditional three-year period of mourning, on the ground that they entailed needless expense. Sports, amusements, and even music met his disapproval because they were unproductive, absorbing energies which might be employed in useful labor. The pressing need, as he saw it, was to increase the supply of food and basic commodities to improve the health, longevity, and numbers of the population; and such a program called for hard work on the part of both common people and officials. His strong denunciation of offensive warfare was also rooted in utilitarianism.

Mo Ti's ethics were by far the boldest of any of the Chinese philosophers. In place of the Confucian system of an expanding series of loyalties beginning with the family and radiating outward, he proclaimed the universal and impartial love of all mankind and declared that there can be no satisfactory community until the distinction between "self" and "other" is completely transcended. Applying his utilitarian yardstick, he reasoned that, by cultivating sympathy and mutual helpfulness with everyone, the individual was ensuring his own welfare as well as contributing to the security of others. But while his doctrine of universal and impartial affection linked altruism to self-interest, it called for a rare degree of discipline and high-mindedness, and its similarity to the ethics of Christianity has often been remarked. Mo Ti believed that the state, like other human institutions, was created by divine ordinance and that it was the duty of the ruler to carry out the will of Heaven, which he interpreted to mean promoting the common welfare. Although the Mohist school, as it is called, was prominent for a while and attracted many adherents, it practically disappeared after the downfall of the Chou Dynasty—partly because of the enmity of the Confucianists—and the teachings of the utilitarian philosopher were almost entirely forgotten until modern times.

A fourth philosophical school, known as the "Legalist," stood far removed both from the bold idealism of Mo Ti and the optimistic humanism of Confucius. Formulated during the hectic period which witnessed the final collapse of the Chou Dynasty and the triumph of the Ch'in, it reflects Hsün-tzu's harsh view of human nature and his emphasis upon coercive discipline. At the same time the Legalists were indebted to Taoism in their contempt for scholarship, the intelligentsia, and conventional ethics; and in their preference for a simple agrarian society over a mobile, sophisticated, and economically diversified one. But, unlike the Taoists, they did not exalt nature or any supernatural agency, and they completely rejected laissez faire. Rather than mystics they were hardheaded realists, or even cynics. Asserting that man is by nature hopelessly selfish and incorrigible, they prescribed complete and unquestioning submission to the ruler. People's behavior, they argued, could be controlled only by carefully defined rewards and punishments, by a code of laws which was fundamentally punitive and which derived not from custom or natural instinct but from the will of the sovereign. Of all the schools of Chinese political thought, the Legalist was the most uncompromisingly authoritarian. Although its principles were systematically applied only during the short-lived Ch'in Dynasty, they exerted a continuing influence upon later dynasties also—tempered somewhat by the opposing Confucian tradition—and they find perhaps more than an echo in the present Chinese totalitarian regime.

Although the later centuries of the Chou Dynasty were marked by strife and unrest and encumbered by the remnants of decaying feudal institutions, the material basis for a productive society had been laid and intellectual progress had reached a high point. An abundant and many-sided literature was in existence. Philosophers had come to grips in mature fashion with fundamental problems of individual and group behavior. Scholarship was an honorable profession, and scholars were considered indispensable to the business of government. There was a growing tradition—not yet very effective—that government entailed moral responsibilities as well as privileges, that those who exercised authority did so on sufferance and only so long as they conformed to the "Decree of Heaven." Moreover, the Chinese had come to think of themselves as composing a unique society, not merely a political affiliation but the "Middle Kingdom"—the heart of civilization as contrasted with outlying "barbarian" areas. They had already mingled with and partially absorbed many non-Chinese tribes, and it is significant that the distinction between their civilization and the "barbarian" regions was not based upon race or nationality. The attitude of superiority which they adopted sometimes made them arrogant, but it gave them a toughness in resisting the shock of invasion and other adversities.

Significance of the Chou period

SELECTED READINGS

• *Items so designated are available in paperback editions.*

   Chang Kwang-chih, *Early Chinese Civilization: Anthropological Perspectives*, Cambridge, Mass., 1972. Provocative essays on Shang and Chou civilizations.

• ———, *The Archaeology of Ancient China*, 3d ed., New Haven, 1977. The best account to date.

• Creel, H. G., *The Birth of China*, New York, 1937. A fascinating account of archeological exploration of Shang civilization, and an excellent introduction to the basic culture pattern of ancient China.

• ———, *Chinese Thought from Confucius to Mao Tse-tung*, Chicago, 1953.

• ———, *Confucius and the Chinese Way*, New York, 1960.

   ———, *The Origins of Statecraft in China*, Vol. I: *The Western Chou Empire*, Chicago, 1970. A valuable contribution.

• Eberhard, Wolfram, *A History of China*, 4th ed., Berkeley, 1977.

• Elvin, Mark, *The Pattern of the Chinese Past*, Stanford, 1975.

   Fairbank, J. K., E. O. Reischauer, and A. M. Craig, *East Asia: Tradition and Transformation*, rev. ed., Boston, 1978. A shortened edition of a major text.

• Fitzgerald, C. P., *China, a Short Cultural History*, 3d ed., New York, 1961. Frequently unconventional in viewpoint.

• Fung Yu-lan, *A Short History of Chinese Philosophy,* ed. Derk Bodde, New York, 1948.
• Goodrich, L. C., *Short History of the Chinese People,* 3d ed., New York, 1959. Brief but informative; fulfills the promise of its title.
Harrison, J. A., *The Chinese Empire: A Short History of China from Neolithic Times to the End of the Eighteenth Century,* New York, 1972. A good synthesis.
Ho Ping-ti, *The Cradle of the East: An Enquiry into the Indigenous Origins of Techniques and Ideas of Neolithic and Early Historic China, 5000–1000 B.C.,* Chicago, 1976.
Hucker, C. O., *China's Imperial Past: An Introduction to Chinese History and Culture,* Stanford, 1975. Remarkably clear, comprehensive, and readable.
• ———, *China to 1850: A Short History,* Stanford, 1978.
Keightley, D. N., *Sources of Shang History: The Oracle Bone Inscriptions of Bronze Age China,* Berkeley, 1978. Synthesizes the research of earlier scholars.
King, F. H., *Farmers of Forty Centuries, or Permanent Agriculture in China, Korea and Japan,* Emmaus, Pa., 1948. A classic description.
• Moore, C. A., ed., *The Chinese Mind: Essentials of Chinese Philosophy and Culture,* Honolulu, 1967.
• Munro, D. J., *The Concept of Man in Early China,* Stanford, 1975.
Ronan, C. A., ed., *The Shorter Science and Civilization in China,* New York, 1978. Abridgement of the first two volumes of a monumental study by Joseph Needham.
Treistman, Judith, *The Prehistory of China: An Archaeological Exploration,* Garden City, N.Y., 1972.
• Watson, Burton, *Early Chinese Literature,* New York, 1962.
Wheatley, Paul, *The Pivot of the Four Quarters: A Preliminary Enquiry into the Origins of the Character of the Ancient Chinese City,* Chicago, 1971.
• Wilhelm, Hellmut, *Change: Eight Lectures on the I Ching,* tr. C. F. Baynes, New York, 1960 (Princeton, 1973).

SOURCE MATERIALS

• de Bary, W. T., ed., *Sources of Chinese Tradition,* "The Classical Period," New York, 1960.
Chai Ch'u, and Winberg Chai, *A Treasury of Chinese Literature,* New York, 1961.
Chan Wing-tsit, ed. and tr., *A Source Book in Chinese Philosophy,* Princeton, 1963. Traces the history of Chinese philosophy from Confucianism to Communism.
• Giles, H. A., ed., *Gems of Chinese Literature,* Shanghai, 1922.
• Legge, James, tr., *The I Ching (The Book of Changes),* Oxford, 1891.
• ———, *The Works of Mencius.*
Lin Yutang, ed., *The Wisdom of China and India,* "Laotse, the Book of Tao," New York, 1942.
Mei, Y. P., tr., *The Ethical and Political Works of Motse,* London, 1929.
Soothill, W. E., tr., *The Analects of Confucius,* Yokohama, 1910.
Waley, Arthur, ed. and tr., *The Book of Songs,* London, 1937.

———, *The Way and Its Power,* London, 1934.

———, *Three Ways of Thought in Ancient China,* London, 1939.

• Watson, Burton, tr., *Mo Tzu: Basic Writings,* New York, 1967.

Wilhelm, Richard, and C. F. Baynes, trs., *The I Ching, or Book of Changes,* Princeton, 1967.

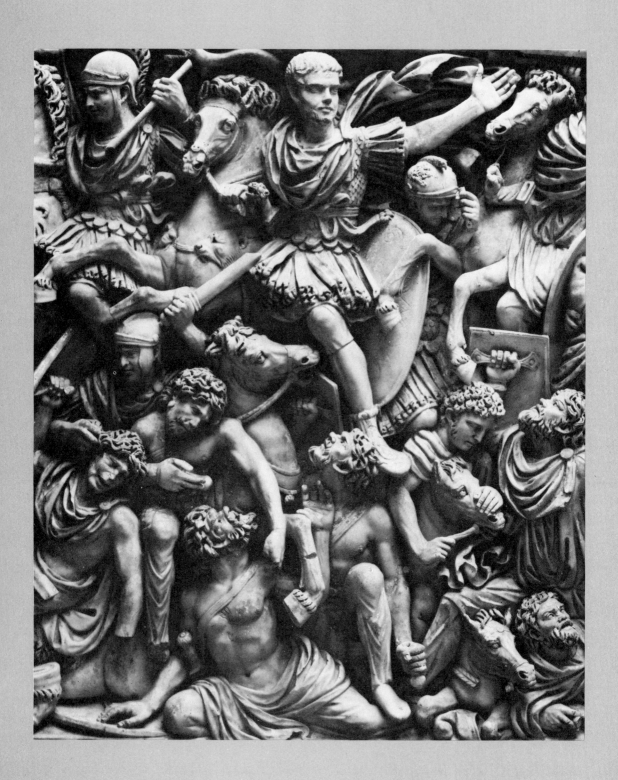

Part Two

THE WORLD IN
THE CLASSICAL ERA

After 600 B.C. the centers of civilization in the Western world were no longer mainly located in the Near East. By that time new cultures were already growing to maturity in Greece and in Italy. Both had started their evolution considerably earlier, but the civilization of Greece did not begin to ripen until about 600 B.C., while the Romans showed little promise of original achievement before 500. About 300 B.C. Greek civilization, properly speaking, came to an end and was superseded by a new culture representing a fusion of elements derived from Greece and the Near East. This was the Hellenistic civilization, which lasted until about the beginning of the Christian era and included not only the Greek peninsula but Egypt and most of Asia west of the Indus River. The outstanding characteristic which serves to distinguish these three civilizations from the ones that had gone before is secularism. No longer does religion absorb the interests of humans to the extent that it did in ancient Egypt or in the nations of Mesopotamia. The state is now above the church, and the power of the priests to determine the direction of cultural evolution has been greatly reduced. Furthermore, ideals of human freedom and an emphasis on the welfare of the individual have largely superseded the despotism and collectivism of the ancient Near East. Only late in Roman history, around the third century A.D., did Near-Eastern despotism begin to reassert itself within the confines of imperial Rome. Around that time too, a new religion, Christianity, began to reshape the life of the West. Somewhat similar developments were taking place in the Far East. In India, Hinduism and the dominance of the Brahman caste were challenged by the ethical and nontheological system of Gautama Buddha. Buddhism also spread to China and Japan and became a major stimulus of cultural vitality in all three countries.

The World in the Classical Era

POLITICS	PHILOSOPHY AND SCIENCE

800 B.C.

Dark Ages of Greek history, 1100–800
Feudalism in China, c. 800–250
Beginning of city-states in Greece, c. 800
Rome founded, c. 750

Thales of Miletus, c. 640–546
Pythagoras, c. 582–c. 507
Confucius, c. 551–479
Lao-tzu, c. 550

Age of the tyrants in Greece, c. 650–c. 500
Reforms of Solon in Athens, 594
Tyranny of Peisistratus, 560
Reforms of Cleisthenes, 508

500 B.C.

Establishment of Roman Republic, c. 500
Greco-Persian War, 490–479

Protagoras, c. 490–c. 420
Socrates, 469–399

Delian League, 479–404
Perfection of Athenian democracy, 461–429
Law of the Twelve Tables, Rome, c. 450
Peloponnesian War, 431–404

Hippocrates, 460–c. 377
Democritus, c. 460–c. 362
The Sophists, c. 450–c. 400
Plato, 427–347

400 B.C.

Aristotle, 384–322

Theban supremacy in Greece, 371–362
Macedonian conquest of Greece, 338–337
Conquests of Alexander the Great, 336–323
Division of Alexander's empire, 323

Mencius, c. 373–288
Epicurus, 342–270
Zeno the Stoic, c. 320–c. 250
Euclid, c. 323–285

300 B.C.

Aristarchus, 310–230

Reign of Emperor Asoka in India, c. 273–232
Punic Wars between Rome and Carthage, 264–146
Ch'in Dynasty in China, 221–207
Building of Great Wall in China, c. 220
Han Dynasty in China, 206 B.C. –220 A.D.

Archimedes, c. 287–212
Eratosthenes, c. 276–c. 195

Herophilus, c. 220–c. 150
Polybius, c. 205–118
The Skeptics, c. 200–c. 100

200 B.C.

Reforms of the Gracchi, 133–121
Beginning of Japanese state, c. 100
Dictatorship of Julius Caesar, 46–44
Principate of Augustus Caesar, 27 B.C.–14 A.D.

Introduction of Stoicism into Rome, c. 140
Cicero, 106–43

100 B.C.

Dictatorship of Julius Caesar, 46–44
Principate of Augustus Caesar, 27 B.C.–14 A.D.

Lucretius, 98–55
Seneca, 34 B.C.–65 A.D.

100 A.D.

"Five Good Emperors," 96–180

Marcus Aurelius, 121–180

200 A.D.

Completion of Roman jurisprudence by great jurists, c. 200
Civil war in Roman Empire, 235–284
Diocletian, 284–305

Galen, 130–c. 200
Plotinus, c. 204–270

300 A.D.

Constantine I, 306–337
Theodosius I, 379–395

400 A.D.

Visigoths sack Rome, 410
West African kingdom of Ghana, c. 450
Deposition of last of Western Roman emperors, 476

500 A.D.

Theodoric the Ostrogoth king of Italy, 493–526
Justinian, 527–565
Corpus of Roman law, c. 550

Boethius, c. 480–524

ECONOMICS	RELIGION	ARTS AND LETTERS	
Rise of caste system in India, 1000–500		*Vedas* in India, 1200–800	
		Upanishads, 800–600	**800 B.C.**
Economic revolution and colonization in Greece, c. 750–c. 600		*Iliad* and *Odyssey,* c. 750	
Rise of middle class in Greece, c. 750–c. 600		Doric architectural style, c. 650–c. 500	
	Gautama Buddha, c. 563–483	Aeschylus, 525–456	
Use of iron in China, c. 500	Orphic and Eleusinian mystery cults, c. 500–c. 100	Phidias, c. 500–c. 432	
		Ionic architectural style, c. 500–c. 400	**500 B.C.**
		Sophocles, 496–406	
		Herodotus, c. 484–c. 420	
		Euripides, 480–406	
		Thucydides, c. 471–c. 400	
		The Parthenon, c. 460	
		Aristophanes, c. 448–c. 380	
Development of coinage in China, c. 400		Corinthian architectural style, c. 400–c. 300	**400 B.C.**
		Praxiteles, c. 370–c. 310	
Hellenistic international trade and growth of large cities, c. 300 B.C.–c. 100 A.D.			**300 B.C.**
Use of iron in sub-Saharan Africa, 200			
Growth of slavery, rise of middle class, decline of small farmer in Rome, c. 250–100	Oriental mystery cults in Rome, c. 250–50		**200 B.C.**
Manufacture of paper in China, c. 100	Spread of Mithraism in Rome, 27 B.C.–270 A.D.		**100 B.C.**
	The Crucifixion, c. 30 A.D.	Virgil, 70–19	
Decline of slavery in Rome, c. 120–c. 476	St. Paul's missionary work, c. 35–c. 67	Horace, 65–8	
Growth of serfdom in Rome, c. 200–500		Livy, 59 B.C.–17 A.D.	
		Ovid, c. 43 B.C.–17 A.D.	
Sharp economic contraction in Rome, c. 200–c. 300		Tacitus, c. 55 A.D.–c. 117 A.D.	**100 A.D.**
Expansion of Bantu people in Africa, 200–900	Development of Buddhism in China, 200–500	The Colosseum, c. 80 A.D.	**200 A.D.**
	Beginning of toleration of Christians in the Roman Empire, 311	The Pantheon, c. 120	
Use of camel for transport in Africa, 300		Height of Roman portrait statuary, c. 120–c. 250	
	St. Augustine, 354–430	Classical age of Hindu culture, c. 300–800	**300 A.D.**
	Christianity made official Roman religion, 380		**400 A.D.**
		Adoption of Chinese system of writing in Japan, c. 405	
Manufacture of glass and invention of gunpowder and magnetic compass in China, c. 500	Benedictine monastic rule, c. 520	Spread of Buddhism in Japan, c. 552	**500 A.D.**

Chapter 8

THE HELLENIC CIVILIZATION

There Lawfulness dwells and her sisters,
Safe foundation of cities,
Justice and Peace, who was bred with her,
Dispensers of wealth to men
Golden daughters of wise-counseling Right.

—Pindar, on the city of Corinth, *Olympian Ode XIII*

Now, what is characteristic of any nature is that which is best for it and
gives most joy. Such to man is the life according to reason, since it is this
that makes him man.

—Aristotle, *Nichomachean Ethics*

Among all the peoples of the ancient world, the one whose culture
most clearly exemplified the spirit of Western man was the
Hellenic or Greek. No one of these nations had so strong a
devotion to liberty, at least for itself, or so firm a belief in the nobility
of human achievement. The Greeks glorified man as the most important creature in the universe and refused to submit to the dictation of
priests or despots or even to humble themselves before their gods.
Their attitude was essentially secular and rationalistic; they exalted the
spirit of free inquiry and made knowledge supreme over faith. It was
largely for these reasons that they advanced their culture to the highest
stage which the ancient world was destined to reach.

The character of Hellenic civilization

1. THE GREEK DARK AGES

The fall of the Mycenaean civilization was a major catastrophe for the
Greek world. It ushered in a period usually called by historians the
Dark Ages, which lasted from about 1100 to 800 B.C. Written records
disappeared, except where accidentally preserved, and culture reverted to simpler forms than had been known for centuries. Toward

The Dark Ages

Bronze Centaur and Man. These figures date from about 750 B.C. They are no more than about five inches high.

Bronze Statuette. Perhaps representing Apollo, this work dates from about 750 B.C.

the end of the period some decorated pottery and skillfully designed metal objects began to appear on the islands of the Aegean Sea, but essentially the period was a long night. Aside from the development of writing at the very end, intellectual accomplishment was limited to ballads, and short epics sung and embellished by bards as they wandered from one village to another. A large part of this material was finally woven into a great epic cycle by one or more poets in the eighth century B.C. Though not all the poems of this cycle have come down to us, the two most important, the *Iliad* and the *Odyssey,* the so-called Homeric epics, provide us with a rich store of information about many of the customs and institutions of the Dark Ages.

The political institutions of the Dark Ages were exceedingly primitive. Each little community of villages was independent of external control, but political authority was so tenuous that it would not be too much to say that the state scarcely existed at all. The *basileus* or ruler was not much more than a tribal leader. He could not make or enforce laws or administer justice. He received no remuneration of any kind, and had to cultivate his farm for a living the same as any other citizen. Practically his only functions were military and priestly. He commanded the army in time of war and offered sacrifices to keep the gods on the good side of the community. Although each little community had its council of nobles and assembly of warriors, neither of these bodies had any definite membership or status as an organ of government. Almost without exception custom took the place of law, and the administration of justice was private. Even willful murder was punishable only by the family of the victim. While it is true that disputes were sometimes submitted to the ruler for settlement, he acted in such cases merely as an arbitrator, not as a judge. As a matter of fact, the political consciousness of the Greeks of this time was so poorly developed that they had no conception of government as an indispensable agency for the preservation of social order. When Odysseus, ruler of Ithaca, was absent for twenty years, no regent was appointed in his place, and no session of the council or assembly was held. No one seemed to think that the complete suspension of government, even for so long a time, was a matter of critical importance.

The pattern of social and economic life was amazingly simple. Though the general tone of the society portrayed in the epics is aristocratic, there was actually no rigid stratification of classes. Manual labor was not looked upon as degrading, and there were apparently no idle rich. That there were dependent laborers of some kind who worked on the lands of the nobles and served them as faithful warriors seems clear from the Homeric epics, but they appear to have been serfs rather than slaves. The slaves were chiefly women, employed as servants, wool-processors, or concubines. Many were war captives, but they do not appear to have been badly treated. Agriculture and herding were the basic occupations of free men. Except for a few skilled crafts like those of wagonmaker, swordsmith, goldsmith, and potter, there was no specialization of labor. For the most part every household made its own tools, wove its own clothing, and raised its own food. So far were the Greeks of this time from being a trading people that they had no word in their language for "merchant," and barter was the only method of exchange that was practiced.

To the Greeks of the Dark Ages religion meant chiefly a system for: (1) explaining the physical world in such a way as to remove its awesome mysteries and give man a feeling of intimate relationship with it; (2) accounting for the tempestuous passions that seized man's nature and made him lose that self-control which the Greeks considered essential for success as a warrior; and (3) obtaining such tangible benefits as good fortune, long life, skill in craftsmanship, and abundant harvests. The Greeks did not expect that their religion would save them from sin or endow them with spiritual blessings. As they conceived it, piety was neither a matter of conduct nor of faith. Their religion, accordingly, had no commandments, dogmas, or sacraments. Every man was at liberty to believe what he pleased and to conduct his own life as he chose without fear of the wrath of the gods.

Religious conceptions in the Dark Ages

As is commonly known, the deities of the early Greek religion were merely human beings writ large. It was really necessary that this should be so if the Greek was to feel at home in the world over which they ruled. Remote, omnipotent beings like the gods of most oriental religions would have inspired fear rather than a sense of security. What the Greek wanted was not necessarily gods of great power, but deities who could be bargained with on equal terms. Consequently gods were endowed with attributes similar to human ones—with human bodies and human weaknesses and wants. The early Greek imagined the great company of divinities as frequently quarreling with one another, needing food and sleep, mingling freely with mortals, and even occasionally procreating children by mortal women. They differed from humans only in the fact that they subsisted on ambrosia and nectar, which made them immortal. They dwelt not in the sky or in the stars but on the summit of Mount Olympus, a peak in northern Greece with an altitude of about 10,000 feet.

Human qualities of the deities

Poseidon or Zeus. Detail from an Athenian statue of about 470 B.C., larger than life size.

The religion was thoroughly polytheistic, and no one deity was elevated very high above any of the others. Zeus, the sky god and wielder of the thunderbolt, who was sometimes referred to as the father of the gods and of men, frequently received less attention than did Poseidon, the sea god, Aphrodite, goddess of love, or Athena, variously considered goddess of wisdom and war and patroness of handicrafts. Since the Greeks had no Satan, their religion cannot be described as dualistic. All of the deities were capable of malevolence as well as good.

The Greeks of the Dark Ages were almost completely indifferent to what happened to them after death. They did assume, however, that shades or ghosts survived for a time after the death of their bodies. All, with a few exceptions, went to the same abode—to the murky realm of Hades situated beneath the earth. This was neither a paradise nor a hell: no one was rewarded for good deeds, and no one was punished for sins. Each of the shades appeared to continue the same kind of life its human embodiment had lived on earth. The Homeric poems make casual mention of two other realms, the Elysian Plain and the realm of Tartarus, which seem at first glance to contradict the idea of no rewards and punishments in the hereafter. But the few individuals who enjoyed the ease and comfort of the Elysian Plain had done nothing to deserve such blessings: they were simply persons whom the gods had chosen to favor. The realm of Tartarus was not really an abode of the dead but a place of imprisonment for rebellious deities.

Worship in early Greek religion consisted primarily of sacrifice. The offerings were made, however, not as an atonement for sin, but chiefly in order to please the gods and induce them to grant favors. In other words, religious practice was external and mechanical and not far removed from magic. Reverence, humility, and purity of heart were not essentials in it. The worshiper just made the proper sacrifice and then hoped for the best. For a religion such as this no elaborate institutions were required. Even a professional priesthood was unnecessary. Since there were no mysteries and no sacraments, one man could perform the simple rites about as well as another. The Greek temple was not a church or place of religious assemblage, and no ceremonies were performed within it. Instead it was a shrine which the god might visit occasionally and use as a temporary house.

As intimated already, the morality of the Greeks in the Dark Ages had only the vaguest connection with their religion. While it is true that the gods were generally disposed to support the right, they did not consider it their duty to combat evil and make righteousness prevail. In meting out rewards to humans, they appear to have been influenced more by their own whims and by gratitude for sacrifices offered than by any consideration for moral character. The only crime they punished was perjury, and that none too consistently. Nearly all the virtues extolled in the epics were those which would make the individual a better soldier—bravery, self-control, patriotism, wisdom (in the sense of cunning), love of one's friends, and hatred of one's enemies. There was no conception of sin in the Christian sense of wrongful acts to be repented of or atoned for.

At the end of the Dark Ages the Greeks were already well started along the road of social ideals that they were destined to follow in later centuries. They were optimists, convinced that life was worth living for its own sake, and could see no reason for looking forward to death as a glad release. They were egotists, striving for the fulfillment of self. As a consequence, mortification of the flesh and all forms of denial which would imply the frustration of life were rejected. They

Man Carrying a Calf for Sacrifice. A life-size Athenian sculpture from about 570 B.C.

Battle between the Gods and the Giants. This frieze dates from before 525 B.C. and is from the sanctuary of Apollo at Delphi.

could see no merit in humility or in turning the other cheek. They were humanists, who worshiped the finite and the natural rather than the otherworldly or sublime. For this reason they refused to invest their gods with awe-inspiring qualities, or to invent any conception of humans as depraved and sinful creatures. Finally, they were devoted to liberty in an even more extreme form than most of their descendants in the classical period were willing to accept.

The basic Greek ideals

2. THE EVOLUTION OF THE CITY-STATES

About 800 B.C. the village communities which had been founded mainly upon tribal or clan organization, began to give way to larger political units. As trade and the need for defense increased, cities grew up around market-places and defensive fortifications as seats of government for whole communities. Thus emerged the city-state, the most famous unit of political society developed by the Greeks. Examples were to be found in almost every section of the Hellenic world. Athens, Thebes, and Megara on the mainland; Sparta and Corinth on the Peloponnesus; Miletus on the shore of Asia Minor; and Mitylene and Samos on the islands of the Aegean Sea—these were among the best known. They varied enormously in both area and population. Sparta with more than 3,000 square miles and Athens with 1,060 had by far the greatest extent; the others averaged less than 100. At the peak of their power Athens and Sparta, each with a population of about 400,000, had approximately three times the numerical strength of most of their neighboring states.

More important is the fact that the Greek city-states varied widely

The origin and nature of the city-states

Variations among the city-states

The evolution of the city-states

The causes of the political cycle; the growth of colonization

The results of Greek expansion

in cultural evolution. From 800 to 500 B.C., commonly called the Archaic period, the Peloponnesian cities of Corinth and Argos were leaders in the development of literature and the arts. In the seventh century Sparta outshone many of its rivals. Preeminent above all were the Greek-speaking cities on the coast of Asia Minor and the islands of the Aegean Sea. Foremost among them was Miletus, where, as we shall see, a brilliant flowering of philosophy and science occurred as early as the sixth century. Athens lagged behind until at least one hundred years later.

With a few exceptions the Greek city-states went through a similar political evolution. They began their histories as monarchies. During the eighth century they were changed into oligarchies. About a hundred years later, on the average, most of the oligarchies were overthrown by dictators, or "tyrants," as the Greeks called them, meaning usurpers who ruled without legal right whether oppressively or not. Finally, in the sixth and fifth centuries, democracies were set up, or in some cases "timocracies," that is, governments based upon a property qualification for the exercise of political rights, or in which love of honor and glory was the ruling principle.

On the whole, it is not difficult to determine the causes of this political evolution. The first change came about as a result of the concentration of landed wealth. As the owners of great estates gained ever greater economic power, they determined to wrest political authority from the ruler, now commonly called king, and vest it in the council, which they generally controlled. In the end they abolished the kingship entirely. Then followed a period of sweeping economic changes and political turmoil.

These developments affected not only Greece itself but many other parts of the Mediterranean world. For they were accompanied and followed by a vast overseas expansion. The chief causes were an increasing scarcity of agricultural land, internal strife, and a general temper of restlessness and discontent. The Greeks rapidly learned of numerous areas, thinly populated, with climate and soil similar to those of the homelands. The parent states most active in the expansion movement were Corinth, Chalcis, and Miletus. Their citizens founded colonies along the Aegean shores and even in Italy and Sicily. Of the latter the best known were Taras (modern Taranto) and Syracuse. They also established trading centers on the coast of Egypt and as far east as Babylon. The results of this expansionist movement were momentous. Commerce and industry grew to be leading pursuits, the urban population increased, and wealth assumed new forms. The rising middle class now joined with dispossessed farmers in an attack upon the landholding oligarchy. The natural fruit of the bitter class conflicts that ensued was dictatorship. By encouraging extravagant hopes and promising relief from chaos, ambitious demagogues attracted enough popular support to enable them to ride into power in defiance of constitutions and laws. Ultimately, however, dissatisfaction with tyrannical rule and the increasing economic power and political conscious-ness of the common citizens led to the establishment of democracies or liberal oligarchies.

Unfortunately space does not permit an analysis of the political his-tory of each of the Greek city-states. Except in the more backward sections of Thessaly and the Peloponnesus, it is safe to conclude that the internal development of all of them paralleled the account given above, although minor variations due to local conditions doubtless oc-curred. The two most important of the Hellenic states, Sparta and Athens, deserve more detailed study.

3. THE ARMED CAMP OF SPARTA

The history of Sparta[1] was the great exception to the political evolu-tion of the city-states. Despite the fact that its citizens sprang from the same origins as most of the other Greeks, Sparta failed to make any progress in the direction of democratic rule. Instead, its government gradually evolved into a form more closely resembling a modern elite dictatorship. Culturally, also, the nation stagnated after the sixth cen-tury. The causes were due partly to isolation. Hemmed in by moun-tains on the northeast and west and lacking good harbors, the Spartan people had little opportunity to profit from the advances made in the outside world. Besides, no middle class arose to aid the masses in the struggle for freedom.

The major explanation is to be found, however, in militarism. The Spartans were originally Dorians who had come into the eastern Pelo-ponnesus as an invading army. At first they attempted to amalgamate with the Mycenaeans they found there. But conflicts arose, and the Spartans resorted to conquest. Though by the end of the ninth century they had gained dominion over all of Laconia, they were not satisfied. West of the Taygetus Mountains lay the fertile plain of Messenia. The Spartans determined to conquer it. The venture was successful, and the Messenian territory was annexed to Laconia. About 640 B.C. the Messenians enlisted the aid of Argos and launched a revolt. The war that followed was desperately fought, Laconia itself was invaded, and apparently it was only the death of the Argive commander and the pa-triotic pleas of the fire-eating poet Tyrtaeus that saved the day for the Spartans. This time the victors took no chances. They confiscated the lands of the Messenians, murdered or expelled their leaders, and turned the masses into serfs called *helots*. Thereafter Spartan foreign policy was defensive. Following the Messenian wars the Spartans feared that further foreign warfare would provide the opportunities

---

[1] Sparta was the leading city of a district called Laconia or Lacedaemonia; sometimes the *state* was referred to by one or the other of these names. The people, also, were frequently called Laconians or Lacedaemonians. (The modern adjective "laconic" comes from the reputation of the ancient Spartans for being sparing with words.)

for a helot uprising; consequently Sparta devoted itself to keeping what it had already gained.

There was scarcely a feature of the life of the Spartans that was not the result of their wars with the Messenians. In subduing and despoiling their enemies they unwittingly enslaved themselves, for they lived through the remaining centuries of their history in deadly fear of insurrections. It was this fear which explains their conservatism, their stubborn resistance to change, lest any innovation result in a fatal weakening of the system. Their provincialism can also be attributed to the same cause. Frightened by the prospect that dangerous ideas might be brought into their country, they discouraged travel and prohibited trade with the outside world. The necessity of maintaining the absolute supremacy of the citizen class over an enormous population of serfs required an iron discipline and a strict subordination of the individual; hence the Spartan collectivism, which extended into every branch of the social and economic life. Finally, much of the cultural backwardness of Sparta grew out of the atmosphere of restraint which inevitably resulted from the bitter struggle to conquer the Messenians and hold them under stern repression.

The Spartan constitution provided for a government preserving the forms of the old system of the Dark Ages. Instead of one king, however, there were two, representing separate families of exalted rank. The Spartan kings enjoyed but few powers and those were chiefly of a military and priestly character. A second branch of the government was the council, composed of the two kings and twenty-eight nobles sixty years of age and over. This body supervised the work of administration, prepared measures for submission to the assembly, and served as the highest court for criminal trials. The third organ of government, the assembly, composed of all adult male citizens, approved or rejected the proposals of the council and elected all public officials except the kings. But the highest authority under the Spartan constitution was vested in a board of five men known as the *ephorate*. The ephors virtually were the government. They presided over the council and the assembly, controlled the educational system and the distribution of property, censored the lives of the citizens, and exercised a veto power over all legislation. They had power also to determine the fate of newborn infants, to conduct prosecutions before the council, and even to depose the kings if the religious omens appeared unfavorable. The Spartan government dominated by the ephors was thus in effect an oligarchy.

The population of Sparta was divided into three main classes. The ruling element was made up of the Spartiates, or descendants of the original conquerors. Though never exceeding one-twentieth of the total population, the Spartiates alone had political privileges. Next in order of rank were the *perioeci,* or "dwellers around." The origin of this class is uncertain, but it was probably composed of peoples that had at one time been allies of the Spartans or had submitted voluntarily to Spartan domination. In return for service as a buffer population between the ruling class and the helots, the perioeci were allowed to carry on trade and to engage in manufacturing. At the bottom of the scale were the helots, or serfs, bound to the soil.

Among these classes only the perioeci enjoyed any appreciable measure of comfort and freedom. While it is true that the economic condition of the helots cannot be described in terms of absolute misery, since they were permitted to keep for themselves a good share of what they produced on the estates of their masters, they were personally subjected to such shameful treatment that they were constantly wretched and rebellious. To guard against rebellion young Spartiates were sometimes sent to live among the helots in disguise and act like a secret police with the power to murder whom they pleased. The brutalizing effects on both sides can be easily imagined.

Perioeci and helots

Those who were born into the Spartiate class were doomed to a respectable slavery for the major part of their lives. Forced to submit to the severest discipline and to sacrifice individual interests, they were little more than cogs in a vast machine. Spartan babies were examined for hardiness at birth and those who were thought to be potential weaklings were carried off to the hills to die of neglect. The education of Spartan males was limited almost entirely to military training, which began at the age of seven, supplemented by merciless floggings to harden the boys for the duties of war. Between the ages of twenty and sixty the men gave almost all their time to state service. Although marriage was practically compulsory there was little family life: young men had to live in barracks, and after the age of thirty they still had to eat in military messes. The husbands carried off their wives on their wedding nights by a show of force. Because they saw so little of them afterwards it sometimes happened that men "had children before they ever saw their wives' faces in daylight."[2] The production of vigorous offspring was the wives' main duty, but mothers had to accept the fact that children were virtually the property of the state. It may be doubted that the Spartiates resented these hardships and deprivations. Pride in their status as the ruling class probably compensated in their minds for harsh discipline and denial of privileges.

Discipline for the benefit of the state

The economic organization of Sparta was designed almost solely for the ends of military efficiency and the supremacy of the citizen class. The best land was owned by the state and was originally divided into equal plots which were assigned to the Spartiate class as inalienable estates. Later these holdings as well as the inferior lands were permitted to be sold and exchanged, with the result that some of the citizens became richer than others. The helots, who did all the work of cultivating the soil, also belonged to the state and were assigned to their mas-

Economic regulations

[2] Plutarch, "Lycurgus," *Lives of Illustrious Men*, I, 81.

ters along with the land. Their masters were forbidden to emancipate them or to sell them outside of the country. The labor of the helots provided for the support of the whole citizen class, whose members were not allowed to be associated with any economic enterprise other than agriculture. The minimal trade and industry of the Spartan state were reserved exclusively for the perioeci.

Description of the Spartan system

The Spartan economic system is frequently described by modern historians as communistic. It is true that some of the means of production (the helots and the land) were collectively owned, in theory at least, and that the Spartiate males contributed from their incomes to provide for their common military messes. But with these exceptions the system was as far removed from communism as it was from anarchy. Essentials of the communist ideal include the doctrines that all the instruments of production shall be owned by the community, that no one shall live by exploiting the labor of others, and that all shall work for the benefit of the community and share the wealth in proportion to need. In Sparta commerce and industry were in private hands; the helots were forced to contribute a portion of what they produced to provide for the subsistence of their masters; and political privileges were restricted to a governing class whose members performed no socially useful labor. With its militarism, its secret police, its minority rule, and its closed economy, the Spartan system resembled fascism more nearly than true communism.

4. THE ATHENIAN TRIUMPH AND TRAGEDY

Athens began its history under conditions quite different from those which prevailed in Sparta. The district of Attica in which Athens is situated had not been the scene of an armed invasion or of bitter conflict between opposing peoples. As a result, no military caste imposed its rule upon a vanquished nation. Furthermore, the wealth of Attica consisted of mineral deposits and splendid harbors in addition to agricultural resources. Athens, consequently, never remained a predominantly agrarian state but rapidly developed a prosperous trade and an essentially urban culture.

Advantages enjoyed by the Athenians

From monarchy to oligarchy in Athens

Until the middle of the eighth century B.C. Athens, like the other Greek states, had a monarchical form of government. During the century that followed, the council of nobles, or Council of the Areopagus, as it came to be called, gradually divested the king of his powers. The transition to rule by the few was both the cause and the result of an increasing concentration of wealth. The introduction of vine and olive culture about this time led to the growth of agriculture as a large-scale enterprise. Since vineyards and olive orchards require considerable time to become profitable, only those farmers with abundant resources were able to survive in the business. Their poorer and less thrifty neighbors sank rapidly into debt, especially since grain was now coming to be imported at ruinous prices. The small farmer had no alternative but to mortgage his land, and then his family and himself, in the vain hope that some day a way of escape would be found. Ultimately many of this class became serfs when the mortgages could not be paid; those without land to mortgage were sold into slavery.

Bitter cries of distress now arose and threats of revolution were heard. The urban middle classes espoused the cause of the peasants in demanding liberalization of the government. Finally, in 594 B.C., all parties agreed upon the appointment of the aristocrat Solon as chief magistrate with absolute power to carry out reforms. The measures Solon enacted provided for both political and economic adjustments. The former included: (1) the establishment of a new council, the Council of Four Hundred, and the admission of the middle classes to membership in it; (2) the enfranchisement of the lower classes by making them eligible for service in the assembly; and (3) the organization of a final court of appeals in criminal cases, open to all citizens and elected by universal manhood suffrage. The economic reforms benefited the poor farmers by canceling existing mortgages, prohibiting enslavement for debt in the future, and limiting the amount of land any one individual could own. Nor did Solon neglect the middle classes. He introduced a new system of coinage designed to give Athens an advantage in foreign trade, imposed heavy penalties for idleness, ordered every man to teach his son a trade, and offered full privileges of citizenship to alien craftsmen who would become permanent residents of the country.

Threats of revolution and the reforms of Solon

Significant though these reforms were, they did not allay the discontent. The nobles were disgruntled because some of their privileges had been taken away. The middle and lower classes were dissatisfied because they were still excluded from the offices of magistracy, and because the Council of the Areopagus was left with its powers intact. The chaos and disillusionment that followed paved the way in 560 B.C. for the triumph of Peisistratus, the first of the Athenian tyrants. Although he proved to be a benevolent despot who patronized culture, reduced the power of the aristocracy, and raised the standard of living of the average Athenian, his son Hippias, who succeeded him, was a ruthless and spiteful oppressor.

The rise of dictatorship

In 510 B.C. Hippias's tyranny was overthrown by a group of nobles with aid from Sparta. Factional conflict raged for another two years until Cleisthenes, an intelligent aristocrat, enlisted the support of the masses to eliminate his rivals from the scene. Having promised concessions to the people as a reward for their help, he proceeded to reform the government in so sweeping a fashion that he has since been known as the father of Athenian democracy. Cleisthenes, who dominated Athenian politics from 508 to 502, enlarged the citizen population by granting full rights to all free men who resided in the country

The reforms of Cleisthenes

Greeks at War. A battle scene from the interior of a drinking cup, done in Athens between about 530 and 500 B.C.

at that time. He established a new council and made it the chief organ of government with power to prepare measures for submission to the assembly and with supreme control over executive and administrative functions. Members of this body were to be chosen by lot. Any male citizen over thirty years of age was eligible. Cleisthenes also expanded the authority of the assembly, giving it power to debate and pass or reject the measures submitted by the Council, to declare war, to appropriate money, and to audit the accounts of retiring magistrates. Lastly, not long after the time of Cleisthenes, in 487, the Athenians instituted the device of ostracism, whereby any citizen who might be dangerous to the state could be sent into honorable exile for a ten-year period. The device was meant to eliminate men who were suspected of cherishing dictatorial ambitions, but too often its effect was to eliminate exceptional personalities and to allow mediocrity to flourish.

The Athenian democracy attained its full perfection in the Age of Pericles (461–429 B.C.). It was during this period that the assembly acquired the authority to initiate legislation in addition to its power to ratify or reject proposals of the council. It was during this time also that the Board of Ten Generals rose to a position roughly comparable to that of the British cabinet. The generals were chosen by the assembly for one-year terms and were eligible for reelection indefinitely. Pericles held the position of chief strategus or president of the Board of Generals for more than thirty years. The generals were not simply commanders of the army but the chief legislative and executive officials in the state. Though wielding enormous power, they could not become tyrants, for their policies were subject to review by the as-

The Owl of Athens. An Athenian silver coin of around 470 B.C., showing the owl, thought to be sacred to Athens's protectress, the goddess Athena. The name Athens appears in the Greek letters ΑΘΣ.

sembly, and they could easily be recalled at the end of their one-year terms or indicted for malfeasance at any time. Finally, it was in the Age of Pericles that the Athenian system of courts was developed to completion. No longer was there merely a supreme court to hear appeals from the decisions of magistrates, but an array of popular courts with authority to try all kinds of cases. At the beginning of each year a list of 6,000 citizens was chosen by lot from the various sections of the country. From this list separate juries, varying in size from 201 to 1,001, were made up for particular trials. Each of these juries constituted a court with power to decide by majority vote every question involved in the case. Although one of the magistrates presided, he had none of the prerogatives of a judge; the jury itself was the judge, and from its decision there was no appeal.

The Athenian democracy differed from the modern form in various ways. First of all, it entirely excluded women. Even taking that into account, it did not extend to the whole population, but only to the citizen class. While it is true that in the time of Cleisthenes the citizens probably included a majority of the inhabitants because of his enfranchisement of resident aliens, in the Age of Pericles the citizens were distinctly a minority. It may be well to observe, however, that within its limits Athenian democracy was more thoroughly applied than is the modern form. The choice by lot of nearly all magistrates except the Ten Generals, the restriction of all terms of public officials to one year, and the uncompromising adherence to the principle of majority rule even in judicial trials were examples of a confidence in the political capacity of the citizen which few modern nations would be willing to accept. The democracy of Athens differed from the contemporary ideal also in the fact that it was direct, not representative. The Athenians were not interested in being governed by a few men of reputation and ability; what vitally concerned them was the assurance to every citizen of an actual voice in the control of all public affairs.

In the century of its greatest expansion and creativity, Athens fought two major wars. The first, the war with Persia, was an outgrowth of the expansion of that empire into the eastern Mediterranean area. The Athenians resented the oppression of the Greek-speaking cities in Asia Minor and aided them in their struggle for freedom. (These cities shared with Athens a common Greek dialect—Ionian—a fact which made the Athenians feel a particularly close kinship with them.) The Persians retaliated by sending a powerful army and fleet to attack the Greeks. Although all Greece was in danger of conquest, Athens bore the chief burden of repelling the invader. The war, which began in 490 B.C. and lasted with interludes of peace until 479, is commonly regarded as one of the most significant in the history of the world. The heroic victories of the Greeks in such battles as Marathon (490) and Salamis (480) put an end to the menace of Persian conquest and forestalled the submergence of Hellenic ideals of freedom in Near-Eastern despotism. The war also had the effect of strengthening democracy in Athens and making that state the leading power in Greece.

The other of the great struggles, the Peloponnesian War with Sparta, had results of a quite different character. Instead of being another milestone in the Athenian march to power, it ended in tragedy. The causes of this war are of particular interest to the student of the downfall of civilizations. First and most important was the growth of Athenian imperialism. In the last year of the war with Persia, Athens had joined with a number of other Greek states in the formation of an offensive and defensive alliance known as the Delian League. When peace was concluded the league was not dissolved, for many of the Greeks feared that the Persians might come back. As time went on, Athens gradually transformed the league into a naval empire for the advancement of its own interests. It used some of the funds in the common treasury for its own purposes. It tried to reduce all the other members to a condition of vassalage, and when one of them rebelled, Athens overwhelmed it by force, seized its navy, and imposed tribute upon it as if it were a conquered state. Such high-handed methods aroused the suspicions of the Spartans, who feared that an Athenian hegemony would soon be extended over all of Greece.

A second major cause was to be found in the social and cultural differences between Athens and Sparta. Athens was democratic, progressive, urban, imperialist, and intellectually and artistically advanced. Sparta was aristocratic, conservative, agrarian, provincial, and culturally backward. Where such sharply contrasting systems exist side by side, conflicts are almost bound to occur. The attitude of the Athenians and Spartans had been hostile for some time. The former looked upon the latter as uncouth barbarians. The Spartans accused the Athenians of attempting to gain control over the northern Peloponnesian states and of encouraging the helots to rebel. Economic factors also played a large part in bringing the conflict to a head. Athens was ambitious to dominate the Corinthian Gulf, the principal avenue of trade with Sicily and southern Italy. This made Athens the deadly enemy of Corinth, the chief ally of Sparta.

The war, which broke out in 431 B.C. and lasted until 404, was a record of frightful calamities for Athens. Athenian trade was destroyed, its democracy overthrown, and the population decimated by a terrible pestilence. Quite as bad was the moral degradation which followed in the wake of the military reverses. Treason, corruption, and brutality were among the hastening ills of the last few years of the conflict. On one occasion the Athenians even slaughtered the whole male population of the island of Melos, and enslaved the women and children, for no other crime than refusing to abandon neutrality. Ultimately, deserted by all its allies except Samos and with its food supply cut off, Athens was left with no alternative but to surrender or starve. The terms imposed upon the Athenians were drastic enough: destruction of their fortifications, surrender of all foreign possessions

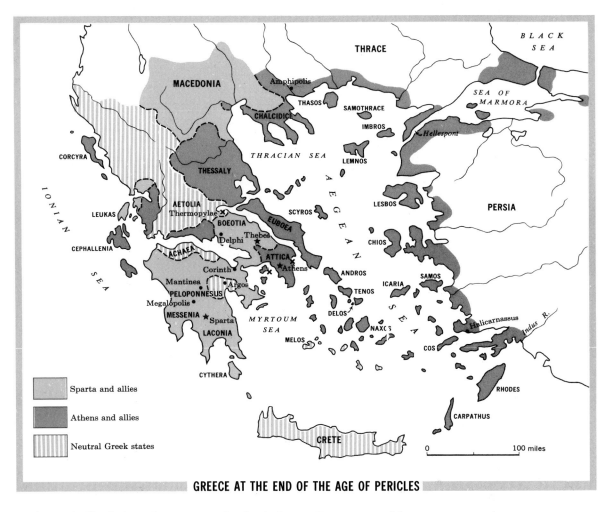

GREECE AT THE END OF THE AGE OF PERICLES

Legend:
- Sparta and allies
- Athens and allies
- Neutral Greek states

0 — 100 miles

and practically their entire navy, and submission to Sparta as a subject state. Though Athens recovered its leadership for a time in the fourth century, its period of glory was approaching its end.

5. POLITICAL DEBACLE—THE LAST DAYS

Not only did the Peloponnesian War put an end to the political supremacy of Athens, it annihilated freedom throughout the Greek world and sealed the doom of the Hellenic political genius. Following the war, Sparta asserted its power over all of Greece. Oligarchies supported by Spartan troops replaced democracies wherever they existed. Confiscation of property and assassination were the methods regularly employed to combat opposition. Although in Athens the tyrants were overthrown after a time and free government restored, Sparta was able to dominate the remainder of Greece for more than thirty years. In 371 B.C., however, Epaminondas of Thebes defeated the Spartan

Continuing conflict among the city-states

army at Leuctra and thereby inaugurated a period of Theban supremacy. Unfortunately Thebes showed little more wisdom and tolerance in governing than Sparta, and nine years later a combination was formed to free the Greek cities from their new oppressor. Failing to break up the alliance, the Thebans gave battle on the field of Mantinea. Both sides claimed the victory, but Epaminondas was slain, and his empire soon afterward collapsed.

The Macedonian conquest

The long succession of wars had now brought the Greek states to the point of exhaustion. Though the glory of their culture was yet undimmed, politically they were prostrate and helpless. Their fate was soon decided for them by the rise of Philip of Macedon. Except for a thin veneer of Hellenic culture, the Macedonians were barbarians; but Philip, before becoming their king, had learned how to lead an army while a hostage at Thebes. Perceiving the weakness of the states to the south, he determined to conquer them. A series of early successes led to a decisive victory in 338 B.C. and soon afterward to dominion over all of Greece except Sparta. Two years later Philip was murdered as the sequel to a family brawl.

Alexander the Great

Rule over Greece now passed into the hands of his son Alexander, a youth of twenty years. After putting to death all possible aspirants to the throne and quelling some feeble revolts of the Greeks, Alexander, subsequently known as "the Great," conceived the grandiose scheme of conquering Persia. One victory followed another until, in the short space of twelve years, all the eastern territory from the Indus River to the Nile had been annexed to Greece as the personal domain of one man. Alexander did not live to enjoy it long. In 323 B.C. he fell ill of Babylonian swamp fever and died at the age of thirty-two.

The significance of Alexander's career

It is difficult to gauge the significance of Alexander's career. Historians have differed widely in their interpretations. Some have seen him as one of the supreme galvanizing forces in history. Others would limit his genius to military strategy and organization and deny that he made a single major contribution of benefit to humanity. There can be no doubt that he was a master of the art of war (he never lost a battle), and that he was intelligent and endowed with charm and physical courage. Unquestionably, also, he was a man of vibrant energy and overpowering ambitions. Just what these ambitions were is not certain. Evidence eludes us that he aspired to conquer the world or to advance the Hellenic ideals of freedom and justice. It seems doubtful that he had much interest in lofty ideals or in using military force to extend them. His main goal was to enhance his own power and glory. The primary significance of his military accomplishment lay in the fact that he carried the Hellenic drive into Asia farther and faster than would otherwise have occurred. He undoubtedly caused the Greek influence to be more widely felt. At the same time he appears to have placed too great a strain upon Hellenism with the result of encouraging a sweeping tide of Eastern influences into the West. Within a short period

Hellenic and Eastern cultures interpenetrated to such an extent as to produce a new civilization. This was the Hellenistic civilization, to be discussed in the chapter that follows.

6. HELLENIC THOUGHT AND CULTURE

From what has been said in preceding chapters it should be clear that the popular notion that all philosophy originated with the Greeks is fallacious. Centuries earlier the Egyptians had given much thought to the nature of the universe and to the social and ethical problems of humanity. The achievement of the Greeks was rather the development of philosophy in a more inclusive manner than it had ever possessed before. They attempted to find answers to every conceivable question about the nature of the universe, the problem of truth, and the meaning and purpose of life. The magnitude of their accomplishment is attested by the fact that philosophy ever since has been largely a debate over the validity of their conclusions.

The antecedents of Greek philosophy

Greek philosophy had its origins in the sixth century B.C. in the work of the so-called Milesian school, whose members were natives of the commercial city of Miletus on the shore of Asia Minor. Their philosophy was fundamentally scientific and materialistic. The problem which chiefly engaged their attention was to discover the nature of the physical world. They believed that all things could be reduced to some primary substance or original matter which was the source of worlds, stars, animals, plants, and men and women, and to which all would ultimately return. Thales, the founder of the school, perceiving that all things contained moisture, taught that the primary substance is water. Anaximander insisted that it could not be any particular thing such as water or fire but some substance "ungendered and imperishable" which "contains and directs all things." He called this substance the Indefinite or the Boundless. A third member of the school, Anaximenes, declared that the original material of the universe is air. Air when rarefied becomes fire; when condensed it turns successively to wind, vapor, water, earth, and stone.

The philosophy of the Milesian school

Although seemingly naive in its conclusions, the philosophy of the Milesian school was of real significance. It broke through the mythological beliefs of the Greeks about the origin of the world and substituted purely rational explanations. It expanded the Egyptian ideas of the eternity of the universe and the indestructibility of matter. It suggested very clearly, especially in the teachings of Anaximander, the concept of evolution in the sense of rhythmic change, of continuing creation and decay.

Significance of the teachings of the Milesian school

Before the end of the sixth century Greek philosophy developed a metaphysical turn; it ceased to be occupied solely with problems of the physical world and shifted its attention to abstruse questions about the nature of being, the meaning of truth, and the position of the divine in the scheme of things. First to exemplify the new tendency were the Pythagoreans, who interpreted philosophy largely in terms of religion. Little is known about them except that their leader, Pythagoras, migrated from the island of Samos to southern Italy and founded a religious community at Croton in 530 B.C. He and his followers taught that the speculative life is the highest good, but that in order to pursue it, the individual must be purified of the evil desires of the flesh. They held that the essence of things is not a material substance but an abstract principle, number. Their chief significance lies in the sharp distinctions they drew between spirit and matter, harmony and discord, good and evil. Perhaps it is accurate to regard the Pythagoreans as the real founders of dualism in Greek thought.

A consequence of the work of the Pythagoreans was to intensify the debate over the nature of the universe. Some of their contemporaries, notably Parmenides, argued that stability or permanence is the real nature of things; change and diversity are simply illusions of the senses. Directly opposed to this conception was the position taken by Heracleitus, who argued that permanence is an illusion, that change alone is real. The universe, he maintained, is in a condition of constant flux; therefore "it is impossible to step twice into the same stream." Creation and destruction, life and death, are but the obverse and reverse sides of the same picture. In affirming such views Heracleitus was really contending that the things we see and hear and feel are all that there is to reality. Evolution or constant change is the law of the universe. The tree or the stone that is here today is gone tomorrow; no underlying substance exists immutable through all eternity.

The eventual answer to the question of the underlying character of the universe was provided by the atomists. The philosopher chiefly responsible for the development of the atomic theory was Democritus, who lived in Abdera on the Thracian coast in the second half of the fifth century. As their name implies, the atomists held that the ultimate constituents of the universe are atoms, infinite in number, indestructible, and indivisible. Although these differ in size and shape, they are exactly alike in composition. Because of the motion inherent in them, they are eternally uniting, separating, and reuniting in different arrangements. Every individual object or organism in the universe is thus the product of a fortuitous concourse of atoms. The only difference between a man and a tree is the difference in the number and arrangement of their atoms. Here was a philosophy which represented the final fruition of the materialistic tendencies of early Greek thought. Democritus denied the immortality of the soul and the existence of any spiritual world. Strange as it may appear to some people, he was a moral idealist, affirming that "Good means not merely not to do wrong, but rather not to desire to do wrong."

About the middle of the fifth century B.C. an intellectual revolution began in Greece. It accompanied the high point of democracy in Athens. The rise in the power of the citizen, the growth of individualism, and the demand for the solution of practical problems produced a reaction against the old ways of thinking. As a result philosophers abandoned the study of the physical universe and turned to consideration of subjects more intimately related to the individual. The first exponents of the new intellectual trend were the Sophists. Originally the term meant "those who are wise," but later it came to be used in the derogatory sense of men who employ specious reasoning. Since most of our knowledge of the Sophists was derived, until comparatively recently, from Plato, one of their severest critics, they were commonly considered to have been the enemies of all that was best in Hellenic culture. Modern research has exposed the fallacy of so extreme a conclusion. Some members of the group, however, did lack a sense of social responsibility and were quite unscrupulous in "making the worse appear the better case."

*The intellectual revolution
begun by the Sophists*

One of the leading Sophists was Protagoras, a native of Abdera who did most of his teaching in Athens. His famous dictum, "Man is the measure of all things," comprehends the essence of the Sophist philosophy. By this he meant that goodness, truth, justice, and beauty are relative to the needs and interests of man. There are no absolute truths or eternal standards of right and justice. Since sense perception is the exclusive source of knowledge, there can be only particular truths valid for a given time and place. Morality likewise varies from one people to another, for there are no absolute canons of right and wrong eternally decreed in the heavens to fit all cases.

*The doctrines of
Protagoras*

Some of the later Sophists went far beyond the teachings of Protagoras. The individualism which was necessarily implicit in the teachings of Protagoras was twisted by Thrasymachus into the doctrine that all laws and customs are merely expressions of the will of the strongest and shrewdest for their own advantage, and that therefore the wise man is the "perfectly unjust man" who is above the law and concerned with the gratification of his own desires. (It should also be mentioned that man, in the sense of the male, was the primary focus of this and all other Greek philosophy dealing with the individual.)

*The extremist doctrines of
the later Sophists*

Yet there was much that was admirable in the teachings of the Sophists, even of those who were the most extreme. Without exception they condemned slavery and the racial exclusiveness of the Greeks. They were champions of liberty, the rights of the common man, and the practical and progressive point of view. They perceived the folly of war and ridiculed the chauvinism of many Athenian citizens. Perhaps their most important work was the extension of philosophy to include not only physics and metaphysics, but ethics and politics as well. As the Roman Cicero expressed it, they "brought philosophy down from heaven to the dwellings of men."

*The valuable
contributions of the
Sophists*

It was inevitable that the relativism, skepticism, and individualism

Socrates. According to Plato, Socrates looked like a goat-man but spoke like a god.

The philosophy of Socrates

Plato

of the Sophists should have aroused strenuous opposition. In the judgment of the more conservative Greeks these doctrines appeared to lead straight to atheism and anarchy. If there is no final truth, and if goodness and justice are merely relative to the whims of the individual, then neither religion, morality, the state, nor society itself can long be maintained. The result of this conviction was the growth of a new philosophic movement grounded upon the theory that truth is real and that absolute standards do exist. The leaders of this movement were perhaps the three most famous individuals in the history of thought—Socrates, Plato, and Aristotle.

Socrates was born in Athens in 469 B.C. of humble parentage; his father was a sculptor, his mother a midwife. How he obtained an education no one knows, but he was certainly familiar with the teachings of earlier Greek thinkers. The impression that he was a mere gabbler in the marketplace is quite unfounded. He became a philosopher on his own account chiefly to combat the doctrines of the Sophists. In 399 B.C. he was condemned to death on a charge of "corrupting the youth and introducing new gods." The real reason for the unjust sentence was the tragic outcome for Athens of the Peloponnesian War. Overwhelmed by resentment, the Athenian citizens turned against Socrates because of his associations with aristocrats, including the traitor Alcibiades, and because of his criticism of popular belief. There is also evidence that he disparaged democracy and contended that no government was worthy of the name except intellectual aristocracy.

Because Socrates wrote nothing himself, historians find it difficult to determine the exact scope of his teachings. He is generally regarded as primarily a teacher of ethics with no interest in abstract philosophy. Certain passages in Plato, however, raise the possibility that Plato's abstract doctrine of Ideas was ultimately of Socratic origin. At any rate we can be reasonably sure that Socrates believed in a stable and universally valid knowledge, which man could possess if he would only pursue the right method. This method would consist in the exchange and analysis of opinions, in the setting up and testing of provisional definitions, until finally an essence of truth recognizable by all could be distilled from them. Socrates argued that in similar fashion man could discover enduring principles of right and justice independent of the selfish desires of human beings. He believed, moreover, that the discovery of such rational principles of conduct would prove an infallible guide to virtuous living, for he denied that anyone who truly knows the good can ever choose the evil.

By far the most distinguished of Socrates's pupils was Plato, who was born in Athens around 429 B.C., the son of noble parents. When he was twenty years old he joined the Socratic circle, remaining a member until the tragic death of his teacher. Unlike his great mentor he was a prolific writer, though some of the works attributed to him are of doubtful authorship. The most noted of his writings are such dialogues as the *Apology,* the *Phaedo,* the *Phaedrus,* the *Symposium,* and the *Republic.* He was engaged in the completion of another great work, the *Laws,* when death overtook him in his eighty-first year.

Plato's objectives in developing his philosophy were similar to those of Socrates although somewhat broader: (1) to combat the theory of reality as a disordered flux and to substitute an interpretation of the universe as essentially spiritual and purposeful; (2) to refute the Sophist doctrines of relativism and skepticism; and (3) to provide a secure foundation for ethics. In order to realize these objectives he developed his doctrine of Ideas. He admitted that relativity and constant change are characteristics of the world of physical things, of the world we perceive with our senses. But he denied that this world is the complete universe. There is a higher, spiritual realm composed of eternal forms or Ideas which only the mind can conceive. These are not, however, mere abstractions invented by the mind, but spiritual things. Each is the pattern of some particular class of objects or relation between objects on earth. Thus there are Ideas of man, tree, shape, size, color, proportion, beauty, and justice. Highest of them all is the Idea of the Good, which is the active cause and guiding purpose of the whole universe. The things we perceive through our senses are merely imperfect copies of the supreme realities, Ideas.

Plato's philosophy of Ideas

Plato's ethical and religious philosophy was closely related to his doctrine of Ideas. Like Socrates he believed that true virtue has its basis in knowledge. But the knowledge derived from the senses is limited and variable; hence true virtue must consist in rational apprehension of the eternal Ideas of goodness and justice. By relegating the physical to an inferior place, he gave to his ethics an ascetic tinge. He regarded the body as a hindrance to the mind and taught that only the rational part of man's nature is noble and good. Yet in contrast with some of his later followers, he did not demand that appetites and emotions should be denied altogether, but urged that they should be strictly subordinated to the reason. Plato never made his conception of God entirely clear, but it is certain that he conceived of the universe as spiritual in nature and governed by intelligent purpose. He rejected both materialism and mechanism. As for the soul, he regarded it not only as immortal but as preexisting through all eternity.

Plato's ethical and religious philosophy

Plato

As a political philosopher Plato was motivated by the ideal of constructing a state which would be free from turbulence and self-seeking on the part of individuals and classes. Neither democracy nor liberty but harmony and efficiency were the ends he desired to achieve. Accordingly, he proposed in his *Republic* a famous plan for society which would have divided the population into three principal classes corresponding to the functions of the soul. The lowest class, representing the appetitive function, would include the farmers, artisans, and merchants. The second class, representing the spirited element or will, would consist of the soldiers. The highest class, representing the func-

Plato as a political philosopher

tion of reason, would be composed of the intellectual aristocracy. Each of these classes would perform those tasks for which it was best fitted. The function of the lowest class would be the production and distribution of goods for the benefit of the whole community; that of the soldiers, defense; the aristocracy, by reason of special aptitude for philosophy, would enjoy a monopoly of political power. The division of the people into these several ranks would not be made on the basis of birth or wealth, but through a sifting process that would take into account the ability of each individual to profit from education. Thus the farmers, artisans, and merchants would be those who had shown the least intellectual capacity, whereas the philosopher-kings would be those who had shown the greatest.

Aristotle

The last of the great champions of the Socratic tradition was Aristotle, a native of Stagira, born in 384 B.C. At the age of seventeen he entered Plato's Academy,[3] continuing as student and teacher there for twenty years. In 343 he was invited by Philip of Macedon to serve as tutor to the young Alexander. History affords few more conspicuous examples of wasted effort, except for the fact that the young prince acquired an enthusiasm for science and for some other elements of Hellenic culture. Seven years later Aristotle returned to Athens, where he conducted a school of his own, known as the Lyceum, until his death in 322 B.C. Aristotle wrote even more voluminously than Plato and on a greater variety of subjects. His principal works include treatises on logic, metaphysics, rhetoric, ethics, natural sciences, and politics.

Aristotle compared with Plato and Socrates

Though Aristotle was as much interested as Plato and Socrates in absolute knowledge and eternal standards, his philosophy differed from theirs in several outstanding respects. To begin with, he had a higher regard for the concrete and the practical. In contrast with Plato, the aesthete, and Socrates, who declared he could learn nothing from trees and stones, Aristotle was an empirical scientist with a compelling interest in biology, medicine, and astronomy. Moreover, he was less inclined than his predecessors to a spiritual outlook. And lastly, he did not share their strong aristocratic sympathies.

Aristotle's conception of the universe

Aristotle agreed with Plato that universals, Ideas (or forms as he called them), are real, and that knowledge derived from the senses is limited and inaccurate. But he refused to go along with his teacher in ascribing an independent existence to universals and in reducing material things to pale reflections of their spiritual patterns. On the contrary, he asserted that form and matter are of equal importance; both are eternal, and neither can exist inseparable from the other. It is the union of the two which gives to the universe its essential character. Forms are the causes of all things; they are the purposive forces that shape the world of matter into the infinitely varied objects and orga-

---

[3] So called from the grove of Academus, where Plato and his disciples met to discuss philosophic problems.

nisms around us. All evolution, both cosmic and organic, results from the interaction of form and matter upon each other. Thus the presence of the form *man* in the human embryo molds and directs the development of the latter until it ultimately evolves as a human being. Aristotle's philosophy may be regarded as halfway between the spiritualism and transcendentalism of Plato, on the one hand, and the mechanistic materialism of the atomists on the other. His conception of the universe was *teleological*—that is, governed by purpose; but he refused to regard the spiritual as completely overshadowing its material embodiment.

That Aristotle should have conceived of God primarily as a First Cause is no more than we should expect from the dominance of the scientific attitude in his philosophy. Aristotle's God was simply the Prime Mover, the original source of the purposive motion contained in the forms. In no sense was he a personal God, for his nature was pure intelligence, devoid of all feelings, will, or desire. Aristotle seems to have left no place in his religious scheme for individual immortality: all the functions of the soul, except the creative reason which is not individual at all, are dependent upon the body and perish with it.

Aristotle's religious doctrines

Aristotle's ethical philosophy was less ascetic than Plato's. He did not regard the body as the prison of the soul, nor did he believe that physical appetites are necessarily evil in themselves. He taught that the highest good consists in self-realization, that is, in the exercise of that part of man's nature which most truly distinguishes him as a human being. Self-realization would therefore be identical with the life of reason. But the life of reason is dependent upon the proper combination of physical and mental conditions. The body must be kept in good health and the emotions under adequate control. The solution is to be found in the *golden mean,* in preserving a balance between excessive indulgence on the one hand and ascetic denial on the other. This was simply a reaffirmation of the characteristic Hellenic ideal of *sophrosyne,* "nothing too much."

Aristotle's ethical philosophy of the golden mean

Although Aristotle included in his *Politics* much descriptive and analytical material on the structure and functions of government, he dealt primarily with the broader aspects of political theory. He considered the state as the supreme institution for the promotion of the good life, and he was therefore vitally interested in its origin and development and in the best forms it could be made to assume. Declaring that man is by nature a political animal, he denied that the state is an artificial product of the ambitions of the few or of the desires of the many. On the contrary, he asserted that it is rooted in the instincts of man himself, and that civilized life outside of its limits is impossible. He considered the best state to be neither a monarchy, an aristocracy, nor a democracy, but a *polity*—which he defined as a commonwealth intermediate between oligarchy and democracy. Essentially it would be a state under the control of the middle class, but Aristotle intended to make sure that the members of that class would be fairly numerous,

The golden mean applied to politics

for he advocated measures to prevent the concentration of wealth. He defended the institution of private property, but he opposed the heaping up of riches beyond what is necessary for intelligent living. He recommended that the government should provide the poor with money to buy small farms or to "make a beginning in trade and husbandry" and thus promote their prosperity and self-respect.

Contrary to a popular belief, the period of Hellenic civilization, strictly speaking, was not a great age of science. The vast majority of *Hellenic science* the scientific achievements commonly thought of as Greek were made during the Hellenistic period, when the culture was no longer predominantly Hellenic but a mixture of Hellenic and Near-Eastern. The interests of the Greeks in the Periclean age and in the century that followed were chiefly speculative and artistic; they were not deeply concerned with material comforts or with mastery of the physical universe. Consequently, with the exception of some important developments in mathematics, biology, and medicine, scientific progress was relatively slight.

The founder of Greek mathematics was apparently Thales of Miletus, who is supposed to have originated several theorems which were *Mathematics* later included in the geometry of Euclid. Perhaps more significant was the work of the Pythagoreans, who developed an elaborate theory of numbers, classifying them into various categories, such as odd, even, prime, composite, perfect, and so forth. They are also supposed to have discovered the theory of proportion and to have proved for the first time that the sum of the three angles of any triangle is equal to two right angles. But the most famous of their achievements was the discovery of the theorem attributed to Pythagoras himself: the square of the hypotenuse of any right-angled triangle is equal to the sum of the squares on the other two sides.

The first of the Greeks to manifest an interest in biology was the philosopher Anaximander, who developed a crude theory of organic *Biology* evolution based upon the principle of survival through progressive adaptations to the environment. The earliest ancestral animals, he asserted, lived in the sea, which originally covered the whole face of the earth. As the waters receded, some organisms were able to adjust themselves to their new environment and became land animals. The final product of this evolutionary process was man himself. The real founder of the science of biology, however, was Aristotle. Devoting many years of his life to painstaking study of the structure, habits, and growth of animals, he revealed many facts which were not destined to be discovered anew until the seventeenth century or later. The metamorphoses of various insects, the reproductive habits of the eel, the embryological development of the dog-fish—these are only samples of the amazing extent of his knowledge. Unfortunately he committed some errors. He denied the sexuality of plants, and although he subscribed to the general theory of evolution, he believed in the spontaneous generation of certain species of worms and insects.

Greek medicine also had its origin with the philosophers. A pioneer was Empedocles, exponent of the theory of the four elements (earth, air, fire, and water). He discovered that blood flows to and from the heart, and that the pores of the skin supplement the work of the respiratory passages in breathing. More important was the work of Hippocrates of Cos in the fifth and fourth centuries. By general consensus he is regarded as the father of medicine. He dinned into the ears of his pupils the doctrine that "Every disease has a natural cause, and without natural causes, nothing ever happens." In addition, by his methods of careful study and comparison of symptoms he laid the foundations for clinical medicine. He discovered the phenomenon of crisis in disease and improved the practice of surgery. Though he had a wide knowledge of drugs, his chief reliances in treatment were diet and rest. The main fact to his discredit was his development of the theory of the four humors—the notion that illness is due to excessive amounts of yellow bile, black bile, blood, and phlegm in the system. The practice of bleeding the patient was the regrettable outgrowth of this theory.

Generally the most common medium of literary expression in the formative age of a people is the epic of heroic deeds. The most famous of the Greek epics, the *Iliad* and the *Odyssey,* were put into written form at the end of the Dark Ages and commonly attributed to Homer. The first, which deals with the Trojan War, has its theme in the wrath of Achilles; the second describes the wanderings and return of Odysseus. Both have supreme literary merit in their carefully woven plots, in the realism of their character portrayals, and in their mastery of the full range of emotional intensity. They exerted an almost incalculable influence upon later writers. Their style and language inspired the fervid emotional poetry of the sixth century, and they were an unfailing source of plots and themes for the great tragedians of the Golden Age of the fifth century.

The three centuries which followed the Dark Ages were distinguished, as we have already seen, by tremendous social changes. The

Medicine

The Homeric epics

Interior of a Greek Cup. Depicted is the friendship of leading characters from the *Iliad:* Patroklus and Achilles. Here Achilles is bandaging Patroklus's wounds.

rural pattern of life gave way to an urban society of steadily increasing complexity. The founding of colonies and the growth of commerce provided new interests and new habits of living. Individuals hitherto submerged rose to a consciousness of their power and importance. It was inevitable that these changes should be reflected in new forms of literature, especially of a more personal type. The first to be developed was the elegy, which was probably intended to be declaimed rather than sung to the accompaniment of music. Elegies varied in theme from individual reactions toward love to the idealism of patriots and reformers. Generally, however, they were devoted to melancholy reflection on the disillusionments of life or to bitter lament over loss of prestige. Outstanding among the authors of elegiac verse was Solon the legislator.

In the sixth century and the early part of the fifth, the elegy was gradually displaced by the lyric, which derives its name from the fact that it was sung to the music of the lyre. The new type of poetry was particularly well adapted to the expression of passionate feelings, the violent loves and hates engendered by the strife of classes. It was employed for other purposes also. Both Alcaeus and Sappho, the latter a woman poet from the island of Lesbos, used it to describe the poignant beauty of love, the delicate grace of spring, and the starlit splendor of a summer night. Meanwhile other poets developed the choral lyric, intended to express the feelings of the community rather than the sentiments of any one individual. Greatest of all the writers of this group was Pindar of Thebes, who wrote during the first half of the fifth century. The lyrics of Pindar took the form of odes celebrating the victories of athletes and the glories of Hellenic civilization.

The supreme literary achievement of the Greeks was the tragic drama. Like so many of their other great works, it had its roots in religion. At the festivals dedicated to the worship of Dionysus, the god of spring and of wine, a chorus of men dressed as satyrs, or goat-men, sang and danced around an altar, enacting the various parts of a dithyramb or choral lyric that related the story of the god's career. In time a leader came to be separated from the chorus to recite the main parts of the story. The true drama was born about the beginning of the fifth century when Aeschylus introduced a second "actor" and relegated the chorus to the background. The name "tragedy," which came to be applied to this drama, was probably derived from the Greek word *tragos* meaning "goat."

Greek tragedy stands out in marked contrast to the tragedies of Shakespeare or modern playwrights. There was, first of all, little action presented on the stage; the main business of the actors was to recite the incidents of a plot which was already familiar to the audience, for the story was drawn from popular legends. Secondly, Greek tragedy devoted little attention to the study of complicated individual personality. There was no development of personal character as

Greek Theater in Epidauros. The construction, to take advantage of the slope of the hill, and the arrangement of the stage are of particular interest. Greek dramas were invariably presented in the open air.

shaped by the vicissitudes of a long career. Those involved in the plot were scarcely individuals at all, but types. On the stage they wore masks to disguise any characteristics which might serve to distinguish them too sharply from the rest of humanity. In addition, Greek tragedies differed from the modern variety in having as their theme the conflict between the individual and the universe, not the clash between personalities, or the internal conflicts of one person. The tragic fate that befell the main characters in these plays was external to individuals. It was brought on by the fact that someone had committed a crime against society, or against the gods, thereby offending the moral scheme of the universe. Punishment must follow in order to balance the scale of justice. Finally, the purpose of Greek tragedies was not merely to depict suffering and to interpret human actions, but to purify the emotions of the audience by representing the triumph of justice.

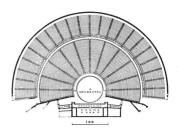

Epidauros Plan

As already indicated, the first of the tragic dramatists was Aeschylus (525–456 B.C.). Though he is known to have written about eighty plays, only seven have survived in complete form, among them *The Persians, Seven against Thebes, Prometheus Bound,* and a trilogy known as *The Oresteia.* Guilt and punishment is the recurrent theme of nearly all of them. The second of the leading tragedians whose works have survived, Sophocles (496–406), is often considered the greatest. His style was more polished and his philosophy more profound than that of his predecessor. He was the author of over a hundred plays. More than any other writer in Greek history, he personified the Hellenic ideal of "nothing too much." His attitude was distinguished by love of harmony and peace, intelligent respect for democracy, and pro-

Aeschylus and Sophocles

found sympathy for human weakness. The most famous of his plays now extant are *Oedipus Rex*, *Antigone*, and *Electra*.

Euripides

The work of the last of the great tragedians, Euripides (480–406), reflects a far different spirit. He was a skeptic, an individualist, a humanist, who took delight in ridiculing the ancient myths and the "sacred cows" of his time. An embittered pessimist who suffered from the barbs of his conservative critics, he loved to humble the proud in his plays and to exalt the lowly. He was the first to give the ordinary man, even the beggar and the peasant, a place in the drama. Euripides is also noted for his sympathy for the slave, for his condemnation of war, and for his protests against the exclusion of women from social and intellectual life. Because of his humanism, his tendency to portray men as they actually were (or even a little worse), and his introduction of the love motif into drama, he is often considered a modernist. It must be remembered, however, that in other respects his plays were perfectly consistent with the Hellenic model. They did not exhibit the evolution of individual character or the conflict of egos to any more notable extent than did the works of Sophocles or Aeschylus. Nevertheless, he has been called the most tragic of the Greek dramatists because he dealt with situations having analogues in real life. Among the best-known tragedies of Euripides are *Alcestis*, *Medea*, and *The Trojan Women*.

Hellenic comedy

Hellenic comedy, in common with tragedy, appears to have grown out of the Dionysiac festivals, but it did not attain full development until late in the fifth century B.C. Its outstanding representative was Aristophanes (448?–380?), a somewhat coarse and belligerent aristocrat who lived in Athens. Most of his plays were written to satirize the political and intellectual ideals of the radical democracy of his time. In *The Knights* he pilloried the incompetent and greedy politicians for their reckless adventures in imperialism. In *The Frogs* he lampooned Euripides for the innovations the latter had made in the drama. *The Clouds* he reserved for ridicule of the Sophists, ignorantly or maliciously classifying Socrates as one of them. While he was undoubtedly a clever poet with a mastery of subtle humor and imaginative skill, his ideas were founded largely upon prejudice. He is deserving of much credit, however, for his sharp criticisms of the policies of the warhawks of Athens during the struggle with Sparta. Though written as a farce, his *Lysistrata* cleverly pointed a way—however infeasible—to the termination of any war: in this play wives refuse to have sexual relations with their husbands until the latter agree to make peace with their foreign enemies.

The Greek historians: Herodotus

No account of Greek literature would be complete without some mention of the two great historians of the Golden Age. Herodotus, the "father of history" (c. 484–c. 420), was a native of Halicarnassus in Asia Minor. He traveled extensively through the Persian empire, Egypt, Greece, and Italy, collecting a multitude of interesting data about various peoples. His famous account of the great war between the Greeks and the Persians included so much background that the work seems almost a history of the world. He regarded that war as an epic struggle between East and West, with Zeus giving victory to the Greeks against a mighty host of barbarians.

If Herodotus deserves to be called the father of history, much more does his younger contemporary, Thucydides (c. 460–c. 400), deserve to be considered the founder of scientific history. Influenced by the skepticism and practicality of the Sophists, Thucydides chose to work on the basis of carefully sifted evidence, rejecting opinion, legends, and hearsay. The subject of his *History* was the war between Sparta and Athens, which he described scientifically and dispassionately, emphasizing the complexity of causes which led to the fateful clash. His aim was to present an accurate record which could be studied with profit by statesmen and generals of all time, and it must be said that he was in full measure successful. If there were any defects in his historical method, they consisted in overemphasizing political factors to the neglect of the social and economic and in failing to consider the importance of emotions in history. He also had a prejudice against the democratic factions in Athens after the death of Pericles.

Thucydides

7. THE MEANING OF GREEK ART

Art as well as literature reflected the basic character of Hellenic civilization. The Greek was essentially a materialist who conceived of the world in physical terms. Plato and the followers of the mystic religions were, of course, exceptions, but few other Greeks had much interest in a universe of spiritual realities. It would be natural therefore to find that the material emblems of architecture and sculpture should exemplify best the ideals the Greek held before him.

Greek art as an expression of the Greek spirit

What did Greek art express? Above all, it symbolized humanism— the glorification of man as the most important creature in the universe. Though much of the sculpture depicted gods, and also goddesses, this did not detract in the slightest from its humanistic quality. The Greek deities existed for the benefit of man; in glorifying them he thus glorified himself. Both architecture and sculpture embodied the ideals of balance, harmony, order, and moderation. Anarchy and excess were abhorrent to the mind of the Greek, but so was absolute repression. Consequently, Greek art exhibited qualities of simplicity and dignified restraint—free from decorative extravagance, on the one hand, and from restrictive conventions on the other. Moreover, Greek art was an expression of the national life. Its purpose was not merely aesthetic but political: to symbolize the pride of the people in their city and to enhance their consciousness of unity. The Parthenon at Athens, for example, was the temple of Athena, the protecting goddess who

The ideals embodied in Greek art

See color plates following page 96

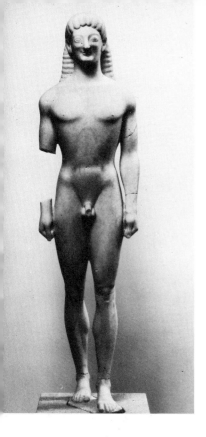

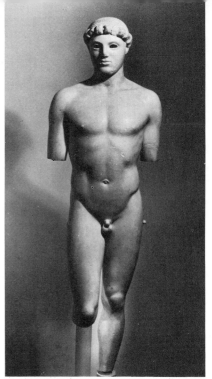

Apollo of Tenea; Apollo of Piombino; "The Critian Boy." These three statues, dating from about 560, 500, and 480 B.C. respectively, display the progressive "unfreezing" of Greek statuary art. The first stiff and symmetrical statue is imitative of Egyptian sculpture (see statue of the Pharoah Mycerinus, p. 38 above). Roughly half a century later it is succeeded by a figure which begins to display motion, as if awakening from a sleep of centuries in a fairy tale. The last figure introduces genuine naturalism in its delicate twists and depiction of the subject's weight resting on one leg.

presided over the corporate life of the state. In providing her with a beautiful shrine which she might frequently visit, the Athenians were giving evidence of their love for their city and their hope for its continuing welfare.

The art of the Greeks differed from that of nearly every people since their time in an interesting variety of ways. Like most of the tragedies of Aeschylus and Sophocles, it was universal. It included few portraits of personalities either in sculpture or in painting. (Most of the portrait busts commonly considered Greek really belong to the Hellenistic Age.) The human beings depicted were generally types, not individuals. Again, Greek art differed from that of most later peoples in its ethical purpose. It was not art for the sake of mere decoration or for the expression of the artist's individual philosophy, but a medium for the ennoblement of humanity. This does not mean that it was didactic in the sense that its merit was determined by the moral lesson it taught, but rather that it was supposed to exemplify qualities of living essentially artistic in themselves. The Athenian, at least, drew no sharp distinction between the ethical and aesthetic spheres; the beautiful and the good were really identical. True morality, therefore, con-

Greek art compared with that of later peoples

sisted in rational living, in the avoidance of grossness, disgusting excesses, and other forms of conduct aesthetically offensive. Finally, Greek art may be contrasted with most later forms in the fact that it was not "naturalistic." Although the utmost attention was given to the depiction of beautiful bodies, this had little to do with fidelity to nature. The Greek was not interested in interpreting nature for its own sake, but in expressing *human* ideals.

The history of Greek art divides itself naturally into three great periods. The first, which can be called the archaic period, covered the seventh and sixth centuries. During the greater part of this age sculpture was dominated by Egyptian influence, as can be seen in the frontality and rigidity of the statues, with their square shoulders and one foot slightly advanced. Toward the end, however, these conventions were thrown aside. The chief architectural styles also had their origin in this period, and several crude temples were built. The second period, which occupied the fifth century, witnessed the full perfection of both architecture and sculpture. The art of this time was completely idealistic. During the fourth century, the last period of Hellenic art, architecture lost some of its balance and simplicity and sculpture assumed new characteristics. It came to reflect more clearly the reactions of the individual artist, to incorporate more realism, and to lose some of its quality as an expression of civic pride.

The three periods of Greek art

For all its artistic excellence, Greek temple architecture was one of the simplest of structural forms. Its essential elements were really only five in number: (1) the cella or nucleus of the building, which was a rectangular chamber to house the statue of the god; (2) the columns, which formed the porch and surrounded the cella; (3) the entablature, which rested upon the columns and supported the roof; (4) the gabled roof itself; and (5) the pediment or triangular section under the gable of the roof. Two different architectural styles were developed, representing modifications of certain of these elements. The more common was the Doric, which made use of a rather heavy, sharply fluted column surmounted by a plain capital. The other, the Ionic, had more slender and more graceful columns with flat flutings, a triple base, and a scroll or volute capital. The so-called Corinthian style, which was chiefly Hellenistic, differed from the Ionic primarily

Greek architecture

Details of the Three Orders of Greek Architecture

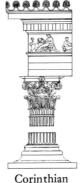

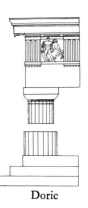

Corinthian   Ionic   Doric

The Parthenon. The largest and most famous of Athenian temples, the Parthenon is considered the classic example of Doric architecture. Its columns were made more graceful by tapering them in a slight curve toward the top. Its friezes and pediments were decorated with lifelike sculptures of prancing horses (see below), fighting giants, and benign and confident deities.

Parthenon Frieze

in being more ornate. The three styles differed also in their treatment of the entablature. In the Ionic style it was left almost plain. In the Doric and Corinthian styles it bore sculptured reliefs. The Parthenon, the best example of Greek architecture, was essentially a Doric building, but it reflected some of the grace and subtlety of Ionic influence.

According to the prevailing opinion among his contemporaries, Greek sculpture attained its acme of development in the work of Phidias (c. 500–c. 432). His masterpieces were the statue of Athena in the Parthenon and the statue of Zeus in the Temple of Olympian Zeus. In addition, he designed and supervised the execution of the Parthenon reliefs. The main qualities of his work are grandeur of conception, patriotism, proportion, dignity, and restraint. Nearly all of his figures are idealized representations of deities and mythological creatures in human form. The second most renowned fifth-century sculptor was Myron, noted for his statue of the discus thrower and for his glorification of other athletic types. The names of three great sculptors in the fourth century have come down to us. The most gifted of them was Praxiteles, renowned for his portrayal of humanized deities with slender, graceful bodies and countenances of philosophic repose. The best known of his works is the statue of Hermes with the infant Dionysus. His older contemporary, Scopas, gained distinction as an emotional sculptor. One of his most successful creations was the statue of a religious ecstatic, a worshiper of Dionysus, in a condition of mystic frenzy. At the end of the century Lysippus introduced even stronger qualities of realism and individualism into sculpture. He was the first great master of the realistic portrait as a study of personal character.

8. ATHENIAN LIFE IN THE GOLDEN AGE

The population of Athens in the fifth and fourth centuries was divided into three distinct groups: the citizens, the metics, and the slaves. The citizens, who numbered at the most about 160,000, included only those males born of citizen parents, except for the few who were occasionally enfranchised by special law. The metics, who probably did not exceed a total of 35,000, were resident aliens, chiefly non-Athenian Greeks. Save for the fact that they had no political privileges and generally were not permitted to own land, male metics had equal opportunities with citizens. They could engage in any occupation they desired and participate in any social or intellectual activities. Contrary to a popular tradition, the slaves in Athens were never a majority of the population. Their maximum number does not seem to have exceeded 110,000. Urban slaves, at least, were very well treated and were sometimes rewarded for faithful service by being set free. The males could work for wages and own property, and some of them

Athenian classes

Left: *The Discobolus or Discus Thrower of Myron.* The statue reflects the glorification of the human body characteristic of Athens in the Golden Age. Now in the Vatican Museum. Right: *Hermes with the Infant Dionysus, by Praxiteles, Fourth Century B.C.* Original in the Olympia Museum, Greece.

held responsible positions as minor public officials and as managers of banks. The treatment of slaves who worked in the mines, however, was often cruel.

Life in Athens stands out in rather sharp contrast to that in most other civilizations. One of its leading features was the amazing degree of social and economic equality that prevailed among all the inhabitants. Although there were many who were poor, there were few who were very rich. Nearly everyone, whether citizen, metic, or slave, ate the same kind of food, wore the same kind of clothing, and participated in the same kind of amusement. This substantial equality was enforced in part by the system of *liturgies,* which were services to the state rendered by wealthy men, chiefly in the form of contributions to support the drama, equip the navy, or provide for the poor.

The amazing degree of social and economic equality

A second outstanding characteristic of Athenian life was its poverty in comforts and luxuries. Part of this was a result of the low income of the mass of the people. Teachers, sculptors, masons, carpenters, and common laborers all received the same standard wage of one drachma per day. Part of it may have been a consequence also of the mild climate, which made possible a life of simplicity. But whatever the cause, the fact remains that, in comparison with modern standards, the Athenians endured an exceedingly impoverished existence. They knew nothing of such common commodities as watches, soap, newspapers, cotton cloth, sugar, tea, or coffee. Their beds had no springs, their houses had no drains, and their food consisted chiefly of barley cakes, onions, and fish, washed down with diluted wine. From the standpoint of clothing they were no better off. A rectangular piece of cloth wrapped around the body and fastened with pins at the shoulders and with a rope around the waist served as the main garment. A larger piece was draped around the body as an extra garment for outdoor wear. No one wore either stockings or socks, and few had any footgear except sandals.

The poverty of Athenian life

But lack of comforts and luxuries was a matter of little consequence to the Athenian citizen. He was totally unable to regard these as the most important things in life. His aim was to live as interestingly and contentedly as possible without spending all his days in grinding toil for the sake of a little more comfort for his family. Nor was he interested in piling up riches as a source of power or prestige. What each citizen really wanted was a small farm or business that would provide him with a reasonable income and at the same time allow him an abundance of leisure for politics, for gossip in the marketplace, and for intellectual or artistic activities if he had the talent to enjoy them.

Indifference toward material comforts and wealth

It is frequently supposed that the Athenian was too lazy or too snobbish to work hard for luxury and security. But this was not quite the case. True, there were some occupations in which he would not engage because he considered them degrading or destructive of moral freedom. He would not break his back digging silver or copper out of

Attitudes toward work

Young Men Baiting a Dog and Cat. This Athenian relief from about 510 B.C. depicts an odd form of leisure-time amusement.

a mine; such work was fit only for slaves. On the other hand, there is plenty of evidence to show that the great majority of Athenian citizens did not look with disdain upon manual labor. Most of them worked on their farms or in their shops as independent craftsmen.

In spite of expansion of trade and increase in population, the economic organization of Athenian society remained comparatively simple. Agriculture and commerce were by far the most important enterprises. Even in Pericles's day the majority of the citizens still lived in the country. Industry was not highly developed. Very few examples of large-scale production are on record, and those chiefly in the manufacture of pottery and implements of war. The largest establishment that ever existed was apparently a shield factory owned by a metic and employing 120 slaves. No other was more than half as large. The enterprises which absorbed the most labor were the mines, but they were owned by the state and were leased in sections to petty contractors to be worked by slaves. The bulk of industry was carried on in small shops owned by individual craftsmen who produced their wares directly to the order of the consumer.

The basic economic activities

Religion underwent some notable changes in the Golden Age of the fifth and fourth centuries. The primitive polytheism and anthropomorphism of the Homeric myths were largely supplanted by a belief in one God as the creator and sustainer of the moral law. Such a doctrine was taught by many of the philosophers, by the poet Pindar, and by the dramatists Aeschylus and Sophocles. Other significant consequences flowed from the mystery cults. These new forms of religion first became popular in the sixth century because of the craving for an emotional faith to make up for the disappointments of life. One was the Orphic cult, which revolved around the myth of the death and resurrection of Dionysus. Another, the Eleusinian cult, had as its central

Changes in religion

theme the abduction of Persephone by Hades, god of the nether world, and her ultimate redemption by Demeter, the great Earth Mother. Both of these cults had as their original purpose the promotion of the life-giving powers of nature, but in time they came to be fraught with a much deeper significance. They expressed to their followers the ideas of vicarious atonement, salvation in an afterlife, and ecstatic union with the divine. Although entirely inconsistent with the spirit of the ancient religion, they made a powerful appeal to certain classes and were largely responsible for the spread of the belief in personal immortality. The more thoughtful Greeks, however, seem to have persisted in their adherence to the worldly, optimistic, and mechanical faith of their ancestors and to have shown little concern about a conviction of sin or a desire for salvation in a life to come.

The family in Athens in the Golden Age

It remains to consider briefly the position of the family in Athens in the fifth and fourth centuries. Though marriage was still an important institution for the procreation of children who would become citizens of the state, there is reason to believe that family life had declined. Men of the more prosperous classes, at least, now spent the greater part of their time away from their families. Wives were relegated to an inferior position and required to remain secluded in their homes. Their place as social and intellectual companions for their husbands was taken by alien women, the *hetaerae,* many of whom were highly cultured natives of the Ionian cities of Asia Minor. Marriage itself assumed the character of a political and economic arrangement devoid of romantic elements. Men married wives so as to ensure that at least some of their children would be legitimate and in order to obtain property in the form of a dowry. It was important also, of course, to have someone to care for the household. But husbands did not consider their wives as their equals and did not appear in public with them or encourage their participation in any form of social or intellectual activity.

9. THE GREEK ACHIEVEMENT AND ITS SIGNIFICANCE FOR US

The magnitude of the Greek achievement

No historian would deny that the achievement of the Greeks was one of the most remarkable in the history of the world. With no great expanse of fertile soil or abundance of mineral resources, they succeeded in developing a higher and more varied civilization than any of the most richly favored nations of the Near East. With only a limited cultural inheritance from the past to build upon as a foundation, they produced intellectual and artistic achievements which have served ever since as models of perfection for the culture of the West. It seems reasonable to conclude also that the Greeks achieved a more normal and more rational mode of living than most other peoples who strutted and fretted their hour upon this planet. The infrequency of brutal crimes and the contentment with simple amusements and modest wealth all point to a comparatively happy and satisfied existence.

It is necessary to be on our guard, however, against uncritical judgments that are sometimes expressed in reference to the achievement of the Greeks. We must not assume that all of the natives of Hellas were as cultured, wise, and free as the citizens of Athens and of the Ionian states across the Aegean. The Spartans, the Arcadians, the Thessalians, and probably the majority of the Boeotians remained much less culturally advanced. Further, the Athenian civilization itself was not without its defects. It permitted some exploitation of the weak, especially of the slaves who toiled in the mines. It was based upon a principle of racial exclusiveness which reckoned every man a foreigner whose parents were not both Athenians, and consequently denied political rights to the majority of the inhabitants. It was also characterized by the overt repression of the female members of the society. Its statecraft was not sufficiently enlightened to avoid the pitfalls of imperialism and even of aggressive war. Finally, the attitude of its citizens was not always tolerant and just. Socrates was put to death for his opinions, and two other philosophers, Anaxagoras and Protagoras, were forced to leave the city. It must be conceded, however, that the record of the Athenians for tolerance was better than that of most other nations, both ancient and modern. There was probably more freedom of expression in Athens during the war with Sparta than there was in the United States during World War I.

Nor is it true that the Hellenic influence has really been as great as is commonly supposed. No well-informed student could accept the sentimental verdict of Shelley: "We are all Greeks; our laws, our literature, our religion, our arts have their roots in Greece." Our laws do not really have their roots in Greece but chiefly in Hellenistic and Roman sources. Much of our poetry is undoubtedly Greek in inspiration, but such is not the case with most of our prose literature. Our religion is no more than partly Greek; except as it was influenced by Plato, Aristotle, and the Romans, it reflects primarily the spirit of the Near East. Even our arts derive from other sources almost as much as from Greece. Actually, modern civilization has been the result of the convergence of numerous influences coming from many different places and periods of time.

In spite of all this, the Hellenic adventure was of profound significance for the history of the world. For the Greeks were the founders of nearly all those ideals we commonly think of as peculiar to the West. The civilizations of the ancient Near East, with the exception, to a certain extent, of the Hebrew and Egyptian, were dominated by absolutism, supernaturalism, ecclesiasticism, the denial of both body and mind, and the subjection of the individual to the group. It is noteworthy that the Greek word for freedom—*eleutheria*—cannot be

*Undesirable features of
Greek life*

*Hellenic influence
sometimes exaggerated*

*The influence of the
Greeks on the West*

The Acropolis Today. Occupying the commanding position is the Parthenon. To the left is the Erechtheum with its Porch of the Maidens facing the Parthenon.

translated into any ancient Near-Eastern language, not even Hebrew. The typical political regime of the Near East was that of an absolute monarch supported by a powerful priesthood. Culture in the Near-Eastern empires served mainly as an instrument to magnify the power of the state and to enhance the prestige of rulers and priests.

Contrast of Greek and Near-Eastern ideals

By contrast, the civilization of Greece, notably in its Athenian form, was founded upon ideals of freedom, optimism, secularism, rationalism, the glorification of both body and mind, and a high regard for the dignity and worth of the individual man. Insofar as the individual was subjected at all, his subjection was to the rule of the majority. This, of course, was not always good, especially in times of crisis, when the majority might be swayed by prejudice. Religion was worldly and practical, serving the interests of human beings. Worship of the gods was a means for the ennoblement of man. As opposed to the ecclesiasticism of the Near East, the Greeks had no organized priesthood at all. They kept their priests in the background and refused under any circumstances to allow them to define dogma or to govern the realm of intellect. In addition, they excluded them from control over the sphere of morality. The culture of the Greeks was the first to be based upon the primacy of intellect—upon the supremacy of the spirit of free inquiry. There was no subject they feared to investigate, or any question they regarded as excluded from the province of reason. To an extent never before realized, mind was supreme over faith, logic and science over superstition.

The tragedy of Hellenic history

The supreme tragedy of the Greeks was, of course, their failure to solve the problem of political conflict. To a large degree, this conflict was the product of social and cultural dissimilarities. Because of different geographic and economic conditions the Greek city-states developed at an uneven pace. Some went forward rapidly to high levels of cultural superiority, while others lagged behind and made little or no intellectual progress. The consequences were discord and suspicion, which gave rise eventually to hatred and fear. Though some of the more advanced thinkers made efforts to propagate the notion that the Hellenes were one people who should reserve their contempt for non-Hellenes, or "barbarians," the conception never became part of a national ethos. Athenians hated Spartans, and vice versa, just as vehemently as they hated Lydians or Persians. Not even the danger of Asian conquest was sufficient to dispel the distrust and antagonism of Greeks for one another. The war that finally broke out between Athenians and Spartans sealed the doom of Hellenic civilization just as effectively as could ever have resulted from foreign conquest.

SELECTED READINGS

• *Items so designated are available in paperback editions.*
• Andrewes, A., *The Greeks,* New York, 1967. An excellent, up-to-date account of archaic and classical Greek history from about 750 to 350 B.C.
• ————, *The Greek Tyrants,* New York, 1956.
• Boardman, J., *Greek Art,* New York, 1964.
————, *The Greeks Overseas,* Baltimore, 1964. The standard treatment of Greek colonization.
Bowra, C. M., *Ancient Greek Literature,* New York, 1960. Bowra is the modern master of this field.
Burn, A. R., *The Lyric Age of Greece,* New York, 1961. A lively introduction to the seventh and sixth centuries.
Dodds, E. R., *The Greeks and the Irrational,* Berkeley, Calif., 1963. A novel approach to classical Greek culture.
Dover, K. J., *Greek Homosexuality,* Cambridge, Mass., 1978. A serious analysis of a basic aspect of classical Greek life.
• Ehrenberg, V., *From Solon to Socrates,* New York, 1967. An excellent treatment of early Athenian history by one of the twentieth-century's leading authorities.
• ————, *The Greek State,* New York, 1960.
Farrington, B., *Greek Science,* rev. ed., Baltimore, 1961.
Finley, M. I., *The Ancient Greeks: An Introduction to Their Life and Thought,* New York, 1963. An expert brief introduction to the Greeks.
• ————, *Early Greece: The Bronze and Archaic Ages,* New York, 1970. The best recent survey of the earlier periods.
————, *The World of Odysseus,* rev. ed., New York, 1965. Attempts to use the Homeric poems as a guide to Dark Ages Greece.
• Forrest, W. G., *A History of Sparta, 950–152 B.C.,* London, 1968.
• Guthrie, W. K. C., *The Greeks and Their Gods,* Boston, 1965.
Jones, A. H. M., *Athenian Democracy,* New York, 1957. Concentrates on actual political practice.
• Kitto, H. D. F., *The Greeks,* Baltimore, 1957. A delightfully written, highly personal interpretation.
• Lloyd, G. E. R., *Early Greek Science: Thales to Aristotle,* London, 1970.

Marrou, H. I., *A History of Education in Antiquity,* New York, 1964. A modern classic that covers the entire ancient world.

Meiggs, R., *The Athenian Empire,* Oxford, 1972. The major study of fifth-century Athenian imperialism. A monumental work.

Michell, H., *The Economics of Ancient Greece,* rev. ed., Cambridge, 1956.

• Nilsson, M. P., *A History of Greek Religion,* New York, 1964.

• Pollitt, J. J., *Art and Experience in Classical Greece,* Cambridge, 1972. The best introduction to the social and intellectual forces behind Greek art.

• Pomeroy, Sarah, B., *Goddesses, Whores, Wives, and Slaves: Women in Classical Antiquity,* New York, 1975. The best treatment of the role of women in Greece and Rome. Relies on a variety of source material and covers women of all classes.

Rose, H. J., *A Handbook of Greek Literature,* New York, 1960.

• ———, *A Handbook of Greek Mythology,* sixth ed., New York, 1960.

• Sealey, R., *A History of the Greek City States, ca. 700–338 B.C.,* Berkeley, Calif., 1977. Provocative essays that reconsider older assumptions about Greek political life.

• Sinclair, T. A., *A History of Greek Political Thought,* London, 1951.

Snell, Bruno, *The Discovery of the Mind: The Greek Origins of European Thought,* Cambridge, Mass., 1953. Stimulating essays.

• Starr, C. G., *The Economic and Social Growth of Early Greece: 800–500 B.C.,* New York, 1978. An excellent study of this difficult but important topic.
———, *The Origins of Greek Civilization, 1100–650 B.C.,* New York, 1961. The best detailed treatment of the early periods.

• Zimmern, A. E., *The Greek Commonwealth,* 5th ed., New York, 1931. A classic study, perhaps too uncritical of the Athenians.

SOURCE MATERIALS

Most Greek authors have been translated in the appropriate volumes of the Loeb Classical Library, Harvard University Press.

In addition the following may be helpful:

• Barnstone, Willis, tr., *Greek Lyric Poetry,* New York, 1962.

Kagan, Donald, *Sources in Greek Political Thought,* Glencoe, Ill., 1965.

• Kirk, G. S., and J. E. Raven, *The Presocratic Philosophers,* Cambridge, 1957.

Chapter 9

THE HELLENISTIC CIVILIZATION

Beauty and virtue and the like are to be honored, if they give pleasure, but if they do not give pleasure, we must bid them farewell.

—Epicurus, "On the End of Life"

I agree that Alexander was carried away so far as to copy oriental luxury. I hold that no mighty deeds, not even conquering the whole world, is of any good unless the man has learned mastery of himself.

—Arrian, *Anabasis of Alexander*

The death of Alexander the Great in 323 B.C. constituted a watershed in the development of world history. Hellenic civilization as it had existed in its prime now came to an end. Of course, the old institutions and ways of life did not suddenly disappear, but Alexander's career had cut so deeply into the old order that it was inconceivable that it could be restored intact. The fusion of cultures and intermingling of peoples resulting from Alexander's conquests accomplished the overthrow of many of the ideals the Greeks had developed in their Golden Age of the fifth and fourth centuries. Gradually a new pattern of civilization emerged, based upon a mixture of Greek and Eastern elements. To this new civilization, which lasted until about the beginning of the Christian era, the name Hellenistic is most commonly applied.

A new stage in world history

Though the break between the Hellenic and Hellenistic eras was as sharp as that between any two other civilizations, it would be a mistake to deny all continuity. The language of the new cultured classes was predominantly Greek, and even the hordes of people whose heritage was non-Greek considered it desirable to have some Hellenic culture. Hellenic achievements in science provided a foundation for the great scientific revolution of the Hellenistic Age. Greek emphasis upon logic was likewise carried over into Hellenistic philosophy, though the objectives of the latter were in many cases quite different.

Comparison of the Hellenistic Age with the Golden Age of Greece

In the spheres of the political, social, and economic the resemblances were few indeed. The classical ideal of democracy was now super-seded by despotism perhaps as rigorous as any that Egypt or Persia had ever produced. The Greek city-state survived in some parts of Greece itself, but elsewhere it was replaced by large-scale monarchy, and in the minds of some leaders by notions of a world state. The Hellenic devotion to simplicity and the golden mean gave way to ex-travagance in the arts and to a love of luxury. In the economic realm there was a growing stress on big business and vigorous competition for profits. In view of these changes it seems valid to conclude that the Hellenistic Age was sufficiently distinct from the Golden Age of Greece to justify its being considered the era of a new civilization.

1. POLITICAL HISTORY AND INSTITUTIONS

The Hellenistic states

When Alexander died in 323 B.C., he left no legitimate heir to succeed him. His nearest male relative was a feeble-minded half-brother. Tra-dition relates that when his friends requested him on his deathbed to designate a successor, he replied "To the strongest." After his death his highest-ranking generals proceeded to divide the empire among them. Some of the younger commanders contested this arrangement, and a series of wars followed which culminated in the decisive battle of Ipsus in 301 B.C. The result of this battle was a new division among the victors. Seleucus took possession of Persia, Mesopotamia, and Syria; Lysimachus assumed control over Asia Minor and Thrace; Cas-

Alexander in Battle. A scene from a sarcophagus of about 300 B.C. Alexander is shown on horseback at the left.

sander established himself in Macedonia; and Ptolemy added Phoenicia and Palestine to his original domain of Egypt. Twenty years later these four states were reduced to three when Seleucus defeated and killed Lysimachus in battle and appropriated his territory in Asia Minor. In the meantime most of the Greek states had revolted against the attempts of Macedon to extend its power over them. By banding together in defensive leagues several of them succeeded in maintaining their independence for nearly a century. Finally, between 146 and 30 B.C. nearly all of the Hellenistic territory passed under Roman rule.

The dominant form of government in the Hellenistic Age was the despotism of rulers who represented themselves as at least semidivine. Alexander himself was recognized as a son of God in Egypt and was worshiped as a god in Greece. His most powerful successors, the Seleucid kings in western Asia and the Ptolemies in Egypt, made systematic attempts to deify themselves. A Seleucid monarch, Antiochus IV, adopted the title "Epiphanes" or "God Manifest." The later members of the dynasty of the Ptolemies signed their decrees "Theos" (God) and revived the practice of sister marriage which had been followed by the pharaohs as a means of preserving the divine blood of the royal family from contamination. Only in the kingdom of Macedonia was despotism tempered by a modicum of respect for the liberties of the citizens.

Two other political institutions developed as by-products of Hellenistic civilization: the Achaean and Aetolian Leagues. We have already seen that most of the Greek states rebelled against Macedonian rule following the division of Alexander's empire. The better to preserve their independence, several of these states formed alliances among themselves, which were gradually expanded to become confederate leagues. The organization of these leagues was essentially the same in all cases. Each had a federal council composed of representatives of the member cities with power to enact laws on subjects of general concern. An assembly which all of the citizens in the federated states could attend decided questions of war and peace and elected officials. Executive and military authority was vested in the hands of a general, elected for one year and eligible for reelection only in alternate years. Although these leagues are frequently described as federal states, they were scarcely more than confederacies. The central authority, like the government of the American States under the Articles of Confederation, was dependent upon the local governments for contributions of revenue and troops. Furthermore, the powers delegated to the central government were limited primarily to matters of war and peace, coinage, and weights and measures. The chief significance of these leagues is to be found in the fact that they constituted the nearest approach ever made in Greece to voluntary national union before modern times.

Alexander the Great. Shown here is a silver coin struck in Thrace by King Lysimachus about 300 B.C.

The Achaean and Aetolian Leagues

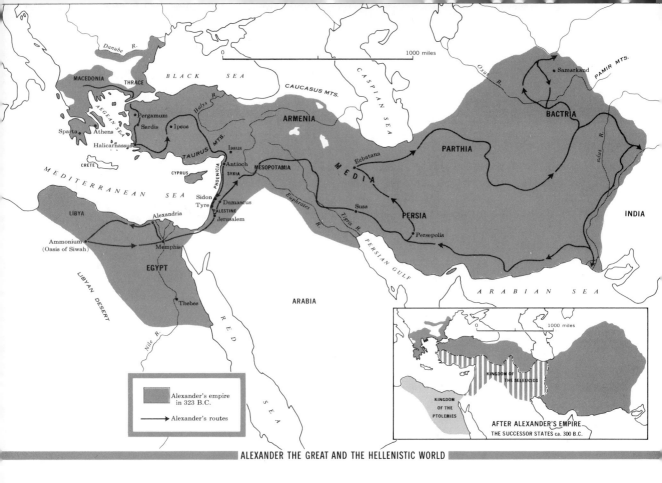

ALEXANDER THE GREAT AND THE HELLENISTIC WORLD

2. SIGNIFICANT ECONOMIC AND SOCIAL DEVELOPMENTS

The economic revolution and its causes

The history of the Hellenistic civilization was marked by economic developments second only in magnitude to the Commercial and Industrial Revolutions of the modern era. Several important causes can be distinguished: (1) the opening up of a vast area of trade from the Indus River to the Nile as a result of the Alexandrian conquests; (2) the rise in prices as a consequence of the release of the enormous Persian hoard of gold and silver into the channels of circulation, resulting in an increase in investment and speculation; and (3) the promotion of trade and industry by governments as a means of augmenting the revenues of the state. The net result was the growth of a system of large-scale production, trade, and finance, with the state as the principal entrepreneur.

The concentration of land ownership

Agriculture was as profoundly affected by the new developments as any other branch of the economic life. The most striking phenomena were the concentration of holdings of land and the degradation of the agricultural population. One of the first things the successors of Alexander did was to confiscate the estates of the chief landowners and add them to the royal domain. The lands thus acquired were either granted to the favorites of the king or leased to tenants under an arrangement calculated to ensure an abundant income for the crown. The tenants were generally forbidden to leave the lands they cultivated until after the harvest and were not allowed to dispose of their grain until after the ruler had had a chance to sell the share he received as rent at the highest price the market would bring. When some of the tenants were on strike or attempted to run away, they were all bound to the soil as hereditary serfs. Many of the small independent farmers also became serfs when they got into debt as a result of inability to compete with large-scale production.

In an effort to make all of the resources of the state contribute to the profit of the government, the rulers of Egypt and the Seleucid Empire promoted and regulated industry and trade. The Ptolemies established factories and shops in nearly every village and town to be owned and operated by the government for its own financial benefit. In addition, they assumed control over all of the enterprises that were privately owned, fixing the prices the owners could charge and manipulating markets to the advantage of the crown. A similar plan of regimentation for industry, although not on quite so ambitious a scale, was enforced by the Seleucid rulers of western Asia. Trade was left by both of these governments very largely in private hands, but it was heavily taxed and regulated in such a way as to make sure that an ample share of the profits went to the ruler. Every facility was provided by the government for the encouragement of new trading ventures. Harbors were improved, warships were sent out to police the seas, and roads and canals were built. Moreover, the Ptolemies employed famous geographers to discover new routes to distant lands and thereby gain access to valuable markets. As a result of such methods Egypt developed a flourishing commerce in the widest variety of products. Into the port of Alexandria came spices from Arabia, copper from Cyprus, gold from Ethiopia and India, tin from Britain, elephants and ivory from Nubia, silver from the northern Aegean and Spain, fine carpets from Asia Minor, and even silk from China. Profits for the government and for some of the merchants were often as high as 20 or 30 percent.

State regimentation of industry and trade

Further evidence of the significant economic development of the Hellenistic Age is to be found in the growth of finance. An international money economy, based upon gold and silver coins, now became general throughout the Near East. Banks, usually owned by the government, developed as the chief institutions of credit for business ventures of every description. Speculation, cornering of markets, intense competition, the growth of large business houses, and the development of insurance and advertising were other significant phenomena of this remarkable age.

The growth of finance

According to the available evidence, the Hellenistic Age, during the first two centuries at least, was a period of prosperity. Although

Hellenistic Coins. Obverse and reverse sides of the silver tetradrachma of Macedon, 336–323 B.C. Objects of common use from this period often show as much beauty of design as formal works of art.

serious crises frequently followed the collapse of speculative booms, they appear to have been of short duration. But the prosperity that existed seems to have been limited chiefly to the rulers, the upper classes, and the merchants. It certainly did not extend to the peasants or even to the workers in the towns. The daily wages of both skilled and unskilled workers in Athens in the third century had dropped to less than half of what they had been in the Age of Pericles. The cost of living, on the other hand, had risen considerably. To make matters worse, unemployment in the large cities was so serious a problem that the government had to provide free grain for many of the inhabitants. Slavery declined in the Hellenistic world, partly because of the influence of the Stoic philosophy, but mainly for the reason that wages were now so low that it was cheaper to hire a free laborer than to purchase and maintain a slave.

An interesting result of social and economic conditions in the Hellenistic Age was the growth of large cities. Despite the fact that a majority of the people still lived in the country, there was an increasing tendency for men to become dissatisfied with the dullness of rural living and to flock into the cities, where life, if not easier, was at least more exciting. But the chief reasons are to be found in the expansion of industry and commerce, in the enlargement of governmental functions, and in the desire of former independent farmers to escape the hardships of serfdom. Cities multiplied and grew in the Hellenistic empires almost as rapidly as in nineteenth- and twentieth-century America. Antioch in Syria quadrupled its population during a single century. Seleucia on the Tigris grew from nothing to a metropolis of several hundred thousand in less than two centuries. The largest and most famous of all the Hellenistic cities was Alexandria in Egypt, with over 500,000 inhabitants and possibly as many as 1,000,000. No other city in ancient times before imperial Rome, surpassed it in size or in magnificence. Its streets were well paved and laid out in regular order. It had splendid public buildings and parks, a museum, and a library of

700,000 scrolls. It was the most brilliant center of Hellenistic cultural achievement, especially in the field of scientific research. The masses of its people, however, had no share in the brilliant and luxurious life around them, although it was paid for in part out of the fruits of their labor.

3. HELLENISTIC CULTURE: PHILOSOPHY, LITERATURE, AND ART

Hellenistic philosophy exhibited two trends that ran almost parallel throughout the civilization. The major trend, exemplified by Stoicism and Epicureanism, showed a fundamental regard for reason as the key to the solution of human problems. This trend was a manifestation of Greek influence, though philosophy and science, as combined in Aristotle, had now come to a parting of the ways. The minor trend, exemplified by the Skeptics, Cynics, and various Asian cults, tended to reject reason, to deny the possibility of attaining truth, and in some cases to turn toward mysticism and a reliance upon faith. Despite the differences in their teachings, the philosophers of the Hellenistic Age were generally agreed upon one thing: the necessity of finding some way of salvation from the hardships and evils of human existence.

Trends in philosophy

The first of the Hellenistic philosophers were the Cynics, who had their origin about 350 B.C. Their foremost leader was Diogenes, who won fame by his ceaseless quest for an "honest" man. Essentially this meant the adoption of the "natural" life and the repudiation of everything conventional and artificial. The Cynics adopted as their principal goal the cultivation of "self-sufficiency": everyone should cultivate within himself the ability to satisfy his own needs. Obviously the Cynics bore some resemblance to other movements that have cropped up through the ages—the hippie movement of the 1960s, for example. There were notable differences, however. The Cynics spurned music and art as manifestations of artificiality, and they were not representative of a youth generation. But all such movements seem to reflect a sense of frustration and hopeless conflict in society. According to one story, Alexander the Great once asked Diogenes's disciple Crates whether the city of Thebes, recently destroyed in war, should be rebuilt: "Why?" replied the Cynic, "another Alexander will surely tear it down again."

The Cynics

Epicureanism and Stoicism both originated about 300 B.C. The founders were, respectively, Epicurus (c. 342–270) and Zeno (fl. after 300), who were residents of Athens. Epicureanism and Stoicism had several features in common. Both were individualistic, concerned not with the welfare of society but with the good of the individual. Both were materialistic, denying categorically the existence of any spiritual substances; even divine beings and the soul were declared to be formed of matter. In Stoicism and Epicureanism alike there were defi-

Epicureanism and Stoicism

nite elements of universalism, since both implied that men are the same the world over and recognized no distinctions between Greeks and "barbarians."

But in many ways the two systems were quite different. Zeno and his disciples taught that the cosmos is an ordered whole in which all contradictions are resolved for ultimate good. Evil is, therefore, relative; the particular misfortunes which befall human beings are but necessary incidents to the final perfection of the universe. Everything that happens is rigidly determined in accordance with rational purpose. No individual is master of his fate; human destiny is a link in an unbroken chain. People are free only in the sense that they can accept their fate or rebel against it. But whether they accept or rebel, they cannot overcome it. Their supreme duty is to submit to the order of the universe in the knowledge that that order is good; in other words, to resign themselves as graciously as possible to their fate. Through such an act of resignation the highest happiness will be attained, which consists in tranquility of mind. The individual who is most truly happy is therefore the one who by the assertion of his rational nature has accomplished a perfect adjustment of his life to the cosmic purpose and has purged his soul of all bitterness and whining protest against evil turns of fortune.

The Stoics' pursuit of tranquility of mind through fatalism

The Stoics developed an ethical and social theory that accorded well with their general philosophy. Believing that the highest good consists in serenity of mind, they naturally emphasized duty and self-discipline as cardinal virtues. Recognizing the prevalence of particular evil, they taught tolerance for and forgiveness of one another. Unlike the Cynics, they did not recommend withdrawal from society but urged participation in public affairs as a duty for the citizen of rational mind. They condemned slavery and war, but it was far from their purpose to preach any crusade against these evils. They were disposed to think that the results that would flow from violent measures of social change would be worse than the diseases they were supposed to cure. Besides, what difference did it make if the body were in bondage so long as the mind was free? Despite its negative character, the Stoic philosophy was the noblest product of the Hellenistic Age. Its equalitarianism, pacifism, and humanitarianism were important factors in mitigating the harshness not only of that time but of later centuries as well.

The ethical and social teachings of the Stoics

The Epicureans derived their metaphysics chiefly from Democritus. Epicurus taught that the basic ingredients of all things are minute, indivisible atoms, and that change and growth are the results of the combination and separation of these particles. Nevertheless, while accepting the materialism of the atomists, Epicurus rejected their absolute mechanism. He denied that an automatic, mechanical motion of the atoms can be the cause of all things in the universe. Though he taught that the atoms move downward in perpendicular lines because

Epicurus and nonmechanistic atomism

of their weight, he insisted upon endowing them with a spontaneous ability to swerve from the perpendicular and thereby to combine with one another. The chief reason for this peculiar modification of the atomic theory was to make possible a belief in human freedom. If the atoms were capable only of mechanical motion, then a human being, who is made up of atoms, would be reduced to the status of an automaton, and fatalism would be the law of the universe. In this repudiation of the mechanistic interpretation of life, Epicurus was probably closer to the Hellenic spirit than either Democritus or the Stoics.

The ethical philosophy of the Epicureans was based upon the doctrine that the highest good is pleasure. But they did not include all forms of indulgence in the category of genuine pleasure. The so-called pleasures of the flesh should be avoided, since every excess of carnality must be balanced by its portion of pain. On the other hand, a moderate satisfaction of bodily appetites is permissible and may be regarded as a good in itself. Better than this is mental pleasure, sober contemplation of the reasons for the choice of some things and the avoidance of others, and mature reflection upon satisfactions previously enjoyed. The highest of all pleasures, however, consists in serenity of soul, in the complete absence of both mental and physical pain. This end can be best achieved through the elimination of fear, especially fear of the supernatural, since that is the sovereign source of mental pain. The individual must recognize from the study of philosophy that the soul is material and therefore cannot survive the body, that the universe operates of itself, and that the gods do not intervene in human affairs. The gods live remote from the world and are too intent upon their own happiness to bother about what takes place on earth. Since they do not reward or punish mortals either in this life or in a life to come there is no reason why they should be feared. The Epicureans thus came by a different route to the same general conclusion as the Stoics—the supreme good is tranquillity of mind.

The ethics of the Epicureans as well as their political theory rested squarely upon a utilitarian basis. In contrast with the Stoics, they did not insist upon virtue as an end in itself but taught that the only reason why one should be good is to increase his own happiness. In like manner, they denied that there is any such thing as absolute justice: laws and institutions are just only insofar as they contribute to the welfare of the individual. Certain rules have been found necessary in every complex society for the maintenance of security and order. These rules are obeyed solely because it is to each individual's advantage to do so. Epicurus held no high regard for either political or social life. He considered the state as a mere convenience and taught that the wise man should take no active part in politics. Unlike the Cynics, he did not propose that civilization should be abandoned; yet his conception of the happiest life was essentially passive and defeatist. Epicurus taught that the thinking person will recognize that evils in the world

The Epicurean pursuit of tranquility of mind through overcoming fear of the supernatural

The ethical and political theories of the Epicureans

cannot be eradicated by human effort; the individual will therefore withdraw to study philosophy and enjoy the fellowship of a few congenial friends.

A more radically defeatist philosophy was that propounded by the Skeptics. Skepticism reached the zenith of its popularity about 200 B.C. under the influence of Carneades. The chief source of its inspiration was the Sophist teaching that all knowledge is derived from sense perception and therefore must be limited and relative. From this was deduced the conclusion that we cannot prove anything. Since the impressions of our senses deceive us, no truth can be certain. All we can say is that things *appear* to be such and such; we do not know what they really *are*. We have no definite knowledge of the supernatural, of the meaning of life, or even of right and wrong. It follows that the sensible course to pursue is suspension of judgment: this alone can lead to happiness. If we will abandon the fruitless quest for absolute truth and cease worrying about good and evil, we will attain that equanimity of mind which is the highest satisfaction that life affords. The Skeptics were even less concerned than the Epicureans with political and social problems. Their ideal was the typically Hellenistic one of escape for the individual from a world neither understandable nor capable of reform.

The nonrational trend in Hellenistic thought reached its farthest extreme in the philosophies of Philo Judaeus and the Neo-Pythagoreans in the last century B.C. and the first century A.D. The proponents of the two systems were in general agreement as to their basic teachings, especially in their predominantly religious viewpoint. They believed in a transcendent God so far removed from the world as to be utterly unknowable to mortal minds. They conceived the universe as being sharply divided between spirit and matter. They considered everything physical and material as evil; the soul is imprisoned in the body, from which an escape can be effected only through rigorous denial and mortification of the flesh. Their attitude was mystical and nonintellectual: truth comes neither from science nor from reason but from revelation. Philo, a Jew who lived in Alexandria, maintained that the books of the Old Testament were of absolute divine authority and contained all truth; the ultimate aim in life is to accomplish a mystic union with God, to lose one's self in the divine. Both Philo and the Neo-Pythagoreans influenced the development of Christian theology—Philo, in particular, with his dualism of matter and spirit and his doctrine of the Logos, the word, or highest intermediary between God and the universe.

Hellenistic literature is significant mainly for the light it throws upon the character of the civilization. Most of the writings showed little originality or depth of thought. But they poured forth from the hands of the copyists in a profusion that is almost incredible when we consider that the art of printing by movable type was unknown. We know the names of at least 1,100 authors. Much of what they wrote was trash, comparable to some of the cheap novels of our own day. Nevertheless, there were several works of more than mediocre quality and a few which met the highest standards ever set by the Greeks.

Among the leading types of Hellenistic literature were the drama and the pastoral. Drama was almost exclusively comedy, represented mainly by the plays of Menander. His plays were very different from the comedy of Aristophanes. They were distinguished by naturalism rather than by satire, by preoccupation with the seamy side of life rather than with political or intellectual issues. Their dominant theme was romantic love, with its pains and pleasures, its intrigues and seductions, and its culmination in happy marriage. The greatest author of pastorals was Theocritus of Syracuse, who wrote in the first half of the third century B.C. His pastorals, as the name implies, celebrate the charm of life in the country and idealize the simple pleasures of rustic folk. Theocritus later found greater imitators in the Roman poet Vergil and the Elizabethan poet Edmund Spenser.

The field of prose literature was dominated by the historians, the biographers, and the authors of utopias. By far the ablest of the writers of history was Polybius of Megalopolis, who lived during the second century B.C. From the standpoint of his scientific approach and his zeal for truth, he probably deserves to be ranked second only to Thucydides among all the historians in ancient times; but he excelled Thucydides in his grasp of the importance of social and economic forces. Although most of the biographies were of a light and gossipy character, their tremendous popularity bears eloquent testimony to the literary tastes of the time. Even more significant was the popularity of the

Hellenistic poetry

Historians, biographers, and authors of utopias

The Dying Gaul. A good example of Hellenistic realism in sculpture, which often reflected a preoccupation with the morbid and sensational. Every detail of the warrior's agony is dramatically portrayed. Now in the Capitoline Museum, Rome.

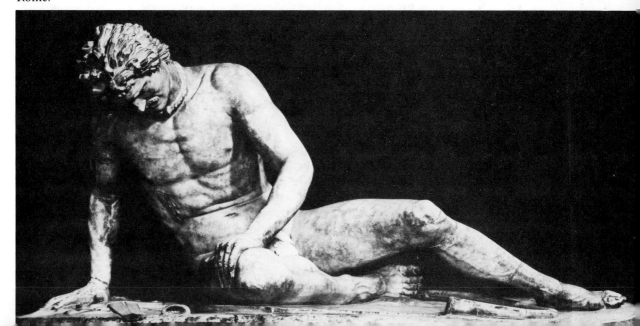

Left: *The Winged Victory of Samothrace*. In this figure, done around 200 B.C., a Hellenistic sculptor preserved some of the calmness and devotion to grace and proportion characteristic of Hellenic art in the Golden Age. Right: *Laocoön*. In sharp contrast to the serenity of the Winged Victory is this famous sculpture group from the late second century B.C., depicting the death of Laocoön. According to legend, Laocoön warned the Trojans not to touch the wooden horse sent by the Greeks and was punished by Poseidon, who sent two serpents to kill him and his sons. The intense emotionalism of this work later had a great influence on western European art from Michelangelo onwards.

utopias, or descriptive accounts of ideal states. Virtually all of them depicted a life of social and economic equality, free from greed, oppression, and strife, on an imaginary island or in some distant, unfamiliar region. Generally in these paradises money was considered to be unknown, trade was prohibited, all property was held in common, and all were required to work with their hands in producing the necessities of life. We are probably justified in assuming that the profusion of this utopian literature was a direct result of the evils and injustices of Hellenistic society and a consciousness of the need for reform.

Hellenistic art   Hellenistic art did not preserve all of the characteristic qualities of the art of the Greeks. In place of the humanism, balance, and restraint which had distinguished the architecture and sculpture of the Golden Age, qualities of exaggerated realism, sensationalism, and voluptuousness now became dominant. The simple and dignified Doric and Ionic temples gave way to luxurious palaces, costly mansions, and elaborate public buildings and monuments symbolic of power and wealth. A typical example was the great lighthouse of Alexandria, which rose to a height of nearly four hundred feet, with three diminishing stories and eight columns to support the light at the top. Sculpture likewise exhibited extravagant and sentimental tendencies. Many of the statues and figures in relief were huge and some of them almost grotesque. Violent emotionalism and exaggerated realism were features common to the majority. But by no means all of Hellenistic sculpture was overwrought and grotesque. Some of it was distinguished by a calmness and poise and compassion for human suffering reminiscent of the best work of the great fourth-century artists. Statues which exemplify these superior qualities include the *Aphrodite of Melos* (*Venus de Milo*) and the *Winged Victory of Samothrace*.

4. THE FIRST GREAT AGE OF SCIENCE

The most brilliant age in the history of science prior to the seventeenth century A.D. was the period of the Hellenistic civilization. Indeed, many of the achievements of the modern age would scarcely have been possible without the discoveries of the scientists of Alexandria, Syracuse, Pergamum, and other great cities of the Hellenistic world. The reasons for the impressive development of science in the centuries after the downfall of Alexander's empire are not difficult to discover. Alexander himself had given some financial encouragement to the progress of research. More important was the stimulus provided for intellectual inquiry by the fusion of Chaldean and Egyptian science with the learning of the Greeks. Possibly a third factor was the new interest in luxury and comfort and the demand for practical knowledge which would enable the scientific thinker to solve the problems of a disordered and unsatisfying existence.

See color plates following page 96

Factors responsible for the remarkable progress of science

The sciences which received major attention in the Hellenistic Age were astronomy, mathematics, geography, medicine, and physics. Chemistry, aside from metallurgy, was practically unknown. Except for the work of Theophrastus, who was the first to recognize the sexuality of plants, biology was also largely neglected. Neither chemistry nor biology bore any definite relationship to trade or to the forms of industry then in existence, and apparently they were not regarded as having much practical value.

The most popular sciences

The most renowned of the earlier astronomers of this time was Aristarchus of Samos (310–230 B.C.), who is sometimes called the "Hellenistic Copernicus." His chief title to fame comes from his deduction that the earth and the other planets revolve around the sun. Unfortunately this deduction was not accepted by his successors. It conflicted with the teachings of Aristotle and with the conviction of the Greeks that man, and therefore the earth, must be at the center of the universe. Besides, it was not in harmony with the beliefs of the Jews and other Eastern peoples who made up so large a percentage of

Astronomy

the Hellenistic population. Another important Hellenistic astronomer was Hipparchus, who did his most valuable work in Alexandria in the latter half of the second century B.C. His chief contributions were the invention of the astrolabe and the approximately correct calculation of the diameter of the moon and its distance from the earth. His fame was eventually overshadowed, however, by the reputation of Ptolemy of Alexandria (second century A.D.). Although Ptolemy made few original discoveries, he systematized the work of others. His principal writing, the *Almagest,* based upon the geocentric theory (the view that all heavenly bodies revolve around the earth), was handed down to medieval Europe as the classic summary of ancient astronomy. Ptolemy's geography too had a considerable influence on medieval and Renaissance thought.

Mathematics and geography

Closely allied with astronomy were two other sciences, mathematics and geography. The Hellenistic mathematician of greatest renown was, of course, Euclid (c. 323–c. 285 B.C.), the master of geometry. Until the middle of the nineteenth century his *Elements of Geometry* remained the accepted basis for the study of that branch of mathematics. Much of the material in this work was not original but was a synthesis of the discoveries of others. The most original of the Hellenistic mathematicians was probably Hipparchus, who laid the foundations of both plane and spherical trigonometry. Hellenistic geography owed most of its development to Eratosthenes (c. 276–c. 196 B.C.), astronomer, poet, philologist, and librarian of Alexandria. By means of sundials placed some hundreds of miles apart, he calculated the circumference of the earth with an error of less than 200 miles. He produced the most accurate map that had yet been devised, with the surface of the earth divided into degrees of latitude and longitude. He propounded the theory that all of the oceans are really one, and he was the first to suggest the possibility of reaching India by sailing west. One of his successors divided the earth into the five climatic zones which are still recognized, and explained the ebb and flow of the tides as due to the influence of the moon.

Medicine: the development of anatomy

Perhaps none of the Hellenistic advances in science surpassed in importance the progress in medicine. Especially significant was the work of Herophilus of Chalcedon, who conducted his researches in Alexandria about the beginning of the second century. Without question he was the greatest anatomist of antiquity and probably the first to practice human dissection. Among his most important achievements were a detailed description of the brain, with an attempt to distinguish between the functions of its various parts; the discovery of the significance of the pulse and its use in diagnosing illness; and the discovery that the arteries contain blood alone, not a mixture of blood and air as Aristotle had taught, and that their function is to carry blood from the heart to all parts of the body. The value of this last discovery in laying the basis for a knowledge of the circulation of the blood can hardly be overestimated.

The ablest of the colleagues of Herophilus was Erasistratus, who flourished in Alexandria about the middle of the third century. He is considered the founder of physiology as a separate science. Not only did he practice dissection, but he is believed to have gained a great deal of his knowledge of bodily functions from vivisection. He discovered the valves of the heart, distinguished between motor and sensory nerves, and taught that the ultimate branches of the arteries and veins are connected. He was the first to reject absolutely the humoral theory of disease and to condemn excessive blood-letting as a method of cure. Unfortunately this theory was revived by Galen, the great encyclopedist of medicine who lived in the Roman Empire in the second century A.D.

Physiology

Prior to the third century B.C. physics had been a branch of philosophy. It was made a separate experimental science by Archimedes of Syracuse (c. 287–212 B.C.). Archimedes discovered the law of floating bodies, or specific gravity, and formulated with scientific exactness the principles of the lever, the pulley, and the screw. Among his memorable inventions were the compound pulley, the tubular screw for pumping water, the screw propeller for ships, and the burning lens. Although he has been called the "technical Yankee of antiquity," there is evidence that he set no high value upon his ingenious mechanical contraptions and preferred to devote his time to pure scientific research.

Physics

Certain other individuals in the Hellenistic Age were quite willing to give all their attention to applied science. Preeminent among them was Hero of Alexandria, who lived in the last century B.C. The record of inventions credited to him almost passes belief. The list includes a fire engine, a siphon, a jet engine, a hydraulic organ, a slot machine, and a catapult operated by compressed air. How many of these inventions were really his own is impossible to say, but there appears to be no question that such contrivances were actually in existence in his time or soon thereafter. Nevertheless, the total progress in applied science was comparatively slight, probably for the reason that human labor continued to be so abundant and cheap that it was not worthwhile to substitute the work of machines.

Applied science

5. RELIGION IN THE HELLENISTIC AGE

If there was one aspect of the Hellenistic civilization which served more than others to accent the contrast with Hellenic culture, it was the new trend in religion. The civic religion of the Greeks as it was in the age of the city-states had now almost entirely disappeared. For the majority of the intellectuals its place was taken by the philosophies of Stoicism, Epicureanism, and Skepticism. Some who were less philosophically inclined turned to the worship of Fortune.

The new trend in religion

Among the common people a tendency to embrace emotional religions was even more clearly manifest. The Orphic and Eleusinian mystery cults attracted more votaries than ever before. The worship of the Egyptian mother-goddess, Isis, threatened for a time to become dominant throughout the Near East. The astral religion of the Chaldeans likewise spread rapidly, with the result that its chief product, astrology, was received with fanatical enthusiasm throughout the Hellenistic world. But the most powerful influence of all came from the offshoots of Zoroastrianism, especially from Mithraism and Gnosticism. While all of the cults of Oriental origin resembled each other in their promises of salvation in a life to come, Mithraism and Gnosticism had a more ethically significant mythology, a deeper contempt for this world, and a more clearly defined doctrine of redemption through a personal savior. These were the ideas which satisfied the emotional cravings of the common people, convinced as they were of the worthlessness of this life and ready to be lured by extravagant promises of better things in a world to come. If we can judge by conditions in our own time, some of the doctrines of these cults must have exerted their influence upon members of the upper classes also. Even the most casual observer of modern society knows that pessimism, mysticism, and otherworldliness are not confined to the downtrodden. In some cases the keenest disgust with this life and the deepest mystical yearnings are to be found among those whose pockets bulge the most.

A factor by no means unimportant in the religious developments of the Hellenistic Age was the dispersion of the Jews. As a result of Alexander's conquest of Palestine in 332 B.C. and the Roman conquest about three centuries later, thousands of Jews migrated to various sections of the Mediterranean world. It has been estimated that 1,000,000 of them lived in Egypt in the first century A.D. and 200,000 in Asia Minor. They mingled freely with other peoples, adopting the Greek language and no small amount of the Hellenic culture which still survived from earlier days. At the same time they played a major part in the diffusion of Eastern beliefs. Some of the Hellenistic Jews eventually became converts to Christianity and were largely instrumental in the spread of that religion outside of Palestine. A notable example, of course, was Saul of Tarsus, known in Christian history as St. Paul.

6. A FORETASTE OF MODERNITY?

With the possible exception of the Roman, no great culture of ancient times appears to suggest the spirit of the modern age quite so emphatically as does the Hellenistic civilization. Here, as in the world of the twentieth century, were to be found a considerable variety of forms of government, the growth of militarism, and a trend in the direction of authoritarian rule. Many of the characteristic economic and social de-

Statue of an Old Market Woman. In the Hellenistic Age the idealism and restraint of Hellenic art were succeeded by a tendency to portray the humble aspects of life and to express compassion for human suffering. Original in the Metropolitan Museum of Art, New York.

velopments of the Hellenistic Age are equally suggestive of contemporary experience: the growth of big business, the expansion of trade, the zeal for exploration and discovery, the interest in technology, the devotion to comfort and the craze for material prosperity, the growth of cities with congested slums, and the widening gulf between rich and poor. In the realms of intellect and art the Hellenistic civilization also bore a distinctly modern flavor. This was exemplified by the emphasis upon science, the narrow specialization of learning, the penchant for realism and naturalism, the vast production of mediocre literature, and the popularity of mysticism side by side with extreme skepticism and dogmatic unbelief.

Because of these resemblances there has been a tendency among certain writers to regard our own civilization as decadent. But this is based partly upon the false assumption that the Hellenistic culture was merely a degenerate phase of Greek civilization. Instead, it was a new social and cultural organism born of a fusion of Greek and Near-Eastern elements. Moreover, the differences between the Hellenistic civilization and that of the contemporary world are perhaps just as important as the resemblances. The Hellenistic political outlook was es-

Basic differences

sentially cosmopolitan; nothing comparable to the national patriotism of modern times really prevailed. Despite the remarkable expansion of trade in the Hellenistic Age, no industrial revolution ever took place, for reasons which have already been noted. Finally, Hellenistic science was more limited than that of the present day. Modern pure science is to a very large extent a species of philosophy—an adventure of the mind in the realm of the unknown. Notwithstanding frequent assertions to the contrary, much of it is gloriously impractical and will probably remain so.

SELECTED READINGS

• *Items so designated are available in paperback editions.*

Burn, A. R., *Alexander the Great and the Hellenistic World,* New York, 1962. A good brief biography.

• Bury, J. B., et al., *The Hellenistic Age,* New York, 1923.

Cary, Max, *The Legacy of Alexander: A History of the Greek World from 323 to 146 B.C.,* New York, 1932. Best on the complicated political history of the period.

Clagett, M., *Greek Science in Antiquity,* New York, 1963.

Festugière, A. J., *Epicurus and His Gods,* Cambridge, Mass., 1956.

• Finley, M. I., *The Ancient Economy,* Berkeley, Calif., 1973. A fundamental topical treatment.

Grant, F. C., *Hellenistic Religions,* New York, 1963.

• Hadas, M., *Hellenistic Culture,* New York, 1964.

Larsen, J. A. O., *Greek Federal States,* Oxford, 1968.

Rostovtzeff, M., *The Social and Economic History of the Hellenistic World,* 3 vols., Oxford, 1941. An authoritative mine of information.

• Tarn, W. W., *Alexander the Great,* Cambridge, 1948. Tarn was the leading English expert on Alexander and the Hellenistic period.

• ———, *Hellenistic Civilization,* 3rd ed., London, 1952. Still indispensible.

• Wilcken, U., *Alexander the Great,* New York, 1932. A fundamental older interpretation, translated from the German.

SOURCE MATERIALS

Greek source materials for the Hellenistic period are available in the appropriate volumes of the Loeb Classical Library, Harvard University Press.

Chapter 10

ROMAN CIVILIZATION

My city and country, so far as I am Antoninus, is Rome, but so far as I am a man, it is the world.

—Marcus Aurelius Antoninus, *Meditations*

For the categories into which you divide the world are not Hellenes and Barbarians. . . . The division which you substituted is one into Romans and non-Romans. To such a degree have you expanded the name of your city.

—Aelius Aristides, *Oration to Rome*

Well before the glory that was Greece had begun to fade, another civilization, ultimately much influenced by Greek culture, had started its growth in the West on the banks of the Tiber. Around the time of Alexander's conquests the new civilization of Rome was already a dominant force on the Italian peninsula. For five centuries thereafter Rome's power increased. By the end of the first century B.C. it had imposed its rule over the entire Hellenistic world as well as over most of modern-day western Europe. By conquering the old Hellenistic states and destroying the North African civilization of Carthage, Rome was able to make the Mediterranean a "Roman lake." In so doing it brought Greek institutions and ideas to the western half of the Mediterranean world. And by pushing northwards to the Rhine and Danube rivers it brought Mediterranean urban culture to lands still sunk in the Iron Age. Rome, then, was the builder of a great historical bridge between East and West.

The rise of Rome

Of course Rome would not have been able to play this role had it not followed its own peculiar course of development. This was marked by the tension between two different cultural outlooks. On the one hand Romans throughout most of their history tended to be conservative: they revered their old agricultural traditions, household gods, and ruggedly warlike ways. But they also wanted to be builders and could not resist the attractions of Greek culture and lux-

The Roman synthesis

ury. For a few centuries their greatness was based on a synthesis of these different traits: respect for tradition, order, and military prowess, together with Greek urbanization and cultivation of the mind. The synthesis could not last forever, but as long as it did the glory that was Greece was replaced by the grandeur that was Rome.

1. EARLY ITALY AND THE ROMAN MONARCHY

The impact of geography on Roman history

The geographical character of the Italian peninsula contributed significantly to the course of Roman history. Except for some excellent marble and small quantities of tin, copper, iron, and gold, Italy has no mineral resources. The extensive coastline is broken by few good harbors. On the other hand, the amount of fertile land is much larger than that of Greece. As a result, the Romans were destined to remain a predominantly agrarian people through the greater part of their history. They seldom enjoyed the intellectual stimulus which comes from extensive trading with other areas. In addition, the Italian peninsula was more open to invasion than was Greece. The Alps posed no effective barrier to the influx of peoples from central Europe, and the low-lying coast in many places invited conquest by sea. Domination of the country by force was therefore more common than peaceful intermingling of immigrants with original settlers. The Romans became absorbed in military pursuits almost from the moment of their settlement on Italian soil, for they were forced to defend their own conquests against other invaders.

The earliest inhabitants of Italy

Archeological evidence indicates that Italy was inhabited at least as far back as the later Paleolithic Age. At this time the territory was occupied by a people closely related to the Cro-Magnons of southern France. In the Neolithic period people of Mediterranean stock entered the land, some coming in from northern Africa and others from Spain and Gaul. The beginning of the Bronze Age witnessed several new incursions. From north of the Alps came the first of the immigrants of

An Etruscan Sarcophagus. The Etruscans often depicted social events, sports, funeral banquets, and processions, either in painting or relief, on their tombs. Seen here are preparations for a funeral.

Etruscan Sarcophagus. This work of the fourth century B.C. depicts a husband and wife: note the sympathetic portrayal of the woman and the sense of equality between the two figures.

the Indo-European language group. They were herdsmen and farmers, who brought the horse and the wheeled cart into Italy. Their culture was based upon the use of bronze, although after about 900 B.C. they appear to have acquired a knowledge of iron. These Indo-Europeans seem to have been the ancestors of most of the so-called Italic peoples, including the Romans, and they were probably related to the Hellenic invaders of Greece.

Probably during the eighth century B.C. two other nations of immigrants occupied different portions of the Italian peninsula: the Etruscans and the Greeks. Where the Etruscans came from is a question which has never been satisfactorily answered, although it is certain that they were not Indo-Europeans. Most authorities believe that they were natives of Asia Minor. Whatever their origins, we know that by the sixth century B.C. they had established a great federation of cities that stretched over most of northern and central Italy. Although their writing has never been completely deciphered, enough materials survive to indicate the nature of their culture. They had an alphabet based upon the Greek, a high degree of skill in metalwork, great artistic talents, a flourishing trade with the East, and a religion based upon the worship of gods in human form. They bequeathed to the Romans a knowledge of the arch and the vault, the cruel amusement of gladiatorial combats, and the practice of foretelling the future by supernatural means such as studying the entrails of animals or the flight of birds. One of their most distinctive traits was the comparatively great respect they showed for women. Etruscan wives, unlike those in other contemporary societies, ate with their husbands, and some Etruscan families listed descent through the maternal line.

The Etruscans and the Greeks

The Greeks settled mainly along the southern and southwestern shores of Italy and the island of Sicily, as well as along the southern coast of Gaul. Their most important settlements were Taranto, Na-

The Greeks in Italy

ples, and Syracuse, each of which was an independent city-state. Greek civilization in Italy and Sicily was as advanced as it was in Greece itself. Such famous Greeks as Pythagoras, Archimedes, and even Plato for a time, actually lived in the Italian West. From the Greeks the Romans derived their alphabet, a number of their religious concepts, and much of their art and mythology.

The founding of Rome

The founders of Rome itself were Italic peoples who lived in the area south of the Tiber River. Though the exact year of the founding of the city is unknown, recent archcological research places the event quite near the traditional date of 753 B.C. By reason of its strategic location, Rome came to exercise an effective suzerainty over several of the most important neighboring cities. One conquest followed another until, by the sixth century B.C., Rome came to dominate most of the surrounding area. But just then Etruscans took over power in Rome.

The government of Rome under the monarchy; the powers of the king

The political evolution of Rome in this early period resembled in some ways the governmental development of the Greek communities, although it was far from being exactly the same. The Romans appear from the first to have had a much stronger interest in authority and stability than in liberty or democracy. Their state was essentially an application of the idea of the patriarchal family to the whole community, with the king exercising a jurisdiction over his subjects comparable to that of the head of the family over the members of his household. But just as the authority of the father was limited by custom and by the requirement that he respect the wishes of his adult sons, the authority of the king was limited by the ancient constitution, which he was powerless to change without the consent of the chief men of the realm. His prerogatives were not primarily legislative but executive, priestly, military, and judicial. He judged all civil and criminal cases, but he had no authority to pardon without the consent of the assembly. Although his accession to office had to be confirmed by the people, he could not be deposed, and there was no one who could really challenge the exercise of his powers.

The Senate and the assembly

In addition to the kingship, the Roman government of this time included an assembly and a Senate. The former was composed of all the male citizens of military age. As one of the chief sources of sovereign power, according to the theory, this body could veto any proposal for a change in the law which the king might make. Besides, it determined whether pardons should be granted and whether aggressive war should be declared. But it was essentially a ratifying body with no right to initiate legislation or recommend changes of policy. The Senate, or council of elders, comprised in its membership the heads of the various clans which formed the community. Even more than the common citizens, the rulers of the clans embodied the sovereign power of the state. The king was only one of their number to whom they had delegated the active exercise of their authority. When the royal office became vacant, the powers of the king immediately reverted to the Senate until the succession of a new monarch had been confirmed by the people. In ordinary times the chief function of the Senate was to examine proposals of the king which had been ratified by the assembly and to veto them if they violated rights established by ancient custom. It was thus almost impossible for fundamental changes to be made in the law even when the majority of the citizens were ready to sanction them. This extremely conservative attitude of the ruling classes persisted until the end of Roman history.

Toward the end of the sixth century (the date traditionally given is 509 B.C.) the monarchy was overthrown and replaced by a republic. Legend has it that this revolution was provoked by the crimes of the Tarquins, an Etruscan family that had taken over the kingship in Rome around the middle of the century. After suffering numerous indignities, the last and worst of which was the rape and subsequent suicide of a virtuous Roman matron, Lucretia, by a lustful Tarquin prince, the native Romans could stand no more and rose up to expel their alien oppressors. In fact the story of the rape of Lucretia is fictional but the change in government was probably in part a native uprising against foreigners, as well as a successful movement of the Roman senatorial aristocracy to gain full power for itself. The result was the beginning of Etruscan decline in Italy, as well as a lasting conviction among Romans that kingship was evil.

End of the monarchy

2. THE EARLY REPUBLIC

The history of the Roman Republic for more than two centuries after its establishment was one of almost constant warfare. Many of the most familiar Roman legends, such as that of the brave Horatio, who with only two friends held off an entire army in front of a bridge, date from this period. At first the Romans were on the defensive. The overthrow of the Tarquins resulted in acts of reprisal by their allies in neighboring regions, and other peoples on the borders took advantage of the confusion accompanying the change of regime to slice off portions of Roman territory. After Rome managed to ward off these attacks it began to expand in order to gain more land and satisfy a rapidly growing population. As time went on Rome steadily conquered all the Etruscan territories and then took over all the Greek cities in the southernmost portion of the Italian mainland. Not only did the latter add to the Roman domain, they also brought the Romans into fruitful contact with Greek culture. The Romans were then frequently confronted with revolts of peoples previously conquered. The suppression of these revolts awakened the suspicions of surrounding states and sharpened the appetite of the victors for further triumphs. New wars followed each other in what seemed an unending succession, until by 265 B.C. Rome had conquered the entire Italian peninsula.

This long series of military conflicts had profound social, economic,

Early Roman expansion

See color map following page 96

Roman Battle Sarcophagus. This relief displays the glories of war and expresses the Roman military ideal.

Effects of the early military conflicts

and cultural effects upon the subsequent history of Rome. It affected adversely the interests of the poorer citizens and furthered the concentration of land in the possession of wealthy proprietors. Long service in the army forced the ordinary farmers to neglect the cultivation of the soil, with the result that they fell into debt and frequently lost their farms. Many took refuge in the city, until they were settled later as tenants on great estates in the conquered territories. The wars had the effect also of confirming the agrarian character of the Roman nation. The repeated acquisition of new lands made it possible to absorb the entire population into agricultural pursuits. As a consequence Romans saw no need for the development of industry and commerce. Lastly, the continual warfare of this formative period served to develop among the Romans a strong military ideal: along with Horatio, another of Rome's great early legendary heroes was Cincinnatus, who supposedly left his farm at a moment's notice for the battlefield.

Political changes following the overthrow of the monarchy

During this same period of the early Republic, Rome underwent some significant political changes. These were not products so much of the revolution of the sixth century as of the developments of later years. The revolution which overthrew the monarchy was about as conservative as it is possible for a revolution to be. Its chief effect was to substitute two elected officials called consuls for the king and to exalt the position of the Senate by granting it control over the public funds and a veto on all actions of the assembly. The consuls themselves were usually senators and acted as the agents of their class. They did not rule jointly, but each was supposed to possess the full executive and judicial authority which had previously been wielded by the king. If a conflict arose between them, the Senate might be called upon to decide; or, in time of grave emergency, a dictator might be appointed for a term not greater than six months. In other respects the government remained the same as in the days of the monarchy.

Not long after the establishment of the Republic a struggle for power began among factions of the common citizens. Before the end of the monarchy the Roman population had come to be divided into two great classes—the patricians and the plebeians. The former were the aristocracy, wealthy landowners who monopolized the seats in the Senate and the offices of magistracy. Among the plebeians were some wealthy families who were barred from the patriciate because they were of recent foreign origin, but most plebeians were common people—small farmers, craftsmen, and tradesmen. Many were clients or dependents of the patricians, obliged to fight for them, to render them political support, and to cultivate their estates in return for protection. The grievances of the plebeians were numerous. Compelled to pay heavy taxes and forced to serve in the army in time of war, they were nevertheless excluded from all part in the government except membership in the assembly. Moreover, they felt themselves the victims of discriminatory decisions in judicial trials. They did not even know what legal rights they were supposed to enjoy, for the laws were unwritten, and no one but the consuls had the power to interpret them. In suits for debt the creditor was frequently allowed to sell the debtor into slavery.

The struggle between patricians and plebeians

In order to obtain a redress of these grievances the plebeians rebelled soon after the beginning of the fifth century B.C. They gained their first victory about 494 B.C., when they forced the patricians to agree to the election of a number of officers known as tribunes with power to protect the citizens by means of a veto over unlawful acts of the magistrates. This victory was followed by a successful demand for codification of the laws about 450 B.C. The result was the publication of the famous Law of the Twelve Tables, so called because it was written on tablets of wood. Although the Twelve Tables came to be revered by the Romans of later times as a kind of charter of the people's liberties, they were really nothing of the sort. For the most part they merely perpetuated ancient custom without even abolishing enslavement for debt. They did, however, enable the people to know where they stood in relation to the law, and they permitted an appeal to the assembly against a magistrate's sentence of capital punishment. About a generation later the plebeians won eligibility to positions as lesser magistrates, and about 367 B.C. the first plebeian consul was elected. Since ancient custom provided that, upon completing their term of office, consuls should automatically enter the Senate, the patrician monopoly of seats in that body was broken. The final plebeian victory came in 287 B.C. with the passage of a law which provided that measures enacted by the assembly should become binding upon the state whether the Senate approved them or not.

The victories of the plebeians

The significance of these changes must not be misinterpreted. They did not constitute a revolution to gain more liberty for the individual but merely to curb the power of the magistrates and to win for the plebeians a larger share in government. The state as a whole remained

Significance of the plebeian victories

as despotic as ever, for its authority over the citizens was not even challenged. Indeed, the Romans of the early Republic "never really abandoned the principle that the people were not to govern but to be governed."[1] Because of this attitude the grant of full legislative powers to the assembly seems to have meant little more than a formality; the Senate continued to rule as before. Nor did the admission of plebeians to membership in the Senate have any effect in liberalizing that body. So high was its prestige and so deep was the veneration of the Roman for authority, that the new members were soon swallowed up in the conservatism of the old. Moreover, the fact that the magistrates received no salaries prevented most of the poorer citizens from seeking public office.

Roman society and culture still rather primitive

Intellectually and culturally the Romans developed very slowly. Life in Rome was still harsh and crude. Though writing had been adopted as early as the sixth century, little use was made of it except for the copying of laws, treaties, and funerary inscriptions. Inasmuch as education was limited to instruction imparted by the father in manly sports, practical arts, and soldierly virtues, the great majority of the people were still illiterate. War and agriculture continued as the chief occupations for the bulk of the citizens. A few craftsmen were to be found in the cities, and a minor development of trade had occurred. But the comparative insignificance of Roman commerce at this time is pretty clearly revealed by the fact that the country had no standard system of coinage until 269 B.C.

The religion of the Romans compared with that of the Greeks

During the period of the early Republic Roman religion assumed the character it was destined to retain through the greater part of Roman history. In several ways this religion resembled that of the Greeks, partly for the reason that the Etruscan religion was deeply indebted to the Greek, and the Romans, in turn, were influenced by the Etruscans. Both the Greek and Roman religions emphasized the performances of rites in order to gain benefits from the gods or keep them from anger. The deities in both religions performed similar functions: Jupiter corresponded roughly to Zeus as god of the sky, Minerva to Athena as goddess of wisdom and patroness of crafts, Venus to Aphrodite as goddess of love, Neptune to Poseidon as god of the sea, and so on. The Roman religion, like the Greek, had no dogmas or sacraments or belief in rewards and punishments in an afterlife.

Contrasts with Greek religion

But there were significant differences also. The Roman religion was distinctly more political and less humanist in purpose. It served not to glorify humanity or establish a comfortable relationship between human beings and their world but to protect the state from its enemies and to augment its power and prosperity. The gods were less human; indeed, it was only as a result of Greek and Etruscan influences that they were made personal deities at all, having previously been worshiped as animistic spirits. The Romans never conceived of their dei-

---

[1] Theodor Mommsen, *The History of Rome,* I, 313.

Intervention of Jupiter. This scene from the first century A.D. depicts Jupiter, god of the sky, supporting the Romans in a battle against Germanic barbarians.

ties as quarreling among themselves or mingling with human beings after the fashion of the Homeric divinities. Finally, the Roman religion contained a much stronger element of priestliness than the Greek. The priests, or pontiffs as they were called, formed an organized class, a branch of the government itself. They not only supervised the offering of sacrifices, they were also guardians of an elaborate body of sacred traditions and laws which they alone could interpret. It must be understood, however, that these pontiffs were not priests in the sense of intermediaries between the individual Roman and the gods; they heard no confessions, forgave no sins, and administered no sacraments.

The morality of the Romans in this as in later periods had almost no connection with religion. The Romans did not ask their gods to make them good, but to bestow upon the community and upon their families material blessings. Morality was a matter of patriotism and of respect for authority and tradition. The chief virtues were bravery, honor, self-discipline, reverence for the gods and for one's ancestors, and duty to country and family. Loyalty to Rome took precedence over everything else. For the good of the state the citizen had to be ready to sacrifice not only his own life but, if necessary, the lives of his family and friends. The courage of certain consuls who dutifully put their sons to death for breaches of military discipline was a subject of profound admiration. Few peoples in European history with the exception of the Spartans and modern totalitarians have ever taken the problems of national interest so seriously or subordinated the individual so completely to the welfare of the state.

Morality in the early Republic

3. THE FATEFUL WARS WITH CARTHAGE

By 265 B.C., as we have already learned, Rome had conquered and annexed the whole mainland of Italy south of the Po. Proud and confident of its strength, it was almost certain to strike out into new fields of empire. The prosperous island of Sicily was not yet within its grasp, nor could it regard with indifference the situation in other parts of the Mediterranean world. Rome was now prone to interpret almost any change in the status quo as a threat to its own power and security. It was for such reasons that Rome after 264 B.C. became involved in a series of wars with other great nations which decidedly altered the course of Roman history.

The first and most important of these wars was the struggle with Carthage, a great maritime empire that stretched along the northern coast of Africa from modern-day Tunisia to the Strait of Gibraltar. Carthage had originally been founded about 800 B.C. as a Phoenician colony. In the sixth century it severed its ties with the homeland and gradually developed into a rich and powerful state. The prosperity of its upper classes was founded upon commerce and upon exploitation of the silver and tin resources of Spain and the tropical products of north central Africa. Carthaginian government was oligarchic. The real rulers were thirty merchant princes who constituted an inner council of the Senate. These men controlled elections and dominated every other branch of the government. The remaining 270 members of the Senate appear to have been summoned to meet only on special occasions. In spite of these political deficiencies and a cruel religion that demanded blood sacrifices, Carthage had a civilization superior in luxury and scientific attainment to that of Rome when the struggle between the two states began.

The initial clash with Carthage started in 264 B.C.[2] The primary cause was Roman jealousy over Carthaginian expansion in Sicily. Carthage already controlled the western portion of the island and was threatening the Greek cities of Syracuse and Messina on the eastern coast. If these cities should be captured, all chances of Roman occupation of Sicily would be lost. Faced with this danger, Rome declared war upon Carthage with the hope of forcing it back into its African domain. Twenty-three years of fighting finally brought victory to the Roman generals. Carthage was compelled to surrender its possessions in Sicily and to pay an indemnity of 3,200 talents, or about 13 million dollars at present silver prices.

But the Romans were unable to stand the strain of this triumph. They had had to put forth such heroic efforts to win that when victory was finally secured it made them more arrogant and acquisitive than

---

[2] The wars with Carthage are known as the Punic Wars. The Romans called the Carthaginians *Poeni*, i.e., Phoenicians, whence is derived the adjective "Punic."

ever. As a result, the struggle with Carthage was renewed on two different occasions thereafter. In 218 B.C., the Romans interpreted the Carthaginian attempt to rebuild an empire in Spain as a threat to their interests and responded with a declaration of war. This struggle raged through a period of sixteen years. Italy was ravaged by the armies of Hannibal, the famous Carthaginian commander, who crossed the Alps with sixty elephants, and whose tactics have been copied by military experts to the present day. Rome escaped defeat by the narrowest of margins. Only the durability of its system of alliances in Italy saved the day. As long as these alliances held, Hannibal dared not besiege the city of Rome itself for fear of being attacked from the rear. In the end Carthage was more completely humbled than before. Carthage was compelled to abandon all its possessions except the capital city and its surrounding territory in Africa, and to pay an indemnity of 10,000 talents, or, very roughly, 39 million dollars.

Hannibal. A coin from Carthage representing Hannibal as a victorious general, with an elephant on the reverse.

Roman vindictiveness reached its peak about the middle of the second century B.C. By this time Carthage had recovered a modicum of its former prosperity—enough to excite the displeasure of its conquerors. Nothing would now satisfy the senatorial magnates but the complete destruction of Carthage and the expropriation of its land. In 149 B.C. the Senate dispatched an ultimatum demanding that the Carthaginians abandon their city and settle at least ten miles from the coast. Since this demand was tantamount to a death sentence for a nation dependent upon commerce, it was refused—as the Romans probably hoped it would be. The result was the Third Punic War, a brutal conflict which was fought between 149 and 146 B.C. The final Roman assault upon the city was carried into the houses of the inhabitants and a frightful butchery took place. When the victorious Roman general saw Carthage going up in flames he said: "It is a glorious moment, but I have a strange feeling that some day the same fate will befall my own homeland." After the resistance of the Carthaginians was finally broken, the few citizens who were left to surrender were sold into slavery, their once magnificent city was razed, and the ground was plowed over with salt. Carthaginian territory was then organized into a Roman province, with the best areas parceled out as senatorial estates.

The Third Punic War and the destruction of Carthage

The wars with Carthage had momentous effects on Rome. First, victory in the Second Punic War led to Roman occupation of Spain. This not only brought great new wealth—above all from Spanish silver—but was the beginning of a policy of westward expansion that was to be one of the great formative influences on the history of Europe. Then too the wars brought Rome into conflict with eastern Mediterranean powers and thereby paved the way for still greater dominion. During the Second Punic War, Philip V of Macedon had entered into an alliance with Carthage and had plotted with the king of Syria to divide Egypt between them. In order to forestall the execution of Philip's plans, Rome sent an army into the East. The result was

Results of the wars with Carthage: (1) conquest of Spain and the Hellenistic East

the conquest of Greece and Asia Minor and the establishment of a protectorate over Egypt. Thus before the end of the second century B.C. virtually the entire Mediterranean area had been brought under Roman control. The conquest of the Hellenistic East led to the introduction of Greek ideas and customs into Rome. Despite formidable resistance, these novelties exerted considerable influence in changing some aspects of social and cultural life.

(2) a social and economic revolution

Still another effect of the Punic Wars was a great social and economic revolution that swept over Rome in the third and second centuries B.C. The changes wrought by this revolution may be enumerated as follows: (1) a marked increase in slavery due to the capture and sale of prisoners of war; (2) the decline of the small farmer as a result of the establishment of the plantation system in conquered areas and the influx of cheap grain from the provinces; (3) the growth of a helpless urban element composed of impoverished farmers and workers displaced by slave labor; (4) the appearance of a middle class comprising merchants, moneylenders, and men who held government contracts to operate mines, build roads, or collect taxes; and (5) an increase in luxury and vulgar display, particularly among the newly rich who fattened themselves on the profits of war.

Cato's attempt to prevent the transformation of Roman society

As a consequence of this social and economic revolution, Rome was changed from a republic of yeoman farmers into a complex society with new habits of luxury and indulgence. Though property had never been evenly distributed, the gulf which separated rich and poor now yawned more widely than before. The old-fashioned ideals of discipline and devotion to the service of the state were weakened, and people began to live more for pleasure. A few members of the senatorial aristocracy exerted efforts to check these tendencies and to restore the simple virtues of the past. The leader of this movement was the dour Cato the Elder, who inveighed against the new rich for their soft living and strove to set an example to his countrymen by performing hard labor on his farm and dwelling in a house with a dirt floor and no plaster on the walls. In addition he was a prude who showed contempt for women and boasted that his wife never came into his arms except when there was great thunder. Cato also strove, often cantankerously, to prevent the influx of Greek intellectual influences. But his efforts on all fronts had no lasting effect because the clock could not be turned back.

4. THE SOCIAL STRUGGLES OF THE LATE REPUBLIC

The new period of turbulence

The period from the end of the Punic Wars in 146 B.C. to about 30 B.C. was one of the most turbulent in the history of Rome. It was between these years that the nation reaped the full harvest of the seeds of violence sown during the wars of conquest. Bitter class conflicts, assassinations, desperate struggles between rival dictators, wars, and insurrections were the all too common occurrences of this time. Even the slaves contributed their part to the general disorder: first, in 104 B.C. when they ravaged Sicily; and again in 73 B.C. when 70,000 of them under the leadership of a slave named Spartacus held the consuls at bay for more than a year. Spartacus was finally slain in battle and 6,000 of his followers were captured and left crucified along the length of a long road to provide a warning for others.

The first stage in the conflict between classes of citizens began with the revolt of the Gracchi brothers. The Gracchi were leaders of the liberal, pro-Greek elements in Rome and had the support of the middle classes and a number of influential senators as well. Though of aristocratic lineage themselves, they strove for a program of reforms to alleviate the country's ills. They considered these to be a result of the decline of the free peasantry, and proposed the simple remedy of dividing state lands among the landless. The first of the brothers to take up the cause of reform was Tiberius. Elected tribune in 133 B.C., he proposed a law that restricted the current renters or holders of state lands to a maximum of 640 acres. The excess was to be confiscated by the government and given to the poor in small plots. Conservative aristocrats bitterly opposed this proposal and brought about its veto by Tiberius's colleague in the tribunate, Octavius. Tiberius removed Octavius from office, and when his own term expired attempted to stand for reelection. Both of these moves were unconstitutional and gave the conservative senators an excuse for violence. Armed with clubs, they went on a rampage during the elections and murdered Tiberius and 300 of his followers.

The revolt of the Gracchi: the land program of Tiberius

Nine years later Gaius Gracchus, the younger brother of Tiberius, renewed the struggle for reform. Though Tiberius's land law had finally been enacted by the Senate, Gaius believed that the campaign had to go further. Elected tribune in 123 B.C., and reelected in 122, he procured the enactment of various laws for the benefit of the less privileged. The first provided for stabilizing the price of grain in Rome. For this purpose great public granaries were built along the Tiber. A second law proposed to extend the franchise to Roman allies, giving them the rights of Latin citizens. Still a third gave the middle class the right to make up the juries that tried governors accused of exploiting the provinces. These and similar measures provoked so much anger and contention among the classes that civil war broke out. Gaius was proclaimed an enemy of the state, and the Senate authorized the consuls to take all necessary steps for the defense of the Republic. In the ensuing conflict Gaius committed suicide and about 3,000 of his followers were killed.

Gaius Gracchus and the renewed fight for reform

The Gracchan revolt had a broad significance. It demonstrated, first of all, that the Roman Republic had outgrown its constitution. Over the years the assembly had gained powers almost equal to those of the Senate. Instead of working out a peaceful accommodation to these changes, both sides resorted to violence. By so doing they set a prece-

Significance of the Gracchan revolt

Pompey

Julius Caesar

Pompey and Julius Caesar

dent for the unbridled use of force by any politician ambitious for supreme power and thereby paved the way for the destruction of the Republic. The Romans had shown a remarkable capacity for organizing an empire and for adapting the Greek idea of a city-state to a large territory, but the narrow conservatism of their upper classes was a fatal hindrance to the health of the state. They appeared to regard all reform as evil. They failed to understand the reasons for internal discord and seemed to think that repression was its only remedy.

After the downfall of the Gracchi, two military leaders who had won fame in foreign wars successively made themselves rulers of the state. The first was Marius, who was elevated to the consulship by the masses in 107 B.C. and reelected six times thereafter. Unfortunately, Marius was no statesman and accomplished nothing for his followers beyond demonstrating the ease with which a general with an army at his back could override opposition. Following his death in 86 B.C. the aristocrats took a turn at government by force. Their champion was Sulla, another victorious commander. Appointed dictator in 82 B.C. for an unlimited term, Sulla ruthlessly proceeded to exterminate his opponents and to restore to the Senate its original powers. Even the senatorial veto over acts of the assembly was revived, and the authority of the tribunes was sharply curtailed. After three years of rule Sulla decided to exchange the pomp of power for the pleasures of the senses and retired to a life of luxury and ease on his country estate.

It was not to be expected that the "reforms" of Sulla would stand unchallenged after he had relinquished his office, for the effect of his decrees was to give control to a selfish aristocracy. Several new leaders now emerged to espouse the cause of the people. The most famous of them were Pompey (106–48 B.C.) and Julius Caesar (100–44 B.C.). For a time they pooled their energies and resources in a plot to gain control of the government, but later they became rivals and sought to outdo each other in bids for popular support. Pompey won fame as the conqueror of Syria and Palestine, while Caesar devoted his talents to a series of brilliant forays against the Gauls, adding to the Roman state the territory of modern Belgium, Germany west of the Rhine, and France. In 52 B.C., after a series of mob disorders in Rome, the Senate turned to Pompey and caused his election as sole consul. Caesar, stationed in Gaul, was eventually branded an enemy of the state, and Pompey conspired with the senatorial faction to deprive him of political power. The result was a deadly war between the two men. In 49 B.C. Caesar crossed the Rubicon River into Italy (ever since then an image for a fateful decision) and marched on Rome. Pompey fled to the East in the hope of gathering a large enough army to regain control of Italy. In 48 B.C. the forces of the two rivals met at Pharsalus in Greece. Pompey was defeated and soon afterward was murdered by agents of the ruler of Egypt.

Caesar then intervened in Egyptian politics at the court of Cleopatra (whom he left pregnant). Then he conducted another military campaign in Asia Minor in which victory was so swift that he could report "I came, I saw, I conquered" (*veni, vidi, vici*). After that Caesar returned to Rome. There was now no one who dared to challenge his power. With the aid of his veterans he cowed the Senate into granting his every desire. In 46 B.C. he became dictator for ten years, and two years later for life. In addition, he assumed nearly every other title that would augment his power. He obtained from the Senate full authority to make war and peace and to control the revenues of the state. For all practical purposes he was above the law, and the other agents of the government were merely his servants. It seems unquestionable that he had little respect for the constitution, and there were rumors that he intended to make himself king. At any rate, it was on such a charge that he was assassinated on the Ides of March in 44 B.C. by a group of conspirators, under the leadership of Brutus and Cassius, who hoped to rid Rome of the dictatorship.

Caesar's achievements

Although Caesar used to be revered by historians as a superhuman hero, it is now customary to dismiss him as insignificant. But both extremes of interpretation should be avoided. Certainly he did not "save Rome" and was not the greatest statesman of all time, for he treated the Republic with contempt and made the problem of governing more difficult for those who came after him. Yet some of the measures he took as dictator did have lasting effects. With the aid of a Greek astronomer he revised the calendar so as to make a year last for 365 days (with an extra day added every fourth year). This "Julian" calendar—subject to adjustments made by Pope Gregory XIII in 1582—is still with us. It is thus only proper that the seventh month is named after Julius as "July." By conferring citizenship upon thousands of Spaniards and Gauls, Caesar took an important step toward eliminating the distinction between Italians and provincials. He also helped relieve economic inequities by settling many of his veterans and some of the urban poor on unused lands. Vastly more important than these reforms, however, was Caesar's far-sighted resolve, made before he seized power, to invest his efforts in the West. While Pompey, and before him Alexander, went to the East to gain fame and fortune, Caesar was the first great leader to recognize the potential significance of northwestern Europe. By incorporating Gaul into the Roman world he brought Rome great agricultural wealth and helped bring urban life and culture to what was then the wild West. Western European civilization, later to be anchored in just those regions that Caesar conquered, might not have been the same without him.

Ides of March Coin. This coin was struck by Brutus to commemorate the assassination of Julius Caesar. Brutus is depicted on the obverse; on the reverse is a liberty cap between two daggers and the Latin abbreviation for the Ides of March.

5. ROME BECOMES SOPHISTICATED

The culture that Rome brought to Gaul was itself taken from the Greek East. During the last two centuries of republican history Rome came under the influence of Hellenistic civilization. The result was a flowering of intellectual activity and a further impetus to social change beyond what the Punic Wars had produced. The fact must be noted, however, that several of the components of the Hellenistic pattern of culture were never adopted by the Romans. The science of the Hellenistic Age, for example, was largely ignored, and the same was true of some of its art.

One of the most notable effects of Hellenistic influence was the adoption of Epicureanism and, above all, Stoicism by numerous Romans of the upper classes. The most renowned of the Roman exponents of Epicureanism was Lucretius (98–55 B.C.), author of a book-length philosophical poem entitled *On the Nature of Things*. In writing this work Lucretius was moved to explain the universe in such a way as to remove all fear of the supernatural, which he regarded as the chief obstacle to peace of mind. Worlds and all things in them, he taught, are the results of fortuitous combinations of atoms. Though he admitted the existence of the gods, he conceived of them as living in eternal peace, neither creating nor governing the universe. Everything is a product of mechanical evolution, including human beings, and their habits, institutions, and beliefs. Since mind is indissolubly linked with matter, death means utter extinction; consequently, no part of the human personality can survive to be rewarded or punished in an afterlife. Lucretius's conception of the good life was simple: what one needs, he asserted, is not enjoyment but "peace and a pure heart." Whether one agrees with Lucretius's philosophy or not, there is no doubt that he was an extraordinarily fine poet. In fact his musical cadences, sustained majesty of expression, and infectious enthusiasm earn him a rank among the greatest poets who ever lived.

Stoicism was introduced into Rome about 140 B.C. and soon came to include among its converts numerous influential leaders of public life. The greatest of these was Cicero (106–43 B.C.), the "father of Roman eloquence." Although Cicero adopted doctrines from a number of philosophers, including both Plato and Aristotle, he derived more of his ideas from the Stoics than from any other source. Cicero's ethical philosophy was based on the Stoic premises that virtue is sufficient for happiness and that tranquility of mind is the highest good. He conceived of the ideal human being as one who has been guided by reason to an indifference toward sorrow and pain. Where Cicero diverged from the Greek Stoics was in his greater approval of the active, political life. To this degree he still spoke for the older Roman tradition of service to the state. Cicero never claimed to be an original philosopher but rather conceived his goal to be that of bringing the best of Greek philosophy to the West. In this he was remarkably successful, for he wrote in a rich and elegant Latin prose style that has never been surpassed. Cicero's prose immediately became a standard for composition and has remained so until the present century. Thus even though not a truly great thinker Cicero was the most influential Latin transmitter of ancient thought to the medieval and modern western European worlds.

Lucretius and Cicero were the two leading exponents of Greek thought but not the only two fine writers of the later Roman Republic. It now became the fashion among the upper classes to learn Greek and to strive to reproduce in Latin some of the more popular forms of Greek literature. Some results of enduring literary merit were the ribald comedies of Plautus (257?–184 B.C.), the passionate love poems of Catullus (84?–54? B.C.), and the crisp military memoirs of Julius Caesar, the opening of which all beginning students of Latin used to know as well as the pledge of allegiance.

Roman literary achievements

The conquest of the Hellenistic world accelerated the process of social change which the Punic Wars had begun. The effects were most clearly evident in the growth of luxury, in a widened cleavage between classes, and in a further increase in slavery. The Italian people, numbering about eight million at the end of the Republic, had come to be divided into four main castes: the aristocracy, the equestrians, the common citizens, and the slaves. The aristocracy included the senatorial class with a total membership of 300 citizens and their families. The majority of them inherited their status, although occasionally a plebeian would gain admission to the Senate through serving a term as consul. Most of the aristocrats gained their living as office-holders and as owners of great landed estates. The equestrian order was made up of government contractors, bankers, and the wealthier merchants. Originally this class had been composed of those citizens with incomes sufficient to enable them to serve in the cavalry at their own ex-

Social conditions in the late Republic

Left: *Atrium of an Upper-class House in Pompeii, Seen from the Interior.* Around the atrium or central court were grouped suites of living rooms. The marble columns and decorated walls still give an idea of the luxury and refinement enjoyed by the privileged minority. Right: *A Street in Ostia.* This town was the seaport of ancient Rome. The round arches and masonry columns form the balcony of a rich man's house.

pense, but the term equestrian had now come to be applied to all out-side of the senatorial class who possessed property in substantial amount. The equestrians were the chief offenders in the indulgence of vulgar tastes and in the exploitation of the poor and the provincials. As bankers they regularly charged exorbitant interest rates whenever they could get them. By far the largest number of the citizens were mere commoners or plebeians. Some of these were independent farmers, a few were industrial workers, but the majority were members of the city mob. When Julius Caesar became dictator, 320,000 citizens were receiving free grain from the state.

The Roman slaves were scarcely considered people at all but in-struments of production like cattle or horses to be worked for the profit of their masters. Notwithstanding the fact that some of them were cultivated foreigners taken as prisoners of war, they had none of the privileges granted to slaves in Athens. The policy of many of their owners was to get as much work out of them as possible during their prime and then to turn them loose to be fed by the state when they be-came old and useless. Of course, there were exceptions, especially as a result of the civilizing effects of Stoicism. Cicero, for example, re-ported himself very fond of his slaves. It is, nevertheless, a sad com-mentary on Roman civilization that nearly all of the productive labor in the country was done by slaves. They produced practically all of the nation's food supply, for the amount contributed by the few surviving independent farmers was quite insignificant. At least 80 percent of the workers employed in shops were slaves or former slaves. But many of the members of the servile population were engaged in nonproductive activities. A lucrative form of investment for the business classes was ownership of slaves trained as gladiators, who could be rented to the government or to aspiring politicians for the amusement of the peo-ple. The growth of luxury also required the employment of thousands of slaves in domestic service. The man of great wealth must have his doorkeepers, his litter-bearers, his couriers (for the government of the Republic had no postal service), his valets, and his tutors for his chil-dren. In some great households there were special servants with no other duties than to rub the master down after his bath or to care for his sandals.

The religious beliefs of the Romans were altered in various ways in the last two centuries of the Republic—again mainly because of the ex-tension of Roman power over most of the Hellenistic states. There was, first of all, a tendency of the upper classes to abandon the tradi-tional religion for the philosophies of Stoicism and, to a lesser degree, Epicureanism. But many of the common people also found worship of the ancient gods no longer satisfying. It was too formal and me-chanical and demanded too much in the way of duty and self-sacrifice to meet the needs of the masses, whose lives were now empty and meaningless. Furthermore, Italy had attracted a stream of immigrants from the East, most of whom had a religious background totally different from that of the Romans. The result was the spread of Eastern mystery cults, which satisfied the craving for a more emotional religion and offered the reward of immortality to the wretched and downtrodden of the earth. From Egypt came the cult of Osiris (or Serapis, as the god was now more commonly called), while from Phrygia in Asia Minor was introduced the worship of the Great Mother, with her eunuch priests and wild, symbolic orgies. So strong was the appeal of these cults that the decrees of the Senate against them proved almost impossible to enforce. In the last century B.C. the Persian cult of Mithraism, which came to surpass all the others in popularity, gained a foothold in Italy.

6. THE PRINCIPATE OR EARLY EMPIRE (27 B.C.–180 A.D.)

Shortly before his death in 44 B.C., Julius Caesar had adopted as his sole heir his grandnephew Octavian (63 B.C.–14 A.D.), then a young man of eighteen quietly pursuing his studies in Illyria across the Adriatic Sea. Upon learning of his uncle's death, Octavian hastened to Rome to take control of the government. He soon found that he had to share his ambition with two of Caesar's powerful friends, Mark Antony and Lepidus. The following year the three men formed an alliance for the purpose of crushing the power of the aristocratic group responsible for Caesar's murder. The methods employed were not to the new leaders' credit. Prominent members of the aristocracy were hunted down and slain and their property confiscated. The most noted of the victims was Cicero, brutally slain by Mark Antony's thugs though he had taken no part in the conspiracy against Caesar's life. The real murderers, Brutus and Cassius, escaped and organized an army, but were finally defeated by Octavian and his colleagues near Philippi in 42 B.C.

An alliance to avenge Caesar's death

Thereafter a quarrel developed between the members of the alliance, inspired primarily by Antony's jealousy of Octavian. The subsequent struggle became a contest between East and West. Antony went to the East and made an alliance with Cleopatra that was dedicated to introducing principles of Oriental despotism into Roman rule. Octavian consolidated the forces of the West and came forward as the champion of Greek cultural traditions. As in the earlier contest between Caesar and Pompey the victory again was for the West. In the naval battle of Actium (31 B.C.) Octavian's forces defeated those of Antony and Cleopatra, both of whom soon afterwards committed suicide. It was now clear that Rome would not be swallowed up by the East. Actium guaranteed that there would be several more centuries for the consolidation of Greek ideals and urban life, a development important above all for the future of western Europe.

The struggle between Antony and Octavian

The victory of Octavian ushered in a new period in Roman history, the most glorious and the most prosperous that the nation experi-

*The revival of
constitutional government*

enced. Although problems of peace and order were still far from being completely solved, the deadly civil strife was ended, and the people now had their first decent opportunity to show what their talents could achieve. Octavian was determined to preserve the forms if not the substance of constitutional government. He accepted the titles of Augustus and emperor (which then only meant "victorious general") conferred upon him by the Senate and the army. He held the authority of proconsul and tribune permanently; but he refused to make himself dictator or even consul for life, despite the pleas of the populace that he do so. In his view the Senate and the people were the supreme sovereigns, as they had been under the early Republic. The title by which he preferred to have his authority designated was princeps, or first citizen of the state. For this reason the period of his rule and that of his successors is properly called the Principate, or early Empire, to distinguish it from the periods of the Republic (sixth century B.C. to 27 B.C.), the time of upheavals (180 A.D. to 284 A.D.), and the period of the late Empire (284 A.D. to 610 A.D.).

The reforms of Augustus

Octavian, or Augustus as he was now more commonly called, ruled over Italy and the provinces for forty-four years (31 B.C.–14 A.D.). At the beginning of the period he governed by military power and by common consent, but in 27 B.C. the Senate bestowed upon him the series of offices and titles described above. His work as a statesman at least equaled in importance that of Julius Caesar. Among the reforms of Augustus were the establishment of a new coinage system, the creation of a centralized system of courts under his own supervision, and the bestowal of a large measure of local self-government upon cities and provinces. He insisted upon experience and intelligence as qualifi-

The Emperor Augustus Receiving the Submission of German Barbarians. A drinking cup of the first century A.D.

Trajan Addressing His Troops. This relief on the column of Trajan dates from the first century A.D.

cations for appointment to administrative office. By virtue of his proconsular authority he assumed direct control over the provincial governors and punished them severely for graft and extortion. He abolished the old system of farming out the collection of taxes in the provinces, which had led to great abuses, and appointed his own personal representatives as collectors at regular salaries. But he did not stop with political reforms. He enacted laws designed to check the more glaring social and moral evils of the time. By his own example of temperate living he sought to discourage luxurious habits and to set the precedent for a return to the ancient virtues.

After the death of Augustus in 14 A.D. until almost the end of the century Rome had no really capable rulers, with the single exception of Claudius (41–54). Several of Augustus's successors, most infamously Caligula (37–41) and Nero (54–68), were brutal tyrants who squandered the resources of the state and kept the city of Rome in an uproar by their deeds of bloody violence. But starting in 96 A.D., a period of strong and stable government returned with the advent of "five good emperors": Nerva (96–98), Trajan (98–117), Hadrian (117–138), Antoninus Pius (138–161), and Marcus Aurelius (161–180). These five ruled in harmony with the Senate, displayed great gifts as administrators, and, each in their turn, were able to bequeath a well-ordered and united realm to their designated successors.

From the time of Augustus until that of Trajan, the Roman Empire continued to expand. Augustus gained more land for Rome than did any other Roman ruler. His generals advanced into central Europe, conquering the territories known today as Switzerland, Austria, and

Augustus

Territorial expansion under the empire

Bulgaria. Only in modern-day central Germany did Roman troops meet defeat, a setback which convinced Augustus to hold the Roman borders at the Rhine and Danube. Subsequently, in 43 A.D., the Emperor Claudius began the conquest of Britain, and at the beginning of the next century Trajan pushed beyond the Danube to add Dacia (now Rumania) to the Roman realms. Trajan also conquered territories in Mesopotamia but thereby incurred the enmity of the Persians, causing his successor Hadrian to embark on a defensive policy. The Roman Empire had now reached its ultimate territorial limits; in the third century these limits would begin to recede.

The Pax Romana

See color map following page 96

Rome's peaceful sway over a vast empire for about two centuries from the time of Augustus to that of Marcus Aurelius was certainly one of its most impressive accomplishments. As the historian Gibbon said, "the Empire of Rome comprehended the fairest part of the earth and the most civilized portion of mankind." The celebrated *Pax Romana,* or Roman peace, was unprecedented. The Mediterranean was now under the control of one power (as it has never been before or since) and experienced the passage of centuries without a single naval battle. On land one rule held without contention from the borders of Scotland to those of Persia. A contemporary orator justly boasted that "the whole civilized world lays down the arms which were its ancient load, as if on holiday . . . all places are full of gymnasia, fountains, monumental approaches, temples, workshops, schools; one can say that the civilized world, which had been sick from the beginning . . . , has been brought by the right knowledge to a state of health." But much of this health, as we will see, proved illusory.

7. CULTURE AND LIFE IN THE PERIOD OF THE PRINCIPATE

From the standpoint of variety of intellectual and artistic interests the period of the Principate outshone all other ages in the history of Rome. From 27 B.C. to about 200 A.D. Roman philosophy attained its most characteristic form. The same period also witnessed the production of outstanding literary works, the growth of a distinctive architecture and art, and the greatest triumphs of Roman engineering.

Cultural progress under the Principate

Roman Stoicism

The form of philosophy that appealed most strongly to the Romans was Stoicism. The reasons for Stoicism's popularity are easy to discover. With its emphasis upon duty, self-discipline, and subjection to the natural order of things, it accorded well with the ancient virtues of the Romans and with their habits of conservatism. Moreover, its insistence upon civic obligations and its doctrine of cosmopolitanism appealed to the Roman political-mindedness and pride in world empire. It is necessary to observe, however, that the Stoicism developed in the days of the Principate was somewhat different from that of

Marcus Aurelius. The mounted figure of the emperor-philosopher, now standing on the Piazza del Campidoglio in Rome, is the only full-sized equestrian statue surviving from the ancient world. The Christians destroyed other such statues because they seemed to stand for ruler worship, but they saved this one on the mistaken assumption that it represented Constantine, the first Christian Roman emperor.

Zeno and his school. The old physical theories borrowed from Heraclitus were now discarded, and in their place was substituted a broader interest in politics and ethics. There was a tendency also for Roman Stoicism to assume a more distinctly religious flavor than that which had characterized the original philosophy.

Three eminent apostles of Stoicism lived and taught in Rome in the two centuries that followed the rule of Augustus: Seneca (4 B.C.–65 A.D.), millionaire adviser for a time to Nero; Epictetus, the slave (60?–120 A.D.); and the Emperor Marcus Aurelius (121–180 A.D.). All of them agreed that inner serenity is the ultimate goal to be sought, that true happiness can be found only in surrender to the benevolent order of the universe. They preached the ideal of virtue for virtue's sake, deplored the sinfulness of human nature, and urged obedience to conscience as the voice of duty. Seneca and Epictetus adulterated their philosophy with such deep mystical yearnings as to make it almost a religion. They worshiped the cosmos as divine, governed by an all-powerful Providence who ordains all that happens for ultimate good. The last of the Roman Stoics, Marcus Aurelius, was more fatalistic and less hopeful. Although he did not reject the conception of an ordered and rational universe, he shared neither the faith nor the dogmatism of the earlier Stoics. He was confident of no blessed immortality to balance the sufferings of one's earthly career and was inclined to think of humans as creatures buffeted by evil fortune for which no distant perfection of the whole could fully atone. He urged, nevertheless, that people should continue to live nobly, that they should neither abandon themselves to gross indulgence nor break down in angry protest, but that they should derive what contentment they could from dignified resignation to suffering and tranquil submission to death.

The literary achievements of the Romans bore a definite relation to

Seneca, Epictetus, and Marcus Aurelius

their philosophy. This was especially true of the works of the most distinguished writers of the Augustan Age. Horace (65–8 B.C.), for example, in his famous *Odes* drew copiously from the teachings of both Epicureans and Stoics. He confined his attention, however, to their doctrines of a way of life, for like most of the Romans he had little curiosity about the nature of the world. He developed a philosophy which combined the Epicurean justification of pleasure with the Stoic bravery in the face of trouble. While he never reduced pleasure to the mere absence of pain, he was sophisticated enough to know that the highest enjoyment is possible only through the exercise of rational control.

Virgil (70–19 B.C.) likewise reflects a measure of the philosophical temper of his age. Though his *Eclogues* convey something of the Epicurean ideal of quiet pleasure, Virgil was much more of a Stoic. His utopian vision of an age of peace and abundance, his brooding sense of the tragedy of human fate, and his idealization of a life in harmony with nature indicate an intellectual heritage similar to that of Seneca and Epictetus. Virgil's most noted work, the *Aeneid,* like several of the *Odes* of Horace, was a purposeful glorification of Roman imperialism. The *Aeneid* in fact was an epic of empire recounting the toils and triumphs of the founding of the state, its glorious traditions, and its magnificent destiny. Other major writers of the Augustan Age were Ovid (43 B.C.?–17 A.D.) and Livy (59 B.C.–17 A.D.). The former was the chief representative of the cynical and individualist tendencies of his day. His brilliant and witty writings often reflected the dissolute tastes of the time. The chief claim of Livy to fame rests upon his skill as a prose stylist. As a historian he was woefully deficient. His main work, a history of Rome, is replete with dramatic and picturesque narrative, designed to appeal to the patriotic emotions rather than to present an accurate record of events.

The literature of the period which followed the death of Augustus also exemplified conflicting social and intellectual tendencies. The novels of Petronius and Apuleius and the epigrams of Martial describe the more exotic and sometimes sordid aspects of Roman life. The attitude of the authors is not to instruct or uplift but chiefly to tell an entertaining story or turn a witty phrase. An entirely different viewpoint is presented in the works of the other most important writers of this age: Juvenal, the satirist (60?–140 A.D.), and Tacitus, the historian (55?–117? A.D.). Juvenal wrote under the influence of the Stoics but with narrow vision. Convinced that the troubles of the nation were due to moral degeneracy, he lashed the vices of his countrymen with the fury of an evangelist. A somewhat similar attitude characterized the writing of his younger contemporary, Tacitus. The best-known of Roman historians, Tacitus described the events of his age not with a view to dispassionate analysis but largely for the purpose of moral indictment. His description of the customs of the ancient Germans in his

Germania served to heighten the contrast between the manly virtues of an unspoiled race and the effeminate vices of the decadent Romans. Whatever his failings as a historian, he was a master of ironic wit and brilliant aphorism. Referring to the boasted *Pax Romana,* he makes a barbarian chieftain say: "They create a wilderness and call it peace."

Roman art first assumed its distinctive character during the period of the Principate. Before this time what passed for an art of Rome was really an importation from the Hellenistic East. Conquering armies brought back to Italy wagonloads of statues, reliefs, and marble columns as part of the plunder from Greece and Asia Minor. These became the property of wealthy businessmen and were used to embellish their sumptuous mansions. As the demand increased, hundreds of copies were made, with the result that Rome came to have by the end of the Republic a profusion of objects of art which had no more cultural significance than the Picassos in the home of some modern stockbroker. The aura of national glory which surrounded the early Principate stimulated the growth of an art that was more indigenous. Augustus himself boasted that he found Rome a city of brick and left it a city of marble. Nevertheless, much of the old Hellenistic influence remained until the talent of the Romans themselves was exhausted.

The arts most truly expressive of the Roman character were architecture and sculpture. Architecture was monumental, designed to symbolize power and grandeur. It contained as its leading elements the round arch, the vault, and the dome, although at times the Corinthian column was employed, especially in the construction of temples. The materials most commonly used were brick, squared stone blocks, and concrete, the last a Roman invention. As a further adornment of public buildings, sculptured entablatures and facades, built up of tiers of colonnades or arcades, were frequently added. Roman architecture was devoted primarily to utilitarian purposes. The foremost examples were government buildings, amphitheaters, baths, race courses, and private houses. Nearly all were of massive proportions and solid construction. Among the largest and most noted were the Pantheon, with its dome having a diameter of 142 feet, and the Colosseum, which

Achievements in art

See color plates following page 96

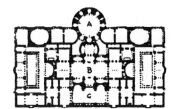

Floor Plan of the Baths of Caracalla

The Baths of Caracalla, Rome. The gigantic scale is typical of late empire buildings. Elaborate and luxurious public baths like these were often presented to the public by the emperor or rich citizens. The floor plan above indicates the separate chambers for hot tub baths.

The Pantheon in Rome. Built by the Emperor Hadrian it boasted the largest dome without interior supports of the ancient world. The dome forms a perfect sphere, exactly as high as it is wide.

could accommodate 65,000 spectators at the gladiatorial combats. Roman sculpture included as its main forms triumphal arches and columns, narrative reliefs, altars, and portrait busts and statues. Its distinguishing characteristics were individuality and naturalism. Sometimes Roman statues and busts served only to express the vanity of the aristocracy, but the best Roman sculptured portraiture succeeded in conveying qualities of simple human dignity similar to those espoused in the philosophy of the Stoics.

Roman engineering

Closely related to their achievements in architecture were Roman triumphs in engineering and public services. The imperial Romans built marvelous roads and bridges, many of which still survive. In the time of Trajan eleven aqueducts brought water into Rome from the nearby hills and provided the city with 300 million gallons daily for drinking and bathing as well as for flushing a well-designed sewage system. Water was cleverly funneled into the homes of the rich for their private gardens, fountains, and pools. Romans also established the first hospitals in the Western world and the first system of state medicine for the benefit of the poor.

As impressive as the Romans were in engineering, they accomplished little in science. They excelled, as has been jokingly but not inaccurately said, in drains, not brains. Scarcely an original discovery of fundamental importance was made by anyone of Latin nationality. This fact seems strange when we consider that the Romans had the advantage of Hellenistic science as a foundation upon which to build. But they neglected their opportunity almost completely because they had no vigorous curiosity about the natural world in which they lived. Roman writers on scientific subjects were hopelessly devoid of critical intelligence. The most renowned and typical of them was Pliny the Elder (23–79 A.D.), who completed about 77 A.D. a voluminous encyclopedia of "science" which he called *Natural History*. The subjects discussed varied from cosmology to economics. Despite the wealth of material it contains, Pliny's work is of limited value. He was totally unable to distinguish between fact and fable. In his estimation, the weirdest tales of wonders and portents were to be accepted as of equal value with the most solidly established facts.

The only real scientific advance made during the period of the Principate was the work of Hellenistic scientists who lived in Italy or in the provinces. One of these was the astronomer Ptolemy, who flourished in Alexandria around the middle of the second century (see above, p. 162). Another was the physician Galen, active in Rome at various times during the latter half of the second century. While Galen's fame rests primarily on his medical encyclopedia, systematizing the learn-

Pliny

Galen

Roman Aqueduct at Segovia, Spain. Aqueducts conveyed water from mountains to the larger cities.

ing of others, he is deserving of more credit for his own experiments which brought him close to a discovery of the circulation of the blood. He not only taught but proved that the arteries carry blood, and that severance of even a small one is sufficient to drain away all of the blood of the body in little more than half an hour.

Roman women

Roman society exhibited the same general tendencies under the Principate as in the last days of the Republic. One of the least attractive of its traits was the low status it accorded to women. The historian M. I. Finley has remarked that the two most famous women in Roman history were Cleopatra, who was not even a Roman, and the fictional Lucretia, who earned her fame by being raped and killing herself. Seldom have women been so confined to domesticity and obscurity. Roman women did not even really have their own names but were given family names with feminine endings—for example, Julia from Julius, Claudia from Claudius, and Livia from Livius. When there were two daughters in a family they would be distinguished only as "Julia the elder" and "Julia the younger," and when several as "Julia the first," "second," and "third." Women were expected to be subservient to their fathers and husbands, were valued to the degree they produced progeny, and were expected to stay at home. A typical tomb epitaph might say: "She loved her husband . . . she bore two sons . . . she was pleasant to talk with . . . she kept the house and worked in wool. That is all." During the Principate Roman women from imperial families not surprisingly tried to escape these limitations by taking a backstage and often literally murderous role in politics. Less highly placed women sought outlets in the excitement of gladiatorial shows—making gladiators the equivalent of modern rock-and-roll stars—or in the ceremonies of religious cults.

Gladiatorial combat

Along with the confinement of women, the most serious indictment which can be brought against the age was the further growth of the passion for cruelty. Whereas the Greeks entertained themselves with theatre, the Romans more and more preferred "circuses," which were really exhibitions of human slaughter. In the period of the Principate the great games and spectacles became bloodier than ever. The Romans could no longer obtain a sufficient thrill from mere exhibitions of athletic prowess: pugilists were now required to have their hands wrapped with thongs of leather loaded with iron or lead. The most popular amusement of all was watching the gladiatorial combats in the Colosseum or in other amphitheaters capable of accommodating thousands of spectators. Fights between gladiators were nothing new, but they were now presented on a much more elaborate scale. Not only the common people attended them, but wealthy aristocrats also, and frequently the head of the government himself. The gladiators fought to the accompaniment of savage cries and curses from the audience. When one went down with a disabling wound, it was the privilege of the crowd to decide whether his life should be spared or whether the weapon of his opponent should be plunged into

The Colosseum. Built by the Roman emperors between 75 and 80 A.D. as a place of entertainment, it was the scene of gladiatorial combats. The most common form of Greek secular architecture was the theater (see p. 197), but the most common Roman form was the amphitheater.

his heart. One contest after another, often featuring the sacrifice of men to wild animals, was staged in the course of a single exhibition. Should the arena become too sodden with blood, it was covered over with a fresh layer of sand, and the revolting performance went on. Most of the gladiators were condemned criminals or slaves, but some were volunteers even from the respectable classes. Commodus, the worthless son of Marcus Aurelius, entered the arena several times for the sake of the plaudits of the mob: this was his idea of a Roman holiday.

Notwithstanding its low moral tone, the age of the Principate was characterized by an even deeper interest in salvationist religions than that which had prevailed under the Republic. Mithraism now gained adherents by the thousands, absorbing many of the followers of the cults of the Great Mother and of Serapis. About 40 A.D. the first Christians appeared in Rome. The new sect grew steadily and eventually succeeded in displacing Mithraism as the most popular of the salvationist faiths. We will read more about its nature and success in the next chapter.

The establishment of stable government by Augustus ushered in a

The spread of Mithraism and Christianity

The Maison Carrée at Nîmes, France. The most perfect example of a Roman temple extant. Reflecting possible Etruscan influence, it was built on a high base or podium with great steps leading to the entrance. It dates from the beginning of the Christian era.

period of prosperity for Italy which lasted for more than two centuries. Trade was now extended to all parts of the known world, even to Arabia, India, and China. Manufacturing increased somewhat, especially in the production of pottery, textiles, and articles of metal and glass. In spite of all this, the economic order was far from healthy. Prosperity was not evenly distributed but was confined primarily to the upper classes. Since the stigma attached to manual labor persisted as strongly as ever, production was bound to decline as the supply of slaves diminished. Perhaps worse was the fact that Italy had a decidedly unfavorable balance of trade. The meager industrial development was by no means sufficient to provide enough articles of export to meet the demand for luxuries imported from the provinces and from the outside world. As a consequence, Italy was gradually drained of its supply of precious metals. By the third century the Western Roman economy began to collapse.

Portrait Bust of a Roman Lady. The ostentatiousness of upper-class culture during the period of the Principate is well displayed by this sculpture, done around 90 A.D.

8. ROMAN LAW

There is general agreement that one of the most important legacies which the Romans left to succeeding cultures was their system of law. This was the result of a gradual evolution which may be considered to have begun with the publication of the Twelve Tables about 450 B.C. In the later centuries of the Republic the law of the Twelve Tables was modified and practically superseded by the growth of new precedents and principles. These emanated from different sources: from changes in custom, from the teachings of the Stoics, from the decisions of judges, but especially from the edicts of the *praetors*. The Roman praetors were magistrates who had authority to define and interpret the law in a particular suit and issue instructions to the jury for the decision of the case. The jury merely decided questions of fact; all issues of law were settled by the praetor, and generally his interpretations became precedents for the decision of similar cases in the future. Thus a system of judicial practice was built up in somewhat the same fashion as the English common law.

The early development of Roman law

It was under the Principate, however, that the Roman law attained its highest stage of development. This later progress was the result in part of the extension of the law over a wider field of jurisdiction, over the lives and properties of aliens in strange environments as well as over the citizens of Italy. But the major reason was the fact that Augustus and his successors gave to certain eminent jurists the right to deliver opinions on the legal issues of cases under trial in the courts. The most prominent of the men thus designated from time to time were Gaius, Ulpian, Papinian, and Paulus. Although most of them held high judicial office, they had gained their reputations primarily as lawyers and writers on legal subjects. The responses of these jurists came to embody a science and philosophy of law and were accepted as the basis of Roman jurisprudence. It was typical of the Roman respect for authority that the ideas of these men should have been adopted so readily even when they upset, as they occasionally did, time-honored beliefs.

Roman law under the Principate; the great jurists

The Roman law as it was developed under the influence of the jurists comprised three great branches or divisions: the civil law, the law of peoples, and the natural law. The civil law was the law of Rome and its citizens. As such it existed in both written and unwritten forms. It included the statutes of the Senate, the decrees of the princeps, the edicts of the praetors, and also certain ancient customs operating with the force of law. The law of peoples, was the law that was held to be common to all people regardless of nationality. It was the law which authorized the institutions of slavery and private ownership of property and defined the principles of purchase and sale, partnership, and contract. It was not superior to the civil law but supplemented it as especially applicable to the alien inhabitants of the empire.

The three divisions of Roman law

The most interesting and in many ways the most important branch of the Roman law was the natural law. This was not a product of judicial practice, but of philosophy. The Stoics had developed the idea of a rational order of nature which is the embodiment of justice and right. They had affirmed that all men are by nature equal, and that

The natural law

they are entitled to certain basic rights which governments have no authority to transgress. The father of the law of nature as a legal principle, however, was not one of the Hellenistic Stoics, but Cicero. "True law," he declared, "is right reason consonant with nature, diffused among all men, constant, eternal. To make enactments infringing this law, religion forbids, neither may it be repealed even in part, nor have we power through Senate or people to free ourselves from it." This law is prior to the state itself, and any ruler who defies it automatically becomes a tyrant. Most of the great jurists subscribed to conceptions of the law of nature very similar to those of the philosophers. Although the jurists did not regard this law as an automatic limitation upon the civil law, they thought of it nevertheless as a great ideal to which the statutes and decrees of men ought to conform. This development of the concept of abstract justice as a legal principle was one of the noblest achievements of the Roman civilization.

9. THE CRISIS OF THE THIRD CENTURY (180–284 A.D.)

The problems of imperial succession

With the death of Marcus Aurelius in 180 A.D. the period of beneficent imperial rule came to an end. One reason for the success of the "five good emperors" was that the first four designated particularly promising young men, rather than sons or close relatives, for the succession. But Marcus Aurelius broke this pattern with results that were to prove fateful. Although he was one of the most philosophic and thoughtful rulers who ever reigned, he was not wise enough to recognize that his son Commodus was a vicious incompetent. Made emperor by his father's wishes, Commodus indulged his taste for perversities, showed open contempt for the Senate, and ruled so brutally that a palace clique finally had him murdered by strangling in 192. Matters thereafter became worse. With the lack of an obvious successor to Commodus, the armies of the provinces raised their own candidates and civil war ensued. Although a provincial general, Septimius Severus (193–211), emerged victorious, it now became clear that provincial armies could interfere in imperial politics at will. Severus and some of his successors aggravated the problem by eliminating even the theoretical rights of the Senate and ruling frankly as military dictators. Once the role of brute force was openly revealed any aspiring general could try his luck at seizing power. Hence civil war became endemic. From 235 to 284 there were no less than twenty-six "barracks emperors," of whom only one managed to escape a violent death.

The half-century between 235 and 284 was certainly the worst for Rome since its rise to world power. In addition to political chaos, a number of other factors combined to bring the empire to the brink of ruin. One was that civil war had disastrous economic effects. Not only did constant warfare interfere with agriculture and trade, but the

Commodus. The self-deluded ruler encouraged artists to portray him as the equal of Hercules.

Arch of Septimius Severus. This monument to the feats of Septimius Severus was constructed about 200 A.D.

rivalry of aspirants to rule led them to drain the wealth of their territories in order to gain favor with their armies. Following the maxim of "enriching the soldiers and scorning the rest," they could only raise funds by debasing the coinage and by nearly confiscatory taxation of civilians. Landlords, small tenants, and manufacturers thus had little motive to produce at a time when production was most necessary. In human terms the poorest, as is usual in times of economic contraction, were hurt the worst. Often they were driven to the most wretched extremes of destitution. In the wake of war and hunger, disease then became rampant. Already in the reign of Marcus Aurelius a terrible plague had swept through the empire, decimating the army and the population at large. In the middle of the third century pestilence returned and struck at the population with its fearful scythe for fifteen years.

Consequences of civil war

The resulting strain on human resources came at a time when Rome could least afford it, for still another threat to the empire in the middle of the third century was the advance of Rome's external enemies. With Roman ranks thinned by disease and Roman armies fighting each other, Germans in the West and Persians in the East were able to break through the old Roman defense lines. In 251 the Goths defeated and slew the Emperor Decius, crossed the Danube, and marauded at will in the Balkans. A more humiliating disaster came in 260 when the Emperor Valerian was captured in battle by the Persians and made to kneel as a footstool for their ruler. When he died his body was stuffed

The Emperor Decius. The extreme naturalism and furrowed brow is typical of the portraits of this period.

The Emperor Philip the Arab. An artistic legacy of the Roman "age of anxiety."

and hung on exhibition. Clearly the days of Caesar and Augustus were very far off.

Understandably enough the culture of the third century was marked by pervasive anxiety. One can even see expressions of worry in the surviving statuary, as in the bust of the Emperor Philip (244–249) who appears almost to realize that he would soon be killed in battle. Suiting the spirit of the age, the Neoplatonic philosophy of otherworldlyism came to the fore. Neoplatonism (meaning "New Platonism") drew the spiritualist tendency of Plato's thought to extremes. The first of its basic teachings was emanationism: everything that exists proceeds from God in a continuing stream of emanations. The initial stage in the process is the emanation of the world-soul. From this come the divine Ideas or spiritual patterns, and then the souls of particular things. The final emanation is matter. But matter has no form or quality of its own; it is simply the privation of spirit, the residue which is left after the spiritual rays from God have burned themselves out. It follows that matter is to be despised as the symbol of evil and darkness. The second major doctrine was mysticism. The human soul was originally a part of God, but it has become separated from its divine source through its union with matter. The highest goal of life should be mystic reunion with the divine, which can be accomplished through contemplation and through emancipation of the soul from bondage to matter. Human beings should be ashamed of the fact that they possess a physical body and should seek to subjugate it in every way possible. Asceticism was therefore the third main teaching of this philosophy.

Plotinus

The real founder of Neoplatonism was Plotinus, who was born in Egypt about 204 A.D. In the later years of his life he taught in Rome and won many followers among the upper classes before he died in 270. His principal successors diluted the philosophy with more and more bizarre superstitions. In spite of its antirational viewpoint and its utter indifference to the state, Neoplatonism became so popular in Rome in the third and fourth centuries A.D. that it almost completely supplanted Stoicism. No fact could have expressed more eloquently the turn of Rome away from the realities of the here and now.

10. CAUSES FOR ROME'S DECLINE

Turning point in 284

As Rome was not built in a day, so it was not lost in one. As we will see in the next chapter, strong rule returned in 284. Thereafter the Roman Empire endured in the West for two hundred years more and in the East for a millennium. But the restored Roman state was extremely different from the old one—so much so that it is proper to end the story of characteristically Roman civilization here and review the reasons for Rome's decline.

More has been written on the fall of Rome than on the death of any other civilization. The theories offered to account for the decline have been many and varied. A popular recent one is that Rome fell from the effects of lead poisoning, but this cannot be accepted for many reasons, one of which is that most Roman pipes were not made of lead but of *terra cotta*. Moralists have found the explanation for Rome's fall in the descriptions of lechery and gluttony presented in the writings of such authors as Juvenal and Petronius. Such an approach, however, overlooks the facts that much of this evidence is patently overdrawn, and that nearly all of it comes from the period of the early Principate: in the later centuries, when the empire was more obviously collapsing, morality became more austere through the influence of ascetic religions. One of the simplest explanations is that Rome fell only because of the severity of German attacks. But barbarians had always stood ready to attack Rome throughout its long history: German pressures indeed mounted at certain times but German invasions would never have succeeded had they not come at moments when Rome was already weakened internally.

It is best then, to concentrate on Rome's most serious internal problems. Some of these were political. The most obvious political failing of the Roman constitution under the Principate was the lack of a clear law of succession. Especially when a ruler died suddenly there was no certainty about who was to follow him. In modern America the deaths of a Lincoln or Kennedy might shock the nation, but people at least knew what would happen next; in imperial Rome no one knew and civil war was generally the result. From 235 to 284 such warfare fed upon itself. Civil war was also nurtured by the lack of constitutional means for reform. If regimes became unpopular, as most did after 180, the only means to alter them was to overthrow them. But the resort to violence always bred more violence. In addition to those problems, imperial Rome's greatest political weakness may ultimately have been that it did not involve enough people in the work of government. The vast majority of the empire's inhabitants were subjects who did not participate in the government in any way. Hence they looked on the empire at best with indifference and often with hostility, especially when tax-collectors appeared. Loyalty to Rome was needed to keep the empire going, but when the tests came such loyalty was lacking.

Even without political problems the Roman Empire would probably have been fated to extinction for economic reasons. Rome's worst economic problems derived from its slave system and from manpower shortages. Roman civilization was based on cities, and Roman cities existed largely by virtue of an agricultural surplus produced by slaves. Slaves were worked so hard that they did not normally reproduce to fill their own ranks. Until the time of Trajan Roman victories in war and fresh conquests provided fresh supplies of slaves to keep the system going, but thereafter the economy began to run out of human fuel. Landlords could no longer be so profligate of human life, barracks slavery came to an end, and the countryside produced less of a surplus to feed the towns. The fact that no technological advance took up the slack may also be attributed to slavery. Later in Western history agricultural surpluses were produced by technological revolutions but Roman landlords were indifferent to technology because interest in it was thought to be demeaning. As long as there were slaves to do the work there was no interest in labor-saving devices, and attention to any sort of machinery was deemed a sign of slavishness. Landlords proved their nobility by their interest in "higher things," but while they were contemplating these heights their agricultural surpluses gradually became depleted.

Manpower shortages greatly aggravated Rome's economic problems. With the end of foreign conquests and the decline of slavery there was a pressing need for people to stay on the farm, but because of constant barbarian pressures there was also a steady need for men to serve in the army. The plagues of the second and third centuries sharply reduced the population just at the worst time. It has been estimated that between the reign of Marcus Aurelius and the restoration of strong rule in 284 the population of the Roman Empire was reduced by one third. (Demoralization seems also to have lowered the birthrate.) The result was that there were neither sufficient forces to work the land nor men to fight Rome's enemies. No wonder Rome began to lose battles as it had seldom lost them before.

Enormous dedication and exertion on the part of large numbers might just possibly have saved Rome, but few were willing to work hard for the public good. For this cultural explanations may be posited. Most simply stated the Roman Empire of the third century could not draw upon commonly shared civic ideals. By then the old republican and senatorial traditions had been rendered manifestly obsolete. Worse, provincials could hardly be expected to fight or work hard for Roman ideals of any sort, especially when the Roman state no longer stood for beneficent peace but only brought recurrent war and oppressive taxation. Regional differences, the lack of public education, and social stratification were further barriers to the development of any unifying public spirit. As the empire foundered new ideals indeed emerged, but they were religious, otherworldly ones. Ultimately, then, the decline of Rome was accompanied by disinterest, and the Roman world slowly came to an end not so much with a bang as with a whimper.

11. THE ROMAN HERITAGE

It is tempting to believe that we today have many similarities to the Romans: first of all, because Rome is nearer to us in time than any of the other civilizations of antiquity; and secondly, because Rome seems to bear such a close kinship to the modern temper. The resemblances between Roman history and the history of Great Britain or the United States in the nineteenth and twentieth centuries have often been noted. The Roman economic evolution progressed all the way from a simple agrarianism to a complex urban system with problems of unemployment, gross disparities of wealth, and financial crises. The Roman Empire, in common with the British, was founded upon conquest. It must not be forgotten, however, that the heritage of Rome was an ancient heritage and that consequently, the similarities between the Roman and modern civilizations are not so important as they seem. As we have noted already, the Romans disdained industrial activities, and they were not interested in science. Neither did they have any idea of the modern national state; the provinces were really colonies, not integral parts of a body politic. The Romans also never developed an adequate system of representative government. Finally, the Roman conception of religion was vastly different from our own. Their system of worship, like that of the Greeks, was external and mechanical, not inward or spiritual. What Christians consider the highest ideal of piety—an emotional attitude of love for the divine—the Romans regarded as gross superstition.

Comparison of Rome with the modern world

The Forum, the Civic Center of Ancient Rome. In addition to public squares, the Forum included triumphal arches, magnificent temples, and government buildings. In the foreground is the Temple of Saturn. Behind it is the Temple of Antoninus and Faustina. The three columns at the extreme right are what is left of the Temple of Castor and Pollux, and in the farthest background is the arch of Titus.

Nevertheless, the civilization of Rome exerted a great influence upon later cultures. The form, if not the spirit, of Roman architecture was preserved in the ecclesiastical architecture of the Middle Ages and survives to this day in the design of many of our government buildings. The sculpture of the Augustan Age also lives on in the equestrian statues, the memorial arches and columns, and in the portraits in stone of statesmen and generals that adorn our streets and parks. Although subjected to new interpretations, the law of the great jurists became an important part of the Code of Justinian and was thus handed down to the Middle Ages and modern times. American judges frequently cite maxims originally invented by Gaius or Ulpian. Further, the legal systems of nearly all continental European countries today incorporate much of the Roman law. This law was one of the grandest of the Romans' achievements and reflected their genius for governing a vast and diverse empire. It should not be forgotten either that Roman literary achievements furnished much of the inspiration for the revival of learning that spread over Europe in the twelfth century and reached its zenith in the Renaissance. Perhaps not so well known is the fact that the organization of the Catholic Church, to say nothing of part of its ritual, was adapted from the structure of the Roman state and the complex of the Roman religion. For example, the pope still bears the title of supreme pontiff (*pontifex maximus*), which was used to designate the authority of the emperor as head of the civic religion.

Most important of all Rome's contributions to the future was the transmission of Greek civilization to the European West. The development in Italy of a culture that was highly suffused by Greek ideals from the second century B.C. onwards was in itself an important counterweight to the earlier predominance of Greek-oriented civilization in the East. Then, following the path of Julius Caesar, this culture advanced still further West. Before the coming of Rome the culture of northwestern Europe (modern France, the Benelux countries, western and southern Germany, and England) was tribal. Rome brought cities and Greek ideas, above all conceptions of human freedom and individual autonomy that went along with the development of highly differentiated urban life. It is true that ideals of freedom were often ignored in practice—they did not temper Roman dependence on slavery and subjugation of women, or prevent Roman rule in conquered territories from being exploitative and sometimes oppressive. Nonetheless, Roman history is the real beginning of Western history as we now know it. Greek civilization brought to the East by Alexander was not enduring, but the same civilization brought West by the work of such men as Caesar, Cicero, and Augustus was the starting point for many of the subsequent accomplishments of western Europe. As we will see, the development was not continuous and there were many other ingredients to later European success, but the influence of Rome was no less profound.

SELECTED READINGS

• *Items so designated are available in paperback editions.*

POLITICAL HISTORY

• Adcock, F. E., *Roman Political Ideas and Practice,* Ann Arbor, Mich., 1964.

Bloch, Raymond, *The Origins of Rome,* New York, 1960.

Cary, M., and H. H. Scullard, *A History of Rome,* 3rd ed., New York, 1975. A basic college-level textbook.

Chambers, M., ed., *The Fall of Rome,* New York, 1970. A collection of readings on this perennially fascinating subject.

Cowell, F. R., *Cicero and the Roman Republic,* New York, 1948.

Gruen, E. S., *The Last Generation of the Roman Republic,* Berkeley, Calif., 1964.

Haywood, R. M., *The Myth of Rome's Fall,* New York, 1962.

Mommsen, Theodor, *The History of Rome,* Chicago, 1957. An abridged reissue of one of the greatest historical works of the nineteenth century. Emphasizes personalities, especially that of Julius Caesar.

Ogilvie, R. M., *Early Rome and the Etruscans,* Atlantic Highlands, N.J., 1976. Now the best specialized review of the earliest period.

• Scullard, H. H., *From the Gracchi to Nero,* New York, 1959. Good survey of events in this central period.

Sinnigen, W., and A. E. R. Boak, *A History of Rome to A.D. 565,* 6th ed., New York, 1977. A good alternative to Cary and Scullard as a basic textbook.

• Starr, C. G., *The Emergence of Rome,* Ithaca, N.Y., 1953. A brief elementary introduction.

• Syme, Ronald, *The Roman Revolution,* New York, 1939. A pathfinding work on the late Republic and early empire that stresses power politics and the role of factions rather than the clash of institutional principles. Also extremely well written.

• Taylor, Lily Ross, *Party Politics in the Age of Caesar,* Berkeley, Calif., 1949. Still the best introduction to society and politics in the late republican period.

Warmington, B. H., *Carthage,* Baltimore, 1965.

CULTURAL AND SOCIAL HISTORY

Africa, T., *Rome of the Caesars,* New York, 1965. An entertaining approach to the history of imperial Rome by means of short biographies.

Arnold, E. V., *Roman Stoicism,* New York, 1911.

• Badian, Ernst, *Roman Imperialism in the Late Republic,* Oxford, 1967. Very sophisticated analysis.

Bailey, Cyril, ed., *The Legacy of Rome,* New York, 1924. An older collection of readings on different aspects of the Roman legacy to later times.

Balston, J. P. V. D., *Life and Leisure in Ancient Rome,* New York, 1969.

• Brunt, P. A., *Social Conflicts in the Roman Republic,* London, 1971.

• Carcopino, Jerome, *Daily Life in Ancient Rome,* New Haven, Conn., 1960.

Dill, Samuel, *Roman Society from Nero to Marcus Aurelius,* New York, 1905.

Duff, J. W., *A Literary History of Rome in the Golden Age,* New York, 1964.

———, *A Literary History of Rome in the Silver Age,* New York, 1960.

Earl, Donald, *The Moral and Political Tradition of Rome,* Ithaca, N.Y., 1967.

Frank, Tenney, *Economic History of Rome,* Baltimore, 1927. Still valuable.

Grant, M., *Roman Literature,* New York, 1954.

Laistner, M. L. W., *The Greater Roman Historians,* Berkeley, Calif., 1947.

McMullen, R., *Enemies of the Roman Order,* Cambridge, Mass., 1966.

———, *Roman Social Relations, 50 B.C. to A.D. 284,* New Haven, Conn., 1974.

Rostovtzeff, M. I., *Social and Economic History of the Roman Empire,* 2nd ed., 2 vols., New York, 1957. By one of the greatest historians of the early twentieth century. Important both for its interpretations and the wealth of information it contains.

• Sandbach, F. H., *The Stoics,* London, 1975.

Scullard, H. H., *The Etruscan Cities and Rome,* Ithaca, N.Y., 1967.

• Starr, C. G., *Civilization and the Caesars,* Ithaca, N.Y., 1954. Surveys Roman intellectual developments in the four centuries after Cicero.

Toynbee, A. J., *Hannibal's Legacy,* 2 vols., London, 1965.

Westermann, W. L., *The Slave Systems of Greek and Roman Antiquity,* Philadelphia, 1955. The best overview of this basic subject.

• Wheeler, Mortimer, *The Art of Rome,* New York, 1964.

Yavetz, Z., *Plebs and Princeps,* London, 1969.

SOURCE MATERIALS

Translations of Roman authors are available in the appropriate volumes of the Loeb Classical Library, Harvard University Press.

See also:

• Lewis, Naphtali, and M. Reinhold, *Roman Civilization,* 2 vols., New York, 1955.

MacKendrick, P., *The Roman Mind at Work,* Princeton, N.J., 1958.

Chapter 11

CHRISTIANITY AND THE TRANSFORMATION OF THE ROMAN WORLD

Who will hereafter credit the fact . . . that Rome has to fight within her own borders not for glory but for bare life? . . . The poet Lucan describing the power of the city in a glowing passage says: "If Rome be weak, where shall we look for strength?" We may vary his words and say: "If Rome be lost, where shall we look for help?"

For mortals this life is a race: we run it on earth that we may receive our crown elsewhere. No man can walk secure amid serpents and scorpions.

—St. Jerome, *Letters*

The Roman Empire declined after 180 A.D. but it did not collapse. In 284 the vigorous soldier-emperor Diocletian began a reorganization of the empire which gave it a new lease on life. Thereafter, throughout the fourth century the Roman state continued to surround the Mediterranean. In the fifth century the western half of the empire did fall to invading Germans, but even then Roman institutions were not entirely destroyed, and in the sixth century the eastern half of the empire managed to reconquer a good part of the western Mediterranean shoreline. Only in the seventh century did it become fully clear that the Roman Empire could only hope to survive by turning away from the West and consolidating its strength in the East. When that happened ancient history clearly came to an end.

The protracted decline of the Roman Empire

Historians used to underestimate the longevity of Roman institutions and begin their discussions of medieval history in the third, fourth, or fifth century. Since historical periodization is always approximate and depends largely on what aspects of development a historian wishes to emphasize, this approach cannot be dismissed. Certainly the transition from ancient to medieval history was gradual and

The age of late antiquity (284–610)

many "medieval" ways were slowly emerging in the West as early as the third century. But it is now more customary to conceive of ancient history continuing after 284 and lasting until the Roman Empire lost control over the Mediterranean in the seventh century. The period from 284 to about 610, although transitional (as, of course, all ages are), has certain common themes of its own and is perhaps best described as neither Roman nor medieval but as the age of late antiquity.

The major cultural trend of late antique history was the spread and triumph of Christianity throughout the Roman world. At first Christianity was just one of several manifestations of the turn toward other-worldlyism, but in the fourth century it was adopted as the Roman state religion and thereafter became one of the greatest shaping forces in the development of the West. While Christianity was spreading, the Roman Empire was indubitably declining. Central to this decline was a contraction of the urban life on which the empire had been based. Once the empire began to experience severe pressures it was inevitable that contraction would be most pronounced in the European northwest because city civilization there was least deeply rooted and because the area was far away from the empire's major trade and communications lifelines on the Mediterranean. Contraction was also felt in parts of the West that were closer to the Mediterranean because western cities depended far more on declining agricultural production than eastern ones. The East relied more on trade in luxury goods and industry. Consequently the entire period saw a steady shift in the weight of civilization and imperial government from West to East. The most visible manifestations of this shift were the German successes of the fifth century. These surely helped open a new chapter in Western political history, but their immediate impact should not be exaggerated. Even with the influx of Germans, Roman institutions continued to decline gradually. Particularly in areas that were on or close to the Mediterranean, Roman city life persisted, albeit with steadily declining vigor, until the Mediterranean was no longer a Roman lake.

1. THE REORGANIZED EMPIRE

Before we examine the emergence and triumph of Christianity, it is best to survey the nature of the government and society in which the new religion became a dominant force. The fifty years of chaos that threatened to destroy Rome in the third century were ended by the energetic work of a remarkable soldier named Diocletian, who ruled as emperor from 284 to 305. Conscious of some of the more obvious problems that had undone his predecessors, Diocletian embarked on a number of fundamental political and economic reforms. Recognizing that the dominance of the army in the life of the state had hitherto been too great, he introduced measures to separate military from civilian administrative chains of command. Aware that new pressures, both external and internal, had made it nearly impossible for one man to govern the entire Roman Empire, he divided his realm in half, granting the western part to a trusted colleague, Maximian, who recognized Diocletian as the senior ruler. The two then chose lieutenants, called *caesars,* to govern large subsections of their territories. This system was also meant to provide for an orderly succession, for the caesars were supposed to inherit the major rule of either East or West and then appoint new caesars in their stead. In the economic sphere Diocletian stabilized the badly debased currency, introduced a new system of taxation, and issued legislation designed to keep agricultural workers and town-dwellers at their jobs so that the basic work necessary to support the empire would continue to be done.

Diocletian. His short hair is in the Roman military style.

Although Diocletian's program of reorganization was remarkably successful insofar as it restored an empire that had been on the verge of expiring, it also helped to transform the empire. Essentially Diocletian changed the empire by "orientalizing" it in three primary and lasting ways. Most literally, he began a geographical orientalization of the empire by shifting its administrative weight toward the East. Since he was a "Roman" emperor we would assume that he must have ruled from Rome, but in fact between 284 and 303 he was never there, ruling instead from Nicomedia, a city in modern-day Turkey. This he did in tacit recognition of the fact that the wealthier and more vital part of the empire was clearly in the East. Second, as befitting one who turned his back on Rome, Diocletian adopted the titles and ceremonies of an Oriental potentate. Probably he did this less because he had Eastern tastes than because he wished to avoid the fate of his predecessors who were insufficiently respected. Most likely he thought that if he were feared and worshiped he would stand a greater chance of dying in bed. Accordingly, Diocletian completely abandoned Augustus's policy of appearing to be a constitutional ruler and came forward as an undisguised autocrat. He took the title not of princeps, or first citizen, but of *dominus,* or lord, and he introduced Oriental ceremony into his court. He wore a diadem and a purple gown of silk interwoven with gold. Those who gained an audience had to prostrate themselves before him; a privileged few were allowed to kiss his robe.

Diocletian's easternizing policy

The third aspect of orientalization in Diocletian's policy was his growing reliance on an imperial bureaucracy. By separating civilian from military commands and legislating on a wide variety of economic and social matters, Diocletian created the need for many new officials. Not surprisingly, by the end of his reign subjects were complaining that "there were more tax-collectors than taxpayers." The officials did keep the empire going but the new bureaucracy was prone—as all are—to graft and corruption; worse, the growth of of-

The growth of imperial bureaucracy

272

*Christianity and the
Transformation of the Roman
World*

The Emperor Honorius. An example of the impassive portrait sculpture brought in by the age of Diocletian. Compare the lack of individuality of this bust to the portraits of Decius and Philip the Arab, above, pp. 261–62.

The reign of Constantine

ficialdom called for reservoirs of manpower and wealth at a time when the Roman Empire no longer had large supplies of either. Taken together, the various aspects of Diocletian's easternizing made him seem more like a pharaoh than a Roman ruler: it was almost as if the defeat of Antony and Cleopatra at Actium was now being avenged.

The new coercive regime of Diocletian left no room for the cultivation of individual spontaneity or freedom. The results can be seen most clearly in the building and art of the age. Diocletian himself preferred a colossal bombastic style of building that was meant to emphasize his own power. The baths he had constructed in Rome, when he finally arrived there in 303, were the largest yet known, encompassing about thirty acres. When he retired in 305 Diocletian built a palace for himself in what is now Split (Yugoslavia) that was laid out along a rectilinear grid like an army camp. A plan of this palace shows clearly how Diocletian favored regimentation in everything.

Also in the age of Diocletian, Roman portrait statuary, which had hitherto featured striking naturalism and individuality, became impersonal. Human faces became impassive and symmetrical rather than reflecting a free play of emotions. Porphyry, a particularly hard and dark stone that had to be imported from Egypt—itself a sign of easternization—often replaced marble for imperial busts. Porphyry groups of Diocletian, Maximian, and their two caesars show the new hardness and symmetry at their fullest, for the figures were made to look so similar that they are indistinguishable from each other.

In 305 Diocletian decided to abdicate to raise cabbages—an unprecedented achievement for a late-Roman ruler. At the same time he obliged his colleague Maximian to retire as well, and their two caesars moved peacefully up the ladders of succession. Such concord, however, could not last. Soon civil war broke out among Diocletian's successors and continued until Constantine, the son of one of the original caesars, emerged victorious. From 312 until 324 Constantine ruled only in the West, but from the latter year until his death in 337 he did

Diocletian's Palace in Split. An artistic reconstruction.

Left: *Porphyry Sculptures of Diocletian and His Colleagues in Rule*. Every effort is made to make the two senior rulers and their two junior colleagues look identical by means of stylization. Note also the emphasis on military strength. Right: *Colossal Head of Constantine*. In the head of Constantine the eyes are enlarged as if to emphasize the ruler's spiritual vision. The head is approximately ten times larger than life.

away with the sharing of powers and ruled over a reunited empire. Except for the fact that he favored Christianity, an epoch-making decision to be treated in the next section, Constantine otherwise continued to govern along the lines laid down by Diocletian. Bureaucracy proliferated and the state became so vigilant in keeping town-dwellers and agricultural laborers at their posts that society began to harden into a caste system. Although Constantine was a Christian, he never thought for a moment of acting with any Christlike humility: on the contrary, he made court ceremonials more elaborate and generally behaved as if he were a god. In keeping with this he built a new capital in 330 and named it Constantinople, after himself. Although he declared that he moved his government from Rome to Constantinople in order to demonstrate his abandonment of paganism, self-esteem was no doubt a major factor, and the shift was the most visible manifestation of the continued move of Roman civilization to the East. Situated on the border of Europe and Asia, Constantinople had commanding advantages as a center for eastern-oriented communications, trade, and defense. Surrounded on three sides by water and protected on land by walls, it was to prove nearly impregnable and would remain the center of "Roman" government for as long as the Roman Empire was to endure.

Constantine also made the succession hereditary. By so doing he

274

*Christianity and the
Transformation of the Roman
World*

Theodosius. Detail from a silver plate. The emperor is shown with an orb in his hand, symbolizing his worldly power, and a halo, symbolizing his supernatural strength.

brought Rome back to the principle of dynastic monarchy that it had thrown off about eight hundred years earlier. But Constantine, who treated the empire as if it were his private property, did not pass on united rule to one son. Instead he divided his realm among three of them. Not surprisingly his three sons started fighting each other upon their father's death, a conflict exacerbated by religious differences. The warfare and succeeding dynastic squabbles that continued on and off for most of the fourth century need not detain us here. Suffice it to say that they were not as serious as the civil wars of the third century, and that from time to time one or another contestant was able to reunite the empire for a period of years. The last to do so was Theodosius I (379–395), who butchered thousands of innocent citizens of Thessalonica in retribution for the death of one of his officers, but whose energies in preserving the empire by holding off Germanic barbarians still gave him some claim to his surname "the Great."

The period between Constantine and Theodosius saw the steady development of earlier tendencies. With Constantinople now the leading city of the empire, the center of commerce and administration was located clearly in the East. Regionalism too was becoming more pronounced: the Latin-speaking West was losing a sense of rapport and contact with the Greek-speaking East, and in both West and East local differences were becoming accentuated. In economic life the hallmark of the age was the growing gap between rich and poor. In the West large landowners were able to consolidate their holdings, and in the East some individuals became prosperous by rising through the bureaucracy and enriching themselves with graft, or by trading in luxury goods. But the taxation system initiated by Diocletian and maintained throughout the fourth century weighed down heavily on the poor, forcing them to carry the burden of supporting the bureaucracy, the army, and the lavish imperial court or courts. The poor, moreover, had no chance to escape their poverty, for legislation demanded that they and their heirs stay at their unrewarding and heavily taxed jobs. Since most people in the fourth century were poor, most people lived in desperate and unrelenting poverty against a backdrop of ostentatious wealth. The Roman Empire may have been restored in the years from 284 to 395, but it was nonetheless a fertile breeding-ground for a new religion of otherworldly salvation.

2. THE EMERGENCE AND TRIUMPH OF CHRISTIANITY

Christian beginnings of course go back several centuries before Constantine to the time of Jesus. Christianity was formed primarily by Jesus and St. Paul and gained converts steadily thereafter. But the new religion only became really widespread during the chaos of the third century and only triumphed in the Roman Empire during the demoralization of the fourth. At the time of its humble beginnings nobody could have known that Christianity would be decreed the sole religion of the Roman Empire by the year 380.

Jesus of Nazareth was born in Bethlehem, a small town of Judea, sometime near the beginning of the Christian era (but not exactly in the "year one"—we owe this mistake in our dating system to a sixth-century monk). While Jesus was growing up Judea was under Roman rule. The atmosphere of the country was charged with religious emotionalism and political discontent. Some of the people, notably the Pharisees, concentrated on preserving the Jewish law and looked forward to the coming of a political messiah who would rescue the country from Rome. Most extreme of those who sought hope in politics were the "Zealots," who wished to overthrow the Romans by means of armed force. Some groups, on the other hand, were not interested in politics at all. Typical of these were the Essenes, who hoped for spiritual deliverance through asceticism, repentance, and mystical union with God. The ministry of Jesus was clearly more allied to this pacific orientation.

Jesus of Nazareth; his milieu

When Jesus was about thirty years old, he was acclaimed by an ascetic evangelist, John the Baptist, as one "mightier than I, whose shoes I am not worthy to bear." Thenceforth for about three years his career, according to the New Testament accounts, was a continuous course of preaching and teaching and of healing the sick, "casting out devils," restoring sight to the blind, and raising the dead. He not only denounced shame, greed, and licentious living but set the example himself by a life of humility and self-denial. Though the conception he held of himself is somewhat obscure, he apparently believed that he had a mission to save humanity from error and sin. His preaching and other activities eventually aroused the antagonism of some of the chief priests and conservative rabbis. They disliked his caustic references to the legalism of the Pharisees, his contempt for form and ceremony, and his scorn for pomp and luxury. They feared also that his active leadership would cause trouble with the Romans. Accordingly, they brought him into the highest court in Jerusalem, where he was solemnly condemned for blasphemy and for setting himself up as "king of the Jews" and turned over to Pontius Pilate, the Roman governor, for execution of the sentence. After hours of agony he died on the cross between two thieves on the hill of Golgotha outside Jerusalem.

Jesus's career

The crucifixion of Jesus marked a great climax in Christian history. At first his death was viewed by his followers as the end of their hopes. Their despair soon vanished, however, for rumors began to spread that the Master was alive, and that he had been seen by certain of his faithful disciples. The remainder of his followers were quickly convinced that he had risen from the dead, and that he was truly a divine being. With their courage restored, they organized their little

Jesus Christ. An artist's conception from a sixth-century mosaic in Ravenna.

Christianity and the Transformation of the Roman World

A Carved Tablet, c. 400 A.D., Depicting Christ's Tomb and Ascension into Heaven

St. Paul. From a Ravenna mosaic.

band and began preaching and testifying in the name of their martyred leader. Thus one of the world's great religions was launched on a career that would ultimately convert an empire no less mighty than Rome.

There has never been perfect agreement among Christians as to the precise teachings of Jesus of Nazareth. The only dependable records are the four Gospels, but the earliest of these was not written until at least a generation after Jesus's death. According to the beliefs of his orthodox followers, the founder of Christianity revealed himself as the Christ, the divine Son of God, who was sent on this earth to suffer and die for the sins of humanity. They were convinced that after three days in the tomb, he had risen from the dead and ascended into heaven, whence he would come again to judge the world. The Gospels at least make it clear that he included the following among his basic teachings: (1) the fatherhood of God and the brotherhood of humanity; (2) the Golden Rule; (3) forgiveness and love of one's enemies; (4) repayment of evil with good; (5) self-denial; (6) condemnation of hypocrisy and greed; (7) opposition to ceremonialism as the essence of religion; (8) the imminent approach of the end of the world; and (9) the resurrection of the dead and the establishment of the kingdom of heaven. Recent research has tended to emphasize the last two of these points as being at the center of Jesus's mission.

Christianity was broadened and invested with a more elaborate theology by some of the successors of Jesus, above all the Apostle Paul, originally known as Saul of Tarsus (10?–67?A.D.). Although of Jewish nationality, Paul was not a native of Palestine but a Jew born in the city of Tarsus in southeastern Asia Minor. Originally a persecutor of Christians, he was later converted to Christianity, and devoted his limitless energy to propagating that faith throughout the Near East. It would be almost impossible to overestimate the significance of his work. Denying that Jesus was sent merely as the redeemer of the Jews, Paul proclaimed Christianity to be a universal religion. But this was not all. He gave major emphasis to the idea of Jesus as the Christ, as the anointed God-man whose death on the cross was an atonement for the sins of humanity. Not only did he reject the works of the Law (i.e., Jewish ritualism) as of primary importance in religion, but he declared them to be utterly worthless in procuring salvation. Human beings are sinners by nature, and can therefore be saved only by faith and by the grace of God "through the redemption that is in Christ Jesus." It follows, according to Paul, that human fate in the life to come is almost entirely dependent upon the will of God; for "Hath not the potter power over the clay, of the same lump to make one vessel unto honor, and another unto dishonor?" (Romans 9:21). God has mercy "on whom he will have mercy, and whom he will he hardeneth" (Romans 9:18).

Although it may be something of a simplification, it seems basically true to say that Jesus proclaimed the imminent coming of the kingdom of God, whereas Paul laid the basis for a religion of personal salvation through Christ and the ministry of the Church. Therefore, after the time of Paul the development of Christianity was marked by the development of ceremonies, or sacraments, to bring the believer closer to Christ, as well as the development of an organization of priests to administer those sacraments. In teaching that priests who administered sacraments were endowed with supernatural powers, Christianity gradually developed a distinction between clergy and laity that was much sharper than that which had existed in most earlier religions. This would become the basis of subsequent Western controversies and divisions between "Church" and "State." In the meantime, Christianity's emphasis on otherworldly salvation ministered by a worldly priestly organization helped it greatly to grow and ultimately to flourish.

Christianity grew steadily in the first two centuries after Christ but only really began to flourish in the third. To understand this we must recall that the third century in Roman history was an "age of anxiety." At a time of extreme political turbulence and economic hardship people understandably began to treat life on earth as an illusion and place their hopes in the beyond. The human body and the material world were more and more regarded as either evil or basically unreal. As the Neoplatonic philosopher and leading thinker of that age, Plotinus, wrote, "when I come to myself, I wonder how it is that I have a body . . . by what deterioration did this happen?" Plotinus devised a whole philosophical system to answer this question, but this system was far too abstruse to have much meaning for large numbers of people. Instead, as we have seen, several religions that emphasized the dominance in this world of spiritual forces and the absolute preeminence of otherworldly salvation gained hold as never before.

At first Christianity was just another of these religions; Mithraism, Gnosticism, and the cults of Isis and Serapis were others. It is natural to ask, therefore, why Christianity gained converts in the third century at the expense of its rivals. A number of answers may be posited. One of the simplest, but not therefore the least important, is that even though Christianity borrowed elements from older religions—above all Judaism and Gnosticism—it was new and therefore possessed of a sense of dynamism that was lacking among the other salvationist religions which had existed for centuries. (It is noteworthy in this regard that one of Christianity's most serious rivals in the period from 276 to about 400 was Manicheanism, which was even newer than itself.) Christianity's dynamism was also enhanced by its rigorous exclusiveness. Hitherto people took on religions as today we might take on insurance policies, piling one on another in order to feel more secure. The fact that Christianity strictly prohibited this, demanding that the Christian God be worshiped alone, made the new religion most ap-

A Medieval Christian Conception of the Torments of the Damned in Hell

An Early-Christian Woman. A wall-painting from the catacomb of Priscilla, Rome, third century A.D.

pealing at a time when people were searching desperately for absolutes. Similarly, Christianity alone among its rivals (with the later exception of Manicheanism) had an all-embracing theory to explain evil on earth, namely as the work of demons governed by the devil. When Christian missionaries sought converts they successfully emphasized the new faith's ability to combat these demons by reputed miracles.

Although Christianity's novelty, exclusiveness, and theory of evil help greatly to explain its success, probably the greatest attractions of the religion had to do with three other traits: its view of salvation, its social dimensions, and its organizational structure. Exorcism of demons might help to make life more tolerable on earth but ultimately people in the later Roman Empire were most concerned with other-worldly salvation. Rival religions also promised an afterlife, but Christianity's doctrine on this subject was the most far-reaching. Christian preachers who warned that nonbelievers would "liquefy in fierce fires" for eternity and that believers would enjoy eternal blessedness understandably made many converts in an age of fears. They made converts too among all classes because Christianity had from its origins been a religion of the humble—carpenters, fishermen, and tent-makers—which promised the exaltation of the lowly. As the religion grew it gained a few wealthy patrons but it continued to find its greatest strength among the lower and middle classes who comprised the greatest numbers in the Roman Empire. Moreover, while Christianity forbade women to become priests or discuss the faith, and, as we will see, took on many attitudes hostile to women, it at least accorded women some rights of participation in worship and equal hope with men for salvation. This fact gave it an advantage over Mithraism, which excluded women from its cult entirely. In addition to all these considerations, a final reason for Christianity's success lay in its organization. Unlike the rival mystery religions, it had by the third century developed an organized hierarchy of priests to direct the life of the faith. More than that, Christian congregations were tightly knit communities that provided services to their members—such as nursing, support of the unprotected, and burial—that went beyond strictly religious concerns. Those who became Christians found human contacts and a sense of mission while the rest of the world seemed to be collapsing about them.

Christianity was never as brutally persecuted by the Roman state as used to be thought. In fact the attitude of Rome was usually one of indifference: Christians were customarily tolerated unless certain magistrates decided to prosecute them for refusing to worship the official state gods. From time to time there were more concerted persecutions, but these were highly intermittent and never lasted long enough to do irreparable damage: on the contrary they served to give Christianity some helpful publicity. To this degree the blood of martyrs really was the seed of the Church, but only because the blood did not flow too freely. One last great persecution took place toward the end of the reign of Diocletian and was continued by one of his immediate successors, a particularly bitter enemy of Christianity named Galerius. But by then the religion was far too strong to be wiped out by persecution, a fact that Galerius finally recognized by issuing an edict of toleration right before his death in 311. Thereafter Christianity was to be supported by the Roman state rather than persecuted by it.

The adoption of Christianity by the Roman Empire was initiated by Constantine and completed by Theodosius. Constantine did not yet make Christianity the official religion of the empire, but he clearly favored it. Probably he did so both because he associated his own conversion to the faith (around the year 312) with a rise of his political for-

Jonah under the Gourd. A Christian marble statue done around the time of Constantine's conversion. Jonah resting after leaving the whale's belly was a symbol for the risen Christ.

Christ and the Apostles in the Heavenly Jerusalem. Noteworthy is how this fourth-century mosaic (heavily restored) portrays Roman dress and Roman buildings, showing how quickly after Constantine's conversion the Romans were able to conceive Jesus as one of their own.

tunes, and because he hoped that Christianity might bring a spiritual unity to an empire that had been badly demoralized and religiously divided. Some of his successors, who were brought up in the Christian religion, went much further to achieve this end by ordering the persecution of pagans more ruthlessly than some pagan emperors had formerly persecuted Christians. Christianity probably would have triumphed anyway merely with official support because aspiring functionaries were usually quick to accept the religion of their rulers. The masses too were easily converts to the faith once it was supported by the state because, even though the fourth century was politically more stable than the third, the reorganization of the empire weighed most heavily on the lower classes and made them as much concerned about otherworldly salvation as they had been in the century before. Substantial numbers, too, simply followed the lead of authority. Christians probably comprised no more than a fifth of the population of the Roman Empire at the time of the conversion of Constantine at the beginning of the fourth century; with state support they quickly became an overwhelming majority. When Theodosius the Great forbade the worship of all religions other than Christianity by an edict of 380, paganism, already disappearing, was soon wiped out in all but the most rural backlands of the Roman realms.

3. THE NEW CONTOURS OF CHRISTIANITY

Changes in the Christian religion

Once the new faith became dominant within the Roman Empire it underwent some major changes in forms of thought, organization, and conduct. These changes all bore relationships to earlier tendencies, but the triumph of the faith greatly accelerated certain trends and altered the course of others. The result was that in many basic respects the

Christianity of the late fourth century was a very different religion from the one persecuted by Diocletian and Galerius.

One consequence of Christianity's triumph was the flaring up of bitter doctrinal disputes. These brought great turmoil to the Church but resulted in the hammering out of dogma and discipline. Before the conversion of Constantine there had of course been disagreements among Christians about doctrinal matters, but as long as Christianity was a minority religion it managed to control its internal divisions in order to present a united front against hostile outsiders. Hardly had the new faith emerged victorious, however, than sharp splits developed within its own ranks. These were due partly to the fact that there had always been a tension between the intellectual and emotional tendencies within the religion which could now come more fully into the open, and partly to the fact that different regions of the empire tried to preserve a sense of their separate identities by preferring different theological formulas.

Controversy over doctrinal matters

The first of the bitter disputes was between the Arians and Athanasians over the nature of the Trinity. The Arians—not to be confused with Aryans (a racial term)—were followers of a priest named Arius and were the more intellectual group. Under the influence of Greek philosophy they rejected the idea that Christ could be equal with God. Instead they maintained that the Son was created by the Father and therefore was not co-eternal with Him or formed of the same substance. The followers of St. Athanasius, indifferent to human logic, held that even though Christ was the Son he was fully God: that Father, Son, and Holy Ghost were all absolutely equal and composed of an identical substance. After protracted struggles Athanasius's side won out and the Athanasian doctrine became the dogma of the Church, as it remains today.

Division between the Arians and Athanasians

The struggle between the Arians and Athanasians was followed by numerous other doctrinal quarrels which succeeded each other for the next few centuries. The issues at stake were generally too abstruse to warrant explaining here, but the results were momentous. One was that the the dogmas of the Catholic faith steadily began to become fixed. It should be emphasized that this was a slow development and that many basic tenets of Catholicism were only defined much later (for example, the theory of the Mass was not formally promulgated until 1215; the doctrine of the Immaculate Conception of the Virgin Mary until 1854; and that of the Bodily Assumption of the Virgin until 1950). Nonetheless the faith was beginning to take on a sharply defined form that was unprecedented in the history of earlier religions. Above all, this meant that any who differed from a certain formulation would be excluded from the community and often persecuted as a heretic. In the subsequent history of Christianity this concern for doctrinal uniformity was to result in both strengths and weaknesses for the Church.

Consequences of persisting doctrinal disputes

282

*Christianity and the
Transformation of the Roman
World*

Other results

*Imperial involvement in
religious conflicts*

*The evolution of Church
organization*

Two other results of the doctrinal quarrels were that they aggravated regional hostilities and provoked secular interference into the government of the Church. In the fourth century differences among Christians increased alienation between West and East and also aggravated hostilities between one region and another within the East. Although the Roman Empire was evolving toward regionalism for many different reasons, including economic and administrative ones, and although regionalism was partly a cause of religious differences, the sharper and more frequent religious quarrels became, the more they serve to intensify regional hostilities.

At the same time the Roman state was inevitably drawn into these religious conflicts. The same Constantine who favored Christianity as a unifying force was horrified by the prompt emergence of the Arian conflict and intervened in it by calling the Council of Nicea (325), which condemned Arius. It is noteworthy that this council—the first general council of the Church—was not only convened by a Roman emperor, but that Constantine served during its meetings as a presiding officer. Thereafter secular interference in Church matters continued, above all in the East. There were two major reasons for this: First, religious disputes were more prevalent in the East than the West and quarreling parties often appealed to the emperor for support. Second, the weight of imperial government was generally heavier in the East, and after 476 there were no Roman emperors in the West at all. When Eastern emperors were not appealed to by quarreling parties they interfered in religious disputes themselves, as Constantine had done before them, in order to preserve unity. The result was that in the East the emperor assumed great religious authority and control, but in the West the future of relations between State and Church was more open.

Even while emperors were interfering in religious matters, however, the Church's own internal organization was becoming more complex and articulated. We have seen that a clear distinction between clergy and laity was already a hallmark of the early Christian religion after the time of St. Paul. The next step was the development of a hierarchical organization within the ranks of the clergy. The superiority of bishops over priests was recognized before Christianity's triumph. Christian organization was centered in cities and one bishop in each important city became the authority to which all the clergy in the surrounding vicinity answered. This organization was sufficient for a minority religion but as the number of congregations multiplied, and as the influence of the Church increased due to the adoption of Christianity as the official religion of Rome, distinctions of rank among the bishops themselves began to appear. Those who had their headquarters in the larger cities came to be called metropolitans (today known in the West as archbishops), with authority over the clergy of an entire province. In the fourth century the still higher rank of patriarch was established to designate those bishops who ruled over the oldest and largest of Christian communities—such cities as Rome, Jerusalem, Constantinople, Antioch, and Alexandria, and their surrounding districts. Thus the Christian clergy by 400 A.D. had come to embrace a definite hierarchy of patriarchs, metropolitans, bishops, and priests.

The climax of all this development—still largely in the future—was the growth of the primacy of the bishop of Rome, or in other words the rise of the papacy. For several reasons the bishop of Rome enjoyed a preeminence over the other patriarchs of the Church. The city in which he ruled was venerated by the faithful as a scene of the missionary activities of the Apostles Peter and Paul. The tradition was widely accepted that Peter had founded the bishopric of Rome, and that therefore all of his successors were heirs of his authority and prestige. This tradition was supplemented by the theory that Peter had been commissioned by Christ as his vicar on earth and had been given the keys of the kingdom of heaven with power to punish people for their sins and even to absolve them from guilt (Matthew 16:18–19). This theory, known as the doctrine of the Petrine Succession, has been used by popes ever since as a basis for their claims to authority over the Church. The bishops of Rome had an advantage also in the fact that after the transfer of the imperial capital to Constantinople there was seldom any emperor with effective sovereignty in the West. Finally, in 445 the Emperor Valentinian III issued a decree commanding all western bishops to submit to the jurisdiction of the pope. It must not be supposed, however, that the Church was by any means yet under a monarchical form of government. The patriarchs in the East regarded the extreme assertions of papal claims as brazen effrontery, and even many bishops in the West continued to ignore them for some time. The clearest example of the papacy's early weakness is the fact that the popes did not even attend the first eight general councils of the Church (from 325 to 869) although later they were to convene and preside over all the others.

The rise of the papacy

The growth of ecclesiastical organization helped the Church to conquer the Roman world in the fourth century and to minister to the needs of the faithful thereafter. The existence of an episcopal administrative structure was particularly influential in the West as the Roman Empire decayed and finally collapsed in the fifth century. Since there was always a bishop in every city who was trained to some degree in the arts of administration, the Church in the West took over many of the functions of government and helped to preserve order amid the deepening chaos. But the new emphasis on administration also had its inevitably deleterious effects: with the Church developing its own rationalized administrative structure it inevitably became more worldly and distant in spirit from the simple faith of Jesus and the Apostles.

Effects of the rationalization of ecclesiastical administration

The clearest reaction to this trend was expressed in the spread of

The rise of monasticism

The extremes of monastic asceticism

The communal monasticism of St. Basil

monasticism. Today we are accustomed to thinking of monks as groups of priests who live communally in order to dedicate themselves primarily to lives of contemplation and prayer. In their origins, however, monks were not priests but laymen, who almost always lived alone and who sought extremes of self-torture rather than ordered lives of spirituality. Monasticism began to emerge in the third century as a response to the anxieties of that age, but it only became a dominant movement within Christianity in the fourth century. Two obvious reasons for this fact stand out. First of all, the choice of extreme hermitlike asceticism was a substitute for martyrdom. With the conversion of Constantine and the abandonment of persecution, most chances of winning a crown of glory in heaven by undergoing death for the faith were eliminated. But the desire to prove one's religious ardor by self-abasement and suffering was still present. Second, as the fourth century progressed the priesthood became more and more enmired in worldly concerns. Those who wished to avoid secular temptations fled to the deserts and woods to practice an asceticism that priests and bishops were forgetting. (Monks customarily became priests only later during the Middle Ages.) In this way even while Christianity was accommodating itself to practical needs, monasticism satisfied the inclinations of ascetic extremists who otherwise might have become Gnostics or Manicheans and who looked forward to lives of torture and deprivation that far outstripped those of Christ and the Apostles.

Monasticism first emerged in the East, where for about one hundred years after Constantine's conversion it spread like a mania. Hermit monks of Egypt and Syria vied with each other in their pursuit of the most inhuman and humiliating excesses. Some grazed in the fields after the manner of cows, others penned themselves into small cages, and others hung heavy weights around their necks. A monk named Cyriacus stood for hours on one leg like a crane until he could bear it no more. The most extravagant of these monastic ascetics was St. Simeon Stylites, who performed self-punishing exercises—such as touching his feet with his head 1,244 times in succession—on top of a high pillar for thirty-seven years, while crowds gathered below to worship "the worms that dropped from his body."

In time such ascetic hysteria subsided and it became recognized that monasticism would be more enduring if monks lived in a community and did not concentrate on self-torture. The most successful architect of communal monasticism in the East was St. Basil (330?–379), who started his monastic career as a hermit and ascetic extremist but came to prefer communal and more moderate forms of life. Basil expressed this preference in writings for monks that laid down the basic guidelines for eastern monasticism from then until the present time. Rather than encouraging extremes of self-torture, Basil encouraged monks to discipline themselves by useful labor. Although his teachings were

A Monastery of the Basilian Order on Mt. Athos. The asceticism of the Basilian monks caused them to build their monasteries in almost inaccessible places on lofty crags or on the steep sides of rugged mountains.

still extremely severe by modern standards, he prohibited monks from engaging in prolonged fasts or lacerating their flesh. In place of that he urged them to submit to obligations of poverty and humility, and to spend many hours of the day in silent religious meditation. With the triumph of St. Basil's ideas, eastern monasticism became more organized and subdued, but even so Basilian monks preferred to live as far away from the "world" as they could and never had the same civilizing influence on external society as did their brothers in western Europe.

Monasticism did not at first spread so quickly in the West as it did in the East because the West was not as attracted by severe asceticism. Most often whatever monasticism was introduced in the West was too ascetic to have any widespread appeal. This situation was only remedied in the sixth century when St. Benedict (480?–547?) drafted his famous Latin rule which ultimately became the guide for nearly all the monks in the West. Recent research has shown that Benedict copied much of his rule from an earlier Latin text, but he still produced a document that is notable for its brevity, flexibility, and moderation. The Benedictine rule imposed obligations similar to those laid down by St. Basil: poverty, obedience, labor, and religious devotion. Yet Benedict prescribed less austerity than Basil did: the monks were granted a sufficiency of simple food, clothing, and enough sleep; they were even allowed to drink a small amount of wine, although meat was only granted to the sick. The abbot's authority was absolute and the abbot was allowed to flog monks for disobedience, yet Benedict urged him

The rule of St. Benedict

286

*Christianity and the
Transformation of the Roman
World*

*The significance of
Benedictine monasticism:
(1) missionary activities
and attitude towards
manual labor*

to try "to be loved rather than feared," and ordained that the abbot take counsel before making decisions "because the Lord often reveals to a younger member what is best." For such reasons the Benedictine monastery became a center of deep religious enrichment rather than a school for punishment.

We will have occasion for continuing the story of Benedictine monasticism later on, but here we may point in advance to some of its greatest contributions to the development of Western civilization. One was that Benedictine monks were committed from an early date to missionary work: they were primarily responsible for the conversion of England and later most of Germany. Such activities not only helped to spread the faith but also served to create a sense of cultural unity for western Europe. Another positive contribution lay in the attitude of the Benedictines towards work. Whereas the highest goal for ancient philosophers and aristocrats was to have enough leisure time for unimpeded contemplation, St. Benedict wanted his monks always to keep busy, for he believed that "idleness is an enemy of the soul." Therefore he prescribed that they should be occupied at certain times in manual labor, a prescription that would have horrified most thinkers of earlier times. Accordingly, early Benedictines worked hard themselves and spread the idea of the dignity of labor to others. With Benedictine support acceptance of this idea would become one of the most distinctive traits of Western culture. We read of Benedictines who gladly milked cows, threshed, plowed, and hammered: in so doing they increased the prosperity of their own monasteries and provided good examples for others. Benedictine monasteries became particularly successful in farming and later in estate-managing. Thus they often helped to advance the level of the western European economy and sometimes even to provide wealth that could be drawn upon by emerging western European states.

The fact that Benedictine monasteries were often islands of culture when literacy and learning were all but forgotten in the secular world is better known. St. Benedict himself was no admirer of classical culture. Quite the contrary, he wanted his monks only to serve Christ—not literature or philosophy. But he did assume that monks would have to read well enough to say their prayers. That meant that there would have to be some teaching in the monasteries because it was seldom available outside, and because boys were often given over from birth to the monastic profession. Once there was teaching there would obviously be at least a few writing implements and books. This explains why Benedictines always maintained some literacy but not why some of them became devoted to perpetuating classical culture. The

A Monk Working in the Fields.
From an eleventh-century manuscript.

impetus behind the latter development was the work of a monastic thinker named Cassiodorus (477?–570?). Inspired by St. Augustine, whom we will treat in more detail later, Cassiodorus believed that some basic classical learning was necessary for the proper understanding of the Bible; this justified the study of the classics by monks. Furthermore, Cassiodorus recognized that copying manuscripts was in itself "manual labor" (literally work with the hands) and might be even more appropriate for monks than hard work in the fields. As Benedictines began to subscribe to these ideas, Benedictine monasteries became centers for learning and transcribing that were without rival for centuries. No work of classical Latin literature, including such "licentious" writings as the poems of Catullus and Ovid, would survive today had they not been copied and preserved during the early Middle Ages by Benedictine monks.

Love of women was of course, however, not a Benedictine preference. Returning to our original subject—the changes that took place in Christian institutions and attitudes during the fourth century—we may count a final fateful trend to have been the development of a negative attitude toward the role of women in human life. Compared to most other religions, Christianity was favorable to women. Female souls were regarded as being equal to male ones in the eyes of God, and human nature was deemed to be complete only in both sexes. St. Paul even went so far as to say that after baptism "there is neither male nor female" (Galatians 3:28), a spiritual equalitarianism which meant that women could be saved as fully as men. But Christians from earliest times shared the view of their contemporaries that in everyday life and in marriage women were to be strictly subject to men. Not only did early Christians believe, with all male supremacists of the ancient world, that women should be excluded from positions of leadership or decision-making, meaning that they should be "silent in Church" (I Corinthians 14:34–35), but they added to this the view that women were more "fleshly" than men and therefore should be subjected to men as the flesh is subjected to the spirit (Ephesians 5:21–33).

With the growth of the ascetic movement in the third and fourth centuries, the denigration of women as dangerously "fleshly" creatures became more and more pronounced. Since sexual abstinence lay at the heart of asceticism, the most perfect men were expected to shun women. Monks, of course, shunned women the most. This was a primary reason why they fled to deserts and forests. One eastern ascetic was struck by the need for virginity in the midst of his marriage ceremony, ran off to a hermit's cell and blocked the entrance; another monk who was forced to carry his aged mother across a stream swaddled her up as thoroughly as he could so that he would not catch any "fire" and no thoughts of other women attack him. With monks taking such an uncompromising attitude, the call for continence was extended to the priesthood. Originally priests could be married; it seems

(2) the preservation of classical culture; Cassiodorus

Christian attitudes toward women

The emergence of the doctrine of celibacy

288

*Christianity and the
Transformation of the Roman
World*

that even some of the Apostles were (I Corinthians 9:5). But in the course of the fourth century the doctrine spread that priests could not be married after ordination, and that if they had been married before then they were expected to live continently with their wives afterwards.

Once virginity was accepted as the highest standard, marriage was taken to be only second-best. St. Jerome expressed this view most earthily when he said that virginity was wheat, marriage barley, and fornication cow-dung: since people should not eat cow-dung he would permit them barley. The major purposes of marriage were to keep men from "burning" and to propagate the species. (St. Jerome went so far as to praise marriage above all because it brought more virgins into the world!) Thus Christianity reinforced the ancient view that woman's major earthly purpose was to serve as mother. Men and women were warned not to take pleasure even in marital intercourse but to indulge in it only for the purpose of procreation. Women were to be "saved in childbearing" (I Timothy 2:15). Since they could not become priests and only a very few could become nuns (female monasticism was regarded as being a very expensive luxury in the premodern world), almost all women were expected to become submissive wives and mothers. As wives they were not expected to have their own careers and were not meant to be educated or even literate. Hence, even though they had full hopes for salvation, they were treated as inferiors in the everyday affairs of the world, a treatment that would endure until modern times.

4. THE GERMANIC INVASIONS AND THE FALL OF THE ROMAN EMPIRE IN THE WEST

While Christianity was conquering the Roman Empire from within, another force, that of the Germanic barbarians, was threatening it from without. The Germans, who had already almost brought Rome to its knees in the third century, were held off from the time of Diocletian until shortly before the reign of Theodosius the Great. But thereafter they demolished Western Roman resistance and, by the end of the fifth century, succeeded in conquering all of the Roman West. Germanic kingdoms then became the new form of government in territories once ruled over by Caesar and Augustus.

It is customary to think, perhaps with the encouragement of grade-B movies, that the Germans who destroyed the Western Roman Empire were fierce and thoroughly uncouth savages. But that is a misunderstanding. The Germans were barbarians in the sense that they did not live in cities and were customarily illiterate, but they were not therefore savages. On the contrary, they often practiced settled agriculture—although they preferred hunting and grazing—and were adept at making iron tools and weapons as well as at other metal and clay crafts. Physically they looked enough like Romans so that they could intermarry without causing much comment, and their language belonged to the Indo-European group, and therefore was related to Latin and Greek. Prolonged interaction with the Romans had a decisive civilizing influence on the Germans before they started their final conquests. Germans and Romans who shared common borders along the Rhine and Danube had steady trading relations with each other. Even during times of war Romans were often allied with some German tribes while they fought others. By the fourth century German tribes often served as auxiliaries of depleted Roman armies and were sometimes allowed to settle on borderlands of the empire where Roman farmers had given up trying to cultivate the land. Many German tribes too had been converted to Christianity in the fourth century, although the Christianity they accepted was of the heretical Arian version. All these interactions made the Germans very familiar with Roman civilization and substantially favorable to it.

The Germans began their final push not to destroy Rome but to find more and better land. The first breakthrough occurred in 378 when one tribe, the Visigoths, who had recently settled on some Roman lands in the Danube region, revolted against mistreatment by Roman officials and then decisively defeated a punitive Roman army in the Battle of Adrianople. The Visigoths did not immediately follow up this victory because they were cleverly bought off and made allies of the empire by Theodosius the Great. But when Theodosius died in 395 he divided his realm between his two sons, neither of whom was as competent as he was, and both halves of the empire were weakened by political intrigues. The Visigoths under their leader Alaric took advantage of this situation to wander through Roman realms almost at will, looking for the best land and provisions. In 410 they sacked Rome itself—a great shock to some contemporaries—and in the following years marched into southern Gaul. Meanwhile, in December of 406, a group of allied German tribes led by the Vandals crossed the frozen Rhine and capitalized on Roman preoccupation with the Visigoths by streaming through Gaul into Spain. Later they were able to cross the straits into northwest Africa, then one of the richest agricultural regions of the empire. From Africa they took control of the central Mediterranean, even sacking Rome from the sea in 455. By 476 the entirely ineffectual Western Roman emperor, a mere boy derisively nicknamed Augustulus ("little Augustus"), was easily deposed by a leader of a mixed band of Germans who then assumed the title of king of Rome. Accordingly, 476 is conventionally given as the date for the end of the Western Roman Empire. But it must be remembered that a Roman emperor, who maintained some claims to authority in the West, continued to rule in Constantinople.

Two questions that historians of the German invasions customarily

The Visigoths and the Vandals

*Christianity and the
Transformation of the Roman
World*

*Reasons for the German
success*

ask are: How did the Germans manage to triumph so easily? Why was it that they were particularly successful in the West rather than the East? The ease of the German victories appears particularly striking when it is recognized that the German armies were remarkably small: the Goths who won at Adrianople numbered no more than 10,000 men, and the total number of the Vandal "hordes" (including women and children) was about 80,000—a population about the same as that of an average-sized American suburb. But the Roman armies themselves were depleted because of declining population and the need for manpower in other occupations, above all in the new bureaucracies. More than that, German armies often won by default (Adrianople was one of the few pitched battles in the history of their advance) because the Romans were no longer zealous about defending themselves. Germans were seldom regarded with horror—many German soldiers had even risen to positions of leadership within Roman ranks—and the coercive regime begun by Diocletian was not deemed to be worth fighting for.

*Why the Eastern Roman
Empire survived and the
Western collapsed*

The reasons why the Germans fared best in the West are complex—some having to do with personalities and mistakes of the moment, and others with geographical considerations. But the primary explanation why the Eastern Roman Empire survived while the Western did not is that the East was simply richer. By the fifth century most Western Roman cities had shrunk both in terms of population and space to a small fraction of their earlier size and were often little more than empty administrative shells or fortifications. The economy of the West was becoming more and more strictly agricultural, and agricultural produce served only to feed farm laborers and keep rich landlords in luxuries. In the East, on the other hand, cities like Constantinople, Antioch, and Alexandria were still teeming metropolises because of their trade and industry. Because the eastern state had greater reserves of wealth to tax, it was more vigorous. It could also afford to buy off the barbarians with tribute money, which it did with increasing regularity. So Constantinople was able to stay afloat while Rome floundered and then sank.

*Consequences of the
Germanic invasions*

The effects of the Germanic conquests in the West were not cataclysmic. The greatest difference between the Germans and the Romans had been that the former did not live in cities, but since the Western Roman cities were already in a state of decline, the invasions only served at most to accelerate the progress of urban decay. On the land Germans replaced Roman landlords without interrupting basic Roman agricultural patterns. Moreover, since the Germans never comprised very large numbers, they usually never took over more than a part of Roman lands. Germans also tried to avail themselves of Roman administrative apparatuses, but these tended to diminish gradually because of the diminishing of wealth and literacy. Thus the only major German innovation was to create separate tribal kingdoms in the West in place of a united empire.

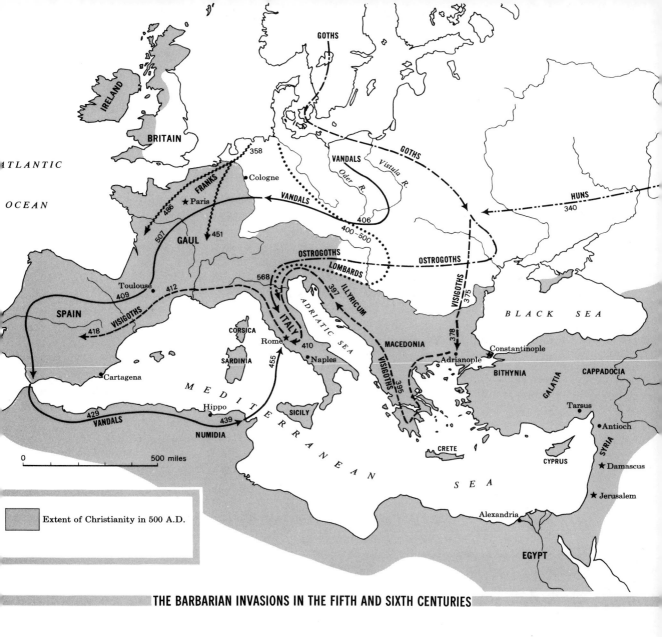

THE BARBARIAN INVASIONS IN THE FIFTH AND SIXTH CENTURIES

The map of western Europe around the year 500 reveals the following major political divisions. Germanic tribes of Anglo-Saxons, who had crossed the English Channel in the middle of the fifth century, were extending their rule on the island of Britain. In the northern part of Gaul, around Paris and east to the Rhine, the growing kingdom of the Franks was ruled over by a crafty warrior named Clovis. South of the Franks were the Visigoths, who ruled the southern half of Gaul and most of Spain. South of them were the Vandals, who ruled throughout previously Roman northwest Africa. In all of Italy the Ostrogoths, eastern relatives of the Visigoths, held sway under their impressive King Theodoric. Of these kingdoms the Frankish would

Germanic kingdoms in the year 500

292

*Christianity and the
Transformation of the Roman
World*

Theodoric the Ostrogoth. The barbarian ruler is shown here in Roman dress, with an ornate Roman hairstyle and a Roman symbol of victory in his hand. The inscription reads REX THEODERICVS PIVS PRINCIS, Latin for King Theodoric, pious prince.

be most promising for the future (for that reason it will be taken up in the next chapter) and the seemingly strongest for the present was that of the Ostrogoths.

Theodoric the Ostrogoth, who ruled in Italy from 493 to 526, was a great admirer of Roman civilization; this he tried to preserve as best he could. He fostered agriculture and commerce, repaired public buildings and roads, patronized learning, and maintained a policy of religious toleration. In short he gave Italy a more enlightened rule than it had known under most of its earlier emperors. But since Theodoric and his sparsely numbered Ostrogoths were Arian Christians while the local bishops and native population were Catholics, his rule, no matter how tolerant and benign, was viewed with some hostility. The "Roman" rulers in Constantinople were also hostile to Theodoric because he was an Arian and because they had not given up hopes of reconquering Italy themselves. All these circumstances led, as we will see, to the demise of Theodoric's Ostrogothic kingdom not long after his death. In fact, all of the continental barbarian kingdoms would not last long except for that of the Franks.

5. THE SHAPING OF WESTERN CHRISTIAN THOUGHT

The period of the decline and fall of the Roman Empire in the West was also the time when a few Western Christian thinkers formulated an approach to the world and to God that was to guide the thought of the West for roughly the next 800 years. This concurrence of political decline and theological advance is not surprising. With the empire falling and being replaced by barbarian kingdoms, it seemed clearer than ever to thinking Christians both that the classical inheritance had to be

Mosaic of Theodoric's Palace at Ravenna. At the right is a stylized conception of the ruler's palace, with the Latin inscription PALA TIVM; to the left of it is a row of saints, who would be indistinguishable were it not for the initials on their clothing: for early Christian artists, supernatural merits rather than individual personality traits were of the essence.

reexamined and that God had not intended the world to be anything more than a transistory testing place. The consequences of these assumptions accordingly became questions of most pressing concern. Between about 380 and 525 answers were worked out by Western Christian thinkers whose thought and accomplishments were intimately interrelated. The towering figure among them was St. Augustine, but some others had great influence as well.

Three contemporaries who all knew and influenced each other—St. Jerome (340?–420), St. Ambrose (340?–397), and St. Augustine (354–430)—count as three of the four greatest "fathers" of the Western, Latin Church. (The fourth, St. Gregory the Great, came later and will be discussed in the next chapter.) St. Jerome's greatest single contribution to the future was his translation of the Bible from Hebrew and Greek into Latin. His version, known as the "Vulgate" (or "common" version), became the standard Latin Bible used throughout the Middle Ages; with minor variations it continued to be used long afterwards by the Roman Catholic Church. Fortunately Jerome was one of the best writers of his day, and endowed his translation with vigorous, often colloquial prose and, occasionally, fine poetry. Since the Vulgate was the most widely read work in Latin for centuries, Jerome's writing had as much influence on Latin style and thought as the King James Bible has had on English literature. Jerome, who was the least original thinker of the great Latin fathers, also influenced the Western Christian future by his contentious but eloquent formulations of contemporary views. Among the most important of these were the beliefs that much of the Bible was to be understood allegorically rather than literally, that classical learning could only be valid for Christians if it was thoroughly subordinated to Christian aims, and that the most perfect Christians were those who were rigorously ascetic. In keeping with the last position Jerome was an avid supporter of monasticism. He also taught that women should not take baths so that they would not see their own bodies naked.

Unlike Jerome, who was primarily a scholar, St. Ambrose was most active in the concerns of the world as archbishop of Milan. In this office he was the most influential Church official in the West—more so even than the pope. Guided by his practical concerns, Ambrose wrote an ethical work, *On the Duties of Ministers,* which followed closely upon Cicero's *On Duties* in title and form, and also drew heavily on Cicero's Stoic ethics. But Ambrose differed from Cicero and most of traditional classical thought on two major points. One was that the beginning and end of human conduct should be the reverence and search for God rather than any self-concern or interest in social adjustment. The other—Ambrose's most original contribution—was that God helps some Christians but not others in this pursuit by the gift of grace, a point that was to be greatly refined and enlarged upon by St. Augustine. Ambrose put his concern for proper conduct into action by his most famous act, his confrontation with the Emperor Theodosius the Great for massacring innocent civilians.

294

*Christianity and the
Transformation of the Roman
World*

Ambrose argued that by violating divine commandments Theodosius had made himself subject to Church discipline. Remarkably the archbishop succeeded in forcing the sovereign emperor to do penance. This was the first time that a churchman had subordinated the Roman secular power in matters of morality. Consequently it symbolized the Church's claim to preeminence in this sphere, and particularly the *Western* Church's developing sense of autonomy and moral superiority that would subsequently make it so much more independent and influential on the secular world than the Eastern Church.

St. Ambrose's disciple, St. Augustine, was the greatest of all the Latin fathers; indeed he was one of the most powerful Christian intellects of all time. Augustine's influence on subsequent medieval thought was incalculable. Even after the Middle Ages his theology had a profound influence on the development of Protestantism; in the twentieth century many leading Christian thinkers have called themselves Neo-Augustinians. It may be that one reason why Augustine's Christianity was so searching was because he began his career by searching for it. Nominally a Christian from birth, he hesitated until he was thirty-three to be baptized but passed from one system of thought to another without being able to find intellectual or spiritual satisfaction in any. Only increasing doubts about all other alternatives, the appeals of St. Ambrose's teachings, and a mystical experience movingly described in his *Confessions* led Augustine to embrace the faith without reserve in 387. Thereafter he advanced rapidly in ecclesiastical positions, becoming bishop of the North African city of Hippo in 395. Although he led a most active life in this office, he still found time to write a large number of profound, complex, and powerful treatises in which he set forth his convictions concerning the most fundamental problems of Christian thought and action.

St. Augustine

St. Augustine's theology revolved around the principles of divine omnipotence and the profound sinfulness of humanity. Ever since humankind turned away from God in the Garden of Eden humans have remained basically sinful. One of Augustine's most vivid examples of this comes from a passage in the *Confessions,* where he tells how he and some other boys once were driven to steal pears from a neighbor's garden, not because they were hungry or because the pears were beautiful, but for the sake of the evil itself. God would be purely just if He condemned all human beings to hell, but since He is also merciful He has elected to save a few. Ultimately human will has nothing to do with this choice: although one has the power to choose between good and evil, one does not have the power to decide whether he will be saved. God alone, from eternity, predestined a portion of the human race to be saved, and left the remainder to be damned. In other words, God fixed for all time the number of human inhabitants of heaven. If any mere mortals were to respond that this seems unfair, the answer is first that strict "fairness" would confine all

Augustine's theology

to perdition, and second that the basis for God's choice is a mystery wrapped up in His omnipotence—far beyond the realm of human comprehension.

Even though it might seem to us that the practical consequences of this rigorous doctrine of predestination would be lethargy and fatalism, Augustine and subsequent medieval Christians did not see it that way at all. Humans themselves must do good, and if they are "chosen" they will do good; since no one knows who is chosen and who is not, all should try to do good in the hope that they are among the chosen. For Augustine the central guide to doing good was the doctrine of "charity," which meant leading a life devoted to loving God and loving one's neighbor for the sake of God. Seen from the opposite, humans should avoid "cupidity," or loving earthly things for their own sake. Put in other terms, Augustine taught that humans should behave on earth as if they were travelers or "pilgrims," keeping their eyes at all times on their heavenly home, and avoiding all materialistic concerns.

The doctrine of predestination

Augustine built an interpretation of history on this view in one of his major works, *On the City of God*. In this, he argued that the entire human race from the Creation until the Last Judgment was and will be composed of two warring societies, those who "live according to man" and love themselves, and those who "live according to God." The former belong to the "City of Earth," and will be damned, while the blessed few who compose the "City of God" will on Judgment Day put on the garment of immortality. This reading of history subsequently went unquestioned throughout the Middle Ages.

On the City of God

Although Augustine worked out for the first time major new aspects of Christian theology, he believed that he was only putting together truths that he found in the Bible. Indeed, he was convinced that the Bible alone contained all the wisdom worth knowing. But he also believed that much of the Bible was expressed very difficultly, and that it was therefore necessary to have a certain amount of education in order to understand it thoroughly. This conviction led him to a modified acceptance of classical learning. The ancient world had already worked out an educational system based on the "liberal arts," or those subjects necessary for the worldly success and intellectual growth of free men. Augustine argued that privileged Christians could learn the fundamentals of these subjects, but only in a limited way and for a completely different end—study of the Bible. Since nonreligious schools existed in his day which taught these subjects, he permitted a Christian elite to attend them; later, when such schools died out, their place was taken by schools in monasteries and cathedrals. Thus Augustine's teaching laid the groundwork for some continuity of educational practice as well as for the theory behind the preservation of some classical treatises. But we must qualify this by remarking that Augustine intended liberal education only for an elite;

Augustine's view of classical learning

296

*Christianity and the
Transformation of the Roman
World*

Boethius

all others were simply to be catechized, or drilled, in the faith. He also thought it far worse that anyone should become engaged in classical thought for its own sake than that someone might not know any classical thought at all. The true wisdom of mortals, he insisted, was piety.

Augustine had many followers, of whom the most interesting and influential was Boethius, a Roman aristocrat who lived from about 480 to 524. To say that Boethius was a follower of St. Augustine might until recently have been regarded as controversial because some of his works make no explicit mention of Christianity. Indeed, since Boethius was indisputably interested in ancient philosophy, wrote in a polished, almost Ciceronian style, and came from a noble Roman family, it has been customary to view him as the "last of the Romans." But in fact he meant the classics to serve Christian purposes, just as Augustine had prescribed, and his own teachings were basically Augustinian.

*Boethius's intellectual
contributions*

Because Boethius lived a century after Augustine he could see far more clearly that the ancient world was coming to an end. Therefore he made it his first goal to preserve as much of the best ancient learning as he could by a series of handbooks, translations, and commentaries. Accepting a contemporary division of the liberal arts into seven subjects—grammar, rhetoric, logic, arithmetic, geometry, astronomy, and music—he wrote handbooks on two: arithmetic and music. These summaries were meant to convey all the basic aspects of the subject matter that a Christian might need to know. Had Boethius lived longer he probably would have written similar treatments of the other liberal arts, but as it was he concentrated his efforts on the subject that was his favorite: logic. In order to preserve the best of classical logic, he translated from Greek into Latin some of Aristotle's logical treatises as well as an introductory work on logic by Porphyry (another ancient philosopher). He also wrote his own explanatory commentaries on these works in order to help beginners. Since Latin writers had never been interested in logic, even in the most flourishing periods of Roman culture, Boethius's translations and commentaries became a crucial link between the Greeks and the Middle Ages. Boethius helped endow the Latin language with a logical vocabulary, and when interest in logic was revived in the twelfth-century West it rested first on a Boethian basis.

Boethius. A twelfth-century artist's conception of Boethius as a musician, a reputation he earned because of his treatise on music.

Although Boethius was an exponent of Aristotle's logic, his worldview was not Aristotelian but Augustinian. This can be seen both in his several orthodox treatises on Christian theology and above all in his masterpiece, *The Consolation of Philosophy*. Boethius wrote the *Consolation* at the end of his life, after he had been condemned to death for treason by Theodoric the Ostrogoth, whom he had served as an official. (Historians are unsure about the justice of the charges.) In it Boethius asks the age-old question of what is human happiness, and concludes that it is not found in earthly rewards such as riches or fame but only in the "highest good," which is God. Human life, then, should be spent in pursuit of God. Since Boethius speaks in the *Consolation* as a philosopher rather than a theologian, he does not refer to Christian revelation or to the role of divine grace in salvation. But his basically Augustinian message is unmistakable. *The Consolation of Philosophy* became one of the most popular books of the Middle Ages because it was extremely well written, because it showed how classical expression and some classical ideas could be appropriated and subordinated into a clearly Christian framework, and most of all, because it seemed to offer a real meaning to life. In times when all earthly things really did seem crude or fleeting it was a genuine consolation to be told eloquently and "philosophically" that life has purpose if it is led for the sake of God.

The Consolation of
Philosophy

At a climactic moment in the *Consolation* Boethius retold in verse the myth of Orpheus in a way that might stand for the common position of the four writers we have just discussed; i.e., how Christian thinkers were willing to accept and maintain some continuity with the classical tradition. But Boethius also made new sense of the story. According to Boethius Orpheus's wife, Eurydice, symbolized hell; since Orpheus could not refrain from looking at her he was forced to die and was condemned to hell himself. In other words, Orpheus was too worldly and material; he should not have loved a woman but instead have sought God. True Christians, on the other hand, know that "happy is he who can look into the shining spring of good [i.e., the divine vision]; happy is he who can break the heavy chains of earth."

*The myth of Orpheus as
a symbol for Christian
truths*

6. EASTERN ROME AND THE WEST

Boethius's execution by Theodoric the Ostrogoth in 524 was in many ways an important historical turning point. For one, Boethius was both the last noteworthy philosopher and last writer of cultivated Latin prose the West was to have for many hundreds of years. Then too Boethius was a layman, and for hundreds of years afterwards almost all western European writers would be priests or monks. In the political sphere Boethius's execution was symptomatic as well because it was the harbinger of the collapse of the Ostrogothic kingdom in Italy. Whether or not he was justly condemned, Boethius's execution showed that the Arian Ostrogoths could not live in perfect harmony with Catholic Christians such as himself. Soon afterwards, therefore, the Ostrogoths were overthrown by the Eastern Roman Empire. That event in turn was to be a major factor in the ultimate divorce between East and West and the consequent final disintegration of the old Roman World.

*Boethius's execution a
turning point*

The conquest of the Ostrogoths was part of a larger plan for Roman revival conceived and directed by the Eastern Roman Emperor Justinian (527–565). Eastern Rome, with its capital at Constantinople, had faced many external pressures from barbarians and internal re-

The Emperor Justinian

Justinian and Theodora. Sixth-century mosaics from the church of San Vitale, Ravenna. The emperor and empress are conceived here to have supernatural, almost priestly powers: they are advancing toward the altar, bringing the communion dish and chalice respectively. Both rulers are set off from their

ligious dissensions since the time of Theodosius. But throughout the fifth century it had managed to weather these, and by the time of Justinian's accession had regained much of its strength. Although the Eastern Roman Empire—which then encompassed the modern-day territories of Greece, Turkey, most of the Middle East, and Egypt— was largely Greek- and Syriac-speaking, Justinian himself came from a westernmost province (modern-day Yugoslavia) and spoke Latin. Not surprisingly, therefore, he concentrated his interests on the West. He saw himself as the heir of imperial Rome, whose ancient power and western territory he was resolved to restore. Aided by his astute and determined wife, Theodora, who, unlike earlier imperial Roman consorts, played an influential role in his reign, Justinian took great strides toward this goal. But ultimately his policy of recovering the West proved unrealistic.

See color map facing page 384

One of Justinian's most impressive and lasting accomplishments was his codification of Roman law. This project was part of his attempt to emphasize continuities with earlier imperial Rome and the Latin legal tradition. It was also meant to enhance his own prestige and absolute power. Codification of the law was necessary because between the third and sixth centuries the volume of statutes had continued to grow, with the result that the vast body of enactments contained many contradictory or obsolete elements. Moreover, conditions had changed so radically that many of the old legal principles could no longer be applied, due to the establishment of an Oriental despotism and the adoption of Christianity as the offical religion.

Codification and revision of Roman law; the Corpus Juris Civilis

retinues by their haloes. The observant viewer is also meant to note the representation of the "three wise kings from the East" at the hem of Theodora's gown: just as the "three magi" once had supernatural knowledge of Christ, so now do their counterparts, Justinian and Theodora.

When Justinian came to the throne in 527, he immediately decided upon a revision and codification of the existing law to bring it into harmony with the new conditions and to establish it as an authoritative basis of his rule. To carry out the actual work he appointed a commission of lawyers under the supervision of his minister, Tribonian. Within two years the commission published the first result of its labors. This was the Code, a systematic revision of all of the statutory laws which had been issued from the reign of Hadrian to the reign of Justinian. The Code was later supplemented by the Novels, which contained the legislation of Justinian and his immediate successors. By 532 the commission had completed the Digest, representing a summary of all of the writings of the great jurists. The final product of the work of revision was the Institutes, a textbook of the legal principles which were reflected in both the Digest and the Code. The combination of all four of these results of the program of revision constitutes the *Corpus Juris Civilis,* or the body of the civil law.

Justinian's *Corpus* was a brilliant achievement in its own terms: the Digest alone has been justly called "the most remarkable and important lawbook that the world has ever seen." In addition, the *Corpus* had an extraordinarily great, often almost monopolistic influence, on subsequent legal and governmental history. Revived and restudied in western Europe from the eleventh century on, Justinian's *Corpus* became the basis of all the law and jurisprudence of European states, exclusive of England (which followed its own "common law"). The nineteenth-century Napoleonic Code, which provided the basis for

General significance of Justinian's Corpus

300

*Christianity and the
Transformation of the Roman
World*

the laws of modern European countries and also of Latin America, is fundamentally the Institutes of Justinian in modern dress.

Only a few of the more specific influences of Justinian's legal work can be alluded to here. One is that in its basic governmental theory it was a bastion of absolutism. Starting from the maxim that "what pleases the prince has the force of law," it granted untrammeled powers to the imperial sovereign and therefore was adopted with alacrity by later European monarchs and autocrats. But the *Corpus* also provided some theoretical support for constitutionalism because it maintained that the sovereign originally obtained his powers from the people rather than from God. Since government came from the people it could in theory be given back to them. Perhaps most important and influential was the *Corpus*'s view of the state as an abstract public and secular entity. In the Middle Ages rival views of the state as the private property of the ruler or as a supernatural creation meant to control sin often predominated. The modern conception of the state as a public entity concerned not with the future life but with secular, everyday affairs gained strength towards the end of the Middle Ages largely because of the revival of assumptions found in Justinian's legal compilations.

Justinian aimed to be a full Roman emperor in geographical practice as well as in legal theory. To this end he sent out armies to reconquer the West. At first they were quickly successful. In 533 Justinian's brilliant general Belisarius conquered the Vandal kingdom in northwest Africa, and in 536 Belisarius seemed to have won all Italy, where he was welcomed by the Catholic subjects of the Ostrogoths. But the first victories of the Italian campaign were illusory. After their initial defeats the Ostrogoths put up stubborn resistance and the war dragged on for decades until the exhausted Eastern Romans finally reduced the last Gothic outposts in 563. Shortly before he died Justinian became master of all Italy as well as northwest Africa and coastal parts of Spain that his troops had also managed to recapture. The Mediterranean was once more briefly a "Roman" lake. But the cost of the endeavor was soon going to call the very existence of the Eastern Roman Empire into question.

There were two major reasons why Justinian's western campaigns were ill-advised. One was that his realm really could not afford them. Belisarius seldom had enough troops to do his job properly: he began his Italian campaign with only 8,000 men. Later, when Justinian did grant his generals enough troops, it was only at the cost of oppressive taxation. But additional troops would probably have been insufficient to hold the new lines in the West because the empire had greater interests, as well as enemies, to the East. While the Eastern Roman Empire was exhausting itself in Italy the Persians were gathering strength. Justinian's successors had to pull away from the West in order to meet the threat of a revived Persia, but even so, by the beginning of the seventh century, it seemed as if the Persians would be able to march all the way to the waters that faced Constantinople. Only a heroic reorganization of the empire after 610 saved the day, but it was one that helped withdraw Eastern Rome from the West and helped the West begin to lead a life of its own.

In the meantime Justinian's wars had left most of Italy in a shambles. In the course of the protracted fighting much devastation had been wrought. Around Rome aqueducts were cut and the countryside returned to marshes that would not be drained until the time of Mussolini. In 568, only three years after Justinian's death, another Germanic tribe, the Lombards, invaded the country and took much of it away from the Eastern Romans. They met little resistance because the latter were now properly paying more attention to the East, but the Lombards were still too weak to conquer the whole Italian peninsula. Instead, Italy became divided between Lombard, Eastern Roman, and papal territories. At the same time Slavs took advantage of Eastern Roman weakness to sweep into the Balkans. Further west the Franks in Gaul were fighting among themselves, and it would be only a matter of time before northwest Africa and most of Spain would fall to Arabs. So the Roman unity had finally come to an end. The future in this decentralized world may have looked bleak, but new forces in the separate areas would soon be gathering strength.

The end of Roman unity

SELECTED READINGS

- *Items so designated are available in paperback editions.*
- Anderson, Hugh, *Jesus,* Englewood Cliffs, N.J., 1967. An excellent collection of readings displaying many different scholarly points of view.

   Bonner, Gerald, *St. Augustine of Hippo,* London, 1963. The best biography for beginners.
- Brown, Peter, *Augustine of Hippo,* Berkeley, Calif., 1967. An extremely subtle study.
- ———, *The World of Late Antiquity,* New York, 1971. A survey that approaches the period in its own terms rather than as a prelude to the Middle Ages.
- Bultmann, Rudolf, *Primitive Christianity in Its Contemporary Setting,* New York, 1956. Summarizes the ideas of one of our century's most important biblical scholars.
- Bury, J. B., *The Invasion of Europe by the Barbarians,* London, 1928. A straightforward narrative.
- Chadwick, Henry, *The Early Church,* Baltimore, 1967.
- Cochrane, C. N., *Christianity and Classical Culture,* Oxford, 1940. Difficult but fundamental.

   Daniélou, J., and H. I. Marrou, *The Christian Centuries; I: The First Six Hundred Years,* London, 1964. A survey from the Roman Catholic perspective.

   Dill, Samuel, *Roman Society in the Last Century of the Western Empire,* London, 1921.
- Dodds, E. R., *Pagan and Christian in an Age of Anxiety,* Cambridge, 1965. A

short but brilliant study of what pagans and Christians had in common as well as what made Christianity ultimately successful.

- Enslin, M. S., *The Prophet from Nazareth,* New York, 1961.

  Gibbon, Edward, *The Decline and Fall of the Roman Empire.* (Many editions, including several abridged ones.)

- Jones, A. H. M., *The Decline of the Ancient World,* New York, 1966. A survey that emphasizes economic and social factors.

- Katz, Solomon, *The Decline of Rome,* Ithaca, N.Y., 1955. The best brief introduction.

- Knowles, David, *Christian Monasticism,* New York, 1969.

- Latourette, K. S., *A History of Christianity,* New York, 1953.

- L'Orange, H. P., *Art Forms and Civic Life in the Late Roman Empire,* Princeton, N.J., 1965. An imaginative and stimulating essay displaying how developments in art reflected developments in political and social life.

- Lot, Ferdinand, *The End of the Ancient World,* New York, 1931. The best detailed treatment of the political history of the period.

- Lyon, Bryce, *The Origins of the Middle Ages,* New York, 1971.

  MacMullen, Ramsay, *Constantine,* New York, 1969. A good popular biography.

  Markus, R. A., *Christianity in the Roman World,* New York, 1974.

- Mattingly, Harold, *Christianity in the Roman Empire,* New York, 1967.

  Momigliano, A., *The Conflict between Paganism and Christianity,* New York, 1963.

  Pelikan, J., *The Christian Tradition; I: The Emergence of the Catholic Tradition,* Chicago, 1971. An advanced survey of doctrine.

- Rand, E. K., *Founders of the Middle Ages,* Cambridge, Mass., 1928. A thoroughly engaging account of the early Christian reactions to the classics.

- Riché, Pierre, *Education and Culture in the Barbarian West,* Columbia, S.C., 1976. A magisterial survey of learning in the Christian West from the fall of Rome to about 800.

- White, Lynn T., Jr., *The Transformation of the Roman World,* Berkeley, Calif., 1966. Stimulating essays.

  Workman, H. B., *The Evolution of the Monastic Ideal,* London, 1913. Highly interpretative but still one of the best works on the subject.

SOURCE MATERIALS

- St. Augustine, *City of God,* tr. H. Bettenson, Baltimore, 1972.
- ———, *Confessions,* tr. R. S. Pine-Coffin, Baltimore, 1961.
- ———, *The Enchiridion on Faith, Hope and Love,* ed. H. Paolucci, Chicago, 1961.
- ———, *On Christian Doctrine,* tr. D. W. Robertson, Jr., New York, 1958.
- Boethius, *The Consolation of Philosophy,* tr. R. Green, Indianapolis, 1962.
- Cassiodorus, *An Introduction to Divine and Human Readings,* tr. L. W. Jones, New York, 1946.
- *Early Christian Writings: The Apostolic Fathers,* tr. M. Staniforth, Baltimore, 1968.
- Eusebius, *The History of the Church,* tr. G. A. Williamson, Baltimore, 1965.

  Procopius, *The Secret History,* tr. G. A. Williamson, Baltimore, 1966.

Chapter 12

THE FAR EAST AND AFRICA IN TRANSITION (c. 200 B.C.-900 A.D.)

If brave and ambitious men have sincere understanding and awareness; if they fear and heed the warnings of disaster and use transcendent vision and profound judgment; if they . . . rid themselves of the blind notion that the mandate of Heaven can be pursued like a deer in chase and realize that the sacred vessel of rule must be given from on high; . . . then will fortune and blessing flow to their sons and grandsons, and the rewards of Heaven will be with them to the end of their days.

—Pan Piao, *History of the Former Han Dynasty*

D uring the period when the Greco-Roman classical civilization was being extended throughout the Mediterranean world under the auspices of the Roman Empire, a high stage of cultural development had been reached in both India and China. The disturbances that characterized the downfall of the Roman Empire in the West had their parallels in Asia too. However, the invasions and political upheavals in the Far East did not produce the same drastic changes as those in the West. The structure of society continued without serious modification in India and China, and the cultures of these two countries attained a brilliant peak while Europe was experiencing its Dark Ages. In India a combination of commercial prosperity—which encouraged the growth of large cities—and the religious enthusiasm accompanying the spread of Buddhism stimulated an outpouring of artistic talent. During this period Indian influence extended far beyond the borders of the country. Buddhism was planted in Central Asia and from there carried to China, Korea, and Japan. Indian colonization led to the introduction of both Buddhism and Hinduism, together with their art and literature, in Southeast Asia and the Malay Archipelago (which is still called Indonesia). China, while importing a major religion from India, showed much greater success in achieving political unification and an effective administrative system. So great was the prestige of imperial China that its culture was studied and eagerly assimilated by the Japanese in the sixth and succeeding centuries A.D. At the same time the West received some impact from the

Contrasts of East and West

civilization of Asia by way of the Hellenistic and imperial Roman commercial centers and, later, through the initiative of the Arabs. In sub-Saharan Africa civilization developed slowly. Geographic isolation limited cultural and commercial exchange to a far greater degree than it did in the case of Japan. Contact with the Romans was negligible and Arab incursions south of the Sahara were intermittent.

1. THE FLOWERING OF HINDU CIVILIZATION

Conflict in post-Maurya India

The Maurya Dynasty, under the energetic and devout King Asoka, had projected a common rule over the greater part of India. Upon the overthrow of this dynasty early in the second century B.C., the empire quickly fell apart, leaving India in a condition of political discord. For the next several hundred years the most powerful kingdoms were centered not in the Indo-Gangetic plain but in the Deccan, where a succession of dynasties contended with one another, and some of them emerged as major states with extensive territories and resources. It is clear that by this time the arts of civilization were well advanced in southern India, even though the most distinctive historic influences—Vedic literature and philosophy, the traditional religious and social concepts of Hinduism, and the creative force of Buddhism—had originated in the north. Moreover, the invasions which began to trouble northern India did not penetrate into the Deccan. The states of the Deccan carried on commercial intercourse with neighboring and even distant areas but were not seriously threatened with hostile assaults from foreign powers. On the contrary, their merchants and missionaries were ensuring the cultural ascendancy of India over Southeast Asia.

The Gupta Dynasty

After a period of domination by nomadic tribes from Turkestan, the political initiative in India was recovered by a native house which established a highly effective rule and was even more remarkable for its advancement of culture. The Gupta Dynasty, as it was called, governed most of northern India during the fourth and fifth centuries A.D. The dynasty's founder, Chandragupta I, was probably not descended from the Chandragupta who had instituted the Maurya Dynasty after the death of Alexander the Great, but the Guptas ruled from the same capital—Pataliputra (Patna) on the Ganges—and also revived some of the principles of the renowned King Asoka. The climax of the Gupta period came in the reign of Vikramaditya ("Sun of Power"), 375–413 A.D., which inaugurated a golden age not unworthy of comparison with Athens' Golden Age in the days of Pericles. Valuable information on conditions in northern India at this time has been preserved in the brief account written by a Chinese pilgrim, Fa Hsien, who spent six years in the realm of Vikramaditya. Buddhism had already spread into China, and the monk Fa Hsien undertook his hazardous journey to acquire sacred texts and firsthand knowledge of the religion in the land of its birth. His comments, however, were not restricted to religious matters, and because he was an intelligent and civilized foreigner, his observations may be taken as objective and generally reliable. The travels of Fa Hsien in themselves represent no mean undertaking. He made his way on foot across Sinkiang and the mountain passes, taking six years to reach India (399–405 A.D.). Here he taught himself the Sanskrit language, procured texts, drawings, and relics at the Gupta capital, and then returned to his native land by sea, spending two years in Ceylon en route and also visiting Java on the voyage. Altogether, during the fiteen years of his pilgrimage he traversed a distance of some 8,000 miles.

According to Fa Hsien's testimony, Buddhism was flourishing in India, especially in the Gupta empire, but all the Hindu cults were tolerated and the rivalry among the different religions was not embittered by persecution. Evidently the impact of Buddhism and the traditions of Asoka had stimulated the growth of humane sentiments, given practical expression in public hospitals, rest houses, and other charitable institutions receiving state support. Fa Hsien asserted that the Indians scrupulously refrained from the use of liquor and were vegetarians to such an extent that they slaughtered no living creatures—undoubtedly a pious exaggeration. Apparently, also, the caste system had not become utterly rigid, probably because Buddhism was still vigorous and also because segregation was impracticable in the cosmopolitan society of the thriving commercial centers. Fa Hsien, who had no reason to bestow unmerited praise (he does not even mention the name of the great king Vikramaditya), described the government as just and beneficent. The roads, he indicated, were well maintained, brigandage was rare, taxes were relatively light, and capital punishment was unknown. He testified to a generally high level of prosperity, social contentment, and intellectual vitality at a time when the nations of western Europe were sinking into a state of semibarbarism.

Another invasion of India destroyed the Gupta power and brought a period of confusion lasting for more than a century. Almost simultaneously with the formal demise of the Roman Empire in the West, a group of nomads called "White Huns" defeated the Gupta forces and made themselves masters of northern India (480 A.D.). By the early sixth century the White Huns had staked out an empire extending from Bengal in the east into Afghanistan and Central Asia. However, it was much more barbaric than its predecessors, and disrupted the splendid administrative system of the Guptas. The Huns in India were gradually absorbed by the native population, but on the northwestern borders a promising artistic movement was blighted before the Hunnish power disintegrated in accordance with the usual cycle of hastily constructed nomadic states. After the Hunnish menace receded, an able government was re-established by one of the most famous rulers in Indian history, King Harsha (606–648 A.D.).

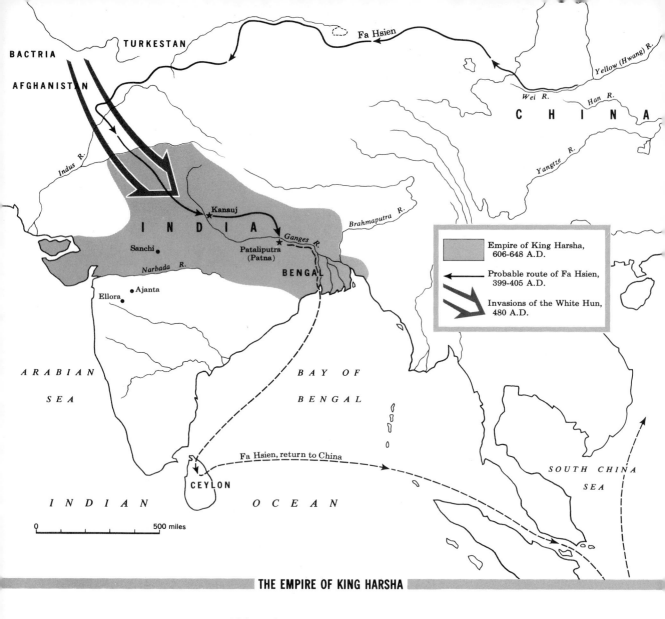

Empire of King Harsha, 606–648 A.D.

Probable route of Fa Hsien, 399–405 A.D.

Invasions of the White Hun, 480 A.D.

THE EMPIRE OF KING HARSHA

The reign of King Harsha (606–648 A.D.)

Although Harsha's state was not literally a continuation of the Gupta, it was so similar in important features that the term "Gupta" is often used to designate the civilization of northern India from the fourth to the seventh century, a period of cultural maturity despite the devastating interlude of the Hunnish invasion. King Harsha was a mighty conqueror who, with a huge army efficiently organized in divisions of infantry, cavalry, and elephants, reunited most of northern India. He was also a capable administrator, an intelligent and prudent statesman, and a generous patron of art, literature, and religion. His capital, Kanauj, extending four miles along the river in the central Ganges valley, was a splendid city, adorned with hundreds of temples and imposing public buildings, and enlivened with festive pageantry. As in the reign of Vikramaditya, the account of a Chinese Buddhist pilgrim throws revealing light upon Harsha's administration.

According to the narrative of this pilgrim (Hsün-tsang or Yuan Chwang) and other contemporary records, Harsha's administration was in the Gupta tradition but slightly less gentle. The state revenue was derived chiefly from taxes on the royal domains, which amounted to one-sixth of the produce of the villages and could hardly be regarded as oppressive. Harsha allotted only one-fourth of his income to administrative expenses, devoting the remainder to the rewarding of public servants, to charity, and to the promotion of education, religion, and the arts. In contrast to the mild punishments employed by the earlier Gupta regime, King Harsha inflicted such severe penalties as mutilation and death through starvation. Nevertheless, crimes of violence seem to have become more numerous. Religious toleration was still the official policy. Although Harsha is supposed to have been converted to the *Mahayana* school of Buddhism, he continued to worship the Sun and Shiva, and no attempt was made to enforce a religious orthodoxy. Despite this policy, the Brahmans were beginning to recover their ascendancy, and it was only a question of time before Buddhism, with its universalist and caste-dissolving tendencies, would be crowded out or absorbed by the cults so deeply rooted in Indian local tradition, literature, and social institutions. During the upheaval which followed the death of Harsha, this trend became more pronounced.

During the first seven or eight centuries of the Christian era, in spite of invasions and disunity, political vigor and artistic and intellectual creativity in India reached their height. This period, in which Hindu civilization attained its full maturity, ranks as a major era in the history of the world's cultures. What the Periclean Age and the Augustan Age were for the classical civilizations of the West the reigns of Vikramaditya and Harsha were for India and, to a considerable extent, for other portions of Southern Asia. Undoubtedly the development of industry and commerce helps explain the generally prosperous state of Indian society and the cultural advances. At this time, and later also, India was the center of an intercontinental market, and her merchants took the initiative in navigation on the high seas. During the first two centuries A.D. there was extensive intercourse between India and the Near East, especially with the city of Alexandria. Many products were also being exported from India to the Roman West, including jewels, ivory, tortoise shells, pepper, cinnamon and other spices, fine muslin cloth, and silks of both Indian and Chinese manufacture. In exchange the Indians imported linens, glass, copper, wines, and other items, but the trade balance was so decidedly in India's favor that the Roman emperors became alarmed at the drainage of gold to the East and tried to curtail the use of silk for wearing apparel. Some of this trade was

overland, but Indian merchants had from early days sailed across the
Arabian Sea and up the Red Sea to Egypt. Not until the first century
A.D. did Western traders discover the monsoon winds which enabled
them to sail east to the Indian coast during the summer and then return
when the wind direction changed in October. Traffic between the
Near Eastern ports and southern India was probably even greater than
with northern India. Pearls and beryls from the Deccan were especially prized, and Roman coins, testifying to a once flourishing trade,
have been discovered along both the southwestern and southeastern
coasts of the Indian peninsula. Apparently no obstacles were placed
by the Indian rulers in the way of foreign intercourse or even against
settlement by foreign traders, some of whom took up permanent residence in India. Southern India acquired small colonies of Romans,
Jews, Nestorian Christians from Syria and Persia (a Syriac-speaking
Christian church still exists in south-western India), and Arabs.

Influence upon the West

Through commercial contacts India probably exerted more influence upon the West than has been generally recognized, although
much of it came somewhat later and with the Arabs as intermediaries.
The Indian numerals ("Arabic"), which were not adopted by Europeans until the late Middle Ages, were perhaps known in Alexandria
as early as the second century A.D. In the eighth and ninth centuries
important scientific and medical treatises were translated from Sanskrit into Arabic. In addition, it is quite possible that familiarity with
Indian philosophy and religion contributed a stimulus to the growth
of Christian monasticism. The earliest Christian hermit-ascetics
appeared in Eygpt, where there was considerable knowledge of Hinduism and Buddhism, both of which religions stressed the concepts
of renunciation and mystic exaltation.

*Buddhist patronage of
education*

The manifold intellectual activity of this period of Indian history
reflected the interests of a cosmopolitan society, the patronage of
wealthy rulers, and—most strongly of all—the incentives of religious
faith. High levels of scholarship were maintained both by the Brahmans and by Buddhist monks, and large libraries came into being.
Particularly noteworthy were the educational foundations, for which
the chief credit should be given to the Buddhists. The role of the
Buddhist monks in education was comparable to that of the Christian
monks of the West during the early Middle Ages, but the scope of
their studies was broader because the general level of knowledge was
far higher in India than in the West at this time. Some Buddhist monasteries were internationally famous centers of learning, unmatched in
Europe until the rise of such universities as Paris, Montpellier, and
Oxford in the late Middle Ages. One of the greatest Buddhist universities, at Nalanda in the Ganges valley (in modern Bihar), was
functioning as early as the fourth or fifth century A.D. Endowed by
the Gupta rulers with a substantial income, it maintained residence
halls for students—with free tuition, board, lodging, and medical care

Ruins at Nalanda. The remains of the ancient university town, early seat of Buddhist learning.

for poor boys who were able to pass the entrance examinations—and had a library that occupied three buildings. Pilgrims visiting the university in the seventh century reported that 5,000 students were in attendance, including some from Tibet, China, and Korea. Although Nalanda was a Buddhist foundation and provided instruction in eighteen different schools of Buddhism, its faculty also offered courses in Hindu philosophy, grammar, medicine, mathematics, and in both Vedic and contemporary literature.

While the literary output was prolific and uninhibited, it betrayed a veneration for the past in that Sanskrit—the ancient language of the Epic Age—became the universally accepted literary vehicle, in the Deccan as well as in Hindustan. Even the Buddhists felt constrained to translate their sacred texts from *Pali* (the dialect of King Asoka's day) into Sanskrit, and it was the Sanskrit versions which were carried by missionaries into Central Asia, China, Korea, and ultimately Japan. Literature of the Gupta Age, in both prose and poetry, ranged from scientific treatises and biographies to tales for popular entertainment. The latter included long romantic narratives suggestive of—and perhaps the prototype of—the *Arabian Nights;* and also "Beast Fables" comparable to those attributed to Aesop. The most impressive literary medium was the drama, which, as in Europe somewhat later, evolved out of a popular type of religious instruction and entertainment. The Sanskrit drama, in its perfected form, combined song, dance, and gesture with narrative and dialogue, and thus resembled the Western opera or cantata more than the typical stage play. The plots, often diffuse, were usually concerned with romantic love, drew heavily upon legendary themes from the epics, and resorted to miracles when-

Literature: romantic narratives, fables, and drama

ever necessary to resolve a difficulty in the story. Although they employed pathos, the dramas were never tragedies, always ending happily. They also utilized the peculiarly artificial device of having the principal characters speak in classical Sanskrit while women and lesser figures used the less elegant dialect of ordinary conversation. Although the Sanskrit drama never provided the suspense or realism characteristic of the modern Western theater, it did attain undeniable beauty, both in descriptions of nature and in lyrical passages expressing human emotions of tenderness and anguish.

The most superb expression of the Indian creative faculties during these centuries was in art, especially architecture and sculpture, although some excellent paintings were also produced. By the Gupta era, architecture was nearing a point of perfection, as evidenced by imposing stone structures in all sections of India. As in so many other fields, the Buddhists pioneered in the development of artistic forms. The evolution of the Buddhist monasteries and temples set the pattern for practically the whole of Hindu architecture (and sculpture also). During the early centuries when *Hinayana* Buddhism was dominant, neither temples nor images of Gautama were made. Hence the first typical Buddhist monument was the *stupa,* a simple burial mound in the shape of a dome or hemisphere crowned with an umbrella—the Indian symbol of sovereignty. Inside the brick- or rock-faced mound was buried a sacred relic, usually some object associated with Gautama or with a revered Buddhist saint. The most famous *stupa* is the large one at Sanchi in the very center of India, still in an excellent state of preservation, although it was begun in Asoka's reign and substantially completed during the first century B.C. More impressive than the stone-faced mound (which has a diameter at the base of 120 feet) are the four carved gateways surrounding the *stupa.* These massive fences of stone are supported by pillars 35 feet high and, in spite of their huge proportions, are adorned with intricate carvings, both pictorial and symbolic, with a profusion of delicately formed human and animal figures. After the *stupa,* the next step in the evolution of religious architecture was the assembly hall, where monks and lay disciples gathered to honor the memory of Gautama, the "Master of the Law." These halls were commonly tunneled out of solid rock in a mountain or the side of a cliff. Their general plan was similar to that of the Roman basilica and early Christian church in that it emphasized a central passageway or nave separated from aisles on either side by round columns. Paralleling the evolution of the temple was the development of the Buddhist monastery. Like the assembly hall or temple, the monastery was often carved out of a single mass of rock, with successive stories of cells or cubicles so arranged that the structure as a whole appeared to be a terraced pyramid. Devotees of the Hindu cults soon began to construct temples in imitation of the Buddhist and eventually even more elaborate.

Buddhist Missionary. A sixth-century carving supposed to represent the first Indian Buddhist missionary to China. Buddhism had probably been introduced into China as early as the first century A.D.

Great Stupa at Sanchi. Begun by Asoka and completed under the Andhra Dynasty (72–25 B.C.), it was originally a burial mound containing relics of the Buddha. The fully developed stupa, designed with mathematical precision, became an architectural symbol of the cosmos. The tiered mast on top of the structure represents the earth's axis penetrating the dome of heaven.

Although some free-standing temples were erected as early as the first century A.D., for several centuries the Indians seemed to prefer the more arduous method of hewing their edifices out of the solid rock of caves and cliffs. More than 1,200 rock-cut temples and monasteries were executed in various sections of India, the larger proportion being along the western coast. The two most remarkable groups of cliff excavations are located at Ajanta and Ellora, about 70 miles apart, in the northern part of what later became Hyderabad. The Ajanta caves were Buddhist sanctuaries, some of them dating from the second century B.C. and some from as late as the fifth century A.D. They include both assembly halls and monasteries, complete with stone beds, tables, water cisterns, and niches for oil reading lamps. The even more splendid caves at Ellora represent about 900 years of architectural and sculptural enterprise, extending from the fourth to the thirteenth century. The Buddhists were the first to utilize the site, but some of the caves were the work of Jains and the largest number were constructed as Hindu temples, of tremendous size and lavish design.

Rock-cut temples and monasteries

Temples composed of separate stone blocks, in contrast to the cave type, began to be more common in Gupta times and were typical of the most active period of Hindu temple building, between the sixth and the thirteenth centuries. The essential architectural features of these free-standing Hindu temples are (1) a base consisting of a square

Ajanta. A section of the gorge from which more than thirty cave chambers of worship, assembly, and residence were cut and decorated over a period of 700 years, beginning in the second century B. C.

or rectangular chamber to house the image of the god, and (2) a lofty tower which rises from the roof of the chamber and dominates the entire edifice. The shape of the tower distinguishes the two main styles of Hindu temples. The "Dravidian" style, found only in the tropics, is identified by a terraced steeple divided into stories like a step pyramid and decidedly reminiscent of the early Buddhist rock-cut monasteries. The "Indo-Aryan" style, prevalent in northern India, has a curvilinear tower with vertical ribs which may possibly be derived from the Buddhist *stupa*.

Sculpture and Indian ideals

Sculpture usually develops in close conjunction with architecture, and this was especially true in India, where so many sacred halls and chambers were literally carved out of stone. Decorative engravings, including figures in relief, were typically an integral part of the building itself. Chiseled decorations were very successfully applied to the gateways and pillars surrounding some of the early Buddhist *stupas*. The figures on the gates of the great *stupa* at Sanchi (first century B.C.) are particularly fine examples. Although they were intended to commemorate events of sacred tradition and embody pious symbolism, they are invested with vigor, freshness, and spontaneity, suggesting an uninhibited delight in the natural world rather than a brooding melancholy. Meanwhile a significant school of sculpture was arising in northwestern India and beyond the borders in Afghanistan and Bactria. The initial stimulus undoubtedly was Greek or Hellenistic, but Persian and other influences played a part, and the school developed its own original characteristics with Buddhist concepts predominant. It was in this region that the figure of Gautama was delineated for the first time, and relief sculptures depicted the legendary incidents of his life from infancy to Enlightenment. The large statues of the Buddha clearly revealed Greek influence at the beginning: the head resembled an Apollo or Zeus and the garment was draped like a toga rather than a monk's robe. However, there was a gradual approach toward the conventional form—in cross-legged posture and an attitude of benign repose—which eventually came to represent the Buddha all over the Far East. This Greco-Buddhist school of sculpture continued to flourish in the border regions of Central Asia, acquiring a more and more hearty realism, until it was snuffed out by the Hun invasions in the early sixth century.

During the Gutpa Age, Indian sculpture largely emancipated itself from foreign influences and assumed characteristics peculiarly expressive of Indian ideals. The treatment of the human form was handled with a subtle delicacy, conveying a sense both of rhythmic movement and tranquility. Garments on the figures were shown as almost transparent or suggested only in faint outline so that the effect is that of nudity, although chaste rather than voluptuous. The harmonious proportions and graceful curves of the limbs were derived from a study of plant forms as well as from human anatomy. Thus Gupta art, particularly as exemplified in the statues of Buddha, was idealistic and spiritual rather than realistic.

The richest creations of the Hindu artistic genius are to be found in the relief sculpture and fresco paintings executed in the rock-cut temples upon which so much energy was expended during the period

Eastern Gateway of the Great Stupa at Sanchi. The relief carvings, depicting incidents from the life of the Buddha, are remarkable for their fine detail, vitality, and naturalism.

Entrance to the Ajanta Caves. The Gupta period (fourth to seventh centuries A.D.) constitutes the Golden Age of Indian art—in sculpture, architecture, and painting—as well as the climax of classical Sanskrit literature.

Left: *Yakshi or "Tree Spirit."* A female figure derived from an early fertility cult but here symbolizing the transition from the sensuous world of illusion to the world of the spirit. Right: *Cast Bronze Buddha from Sultanganj in Bengal.* This 7-foot 6-inch representation of Buddha, dating from the fifth century, is typical of Gupta art and metallurgy at its peak.

corresponding to the Classical and Medieval ages of the West. The Buddhist caves at Ajanta contain the most important surviving collection of wall paintings. Religious in inspiration, they are at the same time spontaneous and unrestrained, proclaiming an unabashed delight in physical beauty. Although long neglected and damaged by the ravages of bats, insects, smoke, and water seepage, they are still magnificent. (The Indian government is taking steps to clean and conserve this priceless heritage.) In the Hindu temples, which increased in number from the seventh century on as Buddhism began to decline, decoration was usually in sculpture rather than painting. Relief sculptures in the Ellora cave temples and in Hindu and Jain temples erected during the tenth and eleventh centuries at Khajuraho in east central India rank among masterpieces of the world's art. In these carvings not only the gods but a galaxy of figures and dramatic episodes out of India's historic and legendary past seem to come alive. Many scenes are boldly realistic, but the Hindu tendency toward abstraction is also evident in the practice of depicting gods with several pairs of arms or several faces to signify their separate attributes. The themes portrayed range from voluptuous ecstasy and heroic struggle to attitudes of piety and mystic contemplation.

While the Indian communities were bringing their civilization to a point of refinement, they were also implanting it among various other peoples of Southeast Asia. Indian navigators and merchants were active in the eastern waters of the Indian Ocean as well as in the Arabian Sea to the west and apparently led the world in maritime enter-

Relief sculpture and painting

The spread of Indian culture

prise during this period. Some of the Indian states maintained navies and had a Board of Shipping as a governmental department. They not only promoted commerce but chartered companies of merchants, giving them trade monopolies in certain areas and authority to establish colonies. During the early centuries A.D. Indian colonies were planted in the Malay Peninsula, Annam (eastern Indochina), Java, Sumatra, and many other islands of the Malay Archipelago. Between the fifth and tenth centuries an empire ruled by a Buddhist dynasty and possessing formidable naval strength was based on the island of Sumatra. It also controlled western Java, extended into the Malay Peninsula, sent colonists to Borneo and from thence to the Philippine Islands. It dominated the Strait of Malacca and effectively policed the waters of this area against piracy. Although weakened by a long struggle with one of the Hindu mainland states, the empire (known as the Srivijaya) remained intact until the fourteenth century. Indian influence was extensive in the peninsula of Indochina—in the Cham state on the southeastern coast (later absorbed into the Annamese empire), in the Cambodian kingdoms of the lower Mekong valley, and among the Thais (Siamese) to the northwest.

The political vicissitudes of these various Eastern states were too complex to be enumerated here, but the entire region long remained an outpost of Indian culture. Sanskrit literature was introduced, along with Buddhism and the leading cults of Hinduism. Art and architecture, originating in Indian prototypes, were assiduously cultivated and attained considerable individuality. During the eighth and ninth centuries the Srivijaya empire in Sumatra and Java was perhaps the foremost center of Buddhist art. The colossal temple of Borobudur in central Java, one of the world's architectural marvels, is actually a

*Art in the Srivijaya and
Khmer Empires*

Relief Sculpture in the Hindu Cave at Ellora, Hyderabad (eighth century A.D.) The central figures are the god Shiva and his consort Parvati.

stone-encased hill rising 150 feet high, with nine terraces, staircases, covered gateways, and four galleries containing 1,500 sculptured panels. This "great picture bible of the Mahayana creed" is currently being restored under the sponsorship of UNESCO. In the ninth century, building on an ambitious scale was in progress in the Cambodian empire established by the Khmers, a native people who wielded dominion over a large part of Indochina between the ninth and the fourteenth centuries, and who responded energetically to the stimulus of Indian cultural contacts. Their capital city, Angkor (recovered from the jungle by French archeologists in the twentieth century), was of almost incredible magnificence in its heyday. Among several huge temples the most imposing was that of Angkor Wat, about a mile south of the capital, built during the twelfth century and said to be the largest work of its kind in the world, surpassing in mass even Luxor and Karnak of ancient Egypt. Angkor Wat was dedicated to the Hindu god Vishnu and was also designed as a tomb for the emperor, who was deified after his death and identified in some way with Vishnu. Eastern Asia for which historical records are available. In addition, it warned sinners of the numerous hells awaiting the wicked, celebrated the king's earthly conquests, and depicted scenes from the classic Sanskrit epics of India. While Hindu influence was ascendant in Cambodia, Buddhism was also a potent force there. Khmer statues of Buddha are distinguished by the "smile of Angkor"—a countenance expressing the height of benevolence and the supreme peace associated with the attainment of an inner state of enlightenment or *nirvana*.

During the Middle Ages the whole region surrounding the Bay of Bengal, while comprising separate political units, was dominated by Indian culture, imparted through commercial contacts and manifest in the fields of religion, literature, and art. The creative activity in this

Flourishing culture of "Greater India"

Angkor Wat. Built in the twelfth century by Suryavarman II as a sepulcher and monument to the divinity of the monarch, this temple is one of the largest religious structures in the world. The architecture of Angkor Wat is derived from the Indian stupa form.

Wall Carvings at Angkor Wat. The walls of this twelfth-century monument to the god Vishnu are covered with bas reliefs of celestial dancers, parading kings, and marching armies.

"Greater India" was not inferior to that of the motherland. In some ways it was even bolder, more vigorous and experimental, and it continued to flourish after the onslaught of fanatical Muslim conquerors from Afghanistan had brought a decay in India. However, a decline finally overtook the Buddhist and Hindu civilizations of Southeast Asia as the result of exhausting struggles among the competing states, pressure from China to the north, and—more decisive—the impact of Arab and other Muslim adventurers who traded, proselytized, and conquered successfully in this area during the fourteenth, fifteenth, and sixteenth centuries.

2. THE TERRITORIAL, POLITICAL, AND CULTURAL GROWTH OF CHINA

The Ch'in Dynasty, inaugurated after the overthrow of the Chou, lasted only fourteen years (221–207 B.C.), but it was one of the most important in Chinese history because it carried out a drastic reorganization of the government with permanent effects upon the character of the state. The founder of the dynasty, who assumed the title of "First Emperor" (Shih Huang Ti), was a man of iron will and administrative genius. He did away with the rival kingdoms, divided the country into provinces, and instituted an elaborate bureaucracy directly responsible to himself. The centralized administration and effective military organization that had been carefully cultivated in the state of Ch'in was now applied to all of China, thus effecting a momentous break with the past. The feudal institutions of 500 years'

The Ch'in Dynasty (*221–207 B.C.*)

standing were almost completely extinguished, and the government was brought into direct contact with the people. Determined to eliminate any competition for authority, the emperor's chief minister forbade the philosophic schools to continue their discussions and commanded their writings to be destroyed. His order for the burning of the books was a sweeping one, carrying the death penalty for disobedience, although copies of the forbidden works were locked up in the imperial library. Some Taoist writings were exempted from the proscription because the emperor was attracted by their reputed magic-working formulas. He was particularly anxious to root out the Confucianist and Mohist teachings because they emphasized moral restraints upon the ruler and his dependence upon the advice of learned counselors.

*Shih Huang Ti, "First
Emperor"*

Every aspect of Shih Huang Ti's reign reveals tremendous force of personality and a ruthless determination. He carried out conquests in all directions. In the south he not only annexed regions but built canals, one of which linked the Yangtze to the West River (of which Canton is the principal port). While raising large armies by conscription he disarmed the bulk of the Chinese people as a precautionary measure. With forced labor he executed an ambitious building program that included a network of military roads radiating from his capital. His most impressive engineering project was to complete and join together the series of fortifications in the north, by which he created the Great Wall of China, reaching from the seacoast some 1,400 miles inland. At his capital (near Sian, the site of the old Western Chou capital) he had constructed a sumptuous palace measuring 2,500 by 500 feet and capable of accommodating 10,000 people. In addition to such undertakings he and his ministers found time to standardize weights, measures, and even the axle length of carts, and—still more important—to unify the style of writing in China, with the result that communication among the various sections was made easy in spite of the diversity of spoken dialects. In his administrative policies the First Emperor probably borrowed some features from the Persian monarchs and from the Indian ruler Chandragupta Maurya. That he made a great impression not only upon the Chinese but upon foreign powers is illustrated by the fact that his country came to be known in other lands as "China"—after the name of his dynasty. This indomitable monarch's chief weakness was his addiction to superstitious fancies. He undertook several journeys in search of the elixir of immortality and died on one of these expeditions. Three years later his dynasty ended in a round of court conspiracies and assassinations, and his great palace was burned to the ground.

The Ch'in emperor had aimed at a social as well as political reconstruction, and although this was a more difficult undertaking it succeeded in part. On the whole his policy was to encourage and promote agriculture above commerce, assisting the farmers and holding the merchant class in check. Officially he abolished serfdom, decreeing that the peasants should be owners of the lands they worked. It is doubtful, however, that their lot was actually much better than before. Not only were there great differences between the small and the large proprietors, but the poor peasants became burdened with debts contracted with the merchants and moneylenders, the very group the government had intended to restrain. The Ch'in ruler exacted heavy taxes of various sorts, including a poll tax, and conscripted men for military and labor service with a callous disregard for human suffering. Thus, while the state was concerning itself more directly and actively than ever before with the welfare of the whole community, it reduced the dignity and freedom of the individual to a minimum. Large numbers of the population were forcibly moved from one region to another and many were made slaves of the state. People's actions and, as far as possible, their thoughts also were controlled by the government. The Ch'in rule carried into practice the Legalist doctrines of coercion, punishment, and fear, and bore a striking resemblance to the European totalitarian regimes of the twentieth century.

The overthrow of the Ch'in Dynasty was followed soon afterward by the establishment of the Han, founded by a military adventurer who had risen from the ranks. In the course of Chinese history many dynasties came and went—some very brief and some with only a local jurisdiction—but most of them tended to follow a similar course and met with a similar fate. From time to time a new ruling house was inaugurated by force or usurpation, sometimes by an alien or by a leader of lowly birth (the founder of the Han Dynasty was said to have come from a poor peasant family). If he could vindicate his authority and maintain order, he was looked upon as a legitimate ruler entitled to all the imperial dignities, regardless of the previous status

Social reforms and totalitarian methods of Shih Huang Ti

The Han Dynasty (206 B.C.–220 A.D.)

The Great Wall of China at Nankow Pass. The wall was erected about 221–207 B.C. for defense against northern invaders.

of his family. To be accepted, however, the dynasty had to promote general prosperity as well as defend the country and suppress internal strife. The typical dynastic cycle of China illustrates not only the rise and fall of successive ruling families but also the close relationship between the condition of society and the durability of a political regime. Usually during the early years of a dynasty vigorous and efficient rule was accompanied by internal peace, prosperity, and an increase in population. When the imperial court and its officers became venal and corrupt, neglected administrative problems, and demanded exorbitant taxes, domestic upheaval ensued, frequently joined to the threat of attack from without. If the dynasty failed to resolve the crisis, it went down in bloodshed, and a new firm hand seized control, cleared away the debris, and began the process all over again under a new dynastic name. The rise and fall of the Han Dynasty (206 B.C.–220 A.D.) illustrates the general pattern which was typical of China's successive political episodes. At the same time the Han Dynasty marks one of the most splendid periods in Chinese history, characterized by cultural progress and by the development of a form of government so satisfactory that its essential features remained unchanged—except for temporary interruptions—until the present century.

Centralized government

The Han government was a centralized bureaucracy but conducted with some regard for local differences and with deference to ancient traditions. Certain aspects of feudalism were reintroduced as the first Han emperor granted estates in the form of fiefs to his relatives and other prominent figures. However, the danger of feudal principalities becoming powerful and independent, as had happened in Chou times, was circumvented by a decree requiring the estates of nobles to be divided among the heirs instead of passing intact to the eldest son. Chinese society was still far from being equalitarian, but its aristocratic structure had been severely jolted. The imperial administration cut across class lines, and there was little danger that it would ever again be constituted on feudal principles. The power of the old Chou states was broken beyond recovery. Obviously, the Han rulers were profiting from and continuing the work begun by the hated house of Ch'in, although they softened the harshest features of the Ch'in regime. Whereas the Ch'in emperor had antagonized the class of scholars, the Han ruler sought their favor and support and instructed his officials to recommend to the public service young men of ability irrespective of birth. The Confucianists profited most from the government's policy of toleration toward the philosophical schools. Some of their books had escaped the flames, and the scholars had long memories. Under the patronage of the emperor, Confucianist teachings were reinterpreted, with more emphasis upon the supremacy of the central authority than Confucius had probably intended. Thus, instead of serving as a stumbling block, they assisted in the creation of an efficient imperial government.

The Han rule, while energetic, efficient, and relatively enlightened, was sufficiently severe. As under the Ch'in, ambitious public works of reclamation and canal- and road-building entailed enormous labor, much of which was performed by slaves. Taxes were high, the salt and iron industries were made state monopolies, and the currency was debased to yield a profit to the government at the expense of the people. At the same time, the emperor attempted to regulate prices, not merely for the protection of the poorer consumers but to divert the middleman's profit into the imperial coffers. The government also participated in the rapidly expanding foreign commerce of the empire.

The severity of Han rule

As under most strong dynasties, efforts were directed to expanding the territorial frontiers. The Huns after many campaigns were forced to acknowledge Han suzerainty and compelled to furnish tribute and military support. Chinese control was established over much of Central Asia, including not only the Tarim basin of Sinkiang but parts of Turkestan beyond the mountains. Southern Manchuria and northern Korea were annexed, and Chinese settlers and culture penetrated this area. The provinces south of the Yangtze were secured and also northeastern Indochina (Tonkin). Both in territorial extent and in power, China under the Han was almost equal to the contemporary Roman Empire. Nor was China isolated from other civilized areas. Her trade connections were far-reaching, especially by the caravan routes which traversed Sinkiang and Turkestan. The Chinese had also begun to venture on the high seas, although ocean traffic was conducted chiefly by Indian navigators who sailed to the South China Sea and the Gulf of Tonkin. Chinese merchants exchanged products not only with India and Ceylon, but also with Japan, Persia, Arabia, Syria, and—indirectly—with Rome. The trade balance was generally favorable to China because of the high price commanded by her leading export, silk, frequently paid for in gold or precious stones.

Expansion of the empire

The Han Dynasty reached its climax in the latter half of the second century B.C., under the able leadership of an emperor who ruled for more than fifty years (Han Wu Ti, 140–87 B.C.). At the opening of the first century A.D. a court minister named Wang Mang, without military backing but with wide popular support, seized the imperial throne and proclaimed a new dynasty, which lasted only until the usurper's death fourteen years later (23 A.D.). During his brief and disastrous reign Wang Mang launched a radical reform program, sometimes described as an abortive attempt to establish a socialist society but which was actually inspired by Confucianist precepts as interpreted by Wang. He tried to re-establish early Chou institutions, including a semifeudal nobility, while at the same time alleviating the condition of slaves. Invoking the ancient doctrine that all land belongs to the ruler, he confiscated the property of great landowners to provide a farm plot for every family. However benevolent in intent, Wang's reforms were vitiated by his own inflexibility, inefficiency, and corruption through the exercise of power. He alienated almost all

*The usurpation of Wang
Mang*

sections of the population, including those he was trying to help, and must go down as one of the supreme failures in the history of public administration. After he was murdered by rebels who broke into the palace, his program was scrapped. In 25 A.D. the Han family recovered the throne and retained it for two more centuries—a period known as the Later or Eastern Han because the capital was moved eastward to the site of Honan. The Later Han period exhibited the typical symptoms of decay at court and within the ruling house, although the administrative system remained intact and China's reputation in foreign parts was upheld by skillful diplomacy and force of arms. The dynasty crumbled as rebellions broke out and power passed into the hands of warlords, one of whom deposed the Han emperor in 220 A.D.

A period of turbulence and disunity

For almost four centuries after the collapse of the Han Dynasty, China was in a state of turbulence and upheaval. The country was divided, warfare was frequent, and it seemed that all the gains of the previous era were in jeopardy. Although the dates are not identical, this period of political disunity in China is comparable to the time of confusion which Europe experienced after the fall of the Roman Empire in the West. As in Europe during the early Middle Ages, the central government was weak or nonexistent; barbarian invasions affected a wide area; and, just as Christianity became rooted among the Latin and Germanic peoples of the West, a new otherworldly religion—Buddhism—made tremendous headway in China. Aside from these parallels, however, China's period of disunion was very different from the early Middle Ages in Europe. In China there was no appreciable decline in commerce or in city life, nor was there a serious modification of culture and institutions. The absence of a strong central authority was the only real disadvantage from which the country suffered, and this defect could be remedied by reviving the administrative machinery which had been temporarily disrupted. The Han state had been a practical and effective expression of Chinese experience, utilizing existing social and economic institutions and emphasizing ancient traditions. Consequently, even a long period of semianarchy could not destroy China's civilization. This period, dismal as it was, gave evidence of the toughness of Chinese society and culture, embodied in the patriarchal family, the village organization, and the sturdy enterprise of farmers who literally worshiped the soil on which they labored and were determined to make it support them regardless of the political controversies that raged on all sides.

Nomadic invaders from the north

As might be expected, the nomadic peoples on China's northern borders took advantage of her internal weakness to overrun the country. For about 250 years, from the fourth to the late sixth century A.D., practically all northern China including the Wei and Yellow River valleys was ruled by nomad dynasties of Hunnish, Turkish, and related stocks. It was not, however, successfully incorporated into any of the extensive but short-lived empires which arose in Central Asia and often impinged upon India as well as China. The dominance of non-Chinese rulers over the Yellow River valley—the historic center of Chinese culture—did not by any means destroy this culture. On the contrary, the rulers seemed eager to be accepted as custodians and defenders of civilization, and in the Far East civilization was synonymous with Chinese institutions. The nomads who settled south of the Great Wall assimilated the speech and customs of the older inhabitants. One of the few permanent changes in the habits of the Chinese people that can be attributed to their contact with the steppe nomads was in costume. During the fourth and fifth centuries they adopted trousers and boots similar to those worn by the northern horsemen, and this style of dress gradually supplanted the flowing tunic even in south China.

*Restoration of power and
unity under the T'ang
Dynasty (618–907)*

The contrast between China and western Europe during the medieval era is accentuated by the fact that four centuries of disunity in China were followed by another vigorous and highly successful dynasty, the T'ang (618–907), which re-established the imperial administration, again pushed back the territorial frontiers, and promoted brilliant cultural achievements. Thus, at the very time when feudalism was taking root in Europe and a new type of civilization was in process of formation there, China was resuming the course that had been marked out in Han times. Although it followed so closely upon the period of invasion and division, the T'ang Dynasty in many respects marked the culmination of China's cultural evolution.[1]

*The height of T'ang
power*

The T'ang Dynasty was at its height during the first half of the eighth century, covered almost entirely by one distinguished reign, when the area under Chinese control was slightly greater than the Han dominions and greater than it has ever been since under a native Chinese monarch. Wars in Mongolia broke the power of the Turks, who had been dominant there for about 150 years, and some of them became allies of the T'ang emperor. Parts of Manchuria were annexed, all Korea was tributary for a brief span, and control was again asserted over northern Indochina. The most redoubtable advances were in Central Asia. Chinese jurisdiction was recognized as far west as the Caspian Sea and the borders of Afghanistan and India, and some of the Indus valley princes accepted Chinese suzerainty. In carrying out their military exploits the T'ang rulers relied heavily upon the assistance of the non-Chinese peoples with whom their subjects were by this time familiar, either as friends or as foes. Now that the Chinese dragon was in the ascendancy, Mongols, Turks, and Huns were glad to be accepted as allies.

[1] Actually the brief Sui Dynasty (589–618) had already reunited China and inaugurated the new era of progess.

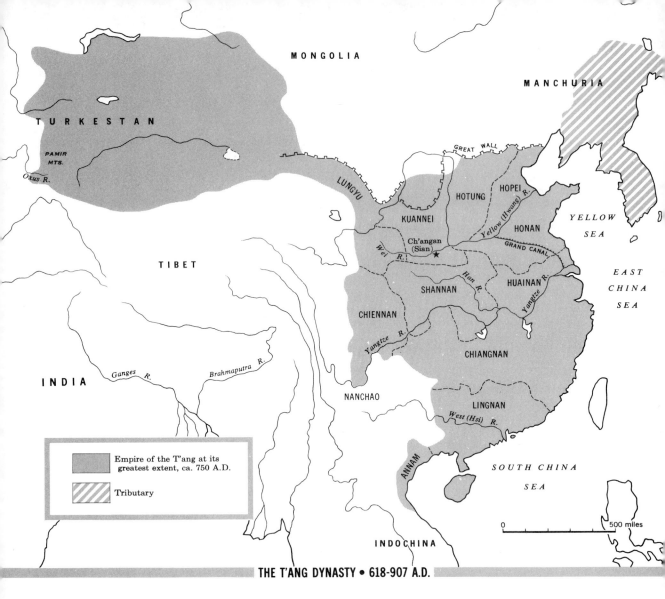

THE T'ANG DYNASTY • 618-907 A.D.

Decline of the T'ang empire

Imposing as was the T'ang hegemony over Central Asia, it could not be maintained indefinitely. When the rapid expansion of Islam began under Arab leadership in the seventh century, it seemed for a while that China, in spite of her remoteness from the West, was the only power to offer effective resistance. The last Sassanid king of Persia, fleeing from the Arabs, sought refuge at the T'ang court, and T'ang forces with the assistance of local princes checked the Muslim advance in Turkestan. The check was only temporary, however. When the T'ang administration passed its zenith (about 750), the Arabs gained control of Turkestan—bequeathing the religion of Islam as a permanent heritage—and for a time their influence extended as far east as the border of China's Kansu province. The T'ang rulers also encountered trouble with Tibet, which previously had remained in isolation from the turbulent politics of Central Asia. Early in the seventh century a kingdom was founded in the highland country by a leader who attained sufficient prestige to be given both a Chinese and an Indian princess in marriage. The Tibetans invaded Chinese territory several times, allied themselves alternately with the Turks and with the Arabs, and interrupted trade between China and Persia by blocking the passes through the Pamir Mountains. In 798 the T'ang court succeeded in obtaining a treaty of alliance with the famous Harun-al-Raschid, caliph of Baghdad, and the Tibetan power subsided in the ninth century. Meanwhile, a division of Turks had reoccupied Mongolia, and in spite of a long struggle the Chinese were unable to hold their northern and western frontiers inviolate. By the end of the ninth century internal rebellions, together with governmental corruption and decadence in the ruling house, had led again to a state of general disorder.

The T'ang administrative machinery, similar to the Han, was centralized under the emperor and staffed by a large bureaucracy. China proper was divided into fifteen provinces, which were subdivided into prefectures, and these again into smaller units or sub-prefectures, and each of the units was headed by an official appointed from the capital. The Han practice of recruiting talent for the imperial service had now developed into a rudimentary civil-service system in which written examinations were offered periodically throughout the provinces, and officeholders were chosen from among the successful candidates. Appointments were not confined solely to those who had taken the examinations, nor were all successful candidates rewarded with positions; but the system did provide opportunities for public service to young men of ability from every class of the population, in keeping with the policy advocated by Confucius a thousand years earlier.

Since the abolition of feudalism and the establishment of peasant proprietorship by the Ch'in emperor, the character of Chinese society had not greatly changed. Many peasants were tenants rather than independent owners, and slavery had not entirely disappeared, although the percentage of slaves in the population was small. Inequalities in wealth and distinctions of rank were conspicuous. The T'ang emperors supported a titled nobility of several grades, but its prestige was based upon governmental favor rather than upon the possession of landed estates. Instead of hereditary titles carrying administrative power as in a feudal regime, the titles were bestowed upon eminent officials as a reward for their services. Ordinarily the emperor did not rule as a military despot but maintained a clear separation between the civil and military authority. It was only during periods of weakness and disorder that warlords usurped political functions. By T'ang times the Chinese had acquired a conviction that military regimes were incompatible with a normal, civilized state of

Development of the civil service

Chinese society under the T'ang

affairs. By tradition society was believed to be properly composed of five classes ranked in the order of their value to the commonwealth. These were, first, scholars; second, farmers; third, artisans; fourth, merchants; and last, soldiers, lumped together with beggars, thieves, and bandits.[2] The notable aspects of this classification are the high recognition granted to intellectual ability, the deprecation of violence and of nonproductive occupations, and the fact that the categories are based upon individual talents and capacities rather than upon birth. The five-class system was never fully realized or perfectly respected, but it was an ideal which tended to lessen the rigidity of Chinese institutions. On the more practical side, the prominence of scholars in the administration and the system of competitive examinations helped to prevent the dominance of aristocratic families. In addition, the circumstance that the imperial throne did not remain in any one family for more than a few centuries provided an object lesson not to be forgotten.

Agriculture

Continuing the policy of encouraging agriculture, every vigorous dynasty gave attention to irrigation works, usually maintained public granaries to provide food distribution in famine years, and sometimes attempted to relieve the farmers from their heavy burden of debt and taxes. Nevertheless, while China was already one of the world's leading agricultural countries, the poorer peasants undoubtedly suffered from a miserably low standard of living as has been the case throughout history. Furthermore, the farmer bore the chief burden of supporting the state. Theoretically the emperor reserved the right to redistribute holdings, but in practice he was usually content to break the power of overly ambitious wealthy houses that might challenge his own authority. Too often the interest of officials in the peasants centered upon the fact that they constituted the most lucrative and dependable source of taxation, collectible either in produce or labor, the latter including conscription for military service.

Commerce and urban growth

Curiously enough, in spite of the honored position of the farmer and the pro-agrarian policies of the government, the merchant class attained a prominence far superior to that of European merchants during this period, and the steady increase of trade induced the growth of thriving cities. During the eighth century the T'ang capital in the Wei valley (on the site of Sian, but known during this period as Ch'ang-an), the eastern terminus of the trans-Asiatic caravan routes, apparently had a population of close to 2 million, while the population of China as a whole was between 40 and 50 million—about 5 percent of the present number. Foreign commerce was greater under the T'ang than ever before, and an increasing proportion of it was oceanic, the leading ports of exchange being Canton and other cities along the

[2] A famous ancient Chinese proverb is "Good iron is not used to make a nail; a good man is not used to make a soldier."

southeast coast, where merchants of various nationalities from the Near and Middle East were to be found. In addition to silk and spices, porcelain ware was becoming a notable item in China's export trade.

Significant developments in religion took place during the period under consideration. The most important was the introduction of Buddhism, which brought the Chinese for the first time into contact with a complex religion with an elaborate theology, ecclesiastical organization, and emphasis upon personal salvation. For several centuries following the life of Gautama, the Buddhist faith gained such momentum in the regions surrounding India that it was bound to reach China. It was brought in over the northern trade routes as early as the first century A.D. and made rapid headway during the period of disunion that followed the collapse of the Han Dynasty. Buddhism met with a mixed reception in China, arousing both enthusiastic interest and repugnance. Mysticism, asceticism, contempt for the physical world, and the concept of transmigration of souls were quite alien to Chinese tradition; and the monastic life seemed to involve a repudiation of sacred family loyalties. On the other hand, Buddhism offered consolations not found in the native Chinese cults or philosophical disciplines. It was nonaristocratic, open to all classes, and—in contrast to the Confucian emphasis upon the inflexible will of Heaven—its *karma* doctrine affirmed that anyone could improve his chances in a future existence by diligent application. Converts were attracted by the rich symbolism of the new religion, and the voluminous scriptures which the Buddhist missionaries brought with them impressed the Chinese, who venerated scholarship. Buddhism's otherworldly orientation appealed particularly to the downtrodden and oppressed. In spite of violent opposition from some Chinese rulers, Buddhism continued to recruit adherents; congregations of women as well as of men were organized; pilgrims went to India to study and returned with copies of the Buddhist canons. By about 500 A.D. China had practically become a Buddhist country.

It might be supposed that after the restoration of a strong monarchy the interest in this imported salvationist faith would have subsided, but such was not the case. Although a few of the T'ang emperors tried to root out Buddhism (one emperor is reputed to have destroyed 40,000 temples), several of them encouraged it, and it was under the T'ang Dynasty that Chinese Buddhism reached its height as a creative influence. Many varieties of the religion had been brought into China—chiefly of the *Mahayana* school—and others were developed on Chinese soil, appealing to different temperaments and degrees of education. One of the most popular sects, called the "Pure Land" or "Lotus" school, promised an easy salvation in a western paradise to all who invoked the name of Amida (or Amitabha). Amida, theoretically an incarnation of Buddha, was actually visualized as a god, alleged to have been born of a lotus in the heavenly western realm of

The introduction of Buddhism

Head of Buddha. T'ang Dynasty (618–907). This stone head was found in the caves of Lung Men.

Varieties of Chinese Buddhism

bliss. Several of the sects, however, encouraged a zeal for scholarship and also stimulated interest in the problems of government and society. The most vigorous philosophical speculation under the T'ang was found in Buddhist circles. But in spite of the great success of Buddhism its triumph was not comparable to the ascendancy of Christianity in western Europe during this same period. The Chinese Buddhists were not united in a common discipline, had no coercive power, and their organization did not replace or challenge the authority of the state as did the Christian hierarchy in the West. And the fact that Buddhism was practiced in almost all parts of the country did not mean that other religions had ceased to exist. The idea of an inclusive universal church was foreign to Chinese conceptions.

Taoism as a religion

Paralleling the spread of Buddhism, Taoism, which had originated as a philosophical school, acquired the characteristic features of an otherworldly religion with wide popular appeal. Taoism developed not only a priesthood but an ecclesiastical hierarchy headed by a "Prince Celestial Master," who established pontifical headquarters in south central China. This Taoist hierarchy was given official recognition in the eighth century and was not formally abolished until 1927. The religion, incorporating many primitive beliefs, expounded the Way (*Tao*), which was interpreted to mean the road to individual happiness defined usually in material terms, although it offered elements to attract intellectuals and encouraged acts of charity. Taoism was greatly affected by Buddhism and borrowed ideas from the foreign faith, including the concepts of *karma* and transmigration and the belief in thirty-three heavens and eighteen hells. Its priesthood was modeled after the Buddhist monastic order, except that the Taoists did not practice celibacy; and the later Taoist scriptures show a strong resemblance to Buddhist texts. Inevitably rivalry sprang up between the two competing religions, but neither was able to eliminate the other and both received imperial as well as popular support. Some Taoist apologists claimed that their master, Lao-tzu, had actually been the Buddha or else had instructed him; while Buddhists countered with the assertion that Lao-tzu had rendered homage to Gautama.

Confucianism as a state cult

In spite of the popularity of Taoism and the temporary ascendancy of Buddhism, Confucianism began to be revived in the later T'ang period and retained its hold upon the allegiance of the Chinese. Although usually described as one of the three great religions of China, Confucianism was not and never became a religion in the strict sense of the term. It was a body of ethical principles, of etiquette and formal ceremony, and also—as a result of the policies of Han and T'ang emperors—a code of government, strengthened by the practice of recruiting officials from scholars versed in the Confucian classics. Veneration for the great teacher finally became part of the state cult and was invested with formal religious observances. The later Han emperors had prescribed sacrifices to Confucius in every large city,

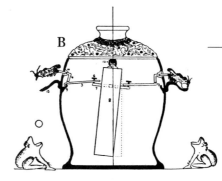

The Ancestor of All Seismographs. Invented by a Chinese mathematician and geographer in 132 A.D., it was described in a contemporary document as an "earthquake weathercock." These conjectural reconstructions show the interior of the bronze, bell-shaped instrument. (A) The pendulum carries jointed arms radiating in eight directions, each arm ending in a crank connected with a dragon head. (B) When an earth tremor causes the pendulum to swing, one of the dragon heads is raised and releases a ball, which drops into the mouth of a toad below. After the swing of the pendulum, a catch mechanism immobilizes the instrument. Thus, by observing which ball has fallen, it is possible to determine the direction of the initial shock wave.

and a T'ang ruler of the seventh century ordered temples to be built in his honor in each prefecture and subprefecture. Thus the sage, together with other famous men of antiquity, revered rulers, outstanding generals, etc., was ensured perpetual homage and respect, but he was not worshiped as were the Buddhist and Taoist deities. The Chinese idea of religion, it should be remembered, was different from that of most other peoples. The typical Chinese would be a Confucianist as a matter of course; but he might also be a Taoist, a Buddhist, or a combination of both.

Many economic and cultural changes took place during the thousand years between the Ch'in Dynasty and the end of the T'ang. Some items were borrowed from Western lands—grapes and alfalfa among the agricultural products, astrological concepts and the seven-day week from the Manicheans. The Chinese began to use coal for fuel and for smelting iron in the fourth century A.D., far in advance of Europeans. Their astrologers had observed sunspots as early as 28 B.C.; a crude seismograph was constructed in 132 A.D. The magnetic compass, apparently developed by the Taoists around 500 A.D., was used chiefly to determine favorable locations for grave sites. The properties of gunpowder had also been discovered. At this time, however, gunpowder was employed not to blow people to bits but in the manufacture of firecrackers to frighten away evil spirits. The highly important invention of paper (made of bark, hemp, and rags) was achieved by the beginning of the second century A.D., and printing from blocks was introduced about 500 years later. By the tenth century the printing of books was common not only in China but in Korea and Japan.

Porcelain Ewer or Pitcher, in the Form of a Court Lady. T'ang Dynasty.

Economic and cultural changes

Two Carved Wood Bodhisattvas. T'ang Dynasty. The bodhisattva, or Buddha-to-be, represented a person eligible for enlightenment but who remained in the world to help others on the upward path. In Mahayana Buddhism a number of bodhisattvas came to be worshiped as deities.

A great deal of the intellectual and artistic progress of this era must be credited to the Buddhists, whose contributions were not confined to religion exclusively. Buddhism enriched Chinese music by the introduction of a liturgy of vocal chants and also with several new musical instruments, including the psaltery, guitar or mandolin and other stringed instruments, the reed organ, clarinet, and a type of flute. It was in the visual arts, however, that the impetus of Buddhism was most notable. The Buddhists of northern India, who had absorbed artistic motifs from the Greeks and Persians, spread them into Central Asia and thence into China. During the period of disunion and the early T'ang Dynasty, Chinese sculpture reached its climax, successfully blending together Indian, Iranian, and Hellenic characteristics into a distinctive Chinese style. Superbly beautiful examples of this sculpture have survived, the best of which were produced in the late sixth and early seventh centuries. The most impressive works of architecture were Buddhist temples or sacred grottoes in northwestern China, carved out of rock caves after the Indian manner. Painting, too, reached a peak of realism and sensitivity which has rarely been surpassed. Skill in this medium was stimulated by the Chinese habit of writing with brush and ink, and pictorial figures or scenes were often combined with masterly specimens of calligraphy executed on scrolls of silk. Some paintings in fresco have been preserved from T'ang times and, like the sculpture, they show Buddhist influence. Outstanding among the minor arts was the production of pottery figurines representing human beings and animals with grace and naturalness, used chiefly as funeral presents to the departed. The manufacture of white porcelain—the beginning of the world-famous "china" ware—apparently began in the sixth or seventh century.

As early as Chou times, the Chinese civilization was highly literary, and by the T'ang period China had probably the most abundant collection of writings of any nation in the world. Philosophical activity did not equal the creative age of Confucius, Mo Ti, and Mencius, but a great variety of literary forms had come into existence, showing maturity of thought, sophistication, and aesthetic sensitivity. Writers of the T'ang period produced histories, essays, dictionaries, short stories and romances for popular entertainers, an embryonic form of the drama, and—outshining all the rest—poetry. Poetry had been developed prolifically during the centuries of disunion and civil strife. The influence of Buddhism and Taoism imparted emotional intensity and a quality of mysticism conducive to lyrical richness. The final result was a flowering in the eighth and ninth centuries which made the T'ang the supreme age of Chinese poetry. The verse forms were usually short, with words carefully chosen to evoke beauty of tone as well as to convey pithy thought and vivid imagery. While sometimes expressing philosophical ideas, they were frequently poignant in mood and romantic in theme, treating especially of nature, love, and friendship. A few of the best examples were tinged with a deep melancholy, expressing compassion for the miserable lot of the poor, distress over abuses in government, revulsion against the senseless brutality of war, and bewilderment at the apparent triumph of evil over good.

3. EARLY CIVILIZATION IN JAPAN

Of the great civilizations of the Far East, Japan's was the latest to develop. In origin it was derived from and was largely an adaptation of cultures from the mainland, especially from China. However, the fact that the Japanese lagged many centuries behind China and India and made their most rapid progress under the stimulus of borrowings from China does not prove that the island dwellers were lacking in ability or originality. Not only did the Japanese display remarkable ingenuity in assimilating foreign elements and in modifying them to meet their particular needs, but during some periods of history they seemed to possess more initiative than any of the other Far Eastern nations. The backwardness of Japan in early times is explained, at least in part, by the geographical circumstance of its isolation from the continent of Asia. Before oceanic commerce was well advanced, the Japanese islands could not be readily affected by political and cultural changes taking place on the mainland. These islands stand in the same relationship to Asia as do the British Isles to Europe. Just as European civilization was slowly extended from the Near Eastern centers westward to Italy and then to the northern countries, reaching Britain last of all, so Far Eastern civilization gradually radiated from the Yellow River valley to the south, west, and northeast, and necessarily reached Japan belatedly. Actually Japan is much more remote from the neighboring continent than is Britain from Continental Europe. At the narrowest point the Strait of Dover is only about 20 miles wide, while more than 100 miles separate the islands of Japan from the closest point on the Korean peninsula.

The retarded development of civilization in Japan

Japan's geographic setting is in some ways very favorable. Of the approximately 3,000 islands composing the group, only about 600 are inhabited, and the bulk of the population is concentrated on the four principal islands. The entire archipelago lies within the temperate zone, and the largest island, Honshu, holding about half of the Japanese people, lies between almost exactly the same latitudes as the state of California. The Black Current, drifting northward from tropical seas, moderates the severity of winter; and cyclonic storms, while sometimes destructive, bring fluctuations in temperature that are conducive to physical and mental vigor. Their proximity to the ocean encouraged the Japanese to develop navigation and to become hardy fishermen. With its expanse of seacoast, mountains, volcanoes and

Geographic advantages and disadvantages

snow-capped peaks, the region is scenically one of the most beautiful in the world, a factor which has undoubtedly contributed to the keen aesthetic sensibilities of the Japanese people. At the same time Japan is by no means perfectly endowed by nature and suffers from several disadvantages. Except for having fair deposits of coal, the islands are poor in mineral resources. Even more serious has been the scarcity of good agricultural land, owing to the rocky or mountainous character of much of the country. Although throughout most of their history the Japanese have been a nation of farmers, only about 16 percent of their soil is cultivable. This sufficed when the population was small and generally stationary; it has posed a tremendous problem in modern times.

Racial stocks in Japan

Small as is the land area of Japan (slightly less than that of California) and in spite of its relative isolation, it was inhabited even in early times by people of various stocks as the result of successive migrations from the continent. The earliest inhabitants, so far as is known, were a primitive people who possessed a Neolithic culture, crude in many respects but distinguished by pottery of striking design and skillfully fashioned weapons. They are represented today by the Ainu, a light-colored, flat-faced, and hairy people, who have largely disappeared except from Hokkaido and the Kuril Islands to the north. For the most part the Japanese nation is descended from Mongoloid invaders who crossed over to the islands at various times during the Neolithic Age and even later, chiefly by way of Korea. From the time of the Ch'in Dynasty on, the settlers in Japan possessed some knowledge of Chinese culture, which had already penetrated into Korea. Bronze mirrors, carved jewels, and swords of Chinese or Mongolian type appear in graves dating from the second and first centuries B.C. By the close of the first century B.C. the Japanese had begun to use iron as well as bronze.

The beginnings of Japanese society

Quite understandably, the leading centers of cultural evolution were in the south and west of Japan—the areas closest to Korea, from which the chief migrations came—and developments in this region gradually spread to the north and east. The real nucleus of the Japanese state was the peninsula of Yamato, on the southeastern side of the great island of Honshu, to which a group of families had migrated from Kyushu (opposite Korea) perhaps as early as the first century A.D. The Japanese communities at this time were very primitive. People wore clothing made from hemp or bark, although silk was not entirely unknown. They carried on trade by barter only and had no system of writing. The chief unit of society was the clan, a group of families claiming to be related by blood. Each clan venerated some particular deity, who was supposed to be the ancestor of the group; but the worship of human ancestors had not yet become an institution. The headship of the clan was vested hereditarily in a specific family, and the clan leader served both as a warrior chieftain and as

EARLY JAPAN

priest. In primitive Japanese society women seem to have held a position of prominence, perhaps even of superiority. The clan head was sometimes a woman, and evidence points to the conclusion that originally the family was matriarchal, with descent traced through the mother—a remarkable circumstance in view of the rigid subordination of women in later times. The transition to a patriarchal system, however, was effected at an early date. According to Chinese accounts from the third century A.D., polygamy was a common practice, especially among men of the higher classes. Various crafts and skills were organized as occupational groups in the form of guilds with hereditary membership. Each guild was attached to a clan and tended to merge with it eventually, although a few guilds whose members performed distinctive services, such as administering religious rites, retained an independent existence and honorable status. Members of the agricultural and artisans' guilds, on the other hand, were practically serfs. Society was decidedly aristocratic, rank was generally hereditary, and slavery existed, although the number of slaves was relatively small.

The foundations of Shintoism

Japanese religion, while comparable to that of other primitive peoples, was in some ways unique. It was basically animistic, a type of unreflecting and almost universal nature worship, with no well-defined conception of the nature of divine being. In a general way it was polytheistic, except that the term probably suggests too definite a catalogue of gods or too precise a theology. The Japanese later gave their religion the name of *Shinto* ("the way of the Gods"), simply because they needed to distinguish it from Buddhism when this articulate and mature faith began to compete with the native cult. Although the Japanese recognized some great deities, associated with the sun, moon, earth, crops, and storms, these were not endowed with distinct personalities and were not represented by images. Objects of worship were designated as *kami,* a term meaning "superior" but which was applied to almost anything having mysterious or interesting properties, ranging from heavenly phenomena to irregularly shaped stones and such lowly objects as sand, mud, and vermin. No sharp line was drawn between the natural and the supernatural or between magic and worship. The notion of life after death was extremely shadowy, and religion was largely devoid of ethical content. It involved taboos and scrupulous concern for ceremonial cleanness, with purification rites to remove contamination, but the requirements were not based on considerations of morality or even always of health. Uncleanness, for example, was associated with childbirth, with contact with the dead, and with wounds whether inflicted honorably or not. To placate the gods, respectful gestures, prayers, and sacrifices were employed. Offerings of food and drink gradually tended to be superseded by symbolic objects—of pottery, wood, and eventually paper.

Attractive elements in native Japanese religion

In spite of its diffuse and elementary character, the native Japanese religion was not lacking in attractive elements. It reflected an attitude of cheerfulness and a rare sympathy for and appreciation of nature. The gods were not thought of as cruel and terrifying creatures; even the god of the storm was generally conceived as benign. On the whole, the religion of the Japanese was one "of love and gratitude rather than of fear, and the purpose of their religious rites was to praise and thank as much as to placate and mollify their divinities."[3] It was

[3]G. B. Sansom, *Japan, a Short Cultural History,* p. 47.

enlivened also with picturesque legends and poetic phrases that suggest a spontaneous delight in the natural world.

The clan which was dominant on the plain of Yamato, and gradually acquired an ascendancy over adjacent regions, probably came from Kyushu and claimed descent from the Sun Goddess. There was nothing remarkable in such a claim because all important families traced their ancestry to gods or goddesses. However, myths associated with the Sun Goddess assumed greater significance as the Yamato clan extended its political power and attempted to secure fuller recognition of its paramountcy over the other clans, for which purpose it was helpful to foster the legend that the Yamato chief had been divinely appointed to rule over Japan (even though most of it was still unconquered from the aborigines). According to this legend the Sun Goddess had sent down to earth her own grandson, Ninigino-Mikoto. Ninigi, "thrusting apart the many-piled clouds of Heaven, clove his way with an awful way-cleaving" to land on the western island of Kyushu, carrying with him the three symbols of Japanese royalty—a jewel, a sword, and a mirror. The grandson of this Ninigi, it was related, advanced along the coast of the larger island to Yamato, where he began to rule as Jimmu, the "first emperor." National tradition dates the empire from February 11, 660 B.C. Actually, it was at least 600 or 700 years later that the Yamato state was established, and then it was anything but imperial. The saga of the Sun Goddess and her descendants did not become a distinctive element in the national cult of Japan until the sixth century A.D., and not until the modern era was it deliberately exploited on a national scale for the purpose of instilling a fanatical and unquestioning patriotism among the people.

For many centuries the Japanese maintained contact with and continued to receive cultural impetus from Korea, which means that they were being influenced indirectly by the older and richer civilization of China of the Han and later dynasties. The Japanese even controlled a small section at the southern tip of Korea from about 100 to 560 A.D. and intervened in Korean politics to maintain a balance of power, siding with one and then another of the three kingdoms into which Korea was divided during this time. Of fundamental importance for the later history of Japan was the introduction, by way of Korea, of the Chinese system of writing (about 405 A.D.) and of Buddhism (about 552 A.D.).

While the technique of writing was essential to the advance of civilization, it was unfortunate for the Japanese that they acquired it from China. If they had been able to devise or borrow a phonetic or alphabetic system, the problem of writing their language would have been comparatively simple. The Chinese characters—fundamentally pictographic or ideographic, with very little apparent relationship to pronunciation of the words for which they stand—had been developed to a state of complexity and utilized in producing masterpieces of Chinese literature; but they were ill suited to represent Japanese. The

Founding of the Japanese state

Japanese Tomb Culture. Clay grave statues of ordinary people, such as this soldier, surrounded the tombs of more important people. This reflects the influence of Korean culture. Such statuary began to appear in the third and fourth centuries A.D.

Japanese writing

Japanese language is phonetically quite different from the Chinese, and the attempt to write it with Chinese characters was a feat as difficult as it would be to try to write English in Chinese characters. Nevertheless, the Japanese struggled heroically with the task and eventually developed a script of their own, or, rather, two varieties of script. Although the original Chinese characters were abbreviated considerably and, during the ninth and tenth centuries, given phonetic value by identification with individual Japanese syllables, the resulting product was still cumbersome. Hence, the process of learning to write Japanese—in which 48 phonetic symbols plus 1,850 Chinese characters must be mastered—was and still is a laborious undertaking. The fact that the system of writing is alien to the structure, inflection, and idiosyncrasies of the spoken language hampered clarity of expression. To compensate for these disadvantages, however, along with the Chinese-derived script a great many Chinese words were adopted bodily by the Japanese, enriching their language in vocabulary and concepts. In view of the circumstances in which writing was introduced in Japan, a person who wished to become educated was almost bound to learn the Chinese language, especially since it was the vehicle of all literature considered worthy of the name. For several centuries Japanese scholars, officials, and men of letters wrote in classical Chinese, in somewhat the same manner that educated Europeans used Latin during the Middle Ages and later—except that while Latin was

JAPANESE TEXT   KAMBUN TEXT

Japanese and Chinese Writing. The text on the right is a passage from Mencius in Chinese with kaeriten added on the left hand side of each column to indicate the sequence in which the characters should be read to transcribe the passage into Japanese. This adaptation of Chinese writing is called Kambun. The text on the left is the same passage in Japanese. The hiragana written between the characters indicate the appropriate verbal inflections and postpositions. The small hiragana beside each character indicate the correct Japanese pronunciation. Note the use of Chinese characters in the Japanese text.

Great Buddha, Todaiji Temple, Nara. This statue, cast in the middle of the eighth century A.D., is one of the two largest bronze statues in the world. The seated Buddha is 53 feet high.

both written and spoken by educated Europeans, few Japanese scholars or literati learned to *speak* Chinese.[4]

In the middle of the sixth century Buddhism began to obtain a foothold in Japan. The first Buddhist missionary is said to have come from Korea; other evangelists of the new faith arrived not only from Korea but from China and even from India. As in the case of China, the *Mahayana* school of Buddhism, with its elaborate theology and emphasis upon the soul's redemption, was most in evidence. And, just as had happened in China, a number of different sects arose in Japan from time to time. The appearance of Buddhism in Japan produced perhaps even greater agitation than had accompanied its introduction into China a few centuries earlier. The Chinese were at least familiar with mystical concepts through Taoism, but the Japanese had had no previous experience either with this type of otherworldly religion or with any analogous philosophy. Part of the appeal of Buddhism to the Japanese lay in its novelty. The Buddhist scriptures raised questions that had apparently never occurred to the Japanese before—as to the soul, the nature of the immaterial world, rewards and punishments after death—and then proceeded to answer them with impressive eloquence. For a while, sharp controversy raged over the acceptability of the foreign faith (the first statue of the Buddha sent from Korea was thrown into a canal when an epidemic of disease broke out). However, one prominent aristocratic family in Yamato, the Soga, adopted and championed the cause of Buddhism and prevailed upon the imperial clan to favor it, so that before the close of the sixth century the success of the religion was assured. To some extent its success was attributable to political maneuvers and expediency. In

The establishment of Buddhism in Japan

[4] For an illuminating discussion of the Japanese language, see E. O. Reischauer, *The Japanese,* chapter 37.

patronizing the scholarly faith the Soga family sought to enhance its own prestige and, through the benefit of whatever supernatural power the religion contained, to secure an advantage in the struggle against rival families. Buddhism rapidly acquired a wide following both among the common people and the aristocracy and became so firmly entrenched that it would survive any shift in equilibrium among the contending clans. Probably its popularity is largely explained by its being interpreted as a miraculous protector against disasters both in this world and the next rather than by its philosophical heritage. Nevertheless, the increasing familiarity with Buddhist doctrines stimulated intellectual activity and was conducive to the cultivation of attitudes of sympathy and humaneness.

Buddhism a medium for disseminating Chinese culture

One of the most significant aspects of the spread of Buddhism in Japan was that it proved to be a highly effective medium for disseminating Chinese culture, especially art, architecture, and literature. Temples and shrines were erected, paintings and images of the Buddha were produced, and libraries of the sacred texts were accumulated. Converts from the aristocratic class frequently went to China to study, returning with a broadened viewpoint and refined tastes. The native Japanese cult, now beginning to be called *Shinto,* was by no means extinguished, but it was influenced considerably by contact with Buddhism. There was very little antagonism between the two religions. Buddhism in Japan became tinged with national traditions, and frequently the same shrine was regarded as sacred to both faiths. The Japanese priests, whether Buddhist or Shinto, did not constitute a hierarchy with coercive powers over the people any more than did the priests in China, although the Buddhist monasteries gained in economic importance as they were endowed with lands.

During the most vigorous period of the T'ang Dynasty, the impact

Horyuji Temple, Nara. The Horyuji Temple, founded in 607 A.D. by Prince Shotoku, Regent of the Empress-Regnant Suiko, is a complex of about forty buildings and includes some of the oldest wooden structures in the world.

of Chinese civilization upon Japan reached such a climax that it marks a turning point in the evolution of Japanese institutions. It is not at all strange that the Japanese turned avidly to China for tutelage at this time. China under the early T'ang rulers was one of the most highly civilized states in the world, as well as the most powerful, and in the Far East had no close rivals for such a distinction. Throughout the seventh and eighth centuries the government in Yamato sent a succession of official embassies to the T'ang court, largely for the purpose of recruiting personnel trained in the sciences, arts, and letters. The result was a wholesale copying of Chinese techniques and ideas, affecting almost every aspect of Japanese life and society. Chinese medical practices, military tactics, and methods of road building were introduced; also styles of architecture, of household furniture, and even of dress. A system of weights and measures was adopted, and copper coins came into limited circulation, although a genuine money economy did not replace barter until centuries later. Many works of art had previously been imported and copied, but now Japanese painters and sculptors began to display both technical proficiency and originality. The Chinese classics, especially the Confucian writings, were studied intently, since every well-bred person was expected to be familiar with them. Along with these concrete and visible innovations came an attempt to fit the social structure into the Chinese pattern. A new emphasis was placed upon family solidarity and filial devotion, including the duty of sacrificing to ancestral spirits.[5] Japanese leaders and intellectuals seemed determined to remake their country in the image of China.

The most comprehensive project involved nothing less than reconstituting the government according to the T'ang model. It was announced by a decree known as the Taika Reform Edict, issued in 645 A.D. by the Yamato ruler at the instigation of a clique of scholar-reformers. This declaration, rather than the mythical events of 660 B.C., represents the founding of the Japanese imperial system. By the Taika Edict the ruler assumed the role not of a mere clan leader but of an emperor, with absolute power, although professedly honoring Confucian principles. All Japan was to be divided into provinces, prefectures, and subprefectures, which would be administered by a centrally appointed bureaucracy recruited from the populace. Faithful to the example of China, the reformers instituted a civil service, offering examinations to candidates for government posts, whose selection would be based not on familiarity with the problems of Japan but on proficiency in Chinese philosophy and classical literature. To give the new administration an economic foundation and to bring it to bear directly upon the people, the Reform Edict proclaimed that all the

Japanese Religious Sculpture. This wooden figure of Bishamon, revered as one of the Four Guardian Kings of the Budhist kingdom, dates from the twelfth century or earlier.

Chinese influence on Japanese government

---

[5] Some Japanese scholars deny that the custom of ancestor worship was an importation; but in any case it was intensified by contacts with the Chinese. An unfortunate consequence was the increasing subordination of women to male authority in the patriarchal family and in society at large.

land belonged to the emperor, and that it would be divided equitably among the farmers and redistributed every six years. In return, every landholder would be required to pay taxes (in commodities, money, or labor) directly to the state.

Altogether, the reform program of the seventh century was one of the most ambitious that any government has ever attempted. It sought to graft upon a still fairly primitive society an administrative system that was the product of almost a thousand years of evolution among a people with cultural maturity and deeply entrenched traditions. Similarly, it involved an effort on the part of one corner of Japan to impose its regime on the entire area, much of which had hardly advanced beyond the Neolithic stage. In adopting the scheme of a centralized paternalism, one aspect of the Chinese prototype was studiously avoided: namely, the concept that imperial authority is conditional upon the promotion of public welfare and that it may be terminated—by rebellion as a last resort—if it fails in this objective. The Yamato group tried to attach a bureaucracy of scholar-officials to a government that called for perpetual rule by one family, whose head occupied a position of inviolable sanctity. To strengthen the prestige of the emperor, greater emphasis than ever before was placed upon his reputed descent from the Sun Goddess. He was represented as the embodiment of a "lineal succession unbroken for ages eternal" and as divine in his own person—a significantly different concept from that of the "Mandate of Heaven," the conditional and temporary divinity that hedged the Chinese emperor. In addition to this fundamental contrast between the official Chinese and Japanese theories as to the ultimate basis and limits of political authority, there was a notable divergence in practice also. China knew many different dynasties, most of them begun through rebellion or usurpation; but when a vigorous emperor sat on the throne, he usually ruled effectively and sometimes autocratically, as is attested by the records of the first few rulers of every major dynasty. In Japan, on the other hand, while the imperial family was never dethroned in spite of violent or revolutionary changes within society and in foreign relations, and while the fiction of imperial sanctity was carefully preserved, the actual power for the most part was exercised by some other family, agency, or clique, using the sacred imperial office as a front. Indirect government, sometimes removed by several stages from the nominal sovereign, has been the rule rather than the exception in Japan ever since its attempt to incorporate the Chinese political machinery.

In view of the inherent difficulties, it is not surprising that the reform program of the seventh century was not entirely successful. The new administrative system existed on paper but not as an operating reality. The imperial clan, which had previously enjoyed only a limited and largely ceremonial authority over the others, could not compel absolute obedience from remote areas, and aristocratic traditions were too strong to be broken immediately. The emperor made it a practice to appoint clan heads as officials in their own territories instead of replacing them by loyal servants sent out from the capital. Thus the local magnates acquired new titles and kept much of their former power. Examinations were provided for candidates desiring posts in the government service, but important positions were almost always reserved for members of the aristocracy, while capable men of the lower class found themselves employed as underlings and clerks. The announced policy of land equalization, which was intended to serve as the basis for a uniform tax system, was the most dismal failure of all. It had been inspired by the Chinese ideal of community interest in the land, a sentiment which condemned the appropriation of land for the exclusive benefit of any individual and taught that it should be distributed equally among the cultivators. This was only a theory in China, and in Japan it was thoroughly unrealistic. Later large proprietors managed to evade taxation and so increased the burden upon the poorer farmers that some of them ran away from their homes in sheer desperation. In this manner the amount of taxable land diminished, and the emperors themselves contributed to the process by giving away estates to courtiers or to endow Buddhist monasteries. Furthermore, the decree regarding periodic redistribution of land applied only to the fields that had already been brought under rice cultivation, a relatively small area. As the frontier clans added to their domains either by conquest from the aborigines or by reclaiming waste lands for cultivation, these new territories were regarded as personal holdings not directly subject to imperial assessment. Consequently, economic progress lessened rather than increased the proportion of the land under effective control by the central government. Instead of securing large funds from taxation, the court became more and more dependent for revenue upon estates that were owned outright by the imperial family.

Although the central government failed in its political objectives, it succeeded in promoting cultural progress to an appreciable degree. Before the seventh century there had been no fixed Japanese capital even in Yamato, or in fact no cities at all. Impressed with the splendor of the T'ang capital, the great city of Ch'ang-an, the Japanese determined to build one like it to serve as the imperial headquarters. Their city, begun in 710 and located near the modern town of Nara, followed the Chinese model faithfully in its broad streets and carefully aligned squares of equal size, although it was unwalled and much smaller than Ch'ang-an. Even so, its plan was too large for the population that occupied it. In 794 a more imposing capital was built at Kyoto, which has been an important city ever since. The construction of these cities under imperial patronage, with palaces, temples, and other public buildings, provided a stimulus to all the arts. Scholarship, bent on the production of histories, treatises, and literary criticism,

Governmental stimulation of culture

Benten Playing on a Biwa. A Japanese painting on silk by an artist of the Heian (Fujiwara) period, 893–1185.

also flourished at the imperial court. If the bureaucracy had little real public responsibility, its members could find satisfaction and enhanced social prestige in polishing their classical Chinese, translating Buddhist sutras, painting, or composing poetry of a rather strained and artificial type. The refinement of ceremony and etiquette also received much attention. Life in court circles tended to become effete and frivolous, but it harbored some artistic and intellectual talent of high caliber. Odd as it may seem, the best Japanese literature of this period was produced by women of the nobility and of the imperial household. Their contributions, outstanding in the tenth and eleventh centuries, were chiefly prose, typically in the form of diaries but including one justly famous romantic novel (*Tale of Genji*). In this instance it was fortunate that women, even of the court, were not held to the same educational standards as men. "While the men of the period were pompously writing bad Chinese, their ladies consoled themselves for their lack of education by writing good Japanese, and created, incidentally, Japan's first great prose literature."[6]

4. THE FOUNDATION OF CIVILIZATIONS IN AFRICA SOUTH OF THE SAHARA

The advance of civilization in sub-Saharan Africa was relatively slow. Africa's lack of early development, like Japan's, may be explained in

[6] E. O. Reischauer, *Japan, the Story of a Nation*, pp. 34–35.

part by its geographical isolation. The continent possessed few natural harbors, leaching of the soil's nutrients contributed to a general scarcity of good agricultural land, and the vast Sahara inhibited meaningful cultural and profitable commercial exchange. Desert transportation was dangerous and unreliable with horses or oxen.

Before 200 B.C. nearly all Africans south of the Sahara functioned on a nomadic hunting and gathering level. Religion, deeply rooted in superstition, remained basically animistic. Leadership was exercised by priests or family elders. Population density was exceedingly low everywhere, obviating the need to form large, centralized governing units. With an abundance of unoccupied land. Africans found permanent settlements unnecessary, and in the absence of external threats, there was no compulsion to organize military cadres for defense. Government was therefore rudimentary. Many clans engaged in ancestor worship for the purpose of establishing a sense of continuity and exerting a measure of moral control. Intermediaries were chosen from among elders in the group to interpret the will of the ancestors and gods and to lead rituals in their honor.

From very early times, some Africans developed exceptionally advanced skills in metallurgy. At least 1,500 years ago Africans on the western shore of Lake Victoria in East Africa produced medium carbon steel in forced-draft furnaces. Their sophisticated technique would not be matched by Europeans for centuries. Inexplicably, the African practice did not seem to have radiated beyond the ancestors of the present Haya people of modern Tanzania. Of greater consequence to Africa was the smelting of iron.

The Iron Age wrought revolutionary changes in African life styles after about 200 B.C. At that time, small bands of Bantu-speaking Negroes living along the modern Nigerian-Cameroon border in West Africa learned how to forge iron ore into spears and hoes. We do not yet know whether they developed the ability to smelt iron independently or whether the technique was introduced by immigrants from North Africa or from the lands of Kush. In any case, it endowed the Bantu with an immediate technological advantage over others. With their superior iron implements they expanded southward into the equatorial woodlands of West Central Africa. Then in approximately 1 A.D., in the watershed of the Congo-Zambezi river systems, they encountered high-yield food crops, including the nutritious banana, coco-yam and plantain. These plants had probably spread up the Zambezi River valley from Madagascar island. They were brought to Madagascar by seaborne southeast Asian immigrants of Javanese origin. The Bantu, possessing sturdy iron hoes, were in an excellent position to cultivate these new food crops.

Iron metallurgy, together with superior southeast Asian crops, greatly accelerated the transition from a food-gathering to a food-producing economy. By 200 A.D. agricultural surpluses had triggered a population explosion among the Bantu, propelling them in easterly

Early mechanisms for social control

Metallurgy

Iron and the Bantu dispersion

The Iron Age in Africa. An iron smelter in Tanzania such as those that enabled th Bantu to create iron tools and weapons.

Southeast Asian food crops trigger population explosions

and westerly directions across the breadth of equatorial Africa from coast to coast. Small, segmented Neolithic populations were either absorbed or eliminated by the Bantu, who enjoyed greater social cohesion and practiced efficient methods of farming and pastoralism. With plentiful food and meat, they could support many wives and large, extended families. Consequently, their numbers quickly multiplied.

The emergence of village life and trading activity

Food-producing economies led to the emergence of village life. Trade became a necessary handmaiden to agriculture as metallurgists bartered their finished tools for iron ore, copper, salt, and other essential commodities. By the close of the tenth century, most Africans were using iron implements; and from the Cameroons to the South African veld they spoke Bantu-related languages. Bantu peoples had thus initiated an agricultural revolution and accelerated the development of new mechanisms for social organization and control in East, Central, and Southern Africa. In effect, they laid the necessary foundations for the civilizations which emerged in the millennium after 900 A.D.

The impact of iron in West Africa

Iron technology brought forth similar changes in West Africa, even though the Bantu diaspora did not extend there. For centuries Nubians from the Upper Nile and Saharan Berbers, bearing iron tools and weapons, had infiltrated Negro cultures of the West African grasslands. Marrying local women, they quickly lost their ethnic identity. An excellent environment for fishing and cereal cultivation in the Niger River area and Chad basin had already stimulated a dramatic growth of the indigenous population.

Before the introduction of the camel, Carthaginians and later Romans had conducted a minuscule Saharan trade by horse-drawn chariot. But few if any of them ever established direct commercial connections with West Africans. Their small purchases of gold, ivory, slaves, and pepper were made through the middlemen of Garamante in the Fezzan oases of central Sahara. The clever Garamantes received glass beads, fine cloth, and dates which they passed on to the West African producers. By 300 A.D. camels had come into wide use in the Sahara as transport vehicles. Camels possessed an exceptional capacity for carrying heavy loads over long distances and maneuvering effectively under sandy conditions. They became, in effect, ships of the desert and greatly facilitated the movement of peoples and goods between North and West Africa. An ensuing revival and expansion of trans-Saharan trade led to the eventual flowering of market centers and coherent civilizations in the grassland expanse between southern Mauretania and Lake Chad.

Roman departure from North Africa in the fourth century A.D. seems to have coincided with the organization by desert Berbers of the first West African kingdom, called Ghana, or Awkar. This Negro-Berber state, located in the southeastern corner of modern Mauretania, thrived on its middleman position between the gold miners of the southern forests and the Berber traders of North Africa. By the eighth century the "Ghana," or king, of Awkar was a Negro, and his people were known in North Africa and the Middle East as the world's major gold exporters.

Trans-Saharan traffic remained small and informally organized until the mid-seventh century when Muslim Arabs overran the strategic Fezzan oases. By 740 A.D. desert Berbers had begun to embrace Islam and to withdraw more deeply into the Sahara where they set up new

Agriculture. A Ndebele granary in southern Zimbabwe. The ability to sustain sedentary village life depended on the community's ability to stockpile foodstuffs.

The Berbers in West Africa

The West African Sudan: Land of the Blacks

Indo-Shirazi penetration along the East African coast

trade centers. At Sijilmasa they exchanged Ghanaian gold with the Arabs for Saharan salt. The salt was resold in the south to perspiring miners while the Arabs carried their gold into North Africa and Europe.

The Arab presence in North Africa encouraged Berbers to probe more deeply into West Africa in search of gold or to seek refuge from Islamic persecution. Zaghawa Berbers established communities of highly cultured farmers and fishermen around Lake Chad. In 846 A.D. they founded a ruling dynasty, based on concepts of divine kingship. Like the Berbers in Ghana, they readily married into local families and were ethnically absorbed within a few generations.

Small chieftaincies were gradually coalescing into larger governing units from the upper Senegal eastward to the shores of Lake Chad. By about 800 A.D. trade routes had reached the upper Niger River, where caravan paths from Morocco, Algeria, Tunis, Tripoli, and Egypt converged at the emporium of Gao. West Africa's rolling grasslands had become famous in Arab commercial circles as the Bilad-as-Sudan or "Land of the Blacks."

Similar commercial and political trends were discernible along the coast of East Africa. The rise of Persian sea power in the late seventh century resulted in the eclipse of Ethiopian trade in the Red Sea and western Indian Ocean. Arabs from the Persian Shiraz swarmed along the Banadir coast of modern Somalia, where they established permanent trading settlements. Within a few generations they turned their sailing boats, or dhows, southward along the coast of modern Kenya and Tanzania. There they encountered Bantu-speaking people who, centuries before, had reached the coast from the equatorial savanna. By 900 A.D. the Bantu were beginning to marry into Arab Shirazi and Indian families, who had only recently converted to Islam. Together

Gateway to a Medieval City in the Sultanate of Morocco. Morocco was a major trading partner of the Western Sudanic cities and had a significant architectural impact on the area.

they founded dynasties and organized a formal seaborne trade propelled by monsoon winds. As of old, turtle shells, ivory, rhinoceros horns, and small numbers of slaves were exported to Arabian ports and northwestern India. But by 900 A.D. increasing quantities of Central African copper had begun to arrive on the Mozambique coast. Growing Asian demands for copper led to trading operations through the Zambezi valley to reach the mines of Katanga. Indian Ocean trade, like that of the Sahara, acted as a powerful catalyst for the centralization of authority among groups engaged in mining and marketing activities.

The catalytic effect of Indian Ocean Trade

Meanwhile, in the sixth century along the upper reaches of the Nile, a number of Christian Nubian kingdoms appeared. The Nubians, though influenced by Byzantine Greece, developed their own language, laid out beautiful cities, constructed impressive brick monasteries and cathedrals, and adorned them with paintings. They also enjoyed a highly sophisticated tradition of ceramic art, with pottery of outstanding design. Their civilization reached its zenith during the ninth and tenth centuries. Powerful Nubian armies were strong enough to resist Muslim intrusions for nearly four centuries afterward.

The flowering of Nubian civilization

SELECTED READINGS

• Items so designated are available in paperback editions.
• Binyon, Laurence, *Painting in the Far East,* 3d ed., New York, 1923.
• ——, *The Spirit of Man in Asian Art,* New York, 1935.
• Nakamura Hajime, *Ways of Thinking of Eastern Peoples: India, China, Tibet, Japan,* ed. P. P. Wiener, Honolulu, 1964.

INDIA—*See also Readings for Chapter 6*

Devahuti, D., *Harsha: A Political Study,* Oxford, 1970.
Panikkar, K. M., *India and the Indian Ocean,* New York, 1945.
Sen, Gertrude E., *The Pageant of India's History,* Vol. I, New York, 1948.
van Leur, J. C., *Indonesian Trade and Society,* New York, 1955.

CHINA—*See also Readings for Chapter 7*

Bagchi, P. C., *India and China, a Thousand Years of Cultural Relations,* rev. ed., New York, 1951.
Balazs, Etienne, *Chinese Civilization and Bureaucracy,* New Haven, 1964. An important interpretation of Chinese society.
Carter, T. F., and L. C. Goodrich, *The Invention of Printing in China and Its Spread Westward,* 2d ed., New York, 1955.
• Ch'en, Kenneth, *Buddhism in China, A Historical Survey,* Princeton, 1974. A solid and lucid study.
Ching, Julia, *Confucianism and Christianity: A Comparative Study,* New York, 1977.

• Lattimore, Owen, *The Inner Asian Frontiers of China*, 2d ed., New York, 1951.

• Levenson, J. R., and F. Schurmann, *China, an Interpretive History: From the Beginnings to the Fall of Han*, Berkeley, 1969.

Schafer, E. H., *The Golden Peaches of Samarkand: A Study of T'ang Exotics*, Berkeley, 1963.

Shryock, J. K., *The Origin and Development of the State Cult of Confucius*, New York, 1932.

Sickman, L., and A. Soper, *The Art and Architecture of China*, Baltimore, 1956. Reliable; richly illustrated.

• Sullivan, Michael, *The Arts of China*, rev. ed., Berkeley, 1978. Incorporates recent archeological discoveries.

Sun, E. Z., and John De Francis, *Chinese Social History*, Washington, 1956. Translations of articles by modern Chinese scholars.

• Wittfogel, K. A., *Oriental Despotism: A Comparative Study of Total Power*, New Haven, 1957. Attempts to explain the despotic character of the Chinese imperial government by the necessities of a "hydraulic society," in which flood control and efficient irrigation systems were imperative.

Wright, Arthur F., *Buddhism in Chinese History*, Stanford, 1959. Brief but good.

Zurcher, E., *The Buddhist Conquest of China: The Spread and Adaptation of Buddhism in Early Medieval China*, 2 vols., Leiden, 1959. An illuminating study of the interaction between Chinese culture and Buddhism to the early fifth century A.D.

JAPAN

Anesaki, Masaharu, *Art, Life and Nature in Japan*, Boston, 1933.

———, *History of Japanese Religion*, London, 1930.

Brower, R. H., and E. Miner, *Japanese Court Poetry*, Stanford, 1961. Covers the period from the sixth to the fourteenth centuries.

Cole, Wendell, *Kyoto in the Momoyama Period*, Norman, Okla., 1967.

Eliot, Charles, *Japanese Buddhism*, New York, 1959. A standard text.

• Fenollosa, E. F., *Epochs of Chinese and Japanese Art*, New York, 1927.

• Hall, J. W., *Japan: From Prehistory to Modern Times*, New York, 1971.

Langer, P. F., *Japan, Yesterday and Today*, New York, 1966. An excellent summary.

• Moore, C. A., ed., *The Japanese Mind: Essentials of Japanese Philosophy and Culture*, Honolulu, 1967.

• Morris, Ivan, *The World of the Shining Prince*, Baltimore, 1969.

• Munsterberg, Hugo, *The Arts of Japan: An Illustrated History*, Rutland, Vt., 1957.

• Reischauer, E. O., *Japan: The Story of a Nation*, New York, 1979. Lucid and well organized.

Sansom, George B., *A History of Japan to 1934*, Stanford, 1958. An outstanding work by an eminent British scholar.

———, *Japan: A Short Cultural History*, rev. ed., New York, 1962.

Swann, Peter C., *An Introduction to the Arts of Japan*, New York, 1958.

• Warner, Langdon, *The Enduring Art of Japan*, Cambridge, Mass., 1952.

Wheatley, Paul, and Thomas See, *From Court to Capital: A Tentative Interpretation of the Origins of the Japanese Urban Tradition*, Chicago, 1978.

Whitney, J. H., and R. K. Beardsley, *Twelve Doors to Japan,* New York, 1965.

AFRICA

Adams, William Y., *Nubia—Corridor to Africa,* London, 1977.
• Bovill, E. W., *The Golden Trade of the Moors.* New York, 1958.
• Oliver, Roland, ed., *The Dawn of African History,* New York, 1968.
Oliver, Roland, and Brian Fagan, eds., *Africa in the Iron Age c. 500 B.C. to A.D. 1400,* Cambridge, 1975.
• Posnansky, Merrick, ed., *Prelude to East African History,* London, 1966.
Shaw, Thurstan C., *Nigeria: Its Archaeology and Early History,* London, 1977.

SOURCE MATERIALS

Aston, W. G., tr., *Nihongi: Chronicles of Japan from the Earliest Times to* A.D. *697,* 2 vols., London, 1896.
Ayscough, Florence, ed., *Tu Fu, the Autobiography of a Chinese Poet,* London, 1934.
Beal, Samuel, tr., *Buddhist Records of the Western World,* 2 vols., London, 1884.
Bynner, Witter, and Kiang Kanghu, trs., *The Jade Mountain, a Chinese Anthology,* New York, 1929.
• de Bary, W. T., ed., *Sources of Chinese Tradition,* "The Imperial Age: Ch'in and Han"; "Neo-Taoism and Buddhism," New York, 1960.
• ———, ed., *Sources of Indian Tradition, "Hinduism,"* New York, 1958.
• ———, ed., *Sources of Japanese Tradition,* "Ancient Japan"; "The Heian Period," New York, 1964.
• Fage, J. D., and R. A. Oliver, eds., *Papers in African Prehistory,* New York, 1979.
• Keene, Donald, ed., *Anthology of Japanese Literature, from the Earliest Era to the Mid-Nineteenth Century,* New York, 1956.
Lu, David, ed., *Sources of Japanese History,* Vol. I, New York, 1973.
Morris, Ivan., tr., *As I Crossed the Bridge of Dreams: Recollections of a Woman in Eleventh-Century Japan.*
Sanskrit Dramas: *Sakuntala, The Little Clay Cart.*
• Thompson, L., and J. Ferguson, eds., *Africa in Classical Antiquity,* New York, 1969.
• van Buitenen, J. A. B., *Tales of Ancient India,* Chicago, 1959.
Waley, Arthur, tr., *Ballads and Stories from Tun-Huang, an Anthology* (T'ang era); *The Tale of Genji; Translations from the Chinese,* New York, 1960.
Watson, Burton, tr., *Records of the Grand Historian of China, Translated from the Shih Chi of Ssu-ma Ch'ien,* 2 vols., New York, 1961.
• Whitehouse, W., and E. Yanagisawa, trs., *The Tale of Lady Ochikubo,* Kobe, 1934.

Part Three

THE WORLD IN
THE MIDDLE AGES

The "Middle Ages" was a term coined by Europeans in the seventeenth century to express their view that a long and dismal period of interruption extended between the glorious accomplishments of classical Greece and Rome and their own "modern age." Because the term became so widespread, it is now an ineradicable part of our historical vocabulary; but no serious scholar uses it with the sense of contempt it once had. Between about 600 and 1500—the rough opening and closing dates of the Middle Ages—too many different things happened to be characterized in any single way. In the eastern parts of the old Roman Empire two new civilizations emerged, the Byzantine and the Islamic, which must rank among the most impressive civilizations of all time. Although the Byzantine civilization came to an end in 1453, the Islamic one has continued to exist without major interruption right up to the present. Seen from an Islamic perspective, therefore, the "Middle Ages" was not a middle period at all but a marvelous time of birth and vigorous early youth. The history of western Europe in the Middle Ages is conventionally divided into three parts: the early Middle Ages; the High Middle Ages; and the later Middle Ages. Throughout the early, High, and later Middle Ages the Christian religion played an extraordinarily important role in human life, but otherwise there are few common denominators. The early Middle Ages, from about 600 to about 1050, came closest to appearing like an interval of darkness, for the level of material and intellectual accomplishment was, in fact, very low. Nonetheless, even during the early Middle Ages important foundations were being laid for the future: above all, western Europe was beginning to develop its own distinct sense of cultural identity. The High Middle Ages, from about 1050 to 1300, was one of the most creative epochs in the history of human endeavor. Europeans greatly improved their standard of living, established enduring national states, developed new institutions of learning and modes of thought, and created magnificent works of literature and art. During the later Middle Ages, from about 1300 to 1500, the survival of many high-medieval accomplishments was called into question by the onslaught of numerous disasters, particularly profound economic depression and lethal plague. But people in the later Middle Ages rose above adversity, tenaciously held on to what was most valuable in their prior inheritance, and, where necessary, created new institutions and thought-patterns to fit their altered circumstances. The Middle Ages thus were really many hundred years of enormous diversity. They may be studied profitably both for their own intrinsic interest and for the fundamental contributions they made to the development of modern times. During these same "medieval" centuries, the great nations of southern and eastern Asia continued their cultural evolution along lines already established. Both India and China were invaded, however, by Mongols from the West and North who introduced alien elements originally derived from Muslim sources. Japan adopted political feudalism and more and more aspects of Chinese culture. The spread of the religion of Islam in Africa promoted political and cultural progress in several regions of that vast continent.

The European Middle Ages

POLITICS	PHILOSOPHY AND SCIENCE	
Byzantine Emperor Heraclius, 610–641		**600**
Muhammad enters Mecca in triumph, 630		
Muslims conquer Syria, Persia, and Egypt, 636–651		
Muslims conquer Spain, 711		
Muslim attack on Constantinople repulsed, 717		**700**
Charles Martel defeats Muslims at Poitiers, 732		
Abbasid dynasty in Islam, 750–1258		
Pepin the Short anointed king of the Franks, 751		
Charlemagne, 768–814		
Charlemagne crowned emperor, 800		**800**
Carolingian Empire disintegrates, c. 850–911		
Alfred the Great of England, 871–899		
High point of Viking raids in Europe, c. 880–911		
	Al-Farabi, d. 950	
Otto the Great of Germany, 936–973	Avicenna, d. 1037	**900**
	Peter Abelard, 1079–1142	**1000**
Norman Conquest of England, 1066		
Seljuk Turks defeat Byzantines at Manzikert, 1071		
Penance of Henry IV at Canossa, 1077		
Henry I of England, 1100–1135	Origins of universities in the West, c. 1100–c. 1300	**1100**
Louis VI of France, 1108–1137	Translation of Aristotle's works into Latin, c. 1140–c. 1260	
Frederick I (Barbarossa) of Germany, 1152–1190	Peter Lombard's *Sentences,* c. 1155	
Henry II of England, 1154–1189	Robert Grosseteste, c. 1168–1253	
Philip Augustus of France, 1180–1223	Windmill invented, c. 1180	
	Averroës, d. 1198	
Crusaders take Constantinople (Fourth Crusade), 1204	Maimonides, d. 1204	**1200**
Spanish victory over Muslims at Las Navas de Tolosa, 1212		
Frederick II of Germany and Sicily, 1212–1250	Roger Bacon, c. 1214–1294	
	St. Thomas Aquinas, 1225–1274	
Magna Carta, 1215	Height of Scholasticism, c. 1250–c. 1277	
Louis IX (St. Louis) of France, 1226–1270	William of Ockham, c. 1285–1349	
	Mechanical clock invented, c. 1290	
Edward I of England, 1272–1307		
Philip IV (the Fair) of France, 1285–1314	Master Eckhart, active c. 1300–c. 1327	**1300**
Hundred Years' War, 1337–1453	Height of nominalism, c. 1320–c. 1500	
Political chaos in Germany, c. 1350–c. 1450		
Appearance of Joan of Arc, 1429–1431		**1400**
Reassertion of royal power in France, c. 1143–c. 1513	Printing with movable type, c. 1450	
Rise of princes in Germany, c. 1450–c. 1500	Heavy artillery helps Turks capture Constantinople and French end Hundred Years' War, 1453	
Capture of Constantinople by Ottoman Turks, 1453		
Wars of the Roses in England, 1455–1485		
Peace among northern Italian states, 1454–1485		
Marriage of Ferdinand and Isabella, 1469		
Strong Tudor dynasty in England, 1485–1603		

The European Middle Ages (continued)

	ECONOMICS	RELIGION	ARTS AND LETTERS
600	Decline of towns and trade in the West, c. 500–c. 700	Muhammad, c. 570–632 Pope Gregory I, 590–604 Muhammad's *Hijrah*, 622	Byzantine church of Santa Sophia, 532–537
700	Height of Islamic commerce and industry, c. 700–c. 1300 Predominantly agrarian economy in the West, c. 700–c. 1050	Split in Islam between Shiites and Sunnites, c. 656 Missionary work of St. Boniface in Germany, c. 715–754 Iconoclasm in Byzantine Empire, 726–843	The Venerable Bede, d. 735 *Beowulf*, c. 750 Irish "Book of Kells," c. 750 Carolingian Renaissance, c. 800–c. 850
800	Height of Byzantine commerce and industry, c. 800–c. 1000	Foundation of Cluny, 910	
900		Byzantine conversion of Russia, c. 988	
1000	Destruction of Byzantine free peasantry, c. 1025–c. 1100 Agricultural advance, revival of towns and trade in the West, c. 1050– c. 1300	Beginning of Reform Papacy, 1046 Schism between Roman and Eastern Orthodox Churches, 1054 Pope Gregory VII, 1073–1085 St. Bernard of Clairvaux, 1090–1153 First Crusade, 1095–1099	Romanesque style in architecture and art, c. 1000–c. 1200
1100		Height of Cistercian monasticism, c. 1115–c. 1153 Concordat of Worms ends investiture struggle, 1122 Crusaders lose Jerusalem to Saladin, 1187 Pope Innocent III, 1198–1216	*Song of Roland*, c. 1095 Troubadour poetry, c. 1100–c. 1220 *Rubaiyat* of Umar Khayyam, c. 1120 Anna Comnena's biography of Alexius, 1148 Gothic style in architecture and art, c. 1150–c. 1500 Poetry of Chretien de Troyes, c. 1165–c. 1190
1200		Albigensian Crusade, 1208–1213 Founding of Franciscan Order, 1210 Fourth Lateran Council, 1215 Founding of Dominican Order, 1216 Fall of last Christian outposts in Holy Land, 1291 Pope Boniface VIII, 1294–1303	Development of polyphony in Paris, c. 1170 Wolfram von Eschenbach, c. 1200 Gottfried von Strassburg, c. 1210 Persian poetry of Sadi, c. 1250
1300	European economic depression, c. 1300–c. 1450 Floods through western Europe, 1315 Black Death, 1347–1350 Height of Hanseatic League, c. 1350–c. 1450 English Peasants' Revolt, 1381 Medici Bank, 1397–1494	Babylonian Captivity of papacy, 1305–1378 John Wyclif, c. 1330–1384 Great Schism of papacy, 1378–1417 John Hus preaches in Bohemia, c. 1408–1415	*Romance of the Rose*, c. 1270 Paintings of Giotto, c. 1305–1337 Dante's *Divine Comedy*, c. 1310 Boccaccio's *Decameron*, c. 1350 Persian poetry of Hafiz, c. 1370 Chaucer's *Canterbury Tales*, c. 1390
1400		Council of Constance, 1414–1417 Hussite Revolt, 1420–1434 *Imitation of Christ*, c. 1427 Council of Basel, defeat of conciliarism, 1431–1449	Paintings of Jan van Eyck, c. 1400–c. 1441

The Nonwestern World, 600–1600

AFRICA	INDIA	THE FAR EAST	
Expansion of Bantu people, 200–900	Great stone temple architecture, c. 550–1250 Sanskrit drama, c. 600–1000 King Harsha, 606–648	T'ang Dynasty in China, 618–907 Taika Reform Edict, creating imperial government in Japan, 645	**600** **700**
			800
		Wood-block printing of books in China, Japan, and Korea, c. 900	**900**
Expansion of Islam, 1000–1500 Consolidation of states, 1000–1500	Muslim invasions, 1000–1500	Sung Dynasty in China, 960–1279	**1000**
Bantu, Arab, and Indian cultures blend in Swahili civilization along eastern coast, c. 1100–1500		Neo-Confucianism, 1130–1200 Highest development of landscape painting in China, 1141–1279 Explosive powder used in weapons in China, c. 1150 Genghis Khan, 1162?–1227 Establishment of Shogunate in Japan, 1192 Zen Buddhism in Japan, c. 1200	**1100**
Decline of Kingdom of Ghana, c. 1224	Turkish Sultanate at Delhi, 1206–1526	Inoculation for smallpox in China, c. 1200 Development of Chinese drama, c. 1235 Marco Polo in China, 1275–1292	**1200**
Mali empire in middle Niger region, c. 1300–1500 University of Timbuktu, c. 1330		Mongol (Yüan) Dynasty in China, 1279–1368 Rise of daimyo in Japan, 1300–1500 Ming Dynasty in China, 1368–1644	**1300**
	Sack of Delhi by Timur, 1398		**1400**
Expansion of Songhay, c. 1493–1582			

AFRICA	INDIA	THE FAR EAST
1500	Founding of Sikh religious sect, c. 1500	
		Introduction of Christianity into Japan, 1549–1551
Decline of Songhay after defeat by Moroccans, 1591		

Chapter 13

ROME'S THREE HEIRS: THE BY-ZANTINE, ISLAMIC, AND EARLY-MEDIEVAL WESTERN WORLDS

Constantinople is a bustling city, and merchants come to it from all over, by sea or land, and there is none like it in the world except Baghdad, the great city of Islam. In Constantinople is the church of Santa Sophia, and the seat of the Pope of the Greeks, since the Greeks do not obey the Pope of Rome. There are also as many churches as there are days of the year. A quantity of wealth is brought to them from the islands, and the like of this wealth is not to be found in any other church in the world.

—Benjamin of Tudela, *Travels*

You have become the best community ever raised up for mankind, enjoining the right and forbidding the wrong, and having faith in God.

—The Koran, III, 110

He who ordains the fate of kingdoms and the march of events, the almighty Disposer, having destroyed one extraordinary image, that of the Romans, which had feet of iron, or even feet of clay, then raised up among the Franks the golden head of a second image, just as remarkable, in the person of the glorious Charlemagne.

—A monk of St. Gall

A new period in the history of Western civilizations began in the seventh century when it became clear that there would no longer be a single empire ruling over all the territories bordering on the Mediterranean. By about 700 A.D., in place of a united Rome, there were three successor civilizations that stood as rivals on different Mediterranean shores: the Byzantine, the Islamic, and the Western Christian. Each of these had its own language and distinctive forms of life. The Byzantine civilization, which descended directly from the Eastern Roman Empire, was Greek-speaking and dedicated to combining Roman governmental traditions with intense pursuit of

The successors of Rome

the Christian faith. The Islamic civilization was based on Arabic and inspired in government as well as culture by the idealism of a dynamic new religion. Western Christian civilization in comparison to the others was a laggard. It was the least economically advanced and faced organizational weaknesses in both government and religion. But it did have some base of unity in Christianity and the Latin language, and it would soon begin to find greater political and religious cohesiveness.

The reappraisal of the Byzantine and Islamic civilizations

Because the Western Christian civilization ultimately outstripped its rivals, Western writers until recently have tended to denigrate the Byzantine and Islamic civilizations as backward and even irrational. Of the three, however, the Western Christian was certainly the most backward from about the seventh to the eleventh centuries. For some four or five hundred years the West lived in the shadow of Constantinople and Mecca. Scholars are only now beginning to recognize the full measure of Byzantine and Islamic accomplishments. These greatly merit our attention both for their own sakes and because they influenced western European development in many direct and indirect ways.

1. THE BYZANTINE EMPIRE AND ITS CULTURE

The Byzantine achievement impressive despite weaknesses

Once dismissed by the historian Gibbon as "a tedious and uniform tale of weakness and misery," the story of Byzantine history is today recognized to be a most interesting and impressive one. It is true that the Byzantine Empire was in many respects not very innovative; it was also continually beset by grave external threats and internal weaknesses. Nonetheless it managed to survive for a millennium. In fact the empire did not just survive, it frequently prospered and greatly influenced the world around it. Among many other achievements, it helped preserve ancient Greek thought, created magnificent works of art, and brought Christian culture to pagan peoples, above all the Slavs. Simply stated it was one of the most enduring and influential empires the world has ever known.

Problems of periodization in Byzantine history

It is impossible to date the beginning of Byzantine history with any precision because the Byzantine Empire was the uninterrupted successor of the Roman state. For this reason different historians prefer different beginnings. Some argue that "Byzantine" characteristics already emerged in Roman history as a result of the easternizing policy of Diocletian, and others that Byzantine history began when Constantine moved his capital from Rome to Constantinople, the city which subsequently became the center of the Byzantine world. (The old name for the site on which Constantinople was built was Byzantium, from which we get the adjective Byzantine; it would be more accurate but cumbersome to say Constantinopolitine.) Diocletian and Constantine, however, continued to rule a united Roman Empire. As we have seen, as late as the sixth century, after the western part of the empire had fallen to the Germans, the Eastern Roman Emperor Justinian thought of himself as an heir to Augustus and fought hard to win back the West. Justinian's reign was clearly an important turning point in the direction of Byzantine civilization because it saw the crystallization of new forms of thought and art that can be considered more "Byzantine" than "Roman." But this still remains a matter of subjective emphasis: some scholars emphasize these newer forms, while others respond that Justinian continued to speak Latin and dreamed of restoring old Rome. Only after 610 did a new dynasty emerge that came from the East, spoke Greek, and maintained a fully Eastern or properly "Byzantine" policy. Hence although good arguments can be made for beginning Byzantine history with Diocletian, Constantine, or Justinian, we will begin here with the accession in 610 of the Emperor Heraclius.

It is also convenient to begin in 610 because from then until 1071 the main lines of Byzantine military and political history were determined by successful resistance against successive waves of invasions from the East. When Heraclius came to the throne the very existence of the Byzantine Empire was being challenged by the Persians, who had conquered almost all of the empire's Asian territories. As a symbol of their triumph the Persians in 614 even carried off the holy relic believed to be part of the original cross from Jerusalem. By enormous effort Heraclius rallied Byzantine strength and quickly turned the tide, fully routing the Persians and retrieving the cross in 627. Persia was then reduced to a subordinate state and Heraclius reigned in glory until 641. But in his last years new armies began to invade eastern Byzantine territory, swarming out of hitherto placid Arabia. Inspired by the new religion of Islam and profiting from Byzantine exhaustion after the struggle with Persia, the Arabs made astonishingly rapid gains. By 650 they had taken most of the Byzantine territories the Persians had occupied briefly in the early seventh century, had conquered all of Persia itself, and were making their way westward across North Africa. Having become a Mediterranean power, the Arabs also took to the sea. In 677 they tried to conquer Constantinople with a fleet. Failing that, they attempted to take the city again in 717 by means of a concerted land and sea operation.

The Arab threat to Constantinople in 717 was a new low in Byzantine fortunes, but the threat was countered by the Emperor Leo the Isaurian (717–741) with as much resolution as Heraclius had met the Persian threat a century before. With the help of a secret incendiary device known as "Greek fire"[1] and great military ability, Leo was able

The reign of Heraclius; the rise of Islam

Byzantine revival prior to the Battle of Manzikert

[1] This is believed to have been a mixture of sulphur, naptha, and quicklime. Bronze tubes placed on the prows of ships, and also on the walls of Constantinople, released this liquid fire at the enemy.

ΠΩΡΙΚΟΡ· Η ρασδὲ και τοσοκλαριῶπρ πολοωπυρί·

τόλεερωμει πυρπολ· τωντωνεΝΑΝΤΙ φελοΝ·

Greek Fire

to defeat the Arab forces on sea and land. Leo's relief of Constantinople in 717 was one of the most significant battles in European history, not just because it allowed the Byzantine Empire to endure for centuries more, but also because it helped to save the West: had the Islamic armies taken Constantinople there would have been little to stop them from sweeping through the rest of Europe. Over the next few decades the Byzantines were able to reconquer most of Asia Minor. This territory, together with Greece, became the heartland of their empire for the next three hundred years. Thereafter the Byzantines achieved a stalemate with Islam until they were able to take the offensive against a decaying Islamic power in the second half of the tenth century. In that period—the greatest in Byzantine history—Byzantine troops reconquered most of Syria. But in the eleventh century a different Islamic people, the Seljuk Turks, cancelled out all the prior Byzantine gains. In 1071 the Seljuks annihilated a Byzantine army at Manzikert in Asia Minor, a stunning victory which allowed them to overrun the remaining Byzantine eastern provinces. Constantinople was now thrown back upon itself more or less as it had been in the days of Heraclius and Leo.

The end of the Byzantine Empire

After Manzikert the Byzantine Empire managed to survive, but never regained its earlier vigor. One major reason for this was the fact that, from 1071 until the final destruction of the empire in 1453, Byzantine fortunes were greatly complicated by the rise of western Europe. Hitherto the West had been far too weak to present any major challenge to Byzantium, but that situation changed entirely in the course of the eleventh century. In 1071, the same year that saw the victory of the Seljuks over the Byzantines in Asia Minor, westerners known as Normans expelled the Byzantines from their last holdings in southern Italy. Despite this clear sign of Western enmity, in 1095 a Byzantine emperor named Alexius Comnenus issued a call for Western help against the Turks. He could hardly have made a worse mistake: his call helped inspire the Crusades, and the Crusades became a major cause for the fall of the Byzantine state. Westerners on the First Crusade did help the Byzantines win back Asia Minor but they also carved out territories for themselves in Syria, which the Byzantines considered to be their own. As time went on frictions mounted and the westerners, now militarily superior, looked more and more upon Constantinople as a fruit ripe for the picking. In 1204 they finally picked it: Crusaders who should have been intent on conquering Jerusalem conquered Constantinople instead and sacked the city with ruthless ferocity. A greatly reduced Byzantine government was able to survive nearby and return to Constantinople in 1261, but thereafter the Byzantine state was an "empire" in name and recollection of past glories only. After 1261 it eked out a reduced existence in parts of Greece until 1453, when powerful Turkish successors to the Seljuks, the Ottomans, completed the Crusaders' work of destruction by conquering the last vestiges of the empire and taking Constantinople. Turks rule in Constantinople—now Istanbul—even today.

That Constantinople was finally taken was no surprise. What *is* a cause for wonder is that the Byzantine state survived for so many centuries in the face of so many different hostile forces. This wonder becomes all the greater when it is recognized that the internal political history of the empire was exceedingly tumultuous. Because Byzantine rulers followed their late-Roman predecessors in claiming the powers of divinely appointed absolute monarchs, there was no way of opposing them other than by intrigue and violence. Hence Byzantine history was marked by repeated palace revolts; mutilations, murders, and blindings were almost commonplace. Byzantine politics became so famous for their behind-the-scenes complexity that we still use the word "Byzantine" to refer to highly complex and devious backstage machinations. Fortunately for the empire some very able rulers did emerge from time to time to wield their untrammeled powers with efficiency, and, even more fortunately, a bureaucratic machinery always kept running during times of palace upheaval.

Factors of the stability of the Byzantine Empire: (1) occasional able rulers

Efficient bureaucratic government indeed was one of the major elements of Byzantine success and longevity. The Byzantines could count on having an adequate supply of manpower for their bureaucracy because Byzantine civilization preserved and encouraged the practice of education for the laity. This was one of the major differences between the Byzantine East and the early Latin West: from about 600 to about 1200 there was practically no literate laity in Western Christendom, while lay literacy in the Byzantine East was the basis of governmental accomplishment. Byzantine officialdom regulated many aspects of life, far more than we would think proper

(2) efficient bureaucratic administration

today. Bureaucrats helped supervise education and religion and presided over all forms of economic endeavor. Urban officials in Constantinople, for example, regulated prices and wages, maintained systems of licensing, controlled exports, and enforced the observance of the Sabbath. What is more, they usually did this with comparative efficiency and did not stifle business initiative. Bureaucratic methods too helped regulate the army and navy, the courts, and the diplomatic service, endowing them with organizational strengths incomparable for their age.

(3) firm economic base

Another explanation for Byzantine endurance was the comparatively sound economic base of the state until the eleventh century. As the historian Sir Steven Runciman has said, "if Byzantium owed her strength and security to the efficiency of her Services, it was her trade that enabled her to pay for them." While long-distance trade and urban life all but disappeared in the West for hundreds of years, commerce and cities continued to flourish in the Byzantine East. Above all, in the ninth and tenth centuries Constantinople was a vital trade emporium for Far Eastern luxury goods and Western raw materials. The empire also nurtured and protected its own industries, most notably that of silk-making, and it was renowned until the eleventh century for its stable gold and silver coinage. Among its great urban centers was not only Constantinople, which at times may have had a population of close to a million, but also in certain periods Antioch, and up until the end of Byzantine history the bustling cities of Thessalonica and Trebizond.

The significance of Byzantine agricultural history

Historians emphasize Byzantine trade and industry because these were so advanced for the time and provided most of the surplus wealth which supported the state. But agriculture was really at the heart of the Byzantine economy as it was of all premodern ones. The story of Byzantine agricultural history is mainly one of a struggle of small peasants to stay free of the encroachments of large estates owned by wealthy aristocrats and monasteries. Until the eleventh century the free peasantry just managed to maintain its existence with the help of state legislation, but after 1025 the aristocracy gained power in the government and began to transform the peasants into impoverished tenants. This had many unfortunate results, not the least of which was that the peasants became less interested in resisting the enemy. The defeat at Manzikert was the inevitable result. The destruction of the free peasantry was accompanied and followed in the last centuries of Byzantine history by foreign domination of Byzantine trade. Primarily the Italian cities of Venice and Genoa established trading outposts and privileges within Byzantine realms after 1204, which channeled off much of the wealth on which the state had previously relied. In this way the empire was defeated by the Venetians from within before it was destroyed by the Turks from without.

So far we have spoken about military campaigns, government, and economics as if they were at the center of Byzantine survival. Seen from hindsight they were, but what the Byzantines themselves cared about most was usually religion. Remarkable as it might seem, Byzantines fought over abstruse religious questions as vehemently as we today might argue about politics and sports—indeed more vehemently because the Byzantines were often willing to fight and even die over some words in a religious creed. The intense preoccupation with questions of doctrine is well illustrated by the report of an early Byzantine writer who said that when he asked a baker for the price of bread, the answer came back, "the Father is greater than the Son," and when he asked whether his bath was ready, was told that "the Son proceeds from nothing." Understandably such zealousness could harm the state greatly during times of religious dissension but endow it with a powerful sense of confidence and mission during times of religious concord.

Preoccupation with religion

Byzantine religious dissensions were greatly complicated by the fact that the emperors took an active role in them. Because the emperors carried great power in the life of the Church—emperors were sometimes deemed by churchmen to be "similar to God"—they exerted great influence in religious debates. Nonetheless, especially in the face of provincial separatism, rulers could never force all their subjects to believe what they did. Only after the loss of many eastern provinces and the refinement of doctrinal formulae did religious peace seem near in the eighth century. But then it was shattered for still another century by what is known as the Iconoclastic Controversy.

Imperial participation in religious controversies

The Iconoclasts were those who wished to prohibit the worship of icons—that is, images of Christ and the saints. Since the Iconoclastic movement was initiated by the Emperor Leo the Isaurian, and subsequently directed with even greater energy by his son Constantine V (740–775), historians have discerned in it different motives. One was certainly theological. The worship of images seemed to the Iconoclasts to smack of paganism. They believed that nothing made by human beings should be worshiped by them, that Christ was so divine that he could not be conceived of in terms of human art, and that the prohibition of worshiping "graven images" in the Ten Commandments (Exodus: 20,4) placed the matter beyond dispute.

Iconoclasts' Cross. The Iconoclasts covered over beautiful apse mosaics with unadorned crosses. This example survives in St. Irene's church, Greece.

In addition to these theological points, there were probably other considerations. Since Leo the Isaurian was the emperor who saved Constantinople from the onslaught of Islam, and since Muslims zealously shunned images on the grounds that they were "the work of Satan" (Koran: V.92), it has been argued that Leo's Iconoclastic policy was an attempt to answer one of Islam's greatest criticisms of Christianity and thereby deprive Islam of some of its appeal. There may also have been certain internal political and financial motives. By proclaiming a radical new religious movement the emperors may have wished to reassert their control over the Church and combat the

Political and financial motives

Christ as Ruler of the Universe. **A twelfth-century Byzantine mosaic from the cathedral of Cefalù in Sicily. Although the Byzantines did not rule in Sicily in the twelfth century, the Norman rulers employed Byzantine workmen. Note the use of Greek—the Byzantine language—on the left-handed Bible page and Latin—the Norman language—on the right.**

growing strength of monasteries. In the event, the monasteries did rally behind the cause of images and as a result were bitterly persecuted by Constantine V, who took the opportunity to appropriate much monastic wealth.

Significance of the Iconoclastic Controversy

The Iconoclastic Controversy was resolved in the ninth century by a return to the status quo, namely the worship of images, but the century of turmoil over the issue had some profound results. One was the destruction by imperial order of a large amount of religious art. Pre-eighth-century Byzantine religious art that survives today comes mostly from places like Italy or Palestine, which were beyond the easy reach of the Iconoclastic emperors. When we see how great this art is we can only lament the destruction of the rest. A second consequence of the controversy was the opening of a serious religious breach between East and West. The pope, who until the eighth century had usually been a close ally of the Byzantines, could not accept Iconoclasm for many reasons. The most important of these was that extreme Iconoclasm tended to question the cult of saints, and the claims of papal primacy were based on an assumed descent from St. Peter. Accordingly, the eighth-century popes combated Byzantine Iconoclasm and turned to the Frankish kings for support. This "about-face of the papacy" was both a major step in the worsening of East-West relations and a landmark in the history of western Europe.

Other results: (1) reaffirmation of tradition

Those were some consequences of Iconoclasm's temporary victory; a major consequence of its defeat was the reassertion of some major traits of Byzantine religiosity, which from the ninth century until the end of Byzantine history remained predominant. One of these was the reemphasis of a faith in traditionalism. Even when Byzantines were experimenting in religious matters they consistently stated that they were only restating or developing the implications of tradition. Now, after centuries of turmoil, they abandoned experiment almost entirely and reaffirmed tradition more than ever. As one opponent of Iconoclasm said: "If an angel or an emperor announces to you a gospel other than the one you have received, close your ears." This view gave strength to Byzantine religion internally by ending controversy and heresy, and helped it gain new adherents in the ninth and tenth centuries. But it also inhibited free speculation not just in religion but also in related intellectual matters.

Allied to this development was the triumph of Byzantine contemplative piety. Supporters defended the use of icons not on the grounds that they were meant to be worshiped for themselves but because they helped lead the mind from the material to the immaterial. The emphasis on contemplation as a road to religious enlightenment thereafter became the hallmark of Byzantine spirituality. While westerners did not by any means reject such a path, the typical Western saint was an activist who saw sin as a vice and sought salvation through good works. Byzantine theologians on the other hand saw sin more as ignorance and believed that salvation was to be found in illumination. This led to a certain religious passivity and mysticism in Eastern Christianity which makes it seem different from Western varieties up to the present time.

(2) the triumph of Byzantine contemplative piety

Since religion was so dominant in Byzantine life, certain secular aspects of Byzantine civilization often go unnoticed, but there are good reasons why some of these should not be forgotten. One is Byzantine cultivation of the classics. Commitment to Christianity by no means inhibited the Byzantines from revering their ancient Greek inheritance. Byzantine schools based their instruction on classical Greek literature to the degree that educated people could quote Homer more extensively than we today can quote Shakespeare. Byzantine scholars studied and commented on the philosophy of Plato and Aristotle, and Byzantine writers imitated the prose of Thucydides. Such dedicated classicism both enriched Byzantine intellectual and literary life, which is too often dismissed entirely by moderns because it generally lacked originality, and helped preserve the Greek classics for later ages. The bulk of classical Greek literature that we have today survives only because it was copied by Byzantine scribes.

Byzantine classicism

Byzantine classicism was a product of an educational system for the laity which extended even to the education of women. Given attitudes and practices in the contemporary Christian West and Islam, Byzantine commitment to female education was truly unusual. Girls from aristocratic or prosperous families did not go to schools but were relatively well educated at home by private tutors. We are told, for example, that one Byzantine woman could discourse like a Plato or a Pythagoras. The most famous Byzantine female intellectual was the Princess Anna Comnena, who described the deeds of her father Alexius in an urbane biography in which she freely cited Homer and the ancient tragedians. In addition to such literary figures there were

The education of women

women doctors in the Byzantine Empire, a fact which may serve to remind us that there have hardly been any in America almost to the present day.

Byzantine achievements in the realms of architecture and art are more familiar. The finest example of Byzantine architecture was the Church of Santa Sophia (Holy Wisdom), built at enormous cost in the sixth century. Even though it was built before the date we have taken here to be the beginning of Byzantine history, it was typically Byzantine in both its style and subsequent influence. Although designed by architects of Hellenic descent, it was vastly different from any Greek temple. Its purpose was not to express human pride in the power of the individual, but to symbolize the inward and spiritual character of the Christian religion. It was for this reason that the architects gave little attention to the external appearance of the building. Nothing but plain brick covered with plaster was used for the exterior walls; there were no marble facings, graceful columns, or sculptured entablatures. The interior, however, was decorated with richly colored mosaics, gold leaf, colored marble columns, and bits of tinted glass set on edge to refract the rays of sunlight after the fashion of sparkling gems. To emphasize a sense of the miraculous, the building was constructed in such a way that no light appeared to come from the outside at all but to be manufactured within.

The structural design of Santa Sophia was something altogether new in the history of architecture. Its central feature was the application of the principle of the dome to a building of square shape. The church was designed, first of all, in the form of a cross, and then over the central square was to be erected a magnificent dome, which would dominate the entire structure. The main problem was how to fit the round circumference of the dome to the square area it was supposed to cover. The solution consisted in having four great arches spring from pillars at the four corners of the central square. The rim of the dome

Santa Sophia. The greatest monument of Byzantine architecture. The four minarets were added after the fall of the Byzantine Empire, when the Turks turned the church into a mosque. As the diagram shows, the central dome rests on four massive arches.

was then made to rest on the keystones of the arches, with the curved triangular spaces between the arches filled in with masonry. The result was an architectural framework of marvelous strength, which at the same time made possible a style of imposing grandeur and even some delicacy of treatment. The great dome of Santa Sophia has a diameter of 107 feet and rises to a height of nearly 180 feet from the floor. So many windows are placed around its rim that the dome appears to have no support at all but to be suspended in mid-air.

As in architecture, so in art the Byzantines profoundly altered the earlier Greek classical style. Byzantines excelled in ivory-carving, manuscript illumination, jewelry-making, and, above all, the creation of mosaics—that is, designs of pictures produced by fitting together small pieces of colored glass or stone. Human figures in these mosaics were usually distorted and elongated in a very unclassical fashion to create the impression of intense piety or extreme majesty. Most Byzantine art is marked by highly abstract, formal, and jewel-like qualities. For this reason many consider Byzantine artistic culture to be a model of timeless perfection. The modern poet W. B. Yeats expressed this point of view most eloquently when he wrote in his "Sailing to Byzantium" of artificial birds made by Byzantine goldsmiths ". . . to sing / To lords and ladies of Byzantium / Of what is past, or passing, or to come."

Probably the single greatest testimony to the vitality of Byzantine civilization at its height was the conversion of many Slavic peoples, especially those of Russia. According to the legend, which has a basic kernel of fact, a Russian ruler named Vladimir decided around 988 to abandon the paganism of his ancestors. Accordingly, he sent emissaries to report on the religious practices of Islam, Roman Catholicism, and Byzantine Christianity. When they returned to tell him that only among the Byzantines did God seem to "dwell among men," he promptly agreed to be baptized by a Byzantine missionary. The event was momentous because Russia thereupon became a cultural province of Byzantium. From then until the twentieth century Russia remained a bastion of the Eastern Orthodox religion.

After Constantinople fell in 1453 Russians began to feel that they were chosen to carry on both the faith and the imperial mission of the fallen Byzantine Empire. Thus their ruler took the title of tsar—which simply means caesar—and Russians asserted that Moscow was "the third Rome": "Two Romes have fallen," said a Russian spokesman, "the third is still standing, and a fourth there shall not be." Such ideology helps explain in part the later growth of Russian imperialism. Byzantine traditions also may help explain the dominance of the ruler in the Russian state. Without question Byzantine stylistic principles influenced Russian religious art, and Byzantine ideas influenced the thought of modern Russia's greatest writers, Dostoevsky and Tolstoy.

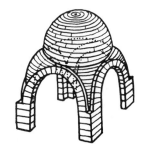

Diagram of Santa Sophia Dome

See color plates following page 384

Byzantine Metalwork. This dish, from about 620, represents literally David and Goliath, and figuratively the New Dispensation (David was the ancestor of Christ) overcoming the Old. The New, Christian, Dispensation is also symbolized by the sun, and the Old by a crescent moon.

Russian Icon. This early–seventeenth-century Russian painting depicts an angel in a distinctly Byzantine style.

Unfortunately, just at the time when relations between Constantinople and Russia were solidifying, relations with the West were deteriorating to a point of no return. After the skirmishes of the Iconoclastic period relations between Eastern and Western Christians remained tense, partly because Constantinople resented Western claims (initiated by Charlemagne in 800) of creating a rival empire, but most of all because cultural and religious differences between the two were growing. From the Byzantine point of view westerners were uncouth and ignorant, while to western European eyes Byzantines were effeminate and prone to heresy. Once the West started to revive, it began to take the offensive against a weakened East in theory and practice. In 1054 extreme papal claims of primacy over the Eastern Church provoked a religious schism which since then has never been healed. Thereafter the Crusades drove home the dividing wedge.

After the sack of Constantinople in 1204 Byzantine hatred of westerners became understandably intense. "Between us and them," one Byzantine wrote, "there is now a deep chasm: we do not have a single thought in common." Westerners called easterners "the dregs of the dregs . . . unworthy of the sun's light," while easterners called westerners the children of darkness, alluding to the fact that the sun sets in the West. The beneficiaries of this hatred were the Turks, who not only conquered Constantinople in 1453, but soon after conquered most of southeastern Europe up to Vienna.

St. Mark's Church, Venice. The most splendid example of Byzantine architecture in Italy.

The Interior of St. Mark's, Venice

In view of this sad history of hostility it is best to end our treatment of Byzantine civilization by recalling how much we owe to it. In simple physical terms the Byzantine Empire acted as a bulwark against Islam from the seventh to the eleventh centuries, thus helping to preserve an independent West. If the Byzantines had not prospered and defended Europe, Western Christian civilization might well have been snuffed out. Then too we owe an enormous amount in cultural terms to Byzantine scholars who helped preserve classical Greek learning. The most famous moment of communication between Byzantine and western European scholars came during the Italian Renaissance, when Byzantines helped introduce Italian humanists to the works of Plato. But westerners were already learning from Byzantines before then, and they continued to gain riches from Byzantine manuscripts until the sixteenth century. Similarly, Byzantine art exerted a great influence on the art of western Europe over a long period of time. To take only some of the most famous examples, St. Mark's basilica in Venice was built in close imitation of the Byzantine style, and the art of such great Western painters as Giotto and El Greco owes much in different ways to Byzantine influences. Nor should we stop at listing influences because the great surviving monuments of Byzantine culture retain their imposing appeal in and of themselves. Travelers who view Byzantine mosaics in such cities as Ravenna and Palermo are continually awe-struck; others who make their way to Istanbul still find Santa Sophia to be a marvel. In such jeweled beauty, then, the light from the Byzantine East, which once glowed so brightly, continues to shimmer.

The Byzantine contribution to Western civilization

2. THE FLOWERING OF ISLAM

In contrast to Byzantine history, which has no clearly datable beginning but a definite end in 1453, the history of Islamic civilization has a clear point of origin, beginning with the career of Muhammad in the seventh century, but no end since Islam, Muhammad's religion, is still a major force in the modern world. Believers in Islam, known as Muslims, currently comprise about one-seventh of the global population: in their greatest concentrations they extend from Africa through the Middle East and the Soviet Union to India, Bangladesh, and Indonesia. All these Muslims subscribe both to a common religion and a common way of life, for Islam has always demanded from its followers not just adherence to certain forms of worship but also adherence to set social and cultural norms. Indeed, more than Judaism or Christianity, Islam has been a great experiment in trying to build a worldwide society based on a full identity between religious requirements and a thoroughgoing code for everyday existence. In practice, of course, that experiment has differed in its success and quality according to time and place, but it is still being tested and it accounts for the fact that there remains an extraordinary sense of community between all Muslims regardless of race, language, and geographical distribution. In this section we will trace the early history of the Islamic experiment with primary emphasis on its orientation toward the West. But it must always be remembered that Islam expanded in many directions and that it ultimately had as much influence on the history of Africa and India as it did on that of Europe or western Asia.

Although Islam spread to many lands it was born in Arabia, so the story of its history must begin there. Arabia, a peninsula of deserts, had been so backward before the founding of Islam that the two dominant neighboring empires, the Roman and the Persian, had not deemed it worthwhile to extend their rule over Arabian territories. Most Arabs were Bedouins, wandering camel herdsmen who lived off the milk of their animals and the produce, such as dates, that was grown in desert oases. In the second half of the sixth century there was a quickening of economic life owing to a shift in long-distance trade routes. The protracted wars between the Byzantine and Persian Empires made Arabia a safer transit route for caravans than other areas, and some towns grew to direct and take advantage of this growth of trade. Most prominent of these was Mecca, which owed its position not just to the fact that it lay on the junction of important trade routes, but also because it had long been a center for local religion. In Mecca was located the Kabah, a pilgrimage shrine which served as a central place of worship for many different Arabian clans and tribes. (Within the Kabah was the Black Stone, a meteorite worshiped as a miraculous relic by adherents of many different divinities.) The men who controlled this shrine and also directed the economic life of the Meccan area belonged to the tribe of Quraish, an aristocracy of traders and entrepreneurs who provided the area with whatever little government it knew.

Muhammad, the founder of Islam, was born in Mecca to a family of

The Kabah. It contains the black stone which was supposed to have been miraculously sent down from heaven, and rests in the courtyard of the great mosque in Mecca.

the Quraish about 570. Orphaned early in life he entered the service of a rich widow whom he later married, thereby attaining financial security. Until middle age he lived as a prosperous trader, behaving little differently from his fellow townsmen, but around 610 he underwent a religious experience which changed the course of his life and ultimately that of a good part of the world. Although most Arabs until then had been polytheists who recognized at most the vague superiority of a more powerful god they called Allah, Muhammad in 610 believed he heard a voice from heaven tell him that there was no god but Allah alone. In other words, as the result of a conversion experience he became an uncompromising monotheist. Thereafter he received further messages which served as the basis for a new religion and which commanded him to accept the calling of "Prophet" to proclaim the monotheistic faith to the Quraish. At first he was not very successful in gaining converts beyond a limited circle, perhaps because the leading Quraish tribesmen believed that establishment of a new religion would deprive the Kabah, and therewith Mecca, of its central place in local worship. The town of Yathrib to the north, however, had no such concerns, and its representatives invited Muhammad to emigrate there so that he could serve as a neutral arbiter of local rivalries. In 622 Muhammad and his followers accepted the invitation. Because their migration—called in Arabic the *Hijrah* (or Hegira)—saw the beginning of a change upward in Muhammad's fortunes, it is considered by Muslims to mark the beginning of their era: as Christians begin their era with the birth of Christ so Muslims begin their dating system with the *Hijrah* of 622.

Muhammad changed the name of Yathrib to Medina (the "city of the Prophet") and quickly succeeded in establishing himself as ruler of

Muhammad

the town. In the course of doing this he consciously began to organize his converts into a political as well as religious community. But he still needed to find some means of support for his original Meccan followers, and he also desired to wreak vengeance on the Quraish for not heeding his calls for conversion. Accordingly, he started leading his followers in raids on Quraish caravans traveling beyond Mecca. The Quraish endeavored to defend themselves, but after a few years Muhammad's band, fired by religious enthusiasm, succeeded in defeating them. In 630, after several desert battles, Muhammad entered Mecca in triumph. The Quraish thereupon submitted to the new faith and the Kabah was not only preserved but made the main shrine of Islam, as it remains today. With the taking of Mecca other tribes throughout Arabia in turn accepted the new faith. Thus, although Muhammad died in 632, he lived long enough to see the religion he had founded become a success.

The doctrines of Islam are very simple. The word *islam* itself means submission, and the faith of Islam called for absolute submission to God. Although the Arabic name for the one God is Allah, it is mistaken to believe that Muslims worship a god like Zeus or Jupiter who is merely one of a pantheon: Allah for Muslims means the Creator God Almighty—the same omnipotent deity worshiped by Christians and Jews. Instead of saying, then, that Muslims believe "there is no god but Allah," it is more correct to say they believe that "there is no divinity but God." In keeping with this, Muslims believe that Muhammad himself was God's last and greatest prophet, but not that he was God himself. In addition to strict monotheism Muhammad taught above all that men and women must surrender themselves entirely to God because divine judgment was imminent. Mortals must make a fundamental choice about whether to begin a new life of divine service: if they decide in favor of this, God will guide them to blessedness, but if they do not, God will turn away from them and they will become irredeemably wicked. On judgment day the pious will be granted eternal life in a fleshly paradise of delights but the damned will be sent to a realm of eternal fire and torture. The practical steps the believer can take are found in the Koran, the purported compilation of the revelations sent by God to Muhammad, and accordingly the definitive Islamic scripture. These steps include thorough dedication to moral rectitude and compassion, and fidelity to set religious observances: i.e., a regimen of prayers and fasts, pilgrimage to Mecca, and frequent recitation of parts of the Koran.

The fact that much in the religion of Islam bears similarity to Judaism and Christianity is not just coincidental; Muhammad was definitely influenced by the two earlier religions. (There were many Jews in Mecca and Medina; Christian thought was also known to Muhammad, although more indirectly.) Islam most resembles the two earlier religions in its strict monotheism, its stress on personal morality and

The Archangel Gabriel Brings Revelation to Muhammad. A much later Persian conception.

compassion, and its reliance on written, revealed scripture. Muhammad proclaimed the Koran as the ultimate source of religious authority but accepted both the Old and New Testaments as divinely inspired books. From Christianity Muhammad seems to have derived his doctrines of the last judgment, the resurrection of the body with subsequent rewards and punishments, and his belief in angels (he thought that God's first message to him had been sent by the angel Gabriel). But although Muhammad accepted Jesus Christ as one of the greatest of a long line of prophets, he did not believe in Christ's divinity and himself laid claim to no miracles other than the writing of the Koran. He also ignored the Christian doctrine of sacrificial love, and, most importantly, preached a religion without sacraments or priests. For Muslims every believer has direct responsibility for living the life of the faith without intermediaries; instead of priests there are only religious scholars who may comment on problems of Islamic faith and law. Muslims are expected to pray together in mosques, but there is nothing like a Muslim mass. The absence of clergy makes Islam more similar to Judaism, a similarity which is enhanced by Islamic stress on the inextricable connection between the religious and sociopolitical life of the divinely inspired community. But, unlike Judaism, Islam laid claim to universalism and a unique role in uniting the world as it started to spread far beyond the confines of Arabia.

The start of this move toward becoming a world force took place immediately upon Muhammad's death. Since he had made no provision for the future, and since the Arabs had no clear concept of political succession, it was unclear whether Muhammad's community would survive at all. But his closest followers, led by his father-in-law Abu-Bakr and a zealous early convert named Umar, forestalled this possibility by quickly taking the initiative and naming Abu-Bakr *ca-*

The unification of Arabia after Muhammad: the caliphs

Two Views of the Dome of the Rock, Jerusalem. According to Muslim tradition, Muhammad made a miraculous journey to Jerusalem before his death and left a footprint in a rock. The mosque which was erected over the site in the seventh century is, after the Kabah, Islam's second holiest shrine.

liph, meaning "deputy of the Prophet." Thereafter, for about three hundred years, the caliph was to serve as the supreme religious and political leader of all Muslims. Immediately after becoming caliph Abu-Bakr began a military campaign to subdue various Arabian tribes which had followed Muhammad but were not willing to accept his successor's authority. In the course of this military action, which was marked by thorough success, Abu-Bakr's forces began to spill northwards over the borders of Arabia. Probably to their surprise they found that they met minimal resistance from Byzantine and Persian forces.

Arab expansion and conquests

Abu-Bakr died two years after his accession but was succeeded as caliph by Umar, who continued to direct the Arabian invasions of the neighboring empires. In the following years triumph was virtually uninterrupted. In 636 the Arabs routed a Byzantine army in Syria and then quickly swept over the entire area, occupying the leading cities of Antioch, Damascus, and Jerusalem; in 637 they destroyed the main army of the Persians and marched into the Persian capital of Ctesiphon. Once the Persian administrative center was taken, the Persian Empire offered scarcely any more resistance: by 651 the Arabian conquest of the entire Persian realm was complete. Since Byzantium was centered around distant Constantinople, the Arabs were not similarly able to stop its imperial heart from beating. But they did quickly manage to deprive the Byzantine Empire of Egypt by 646 and then swept west across North Africa. In 711 they crossed from there into Spain and quickly took almost all of that area too. Thus within less than a century all of ancient Persia and much of the old Roman world was conquered by Islam.

How can we explain this prodigious expansion? The best approach is to see first what impelled the conquerors and then to see what circumstances helped to ease their way. Contrary to widespread belief the early spread of Islam was not achieved through a religious crusade. At first the Arabs were not at all interested in converting other peoples: to the contrary, they hoped that conquered populations would not convert so that they could maintain their own identity as a community of rulers and tax-gatherers. But although their motives for expansion were not religious, religious enthusiasm played a crucial role in making the hitherto unruly Arabs take orders from the caliph and in instilling a sense that they were carrying out the will of God. What really moved the Arabs out of the desert was the search for richer territory and booty, and what kept them moving ever farther was the ease of acquiring new wealth as they progressed. Fortunately for the Arabs their inspiration by Islam came just at the right time in terms of the weakness of their enemies. The Byzantines and Persians had become so exhausted by their long wars that they could hardly rally for a new effort. Moreover, Persian and Byzantine local populations were hostile to the financial demands made by their bureaucratic empires; also, in the Byzantine lands of Syria and Egypt "heretical" Christians were at odds with the persecuting orthodoxy of Constantinople. Because the Arabs did not demand conversion and exacted fewer taxes than the Byzantines and Persians, they were often welcomed as preferable to the old rulers. One Christian writer in Syria went so far as to say "the God of vengeance delivered us out of the hands of the Romans [i.e., the Byzantine Empire] by means of the Arabs." For all these reasons Islam quickly spread over the vast extent of territory between Egypt and Iran, and has been rooted there ever since.

While the Arabs were extending their conquests they ran into their first serious political divisions. In 644 the Caliph Umar died; he was replaced by one Uthman, a weak ruler who had the added drawback for many of belonging to the Umayyad family, a wealthy clan from Mecca which had not at first accepted Muhammad's call. Those dissatisfied with Uthman rallied around the Prophet's cousin and son-in-law Ali, whose blood, background, and warrior spirit made him seem a more appropriate leader of the cause. When Uthman was murdered in 656 by mutineers, Ali's partisans raised him up as caliph. But Uthman's powerful family and supporters were unwilling to accept Ali. In subsequent disturbances Ali was murdered and Uthman's party emerged triumphant. In 661 a member of the Umayyad family took over as caliph and that house ruled Islam until 750. Even then, however, Ali's followers did not accept defeat. As time went on they har-

Reasons for the spread of Islam

Division between Shiites and Sunnites

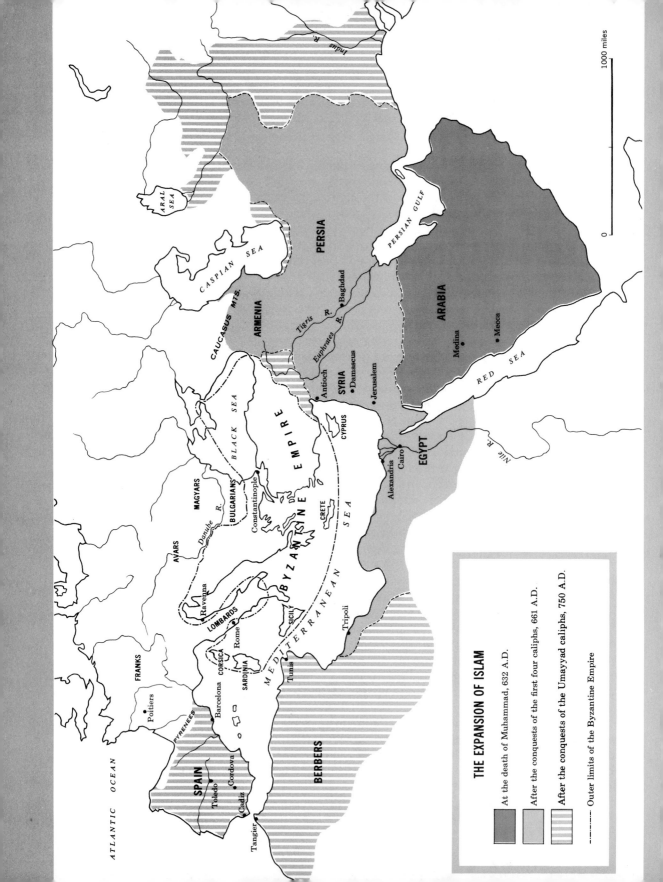

ATLANTIC OCEAN

SPAIN
Toledo
Cordova
Cadiz
Tangier

FRANKS
Poitiers
PYRENEES
Barcelona

BERBERS

CORSICA
SARDINIA
Tunis

MEDITERRANEAN SEA

LOMBARDS
Ravenna
Rome
SICILY

AVARS
MAGYARS
BULGARIANS
Danube R.
Constantinople

BYZANTINE EMPIRE

BLACK SEA

CRETE
CYPRUS

Tripoli

EGYPT
Alexandria
Cairo

Nile R.

RED SEA

ARABIA
Medina
Mecca

SYRIA
Antioch
Damascus
Jerusalem

PERSIA
Baghdad
Tigris R.
Euphrates R.

ARMENIA

CAUCASUS MTS.

CASPIAN SEA

ARAL SEA

Indus R.

PERSIAN GULF

1000 miles
0

THE EXPANSION OF ISLAM

At the death of Muhammad, 632 A.D.

After the conquests of the first four caliphs, 661 A.D.

After the conquests of the Umayyad caliphs, 750 A.D.

Outer limits of the Byzantine Empire

dened into a minority religious party known as Shiites; this group insisted that only descendants of Ali could be caliphs or have any authority over the Muslim community. Those who stood instead for the actual historical development of the caliphate and became committed to its customs were called Sunnites. The cleft between the two parties has been a lasting one in Islamic history. Often persecuted, Shiites developed great militancy and a deep sense of being the only true preservers of the faith. From time to time they were able to seize power in one or another area, but they never succeeded in converting the majority of Muslims. Today they rule in Iran and are very numerous in Iraq but comprise only about one-tenth of the worldwide population of Islam.

The triumph of the Umayyads in 661 began a more settled period in the history of the caliphate, lasting until 945. During that time there were two major governing orientations: that represented by the rule of the Umayyads, and that represented by their successors, the Abbasids. The Umayyads centered their strength in the old Byzantine territories in Syria and continued to use local officials who were not Muslims for their administration. For these reasons the Umayyad caliphate appears to some extent like a Byzantine successor state. With their more Western orientation the Umayyads concentrated their energies on dominating the Mediterranean and conquering Constantinople. When their most massive attack on the Byzantine capital failed in 717, Umayyad strength was seriously weakened; it was only a matter of time before a new orientation would develop.

The Umayyads

This was represented by the takeover of a new family, the Abbasids, in 750. Their rule may be said to have stressed Persian more than Byzantine elements. Characteristic of this change was a shift in capitals, for the second Abbasid caliph built his new capital of Baghdad in Iraq near the ruins of the old Persian capital and even appropriated stones from the ruins. The Abbasids developed their own Muslim administration and imitated Persian absolutism. Abbasid caliphs ruthlessly cut down their enemies, surrounded themselves with elaborate court ceremonies, and lavishly patronized sophisticated literature. This is the world described in the *Arabian Nights,* a collection of stories of dazzling Oriental splendor written in Baghdad under the Abbasids. The dominating presence in those stories, Harun al-Rashid, actually reigned as caliph from 786 to 809 and behaved as extravagantly as he was described, tossing coins in the streets, passing out sumptuous gifts to his favorites and severe punishments to his enemies. From a Western point of view the Abbasid caliphate was of significance not just in creating legends and literature but also because its Eastern orientation took much pressure off the Mediterranean. The Byzantine state, accordingly, was able to revive and the Franks in the far West began to develop some strength of their own. (The greatest Frankish ruler, Charlemagne, maintained diplomatic relations with the cali-

The Abbasids

*Islamic political history
after the fall of the
Abbasid Empire*

phate of Harun al-Rashid, who patronizingly sent the much poorer westerner a gift of an elephant.)

When Abbasid power began to decline in the tenth century there followed an extended period of decentralization. The major cause for growing Abbasid weakness was the gradual impoverishment of their primary economic base, the agricultural wealth of the Tigris-Euphrates basin. Their decline was further accelerated by the later Abbasids' practice of surrounding themselves with Turkish soldiers, who soon realized that they could take over actual power in the state. In 945 the Abbasid Empire fell apart when a Shiite tribe seized Baghdad. Thereafter the Abbasids became powerless figureheads until their caliphate was completely destroyed with the destruction of Baghdad by the Mongols in 1258. From 945 until the sixteenth century Islamic political life was marked by localism, with different petty rulers, most often Turkish, taking command in different areas. It used to be thought that this decentralization also meant decay, but in fact Islamic civilization greatly prospered in the "middle period," above all from about 900 to about 1250, a time also when Islamic rule expanded into modern-day Turkey and India. Later, new Islamic empires developed, the leading one in the West being that of the Ottoman Turks, who controlled much of eastern Europe and the Near East from the fifteenth century until 1918. It is therefore entirely false to believe that Islamic history descended upon an ever downward course sometime shortly after the reign of Harun al-Rashid.

*The character of Islamic
culture and society*

For those who approach Islamic civilization with modern preconceptions, the greatest surprise is to realize that from the time of Muhammad until at least about 1500 Islamic culture and society was extraordinarily cosmopolitan and dynamic. Muhammad himself was not a desert Arab but a town-dweller and trader imbued with advanced ideals. Subsequently, Muslim culture became highly cosmopolitan for several reasons: it inherited the sophistication of Byzantium and Persia; it remained centered at the crossroads of long-distance trade between the Far East and West; and the prosperous town life in most Muslim territories counterbalanced agriculture. Because of the importance of trade there was much geographical mobility. Muhammad's teachings furthermore encouraged social mobility because the Koran stressed the equality of all Muslims. The result was that at the court of Baghdad, and later at those of the decentralized Muslim states, careers were open to those with talent. Since literacy was remarkably widespread—a rough estimate for around the year 1000 is 20 percent of all Muslim males—many could rise through education. Offices were seldom regarded as being hereditary and "new men" could arrive at the top by enterprise and skill. Muslims were also remarkably tolerant of other religions. As stated above, they rarely sought forced conversions, and they generally allowed a place within their own states for Jews and Christians, whom they accepted as "people of the book" because the Bible was seen as a precursor of the Koran. In keeping with this attitude of toleration an early caliph employed a Christian as his chief secretary, the Umayyads patronized a Christian who wrote poetry in Arabic, and Muslim Spain saw the greatest flowering of Jewish culture between ancient and modern times. The greatest fruit of this Jewish flowering was the work of Moses Maimonides (1135–1204), a profound religious thinker, sometimes called "the second Moses," who wrote both in Hebrew and Arabic.

There was one major exception to this rule of Muslim equalitarianism and tolerance: the treatment of women. Perhaps because social status was so fluid, successful men were extremely anxious to preserve and enhance their positions and their "honor." They could accomplish this by maintaining and/or expanding their worldly possessions, which category included women. For a man's females to be most "valuable" to his status, their inviolability had to be assured. The Koran allowed a man to marry four wives, so women were at a premium, and married ones were segregated from other male society. A prominent man would also have a number of female servants and concubines, and he kept all these women in a part of his residence called the harem, where they were guarded by eunuchs, i.e., castrated men. Within these enclaves women vied with each other for preeminence and engaged in intrigues to advance the fortunes of their children. Although large harems could be kept only by the wealthy, the system was imitated so far as possible by all classes. Based on the principle that women were chattel, these practices did much to debase women and to emphasize attitudes of domination in sexual life. Male homosexual relations were tolerated in upper-class society, yet they too were based on patterns of domination, usually that of a powerful adult over an adolescent.

The treatment of women

There were two major Islamic avenues for devotion to the particularly religious life. One was that of the *ulama,* learned men who came closest to being like priests. Their job was to study and offer advice on all aspects of religion and religious law. Not surprisingly they usually stood for tradition and rigorous maintenance of the faith; most often they exerted great influence on the conduct of public life. But complementary to them were the *sufis,* religious mystics who might be equated with Christian monks, were it not for the fact that they were not committed to celibacy and seldom withdrew from the life of the community. Sufis stressed contemplation and ecstasy as the ulama stressed religious law: they had no common program and in practice behaved very differently. Some sufis were "whirling dervishes," known in the West as such because of their dances; others were *faqirs,* associated in the West with snake-charming in marketplaces; and others were quiet meditative men who practiced no exotic rites. Sufis were usually organized into "brotherhoods," which did much to con-

Islamic religious life: the
ulama *and the* sufis

vert outlying areas such as Africa and India. Within all of Islamdom sufism provided a channel for the most intense religious impulses. The ability of the ulama and sufis to coexist is in itself a remarkable index of Islamic cultural pluralism.

Islamic philosophy

More remarkable still is the fact that these two groups often coexisted with representatives of yet another worldview, students and practitioners of philosophy and science. Islamic philosophers were actually called *faylasufs* in Arabic because they were dedicated to the cultivation of what the Greeks had called *philosophia*. Islamic philosophy was based on the study of earlier Greek thought, above all the Aristotelian and Neoplatonic strains. Around the time when the philosophical schools were closed in Athens by order of the Emperor Justinian, Greek philosophers migrated east, and the works of Aristotle and others were translated into Syriac, a Semitic dialect. From that point of transmission Greek philosophy gradually entered the life of Islam and became cultivated by the class of faylasufs, who believed that the universe is rational and that a philosophical approach to life was the highest god-given calling. The faylasufs' profound knowledge of Aristotle can be seen, for example, in the fact that Avicenna (d. 1037), one of the greatest of them, read practically all of Aristotle's works in the Far-Eastern town of Bukhara before he reached the age of eighteen.

The problem of reconciling Greek ideas with Islamic religion

The most serious problem faced by the faylasufs was that of reconciling Greek philosophy with Islamic religion because they followed their Greek sources in believing—in opposition to Islamic doctrine—that the world is eternal and that there is no immortality for the individual soul. Different faylasufs reacted to this problem in different ways. Of the three greatest, Al-Farabi (d. 950), who lived mainly in Baghdad, was least concerned by it; he taught that an enlightened elite could philosophize without being distracted by the binding common beliefs of the masses. Even so, he never attacked these beliefs, considering them necessary to hold society together.

Avicenna and Averroës

Unlike Al-Farabi, Avicenna, who was active further east, taught a less rationalistic philosophy that came close in many points to sufi mysticism. (A later story held that Avicenna said of a sufi "all I know, he sees," while the sufi replied "all I see, he knows.") Finally, Averroës (1126–98) of Cordova, in Spain, was a thoroughgoing Aristotelian who led two lives, one in private as an extreme rationalist and the other in public as a believer in the official faith, indeed even as an official censor. Averroës was the last really important Islamic philosopher: after him rationalism either blended into sufism, the direction pointed to by Avicenna, or became too constrained by religious orthodoxy to lead an independent existence. But in its heyday between about 850 and 1200 Islamic philosophy was far more advanced and sophisticated than anything found in either the Byzantine or Western Christian realms.

Before their decline Islamic faylasufs were as distinguished in studying natural science as they were in philosophical speculation. Usually the same men were both philosophers and scientists because they could by no means make a living by commenting on Aristotle (there were no universities in which to teach) but could rise to positions of wealth and power by practicing astrology and medicine. Astrology sounds to us today less like science than superstition, but among the Muslims it was an "applied science" intimately related to accurate astronomical observation: after an Islamic astrologer carefully studied and foretold the courses of the heavenly bodies, he would endeavor to apply his knowledge to the course of human events, particularly the fortunes of wealthy patrons. In order to account most simply for heavenly motions, some Muslims considered the possibilities that the earth rotates on its axis and revolves around the sun, but these theories were not accepted because they did not fit in with ancient preconceptions such as the assumption of circular planetary orbits. It was therefore not in these suggestions that Muslim astrologers later influenced the West, but rather in their extremely advanced observations and predictive tables that often went beyond the most careful work of the Greeks.

Islamic science; the practice of astrology

Islamic accomplishments in medicine were equally remarkable. Faylasufs serving as physicians appropriated the knowledge contained in the medical writings of the Hellenistic Age but were rarely content with that. Avicenna discovered the contagious nature of tuberculosis, described pleurisy and several varieties of nervous ailments, and pointed out that disease can be spread through contamination of water and soil. His chief medical writing, the *Canon,* was accepted in Europe as authoritative until late in the seventeenth century. Avicenna's older contemporary, Rhazes (865–925), was the greatest clinical physician of the medieval world. His major achievement was the discovery of the difference between measles and smallpox. Other Islamic physicians discovered the value of cauterization and of styptic agents, diagnosed cancer of the stomach, prescribed antidotes for cases of poisoning, and made notable progress in treating diseases of the eyes. In addition, they recognized the infectious character of bubonic plague, pointing out that it could be transmitted by clothes. Finally, the Muslims excelled all other medieval peoples in the organization of hospitals and in the control of medical practice. There were at least thirty-four great hospitals located in the principal cities of Persia, Syria, and Egypt, which appear to have been organized in a strikingly modern fashion. Each had wards for particular cases, a dispensary, and a library. The chief physicians and surgeons lectured to the students and graduates, examined them, and issued licenses to practice. Even the owners of leeches, who in most cases were also barbers, had to submit them for inspection at regular intervals.

Islamic contributions to medicine

Other great Islamic scientific achievements were in optics, chemis-

Optics, chemistry, and mathematics

try, and mathematics. Islamic physicists founded the science of optics and drew a number of significant conclusions regarding the theory of magnifying lenses and the velocity, transmission, and refraction of light. Islamic chemistry was an outgrowth of alchemy, an invention of the Hellenistic Greeks, the system of belief that was based upon the principle that all metals were the same in essence, and that baser metals could therefore be transmuted into gold if only the right instrument, the philosopher's stone, could be found. But the efforts of scientists in this field were by no means confined to this fruitless quest; some even denied the whole theory of transmutation of metals. As a result of innumerable experiments by Muslim scientists, various new substances and compounds were discovered; among them carbonate of soda, alum, borax, bichloride of mercury, nitrate of silver, saltpeter, and nitric and sulphuric acids. In addition, Islamic scientists were the first to describe the chemical processes of distillation, filtration, and sublimation. In mathematics Islam's greatest accomplishment was to unite the geometry of the Greeks with the number science of the Hindus. Borrowing what westerners know as "Arabic numerals," including the zero, from the Hindus, Islamic mathematicians were able to develop an arithmetic based on the decimal system and also make advances in algebra (itself an Arabic word). Building upon Greek geometry with reference to heavenly motions, they made great progress in spherical trigonometry. Thus they brought together and advanced all the areas of mathematical knowledge which would later be further developed in the Christian West.

In addition to its philosophers and scientists Islam had its poets too. The primitive Arabs themselves had excelled in writing poetry, and literary accomplishment became recognized as a way to distinguish oneself at court. Probably the greatest of Islamic poets were the Persians (who wrote in their own language), the best known of whom in the West is Umar Khayyam (d. 1123) because his *Rubaiyat* was turned into a popular English poem by the Victorian Edward Fitzgerald. Although Fitzgerald's translation distorts much, Umar's hedonism ("a jug of wine, a loaf of bread—and thou") shows us that all Muslims were by no means dour puritans. Actually Umar's poetry was excelled by the works of Sadi (1193–1292) and Hafiz (d. 1389). And far from Persia lush poetry was cultivated as well in the courts of Muslim Spain. This poetry too was by no means inhibited, as can be seen from lines like "such was my kissing, such my sucking of his mouth / that he was almost made toothless."

In their artistic endeavors Muslims were highly eclectic. Their main source of inspiration came from the art of Byzantium and Persia. The former contributed many of the structural features of Islamic architecture, especially the dome, the column, and the arch. Persian influence was probably responsible for the intricate, nonnaturalistic designs which were used as decorative motifs in practically all of the arts.

The Great Mosque, Qayrawan, Tunisia. This ninth century minaret, from which the criers call the faithful to prayer, is a leading monument of the North African Islamic architectural style.

The Court of the Lions in the Al-hambra, Granada, Spain. The palace-fortress of the Alhambra is one of the finest monuments of the Islamic architectural style. Notable are the graceful columns, the horseshoe arches, and the delicate tracery in stone that surmounts the arches.

From both Persia and Byzantium came the tendency to subordinate form to rich and sensuous color. Architecture was the most important of the Islamic arts; the development of both painting and sculpture was inhibited by religious prejudice against representation of the human form. By no means all of the examples of this architecture were mosques; many were palaces, schools, libraries, private dwellings, and hospitals. Indeed, Islamic architecture had a much more decidedly secular character than any in medieval Europe. Among its principal elements were bulbous domes, minarets, horseshoe arches, and twisted columns, together with the use of tracery in stone, alternating stripes of black and white, mosaics, and Arabic script as decorative devices. As in the Byzantine style, comparatively little attention was given to exterior ornamentation. The so-called minor arts of the Muslims included the weaving of gorgeous pile carpets and rugs, magnificent leather tooling, and the making of brocaded silks and tapestries, inlaid metalwork, enameled glassware, and painted pottery. Most of the products of these arts were embellished with complicated patterns of interlacing geometric designs, plants and fruits and flowers, Arabic script, and fantastic animal figures. In general, art laid particular emphasis on pure visual design. Separated from any role in religious teaching, it became highly abstract and nonrepresentational. For these reasons Islamic art often seems more secular and "modern" than any other art of premodern times.

The eclectic art of the Muslims

The economic life of the Islamic world varied greatly according to time and place, but underdevelopment was certainly not one of its primary characteristics. On the contrary, in the central areas of Islamic civilization from the first Arab conquests until about the fourteenth century mercantile life was extraordinarily advanced. The principal reason for this was that the Arabs inherited in Syria and Persia an area that was already marked by an enterprising urban culture and that was at the crossroads of the world, lying athwart the major trade routes between Africa, Europe, India, and China. Islamic traders and entrepreneurs built venturesomely on these earlier foundations. Muslim merchants penetrated into southern Russia and even into the equatorial regions of Africa, while caravans of thousands of camels traveled to the gates of India and China. (The Muslims used camels as pack animals instead of building roads and drawing wheeled carts.) Ships from Islam established new routes across the Indian Ocean, the Persian Gulf, and the Caspian Sea. For periods of time Islamic ships also dominated parts of the Mediterranean. Indeed, one reason for subsequent Islamic decline was that the Western Christians took hold of the Mediterranean in the eleventh and twelfth centuries and wrested control of the Indian Ocean in the sixteenth century.

(2) industry

The great Islamic expansion of commerce would scarcely have been possible without a corresponding development of industry. It was the ability of the people of one region to turn their natural resources into finished products for sale to other regions which provided a basis for a large part of the trade. Nearly every one of the great cities specialized in some particular variety of manufactures. Mosul, in Syria, was a center of the manufacture of cotton cloth; Baghdad specialized in glassware, jewelry, pottery, and silks; Damascus was famous for its fine steel and for its "damask" or woven figured silk; Morocco was noted for the manufacture of leather; and Toledo, in Spain, for its excellent swords. The products of these cities did not exhaust the list of manufactures. Drugs, perfumes, carpets, tapestries, brocades,

Interior of the Great Mosque at Cordova, Spain. This splendid specimen of Moorish architecture gives an excellent view of the cusped arches and alternating stripes of black and white so commonly used by Islamic architects.

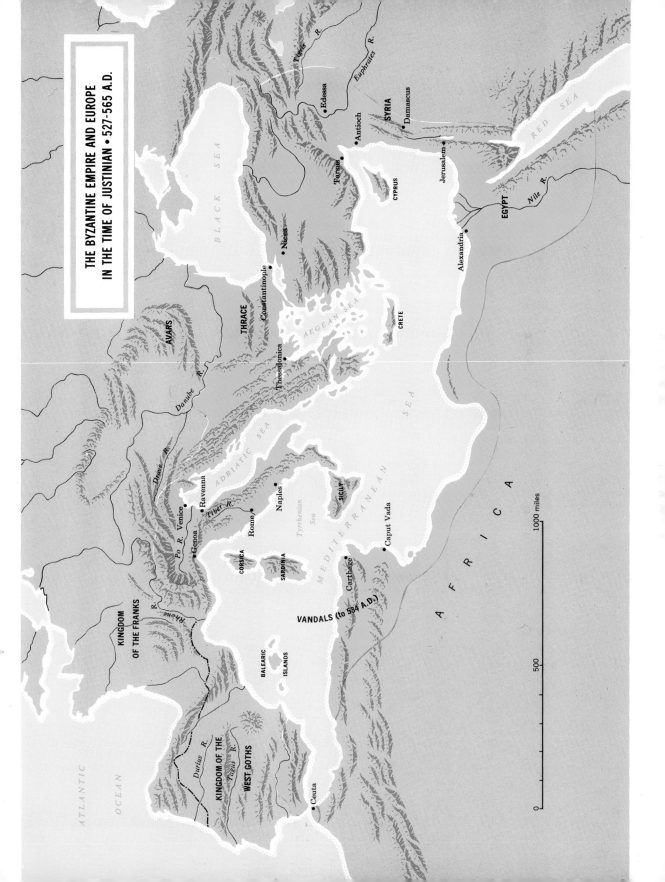

THE BYZANTINE EMPIRE AND EUROPE
IN THE TIME OF JUSTINIAN · 527-565 A.D.

ATLANTIC OCEAN

KINGDOM OF THE FRANKS

Rhône R.

Ebro R.

Durius R.

Tagus R.

KINGDOM OF THE WEST GOTHS

BALEARIC ISLANDS

Ceuta

AFRICA

VANDALS (to 534 A.D.)

Carthage

Caput Vada

CORSICA

SARDINIA

MEDITERRANEAN SEA

Tyrrhenian Sea

SICILY

Naples

Rome

Tiber R.

Genoa

Venice

Po R.

Ravenna

Drave R.

Danube R.

AVARS

ADRIATIC SEA

Thessalonica

THRACE

Constantinople

Nicæa

AEGEAN SEA

CRETE

BLACK SEA

Tigris R.

Edessa

Euphrates R.

Tarsus

Antioch

SYRIA

Damascus

CYPRUS

Jerusalem

EGYPT

Alexandria

Nile R.

RED SEA

AFRICA

0   500   1000 miles

Gold Cup, Byzantine, VI–IX cent. The figure is a personification of Constantinople, a queen or goddess holding the scepter and orb of imperial rule. (MMA)

Saint John Writing His Gospel. From an Anglo-Frankish illuminated manuscript, c. 850, produced in a Carolingian monastery. The unknown artist knew nothing of perspective, but excelled in coloring and conveying a sense of vitality and energy. (Morgan Library)

Merovingian Fibula or Brooch, VII cent. A fabulous gold-plated animal set with garnets and colored paste reveals the lively imagination of the early Middle Ages. (MMA)

Enthroned Madonna and Child, Byzantine School, XIII cent. The painters of Siena followed the opulent and brilliant style of Byzantine art. Their madonnas were not earthly mothers, but celestial queens reigning in dignified splendor. (National Gallery)

The Young King, Louis IX, XIII cent. Though Louis was widely revered as a saint, the artist has endowed him with distinctively human features. (Morgan Library)

Aquamanile, German, XII–XIII cent. Aquamaniles were water jugs used for handwashing during church ritual, or at meal times. (MMA)

Ivory Plaque, German, X cent. The plaque shows Otto the Great presenting a church to Christ while St. Peter watches, a reference to Otto's building an empire by cooperating with the Church. (MMA)

Kings in Battle, French, c. 1250. A scene depicting, with the trappings of knighthood, Joshua's fight against the five kings of Canaan. In the center Joshua raises his hand, commanding the sun and moon to stand still to enable him to complete his victory. (Morgan Library)

Chalice, German, XIII cent. A beautifully embellished wine cup used in the sacrament of the Eucharist. (MMA)

Building Operations. From a French picture Bible, c. 1250. Note the treadmill, with wheel, ropes, and pulley, by means of which a basket of stones is brought to the construction level. (Morgan Library)

Above: Siege of a City. From the *Universal Chronicle* by Jean de Courcy, Flemish, c. 1470. The cannon meant the end of feudal knights and medieval towered fortresses. (Morgan Library)

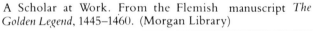

A Scholar at Work. From the Flemish manuscript *The Golden Legend*, 1445–1460. (Morgan Library)

Stained Glass, German, c. 1300. Some stained-glass windows were purely decorative; others told a story. (MMA)

Vespers of the Holy Ghost, with a View of Paris,
Jean Fouquet. From the *Book of Hours* of
Etienne Chevalier, 1461. Demons in the sky are
sent flying by the divine light from Heaven.
The cathedral is Notre Dame. (Robert Lehman)

A Sixteenth-Century Map of the World by Paolo dal Toscanelli, Adviser to Columbus. The European continent
is in the upper left. (Scala)

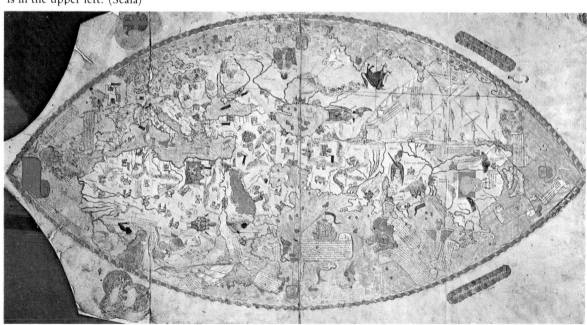

St. Lawrence Enthroned, Fra Lippo Lippi (1406–1469). One of the first of the psychological painters, Fra Lippo Lippi exhibited in this work his gift for portraying pensive melancholy. (MMA)

The Flight into Egypt, Giotto (1276–1337). Giotto is regarded as the founder of the modern tradition in painting. A fresco in the Arena Chapel, Padua. (MMA)

The Birth of Venus, Sandro Botticelli (1444–1510). Botticelli was a mystic as well as a lover of beauty whose works suggest a longing for the glories of the classical world. (Scala)

The Virgin of the Rocks, Leonardo da Vinci. This painting reveals not only Leonardo's interest in human character, but also his absorption in the phenomena of nature. (Louvre)

Mona Lisa, Leonardo da Vinci (1452–1519). Unlike most other Renaissance painters who sought to convey an understandable message, Leonardo created questions to which he gave no answer. Nowhere is this more evident than in the enigmatic countenance of Mona Lisa. (Louvre)

The Last Supper, Leonardo da Vinci. This great fresco depicts the varying reactions of Jesus' disciples when He announces that one of them will betray Him. (Santa Maria della Grazie, Milan)

THE RISE OF THE MEDIEVAL UNIVERSITY

△ Founded in the 12th century
■ Founded in the 13th century
● Founded in the 14th century   — · · — · · —
△ Founded in the 15th century   Boundaries ca. 1500 A.D.

woolens, satins, metal products, and a host of others were turned out by the craftsmen of many cities. From the Chinese the Muslims learned the art of papermaking, and the products of that industry were in great demand, not only within the empire itself but in Europe as well.

In all the areas we have reviewed Islamic civilization so overshadowed that of the Christian West until about the twelfth century that there can be no comparison. When the West did move forward it was partly able to do so because of what it learned from Islam. In the economic sphere westerners profited from absorbing many accomplishments of Islamic technology, such as irrigation techniques, the raising of new crops, papermaking, and the distillation of alcohol. The extent of our debt to Islamic economic influence is well mirrored in the large number of common English words which were originally of Arabic or Persian origin. Among these are traffic, tariff, magazine, alcohol, muslin, orange, lemon, alfalfa, saffron, sugar, syrup, and musk. (Our word admiral also comes from the Arabic—in this case deriving from the title of emir.)

The West was as much indebted to Islam in intellectual and scientific as in economic life. In those areas, too, borrowed words tell some of the story: algebra, cipher, zero, nadir, amalgam, alembic, alchemy, alkali, soda, almanac, and names of many stars such as Aldebaran and Betelgeuse. Islamic civilization both preserved and expanded Greek philosophical and scientific knowledge when such knowledge was almost entirely forgotten in the West. All the important Greek scientific works surviving from ancient times were translated into Arabic and most of these in turn were translated in the medieval West from Arabic into Latin. Above all, the preservation and interpretation of the works of Aristotle was one of Islam's most enduring accomplishments. Not only was Aristotle first reacquired in the West by means of the Arabic translations, but Aristotle was interpreted with Islamic help, above all that of Averroës, whose prestige was so great that he was simply called "the Commentator" by medieval Western writers. Of course Arabic numerals, too, rank as a tremendously important intellectual legacy, as anyone will discover by trying to balance a checkbook with Roman ones.

Aside from all these specific contributions, the civilization of Islam probably had its greatest influence on the West merely by standing as a powerful rival and spur to the imagination. Byzantine civilization was too closely related to the Christian West and ultimately not strong enough to serve this function. Westerners usually, for right or wrong, looked down on the Byzantine Greeks, but they more often respected and feared the Muslims. And right they were as well, for Islamic civilization at its zenith (to use another Arabic word) was surely one of the world's greatest. Though loosely organized, it united peoples as diverse as Arabs, Persians, Turks, various African tribes, and Hindus by means of a great religion and common institutions. Unity within multiplicity was an Islamic hallmark, which created both a splendid diverse society and a splendid legacy of original discoveries and achievements.

3. WESTERN CHRISTIAN CIVILIZATION IN THE EARLY MIDDLE AGES

The shaping of a cultural unity in the early-medieval West

Western Europeans in the early Middle Ages (the period between about 600 and 1050) were so backward in comparison to their Byzantine and Islamic neighbors that a tenth-century Arabic geographer could write of them that "they have large bodies, gross natures, harsh manners, and dull intellects . . . those who live farthest north are particularly stupid, gross, and brutish." Material conditions throughout this period were so primitive that we can almost speak of five centuries of camping-out. Yet new and promising patterns were definitely taking shape. Above all, a new center of civilization was emerging in the north Atlantic regions. Around 800 the Frankish monarchy, based in agriculturally rich northwestern Europe, managed to create a western European empire in alliance with the Western Christian Church. Although this empire did not last long, it still managed to hew out a new Western cultural unity that was to be an important building block for the future.

The kingdom of the Franks: the Merovingian period

Once the Eastern Romans under Justinian had destroyed the Ostrogothic and Vandal kingdoms in Italy and Africa, and the Arabs had eliminated the Visigothic kingdom in Spain, the Frankish rulers in Gaul remained as the major surviving barbarian power in western Europe. But it took about two centuries before they began to exercise their full hegemony. The founder of the Frankish state was the brutal and wily chieftain Clovis, who conquered most of modern-day France and Belgium around 500 and cleverly converted to Catholic Christianity, the religion of the local bishops and indigenous population. Clovis founded the Merovingian dynasty (so called from Merovech, the founder of the family to which he belonged). He did not, however, pass on a united realm but followed the typical barbarian custom of dividing up his kingdom among his sons. More or less without interruption for the next two hundred years sons fought sons for a larger share of the Merovingian inheritance. Toward the end of that period the line also began to degenerate and numerous so-called do-nothing kings left their government and fighting to their chief ministers, known as "mayors of the palace." Throughout this era, one of the darkest in the recorded history of Europe, trade contracted, towns declined, literacy was almost forgotten, and violence was endemic. Minimal agricultural self-sufficiency coexisted with the rule of the battle-axe.

Largely unnoticed, however, some hope for the future was coalescing around the institutions of the Roman papacy and Benedictine monasticism. The architect of a new western European religious policy that was based on an alliance between these two institutions was Pope Gregory I (reigned 590–604), known as St. Gregory the Great. Until his time the Roman popes were generally subordinate to the emperors in Constantinople and to the greater religious prestige of the Christian East, but Gregory sought to counteract this situation by creating a more autonomous western-oriented Latin Church. This he tried to do in many ways. As a theologian—the fourth great "Latin father" of the Church—he built upon the work of his three predecessors, Jerome, Ambrose, and especially Augustine, in articulating a theology that had its own distinct characteristics. Among these were emphasis on the idea of penance and the concept of purgatory as a place for purification before admission into heaven. (Western belief in purgatory was thereafter to become one of the major differences in the dogmas of the Eastern and Western Churches.) In addition to his theological work, Gregory pioneered in the writing of a simplified unadorned Latin prose that corresponded to the actual spoken language of his contemporaries, and presided over the creation of a powerful Latin liturgy. If Gregory did not actually invent the "Gregorian chant," it was under his impetus that this new plainsong—forever after a central part of the Roman Catholic ritual—developed. All of these innovations helped to make the Christian West religiously and culturally more independent of the Greek-speaking East than it had ever been before.

Gregory the Great was as much a statesman as he was a theologian and shaper of Latin. Within Italy he assured the physical survival of the papacy in the face of the barbarian Lombard threat of his day (the Lombards were natural enemies of the papacy because they were Arian heretics) by clever diplomacy and expert management of papal landed estates. He also began to reemphasize earlier claims of papal primacy, especially over Western bishops, that were in danger of being forgotten. Above all, he patronized the order of Benedictine monks and used them to help evangelize new Western territories. Gregory himself had been a Benedictine—perhaps the first Benedictine monk to become pope—and he wrote the standard life of St. Benedict. Because the Benedictine order was still very young and the times were turbulent, Gregory's patronage helped the order to survive and later to become for centuries the only monastic order in the West. In return the pope could profit from using the Benedictines to carry out special projects. The most significant of these was the conversion of Anglo-Saxon England to Christianity. This was a long-term project which took about a century to complete, but its great result was that it left a Christian outpost to the far northwest that was thoroughly loyal to the papacy and that would soon help to bring together the papacy and the Frankish state. Gregory the Great himself did not live to see that union but it was his policy of invigorating the Western Church that most helped to bring it about.

Pope Gregory the Great. In this tenth-century German ivory panel the pope is receiving inspiration from the Holy Spirit in the form of a dove.

Gregory's religious policies

*Factors in the increasing
stability of Frankish Gaul*

Around 700, when the Benedictines were completing their conversion of England, the outlook for Frankish Gaul was becoming somewhat brighter. The most profound reason for this was that the long, troubled period of transition between the ancient and medieval worlds was finally coming to an end. The ancient Roman civilization of cities and Mediterranean trade was in its last gasps in Gaul in the time after Clovis. Then, when the Arabs conquered the southern Mediterranean shore and took to the sea in the seventh century, Gaul and western Europe was finally thrown back upon itself and forced to look away from the Mediterranean. In fact the lands of the north—modern-day northern France, the Low Countries, Germany, and England—were extremely fertile: with adequate farming implements they could yield great natural wealth. Given the proper circumstances, a new power could emerge in the north to make the most of a new pattern of life based predominantly on agrarianism instead of urban commerce and Mediterranean trade. Around 700 that is exactly what happened in Merovingian Gaul.

*The alliance between
Frankish rulers and the
Church; Charles Martel
and St. Boniface*

The proper circumstances were the triumph of a succession of able rulers and their alliance with the Church. In 687 an energetic Merovingian mayor of the palace, Pepin of Heristal, managed to unite all the Frankish lands under his rule and build a new power base for his own family in the region of Belgium and the Rhine. He was succeeded by his aggressive son, Charles Martel ("the Hammer"), who is sometimes considered a second founder of the Frankish state. Charles's claim to this title is twofold. First, in 732 he turned back a Muslim force from Spain at the Battle of Poitiers, some 150 miles from Paris. Although the Muslim contingent was not a real army but merely a marauding band, the incursion was the high-water mark of their progress toward the northwest and Charles's victory won him great prestige. Equally important, around the end of his reign Charles began to develop an alliance with the Church, particularly with the Benedictines of England. Having finished most of their conversion work on their island, the Benedictines, under their idealistic leader St. Boniface, were moving across the English Channel in an attempt to convert central Germany. Charles Martel realized that he and they had common interests, for after he had guarded his southern flank against the Muslims he was seeking to direct Frankish expansion eastward in the direction of Germany. Missionary work and Frankish expansion could go hand in hand, so Charles offered St. Boniface and his Benedictines material aid in return for their support of his territorial aims.

*Solidification of the
alliance in the time of
Pepin the Short*

Once allied with the Franks, St. Boniface provided further service in the next reign in helping to contribute to one of the most momentous events in Western history. Charles Martel had never assumed the royal title, but his son, Pepin the Short, wished to take it. Even though Pepin and not the reigning "do-nothing king" was the real power, Pepin needed the prestige of the Church for supporting a change in dynasties. Fortunately for him the times were highly propitious for obtaining Church support. St. Boniface supported Pepin because the young ruler continued his father's policy of collaborating with the Benedictines in Germany. And Boniface had great influence in Rome because the Anglo-Saxon Benedictines had remained in the closest touch with the papacy since the time of Gregory the Great.

The papacy was now fully prepared to cast its own lots with a strong Frankish ruler because it was in the midst of a bitter fight with the Byzantine emperors over Iconoclasm. The Byzantines until then had offered papal territories in Italy some protection against the Lombards, but the increasingly powerful Franks were now fully able to take over that role. The papacy accordingly made an epochal about-face, turning fully and lastingly to the West. In 750 the pope encouraged Pepin to depose the Merovingian figurehead, and in 751 St. Boniface, acting as papal emissary, anointed Pepin as a divinely sanctioned king. Thus the Frankish monarchy attained a spiritual mandate and was fully integrated into the papal-Benedictine orbit. Shortly afterwards Pepin paid his debt to the pope by conquering the Lombards in Italy. The West was now achieving its own unity based on the Frankish state and the Latin church, not coincidentally just at the time when the Abbasid caliphate was being founded in the East and the Byzantines were going their own fully Greek way.

The ultimate consolidation of the new pattern took place in the reign of Pepin's son, Carolus Magnus or Charlemagne (768–814), from whom the new dynasty takes its name of "Carolingian." Without question Charlemagne ranks as one of the most important rulers of the whole medieval period. Had it been possible to ask him what his greatest accomplishment was, he almost certainly would have replied that it lay in greatly increasing the Frankish realm. Except for the English, there was scarcely a people of western Europe against whom he did not fight. Most of his campaigns were successful; he annexed the greater part of central Europe and northern and central Italy to the Frankish domain. To rule this vast area he bestowed all the powers of local government upon his own appointees, called counts, and tried to remain in control of them by sending representatives of the court to observe them. Among the counts' many duties were the administration of justice and the raising of armies. Although Charlemagne's system in practice was far from perfect, it led to the best government that Europe had seen since the Romans. Because of the military triumphs and internal peace of his reign, Charlemagne was long remembered and revered as a western European folk hero.

Charlemagne. A silver penny struck between 804 and 814 showing Charlemagne in a highly stylized fashion as emperor with Roman toga and laurel. The inscription reads KAROLVS IMP AVG (Charles, Emperor, Augustus).

Primarily to aid his territorial expansion and help administer his realm Charlemagne presided over a revival of learning known as the "Carolingian Renaissance." Charlemagne extended his rule into Germany in the name of Christianity, but in order to proselytize he needed educated monks and priests. More than that, in order to ad-

*The Carolingian
Renaissance*

minister his far-flung territories he needed at least a few people who could read and write. Amazing as it may seem to us, there were hardly any at first in his entire realm who were literate, so thoroughly had the rudiments of learning been forgotten since the decay of Roman city life. Only in Anglo-Saxon England had literacy been cultivated by the Benedictine monks. The reason for this was that the Anglo-Saxons spoke a form of German but the monks needed to learn Latin in order to say their offices and study the Bible. Since they knew no Latin to begin with they had to go about learning it by a very self-conscious program of studies. The greatest Anglo-Saxon Benedictine scholar before Charlemagne's time was the Venerable Bede (d. 735), whose *History of the English Church and People,* written in Latin, was one of the best historical writings of the early-medieval period and can still be read with pleasure. When Charlemagne came to the throne he invited the Anglo-Saxon Benedictine Alcuin—a student of one of Bede's students—to direct a revival of studies on the continent. With Charlemagne's active support Alcuin helped establish new schools to teach reading, directed the copying and correcting of important Latin works, including many Roman classics, and inspired the formulation of a new clear handwriting that is the ancestor of our modern "Roman" print. These were the greatest achievements of the Carolingian Renaissance, which stressed practicality rather than original literary or intellectual endeavors. Thoroughly unpretentious as they were, they established a bridgehead for literacy on the Continent which thereafter would never be completely lost. They also helped to preserve Latin literature, and they made the Latin language the language of state and diplomacy for all of western Europe, as it remained until comparatively modern times.

The climax of Charlemagne's career came in the year 800 when he was crowned emperor on Christmas Day in Rome by the pope. His-

Carolingian Handwriting. Even the untrained reader has no difficulty in reading this excerpt from a Carolingian manuscript.

torians continue to debate whether this was Charlemagne's or the pope's idea, but there is no doubt that the pope did not gain any immediate power from it. Once the Franks ruled Italy they came to dominate the papacy, and indeed the whole Church, to such a degree that by 800 the pope was very close to being Charlemagne's puppet. Charlemagne did not gain any actual new power by taking the imperial title either, but the significance of the event is nonetheless great. Up until 800 the only emperor ruled in Constantinople and could lay claim to being the direct heir of Augustus. Although the Byzantines had lost most of their interest in the West, they still continued to regard it vaguely as an outlying province and were actively opposed to any westerner calling himself emperor. Charlemagne's assumption of the title was virtually a declaration of Western self-confidence and independence. Since Charlemagne's vast realm was fully as large as that of the Byzantines, had great reserves of agricultural wealth, and was defining its own culture based on Western Christianity and the Latin linguistic tradition, the claim to empire was largely justified. More than that, it was never forgotten. Both for its symbolism and its contribution toward giving westerners a sense of unity and purpose it was a major landmark on the road to the making of a great western Europe.

*Charlemagne's coronation
as emperor*

Although the claim to empire was bold and memorable, Charlemagne's actual empire disintegrated quickly after his death for many reasons. The simplest was that hardly any of his successors were as competent and decisive as he was. In order to rule an empire in those still extremely primitive times, one had to have enormous reserves of strength and energy—one had to travel on horseback over enormous distances, fight and win battles at the head of unruly armies, and know how to delegate power to others with vigilance against its abuse. Unfortunately for western Europe few of Charlemagne's heirs had such combinations of energy and talent. To make matters worse, Charlemagne's sole surviving son, Louis the Pious, who inherited the Frankish realm intact, divided his inheritance among his own three sons, thereby bringing civil war back to Frankish Europe. And to make matters worst of all, new waves of invasions began just as Charlemagne's grandsons and great-grandsons started fighting each other: from the north came the Scandinavian Vikings; from the east came the Asiatic Magyars (or Hungarians); and from the south came new attacks by marauding Muslims, attacking now from the sea. Under these pressures the Carolingian Empire completely fell apart and a new political map of Europe was drawn in the tenth century.

*The disintegration of
Charlemagne's empire*

As the Carolingian period was crucial for marking the beginnings of a common north Atlantic western European civilization, so the tenth century was crucial for marking the beginnings of the major modern European political entities. England, which never had been part of Charlemagne's empire, and which hitherto had been divided among

*England in the time of
Alfred the Great*

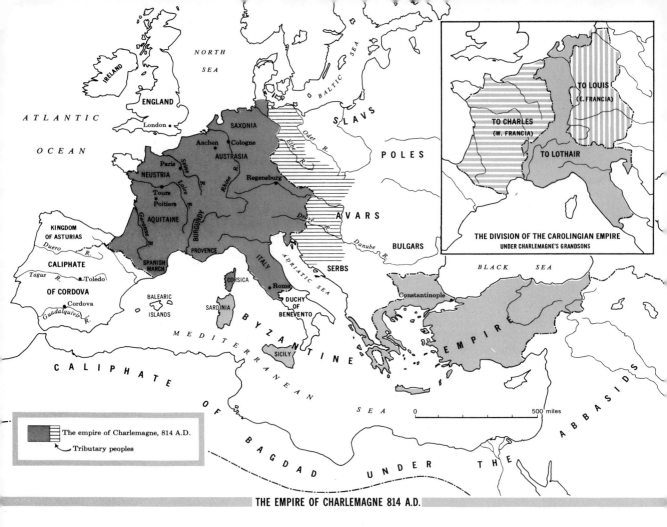

NORTH SEA

ATLANTIC OCEAN

IRELAND

ENGLAND
London

BALTIC SEA

SLAVS

POLES

AVARS

BULGARS

SERBS

NEUSTRIA
Paris
Tours
Poitiers
AQUITAINE
Garonne R.
BURGUNDY
PROVENCE
SPANISH MARCH

Aachen · Cologne
SAXONIA
AUSTRASIA
Regensburg
Seine R.
Loire R.
Rhine R.
Elbe R.
Oder R.
Drave R.
Danube R.

KINGDOM OF ASTURIAS
Duero R.

CALIPHATE OF CORDOVA
Tagus R. · Toledo
Cordova
Guadalquivir R.

BALEARIC ISLANDS

CORSICA
SARDINIA
SICILY
Rome
DUCHY OF BENEVENTO
ITALY

MEDITERRANEAN SEA

BLACK SEA
Constantinople

BYZANTINE EMPIRE

CALIPHATE OF BAGDAD UNDER THE ABBASIDS

0   500 miles

The empire of Charlemagne, 814 A.D.
Tributary peoples

THE DIVISION OF THE CAROLINGIAN EMPIRE
UNDER CHARLEMAGNE'S GRANDSONS

TO CHARLES (W. FRANCIA)
TO LOUIS (E. FRANCIA)
TO LOTHAIR

THE EMPIRE OF CHARLEMAGNE 814 A.D.

smaller warring Anglo-Saxon states, became unified in the late ninth and the tenth century owing to the work of King Alfred the Great (871–899) and his direct successors. Alfred and his heirs reorganized the army, infused new vigor into local government, and codified the English laws. In addition, Alfred founded schools and fostered an interest in Anglo-Saxon writing and other elements of a national culture.

Political conditions in France and Germany

Across the Channel, France (now the name for the main part of Roman Gaul because it was the original seat of the Frankish monarchy) was most devastated by the invasions of Vikings, who had sailed up the French rivers. For that reason France broke up into small principalities rather than developing a strong national monarchy on the pattern of England. Nonetheless there was a king in France, who, however weak, was recognized as the ruler of the western part of Charlemagne's former territories. Directly to the east, the kings of Germany were the strongest continental monarchs of the tenth century, ruling over an essentially united realm. In addition to Germany, their lands encompassed most of the Low Countries and a good part of modern eastern France.

The most important German ruler of the period was Otto the Great. He became king in 936, resoundingly defeated the Hungarians in 955—thereby relieving Germany of its greatest foreign threat—and took the title of emperor in Rome in 962. By this last act Otto strengthened his claim to being the greatest continental monarch since Charlemagne. Otto and his successors, who continued to call themselves emperors, tried to rule over Italy but barely succeeded in doing so. Instead, Italy in the tenth century saw the greatest western European development of urban life, a pattern on which the Italians would subsequently build.

Otto the Great of Germany

Although Italy did develop some city life in the tenth century, this was by no means typical of the early-medieval period in western Europe as a whole. Quite to the contrary, from the eighth to the eleventh century the European economy was based almost entirely on agriculture and very limited local trade. Roads deteriorated and barter widely replaced the use of money. Whatever cities survived from Roman days were usually empty shells that served at most as administrative centers for bishops and fortified places in case of common danger. The main economic unit throughout the period was the self-supporting large landed estate, usually owned by kings, warrior aristocrats, or large-scale monasteries. Although the northern European soil was rich, farming tools in most places were still too primitive to bring in a fully adequate return on the enormous investment of effort expended by the laboring masses. Agricultural yields in all but the most fertile Carolingian heartlands (and often even in them) were pitifully low, and Europeans, except the rulers and the higher clergy, lived on the edge of subsistence. It is true that some increase in agricultural income had underpinned the Carolingian successes and some progress in farming might have continued had the peace of Charlemagne's reign endured. But the subsequent invasions of the ninth and tenth centuries set agricultural life back and new beginnings would have to be made in the years thereafter.

The economy of western Europe in the early Middle Ages

Given the low level of early-medieval economic life, it is not surprising that the age was not a prosperous time for learning or the arts: if there is scarcely enough wealth to keep most people alive, there is not going to be much to support schools or major artistic projects. Throughout the period, even in the best of years, learning was a privilege for the few: the masses received no formal education, and even most members of the secular aristocracy were illiterate. Learning also consisted mostly of memorization, without regard for criticism or refutation. We have seen that there was some revival of learning under Charlemagne that may be called a "renaissance" but that it did not issue into any real intellectual creativity. Its major accomplishment was the founding of enough schools to educate the clergy in the rudi-

The low level of intellectual life

ments of reading and the training of enough monastic scribes to re-copy and preserve some major works of Roman literature. Even this accomplishment was jeopardized in the period of invasions that accompanied the fall of the Carolingian Empire. Fortunately just enough schools and manuscripts survived to become the basis for another—far greater—revival of learning that began in the eleventh and twelfth centuries.

Literature

In the realm of literature the early Middle Ages had an extremely meager production. This was because few Christians could write and those who could were usually monks and priests, who were not supposed to engage in purely literary endeavors. There was some impressive writing of history in Latin, most notably that of Bede and Charlemagne's eloquent biographer, Einhard, but otherwise Latin composition was little cultivated. Toward the close of the period, however, the vernacular languages, which were either Germanic or based on different regional dialects of Latin (the "Romance" languages, so-called because they were based on "Roman" speech) began to be employed for crude poetic expression, usually first by oral transmission.

Beowulf

The best-known example of this literature in the vernacular is the Anglo-Saxon epic poem *Beowulf.* First put into written form about the eighth century, this poem incorporates ancient legends of the Germanic peoples of northwestern Europe. It is a story of fighting and seafaring and of heroic adventure against deadly dragons and the forces of nature. The background of the epic is pre-Christian, but the author of the work introduced into it some qualities of Christian idealism. *Beowulf* is important not only as one of the earliest specimens of Anglo-Saxon or Old English poetry, but also for the picture it gives of the society of the English and their ancestors in the early Middle Ages.

The artistic history of the early Middle Ages was a story of isolated and interrupted accomplishments because artistic life relied most of all on brief moments of local peace or royal patronage. The earliest enduring monuments of early-medieval art were those created by monks in Ireland—which had its own unique culture—between the sixth and the eighth centuries. Above all in manuscript illumination (i.e., painted illustrations) the Irish monks developed a thoroughly anticlassical and almost surrealistic style, whose origins are most difficult to account for. The greatest surviving product from this school is the stunning "Book of Kells," an illuminated Gospel book that has been called "the most sophisticated work of decorative art in the history of painting." The Irish school declined without subsequent influence and was followed by artistic products of the Carolingian Renaissance.

Irish Art. The opening of a gospel page that shows the Irish style at its most surrealistic.

The art of Charlemagne's period returned for much of its inspiration to classical models, yet it also retained some of the spontaneous vitality of barbarian decoration. When Charlemagne's empire declined and disintegrated there was a corresponding decline and then interruption in the history of Western art. In the tenth century, however, new

Carolingian Art. The fountain of life: an illuminated manuscript page from Gottschalk's Evangeliary (book with four gospels), dating from 781.

regional schools emerged. The greatest of these were the English, which emphasized restless fluency in manuscript illumination; the German, which was more grave but still managed to communicate extreme religious ecstasy; and the northern Spanish, which, though Christian, created a rather strange and independent style mostly influenced by the decorative style of Islamic art. By the very end of the early-medieval period a new European international style was emerging that would be called "Romanesque," but that is a subject for later consideration.

Regional variations in early-medieval art

Just as the Romanesque style bridged the early and subsequent medieval periods, there is no single, obvious terminal date for early-medieval history as a whole. The date 1000 is sometimes given, most of all because it is a convenient round number, but even as late as 1050 Europe had not changed on the surface very much from the way it had been since the end of the Carolingian period. Indeed, looking at Europe as late as 1050 it would at first seem that not much progress had been made over the entire course of the early-medieval centuries. Except for Germany there was hardly any centralized government, because by 1050 the Anglo-Saxon English state created by King Alfred and his successors was falling apart. Throughout Europe, all but the most privileged individuals continued to live on the brink of starvation and cultural attainments were minimal and sparse. But actually much had been accomplished. By shifting its main weight to the Atlantic northwest, European civilization became centered in lands that would soon harvest great agricultural wealth. By preserving some of the traditions developed by Gregory the Great, St. Boniface,

A distinct western European civilization evident in 1050

Left: *Utrecht Psalter.* This Carolingian manuscript of the Psalms from about 820 later provided the basis for the "nervous expressiveness" of the tenth-century English regional school. Right: *Bamberg Apocalypse.* In this manuscript illumination from about 1000 A.D. the fall of Babylon in the Book of Revelation (18: 1–20) is displayed by depicting the city upside down. An example of the grave regional German style.

Pepin, and Charlemagne, European civilization had also developed an enduring sense of cultural unity based on Western Christianity and the Latin inheritance. And in the tenth century the beginnings of the future European kingdoms and city-states started to coalesce. Western European civilization was thus for the first time becoming autonomous and distinctive. From then until now it would become a leading force in the history of the world.

SELECTED READINGS

- *Items so designated are available in paperback editions.*

BYZANTINE CIVILIZATION

Beckwith, John, *The Art of Constantinople,* 2nd ed., London, 1968. A standard account.
- Diehl, Charles, *Byzantium: Greatness and Decline,* New Brunswick, N.J., 1957. Evaluates strengths and weaknesses of Byzantine civilization.
Geanakoplos, D. J., *Byzantine East and Latin West,* New York, 1966.
Hussey, J. M., *The Byzantine World,* London, 1957. Half-narrative, half-topical; a useful short introduction.
- Krautheimer, R., *Early Christian and Byzantine Architecture,* Baltimore, 1970.

Magoulias, H. J., *Byzantine Christianity: Emperor, Church and the West*, Chicago, 1970. Limited to three themes mentioned in title.

Miller, D. A., *The Byzantine Tradition*, New York, 1966. The briefest introduction.

Ostrogorsky, George, *History of the Byzantine State*, New Brunswick, N.J., 1957. The most authoritative longer account of political developments; very scholarly.

• Pelikan, J., *The Christian Tradition; II: The Spirit of Eastern Christendom*, Chicago, 1974. An advanced treatment of religious doctrines.

• Runciman, S., *Byzantine Civilization*, New York, 1933. A topical approach; well written but in parts outdated.

• ———, *Byzantine Style and Civilization*, Baltimore, 1975. A fine study of Byzantine art.

• Vasiliev, A. A., *History of the Byzantine Empire*, 2 vols., Madison, Wisc., 1928. Supplements Ostrogorsky; valuable for its detail on social and intellectual as well as political history.

Vryonis, S., *Byzantium and Europe*, New York, 1967. Noteworthy for its illustrations.

ISLAMIC CIVILIZATION

Arnold, Thomas, and A. Guillaume, *The Legacy of Islam*, New York, 1931.

Gabrieli, F., *Muhammad and the Conquests of Islam*, New York, 1968.

• Gibb, H. A. R., *Arabic Literature: An Introduction*, 2nd ed., Oxford, 1963. An excellent survey.

———, *Mohammedanism: An Historical Survey*, 2nd ed., Oxford, 1953. The best brief interpretation of Islamic religion.

• Goitein, S. D., *Jews and Arabs, Their Contacts through the Ages*, New York, 1955.

Grube, E. J., *The World of Islam*, New York, 1966.

• Hodgson, M., *The Venture of Islam*, 3 vols., Chicago, 1974. A masterwork. One of the greatest works of history written by a modern American. Advanced and sometimes difficult, but always rewarding.

• Lewis, Bernard, *The Arabs in History*, rev. ed., New York, 1966. The best short survey of the conquests and political fortunes of the Arabs.

• Lombard, Maurice, *The Golden Age of Islam*, New York, 1975.

Peters, F. E., *Aristotle and the Arabs*, New York, 1968. A well-written and engaging account.

Watt, W. Montgomery, *Islamic Philosophy and Theology*, Edinburgh, 1962.

• ———, *Muhammad: Prophet and Statesman*, Oxford, 1961. A good short biography.

Watt, W. M., and P. Cachia, *A History of Islamic Spain*, Edinburgh, 1965. Briefly covers an undeservedly neglected subject.

EARLY-MEDIEVAL WESTERN CHRISTIAN CIVILIZATION

• Barraclough, G., *The Crucible of Europe: The Ninth and Tenth Centuries in European History*, Berkeley, Calif., 1976. A controversial and sometimes wrongheaded but clear and stimulating interpretation of political developments.

• Dawson, Christopher, *The Making of Europe,* London, 1932. A brilliant interpretation that emphasizes cultural and religious developments by one of this century's most eminent Catholic historians.
• Duby, G., *The Early Growth of the European Economy,* Ithaca, N.Y., 1974. Emphasizes role of lords and peasants; very sophisticated economic history.
  Fichtenau, H., *The Carolingian Empire,* Oxford, 1957. A highly interpretative account that aims to whittle its subject down to size.
• Ganshof, F. L., *Frankish Institutions under Charlemagne,* Providence, 1958. A straightforward technical exposition.
  Halphen, L., *Charlemagne and the Carolingian Empire,* New York, 1977. An older French survey recently translated into English.
• Kitzinger, Ernst, *Early Medieval Art,* London, 1940. A very short but masterful introduction.
• Laistner, M. L. W., *Thought and Letters in Western Europe, A.D. 500–900,* rev. ed., Ithaca, N.Y., 1957. An old-fashioned but standard account; should be supplemented by Wolff.
• Pirenne, Henri, *Mohammed and Charlemagne,* New York, 1939. A bold interpretation, now no longer widely accepted but still thought provoking.
  Stenton, Frank, *Anglo-Saxon England,* 3rd ed., Oxford, 1971. A standard work.
• Sullivan, Richard E., *Heirs of the Roman Empire,* Ithaca, N.Y., 1960. An elementary introduction.
• Wallace-Hadrill, J. M., *The Barbarian West, A. D. 400–1000,* 2nd ed., London, 1962. A sophisticated short account that emphasizes analysis of the historical sources and questions earlier scholarly assumptions.
  Wolff, Philippe, *The Awakening of Europe,* Baltimore, 1968. The "new intellectual history": emphasizes interrelations between the development of thought and material foundations. Masterfully written and organized.

SOURCE MATERIALS

• Arberry, A. J., *The Koran Interpreted,* 2 vols., London, 1955.
• Bede, *A History of the English Church and People,* tr. L. Sherley-Price, Baltimore, 1955.
• Brand, Charles M., ed., *Icon and Minaret: Sources of Byzantine and Islamic Civilization,* Englewood Cliffs, N.J., 1969.
• Brentano, Robert, ed., *The Early Middle Ages: 500–1000,* New York, 1964. The best shorter anthology of the Western Christian sources, enlivened by the editor's subjective commentary.
  Davis, Charles T., ed.; *The Eagle, the Crescent, and the Cross,* New York, 1967.
• Einhard and Notker the Stammerer, *Two Lives of Charlemagne,* tr. L. Thorpe, Baltimore, 1969.
• Gregory Bishop of Tours, *History of the Franks,* tr. E. Brehaut, New York, 1965.

Chapter 14

THE HIGH MIDDLE AGES (1050–1300): ECONOMIC, SOCIAL, AND POLITICAL INSTITUTIONS

I judge those who write at this time to be in a certain measure happy. For, after the turbulence of the past, an unprecedented brightness of peace has dawned again.

—The historian Otto of
Freising, writing around 1158

The period between about 1050 and 1300, termed by historians the High Middle Ages, was the time when western Europe first clearly emerged from backwardness to become one of the greatest powers on the globe. Around 1050 the West was still less developed in most respects than the Byzantine Empire or the Islamic world, but by 1300 it had forged ahead of these two rivals. From a global perspective, only China was its equal in economic, political, and cultural prosperity. Given the sorry state of western Europe around 1050, this startling leap forward was certainly one of the most impressive achievements of human history. Those who think that the entire Middle Ages were times of stagnation could not be more wrong.

Western Europe emerges from backwardness

The reasons for Europe's enormous progress in the High Middle Ages are predictably complex, yet medieval historians agree upon certain broad lines of interpretation. One is that Europe between 900 and 1050 was already poised for growth and could finally begin to live up to its potential once the devastating invasions of Vikings, Hungarians, and Muslims had ceased. Most of these invasions had tapered off by around 1000, but in the eleventh century England was still troubled by the Danes: the year 1066, more famous as the year of the Norman Conquest, was also the year of the last Viking invasion of England.

Reasons for the "great leap forward"

Once foreign invasions were no longer imminent, western Europeans could concentrate on developing their economic life with much less fear of interruption than before. Because of the relative continuity allowed by this change, extraordinarily important technological breakthroughs were made, above all those that contributed to the first great western European "agricultural revolution." The revolution in agriculture made food more bountiful and provided a solid basis for economic development and diversification in other spheres. Population grew rapidly and towns and cities grew to such a degree that we can speak also of an "urban revolution." At the same time political life in the West became more stable. In the course of the High Middle Ages strong new secular governments began to provide more and more internal peace for their subjects and became the foundations of our modern nation-states. In addition to all these advances, there were also striking new religious and intellectual developments, to be treated in the next chapter, which helped give the West a new sense of mission and self-confidence. Although in this chapter we will treat only the economic, social, and political accomplishments of the High Middle Ages, it is well to bear in mind that religion played a pervasive role in all of medieval life, and that all aspects of the high-medieval "great leap forward" were inextricably interrelated.

1. THE FIRST AGRICULTURAL REVOLUTION

The state of agriculture before 1050

The agricultural worker, the "Man with the Hoe," supported European civilization materially by his labors more than anyone else until the industrialization of modern times. Yet, amazing as it seems, until about 1050 he had hardly so much as a hoe. Inventories of farm implements from the Carolingian period reveal that metal tools on the wealthiest rural estates were extremely rare and even wooden implements were so few in number that many laborers must have had to grapple with nature quite literally with only their bare hands. Between about 1050 and 1250 all that changed. In roughly those two centuries an agricultural revolution took place which entirely altered the nature and vastly increased the output of western European farming.

Prerequisities for the medieval agricultural revolution: (1) shift in area of cultivation

Many of the prerequisites for the medieval agricultural revolution had been present before the middle of the eleventh century. The most important was the shift in the weight of European civilization from the Mediterranean to the north Atlantic regions. Most of northern Europe from southern England to the Urals is a vast, wet, and highly fertile alluvial plain. The Romans had hardly begun to cultivate this area because they only ruled part of it, because it lay too far away from the center of their civilization, and because they did not have the proper tools and systems to work the soil. Starting around the time of the Carolingians much more attention was paid to colonizing and cultivating the great alluvial plain. The Carolingians opened up all of western and central Germany to agricultural settlement and started experimenting with new tools and methods that would be most appropriate for cultivating the newly settled lands. The results helped support other Carolingian achievements, but the Carolingian peace, as we have seen, was too brief to allow for any cumulative development. After the invasions of the tenth century, it was necessary to start again in a systematic attempt to exploit the potential wealth of the north. As long as Western civilization was centered in England, northern France, the Low Countries, and Germany, however, the rich lands were right there to be cultivated.

Another prerequisite for agricultural development was improved climate. We know far less about European climatic patterns in past centuries than we would like to, but historians of climate are reasonably certain that there was an "optimum," or period of improved climate for western Europe, lasting from about 700 to 1200. This meant not only that during those centuries the temperature on the average was somewhat warmer than it had been before (at most only a rise of about 1° Centigrade), but also that the weather was somewhat drier. Dryness was of primary advantage to northern Europe, where lands were, if anything, usually too wet for good farming, whereas it was disadvantageous to the Mediterranean south, which was already dry enough. Among other things, the occurrence of this optimum helps explain why there was more agricultural cultivation in northern climes such as Iceland than there has been since then. (Also, with fewer icebergs in the northern seas, Norsemen were able to reach Greenland and Newfoundland, and Greenland then was probably indeed more green than white.) Although the optimum began around 700 and continued through the ninth and tenth centuries, it could not by itself counteract the deleterious effects of the tenth-century invasions. Fortunately the weather stayed propitious when Europeans again were able to take advantage of it.

(2) improved climate

Similar remarks apply to the fact that the Carolingians knew about many of the technological devices to be discussed presently that later most helped western Europeans accomplish their first agricultural revolution. Although the most basic new devices were known before 1050, all came into widespread use and were brought to greatest perfection between then and about 1200 because only then was there a conjunction of the most favorable circumstances. Not only did the invasions end and good climate continue, but better government gradually provided the more lasting peace necessary for agricultural expansion. Landlords too became more interested in profit-making than mere consumption. Above all, from about 1050 to 1200 there was a greater consolidation of wealth for further investment as one advance helped support another; quite simply, technological devices could now be afforded.

(3) technology in conjunction with favorable circumstances

Light Plow and Heavy Plow. Note that the peasant using the light plow has to press his foot on it to give it added weight. The major innovation of the heavy

Technological innovations: (1) the heavy plow

One of the first and most important breakthroughs in agriculture was the use of the heavy plow. The plow itself, of course, is an ancient tool, but the Romans knew only a light "scratch plow" that broke up the surface of the ground without fully turning it over. This implement was sufficient for the light soil of the Mediterranean regions but was virtually useless with the much heavier, wetter soil of the European north. During the course of the early Middle Ages a much heavier and more efficient plow was developed that could cultivate the northern lands. Not only could this heavier plow deal with heavier soils, but it was fitted with new parts that enabled it to turn over furrows and fully aerate the ground. The benefits were immeasurable. In addition to the fact that the plow allowed for the cultivation of hitherto unworkable lands, the furrows it made provided excellent drainage systems for water-logged territories. It also saved labor: whereas the Roman scratch plow had to be dragged over the fields twice in two different directions, the heavy plow did more thorough work in one operation. In short, the opening up of northern Europe for intensive agriculture and everything that followed would have been inconceivable without the heavy plow.

(2) the three-field system

Closely allied to the use of the heavy plow was the introduction of the three-field system of crop rotation. Before modern times, farmers always let a large part of their arable land lie fallow for a year to avoid exhaustion of the soil because there was not enough fertilizer to support more intensive agriculture, and nitrogen-fixing crops such as clover and alfalfa were almost unknown. But the Romans represented an unproductive extreme in their inability to cultivate any more than half of their arable land in any year. The medieval innovation was to reduce the fallow to one-third by introducing a three-field system. In a given year one third of the land would lie fallow, one third would be given to cereal that was sown in the fall and harvested in early sum-

plow was the long moldboard, which turned over the ground after the plowshare cut into it.

mer, and one third to a new crop—oats, barley, or legumes—that would be planted in the late spring and harvested in August or September. The fields were then rotated over a three-year cycle. The major innovation was the planting of the new crop which grew over the summer. The Romans could not have supported this system because their lands were poorer and especially because the Mediterranean area is too dry to support much summer growth at all. In this respect the wetter north obviously had a great advantage. The benefits of the new crop were that it did not deplete the soil as much as cereal like wheat and rye (in fact, it restored nitrogen taken from the soil by these crops); that it provided some insurance against loss from natural disasters by diversifying the growth of the fields; and that it produced new types of food. If the third field was planted with oats, the crop could be consumed by both humans and horses; if planted with legumes, it helped to balance the human diet by providing a source of protein to balance the major intake of cereal carbohydrates. Since the new system also helped to diversify labor over the course of the year and raised production from one-half to two-thirds, it was nothing short of an agricultural miracle.

A third major innovation was the use of mills. The Romans had known about water mills but hardly used them, partly because they had enough slaves to be indifferent to labor-saving devices and partly because most Roman territories were not richly endowed with swiftly flowing streams. Starting around 1050, however, there was a veritable craze in northern Europe for building increasingly efficient water mills. One French area we know of saw a growth from 14 water mills in the eleventh century to 60 in the twelfth; in another part of France about 40 mills were built between 850 and 1080, 40 more between 1080 and 1125, and 245 between 1125 and 1175. Once Europeans had mastered the complex technology of building water mills, they turned

(3) use of mills

*(4) other technological
developments*

their attention to harnessing the power of wind: around 1170 they constructed the first European windmills. Thereafter, in flat lands like Holland that had no swiftly flowing streams, windmills proliferated as rapidly as water-powered ones had spread elsewhere. Although the major use of mills was to grind grain, they were soon adapted for a variety of other important functions: for example, they were employed to drive saws, process cloth, press oil, brew beer, provide power for iron forges, and crush pulp for manufacturing paper. Paper had been made in China and the Islamic world before this but never with the aid of paper mills, which is evidence of the technological sophistication the West was achieving in comparison to other advanced civilizations.

There were other important technological breakthroughs that gathered force around 1050 which should be mentioned. Several related to providing the means for using horses as farm animals. Around 800 a padded collar was first introduced into Europe; this allowed the horse to put his full weight into pulling without choking himself. Roughly a century later iron horseshoes were first used to protect hooves, and perhaps around 1050 tandem harnessing was developed to allow horses to pull behind each other. With these advances and the greater abundance of oats due to the three-field system, horses replaced oxen as farm animals in some parts of Europe and brought with them the advantages of working more quickly and working longer hours. Further inventions were the wheelbarrow and the harrow, a tool drawn over the field after the plow to level the earth and mix in the seed. Important for most of these inventions was the greater use of iron in the High Middle Ages to reinforce all sorts of agricultural implements, most crucially the parts of the heavy plow that came into contact with the soil.

So far we have been speaking of technological developments as if they alone account for the high-medieval agricultural revolution. But that is by no means the case. Along with improved technology came a

Peasants Bringing Grain to Windmills. Shown here are two different kinds of mills: those set to operate by prevailing winds and those that are pivoted to face into chance winds. Note how windmills dot the landscape.

great extension in the amount of land made arable and more intensive cultivation of the land already cleared. Although the Carolingians had begun to open the rich plain of northwestern Europe to tillage, they had only chosen to clear the most easily workable patches: a map of Carolingian agricultural settlements would show numerous tiny islands of cultivated lands surrounded by vast stretches of forests, swamps, and wastes. Starting around 1050, and greatly accelerating in the twelfth century, movements of land-clearing entirely changed the topography of northern Europe. First, greater peace and stability allowed farm workers in northern France and western Germany to begin pushing beyond the islands of settlement, clearing little bits of land at a time. At first they did this surreptitiously because they were poaching on territories that were actually owned by aristocratic lords. But then the aristocratic landowners gave their support to the clearing activities because they demanded their own profits from them. When that happened the work of clearing forests and draining swamps was carried on more swiftly. Thus, as the twelfth century progressed the isolated arable islands of Carolingian times expanded to meet each other. While this was going on, and continuing somewhat later, entirely new areas were colonized and opened to cultivation, for example, in northern England, Holland, and above all the eastern parts of Germany. Finally, in the twelfth and thirteenth centuries, peasants began working all the lands they had cleared more efficiently and intensively in order to gain more income for themselves. They harrowed after plowing, hoed frequently to keep down weeds, and added extra plowings to their yearly cycle, thereby greatly helping to renew the fertility of the soil.

Extension and intense cultivation of arable land

The result of all these changes was an enormous increase in agricultural production. With more land opened for cultivation obviously more crops were raised, but the increase was magnified by the introduction of more efficient farming methods. Thus, average yields from grains of seed sown increased from at best twofold in Carolingian times to three- or fourfold by around 1300. And all the additional grain could be ground far more rapidly than before because a mill could grind grain in the same time that it would have taken forty men to do the same job. Europeans, therefore, could for the first time begin to rely on a regular and stable food supply.

Enormous increase in agricultural productivity

That fact in turn had the profoundest consequences for the further development of European history. To begin with, it meant that more land could be given over to uses other than raising grain. Accordingly, as the High Middle Ages progressed, there was greater agricultural diversification and specialization. Large areas were turned over to sheep-raising, others to viniculture, and others to raising cotton and dyestuffs. Many of the products of these new enterprises were consumed locally, but many were also traded over long distances or used to provide the raw materials for new industries—above all those of cloth-making. The growth of this trade and manufacturing helped ini-

Consequences of the agricultural revolution

tiate and support, as we will see, the growth of towns. The agricultural boom also helped sustain the growth of towns in another way: by supporting a great spurt in population. With more food and a better diet (above all the increase in proteins) life expectancy increased from perhaps as low as an average of thirty years for the poor of Carolingian Europe to between forty and fifty years in the High Middle Ages. Healthier people also increased their birthrate. For these reasons the population of the West grew about threefold between about 1050 and 1300. More people and more labor-saving devices meant that not everybody had to stay on the farm: some could migrate to new towns and cities where they found a new way of life.

Other results

Still other results of the agricultural revolution were that it raised the incomes of lords, thereby underpinning a great increase in the sophistication of aristocratic life, and raised the incomes of monarchs, underpinning the growth of states. European-wide prosperity also helped support the growth of the Church and paid the way for the burgeoning of schools and intellectual enterprises. One final, more intangible, result was that Europeans apparently became more optimistic, more energetic, and more willing to experiment and take risks than any of their rivals on the world scene.

2. LORD AND SERF: SOCIAL CONDITIONS AND QUALITY OF LIFE IN THE MANORIAL REGIME

The meaning of the term manorialism

While the agricultural revolution was going on, social and economic conditions began to change for both landowners and agricultural laborers. Since for much of the High Middle Ages, however, rural life revolved around the institution of the manor owned by lords and worked by serfs, it is best to describe this manorial regime in its most typical form before describing basic changes. In reading the following it should be understood that the term manorialism is not synonymous with feudalism: manorialism was an economic system in which large agricultural estates were worked by serfs, whereas feudalism, in the sense the word is used by most medieval historians, was a political system in which government was greatly decentralized (see the fourth section of this chapter). It should also be borne in mind that when scholars talk about manorialism based on a "typical manor" they are resorting to a historical approximation: no two manors were ever exactly alike, and many differed enormously in size and basic characteristics. Moreover, in those parts of Europe furthest away from the original centers of Carolingian settlement between the Seine and the Rhine, there were few, if any, manors at all. In Italy there was still much agriculture based on slavery, and in central and eastern Germany there were many smaller farms worked by free peasants.

The manor first clearly emerged in Carolingian times and continued

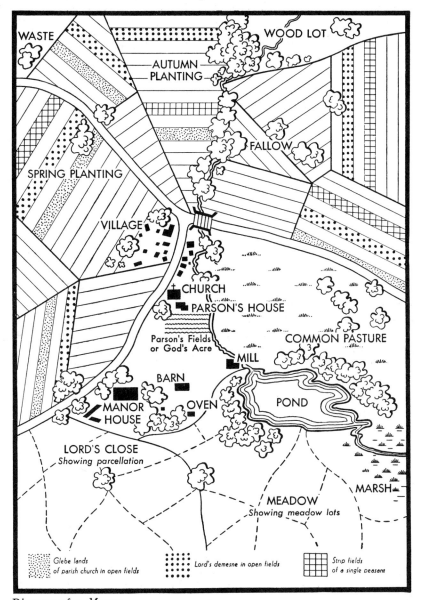

Within the diagram:

WASTE

WOOD LOT

AUTUMN PLANTING

FALLOW

SPRING PLANTING

VILLAGE

CHURCH

PARSON'S HOUSE

Parson's Fields or God's Acre

COMMON PASTURE

MILL

BARN

OVEN

POND

MANOR HOUSE

LORD'S CLOSE
Showing parcellation

MARSH

MEADOW
Showing meadow lots

Glebe lands
of parish church in open fields

Lord's demesne in open fields

Strip fields
of a single peasant

Diagram of a Manor

to be the dominant form of agrarian social and economic organization in most of northwestern Europe until about the thirteenth century. It descended from the large Roman landed estate, but, unlike the Roman estate, the manor was worked by serfs (sometimes called villeins) and not slaves. Serfs were definitely not free in the modern sense: above all, they could not leave their lands, were forced to work for their lords regularly without pay, were subject to numerous humiliating dues, and were most often subject to the jurisdiction of the lord's court. But they were much better off than slaves insofar as they were allocated

The manor; serfs

*The manorial system of
agriculture*

land which they cultivated to support themselves and which normally could not be taken away from them. Thus, when there were agricultural improvements the serfs themselves could hope to profit at least a little from them. More than that, although the lord theoretically had the right to levy dues at will, in practice obligations tended to remain fixed. Although the lot of the serf was surely terribly hard, he was seldom entirely at his lord's whim.

The lands of the manor, which might run from several hundred to several thousand acres, were divided into those that belonged to the lord and those that were allocated to the serfs. The former, called the lord's *demesne* (pronounced demean), usually comprised between a third and a half of the arable land. It was worked by the serfs on certain days, perhaps three days a week. The demesne did not consist of big parcels but was made up of narrow strips alternating with strips belonging to different peasants (and sometimes also strips set aside for the Church). All these strips were long and narrow because a heavy plow drawn by a yoke of horses or oxen could not be turned around easily. Because all the strips were generally separated only by a narrow band of unplowed turf, the whole regime is sometimes called the *open-field system*. Even when the serfs were working their own lands they almost always worked together because they usually owned farm animals and implements in common. For the same reason, grazing lands were called "commons" because the commonly owned herds grazed there together. In addition to cultivated fields and pastures, the serfs usually had their own small gardens. Most manors also had forests set aside primarily for the lord's hunting but which were also useful for the foraging of pigs and the gathering of firewood. Insofar as serfs were allowed to take advantage of such opportunities they did that too in common: indeed, the entire manorial system emphasized communal enterprise and solidarity.

Living conditions of serfs

Communalism must have helped make a barely endurable life seem slightly more bearable. Even though the lot of the medieval serf was surely far superior to that of the Roman slave, and even though it improved from around 1050 to 1300, it was still primitive and pitiful beyond modern comprehension. Dwellings were usually miserable hovels constructed of wattle—braided twigs—smeared over with mud. As late as the thirteenth century an English peasant was convicted of destroying his neighbor's house simply by sawing apart one central beam. The floors of most huts were usually no more than the bare earth, often cold or damp. For beds there was seldom more than bracken, and beyond that there was hardly any furniture. Not entirely jokingly it may be said that a good meal often consisted of two courses: one a porridge very much like gruel and the other a gruel very much like porridge. Fruit was almost unheard of and meager vegetables were limited to such fare as onions, leeks, turnips, and cabbages—all boiled to make a thin soup. Meat came at most a few times a year, either on holidays or deep in winter, when all the fodder for a scrawny ox or pig had run out. Cooking utensils were never cleaned, so as to make sure that there was never any waste. In addition, there was always the possibility of crop failures, which affected the serfs far more than their lords, since the lords demanded the same income as always. At such times the serfs were forced to surrender whatever grain they had and watched their children die slowly of starvation. It is particularly heart-rending to realize that children might be dying while there was still a bit of grain in the granaries: but that grain could not be touched because it was set aside as next year's seed, and without that there would be no future at all.

To counterbalance this grim picture we may now turn to patterns of change and improvement. One, as we have already seen, was dietary. In the High Middle Ages famines were actually far rarer than before and people grew stronger because some protein, mostly in the form of legumes, was added to their fare. There was also a widespread enfranchisement (i.e., freeing) of serfs for many reasons. Once landlords started opening up new lands, they could only attract laborers by guaranteeing their freedom. New centers of free labor usually attracted runaway serfs and became models of a new system whereby landlords asked for fixed rents rather than demanding services. Then, even on the old manors, lords began to realize that they might be able to raise profits by demanding rents instead of duties. Alternatively, serfs might become sufficiently rich by selling their excess produce at free markets to buy their freedom.

Improvements in the condition of serfs

In these different ways serfdom gradually came to an end throughout most of Europe in the course of the thirteenth century. The process, however, moved more or less swiftly in different areas—it was somewhat delayed in England and was seldom so complete that former serfs did not owe some remnant of labor service and dues to powerful local lords. In France some of these continued to exist as nagging indignities right up to the French Revolution in 1789. Serfs who became enfranchised often continued to work communally, but they were now free peasants who produced more for the open market than for their own subsistence.

The lords profited even more than their serfs from the agricultural revolution for several reasons. One was that whenever lords enfranchised serfs they obtained large sums of cash, usually about all the wealth that the serfs had hitherto amassed. Afterwards the lords lived mainly on their rents. Since some of these were levied on lands that the lords had once owned but had never been cultivated, noble income rose greatly. Even more than that, once the lords began to prefer rents to services, they found that rents were easier to increase. In their capacity as rent-collectors the lords did not personally supervise their lands as much as before but traveled more freely, sometimes going off crusading and sometimes living at royal courts. Consequently, added

Benefits of the agricultural revolution for lords

*The medieval nobility;
the rise of chivalry*

wealth allowed them to live better, and greater mobility gave them new ideas for improving their style of life.

Increased sophistication of the nobility was much enhanced by the fact that in the High Middle Ages there was less tumultuous local warfare than before. Until around 1100 the typical European noble was a crude and brutal warrior who spent most of his time engaging in combat with his neighbors and pillaging the defenseless. Much of this violence slackened off in the twelfth century as a result of ecclesiastical constraints, because emerging states were more effectively enforcing local peace, and because the nobles themselves were beginning to enjoy a more settled existence. Nobles continued to go on crusades and to fight in national wars, but they engaged in petty quarrels with each other less frequently. Apparently as an unconscious surrogate for the old fighting spirit the code of *chivalry* was developed. This channeled martial conduct into relatively benign activities. Chivalry literally means "horsemanship," and the chivalrous noble was expected to be thoroughly adept at the equestrian arts. Chivalry also imposed the obligation of fighting in defense of honorable causes; if none were to be found there were opportunities for combat in tournaments, mock battles that at first were quite savage but later became elaborate ceremonial affairs. Above all, the chivalric lord—typically a "knight" who owned less land than the upper aristocracy—was expected to be not only brave and loyal but generous, truthful, reverent, kind to the poor, and disdainful of unfair advantage or sordid gain.

By-products of the increase in noble wealth and the rise of chivalry

Jousting in a Tournament

Aristocratic Table Manners. There are knives but no forks or napkins on the table. The large stars mark these nobles as members of a chivalric order.

were improvements in the quality of living conditions and the treatment of women. Until around 1100 most noble dwellings were made of wood, and burned down frequently because of primitive heating and cooking methods. With increasing wealth and more advanced technology, castles after 1100 were usually built of stone and were thus far less flammable. Moreover, they were now equipped with chimneys and mantled fireplaces, both medieval inventions, which meant that instead of having one large fire in a central great hall, individual rooms could be heated and individuals gained some privacy. Nobles customarily ate fewer vegetables than peasants, but their diet was laden with meat; increased luxury trade also brought costly exotic spices like pepper and saffron to their tables. Although table manners were still atrocious—all used only knives and spoons but no forks and blew their noses on their sleeves—nobles tried to show their superiority to others by dressing elegantly, indeed ostentatiously. During this period snug-fitting clothing also became available because both knitting and the button and buttonhole had just been invented. *Improvements in the quality of noble life*

The history of noble attitudes toward women in the High Middle Ages is somewhat controversial for two reasons. One is that most of our evidence comes from literature, and historians differ as to what degree literature actually reflects life. The other is that according to some scholars women were at best put on a pedestal, whereas modern women rightly prefer to move "up from the pedestal." Nonetheless, there can be no question that as the material quality of noble life improved it did so for women as well as men. More than that, there definitely was a revolution in some verbalized attitudes toward the female sex. Until the twelfth century, aside from a few female saints, women were virtually ignored in literature: the typical French epic told of bloody warlike deeds that either made no mention of women or portrayed them only in passing as being totally subservient. But within a few decades after 1100 noblewomen were suddenly turned into objects of veneration by lyric poets and writers of romances (see the following chapter). A typical troubadour poet could write of his lady *Changes in noble attitudes toward women* that "all I do that is fitting I infer from her beautiful body," and that "she is the tree and the branch where joy's fruit ripens."

Although the new "courtly" literature was extremely idealistic and somewhat artificial, it surely expressed the values of a gentler culture wherein upper-class women were in practice more respected than before. Moreover, there is no question that certain royal women in the twelfth and thirteenth centuries actually did rule their states on various occasions when their husbands or sons were dead or unable to do so. The indomitable Eleanor of Aquitaine, wife of Henry II, for example, helped rule England even though she was over seventy years old when her son Richard I went on a crusade from 1190 to 1194, and the strong-willed Blanche of Castile ruled France extremely well twice in the thirteenth century, once during the minority of her son Louis IX and again when he was off crusading. No doubt from a modern perspective high-medieval women were still very constrained, but from the point of view of the past the High Middle Ages was a time of progress for the women of the upper classes. The most striking symbol comes from the history of the game of chess: before the twelfth century chess was played in Eastern countries, but there the equivalent of the queen was a male figure, the king's chief minister, who could only move diagonally one square at a time; in twelfth-century western Europe, however, this piece was turned into a queen, and sometime before the end of the Middle Ages she began to move all over the board.

3. THE REVIVAL OF TRADE AND THE URBAN REVOLUTION

Inseparable from the agricultural revolution, the enfranchisement of serfs, and the growing sophistication of noble life was the revival of trade and the burgeoning of towns. Reviving trade was of many different sorts. Most fundamental was the mundane trade at local markets, where serfs or free peasants sold their excess grain or perhaps a few dozen eggs. But with growing specialization, produce like wine or cotton might be shipped over longer distances. River and sea routes were used wherever possible, but land transport was also necessary and this was aided by improvements in road-building, the introduction of packhorses and mules, and the building of bridges. Whereas the Romans were really only interested in land *communications,* medieval people, starting in the eleventh century, concentrated on land *transport* to the degree that they were much better able to maintain a vigorous land-based trade. And that is not to say that they ignored Mediterranean communications either. On the contrary, starting again in the eleventh century they began to make the former Roman "lake" the intermediary for an extensive seaborne trade that stretched over shorter and longer distances. Between 1050 and 1300 the Italian

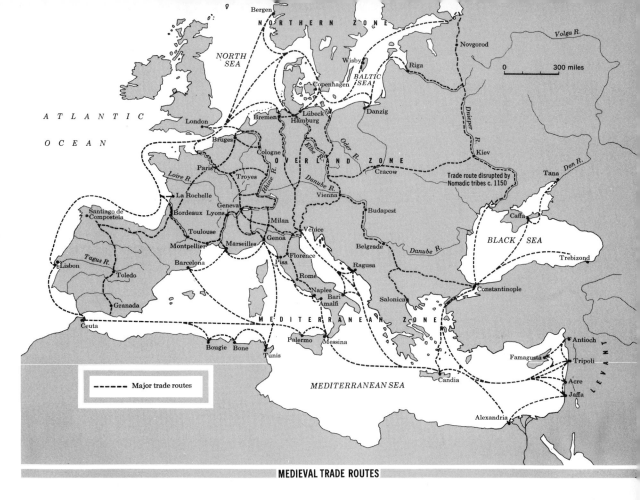

MEDIEVAL TRADE ROUTES

city-states of Genoa, Pisa, and Venice freed much of the Mediterranean from Muslim control, started monopolizing trade on formerly Byzantine waters, and began to establish in eastern Mediterranean outposts a flourishing commerce with the Orient. As a result, luxury goods such as spices, gems, perfumes, and fine cloths began to appear in Western markets and stimulated economic life by inspiring nobles to accelerate the agricultural revolution in order to pay for them.

This revival of trade called for new patterns of payment and the development of new commercial techniques. Most significantly, western Europe returned to a money economy after about four centuries when coined money was hardly used as a medium of exchange. The traditional manor had been almost self-sufficient and the few external items needed could be bartered for. But with the growth of markets coins became indispensable. At first these were coins of only the smallest denominations, but as luxury trade grew in the West the denominations increased apace; by the thirteenth century gold coins were minted by Italian states such as Florence and Venice.

In a similar pattern of development, long-distance traders were first itinerant merchants, often not unlike peddlers, but gradually they

The revival of a money economy

found it best to exhibit and sell their wares at international trade fairs. The most prosperous of these fairs were held in the French province of Champagne, where, for example, cloths from Flanders and spices brought by Italians from the East were exhibited and sold. Later, by around 1300, trade fairs declined because prosperous merchants were now sending out whole fleets from Italy to the north Atlantic and staying at home themselves. To facilitate this more sedentary pattern of business life, merchants perfected modern techniques of business partnerships, letters of credit, and accounting. Because such entrepreneurs invested in trade intentionally for profit and devised and used sophisticated credit mechanisms, most modern historians agree in calling them the first Western commercial capitalists.

In addition to the expansion of money and credit, trade was vastly facilitated by the rapid growth of towns. If we could imagine an aerial view of twelfth-century Europe, the mushrooming of towns would be the most strikingly visible phenomenon after the clearing of forests and wastes. Some historians misleadingly include under the heading of towns the numerous new agricultural village communities of peasants that were established in clearings. These, however, were not really urban in any sense. Putting them aside, many urban agglomerations were built from the ground up in the High Middle Ages, and existing towns that had barely survived from the Roman period grew enormously in size. To take some examples, in central and eastern Germany, which had not been part of the old Roman area of settlement, new towns such as Freiburg, Lübeck, Munich, and Berlin were founded in the twelfth century. Further west, where old Roman towns had become little more than episcopal residences or stockades, formerly insignificant towns like Paris, London, and Cologne roughly doubled in size between 1100 and 1200 and doubled again in the next century. Urban life was above all concentrated in Italy, which encompassed most of Europe's largest cities: Venice, Genoa, Milan, Bologna, Palermo, Florence, and Naples. In the thirteenth century the population of the largest of these—Venice, Genoa, and Milan—was in the range of 100,000. We lack accurate growth figures for other Italian cities, but it seems likely that many at least trebled in population between about 1150 and 1300 because we do know that the smaller Italian town of Imola, near Bologna, grew from some 4,200 in 1210 to 11,500 in 1312. Considering that town life had come very close to disappearing in most of Europe between 750 and 1050, it is warranted to speak of a high-medieval urban revolution. Moreover, from the High Middle Ages until now a vigorous urban life has been a major characteristic of western European and subsequently modern world civilization.

It used to be thought that the primary cause of the medieval urban revolution was the revival of long-distance trade. Theoretically, itinerant peddlers, who had no secure place in the dominantly agrarian so-

View of Paris. The city looked this way at the end of the Middle Ages, around 1480. Note the prominence of the cathedral of Notre Dame in the center and the large number of other church spires; note, too, how closely all the buildings are packed behind the walls.

ciety of Europe, gradually settled together in towns in order to offer each other much-needed protection and establish markets to sell their wares. In fact, the picture is far more complicated than that. While some towns did receive great stimulus from long-distance trade, and the growth of a major city such as Venice would have been unthinkable without it, most towns relied for their origin and early economic vitality far more on the wealth of their surrounding areas. These brought them surplus agricultural goods, raw materials for manufacture, and an influx of population. In other words, the quickening of economic life in general was the major cause of urban growth: towns existed in a symbiotic relationship with the countryside by providing markets and also wares made by artisans, while they lived off the rural food surplus and grew with the migration of surplus serfs or peasants who were seeking a better life. (Escaped serfs were guaranteed their freedom if they stayed in a town a year and a day.) Once towns started to flourish, many of them began to specialize in certain enterprises. Paris and Bologna gained considerable wealth by becoming the homes of leading universities; Venice, Genoa, Cologne, and London became centers of long-distance trade; and Milan, Ghent, and Bruges specialized in manufactures. The most important urban industries were those devoted to cloth-making. Cloth manufacturers sometimes developed techniques of large-scale production and investment that are ancestors of the modern factory system and industrial capitalism. But it must be emphasized that large industrial enterprises were atypical of medieval economic life as a whole.

Medieval cities and towns were not smaller-scale facsimiles of modern ones, and to our own eyes would have still seemed half-rural and uncivilized. Streets were often unpaved, houses had gardens for rais-

Causes of the urban revolution

Old Houses in Strassburg. In the Middle Ages food was stored in attics, with special openings for ventilation, as insurance against famine. Of course there was still much spoilage.

The Great Crane at Bruges. A pulley device operated by human energy. Animals wander through the narrow street in the background.

A Medieval Shoemaker

Life in medieval towns

ing vegetables, and cows and pigs were kept in stables and pigsties. Passing along the streets of a major metropolis one might be stopped by a flock of bleating sheep or a crowd of honking geese. Sanitary conditions were often very poor and the air must often have reeked of excrement—both animal and human. Town-dwellers were cursed by the frequency of fires that swept quickly through closely settled wooden or straw quarters and went unstopped by the lack of fire stations. People were also highly susceptible to contagious diseases bred by unsanitary conditions and crowding. Still another problem was that economic tensions and family rivalries could lead to bloody riots. Yet for all this, urban folk took great pride in their new cities and ways of life. A famous paean to London, for example, written by a twelfth-century denizen of that city, boasted of its prosperity, piety, and perfect climate (!), and claimed that except for frequent fires, London's only nuisance was "the immoderate drinking of fools."

The most distinctive form of economic and social organization in the medieval towns was the guild. This was, roughly speaking, a professional association organized to protect and promote special interests. The main types were merchant guilds and craft guilds. The primary functions of the merchant guild were to maintain a monopoly of the local market for its members and to preserve a stable economic system. To accomplish these ends the merchant guild severely restricted trading by foreigners in the city, guaranteed to its members the right to participate in sales offered by other members, enforced uniform pricing, and did everything possible to ensure that no individual would corner the market for goods produced by its members.

Craft guilds similarly regulated the affairs of artisans. Usually their only full-fledged voting members were so-called master craftsmen, who were experts at their trades and ran their own shops. Hence if these guilds were anything like modern trade unions, they were unions of bosses. Second-class members of craft guilds were journeymen, who had learned their trades but still worked for the masters (*journeyman* is from the French *journée,* meaning "day," or by extension "day's work"), and apprentices. Terms of apprenticeship were carefully regulated: if an apprentice wished to become a master he often had to produce a "masterpiece" for judging by the masters of the guild. Craft guilds, like merchant guilds, sought to preserve monopolies and to limit competition. Thus they established uniformity of prices and wages, prohibited working after hours, and formulated detailed regulations governing methods of production and quality of materials. In addition to all their economic functions, both kinds of guilds served important social ones. Often they acted in the capacity of religious associations, benevolent societies, and social clubs. Wherever possible guilds tried to minister to the human needs of their members. Thus in some cities they came close to becoming miniature governments.

A Medieval Weaver

Town merchants and artisans were particularly concerned to protect themselves because they had no accepted role in the older medieval scheme of things. Usually merchants were disdained by the landed aristocracy because they could claim no ancient lineages and were not versed in the ways of chivalry. Worst of all, they were too obviously concerned with pecuniary gain. Although nobles too were gradually becoming interested in making profits, they displayed this less openly: they paid little attention in their daily lives to accounts and made much of their free-spending largesse. Still another reason why medieval

Medieval attitudes toward merchants

Medieval Walled City of Carcassonne, France. These walls date from 1240 to 1285.

A Medieval Tailor

Significance of the urban revolution: (1) development of the economy and government

(2) towns as a foundation for intellectual life

merchants were on the defensive was that the Church, opposed to illicit gain, taught a doctrine of the "just price" that was often at variance with what the merchants thought they deserved. Clergymen too condemned usury—i.e., the lending of money for interest—even though it was often essential for doing business. A decree of the Second Lateran Council of 1139, to take one example, excoriated the "detestable, shameful, and insatiable rapacity of moneylenders." As time went on, however, attitudes slowly changed. In Italy it often became hard to tell merchants from aristocrats because the latter customarily lived in towns and often engaged in trade themselves. In the rest of Europe, the most prosperous town-dwellers, called patricians, developed their own sense of pride verging on that of the nobility. The medieval Church never abandoned its prohibition of usury, but it did come to approve making profits on commercial risks, which was often close to the same thing. Moreover, starting around the thirteenth century leading churchmen came to speak more favorably of merchants. St. Bonaventure, a leading thirteenth-century churchman, argued that God showed special favors to shepherds like David in the time of the Old Testament, to fishers like Peter in the time of the New, and to merchants like St. Francis in the thirteenth century.

All in all, the importance of the high-medieval urban revolution can scarcely be overestimated. The fact that the new towns were the vital pumps of the high-medieval economy has already been sufficiently emphasized: in providing markets and producing wares they kept the entire economic system thriving. In addition, cities and towns made important contributions to the development of government because in many areas they gained their own independence and ruled themselves as city-states. Primarily in Italy, where urban life was by far the most advanced, city governments experimented with new systems of tax-collecting, record-keeping, and public participation in decision-making. Italian city-states were particularly advanced in their administrative techniques and thereby helped influence a general European-wide growth in governmental sophistication.

Finally, the rise of towns contributed greatly to the quickening of intellectual life in the West. New schools were invariably located in towns because towns afforded domiciles and legal protection for scholars. At first, students and teachers were always clerics, but by the thirteenth century the needs of merchants to be trained in reading and accounting led to the foundation of numerous lay primary schools. Equally momentous for the future was the fact that the stimulating urban environment helped make advanced schools more open to intellectual experimentation than any in the West since those of the Greeks. Not coincidentally, Greek intellectual life too was based on thriving cities. Thus it seems that without commerce in goods there can be little exciting commerce in ideas.

4. FEUDALISM AND THE RISE OF THE NATIONAL MONARCHIES

If any western European city of around 1200 epitomized Europe's greatest new accomplishments it was Paris: that city was not only a bustling commercial center and an important center of learning, it was also the capital of what was becoming Europe's most powerful government. France, like England and the new Christian kingdoms of the Iberian peninsula, was taking shape in the twelfth and thirteenth centuries as a *national monarchy,* a new form of government which was to dominate Europe's political future. Because the developing national monarchies were the most successful and promising European governments we must concentrate on them, but before we do it is well to see what was happening from the political point of view in Germany and Italy.

*The national monarchy as
a political innovation*

Around 1050 Germany was unquestionably the most centralized and best-ruled territory in Europe, but by 1300 it had fallen into a congeries of warring petty states. Since most other areas of Europe were gaining stronger rule in the very same period, the political decline of Germany becomes an intriguing historical problem. It is also a problem of fundamental importance because from a political point of view Germany only caught up with the rest of Europe in the nineteenth century: in trying to gain its full place in the European political system as late as then it created difficulties that have just come to be resolved in our own age.

*The political decline of
medieval Germany an
intriguing historical
problem*

The major sources of Germany's strength from the reign of Otto the Great in the middle of the tenth century until the latter part of the eleventh century were its succession of strong rulers, its resistance to political fragmentation, and the close alliance of its crown with the Church. By resoundingly defeating the Hungarians and taking the title of emperor, Otto kept the country from falling prey to further invasions and won great prestige for the monarchy. For over a century afterwards there was a nearly uninterrupted succession of rulers as able and vigorous as Otto. Their nearest political rivals were the dukes, military leaders of five large German territories (Lorraine, Saxony, Franconia, Swabia, and Bavaria), but throughout most of this period the dukes were overawed by the emperors' greater power. The latter, in order to rule their wide territories—which included Switzerland, eastern France, and most of the Low Countries, as well as claims to northern Italy—relied heavily on cooperation with the Church. The leading royal administrators were archbishops and bishops whom the emperors appointed without interference from the pope and who often came from their own families. The German emperors were so strong that, when they chose to do so, they could come down to Italy

*The German monarchy in
the tenth and eleventh
centuries*

and name their own popes. The archbishops and bishops ran the German government fairly well for the times without any elaborate administrative machinery, and they counterbalanced the strength of the dukes. In the course of the eleventh century the emperors were starting tentatively to develop their own secular administration. Had they been allowed to continue this policy, it might have provided a really solid governmental foundation for the future. But just then the whole system shaped by Otto the Great and his successors was dramatically challenged by a revolution within the Church.

The challenge to the German government came in the reign of Henry IV (1056–1106) and was directed by Pope Gregory VII (1073–1085). For reasons that will be discussed in the next chapter, Gregory wished to free the Church from secular control and launched a struggle to achieve this aim against Henry IV. Gregory immediately placed Henry on the defensive by forging an alliance with the dukes and other German princes, who only needed a sufficient pretext to rise up against their ruler. When the princes threatened to depose Henry because of his disobedience to the pope, the hitherto mighty ruler was forced to seek absolution from Gregory VII in one of the most melodramatic scenes of the Middle Ages. In the depths of winter in 1077 Henry hurried over the Alps to abase himself before the pope in the north Italian castle of Canossa. As Gregory described the scene in a letter to the princes: ❡There on three successive days, standing before the castle gate, laying aside all royal insignia, barefooted and in coarse attire, Henry ceased not with many tears to beseech the apostolic help and comfort.❡ No German ruler had ever been so humiliated. Although the events at Canossa forestalled Henry's deposition, they robbed him of his great prestige. By the time his struggle with the papacy, continued by his son, was over, the princes had won far more practical independence from the crown than they had ever had. More than that, in 1125 they made good their claims to be able to elect a new ruler regardless of hereditary succession—a principle that would thereafter often lead them to choose the weakest successors or to embroil the country in civil war. Meanwhile, the crown had lost much of its control of the Church and thus in effect had its administrative rug pulled out from under it. While France and England were gradually consolidating their centralized governmental apparatuses, Germany was losing its own.

A major attempt to stem the tide running against the German monarchy was made in the twelfth century by Frederick I (1152–1190), who came from the family of Hohenstaufen. Frederick, called "Barbarossa" (meaning "red beard"), tried to reassert his imperial dignity by calling his realm the "Holy Roman Empire," on the theory that it was a universal empire descending from Rome and blessed by God. Laying claim to Roman descent, he promulgated old Roman imperial laws—preserved in the Code of Justinian—that gave him much theoretical power. But he could not hope to enforce such laws unless he had his own material base of support. Therefore the major policy of his reign was to balance the power of the princes by carving out his own geographical domain from which he might draw wealth and strength.

Unfortunately for Frederick, his ancestral lands were located in Swabia, a poorer part of Germany that even today still consists of relatively unproductive hill country and the Black Forest. So Frederick decided to make northern Italy his power base in addition to Swabia. In this he could hardly have made a worse decision. Northern Italy was certainly wealthy, but it was also fiercely independent. Its rich towns and cities, led by Milan, offered stiff resistance. They were further lent helpful moral support by the papacy, which had no wish to see a strong German emperor ruling powerfully in Italy. Frederick came very close to overpowering the urban-papal alliance but ultimately the Alps proved to be too great a barrier to allow him to enforce his will in Italy and hope to rule in Germany as well. Whenever he subdued the towns he would shortly afterwards have to leave for home, and the towns, with papal encouragement, would then rise up again. Finally, in 1176, insufficient German imperial forces were resoundingly defeated by the troops of a north Italian urban coalition at Legnano, and Barbarossa was forced to concede the area's de facto independence. In the meantime, the princes in Germany were continuing to gather strength, especially by colonizing the rich agricultural lands east of the Elbe where Frederick really should have busied himself, and the emperor's struggle with the popes further alienated elements within the German church. Because Barbarossa was a dashing figure he was well remembered by Germans, but his reign virtually made it certain that the German empire would not rise again during the medieval period.

The reign of Barbarossa's equally famous grandson, Frederick II (1212–1250), was merely a playing out of Germany's fate. In terms of his personality Frederick was probably the most fascinating of all medieval rulers. Because his father, Henry VI, had inherited through marriage the kingdom of southern Italy and Sicily (later called the Kingdom of the Two Sicilies), Frederick grew up in Palermo, where he absorbed elements of Islamic culture. (Arabs had ruled in Sicily for two and a half centuries, from 831 to 1071.) Frederick II spoke five or six languages, was a patron of learning, and wrote his own book on falconry, which takes an honored place in the early history of Western observational science. He also performed bizarre and brutal "experiments," such as disemboweling men to observe the comparative effects of rest and exercise upon digestion. Such practices corresponded to Frederick's overall policy of trying to rule like an Oriental despot. In his autonomous kingdom of southern Italy he introduced Eastern forms of absolutist and bureaucratic government. He established a

Frederick's Italian policy

Frederick Barbarossa. A stylized contemporary representation.

Frederick II; his personality and policies

The Emperor Frederick II. He is shown holding a *fleur de lis,* as a symbol of rule, with a falcon, his favorite bird, at his side.

The political situation in high-medieval Italy

professional army, levied direct taxation, and promulgated uniform Roman law. Typically, Frederick tried to create a ruler cult and decreed it an act of sacrilege even to discuss his statutes or judgments. For a while these policies seemed successful in ruling southern Italy, but Frederick's power base in Italy led to renewed conflicts with the papacy and the north Italian cities. These dragged on indecisively until his death, but thereafter the papacy was resolved to see no further Hohenstaufens ruling in Italy and proceeded to eliminate the remaining contenders from the line by calling crusades against them. Overtaxed by Frederick's ruthlessness and subsequent wars, southern Italy gradually sank into the backwardness from which it is only barely emerging today. And Frederick's reign was as damaging to Germany as well. Bent on pursuing his Italian policies without hindrance, Frederick formally wrote Germany off to the princes by granting them large areas of sovereignty. Although titular "emperors" afterwards continued to be elected, the princes were the real rulers of the country. Yet they fought with each other so much that peace was rare, and they subdivided their lands among their heirs to such an extent that the map of Germany began to look like a jig-saw puzzle. As the French philosopher Voltaire later said, the German "Holy Roman Empire" had become neither holy, nor Roman, nor an empire.

The story of high-medieval Italian politics may be told more quickly. Southern Italy and Sicily had been welded together into a strong monarchical state in the twelfth century by Norman-French descendants of the Vikings. But then, as we have seen, the area went to the Hohenstaufens and was subsequently brought to ruin. Central Italy was largely ruled by the papacy in the High Middle Ages, but the popes were seldom strong enough to create a really well-governed state, partly because they were at constant loggerheads with the German emperors. Farthest north were the rich commercial and manufacturing cities which had successfully fought off Barbarossa. These were usually organized politically in the form of republics or "communes." They offered much participation in governmental life to their more prosperous inhabitants. But because of diverse economic interests and family antagonisms, the Italian cities were usually riven with internal strife. Moreover, although they could unite in leagues against foreign threats such as those represented by Barbarossa or Frederick II, the cities often fought each other when foreign threats were absent. The result was that although economic and cultural life was very far advanced in the Italian cities, and although the cities made important experiments in administrative techniques, political stability was widely lacking in northern Italy throughout most of the high-medieval period.

If one looks for the centers of growing political stability in Europe, then one has to seek them in high-medieval France and England. Ironically, some of the most basic foundations for future political achievement in France were established without any planning just

GERMAN EMPIRE c. 1200 A.D.

when that area was most politically unstable. These foundations were aspects of a level of political decentralization often referred to by historians as the system of "feudalism." The use of this word is controversial because ever since Marx some historians prefer to use it as a term to describe an agrarian economic and social system wherein large estates are worked by a dependent peasantry. The difficulty with this usage is that it is too imprecise, for such large estates existed in many times and places beyond the European Middle Ages and the medieval agrarian system can best be called manorialism. Some historians on

Feudalism: a controversial term

the other extreme argue that even if the word feudalism is used to describe a medieval political system, medieval realities were so diverse that no one definition of feudalism can accurately or even usefully be extended to cover more than a single case. Nonetheless, for convenience we can retain the use of the word here and apply it to a specific point in medieval political development so long as we bear in mind that, like manorialism, it is only meant to serve as any approximation and that other historians may use it as a term for economic or sociological analysis.

Political feudalism was essentially a system of extreme political decentralization wherein what we today would call public power was widely vested in private hands. From a historical perspective it was most fully experienced in France during the tenth century when the Carolingian empire had disintegrated and the area was being buffeted by devastating Viking invasions. The Carolingians had maintained a modicum of public authority, but they proved to be no help whatsoever in warding off the invasions. So local landlords had to fend for themselves. In the end, the landlords turned out to offer the best defense against the Vikings and accordingly were able to acquire practically all the old governmental powers. They raised their own small armies, dispensed their own crude justice, and occasionally issued their own primitive coins. Despite such decentralization, however, it was never forgotten that there once had been higher and larger units of government. Above all, no matter how weak the king was (and he was indeed usually very weak), there always remained a king in France who descended directly or indirectly from the western branch of the Carolingians. There also were scattered remaining dukes or counts, who in theory were supposed to have more power and authority than petty landlords or knights. So, by a complicated and hard-to-trace process of rationalization, a vague theory was worked out in the course of the tenth and eleventh centuries that tried to establish some order within feudalism. According to this, minor feudal lords did not hold their powers outright but only held them as so-called *fiefs* (rhymes with reefs), which could be revoked upon noncompliance with certain obligations. In theory—and much of this theory was ignored in practice for long periods of time—the king or higher lords granted fiefs, that is, governmental rights over various lands, to lesser lords in return for a stipulated amount of military service. In turn, the lesser lords could grant some of those fiefs to still lesser lords for military services until the chain stopped at the lowest level of knights. The holder of a fief was called a *vassal* of the granter, but this term had none of the demeaning connotations that it has gained today. Vassalage—much unlike serfdom—was a purely honorable status and all fief-holders were "noble."

Since feudalism was originally a form of decentralization, it once was considered by historians to have been a corrosive or divisive historical force; in common speech today many use the word feudal as a synonym for backward. But scholars more recently have come to the conclusion that feudalism was a force for progress and a fundamental point of departure for the growth of the modern state. They note that in areas such as Germany and Italy, where there was hardly any feudalism, political stabilization and unification came only in later times, whereas in the areas of France and England, which saw full feudalization, stabilization and governmental centralization came rapidly afterwards. Scholars now posit several reasons for this. Because feudalism was originally spontaneous and makeshift, it was highly flexible. Local lords, instead of being bound by anachronistic, procrustean principles, could rule as seemed best at the moment, or could bend to the dictates of particular local customs. Thus their governments, however crude, worked the best for their times and could be used for building an even stronger government as time went on. A second reason for the effectiveness of feudalism was that it drew more people into direct contact with the actual workings of political life than had the old Roman or Carolingian systems. Government on the most local level could most easily be seen or experienced; as it became tangible people began to appreciate and identify with it far more than they had appreciated empires. The result was that feudalism inculcated growing governmental loyalty, and once that loyalty was developed it could be drawn upon by still larger units. Thirdly, feudalism helped lead to certain more modern institutions by its emphasis on courts. As the feudal system became more regularized, it became customary for vassals to appear at the court of their overlords at least once a year. There they were expected to "pay court," i.e., show certain ceremonial signs of loyalty, and also to serve on "courts" in the sense of participating in trials and offering counsel. Thus they became more and more accustomed to performing governmental business and began to behave more like courtiers or politicians. As the monarchical states of France and England themselves developed, kings saw how useful the feudal court was and made it the administrative kernel of their expanding governmental systems. A final reason why feudalism led to political progress is not really intrinsic to the system itself. Because the theory of larger units was never forgotten, it could be drawn upon by greater lords and kings when the right time came to reacquire their rights.

The greatest possibilities for the use of feudalism were first demonstrated in England after the Norman Conquest of 1066. We have seen that England became unified and enjoyed strong kingship under the Saxon Alfred and his successors in the late ninth and tenth centuries. But then the Saxon kingship began to weaken, primarily as the result of renewed Viking invasions and poor leadership. In 1066 William, the duke of Normandy (in western France), laid claim to the English crown and crossed the Channel to conquer what he had claimed. For-

Feudalism as a cause of political progress

The Norman Conquest

Battle of Hastings. A scene from the Bayeux tapestry, embroidered shortly after William the Conqueror's victory. The inscription reads in translation: "Here the English and French have fallen together in battle."

tunately for him the newly installed English king, Harold, had just warded off a Viking attack in the north and thus could not offer resistance at full strength. At the Battle of Hastings Harold and his Saxon troops fought bravely, but ultimately could not withstand the onslaught of the fresher Norman troops. As the day waned Harold fell, mortally wounded by a random arrow, his forces dispersed, and the Normans took the field and with it, England. Duke William now became King William, the Conqueror, and proceeded to rule his new prize as he wished.

The feudal system in Norman England

With hindsight we can say that the Norman Conquest came at just the right time to preserve and enhance political stability. Before 1066 England was threatened with disintegration under warrior aristocrats called earls, but William destroyed their power entirely. In its place he substituted the feudal system, whereby all the land in England was newly granted in the form of fiefs held directly or indirectly from the king. Fief-holders had most of the governmental rights they had obtained less formally on the Continent, but William retained the prerogatives of coining money, collecting a land tax, and supervising justice in major criminal cases. He also retained the Anglo-Saxon officer of local government, known as the sheriff, to help him administer and enforce these rights. In order to make sure that none of his barons (the English term for major fief-holders) became too powerful, William was careful to scatter the fiefs granted to them throughout various parts of the country. In these ways William used feudal practices to help govern England when there were not yet enough trained administrators to allow any real governmental professionalization. But he also retained much royal power and kept the country thoroughly unified under the crown.

The history of English government in the two centuries after William is primarily a story of kings tightening up the feudal system to their advantage until they superseded it and created a strong national monarchy. The first to take steps in this direction was the Conqueror's energetic son Henry I (1100–1135). One of his most important accomplishments was to start a process of specialization at the royal court whereby certain officials began to take full professional responsibility for supervising financial accounts; these officials became known as clerks of the *Exchequer*. Another accomplishment was to institute a system of traveling circuit-judges to administer justice as direct royal representatives in various parts of the realm.

After an intervening period of civil war Henry I was succeeded by his grandson Henry II (1154–1189), who was very much in his grandfather's activist mold. Henry II's reign was certainly one of the most momentous in all of English history. One reason for this was that it saw a great struggle between the king and the flamboyant archbishop of Canterbury, Thomas Becket, over the status of Church courts and Church law. In Henry's time priests and other clerics were tried for any crimes in Church courts under the rules of canon law. Punishment in these courts was notoriously lax. Even murderers were seldom sentenced to more than penance and loss of their clerical status. Also, decisions handed down in English Church courts could be appealed to the papal *curia* in Rome. Henry, who wished to have royal law prevail as far as possible and maintain judicial standards for all subjects in his realm, tried to limit these practices by the Constitutions of Clarendon of 1164. On the matter of clerics accused of crime he was willing to compromise by allowing them to be judged in Church courts but then

The growth of national monarchy in England; the reign of Henry I

The struggle between Henry II and Thomas Becket

Martyrdom of Thomas Becket. From a thirteenth-century English Psalter. One of the knights has struck Becket so mightily that he has broken his sword.

have them sentenced in royal ones. Becket, however, resisted all attempts at change with great determination. The quarrel between king and archbishop was made more bitter by the fact that the two had earlier been close friends. It reached a tragic climax when Becket was murdered in Canterbury Cathedral by four of Henry's knights, after the king, in an outburst of anger, had rebuked them for doing nothing to rid him of his antagonist. The crime so shocked the English public that Becket was quickly revered as a martyr and became the most famous English saint. More important for the history of government, Henry had to abandon most of his program of bringing the Church courts under royal control, and his aims were only fulfilled in the sixteenth century with the coming of the English Reformation.

Despite this major setback, Henry II made enormous governmental gains in other areas, so much so that some historians maintain that Henry was the greatest king that England has ever known. His most important contributions were judicial. He greatly expanded the use of the itinerant judges instituted by Henry I and began the practice of commanding sheriffs to bring before these judges groups of men who were familiar with local conditions. These were then required to report under oath every case of murder, arson, robbery, or other major crimes known to them to have occurred since the judges' last visit. This was the origin of the grand jury. Henry also for the first time allowed parties in civil disputes to obtain royal justice. In the most prevalent type of case, someone who claimed to have been recently dispossessed of his land could obtain a writ from the crown, which would order the sheriff to bring twelve men who were assumed to know the facts before a judge. The twelve were then asked under oath if the plaintiff's claim was true, and the judge rendered his decision in accordance with their answers. Out of such practices grew the institution of the trial jury.

Henry II's legal innovations benefited both the crown and the country in several ways. Most obviously, they made justice more uniform and equitable throughout the realm. They also thereby made royal justice sought after and popular. Particularly in disputes over land—the most important and frequent disputes of the day—the weaker party was no longer at the mercy of a strong-arming neighbor. Usually the weaker parties were knights, with whom the crown before then had not been in close touch. In helping defend their rights Henry gained valuable allies in his policy of keeping the stronger barons in tow. Finally, the widespread use of juries in Henry's reign brought more and more people into actual participation in royal government. In so doing it got them more interested in government and more loyal to government. Since these people served without pay, Henry brilliantly managed to expand the competence and popularity of his government at very little cost.

The most concrete proof of Henry II's success is that after his death his government worked so well that it more or less ran on its own.

Henry's son, the swashbuckling Richard I, the "Lionhearted," ruled for ten years, from 1189 to 1199, but in that time he only stayed in England for six months because he was otherwise engaged in crusading or defending his possessions on the Continent. Throughout the time of Richard's absence governmental administration actually became more efficient, owing to the work of capable ministers. The country also raised two huge sums for Richard by taxation: one to pay for his crusade to the Holy Land and the other to buy his ransom when he was captured by an enemy on his return. But later when a new king needed still more money, most Englishmen were disinclined to pay it.

The new king was Richard's brother, John (1199–1216), who has the reputation of being a villain but was more a victim of circumstances. Ever since the time of William the Conqueror, English kings had continued to rule in large portions of modern-day France, but by John's reign the kings of France were becoming strong enough to take back much of these territories. John had the great misfortune of facing the able French King Philip Augustus, who won back Normandy and neighboring lands by force of arms in 1204 and reinsured this victory by military successes in 1214. John needed money both to govern England and to fight in France, but his defeats made his subjects disinclined to give it to him. The barons particularly resented John's financial exigencies and in 1215 they made him renounce these in the subsequently famous Magna Carta (Great Charter), a document which was also designed to redress all the other abuses the barons could think of. Most common conceptions of Magna Carta are erroneous. It was not intended to be a bill of rights or a charter of liberties for the common man. On the contrary, it was basically a feudal document in which the king as overlord pledged to respect the traditional rights of his vassals. Nonetheless, it did enunciate in writing the important principles that large sums of money could not be raised by the crown without consent given by the barons in a common council, and that no free man could be punished by the crown without judgment by his equals and by the law of the land. Above all, Magna Carta was important as an expression of the principle of limited government and of the idea that the king is bound by the law.

As the contemporary American medievalist J. R. Strayer has said, "Magna Carta made arbitrary government difficult, but it did not make centralized government impossible." In the century following its issuance, the progress of centralized government continued apace. In the reign of John's son, Henry III (1216–1277), the barons vied with the weak king for control of the government but did so on the assumption that centralized government itself was a good thing. Throughout that period administrators continued to perfect more efficient legal and administrative institutions. Whereas in the reign of Henry I financial administration began to become a specialized bureau of the royal court, in the reign of Henry III this became true of legal administration (the creation of permanent High Courts) and adminis-

King John. An effigy in Worcester cathedral.

The reign of John; Magna Carta

The progress of centralized government in the reign of Henry III

tration of foreign correspondence (the so-called Chancery). English central government was now fully developing a trained officialdom.

The last and most famous branch of the medieval English governmental system was Parliament. This gradually emerged as a separate branch of government in the decades before and after 1300, above all owing to the wishes of Henry III's son, Edward I (1272–1307). Although Parliament later became a check against royal absolutism, nothing could be further from the truth than to think that its first meetings were "demanded by the people." In its origins Parliament actually had little to do with popular representation, but was rather the king's feudal court in its largest gathering. Edward I was a strong king who called Parliaments frequently to raise money as quickly and efficiently as possible in order to help finance his foreign wars. Those present at Parliaments were not only expected to give their consent to taxation—in fact, it was virtually inconceivable for them to refuse—but while they were there they were told why taxes were necessary so that they would pay them less grudgingly. They could also agree upon details of collection and payment. At the same meetings Edward could take advice about pressing concerns, have justice done for exceptional cases, review local administration, and promulgate new laws. Probably the most unusual trait of Edward's Parliaments in comparison to similar assemblies on the Continent was that they began to include representatives from the counties and towns in addition to the higher nobility. These representatives, however, scarcely spoke for "the people" because most of the people of England were unfranchised serfs and peasants—not to mention women, who were never consulted in any way. Most likely, Edward had predominantly financial motives for calling representatives from the "commons." He probably also realized the propaganda value of overawing local representatives with royal grandeur at impressive parliamentary meetings so that they would then spread a favorable impression of the monarchy back home. As time went on, commoners were called to Parliament so often that they became a recognized part of its organization: by the middle of the fourteenth century they sat regularly in their own "house." But they still represented only the prosperous people of countryside and towns and were usually manipulated by the crown or the nobles.

Edward I's reign also saw the culmination of the development of a strong national monarchy in other aspects. By force of arms Edward nearly unified the entire island of Britain, conquering Wales and almost subduing Scotland (which, however, was to rise up again soon after his death). Edward began the practice of regularly issuing statute law, that is, original public legislation designed to apply indefinitely to the entire realm. Because of his role as a law-giver, Edward is sometimes referred to as the "English Justinian." Most important, Edward also curtailed the feudal powers of his barons by limiting their rights

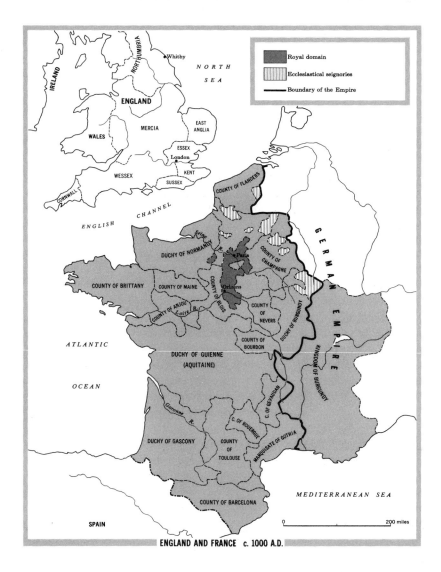

ENGLAND AND FRANCE c. 1000 A.D.

to hold private courts and to grant their own lands as fiefs. Thus, by the end of his reign much of the independent power once consciously vested with the barons by William the Conqueror was being taken away from them. The explanation for this is that in the intervening high-medieval centuries the king was developing his own royal institutions of government to the degree that old-fashioned feudalism was now no longer of any real service. Because Edward pressed his strong government and financial demands somewhat excessively for the spirit of the age, there was an antimonarchical reaction after his death. But it is striking that after Edward's time whenever there were baronial rebellions they were always made on the assumption that England would remain a unified country, governed by the basic high-medieval monarchical institutions. England was unified around the crown in

*The process of political
centralization in France*

the High Middle Ages and would remain a basically well-governed and unified country right up to modern times.

While the process of governmental centralization was making impressive strides in England, it developed more slowly in France. But by around 1300 it had come close to reaching the same point of completion. French governmental unification proceeded more slowly because France in the eleventh century was more decentralized than England and faced greater problems. The last of the weak Carolingian monarchs was replaced in 987 by Hugh Capet, the count of Paris, but the new Capetian dynasty—which was to rule without interruption until 1328—was at first no stronger than the old Carolingian one. Even through most of the twelfth century the kings of France ruled directly only in a small area around Paris known as the Ile-de-France, roughly the size of Vermont. Beyond that territory the kings had shadowy claims to being the feudal overlords of numerous counts and dukes throughout much of the area of modern France, but for practical purposes those counts and dukes were almost entirely independent. It was said that when the king of France demanded homage from the first duke of Normandy, the duke had one of his warriors pretend to kiss the king's foot but then seize the royal leg and pull the king over backwards, to the mockery of all those present. While the French kingship was so weak, the various parts of France were developing their own distinct local traditions and dialects. Thus, whereas William the Conqueror inherited in England a country that had already been unified and was just on the verge of falling apart, the French kings of the High Middle Ages had to unify their country from scratch, with only a vague reminiscence of Carolingian unity to build upon.

*Factors facilitating the
growth of the French
monarchy*

In many respects, however, luck was on their side. First of all, they were fortunate for hundreds of years in having direct male heirs to succeed them. Consequently, there were no deadly quarrels over the right of succession. In the second place, most of the French kings lived to an advanced age, the average period of rule being about thirty years. That meant that sons were already mature men when they came to the throne and there were few regencies to squander the royal power during the minority of a prince. More than that, the kings of France were always highly visible, if sometimes not very imposing, when there were power struggles elsewhere, so people in neighboring areas became accustomed to thinking of the kingship as a force for stability in an unstable world. A third favorable circumstance for the French kings was the growth of agricultural prosperity and trade in their home region; this provided them with important sources of revenue. A fourth fortuitous development was that the kings were able to gain the support of the popes because the latter usually needed allies in their incessant struggles with the German emperors. The popes lent the French kings prestige, as they earlier had done for the Carolingians, and they also allowed them much direct power over the local

Church, thereby bringing the kings further income and influence from patronage. A fifth factor in the French king's favor was the growth in the twelfth and thirteenth centuries of the University of Paris as the leading European center of studies. As foreigners came flocking to the university, they learned of the French king's growing authority and spread their impressions when they returned home. Finally, and by no means least of all, great credit must be given to the shrewdness and vigor of several of the French kings themselves.

The first noteworthy Capetian king was Louis VI, "the Fat" (1108–1137). While accomplishing nothing startling, Louis at least managed to pacify his home base, the Ile-de-France, by driving out or subduing its turbulent "robber barons." Once this was accomplished, agriculture and trade could prosper and the intellectual life of Paris could start to flourish. Thereafter, the French kings had a geographical source of power of exactly the kind that the German ruler Barbarossa sought but never found. The really startling additions to the realm were made by Louis's grandson, Philip Augustus (1180–1223). Philip was wily enough to know how to take advantage of certain feudal rights in order to win large amounts of western French territory from the English King John. He was also decisive enough to know how to defend his gains in battle. Most impressive of all, Philip worked out an excellent formula for governing his new acquisitions. Since these increased his original lands close to fourfold, and since each new area had its own highly distinct local customs, it would have been hopeless to try to enforce strict governmental standardization by means of what was then a very rudimentary administrative system. Instead, Philip allowed his new provinces to maintain most of their indigenous governmental practices but superimposed on them new royal officials known as *baillis*. These officials were entirely loyal to Philip because they never came from the regions in which they served and were paid impressive salaries for the day. They had full judicial, administrative, and military authority in their bailiwicks: on royal orders they tolerated regional diversities but guided them to the king's advantage. Thus there were no revolts in the conquered territories and royal power was enhanced. This pattern of local diversity balanced against bureaucratic centralization was to remain the basic pattern of French government. Thus Philip Augustus can be seen as an important founder of the modern French state.

In the brief reign of Philip's son, Louis VIII (1223–1226), almost all of southern France was added to the crown in the name of intervention against religious heresy. Once incorporated, this territory was governed largely on the same principles laid down by Philip. The next king, Louis IX (1226–1270), was so pious that he was later canonized by the Church and is commonly referred to as St. Louis. He ruled strongly and justly (except for great intolerance of Jews and heretics), decreed a standardized coinage for the country, perfected the judicial

Foundations of the French monarchy; Louis VI and Philip Augustus

A Seal Depicting Philip Augustus

St. Louis

King Philip the Fair of France

Comparison of England
and France

system, and brought France a long, golden period of internal peace. Because he was so well-loved, the monarchy lived off his prestige for many years afterwards.

That prestige, however, came close to being squandered by St. Louis's more ruthless grandson, Philip IV, "the Fair" (1285–1314). Philip fought many battles at once, seeking to round out French territories in the northeast and southwest and to gain full control over the French Church instead of sharing it with the pope in Rome. All these activities forced him to accelerate the process of governmental centralization, especially with the aim of trying to raise money. Thus his reign saw the quick formulation of many administrative institutions that came close to completing the development of medieval French government, as the contemporary reign of Edward I did in England. Philip's reign also saw the calling of assemblies that were roughly equivalent to the English Parliaments, but these—later called "Estates General"—never played a central role in the French governmental system. Philip the Fair was successful in most of his ventures; above all, as we will later see, in reducing the pope to the level of a virtual French figurehead. After his death there would be an antimonarchical reaction, as there was at the same time in England, but by his reign France was unquestionably the strongest power in Europe. With only a sixteenth-century interruption, it would remain so until the nineteenth century.

While England and France followed certain similar processes of monarchical centralization and nation-building, they were also marked by basic differences that are worth describing because they were to typify differences in development for centuries after. England, a far smaller country than France, was much better unified. Aside from Wales and Scotland, there were no regions in Britain that had such different languages or traditions that they thought of themselves as separate territories. Correspondingly, there were no aristocrats who could move toward separatism by drawing on regional resentments. This meant that England never really had to face the threat of internal division and could develop strong institutions of united national government such as Parliament. It also meant that the English kings, starting primarily with Henry II, could rely on numerous local dignitaries, above all, the knights, to do much work of local government without pay. The obvious advantage was that local government was cheap, but the hidden implication of the system was that government also had to be popular, or else much of the voluntary work would grind to a halt. This doubtless was the main reason why English kings went out of their way to seek formal consent for their actions. When they did not they could barely rule, so wise kings learned the lesson and as time went on England became most clearly a limited monarchy. The French kings, much to the contrary, ruled a richer and larger country, which gave them—at least in times of peace—sufficient wealth to pay for a more bureaucratic, salaried administration at both the central and local levels. French kings therefore could rule more absolutely. But they were continually faced with serious threats of regional separatism. Different regions continued to cherish their own traditions and often supported centrifugalism in league with the upper aristocracy. So French kings often had to struggle with attempts at regional breakaways and take various measures to subdue their aristocrats. Up to around 1700 the monarchy had to fight a steady battle against regionalism, but it had the resources to win consistently and thereby managed to grow from strength to strength.

The only continental state that would rival France until the rise of Germany in the nineteenth century was Spain. The foundations of Spain's greatness were also laid in the High Middle Ages on the principle of national monarchy, but in the Middle Ages there was not yet one monarchy that ruled through most of the Iberian peninsula. After the Christians started pushing back the forces of Islam around 1100 there were four Spanish Christian kingdoms: the tiny northern mountain state of Navarre, which would always remain comparatively insignificant; Portugal in the west; Aragon in the northeast; and Castile in the center. The main Spanish occupation in the High Middle Ages was the *Reconquista*, i.e., the reconquest of the peninsula for Christianity. This reached its culmination in the year 1212 in a major victory of a combined Aragonese-Castilian army over the Muslims at Las Navas de Tolosa. The rest was mostly mopping up. By the end of the thirteenth century all that remained of earlier Muslim domination was the small state of Granada in the extreme south, and Granada existed largely because it was willing to pay tribute to the Christians. Because Castile had the largest open frontier, it became by far the largest Spanish kingdom, but it was balanced in wealth by the more urban and trade-oriented Aragon. Both kingdoms developed institutions in the thirteenth century that roughly paralleled those of France. But until the union of Aragon and Castile under King Ferdinand and Queen Isabella in the fifteenth century, the Iberian states individually could not hope to be as strong as the much richer and more populous France.

Medieval Spain

Before concluding this chapter it is best to assess the general significance of the rise of the national monarchies in high-medieval western Europe. Until their emergence there had been two basic patterns of government in Europe: city-states and empires. City-states had the advantage of drawing heavily upon citizen participation and loyalty and thus were able to make highly efficient use of their human potential. But they were often divided by economic rivalries and they were not sufficiently large or militarily strong to defend themselves against imperial forces. The empires, on the other hand, could win battles and often had the resources to support an efficient bureaucratic administrative apparatus, but they drew on little voluntary participation and were too far-flung or rapacious to inspire any deep loyal-

*Historical role of the
national monarchies*

ties. The new national monarchies were to prove the "golden mean" between these extremes. They were large enough to have adequate military strength and they developed administrative techniques that would rival and eventually surpass those of the Roman or Byzantine Empires. More than that, building at first upon the bases of feudalism, they drew upon sufficient citizen participation and loyalty to help support them in times of stress when empires would have foundered. By about 1300 the monarchies of England, France, and the Iberian peninsula had gained the primary loyalties of their subjects, superseding loyalties to communities, regions, or to the government of the Church. For all these reasons they brought much internal peace and stability to large parts of Europe where there had been little stability before. Thus they contributed greatly to making life fruitful. The medieval national monarchies were also the ancestors of the modern nation-states—the most effective and equitable governments of our day (the current Soviet Union being something more like an empire). In short, they were one of the Middle Ages' most beneficial bequests to modern times.

SELECTED READINGS

• *Items so designated are available in paperback editions.*

GENERAL STUDIES

• Bloch, Marc, *Feudal Society,* Chicago, 1961. A modern classic, first published in France in 1940. Full of valuable insights but outdated in some respects.
• Heer, Friedrich, *The Medieval World,* London, 1961. A controversial interpretation that opposes an "open" twelfth century to a "closed" thirteenth century. Very detailed.
• Southern, R. W., *The Making of the Middle Ages,* New Haven, Conn., 1953. A subtle and brilliant reading of eleventh- and twelfth-century developments. Difficult but most rewarding.
• Strayer, J. R., *Western Europe in the Middle Ages,* 2nd ed., Pacific Palisades, Calif., 1974. In a class by itself as the best short introduction to medieval political and cultural history.
  Wood, Charles T., *The Age of Chivalry* (also published as *The Quest for Eternity*), London, 1970. A lively work for the beginner that supplements Strayer in its emphasis on economic and social history.

ECONOMIC AND SOCIAL CONDITIONS

• Bautier, R. H., *The Economic Development of Medieval Europe,* London, 1971.
• Duby, G., *Rural Economy and Country Life in the Medieval West,* London, 1968. The best work on agrarian history. Highly recommended as an example of recent French historiography at its highest level.

- Gies, J. and F., *Life in a Medieval City,* New York, 1973. An engaging popular account concentrating on life in thirteenth-century Troyes.

  Labarge, M. W., *A Baronial Household of the Thirteenth Century,* New York, 1965. Particularly valuable for its emphasis on the career of a woman.
- Lopez, Robert S., *The Commercial Revolution of the Middle Ages,* Englewood Cliffs, N.J., 1971.
- Painter, Sidney, *French Chivalry,* Baltimore, 1940.
- Pirenne, H., *Economic and Social History of Medieval Europe,* London, 1936. Many of Pirenne's ideas are no longer accepted but this is still an extremely useful brief account.

  Postan, M. M., *The Medieval Economy and Society: An Economic History of Britain, 1100–1500,* Berkeley, Calif., 1972.
- Power, Eileen, *Medieval Women,* Cambridge, 1975. Very brief but informative.
- White, Lynn, Jr., *Medieval Technology and Social Change,* Oxford, 1962. Controversial but excellently written and thought-provoking.

POLITICAL DEVELOPMENTS

- Barraclough, G., *The Origins of Modern Germany,* 2nd ed., Oxford, 1947. Highly interpretative, should be read in conjunction with Hampe.

  Douglas, David, *The Norman Achievement, 1050–1100,* Berkeley, Calif., 1969.

  ———, *The Norman Fate, 1100–1154,* Berkeley, Calif., 1976.
- Fawtier, R., *The Capetian Kings of France,* London, 1962. The best single volume on medieval French politics.

  Hampe, K., *Germany under the Salian and Hohenstaufen Emperors,* Totowa, N.J., 1973. An older, reliable German work recently translated.

  Hyde, J. K., *Society and Politics in Medieval Italy,* New York, 1973. An excellent survey that integrates political and social history.

  Loyn, H. R., *The Norman Conquest,* London, 1965.

  O'Callaghan, Joseph F., *A History of Medieval Spain,* Ithaca, N.Y., 1975.

  Petit-Dutaillis, Charles, *The Feudal Monarchy in France and England,* London, 1936. An excellent essay in comparative history.
- Poole, Austin L., *From Domesday Book to Magna Carta, 1087–1216,* 2nd ed., Oxford, 1955. Very detailed yet clear.
- Sayles, G. O., *The King's Parliament of England,* New York, 1974. Emphasizes the role of the crown and downplays the importance of the commons.

  ———, *The Medieval Foundations of England,* London, 1952. An excellent interpretation of medieval English political developments.
- Stephenson, Carl, *Mediaeval Feudalism,* Ithaca, N.Y., 1942. Very elementary.
- Strayer, J. R., *On the Medieval Origins of the Modern State,* Princeton, N.J., 1970. A distillation of the ideas of one of America's greatest medievalists.

SOURCE MATERIALS

  Herlihy, David, ed., *The History of Feudalism,* New York, 1970.
- Lopez, Robert S., and I. W. Raymond, eds., *Medieval Trade in the Mediterranean World,* New York, 1955.

- Lyon, Bryce, ed., *The High Middle Ages,* New York, 1964.
- Otto of Freising, *The Deeds of Frederick Barbarossa,* tr. C. C. Mierow, New York, 1953. A contemporary chronicle that is interesting enough to read from start to finish.

Strayer, J. R., ed., *Feudalism,* Princeton, N.J., 1965.

Chapter 15

THE HIGH MIDDLE AGES (1050–1300): RELIGIOUS AND INTELLECTUAL DEVELOPMENTS

You would see men and women dragging carts through marshes . . . everywhere miracles daily occurring, jubilant songs rendered to God. . . . You would say that the prophecy was fulfilled, "The Spirit of Life was in the wheels."

> —Abbot Robert of Torigni,
> on the building of the cathedral
> of Chartres, 1145

The religious and intellectual changes that transpired in the West between 1050 and 1300 were as important as the economic, social, and political ones. In the sphere of religion, the most fundamental organizational development was the triumph of the _papal monarchy_. Before the middle of the eleventh century certain popes had laid claim to primacy within the Church, but very few were able to come close to making good on such claims. Indeed, most popes before about 1050 were hardly able to rule effectively as bishops of Rome. But then, most dramatically, the popes emerged as the supreme religious leaders of Western Christendom. They centralized the government of the Church, challenged the sway of emperors and kings, and called forth the crusading movement. By 1300 the temporal success of the papacy had proven to be its own nemesis, but the popes still ruled the Church internally, as they continue to rule the Roman Catholic Church today.

Religious changes

While the papacy was assuming power, a new vitality infused the Christian religion itself, enabling Christianity to capture the human imagination as never before. At the same time too there was a remarkable revival of intellectual and cultural life. In education, thought, and

Intellectual changes

the arts, as in economics and politics, the West before 1050 had been a backwater. Thereafter it emerged swiftly from backwardness to become an intellectual and artistic leader of the globe. Westerners boasted that learning and the arts had moved northwest to them from Egypt, Greece, and Rome—a boast that was largely true. In the High Middle Ages Europeans first started building on ancient intellectual foundations and also contributed major intellectual and artistic innovations of their own.

1. THE CONSOLIDATION OF THE PAPAL MONARCHY

The sorry state of religious life in the tenth and early eleventh centuries

To understand the origins and appreciate the significance of the western European religious revival of the High Middle Ages it is necessary to have some idea of the level to which religion had sunk in the tenth and early eleventh centuries. Around 800 the Emperor Charlemagne had made some valiant attempts to enhance the religious authority of bishops, introduce the parish system into rural regions where there had hardly been any priests before, and provide for the literacy of the clergy. But with the collapse of the Carolingian Empire, religious decentralization and ensuing corruption prevailed throughout most of Europe. Most churches and monasteries became the private property of strong local lords. The latter disposed of Church offices under their control as they wished, often by selling them or by granting them to close relatives. Obviously this was not the best way to find the most worthy candidates, and many priests were quite unqualified for their jobs. They were almost always illiterate, and often they lived openly with concubines. When archbishops or bishops were able to control appointments the results were not much better because such officials were usually close relatives of secular lords and followed their practices of financial or family aggrandizement. As for the popes, they were usually incompetent or corrupt, the sons or tools of powerful families who lived in or around the city of Rome. Some were astonishingly debauched. John XII may have been the worst of them. He was made pope at the age of eighteen in 955 because of the strength of his family. It is certain that he ruled for nine years as a thorough profligate, but there is some uncertainty about the cause of his death: either he was caught *in flagrante delicto* by a jealous husband and murdered on the spot, or else he died in the midst of a carnal act from sheer amorous exertion.

Religious revival: (1) Cluny and monastic reform

Once Europe began to catch its breath from the wave of external invasions that peaked in the tenth century, the wide extent of religious corruption or indifference was bound to call forth some reaction. The first successful measures of reform were taken in the monasteries because the work of a bishop was limited to what he could do in his lifetime, and even more because most archbishops and bishops were unable to disentangle themselves from the political affairs of their day. Monasteries could be somewhat more independent and could count more on the support of their reforms by lay lords, insofar as lords feared for the health of their souls if monks did not serve their proper function in saying offices (i.e., prayers). The movement for monastic reform began with the foundation of the monastery of Cluny in Burgundy in 910 by a pious nobleman. Cluny was a Benedictine house but it introduced two constitutional innovations. One was that, in order to remain free from domination by either local secular or ecclesiastical powers, it was made directly subject to the pope. The other was that it undertook the reform or foundation of numerous "daughter monasteries": whereas formerly all Benedictine houses had been independent and equal, Cluny founded a monastic "family," whose members were subordinate to it. Owing to the succession of a few extremely pious, active, and long-lived abbots, the congregation of Cluniac houses grew so rapidly that there were sixty-seven by 1049. In all of them dedicated priors were chosen who followed the dictates of the abbot of Cluny rather than being responsible to local potentates. Cluniac monks accordingly became famous for their industry in the saying of offices. And Cluny was only the most famous of the new congregations. Other similar ones spread just as rapidly in the years around 1000 and succeeded in making the reformed monasteries vital centers of religious life and prayer.

Around the middle of the eleventh century, after so many monasteries had been taken out of the control of secular authorities, the leaders of the monastic reform movement started to lobby for the reform of the secular clergy as well. They centered their attacks upon *simony*—i.e., the buying and selling of positions in the Church—and they also demanded celibacy for all levels of clergy. Their entire program was directed toward depriving secular powers of their ability to dictate appointments of bishops, abbots, and priests, and toward making the clerical estate as "pure" and as distinct from the secular one as possible. Once this reform program was appropriated by the papacy, it would begin to change the face of the entire Church.

*(2) reform of the
secular clergy*

Considering that the reformers were greatly opposed to lay interference, it is ironic that their party was first installed in the papacy by a German emperor, namely Henry III. In 1046 this ruler came to Italy, deposed three rival Italian claimants to the papal title, and named as pope a German reformer from his own retinue. Henry III's act brought in a series of reforming popes, who started to promulgate decrees against simony, clerical marriage, and immorality of all sorts throughout the Church. These popes also insisted upon their own role as primates and universal spiritual leaders in order to give strength to their actions. One of the most important steps they took was the issuance in 1059 of a decree on papal elections. This vested the right of naming a new pope solely with the cardinals, thereby depriving the

*Emperor Henry III and
reform of the papacy*

Roman aristocracy or the German emperor of the chance to interfere in the matter. The decree preserved the independence of papal elections thereafter. In granting the right of election to cardinals the decree also became a milestone in the evolution of a special body within the Church. Ever since the tenth century a number of bishops and clerics, known as cardinals, from sees in and near Rome had taken on an important role as advisors and administrative assistants of the popes, but the election decree of 1059 first gave them their clearest powers. Thereafter the "college of cardinals" took on more and more administrative duties and helped create continuity in papal policy, especially when there was a quick succession of pontiffs. The cardinals still elect the pope today.

*The ideals of Pope
Gregory VII*

A new and most momentous phase in the history of the reform movement was initiated during the pontificate of Gregory VII (1073–1085). Scholars disagree about how much Gregory was indebted to the ideas and policies of his predecessors in the reform movement and how much he departed from them. The answer seems to be that Gregory supported reform as much as others, indeed he explicitly renewed his predecessors' decrees against simony and clerical marriage. Yet he was not only more zealous in trying to enforce these decrees—a contemporary even called him a "Holy Satan"—but he brought with him a basically new conception of the role of the Church in human life. Whereas the older Christian ideal had been that of withdrawal, and the perfect "athlete of Christ" had been a passive contemplative, or ascetic monk, Gregory VII conceived of Christianity as being much more activist and believed that the Church was responsible for creating "right order in the world." To this end he demanded absolute obedience and strenuous chastity from his clergy: some of his clerical opponents complained that he wanted clerics to live like angels. Equally important, he thought of kings and emperors as his inferiors, who would carry out his commands obediently and help him reform and evangelize the world. Gregory allowed that secular princes would continue to rule directly and make their own decisions in purely secular matters, but he expected them to accept ultimate papal overlordship. Put in other terms, in contrast to his predecessors who had sought merely a duality of ecclesiastical and secular authority, Gregory VII wanted to create a papal monarchy over both. When told that his ideas were novel, he and his immediate followers replied: "The Lord did not say 'I am custom'; the Lord said 'I am truth.'" Since no pope had spoken like this before, it is proper to accept the judgment of a modern historian who called Gregory "the great innovator, who stood quite alone."

The investiture struggle

Gregory's actual conduct as pope was nothing short of revolutionary. From the start he was determined to enforce a decree against "lay investiture," the practice whereby secular rulers ceremonially granted clerics the symbols of their office. The German Emperor

Henry IV was bound to resist this because the ceremony was a manifestation of his long-accepted rights to appoint and control churchmen: without these his own authority would be greatly weakened. The ensuing fight is often called "the investiture struggle" because the problem of investitures was a central one, but the struggle was really about the relative obedience and strength of pope and emperor. The larger issue was immediately joined when Henry IV flouted Gregory's injunctions against appointing prelates. Whereas earlier popes might have tried to deal with such insubordination diplomatically, Gregory rapidly took the entirely unprecedented step of excommunicating the emperor and suspending him from all his powers as an earthly ruler. This bold act amazed all who learned of it. Between 955 and 1057 German emperors had deposed five and named twelve out of twenty-five popes; now a pope dared to dismiss an emperor! We have seen in the previous chapter that in 1077 Henry IV abased himself before the pope in order to forestall a formal deposition: that act amazed contemporaries even more. Thereafter Henry was able to rally some support and sympathy for himself and a terrible war of words ensued, while on the actual battlefield the emperor was able to place troops supporting the pope on the defensive. In 1085 Gregory died, seemingly defeated. But Gregory's successors continued the struggle with Henry IV and later with his son, Henry V.

The long and bitter contest on investiture only came to an end with the Concordat of Worms (a city in Germany) of 1122. Under this compromise the German emperor was forbidden to invest prelates with the religious symbols of their office but was allowed to invest them with the symbols of their rights as temporal rulers because the emperor was recognized as their temporal overlord. That settlement was ultimately less significant than the fact that the struggle had lastingly impaired the prestige of the emperors and raised that of the popes. In addition, the dramatic struggle helped rally the Western clergy behind the pope and galvanized the attentions of all onlookers. As one chronicler reported, nothing else was talked about "even in the women's spinning-rooms and the artisans' workshops." This meant that people who had earlier been largely indifferent to or excluded from religious issues became much more absorbed by them.

Results of the conflict

Gregory VII's successors and most of the popes of the twelfth century were fully committed to the goal of papal monarchy. But they were far less impetuous than Gregory had been and were more interested in the everyday administration of the Church. They apparently recognized that there was no point in claiming to rule as papal monarchs unless they could avail themselves of a governmental apparatus to support their claims. To this end they presided over an impressive growth of law and administration. Under papal guidance the twelfth century saw the basic formulation of the canon law of the Church. Canon law claimed ecclesiastical jurisdiction for all sorts of cases per-

The growth of papal monarchy

taining not only to the clergy but also to problems of marriage, inheritance, and rights of widows and orphans. Most of these cases were supposed to originate in the courts of bishops, but the popes insisted that they alone could issue dispensations from the strict letter of the law and that the papal *consistory*—comprised of the pope and cardinals—should serve as a final court of appeals. As the power of the papacy and the prestige of the Church mounted, cases in canon law courts and appeals to Rome rapidly increased; after the middle of the twelfth century legal expertise became so important for exercising the papal office that most popes were trained canon lawyers, whereas previously they had usually been monks. Concurrent with this growth of legalism was the growth of an administrative apparatus to keep records and collect income. As the century wore on, the papacy developed a bureaucratic government that was far in advance of most of the secular governments of the day. This allowed it to become richer, more efficient, and ever stronger. Finally, the popes asserted their powers within the Church by gaining greater control over the election of bishops and by calling general councils in Rome to promulgate laws and demonstrate their leadership.

Pope Innocent III

By common consent the most capable and successful of all high-medieval popes was Innocent III (1198–1216). Innocent, who was elected at the age of thirty-seven, was extremely young and vigorous for a high-medieval pope; more than that, he was expertly trained in both theology and canon law. His major goal was to unify all Christendom under papal hegemony and to bring in the "right order in the world" so fervently desired by Gregory VII. He never questioned the right of kings and princes to rule directly in the secular sphere but believed that he could step in and discipline kings whenever they "sinned," a wide opening for interference. Beyond that, he saw himself as the ultimate overlord of all. In his own words he said that "as every knee is bowed to Jesus . . . so all men should obey His Vicar [i.e., the pope]."

Innocent sought to implement his goals in many different ways. In order to give the papacy a solid territorial base of support, like the one drawn upon by the French kings, he tried to initiate strong rule in the papal territories around Rome by consolidating them where possible and providing for efficient and vigilant administration. For this reason Innocent is often considered to be the real founder of the Papal States. But because some urban communities tenaciously sought to maintain their independence, he never came close to dominating the papal lands in Italy so completely as the French kings controlled the Ile-de-France. In other projects he was more completely successful. He intervened in German politics assertively enough to engineer the triumph of his own candidate for the imperial office, the Hohenstaufen Frederick II. He disciplined the French King Philip Augustus for his marital misconduct and forced John of England to accept an unwanted candidate as archbishop of Canterbury. To demonstrate his superiority and also

Pope Innocent III. A mosaic dating from the thirteenth century.

gain income, Innocent forced John to grant England to the papacy as a fief, and he similarly gained the feudal overlordship of Aragon, Sicily, and Hungary. When southern France was threatened by the spread of the Albigensian heresy (to be discussed later) the pope effectively called a crusade that would extinguish it by force. He also levied the first income tax on the clergy to support a crusade to the Holy Land. The crown of Innocent's religious achievement was the calling of the Fourth Lateran Council in Rome in 1215. This defined central dogmas of the faith and made the leadership of the papacy within Christendom more apparent than ever. The pope was now clearly both disciplining kings and ruling over the Church without hindrance.

Innocent's reign was certainly the zenith of the papal monarchy, but it also sowed some of the seeds of future ruin. Innocent himself could administer the Papal States and seek new sources of income without seeming to compromise the spiritual dignity of his office. But future popes who followed his policies had less of his stature and thus began to appear more like ordinary acquisitive rulers. Moreover, because the Papal States bordered on the Kingdom of Sicily, Innocent's successors quickly came into conflict with the neighboring ruler, who was none other than Innocent's protegé Frederick II. Although Innocent had raised up Frederick, he never dreamed that Frederick would later become an inveterate opponent of paper power in Italy.

Problems for Innocent's successors

At first these and other problems were not fully apparent. The popes of the thirteenth century continued to enhance their powers and centralize the government of the Church. They gradually asserted the right to name candidates for ecclesiastical benefices, both high and low, and they asserted control over the curriculum and doctrine taught at the University of Paris. But they also became involved in a protracted political struggle which led to their own demise as temporal powers. This struggle began with the attempt of the popes to destroy Frederick II. To some degree they were acting in self-defense because Frederick threatened their own rule in central Italy. But in combating him they overemployed their spiritual weapons. Instead of merely excommunicating and deposing Frederick, they also called a crusade against him—the first time a crusade was called on a large scale for blatantly political purposes.

The papacy's struggle with Frederick II and his heirs; political crusades

After Frederick's death in 1250 a succession of popes made a still worse mistake by renewing and maintaining their crusade against all of the emperor's heirs, whom they called the "viper brood." In order to implement this crusade they became preoccupied with raising funds, and they sought and won as their military champion a younger son from the French royal house, Charles of Anjou. But the latter only helped the popes for the purely political motive of winning the Kingdom of Sicily for himself. Charles in fact won Sicily in 1268 by defeating the last of Frederick II's male heirs. But he then taxed the realm so excessively that the Sicilians revolted in the "Sicilian Vespers" of 1282 and offered their crown to the king of Aragon, who had married Fred-

The effects of the political crusades

Pope Boniface VIII. From a portrait by Giotto.

erick II's granddaughter. The king of Aragon accordingly entered the Italian arena and came close to winning Frederick's former kingdom for himself. To prevent this Charles of Anjou and the reigning pope prevailed upon the king of France—then Philip III (1270–1285)—to embark on a crusade against Aragon. This crusade was a terrible failure and Philip III died on it. In the wake of these events Philip's son, Philip IV, resolved to alter the traditional French pro-papal policy. By that time France had become so strong that such a decision was fateful. More than that, by misusing the institution of the crusade and trying to raise increasingly large sums of money to support it, the popes had lost much of their prestige. The denouement would be played out at the very beginning of the next century.

The temporal might of the papacy was toppled almost melodramatically in the reign of Boniface VIII (1294–1303). Many of Boniface's troubles were not of his own making. His greatest obstacle was that the national monarchies had gained more of their subjects' loyalties than the papacy could draw upon because of the steady growth of royal power and erosion of papal prestige. Boniface also had the misfortune to succeed a particularly pious, although inept, pope who resigned his office within a year. Since Boniface was entirely lacking in conventional piety or humility, the contrast turned many Christian observers against him. Some even maintained—incorrectly—that Boniface had convinced his predecessor to resign and had murdered him shortly afterwards. Boniface ruled assertively and presided over the first papal "jubilee" in Rome in 1300. This was an apparent, but, as events would show, hollow demonstration of papal might.

Two crucial disputes: (1) the issue of clerical taxation

Two disputes with the kings of England and France proved to be Boniface's undoing. The first concerned the clerical taxation that had been initiated by Innocent III. Although Innocent had levied this tax to support a crusade and had collected it himself, in the course of the thirteenth century the kings of England and France had begun to levy and collect clerical taxes on the pretext that they would use them to help the popes on future crusades to the Holy Land or aid in papal crusades against the Hohenstaufens. Then, at the end of the century, the kings started to levy their own war taxes on the clergy without any pretexts at all. Boniface understandably tried to prohibit this step, but quickly found that he had lost the support of the English and French clergy. Thus when the kings offered resistance he had to back down.

(2) quarrel with the king of France

Boniface's second dispute was with the king of France alone. Specifically it concerned Philip IV's determination to try a French bishop for treason. As in the earlier struggle between Gregory VII and Henry IV of Germany, the real issue was the comparative strength of papal and secular power, but this time the papacy was decisively defeated. As before, there was a bitter propaganda war, but now hardly anyone listened to the pope. The king instead pressed absurd charges of heresy against Boniface and sent his minions to arrest the pope to stand trial. At the papal residence of Anagni in 1303 Boniface, who was in his eighties, was captured and mistreated before he was released by the local citizens. These events exhausted the old man's strength and he died a month later. Immediately thereupon it was said that he had entered the papacy like a fox, reigned like a lion, but died like a dog.

After Boniface VIII's death the papacy became virtually a pawn of French temporal authority for most of the fourteenth century. But the emergence and success of the papal monarchy in the High Middle Ages had several beneficial effects during the course of that period. One was that the international rule of the papacy over the Church enhanced international communications and uniformity of religious practices. Another was that the papal cultivation of canon law aided a growing respect for law of all sorts and often helped protect the causes of otherwise defenseless subjects, like widows and orphans. The popes also managed to advance very far in their campaigns to eliminate the sale of Church offices and to raise the morals of the clergy. By centralizing appointments they made it easier for worthy candidates who had no locally influential relatives to gain advancement. There was of course corruption in the papal government too, but in an age of entrenched localism the triumph of an international force was mainly beneficial. Finally, as we will see later, the growth of the papal monarchy helped bring vitality to popular religion and helped support the revival of learning.

Beneficial effects of the papal monarchy

2. THE CRUSADES

The rise and fall of the crusading movement was closely related to the fortunes of the high-medieval papal monarchy. The First Crusade was initiated by the papacy, and its success a great early victory for the papal monarchy. But the later decline of the crusading movement helped undermine the pope's temporal authority. Thus the Crusades can be seen as part of a chapter in papal and religious history. In addition, the Crusades opened the first chapter in the history of Western imperialism.

Two themes of the crusading movement

The immediate cause of the First Crusade was an appeal for aid in 1095 by the Byzantine Emperor Alexius Comnenus. Alexius hoped to reconquer Byzantine territory in Asia Minor which had recently been lost to the Turks. Since he had already become accustomed to using Western mercenaries as auxiliary troops, he asked the pope to help rally some Western military support. But the emperor soon found, no doubt to his great surprise, that he was receiving not just simple aid but a *crusade*. In other words, instead of a band of mercenaries to fight in Asia Minor, the West sent forth an enormous army of volunteers whose goal was to wrest Jerusalem away from Islam. Since the decision to turn Alexius's call for aid into a crusade was made by the pope, it is well to examine the latter's motives.

The direct cause of the First Crusade

The Roman pope in 1095 was Urban II, an extremely competent

THE MAJOR CRUSADES

Population predominantly Christian
Population predominantly Moslem
First Crusade
Second Crusade
Third Crusade
Fourth Crusade

Political boundaries are those shown at the time of the First Crusade

0   300 miles

The Gregorian theory of Christian Warfare

disciple of Gregory VII. Without question, Urban called the First Crusade to help further the policies of the Gregorian papacy. Urban's very patronage of Christian warfare was Gregorian. Early Christianity had been pacifistic: St. Martin, for example, a revered Christian saint of the fourth century, gave up his career as a soldier when he converted with the statement "I am Christ's soldier; I cannot fight." The Latin fathers St. Augustine and St. Gregory worked out theories to justify Christian warfare but only in the eleventh century, with the triumph of the Gregorian movement, were these put into practice. Gregory VII engineered papal support for the Norman Conquest even before he became pope, and he, or popes under his influence, blessed Christian campaigns against Muslims in Spain, Greeks in Italy, and Slavs in the German east. All these campaigns were considered by Gregory VII and his followers to be steps toward gaining "right order in the world."

Following in Gregory VII's footsteps, Urban II probably conceived of a great crusade to the Holy Land as a means for achieving at least four ends. One was to bring the Greek Orthodox Church back into the fold. By sending a mighty volunteer army to the East, Urban might overawe the Byzantines with Western strength and convince them to reaccept Roman primacy. If he was successful in that, he would gain a great victory for the Gregorian program of papal monarchy. A second motive was to embarrass the pope's greatest enemy, the German emperor. In 1095 Henry IV had become so militarily strong that Urban had been forced to flee Italy for France. By calling a mighty crusade of all westerners but Germans, Urban might hope to show up the emperor as a narrow-minded, un-Christian persecutor, and demonstrate his own ability to be the spiritual leader of the West. Thirdly, by sending off a large contingent of fighters Urban might help to achieve peace at home. Earlier, the local French Church had supported a "peace movement" which prohibited attacks on noncombatants (the "Peace of God") and then prohibited fighting on certain holy days (the "Truce of God"). Right before he called the First Crusade Urban promulgated the first full papal approval and extension of this peace movement. Clearly the crusade was linked to the call for peace: in effect, Urban told unruly warriors that if they really wished to fight they could do so justly for a Christian cause overseas. Finally, the goal of Jerusalem itself must have genuinely inspired Urban. Jerusalem was thought to be the center of the earth and was the most sacred shrine of the Christian religion. It must have seemed only proper that pilgrimages to Jerusalem should not be impeded and that Christians should rule the city directly. "Right order in the world" could scarcely mean less.

Urban II's motives

When Urban called his crusade at a Church council in the French town of Clermont in 1095, the response was more enthusiastic than he could possibly have expected. Many in the crowd interrupted the pope's speech with spontaneous cries of "God wills it," and many impetuously rushed off to the East shortly thereafter. All told, there were

Economic and political causes of the First Crusade

French Knights about to Depart on a Crusade. The chief weapons are the long bow and the spear.

probably about a hundred thousand men in the main crusading army, an enormous number for the day. Accordingly, the question arises as to why Urban's appeal was so remarkably successful. Certainly there were economic and political reasons. Many of the poorer people who went crusading came from areas that by 1095 were already becoming overpopulated: these crusaders may have hoped to do better for themselves in the East than they could on their crowded lands. Similarly, some lords were feeling the pressures of growing political stability and a growing acceptance of *primogeniture* (inheritance limited to the eldest male heir). Hitherto younger sons might have hoped to make their own fortune in endemic warfare, or at least inherit a small piece of territory for themselves, but now there were more and longer-lived siblings, warfare was becoming limited, and only the eldest son inherited his father's lands. Clearly, leaving for the East was an attractive alternative to chafing at home.

*Religion the dominant
motive: crusades as armed
pilgrimages*

But the dominant motive for going on the First Crusade was definitely religious. Nobody could have gone crusading out of purely calculating motives because nobody could have predicted for certain that new lands would be won. Indeed, any rational caculation would have predicted at best an unremunerative return trip, or, more likely, death at the hands of the Muslims. But the journey offered great solace for the Christian soul. For centuries pilgrimages had been the most popular type of Christian penance, and the pilgrimage to Jerusalem was considered to be the most sacred and efficacious one of all. Obviously the greatest of all spiritual rewards would come from going on an armed pilgrimage to Jerusalem in order to win back the holiest of sacred places for Christianity. To make this point explicit, Urban II at Clermont promised that Crusaders would be freed from all other penances imposed by the Church. Immediately afterwards some Crusade preachers went even further by promising, without Urban's authorization, what became known as a *plenary indulgence.* This was the promise that all Crusaders would be entirely freed from otherworldly punishments in pugatory and that their souls would go straight to heaven if they died on the Crusade. The plenary indulgence was a truly extraordinary offer and crowds streamed in to take advantage of it. As they flocked together they were further whipped up by preachers into a religious frenzy that approached mass hysteria. They were convinced that they had been chosen to cleanse the world of unbelievers. One terrible consequence was that even before they had fully set out for the East they started slaughtering European Jews in the first really virulent outbreak of Western anti-Semitism.

*The brutal conduct of the
Crusaders*

Against great odds the First Crusade was a thorough success. In 1098 the Crusaders captured Antioch and with it most of Syria; in 1099 they took Jerusalem. Their success came mainly from the facts that their Muslim opponents just at that time were internally divided and that the appearance of the strange, uncouth, and terribly savage

Burning of Jews. From a late-medieval German manuscript. After the persecutions of the First Crusade, treatment of Jews in western Europe became worse and worse. These Jews were set upon by the populace because they were suspected of poisoning wells.

westerners took the Muslims by surprise. From the start the Crusaders in the Holy Land acted like imperialists. As soon as they conquered new territories they claimed them as property for themselves, carving out their acquisitions into four different principalities. They also exulted in their own ferocity. When they captured Antioch, instead of taking prisoners they killed all the Turks they laid their hands on. Similarly, when they conquered Jerusalem they ignored Christ's own pacifistic precepts, mercilessly slaughtering all the Muslim inhabitants of the city. Some Crusaders actually boasted in a joint letter home that "in Solomon's Porch and in his temple our men rode in the blood of the Saracens up to the knees of their horses." Those Crusaders who stayed on in the Holy Land gradually became more civilized and tolerant, but new waves of armed pilgrims from the West continued to act brutally. Moreover, even the settled Crusaders never became fully integrated with the local population but remained a separate, exploiting foreign element in the heart of the Islamic world.

Given the fact that the Christian states comprised only an underpopulated, narrow strip of colonies along the coastline of Syria and Palestine, it was only a matter of time before they would be won back for Islam. By 1144 the northernmost principality fell. When Christian warriors led by the king of France and emperor of Germany came East in the Second Crusade to recoup the losses, they were too internally divided to win any victories. Not long afterwards the Islamic lands of the region were united from Egypt by the Sultan Saladin, who recaptured Jerusalem in 1187. Again a force from the West tried to repair the damages: this was the Third Crusade, led by the German Em-

Failure of subsequent crusades; the triumph of Frederick II's diplomacy

Krak des Chevaliers, Northern Syria. This Castle of the Knights is considered the most magnificent of all the Crusader fortresses and one of the best preserved relics of the Middle Ages.

peror Frederick Barbarossa, the French King Philip Augustus, and the English King Richard the Lionhearted. Even this glorious host, however, could not triumph, above all because rival leaders again quarreled among themselves. When Innocent III became pope his main ambition was to win back Jerusalem. He called the Fourth Crusade to that end, but that Crusade was an unprecedented disaster from the point of view of a united Christendom. The pope could not control its direction and the Crusaders in 1204 wound up seizing Orthodox Christian Constantinople instead of marching on the Holy Land. As we have seen, the ultimate result of this act was to help destroy the Byzantine Empire and open up eastern Europe to the Ottoman Turks. Innocent convened the Fourth Lateran Council in 1215 partially to prepare for yet another crusade that would be more directly under papal guidance. That crusade, the fifth, was launched from the sea against Egypt in order to penetrate Muslim power at its base, but after a promising start it too was a failure. Only the Sixth Crusade, led from 1228 to 1229 by the Emperor Frederick II, was a success; this, however, was not for any military reasons. Frederick, who knew Arabic and could communicate easily with the Egyptian sultan, did not fight but skillfully negotiated a treaty whereby Jerusalem and a narrow access route were restored to the Christians. Thus diplomacy triumphed where warfare had failed. But the Christians could not hold on to their gains and Jerusalem fell again in 1244, never to be recaptured by the West until 1917. The Christian "states" were now only a small enclave around the Palestinian city of Acre.

While Frederick II was negotiating for Jerusalem, he was under excommunication by the pope; therefore, when he entered the city, he had to crown himself king of Jerusalem in the Church of the Holy Sepulcher with his own hands. This was indicative of the fact that by then the papacy was becoming more intent on advancing European

The papacy's sacrifice of the crusading ideal to political interests

political aims than on reconquering the Holy Land. The victory of the First Crusade had greatly enhanced the prestige and strength of the papal monarchy, but the subsequent failures were increasingly calling into question the papal ability to unite the West for a great enterprise. The Albigensian Crusade, called by Innocent III in 1208, established the crucial precedent that a believer could receive the same spiritual rewards by crusading within Europe as by going on a much longer and more risky crusade to the East. The Albigensian Crusade did not damage the papacy's religious image, however, because the Albigensian heretics (whose beliefs will be discussed later) were a clear religious threat to the Church. Once the papacy launched its crusade against Frederick II and his heirs, however, it fully sacrificed the crusading ideal to political interests.

It was then that the decline of the crusading movement and the decline of the papacy became most closely interrelated. In the crusades against Frederick and his successors, and later against the king of Aragon, the popes offered the same plenary indulgence that was by then officially offered to all Crusaders against Islam. Worse, they granted the same indulgence to anyone who simply contributed enough money to arm a Crusader for the enterprise. This created a great inflation in indulgences. By 1291 the last Christian outposts in the Holy Land had fallen without any Western help while the papacy was still trying to salvage its losing crusade against Aragon. Boniface VIII's papal jubilee of 1300, which offered a plenary indulgence to all those who made a pilgrimage to Rome, was a tacit recognition that the Eternal City and not the Holy Land would henceforth have to be the central goal of Christian pilgrimage. Boniface fell from power three years later for many reasons, but one was certainly that the prestige of the papacy had become irreparably damaged by the misuses and failures of crusading.

The decline of the crusading movement and the decline of the papacy interrelated

So, while the crusading idea helped build up the papal monarchy, it also helped destroy it. Other than that, what practical significance did the Crusades have? On the credit side, the almost incredible success of the First Crusade greatly helped raise the self-confidence of the medieval West. For centuries western Europe had been on the defensive against Islam; now a Western army could march into a center of Islamic power and take a coveted prize seemingly at will. This dramatic victory contributed to making the twelfth century an age of extraordinary buoyancy and optimism. To Western Christians it must have seemed as if God was on their side and that they could accomplish almost anything they wished. The Crusades also helped broaden Western horizons. Few westerners in the Holy Land ever bothered to learn Arabic or profit from specific Islamic institutions or ideas—the most profitable cultural communications between Christians and Muslims took place in Spain and Sicily—but Crusaders who traveled long distances through foreign lands were bound to become somewhat more sophisticated. The Crusades certainly stimulated interest in hitherto

Positive effects of the Crusades

unknown luxury goods and presented a wealth of subjects for literature and fable.

Commerce and Taxation

From an economic point of view, the success of the First Crusade
helped open up the eastern Mediterranean to Western commerce. The
Italian cities of Venice and Genoa particularly began to dominate trade
in that area, thereby helping to enhance Western prosperity as a
whole. The need to transfer money over long distances also stimulated
early experiments in banking techniques. Politically, the precedent of
taxing the clergy for financing crusades was not only quickly turned
to the advantage of the Western monarchies, it also stimulated the development of various forms of national taxation. More than that, the
very act of organizing a country to help support a royal crusade by
raising funds and provisions was an important stimulus to the development of efficient administrative institutions in the emerging nation-
states.

Negative consequences

But there was a debit as well as a credit side to the crusading balance
sheet. There is no excusing the Crusaders' savage butchery—of Jews
at home and of Muslims abroad. As we have seen too in Chapter 10,
the Crusades greatly accelerated the deterioration of Western relations
with the Byzantine Empire and contributed fundamentally to the destruction of that realm, with all the disastrous consequences that followed. And Western imperialism in the Holy Land was only the
beginning of a long history of imperialism that has continued until
modern times.

3. THE OUTBURST OF RELIGIOUS VITALITY

*The awakening of
religious interest*

The First Crusade would never have succeeded if westerners had not
become enthusiastic about religion. The growth of that enthusiasm itself was a most remarkable development. Had the First Crusade been
called about fifty years earlier it is doubtful that many people would
have joined it. But the eleventh-century reform movement and the
pontificate of Gregory VII awakened interest in religion in all quarters. Thereafter the entire high-medieval period was to be marked by
extraordinary religious vitality.

*The impact of the
Gregorian reform
movement on religious
revival*

The reformers and Gregory VII stimulated a European religious revival for two reasons. One was that the campaign to cleanse the
Church actually achieved a large measure of success: the laity could
now respect the clergy more and increasingly large numbers of people
were inspired to join the clergy themselves. According to a reliable estimate, the number of people who joined monastic orders in England
increased tenfold between 1066 and 1200, a statistic that does not
include the increase in priests. The other reason why the work of
Gregory VII in particular helped inspire a revival was that Gregory explicitly called upon the laity to help discipline their priests. In letters of

great propagandistic power he denounced the sins of "fornicating priests" (by which he really meant just married ones) and urged the laity to drive them from their pulpits or boycott their services. Not surprisingly, this touched off something close to a vigilante movement in many parts of Europe. This excitement, taken together with the fact that the papal struggle with Henry IV was really the first European event of universal interest, increased religious commitment immensely. Until about 1050 most western Europeans were Christians in name, but religiosity seems to have been lukewarm and attendance at church services quite rare; after the Gregorian period Christianity was becoming an ideal and practice which really began to direct human lives.

One of the most visible manifestations of the new religiosity was the spread of the Cistercian movement in the twelfth century. By around 1100 the Cluniac monks had begun to sink into the same morass of worldliness and corruption that had engulfed their older Benedictine brothers whom they had set about to reform. The result was the founding of new orders to provide for the fullest expression of monastic idealism. One was the Carthusian order, whose monks were required to live in separate cells, abstain from meat, and fast three days each week on bread, water, and salt. The Carthusians never sought to attract great numbers and therefore remained a small group. But the same was by no means true of the Cistercians. The latter were monks who were first organized around 1100 and who sought to follow the Benedictine Rule in the purest and most austere way possible. In order

The new religiosity: the Carthusian and Cistercian orders; St. Bernard of Clairvaux

St. Bernard of Clairvaux. Here the saint, in the white habit of the Cistercians, has a miraculous vision of Christ during Mass. From a manuscript of about 1290.

to avoid the worldly temptations to which the Cluniacs had succumbed, they founded new monasteries in forests and wastelands as
far away from civilization as possible. They shunned all unnecessary
church decoration and ostentatious utensils, abandoned the Cluniac
stress on an elaborate liturgy in favor of more contemplation and
private prayer, and seriously committed themselves to hard manual
labor. Under the charismatic leadership of St. Bernard of Clairvaux
(1090–1153), a spellbinding preacher, brilliant writer, and the most influential European religious personality of his age, the Cistercian order
grew exponentially. There were only 5 houses in 1115 but no less than
343 on St. Bernard's death in 1153. This growth not only meant that
many more men were becoming monks—the older houses did not
disappear—but that many pious laymen were donating funds and
lands to support the new monasteries.

*New forms of religious
belief and practice*

As more people were entering or patronizing new monasteries, the
very nature of religious belief and devotion was changing. One of
many examples was a shift away from the cult of saints to emphasis on
the worship of Jesus and veneration of the Virgin Mary. Older Benedictine monasteries encouraged the veneration of the relics of local
saints that they housed in order to attract pilgrims and donations. But
the Cluniac and Cistercian orders were both centralized congregations
that allowed only one saintly patron for all their houses: respectively,
St. Peter (to honor the founder of the papacy) and the Virgin. Since
these monasteries contained few relics (the Virgin was thought to have
been taken bodily into heaven, so there were no corporeal relics for
her at all) they deemphasized their cult. The veneration of relics was
replaced by a concentration on the Eucharist, or the sacrament of the
Lord's Supper. Of course celebration of the Eucharist had always been
an important part of the Christian faith, but only in the twelfth century was it made really central, for only then did theologians fully
work out the doctrine of *transubstantiation*. According to this the priest
during mass cooperates with God in the performance of a miracle
whereby the bread and wine on the altar are changed or "transubstantiated" into the body and blood of Christ. Popular reverence for the
Eucharist became so great in the twelfth century that for the first time
the practice of elevating the consecrated host was initiated so that the
whole congregation could see it. The new theology of the Eucharist
greatly enhanced the dignity of the priest and also encouraged the
faithful to meditate on the Passion of Christ. As a result many developed an intense sense of identification with Christ and tried to imitate
his life in different ways.

*The cult of the Virgin
Mary*

Coming a very close second to the renewed worship of Christ in
the twelfth century was veneration of the Virgin Mary. This development was more unprecedented because until then the Virgin had
been only negligibly honored in the Western Church. Exactly why
veneration of the Virgin became so pronounced in the twelfth century

Christ Blessing the Coronation of His Mother, the Virgin Mary. A relief from the cathedral of Notre Dame, Paris.

is not fully clear, but, whatever the explanation, there is no doubt that in the twelfth century the cult of Mary blossomed throughout all of western Europe. Not only did the Cistercians make her their patron saint, but St. Bernard constantly taught about her life and virtues, and practically all the magnificent new cathedrals of the age were dedicated to her: there was Notre Dame ("Our Lady") of Paris, and also a "Notre Dame" of Chartres, Rheims, Amiens, Rouen, Laon, and many other places. Theologically, Mary's role was that of intercessor with her son for the salvation of human souls. It was held that Mary was the mother of all, an infinite repository of mercy who urged the salvation even of sinners so long as they were loving and ultimately contrite. Numerous stories circulated about seeming reprobates who were saved because they venerated Mary and because she then spoke for them at the hour of death.

The significance of the new cult was manifold. It was the first time that a woman was given such a central and honored place in the Christian religion. The fathers of the church still taught that sin had entered the world through the woman Eve; they now counterbalanced this by explaining how the triumph over sin came about with the help of Mary. Then too, this emphasis gave women a religious figure with whom they could identify, thereby enhancing their own religiosity. A third result was that artists and writers who portrayed Mary were able to concentrate on femininity and scenes of human tenderness and family life. This contributed greatly to a general softening of artistic and literary style. But perhaps most important of all, the rise of the cult of Mary was closely associated with a general rise of hopefulness and optimism in the twelfth-century West.

Significance of the cult

The Virgin in Majesty. A representation from a stained-glass window in the cathedral of Chartres.

Innocent III's response to heresy

Sometimes the great religious enthusiasm of the twelfth century went beyond the bounds approved by the Church. After Gregory VII had called upon the laity to help discipline their clergy it was difficult to control lay enthusiasm. As the twelfth century progressed and the papal monarchy concentrated on strengthening its legal and financial administration, some lay people began to wonder whether the Church, which had once been so inspiring, had not begun to lose sight of its idealistic goals. Another difficulty was that the growing emphasis on the miraculous powers of priests tended to inhibit the religious role of the laity and place it in a distinct position of spiritual inferiority. The result was that in the second half of the twelfth century large-scale movements of popular heresy swept over western Europe for the first time in its history. The two major twelfth-century heresies were Albigensianism and Waldensianism. The former, which had its greatest strength in Italy and southern France was a recrudescence of Eastern dualism. Like the Zoroastrians, Gnostics, and Manicheans before them, the Albigensians believed that all matter was created by an evil principle and that therefore the flesh should be thoroughly mortified. This teaching was completely at variance with Christianity, but it seems that most Albigensians believed themselves to be Christians and subscribed to the heresy mainly because it challenged the authority of insufficiently zealous Catholic priests and provided an outlet for intense lay spirituality. More typical of twelfth-century mainstream religious protest was Waldensianism, a heresy that originated in southern France and spread throughout most of Europe. Waldensians wished to imitate the life of Christ and the Apostles to the fullest possible extent. Therefore, they translated and studied the Gospels, and dedicated themselves to lives of poverty and preaching. Since the Waldensians did not attack any actual doctrines or practices of the Church, the ecclesiastical hierarchy did not at first interfere with them. But it was soon recognized that they were becoming too independent and that their simple piety could prove an embarrassing contrast to the life of worldly prelates. So the papacy forbade them to preach without authorization; when they refused to accept this they were condemned for heresy. This only made them more radical and they began to teach that men could be saved by living the simple apostolic life without any need for the sacraments administered by priests.

When Innocent III became pope in 1198 he was faced with a very serious challenge from growing heresies. His response was characteristically decisive and fateful for the future of the Church. Simply stated it was two-pronged. On the one hand, Innocent resolved to crush all disobedience to papal authority, but on the other, he decided to patronize whatever idealistic religious groups he could find that were willing to acknowledge obedience. Papal monarchy would hence no longer be threatened, but there would still be some dynamic spirituality within the Church. Innocent not only launched a full-scale crusade against the Albigensians, he also encouraged the use of judicial procedures against heresy that included ruthless techniques of religious "inquisition." In 1252 the papacy first approved the use of torture in inquisitorial trials, and burning at the stake became the prevalent punishment for religious disobedience. Neither the crusade nor the inquisitorial procedures were fully successful in uprooting the Albigensian heresy in Innocent's own lifetime, but the extension of such measures did result in destroying the heresy by fire and sword after about the middle of the thirteenth century. Waldensians, like Albigensians, were hunted down by inquisitors and their numbers reduced, but scattered Waldensian groups did manage to survive until modern times.

Another aspect of Innocent's program was to pronounce formally the new religious doctrines that enhanced the special status of priests and the ecclesiastical hierarchy. Thus at the Fourth Lateran Council of 1215 he reaffirmed the doctrine that the sacraments administered by the Church were the indispensable means of procuring God's grace, and that no one could be saved without them. The decrees of the Lateran Council emphasized two sacraments: the Eucharist and Penance. The doctrine of transubstantiation was formally defined and it was made a requirement—as it remains today—that all Catholics confess their sins to a priest at least once a year. The council also promulgated other doctrinal definitions and disciplinary measures which served both to oppose heresy and assert the unique dignity of the clergy.

Innocent III's emphasis on the sacraments

As stated above, the other side of Innocent's policy was to support obedient idealistic movements within the Church. The most important of these were the new orders of *friars*—the Dominicans and the Franciscans. Friars were like monks in vowing to follow a rule but they differed greatly from monks in their actual conduct. Above all, they did not retreat from society into monasteries. Assuming that the way of life originally followed by Christ and the Apostles was the most holy, they wandered through the countryside and especially the towns ministering to the sick and poor, preaching, and teaching. In imitation of Christ they also resolved to wed themselves to poverty. In many respects they resembled the Waldensian heretics but they professed absolute obedience to the pope and sought to fight heresy themselves.

The new orders of friars

The Dominican order, founded by St. Dominic in 1216 with Innocent III's approval, was particularly dedicated to the fight against heresy and also to the conversion of Jews and Muslims. At first the Dominicans hoped to achieve this end by preaching and public debate. Hence they became intellectually oriented. Many members of the order gained teaching positions in the infant European universities and contributed much to the development of philosophy and theology. The most influential thinker of the thirteenth century, St. Thomas

The Dominican order

St. Francis of Assisi. By the great
Italian painter of the late thirteenth century, Cimabue.

*The working relationship
between the papal
monarchy and the friars*

The age of faith

Aquinas, was a Dominican who addressed one of his major theological works to converting the "gentiles" (i.e., all non-Christians). The
Dominicans always retained their reputation for learning, but they
also came to believe that stubborn heretics were best controlled by
legal procedures. Accordingly, they became the leading medieval administrators of inquisitorial trials.

The Franciscan order was in many respects quite different and more
radical. Its founder, St. Francis of Assisi (1182–1226), behaved at first
remarkably like a social rebel and heretic. The son of a rich Italian
merchant, he became dissatisfied with the values of his father and determined to become a servant of the poor. Giving away all of his property, he threw off all of his clothes in public, donned the simple garb
of a beggar, and began to preach salvation and minister to outcasts in
the darkest corners of Italian cities. He rigorously imitated the life of
Christ and displayed indifference to doctrine, form, and ceremony.
But he did wish to gain the support of the pope. One day in 1210 he
appeared in Rome with a small ragged band to request that Innocent
III approve a primitive "rule" that was little more than a collection of
Gospel precepts. Some other pope might have rejected the layman
Francis as a hopelessly unworldly, perhaps even demented, religious
anarchist. But Francis was thoroughly willing to profess obedience,
and Innocent had the genius to approve Francis's rule and give him
permission to preach. With papal support the Franciscan movement
spread rapidly. Thus Innocent managed to harness a vital new force
that would help maintain a sense of religious enthusiasm within the
Church.

Until the end of the thirteenth century both the Franciscans and
Dominicans worked closely together with the papal monarchy in a
mutually supportive relationship. The popes helped the friars establish
themselves throughout Europe and often allowed them to infringe on
the duties of parish priests. On their side the friars combated heresy,
helped preach papal crusades, were active in missionary work, and
otherwise undertook special missions for the popes. Above all, by the
power of their examples and by their vigorous preaching the friars
helped maintain religious intensity throughout the thirteenth century.

The entire period from 1050 to 1300 was hence unquestionably a
great "age of faith." The products of this faith were both tangible and
intangible. We will examine the tangible products—works of theology, literature, art, and architecture—presently. Great as these were,
the intangible products were equally important. Until the Christian
religion became deeply felt in the High Middle Ages there were hardly
any common ideals to inspire average men and women. Life in the
Middle Ages was extraordinarily hard, and until about 1050 there was
not much to give it meaning. Then, when people began to take Christianity more seriously, an impetus was provided for performing hard
work of all sorts. As we have seen in the last chapter, Europeans after

1050 literally had better food than before, and now we have seen that
they were better fed figuratively as well. With more spiritual as well as
material nourishment they accomplished great feats in all forms of
human endeavor.

4. THE MEDIEVAL INTELLECTUAL REVIVAL

The major intellectual accomplishments of the High Middle Ages
were of four related but different sorts: the spread of primary education and literacy; the origin and spread of universities; the acquisition
of classical and Islamic knowledge, and the actual progress in thought
made by westerners. Any one of these accomplishments would have
earned the High Middle Ages a signal place in the history of Western
learning; taken together they began the era of Western intellectual predominance which became a hallmark of modern times.

Four major intellectual accomplishments

Around 800 Charlemagne ordered that primary schools be established in every bishopic and monastery in his realm. Although it is
doubtful that this command was carried out to the letter, many
schools were certainly founded during the Carolingian period. But
their continued existence was later endangered by the Viking invasions. Primary education in some monasteries and cathedral towns
managed to survive, but until around 1050 the extent and quality of
basic education in the European West was meager. Thereafter, however, there was a blossoming that paralleled the efflorescence we have
seen in other human activities. Even contemporaries were struck by
the rapidity with which schools sprang up all over Europe. One
French monk writing in 1115 stated that when he was growing up
around 1075 there was "such a scarcity of teachers that there were almost none in the villages and hardly any in the cities," but that by his
maturity there was "a great number of schools," and the study of
grammar was "flourishing far and wide." Similarly, a Flemish chronicle reported that around 1120 there was an extraordinary new passion
for the study and practice of rhetoric. Clearly, the economic revival,
the growth of towns, and the emergence of strong government allowed Europeans to dedicate themselves to basic education as never
before.

The spread of primary education

The high-medieval educational boom was more than just merely a
growth of schools, for the nature of the schools changed, and as time
went on so did the curriculum and the clientele. The first basic mutation was that monasteries in the twelfth century abandoned their practice of educating outsiders. Earlier, monasteries had taught only a privileged few who were not monks how to read, solely because there were
no other schools where those outsiders could go. But by the twelfth
century there were sufficient alternatives. The main centers of European education became the cathedral schools located in the growing

Changes in medieval education: (1) the development of cathedral schools

A Woman Representing Grammar Leading a Young Boy into the Palace of the Liberal Arts

towns. The papal monarchy energetically supported this development by ordering in 1179 that all cathedrals should set aside income for one schoolteacher, who could then instruct all who wished, rich or poor, without fee. The papacy believed correctly that this measure would enlarge the number of well-trained clerics and potential administrators.

(2) the broadening of the curriculum

At first the cathedral schools existed almost exclusively for the basic training of priests, and the curriculum was designed to teach only the literacy necessary for reading the Church offices. But soon after 1100 the curriculum was broadened. With the growth of both ecclesiastical and secular governments there was a growing demand for trained officials who had to know more than how to read a few prayers. The revived reliance on law especially made it imperative to improve the quality of primary education in order to train future lawyers. Above all, a thorough knowledge of Latin grammar and composition began to be inculcated, often by studying some of the Roman classics such as the works of Cicero and Vergil. The revived interest in these texts, and attempts to imitate them, has led scholars to refer to a "Renaissance of the Twelfth Century."

(3) the growth of lay education

Until about 1200 the students in the urban schools remained predominantly clerical. Even those who hoped to become lawyers or administrators rather than mere priests usually found it advantageous to take Church orders. But afterwards more pupils entered schools who were not in the clergy and never intended to be. Some were children of the upper classes who began to regard literacy as a badge of status.

Others were future notaries (i.e., men who drew up official documents) or merchants who needed some literacy and/or computational skills to advance their own careers. Customarily, the latter groups would not go to cathedral schools but to alternate ones which were more practically oriented. Such schools grew rapidly in the course of the thirteenth century and became completely independent of ecclesiastical control. Not only were their students recruited from the laity, their teachers were usually laymen as well. At time went on instruction ceased being in Latin, as had hitherto been the case, and was offered in the European vernacular languages instead.

The rise of lay education was an enormously important development in western European history for two related reasons. The first was that the Church lost its monopoly over education for the first time in almost a millennium. Learning and resultant attitudes could now become more secular, and they did just that increasingly over the course of time. Laymen could not only evaluate and criticize the ideas of priests, they could also pursue entirely secular lines of inquiry. Western culture therefore ultimately became more independent of religion, and much of the traditionalism associated with religion, than any other culture in the world. Secondly, the growth of lay schools, taken together with the growth of church schools which trained the laity, led to an enormous growth of lay literacy: by 1340 roughly 40 percent of the Florentine population could read; by the later fifteenth century about 40 percent of the total population of England was literate as well. (These figures include women, who were usually taught to read by tutors at home rather than in schools.) When one considers that literacy around 1050 was almost entirely limited to the clergy, and that the literate comprised less than 1 percent of the population of western Europe, it can be appreciated that an astonishing revolution had taken place. Without it, many of Europe's other accomplishments would have been inconceivable.

*Significance of the rise of
lay education*

The emergence of universities was part of the same high-medieval educational boom. Originally, universities were institutions that gave specialized instruction in advanced studies which could not be pursued in average cathedral schools. In Italy the earliest universities took shape in the eleventh and twelfth centuries. They were those of Salerno, which specialized in medicine, and Bologna, which specialized in law—both Roman law and the canon law of the Church. North of the Alps the earliest and for a long time the most prominent university was that of Paris. The University of Paris started out as a cathedral school like many others, but in the twelfth century it began to become a recognized center of northern intellectual life. One reason for this was that scholars there found necessary conditions of peace and stability provided by the increasingly strong French kingship; another was that food was plentiful because the area was rich in agricultural produce; and another was that the cathedral school of Paris in the first half of the twelfth century boasted the most charismatic and controversial

The origins of universities

See color map following
page 384

teacher of the day, Peter Abelard (1079–1142). Abelard, whose intellectual accomplishments we will discuss later, attracted students from all over Europe in droves. According to an apocryphal story that was told at the time, he was such an exciting teacher that when he was forbidden to teach in French lands, because of his controversial views, he climbed a tree and students flocked under it to hear him lecture; when he was then forbidden to teach from the air he started lecturing from a boat and students massed to hear him from the banks. As a result of his reputation many other teachers settled in Paris and began to offer much more varied and advanced instruction than anything offered in other French cathedral schools. By 1200 Paris was evolving into a university that specialized in liberal arts and theology. Around then Innocent III, who had studied in Paris himself, called the school "the oven that bakes the bread for the entire world."

Nature of the medieval university

It should be emphasized that the institution of the university was really a medieval invention. Of course advanced schools existed in the ancient world, but they did not have fixed curricula or organized faculties, and they did not award degrees. At first, medieval universities themselves were not so much places as groups of scholars. The term university originally meant a corporation or guild. In fact, all of the medieval universities were corporations, either of teachers or students, organized like other guilds to protect their interests and rights. But gradually the word university came to mean an educational institution with a school of liberal arts and one or more faculties in the professional subjects of law, medicine, and theology. Salerno never became more than a medical school, but Bologna and Paris after about 1200 were regarded as the prototypic universities. During the thirteenth century such famous institutions as Oxford, Cambridge, Montpellier, Salamanca, and Naples were founded or granted formal recognition. In Germany there were no universities until the fourteenth century—a reflection of the disorganized condition of that area—but in 1385 Heidelberg, the first university on German soil, was founded and many others quickly followed.

Organization of universities

Every university in medieval Europe was patterned after one or the other of two different models. Throughout Italy, Spain, and southern France the standard was generally the University of Bologna, in which the students themselves constituted the corporation. They hired the teachers, paid their salaries, and fined or discharged them for neglect of duty or inefficient instruction. The universities of northern Europe were modeled after Paris, which was not a guild of students but of teachers. It included four faculties—arts, theology, law, and medicine—each headed by a dean. In the great majority of the northern universities arts and theology were the leading branches of study. Before the end of the thirteenth century separate colleges came to be established within the University of Paris. The original college was nothing more than an endowed home for poor students, but eventually the colleges become centers of instruction as well as residences. While most of these colleges have disappeared from the Continent, the universities of Oxford and Cambridge still retain the pattern of federal organization copied from Paris. The colleges of which they are composed are semi-independent educational units.

Most of our modern degrees as well as our modern university organization derive from the medieval system, but actual courses of study have been greatly altered. No curriculum in the Middle Ages included history or anything like the modern social sciences. The medieval student was assumed to know Latin grammar thoroughly before entrance into a university—this he learned in the primary, or "grammar," schools. Upon admission, limited to males, he was required to spend about four years studying the basic liberal arts, which meant doing advanced work in Latin grammar and rhetoric, and mastering the rules of logic. If he passed his examinations he received the preliminary degree of bachelor of arts (the prototype of our B.A.), which conferred no unusual distinction. To assure himself a place in professional life he then usually had to devote additional years to the pursuit of an advanced degree, such as master of arts (M.A.), or doctor of laws, medicine, or theology. For the M.A. degree three or four years had to be given to the study of mathematics, natural science, and philosophy. This was accomplished by reading and commenting on standard ancient works, such as those of Euclid and especially Aristotle. Abstract analysis was emphasized and there was no such thing as laboratory science. The requirements for the doctors' degrees included more specialized training. Those for the doctorate in theology were particularly arduous: by the end of the Middle Ages the course for the doctorate in theology at the University of Paris had been extended to twelve or thirteen years after the roughly eight years taken for the M.A.! Continuous residence was not required and it was accordingly

The courses of study

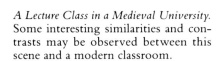

A Lecture Class in a Medieval University. Some interesting similarities and contrasts may be observed between this scene and a modern classroom.

rare to become a doctor of theology before the age of forty; statutes in fact forbade awarding the degree to anyone under thirty-five. Strictly speaking, doctor's degrees, including even the one in medicine, only conferred the right to teach. But in practice university degrees of all grades were recognized as standards of attainment and became pathways to nonacademic careers.

Student life

Student life in medieval universities was often very rowdy. Many students were very immature because it was customary to begin university studies between the ages of twelve and fifteen. Moreover, all university students believed that they comprised an independent and privileged community, set aside from that of the local townspeople. Since the latter tried to reap financial profits from the students, and the students were naturally boisterous, there were frequent riots and sometimes pitched battles between "town" and "gown." But actual study was very intense. Because the greatest emphasis was placed on the value of authority and also because books were prohibitively expensive (they were handwritten and made from rare parchment), there was an enormous amount of rote memorization. As students advanced in their disciplines they were also expected to develop their own skills in formal, public disputations. Advanced disputations could become extremely complex and abstract; sometimes they might also last for days. The most important fact pertaining to medieval university students was that, after about 1250, there were so many of them. The University of Paris in the thirteenth century numbered about seven thousand students and Oxford somewhere around two thousand in any given year. This means that a relatively appreciable proportion of male Europeans who were more than peasants or artisans were gaining at least some education at the higher levels.

Acquisition of Greek and Arabic knowledge

As the numbers of those educated at all levels vastly increased during the High Middle Ages, so did the quality of learning. This was owing first and foremost to the reacquisition of Greek knowledge and to the absorption of intellectual advances made by the Muslims. Since practically no western Europeans knew Greek or Arabic, works in those languages had to be transmitted by means of Latin translations. But there were very few of these before about 1140: of all the many works of Aristotle only a few logical treatises were available in Latin translations before the middle of the twelfth century. But then, suddenly, an enormous burst of translating activity made almost all of ancient Greek and Arabic scientific knowledge accessible to western Europeans. This activity transpired in Spain and Sicily because Christians there lived in close proximity with Arabic speakers, or Jews who knew Latin and Arabic, either of whom could aid them in their tasks. Greek works were first translated into Latin from earlier Arabic translations; then many were retranslated directly from the Greek by a few westerners who had managed to learn that language, usually by traveling in Greek-speaking territories. The result was that by about 1260 almost the entire Aristotelian corpus that is known today was made available in Latin. So also were basic works of such important Greek scientific thinkers as Euclid, Galen, and Ptolemy. Only the milestones of Greek literature and the works of Plato were not yet translated because they had not been made available to the Arabs; they existed only in inaccessible Byzantine manuscripts. But in addition to the thought of the Greeks, Western scholars became familiar with the accomplishments of all the major Islamic philosophers and scientists such as Avicenna and Averroës.

The growth of western scientific and speculative thought; Robert Grosseteste and Roger Bacon

Having acquired the best of Greek and Arabic scientific and speculative thought, the West was able to build on it and make its own advances. This progress transpired in different ways. When it came to natural science, westerners were able to start building on the acquired learning without much difficulty because it seldom conflicted with the principles of Christianity. But when it came to philosophy, the basic question arose as to how thoroughly Greek and Arabic thought was compatible with the Christian faith. The most advanced thirteenth-century scientist was the Englishman Robert Grosseteste (c. 1168–1253), who was not only a great thinker but was also very active in public life as bishop of Lincoln. Grosseteste became so proficient at Greek that he translated all of Aristotle's *Ethics*. More important, he made very significant theoretical advances in mathematics, astronomy, and optics. He formulated a sophisticated scientific explanation of the rainbow and he posited the use of lenses for magnification. Grosseteste's leading disciple was Roger Bacon (c. 1214–1294), who is today more famous than his teacher because he seems to have predicted automobiles and flying machines. Bacon in fact had no real interest in machinery, but he did follow up on Grosseteste's work in optics, discussing, for example, further properties of lenses, the rapid speed of light, and the nature of human vision. Grosseteste, Bacon, and some of their followers at the University of Oxford argued that natural knowledge was more certain when it was based on sensory evidence than when it rested on abstract reason. To this degree they can be seen as early forerunners of modern science. But the important qualification remains that they did not yet perform any real laboratory experiments.

The meaning of Scholasticism

The story of the high-medieval encounter between Greek and Arabic philosophy and Christian faith is basically the story of the emergence of Scholasticism. This word can be, and has been, defined in many ways. In its root meaning Scholasticism was simply the method of teaching and learning followed in the medieval schools. That meant that it was highly systematic and also that it was highly respectful of authority. Yet Scholasticism was not only a method of study: it was a worldview. As such, it taught that there was a fundamental compatability between the knowledge humans can obtain naturally, i.e., by experience or reason, and the teachings imparted by

Divine Revelation. Since medieval scholars believed that the Greeks were the masters of natural knowledge and that all revelation was in the Bible, Scholasticism consequently was the theory and practice of reconciling classical philosophy with Christian faith.

Peter Abelard

One of the most important thinkers who paved the way for Scholasticism without yet being fully a Scholastic himself was the stormy petrel Peter Abelard. As a student Abelard was so adept in logic and theology that he publicly humiliated his teachers in and around Paris in debate. Such arrogant conduct made him many enemies. These engineered his first conviction for heresy in 1121. To complicate matters, Abelard entered upon an affair with a young woman, Heloise, herself a scholar, without marrying her. Abelard had been hired to be Heloise's tutor by her uncle, Fulbert, canon of Notre Dame of Paris. A child was the result of the affair, and Heloise's uncle took revenge upon Abelard by having him castrated. Heloise became a nun and Abelard a monk, but Abelard was too restless and cantankerous a personality to find real peace in a monastery. After quarreling and breaking with the monks of two different communities, he set himself up as a teacher in Paris from about 1132 until 1141. This was the peak of his career. In 1141, however, he was again charged with heresy, this time by the highly influential St. Bernard, and condemned by a Church council. Not long afterwards the persecuted thinker abjured, and in 1142 he died in retirement. Abelard recounted many of these trials in a letter called *The Story of My Calamities,* one of the first autobiographical accounts written in the West since St. Augustine's *Confessions.*

The life of the mind as a profession

On first reading, this work appears "modern" because Abelard seems to revel in himself and boast a great deal. But actually he did not write about his calamities in order to boast. Rather, his main intention was to moralize about how he had been appropriately punished for his intellectual pride by his first condemnation, and for his "lechery" by the loss of those parts which had "offended." Abelard certainly represents a reawakening interest in personal introspection, but in this he did not differ much from St. Augustine. More important is the fact that he was the first westerner who sought to make a full profession out of the life of the mind.

Sic et Non and the Scholastic method

Abelard's greatest contributions to the subsequent development of Scholasticism were made in his *Sic et Non* (Yes and No) and in a number of original theological works. In the *Sic et Non* Abelard prepared the way for the Scholastic method by gathering a collection of statements from the Bible and the church fathers that spoke for both sides of 150 theological questions. It used to be thought that the brash Abelard did this in order to embarrass authority, but the contrary is true. What Abelard really hoped to do was begin a process of careful study, whereby it could be shown that the highest authority of the Bible was infallible, and that the best authorities, despite any appearances to the contrary, really agreed with each other. Later Scholastics would follow his method of studying theology by raising fundamental questions and arraying the answers that had been put forth in authoritative texts. Abelard did not propose any solutions of his own in the *Sic et Non,* but he did start to do this in his original theological writings. In these he proposed to treat theology like a science, by studying it as comprehensively as possible and by applying to it the tools of logic, of which he was a master. He did not even shrink from applying logic to the mystery of the Trinity, one of the excesses for which he was condemned. Thus he was one of the first to try to harmonize religion with rationalism and was in this capacity a herald of the Scholastic outlook.

Immediately after Abelard's death two important steps were taken to further prepare for mature Scholasticism. One was the writing of the *Book of Sentences* between 1155 and 1157 by Abelard's student Peter Lombard. This raised all the most fundamental theological questions in rigorously consequential order, adduced answers from the Bible and Christian authorities on both sides of each question, and then proposed a judgment on every case. Within a short time Peter Lombard's work became a standard text. Once formal schools of theology were established in the universities, all aspirants to the doctorate were required to study and comment upon it; not surprisingly theologians also followed its organizational procedures in their own writings. Thus the full Scholastic method was born.

The other basic step in the development of Scholasticism, as mentioned above, was the reacquisition of classical philosophy that occurred after about 1140. Abelard would probably have been glad to have drawn upon the thought of the Greeks, but he could not because few Greek works were yet available in translation. Later theologians, however, could avail themselves fully of the new knowledge, above all, the works of Aristotle and his Arabic commentators. By around 1250 Aristotle's authority in purely philosophical matters became so great that he was referred to as "the Philosopher" pure and simple. Scholastics of the mid–thirteenth century accordingly adhered to Peter Lombard's organizational method, but added the consideration of Greek and Arabic philosophical authorities to that of purely Christian theological ones. In doing this they tried to construct systems of understanding the entire universe that most fully harmonized the earlier separate realms of faith and natural knowledge.

By far the greatest accomplishments in this endeavor were made by St. Thomas Aquinas (1225–1274), the leading Scholastic theologian of the University of Paris. As a member of the Dominican order, St. Thomas was committed to the principle that faith could be defended by reason. More important, he believed that natural knowledge and the study of the created universe were legitimate ways of approaching theological wisdom because "nature" complements "grace." By this

Peter Lombard's Book of Sentences

Influence of Aristotle

St. Thomas Aquinas

St. Thomas Aquinas. A fifteenth-century painting by Justus of Ghent, after an earlier copy.

The achievements of the thirteenth century

he meant to say that because God created the natural world He can be approached through its terms even though ultimate certainty about the highest truths can only be obtained through the supernatural revelation of the Bible. Imbued with a deep confidence in the value of human reason and human experience, as well as in his own ability to harmonize Greek philosophy with Christian theology, Thomas was the most serene of saints. In a long career of teaching at the University of Paris and elsewhere he indulged in few controversies and worked quietly on his two great *Summaries* of theology: the *Summa contra Gentiles* and the much larger *Summa Theologica*. In these he hoped to set down all that could be said about the faith on the firmest of foundations.

Most experts think that St. Thomas came extremely close to fulfilling this extraordinarily ambitious goal. His vast *Summaries* are awesome for their rigorous orderliness and intellectual penetration. He admits in them that there are certain "mysteries of the faith," such as the doctrines of the Trinity and the Incarnation, that cannot be approached by the unaided human intellect; otherwise, he subjects all theological questions to philosophical inquiry. In this, St. Thomas relied heavily on the work of Aristotle, but he is by no means merely "Aristotle baptized." Instead, he fully subordinated Aristotelianism to basic Christian principles and thereby created his own original philosophical and theological system. Scholars disagree about how far this system diverges from the earlier Christian thought of St. Augustine, but there seems little doubt that Aquinas placed a higher value on human reason, on human life in this world, and on the abilities of humans to participate in their own salvation. Not long after his death St. Thomas was canonized, for his intellectual accomplishments seemed like miracles. His influence lives on today insofar as he helped to revive confidence in rationalism and human experience. More directly, philosophy in the modern Roman Catholic Church is supposed to be taught according to the Thomistic method, doctrine, and principles.

With the achievements of St. Thomas Aquinas in the middle of the thirteenth century, Western medieval thought reached its pinnacle. Not coincidentally, other aspects of medieval civilization were reaching their pinnacles at the same time. France was enjoying its ripest period of peace and prosperity under the rule of St. Louis, the University of Paris was defining its basic organizational forms, and the greatest French Gothic cathedrals were being built. Some ardent admirers of medieval culture have fixed on these accomplishments to call the thirteenth the "greatest of centuries." Such a judgment, of course, is a matter of taste, but many of us might respond that life was still too harsh and requirements for religious orthodoxy too great to justify this extreme celebration of the lost past. Whatever our individual judgments, it seems wise to end this section by correcting some false impressions about medieval intellectual life.

It is often thought that medieval thinkers were excessively conservative, but in fact the greatest thinkers of the High Middle Ages were astonishingly receptive to new ideas. As committed Christians they could not allow doubts to be cast upon the principles of their faith, but otherwise they were glad to accept whatever they could from the Greeks and Arabs. Considering that Aristotelian thought was radically different than anything accepted before in its emphasis on rationalism and the fundamental goodness and purposefulness of nature, its rapid acceptance by the Scholastics was a philosophical revolution. Another false impression is that Scholastic thinkers were greatly constrained by authority. Certainly they revered authority more than we do today, but Scholastics like St. Thomas did not regard the mere citation of texts—except biblical revelation concerning the mysteries of the faith—as being sufficient to clinch an argument. Rather, the authorities were brought forth to outline the possibilities, but reason and experience then demonstrated the truth. Finally, it is often believed that Scholastic thinkers were "antihumanistic," but modern scholars are coming to the opposite conclusion. Scholastics unquestionably gave primacy to the soul over the body and to otherworldly salvation over life in the here and now. But they also exalted the dignity of human nature because they viewed it as a glorious divine creation, and they believed in the possibility of a working alliance between themselves and God. Moreover, they had extraordinary faith in the powers of human reason—probably more than we do today.

5. THE BLOSSOMING OF LITERATURE, ART, AND MUSIC

The literature of the High Middle Ages was as varied, lively, and impressive as that produced in any other period in Western history. The revival of grammatical studies in the cathedral schools and universities led to the production of some excellent Latin poetry. The best examples were secular lyrics, especially those written in the twelfth century by a group of poets known as the Goliards. How these poets got their name is uncertain, but it possibly meant followers of the devil. That would have been appropriate because the Goliards were riotous poets who wrote parodies of the liturgy and burlesques of the Gospels. Their lyrics celebrated the beauties of the changing seasons, the carefree life of the open road, the pleasures of drinking and sporting, and especially the joys of love. The authors of these rollicking and satirical songs were mainly wandering students, although some were men in more advanced years. The names of most are unknown. Their poetry is particularly significant both for its robust vitality and for being the first clear counterstatement to the ascetic ideal of Christianity.

In addition to the use of Latin, the vernacular languages of French,

Charlemagne Weeping for His Knights. A scene from the *Song of Roland.*

The growth of vernacular literature; the epic

German, Spanish, and Italian became increasingly popular as media of literary expression. At first, most of the literature in the vernacular languages was written in the form of the heroic epic. Among the leading examples were the French *Song of Roland,* the Norse eddas and sagas, the German *Song of the Nibelungs,* and the Spanish *Poem of the Cid.* Practically all of these works were originally composed between 1050 and 1150, although some were first set down in writing afterwards. These epics portrayed a virile but unpolished warrior society. Blood flowed freely, skulls were cleaved by battleaxes, and heroic warfare, honor, and loyalty were the major themes. If women were mentioned at all, they were subordinate to men. Brides were expected to die for their betrotheds, but husbands were free to beat their wives. In one French epic a queen who tried to influence her husband met with a blow to the nose; even though blood flowed she replied: "Many thanks, when it pleases you, you may do it again." Despite the repugnance we find in such passages, the best of the vernacular epics have much unpretentious literary power. Above all, the *Song of Roland,* though crude, is like an uncut gem.

The love songs of the troubadours

In comparison to the epics, an enormous change in both subject matter and style was introduced in twelfth-century France by the troubadour poets and the writers of courtly romances. The dramatic nature of this change represents further proof that high-medieval culture was not at all conservative. The troubadours were courtier poets who came from southern France and wrote in the dialect of French known as Provençal. The origin of their inspiration is debated, but there can be no doubt that they initiated a movement of profound importance for all subsequent Western literature. Their style was far more finely wrought and sophisticated than that of the epic poets, and the most eloquent of their lyrics, which were meant to be sung to music, originated the theme of romantic love. The troubadours idealized women as marvelous beings who could grant intense spiritual and sensual gratification. Whatever greatness the poets found in themselves they usually attributed to the inspiration they found in love. But they also assumed that their love would lose its magic if it were too easily or frequently gratified. Therefore, they wrote more often of longing than of romantic fulfillment.

In addition to their love lyrics, the troubadours wrote several other kinds of short poems. Some were simply bawdy. In these, love is not mentioned at all but the poet revels in thoughts of carnality, comparing, for example, the riding of his horse to the "riding" of his mistress. Other troubadour poems treat of feats of arms, others comment on contemporary political events, and a few even meditate on matters of religion. But whatever the subject matter, the best troubadour poems were always cleverly and innovatively expressed. The literary tradition originated by the southern French troubadours was continued by the _trouvères_ in northern France and by the _minnesingers_ in Germany. Thereafter many of their innovations were developed by later lyric poets in all Western languages. Some of their poetic devices were consciously revived in the twentieth century by such "modernists" as Ezra Pound.

An equally important twelfth-century French innovation was the composition of longer narrative poems known as romances. These were the first clear ancestors of the modern novel: they told engaging stories, they often excelled in portraying character, and their subject matter was usually love and adventure. Some romances elaborated on classical Greek themes, but the most famous and best were "Arthurian." These took their material from the legendary exploits of the Celtic hero King Arthur and his many chivalrous knights. The first great writer of Arthurian romances was the northern Frenchman Chrétien de Troyes, who was active between about 1165 and 1190. Chrétien did much to help create and shape the new form, and he also introduced innovations in subject matter and attitudes. Whereas the troubadours exalted unrequited, extramarital love, Chrétien was the first to hold forth the ideal of romantic love within marriage. He also described not only the deeds but the thoughts and emotions of his characters.

A generation later, Chrétien's work was continued by the great German poets Wolfram von Eschenbach and Gottfried von Strassburg. These are recognized as the greatest writers in the German language before the eighteenth century. Wolfram's _Parzival,_ a story of love and the search for the Holy Grail, is more subtle, complex, and greater in scope than any other high-medieval literary work except Dante's _Divine Comedy_. Like Chrétien, Wolfram believed that true love could

Other troubadour poems

_The Arthurian romances;
Chrétien de Troyes_

A Thirteenth-Century Miniature.
From a Manuscript of Wolfram
von Eschenbach's _Parzival._

only be fulfilled in marriage, and in *Parzival,* for the first time in Western literature since the Greeks, one can see a full psychological development of the hero. Gottfried von Strassburg's *Tristan* is a more somber work, which tells of the hopeless adulterous love of Tristan and Isolde. Indeed, it might almost be regarded as the prototype of modern tragic romanticism. Gottfried was one of the first to develop fully the idea of individual suffering as a literary theme and to point out the indistinct line which separates pleasure from pain. For him, to love is to yearn, and suffering and unfulfilled gratification are integral chapters of the book of life. Unlike the troubadours, he could only see complete fulfillment of love in death. *Parzival* and *Tristan* have become most famous today in the form of their operatic reconceptions by the nineteenth-century German composer Richard Wagner.

Not all high-medieval narratives were so elevated as the romances in either form or substance. A very different new narrative form was the *fabliau,* or verse fable. Although *fabliaux* derived from the moral animal tales of Aesop, they quickly evolved into short stories that were written less to edify or instruct than to amuse. Often they were very coarse, and sometimes they dealt with sexual relations in a broadly humorous and thoroughly unromantic manner. Many were also strongly anticlerical, making monks and priests the butts of their jokes. Because the *fabliaux* are so "uncourtly" it used to be thought that they were written solely for the new urban classes. But there is now little doubt that they were addressed at least equally to the "refined" aristocracy who liked to have their laughs too. They are significant as expressions of growing worldliness and as the first manifestations of the robust realism which was later to be perfected by Boccaccio and Chaucer.

Completely different in form but similar as an illustration of growing worldliness was the sprawling *Romance of the Rose.* As its title indicates, this was begun as a romance, specifically around 1230 by the courtly Frenchman William of Lorris. But William left his rather flowery, romantic work unfinished, and it was completed around 1270 by another Frenchman, John of Meun. The latter changed its nature greatly. He inserted long, biting digressions in which he skewered religious hypocrisy, and made his major theme the need for procreation. Not love, but the service of "Dame Nature" in sexual fecundity is urged in numerous witty but extremely earthy images and metaphors. At the climax the originally dreamy hero seizes his mistress, who is allegorically depicted as a rose, and rapes her. Since the work became enormously popular, it seems fair to conclude that tastes, then as now, were very diverse.

In a class by itself as the greatest work of medieval literature is Dante's *Divine Comedy.* Not much is known about the life of Dante Alighieri (1265–1321), except that he was active during the early part of his career in the political affairs of his native city of Florence. Despite

Nature Perpetuates the Species. A miniature from a manuscript of the *Romance of the Rose.*

his engagement in politics and the fact that he was a layman, he managed to acquire an awesome mastery of the religious, philosophic, and literary knowledge of his time. He not only knew the Bible and the church fathers, but—most unusual for a layman—he also absorbed the most recent Scholastic theology. In addition, he was thoroughly familiar with Virgil, Cicero, Boethius, and numerous other classical writers, and was fully conversant with the poems of the troubadours and the Italian poetry of his own day. In 1302 he was expelled from Florence after a political upheaval and was forced to live the rest of his life in exile. The *Divine Comedy*, his major work, was written during this final period.

Dante

Dante's *Divine Comedy* is a monumental narrative in powerful rhyming Italian verse, which describes the poet's journey through hell, purgatory, and paradise. At the start Dante tells of how he once found himself in a "dark wood," his metaphor for a deep personal mid-life crisis. He is led out of this forest of despair by the Roman Virgil, who stands for the heights of classical reason and philosophy. Virgil guides Dante on a trip through hell and purgatory, and afterwards Dante's deceased beloved, Beatrice, who stands for Christian wisdom and blessedness, takes over and guides him through paradise. In the course of this progress Dante meets both historical beings and the poet's contemporaries, all of whom have already been assigned places in the afterlife, and he is instructed by them and his guides as to why they met their several fates. As the poem progresses the poet himself leaves the condition of despair to grow in wisdom and ultimately to reach assurance of his own salvation.

The Divine Comedy

Every reader finds a different combination of wonder and satisfaction in Dante's magnificent work. Some—especially those who know Italian—marvel at the vigor and inventiveness of Dante's language and images. Others are awed by his subtle complexity and poetic symmetry; others by his array of learning; others by the vitality of his characters and individual stories; and still others by his soaring imagination. The historian finds it particularly remarkable that Dante could sum up the best of medieval learning in such an artistically satisfying manner. Dante stressed the precedence of salvation, but he viewed the earth as existing for human benefit. He allowed humans free will to choose good and avoid evil, and accepted Greek philosophy as authoritative in its own sphere; for example, he called Aristotle "the master of them that know." Above all, his sense of hope and his ultimate faith in humanity—remarkable for a defeated exile—most powerfully expresses the dominant mood of the High Middle Ages and makes Dante one of the two or three most stirringly affirmative writers who ever lived.

Quarter Barrel Vaults, Typical of Romanesque Architecture. St. Etienne, Nevers.

The closest architectural equivalents of the *Divine Comedy* are the great high-medieval Gothic cathedrals, for they too have qualities of vast scope, balance of intricate detail with careful symmetry, soaring

*Medieval architecture: (1)
the Romanesque style*

Worms Cathedral, Eleventh-Century Romanesque

Romanesque Sculpture. Shown here is Jesus with two of his Apostles. The elongation and distortion is typical. From a church in Spain.

height, and affirmative religious grandeur. But before we approach the Gothic style, it is best to introduce it by means of its high-medieval predecessor, the style of architecture and art known as the Romanesque. This style had its origins in the tenth century, but became fully formed in the eleventh and first half of the twelfth centuries, when the religious reform movement led to the building of many new monasteries and large churches. The Romanesque was primarily a building style: it aimed to manifest the glory of God in ecclesiastical construction by rigorously subordinating all architectural details to a uniform system. In this it was very severe: we may think of it as the architectural analogue of the unadorned hymn. Aside from its primary stress on systematic construction, the essential features of the Romanesque style were the rounded arch, massive stone walls, enormous piers, small windows, and the predominance of horizontal lines. The plainness of interiors was sometimes relieved by mosaics or frescoes in bright colors, and, a very important innovation for Christian art, the introduction of sculptural decoration, both within and without. For the first time, full-length human figures appeared on facades. These are usually grave and elongated far beyond natural dimensions, but they have much evocative power and represent the first manifestations of a revived interest in sculpting the human form.

In the course of the twelfth and thirteenth centuries the Romanesque style was supplanted throughout most of Europe by the Gothic. Although trained art historians can see how certain traits of the one style led to the development of the other, the actual appearance of the two styles is enormously different. In fact, the two seem as different as the epic is different from the romance, an appropriate analogy because the Gothic style emerged in France in the mid–twelfth century exactly when the romance did, and because it was far more sophisticated, graceful, and elegant than its predecessor, in the same way that the romance compared with the epic. The rapid development and acceptance of the Gothic shows for a last time—if any more proof be needed—that the twelfth century was experimental and dynamic, arguably at least as much as the twentieth. When the abbey church of St. Denis, venerated as the shrine of the French patron saint and burial place of French kings, was torn down in 1144 in order to make room for a much larger one in the strikingly new Gothic style, it was as if the president of the United States were to tear down the White House and replace it with a Mies van der Rohe or Frank Lloyd Wright edifice. Such an act today would be highly improbable, or at least would create an enormous uproar. But in the twelfth century the equivalent act actually happened and was taken in stride.

Gothic architecture was one of the most intricate of building styles. Its basic elements were the pointed arch, groined and ribbed vaulting, and the flying buttress. These devices made possible a much lighter and loftier construction than could ever have been achieved with the round arch and the engaged pier of the Romanesque. In fact, the

(2) the development of the Gothic style

Elements of the Gothic style

Left: *Rheims Cathedral.* Built between 1220 and 1299, this High Gothic cathedral places great stress on the vertical elements. The gabled portals, the windows above the doorways, the gallery of royal statues, and the multitude of pinnacles all accentuate the height of the structue. Right: *The High Chapel of La Sainte-Chapelle, Paris.* High Gothic is here carried to its logical extreme. Slender columns, tracery, and stained-glass windows take the place of walls.

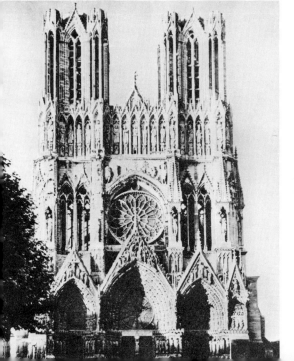

See color plates following
page 384

*The significance of Gothic
architecture*

Gothic cathedral could be described as a skeletal framework of stone enclosed by enormous windows. Other features included lofty spires, rose windows, delicate tracery in stone, elaborately sculptured facades, multiple columns, and the use of gargoyles, or representations of mythical monsters, as decorative devices. Ornamentation in the best of the cathedrals was generally concentrated on the exterior. Except for the stained glass windows and the intricate carving on woodwork and altars, interiors were kept rather simple and occasionally almost severe. But the inside of the Gothic cathedral was never somber or gloomy. The stained glass windows served not to exclude the light but to glorify it, to catch the rays of sunlight and suffuse them with a richness and warmth of color which nature itself could hardly duplicate even in its happiest moods.

Many people still think of the Gothic cathedral as the expression of purely ascetic otherworldliness, but this estimation is highly inaccurate. Certainly all churches are dedicated to the glory of God and hope for life everlasting, but Gothic ones sometimes included stained glass scenes of daily life that had no overt religious significance at all. More important, Gothic sculpture of religious figures such as Jesus, the Virgin, and the saints was becoming far more naturalistic than anything hitherto created in the medieval West. So also was the sculptural representation of plant and animal life, for interest in the human person and in the world of natural beauty was no longer considered sinful. Moreover, Gothic architecture was also an expression of the medieval intellectual genius. Each cathedral, with its mass of symbolic figures, was a kind of encyclopedia of medieval knowledge carved in stone for

Gothic Sculpture. The three kings bearing gifts, from the thirteenth-century cathedral of Amiens. Note the greater naturalism in comparison to the Romanesque sculpture shown on p. 476.

those who could not read. Finally, Gothic cathedrals were manifestations of urban pride. Always located in the growing medieval cities, they were meant to be both centers of community life and expressions of a town's greatness. When a new cathedral went up the people of the entire community participated in erecting it, and rightfully regarded it as almost their own property. Many of the Gothic cathedrals were the products of urban rivalries. Each city or town sought to overawe its neighbor with ever bigger or taller buildings, to the degree that ambitions sometimes got out of bounds and many of the cathedrals were left unfinished. But most of the finished ones are still vast enough. Built to last into eternity, they provide the most striking visual manifestation of the soaring exuberance of their age.

Surveys of high-medieval accomplishments often omit drama and music, but such oversights are unfortunate. Our own modern drama descends at least as much from the medieval form as from the classical one. Throughout the medieval period some Latin classical plays were known in manuscript but were never performed. Instead drama was born all over again within the Church. In the early Middle Ages certain passages in the liturgy began to be acted out. Then, in the twelfth century, primarily in Paris, these were superseded by short religious plays in Latin, performed inside the Church. Rapidly thereafter, and still in twelfth-century Paris, the Latin plays were supplemented or supplanted by ones in the vernacular so that the whole congregation could understand them. Then, around 1200, these started to be performed outside, in front of the Church, so that they would not take time away from the services. As soon as that happened, drama entered the everyday world: nonreligious stories were introduced, character portrayal was expanded, and the way was fully prepared for the Elizabethans and Shakespeare.

The revival of drama

As the drama grew out of developments within the liturgy and then moved far beyond them, so did characteristically Western music. Until the High Middle Ages Western music was *homophonic,* as is most non-Western music even today. That is, it developed only one melody at a time without any harmonic background. The great high-medieval invention was *polyphony,* or the playing of two or more harmonious melodies together. Some experiments along these lines may have been made in the West as early as the tenth century, but the most fundamental breakthrough was achieved in the cathedral of Paris around 1170, when the Mass was first sung by two voices weaving together two different melodies in "counterpoint." Roughly concurrently, systems of musical notation were invented and perfected so that performance no longer had to rely on memory and could become more complex. All the greatness of Western music followed from these first steps.

*Medieval music:
polyphony*

It may have been noticed that many of the same people who made such important contributions to learning, thought, literature, architecture, drama, and music, must have intermingled with each other in the Paris of the High Middle Ages. Some of them no doubt prayed together in the cathedral of Notre Dame. The names of the leading scholars are remembered, but the names of most of the others are forgotten. Yet taken together they did as much for civilization and created as many enduring monuments as their counterparts in ancient Athens. If their names are forgotten, their achievements in many different ways live on still.

SELECTED READINGS

• *Items so designated are available in paperback editions.*

RELIGION AND THE CRUSADES

• Barraclough, G., *The Medieval Papacy*, New York, 1968. A forcefully argued analytical treatment. Noteworthy too for its illustrations.

Daniel-Rops, H., *Cathedral and Crusade*, 2 vols., New York, 1963. The best survey from a Roman Catholic perspective.

Erdmann, Carl, *The Origin of the Idea of Crusade*, Princeton, N.J., 1978. A brilliant advanced work on the background to the First Crusade.

Lambert, Malcolm, *Medieval Heresy*, London, 1977. A masterful synthesis.

Leclercq, Jean, *Bernard of Clairvaux and the Cistercian Spirit*, Kalamazoo, Mich., 1976.

• Mayer, Hans Eberhard, *The Crusades*, New York, 1972. The best one-volume survey.

Moorman, J. R. H., *A History of the Franciscan Order from its Origins to the Year 1517*, Oxford, 1968. Exhaustive.

Runciman, S., *A History of the Crusades*, 3 vols., Cambridge, 1951–54. Colorful and engrossing.

Southern, R. W., *Western Society and the Church in the Middle Ages*, Baltimore, 1970. An extremely insightful and well-written interpretation of the interplay between society and religion.

Tellenbach, G., *Church, State and Christian Society at the Time of the Investiture Contest*, Oxford, 1940. Stresses revolutionary aspects of Gregory VII's thought and career.

Ullmann, Walter, *A Short History of the Papacy in the Middle Ages*, 2nd ed., London, 1974.

THOUGHT, LETTERS, AND THE ARTS

• Baldwin, John W., *The Scholastic Culture of the Middle Ages*, Lexington, Mass., 1971. A fine introduction.

Bergin, T. G., *Dante*, New York, 1965.

Chenu, M. D., *Toward Understanding St. Thomas*, Chicago, 1964. An excellent approach to St. Thomas's work by a contemporary Dominican.

Cobban, Alan B., *The Medieval Universities*, London, 1975. The best shorter treatment in English.

• Crombie, A. C., *Medieval and Early Modern Science*, Vol. I, rev. ed., New York, 1959.

Curtius, E. R., *European Literature and the Latin Middle Ages,* New York, 1953. An exhaustive treatment of medieval Latin literature in terms of its classical background and influence on later times.

Frankl, P., *Gothic Architecture,* Baltimore, 1962.

Gilson, E., *Reason and Revelation in the Middle Ages,* New York, 1938. A brief but illuminating treatment by the greatest modern student of Scholasticism.

• Haskins, C. H., *The Renaissance of the Twelfth Century,* Cambridge, Mass., 1927. Treats Latin writings in many different genres.

• Henderson, George, *Gothic,* Baltimore, 1967.

Holmes, Urban T., *A History of Old French Literature,* 2nd ed., London, 1948.

Hoppin, Richard H., *Medieval Music,* New York, 1978.

• Knowles, David, *The Evolution of Medieval Thought,* New York, 1962. A very authoritative and well-written but often difficult survey.

Leclercq, Jean, *The Love of Learning and the Desire for God,* New York, 1961. About monastic culture, with special reference to St. Bernard.

Leff, G., *Paris and Oxford Universities in the Thirteenth and Fourteenth Centuries,* New York, 1968. Covers both thought and institutions of learning.

• Lewis, C. S., *The Discarded Image,* Cambridge, 1964.

• Mâle, E., *The Gothic Image,* New York, 1913.

• Morris, Colin, *The Discovery of the Individual,* London, 1972. A provocative interpretation which sees "individualism" as a twelfth-century discovery.

Reese, Gustave, *Music in the Middle Ages,* New York, 1940.

Southern, R. W., *Medieval Humanism,* New York, 1970. A collection of essays, almost all of which are exciting. Most exciting is the title piece.

• Ullmann, W., *Medieval Political Thought,* rev. ed., Baltimore, 1976. The best short survey.

Van Steenberghen, F., *Aristotle in the West,* New York, 1970. A short account of the recovery of Aristotelian thought in the High Middle Ages.

• Von Simson, O., *The Gothic Cathedral,* New York, 1956. A controversial argument that Gothic architecture was meant to be "scientific."

SOURCE MATERIALS

• *An Aquinas Reader,* ed. Mary T. Clark, New York, 1972.

• Chrétien de Troyes, *Arthurian Romances,* tr. W. W. Comfort, New York, 1914.

• Dante, *The Divine Comedy,* tr. J. Ciardi, New York, 1977.

• Goldin, F., ed., *Lyrics of the Troubadours and Trouvères,* New York, 1973.

• Gottfried von Strassburg, *Tristan,* tr. A. T. Hatto, Baltimore, 1960.

• Joinville and Villehardouin, *Chronicles of the Crusades,* tr. M. R. B. Shaw, Baltimore, 1963.

• *The Letters of Abelard and Heloise* (includes Abelard's *Story of My Calamities*), tr. B. Radice, Baltimore, 1974.

• Peters, Edward, ed., *The First Crusade: The Chronicle of Fulcher of Chartres and Other Source Materials,* Philadelphia, 1971.

The Romance of the Rose, tr. Harry W. Robbins, New York, 1962.
- *The Song of Roland,* tr. F. Goldin, New York, 1978.
- Thorndike, Lynn, ed., *University Records and Life in the Middle Ages,* New York, 1944.
- Tierney, Brian, ed., *The Crisis of Church and State, 1050–1300,* Englewood Cliffs, N.J., 1964. An excellent anthology of readings introduced and connected by masterful commentary.
- Wolfram von Eschenbach, *Parzival,* tr. H. M. Mustard and C. E. Passage, New York, 1961.

Chapter 16

THE LATER MIDDLE AGES
(1300–1500)

My lot has been to live amidst a storm
Of varying disturbing circumstances.
For you . . . a better age awaits.
Our descendants—the darkness once dispersed—
Can come again to the old radiance.

> —The poet Petrarch,
> writing in the 1340s

If the High Middle Ages were "times of feasts," then the late Middle Ages were "times of famine." From about 1300 until the middle or latter part of the fifteenth century calamities struck throughout western Europe with appalling severity and dismaying persistence. Famine first prevailed because agriculture was impeded by soil exhaustion, colder weather, and torrential rainfalls. Then, on top of those "acts of God," came the most terrible natural disaster of all: the dreadful plague known as the "Black Death," which cut broad swaths of mortality throughout western Europe. As if all that were not enough, incessant warfare continually brought hardship and desolation. Common people suffered most because they were most exposed to raping, stabbing, looting, and burning by soldiers and organized bands of freebooters. After an army passed through a region one might see miles of smoldering ruins littered with putrefying corpses; in many places the desolation was so great that wolves roamed the countryside and even entered the outskirts of the cities. In short, if the serene Virgin symbolized the High Middle Ages, the grinning death's-head symbolized the succeeding period. For these reasons we should not look to the later Middle Ages for the dramatic progress we saw transpiring earlier; but this is not to say that there was no progress at all. In the last two centuries of the Middle Ages Europeans dis-

The later Middle Ages: castastrophe and adaptation

played a tenacious perseverance in the face of adversity. Instead of abandoning themselves to apathy, they resolutely sought to adjust themselves to changed circumstances. Thus there was no collapse of civilization as there was with the fall of the Roman Empire, but rather a period of transition that resulted in preserving and building upon what was most solid in Europe's earlier legacy.

1. ECONOMIC DEPRESSION AND THE EMERGENCE OF A NEW EQUILIBRIUM

Economic crisis

By around 1300 the agricultural expansion of the High Middle Ages had reached its limits. Thereafter yields and areas under cultivation began to decline, causing a decline in the whole European economy that was accelerated by the disruptive effects of war. Accordingly, the first half of the fourteenth century was a time of growing economic depression. The coming of the Black Death in 1347 made this depression particularly acute because it completely disrupted the affairs of daily life. Subsequent recurrences of the plague and protracted warfare continued to depress most of the European economy until deep into the fifteenth century. But between roughly 1350–1450 Europeans learned how to adjust to the new economic circumstances and succeeded in placing their economy on a sounder basis. This became most evident after around 1450, when the tapering off of disease and warfare permitted a slow, but steady economic recovery. All told, therefore, despite a prolonged depression of roughly 150 years, Europe emerged in the later fifteenth century with a healthier economy than it had known earlier.

Agricultural adversity

The limits to agricultural expansion reached around 1300 were natural ones. There was a limit to the amount of land that could be cleared and a limit to the amount of crops that could be raised without the introduction of scientific farming. In fact, Europeans had gone further in clearing and cultivating than they should have: in the enthusiasm of the high-medieval colonization movement, marginal lands had been cleared that were not rich enough to sustain intense cultivation. In addition, even the best plots were becoming overworked. To make matters worse, after around 1300 the weather deteriorated. Whereas western Europe had been favored with a drying and warming trend in the eleventh and twelfth centuries, the fourteenth century saw the climate become colder and wetter. Although the average decline in temperature over the course of the century was only at most 1° Centigrade, this was sufficient to curtail viticulture in many northern areas such as England. Cereal farming too became increasingly impractical in far northern regions because the growing season became too short: in Greenland and parts of Scandinavia agricultural settlements were abandoned entirely. Increased rainfall also took its toll.

Terrible floods that deluged all of northwestern Europe in 1315 ruined crops and caused a prolonged, deathly famine. For three years peasants were so driven by hunger that they ate their seed grain, ruining their chances for a full recovery in the following season. In desperation they also ate cats, dogs, and rats. Many peasants were so exposed to unsanitary conditions and weakened by malnutrition that they became highly susceptible to disease. Thus there was an appalling death rate. In one Flemish city a tenth of the population was buried within a six-month period of 1316 alone. Relatively settled farming conditions returned after 1318, but in many parts of Europe heavy rains or other climatic disasters came again. In Italy floods swept away Florentine bridges in 1333 and a tidal wave destroyed the port of Amalfi in 1343. With nature so recurrently capricious economic life could only suffer.

Although ruinous wars combined with famine to kill off many, Europe remained overpopulated until the middle of the fourteenth century. The reason for this was that population growth was still outstripping food supply. Since people continued to multiply while cereal production declined, there was just not enough food to go around. Accordingly, grain prices soared and the poor throughout Europe paid the penalty in hunger. And then a disaster struck which was so appalling that it seemed to many to presage the end of the world.

This was the Black Death, a combined onslaught of bubonic and pneumonic plague which first swept through Europe from 1347 to 1350, and returned at periodic intervals for roughly the next hundred years. This calamity was fully comparable—in terms of the death, dislocation, and horror it wrought—to the two world wars of the twentieth century. The clinical effects of the plague were hideous. Once infected with bubonic plague by a flea-bite, the diseased person would develop enormous swellings in the groin or armpits; black spots might appear on the arms and legs, diarrhea would ensue, and the victim would die between the third and fifth day. If the infection came in the pneumonic form, i.e., caused by inhalation, there would be coughing of blood instead of swellings, and death would follow within three days. Some people went to bed healthy and were dead the next morning after a night of agony; ships with dead crews floated aimlessly on the seas. Although the successive epidemics left a few localities unscathed, the overall demographic effects of the plague were devastating. To take just a few examples: the population of Toulouse declined from roughly 30,000 in 1335, to 26,000 in 1385, to 8,000 in 1430; the total population of eastern Normandy fell by 30 percent between 1347 and 1357, and again by 30 percent before 1380; in the rural area around Pistoia a population depletion of about 60 percent occurred between 1340 and 1404. Altogether, the combined effects of famine, war, and, above all, plague reduced the total population of western Europe by at least one half and probably more like two-thirds between 1300 and 1450.

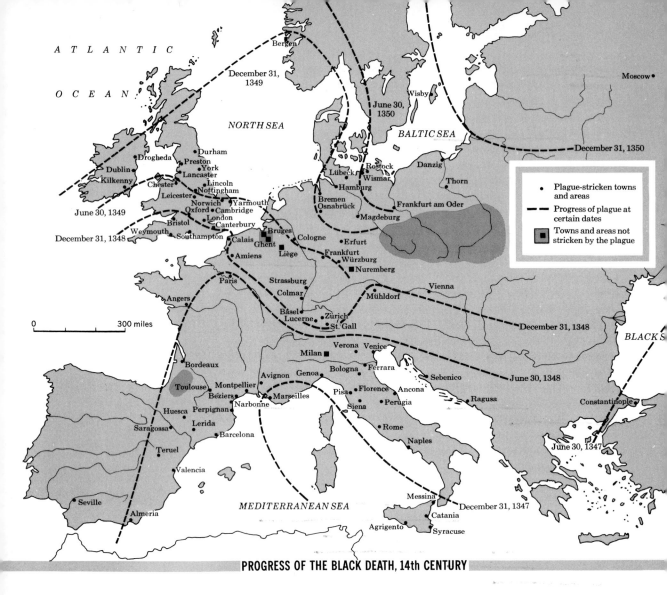

ATLANTIC
OCEAN

NORTH SEA

BALTIC SEA

MEDITERRANEAN SEA

BLACK S

Bergen

December 31,
1349

Wisby

June 30,
1350

Moscow

December 31, 1350

Drogheda
Dublin
Kilkenny
Chester
June 30, 1349

Durham
Preston
York
Lancaster
Lincoln
Nottingham

Rostock
Lübeck
Wismar
Hamburg

Danzig

Thorn

December 31, 1348
Weymouth
Bristol

Leicester
Norwich
Oxford · Cambridge
London
Southampton Canterbury
Calais
Amiens
Paris

Yarmouth

Bremen
Osnabrück
Bruges
Ghent
Liège

Magdeburg

Frankfurt am Oder

Cologne
Frankfurt
Würzburg
Nuremberg

Erfurt

Angers

Strassburg
Colmar
Bâsel
Lucerne
St. Gall

Zürich

Mühldorf

Vienna

December 31, 1348

Bordeaux

Toulouse

Milan

Verona Venice

December 31, 1347

Montpellier
Béziers
Narbonne
Huesca
Perpignan
Lerida
Saragossa
Teruel
Valencia

Avignon Genoa

Marseilles

Pisa

Bologna
Florence
Siena
Perugia
Rome

Ferrara

Ancona

Sebenico

Ragusa

June 30, 1348

Constantinople

June 30, 1347

Seville
Almeria

Barcelona

Naples

Messina
Catania
Agrigento Syracuse

Legend:

- Plague-stricken towns and areas
- Progress of plague at certain dates
- Towns and areas not stricken by the plague

0   300 miles

PROGRESS OF THE BLACK DEATH, 14th CENTURY

The Black Death disrupts society and economy

At first, the Black Death caused great hardships for most of the survivors. Since panic-stricken people wished to avoid contagion, many fled from their jobs to seek isolation. Town-dwellers fled to the country and country-dwellers fled from each other. Even the pope retreated to the interior of his palace and allowed no one entrance. With large numbers dead and others away from their posts, harvests were left rotting, manufacturing was disrupted, and conveyance systems were abandoned. Hence basic commodities became scarcer and prices rose. For these reasons the onslaught of the plague greatly intensified Europe's economic crisis.

But after around 1400 the new demographic realities began to turn prices around and alter basic economic patterns. Particularly, the prices of staple foodstuffs began to decline because production gradually returned to normal and there were fewer mouths to feed. Recurrent reappearances of the plague or natural disasters sometimes caused prices to fluctuate greatly in certain years, but overall prices of basic commodities throughout most of the fifteenth century went down or remained stable. This trend led to new agricultural specialization. Since cereals were cheaper, people could afford to spend a greater percentage of their income on comparative luxuries such as dairy products, meat, and wine. Hitherto farmers all over Europe had concentrated on cereals because bread was the staff of life, but now it was wisest, particularly in areas of poorer soil or unpropitious climate, to shift to specialized production. Depending upon whatever seemed most feasible, land might be used for the raising of livestock for milk, grapes for wine, or malt for beer. Specialized regional economies resulted: parts of England were given over to sheep-raising or beer production, parts of France concentrated on wine, and Sweden traded butter for cheap German grain. Most areas of Europe turned to what they could do best, and reciprocal trade of basic commodities over long distances created a sound new commercial equilibrium.

Economic consequences of the Black Death: (1) agricultural specialization

Another economic result of the Black Death was an increase in the relative importance of towns and cities. Urban manufacturers usually could respond more flexibly than landlords to drastically changed economic conditions because their production capabilities were more elastic. When markets shrank, manufacturers could cut back supply more easily to match demand; they could also raise production more easily when circumstances warranted. Thus urban entrepreneurs bounced back from disaster more quickly than landowners. Often

(2) the growth in importance of urban centers

The Four Horsemen of the Apocalypse. This woodcut, done by Albrecht Dürer at the end of the fifteenth century, well illustrates the mood of the later Middle Ages, when humans were overwhelmed by war, famine, and disease.

they took advantage of their greater strength to attract rural labor by means of higher salaries. Thereby the population balance between countryside and town was shifted slightly in favor of the latter.

Certain urban centers, especially those in northern Germany and northern Italy, profited the most from the new circumstances. In Germany a group of cities and towns under the leadership of Lübeck and Bremen allied in the so-called Hanseatic League to control long-distance trade in the Baltic and North Seas. Their fleets transported German grain to Scandinavia and brought back dairy products, fish, and furs. The enhanced European per capita ability to buy luxury goods brought new wealth to the northern Italian trading cities of Genoa and, especially, Venice because these cities controlled the importation of spices from the East. Greater expenditures on luxury also aided the economies of Florence, Venice, Milan, and other neighboring cities because those cities concentrated on the manufacture of silks and linens, light woolens, and other fine cloths. Milan, in addition, prospered from its armaments industry, which kept the warring European states supplied with armor and weapons. Because of varying local conditions, some cities and towns, above all those of Flanders, became economically depressed, but altogether European urban centers profited remarkably well from the new economic circumstances and emphasis on specialization.

The changed circumstances also helped stimulate the development of sophisticated business, accounting, and banking techniques. Because sharp fluctuations in prices made investments precarious, new forms of partnerships were created to minimize risks. Insurance contracts were also invented to take some of the risk out of shipping. Europe's most useful accounting invention, double-entry bookkeeping, was first put into use in Italy in the mid–fourteenth century and spread rapidly thereafter north of the Alps. This allowed for quick dis-

A Late-Medieval Italian Town. By Ambrogio Lorenzetti.

covery of computational errors and easy overview of profits and losses, credits and debits. Large-scale banking had already become common after the middle of the thirteenth century, but the economic crises of the later Middle Ages encouraged banks to alter some of their ways of doing business. Most important was the development of prudent branch-banking techniques, especially by the Florentine house of the Medici. Earlier banks had built branches, but the Medici bank, which flourished from 1397 to 1494, organized theirs along the lines of a modern holding company. The Medici branches, located in London, Bruges, and Avignon, as well as several Italian cities, were dominated by senior partners from the Medici family who followed common policies. Formally, however, each branch was a separate partnership which did not carry any other branch down with it if it collapsed. Other Italian banks experimented with advanced credit techniques. Some even allowed their clients to transfer funds between each other without any real money changing hands. Such "book transfers" were at first executed only by oral command, but around 1400 they started to be carried out by written orders. These were the earliest ancestors of the modern check.

In surveying the two centuries of late-medieval economic history, both the role of nature and that of human beings must be emphasized. The premodern history of all parts of the globe tends to show that whenever population becomes excessive natural controls manage to reduce it. Bad weather and disease may come at any time, but when humans are already suffering from hunger and conditions of overcrowding, the results of natural disasters will be particularly devastating. That certainly is what happened in the fourteenth century. Nature intervened cruelly in human affairs, but no matter how cruel the immediate effects were, the results were ultimately beneficial. By 1450 a far smaller population had a higher average standard of living than the population of 1300. In this result humans too played their part. Because people were determined to make the best of the new circumstances and avoid a recurrence of economic depression, they managed to reorganize their economic life and place it on a sounder footing. The gross European product of about 1450 was probably smaller than it was in 1300, but this is not surprising given the much smaller population. In fact, per capita output had risen with per capita income, and the European economy was ready to move on to new conquests.

The interaction of man and nature in late-medieval economic history

2. SOCIAL AND EMOTIONAL DISLOCATION

Before the healthy new equilibrium was reached, the economic crises of the later Middle Ages contributed from about 1300 to 1450 to provoking a rash of lower-class rural and urban insurrections more numerous than Europe had ever known before or has ever known since.

Social crisis: lower-class revolts

Rural insurrections: the
Jacquerie

It used to be thought that these were all caused by extreme deprivation, but as we will see, that was not always the case.

The one large-scale rural uprising that was most clearly caused by extreme poverty was the northern French "Jacquerie" of 1358. This took its name from the prototypical French peasant, "Jacques Bonhomme," who had finally suffered more than he could endure. In 1348 and 1349 the Black Death had brought its terror and wreaked havoc with the economy and with people's lives. Then a flare-up of war between England and France had spread great desolation over the countryside. The peasants, as usual in late-medieval warfare, suffered most from the pillaging and burning carried out by the rapacious soldiers. To make matters even less endurable, after the English decisively defeated the French in 1356 at the Battle of Poitiers the French king, John II, and numerous aristocrats had to be ransomed. As always in such cases, the peasants were asked to bear the heaviest share of the burden, but by 1358 they had had enough and rose up with astounding ferocity. Without any clear program they burned down castles, murdered their lords, and raped their lords' wives. Undoubtedly their intense (and justified) economic resentments were the major cause for the uprising, but it should be said too that 1358 was a year of deep political uncertainty for northern France, thus making an uprising of peasants possible. While the king was in captivity in England, groups of townsmen were trying to reform the governmental system by limiting monarchical powers, and certain aristocrats were plotting to seize power. In the meantime, John II's son, Charles, was trying both to raise a large ransom for his father and subdue the crown's enemies. Although we can never be certain, it seems unlikely that the peasants would have revolted had they not sensed an opportunity to take advantage of France's political confusion. But in fact the opportunity was not as great as they may have thought: within a month the privileged powers closed ranks, massacred the rebels, and quickly restored order.

Background of the English
Peasants' Revolt

The English Peasants' Revolt of 1381—the most serious lower-class rebellion in English history—is frequently bracketed with the Jacquerie, but its causes were very different. Instead of being a revolt of abject desperation, it was one of frustrated rising expectations. By 1381 the effects of the Black Death should have been working in favor of the peasants. Above all, a shortage of labor should have placed their services in demand. In fact, the incidence of the plague did help to increase manumissions (i.e., freeings) of serfs and raise salaries or lower rents of free farm laborers. But aristocratic landlords fought back to preserve their own incomes. They succeeded in having legislation passed that aimed to keep wages at pre-plague levels and force landless laborers to work at the lower rates. Aristocrats furthermore often tried to exact all their old dues and unpaid services. Because the peasants were unwilling to be pushed down into their previous poverty and subservience, a collision was bound to take place.

The spark that ignited the great revolt of 1381 was an attempt to collect a national tax levied equally on every head instead of being made proportional to wealth. This was an unprecedented development in English tax-collecting that the peasants understandably found unfair. Two head-taxes were levied without resistance in 1377 and 1379, but when agents tried to collect a third in 1381 the peasantry rose up to resist and seek redress of all their grievances. First they burned local records and sacked the dwellings of those they considered their exploiters; then they marched on London, where they executed the lord chancellor and treasurer of England. Recognizing the gravity of the situation, the fifteen-year-old king, Richard II, went out to meet the peasants and won their confidence by promising to abolish serfdom and keep rents low; meanwhile, during negotiations, the peasant leader, Wat Tyler, was murdered in a squabble with the king's escort. Lacking leadership, the peasants, who mistakenly thought they had achieved their aims, rapidly dispersed. But once the boy-king was no longer in danger of his life he kept none of his promises. Instead, the scattered peasant forces were quickly hunted down and a few alleged trouble-makers were executed without any mass reprisals. The revolt itself therefore accomplished nothing, but within a few decades the natural play of economic forces caused serfdom to disappear and considerably improved the lot of the rural wage laborer.

The course of the revolt

Other rural revolts took place in other parts of Europe, but we may now look at some urban ones. Conventionally, the urban revolts of the later Middle Ages are viewed as uprisings of exploited proletarians who were more oppressed than ever because of the effects of economic depression. But this is probably too great a simplification because each case differed and complex forces were always at work. For example, an uprising in the north German town of Brunswick in 1374 was much less a movement of the poor against the rich than a political upheaval in which one political alliance replaced another. A different north German uprising, in Lübeck in 1408, has been aptly described as a "taxpayer's" revolt. This again was less a confrontation of the poor versus the rich than an attempt of a faction that was out of power to initiate less costly government.

The character of urban uprisings

The nearest thing to a real proletarian revolt was the uprising in 1378 of the Florentine *Ciompi* (pronounced "cheeompi"). The Ciompi were wool-combers who had the misfortune to be engaged in an industry that had become particularly depressed. Some of them had lost their jobs and others were frequently cheated or underpaid by the masters of the woolen industry. The latter wielded great political power in Florence, and thus could pass economic legislation in their own favor. This fact in itself meant that if there were to be economic reforms, they would have to go together with political changes. As events transpired it was a political crisis that called the Ciompi into direct action. In 1378 Florence had become exhausted by three years of war with the papacy. Certain patrician leaders overthrew the old

The Ciompi Revolt

regime to alter the war policy and gain their own political advantage. Circumstances led them to seek the support of the lower classes and, once stirred up, the Ciompi became emboldened after a few months to launch their own far more radical rebellion. This was inspired primarily by economic hardship and grievances, but personal hatreds also played a role. The Ciompi gained power for six weeks, during which they tried to institute tax relief, fuller employment, and representation of themselves and other proletarian groups in the Florentine government. But they could not maintain their hold on power and a new oligarchical government revoked all their reforms.

General observations on the nature of popular uprisings

If we try to draw any general conclusions about these various uprisings, we can certainly say that few if any of them would have occurred had there not been an economic crisis. But political considerations always had some influence, and the rebels in some uprisings were more prosperous than in others. It is noteworthy that all the genuinely lower-class uprisings of economically desperate groups quickly failed. This was certainly because the upper classes were more accustomed to wielding power and giving orders; even more important, they had access to the money and troops necessary to quell revolts. Sometimes elements within the lower classes might fight among themselves, whereas the privileged always managed to rally into a united front when faced by a lower-class threat to their domination. In addition, lower-class rebels were usually more intent on redressing immediate grievances than on developing fully coherent long-term governmental programs; inspiring ideals for cohesive action were generally lacking. The case of the Hussite Revolution in Bohemia—to be treated later— shows that religion in the later Middle Ages was a more effective rallying ground for large numbers of people than were political, economic, and social demands.

The crisis of the late-medieval aristocracy

Although the upper classes succeeded in overcoming popular uprisings, they perceived the economic and emotional insecurities of the later Middle Ages and the possibility of revolt as a constant threat, and became obsessed with maintaining their privileged social status. Late-medieval aristocrats were in a precarious economic position because they gained most of their income from land. In times when grain prices and rents were falling and wages rising, landowners were obviously in economic trouble. Some aristocrats probably also felt threatened by the rapid rise of merchants and financiers who could make quick killings because of sharp market fluctuations. In practice, really wealthy merchants bought land and were absorbed into the aristocracy. Moreover, most landowning aristocrats were able to stave off economic threats by expert estate management; in fact, many of them actually became richer than ever. But most still felt more exposed to social and economic insecurities than before. The result was that they tried to set up artificial barriers behind which they separated themselves from other classes.

A Party of Late Medieval Aristocrats. Notice the pointed shoes and the women's pointed hats, twice as high as their heads.

Two of the most striking examples of this separation were the aristocratic emphasis on luxury, and the formation of exclusive chivalric orders. The late Middle Ages was the period par excellence of aristocratic ostentation. While famine or disease raged, aristocrats regaled themselves with lavish banquets and magnificent pageants. At one feast in Flanders in 1468 a table decoration was forty-six feet high. Aristocratic clothing too was extremely ostentatious: men wore long, pointed shoes, and women ornately festooned headdresses. Throughout history rich people have always enjoyed dressing up, but the aristocrats of the later Middle Ages seem to have done so obsessively to comfort themselves and convey the message that they were entirely different from others. The insistence on maintaining a sharply defined social hierarchy also accounts for the late-medieval proliferation of chivalric orders, such as those of the Knights of the Garter or the Golden Fleece. By joining together in exclusive orders which prescribed special conduct and boasted special insignia of membership, aristocrats who felt threatened by social pressures again tried to set themselves off from others, in effect, by putting up a sign that read "for members only."

Another explanation for the exorbitant stress on luxury is that it was a form of escapism. Aristocrats who were continually exposed to the sight and smell of death must have found it emotionally comforting to retreat into a dream-world of elegant manners, splendid feasts, and multicolored clothes. In a parallel fashion, nonaristocrats who

Duke Philip the Good of Burgundy. The duke proudly wears the emblem of the Order of the Golden Fleece around his neck.

A Late-Medieval Crucifixion Scene. The Virgin has to be held up to keep from swooning, and the angels are weeping.

could not afford such luxuries often sought relief from the vision of death in crude public entertainments: for example, crowds would watch blind beggars try to catch a squealing pig but beat each other with clubs instead, or they would cheer on boys to clamber up greasy poles in order to win prizes of geese.

It must not be thought, however, that late-medieval people gave themselves over to riotous living without interruption. In fact, the very same people of all classes who sought elegant or boisterous diversions just as often went to the other emotional extreme when faced by the psychic stress caused by the troubles of the age, and abandoned themselves to sorrow. Throughout the period grown men and women shed tears in abundance. The queen mother of France wept in public when she first viewed her grandson; the great preacher Vincent Ferrer had to interrupt his sermons on Christ's Passion and the Last Judgment because he and his audience were sobbing too convulsively; and the English king, Edward II, supposedly wept so much when imprisoned that he gushed forth enough hot water for his own shave. The last story taxes the imagination, but it does illustrate well what contemporaries thought was possible. We know for certain that the Church encouraged crying because of the survival of moving statuettes of weeping St. Johns, which were obviously designed to call forth tears from their viewers.

People also were encouraged by preachers to brood on the Passion of Christ and on their own mortality. Fearsome crucifixes abounded,

A Dead Man Before His Judge. A late-medieval reminder of human mortality.

and the figure of the Virgin Mary was less a smiling madonna than a sorrowing mother: now she was most frequently depicted slumping with grief at the foot of the cross, or holding the dead Christ in her lap. The late-medieval obsession with mortality can also still be seen in sculptures, frescoes, and book illustrations that reminded viewers of the brevity of life and the torments of hell. The characteristic tombs of the High Middle Ages were mounted with sculptures that either showed the deceased in some action that had been typical of his or her accomplishments in life, or else in a state of repose that showed death to be nothing more than peaceful sleep. But in the late fourteenth century, tombs appeared that displayed the physical ravages of death in the most gruesome ways imaginable: emaciated corpses were displayed with protruding intestines or covered with snakes or toads. Some tombs bore inscriptions stating that the viewer would soon be "a fetid cadaver, food for worms"; some warned chillingly: "What you are, I was; what I am, you will be." Omnipresent illustrations displayed figures of grinning death, with his scythe, carrying off elegant and healthy men and women, or sadistic devils roasting pain-wracked humans in hell. Because people who painted or brooded on such pictures might the next day indulge in excessive revels, late-medieval culture often seems to border on the manic-depressive. But apparently such extreme reactions were necessary to help people cope with their fears.

3. TRIALS FOR THE CHURCH AND HUNGER FOR THE DIVINE

The intense concentration on the meaning of death was also a manifestation of a very deep and pervasive religiosity. The religious enthusiasm of the High Middle Ages by no means flagged after 1300; if anything, it became more intense. But religious enthusiasm took on new forms of expression because of the institutional difficulties of the Church and the turmoils of the age.

After the humiliation and death of Pope Boniface VIII in 1303, the Church experienced a period of institutional crisis that was as severe and prolonged as the contemporary economic crisis. We may distinguish three phases: the so-called Babylonian Captivity of the papacy, 1305–1378; the Great Schism, 1378–1417; and the period of the Italian territorial papacy, 1417–1517. During the Babylonian Captivity the papacy was located in Avignon instead of Rome and was generally subservient to the interests of the French crown. There were several reasons for this: the most obvious was that since the test of strength between Philip the Fair and Boniface VIII had resulted in a clear victory for the French king, subsequent popes were unwilling to risk French royal ire. In fact, once the popes recognized that they could not give orders to the French kings, they found that they had certain ad-

The Prince of the World. A stone figure from the church of St. Sebald, Nuremberg, from about 1330. From the front the man is smiling and master of all he surveys; from the rear he is crawling with vermin.

vantages to gain from currying their favor. One was a safe home in southern France, away from the tumult of Italy. Central Italy and the city of Rome in the fourteenth century had become so politically turbulent and rebellious that the pope could not even count on finding personal safety there, let alone sufficiently peaceful conditions to maintain orderly ecclesiastical administration. But no such danger existed in Avignon. Even though Avignon was not then part of the French kingdom—it was the major city of a small papal territory—French military might was close enough to guarantee the pope his much needed security. Another advantage of papal subservience to French power was help from the French in pursuing mutually advantageous policies in Germany and southern Italy. Perhaps most important was a working agreement whereby the French king would propose his own candidates to become bishops and the pope would then name them, thereby gaining sizable monetary payments. After 1305 the pro-French system became so entrenched that a majority of cardinals and all the popes until 1378 were themselves French.

At Avignon the popes were more successful than ever in pursuing their policy of centralizing the government of the Church. For the first time they worked out a really sound system of papal finance, based on the systematization of dues collected from the clergy throughout Europe. The papacy also succeeded in appointing more candidates to vacant benefices than before (in practice often naming candidates proposed by the French and English kings), and they proceeded against heresy with great determination, indeed with ruthlessness. But whatever the popes achieved in power they lost in respect and loyalty. The clergy became alienated as a result of being asked to pay so much money, and much of the laity was horrified by the corruption and unbridled luxury displayed at the papal court: there the cardinals lived more splendidly than lords, dining off peacocks, pheasants, grouse, and swans, and drinking from elaborately sculptured fountains that spouted the finest wines. Most of the Avignonese popes themselves were personally upright and abstemious, but one, Clement VI (1342–1352), was worse than his cardinals. Clement was ready to offer any spiritual benefit for money, boasted that he would appoint even a jackass as bishop if political circumstances warranted, and defended his incessant sexual transgressions by insisting that he fornicated on doctors' orders.

As time went on the pressures of informed public opinion forced the popes to promise that they would return to Rome. After one abortive attempt by Urban V in 1367, Pope Gregory XI finally did return to the Holy City in 1377. But he died a year later and then disaster struck. The college of cardinals, surrounded in Rome by clamoring Italians, yielded to local sentiment by naming an Italian as pope, who took the title of Urban VI. But most of the cardinals were Frenchmen and quickly regretted their decision, especially because Urban VI immediately began quarreling with them and revealing what were probably paranoid tendencies. Therefore, after only a few months, the French cardinals met again, declared the previous election void, and replaced Urban with one of their own number, who called himself Clement VII.

Unfortunately, however, Urban VI did not meekly resign. On the contrary, he named an entirely new Italian college of cardinals and remained entrenched in Rome. Clement VII quickly retreated with his own party to Avignon and the so-called Great Schism ensued. France and other countries in the French political orbit—such as Scotland, Castile, and Aragon—recognized Clement, while the rest of Europe recognized Urban as the true pope. For three decades Christians looked on helplessly while the rival pontiffs hurled curses at each other and the international monastic orders became divided into Roman and Avignonese camps. The death of one or the other pope did not end the schism; each camp had its own set of cardinals which promptly named either a French or Italian successor. The desperateness of the situation led a council of prelates from both camps to meet in Pisa in 1409 to depose both popes and name a new one instead. But neither the Italian nor the French pope accepted the council's decision and both had enough political support to retain some obedience. So after 1409 there were three rival claimants hurling curses instead of two.

The Great Schism was finally ended in 1417 by the Council of Constance, the largest ecclesiastical gathering in medieval history. This time the assembled prelates made certain to gain the crucial support of secular powers and also to eliminate the prior claimants before naming a new pope. After the council's election of Martin V in 1417, European ecclesiastical unity was thus fully restored. But a struggle over the nature of Church government followed immediately. The members of the Council of Constance challenged the prevailing medieval theory of papal monarchy by calling for balanced, "conciliar," government. In two momentous decrees they stated that a general council of prelates was superior in authority to the pope, and that such councils should meet regularly to govern the Church. Not surprisingly, subsequent popes—who had now returned to Rome—sought to nullify these decrees. When a new council met in Basel in 1431, in accordance with the principles laid down at Constance, the reigning pope did all he could to sabotage its activities. Ultimately he was successful: after a protracted struggle the Council of Basel dissolved in 1449 in abject failure, and the attempt to institute constitutional government in the Church was completely defeated. But the papacy only won this victory over conciliarism by gaining the support of the rulers of the European states. In separate concordats with kings and princes, the popes granted the secular rulers much authority over the various local churches. The popes thus became assured of theoretical supremacy at the cost of surrendering much real power. To compensate for this they concentrated on consolidating their own direct rule in central Italy. Most of the fifteenth-century popes ruled very much like any other princes, leading

The decline of clerical prestige

armies, jockeying for alliances, and building magnificent palaces. Hence, although they did succeed for the first time in creating a viable political state, their reputation for disinterested piety remained low.

While the papacy was undergoing these vicissitudes, the local clergy throughout Europe was undergoing a loss of prestige for several reasons. One was that the pope's greater financial demands forced the clergy to demand more from the laity, but such demands were bitterly resented, especially during times of prevailing economic crisis. Then too during outbreaks of plague the clergy sometimes fled their posts just like everyone else, but in so doing they lost whatever claim they had for being morally superior. Probably the single greatest reason for growing dissatisfaction with the clergy was the increase in lay literacy. The continued proliferation of schools and the decline in the cost of books—a subject we will treat later—made it possible for large numbers of lay people to learn how to read. Once that happened, the laity could start reading parts of the Bible, or, more frequently, popular religious primers. These made it clear that their local priests were not living according to the standards set by Jesus and the Apostles. In the meantime, the upheavals and horrors of the age drove people to seek religious solace more than ever. Finding the conventional channels of church attendance, confession, and submission to clerical authority insufficient, the laity sought supplementary or alternate routes to piety. These differed greatly from each other, but they all aimed to satisfy an immense hunger for the divine.

The most widely-traveled route was that of performing repeated acts of external devotion in the hope that they would gain the devotee divine favor on earth and salvation in the hereafter. People flocked to go on pilgrimages as never before and participated regularly in bare-

A German Flagellant Procession. These penitents hoped they could ward off the Black Death by their mutually inflicted tortures.

footed religious processions: the latter were often held twice a month and occasionally as often as once a week. Men and women also eagerly bought indulgences, i.e., papal grants, that were supposed to free them from time in purgatory, and they paid in advance for the reading of numerous requiem masses to save their souls after death. Obsession with repeating prayers reached a peak when some pious individuals tried to compute the number of drops of blood that Christ shed on the cross so that they could say the same number of Our Fathers. The most excessive and repugnant form of religious ritual in the later Middle Ages was flagellation. Some women who lived in communal houses beat themselves with the roughest animal hides, chains, and knotted thongs. A young girl who entered such a community in Poland in 1331 suffered extreme internal injuries and became completely disfigured within eleven months. Flailings were not usually performed in public, but during the first onslaught of the Black Death in 1348 and 1349, whole bands of lay people marched through northern Europe chanting and beating each other with metal-tipped scourges in the hope of appeasing the apparent divine wrath.

The growth of lay piety: (1) devotional practices

An opposite route to godliness was the inward path of mysticism. Throughout the European continent, but particularly in Germany and England, male and female mystics, both clerical and lay, sought union with God by means of "detachment," contemplation, or spiritual exercises. The most original and eloquent late-medieval mystical theorist was the German Dominican, Master Eckhart (c. 1260–1327), who taught that there was a power or "spark" deep within every human soul that was really the dwelling-place of God. By renouncing all sense of selfhood one could retreat into one's innermost recesses and there find divinity. Eckhart did not recommend ceasing attendance at church—he hardly could have because he preached in churches—but he made it clear that outward rituals were of comparatively little importance in reaching God. He also gave the impression to his lay audiences that they might attain godliness largely on their own volition. Thus he was charged by ecclesiastical authorities with inciting "ignorant and undisciplined people to wild and dangerous excesses." Although Eckhart pleaded his own doctrinal orthodoxy, some of his teachings were condemned by the papacy.

(2) mysticism

That Eckhart's critics were not entirely mistaken in their worries is shown by the fact that some lay people in Germany who were influenced by him did fall into the heresy of believing that they could become fully united with God on earth without any priestly intermediaries. But these so-called heretics of the Free Spirit were few in number. Much more numerous were later orthodox mystics, sometimes influenced by Eckhart and sometimes not, who placed greater emphasis on the divine initiative in the meeting of the soul with God and made certain to insist that the ministrations of the Church were a necessary contribution to the mystic way. Even they, however, believed that "churches make no man holy, but men make churches holy."

Heterodox and orthodox mysticism

Most of the great teachers and practitioners of mysticism in the fourteenth century were clerics, nuns, or hermits, but in the fifteenth century a modified form of mysticism was spread among lay people. This "practical mysticism" did not aim for full ecstatic union with God, but rather for an ongoing sense of some divine presence during the conduct of daily life. The most popular manual that pointed the way to this goal was the Latin *Imitation of Christ,* written around 1427, probably by the north German canon Thomas à Kempis. Because this was written in a simple but forceful style and taught how to be a pious Christian while still living actively in the world, it was particularly attractive to lay readers. Thus it quickly became translated into the leading European vernaculars. From then until today it has been more widely read by Christians than any other religious work outside of the Bible. The *Imitation* urges its readers to participate in one religious ceremony—the sacrament of the Eucharist—but otherwise it emphasizes inward piety. According to its teachings, the individual Christian is best able to become the "partner" of Jesus Christ both by taking communion and also by engaging in Biblical meditation and leading a simple, moral life.

A third distinct form of late-medieval piety was outright religious protest or heresy. In England and Bohemia especially, heretical movements became serious threats to the Church. The founder of heresy in late-medieval England was an Oxford theologian named John Wyclif (c. 1330–1384). Wyclif's rigorous adherence to the theology of St. Augustine led him to believe that a certain number of humans were predestined to be saved while the rest were irrevocably damned. He thought the predestined would naturally live simply, according to the standards of the New Testament, but in fact he found most members of the Church hierarchy indulging in splendid extravagances. Hence he concluded that most Church officials were damned. For him the only solution was to have secular rulers appropriate ecclesiastical wealth and reform the Church by replacing corrupt priests and bishops with men who would live according to apostolic standards. This position was obviously attractive to the aristocracy of England, who may have looked forward to enriching themselves with Church spoils and at least saw nothing wrong with using Wyclif as a bulldog to frighten the pope and the local clergy. Thus, Wyclif at first received influential aristocratic support. But towards the end of his life he moved from merely calling for reform to attacking some of the most basic institutions of the Church, above all the sacrament of the Eucharist. This radicalism frightened off his influential protectors, and Wyclif probably would have been formally condemned for heresy had he lived longer. His death brought no respite for the Church, however, because he had attracted numerous lay followers—called Lollards—who zealously continued to propagate some of his most radical ideas. Above all, the Lollards taught that pious Christians should shun the corrupt Church and instead study the Bible and rely as far as possible on their individual consciences. Lollardy gained many adherents in the last two decades of the fourteenth century, but after the introduction in England of the death penalty for heresy in 1399 and the failure of a Lollard uprising in 1414 the heretical wave greatly receded. Nonetheless, a few Lollards did continue to survive underground, and their descendants helped contribute to the Protestant Revolution of the sixteenth century.

Much greater was the influence of Wyclifism in Bohemia. Around 1400, Czech students who had studied in Oxford brought back Wyclif's ideas to the Bohemian capital of Prague. There Wyclifism was enthusiastically received by an eloquent preacher named John Hus (c. 1373–1415), who had already been inveighing in well-attended sermons against "the world, the flesh, and the devil." Hus employed Wyclifite theories to back up his own calls for the end of ecclesiastical corruption, and rallied many Bohemians to the cause of reform in the years between 1408 and 1415. Never alienating anyone as Wyclif had done by criticizing the doctrine of the Eucharist, Hus gained support from many different directions. The politics of the Great Schism prompted the king of Bohemia to lend Hus his protection, and influential aristocrats supported Hus for motives similar to those of their English counterparts. Above all, Hus gained a mass following because of his eloquence and concern for social justice. Accordingly, most of Bohemia was behind him when Hus in 1415 agreed to travel to the Council of Constance to defend his views and try to convince the assembled prelates that only thoroughgoing reform could save the Church. But although Hus had been guaranteed his personal safety, this assurance was revoked as soon as he arrived at the Council: rather than being given a fair hearing, the betrayed idealist was tried for heresy and burned.

Hus's supporters in Bohemia were justifiably outraged and quickly raised the banner of open revolt. The aristocracy took advantage of the situation to seize Church lands, and poorer priests, artisans, and peasants rallied together in the hope of achieving Hus's goals of religious reform and social justice. Between 1420 and 1424 armies of lower-class Hussites, led by a brilliant blind general, John Zizka, amazingly defeated several invading forces of well-armed "crusading" knights from Germany. In 1434 more conservative, aristocratically dominated Hussites overcame the radicals, thereby ending attempts to initiate a purified new religious and social dispensation. But even the conservatives refused to return to full orthodoxy. Thus Bohemia never came back to the Catholic fold until after the Catholic Reformation in the seventeenth century. The Hussite declaration of religious independence was both a foretaste of what was to come one hundred years later with Protestantism and the most successful late-medieval expression of dissatisfaction with the government of the Church.

4. POLITICAL CRISIS AND RECOVERY

The story of late-medieval politics at first seems very dreary because throughout most of the period there was incessant strife. Almost everywhere neighbors fought neighbors and states fought states. But on closer inspection it becomes clear that despite the turmoil there was ultimate improvement in almost all the governments of Europe. In the course of the fifteenth century peace returned to most of the continent, the national monarchies in particular became stronger, and the period ended on a new note of strength just as it had from the point of view of economics.

Starting our survey with Italy, it must first be explained that the Kingdom of Naples in the extreme south of the Italian peninsula was sunk in endemic warfare or maladministration more or less without interruption throughout the fourteenth and fifteenth centuries. Otherwise, Italy emerged from the prevailing political turmoil of the late Middle Ages earlier than any other part of Europe. The fourteenth century was a time of troubles for the Papal States, comprising most of central Italy, because forces representing the absent or divided papacy were seldom able to overcome the resistance of refractory towns and rival leaders of marauding military bands. But after the end of the Great Schism in 1417 the popes concentrated more on consolidating their own Italian territories and gradually became the strong rulers of most of the middle part of the peninsula. Further north some of the leading city-states—such as Florence, Venice, Siena, and Genoa—had experienced at least occasional and most often prolonged social warfare in the fourteenth century because of the economic pressures of the age. But sooner or later the most powerful families or interest groups overcame internal resistance. By around 1400 the three leading cities of the north—Venice, Milan, Florence—had fixed definitively upon their own different forms of government: Venice was ruled by a merchant oligarchy, Milan by a dynastic despotism, and Florence by a complex, supposedly republican system that was actually controlled by the rich. (After 1434 the Florentine republic was in practice dominated by the banking family of the Medici.)

Having settled their internal problems, Venice, Milan, and Florence proceeded from about 1400 to 1454 to expand territorially and conquer almost all the other northern Italian cities and towns except Genoa, which remained prosperous and independent but gained no new territory. Thus, by the middle of the fifteenth century Italy was divided into five major parts: the states of Venice, Milan, and Florence in the north; the Papal States in the middle; and the backward Kingdom of Naples in the south. A treaty of 1454 initiated a half-century of peace between these states: whenever one threatened to upset the "balance of power," the others usually allied against it before serious warfare could break out. Accordingly, the last half of the fifteenth century was a fortunate age for Italy. But in 1494 a French invasion initiated a period of renewed warfare in which the French attempt at dominating Italy was successfully countered by Spain.

North of the Alps political turmoil prevailed throughout the fourteenth century and lasted longer into the fifteenth. Probably the worse instability was experienced in Germany. There the virtually independent princes continually warred with the greatly weakened emperors, or else they warred with each other. Between about 1350 and 1450 near-anarchy prevailed, because while the princes were warring and subdividing their inheritances into smaller states, petty powers such as free cities and knights who owned one or two castles were striving to shake off the rule of the princes. Throughout most of the German west these attempts met with enough success to fragment political authority more than ever, but in the east after about 1450 certain stronger German princes managed to assert their authority over divisive forces. After they did so they started to govern firmly over middle-sized states on the model of the larger national monarchies of England and France. The strongest princes were those who ruled in eastern territories such as Bavaria, Austria, and Brandenburg, because there towns were fewer and smaller and the princes had earlier been able to take advantage of imperial weakness to preside over the colonization of large tracts of land. Especially the Hapsburg princes of Austria and the Hohenzollern princes of Brandenburg—a territory joined in the sixteenth century with the easternmost lands of Prussia—would be the most influential powers in Germany's future.

Germany: the triumph of the princes

The great nation-states did not escape unscathed from the late-medieval turmoil either. France was strife-ridden for much of the period, primarily in the form of the Hundred Years' War between France and England. The Hundred Years' War was actually a series of conflicts that lasted for even more than one hundred years—from 1337 to 1453. There were several different causes for this prolonged struggle. The major one was the long-standing problem of French territory held by the English kings. At the beginning of the fourteenth century the English kings still ruled much of the rich southern French lands of Gascony and Aquitaine as vassals of the French crown. The French, who since the reign of Philip Augustus had been expanding and consolidating their rule, obviously hoped to expel the English, and war was therefore inevitable. Another cause for strife was that the English economic interests in the woolen trade with Flanders led them to support the frequent attempts of Flemish burghers to rebel against French rule. Finally, the fact that the direct Capetian line of succession to the French throne died out in 1328, to be replaced thereafter by the related Valois dynasty, meant that the English kings, who themselves descended from the Capetians as a result of intermarriage, laid claim to the French crown itself.

France: causes of the Hundred Years' War

France should have had no difficulty in defeating England at the start: it was the richest country in Europe and outnumbered England

*The course of the war:
factors in the initial
English success*

in population by some fifteen million to fewer than four million. Nonetheless, throughout most of the first three-quarters of the Hundred Years' War the English won most of the pitched battles. One reason for this was that the English had learned superior military tactics, using well-disciplined archers to fend off and scatter the heavily armored mounted French knights. In the three greatest battles of the long conflict—Crécy (1346), Poitiers (1356), and Agincourt (1415)—the outnumbered English relied on tight discipline and effective use of the longbow to inflict crushing defeats on the French. Another reason for English success was that the war was always fought on French soil. That being the case, English soldiers were eager to fight because they could look forward to rich plunder, while their own homeland suffered none of the disasters of war. Worst of all for the French was the fact that they often were badly divided. The French crown had always had to fear provincial attempts to assert autonomy: especially during the long period of warfare, when there were several highly inept kings and the English encouraged internal French dissensions, many aristocratic provincial leaders took advantage of the confusion to ally with the enemy and seek their own advantage. The most dramatic and fateful instance was the breaking away of Burgundy, whose dukes from 1419 to 1435 allied with the English, an act which called the very existence of an independent French crown into question.

It was in this dark period that the heroic figure of Joan of Arc came forth to rally the French. In 1429 Joan, an illiterate but extremely devout peasant girl, sought out the uncrowned French ruler, Charles VII, to announce that she had been divinely commissioned to drive the English out of France. Charles was persuaded to let her take command of his troops, and her piety and sincerity made such a favorable impression on the soldiers that their morale was raised immensely. In a few months Joan had liberated much of central France from English domination and had brought Charles to Rheims, where he was crowned king. But in May 1430 she was captured by the Burgundians and handed over to the English, who accused her of being a witch and tried her for heresy. Condemned in 1431 after a predetermined trial, she was publicly burned to death in the market square at Rouen. Nonetheless, the French, fired by their initial victories, continued to move on the offensive. When Burgundy withdrew from the English alliance in 1435, and the English king, Henry VI, proved to be totally incompetent, there followed an uninterrupted series of triumphs for the French side. In 1453 the capture of Bordeaux, the last of the English strongholds in the southwest, finally brought the long war to an end. The English now held no land in France except for the Channel port of Calais, which they ultimately lost in 1558.

More than merely expelling the English from French territory, the Hundred Years' War resulted in greatly strengthening the powers of the French crown. Although many of the French kings during the long war had been ineffective personalities—one, Charles VI, was even insane—the monarchy demonstrated remarkable staying power because it provided France with the strongest institutions it knew and therefore offered the only realistic hope for lasting stability and peace. Moreover, warfare emergencies allowed the kings to gather new powers, above all, the rights to collect national taxes and maintain a standing army. Hence after Charles VII succeeded in defeating the English, the crown was able to renew the high-medieval royal tradition of ruling the country assertively. In the reigns of Charles's successors, Louis XI (1461–1483) and Louis XII (1498–1515), the monarchy became ever stronger. Its greatest single achievement was the destruction of the power of Burgundy in 1477 when the Burgundian duke, Charles the Bold, fell in the battle of Nancy at the hands of the Swiss, whom Charles had been trying to dominate. Since Charles died without a male heir, Louis XI of France was able to march into Burgundy and reabsorb the breakaway duchy. Later, when Louis XII gained Brittany by marriage, the French kings ruled powerfully over almost all of what is today included in the borders of France.

Although the Hundred Years' War was fought on French instead of English soil, England also experienced great turmoil during the later Middle Ages because of internal instability. Indeed, England was a hotbed of insurrection: of the nine English kings who came to the throne between 1307 and 1485, five died violently because of revolts or conspiracies. Most of these slain kings had proven themselves to be incapable rulers, but there were other reasons for England's political troubles as well. One was that the crown had been too ambitious in trying both to hold on to its territories in France and also subdue Scotland. This policy often made it necessary to resort to heavy taxation and to grant major political concessions to the aristocracy. When English arms in France were successful, the crown rode the crest of popularity and the aristocracy prospered from military spoils and ransoms; but whenever the tides of battle turned to defeat, the crown became financially embarrassed and thrown on the political defensive. To make matters worse, the English aristocracy was particularly unruly throughout the period, not just because the aristocrats often had reason to distrust the inept kings, but because the economic pressures of the age made them seek to enlarge their agricultural estates at the expense of each other. This led to factionalism, and factionalism often led to civil war.

After the English presence in France was virtually eradicated and the aristocracy could no longer hope to enrich itself on the spoils of foreign warfare, England's political situation became particularly desperate. As bad luck would have it, the reigning king, Henry VI (1422–1461), was one of the most incompetent that England has ever had. According to one recent authority, Henry "paralyzed and con-

Louis XI of France. A portrait by Fouquet.

England: internal turmoil

The Wars of the Roses

The positive aspects of English political developments, 1307–1485

fused the whole process of English government with a royal irresponsibility and inanity which had no precedent." Henry's willfulness helped provoke the Wars of the Roses that flared on and off from 1455 to 1485. These wars received their name from the emblems of the two competing factions: the red rose of Henry's family of Lancaster and the white rose of the rival house of York. The Yorkists for a time gained the kingship, under such monarchs as Richard III, but in 1485 they were replaced by a new dynasty, that of the Tudors, who began a new period in English history. The first Tudor king, Henry VII, steadily eliminated rival claimants to the throne, avoided expensive foreign wars, built up a financial surplus, and gradually reasserted royal power over the aristocracy. When he died in 1509 he was therefore able to pass on to his son, Henry VIII (1509–1547), a royal power that was as great as it had ever been before.

It is tempting to view the entire period of English history between 1307 and the accession of Henry VII in 1485 as one long, dreary interregnum which accomplished nothing positive. But that would not quite be doing justice to the time: in the first place, the fact that England did not entirely fall apart during the recurrent turbulence was an accomplishment in itself. Remarkably, the rebellious aristocrats of the later Middle Ages never tried to proclaim the independence of any of their regions; only once, in 1405, did they seek unsuccessfully to divide the country between them. Discounting that insignificant exception, aristocratic rebels always sought to control the central government rather than destroy or break away from it. Thus when Henry VII came to the throne, he did not have to win back any English territories as Louis XI of France had had to win back Burgundy. More than that, the antagonisms of the Hundred Years' War had the ultimately beneficial effect of enhancing an English sense of national identity. From the Norman Conquest until deep into the fourteenth century, French was the preferred language of the English crown and aristocracy, but mounting anti-French sentiment contributed to the complete triumph of English by around 1400. The loss of lands in France was also ultimately beneficial because thereafter the crown was freed from the inevitability of war with the French. This freedom gave England more diplomatic maneuverability in sixteenth-century continental politics and later helped strengthen England's ability to invest its energies in overseas expansion in America and elsewhere. Yet another positive development was the steady growth of effective governmental institutions; despite the shifting fortunes of kings, the central governmental administration expanded and became more sophisticated. Parliament too became stronger, largely because both the crown and the aristocracy believed that they could use it for their own ends. In 1307 Parliament had not yet become a regular part of the English governmental system, but by 1485 it definitely had. Later kings who tried to govern without it ran into severe difficulties.

Around the time when Louis XI of France and Henry VII of England were reasserting royal power in their respective countries, the Spanish monarchs, Ferdinand and Isabella, were doing the same on the Iberian peninsula. In the latter area there had also been incessant strife in the later Middle Ages; Aragon and Castile had often fought each other, and aristocratic factions within those kingdoms had continually fought the crown. But in 1496 Ferdinand, the heir of Aragon, married Isabella, the heiress of Castile, and thereby created a union which laid the basis for modern Spain.

Although Spain did not become a fully united nation until 1716 because Aragon and Castile retained their separate institutions, at least warfare between the two previously independent kingdoms ended and the new country was able to embark on united policies. Isabella and Ferdinand, ruling respectively until 1504 and 1516, annexed Granada, the last Muslim state in the peninsula, expelled the Jews, whom they regarded as a divisive element in their society, and thoroughly subdued their aristocracies. Having dealt with their major internal obstacles, the Spanish rulers also started to embark on an ambitious foreign policy: not only did they turn to overseas expansion, as most famously in their support of Christopher Columbus, but they also entered decisively into the arena of Italian politics. Enriched by the influx of American gold and silver after the conquest of Mexico and Peru, and nearly invincible on the battlefields, Spain quickly became Europe's most powerful state in the sixteenth century.

Ultimately the clearest result of political developments throughout Europe in the late Middle Ages was the preservation of basic high-medieval patterns. The areas of Italy and Germany which had been politically divided before 1300 remained politically divided thereafter. The emergence of middle-sized states in both of these areas in the fifteenth century brought more stability than had existed before, but events would show that Italy and Germany would still be the prey of the Western powers. The latter were clearly much stronger because they were consolidated around stronger national monarchies. The trials of the later Middle Ages put the existence of these monarchies to the test, but after 1450 they emerged stronger than ever. The clearest illustration of their superiority is shown by the history of Italy in the years immediately following 1494. Until then the Italian states appeared to the relatively well-governed and prosperous. They experimented with advanced techniques of administration and diplomacy. But when France and Spain invaded the peninsula the Italian states fell over like houses of cards. The Western monarchies could simply draw on greater resources and thus inherited the future of Europe.

5. THOUGHT, LITERATURE, AND ART

Although it might be guessed that the extreme hardships of the later Middle Ages should have led to the decline or stagnation of intellectual and artistic endeavors, in fact the period was an extremely fruitful one in the realms of thought, literature, and art. In this section we will postpone treatment of certain developments most closely related to the early history of the Italian Renaissance, but will discuss some of western Europe's other important late-medieval intellectual and artistic accomplishments.

Crisis in theology and philosophy

Theology and philosophy after about 1300 faced a crisis of doubt. This doubt did not concern the existence of God and His supernatural powers, but was rather doubt about human ability to comprehend the supernatural. Whereas St. Thomas Aquinas and other Scholastics in the High Middle Ages had serenely delimited the number of "mysteries of the faith" and believed that everything else, both in heaven and earth, could be thoroughly understood by humans, the floods, frosts, wars, and plagues of the fourteenth century helped undermine such confidence in the powers of human understanding. Once human beings experienced the universe as arbitrary and unpredictable, fourteenth-century thinkers began to wonder whether there was not far more in heaven and earth than could be understood by their philosophies. The result was a thoroughgoing reevaluation of the prior theological and philosophical outlook.

William of Ockham; nominalism

The leading late-medieval abstract thinker was the English Franciscan William of Ockham, who was born around 1285 and died in 1349, apparently from the Black Death. Traditionally, Franciscans had always had greater doubts than Dominicans like St. Thomas concerning the abilities of human reason to comprehend the supernatural; Ockham, convinced by the events of his age, expressed these most formidably. He denied that the existence of God and numerous other theological matters could be demonstrated apart from scriptural revelation, and he emphasized God's freedom and absolute power to do anything He wished. In the realm of human knowledge per se Ockham's searching intellect drove him to look for absolute certainties instead of mere theories. In investigating earthly matters he developed the position, known as *nominalism*, that only individual things, but not collectivities, are real, and that one thing therefore cannot be understood by means of another: to know a chair one has to see and touch it rather than just know what several other chairs are like. Ockham also formulated a logic which was based on the assumption that words stood only for themselves rather than for real things. Such logic might not say much about the real world, but at least it could not be refuted, since it was as internally valid in its own terms as Euclidean geometry.

The significance of Ockham's thought

Ockham's outlook, which gained widespread adherence in the late-medieval universities, today oftens seems overly methodological and verging on the arid, but it had several important effects on the development of Western thought. Ockham's concern about what God *might* do led to the raising by his followers of some of the seemingly absurd questions for which medieval theology has been mocked, for example, asking whether God can undo the past, or whether an infinite number of pure spirits can simultaneously inhabit the same place (the nearest medieval thinkers actually came to asking how many angels can dance on the head of a pin). Nonetheless, Ockham's emphasis on preserving God's autonomy led to a stress on divine omnipotence that became one of the basic presuppositions of sixteenth-century Protestantism. Further, Ockham's determination to find certainties in the realm of human knowledge ultimately helped make it possible to discuss human affairs and natural science without reference to supernatural explanations—one of the most important foundations of the modern scientific method. Finally, Ockham's opposition to studying collectivities and his refusal to apply logic to real things helped encourage *empiricism,* or the belief that knowledge of the world should rest on sense experience rather than abstract reason. This too is a presupposition for scientific progress: thus it is probably not coincidental that some of Ockham's fourteenth-century followers made significant advances in the study of physics.

Ockham's search for reliable truths finds certain parallels in the realm of late-medieval literature, although Ockham surely had no direct influence in that field. The major trait of the best late-medieval literature was *naturalism,* or the attempt to describe things the way they really are. This was more a development from high-medieval precedents—such as the explorations of human conduct pursued by Chrétien de Troyes, Wolfram von Eschenbach, and Dante—than a reaction against them. The steady growth of a lay reading public furthermore encouraged authors to avoid theological and philosophical abstractions and seek more to entertain by portraying people realistically with all their strengths and foibles. Another main characteristic of late-medieval literature, the predominance of composition in the European vernaculars instead of Latin, also developed out of high-medieval precedents but gained great momentum in the later Middle Ages for two different reasons. One was that international tensions and hostilities, including the numerous wars of the age and the trials of the universal papacy, led to need for security and a pride of self-identification reflected by the use of vernacular tongues. Probably more important was the fact that continued spread of education for the laity greatly increased a public that could read in a given vernacular language but not in Latin. Hence although much poetry was written during the High Middle Ages in the vernacular, in the later Middle Ages use of the vernacular was widely extended to prose. Moreover, countries such as Italy and England, which had just begun to cultivate their own vernacular literatures around 1300, subsequently began to employ their native tongues to the most impressive literary effect.

The greatest writer of vernacular prose fiction of the later Middle Ages was the Italian Giovanni Boccaccio (1313–1375). Although

The naturalism of late-medieval literature

Boccaccio

Boccaccio would have taken an honored place in literary history for some of his lesser works, which included courtly romances, pastoral poems, and learned treatises, by far the most impressive of his writings is the *Decameron,* written between 1348 and 1351. This is a collection of one hundred stories, mostly about love and sex, adventure, and clever trickery, supposedly told by a sophisticated party of seven young ladies and three men who are sojourning in a country villa outside Florence in order to escape the ravages of the Black Death. Boccaccio by no means invented all one hundred plots, but even when he borrowed the outlines of his tales from earlier sources he retold the stories in his own characteristically exuberant, masterful, and extremely witty fashion. There are many reasons why the *Decameron* must be counted as epoch-making from a historical point of view. The first is that it was the earliest ambitious and successful work of vernacular creative literature ever written in western Europe in narrative prose. Boccaccio's prose is "modern" in the sense that it is brisk, for unlike the medieval authors of flowery romances, Boccaccio purposely wrote in an unaffected, colloquial style. Simply stated, in the *Decameron* he was less interested in being "elevated" or elegant than in being unpretentiously entertaining. From the point of view of content, Boccaccio wished to portray men and women as they really are rather than as they ought to be. Thus when he wrote about the clergy he showed them to be as susceptible to human appetites and failings as other mortals. His women are not pallid playthings, distant goddesses, or steadfast virgins, but flesh-and-blood creatures with intellects, who interact more comfortably and naturally with men and with each other than any women in Western literature had ever done before. Boccaccio's treatment of sexual relations is often graphic, often witty, but never demeaning. In his world the natural desires of both women and men are not meant to be thwarted. For all these reasons the *Decameron* is a robust and delightful appreciation of all that is human.

Chaucer

Similar in many ways to Boccaccio as a creator of robust, naturalistic vernacular literature was the Englishman Geoffrey Chaucer (c. 1340–1400). Chaucer was the first major writer of an English that can still be read today with relatively little effort. Remarkably, he was both a founding father of England's mighty literary tradition and one of the four or five greatest contributors to it: most critics rank him just behind Shakespeare, and in a class with Milton, Wordsworth, and Dickens. Chaucer wrote several highly impressive works, but his masterpiece is unquestionably the unfinished *Canterbury Tales,* dating from the end of his career. Like the *Decameron,* this is a collection of stories held together by a frame, in Chaucer's case the device of having a group of people tell stories while on a pilgrimage from London to Canterbury. But there are also differences between the *Decameron* and the *Canterbury Tales.* Chaucer's stories are told in sparkling verse instead of prose and they are recounted by people of all different classes—from a chivalric knight to a dedicated university student to a thieving miller with a wart on his nose. Lively women are also represented, most memorably the gap-toothed, oft-married "Wife of Bath," who knows all "the remedies of love." Each character tells a story which is particularly illustrative of his or her own occupation and outlook on the world. By this device Chaucer is able to create a highly diverse "human comedy." His range is therefore greater than Boccaccio's and although he is as witty, frank, and lusty as the Italian, he is sometimes more profound.

As naturalism was a dominant trait of late-medieval literature, so it was of late-medieval art. Already by the thirteenth century Gothic sculptors were paying far more attention than their Romanesque predecessors had done to the way plants, animals, and human beings really looked. Whereas medieval art had previously emphasized abstract design, the stress was now increasingly on realism: thirteenth-century carvings of leaves and flowers must have been done from direct observation and are the first to be clearly recognizable as distinct species. Statues of humans also gradually became more naturally proportioned and realistic in their portrayals of facial expressions. By around 1290 the concern for realism had become so great that a sculptor working on a tomb-portrait of the German Emperor Rudolf of Hapsburg allegedly made a hurried return trip to view Rudolf in person, because he had heard that a new wrinkle had appeared on the emperor's face.

In the next two centuries the trend toward naturalism continued in sculpture and was extended to manuscript illumination and painting. The latter was in certain basic respects a new art. Ever since the caveman, painting had been done on walls, but walls of course were not easily movable. The art of wall-painting continued to be cultivated in the Middle Ages and long afterwards, especially in the form of *frescoes, or paintings done on wet plaster*. But in addition to frescoes, Italian artists in the thirteenth century first started painting pictures on pieces of wood or canvas. These were first done in tempera (pigments mixed with water and natural gums or eggwhites), but around 1400 painting in oils was introduced in the European north. These new technical developments created new artistic opportunities. Artists were now able to paint religious scenes on altarpieces for churches and for private devotions practiced by the wealthier laity at home. Artists also painted the first Western portraits, which were meant to gratify the self-esteem of monarchs and aristocrats. The earliest surviving example of a naturalistic painted portrait is one of a French king, John the Good, executed around 1360. Others followed quickly, so that within a short time the art of portraiture done from life was highly developed. Visitors to art museums will notice that some of the most realistic and sensitive portraits of all time date from the fifteenth century.

The most pioneering and important painter of the later Middle Ages was the Florentine Giotto (c. 1267–1337). He did not engage in indi-

The Meeting of Joachim and Anna at the Golden Gate. A fresco by Giotto. Note how the haloes merge: this old and barren couple will soon miraculously have a child, none other than Mary, the mother of Jesus.

The naturalistic style of Giotto

vidual portraiture, but he brought deep humanity to his religious images done on both walls and movable panels. Giotto was preeminently a naturalist, i.e., an imitator of nature. Not only do his human beings and animals look more natural than those of his predecessors, they seem to do more natural things. When Christ enters Jerusalem on Palm Sunday, boys climb trees to get a better view; when St. Francis is laid out in death, one onlooker takes the opportunity to see whether the saint had really received Christ's wounds; and when the Virgin's parents, Joachim and Anna, meet after a long separation, they actually embrace and kiss—perhaps the first deeply tender kiss in Western art. It was certainly not true, as one fanciful storyteller later reported, that an onlooker found a fly Giotto had painted so real that he attempted to brush it away with his hand, but Giotto in fact accomplished something more. Specifically, he was the first to conceive of the painted space in fully three-dimensional terms: as one art historian has put it, Giotto's frescoes were the first to "knock a hole into the wall." After Giotto's death a reaction in Italian painting set in. This was probably caused by a new reverence for the awesomely supernatural brought about by the horrors of the plague. Whatever the explanation, artists of the mid–fourteenth century briefly moved away from naturalism and painted stern, forbidding religious figures who seemed to float in space. But by around 1400 artists came back down to earth and started to build upon Giotto's influence in ways that led to the great Italian renaissance in painting.

See color plates following page 384

In the north of Europe painting did not advance impressively beyond manuscript illumination until the early fifteenth century, but then it suddenly came very much into its own. The leading northern

European painters were Flemish, first and foremost the brothers Hubert and Jan van Eyck (c. 1366–1426; c. 1380–1441), Roger van der Weyden (c. 1400–1464), and Hans Memling (c. 1430–1494). The van Eycks used to be credited with the invention of oil painting; while that is now open to question, they certainly were its greatest early practitioners. The use of oils allowed them and the other fifteenth-century Flemish painters to engage in brilliant coloring and sharp-focused realism. The van Eycks and van der Weyden excelled most at two things: communicating a sense of deep religious piety and portraying minute details of familiar everyday experience. These may at first seem incompatible, but it should be remembered that contemporary manuals of practical mysticism such as *The Imitation of Christ* also sought to link deep piety with everyday existence. Thus it was by no means blasphemous when a Flemish painter would portray behind a tender Madonna and Child a vista of contemporary life with people going about their usual business and a man even urinating against a wall. This union between the sacred and profane tended to fall apart in the work of Memling, who excelled in either straightforward religious pictures or secular portraits, but it would return in the work of the greatest painters of the Low Countries, Brueghel and Rembrandt.

The Flemish painters

6. ADVANCES IN TECHNOLOGY

No account of enduring late-medieval accomplishments would be complete without mention of certain epoch-making technological advances. Sadly, but probably not unexpectedly, treatment of this subject has to begin with reference to the invention of artillery and firearms. The prevalence of warfare stimulated the development of new weaponry. Gunpowder itself was a Chinese invention, but it was first put to particularly devastating uses in the late-medieval West. Heavy cannons, which made terrible noises "as though all the dyvels of hell had been in the way," were first employed around 1330. The earliest cannons were so primitive that it often was more dangerous to stand behind than in front of them, but by the middle of the fifteenth century they were greatly improved and began to revolutionize the nature of warfare. In one year, 1453, heavy artillery played a leading role in determining the outcome of two crucial conflicts: the Ottoman Turks used German and Hungarian cannons to breach the defenses of Constantinople—hitherto the most impregnable in Europe—and the French used heavy artillery to take the city of Bordeaux, thereby ending the Hundred Years' War. Cannons thereafter made it difficult for rebellious aristocrats to hole up in their stone castles, and thus they aided in the consolidation of the national monarchies. Placed aboard ships, cannons enabled European vessels to dominate foreign waters in the subsequent age of overseas expansion. Guns were also invented in the fourteenth century, to be gradually perfected afterwards.

Late-medieval technological achievements: (1) the weapons of war

Cannons Being Used to Breach the Walls of a Castle. This scene depicts a late engagement of the Hundred Years' War.

Shortly after 1500 the most effective new variety of gun, the musket, allowed foot-soldiers to end once and for all the earlier military dominance of heavily armored mounted knights. Once lance-bearing cavalries became outmoded and fighting could more easily be carried on by all, the monarchical states that could turn out the largest armies completely subdued internal resistance and dominated the battlefields of Europe.

Other late-medieval technological developments were more life-enhancing. Eyeglasses, first invented in the 1280s, were perfected in the fourteenth century. These allowed older people to keep on reading when nearsightedness would otherwise have stopped them. For example, the great fourteenth-century scholar Petrarch, who boasted excellent sight in his youth, wore spectacles after his sixtieth year and was thus enabled to complete some of his most important works. Around 1300 the use of the magnetic compass helped ships to sail further away from land and venture out into the Atlantic. One immediate result was the opening of direct sea commerce between Italy and the North. Subsequently, numerous improvements in shipbuilding, map making, and navigational devices contributed to Europe's ability to start expanding overseas. In the early fourteenth century the Azores and Cape Verde Islands were reached; then, after a long pause caused by Europe's plagues and wars, the African Cape of Good Hope was rounded in 1488, the West Indies discovered in 1492, India reached by the sea route in 1498, and Brazil discovered in 1500. Partly as a result of technology the world was thus suddenly made much smaller.

Among the most familiar implements of our modern life that were invented by Europeans in the later Middle Ages were clocks and printed books. Mechanical clocks were invented shortly before 1300

(2) optical and navigational instruments

and proliferated in the years immediately thereafter. The earliest clocks were too expensive for private purchase, but towns quickly vied with each other to install the most elaborate clocks in their prominent public buildings. These clocks not only told the time but showed the courses of sun, moon, and planets, and performed mechanical tricks on the striking of the hours. The new invention ultimately had two profound effects. One was the further stimulation of European interest in complex machinery of all sorts. This interest had already been awakened by the high-medieval proliferation of mills, but clocks ultimately became even more omnipresent than mills because after about 1650 they became quite cheap and were brought into practically every European home. Household clocks served as models of marvelous machines. Equally if not more significant was the fact that clocks began to rationalize the course of European daily affairs. Until the advent of clocks in the late Middle Ages time was flexible. Men and women had only a rough idea of how late in the day it was and rose and retired more or less with the sun. Especially people who lived in the country performed different jobs at different rates according to the rhythm of the seasons. Even when hours were counted, they were measured at different lengths according to the amount of light in the different seasons of the year. In the fourteenth century, however, clocks first started relentlessly striking equal hours through the day and night. Thus they began to regulate work with new precision. People were expected to start and end work "on time" and many came to believe that "time is money." This emphasis on time-keeping brought new efficiencies but also new tensions: Lewis Carroll's white rabbit, who is always looking at his pocket watch and muttering, "how late it's getting," is a telling caricature of time-obsessed Western man.

The invention of printing with movable type was equally momentous. The major stimulus for this invention was the replacement of

(3) mechanical clocks

Horloge de Sapience. This miniature, from an early–fifteenth-century French manuscript, reflects the growing fascination with machines of all sorts and clocks in particular.

Left: *Paper-Making at a Paper Mill*. Right: *A Printing Press*. From a title page of a Parisian printer, 1520.

(4) the invention of printing

parchment by paper as Europe's primary writing material between 1200 and 1400. Parchment, made from the skins of valuable farm animals, was extremely expensive: since it was possible to get only about four good parchment leaves from one animal, it was necessary to slaughter between two to three hundred sheep or calves to gain enough parchment for a Bible! Paper, made from rags turned into pulp by mills, brought prices down dramatically. Late-medieval records show that paper sold at one-sixth the price of parchment. Accordingly, it became cheaper to learn how to read and write. With literacy becoming ever more widespread, there was a growing market for still cheaper books, and the invention of printing with movable type around 1450 fully met this demand. By greatly saving labor, the invention made printed books about one-fifth as expensive as handwritten ones within about two decades.

The effects of printing

As soon as books became easily accessible, literacy increased even more and book-culture became a basic part of the European way of life. After about 1500 Europeans could afford to read and buy books of all sorts—not just religious tracts, but instructional manuals, light entertainment, and, by the eighteenth century, newspapers. Printing insured that ideas would spread quickly and reliably; moreover, revolutionary ideas could no longer be easily extinguished once they were set down in hundreds of copies of books. Thus the greatest religious reformer of the sixteenth century, Martin Luther, gained an immediate following throughout Germany by employing the printing press to run off pamphlets: had printing not been available to him, Luther might have died like Hus. The spread of books also helped stimulate the growth of cultural nationalism. Before printing, regional dialects in most European countries were often so diverse that people who supposedly spoke the same language often could barely understand each other. Such a situation hindered governmental centralization because a royal servant might be entirely unable to communicate with inhabitants of the provinces. Shortly after the invention of printing, however, each European country began to develop its own linguistic standards which were disseminated uniformly by books. The "King's English" was what was printed in London and carried to Yorkshire or Wales. Thus communications were enhanced and governments were able to operate ever more efficiently.

In conclusion it may be said that clocks and books as much as guns and ocean-going ships helped Europe to dominate the globe after 1500. The habits inculcated by clocks encouraged Europeans to work efficiently and to plan precisely; the prevalence of books enhanced communications and the flow of progressive ideas. Once accustomed to reading books, Europeans communicated and experimented intellectually as no other peoples in the world. Thus it was not surprising that after 1500 Europeans could start to make the whole world their own.

Technological advancement a factor in Europe's subsequent global preeminence

SELECTED READINGS

• *Items so designated are available in paperback editions.*

Breisach, E., *Renaissance Europe, 1300–1517,* New York, 1973. The best college-level textbook on the period.

Bridbury, A. R., *Economic Growth: England in the Later Middle Ages,* 2nd ed., New York, 1975. A controversial argument against the dominant theory of economic depression.

• Brucker, G., *Renaissance Florence,* New York, 1969. An excellent introduction by one of America's foremost experts.

• Cipolla, C. M., *Clocks and Culture, 1300–1700,* London, 1967. Treats both technological developments and the importance of clocks as items of trade.

• Cole, Bruce, *Giotto and Florentine Painting, 1280–1375,* New York, 1976. A clear and stimulating introduction.

Dollinger, P., *The German Hansa,* Stanford, 1970.

Fourquin, G., *The Anatomy of Popular Rebellion in the Middle Ages,* New York, 1978.

Hale, John R., et al., *Europe in the Late Middle Ages,* Evanston, Ill., 1965. Specialized essays on numerous subjects.

Herlihy, David, *Medieval and Renaissance Pistoia: The Social History of an Italian Town,* New Haven, Conn., 1967. Important for its use of statistical evidence.

• Holmes, George, *The Later Middle Ages, 1272–1485,* New York, 1962.

• Huizinga, J., *The Waning of the Middle Ages,* London, 1924. A beautifully written classic on forms of thought and art in the Low Countries.

• Johnson, Jerah, and W. Percy, *The Age of Recovery: The Fifteenth Century,* Ithaca, N.Y., 1970.

Kaminsky, H., *A History of the Hussite Revolution*, Berkeley, Calif., 1967. Detailed and difficult but far and away the best treatment of the subject.

• Lerner, R., *The Age of Adversity: The Fourteenth Century*, Ithaca, N.Y., 1968.

Lewis, P. S., *Later Medieval France: The Polity*, London, 1968.

McFarlane, K. B., *The Nobility of Later Medieval England*, Oxford, 1973. An excellent collection of essays by a late master of the field.

• Meiss, M., *Painting in Florence and Siena After the Black Death*, Princeton, N.J., 1951. A stimulating attempt to relate art history to the spirit of an age.

• Miskimin, H. A., *The Economy of Early Renaissance Europe, 1300–1460*, Englewood Cliffs, N.J., 1969. The best short work on the subject.

Mollat, G., *The Popes at Avignon, 1305–1378*, London, 1963.

• Panofsky, E., *Early Netherlandish Painting*, 2 vols., Cambridge, Mass., 1953. A brilliant specialized history by a master art historian.

• Pernoud, R., *Joan of Arc*, New York, 1966. Joan viewed through the eyes of her contemporaries.

Perroy, E., *The Hundred Years War*, Bloomington, Ind., 1959. The standard account.

Scaglione, A., *Nature and Love in the Late Middle Ages*, Berkeley, Calif., 1963.

• Smart, Alastair, *The Dawn of Italian Painting, 1250–1400*, Ithaca, N.Y., 1978. More detailed than Cole.

Trinkaus, C., and H. A. Oberman, eds., *The Pursuit of Holiness in Late Medieval and Renaissance Religion*, Leiden, 1974. Essays that reveal the most recent trends in research.

Vaughan, Richard, *Valois Burgundy*, London, 1975.

• Waley, D., *Later Medieval Europe*, 2nd ed., London, 1975.

SOURCE MATERIALS

Allmand, C. T., ed., *Society at War: The Experience of England and France During the Hundred Years War*, Edinburgh, 1973. An outstanding collection of documents.

• Boccaccio, G., *The Decameron*, tr. M. Musa and P. E. Bondanella, New York, 1977.

• Chaucer, G., *The Canterbury Tales*. (Many editions.)

Colledge, E., ed., *The Mediaeval Mystics of England*, New York, 1961.

• Froissart, J., *Chronicles*, tr. G. Brereton, Baltimore, 1968. A selection from the most famous contemporary account of the Hundred Years' War. Reads more like a novel than like history.

The Imitation of Christ, tr. L. Sherley-Price, Baltimore, 1952.

John Hus at the Council of Constance, tr. M. Spinka, New York, 1965. The translation of a Czech chronicle with an expert introduction and appended collection of documents.

Meister Eckhart, tr. R. B. Blakney, New York, 1941.

Memoirs of a Renaissance Pope: The Commentaries of Pius II (abridged ed.), tr. F. A. Gragg, New York, 1959. A fascinating insight into the Renaissance papacy.

A Parisian Journal, 1405–1449, tr. J. Shirley, Oxford, 1968. A marvelous panorama of Parisian life recorded by an eyewitness.

• Pitti, B., and G. Dati, *Two Memoirs of Renaissance Florence*, tr. J. Martines, New York, 1967.

Chapter 17

INDIA, THE FAR EAST, AND AFRICA IN THE LATER MIDDLE AGES

Seldom [have] two civilizations, so vast and so strongly developed, yet so radically dissimilar as the Muhammadan and Hindu, [met and mingled] together. The very contrasts which existed between them, the wide divergences in their culture and their religions, make the history of their impact peculiarly instructive and lend an added interest to the art and above all to the architecture which their united genius called into being.

—Sir John Marshall, in *Cambridge History of India,* Vol. III

The centuries which are known in the West as the Middle Ages did not have quite the same importance for the civilizations of the Eastern lands as they did for the evolution of European civilization. The cultures of India and China were already highly advanced, while the western Europeans were only beginning to develop a stabilized society and to utilize their intellectual resources to a significant degree. In contrast to western Europe, which during the late medieval centuries was relatively free from external disturbances, both India and China experienced fresh invasions more sweeping in character than any they had known since the beginnings of their recorded history. They were able to survive the shock of these invasions with the essential features of their cultures intact, although permanent modifications took place in Indian society. Japan was unique among the principal Asian states in the fact that she was not subjected to foreign conquest. The tensions and conflicts within her own society, however, were tremendous, and they gradually produced a type of social and political organization which was remarkably similar to the feudal system of western Europe. The face of black Africa changed dramatically with the expansion of trade. Great kingdoms and empires encompassing diverse cultures, languages, and religious systems arose and urban centers of high civilization reflecting the convergence of Islamic and African cultures flourished.

Contrasts with the European Middle Ages

1. THE ESTABLISHMENT OF MUSLIM KINGDOMS IN INDIA (c. 1000–1500)

The Muslim invaders of India

About the same time that the nations of western Europe were initiating the economic and intellectual progress which distinguished the later Middle Ages and which made possible the brilliant culture of the Renaissance, the peoples of India were harried by a series of marauding raids that devastated their society and sorely impaired their creative talents. The invaders of this period were devotees of Islam. They implanted the Muslim religion in India so firmly that it has ever since been the faith of a substantial minority of the population. But while the expansion of Islam in Africa, Spain, and the Middle East was associated with the quickening of cultural activities and with the attainment of relatively harmonious relations between the conquerors and their subject peoples, the Muslim conquests in India led to wanton destruction and created a deep and abiding cleavage between the opposing religious groups.

The conquests of the Turks and Afghans

The first of the Muslim conquerors of India were Turks from Afghanistan. They did not come in numberless hordes, nor were they unresisted by native troops. The fact that they were able to sweep across the country and work such havoc is a commentary on the fateful political division of India and the lack of solidarity among her people. Ever since the decay of Harsha's empire in the seventh century, Hindustan had been disunited and subject to contention among various states. The strongest of the Hindu states were those inhabited by a group known as Rajputs. The origin of the Rajputs (the word means literally "sons of kings") is not known. It is probable that they were not Indians to begin with but the descendants of Huns and other invaders of the fifth and sixth centuries who had become assimilated into Hindu society. Generally they were regarded as belonging to the *kshatriya* (warrior) caste, and they prided themselves on their military traditions. The rulers and nobility of the Rajput kingdoms had developed a code of chivalrous conduct somewhat like the cult of chivalry of the medieval European knights. They were redoubtable horsemen, proud of their skill with the sword, and hypersensitive to insult. The Rajputs were the fiercest and bravest fighters in India, but they were unable to stem the Muslim advance.

Factors aiding the conquerors

Undoubtedly the helplessness of the Indian people during this time of invasion was intensified by the caste system, which was now exacting a heavy penalty. Each stratum of the population was hedged in by its own prescribed activities and loyalties—military defense was considered to be the function of the *kshatriyas* alone. The lower classes were impoverished and dispirited, and there was little incentive for concerted action in the common interest. By contrast, the Muslim invaders were a fresh and energetic people, excited by the prospect of rich spoils and inspired by an activist creed that promised certain

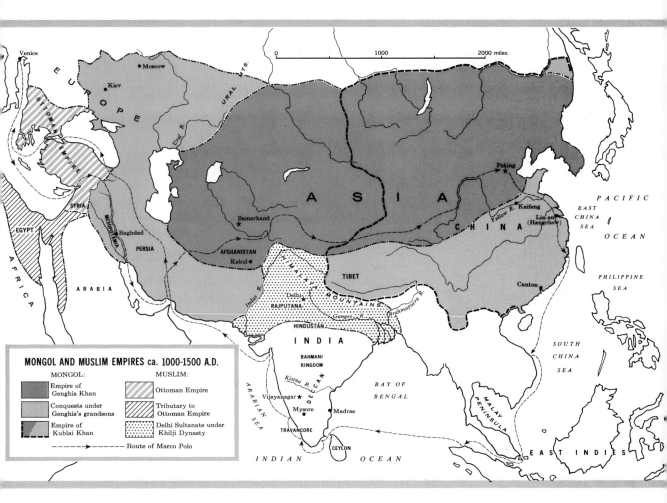

recompense for service in a holy war against idolators. The Hindus
were not prepared to cope with such fanatical zeal as their adversaries
displayed. Nevertheless, the Rajputs gave a good account of themselves in combat; and some of them, when they saw that opposition
was useless, removed with their retainers into the heart of the Indian
desert to rebuild their shattered communities in the region which
came to be called Rajputana.

After its initial impact the Muslim conquest of northern India
entered a new phase, characterized by the establishment of governmental centers and permanent residences on Indian soil. The most
important kingdom founded by the Turks, with Delhi as its capital,
gradually acquired control over all of Hindustan and even penetrated
into the Deccan. Between the thirteenth and the sixteenth centuries,
five successive dynasties of Turks or Afghans ruled from Delhi. The
fortunes of the kingdom and the character of the rulers during these

*Extension of the Muslim
conquests*

Kutb Minar, near Delhi. This magnificent "pillar of victory," 238 feet high, was erected in the early thirteenth century by Kutb-ud-din, the founder of a Muslim sultanate at Delhi.

300 years cannot be detailed here, but they varied tremendously. In one instance the sultan was a woman named Raziya, who demonstrated great energy and ability but was murdered with her husband—an Ethiopian—by jealous nobles (in 1240). Intrigues and assassinations were frequent because of the absence of an established rule of succession to the throne. By comparison with the Hindu caste-bound society, the Islamic community was democratic, and even an upstart who seized the throne by violence might be accepted as a legitimate sovereign if he proved capable. It was not uncommon for a slave who had been trained for administrative work to be entrusted with large responsibilities both civil and military and finally to usurp authority when a favorable opportunity arose. In fact, one line of Delhi rulers is known as the "Slave Kings" (1206–1290) because its founder had been a slave and viceroy of an early sultan.

In spite of the fact that high positions were open to men of low birth, the administration was thoroughly autocratic in operation, and it derived its character from the personality, the ambitions, or the whims of the ruler. Cruelty, depravity, enlightened statesmanship, and humanitarian sensibilities were all exemplified in erratic sequence. For example, the founder of the Khilji Dynasty (1290–1318) was a benevolent and mild-tempered old gentleman who hated to shed the

Characteristics of Muslim rule

blood even of criminals. The nephew who assassinated and succeeded him was a monster of treachery and cruelty, and so extortionate that he reduced his Hindu subjects to poverty. The next sultan, although scholarly and abstinent by habit, was in some ways even worse than his predecessor. He compelled the entire population of Delhi to move to another site 600 miles distant, leaving the great city desolate. He disrupted commerce by debasing the currency, exacted such heavy taxes that whole villages were abandoned, hunted down men like wild beasts for sport, and dreamed of conquering Persia and China. But this dismal tyrant's successor (promoted to the throne by the army chiefs) during a long and peaceful reign of thirty-seven years adhered to principles of justice and benevolence considerably above the general standard of fourteenth-century states the world over. He reduced taxes, provided poor relief, granted loans to the peasants, and promoted prosperity by reclaiming wastelands and by building extensive irrigation works.

The five-century period of the Turkish invasions and the Delhi Sultanate witnessed many changes in India but few original or constructive cultural developments. The central fact, of course, was the introduction of the Muslim religion and its gradual accommodation to the conditions of the country. At the outset, reconciliation between Islam and Hinduism seemed impossible. Islam was strictly monotheistic, possessed a clear-cut and simple but dogmatic creed, regarded graven images as sinful, and emphasized the equality of believers. Hinduism was polytheistic (although tending toward monotheism or pantheism in its philosophy), taught that there are many equally valid approaches to an understanding of the divine being, delighted in symbols, pictorial forms, and architectural profusion, and carried the concept of human inequality to extremes. The Hindus were noncredal and disposed to tolerance; the Muslims considered it their sacred duty to spread the one true faith of Allah and his Prophet. Nevertheless, the two peoples gradually drew closer together. The Muslim sovereigns did not exterminate the Hindus whom they had subjected. They followed the shrewder policy of laying discriminatory assessments upon the "unbelievers"—a poll tax and a tax on Hindu religious festivals and pilgrimages. Naturally, a good many Hindus became converts to Islam, and those who did so were accepted on an equal basis by the dominant Muslim faction. Moreover, intermarriage took place between Hindus and Muslims in spite of religious scruples on both sides. As already indicated, some of the sultans and their officials were intelligent and progressive in outlook. The best of them tried to improve economic conditions; some were patrons of literature and the arts, encouraged scholarship, and erected splendid monuments.

It is apparent, however, that the general effects of the Turkish conquests were depressing. They were accompanied by orgies of slaughter and spoliation. They threw a pall over the creative spirit of the Hindus, bringing a marked decline in a tradition of intellectual and

*Contrasts between Islam
and Hinduism*

General effects of the Turkish conquests

The Great Mongol Conqueror Genghis Khan, Grandfather of the Founder of the Mongol (Yüan) Dynasty in China.

Mongol invaders: Timur

artistic enterprise that had once been vigorous. Turko-Afghan forces destroyed the major centers of Buddhism, including the great university at Nalanda, and almost completely wiped out the remnants of Buddhism in India. Mosques of excellent workmanship were constructed—often from the stones of demolished Hindu temples—and not all the existing Indian temples were destroyed; but the building of new Hindu religious edifices was prohibited under severe penalties. It is doubtful whether the equalitarian aspects of the teachings of Islam produced any ameliorative effects upon the Indian population. The immediate result, at least, was to create new divisions in an already too sharply divided society. One social effect of the Muslim impact was the subjection of women to a greater degree than ever before. The custom of *purdah* (the veiling and seclusion of women) dates from this era.

After the Turkish sultans had established themselves as sovereigns in Hindustan, they found their position threatened not only by potential Hindu rebellion and by intrigues among their own viceroys but also by new invasions from Central Asia, that inexhaustible reservoir of nomadic peoples. At this time the chief source of disturbance was the expansion of the Mongols, whose force was felt throughout the breadth of Asia and even in Europe. Early in the thirteenth century the famous Mongol chieftain and empire builder Genghis Khan made a brief foray into the Indus valley. His raid was only an incident, but the danger of a Mongol attack upon India persisted. Gradually groups of Mongols settled in northern India and adopted agricultural or industrial pursuits, most of them embracing the Muslim religion. So numerous were they in Delhi in the late thirteenth century that a section of the city was called "Mongol Town." Mongols were employed by the sultan as mercenary troops, in which capacity they were sometimes victimized by his suspicion of their loyalty, and tens of thousands of them were massacred.

Near the end of the fourteenth century northern India was visited by the most devastating raid in all its history, led by Timur the Lame (Tamerlane). Timur, of Turkish descent, had started his career as the chieftain of a small tribal state in Turkestan. After misfortunes and amazing adventures he had welded together a powerful force of cavalry and embarked on a sensational career of conquest. Although he never assumed the title of Khan, he won recognition as overlord from most of the Mongols who had previously followed Genghis Khan. He overran Afghanistan, Persia, and Mesopotamia; then he invaded India with the avowed intention of converting infidels to Islam and procuring booty. He and his troops spent less than a year in India (1398–1399) but left a ruin behind them. The city of Delhi, sacked in a three-day orgy, was turned into a ghost town, so destitute that—to quote a contemporary—"for two whole months not a bird moved a wing in the city." Any place that offered resistance was destroyed and its inhabitants slaughtered or enslaved. Lord Timur carried off with him inestimable quantities of gold and precious stuffs, slaves for all his soldiers, and thousands of skilled craftsmen, including stonemasons to build a great mosque at his capital city of Samarkand in Turkestan. The Delhi Sultanate never fully recovered from the blow dealt to it and to its helpless Hindu subjects by Timur, the "Earth Shaker."

Throughout this period India embraced a number of states, both Muslim and Hindu, which were not included in the Delhi Sultanate. In the fourteenth century two large kingdoms came into existence in the Deccan. Ruled by Muslims, the Bahmani kingdom at its height included about half the Deccan, stretching from sea to sea, and was divided into four provinces. Some of the Bahmani sultans were well-educated and intelligent men, who built lavishly, encouraged trade, and maintained a cosmopolitan atmosphere at their court. In the late fifteenth century the administration deteriorated and the kingdom was broken up into five separate states.

The Bahmani kingdom

Turkish Prisoners before Timur. An Indian painting from the period of Akbar (1556–1605). The use of Arabic script as a decorative device in Indian painting reflects the Muslim influence.

Even more splendid than the Bahmani kingdom was the Hindu empire of Vijayanagar, which at one time dominated the whole southern end of the peninsula as far north as the Kistna River (including, roughly, Madras, Travancore, and Mysore). The capital city, also named Vijayanagar ("City of Victory"), was strongly fortified, heavily populated, and probably—on the testimony of Italian, Portuguese, and Afghan visitors—one of the greatest cities in the world during the fifteenth century. The commerce of the kingdom was eagerly sought. Several kinds of precious stones, particularly large diamonds, were prominent among its exports. The court was sumptuous and the palaces magnificent. Architecture flourished on a grand scale and with an imaginative boldness reminiscent of the classical Sanskrit age. The foundations which underlay the brilliant culture of this last great Hindu empire, however, were not sound. In spite of an orderly government and in the midst of great wealth, the common people suffered from extreme privation and were fleeced by avaricious officials. Luxurious and profligate courts, the encouragement of prostitution in the temples, and the compulsory burning of widows (requiring the mass immolation of thousands of women on the death of a king) were hardly evidences of a healthy society. Unfortunately, a haughty and embittered rivalry between the Hindu and the Bahmani kingdoms weakened both states. In 1565 the almost impregnable city of Vijayanagar was taken and wantonly destroyed by troops from a league of neighboring Muslim powers, and the southern Hindu empire sank into a permanent decline.

2. CHINA UNDER THE SUNG, MONGOL, AND MING DYNASTIES (960–1644)

For about fifty years following the collapse of the great T'ang Dynasty in the early tenth century, China was a divided country with power in the hands of military dictators. After this chaotic but relatively brief interregnum (known to Chinese tradition as the "Five Dynasties"), unity and a strong central government were re-established by an able general who assumed the imperial title and founded the Sung Dynasty. This dynasty, like its predecessor, the T'ang, endured for about three centuries (960–1279). Although the first Sung had been an army officer, he revived the ancient administrative system and restored the power of the civilian bureaucracy. In contrast to the T'ang, the Sung rulers did not adopt a policy of imperialism, and even relinquished control over portions of the empire. Territories in the north and the northwest were lost to seminomadic peoples who, while founding independent kingdoms, assimilated many aspects of Chinese culture. One of these northern groups, the Khitan, established a kingdom in southern Manchuria, annexed territory south of the Great Wall in the Peking area, and collected tribute from the Sung emperors. Although the Khitan were entirely separate from the Chinese in origin, a corruption of their name—"Cathay"—came to be a Western designation for China, a circumstance which indicates that the Khitan did not long retain their distinctive traits after coming into close contact with China's mature civilization.

Early in the twelfth century the Khitan state (Liao) was overthrown by a people of similar stock, the Juchên, who not only occupied Manchuria and Mongolia but also conquered the greater part of northern China. Thus, beginning about 1141, the Sung actually controlled only the Yangtze valley and regions to the south. They established their capital at Hangchow (then known as Lin-an), a magnificent port but far distant from the traditional centers of imperial administration. The later, or southern, Sung period was characterized by a less vigorous administration and by the familiar but depressing symptoms of dynastic decay. These disadvantages, however, were to some extent counterbalanced by the fact that southern China felt the influence of Chinese culture more fully than it had before. The peoples of the south and southwest not only became more completely incorporated into Chinese society but also began to contribute leadership to the state. The center of population was shifting to the south, and there was evidence also that originality and initiative were abundant in this area. During the Southern Sung period (1141–1279) northern China continued to be ruled by the Juchên from the old Sung capital at Kaifeng on the Yellow River. While the loss of so much territory to alien conquerors was humiliating to the Sung emperors, it produced no appreciable permanent changes in the north. The Juchên adapted themselves to Chinese ways as readily as had the Khitan. Both Buddhism and Confucianism obtained a strong hold upon them, and the rulers, following the established convention, adopted a Chinese dynastic title (*Chin* or *Kin,* meaning "Gold").

Peace, internal stability, and prolific cultural activity were characteristic of the Sung period, especially during the first century and a half. As earlier, a flourishing commerce contributed to an increase in wealth and promoted a knowledge of foreign lands. Overland trade declined, partly because the caravan routes were no longer controlled by the Chinese, but business was brisk in port cities of the southeastern coast. Foreign merchants, among whom the Arabs still predominated, were granted the right of residence in the trading centers, subject to the jurisdiction of an Inspector of Foreign Trade. At the same time the Chinese themselves were beginning to participate more extensively in oceanic commerce. The early Sung emperors undertook ambitious public works, including irrigation projects. Apparently society as a whole attained a fair level of prosperity, as evidenced by an increase in population.

The late eleventh century was significant for a reform movement

The Southern Sung period

Heavy Porcelain Vase with Simple Design. Sung Dynasty (960– 1279).

launched by a scholar-official, Wang An-shih (1021–1086), who held the position of chief minister for a number of years. His proposals were the subject of acrimonious controversy and never were carried out in entirety, but they represented a realistic attempt to improve the administration, and they focused attention upon the plight of the common man. Wang promoted the establishment of public schools endowed with state lands, and he advocated revision of the civil-service examinations to encourage a knowledge of practical problems instead of proficiency in classical literary forms. His most determined efforts were directed toward a program of relief for the poor farmers by direct government assistance, by revision of the inequitable tax system and the abolition of forced labor, and by a redistribution of land. He wanted the government to control commerce, fix prices, buy up farm surpluses, and make loans to farmers at a low rate of interest on the security of their growing crops. Wang An-shih's proposals for agrarian relief anticipated some of the measures inaugurated by governments in recent times, and his overall program approximated a kind of state socialism. Although he insisted that he was merely adapting genuine Confucian principles to the needs of the time, his opponents branded him as a dangerous innovator. The contest between the Innovators (Wang's disciples) and the Conservatives continued into the next century, with the emperors favoring sometimes one and sometimes the other group; but the conservative faction ultimately prevailed. Wang's radical proposals, however, have been studied with interest by modern reformers in China and elsewhere.

An invasion by the Mongols brought about the final collapse of the Sung Dynasty and subjected all China, for the first time in its history, to the rule of a foreign conqueror. The Mongol Asiatic empire, like so many of its predecessors, was established with almost incredible swiftness in a series of military campaigns, but it was for a brief period one of the largest ever known. In the early thirteenth century the great Mongol conqueror Genghis Khan overthrew the kingdoms adjacent to China on the north and then swept westward across all Asia. After making a brief foray into India he subdued Persia and Mesopotamia and occupied large stretches of Russian territory north and west of the Caspian Sea. Although the invasion of China was probably inevitable, the Sung emperor contributed to his own downfall by playing a double game with the Mongols. So eager was he to get rid of the Juchên rulers in north China that he sent troops to help the Mongols against them; then he rashly attacked the Mongol forces and exposed his own dominions to the fury of the ruthless and swift-riding horsemen. The conquest of southern China was completed by Genghis Khan's grandson, Kublai Khan, after many years of hard fighting, during which the Mongols not only had to occupy the coastal cities but also had to accustom themselves to naval warfare. In 1279 the last Chinese army was defeated (the commanding general is said to have jumped into the sea with the infant Sung prince in his arms), and Kublai became the master of China.

The huge Asiatic empire of the Mongols, which reached from the China Sea to eastern Europe, was too large to be administered effectively as a unit and did not long remain intact. Religious differences contributed to its dissolution. Before the end of the thirteenth century most of the western princes (khans) had become Muslims and repudiated the authority of Kublai's family, who favored a Tibetan form of Buddhism. Kublai's descendants, however, from their imperial capital of Peking, governed China for the better part of a century (1279–1368).

The dissolution of Kublai's empire

The accession of the Mongol (or Yüan) Dynasty seemed to threaten a serious interruption in the normal course of Chinese civilization. Mongol rule remained essentially a military occupation imposed upon traditional Chinese institutions. Fortunately the damage inflicted was only temporary, and there was actually some progress during this period of foreign domination. The Mongols were notoriously cruel conquerors, leaving ruined cities and mutilated corpses as monuments to the folly of those who resisted them. The bitterly contested occupation of southern China was accompanied by a decimation of the native population in some areas. Nevertheless, the Mongol rulers were wise enough to recognize the desirability of preserving such a great state as China and the advantage to be gained from taxing its people instead of exterminating them. The nomad warriors could not resist the influence of Chinese culture, and the traditional Chinese administrative system was not completely uprooted. The civil-service examinations were suspended for a time, and Chinese were excluded from most governmental posts, although the Mongol emperors employed foreigners of various nationalities in high positions at court. In the fourteenth century, when the dynasty showed signs of weakening and native unrest became ominous, the emperor reinstituted the examination system and admitted Chinese to office, chiefly at the lower level.

The rule of the Mongol emperors

While the Mongol emperors patronized Buddhism, they did not seriously interfere with other native cults and they permitted the introduction of Western religions, although Islam was the only one of these to retain a permanent place. The emperors' lavish endowment of temples and monasteries strained the economy by removing tracts of land from the tax registers and impoverished the peasants, whose holdings had been confiscated. Many peasants lost their lands when conscripted as laborers for the construction of palaces, irrigation works, and an improved transportation system. A notable undertaking was the rebuilding and extension of the Grand Canal linking the capital city of Peking to the Yangtze valley by an inland waterway.

Religious and economic policies

During the Mongol period China was by no means isolated from other regions. The area under the jurisdiction of Peking was consid-

The Imperial Post Road. This road, through a valley west of Chunking, is part of the old Imperial Post Road connecting Peking with the Tibetan capital, Lhasa.

Extension of foreign contacts

erably larger than the empire of the Sung, and the emperors attempted to increase it still further by schemes of conquest of dubious value. Kublai Khan made two attempts to invade Japan (in 1274 and 1281), employing both Chinese and Korean vessels, but a typhoon wrecked many of his ships and the Japanese annihilated the landing party. Fortunately, peaceful intercourse was continued with other nations, near and far. Overland commerce was facilitated by imperial highways which the Mongols built deep into Central Asia and even to Persia. That travel was comparatively safe is indicated by the large number of foreign visitors in China during this period. Foreign merchants enjoyed special privileges in the Mongol empire, while Chinese were discriminated against. Russians, Arabs, and Jews entered China for purposes of trade, as did Genoese and Venetians. The effects of this extensive commerce was to impair rather than strengthen the economy because it drained precious metals out of China and led to inflation of the currency. Marco Polo, the most famous of many European visitors, who lived and traveled widely in China for seventeen years (1275–1292), astonished his countrymen with his glowing report upon returning home (he described Hangchow, the Southern Sung capital, as "the finest and noblest city in the world"). But Marco Polo moved in privileged circles and failed to notice the condition of the common people. By the fourteenth century starvation was widespread and more Chinese had been reduced to slavery than at any other time in history.

In the fourteenth century, Mongol power was undermined by the decadence of the ruling house and by the growing discontent of the Chinese people, who never forgot that they had been subjugated by a barbarian conqueror. Rebellion was brought to a successful conclusion under the leadership of a dynamic, if somewhat grotesque, soldier of fortune, who captured Peking in 1368 and drove the last Mongol emperor into the wastes of Mongolia. This rebel leader was a man of low birth who had been orphaned at an early age and had exchanged the life of a Buddhist monk for that of a bandit. Nevertheless, he was accepted as having won the Mandate of Heaven and became the first emperor of the Ming ("Brilliant" or "Glorious") Dynasty, which lasted from 1368 to 1644. The dynasty proved to be extremely successful and gave renewed proof of the potency of Chinese institutions, although it added little that was new. The government adhered to the Sung patterns, or in some ways more closely to the T'ang, particularly in its emphasis upon the forceful expansion of territorial boundaries. Ming China was a large state, with its authority extending into Manchuria, Mongolia, Indochina, Burma, and the southwestern region facing Tibet. While the great Mongol empire of the thirteenth century had fallen to pieces, it gave promise of being resurrected by Timur (Tamerlane), the master of Turkestan and scourge of India. Although the Ming court regarded Timur's emissaries as tribute bearers, the "Earth Shaker" was actually setting forth on an expedition to conquer China when he died prematurely in 1405. In spite of this stroke of fortune, the Ming emperors made little effort to recover either Turkestan or Sinkiang.

A noteworthy aspect of the early Ming period was the development and rapid expansion of Chinese navigation. The mariner's compass had been in use perhaps since the eleventh century, and some large ships had been constructed; but now maritime enterprise was given tremendous impetus. Chinese sailing vessels, equipped with as many as four decks and comfortable living quarters, undertook voyages to the East Indies, the Malay Peninsula, Ceylon, India, and Arabia, returning with merchandise, tribute, and valuable geographical information. They may have ventured westward around Africa's Cape of Good Hope. In its heyday the Ming navy was more than equal to that of any contemporary European state, although when stationed in the home waters of the Yangtze region it was exposed to attacks from Japanese pirates. Overseas expeditions were discontinued after the demise of Timur and the decay of Mongol power in Central Asia reopened the caravan routes to the West. From about 1424 the government restricted Chinese shipping to coastal waters and the network of canals and discouraged foreign travel on the part of its subjects. The

The overthrow of the Mongols and establishment of the Ming Dynasty

Maritime achievements under the Ming Dynasty

Fall of the Ming Dynasty. The death of the last of the Ming emperors at the hands of the invading Manchus when they captured Peking in 1644.

result was not only a loss of revenue from commerce but also an unfortunate isolation of China at the very time when the Western peoples were beginning to emerge from their provincialism. Instead of retaining the initiative on the high seas, the later Ming rulers proved inefficient in defending their own coasts.

Decline of the Ming Dynasty

A decline in the vitality of the administration was apparent long before the Ming Dynasty came to a close. Officials became lazy and corrupt; power passed into the hands of court favorites and eunuchs; and exorbitant taxes oppressed the peasants to the point of ruin. While the costs of government mounted dizzily—in 1639 military expenditures alone were ten times greater than the entire revenue of the first Ming emperor—territories were being lost through incompetence and rebellion. Although the dynasty finally succumbed to another foreign invasion, internal dissension was the real cause of its collapse.

Cultural developments under the Sung and Ming: Neo-Confucianism

In turning from the political to the cultural developments that took place in China during the Sung, Mongol, and Ming dynasties, we may note that a renewal of interest in philosophical speculation occurred, reaching a climax in the latter half of the twelfth century. This revival represented a return to the fountainhead of Chinese thought—the sages of antiquity, particularly Confucius—but it introduced several new ideas and was not a mere repetition of ancient formulas. The most noted Chinese thinker of this period was Chu Hsi (1130–1200), who held a position at the Sung court and was an opponent of the so-called Innovators (disciples of Wang An-shih). Although Chu Hsi claimed to be interpreting Confucius' teachings in accordance with their original and uncorrupted meaning, he and his associates actually founded a Neo-Confucian school, with a metaphysics which incorporated elements of Taoism and Buddhism. They stressed the concept of the "Supreme Ultimate" or Absolute, a Final Cause which underlies the whole material universe and is antecedent to every rational or moral principle. Nevertheless, Chu Hsi, like his ancient master Confucius, was chiefly interested in human nature and its proper development in an ethical and social order. He reaffirmed Mencius' faith in man's natural capacity for good and upheld the traditional ethical system exemplified by the family and embodied in a paternalistic state administered by a bureaucracy of scholar-officials. The teachings of Chu Hsi, although stoutly contested by rival scholars in his day, eventually came to be regarded as the definitive commentary on the doctrines of the ancient sage. Venerated as orthodoxy, they discouraged creative thought among later scholars and administrators.

A prodigious output of literature has been characteristic of Chinese civilization during almost every period except the most ancient. Printing was very common from Sung times on. Books were printed from wooden blocks, from metal plates, and from movable type made of earthenware, tin, and wood. Poetry seldom equaled the best of the T'ang age in beauty or spontaneity, but lengthy histories, encyclopedias, dictionaries, geographies, and scientific treatises were produced. The most original literary developments were in the fields of the drama and the novel. The Chinese drama attained the level of a major art form during the Mongol Dynasty, partly because the suspension of the civil-service examinations, by cutting off opportunities for official careers, prompted men of talent to turn their attention to a medium of popular entertainment which they had previously considered unworthy of notice. The dramas of the Mongol period, of which more than a hundred have survived, combined lively action with vivid portrayal of character, and they were written in the common idiom of the people rather than in the classical language of scholars. The Chinese theater, like the English theater of Shakespeare's day, was largely devoid of scenery and properties, although the performers made use of elaborate costumes and heavy make-up. Ordinarily all the parts were filled by male actors. The plays were in verse, but, in contrast to the Elizabethan and modern Western drama, the speeches were sung rather than recited and the orchestra (placed directly on the stage) contributed an essential element to the production.

The Chinese novel, originating apparently in the tales of public storytellers, developed contemporaneously with the drama but matured a little later. Its growth was aided indirectly by the sterility of the academic atmosphere that pervaded the court and the bureaucracy of the Ming Dynasty. In the fifteenth century, veneration for Confucian

Fantastic Ceramic Figure of a Deity. Ming Dynasty (1368–1644).

Sung Printed Book. A page from the *Fa-yuan chu-lin* ("Forest of Pearls in the Garden of the Law"). The book was compiled by the Buddhist monk and scholar Tao-Shih in 688. It was printed in 1124, fully three centuries earlier than the Gutenberg Bible.

Development of the Chinese novel

Wooden Statue of Kuan-yin, "Goddess of Mercy." This popular deity, usually represented in female form, was actually derived from a legendary Indian bodhisattva. (In Mahayana Buddhism a bodhisattva was one who had attained enlightenment but chose to remain in the world to help others.)

orthodoxy, especially as embodied in the teachings of Chu Hsi, had become such a fetish among the official coterie of scholars that one of them declared: "The truth has been made manifest. . . . No more writing is needed.".[1] Some men of letters sought a creative outlet by composing narratives in the plain language of the people. In their hands the novel became a highly successful literary medium, skillfully contrived but purveying robust adventure, humor, warm feeling, and salty realism. Frequently historical themes were chosen for subject matter, but the tales also provided commentary—sometimes satirical—upon contemporary society and government.

Sung painting   A large proportion of the Chinese works of art still extant was produced during the period which is being reviewed here. Sculpture had declined in quality since T'ang times, but painting reached its highest peak of excellence under the Sung. The most beautiful and typical Sung paintings are landscapes, frequently executed in only one color but conveying the impression of an intimate understanding of nature in her various moods. Through economy of line, omission of nonessentials, and painstaking treatment of significant detail, the artists sought to bring to light the reality which lies hidden behind the world of appearances. Their dreamy creations were obviously influenced by the mystical teachings of Buddhism and Taoism. Landscape painting was at its ripest during the Southern Sung period, when the leading artists took full advantage of the natural beauty of the Hangchow region. They sometimes painted panoramic scenes on long strips of

[1] L. C. Goodrich, *A Short History of the Chinese People*, p. 196.

Spring Morning at the Palace of Han. Sung Dynasty. Chinese painting emphasized landscapes rather than people and the representation of poetic or philosophic ideas rather than facts.

silk. These were fastened to rollers and could be viewed leisurely by simply holding the rollers in one's hands and winding the painted scroll from one roller to the other.

Architecture attained particular pre-eminence under the Ming, a dynasty which delighted in glorifying and embellishing the visible aspects of Chinese culture. Ming architecture was by no means new in conception, but it was prolific and has left many impressive monuments. The popularity of elaborate gardens, summer residences, game preserves, and hunting lodges among the aristocracy provided opportunities for the designing of graceful pavilions and arched bridges. Fully developed by this period was the pagoda style of temple, distinguished by curving roofs which were usually of tile and frequently in brilliant colors.

China has only rarely been isolated from other parts of the world, and many of her cultural changes were the result of foreign contacts.

Ming architecture

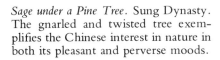

Sage under a Pine Tree. Sung Dynasty. The gnarled and twisted tree exemplifies the Chinese interest in nature in both its pleasant and perverse moods.

"War Spirit." A Ming Dynasty painting.

Achievements in agriculture and in the applied sciences

The Chinese were indebted to the Arabs for contributions in the field of mathematics and probably also in medicine, although the Chinese had themselves accumulated a considerable store of medical data. Inoculation against smallpox seems to have been practiced before the end of the Sung Dynasty. Eyeglasses came into use (from Italy) during the Ming period. New crops of Western origin began to be cultivated in China. Sorghum, introduced in the thirteenth century, and maize in the sixteenth have been raised extensively in northern China ever since. Cotton production, which also began in the thirteenth century, was greatly expanded under the Ming. One innovation which may have been of domestic rather than foreign inspiration was in the technique of warfare. The explosive properties of gunpowder had long been known, but not until the eleventh century were they utilized for the manufacture of lethal weapons. The Mongols, in the thirteenth and fourteenth centuries, employed bombs that perhaps were propelled by primitive cannons. Although these early artillery pieces were crude, they foreshadowed the increasingly destructive character of modern warfare.

3. THE RISE OF FEUDALISM AND MILITARY DICTATORS IN JAPAN (c. 900–1600)

Contrasts between Japan and China

Even though Chinese culture had been incorporated into the foundations of Japanese civilization and exerted a lasting influence, social and political trends in Japan during the medieval era were very different from those in the great mainland state. While China was frequently harassed by nomadic invaders and was temporarily subjugated by a foreign dynasty, her society and culture departed little from the ancient pattern. By contrast, Japan, enjoying the natural protection of her insular position, was not seriously affected by disturbances from without; yet her institutions were profoundly altered as the result of conflicts taking place within her own society. A theoretical unity and an arbitrary and artificial scheme of government had been imposed upon Japan by the reform of the mid-seventh century, which attempted to introduce the Chinese imperial system in its entirety. How completely the attempt had failed is illustrated by the events of the next thousand years. Only belatedly, and after indecisive and exhausting strife, was the basis discovered for a stable and unified society. And when stability was achieved, it was through improvised institutions which were inadequate to solve the problems certain to arise in the wake of economic and cultural change.

The political history of Japan during this period is characterized mainly by two factors: (1) the persistence of an indirect method of government, with the actual power shifting from one family to another but exercised in the name of an inviolate emperor, whose effective authority rarely extended beyond the environs of Kyoto; (2) the feudalization of society and the growth of extralegal military units which imposed their will upon territories under their control. To the end of the sixteenth century the technique of government was variable and uncertain, although the trend from civilian to military authority was unmistakable. At the opening of the seventeenth century a centralized administration was finally established which ended a long period of civil wars, enforced a coherent national policy, and endured almost unshaken until the middle of the nineteenth century. Even when it was overthrown, the habits which it had instilled in the Japanese people could not easily be uprooted.

Character of Japanese political history

In the ninth century the Fujiwara family, through intermarriage with the imperial family and through possession of the office of

A Feudal Stronghold. Hirosaki Castle, in northern Japan, was the residence of one of the "outer daimyo" during the Tokugawa Shogunate. The castle grounds are now a popular resort for cherry-blossom viewing.

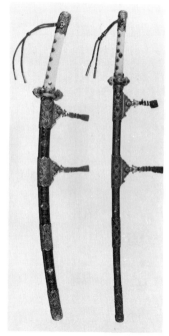

Swords of the Feudal Nobility. This type of curved sword, of fine steel, was worn suspended from the girdle by great daimyo or court nobles during Japan's early feudal age (twelfth to fourteenth centuries). Note the jewelel hilts, the ornately decorated scabbards, and the loops for hanging the swords.

regent, had acquired a dominant position in the government, reducing the emperor to a figurehead. The Fujiwara retained their ascendancy until the twelfth century, but their rule over the outlying sections became more and more nominal as new lands were brought into production by reclamation or by conquest of the aborigines, and as aggressive landowners succeeded in withdrawing their estates from the jurisdiction of the imperial tax collectors. The men who possessed estates in these frontier regions were not hampered by the elaborate rules of etiquette or by the mania for classical Chinese studies that absorbed the energies of the courtiers at Kyoto. They formulated their own standards of conduct, largely dictated by the desire to preserve and extend their holdings, and quarreled with one another over conflicting claims. Naturally, many small farmers relinquished their property to powerful neighbors in return for protection and sank to a position of serfdom. Gradually a manorial economy came into existence, showing some points of similarity to the manorial regime in western Europe during the later Middle Ages.

By a remarkable coincidence of history Japanese society took on aspects of feudalism at the very time when feudal institutions were evolving in western Europe. Of course it would be a mistake to assume that Japanese and Western feudalism were identical, but the parallels between them are striking. In Japan and western Europe alike, leadership was passing to a class of mounted warriors who owned land, dominated the peasantry, and exercised governmental power as a private right. In Japan the rising class of warrior-landlords was derived partly from clan chieftains, partly from adventurers who had established title purely by the sword, and partly from imperial officials who had converted an administrative office into a family possession. The members of the landed class established hereditary claims to their holdings and entered into binding agreements with one another, creating a series of dependent relationships equivalent to a system of lords and vassals. As in the case of European feudalism, the system was extended partly through the voluntary surrender of property by small landowners who sought a noble's protection, and partly through the granting of benefices or fiefs by great lords to lesser men in order to secure their services as vassals. Another parallel to the growth of European feudalism is seen in the fact that property belonging to religious foundations was frequently converted into fiefs. Some Buddhist monasteries and temples became formidable military units, but Japanese religious orders never attained an independence like that of the higher clergy in medieval Europe. They remained generally subservient to the aristocracy.

The Japanese warriors, who corresponded in status and in profession to the medieval knights, were known as samurai, or bushi. The samurai developed a fraternal spirit and a code of conduct to which they jealously clung as their special prerogative and which they called "the way of the horse and the bow." (The term *bushido,* not used before the eighteenth century, denoted a romantic and artificial version of the old feudal code.) Like the European code of chivalry it stressed valor, loyalty, and the necessity of preferring death to dishonor. The samurai was bound above all else to protect, defend, or avenge his lord, to this end sacrificing his own life and, if need be, the lives of his family—a remarkable ideal in view of the sacredness of family ties in Japan. So sensitive was the samurai to any taint of dishonor that he was expected to commit suicide (by a ritual of falling on one's sword, known as hara-kiri) if there was no other way to wipe out the stain on his reputation.

In the twelfth century, feudal warfare culminated in a struggle between two powerful families, the Taira and the Minamoto. With the victory of the Minamoto, their leader reorganized the government on a basis which frankly recognized the paramount role of the landowning warrior-nobility. To avoid appearing as a usurper, the head of the Minamoto family assumed only a military title, becoming known as Shogun, and pretended to be acting as the agent of the emperor. In reality, for the next six and one-half centuries (1192–1867) Japan had a dual government: the civil authority at Kyoto headed by the emperor and embracing various ranks of court nobility whose functions were ornamental rather than essential, and the Bakufu ("Tent Government") headed by the Shogun and commanding the services of the powerful military leaders who owned most of the land. The creation of the Shogunate, as this military-feudal government came to be called, indicates how thoroughly feudalism had permeated Japanese society. The real governors of the country now were not the imperial bureaucracy but the vassals of the Shogun.

Although the Shogunate proved to be a durable institution, it did not remain perpetually in the hands of any one family. On the death of the first Shogun his widow's relatives seized control, with her connivance. This extremely capable woman became known as the "Nun Shogun," because she wielded political influence even after she had nominally retired into holy orders, and with her help the Hojo family came into power. For more than a century the Hojo appointed puppet Shoguns over whom they maintained a regency. Thus, by the early thirteenth century the government of Japan was a confusing series of subterfuges. The central authority (so far as any existed) was exercised by a regent in the name of a puppet general (the Shogun) who, in turn, was theoretically an underling of an emperor, who was himself controlled by a regent (or, in some cases, by an elder member of the imperial family living in retirement). Because the Hojo family had no inherent claim to superiority over other great feudal houses, its ascendancy created jealous dissatisfaction and led inevitably to further conflict. A remarkable incident occurred in 1333 when the Emperor Daigo II attempted to cut through the sham governmental fabric and

The Golden Pavilion (Kiukakuji). A residence built by Yoshimitsu, third Ashikaga Shogun in 1397.

assert his right to rule as well as reign. He mustered sufficient military forces to capture and burn the Shogun's headquarters at Kamakura and ended the Hojo regency. The sequel to this bold stroke, however, was simply a half century of civil war, with two rival emperors, each bidding for support. The schism in the imperial household was healed and order temporarily restored with the triumph of another great military family, the Ashikaga, who again reduced the emperor to a position of impotence.

The period of feudal warfare

The Ashikaga Shoguns (1392–1573) made the serious mistake of taking up residence in Kyoto, where they were exposed to the softening influence of court society and, by relaxing their vigilance, lost effective control over the turbulent lords of outlying districts. Feudal rivalry became increasingly unrestrained until, beginning in the late fifteenth century, Japan experienced 100 years of almost continual warfare. Robbery and pillage were rampant; almost all vestiges of a central government disappeared; even the private estates which the emperor had owned in various parts of the country were absorbed into the feudal domains. The imperial family as well as the Kyoto courtiers were subjected to humiliation by swaggering soldiers. Reduced to poverty, one emperor eked out a living by selling his autograph. In 1500 an imperial corpse lay unburied for six weeks because there was no money in the treasury. The Ashikaga Shogun was almost as impotent as the emperor and quite unable to stop the brigandage and slaughter carried on wantonly by feudal retainers and robber monks. Conditions in Japan seemed to be fast approaching anarchy when, at the close of the sixteenth century, the Shogunate was drastically and effectively reorganized by the Tokugawa family.

In spite of all the confusion and turmoil, however, there were constructive forces at work. The character of Japanese feudalism was changing in a significant direction. Large territorial units were taking shape under fairly competent administrative systems. This trend was the result partly of natural evolution and partly of the policy of the Shoguns. At the outset the Shogun had attempted to control the various fiefs by sending out officials responsible to him and appointed from the military capital at Kamakura; but these officials acquired hereditary status and merged into the hierarchy. The Constable in particular—an officer who was given administrative authority over a province—gradually became a great baron or magnate, absorbing into his own dominion the estates within his jurisdiction. The great lords grew in prestige and material resources at the expense of the lesser fiefholders. During the almost constant warfare of the fifteenth and sixteenth centuries, peasants were pressed into military service, and consequently the importance of the knights began to decline. The appearance of mass armies composed of commoners was comparable to the trend in European countries during this same period; but, while the European armies were recruited chiefly by the kings of national states, the Japanese forces were under the control of feudal lords.

*The ascendancy of the
great lords*

Leadership was passing from the knightly (samurai) class as a whole to the great lords, who were known as daimyo ("Great Names"). The daimyo incorporated many small estates into their own possessions and employed the samurai as managers and as subordinate military commanders. The families which attained the status of daimyo came to be referred to as clans, but they were actually very different from the clans of early Japanese society. Their territories were feudal provinces, and the people under their rule were bound by vassalage or servitude rather than by blood relationship. The ascendancy of the daimyo, while it by no means eliminated feudal dissension, greatly reduced the number of rival units and also ensured a considerable measure of stability within each unit.

The daimyo

Economically and culturally, Japan's feudal age was a period, not of retrogression or stagnation, but of progress. That this was so may seem strange in view of the roughness of the times and the instability of political institutions, but the evidence is undeniable. The Japanese maintained commercial contacts with other Far Eastern countries and continued to receive stimulating influences from China. Foreign trade, increasing steadily from the twelfth century, led to the substitution of money for rice or cloth as a medium of exchange and promoted diversified economic activity. By the fifteenth century the Japanese were exporting not only raw materials, such as lumber, gold, and pearls, but also manufactured goods. Japanese folding fans and screens were in great demand in China, and steel swords were exported by the thousands to a large Far Eastern market. The curved swords forged by Japanese craftsmen in the thirteenth century are said to have been unsurpassed even by the famous blades of Toledo and Damascus.

*Economic progress during
the feudal age*

The samurai and Zen Buddhism

Costume for the No *Dance Drama* (seventeenth century). Lavish and colorful pictorial decoration was characteristic of the costumes worn by *No* actors.

Society during Japan's feudal period was far from being purely agrarian. Commercial and industrial centers came into being, and a few developed into populous cities. Groups of merchants organized guilds for mutual protection and to promote the marketing of their wares. Moreover, in contrast to most of western Europe, the feudal classes participated in capitalistic enterprises. In addition to professional merchants, monastic orders, samurai, great nobles, and occasionally even the Shogun invested in trade.

As in earlier times, various schools of Buddhism contributed to cultural development, largely because they continued to serve as channels for intellectual and aesthetic currents from China. One of the most prominent sects, the Zen (from the Chinese *Ch'an*), was introduced at the close of the twelfth century and spread rapidly among the samurai. Zen Buddhism taught that enlightenment would come to the individual not through study or any intellectual process, but by a sudden flash of insight experienced when one was in tune with nature. Because it stressed physical discipline, self-control, and the practice of meditation in place of formal scholarship, the sect appealed to the warrior class, who felt that Zen teachings gave supernatural sanction to the attitudes which they had already come to regard as essential to their station. Though its doctrines were fundamentally anti-intellectual, its monks fostered both learning and art and injected several refinements into Japanese upper-class society. Among these were an unrivaled type of landscape architecture, the art of flower arrangement, and a delicate social ritual known as the tea ceremony—all of which were Chinese importations but elaborated with great sensitivity in Japan.

Religious developments in Japan during the medieval period were in many ways distinctive. New sects sprang up and caught the imagination of the common people. Some of them proposed the elimination of ceremony and the abolition of distinctions between clergy and laity. Others encouraged a fierce intolerance and a worship of national greatness. That the Japanese lower classes were aroused and encouraged by the new teachings is certain. During the tumultuous fifteenth and sixteenth centuries uprisings against the feudal nobles were instigated by religious congregations, and in a few instances the revolts were successful. These manifestations of popular intransigence, though, had little or no permanent effect upon Japanese society, which remained predominantly aristocratic in structure and tone.

Many other cultural changes resulted from the growth of a productive and diversified economy and from the mutual stimulation among competing religious sects. While sacred writings were being collected and translated in the monasteries, and while courtiers continued to write in the polished but lifeless classical manner, literature was enriched by the addition of tales of daring and high adventure conceived for the entertainment and edification of men of arms. These

The No *Drama*. This art form is characterized by rhythmical recitation of texts, traditional music, and symbolic movement of players.

stories of knightly prowess, composed in a flowing poetical prose and sometimes sung to the accompaniment of a lute, are comparable to the heroic epics of medieval European chivalry. No counterpart of the European poems of romantic love, however, arose in fuedal Japan, where women had sunk to a position of abject subordination to male authority. All the arts were influenced by Chinese models, but the Japanese had long since demonstrated their originality in adapting styles to their own tastes. Particularly impressive were the paintings executed by monks of the Zen sect in the fifteenth and sixteenth centuries. These were chiefly landscapes and similar in style to those of the Chinese artists of the Ming Dynasty, but they possessed an individuality and freshness of their own.

The exacting aesthetic standards of the aristocratic patrons of the Zen sect are also evident in a specialized form of dramatic art, the *No,* which emerged during this period. The *No* "lyric-drama" or "dance-drama" was not a foreign importation but almost purely a native product. Its origins can be traced to ancient folk dances and also to ritualistic dances associated with both Shintoist and Buddhist modes of worship. In its perfected form, it became a unique vehicle of artistic expression and entertainment, which heightened the appeal of rhythm and graceful postures by relating them to dramatic incidents. The themes of the dance-dramas were traditional narratives, but they were presented with great restraint and by suggestive symbolism rather than by literal re-enactment, somewhat in the manner of a series of tableaux. The performers wore masks as well as rich costumes and chanted their lines to the accompaniment of drums and flutes. The *No* drama achieved great popularity among the samurai class and was at its height from the fourteenth to the sixteenth centuries. In spite of its extremely stylized character, it has never entirely disappeared from the artistic heritage of Japan.

4. THE EMERGENCE OF CIVILIZATIONS IN SUB-SAHARAN AFRICA

The period 1000 to 1500 A.D. represented a time of state formation in black Africa. Chieftaincies in many areas were consolidated under divine kings. Numerous kingdoms evolved into expansive territorial empires, embracing a rich diversity of cultures, languages, and religious systems. The process of empire-building was most pronounced in the savanna, or Sudanic zone of West Africa.

*Dramatic growth in the
trans-Saharan trade leads
to state formation in the
West African Sudan*

Trans-Saharan trade expanded at a rapid rate after the eighth century, due in large measure to the initiative of Arabs and Berbers. Concurrently, growing demands from European and North African merchants for gold motivated West Africans to organize themselves on a larger, more efficient scale in order to meet these demands. Ghana's armies, under a black Soninke dynasty, captured the prosperous Berber trading center of Audoghast in the tenth century. Successive Ghanaian monarchs grew immensely rich by tightly controlling the flow of gold across their territory. A production tax was placed on gold exports and nuggets of a certain size were hoarded in order to keep the mineral rare. Ghana's hegemony extended to the upper Niger and Senegal rivers and to the burgeoning commercial centers of Timbuktu, Jenné, and Gao.

*Ghana's wealth based
mainly on gold exports*

Ghana was not a Muslim empire, but its principal customers and those who controlled the strategic desert oases had become Muslims by the tenth century. Rulers in neighboring Takrur accepted Islam about 1000 A.D. and thus became West Africa's first kingdom to do so. Ghana itself had become dangerously dependent on Muslim financial advisers and merchants. Its pagan king was eventually forced to divide the capital city of Kumbi-Saleh into two parts, one for Muslims, the other for pagans.

*The Almoravids overrun
Ghana*

Islam, the handmaiden of West African commerce, could not be contained. By 1054, large bands of nomadic Muslim Berbers had declared a holy war, or *jihad,* and succeeded in recapturing the vital Audoghast markets. Ghana, on the Saharan fringe, had already been weakened by environmental deterioration brought on by overgrazing of pastures and failure to rotate crops. Its capitulation to these puritanical Berber Muslims, called Almoravids, seemed almost inevitable. But the Almoravids brought insecurity to Ghanaian market places and fear along the caravan routes. This condition upset the delicate trade balance between the forest gold miners, the Ghanaian middlemen, and

The Almoravid movement

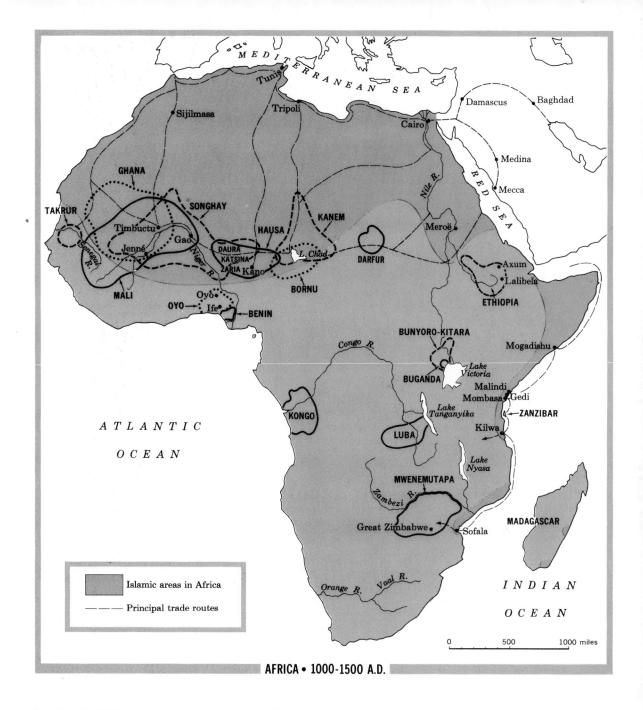

MEDITERRANEAN SEA

Damascus

Baghdad

Sijilmasa

Tripoli

Tunis

Cairo

RED SEA

Medina

Mecca

GHANA

TAKRUR

Senegal R.

SONGHAY

Timbuctu

Jenné

Gao

Niger R.

MALI

HAUSA

DAURA
KATSINA
ZARIA Kano

BORNU

KANEM

L. Chad

DARFUR

Nile R.

Meroë

Axum

Lalibela

ETHIOPIA

Oyo

OYO → Ife

BENIN

Congo R.

BUNYORO-KITARA

BUGANDA

Lake Victoria

Mogadishu

Malindi
Mombasa Gedi

ZANZIBAR

ATLANTIC

OCEAN

KONGO

LUBA

Lake Tanganyika

Kilwa

Lake Nyasa

MWENEMUTAPA

Zambezi R.

Great Zimbabwe

Sofala

MADAGASCAR

INDIAN

OCEAN

Orange R. Vaal R.

Islamic areas in Africa

Principal trade routes

0   500   1000 miles

AFRICA • 1000-1500 A.D.

the North African caravan operators. Indeed, Ghana emerged from
the Almoravid movement in such a weakened condition that peripheral chieftaincies were able to secede. One of these vassal chieftaincies
sacked the Ghanaian capital in 1224 and enslaved the ruling family. A
decade later the victor himself succumbed to the superior magic of a
Ghanaian royal hostage, named Sunjata.

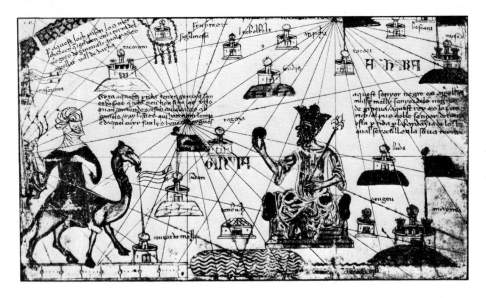

Mansa Musa of Mali Waiting to Receive a Muslim Trader. Detail of the Catalan Atlas, a map drawn on the island of Majorca in 1375.

The rise of Mali

Ghana was finished, but a new territorial empire called Mali was forged by the magician Sunjata, who is still regarded in Western Sudanic folk traditions as a god-hero and founding father. By gaining control of the gold-producing regions, Sunjata could attract the caravan traffic formerly monopolized by Ghana. The oral record also reveals that Sunjata expanded agriculture by introducing the cultivation and weaving of cotton.

Mansa Musa

Under Mansa Musa (1312–1337) Mali's authority reached into the middle Niger city-states of Timbuktu, Jenné, and Gao. He put Mali on the European world maps by performing a stunning gold-laden pilgrimage to Mecca, Islam's spiritual capital in the Middle East. Upon returning, Mansa Musa fostered the growth of Islam by constructing magnificent mosques in the major urban centers. With his seemingly inexhaustible supply of gold he commissioned Spanish and Middle Eastern scholars and architects to transform Malian cities into great seats of Islamic learning. Leading intellectuals were sent to Morocco and Egypt for higher studies, and at Timbuktu foundations were laid for a university at the famed Sankoré mosque. For decades after Musa, Mali enjoyed a reputation in the Muslim world for high standards of public morality and scholarship as well as for law, order, and security. People and goods flowed freely, enabling the cosmopolitan cities of Timbuktu, Jenné, and Gao to flower into major market centers. Through the leadership of Sunjata and Mansa Musa Islam became more deeply implanted among the elite and spread widely in the important towns.

Sunni Ali and the formation of Songhay

While Mansa Musa made great advances in establishing an efficient administrative bureaucracy, he neglected to develop a formula for succession. Court intrigue and factional disputes followed the death of each Mansa. Inevitably, central authority weakened. Gao seceded in 1375 and under Sunni Ali (1464–1492) it blossomed into an expansive territorial empire called Songhay.

As in Muslim India, it was not uncommon for slaves in Africa to assume considerable administrative and military responsibilities and on occasion to usurp authority. This happened in Songhay in 1493 when a high-ranking Muslim slave, named Muhammad Touré, staged a brilliant palace coup. Lacking traditional legitimacy rooted in a pagan past, he promoted Islamic practices and found Islam an invaluable instrument for political and cultural control. Using the praise-title of "Askia," Muhammad Touré (1493–1528) extended Songhay's frontiers deep into the strategic Saharan oases, across the middle Niger to include Mali, and eastward to the emporiums of Hausaland. He then created a labyrinthine bureaucracy with ministries for the army, navy, fisheries, forests, and taxation. Songhay itself was decentralized into provinces, each ruled by a governor chosen from among the Askia's family or royal followers. Muhammad Touré also established vast plantations, worked by slaves under conditions sometimes approaching those in the southern United States before the Civil War.

To facilitate commerce, Muhammad Touré introduced a unified system of weights and measures and appointed market inspectors to protect consumers. The Sankoré mosque at Timbuktu was transformed into an institution comparable to the great European universities of the later Middle Ages, with schools of theology, jurisprudence, mathematics, and medicine. On his pilgrimage to Mecca in 1497 he befriended world-famous Muslim scholars. A few

Askia Muhammad Touré and the growth of Islamic institutions

Songhay's cultural ascendancy

The Old Mosque at Timbuktu. Between the fourteenth and sixteenth centuries, Timbuktu was one of the leading Muslim centers of learning in the Western Sudan.

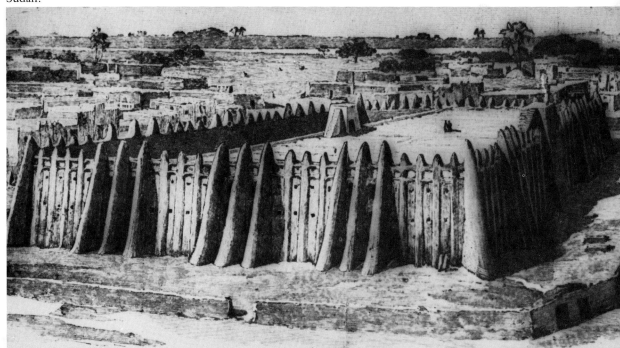

Islam a thin veneer

The Moroccan invasion and Songhay's demise

The emergence of Hausa kingdoms

Islamic penetration and commercial expansion

of them returned with him to Songhay as advisers on government and religion. And like the earlier Mali empire, Songhay established diplomatic relations with Morocco and Egypt, its major trading partners.

Islamic institutions of law, education, and taxation were deeply rooted in the major urban areas by the close of Askia Muhammad's rule in 1528. However, Islam was but a thin veneer elsewhere. Fully 95 percent of the population, consisting of rural peasants and petty chiefs, continued to follow traditional animistic beliefs and life styles. Nevertheless, in spite of serious internal divisions between Islam and the traditional ways. Songhay continued to prosper, reaching its zenith under Askia Daud (1549–1582). Stretching from the snow-capped Atlas Mountains of North Africa to the tropical Cameroon forests and embracing thousands of different cultures, it was clearly one of the world's most expansive empires.

Songhay had overextended itself; and although its armies numbered more than 35,000, it could not keep the outlying regions in subjection. Its vital eastern markets were lost when several Hausa city-states reasserted their independence. In the northwest, Morocco, after defeating the Portuguese, sought direct control over Songhay's mines. Crack Songhay cavalry and archers were no match for Moroccan cannons and imported European arquebuses. After Songhay's defeat by the Moroccans in 1591, the empire—and indeed western Sudanic civilization—rapidly disintegrated. The Moroccans and their Portuguese mercenaries, unable to locate the gold mines or to maintain security on the roads and in the markets, abandoned Songhay altogether in 1612. Political anarchy filled the vacuum, the great cities declined, and trade and Muslim scholarship drifted eastward to the city-states of Hausaland in what is today northern Nigeria and the Niger Republic.

By the twelfth century, uncoordinated self-governing villages in Hausaland had coalesced into centralized kingdoms under semidivine dynasties. These kingdoms, though politically autonomous, shared a common Hausa language and cultural heritage. Daura, the founding kingdom, exercised a vague spiritual suzerainty over the others.

Islam had begun to penetrate Hausa aristocratic and trading circles in the fourteenth century. After 1452, the rural areas experienced a steady influx of red-skinned Fulani herdsmen, who for centuries had been migrating eastward from the Senegal River. The Fulani, who were fervent Muslims brought religious books and established new centers of Islamic learning. At this time, Hausaland was experiencing a commercial revolution with the opening of the kola trade with farmers of the southern forests. In Kano, Katsina, and Zaria, huge markets emerged as traders from disintegrating Songhay shifted their operations to the more secure walled towns of Hausaland.

Hausaland was exceptionally secure, thanks to the military protection offered by the wealthy and powerful kingdom of Kanem-Bornu, lying eastward near Lake Chad. Kanem-Bornu's geographical posi-

Gobirau Mosque, Katsina (northern Nigeria). This mosque was built in the fifteenth century, when the Hausa kingdoms shared strong cultural and economic ties with Songhay. It is constructed of mud mixed with a vegetable matter (katse) and oxen blood.

tion placed it at the gateway to the West African Sudan. Its stable dynasty gained power in 846 A.D. and embraced Islam in 1087. Under Mai Idris Alooma (1580–1617) Kanem-Bornu reached its peak. Alooma established diplomatic relations with Turkey, which had recently captured Tunis in North Africa from Spain. With Turkish advisers, Alooma bureaucratized his government and set it on firm Islamic foundations. A high court of law was organized and staffed by judges who dispensed only Muslim law. The army was equipped with Turkish muskets. The thirteenth-century hostel in Cairo for Bornuese pilgrims and scholars was greatly expanded. Hausaland, sandwiched between Songhay and Bornu, was commercially exploited by both neighbors, but it received considerable cultural enrichment from pilgrims passing through en route to Mecca.

Kanem-Bornu

After Songhay's collapse in 1591, trade shifted not only to Hausaland but also toward the southern forests. Between 1000 and 1500 A.D. the forest people of modern Nigeria experienced new infusions of grasslanders from the Sudanic zone. Leading lineages were transformed into ruling dynasties. They in turn fused scattered villages under priests and elders into small city-states. Ile Ife exercised the same kind of spiritual hegemony for the Yoruba settlers that Daura held for the Hausa in the north. Yoruba warriors from Ile Ife fanned out and established subordinate dynasties at Oyo, Benin, and elsewhere. Under Eware the Great (1440–1473) Benin city expanded into a territorial forest empire. Benin and Ife became centers of high civi-

The rise of forest civilizations

The Griot, Africa's Historian, Daura Emirate. The Praise Singer is the traditional oral historian of African societies. African history has been passed from generation to generation by griots.

lization. Their craft guilds produced naturalistic busts and plaques cast in bronze through the lost wax process. Eware encouraged ivory and wood carving and created a national orchestra. All these secular innovations were aimed at glorifying the ruling families. Art was no longer simply for life's adornment. It now upheld authority and graced the hallways of the sprawling Yoruba palaces.

The Akan forest states

In the hinterlands of modern Ghana, a similar though unrelated political process had begun not long before 1400. Mande traders from old Mali and Songhay pushed southward in a quest for more gold. Stronger demands from North Africa and Europe encouraged them to establish small centers of exchange at the forest's edge. These burgeoning communities represented a curious blend of pagan and Islamic, of forest and Sudanic cultures. The forest people, called the Akan, reacted to this commercial challenge by forging mini-kingdoms at the crossroads of trading activity. Thus, the southward movement of trade stimulated the rise of forest-based states, which in the sixteenth century reached their zenith as new commercial opportunities emanated from Europeans on the coast.

The emergence of Swahili civilization

In chapter 12 it was shown that after the ninth century A.D. the East African coast from Somalia southward received new arrivals. Some were Bantu from the interior, others were Shirazi Arabs from the Somali coast and Persian Gulf, and a few were from northwestern India. The non-African immigrants were sea-oriented merchants in search of African minerals, ivory, and slaves. The Bantu, with inland connections, were in an excellent position to supply their needs. By the twelfth century the Shirazi had founded a series of coastal Muslim city-states, extending southward to modern Mozambique. They married into local Bantu ruling families and initiated Islamic dynasties. Sofala and Kilwa became leading Afro-Asian towns and served as major outlets for gold and copper from the Rhodesian and Katangan plateaus of the interior. Between the twelfth and fifteenth centuries a distinctive Swahili coastal civilization emerged. Swahili civilization grew out of the convergence of Bantu, Arab, and Indian cultures and languages. Swahili mosques, though reminiscent of those gracing the southern Arabian shores, were unique in form and construction. The Swahili language, written in Arabic characters, was soft and melodic.

The Swahili city-states, like their Hausa counterparts, were Muslim, cosmopolitan, culturally homogeneous, yet politically independent of one another. They thrived on their middleman position between producers and consumers. Although Kilwa held commercial sway over Sofala intermittently from 1131 to 1333, it did not exhibit any expansionist tendencies. Rather, the various towns, like Mogadishu and Barawa (in modern Somalia), Gedi, Pate, Malindi, and Mombasa (Kenya), Zanzibar and Kilwa (Tanzania), and Sofala (Mozambique) engaged in vigorous competition with one another. Some towns even minted their own coins and maintained huge treasuries.

Indian Ocean trade, like that of the trans-Sahara, encouraged African rulers to centralize their societies in order to better meet foreign demands. Indeed, coastal requests for Katangan copper and Rhodesian gold led to a transition in leadership from ritual-bearing priests to secular kings commanding enormous military and economic power. Katanga in the thirteenth century was the first state to consolidate.

Middleman position of the Swahili city-states

The Mwenemutapa empire and Great Zimbabwe

Gedi. The ruins of this Afro-Arab town, founded in the early fourteenth century on the Kenya coast. This was the main entrance to the Sultan's palace.

Within two hundred years Katangans had carried their ideas of divine kingship to other societies in the Zambezi valley. On the cool Rhodesian plateau a powerful Katangan kingdom arose, with its ruler assuming the praise name of "Mwenemutapa." His capital at Great Zimbabwe was fortified with massive elliptical walls of cut stone laid in place without mortar.

The Christian kingdoms of Northeast Africa

In the mid-fourth century A.D. the Axumite king Ezana converted to Christianity and made the faith the state religion in what then came to be called Ethiopia. Ethiopian clerics established churches and monasteries and received large tracts of land as gifts from the nobility and successive monarchs. Coptic Christianity, along with the institution of the monarchy, became powerful unifying forces. The monasteries emerged as centers of learning, and important religious texts were translated into Ge'ez, the language of the church hierarchy.

Ethiopian expansion

Shortly after Christianity became the state religion, Ethiopia conquered the neighboring empire of Kush, which was replaced by a number of smaller kingdoms collectively called Nubia. The seventh-century-A.D. Islamic expansion in North Africa led to the collapse of Christian Egypt and to Arab occupation of Persia and of Red Sea ports. In the same century, Beja nomads swept across the Eritrean plateau and cut Ethiopia off from Mediterranean and Middle Eastern trade and civilization. Ethiopia now expanded into the interior. In about 1100 A.D. its political center shifted southward from Axum to Lalibela in the almost inaccessible northwestern highlands. It became even more isolated from the Greco-Roman world after the conquest

Great Zimbabwe. This 34-foot-high conical tower was probably a shrine in the heart of the Mwenemutapa Empire (fifteenth century). The tower and adjacent wall were constructed by placing stone upon stone without mortar.

of the Nubian kingdoms by Arab rulers of Egypt in the late thirteenth and early fourteenth centuries. The early kingdom of Ethiopia reached its zenith in the fourteenth and fifteenth centuries with the conquest of non-Christian and non-Islamic states to the west. The church became a missionary agent for the monarchy by proselytizing and assimilating these conquered areas.

Islamic populations, both internal and foreign, continued to pressure the Christian regime. In the early fifteenth century centrifugal tendencies developed among local nobility. The neighboring state of Adal took advantage of this and proclaimed a jihad in 1529. It achieved a decisive victory over the Ethiopian emperor and brought much of his country under Muslim rule. Christian Ethiopia was saved from complete annihilation when Emperor Lebna Dengel, with the assistance of foreign Portuguese mercenaries, defeated the Muslims in 1541. With mixed success they also halted an invasion of pastoral Kushitic-speaking Galla peoples but were forced over subsequent centuries to share their lands with them. For the next three centuries, Ethiopia retreated into a sullen xenophobia, marked by civil strife, warlords, economic stagnation, and ultimately the disintegration of central authority.

The Muslim threat

Unrelated to these developments was the migration of Nilotic pastoralists into the fertile lands northwest of Lake Victoria in modern Uganda. Between the fourteenth and sixteenth centuries these immigrants, imbued with notions of divine kingship, married Bantu cultivators and established powerful kingdoms. These highly centralized polities, such as Bunyoro, Buganda, and Ankole, were non-Islamic, purely African creations.

SELECTED READINGS

• *Items so designated are available in paperback editions.*

INDIA—*See also Readings for Chapters 6 and 12*

Cambridge History of India, Vol. III, Cambridge, 1937.

Ikram, Mohamad, *Muslim Civilization in India,* ed. A. T. Embree, New York, 1964. Scholarly and readable.

Phillips, C. H., *India,* London, 1949. A useful survey, although devoting little space to the period before the coming of Europeans.

Sharma, S. R., *The Crescent in India,* Bombay, 1954.

CHINA—*See also Readings for Chapters 7 and 12*

Bruce, J. P., *Chu Hsi and His Masters,* London, 1923.

Fairbank, J. K., ed., *Chinese Thought and Institutions,* Chicago, 1957.

Fitzgerald, C. P., *The Southern Expansion of the Chinese People,* New York, 1972.

• Gernet, Jacques, *Daily Life in China (On the Eve of the Mongol Invasion 1250–1276),* Stanford, 1970.

Hucker, C. O., *The Traditional Chinese State in Ming Times (1368–1644),* Tucson, 1961. Brief but informative on political structure and operation.

———, *The Ming Dynasty: Its Origins and Evolving Institutions,* Ann Arbor, 1978. Readable and reliable.

• Hudson, G. F., *Europe and China: A Survey of Their Relations from the Earliest Times to 1800,* London, 1930. Interestingly presented.

Liu, James T. C., *Reform in Sung China: Wang An-shih (1021–1086) and His New Policies,* Cambridge, Mass., 1959. A good, brief interpretive study.

Parsons, J. B., *The Peasant Rebellions of the Late Ming Dynasty,* Tucson, 1970.

• Prawdin, Michael, *The Mongol Empire: Its Rise and Legacy,* tr. E. and C. Paul, London, 1940.

Shih Chung-wen, *The Golden Age of Chinese Drama: Yüan Tsa-chü,* Princeton, 1976.

Sowerby, A. deC., *Nature in Chinese Art,* New York, 1940.

Waley, Arthur, *An Introduction to the Study of Chinese Painting,* New York, 1958.

Williamson, H. R., *Wang An Shih, a Chinese Statesman and Educationalist of the Sung Dynasty,* 2 vols., London, 1935–1937.

Wright, Arthur F., ed., *Studies in Chinese Thought,* Chicago, 1953.

———, ed., *The Confucian Persuasion,* Stanford, 1960.

JAPAN—*See also Readings for Chapter 12*

• Duus, Peter, *Feudalism in Japan,* 2d ed., New York, 1975. Concise account of political developments from the sixth through the nineteenth century.

Sansom, George B., *A History of Japan, 1334–1615,* Stanford, 1961. A major contribution.

———, *The Western World and Japan,* New York, 1950.

Suzuki, D. T., *Zen and Japanese Culture,* New York, 1959.

• Waley, Arthur, *No Plays of Japan,* New York, 1922.

AFRICA

Ade Ajayi, J. F., and I. Espie, eds., *A Thousand Years of West African History,* Ibadan, 1967.

Boahen, Adu, *Topics in West African History,* London, 1968.

Davidson, Basil, *et al., The Growth of African Civilization: A History of West Africa 1000–1800,* London, 1966.

Denyer, Susan, *African Traditional Architecture,* New York, 1978.

Gray, Richard, and David Birmingham, eds., *Pre-Colonial African Trade,* New York, 1970.

• Hull, Richard W., *African Cities and Towns before the European Conquest,* New York, 1976.

———, *Munyakare: African Civilization before the Batuuree,* New York, 1972.

Kilson, Martin, and Robert I. Rotberg, eds., *The African Diaspora,* Cambridge, 1977.

Mair, Lucy, *African Kingdoms,* Oxford, 1977.

Maquet, Jacques, *Civilizations of Black Africa,* New York, 1972.

Ogot, B. A., and J. A. Kieran, eds., *Zamani: A Survey of East African History,* Nairobi, 1968.

Oliver, Roland, ed., *The Middle Age of African History,* New York, 1967.

Ranger, T. O., ed., *Aspects of Central African History,* London, 1969.

SOURCE MATERIALS

Boxer, C. R., ed., *South China in the Sixteenth Century* (narratives of Portuguese and Spanish visitors, 1550–1575).

Chinese Novels and Short Stories: Buck, Pearl, tr., *All Men Are Brothers;* Howell, E. B., tr., *Inconstancy of Madam Chuang and Other Stories;* Waley, Arthur, tr., *The Monkey.*

• de Bary, W. T., ed., *Sources of Chinese Tradition,* "The Confucian Revival," New York, 1960.

• ———, ed., *Sources of Indian Tradition,* "Islam in Medieval India," New York, 1950.

• ———, ed., *Sources of Japanese Tradition,* "Medieval Japan," New York, 1958.

Gallagher, L. J., tr., *China in the Sixteenth Century: The Journals of Matthew Ricci. 1583–1610* (a Jesuit missionary), Milwaukee, 1942.

• Hall, J. W., and T. Toyoda, eds., *Japan in the Muromachi Age,* New Haven, Conn., 1974.

Hodgkin, Thomas, ed., *Nigerian Perspectives,* London, 1960.

• Hsiung, S. I., tr., *The Romance of the Western Chamber,* London, 1935.

• Keene, Donald, ed., *Twenty Plays of the No Theatre,* New York, 1970.

• Ma, Y. W., and J. S. M. Lau, *Traditional Chinese Stories: Themes and Variations,* New York, 1978.

McCullough, H. C., *The Taiheiki: A Chronicle of Medieval Japan,* New York, 1959.

McEwan, P. J. M., ed., *Africa from Early Times to 1800,* London, 1968.

Oliver, R., and G. Mathew, eds., *History of East Africa,* Vol. I, Oxford, 1968.

Reischauer, E. O., and Y. K. Yamagiwa, *Translations from Early Japanese Literature* (eleventh to thirteenth centuries), Cambridge, Mass., 1951.

Waley, Arthur, tr., *The Travels of an Alchemist, the Journeys of the Taoist Ch'ang Ch'un,* London, 1931.

Yule, Henry, tr., *The Book of Ser Marco Polo,* London, 1903.

Part Four

THE EARLY MODERN WORLD

Historians tend to agree that the European Middle Ages ended sometime roughly around 1500. As early as about 1350 in Italy a new movement, usually called the Renaissance, began to challenge and triumph over certain basic medieval assumptions. Around 1500, the Italian Renaissance spread to northern Europe and thereafter led to important achievements in science, which became basic foundations of modern European thought and civilization. Concurrently, in the sixteenth century a religious upheaval, known as the Protestant Revolution, began in Germany and spread to many other countries. This upheaval contributed to the beginnings of the modern era by ending the religious uniformity of the Middle Ages and fostering an upsurge of individualism and rational consciousness. In the economic realm, Europeans around 1500 sailed to distant continents and began to gain new sources of supply. Overseas discovery and colonization contributed to the Commercial Revolution, lasting from about 1450 to 1800, which established a dynamic regime of business for profit. From the point of view of politics, the period around 1500 ushered in an age of absolutism that lasted until about 1800: this was marked by the growth of absolute governments, headed in some instances by kings who equated themselves with the state and professed to rule by divine right. Finally, during the years from 1600 to 1789, there occurred an intellectual revolution, culminating in the "Enlightenment," or enthronement of reason. In Asia as in Europe, a rise in the level of civilization was accompanied by the establishment of autocratic centralized governments. The Mogul rulers of India and the Manchu Dynasty in China brought a large measure of stability and prosperity to those countries, but extravagance and a series of disastrous wars led the Mogul Dynasty to an early decline. In Japan, although feudalism remained intact, the rise of the Tokugawa Shoguns in 1603 provided the substance if not the form of absolute government. In contrast with western European varieties, both Chinese and Japanese despotism survived into the twentieth century. Meanwhile, the maritime supremacy and commercial initiative of western Europeans enabled them to exploit the riches of Africa. The widespread trade in African slaves, while swelling the coffers of European merchants, not only intensified conflict among and within African states but also hastened the decline of brilliant civilizations on that continent.

The Early Modern World

POLITICS	PHILOSOPHY AND SCIENCE	
	Civic humanism in Italy, c. 1380–c. 1450	
		1400
Renaissance popes, 1447–1521	Florentine Neoplatonism, c. 1450–c. 1600	
French invade Italy, 1494		
	Machiavelli, 1469–1527	*1500*
Henry VIII of England, 1509–1547	Vesalius, 1514–1564	
Francis I of France, 1515–1547	More's *Utopia,* 1516	
Charles V, Holy Roman Emperor, 1519–1546	Index of Prohibited Books, 1559	
Troops of Charles V sack Rome, 1527	Francis Bacon, 1561–1626	
Spanish gain supremacy in Italy, 1529	Galileo, 1564–1642	
Philip II of Spain, 1556–1598	Johann Kepler, 1571–1630	
Elizabeth I of England, 1558–1603	Hugo Grotius, 1583–1645	
Defeat of Spanish Armada, 1588	Thomas Hobbes, 1588–1679	
Henry IV of France, 1589–1610		
Edict of Nantes, 1598	René Descartes, 1596–1650	
Thirty Years' War, 1618–1648		
Supremacy of Richelieu in France, 1624–1642		
Louis XIV of France, 1643–1715		
	Bacon's *Novum Organum,* 1620	*1600*
	John Locke, 1632–1704	
	Descarte's *Discourse on Method,* 1637	
English Civil War, 1642–1649	Isaac Newton, 1642–1727	
Commonwealth and Protectorate in England, 1649–1660		
Age of Restoration in England, 1660–1688	Royal Society founded, 1662	
Peter the Great of Russia, 1682–1725		
Revocation of Edict of Nantes, 1685	Newton's *Mathematical Principles of Natural Philosophy,* 1687	
Glorious Revolution in England, 1688–1689		
War of the Spanish Succession, 1702–1714		*1700*
Frederick William I of Prussia, 1713–1740	Linnaeus, 1707–1778	
	Jean-Jacques Rousseau, 1712–1778	
Development of Cabinet system in England, 1714–1742		
Louis XV of France, 1715–1774		
Maria Theresa of Austria, 1740–1780		
Frederick the Great of Prussia, 1740–1786		
Seven Years' War, 1756–1763		
George III of England, 1760–1820		
Catherine the Great of Russia, 1762–1796		
Louis XVI of France, 1774–1792		
Joseph II of Austria, 1780–1790		
Outbreak of French Revolution, 1789		

ECONOMICS	RELIGION	ARTS AND LETTERS
		Francis Petrarch, 1304–1374
		Italian Renaissance, c. 1400– c. 1550
Prosperity in Italy, c. 1450– c. 1550	Martin Luther, 1483–1546	Masaccio, 1401–1428
Commercial Revolution, c. 1450–c. 1800	Ulrich Zwingli, 1484–1531	Botticelli, 1444–1510
European voyages of discovery, c. 1450–c. 1650	Ignatius Loyola, 1491–1556	Leonardo da Vinci, 1452–1519
		Erasmus, c. 1467–1536
		Albrecht Dürer, 1471–1528
		Ariosto, 1474–1533
	John Calvin, 1509–1564	Raphael, 1483–1520
	Luther attacks indulgences, 1517	Michelangelo, 1485–1564
	Henry VIII of England breaks with Rome, 1527–1534	Rabelais, c. 1490–1553
	Loyola founds Society of Jesus, 1534	Northern Renaissance, c. 1500– c. 1600
	Anabaptists seize Münster, 1534	Michelangelo's main work on Sistine Chapel, 1508–1512
Peasants' Revolt in Germany, 1524–1525	Calvin's *Institutes,* 1536	Peter Brueghel, c. 1525–1569
"Age of Silver" c. 1540–c. 1620	Calvin takes over Geneva, 1541	Palestrina, 1525–1594
	Council of Trent, 1545–1563	Montaigne, 1533–1592
	Peace of Augsburg divides Germany into Lutheran and Catholic areas, 1555	El Greco, c. 1541–c. 1614
		Cervantes, 1547–1616
	Elizabethan religious compromise in England, c. 1558– c. 1570	Edmund Spenser, c. 1552–1599
	Revolt of the Netherlands, 1567–1609	Shakespeare, 1564–1616
		Claudio Monteverdi, 1567–1643
		Rubens, 1577–1640
		Bernini, 1598–1680
		Velásquez, 1599–1660
		Rembrandt, 1606–1669
Economic decline of Italy, c. 1600–c. 1800		John Milton, 1608–1674
Height of mercantilism, c. 1600–c. 1700		Christopher Wren, 1632–1723
	Spread of religious toleration, c. 1650–c. 1800	The Enlightenment, c. 1680– c. 1800
		J. S. Bach, 1685–1750
		G. F. Handel, 1685–1759
		Voltaire, 1694–1778
Spread of scientific farming, c. 1700–c. 1800	John Wesley, 1703–1789	Rococo architecture, c. 1700– c. 1800
Height of enclosures in England, c. 1710–c. 1810		
South Sea Bubble, 1720		Joseph Haydn, 1732–1809
		W. A. Mozart, 1756–1791

1400

1500

1600

1700

AFRICA AND THE AMERICAS	INDIA AND THE FAR EAST	

Height of West African forest civilizations,
1400–1472

1400

Voyages of discovery and exploration, 1450–1600

European maritime activity along African coasts,
1500–1800
Growth of African slave trade, 1500–1800
Portuguese dominance of East Coast city-states,
1505–1650

1500

Conquest of Mexico, 1522
Conquest of Peru, 1537

Arrival of Portuguese traders in China
and Japan, 1537–1542
Jesuit missionaries active in China and
Japan, 1550–1650
Akbar the Great Mogul, 1556–1605

British East India Co., chartered, 1600
Tokugawa Shogunate, 1603–1867

1600

Founding of Jamestown, 1607

Landing of Pilgrims, 1620

Taj Mahal, 1632–1647
Japanese isolation, 1637–1854

Downfall of kingdoms of Kongo and Ngola,
1665–1671

Manchu Dynasty in China, 1644–1912
Maratha Confederacy in India, 1650–1760

Rise of Asante empire, founded on Gold Coast
trade, 1700–1750

Decline of Mogul Empire in India, 1700
–1800

1700

Chapter 18

THE CIVILIZATION
OF THE RENAISSANCE
(c. 1350 – c. 1600)

What a piece of work is man, how noble in reason, how infinite in faculty, in form and moving, how express and admirable in action, how like
an angel in apprehension, how like a God: the beauty of the world, the
paragon of animals.

—Shakespeare,
Hamlet, II, 2.

Historians disagree about whether there was a fully defined
period between medieval and modern times that should be
called the "Renaissance." The reason for this is that it is
doubtful whether there was any truly distinctive "Renaissance" politics or economics. Most recent scholars believe that there was not, and
argue that the term "Renaissance" should be reserved for the exciting
developments in thought, literature, and art that transpired between
roughly 1350 and 1600. That is the approach that will be followed
here. When we talk about a "Renaissance period" we mean to refer to
a period in intellectual and cultural history. The following chapter will
accordingly concentrate on intellectual and artistic trends.

*The Renaissance as a
period of distinct cultural
developments*

The term "Renaissance" is hardly accurate from the standpoint of
historical research. It literally means rebirth, and is commonly taken
to imply that in the fourteenth century there was a sudden revival of
interest in the classical learning of Greece and Rome. But this implication is not strictly true because interest in the classics was by no means
rare in the Middle Ages. Dante, for example, revered Vergil, and St.
Thomas Aquinas considered Aristotle to be "the Philosopher."

*The Renaissance no
sudden development*

What, then, was the Renaissance? While no two historians will ever
agree on a single precise answer, certain major trends are clear. De-

*The extension of classical
learning beyond medieval
accomplishments*

*Knowledge of the classics
a foundation for new
achievements*

spite what we have just said, a distinct feature of this period was the growth of classical learning; a growth which was not sudden but gradual and steady. Medieval scholars knew many Roman authors, such as Virgil, Ovid, and Cicero, but in the Renaissance the works of others such as Livy, Tacitus, and Lucretius were discovered and made familiar. Equally, if not more important was the Renaissance discovery of the literature of classical Greece. In the twelfth and thirteenth centuries Greek scientific and philosophical treatises were made available to westerners in Latin translations, but none of the great Greek literary masterpieces and practically none of the major works of Plato were yet known. Moreover, very few medieval westerners could read the Greek language. In the Renaissance, on the other hand, large numbers of Western scholars learned Greek and mastered almost the entire Greek literary heritage that is known today.

Ancient artistic monuments too were studied more carefully. Once Renaissance scholars, writers, and artists became thoroughly familiar with ancient accomplishments, they drew on them to reconsider and alter their own ideas and modes of expression. Thus greater knowledge of the classics contributed to important new accomplishments in the realms of thought, literature, and art.

Although the foundation of many Renaissance achievements was classical, the period can by no means be measured strictly in terms of Greek and Latin influences. The steady growth of urban society—particularly in the Italian city-states—led to the development of an urbane society, i.e., one which delighted in experimenting with new ideas and developing ever more sophisticated expressions of thought and art. This growth also helped create a culture that was increasingly nonecclesiastical, although the Church retained its power and influence to a large extent, and in fact adjusted to the spread of urbanity by becoming more urbane itself. Accordingly, the greatest accomplishments of the Renaissance were shared between the laity and the clergy, with the former achieving and maintaining an edge over the latter. The universities, dominated by the clergy in earlier times, now went into a temporary decline, with the concurrent rise of secular centers of learning—for example, academies and courts. An extremely important development which originated in this move toward secular intellectualism and urbanity was the spread of work in the vernacular as opposed to Latin, the language of the Church. This is not to say, however, that important work was not still written in Latin; on the contrary, we will see that humanism depended in large part on this ancient language. But Latin itself underwent important changes during the period.

It was once thought that Renaissance culture was fundamentally anti-Christian and almost "pagan" in its outlook because it was shaped so much by the ancient classics and by the laity. That interpretation, however, is now universally rejected. Many of the greatest

Renaissance thinkers and artists explicitly emphasized Christian beliefs in their work and most of the others took them for granted. Certainly no one before 1600 admitted to preferring Greek gods to Christ, let alone to espousing atheism. Aside from the common denominator of religious faith, it is difficult to speak of common Renaissance points of view because over the course of two and a half centuries writers and artists were bound to differ greatly in their opinions and outlooks. Some Renaissance figures continued to uphold the medieval tradition of emphasizing humanity's hope for otherworldly salvation and the precedence of the soul over the body, while others paid more "modern" attention to human life in this world. It does seem true, however, that there was a growth in the Renaissance period of optimism, naturalistic modes of expression, and individualism.

One word above all comes closest to summing up the most common and basic Renaissance intellectual ideals, namely humanism. This word has two different meanings, one technical and one general, but both apply to the cultural goals and ideals of a large number of Renaissance thinkers. In its technical sense humanism was a program of studies which aimed to replace the medieval Scholastic emphasis on logic and metaphysics with the study of language, literature, history, and ethics. Ancient literature was always preferred: the study of the Latin classics was at the core of the curriculum, and, whenever possible, the student was expected to advance to Greek. Humanist teachers argued that Scholastic logic was too arid and irrelevant to the practical concerns of life; instead, they preferred the "humanities," which were meant to make their students virtuous and prepare them for contributing best to the public functions of the state. (Women, as usual, were generally ignored, but sometimes aristocratic women were given humanist training in order to make them appear more polished.) The broader sense of humanism lies in a stress on the "dignity of man" as the most excellent of all God's creatures below the angels. Some Renaissance thinkers argued that man was excellent because he alone of earthly creatures could obtain knowledge of God; others stressed man's ability to master his fate and live happily in the world. Either way Renaissance humanists had a firm belief in the nobility and possibilities of the human race.

1. THE RENAISSANCE OF THOUGHT AND LITERATURE IN ITALY

The Renaissance had its beginnings in Italy for several reasons. One was that Italy had a stronger classical tradition than any other country of western Europe. Throughout the Middle Ages the Italians had managed to preserve the belief that they were descendants of the ancient Romans. In some Italian cities traces of the old Roman system of

THE STATES OF ITALY DURING THE RENAISSANCE c. 1494

Lorenzo de' Medici. The leading patron of Florentine art and literature in the latter part of the fifteenth century.

education still survived in the municipal schools. It is likewise true that Italy had a more secular culture than most other regions of Latin Christendom. The Italian universities were founded primarily for the study of law or medicine rather than theology.

Italian economic developments also played a role in underwriting Renaissance cultural accomplishments. As we have seen, the Italian cities were the largest and richest of Europe; therefore they had the most funds to patronize the arts. At first urban governments and corporate organizations patronized artists who worked on churches and public monuments; public funds also helped support writers whose role was to glorify cities in letters and speeches. After about 1450 patronage was monopolized by the private sector: leading aristocratic families—for example, the Sforza in Milan, the Medici in Florence, the Este in Ferrara, and the Gonzaga in Mantua—became patrons of art and literature in order to glorify themselves. These families may not have been richer than their counterparts in northern Europe, but they turned to the patronage of Renaissance culture earlier. The main reason for this was that they had always lived in urban centers—as opposed to the northern aristocrats who customarily lived in country castles or on estates—and therefore became imbued with Renaissance ideals at an earlier date.

Patronage was not limited to the secular sphere: after about 1450, the papacy began to support scholarship and the arts in order to enhance the reputation of Rome and the Papal States. Nicholas V (1447–1455), called the "humanist pope," founded the Vatican Library. He was praised by a contemporary for "the high estimation he gained for books and writers everywhere." Later popes—including Alexander VI (1492–1503), Julius II (1503–1513; the "warrior pope"), and Leo X (1513–1521), the most worldly of the Renaissance popes—obtained the services of the greatest artists of their day, including Raphael and Michelangelo, and made Rome for a few decades the unrivaled artistic capital of the world.

We will return to art presently, but first let us survey the greatest accomplishments of Italian Renaissance scholars and writers. The history of Renaissance scholarship and literature must begin with Francis Petrarch (1304–1374), the earliest of the humanists in the technical sense of the word. Petrarch was a deeply committed Christian who believed that Scholastic theology and philosophy was entirely on the wrong track because it concentrated on abstract speculation rather than teaching people how to behave properly and attain salvation. Petrarch thought that the Christian writer must above all cultivate literary eloquence so that he could inspire people to do good. For him the only models of true eloquence were to be found in the ancient literary classics, which, in addition, were filled with ethical wisdom. So Petrarch dedicated himself to searching for undiscovered ancient Latin texts and writing his own moral treatises in which he imitated their style and quoted their phrases. Thereby he initiated a program of "humanist" studies that was to be influential for centuries. Petrarch also has a place in purely literary history because of his poetry. Although he prized his own Latin poetry over the poems he wrote in the Italian vernacular, only the latter have proved enduring. Above all, the Italian sonnets, later called Petrarchan sonnets, which he wrote for his beloved Laura in the chivalrous style of the troubadours, were widely imitated in form and content throughout the Renaissance period.

Because he was a committed Christian, Petrarch's ultimate ideal for human conduct was the solitary life of contemplation and asceticism. But in subsequent generations, from about 1400 to 1450, a number of Italian thinkers and scholars developed the alternative of what is customarily called "civic humanism." Two of the leading civic humanists were the Florentines, Leonardo Bruni (c. 1370–1444) and Leon Battista Alberti (1404–1472), but there were many others. The civic humanists agreed with Petrarch on the need for eloquence and the study of classical literature, but they also taught that man's nature equipped him for action, for usefulness to his family and society, and for serving the state. In their view ambition and the quest for glory were noble impulses which ought to be encouraged. They refused to condemn the

Pope Julius II. A portrait by Raphael.

Petrarch, the first humanist

Civic humanism

striving for material possessions, for they argued that the history of man's progress is inseparable from his success in gaining mastery over the earth and its resources. None of the civic humanists were anti-religious: most of them merely took Christianity for granted and were concerned primarily with worldly affairs. In addition to differing with Petrarch in their preference for the active over the solitary or contemplative life, the civic humanists went far beyond him in their study of the ancient literary heritage. Many of them discovered important new Latin texts, but far more important was their success in opening up the field of classical Greek studies. In this they were greatly aided by the cooperation of several Byzantine scholars who had migrated to Italy in the first half of the fifteenth century. These men gave instruction in the Greek language and taught about the achievements of their ancient forebears. In doing so they inspired Italian scholars to make trips to Constantinople and other cities in the Near East in search of Greek manuscripts. In 1423 one Italian humanist, Giovanni Aurispa, alone brought back 238 manuscript books, including works of Sophocles, Euripides, and Thucydides. In this way most of the Greek classics, particularly the writings of Plato, the dramatists, and the historians, were first made available to the modern world.

After about 1450 until about 1600 the dominance of the civic humanists in the world of Italian thought gave way to that of a school of Neoplatonists, who sought to blend the thought of Plato, Plotinus, and various strands of ancient mysticism with Christianity. Foremost among these were Marsilio Ficino (1433–1499) and Giovanni Pico della Mirandola (1463–1494), both of whom were members of the Platonic Academy founded by Cosimo de' Medici in Florence. The academy was a loosely organized society of scholars who met to hear readings and lectures. Their hero was unquestionably Plato: sometimes they celebrated Plato's birthday by holding a banquet in his honor, after which everybody gave speeches as if they were characters in a Platonic dialogue. Ficino's greatest achievement was the translation of Plato's works into Latin by 1469, thereby making them widely available to western Europeans for the first time. It is debatable whether Ficino's own philosophy may be called humanist, because he moved away from ethics to metaphysics and taught that the individual should look primarily to the other world. In Ficino's opinion "the immortal soul is always miserable in its mortal body." The same problem holds for Ficino's disciple Giovanni Pico della Mirandola, whose most famous work is the *Oration on the Dignity of Man*. Pico was certainly not a civic humanist because he saw little worth in mundane public affairs. But he did believe that there is "nothing more wonderful than man" because he believed that man is endowed with the capacity to achieve union with God if he so wills.

Hardly any of the Italian thinkers between Petrarch and Pico were really original: their greatness lay mostly in their manner of expression and in their popularization of different themes of ancient thought. The same, however, can no means be said of Renaissance Italy's greatest political philosopher, Niccolò Machiavelli (1469–1527). He belonged to no school but stood in a class by himself. No man did more than Machiavelli to overturn all earlier views of the ethical basis of politics or to pioneer in the dispassionate direct observation of political life. In his *Discourses on Livy* he praised the ancient Roman republic as a model for all time. He lauded constitutionalism, equality, liberty, in the sense of freedom from outside interference, and subordination of religion to the interests of the state. But Machiavelli also wrote *The Prince,* which reflects the unhappy condition of Italy in his time. At the end of the fifteenth century Italy had become the cockpit of international struggles. Both France and Spain had invaded the peninsula and were competing with each other for the allegiance of the Italian states. The latter, in many cases, were torn by internal dissension which made them an easy prey for foreign conquerors. In 1498 Machiavelli entered the service of the newly founded republic of Florence as second chancellor and secretary. His duties largely involved diplomatic missions to other states. While in Rome he became fascinated with the achievements of Cesare Borgia, son of Pope Alexander VI, in cementing a solidified state out of scattered elements. He noted with approval Cesare's combination of ruthlessness with shrewdness and his complete subordination of morality to political ends. In 1512 the Medici returned to overthrow the republic of Florence, and Machiavelli was deprived of his position. Disappointed and embittered, he spent the remainder of his life in exile, devoting his time primarily to writing. In his books, especially in *The Prince,* he described the policies and practices of government, not in accordance with some lofty ideal, but as they actually were. The supreme obligation of the ruler, he avowed, was to maintain the power and safety of the country over which he ruled. No consideration of justice or mercy or the sanctity of treaties should be allowed to stand in his way. Cynical in his views of human nature, Machiavelli maintained that all men are prompted exclusively by motives of self-interest, particularly by desires for personal power and material prosperity. The head of the state should therefore take nothing for granted as to the loyalty or affection of his subjects. The one ideal Machiavelli kept before him in his later years was the unification of Italy. But this he believed had no chance of accomplishment except by the methods of ruthlessness.

In addition to the work of Machiavelli, numerous other accomplishments were made in the realm of Italian literature in the years after 1500. One was *The Book of the Courtier,* published in 1516 by the diplomat and count Baldesar Castiglione. This vividly described Renaissance Italian court life with the aim of describing all the qualities necessary for becoming a "gentleman." More than any other book, it

The political thought of Machiavelli

Niccolò Machiavelli.

set forth and popularized the ideal of the typical "Renaissance man": one who is accomplished in many different pursuits and is also brave, witty, and "courteous," meaning civilized and learned. *The Courtier's* popularity became so great that it was quickly translated into many other European languages and ran through more than a hundred editions. More deeply serious was the work of the historian Francesco Guicciardini (1483–1540). Having served many years as an ambassador of Florence and as a governor of papal territories, Guicciardini enjoyed a unique advantage in acquiring familiarity with the tortuous political life of his day. His special gifts as a historian were a capacity for minute and realistic analysis and an uncanny ability in disclosing the springs of human action. His masterpiece was his *History of Italy*, a detailed and dispassionate account of the varying fortunes of that country from 1492 to 1534.

Neither Castiglione nor Guicciardini were imaginative writers, but sixteenth-century Italians were accomplished in poetry as well, above all in the genre of vernacular epics. The most eminent of the writers of epics was Ludovico Ariosto (1474–1533), author of a lengthy poem entitled *Orlando Furioso (The Madness of Roland)*. Although woven largely of materials taken from the romances of adventure and the legends of the Charlemagne cycle, this work differed radically from any of the medieval epics. It incorporated much that was derived from classical sources; it lacked the impersonal quality of the medieval romances; and it was totally devoid of idealism. Ariosto, who was probably the greatest of Italian poets after Dante, wrote to make readers laugh and to charm them with felicitous descriptions of the quiet splendor of nature and the passionate beauty of love. His work represents the disillusionment of the late Renaissance, the loss of hope and faith, and the tendency to seek consolation in the pursuit of aesthetic pleasure.

2. THE ARTISTIC RENAISSANCE IN ITALY

Despite numerous intellectual and literary advances, the most long-lived achievements of the Italian Renaissance were made in the realm of art. Of all the arts, painting was undoubtedly supreme. We have already seen that around 1300 very impressive beginnings were made in the history of Italian painting by the artistic genius of Giotto, but it was not until the fifteenth century that Italian painting began to attain its majority. One reason for this was that in the early fifteenth century the laws of linear perspective were discovered and first employed to give the fullest sense of three dimensions. Fifteenth-century artists also experimented with effects of light and shade (*chiaroscuro*) and for the first time carefully studied the anatomy and proportions of the human body. By the fifteenth century, too, increase in private wealth and the partial triumph of the secular spirit had freed the domain of art to a large extent from the service of religion. As we have noted above, the Church was no longer the only patron of artists. While subject matter from biblical history was still commonly employed, it was frequently infused with nonreligious themes. The painting of portraits for the purpose of revealing the hidden mysteries of the soul now became popular. Paintings intended to appeal primarily to the intellect were paralleled by others whose main purpose was to delight the eye with gorgeous color and beauty of form. The fifteenth century was characterized also by the introduction of painting in oil, probably from Flanders. The use of the new technique doubtless had much to do with the artistic advance of this period. Since oil does not dry so quickly as fresco pigment, the painter could now work more leisurely, taking time with the more difficult parts of the picture and making corrections if necessary as he went along.

The majority of the painters of the fifteenth century were Florentines. First among them was the precocious Masaccio (1401–1428). Although he died at the age of twenty-seven, Masaccio inspired the work of Italian painters for a hundred years. Masaccio's greatness as a painter is based on his success in "imitating nature," which became a primary value in Renaissance painting. To achieve this effect he employed perspective, perhaps most dramatically in his fresco of the *Trinity;* he also used *chiaroscuro* with originality, leading to a dramatic and moving outcome. In the *Expulsion of Adam and Eve from the Garden*, he records the shame and guilt felt by the individuals in the biblical story.

The best known of the painters who directly followed the tradition begun by Masaccio was the Florentine Sandro Botticelli (1444–1510), who depicted both religious and classical themes. Botticelli's work excels in beautiful and accurate depiction of natural detail; he is a master, for example, at painting the female nude. But his major contribution to Renaissance painting derives from the philosophical basis of much of his work. In Florence he attracted the attention of the Medici, for whom he painted several portraits. Botticelli was also closely associated with the Florentine Neoplatonists. Two of his most famous paintings are *Primavera (Spring)* and *The Birth of Venus*, which illustrate Neoplatonic concepts regarding the classical goddess of love, Venus or Aphrodite. Later in his life Botticelli became a follower of the evangelical priest Savonarola, who came to Florence from Ferrara to preach fire-and-brimstone sermons against worldiness and paganism. Botticelli's *Mystic Nativity* was probably painted as a result of Savonarola's influence; it is a profoundly moving religious painting, in which he anticipates the apocalypse. The last years of Botticelli's life are shadowy; his popularity declined and it is believed he died in poverty.

Perhaps the greatest of the Florentine artists was Leonardo da Vinci

The Expulsion of Adam and Eve from the Garden. Masaccio's painting departed from the tradition of Giotto by introducing emotion and psychological study.

Botticelli

See color plates following page 384

Leonardo da Vinci

See color plates following page 384

The High Renaissance: Leonardo's naturalism

Studies of the Shoulder by Leonardo da Vinci

(1452–1519), one of the most talented and versatile people who ever lived. Leonardo was practically the personification of the "Renaissance man": he was a painter, musician, architect, writer, engineer, and inventor. The illegitimate son of a lawyer and a peasant woman, he was raised by his father and placed at an early age in the studio of Verrocchio, a Florentine artist of considerable repute. By the time he reached twenty-five, Leonardo set up his own artist's shop in Florence and gained the patronage of Lorenzo the Magnificent, the Medici ruler. But if Leonardo can be said to have had any weakness, it was his slowness in working and his difficulty in finishing anything. This displeased Lorenzo and other Florentine patrons, who thought an artist was little more than an artisan, commissioned to produce a certain piece of work for a certain price and on a certain date. Leonardo, however, strongly objected to this view—to him the artist was the equivalent of a philosopher. Therefore, in 1482 he left Florence for the Sforza court of Milan where he was given a freer rein in structuring his time and work. He remained there until the French invaded Milan in 1499; after that he wandered over the Italian peninsula, finally accepting the patronage of the French king, Francis I, under whose auspices Leonardo lived until his death.

The paintings of Leonardo da Vinci began what is known as the High Renaissance in Italy. His approach to painting was that it should be the most accurate possible imitation of nature. Leonardo was like a naturalist, basing his work on his own detailed observations of a blade of grass, the wing of a bird, a waterfall. He obtained human corpses for dissection—by which he was breaking the law—and reconstructed in drawing the minutest features of anatomy, which knowledge he carried over to his paintings. Leonardo worshiped nature, and was convinced of the essential divinity in all living things. It is not surprising, therefore, that he was a vegetarian, and that he went to the marketplace to buy caged birds which he released to their native habitat.

It is generally agreed that Leonardo's masterpieces are the *Virgin of the Rocks* (which exists in two versions), the *Last Supper,* and the *Mona Lisa.* The first represents not only his marvelous technical skill but also his passion for science and his belief in the universe as a well-ordered place. The figures are arranged in geometric composition with every rock and plant depicted in accurate detail. The *Last Supper,* painted on the walls of the refectory of Santa Maria delle Grazie in Milan, is a study of psychological reactions. A serene Christ, resigned to his terrible fate, has just announced to his disciples that one of them will betray him. The purpose of the artist is to portray the mingled emotions of surprise, horror, and guilt revealed in the faces of the disciples as they gradually perceive the meaning of their master's statement. The third of Leonardo's major triumphs, the *Mona Lisa,* reflects a similar interest in the varied moods of the human soul. Although it is true that the *Mona Lisa* is a portrait of an actual woman, the wife of

Francesco del Giocondo, a Neapolitan, it is more than a mere photographic likeness. The distinguished art critic Bernard Berenson has said of it, "Who like Leonardo has depicted . . . the inexhaustible fascination of the woman in her years of mastery? . . . Leonardo is the one artist of whom it may be said with perfect literalness: 'Nothing that he touched but turned into a thing of eternal beauty.' "

The beginning of the High Renaissance around 1490 was also marked by the rise of the so-called Venetian school. Its chief representatives included Giorgione (1478–1510), Titian (c. 1477–1576), and Tintoretto (1518–1594). The work of all these men reflected the luxurious life and the pleasure-loving interests of the thriving commercial city of Venice. Most Venetian painters had none of the preoccupation with philosophical and psychological themes that had characterized the Florentine school. Their aim was to appeal to the senses rather than to the mind. They delighted in painting idyllic landscapes and gorgeous symphonies of color. For their subject matter they chose not merely the opulent beauty of Venetian sunsets and the shimmering silver of lagoons in the moonlight but also the manmade splendor of sparkling jewels, richly colored satins and velvets, and gorgeous palaces. Their portraits were invariably likenesses of the rich and the powerful. In the subordination of form and meaning to color and elegance there were mirrored not only the sumptuous tastes of wealthy merchants, but also definite traces of Eastern influence which had filtered through from Byzantium during the late Middle Ages.

The Venetian painters

The remaining great painters of the High Renaissance all lived their active careers in the sixteenth century. It was in this period that the evolution of art reached its peak, and the first signs of decay began to appear. Rome was now almost the only artistic center of importance on the mainland of the Italian peninsula, although the traditions of the Florentine school still exerted a potent influence. Among the eminent painters of this period at least two must be given more than passing attention. One of the most noted was Raphael (1483–1520), a native of Urbino, and perhaps the most popular artist of the entire Renaissance. The lasting appeal of his style is due primarily to his intense humanism. He developed a conception of a spiritualized and ennobled humanity. He portrayed the members of the human species, not as dubious, tormented creatures, but as temperate, wise, and dignified beings. Although he was influenced by Leonardo da Vinci and copied many features of his work, he cultivated to a much greater extent than Leonardo a symbolical or allegorical approach. His *Disputà* symbolized the dialectical relationship between the Church in heaven and the Church on earth. In a wordly setting against a brilliant sky, doctors and theologians debate the meaning of the Eucharist, while in the clouds above, saints and the Trinity repose in the possession of a holy mystery. Raphael's *School of Athens* is an allegorical representation of the conflict between the Platonist and Aristotelian philosophies. Plato

The painters of the late Renaissance: Raphael

See color plates facing page 576

(painted as a portrait of Leonardo) is shown pointing upward to emphasize the spiritual basis of his world of Ideas, while Aristotle gestures toward the earth to exemplify his belief that concepts or ideas are inseparably linked with their material embodiments. Raphael is noted also for his portraits and Madonnas. To the latter, especially, he gave a softness and warmth that seemed to endow them with a sweetness and piety quite different from the enigmatic and analytical Madonnas of Leonardo da Vinci.

Michelangelo

The last towering figure of the High Renaissance was Michelangelo (1475–1564) of Florence. If Leonardo was a naturalist, Michelangelo was an idealist; where the former looked down to nature to record and reproduce natural phenomena, Michelangelo, who embraced Neoplatonism as a philosophy, was more concerned with metaphysical truths. But both were similar in their belief in the artist as more than an artisan. Michelangelo was a painter, sculptor, architect, and poet—and he expressed himself in all these with a similar power and in a similar manner. At the center of all of Michelangelo's paintings is the human figure, which is always powerful, colossal, magnificent. If man, and the potential of the individual, lay at the center of Italian Renaissance culture, then Michelangelo, who depicted the human, and particularly the male, figure without cease, is the supreme Renaissance artist. Michelangelo's greatest achievement in painting is the ceiling of the Sistine Chapel in Rome, which he worked on from 1508 to 1512 for Pope Julius II. The ceiling is a series of scenes which represent the history of humanity as portrayed in the Old Testament: among these are(*God Dividing the Light from Darkness, God Creating the Earth, The Creation of Adam, The Creation of Eve, The Drunkenness of Noah*) Thirty years later Michelangelo finished the terrifying and monumental *Last Judgment,* also in the chapel, at the center of which is

See color plates following page 576

The School of Athens by Raphael

The Creation of Adam by Michelangelo. One of a series of frescoes on the ceiling of the Sistine Chapel in Rome. Suggesting philosophical inquiries into the meaning of life and the universe, it represents Renaissance realism at its height.

a figure of Christ who appears more like Hercules in his size and power.

In the realm of sculpture the Italian Renaissance took a great step forward by creating statues that were no longer carved as parts of columns or doorways on church buildings or as effigies on tombs. Instead, Italian sculptors for the first time since antiquity carved free-standing statues "in the round." These freed sculpture from its bondage to architecture and established its status as a separate art frequently devoted to secular purposes.

The first great master of Renaissance sculpture was Donatello (1386?–1466). He emancipated his art from Gothic mannerisms and introduced a more vigorous note of individualism than did any of his predecessors. His statute of David triumphant over the body of the slain Goliath, the first free-standing nude since antiquity, established a precedent of naturalism and of glorification of the nude which sculptors for many years afterward were destined to follow. Donatello also produced the first monumental equestrian statue in bronze since the time of the Romans, a commanding figure of the proud warrior, Gattamelata.

One of the greatest sculptors of the Italian Renaissance, and probably of all time, was Michelangelo. Sculpture, in fact, was the artistic field of Michelangelo's personal preference. Despite his success as a painter, he considered himself unfitted for that work. The dominant purpose which motivated all of his sculpture was the expression of thought in stone. His art was above mere naturalism, for he subordinated nature to the force and sweep of his ideas. (He wrote of releasing the "pure forms" which are trapped in the stone.) Other features of his work included the use of distortion for powerful effect, and a ten-

David by Donatello

Pietà by Michelangelo. This portrayal of tragedy was made by the sculptor for his own tomb. Note the distortion for effect exemplified by the elongated body and left arm of the figure of Christ. The figure in the rear is Nicodemus, but was probably intended to represent Michelangelo himself. Original in the cathedral of Florence.

dency to express his philosophical ideas in allegorical form. Most of his masterpieces were done for the embellishment of tombs, a fact significantly in harmony with his absorbing interest in death, especially in his later career. For the tomb of Pope Julius II, which was never finished, he carved his famous figures of the *Bound Slave and Moses*. The first, which is probably in some degree autobiographical, represents tremendous power and talent restrained by the bonds of fate. The statue of Moses is perhaps the leading example of Michelangelo's sculpture, showing his use of anatomical distortion to heighten the effect of emotional intensity. Its purpose was evidently to express the towering rage of the prophet on account of the disloyalty of the children of Israel to the faith of their fathers.

Some other examples of Michelangelo's work as a plastic artist create an even more striking impression. On the tombs of the Medici in Florence he produced a number of allegorical figures, two of which are known by the traditional titles of *Dawn* and *Sunset*. The first is that of a female figure, turning and raising her head like someone called from a dreamless sleep. *Sunset* is the figure of a powerful man who appears to sink under the load of human misery around him.

As Michelangelo's life drew toward its close, he tended to introduce into his sculpture a more exaggerated and spectacular emotional quality, and his figures tended to be more abstract. This was especially true of the *Pietà* intended for his own tomb. The *Pietà* is a statue of the Virgin Mary grieving over the body of the dead Christ. The figure standing behind the Virgin is probably a self-portrait. It is perhaps fitting that this profound but overwrought interpretation of human existence should have brought the Renaissance epoch in sculpture to a close.

To a much greater extent than either sculpture or painting, Renaissance architecture had its roots in the past. The new building style was eclectic, a compound of elements derived from the Middle Ages and from antiquity. It was not the Greek or the Gothic, however, but the Roman and the Romanesque which provided the inspiration for the architecture of the Italian Renaissance. Neither the Greek nor the Gothic had ever found a congenial soil in Italy. The Romanesque, by

The Villa Rotonda of Palladio. A highly influential Renaissance private dwelling near Vicenza. Note how Palladio drew for inspiration on the Roman Pantheon, pictured above, p. 254.

Above: *The Madonna of the Chair*, Raphael (1483–1520). Raphael's art was distinguished by warmth and serenity, and by an uncritical acceptance of the traditions and conventions of his time. (Pitti Palace, Florence) Right: "Christ and Madonna." From *The Last Judgment*, Michelangelo (1475–1564). This painting above the altar in the Sistine Chapel, Rome, shows Christ as judge condemning sinners to perdition. Even the Madonna at His side seems to shrink from His wrath. (Sistine Chapel)

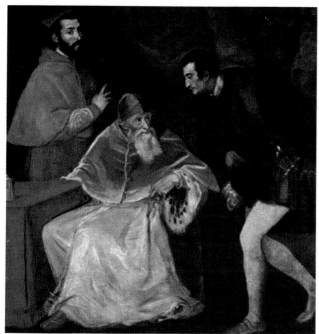

Pope Paul III and His Nephews, Titian (1477–1576). This painting, with its rich harmony of color, is unusual in being both a group portrait and a study of action. (National Museum, Naples)

Charles V, Titian (1488–1576). (Alte Pinakothek)

The Harvesters, Peter Breughel the Elder (1520–1569). Breughel chose to depict the life of humble people. (MMA)

The Virgin and Chancellor Rolin, Jan van Eyck (1390–1444). The early Flemish painters loved to present scenes of piety in the sumptuous surroundings of wealthy burghers. (Louvre)

Erasmus, Hans Holbein the Younger (1497–1543). This portrait is generally regarded as the best representation of the character and personality of the Prince of the Humanists. (Louvre)

St. Andrew and St. Francis, El Greco (1541–1614).
(The Prado)

Burial of the Count of Orgaz, El Greco (1541–1614). El
Greco's masterpiece immortalizes the character of the
people among whom he dwelt. The elongated figures,
gaunt faces, and bold and dramatic colors are typical of
his work. (Iglesia S. Tomé, Toledo, Spain)

An Interior with a Woman Drinking, with Two Men and a Maidservant, Pieter de Hooch (1629–1677?). The subjects and setting contrast strongly with those of the Italian artists. (National Gallery, London) Below: *Crucifixion*, Matthias Grünewald (?–1528). This work is the central panel of the Isenheim Altarpiece, in the Unterlinden Museen, Colmar. (Scala)

Landscape with the Burial of Phocion, Nicolas Poussin (1594–1665). Many consider his paintings of the Roman hills to be models of French classicism. (Louvre)

The Calling of St. Matthew, Caravaggio (1573–1610). Painted for the altarpiece of the Church of San Luigi dei Francesci, Rome. (Scala)

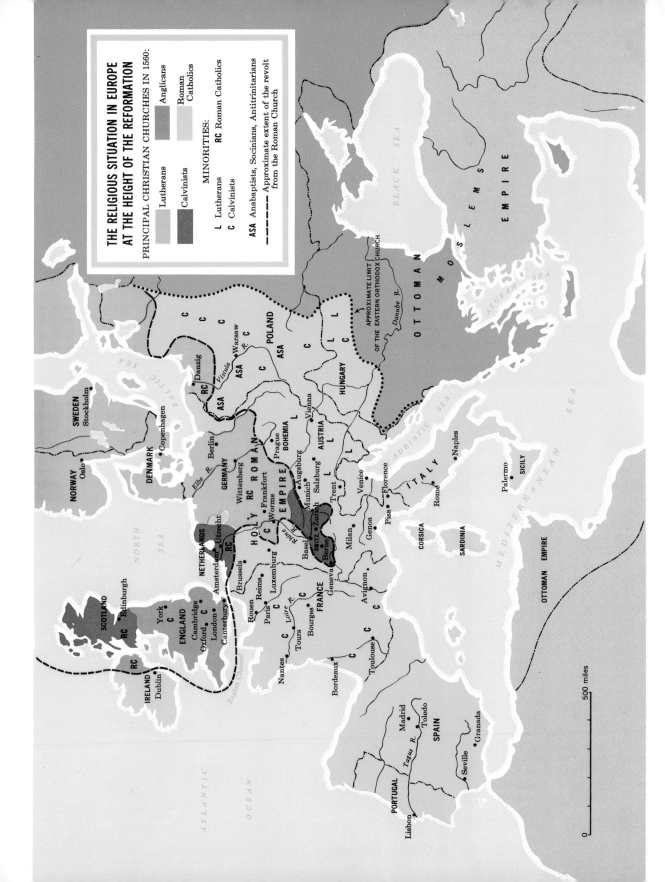

THE RELIGIOUS SITUATION IN EUROPE
AT THE HEIGHT OF THE REFORMATION

PRINCIPAL CHRISTIAN CHURCHES IN 1560:

Lutherans
Anglicans
Calvinists
Roman Catholics

MINORITIES:
L Lutherans   RC Roman Catholics
C Calvinists

ASA Anabaptists, Socinians, Antitrinitarians
---- Approximate extent of the revolt
from the Roman Church

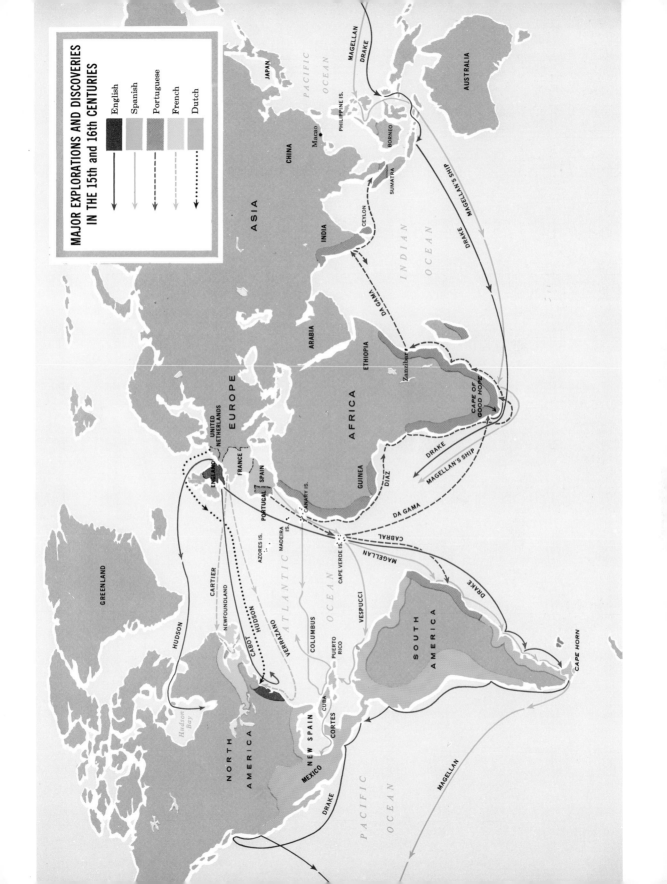

MAJOR EXPLORATIONS AND DISCOVERIES
IN THE 15th and 16th CENTURIES

English
Spanish
Portuguese
French
Dutch

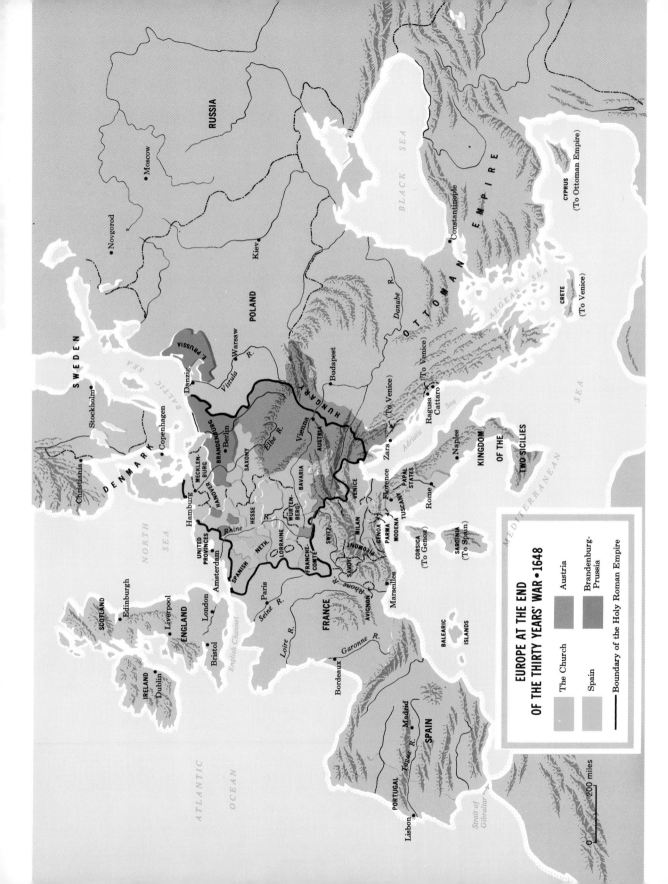

EUROPE AT THE END
OF THE THIRTY YEARS' WAR • 1648

The Church

Spain

Austria

Brandenburg-
Prussia

Boundary of the Holy Roman Empire

0   200 miles

RUSSIA

Moscow

Novgorod

Kiev

SWEDEN

Stockholm

Christiania

DENMARK

Copenhagen

BALTIC SEA

POLAND

Warsaw

E. PRUSSIA

Danzig

Vistula R.

Visula

BRANDENBURG

Berlin

MECKLEN-
BURG

HANOVER

Hamburg

SAXONY

Elbe R.

HESSE

WÜRTEN-
BERG

Rhine

R.

BAVARIA

AUSTRIA

HUNGARY

Vienna

Budapest

Danube R.

BLACK SEA

OTTOMAN EMPIRE

Constantinople

AEGEAN SEA

CRETE
(To Venice)

CYPRUS
(To Ottoman Empire)

NORTH SEA

SCOTLAND

Edinburgh

IRELAND

Dublin

ENGLAND

Liverpool

London

Bristol

English Channel

UNITED
PROVINCES

Amsterdam

SPANISH
NETH.

LORRAINE

FRANCHE-
COMTÉ

SWITZ.

MILAN

PIEDMONT

SAVOY

GENOA

PARMA

MODENA

TUSCANY

PAPAL
STATES

Florence

Rome

VENICE

Zara
(To Venice)

Ragusa
Cattaro
(To Venice)

Adriatic
Sea

Naples

KINGDOM
OF THE
TWO SICILIES

MEDITERRANEAN SEA

CORSICA
(To Genoa)

SARDINIA
(To Spain)

FRANCE

Paris

Seine R.

Loire R.

Garonne R.

Bordeaux

Rhône R.

Marseilles

AVIGNON

BALEARIC
ISLANDS

ATLANTIC
OCEAN

PORTUGAL

Lisbon

SPAIN

Madrid

Tagus R.

Strait of
Gibraltar

St. Peter's, Rome. Built to a square cross plan originally conceived by Bramante and revised by Michelangelo. Completed in 1626, the church rises to a total height of 450 feet.

contrast, was able to flourish there, since it was more in keeping with Italian traditions, while the persistence of a strong admiration for Latin culture made possible a revival of the Roman style. Accordingly, the great architects of the Renaissance generally adopted their building plans from the Romanesque churches and monasteries and copied their decorative devices from the ruins of ancient Rome. The result was an architecture based upon the cruciform floor plan of transept and nave and embodying the decorative features of the column and arch, or the column and lintel, the colonnade, and frequently the dome. Horizontal lines predominated; and, though many of the buildings were churches, the ideals they expressed were the purely secular ones of joy in this life and pride in human achievement. Renaissance architecture emphasized harmony and proportion to a much greater extent than did the Romanesque style. Under the influence of Neoplatonism, Italian architects concluded that perfect proportions in man reflect the harmony of the universe, and that, therefore, the parts of a building should be related to each other and to the whole in the same way as the parts of the human body. A fine example of Renaissance architecture is St. Peter's Church in Rome, built under the patronage of Popes Julius II and Leo X and designed by some of the most celebrated architects of the time, including Donato Bramante (c. 1444–1514) and Michelangelo.

The eclecticism of Renaissance architecture

3. THE WANING OF THE ITALIAN RENAISSANCE

Around 1550 the Renaissance in Italy came to an end after some two centuries of glorious history. The causes of its demise were varied. Possibly at the head of the list should be placed the French invasion of

The Entrance of Charles VIII into Florence. A painting by Francesco Granacci.

Political factors in the decline of the Italian Renaissance: the French invasion of 1494

1494 and the chaos that quickly ensued. The French monarch, Charles VIII, ruled over the richest and most powerful kingdom in Europe. Italy seemed an attractive prey for his grandiose ambitions. Accordingly, in 1494 he led an army of 30,000 well-trained troops across the Alps. The Medici of Florence fled before him, leaving their city to immediate capture. Halting only long enough to establish peace with a subservient new republican government, the French resumed their advance and conquered Naples. By so doing, however, they aroused the suspicions of the rulers of Spain, who feared an attack on their own possession of Sicily. An alliance of Spain, the Papal States, the Holy Roman Empire, Milan, and Venice finally forced Charles to abandon his project. Yet upon his death his successor, Louis XII, repeated the invasion of Italy, and from 1499 until 1529 warfare in Italy was virtually uninterrupted. Alliances and counteralliances followed each other in bewildering succession, but they only managed to prolong the warfare. The French won a great victory at Marignano in 1515, but they were decisively defeated by the Spanish at Pavia in 1525. The worst disaster came in 1527 when unruly Spanish and German troops, nominally under the command of the Spanish ruler Charles V but in fact entirely out of control, sacked the city of Rome, causing irreparable destruction. Only by 1529 did Charles finally manage to gain control over most of the Italian peninsula, putting the fighting to an end for a time. Once triumphant, Charles made a practice of restoring favorite princes as the rulers of Italian states. They continued to preside over their courts, to patronize the arts, and to adorn their cities with luxurious buildings, but in fact they were Spanish puppets and the greatest days of Italy were now clearly over.

To the political disorders was added a waning of Italian prosperity. This apparently brought no severe hardships until after 1600, but the shift of trade routes from the Mediterranean to the Atlantic region, following the discovery of America, was bound ultimately to have its effect. Italian cities gradually lost their supremacy as the centers of world trade. The prosperity they had enjoyed from a monopoly of commerce with the East had been one of the chief nourishing influences in the development of their brilliant culture. An important source of strength was now being drained away. (The effect of this "Commercial Revolution" is the subject of Chapter 16.)

A final cause of the decline of the Italian Renaissance was the Catholic Reformation. During the sixteenth century the Roman Church sought increasingly to exercise firm control over thought and art as part of a campaign to combat worldliness and the spread of Protestantism. In 1542 the Roman Inquisition was established; in 1559 Pope Paul IV issued the first Index of Prohibited Books. The effects of ecclesiastical interference in artistic life were devastating. Michelangelo's great *Last Judgment* in the Sistine Chapel—even though inspired by the thought of the Catholic Reformation—was criticized by some strait-laced fanatics for looking like a bordello because it showed too many naked bodies. Therefore, Paul IV ordered a second-rate artist to paint in clothing wherever possible. (The unfortunate artist was afterwards known as "the underwear-maker.") The most notorious example of inquisitorial censorship of free intellectual speculation was the disciplining of the great scientist Galileo, whose achievements we will discuss more carefully later on. In 1616 the Holy Office in Rome condemned the new astronomical theory that the earth moves around the sun as "foolish, absurd, philosophically false, and formally heretical." Accordingly, the Inquisition proceeded immediately against Galileo when he published a brilliant defense of the heliocentric system in 1632. In short order the Inquisition made Galileo recant his "errors" and sentenced him to house arrest for the duration of his life. Galileo was not willing to face death for his beliefs, but after he publicly retracted his view that the earth revolves around the sun he supposedly whispered, "despite everything, it still moves." Not surprisingly, Galileo was the last great Italian contributor to the development of modern astronomy and physics until modern times. It should not be thought that cultural and artistic achievement in Italy in the seventeenth century was completely extinguished. On the contrary, a great new style of architecture and sculpture known as the baroque was born and flourished in Rome under ecclesiastical auspices. Great advances were also made by Italian musicians without interruption from the sixteenth to the nineteenth century. But whatever seemed threatening to the Church could not be tolerated and the free spirit of Renaissance culture was found no more.

4. THE RENAISSANCE IN THE NORTH

The diffusion of the
Renaissance outside Italy

It was inevitable that after about 1500 the Renaissance which began in Italy should have spread to other European countries. Throughout the fifteenth century there had been a continuous procession of northern European students coming down into Italy to study in Italian universities such as Bologna or Padua, and there were also occasional Italians who traveled north of the Alps. Such interchanges helped spread ideas, but only after around 1500 did most of northern Europe become sufficiently prosperous and politically stable to provide a truly congenial environment for the widespread cultivation of art and literature. Intellectual interchanges, moreover, became much more extensive after 1494, when France and Spain started fighting on Italian battlefields. The result of this development was that more and more northern Europeans began to learn what the Italians had been accomplishing (Spain's forces came not just from Spain but also from Germany and the Low Countries). Then too leading Italian thinkers and artists, like Leonardo, began to enter the retinues of northern kings or aristocrats. Accordingly, the Renaissance became an international movement and continued to be vigorous in the north even after it started to wane on its native ground.

The character of the
northern Renaissance

It must not be supposed, however, that the Renaissance outside of Italy was the same in quality as the Renaissance within Italy. Above all, the northern European Renaissance was generally less secular. It is hard to account for this fully, but several reasons might be hazarded. One is that Italy had always had a more vigorous and independent urban society than the north. Even during the Middle Ages the Italian cities had patronized a more secular educational system in order to provide training for younger generations in business, law, and municipal public affairs. Since Italians could see Roman ruins all around them, they also developed greater familiarity at an earlier date with the classical tradition. That in turn allowed them to develop a more secular vocabulary and encouraged greater interest in depicting non-Christian themes in art. The north, on the other hand, had always focused on theological studies and had become more deeply imbued with religious mysticism. Northern Renaissance culture was never predominantly theological or mystical but it did emphasize religion to a greater degree than its Italian progenitor.

The limited scope of the
German Renaissance

One of the first countries to receive the full impact of the Italian humanist movement was Germany. This was a natural development, not only because of the proximity of the two countries, but also because of the steady migration of German students to the Italian universities. But the long-range influence of this humanism was not profound. What the results might have been if Germany had not been hurled so soon into the maelstrom of religious contention cannot be determined. The fact remains, however, that the Protestant Revolution stirred up extreme passions of intolerance which could not be other than inimical to the humanist ideal. A premium was now set upon faith, while anything resembling the worship of man or reverence for pagan antiquity was almost certain to be regarded as a work of the devil.

To fix a date for the beginning of the German Renaissance is practically impossible. In such prosperous cities of the south as Augsburg, Nuremberg, and Vienna there was a humanist movement, imported from Italy, as early as 1450. By the beginning of the sixteenth century it had spread elsewhere. Among its most notable representatives were Ulrich von Hutten (1488–1523) and Crotus Rubianus (1480–1523). Typical of the German humanist movement, both were less interested in the literary aspects of humanism than in its possibilities for the expression of religious and political protest. Hutten, especially, made use of his gifts as a writer to satirize the worldliness and greed of the clergy and to compose fiery defenses of the German people against foreigners. He was an embittered rebel against almost every institution of the established order.

German humanism

The chief claim to fame of Hutten and Rubianus is their joint authorship of the *Letters of Obscure Men* of 1515, one of the wittiest satires in the history of literature. This was written as a part of a propaganda war in favor of a humanist named Johann Reuchlin who wished to pursue his study of Hebrew writings, above all, the Talmud. When theologians from the University of Cologne and the German inquisitor general tried to have all Hebrew books in Germany destroyed, Reuchlin and his party strongly opposed the move. After a while it became apparent that direct argument was accomplishing nothing, so Reuchlin's supporters resorted to ridicule. Rubianus and Hutten published a series of letters, written in intentionally bad Latin, purportedly by some of Reuchlin's opponents from the University of Cologne. These were given such ridiculous names as Goatmilker, Goosepreacher, Baldpate, and Dungspreader, and shown to be learned fools who paraded forth examples of absurd religious literalism or grotesque erudition. Heinrich Sheep's-mouth, the supposed writer of one of the letters, professed to be worried that he had sinned grievously by eating on Friday an egg that contained the yolk of a chick. The author of another boasted of his "brilliant discovery" that Julius Caesar could not have written the *Commentaries on the Gallic Wars* because he was too busy with his military exploits ever to have learned Latin. Although immediately banned by the Church, the letters circulated nonetheless and were widely read. It is even possible that they helped prepare the way for the Protestant Revolution in Germany.

The Letters of Obscure Men

The German Renaissance in art was limited primarily to painting and engraving, represented chiefly by the work of Albrecht Dürer

Dürer's *Melancholy.* Ponderous "Melancholy" represents "theoretical insight which thinks but cannot act." Compare Dürer's more affirmative view of human potentialities shown on p. 584.

(1471–1528) and Hans Holbein (1497–1543). Both of these artists were profoundly influenced by Italian traditions, though much of the Germanic spirit of somber realism is also expressed in their work. Dürer's best-known paintings are his *Adoration of the Magi, The Four Apostles,* and *The Crucified Christ.* The last is a study in tragic gloom. It shows the body of Jesus stretched on the cross against a bleak and sinister sky. The glimmer of light on the horizon merely adds to the somber effect of the scene. Some of Dürer's best-known engravings exhibit similar qualities. His *Melancholy* represents a female figure, a personification of the creative temperament, meditating on the limited nature of human creativity and knowledge, surrounded by the traditional instruments of learning, which seem useless.

Hans Holbein the Younger, the other great artist of the German Renaissance, derives his renown primarily from his portraits and drawings. His portraits of Erasmus and of Henry VIII of England are among the most famous in the world. An impressive example of his drawings is the one known as *Christ in the Tomb.* It depicts the body of Jesus, with staring eyes and mouth half-open, as neglected in death as the corpse of an ordinary criminal. The artist's purpose was to express the utter degradation which Christ had suffered for the redemption of humans. In his later career Holbein also drew many religious pictures satirizing the abuses in the Catholic Church which were believed to be

German painting: Dürer

Erasmus

See color plates following page 576

the chief justification for the Protestant Revolution. He was one of the few prominent artists to devote his talents to the Protestant cause.

The history of Renaissance literature and philosophy in the Low Countries begins and ends with Desiderius Erasmus (1467?–1536), universally acclaimed as the prince of the humanists. The son of a priest and a servant girl, Erasmus was born near Rotterdam. For his early education he had the benefit of the excellent training given in a school of the Brethren of the Common Life. Later, after his father and mother were both dead, his guardians placed him in a monastery. Here the young Erasmus found little religion or formal instruction of any kind but plenty of freedom to read what he liked. He devoured all the classics he could get his hands on and the writings of many of the church fathers. When he was about thirty years of age, he obtained permission to leave the monastery and enroll in the University of Paris, where he completed the requirements for the degree of bachelor of divinity. But Erasmus subsequently revolted against what he considered to be the arid learning of Parisian Scholasticism. In one of his later writings he reported the following exchange: "Q. Where do you come from? A. The College of Montaigu. Q. Ah, then you must be bowed down with learning. A. No, with lice." Erasmus also never entered into the active duties of a priest, choosing rather to make his living by teaching and writing. By extensive reading of the classics he achieved a style of Latin expression so remarkable for its wit and urbanity that everything he wrote was widely read. But Erasmus's love of the classics was not born of pedantic interest. He admired the ancient authors because they gave voice to the very ideals of tolerance and humanitarianism which held so exalted a place in his own mind. He was wont to believe that Cicero and Socrates were far more deserving of the title of saint than many a Christian canonized by the pope. Erasmus died in Basel at the end of a long and unfaltering career in defense of scholarship, high standards of literary taste, and the life of moderation. He has been called the most civilized man of his age.

Erasmus. A woodcut by Hans Holbein the Younger.

As a philosopher of humanism Erasmus was the incarnation of the finest ideals of the northern Renaissance. Convinced of the inherent goodness of humanity, he believed that all misery and injustice would eventually disappear if only the pure sunlight of reason could be allowed to penetrate the noisome caverns of ignorance, superstition, and hate. With nothing of the fanatic about him, he stood for liberality of mind, for reasonableness and conciliation, rather than for fierce intolerance of evil. He shrank from the violence and passion of war, whether between systems, classes, or nations. Much of his teaching and writing was dedicated to the cause of religious reform. The ceremonial and superstitious extravagances in sixteenth-century Catholic life repelled him. But it was alien to his temper to lead any crusade against them. He sought rather by gentle irony, and occasionally by stinging satire, to expose irrationalism in all of its forms and to propa-

The tolerant thought of Erasmus

gate a humanist religion of simple piety and noble conduct based upon what he called the "philosophy of Christ." Although his criticism of the Catholic faith had some effect in hastening the Protestant Revolution, he recoiled in disgust from the intolerance of the Lutherans. Neither did he have much sympathy for the scientific revival of his time. Like most of the humanists he believed that an emphasis upon science would serve to promote a crude materialism and to distract men's interests from the ennobling influences of literature and moral philosophy. The best-known writings of Erasmus were his *Praise of Folly*, in which he satirized pedantry, the dogmatism of theologians, and the ignorance and credulity of the masses, and his *Colloquies* and *The Handbook of the Christian Knight,* in which he condemned ecclesiastical Christianity and argued for a return to the simple teachings of Jesus, "who commanded us nothing save love for one another." In a less noted, but nonetheless brilliant, work entitled *The Complaint of Peace*, he expressed his abhorrence of war and his contempt for despotic princes.

The art of the Low Countries during the Renaissance period found its greatest practitioner in Peter Brueghel the Elder (c. 1525–1569). Brueghel spent a few years in Italy studying the accomplishments of the Italian Renaissance masters, but his own work remained distinctively Flemish in both subject matter and style. Brueghel continued the tradition of earlier Flemish artists like the van Eycks in realistically portraying scenes from everyday life, but he was one of the earliest painters to pay particular attention to the life of the peasantry. Although he never idealized the roughness of peasants, his attitude to-

Knight, Death, and Devil by Dürer. This engraving of 1513 illustrates the ideal figure of Erasmus's *Handbook of a Christian Knight*. The steadfast knight is able to advance through the world on his charger, his loyal dog at his side, despite intimations of mortality and the snares of the devil.

The Massacre of the Innocents. This painting by Brueghel shows how effectively art can be used as a means of social commentary.

ward them was definitely sympathetic. At first glance many of his paintings look like they are merely trying to recapture the world of nature and humanity without any comment, but closer inspection usually shows that initial appearances are deceptive. In fact, Brueghel was clearly a deeply moral and religious person. His *Land of Cockaigne,* which depicts fat people reclining in languid stupor after a great feast, is clearly meant to show that they are only living in a fool's paradise. His great *Massacre of the Innocents* is particularly moving in its quiet indictment of war and brutality. From a distance this looks like a simple scene of a wintry Flemish town buried in snow, but in fact heartless soldiers are methodically breaking into homes and slaughtering babies. The simple townspeople are helpless to stop them, and the artist seems to be saying: as it happened in the time of Christ, so it happens now.

See color plates following page 576

In France during the time of the Renaissance, there were outstanding achievements in literature and philosophy, illustrated especially by the writings of François Rabelais (1490?–1553) and Michel de Montaigne (1533–1592). Like Erasmus, Rabelais was educated as a monk, but soon after taking holy orders he left the monastery to study medicine at the University of Montpellier. He finished the course for the bachelor's degree in the short space of six weeks and obtained his doc-

The Renaissance in France: Rabelais

Rabelais

Montaigne

torate about five years later, in the meantime having served for a period as public physician in Lyon in addition to lecturing and editing medical writings. He seems from the start to have interspersed his professional activities with literary endeavors of one sort or another. He wrote almanacs for the common people, satires against quacks and astrologers, and burlesques of popular superstitions. In 1532 Rabelais published his first edition of *Gargantua,* which he later revised and combined with another book bearing the title of *Pantagruel.* Gargantua and Pantagruel were originally the names of legendary medieval giants noted for their prodigious strength and gross appetites. Rabelais's account of their adventures served as a vehicle for his robust, sprawling wit and for the expression of his philosophy of exuberant naturalism. In language far from delicate he satirized the practices of the Church, ridiculed Scholasticism, scoffed at superstitions, and pilloried every form of bigotry and repression. No man of the Renaissance was a more uncompromising individualist or exhibited more zeal in glorifying the human and the natural. For him every instinct of man was healthy, provided it was not directed toward tyranny over others. His celebrated description of the abbey of Thélème, built by Gargantua, was intended to show the contrast between his conception of freedom and the Christian ascetic ideal. At Thélème there were no clocks summoning to duties and no vows of celibacy or perpetual membership. The inmates could leave when they liked; but while they remained they dwelt together "according to their own free will and pleasure. They rose out of their beds when they thought good; they did eat, drink, labor, sleep, when they had a mind to it, and were disposed for it. None did awake them, none did offer to constrain them . . . for so Gargantua had established it. In all their Rule and strictest tie of their order there was but this one clause to be observed, *Do what thou wilt.*"

A man of far different temperament and background was Michel de Montaigne (1533–1592). His father was a Catholic, his mother a Jew who had become a Protestant. Almost from the day of his birth their son was subjected to an elaborate system of training. Every morning he was awakened by soft music, and he was attended throughout the day by servants who were forbidden to speak any language but Latin. When he was six years old he was ready for the College of Guienne at Bordeaux and at the age of thirteen began the study of law. After practicing law for a time and serving in various public offices, he retired at thirty-seven to his ancestral estate to devote the remainder of his life to study, contemplation, and writing. Always in delicate health, Montaigne found it necessary now more than ever to conserve his strength. Besides, he was repelled by the bitterness and strife he saw all around him and was for that reason all the more anxious to find a refuge in a world of intellectual seclusion.

Montaigne's ideas are contained in his famous *Essays,* written during his years of retirement. The essence of his philosophy is skepticism in regard to all dogma and final truth. He knew too much about the diversity of beliefs, the welter of foreign customs revealed by geographic discoveries, and the disturbing conclusions of the new science ever to accept the idea that any one sect had exclusive possession of "the Truth delivered once for all to the saints." It seemed to him that religion and morality were as much the product of custom as styles of dress or habits of eating. He taught that God is unknowable, and that it is as foolish to "weep that we shall not exist a hundred years hence as it would be to weep that we had not lived a hundred years ago." Man should be encouraged to despise death and to live nobly and delicately in this life rather than to yearn piously for an afterlife. Montaigne was just as skeptical in regard to assumptions of final truth in philosophy or science. The conclusions of reason, he taught, are sometimes fallacious, and the senses often deceive us. The sooner men come to realize that there is no certainty anywhere, the better chance they will have to escape the tyranny which flows from superstition and bigotry. The road to salvation lies in doubt, not in faith.

The thought of Montaigne:
(1) skepticism

A second element in Montaigne's worldview was tolerance. He could see no real difference between the morals of Christians and those of infidels. All sects, he pointed out, fight each other with equal ferocity, except that "there is no hatred so absolute as that which is Christian." Neither could he see any value in crusades or revolutions for the purpose of overthrowing one system and establishing another. All human institutions in his judgment were about equally futile, and he therefore considered it fatuous that man should take them so seriously as to wade through slaughter in order to substitute one for its opposite. No ideal, he maintained, is worth burning your neighbor for. In his attitude toward questions of ethics Montaigne was not so ribald a champion of carnality as Rabelais, yet he had no sympathy for asceticism. He believed it ridiculous that men should attempt to deny their physical natures and pretend that everything connected with sense is unworthy. "Sit we upon the highest throne in the world," he declared, "yet we do but sit upon our own behind." But in spite of his primarily negative attitude Montaigne did more good in the world than most of his contemporaries who founded new faiths or invented new excuses for absolute monarchs to enslave their subjects. Not only did his ridicule help to quench the flames of the cruel hysteria against witches, but the influence of his skeptical teachings had no small effect in combating fanaticism generally and in paving the way for a more generous tolerance in the future.

(2) tolerance

Despite the strong aesthetic interests of the French, as evidenced by their perfection of Gothic architecture during the Middle Ages, the achievements of their artists in the age of the Renaissance were of comparatively little importance. There was some minor progress in sculpture and a modest advancement in architecture. It was during this

Reasons for the backwardness of Spain in the Renaissance

The character of Spanish painting; El Greco

See color plates following page 576

Spanish drama

time that the Louvre was built, on the site of an earlier structure bearing the same name, while numerous châteaux erected throughout the country represented a more or less successful attempt to combine the grace and elegance of the Italian style with the solidity of the medieval castle. Nor was science entirely neglected, although the major accomplishments were few.

During the sixteenth and early seventeenth centuries Spain was at the height of its glory. Spanish conquests in the Western Hemisphere brought wealth to nobles and merchants and gave Spain a proud position in the front rank of European states. Notwithstanding these facts, the Spanish nation was not one of the leaders in Renaissance culture. The long war with the Moors had engendered a spirit of bigotry, the position of the Church was too strong, and the expulsion of the Jews at the end of the fifteenth century had deprived the country of talent it could ill afford to lose. For these reasons the Spanish Renaissance was limited to a few achievements in painting and literature, albeit some of these rank in brilliance with the best that other countries produced.

Spanish painting bore the deep impression of the bitter struggle between Christian and Moor. As a result it expressed an intense preoccupation with religion and with themes of anguish and tragedy. Its background was medieval; upon it were grafted influences from Flanders and from Italy. The most talented artist of the Spanish Renaissance was not a native of Spain at all, but an immigrant from the island of Crete. His real name was Domenico Theotocopuli, but he is commonly called El Greco (1541?–1614?). After studying for some time under Titian in Venice, El Greco settled in Toledo about 1575, to live there until his death. A stern individualist in temperament, he seems to have imbibed little of the warmth of color and sensuality of the Venetian school. Instead, nearly all of his art is characterized by emotionalism, stark tragedy, or enraptured flights into the supernatural and mystical. He often portrayed gaunt, ascetic-looking figures; his colors sometimes were cold and severe. His scenes of suffering and death seem deliberately contrived to produce an impression of horror. Among his famous works are *The Burial of the Count of Orgaz, Pentecost,* and *The Apocalyptic Vision.* Better than any other artist, El Greco expresses the fiery religious zeal of the Spanish people during the heyday of the Inquisition.

Literature in the Spanish Renaissance displayed tendencies not dissimilar to those in painting. This was notably true of drama, which frequently took the form of allegorical plays depicting the mystery of transubstantiation or appealing to some passion of religious fervor. Other dramatic productions dwelt upon themes of political pride or romance. The colossus among the Spanish dramatists was Lope de Vega (1562–1635), the most prolific author of plays the literary world has seen. He is supposed to have written no fewer than 1,500 comedies and more than 400 religious allegories. Of the total about 500 survive to this day. His secular dramas fall mainly into two classes: (1) the "cloak and sword plays," which depict the violent intrigues and exaggerated ideals of honor among the upper classes; and (2) the plays of national greatness, which celebrate the glories of Spain in its prime and represent the king as the protector of the people against a vicious and degenerate nobility.

Few would deny that the most gifted writer of the Spanish Renaissance was Miguel de Cervantes (1547–1616). His great masterpiece, *Don Quixote,* has even been described as "incomparably the best novel ever written." Composed in the best tradition of Spanish satirical prose, it recounts the adventures of a Spanish gentleman (Don Quixote) who has been slightly unbalanced by constant reading of chivalric romances. His mind filled with all kinds of fantastic adventures, he finally sets out at the age of fifty upon the slippery road of knight-errantry. He imagines windmills to be glowering giants and flocks of sheep to be armies of infidels, whom it is his duty to rout with his spear. In his disordered fancy he mistakes inns for castles and the serving-wenches within them for courtly ladies on fire with love of him. Set off in bold contrast to the ridiculous knight-errant is the figure of his faithful squire, Sancho Panza. The latter represents the ideal of the practical man, with his feet on the ground and content with the substantial pleasures of eating, drinking, and sleeping. The book as a whole is a pungent satire on chivalry, especially on the pretensions of the nobles as the champions of honor and right. Its enormous popularity was convincing proof that medieval civilization was approaching extinction even in Spain.

In common with Spain, England also enjoyed a golden age in the sixteenth and early seventeenth centuries. Though its vast colonial empire had not yet been established, England was nevertheless reaping big profits from the production of wool and from trade with the Continent. The government, recently consolidated under the rule of the Tudors, was enhancing the prosperity of the merchants. Through the elimination of foreign traders, the granting of favors to English shipping, and the negotiation of reciprocal commercial treaties, the English merchant classes were given exceptional advantages over their rivals in other countries. The growth of a national consciousness, the awakening of pride in the power of the state, and the spread of humanism from Italy, France, and the Low Countries also contributed toward the flowering of a brilliant culture in England. Nevertheless, the English Renaissance was confined primarily to literature; the fine arts did not flourish.

The earliest writers of the English Renaissance may best be described as humanists. Although not unmindful of the value of classical studies, they were interested chiefly in the more practical aspects of humanism. Most of them desired a simpler and more rational Christianity and looked forward to an educational system freed from the

Cervantes

Don Quixote

The economic and political foundations of the Renaissance in England

The early English humanists; Thomas More

Sir Thomas More. Portrait by Hans Holbein the Younger.

English Renaissance literature

The Elizabethan dramatists; Marlowe

dominance of Scholastic logic. Others were concerned primarily with individual freedom and the correction of social abuses. The greatest of these early thinkers was Sir Thomas More (1478–1535), esteemed by contemporary humanists as "excellent above all his nation." Following a successful career as a lawyer and as speaker of the House of Commons, More was appointed in 1529 lord chancellor of England. He was not long in this position, however, before he incurred the enmity of his royal master, Henry VIII. More was loyal to Catholic universalism and did not sympathize with the king's design to establish a national church under subjection to the state. When, in 1534, he refused to take the Oath of Supremacy acknowledging the king as the head of the Church of England, he was thrown into the Tower. A year later he was tried for treason on perjured evidence, convicted, and beheaded. More's philosophy is contained in his *Utopia,* which he published in 1516. Purporting to describe an ideal society on an imaginary island, the book is really an indictment of the glaring abuses of the time—of poverty undeserved and wealth unearned, of drastic punishments, religious persecution, and the senseless slaughter of war. The inhabitants of Utopia hold all their goods in common, work only six hours a day so that all may have leisure for intellectual pursuits, and practice the natural virtues of wisdom, moderation, fortitude, and justice. Iron is the precious metal "because it is useful," war and monasticism are abolished, and tolerance is granted to all who recognize the existence of God and the immortality of the soul. Despite criticism of the *Utopia* as conservative in many respects, the conclusion seems justified that the author's ideals of humanity and tolerance were considerably in advance of those of most other men of his time.

If there were any essential differences between the English literature of the Renaissance and that produced during the late Middle Ages, they would consist in a bolder individualism, a stronger sense of national pride, and a deeper interest in themes of philosophic import. The first great poet in England after the time of Chaucer was Edmund Spenser (1552?–1599). His immortal creation, *The Faerie Queene,* is a colorful epic of England's greatness in the days of Elizabeth I. Though written as a moral allegory to express the author's desire for a return to the virtues of chivalry, it celebrates also the joy in conquest and much of the gorgeous sensuousness typical of Renaissance culture.

But the most splendid achievements of the English in the Elizabethan Age were in the realm of drama. Not since the days of the Greeks had the writing of tragedies and comedies attained such heights as were reached in England during the sixteenth and early seventeenth centuries. Especially after 1580 a galaxy of playwrights appeared whose work outshone that of all their predecessors in two thousand years. Included in this galaxy were such luminaries as Christopher Marlowe (1564–1593), John Webster (c. 1580–c. 1625), Ben Jonson (1573?–1637), and William Shakespeare (1564–1616), of whom the first and last are chiefly significant to the historian. Better than

A Map of Thomas More's Imaginary Island of Utopia. "Utopia's" fictional discoverer, Hythlodaeus, whose name means "dispenser of nonsense" in Greek, points to the island of Utopia, which means "no place." From an early edition.

anyone else in his time, Christopher Marlowe embodied the insatiable egoism of the Renaissance—the everlasting craving for the fullness of life, for unlimited knowledge and experience. His brief but stormy life was a succession of scandalous escapades and fiery revolts against the restraints of convention until it was terminated by his death in a tavern brawl before he was thirty years old. The best known of his plays, entitled *Doctor Faustus,* is based upon the legend of Faust, in which the hero sells his soul to the devil in return for the power to feel every possible sensation, experience every possible triumph, and know all the mysteries of the universe.

William Shakespeare, the most talented genius in the history of drama since Euripides, was born into the family of a petty tradesman in the provincial market town of Stratford-on-Avon. His life is enshrouded in more mists of obscurity than the careers of most other great men. It is known that he left his native village when he was about twenty years old, and that ultimately he drifted to London to find employment in the theater. Tradition relates that for a time he earned his living by holding the horses of the more prosperous patrons of the drama. How he eventually became an actor and still later a writer of plays is unknown, but there is evidence that by the time he was twenty-eight he had already acquired a reputation as an author sufficient to excite the jealousy of his rivals. Before he retired to his

The life and writings of William Shakespeare

native Stratford about 1610 to spend the rest of his days in ease, he had written or collaborated in writing nearly forty plays, to say nothing of 150 sonnets and two long narrative poems.

In paying homage to the universality of Shakespeare's genius, we must not lose sight of the fact that he was also a child of the Renaissance. His work bore the deep impression of most of the virtues and defects of Renaissance humanism. Almost as much as Boccaccio or Rabelais, he personified that intense love of things human and earthly which had characterized most of the great writers since the close of the Middle Ages. Moreover, like the majority of the humanists, he showed a limited concern with the problems of politics and scientific thought. Virtually the only political theory that interested him greatly was whether a nation had a better chance of prospering under a good king who was weak or under a bad king who was strong. His knowledge of science was limited primarily to alchemy, astrology, and medicine. But the force and range of Shakespeare's intellect were far from bounded by the narrow horizons of the age in which he lived. While few of the works of his contemporaries are now widely read, the plays of Shakespeare still hold their rank as a kind of secular Bible wherever the English language is spoken. The reason lies not only in the author's unrivaled gift of expression, but especially in his scintillating wit and primarily in his profound analysis of human character assailed by passion and tried by fate.

Shakespeare's dramas fall rather naturally into three main groups. Those written during his earlier years conformed to the traditions of existing plays and generally reflected his own confidence in personal

Mr. WILLIAM
SHAKESPEARES
COMEDIES,
HISTORIES, &
TRAGEDIES.
Published according to the True Originall Copies.

William Shakespeare. Portrait made for the First Folio edition of his works, 1623.

success. They include such comedies as _A Midsummer Night's Dream_ and _The Merchant of Venice,_ a number of historical plays, and the lyrical tragedy, _Romeo and Juliet._ Shortly before 1600 Shakespeare seems to have experienced a change of mood. The restrained optimism of his earlier plays was supplanted by some deep disillusion which led him to distrust human nature and to indict the whole scheme of the universe. The result was a group of dramas characterized by bitterness, overwhelming pathos, and a troubled searching into the mysteries of things. The series begins with the tragedy of intellectual idealism represented by _Hamlet,_ goes on to the cynicism of _Measure for Measure_ and _All's Well That Ends Well,_ and culminates in the cosmic tragedies of _Macbeth_ and _King Lear._ The final group of dramas includes those written during the closing years of Shakespeare's professional life. Among these are _The Winter's Tale_ and _The Tempest._ All of them may be described as idyllic romances. Trouble and grief are now assumed to be only the shadows in a beautiful picture. Despite individual tragedy, the divine plan of the universe is somehow benevolent and just.

5. RENAISSANCE DEVELOPMENTS IN MUSIC

Music in western Europe in the fifteenth and sixteenth centuries reached such a high point of development that it constitutes, together with painting and sculpture, one of the most brilliant aspects of Renaissance activity. While the visual arts were stimulated by the study of ancient models, music flowed naturally from an independent evolution which had long been in progress in medieval Christendom. As earlier, leadership was supplied by men trained in the service of the Church, but the value of secular music was now appreciated, and its principles were combined with those of sacred music to bring a decided gain in color and emotional appeal. The distinction between sacred and profane became less sharp; most composers did not restrict their activities to either field. Music was no longer regarded merely as a diversion or an adjunct to worship but as an independent art.

Different sections of Europe vied with one another for musical leadership. As with the other arts, advance was related to the increasingly generous patronage made possible by the expansion of commerce, and was centered in the prosperous towns. During the fourteenth century a pre- or early Renaissance musical movement called Ars Nova (new art) flourished in Italy and France. Its outstanding composers were Francesco Landini (c. 1325–1397) and Guillaume de Machaut (1300–1377). The madrigals, ballads, and other songs composed by the Ars Nova musicians testify to a rich secular art, but the greatest achievement of the period was a highly complicated yet delicate contrapuntal style adapted for motet and chanson. With Machaut we reach the first integral polyphonic setting of the Ordinary of the Mass.

Renaissance Trumpeters and Singers. Reliefs by Luca della Robbia.

Synthesis of national elements

The fifteenth century was ushered in by a synthesis of English, French, Flemish, and Italian elements that took place in the Duchy of Burgundy. It produced a remarkable school of music inspired by the cathedral of Cambrai and the ducal court at Dijon. This music was gentle, melodious, and euphonious, but in the second half of the century it hardened a little as the northern Flemish element gained in importance. As the sixteenth century opened we find these Franco-Flemish composers in every important court and cathedral choir all over Europe, gradually establishing regional-national schools, usually in attractive combinations of Flemish with German, Spanish, and Italian musical cultures. The various genres thus created show a close affinity with Renaissance art and poetry. In the second half of the sixteenth century the leaders of the nationalized Franco-Flemish style were the Italian Palestrina (c. 1525–1594), who, by virtue of his position as papal composer and his devotion to a subtle and crystal-clear vocal style, became the venerated symbol of church music; the Flemish Roland de Lassus (1532–1594), the most versatile composer of the age; and Tomas Luis de Victoria (c. 1540–1611), the glowing mystic of Spanish music. Music also flourished in England, for the Tudor monarchs were active in patronizing the arts; several of them were accomplished musicians. It was inevitable that the reigning Franco-Flemish style should reach England, where it was superimposed upon an ancient and rich musical culture. The Italian madrigal, imported toward the end of the sixteenth century, found a remarkable second flourishing in England, but songs and instrumental music of an original cast anticipated future developments on the Continent. In William Byrd (1543–1623) English music produced a master fully the equal of the great Flemish, Roman, and Spanish composers of the Renaissance. The general level of music proficiency seems to have been higher in Queen Elizabeth's day than in ours: the singing of part-songs was a popular pastime in homes and at informal social gatherings, and the ability to read a part at sight was expected of the educated elite.

In conclusion, it may be observed that while counterpoint had matured, our modern harmonic system had been born, and thus a way was opened for fresh experimentation. At the same time one should realize that the music of the Renaissance constitutes not merely a stage in evolution but a magnificent achievement in itself, with masters who rank among the great of all time. The composers Palestrina and Lassus are as truly representative of the artistic triumph of the Renaissance as are the painters Raphael and Michelangelo. Their heritage, long neglected except at a few ecclesiastical centers, has within recent years begun to be appreciated, and is now gaining in popularity as interested groups of musicians devote themselves to its revival.

*The greatness of the
Renaissance musical
achievement*

6. THE SCIENTIFIC ACCOMPLISHMENTS OF THE RENAISSANCE PERIOD

Some extraordinarily important accomplishments were made in the history of science during the sixteenth and early seventeenth centuries, but these were not preeminently the achievements of Renaissance humanism. The educational program of the humanists placed a low value on science because it seemed irrelevant to their aim of making people more eloquent and moral. Science for humanists like Petrarch, Leonardo Bruni, or Erasmus was part and parcel of the "vain speculation" of the Scholastics which they attacked and held up to ridicule. Accordingly, none of the great scientists of the Renaissance age belonged to the humanist movement.

*The nonscientific
orientation of Renaissance
humanism*

Nonetheless, at least two intellectual trends of the period did prepare the way for great new scientific advances. One was the popularity of Neoplatonism. The importance of this philosophical system to science was that it proposed certain ideas, such as the central position of the sun and the supposed divinity of given geometrical shapes, that would help lead to crucial scientific breakthroughs. It is ironic that Neoplatonism seems very "unscientific" from the modern perspective because it emphasizes mysticism and intuition instead of empiricism or strictly rational thought. Yet it helped scientific thinkers to reconsider older notions which had impeded the progress of medieval science; in other words, it helped them to put on a new "thinking cap." Among

*Renaissance foundations of
modern science: (1)
Neoplatonism*

*A Cannon Foundry by Leonardo
da Vinci*

the most important of the scientists who were influenced by Neoplatonism were Copernicus and Kepler.

A second trend that contributed to the advance of science was very different. This was the growth in popularity of a *mechanistic* interpretation of the universe. Renaissance mechanism owed its greatest impetus to the publication in 1543 of the works of the great Greek mathematician and physicist Archimedes. Not only were his concrete observations and discoveries among the most advanced and reliable in the entire body of Greek science, but Archimedes taught the view that the universe operates on the basis of mechanical forces, like a great machine. Because his view was diametrically opposed to the occult outlook of the Neoplatonists, who saw the world inhabited by spirits and driven by supernatural forces, it took some time to gather strength. Nonetheless, mechanism did gain some very important early adherents, foremost among whom was the Italian scientist Galileo. Ultimately mechanism played an enormous role in the development of modern science because it insisted upon finding observable and measurable causes and effects in the world of nature.

One other Renaissance development which helped lead to the rise of modern science was the breakdown of the medieval separation between the realms of theory and practice. In the Middle Ages the only "scientists" were Scholastically trained clerics who never for a moment thought of tinkering with machines, mixing chemicals, or dissecting corpses because this empirical approach to science lay outside the Scholastic framework. On the other hand, there were numerous technicians who had little formal education and knew little of abstract theories. But starting in the fifteenth century there was a growing integration of theory and practice. One reason for this was that the highly respected Renaissance artists bridged both areas of endeavor: not only were they marvelous craftsmen, but they studied and made advances in mathematics and science when they investigated the laws of perspective and optics, worked out geometric methods for supporting the weight of enormous architectural domes, and studied the dimensions and details of the human body. In general, they helped make science more empirical and practically oriented than it had been before. Other reasons for the integration were the decline in prestige of the overly theoretical universities and a growing interest in alchemy and astrology among the leisured classes. Here again we can see some irony: alchemy and astrology are today properly dismissed as unscientific superstitions, but in the sixteenth and seventeenth centuries their vogue led some wealthy amateurs to start building laboratories and measuring the courses of the stars. Thereby scientific practice was made eminently respectable. When that happened modern science was on the way to some of its greatest triumphs.

The actual scientific accomplishments of the Renaissance period were international in scope. The achievement par excellence in as-

Alchemists in Their Laboratory. This artist is clearly unsympathetic to the enterprise, but great earlymodern scientists such as Kepler and Newton took alchemy very seriously.

tronomy—the formulation and proof of the heliocentric theory that the earth revolves around the sun—was primarily the work of the Pole Copernicus, the German Kepler, and the Italian Galileo. Until the sixteenth century the Ptolemaic theory that the earth stands still and is the center of the universe went virtually unchallenged in western Europe. Nicholas Copernicus (1473–1543), a Polish clergyman who had absorbed Neoplatonism while studying in Italy, was the first to posit an alternate system. Copernicus made no new observations, but he thoroughly reinterpreted the significance of the old astronomical evidence. Inspired by the Neoplatonic assumptions that the sphere is the most perfect shape, that motion is more nearly divine than rest, and that the sun sits "enthroned" in the midst of the universe, "ruling his children the planets which circle around him," Copernicus worked out a new heliocentric theory. Specifically, in his *On the Revolutions of the Heavenly Spheres*—which he completed around 1530 but did not publish until 1543—he argued that the earth and the planets move around the sun in concentric circles. Copernicus's system itself was still highly imperfect: by no means did it account without difficulties for all the known facts of planetary motion. Moreover, it asked people to reject their commonsense assumptions that the sun moves because it gives the illusion of moving across the sky and that the earth stands still because no movement can be detected. More serious, Copernicus contradicted passages in the Bible, such as the one wherein Joshua commands the sun to stand still. Accordingly, believers in Copernicus's heliocentric theory remained distinctly in the minority until the early seventeenth century.

It was Kepler and Galileo who ensured that Copernicus's revolution in astronomy would become triumphant. Johann Kepler (1571–1630), a mystical thinker who was in many ways more like a magician than a modern scientist, studied astronomy in order to probe the hidden

Progress in astronomy: Copernicus's heliocentric theory

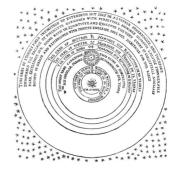

"A Perfect Description of the Celestial Orbes." A diagram by Copernicus, showing the relationship of stars, the planets, and the sun.

*Kepler's laws of planetary
motion*

secrets of God. His basic conviction was that God had created the universe on the basis of mathematical laws. Relying on the new and impressively accurate astronomical observations of the Dane Tycho Brahe (1546–1601), Kepler was able to recognize that two assumptions about planetary motion that Copernicus had taken for granted were simply not in accord with the observable facts. Specifically, Kepler replaced Copernicus's belief in uniform planetary velocity with his own "First Law" that the speed of planets varies with their distance from the sun, and he replaced Copernicus's view that planetary orbits were circular with his "Second Law" that the earth and the other planets travel in *elliptical* paths around the sun. He also argued in favor of magnetic attractions between the sun and the planets which keep the planets in orbital motion. That approach was rejected by most seventeenth-century mechanistic scientists as being far too magical, but in fact it paved the way for the law of universal gravitation formulated by Isaac Newton at the end of the seventeenth century.

*Galileo's confirmation of
the Copernican revolution*

As Kepler perfected Copernicus's heliocentric system from the point of view of mathematical theory, so Galileo Galilei (1564–1642) helped gain acceptance for it by gathering further astronomical evidence. With a telescope which he manufactured himself and raised to a magnifying power of thirty times, he discovered the moons of Jupiter, the rings of Saturn, and spots on the sun. He was able also to determine that the Milky Way is a collection of celestial bodies independent of our solar system and to form some idea of the enormous distances of the fixed stars. Though there were many who held out against them, these discoveries of Galileo gradually convinced the majority of scientists that the main conclusion of Copernicus was true. The final triumph of this idea is commonly called the Copernican Revolution. Few more significant events have occurred in the intellectual history of the world, for it overturned the medieval worldview and paved the way for modern conceptions of mechanism, skepticism, and the infinity of time and space. Some thinkers believe that it contributed also to the degradation of man, since it swept man out of his majestic position at the center of the universe and reduced him to a mere particle of dust in an endless cosmic machine.

In the front rank among the physicists of the Renaissance were Leonardo da Vinci and Galileo. If Leonardo da Vinci had failed completely as a painter, his contributions to science would entitle him to considerable fame. Not the least of these were his achievements in physics. Though he actually made few complete discoveries, his conclusion that "every weight tends to fall toward the center by the shortest way" contained the kernel of the law of gravity. In addition, he worked out the principles of an astonishing variety of inventions, including a diving boat, a steam engine, an armored tank, and a helicopter. Galileo is especially noted as a physicist for his law of falling bodies. Skeptical of the traditional theory that bodies fall with a speed

Galileo

directly proportional to their weight, he taught that bodies dropped from various heights would fall at a rate of speed which increases with the square of the time involved. Rejecting the Scholastic notions of absolute gravity and absolute levity, he taught that these are purely relative terms, that all bodies have weight, even those which, like the air, are invisible, and that in a vacuum all objects would fall with equal velocity. Galileo seems to have had a broader conception of a universal force of gravitation than Leonardo da Vinci, for he perceived that the power which holds the moon in the vicinity of the earth and causes the satellites of Jupiter to circulate around that planet is essentially the same as the force which enables the earth to draw bodies to its surface. He never formulated this principle as a law, however, nor did he realize all of its implications, as did Newton some fifty years later.

The record of Italian achievements in the various sciences related to medicine is also an impressive one. A number of Italian physicians contributed valuable information pertaining to the circulation of the blood. One of them described the valves of the heart, the pulmonary artery, and the aorta, while another located the valves in the veins. Equally significant was the work of certain foreigners who lived and taught in Italy. Andreas Vesalius (1514–1564), a native of Brussels, issued the first careful description of the human body based upon actual investigation. As a result of his extensive dissections he was able to correct many ancient errors. He is commonly considered the father of the modern science of anatomy.

Three other great Renaissance physicians were the German Paracelsus (1493–1547), the Spaniard Michael Servetus (1511–1553), and the Englishman William Harvey (1578–1657). Paracelsus resembled Copernicus and Kepler in believing that spiritual rather than material forces governed the workings of the universe. Hence he was a firm believer in alchemy and astrology. Nevertheless, Paracelsus relied on observation for his knowledge of diseases and their cures. Instead of following the teachings of ancient authorities, he traveled widely, studying cases of illness in different environments and experimenting with many drugs. Above all, his insistence on the close relationship of chemistry and medicine foreshadowed and sometimes directly influenced important modern achievements in pharmacology and healing. Michael Servetus, whose major interest was theology, but who practiced medicine for a living, discovered the lesser or pulmonary circulation of the blood, in an attempt to prove the veracity of the Virgin birth. He described how the blood leaves the right chambers of the heart, is carried to the lungs to be purified, then returns to the heart and is conveyed from that organ to all parts of the body. But Servetus had no idea of the return of the blood to the heart through the veins. It was left for William Harvey, who had studied under Italian physicians at Padua, to complete the discovery. This he did after his return to England about 1610. In his *Dissertation upon the Movement of the Heart* he

An Anatomical Demonstration. This Dutch engraving from 1610 combines a presentation of scientific inquiry with attitudes associated with late-medieval moralizing. The skeletons hold up signs which remind humans that they will return to dust.

described how an artery bound by a ligature would fill with blood in the section nearer the heart, while the portion away from the heart would empty, and how exactly the opposite results would occur when a ligature was placed on a vein. By such experiments he reached the conclusion that the blood is in constant process of circulation from the heart to all parts of the body and back again. Thus while thinkers and writers like Montaigne, Cervantes, and Shakespeare were probing into the mainsprings of human action, contemporary anatomists and physicians were literally taking humans apart and discovering their motive forces.

SELECTED READINGS

• *Items so designated are available in paperback editions.*

Baker, Herschel, *The Image of Man: A Study of the Idea of Human Dignity in Classical Antiquity, the Middle Ages, and the Renaissance,* Cambridge, Mass., 1947. An outstanding and engagingly written survey from the perspective of a modern liberal.

• Baxandall, Michael, *Painting and Experience in Fifteenth Century Italy,* Oxford, 1972.

Benesch, O., *The Art of the Renaissance in Northern Europe,* rev. ed., New York, 1965.

• Berenson, B., *The Italian Painters of the Renaissance,* New York, 1952.

• Burckhardt, J., *The Civilization of the Renaissance in Italy,* many eds. The nineteenth-century work that formulated the modern view of the Renaissance.

- Bush, D., *The Renaissance and English Humanism,* Toronto, 1939.

  Butterfield, H., *The Origins of Modern Science,* London, 1949. Clear and wide ranging. Shows how science developed from major changes in intellectual orientations.

  Chabod, F., *Machiavelli and the Renaissance,* London, 1958.

  Chambers, R. W. *Thomas More,* London, 1936. A spirited defense of the view that More was a life-long committed Catholic.

- Chute, M., *Shakespeare of London,* New York, 1949. The best popular biography.

- Clark, Kenneth M., *Leonardo da Vinci,* 2nd ed., Cambridge, 1952.

- Dean, Leonard F., ed., *Shakespeare: Modern Essays in Criticism,* New York, 1957.

- Ferguson, W., ed., *The Renaissance: Six Essays,* rev. ed., New York, 1962.

- Ford, Boris, ed., *The Age of Shakespeare,* Baltimore, 1955. A good shorter handbook.

- Gilbert, Felix, *Machiavelli and Guicciardini,* Princeton, N.J., 1965. Examines the thought of these writers in terms of the political realities of their day.

- Gilmore, M., *The World of Humanism,* New York, 1952. A well-written survey.

  Gould, Cecil, *An Introduction to Italian Renaissance Painting,* London, 1957.

  Hale, J. R., *Machiavelli and Renaissance Italy,* New York, 1960.

  ———, *Renaissance Europe: The Individual and Society, 1480–1520,* London, 1971. A different kind of survey that does not treat the great events but examines the quality of life.

- Hay, D., ed., *The Renaissance Debate,* New York, 1965. A collection of readings on the question of how to define the Renaissance.

- Kearney, H., *Science and Change, 1500–1700,* New York, 1971. Supplements Butterfield in arguing that science progressed as the result of contributions made by three different "schools."

- Kristeller, P. O., *Renaissance Thought: The Classic, Scholastic, and Humanist Strains,* New York, 1961. Very helpful in defining main trends of Renaissance thought.

- ———, *Eight Philosophers of the Italian Renaissance,* Stanford, Calif., 1964. Admirably clear.

  Lang, Paul H., *Music in Western Civilization,* New York, 1941.

- Levey, M., *Early Renaissance (Style and Civilization),* Baltimore, 1967. Art history.

- Panofsky, E., *Renaissance and Renascences in Western Art,* Stockholm, 1960. A difficult but rewarding attempt to distinguish the Italian Renaissance from its medieval predecessors.

  Phillips, Margaret M., *Erasmus and the Northern Renaissance,* London, 1949.

- Ralph, Philip L., *The Renaissance in Perspective,* New York, 1973.

  Reese, Gustave, *Music in the Renaissance,* rev. ed., New York, 1959. The leading work on the subject.

- Rice, E. F., Jr., *The Foundations of Early Modern Europe, 1460–1559,* New York, 1970.

- ———, *The Renaissance Idea of Wisdom,* Cambridge, Mass., 1958.

  Seigel, J., *Rhetoric and Philosophy in Renaissance Humanism,* Princeton, N.J., 1968. Treats a basic tension in the thought of early Renaissance thinkers.

  Simone, F., *The French Renaissance,* London, 1969.

  Stechow, W., *Northern Renaissance Art: 1400–1600,* Englewood Cliffs, N.J., 1966.

Tolnay, C. de, *The Art and Thought of Michelangelo,* New York, 1964.

Tracy, James, *Erasmus: The Growth of a Mind,* Geneva, 1972. The best intellectual biography.

Whitfield, J. H., *A Short History of Italian Literature,* Baltimore, 1960.

• Wittkower, R., *Architectural Principles in the Age of Humanism,* rev. ed., New York, 1965. An art-historical classic.

SOURCE MATERIALS

Alberti, Leon Battista, *The Family in Renaissance Florence,* tr. R. N. Watkins, Columbia, S.C., 1969.

• Cassirer, E., et al., eds., *The Renaissance Philosophy of Man,* Chicago, 1948. Leading works of Petrarch, Pico, etc.

• Castiglione, B., *The Book of the Courtier,* tr. C. S. Singleton, New York, 1959.

• Erasmus, D., *The Praise of Folly,* tr. J. Wilson, Ann Arbor, Mich., 1958.

Kohl, B. G., and R. G. Witt, eds., *The Earthly Republic: Italian Humanists on Government and Society,* Philadelphia, 1978. New translations with excellent introductions.

• Machiavelli, N., *The Prince,* tr. R. M. Adams, New York, 1976. In addition to Machiavelli's text, this edition provides related documents and an excellent selection of scholarly interpretations.

• Montaigne, M. de, *Essays,* tr. J. M. Cohen, Baltimore, 1958.

• More, Sir Thomas, *Utopia,* tr. R. M. Adams, New York, 1975. In the same series as Adams's translation of Machiavelli's *Prince;* provides background materials and selected scholarly interpretations as well as the text.

• Rabelais, F., *Gargantua and Pantagruel,* tr. J. M. Cohen, Baltimore, 1955. A robust modern translation.

Chapter 19

THE AGE OF
THE REFORMATION
(1517–c. 1600)

For the word of God cannot be received and honored by any works, but by faith alone.

—Martin Luther, *On Christian Liberty*

In conformity to the clear doctrine of the Scripture, we assert that by an eternal and immutable counsel, God has once for all determined both whom He would admit to salvation and whom He would condemn to destruction. . . . In the elect, we consider calling as an evidence of election, and justification as another token of its manifestation, till they arrive in glory, which constitutes its completion.

—John Calvin, *Institutes* III.xxi

The preceding chapter has described the unfolding of a marvelous culture which marked the transition from the Middle Ages to the modern world. It became apparent that this culture, the Renaissance, was almost as peculiarly an echo of the past as a herald of the future. Much of its literature, art, and philosophy, and all of its superstitions, had roots that were deeply buried in classical antiquity or in the centuries of the Middle Ages. Even its humanism breathed veneration for the past. Only in science and political thought and in the vigorous assertion of the right of the individual to pursue his own quest for freedom and dignity was there much that was really new. But the Renaissance in its later stages was accompanied by the growth of another movement, the Reformation, which somewhat more accurately foreshadowed the modern age. This movement included two principal phases: the Protestant Revolution, which broke out in 1517 and resulted in the secession of most of northern Europe from the Roman faith; and the Catholic Reformation, which reached its height about 1560. Although the latter is not called a revolution, it really was

The later stages of the Renaissance accompanied by a religious revolution

such in nearly every sense of the term; for it effected a profound alteration of some of the notable features of late-medieval Catholicism.

In a number of ways the Renaissance and the Reformation were closely related. Both were products of the powerful current of individualism which gained momentum in the fourteenth and fifteenth centuries. Each had a similar background of economic causes in the growth of trade and in the rise of an urban society. Both partook of the character of a return to original sources: in the one case, to the literary and artistic achievements of the Greeks and Romans; in the other, to the Scriptures and the doctrines of the church fathers. But in spite of these important similarities, it is misleading to think of the Reformation as merely the religious aspect of the Renaissance. The guiding principles of the two movements had comparatively little in common. The essence of the Renaissance was devotion to the human and the natural, with religion relegated to a relatively subordinate place. The spirit of the Reformation was characterized by otherworldliness and contempt for the things of this life as inferior to the spiritual. In the mind of the humanist, man's nature was generally considered good; in the view of the Reformer it was unspeakably corrupt and depraved. The leaders of the Renaissance believed in urbanity and tolerance; the followers of Luther and Calvin emphasized faith and conformity. While both the Renaissance and the Reformation aimed at a recovery of the past, they were really oriented in different directions. The past the humanists strove to revive was Greek and Roman antiquity, though a few were concerned with the original Gospels as sources of an unspoiled religion. The Reformers, by contrast, were interested chiefly in a return to the teachings of St. Paul and St. Augustine. It goes without saying that the Renaissance, being an aristocratic movement, had less influence on the common man than did the Reformation.

For reasons such as these, it seems justifiable to conclude that the Reformation was not really a part of the Renaissance. In actual fact, it represented a much sharper break with the civilization of the Middle Ages than the movement led by the humanists ever did. The radical Reformers would have nothing to do with the basic theories and practices of thirteenth-century Christianity. Even the simple religion of love and selflessness for the betterment of the soul, as taught by St. Francis of Assisi, appeared to repel them almost as much as the mysteries of the sacramental dogma or the claims of Innocent III to spiritual and temporal power. In the main, the religious results of this clash with medieval Christianity have endured to this day. Moreover, the Reformation was intimately bound up with certain political trends which have persisted throughout the modern era. National consciousness, as we shall see, was one of the principal causes of the Protestant Revolution. While it is true that several of the humanists wrote under the influence of national pride, the majority were swayed by altogether different considerations. Many were scornful of politics, being interested solely in the individual; others, Erasmus among them, were thoroughly international in their outlook. But the Protestant Reformers could scarcely have gained much of a following if they had not associated their cause with the powerful groundswell of national resentment in northern Europe against an ecclesiastical system that had come to be recognized as largely Italian in character. For this reason, as well as for the reasons mentioned previously, it would seem warranted to regard the Reformation as one gateway to the modern world.

I. THE PROTESTANT REVOLUTION

The Protestant Revolution sprang from a multiplicity of causes, most of them closely related to the political and economic conditions of the age. Nothing could be more inaccurate than to think of the revolt against the Roman Church as exclusively a religious movement, though religious ideas occupied a prominent place in the minds of sixteenth-century Europeans. But without the basic political changes in northern Europe and the growth of new economic interests, Roman Catholicism would probably have undergone no more than a gradual evolution. Nevertheless, since religious causes were the most obvious ones, it will be appropriate to consider them first.

The multiplicity of causes of the Protestant Revolution

To the majority of Martin Luther's early followers the movement he launched was chiefly a rebellion against abuses in the Catholic Church. That such abuses existed no historian would deny. For example, many of the clergy at this time were poorly educated. Some, having obtained their positions through irregular means, were unable to understand the Latin of the Mass they were required to celebrate. Further, a considerable number of the clergy led extremely worldly lives. While some of the popes and bishops were living in princely magnificence, the lowly priests occasionally sought to eke out the incomes from their parishes by keeping taverns, gaming houses, or other establishments for profit. Not only did some monks habitually ignore their vows of chastity, but a few indifferent members of the secular clergy surmounted the hardships of the rule of celibacy by keeping mistresses. Pope Innocent VIII, who reigned about twenty-five years before the beginning of the Protestant Revolution, was known to have had eight illegitimate children, several born before his election to the papacy. There were numerous evils also in connection with the sale of religious offices and dispensations. As in the case of most civil positions, offices in the Church during the Renaissance period were commonly sold to the highest bidder. It is estimated that Pope Leo X enjoyed an income of more than a million dollars a year from the sale of more than two thousand ecclesiastical offices. This abuse was rendered more serious by the fact that the men who bought these positions were under a strong temptation to make

Religious causes: abuses in the Catholic Church

Pope Leo X. From an Italian miniature.

up for their investment by levying high fees for their services. The sale of dispensations was a second malodorous form of ecclesiastical graft. A dispensation may be defined as an exemption from a law of the Church or from some vow previously taken. On the eve of the Reformation the dispensations most commonly sold were exemptions from fasting and from the marriage laws of the Church. By way of illustration, first cousins would be permitted to marry for the payment of a fee of one ducat.

But the abuses which aroused the most outrage and brought pressure for reform were the sale of indulgences and the veneration of relics. An indulgence is a remission of all or of part of the temporal punishment due to sin—that is, of the punishment in this life and in purgatory. The theory upon which the indulgence rests is the famous doctrine of the Treasury of Merits developed by Scholastic theologians in the thirteenth century. According to this doctrine, Jesus and the saints, by reason of their "superfluous" virtues on earth, accumulated an excess of merit in heaven. This excess constitutes a treasure of grace upon which the pope can draw for the benefit of ordinary mortals. Originally, indulgences were not issued for payments of money, but only for works of charity, fasting, going on crusades, and the like. It was the Renaissance popes, with their insatiable desire for revenue, who first embarked upon the sale of indulgences as a profitable business. The methods they employed were far from scrupulous. The traffic in "pardons" was often turned over to bankers on a commission basis. As an example, the Fuggers in Augsburg had charge of the sale of indulgences for Leo X, with permission to pocket one-third of the proceeds. Naturally, only one motive dominated the business—to raise as much money as possible.

For centuries before the Reformation the veneration of sacred relics had been an important element in Catholic worship. It was believed that objects used by Christ or the Virgin, or the bodily remains of the saints possessed a miraculous healing and protective virtue for anyone who touched them or came into their presence. It was inevitable that this belief should open the way for innumerable frauds. Superstitious peasants could be easily convinced that almost any splinter of wood was a fragment of the true cross. And there was no dearth of relic-mongers quick to take advantage of such credulity. The results were fantastic. According to Erasmus, the churches of Europe contained enough wood of the true cross to build a ship. No fewer than five shinbones of the ass on which Jesus rode to Jerusalem were on exhibition in different places, to say nothing of twelve heads of John the Baptist. Martin Luther declared in a pamphlet lampooning his enemy, the archbishop of Mainz, that the latter claimed to possess "a whole pound of the wind that blew for Elijah in the cave on Mount Horeb and two feathers and an egg of the Holy Ghost."

Modern historians agree, however, that abuses in the Catholic

The sale of indulgences

Abuses connected with the veneration of sacred relics

Church were not the primary religious cause of the Protestant Revolution. It was medieval Catholicism itself, not the abuses therein, to which the Reformers objected. Moreover, just before the revolt broke out, conditions had begun to improve. Many pious Catholics themselves had started an agitation for reform, which in time would probably have eliminated most of the glaring evils in the system. But as so often happens in the case of revolutions, the improvement came too late. Other forces more irresistible in character had been gradually gathering momentum. Conspicuous among these was the growing reaction against Scholastic theology, with its elaborate sacramental theory, its belief in the necessity of good works to supplement faith, and its doctrine of divine authority in the hands of the priests.

Abuses not the primary causes of the Protestant Revolution

From preceding chapters the reader will recall that two different systems of theology had developed within the medieval Church. The first was formulated by St. Augustine around 400 A.D, on the basis of teachings in the Pauline Epistles. It was predicated on the assumption of an omnipotent God, who sees the whole drama of the universe in the twinkling of an eye. Not even a sparrow falls to the ground except in accordance with divine decree. Human nature is hopelessly depraved, and it is therefore as impossible for human beings to perform good works of their own volition as for thistles to bring forth figs. Only those mortals can be saved whom God for reasons of His own has predestined to inherit eternal life. Such in its barest outlines was the system of doctrine commonly known as Augustinianism. It was a theology well suited to the age of chaos which followed the breakup of the classical world. People in this time were prone to fatalism and otherworldliness, for they seemed to be at the mercy of forces beyond their control. But the doctrine continued to be taught throughout the Middle Ages, especially in parts of Germany, where the impact of high-medieval civilization was comparatively weak. To Luther and many of his followers it seemed the most logical interpretation of Christian belief.

The clash between two different systems of theology: the Augustinian system

With the growth of a more abundant life in southern and western Europe, it was natural that the pessimistic philosophy of Augustinianism should have been replaced by a system which would restore to humans some measure of pride in their own estate. The change was accelerated also by the growth of a dominant Church organization. The theology of Augustinianism, by placing human fate in the hands of God, had seemed to imply that the functions of an organized Church were comparatively unnecessary. Certainly no sinners could rely upon the ministrations of priests to improve their chances of salvation, since those who were to be saved had already been "elected" by God from all eternity. The new system of belief was finally crystallized in the Scholastic writings of Peter Lombard and St. Thomas Aquinas in the twelfth and thirteenth centuries. Its cardinal premise was the idea that humans had been endowed by God with freedom of

The late-medieval theology of Peter Lombard and St. Thomas Aquinas

will, with power to choose the good and avoid the evil. However, men could not make this choice entirely unaided, for without the support of heavenly grace they would be likely to fall into sin. It was therefore necessary for them to receive the sacraments, the indispensable means for communicating the grace of God to humanity. Of the seven sacraments of the Church, the three most important for the layperson were baptism, penance, and the Eucharist. The first wiped out the stain of previous sin; the second absolved the contrite sinner from guilt; the third was especially significant for its effect in renewing the saving grace of Christ's sacrifice on the cross. Except in emergencies, none of the sacraments could be administered by persons outside the ranks of the priesthood. The members of the clergy, having inherited this power from the Apostle Peter, alone had the authority to cooperate with God in forgiving sins and in performing the miracle of the Eucharist, whereby the bread and wine were transubstantiated into the body and blood of the Savior.

The Protestant Revolution a rebellion against the late-medieval system of theology

The Protestant Revolution was in large measure a rebellion against the second of these systems of theology. Although the doctrines of Peter Lombard and St. Thomas Aquinas had virtually become part of the theology of the Church, they had never been universally accepted. To some Christians who favored Augustinianism, they seemed to detract from the sovereignty of God and to contradict the plain teachings of Paul that human will is in bondage and human nature unspeakably vile. Worse still, in the opinion of these critics, was the fact that Scholastic theology greatly strengthened the authority of the priesthood. In sum, what the Reformers wanted was a return to a more primitive Christianity than that which had prevailed since the thirteenth century. Any doctrine or practice not expressly sanctioned in the Bible, especially in the Pauline Epistles, or not recognized by the fathers of the Church, they were strongly inclined to reject. It was for this reason that they condemned not only the theory of the priesthood and the sacramental system of the Church, but also such medieval additions to the faith as the veneration of the Virgin, the belief in purgatory, the invocation of saints, the cult of relics, and the rule of celibacy for the clergy. The Reformers were by no means rationalists: in fact, they were far more suspicious of reason than the Catholics. Their religious ideal rested upon the Augustinian dogmas of original sin, the total depravity of humanity, predestination, and the bondage of the will— all of which were far more difficult to justify by rationalism than the liberalized Scholastic teachings of St. Thomas Aquinas.

The political causes of the Protestant Revolution: the growth of national consciousness

As a political movement the Protestant Revolution was mainly the result of two developments: first, the growth of a national consciousness in northern Europe; and second, the rise of absolute monarchs. Ever since the late Middle Ages there had been a growing spirit of independence among many of the peoples outside of Italy. They had come to regard their own national life as unique and to resent interference from any external source. Although they were not nationalists in the modern sense, they tended to view the pope as a foreigner who had no right to meddle with local affairs in England, France, or Germany. This feeling was manifested in England as early as the middle of the fourteenth century, when the Statutes of Provisors and Praemunire were passed. The first prohibited appointments by the pope to Church offices in England; the second forbade the appeal of cases from the English courts to Rome. A law more extreme than either of these was issued by the king of France in 1438. The French law practically abolished all papal authority in the country, including the appointive authority and the right to raise revenue. To the civil magistrates was given the power to regulate religious affairs within their own districts. In Germany, despite the fact that there was no political unity, national feeling was by no means absent. It expressed itself in attacks upon the clergy by the Imperial Diet and in numerous decrees by the princes of separate states prohibiting ecclesiastical appointments and the sale of indulgences without their consent.

The growth of a national consciousness in all of these countries went hand in hand with the rise of absolute monarchs. Indeed, it would be difficult to say how much of the sense of nationality was spontaneous and how much of it was stimulated by ambitious rulers intent upon increasing their power. At any rate, it is certain that the claims of rulers to absolute authority were bound to result in defiance of Rome. No despot could be expected to tolerate long the exclusion of religion from his sphere of control. He could not *be* a despot so long as there was a double jurisdiction within his realm. The appetite of princes for control over the Church was whetted originally by the revival of the Roman law, with its doctrine that the people had delegated *all* of their power to the secular ruler. From this doctrine it was a comparatively easy step to the idea that all of the pope's authority could be properly assumed by the head of the state. But whatever the reasons for its growth, there can be no doubt that the ambition of secular princes to establish churches under their own control was a primary cause of the mounting antagonism toward Rome.

The rise of absolute monarchs

Historians disagree as to the importance of economic causation of the Protestant Revolution. Those who conceive of the movement as primarily a religious one think of the sixteenth century as a period of profound and agonized concern over spiritual problems. Such a condition may well have characterized the mass of the people. But it does not alter the fact that in the sixteenth century, as in all ages, there were ruling groups hungry for wealth and quite willing to use popular beliefs for their own advantage. Prominent among the economic objectives of such groups were acquisition of the wealth of the Church and elimination of papal taxation. In the course of its history the Church had grown into a vast economic empire. It was by far the largest landowner in western Europe, to say nothing of its enormous movable wealth in the form of rich furnishings, works of art, jewels, precious metals, and the like. Some of these possessions had been

Economic causes: the desire to confiscate the wealth of the Catholic Church

acquired by the Church through grants by kings, nobles, and other pious layfolk. Religious restrictions on taxation were also a galling grievance to secular rulers. Kings, eager for big armies and navies, had an urgent need for more revenue. But Catholic law prohibited the taxing of Church property. The exemption of episcopal and monastic property from taxation meant a heavier burden on the possessions of individual owners, especially on the property of merchants and bankers. Moreover, the lesser nobles in Germany were being threatened with extinction on account of the collapse of the manorial economy. Many of them looked with covetous eyes upon the lands of the Church. If only some excuse could be found for expropriating these, their difficult situation might be relieved.

Papal taxation, by the eve of the Protestant Revolution, had assumed a baffling variety of irritating forms. First came the *tithe,* which was supposed to be one-tenth of every Christian's income paid for the support of the parish church. Then there were innumerable fees paid into the papal treasury for indulgences, dispensations, appeals of judicial decisions, and so on. In a very real sense the moneys collected for the sale of Church offices and the *annates,* or commissions levied on the first year's income of every bishop and priest, were also forms of papal taxation, since the officials who paid them eventually reimbursed themselves through increased collections from the people. But the main objection to these taxes was not that they were so numerous and burdensome. The real basis of grievance against the papal levies was their effect in draining the northern countries of so much of their wealth for the enrichment of Italy. Economically, the situation was almost exactly the same as if the nations of northern Europe had been conquered by a foreign prince and tribute imposed upon them. Some Germans and Englishmen were scandalized also by the fact that most of the money collected was not being spent for religious purposes, but was being squandered by worldly popes to maintain luxurious courts. The reason for the resentment, however, was probably as much financial as moral.

A third important economic cause of the Protestant Revolution was the conflict between the ambitions of the new merchant class and the ascetic ideals of medieval Christianity. Medieval Scholastic philosophers had argued that business for the sake of great profit is essentially immoral. No one has a right to any more than a reasonable wage for the service he renders to society. All wealth acquired in excess of this amount should be given to the Church to be distributed for the benefit of the needy. The merchant or craftsman who strives to get rich at the expense of the people is really no better than a common thief. To gain an advantage over a rival in business by cornering the market or beating down wages is contrary to all law and morality. Equally sinful is the practice of usury—the charging of interest on loans where no actual risk is involved. This is sheer robbery, the Scholastics argued, for it deprives the person who uses the money of earnings that are justly his; it is contrary to nature, for it enables the man who lends the money to live without labor.

While it is far from true that these doctrines were universally honored even by the Church itself, they nevertheless remained an integral part of the Catholic ideal, at least to the end of the Middle Ages. However, from the later Middle Ages onwards dynamic capitalism was beginning to supplant the old static economy of the medieval guilds. No longer were merchants and manufacturers content with a mere "wage" for the services they rendered to society. They demanded profits, and they could not see that it was any business of the Church to set limits on their earnings. Wages were fit only for hirelings, who had neither the wit nor the industry to go after the big rewards. In addition to all this, the growth of banking meant an even more violent conflict with the ascetic ideal of the Church. As long as the business of moneylending was in the hands of Jews and Muslims, it mattered little that usury should be branded as a sin. But now that Christians were piling up riches by financing the exploits of kings and merchants, the shoe was on another foot. The new crop of bankers resented being told that their lucrative trade in cash was contrary to the laws of God. This seemed to them an attempt of spokesmen for an outmoded past to dictate the standards for a new age of progress. But how was it that Italy did not break with the Catholic Church in view of the extensive development of banking and commerce in such cities as Florence, Genoa, Milan, and Venice? Perhaps one explanation is to be found in the fact that such business activities had taken earlier and deeper roots in Italy than in most parts of Germany. They had been established for so long a time that any possible conflict between them and religious ideals had been largely ignored. Besides, the religion of many Italians tended to approximate that of the ancient Romans; it was external and mechanical rather than profoundly spiritual. To many northern Europeans, by contrast, religion had a deeper significance. It was a system of dogmas and commandments to be observed literally under pain of the awful judgment of a wrathful God. They were, therefore, more likely to be disturbed by inconsistencies between worldly practices and the doctrines of the faith.

Effects of the rise of competitive capitalism

The full story of why the Protestant Revolution began in Germany is so complex that only a few of the possible reasons can be suggested as ideas for the student to consider. Was Germany relatively more backward than most other areas of western Europe? Had the Renaissance touched it so lightly that medieval religiosity remained quite pervasive? Or did economic factors operate more strongly in Germany than elsewhere? The Church in Germany held an enormous proportion of the best agricultural lands, and evidence exists that the country was seething with discontent on account of a too rapid transition from a static economy to an economy of profits and wages. It

Why the Protestant Revolution began in Germany

Martin Luther. A portrait by Melchior Lorch.

The doctrine of justification by faith alone

seems to be true, finally, that Germany was the victim of Catholic abuses to a greater extent than most other countries. How crucial was the shock resulting from these is impossible to say, but at least they provided the immediate impetus for the outbreak of the Lutheran revolt. Unlike England and France, Germany had no powerful king to defend its interests against the papacy. The country was weak and divided. At least partly for this reason, Pope Leo X selected German territory as the most likely field for the sale of indulgences.

I. THE LUTHERAN REVOLT IN GERMANY   By the dawn of the sixteenth century Germany was ripe for religious revolution. All that was necessary was to find a leader who could unite the dissatisfied elements and give a suitable theological gloss to their grievances. Such a leader was not long in appearing. His name was Martin Luther, and he was born in Thuringia in 1483. His parents were originally peasants, but his father had left the soil soon after his marriage to work in the mines of Mansfeld. Here he managed to become moderately prosperous and served in the village council. Nevertheless, young Martin's early environment was far from ideal. He was whipped at home for trivial offenses until he bled, and his mind was filled with hideous terrors of demons and witches. Some of these superstitions clung to him until the end of his life. His parents intended that he should become a lawyer, and with this end in view they placed him at the age of eighteen in the University of Erfurt. During his first four years at the university, Luther worked hard, gaining more than an ordinary reputation as a scholar. But in 1505, while returning from a visit to his home, he was overtaken by a violent storm and felled to the ground by a bolt of lightning. In terror lest an angry God strike him dead, he vowed to St. Anne to become a monk. Soon afterward he entered the Augustinian monastery at Erfurt.

Here he gave himself up to earnest reflection on the state of his soul. Obsessed with the idea that his sins were innumerable, he strove desperately to attain a goal of spiritual peace. He engaged in long vigils and went for days on end without a morsel of food. But the more he fasted and tortured himself, the more his anguish and depression increased. Told that the way of salvation lies in love of God, he was ready to give up in despair. How could he love a Being who is not even just, who saves only those whom it pleases Him to save? "Love Him?" he said to himself, "I do not love Him. I hate Him." But in time, as he pondered the Scriptures, especially the story of the Crucifixion, he gained a new insight into the mysteries of the Christian theology. He was profoundly impressed by the humiliation of the Savior's death on the cross. For the benefit of sinful humanity, the Christ, the God-man, had shared the fate of common criminals. Why had He done so except out of love for His creatures? The God of the storm whose chief attribute appeared to be anger had revealed Himself as a father who pities His children. Here was a miracle which no human

Luther Preaching. With one hand he points to popes, monks, and cardinals going into the mouth of hell. Hell is a beast with a snout, tusk, and eye. With the other hand Luther points to the crucifix. The Lord's Supper is being administered, both the bread and the wine, to the laity.

reason could understand. It must be taken on faith; and by faith alone, Luther concluded, can human beings be justified in the sight of God. This doctrine of justification by faith alone, as opposed to salvation by "good works," quickly became the central doctrine of the Lutheran theology.

But long before Luther had completed his theological system, he was called to lecture on Aristotle and the Bible at the University of Wittenberg, which had recently been founded by Frederick the Wise of Saxony. While serving in this capacity, he was confronted by an event which furnished the spark for the Protestant Revolution. In 1517 an unprincipled Dominican friar by the name of Tetzel appeared in Germany as a hawker of indulgences. Determined to raise as much money as possible for Pope Leo X and the archbishop of Mainz who had employed him, Tetzel deliberately represented the indulgences as tickets of admission to heaven. Though forbidden to enter Saxony, he came to the borders of that state, and many natives of Wittenberg rushed out to buy salvation at so attractive a price. Luther was appalled by such brazen deception of ignorant people. Accordingly, he drew up a set of ninety-five theses or statements attacking the sale of indulgences, and posted them, after the manner of the time, on the door of the castle church on October 31, 1517. Later he had them printed and sent to his friends in a number of cities. Soon it became evident that the Ninety-five Theses had voiced the sentiments of a nation. All over Germany, Luther was hailed as a leader whom God had raised to break the power of an arrogant and hypocritical clergy. A violent reaction against the sale of indulgences was soon in full swing. Tetzel was mobbed and driven from the country. The revolt against Rome had begun.

With the revenue from indulgences cut off, it was inevitable that the pope should take action. Early in 1518 he commanded the general of the Augustinian order to make the rebellious friar recant. Luther not

Luther's revolt against the sale of indulgences

only refused, but published a sermon stating his views more strongly than ever. Forced by his critics to answer questions on many points other than indulgences, he gradually came to realize that his own religion was utterly irreconcilable with that of the Roman Church. There was no alternative except to break with the Catholic faith entirely. In 1520 his teachings were formally condemned in a bull promulgated by Leo X, and he was ordered to recant within sixty days or be dealt with as a heretic. Luther replied by publicly burning the pope's proclamation. For this he was excommunicated and ordered to be turned over to the secular arm for punishment. Germany at this time was still technically under the rule of the Holy Roman Empire. Charles V, who had recently been elevated to the throne of this ramshackle government, was anxious to be rid of the insolent rebel at once, but he dared not act without the approval of the Imperial Diet. Accordingly, in 1521, Luther was summoned to appear before a meeting of this body at Worms. Since many of the princes who composed the Diet were themselves hostile toward the Church, nothing in particular was done, despite Luther's refusal to retract anything he had said. Finally, after a number of the members had gone home, the emperor forced through an edict branding the obstreperous friar as an outlaw. But Luther had already been hidden away in the castle of his friend, Frederick of Saxony. Here he remained until all danger of arrest by the emperor's soldiers had passed. Charles soon afterward withdrew to conduct his war with France, and the Edict of Worms was never enforced.

Thenceforth until his death in 1546 Luther was occupied with his work of building an independent German Church. Despite the fundamental conflict between his own beliefs and Catholic theology, he nevertheless retained a good many of the elements of the Roman system. With the passing of the years he became more conservative than many of his own followers. Though he had originally denounced transubstantiation, he eventually came around to adopting a doctrine which bore at least a superficial resemblance to the Catholic theory. He denied, however, that any change in the substance of the bread and wine occurs as the result of a priestly miracle. The function of the clergyman is simply to *reveal* the presence of God in the bread and wine. Still, the changes he made were drastic enough to preserve the revolutionary character of the new religion. He substituted German for Latin in the services of the Church. He rejected the entire ecclesiastical system of pope, archbishops, bishops, and priests as custodians of the keys to the kingdom of heaven. By abolishing monasticism and insisting upon the right of priests to marry, he went far toward destroying the barrier which had separated clergy from laity and given the former their special status as representatives of God on earth. He recognized only baptism and the Eucharist as sacraments, and he denied that even these had any supernatural effect in bringing down

The Pope as Antichrist. Belching forth toads and scorpions, the beast-man spreads fire and destruction. This drawing by Melchior Lorch is dedicated to Martin Luther and dated 1545.

grace from heaven. Since he continued to emphasize faith rather than good works as the road to salvation, he naturally discarded such formalized practices as fasts, pilgrimages, the veneration of relics, and the invocation of saints. On the other hand, the doctrines of predestination and the supreme authority of the Scriptures were given in the new religion a higher place than they had ever enjoyed in the old. Last of all, Luther abandoned the Catholic idea that the Church should be supreme over the state. Instead of having bishops subject to the pope as the Vicar of Christ, he organized his church under superintendents who were essentially agents of the government.

Founding the Lutheran church; Luther's doctrines

Of course, Luther was not alone responsible for the success of the Protestant Revolution. The overthrow of Catholicism in Germany was also abetted by the outbreak of social revolt. In 1522–1523 there occurred a ferocious rebellion of the knights. These petty nobles were being impoverished by competition from the great estates and by the change to a capitalist economy. They saw as the chief cause of their misery the concentration of landed wealth in the hands of more powerful princes and the Church. Obsessed with national sentiments, they dreamed of a united Germany free from the domination of powerful landlords and grasping priests. The leaders of the movement were Ulrich von Hutten, who had turned from a humanist into a fierce partisan of Luther, and Franz von Sickingen, a notorious robber baron and soldier of fortune. To these men the gospel of Luther seemed to provide an excellent program for a war on behalf of German liberty. Although their rebellion was speedily crushed by the armies of the archbishops and richer nobles, it had considerable effect in persuading the pillars of the old regime that too much resistance to the Lutheran movement would scarcely be wise.

The outbreak of social revolution; the revolt of the knights

The revolt of the knights was followed by a much more violent uprising of the lower classes in 1524–1525. Though most who took part were peasants, a great many poor workers from the cities were attracted to the movement also. The causes of this second rebellion were somewhat similar to those of the first: the rising cost of living, the concentration of holdings of land, and the religious radicalism inspired by Luther's teachings. But the peasants and urban workers were stirred to action by many other factors as well. The decay of the regime had eliminated the paternal relationship between noble and serf. In its place had grown up a mere cash nexus between employer and worker. The sole obligation now of the upper classes was to pay a wage. When sickness or unemployment struck, laborers had to make do with their slender resources as best they could. Furthermore, most of the old privileges which the serf had enjoyed on the manorial estate, of pasturing flocks on the common lands and gathering wood in the forest, were being rapidly abolished. To make matters worse, landlords were attempting to meet advancing prices by exacting higher rents from the peasants. Finally, the lower classes were angered by the

The uprising of the lower classes

Pages from a Bible Translated by Martin Luther, 1534. Left: The title page. Right: An illustration showing several episodes from the story of Jonah in a single composite picture.

fact that the revival of Roman law had the effect of bolstering property rights and of strengthening the power of the state to protect the interests of the rich.

Outcome of the Peasants' Revolt

The Peasants' Revolt of 1524–1525 began in southern Germany and spread rapidly to the north, until large parts of the country were involved. At first it was more like a strike than an insurrection. The rebels contented themselves with drafting petitions and attempting peaceably to persuade their masters to grant them relief from oppression. But before many months had passed the movement came under the influence of such radical leaders as Thomas Münzer (c. 1490–1525), who urged the use of fire and sword against the wicked nobles and clergy. In the spring of 1525 the peasants began plundering and burning cloisters and castles and even murdering some of their more hated opponents. The nobles now turned against them with fiendish fury, slaughtering indiscriminately both those who resisted and those who were helpless. In this they were encouraged by none other than Martin Luther himself. Because Luther had become a staunch ally of the German princes and was a thoroughgoing opponent of social reform, he wrote a violent pamphlet, *Against the Thievish, Murderous Hordes of Peasants,* in which he urged everyone who could to hunt the rebels down like mad dogs, to "strike, strangle, stab secretly or in public, and remember that nothing can be more poisonous, harmful, or devilish than a man in rebellion." The firm alliance of Lutheranism with the powers of the state thereafter helped insure social peace. In fact, after the bloody punishment of the peasant rebels there was never again to be a mass lower-class uprising in all of German history.

II. THE ANABAPTIST MOVEMENT   Shortly after the failure of the Peasants' Revolt a group of radical reformers who were dissatisfied with Luther's growing conservatism, but who did not wish to take up the sword, began to coalesce into the loosely organized movement called Anabaptism. The name means "re-baptism" and was derived from the fact that the Anabaptists held infant baptism to be ineffectual and insisted that the rite should be administered only when the individual had reached the age of reason. But a belief in adult baptism was not really their principal doctrine. The Anabaptists were extreme individualists in religion. Luther's teaching that all have a right to follow the dictates of their own conscience the Anabaptists took exactly as it stood. Not only did they reject the Catholic theory of the priesthood, but they denied the necessity of any clergy at all, maintaining that every individual should follow the guidance of the "inner light." They refused to agree that God's revelation to humanity had ceased with the writing of the last book of the New Testament, but insisted that He continues to speak directly to certain of His chosen followers. They attached much importance to literal interpretation of the Bible, even of its most occult portions. They believed that the Church should be a community of saints and required of their followers abstention from lying, profanity, gluttony, lewdness, and drinking intoxicating liquors. Many of the members looked forward to the early destruction of this world and the establishment of Christ's kingdom of justice and peace, in which they would have a prominent place. But the Anabaptists were not merely a group of religious extremists; they represented as well the most radical social tendencies of their time. Though it is certainly an exaggeration to call them communists, they did denounce the accumulation of wealth and taught that it was the duty of Christians to share their goods with one another. In addition, they declined to recognize any distinctions of rank or class, declaring everyone equal in the sight of God. Many also abominated the taking of oaths, condemned military service, and refused to pay taxes to governments that engaged in war. They abstained in general from political life and demanded the complete separation of Church and State. Their doc-

*The nature of
Anabaptism*

The Siege of Münster in 1534

The siege of Münster

trines represented the extreme manifestation of the revolutionary fervor generated by the Protestant movement.

Unhappily for the fortunes of Anabaptism, a highly unrepresentative group of Anabaptist extremists managed to gain control of the city of Münster in northwestern Germany in 1534. Some of their fellow extremists from surrounding areas came pouring in, and Münster became a new Jerusalem where all of the vagaries of the lunatic fringe of the movement were put into practice. The property of unbelievers was confiscated and polygamy was introduced. A former tailor named John of Leyden assumed the title of king, proclaiming himself the successor of David, with a mission to conquer the world and destroy the heathen. But after a little more than a year Münster was recaptured by Catholic forces and the leaders of Zion were put to death by horrible tortures. As a result of this episode, Anabaptism was thoroughly discredited and all of its adherents were subjected to ruthless persecution throughout Germany and wherever else they could be found. Among the very few who survived were some who banded together in the Mennonite sect, named for its founder, the Dutchman Menno Simons (1492–1559). This sect, dedicated to the pacifism and simple "religion of the heart" of original Anabaptism has continued to exist until the present. Various Anabaptist tenets were also revived later by religious groups such as the Quakers and different Baptist and Pentecostal sects.

III. THE ZWINGLIAN AND CALVINIST REVOLTS IN SWITZERLAND   The special form of Protestantism developed by Luther did not prove to be particularly popular beyond its native environment. Even in Germany it by no means triumphed everywhere (most of southern Germany remained Catholic), and outside of Germany Lutheranism became the official religion only in Denmark, Norway, and Sweden. But the force of the Protestant revolt made itself felt in a number of other lands. Such was especially the case in Switzerland, where national consciousness had been gathering strength for centuries. At the close of the Middle Ages the shepherds and peasants of the Swiss cantons had challenged the right of the Austrians to rule over them, and finally in 1499 had compelled the Emperor Maximilian to recognize their independence, not only of the house of Hapsburg but of the Holy Roman Empire as well. Having thrown off the yoke of a foreign emperor, the Swiss were not likely to submit indefinitely to an alien pope. Moreover, the cities of Zürich, Basel, Berne, and Geneva had grown into flourishing centers of trade. Their populations were dominated by prosperous merchants who were becoming increasingly contemptuous of the Catholic ideal of glorified poverty. Here also northern humanism had found acceptance in cultivated minds, with the effect of creating a healthy distrust of priestly superstitions. Erasmus had lived for a number of years in Basel. Lastly, Switzerland had been exploited by the indulgence peddlers to an extent only less grievous than that in Germany.

The father of the Protestant Revolution in Switzerland was Ulrich Zwingli (1484–1531). Only a few weeks younger than Luther, he was the son of a well-to-do magistrate, who was able to provide him with an excellent education. As a student he devoted nearly all of his time to philosophy and literature, with no interest in religion save in the practical reforms of the Christian humanists. Although he took holy orders at the age of twenty-two, his purpose in entering the priesthood was mainly the opportunity it would give him to cultivate his literary tastes. Ultimately, he turned his interest to religion and devoted his energies to reform of the Church. He accepted nearly all of the teachings of Luther except that he regarded the bread and wine as mere symbols of the body and blood, and he reduced the sacrament of Holy Communion to a simple memorial service. So ably did he marshal the anti-Catholic forces that by 1528 nearly all of northern Switzerland had deserted the ancient faith.

From the northern cantons the Protestant Revolution in Switzerland spread to Geneva. This city, located on a lake of the same name near the French border, had the doubtful advantage of a double government. The people owed allegiance to two suzerains, the local bishop and the count of Savoy. When these high-born chieftains conspired to make their power more absolute, the citizens rebelled against them. The result was their expulsion from the town about 1530 and the establishment of a free republic. But the movement could hardly have been successful without some aid from the northern cantons. Thus, it was not long until Protestant preachers from Zürich and Berne began arriving in Geneva.

Causes of the Protestant Revolution in Switzerland

Zwingli

Ulrich Zwingli. A sixteenth-century woodcut.

John Calvin. This woodcut shows the stern reformer in old age.

Calvin's rule at Geneva

Calvin's theology

It was soon after these events that John Calvin (1509–1564) arrived in Geneva. Although destined to play so prominent a role in the history of Switzerland, he was not a native of that country but of France. He was born at Noyon in Picardy. His mother died when he was very young, and his father, who did not like children, turned him over to the care of an aristocratic friend. For his higher education Calvin was sent to the University of Paris, where, because of his bilious disposition and fault-finding manner, he was dubbed "the accusative case." Later, he shifted at his father's wish to study of law at Orléans. Here he came under the influence of disciples of Luther, evidently to a sufficient extent to cause him to be suspected of heresy. Consequently, in 1534 Calvin fled to Switzerland. He settled for a time in Basel and then moved on to Geneva, which was still in the throes of political revolution. He began preaching and organizing at once, and by 1541 both government and religion had fallen completely under his sway. Until his death in 1564 he ruled the city with a rod of iron. History contains few examples of men more dour in temperament and more stubbornly convinced of the rightness of their own ideas.

Under Calvin's rule Geneva was transformed into a religious oligarchy. The supreme authority was vested in the Congregation of the Clergy, who prepared all legislation and submitted it to the Consistory to be ratified. The latter body, composed, in addition to the clergy, of twelve elders representing the people, had as its principal function the supervision of public and private morals. This function was carried out, not merely by the punishment of antisocial conduct but by a persistent snooping into the private life of every individual. The city was divided into districts, and a committee of the Consistory visited each household without warning to conduct an inquisition into the habits of its members. Even the mildest forms of self-indulgence were strictly prohibited. Dancing, card-playing, attending the theater, working or playing on the Sabbath—all were outlawed as works of the Devil. Innkeepers were forbidden to allow anyone to consume food or drink without first saying grace, or to permit any patron to sit up after nine o'clock unless he was spying on the conduct of others. Needless to say, penalties were severe. Not only were murder and treason classified as capital crimes, but also adultery, witchcraft, blasphemy, and heresy; and the last of these especially was susceptible to a broad interpretation. During the first four years after Calvin became ruler of Geneva, there were no fewer than 58 executions out of a total population of only 16,000.

The essentials of Calvin's theology are contained in his *Institutes of the Christian Religion*, which was originally published in 1536 and revised and enlarged several times thereafter. His ideas resemble those of St. Augustine more than any other theologian. He conceived of the universe as utterly dependent upon the will of an Almighty God, who created all things for his greater glory. Because of the original fall from grace all human beings are sinners by nature, bound hand and foot to an evil inheritance they cannot escape. Nevertheless, God for reasons of His own has predestined some for eternal salvation and damned all the rest to the torments of hell. Nothing that human beings may do can alter their fate; their souls are stamped with God's blessing or curse before they are born. But this did not mean, in Calvin's opinion, that Christians could be indifferent to their conduct on earth. If they were among the elect, God would have implanted in them the desire to live right. Upright conduct is a sign, though not an infallible one, that whoever practices it has been chosen to sit at the throne of glory. Public profession of faith and participation in the sacraments are also presumptive evidences of election to be saved. But most of all, the Calvinists required an active life of piety and good morality as a solemn obligation resting upon members of the Christian commonwealth. Like the ancient Hebrews, they conceived of themselves as chosen instruments of God with a mission to help in the fulfillment of His purposes on earth. Their duty was not to strive for their souls' salvation but for the glory of God. Thus it will be seen that the Calvinist system did not encourage its followers to sit with folded hands, serene in the knowledge that their fate was sealed. No religion has fostered a more abundant zeal in the conquest of nature, in missionary activity, or in the struggle against political tyranny. Doubtless the reason lies in the Calvinist's belief that as the chosen instrument of God he must play a part in the drama of the universe worthy of his exalted status. And with the Lord on his side he was not easily frightened by whatever lions lurked in his path.

The religion of Calvin differed from that of Luther in a number of ways. First, it was more legalistic. Whereas the Wittenberg Reformer had emphasized the guidance of individual conscience, the dictator of Geneva stressed the sovereignty of law. He thought of God as a mighty legislator who had handed down a body of rules in the Scriptures which must be followed to the letter. Secondly, the religion of Calvin was more nearly an Old Testament faith than that of Luther. This can be illustrated in the attitude of the two men toward Sabbath observance. Luther's conception of Sunday was similar to that which prevails in modern continental Europe. He insisted, of course, that his followers should attend church, but he did not demand that during the remainder of the day they should refrain from all pleasure or work. Calvin, on the other hand, revived the Jewish Sabbath with its strict taboos against anything faintly resembling worldliness. In the third place, the religion of Geneva was more closely associated with the ideals of the new capitalism. Luther's sympathies lay with the princes, and on at least one occasion he sharply censured the tycoons of finance for their greed. Calvin sanctified the ventures of the trader and the moneylender and gave an exalted place in his ethical system to the business virtues of thrift and diligence. Finally, Calvinism as com-

The religion of Calvin compared with that of Luther

pared to Lutheranism represented a more radical phase of the Protestant Revolution. As we have seen, the Wittenberg friar retained a good many features of Roman worship and even some Catholic dogmas. Calvin rejected everything he could think of that smacked of "popery." The organization of his church was constructed in such a way as to exclude all traces of the episcopal system. Congregations were to choose their own elders and preachers, while an association of ministers at the top would govern the entire church. Ritual, instrumental music, stained-glass windows, pictures, and images were ruthlessly eliminated, with the consequence that the religion was reduced to "four bare walls and a sermon." Even the observance of Christmas and Easter was sternly prohibited.

The spread of Calvinism

The popularity of Calvinism was not limited to Switzerland. It spread into most countries of western Europe where trade and finance had become leading pursuits. The Huguenots of France, the Puritans of England, the Presbyterians of Scotland, and the members of the Reformed Church in Holland were all Calvinists. It was preeminently the religion of city people; though, of course, it drew converts from other strata as well. Its influence in molding the ethics of modern times was enormous. Members of this faith had much to do with the initial revolts against despotism in England and France, as well as in overthrowing Spanish tyranny in the Netherlands.

IV. THE PROTESTANT REVOLUTION IN ENGLAND   The original blow against the Roman Church in England was not struck by a religious enthusiast like Luther or Calvin but by the head of the government. This does not mean, however, that the English Reformation was ex-

Contrast between Catholic and Protestant Churches. At the left is a Catholic church, showing the profusion of religious ceremonies, church adornments, and ecclesiastical vestments. At the right is a "reformed" Protestant church where most people are listening to a sermon in surroundings of stark simplicity.

clusively a political movement. Henry VIII could not have succeeded in establishing an independent English Church if such action had not had the endorsement of large numbers of his subjects. And there were plenty of reasons why this endorsement was readily given. Though the English had freed themselves in some measure from papal domination, national pride had reached such a point that any degree of subordination to Rome was resented. Besides, England had been the scene for some time of lively agitation for religious reform. The memory of Wyclif's scathing attacks upon the avarice of the priests, the temporal power of popes and bishops, and the sacramental system of the Church had lingered since the fourteenth century. The influence of the Christian humanists, notably Thomas More, in condemning the superstitions in Catholic worship, had also been a factor of considerable importance. Finally, soon after the outbreak of the Protestant Revolution in Germany, Lutheran ideas were brought into England by wandering preachers and through the circulation of printed tracts. As a result, the English monarch, in severing the ties with Rome, had no lack of sympathy from some of the most influential of his subjects.

The clash with the pope was precipitated by Henry VIII's domestic difficulties. For eighteen years he had been married to Catherine of Aragon and had only a sickly daughter, the future Queen Mary, to succeed him. The death of all the sons of this marriage in infancy was a grievous disappointment to the king, who desired a male heir to perpetuate the Tudor dynasty. But this was not all, for Henry had become deeply infatuated with the dark-eyed lady-in-waiting, Anne Boleyn, and was determined to make her his queen. He therefore appealed in 1527 to Pope Clement VII for an annulment of the marriage to Catherine. The law of the Church did not sanction divorce, but it did provide that a marriage could be annulled if proof could be presented that conditions existing at the time of the marriage made it unlawful. Queen Catherine had previously been married to Henry's older brother, Arthur, who had died a few months after the ceremony was performed. Recalling this fact, Henry's lawyers found a passage in the Book of Leviticus which pronounced a curse of childlessness upon the man who should marry his deceased brother's wife. The pope was in a difficult position. If he rejected the king's appeal, England would probably be lost to the Catholic faith, for Henry was apparently firmly convinced that the Scriptural curse had blighted his chances of perpetuating his dynasty. On the other hand, if the pope granted the annulment he would provoke the wrath of the Emperor Charles V, a nephew of Catherine. Charles had already invaded Italy and was threatening the pope with a loss of his temporal power. There seemed nothing for Clement to do but to procrastinate. At first he made a pretense of having the question settled in England, and empowered his own legate and Cardinal Wolsey to hold a court of inquiry to determine whether the marriage to Catherine had been legal.

Underlying causes of the Protestant Revolution in England

Henry VIII. Portrait by Hans Holbein.

Proclamation of the Anglican Church as an independent national unit

After long delay the case was suddenly transferred to Rome. Henry lost patience and resolved to take matters into his own hands. In 1531 he convoked an assembly of the clergy and, by threatening to punish them for violating the Statute of Praemunire in submitting to the papal legate, he induced them to recognize himself as the head of the English Church, "as far as the law of Christ allows." Next he persuaded Parliament to enact a series of laws abolishing all payments of revenue to the pope and proclaiming the Anglican Church an independent, national unit, subject to the exclusive authority of the king. By 1534 the last of the bonds uniting the English church to Rome had been cut.

But the enactments put through by Henry VIII did not really make England a Protestant country. Though the abolition of papal authority was followed by the dissolution of the monasteries and confiscation of their wealth, the Church remained Catholic in doctrine. The Six Articles, adopted by Parliament at the king's behest in 1539, left no room for doubt as to official orthodoxy. Auricular confession, Masses for the dead, and clerical celibacy were all confirmed; death by burning was made the penalty for denying the Catholic dogma of the Eucharist. Yet the influence of a minority of Protestants at this time cannot be ignored. Their numbers were steadily increasing, and during the reign of Henry's successor, Edward VI (1547–1553), they actually gained the ascendancy. Since the new king was only nine years old when he inherited the crown, it was inevitable that the policies of the government should be dictated by powers behind the throne. The men most active in this work were Thomas Cranmer, archbishop of Canterbury, and the dukes of Somerset and Northumberland, who successively dominated the council of regency. All three of these officials had strong Protestant leanings. As a result, the creeds and ceremonies of the Church of England were given some drastic revision. Priests were permitted to marry; English was substituted for Latin in the services; the use of images was abolished; and new articles of belief were drawn up repudiating all sacraments except baptism and communion and affirming the Lutheran dogma of justification by faith alone. When the youthful Edward died in 1553, it looked as if England had definitely entered the Protestant camp.

Surface appearances, however, are frequently deceiving. They were never more so than in England at the end of Edward's reign. The majority of the people had refused to be weaned away from the usages of their ancient faith, and a reaction had set in against the high-handed methods of the radical Protestants. Moreover, the English during the time of the Tudors had grown accustomed to obeying the will of their sovereign. It was an attitude fostered by national pride and the desire for order and prosperity. The successor of Edward VI was Mary (1553–1558), the forlorn and pious daughter of Henry VIII and Catherine. It was inevitable that Mary should have been a Catholic, and that she should have abhorred the revolt against Rome, for the origin of the movement was painfully associated with her mother's sufferings. Consequently, it is not strange that upon coming to the throne she should have attempted to turn the clock back. Not only did she restore the celebration of the Mass and the rule of clerical celibacy, but she prevailed upon Parliament to vote the unconditional return of England to papal allegiance. But her policies ended in lamentable failure for several reasons. First of all, she fell into the same error as her predecessors in forcing through changes that were too radical for the temper of the times. The people of England were not ready for a Lutheran or Calvinist revolution, but neither were they in a mood to accept immediate subjection to Rome. Probably a more serious cause of her failure was her marriage to Philip, the ambitious heir to the Spanish throne. Her subjects feared that this union might lead to unfortunate foreign complications, if not actual annexation by Spain. When the queen allowed herself to be drawn into a war with France, in which England was compelled to surrender Calais, its last foothold on the Continent, the nation was almost ready for rebellion. Death ended Mary's inglorious reign in 1558.

The question whether England was to be Catholic or Protestant was left to be settled by Mary's successor, her half-sister Elizabeth (1558–1603), daughter of Anne Boleyn. Though reared as a Protestant, Elizabeth had no deep religious convictions. Her primary interest was statecraft, and she did not intend that her kingdom should be rent in twain by sectarian strife. Therefore, she decided upon a policy of moderation, refusing to ally herself with either the extreme Catholics or the fanatical Protestants. So carefully did she hew to this line that for some years she deceived the pope into thinking that she might turn Catholic. Nevertheless, she was enough of a nationalist to refuse even to consider a revival of allegiance to Rome. One of the first things she did after becoming queen was to order the passage of a new Act of Supremacy, declaring the English sovereign to be the "supreme governor" of the independent Anglican church. The final settlement, completed about 1570, was a typical English compromise. The church was made Protestant, but certain articles of the creed were left vague enough so that former Catholics might accept them without too much shock to their conscience. Moreover, the episcopal form of organization and much of the Catholic ritual was retained. Long after Elizabeth's death this settlement remained in effect. Indeed, most elements in it have survived to this day. And it is a significant fact that the modern Church of England is broad enough to include within its ranks such diverse factions as the Anglo-Catholics, who differ from Roman Catholics only in rejecting papal supremacy, and the "low-church" Anglicans, who are as radical in their Protestantism as the Lutherans.

The Elizabethan compromise

2. THE CATHOLIC REFORMATION

*The beginnings of
Catholic reform*

As noted at the beginning of this chapter, the Protestant Revolution was only one of the phases of the great movement known as the Reformation. The other was the Catholic Reformation, or the Counter-Reformation as it used to be called, on the assumption that the primary purpose of its leaders was to cleanse the Catholic Church in order to check the growth of Protestantism. Modern historians have shown, however, that the beginnings of the movement for Catholic reform were entirely independent of the Protestant revolt. In Spain, during the closing years of the fifteenth century, a religious revival inaugurated by Cardinal Ximenes, with the approval of the monarchy, stirred that country to the depths. Schools were established, abuses were eliminated from the monasteries, and priests were goaded into accepting their responsibilities as shepherds of their flocks. Though the movement was launched primarily for the purpose of strengthening the Church in the war against heretics, Jews, and Muslims, it nevertheless had considerable effect in regenerating the spiritual life of the nation. In Italy also, since the beginning of the sixteenth century, a number of earnest clerics had been laboring to make the priests of their Church more worthy of their calling. The task was a difficult one on account of the entrenchment of abuses and the example of profligacy set by the papal court. In spite of these obstacles the movement did lead to the founding of several religious orders dedicated to high ideals of piety and social service.

*The climax of the
Catholic Reformation; the
reform popes*

But the fires of Catholic reform burned rather low until after the Protestant Revolution began to make serious inroads. Not until it appeared that the whole German nation was likely to be swept into the Lutheran orbit did any of the popes become seriously concerned about the need for reform. The first to attempt a purification of the Church was Adrian VI, of Utrecht, the only non-Italian to be elected to the papal throne in nearly a century and a half, and the last until 1978. But his reign of only twenty months was too short to enable him to accomplish much, and in 1523 he was succeeded by a Medici (Clement VII), who ruled for eleven years. The campaign against abuses in the Church was not renewed until the reign of Paul III (1534–1549). He and three of his successors, Paul IV (1555–1559), Pius V (1566–1572), and Sixtus V (1585–1590), were the most zealous crusaders for reform who had presided over the Vatican since the days of Gregory VII. They reorganized the papal finances, filled the Church offices with priests renowned for austerity, and dealt drastically with those clerics who persisted in idleness and vice. It was under these popes that the Catholic Reformation reached its height.

These direct activities of the popes were supplemented by the decrees of a Church council convoked in 1545 by Paul III, which met in the Italian city of Trent at intervals between 1545 and 1563. This council was one of the most important in the history of the Church. The main purpose for which it had been summoned was to redefine the doctrines of the Catholic faith, and several of the steps in this direction were highly significant. Without exception, the dogmas challenged by the Protestant Reformers were reaffirmed. Good works were held to be as necessary for salvation as faith. The theory of the sacraments as indispensable means of grace was upheld. Likewise, transubstantiation, the apostolic succession of the priesthood, the belief in purgatory, the invocation of saints, and the rule of celibacy for the clergy were all confirmed as essential elements in the Catholic system. On the much-debated question as to the proper source of Christian belief, the Bible and the traditions of apostolic teaching were held to be of equal authority. Not only was papal supremacy over every bishop and priest expressly maintained, but there was more than a faint suggestion that the authority of the pope transcended that of the Church council itself. Thus the monarchical government of the Church was strongly reaffirmed. The Council of Trent also reaffirmed the doctrine of indulgences which had touched off the Lutheran revolt, although it did condemn the worst scandals connected with the selling of indulgences.

The legislation of Trent was not confined to matters of dogma, but also included provisions for the elimination of abuses and for reinforcing the discipline of the Church over its members. Bishops and priests were forbidden to hold more than one benefice, so that none could grow rich from a plurality of incomes. To eliminate the evil of an ignorant priesthood it was provided that a theological seminary must be established in every diocese. Toward the end of its deliberations the council decided upon a censorship of books to prevent heretical ideas from corrupting the minds of those who still remained in the faith. A commission was appointed to draw up an index or list of writings which ought not to be read. The publication of this list by the pope in 1564 resulted in the formal establishment of the Index of Prohibited Books as a part of the machinery of the Church. Later, a permanent agency known as the Congregation of the Index was set up to revise the list from time to time. Altogether more than forty such revisions have been made. The majority of the books condemned have been theological treatises, and probably the effect in retarding the progress of learning has been slight. Nonetheless, the establishment of the index must be taken as a symptom of the intolerance which had come to infect both Catholics and Protestants.

The Catholic Reformation would never have been as thorough or as successful as it was had it not been for the activities of the Jesuits, or members of the Society of Jesus. They did most of the rough political work in the Council of Trent, which enabled the popes to dominate that body in its later and more important sessions. The Jesuits also were largely responsible for winning areas that had fallen to Protestantism, such as Poland and parts of southern Germany, back into the

The Council of Trent

Reforms of the Council of Trent

Ignatius Loyola. Engraving by Lucas Vorstiman, 1621.

Catholic fold. The founder of the Society of Jesus was Ignatius Loyola (1491–1556), a Spanish nobleman from the Basque country. His early career seems not to have been particularly different from that of other Spaniards of his class—a life of philandering and marauding as a soldier of the king. But about the time the Protestant Revolution was getting well under way in Germany, he was painfully wounded in a battle with the French. While waiting for his injuries to heal, he read a pious biography of Jesus and some legends of the saints which profoundly changed his emotional nature. Overwhelmed by a consciousness of his wasted life, he determined to become a soldier of Christ. After a period of morbid self-tortures, in which he saw visions of Satan, Jesus, and the Trinity, he went to the University of Paris to learn more about the faith he intended to serve. Here he gathered around him a small group of devoted disciples, with whose aid in 1534 he founded the Society of Jesus. The members took monastic vows and pledged themselves to go on a pilgrimage to Jerusalem. In 1540 their organization was approved by Pope Paul III. From then on it grew rapidly. When Loyola died it already boasted no fewer than 1,500 members.

The Society of Jesus was by far the most militant of the religious orders fostered by the spiritual zeal of the sixteenth century. It was not merely a monastic society but a company of soldiers sworn to defend the faith. Their weapons were not to be bullets and spears but eloquence, persuasion, instruction in the right doctrines, and if necessary more worldly methods of exerting influence. The organization was patterned after that of a military company, with a general as commander-in-chief and an iron discipline enforced on the members. All individuality was suppressed, and a soldierlike obedience to the general was exacted of the rank and file. Only the highest of the four classes of members had any share in the government of the order. This little group, known as the Professed of the Four Vows, elected the general for life and consulted with him on important matters. They were also bound to implicit obedience.

As suggested already, the activities of the Jesuits were numerous and varied. First and foremost, they conceived of themselves as the defenders of true religion. For this object they obtained authority from the pope to hear confessions and grant absolution. Many of them became priests in order to gain access to the pulpit and expound the truth as the oracles of God. Still others served as agents of the Inquisition in the relentless war against heresy. In all of this work they followed the leadership of the Church as their infallible guide. They raised no questions and attempted to solve no mysteries. Loyola taught that if the Church ruled that white was black, it would be the duty of its followers to believe it. But the Jesuits were not satisfied merely to hold the field against the attacks of Protestants and heretics; they were anxious to propagate the faith in the farthest corners of the earth—to make Catholics out of Buddhists, Muslims, the Parsees of

India, and the indigenous peoples of the newly discovered continents. Long before the Reformation had ended, there were Jesuit missionaries in Africa, in Japan and China, and in North and South America. Yet another important activity of Loyola's soldiers was education. They founded colleges and seminaries by the hundreds in Europe and America and obtained positions in other institutions as well. Until the eighteenth century the society had a monopoly of education in Spain and a near-monopoly in France. That the Catholic Church recovered so much of its strength in spite of the Protestant secession was due in large measure to the manifold and aggressive activities of the Jesuits.

3. THE REFORMATION HERITAGE

The most immediate effects of the Reformation were a sharp rise in religious persecution and the onset of religious warfare throughout much of Europe. Both Catholics and Protestants took it for granted that diversity of religious belief within any country's boundaries simply could not be tolerated. Therefore religious dissenters were ruthlessly persecuted wherever they were found. In several instances the victims included leading intellects who let their religious speculations or researches carry them in new directions. The most eminent of the original thinkers put to death by the Catholics was Giordano Bruno, an early supporter of the Copernican heliocentric theory. Because Bruno taught the doctrine of a plurality of worlds, which offended biblical orthodoxy, he was haled before the Roman Inquisition (founded in 1542) and burned at the stake in 1600. One of the victims of Calvinist persecution at Geneva was Michael Servetus, the discoverer of the pulmonary circulation of the blood. In 1553 Servetus was condemned for rejecting the doctrine of the Trinity; after some discussion, John Calvin's own recommendation of "merciful" beheading was rejected by Servetus's other Calvinist judges and the daring thinker, whose ideas prefigured modern Unitarianism, was burned slowly at the stake, his major work tied around his arm.

Not surprisingly, the prevalent attitudes of intolerance led to prolonged religious warfare between Catholics and Protestants. The first major religious struggle to break out was the Schmalkaldic War (1546–1547), waged by Charles V in an effort to restore the unity of the Holy Roman Empire under the Catholic faith. In a few months he succeeded in cowing the Protestant princes of Germany into submission, but he was unable to force their subjects back into the Roman religion. The strife was ultimately settled by a compromise treaty, the Religious Peace of Augsburg (1555), under which each German prince was to be free to choose either Lutheranism or Catholicism as the faith of his people. The religion of each state was thus made to depend upon the religion of its ruler. A much more prolonged and bloody struggle

Giordano Bruno

Michael Servetus

Religious wars

took place in France between 1562 and 1593. Here the Protestants, or Huguenots as they were called, were decidedly in the minority, but they included some of the ablest and most influential members of the commercial and financial classes. Besides, they composed a political party involved in machinations against the Catholics for control of the government. In 1562, a faction of ultra-Catholics under the leadership of the duke of Guise forced its way into power and, by its threats of persecution of the Huguenots, plunged the country into civil war. The struggle culminated ten years later in the frightful massacre of St. Bartholomew's Day. The regent, Catherine de' Medici, in a desperate effort to put an end to the strife, plotted with the Guises to murder the Protestant leaders. The conspiracy unloosed the ugly passions of the Paris mob, with the result that in a single night 2,000 Huguenots were slain. The war dragged on until 1593 when Henry IV became a Catholic in order to please the majority of his subjects, but the religious issue did not approach a settlement until 1598 when Henry issued the Edict of Nantes guaranteeing freedom of conscience to Protestants.

The St. Bartholomew's Day Massacre. Thousands of Huguenots were killed in France in the continuing religious strife of the sixteenth century.

To a large extent the Revolt of the Netherlands was also an episode in the religious strife stirred up by the Reformation. Long after the Protestant Revolution began in Germany, the countries now known as Belgium and Holland were still being governed as dominions of the Spanish crown. Though Lutheranism and Calvinism had gained a foothold in the cities, the Protestants of the Netherlands were yet but a fraction of the total population. With the passage of time, however, the numbers of Calvinists increased until they included a majority of the townspeople, at least in the Dutch provinces of the north. Interference by the Spanish government with their freedom of religion led to a desperate revolt in 1565. Religious causes were, of course, not the only ones. Nationalist feeling was a leading factor also, particularly since the Spanish king, Philip II, persisted in treating the Netherlands as mere subject provinces. In addition, there were serious economic grievances—high taxation and the restriction of commerce for the benefit of Spanish merchants. On the other hand, it was religious hatred that was largely responsible for the bitterness of the struggle. Philip II regarded all Protestants as traitors, and he was determined to root them out of every territory over which he ruled. In 1567 he sent the violently anti-Protestant duke of Alva with 10,000 soldiers to quell the revolt in the Netherlands. For six years Alva terrorized the land, putting hundreds of the rebels to death and torturing or imprisoning thousands of others. The Protestants retaliated with almost equal savagery, and the war continued its barbarous course until 1609. It ended in victory for the Protestants, largely through the bravery and self-sacrifice of their original leader, William the Silent. The chief result of the war was the establishment of an independent Dutch Republic comprising the territories now included in Holland. The southern or Belgian provinces, where the majority of the people were Catholics, returned to Spanish rule.

The Revolt of the Netherlands

See color map following page 576

Severe religious warfare continued in the seventeenth century in the form of the Thirty Years' War and the English Civil War, both of which will be treated later on. By around 1650, however, men finally stopped slaughtering each other in the name of salvation, and a new age of toleration slowly began to dawn. The prolonged upheavals had left most of northern Germany and all of the Scandinavian countries Lutheran; Scotland, Holland, and parts of northern Germany and Switzerland Calvinist; England a compromise Protestant country; and the rest of Europe predominantly Catholic. These are roughly the religious divisions of Europe today. It would be a mistake to think that such diversity served to promote religious freedom: on the contrary, religious minorities were outlawed in almost all European countries until about 1800. After about 1650, however, countries at least stopped fighting each other on religious grounds.

End of religious warfare

Among the more clearly modernizing effects of the Reformation were the added momentum the movement gave to the rise of individualism and to the expansion of popular education. By simplifying rit-

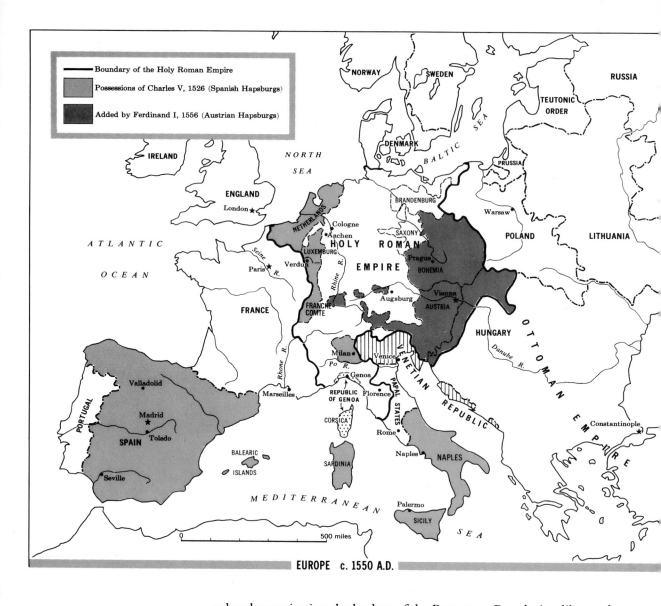

EUROPE c. 1550 A.D.

Legend:
— Boundary of the Holy Roman Empire
Possessions of Charles V, 1526 (Spanish Hapsburgs)
Added by Ferdinand I, 1556 (Austrian Hapsburgs)

Increase in individualism

ual and organization the leaders of the Protestant Revolution liberated people from some of the collective constraints of the medieval Church. More importantly, Protestantism tended to assert the rights of private judgment. When Luther boldly resisted the claims of religious authority at the Diet of Worms by proclaiming, "Here I stand, I cannot do otherwise," he set a precedent for the autonomy of the individual conscience which would never be forgotten.

Growth in education

In addition, the Reformation had some effect in promoting the education of the masses. The Renaissance, with its absorbing interest in the classics, had had the unfortunate result of distorting the curricula of the schools into an exaggerated emphasis upon Greek and Latin and of restricting education to the aristocracy. The Lutherans, Calvinists, and Jesuits changed all of this. Ambitious to propagate their respective doctrines, they established schools for the masses, where even the son of the cobbler or peasant might learn to read the Bible and theological tracts in the vernacular. Practical subjects were often introduced in place of Greek and Latin, and it is a significant fact that some of these schools eventually opened their doors to the new science.

Certain tendencies of Reformation thought also helped ultimately to limit political absolutism. These tendencies were by no means to be found in Lutheranism. Quite to the contrary, Luther was a fervent adherent of St. Paul's doctrine that "the powers that be are ordained of God." Luther insisted that political disobedience was a greater sin than murder, unchastity, dishonesty, or theft, and held that the authority of kings and princes was never to be questioned by their subjects. Some observers indeed see in Luther's influence a powerful stimulus to the growth of authoritarian government in Germany. But Jesuit philosophers, on the other hand, attempted to revive the medieval idea of a higher "law of nature." This natural law embodied divinely shaped principles of right and justice which should be recognized as providing certain limitations upon the power of rulers. Certain Jesuits, moreover, taught that the authority of the secular ruler is derived from the people, and some even affirmed the right of the ordinary citizen to kill a tyrant in extraordinary circumstances. Going still further than the Jesuits, some Calvinists in France, England, and the Low Countries not only asserted the right of revolution but actively practiced it. In England too Protestant "Congregationalists" in the seventeenth century introduced the principle of democracy into their Church government and began to argue that such principles might be extended to the government of the state. Some went so far as to maintain that "the meanest man in England ought to have a voice in the election of the government he lives under." Such arguments were among the earliest expressions of truly democratic thought in modern times.

Religious controls on authoritarian governments

SELECTED READINGS

• *Items so designated are available in paperback editions.*
  Allen, J. W., *A History of Political Thought in the Sixteenth Century*, London, 1928. A very exhaustive older survey.
• Bainton, R. H., *Here I Stand: A Life of Martin Luther*, Nashville, Tenn., 1500. The best introductory biography in English: lively and authoritative. •
• ———, *Women of the Reformation*, Minneapolis, 1977.
  Brodrick, James, *The Origins of the Jesuits*, London, 1940.
• Dickens, A. G., *The Counter Reformation*, London, 1968.
• ———, *The English Reformation*, New York, 1964.
• ———, *Reformation and Society in Sixteenth-Century Europe*, London, 1966.
• Elliott, J. H., *Europe Divided: 1559–1598*, London, 1968. An excellent survey.

• Erikson, E. H., *Young Man Luther,* New York, 1958. A classic psychobiography that analyzes the young Luther's "identity crisis."

Geyl, P., *The Revolt of the Netherlands,* London, 1932.

Grimm, Harold J., *The Reformation Era: 1500–1650,* 2nd ed., New York, 1973. The best college-level text.

Gritsch, E. W., *Reformer without a Church: The Life and Thought of Thomas Muentzer,* Philadelphia, 1967.

• Harbison, E. H., *The Age of Reformation,* Ithaca, N.Y., 1955. An expert elementary introduction.

———, *The Christian Scholar in the Age of the Reformation,* New York, 1956. Treats the relation of scholarship to the Christian calling.

Hillerbrand, Hans J., *Men and Ideas in the Sixteenth Century,* Chicago, 1969.

• Hurstfield, Joel, ed., *The Reformation Crisis,* London, 1965. Stimulating essays.

Jones, Rufus M., *The Spiritual Reformers of the Sixteenth and Seventeenth Centuries,* New York, 1914. A lively account by a modern Quaker.

• McNeill, J. T., *The History and Character of Calvinism,* New York, 1954.

Monter, E. William, *Calvin's Geneva,* New York, 1967.

• O'Connell, M. R., *The Counter Reformation: 1560–1610,* New York, 1974.

Parker, G., *The Dutch Revolt,* Ithaca, N.Y., 1977.

• Spitz, Lewis W., *The Reformation: Basic Interpretations,* 2nd ed., Lexington, Mass., 1972. A collection of readings on points of scholarly dispute.

• Tawney, R. H., *Religion and the Rise of Capitalism,* New York, 1926. The most sophisticated and elegantly written defense of the "Weber thesis."

Trevor-Roper, H., *Religion, The Reformation and Social Change,* London, 1967.

• Troeltsch, E., *Protestantism and Progress,* New York, 1931. Argues the view that Protestants were not "modern."

• Weber, Max, *The Protestant Ethic and the Spirit of Capitalism,* London, 1930. Argues the thesis that Calvinism led to the triumph of the capitalist spirit.

Williams, George H., *The Radical Reformation,* Philadelphia, 1962. Detailed account of the "left-wing" Reformers.

SOURCE MATERIALS

Dillenberger, J., ed., *John Calvin: Selections from His Writings,* Garden City, N.Y., 1971.

———, *Martin Luther: Selections from His Writings,* Garden City, N.Y., 1961.

St. Ignatius Loyola, *The Spiritual Exercises,* tr. R. W. Gleason, Garden City, N.Y., 1964.

Ziegler, D. J., *Great Debates of the Reformation,* New York, 1969.

Chapter 20

THE COMMERCIAL REVOLUTION AND THE NEW SOCIETY (c. 1450 – c. 1800)

Although a Kingdom may be enriched by gifts received, or by purchases taken from some other Nations, yet these are things uncertain and of small consideration when they happen. The ordinary means therefore to encrease our wealth and treasure is by *Forraign Trade,* wherein wee must ever observe this rule: to sell more to strangers yearly than wee consume of theirs in value.

—Thomas Mun, *England's Treasure by Forraign Trade*

In the three and a half centuries between 1450 and 1800 enormous changes took place in European economic life which are often described as the Commercial Revolution. While there is much room for disagreement in detail about what these changes entailed, certain basic generalizations are commonly agreed upon. Above all, the Commercial Revolution encompassed a change from the semi-static, localized, and largely subsistence economy of the Middle Ages to the dynamic, worldwide, capitalist regime of modern times. Recovery from the fourteenth-century economic catastrophes was spurred by overseas discoveries, the influx of new articles of consumption and precious metals, the establishment of overseas markets, and advances in banking and trade. Larger numbers of people began to live off commerce and industry, and the profit motive became more pronounced than ever before. Also during the period of the Commercial Revolution, first Spain and Portugal, and then the north Atlantic states of England, France, and Holland replaced the northern Italian cities as the centers of European economic initiative and prosperity. Finally, in the eighteenth century revolutionary developments in European agriculture brought the European economy to the threshold of the Industrial Revolution. Taken together, all these changes meant unprecedented

Major changes in European economic life

new wealth for Europe and carried in their train important changes in social organization and material culture.

1. THE NATURE AND EFFECTS OF OVERSEAS EXPANSION

We have already seen in Chapter 13 that the European economy was beginning to expand around 1450 after about a century and a half of severe depression. No doubt expansion would have progressed steadily, but it was greatly accelerated in the sixteenth and subsequent centuries by the effects of overseas discoveries and conquests. The initial voyages of discovery were due primarily to Spanish and Portuguese ambitions for a share in the trade with the Orient. For some time this trade had been monopolized by the Italian cities of Venice and Genoa, with the result that the people of the Iberian peninsula had to pay high prices for the spices, silks, and drugs that were imported from the East. It was therefore quite natural that attempts should be made by sailors commissioned by Spanish and Portuguese monarchs to discover a new route to the Orient independent of Italian control. A second cause of the voyages of discovery was the missionary fervor of the Spaniards. The successful Spanish reconquest of the Iberian peninsula from the forces of Islam had generated a surplus of religious zeal, which spilled over into a desire to convert the overseas "heathen." To these causes should be added the fact that advances in geographical knowledge and technological expertise allowed mariners to venture more fearlessly into the open seas. It should be borne in mind, however, that these advances did not all transpire suddenly around 1490. The popular idea that all Europeans before Columbus believed that the earth was flat is simply not true: it would have been impossible after the twelfth century to have found an educated person who did not accept the fact that the earth is a sphere. Furthermore, technological aids like the compass and the astrolabe (a device used for measuring the position of heavenly bodies) were known long before Columbus's voyage. In fact, the Portuguese had already sailed boldly out into the Atlantic to reach the Azores Islands (one-third of the way to the New World) before 1350. Most likely, Europeans would have reached America and the Far East much earlier than they actually did had they not been held back by the depression and political upheavals of the later Middle Ages.

If we except the Norsemen, who discovered the North American continent about 1000 A.D., the pioneers in oceanic navigation were the Portuguese. By the middle of the fifteenth century they had explored the African coast as far south as Guinea. In 1497 their most successful navigator, Vasco da Gama, rounded the tip of Africa and sailed on the next year to India. In the meantime, the Genoese mariner, Christopher Columbus (1451–1506), became convinced of the feasibility of reaching India by sailing west. Rebuffed by the Portuguese, he turned to the Spanish sovereigns, Ferdinand and Isabella, and enlisted their support of his plan. The story of his epochal voyage and its result is a familiar one and need not be recounted here. Though he died ignorant of his real achievement, his discoveries laid the foundations for the Spanish claim to nearly all of the New World. Other discoverers representing the Spanish crown followed Columbus, and soon afterward the conquerors, Cortes and Pizarro. The result was the establishment of a vast colonial empire including what is now the southwestern portion of the United States, Florida, Mexico, and the West Indies, Central America, and all of South America with the exception of Brazil, which was taken by Portugal.

Cortes

The English and the French were not slow in following the Spanish example. The voyages of John Cabot and his son Sebastian in 1497–1498 provided the basis for the English claim to North America, though there was nothing that could be called a British empire in the New World until after the settlement of Virginia in 1607. Early in the sixteenth century the French explorer Cartier sailed up the St. Lawrence, thereby furnishing his native land with some shadow of a title to eastern Canada. More than a hundred years later the explorations of Joliet, La Salle, and Father Marquette gave the French a foothold in the Mississippi valley and in the region of the Great Lakes. Following their victory in their war for independence in the early seventeenth century, the Dutch also took a hand in the struggle for colonial empire. The voyage of Henry Hudson up the river which bears his name enabled them to found New Netherland in 1623, which they were forced to surrender to the English some forty years later. But the most valuable possessions of the Dutch were Malacca, the Spice Islands, and the ports of India and Africa taken from Portugal in the early seventeenth century.

*The British, French, and
Dutch*

The results of these voyages of discovery and the founding of colonial empires were almost incalculable. To begin with, they expanded commerce from its narrow limits of Mediterranean trade into a world enterprise. For the first time in history the ships of the great maritime powers now sailed the seven seas. The tight little monopoly of Oriental trade maintained by the Italian cities was thoroughly punctured. Genoa and Venice gradually sank into relative obscurity, while the harbors of Lisbon, Bordeaux, Liverpool, Bristol, and Amsterdam were crowded with vessels and the shelves of their merchants piled high with goods. A second result was a tremendous increase in the volume of commerce and in the variety of articles of consumption. To the spices and textiles from the Orient were now added tobacco from North America; molasses and rum from the West Indies; cocoa, chocolate, quinine, and cochineal dye from South America; and ivory, slaves, and ostrich feathers from Africa. In addition to these commod-

*The expansion of
commerce into a world
enterprise*

Aden. A sixteenth-century woodcut of the seaport which was a base for merchants and travelers sailing to India.

ities hitherto unknown or obtainable only in limited quantities, the supply of certain older products was greatly increased. This was especially true of sugar, coffee, rice, and cotton, which were imported in such amounts from the Western Hemisphere that they ceased to be articles of luxury.

The increase in the supply of precious metals

    Another significant result of the discovery and conquest of lands overseas was an expansion of the supply of precious metals. When Columbus first sailed to America, the quantities of gold and silver in Europe were scarcely sufficient to support a dynamic economy. Indeed, it was nearly fifty years before the full impact of wealth from America made itself felt. For some time gold was the more abundant metal and was relatively cheap in relation to silver. About 1540 this relation was reversed. Massive imports of silver from the mines of Mexico, Bolivia, and Peru produced such a depreciation in the value of silver that quantities of gold had to be hoarded for critical transactions. Henceforth, for about eighty years, the European economy ran on silver. The result was a tremendous inflation. Prices and wages rose to fantastic heights in what may be considered an artificial prosperity. It did not affect all parts of Europe alike. The German silver-mining industry was ruined by the flood of silver from the Americas. As a consequence, the position of Germany declined, while England and the Netherlands rose to preeminence. For a brief period Spain shared this preeminence, but it was ill-fitted to continue it. Spanish industrial development was too feeble to supply the demand for manufactured products from the European settlers in the Western Hemisphere. Accordingly, they turned to the north of Europe for the textiles, cutlery, and similar products they urgently needed. By the end of the sixteenth century the Spanish economy, which had first seemed to be prospering greatly from the discoveries, lay almost completely in ruins.

2. THE MAIN FEATURES OF THE COMMERCIAL REVOLUTION

The major traits of the Commercial Revolution have been partly suggested by the foregoing discussion of overseas expansion. The outstanding characteristic was the rise of capitalism. Reduced to its simplest terms, capitalism may be defined as a system of production, distribution, and exchange, in which accumulated wealth is invested by private owners for the sake of gain. Its essential features are private enterprise, competition for markets, and business for profit. Generally it involves also the wage system as a method of payment of workers; that is, a mode of payment based not upon the amount of wealth they create, but rather upon their ability to compete with one another for jobs. As indicated already, capitalism is the direct antithesis of the semi-static economy of the medieval guilds, in which production and trade were supposed to be conducted for the benefit of society and with only a reasonable charge for the service rendered, instead of unlimited profits. Although capitalism did not come to its full maturity until the nineteenth century, most of its cardinal features were developed during the Commercial Revolution.

*Incidents of the
Commercial Revolution:
(1) the rise of capitalism*

A second important feature of the Commercial Revolution was the growth of banking. Because of the strong religious and moral disapproval of usury, banking had scarcely been a respectable business during the Middle Ages. For centuries the little that was carried on was

(2) the growth of banking

Sixteenth-Century Mining. The greater complexity of new mining techniques called for greater sophistication of capitalistic organization.

Jacob Fugger

(3) the expansion of credit facilities

virtually monopolized by Jews. Nevertheless, exceptions did exist. As we have seen in Chapter 11, the Church did come to allow profit-making on commercial risks. The result was that several Italian families began to profit greatly from banking enterprises as early as the thirteenth century. The greatest Italian banks were ruined by the blows of the fourteenth-century depression, but afterwards newer and better managed Italian houses, like the bank of the Medici, took their place. By the fifteenth century the banking business had spread to southern Germany and France. The leading firm in the north was that of the Fuggers of Augsburg. The Fuggers lent money to kings and bishops, served as brokers for the pope in the sale of indulgences, and provided the funds that enabled Charles V to buy his election to the throne of the Holy Roman Empire. The rise of these private financial houses was followed by the establishment of government banks, intended to serve the monetary needs of the national states. The first in order of time was the Bank of Sweden (1657), but the one which was destined for the role of greatest importance in economic history was the Bank of England, founded in 1694. Although not technically under government control until 1946, it was the bank of issue for the government and the depositary of public funds.

The growth of banking was necessarily accompanied by the adoption of various aids to financial transactions on a large scale. Credit facilities were extended in such a way that a merchant in Amsterdam could purchase goods from a merchant in Venice by means of a bill of exchange issued by an Amsterdam bank. The Venetian merchant would obtain his money by depositing the bill of exchange in his local bank. Later, the two banks would settle their accounts by comparing balances. Among the other facilities for the expansion of credit were the adoption of a system of payment by check in local transactions and the issuance of bank notes as a substitute for gold and silver. Both of these devices were invented by the Italians and were gradually adopted

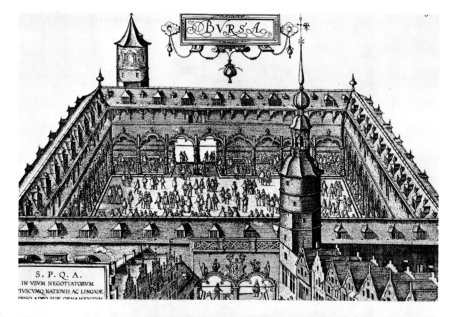

The Antwerp Bourse. Built in the sixteenth century, this was the place of exchange for merchants from all countries.

in northern Europe. The system of payment by check was particularly important in increasing the volume of trade, since the credit resources of the banks could now be expanded far beyond the actual amounts of cash in their vaults.

The Commercial Revolution was not confined, of course, to the growth of trade and banking. Included in it also were fundamental changes in methods of production. The system of manufacture developed by the craft guilds in the later Middle Ages was rapidly becoming defunct. The guilds themselves, dominated by the master craftsmen, had grown selfish and exclusive. Membership in them was commonly restricted to a few privileged families. Besides, they were so completely choked by tradition that they were unable to make adjustments to changing conditions. Moreover, new industries had sprung up entirely outside the guild system. Characteristic examples were mining and smelting and the woolen industry. The rapid development of these enterprises was stimulated by technological advances, such as the invention of the spinning wheel and the stocking frame and the discovery of a new method of making brass, which saved about half of the fuel previously used. In the mining and smelting industries a form of organization was adopted similar to that which has prevailed ever since. The tools and plant facilities belonged to capitalists, while the workers were mere wage-laborers subject to hazards of accident, unemployment, and occupational disease.

(4) the decline of the craft guilds and the rise of new industries

But the most typical form of industrial production in the period of the Commercial Revolution was the domestic system, developed first of all in the woolen industry. The domestic system derives its name from the fact that the work was done in the homes of individual artisans instead of in the shop of a master craftsman. Since the various jobs in the manufacture of a product were given out on contract, the system is also known as the putting-out system. Notwithstanding the petty scale of production, the organization was basically capitalist. The raw material was purchased by an entrepreneur (known as a clothier in the woolen industry) and assigned to individual workers, each of whom would complete his or her allotted task for a stipulated payment. In the case of the woolen industry the yarn would be given out first of all to the spinners, then to the weavers, fullers, and dyers in succession. When the cloth was finally finished, it would be taken by the clothier and sold in the open market for the highest price it would bring. The domestic system was, of course, not restricted to the manufacture of woolen cloth. As time went on, it was extended into many other fields of production. It tied in well with the new glorification of riches and with the conception of a dynamic economy. The capitalist could now thumb his nose at the old restrictions on profits. No association of his rivals could judge the quality of his product or the wages he paid to his workers. Perhaps best of all he could expand his business as he saw fit and introduce new techniques that would reduce costs or increase the volume of production.

(5) the domestic, or putting-out system

Merchants' Houses in Amsterdam, Seventeenth Century. Several of the principal thoroughfares of Amsterdam are canals.

Advantages and disadvantages of the domestic system

Undoubtedly, the domestic system had advantages for the workers themselves, especially as compared to its successor, the factory system. Though wages were low, there was no regular schedule of hours, and it was generally possible for the laborer to supplement the family income by cultivating a small plot of land and raising a few vegetables. Furthermore, conditions of work in the homes were more healthful than in factories, and the artisan had his family to assist him with the simpler tasks. Freedom from the supervision of a foreman and from the fear of discharge for petty reasons were also definite advantages. On the other hand, it must not be forgotten that the workers were too widely scattered to organize effectively for common action. As a consequence they had no means of protecting themselves from dishonest employers, who cheated them out of part of their wages or forced them to accept payment in goods. It is also true that toward the end of the Commercial Revolution the workers became more and more dependent upon the capitalists, who now furnished not only the raw materials but the tools and equipment as well. In some cases the laborers were herded into large central shops and compelled to work under a fixed routine. The difference between this and the high-pressure methods of the factory system was only a matter of degree.

That the Commercial Revolution would involve extensive changes in business organization was practically assured from the start. The prevailing unit of production and trade in the Middle Ages was the shop or store owned by an individual or a family. The partnership was also quite common, in spite of its grave disadvantage of unlimited liability of each of its members for the debts of the entire firm. Obviously no one of these units was well adapted to business involving heavy risks and a huge investment of capital. The first result of the attempt to devise a more suitable business organization was the formation of *regulated companies.* The regulated company was an association of merchants banded together for a common venture. The members did not pool their resources but agreed merely to cooperate for their mutual advantage and to abide by certain definite regulations. Usually the purpose of the combination was to maintain a monopoly of trade in some part of the world. Assessments were often paid by the members for the upkeep of docks and warehouses and especially for protection against "interlopers," as those traders were called who attempted to break into the monopoly. A leading example of this type of organization was an English company known as the Merchant Adventurers, established for the purpose of trade with the Netherlands and Germany.

(6) *changes in business
organization; the growth
of regulated companies*

In the seventeenth century the regulated company was largely superseded by a new type of organization at once more compact and broader in scope. This was the *joint-stock company,* formed through the issuance of shares of capital to a considerable number of investors. Those who purchased the shares might or might not take part in the work of the company, but whether they did or not they were joint owners of the business and therefore entitled to share in its profits in accordance with the amount they had invested. The joint-stock company had numerous advantages over the partnership and the regulated company. First, it was a permanent unit, not subject to reorganization every time one of its members died or withdrew. And second, it made possible a much larger accumulation of capital, through a wide distribution of shares. In short, it possessed nearly every advantage of the modern corporation except that it was not a person in the eyes of the law with the rights and privileges guaranteed to individuals. While most of the early joint-stock companies were founded for commercial ventures, some were organized later in industry. A number of the outstanding trading combinations were also *chartered companies.* This means that they held charters from the government granting a monopoly of the trade in a certain locality and conferring extensive authority over the inhabitants. Through a charter of this kind the British East India Company ruled over India as if it were a private estate until 1784, and even in a sense until 1858. Other famous chartered companies were the Dutch East India Company, the Hudson's Bay Company, the Plymouth Company, and the London Company. The last of these founded the colony of Virginia and governed it for a time as company property.

(7) *the joint-stock
company*

The remaining feature of the Commercial Revolution which needs to be considered was the growth of a more efficient money economy. Money, of course, had been widely in use ever since the revival of

*The Spanish Milled Dollar or
"Piece of Eight."* This was one of
the first coins to have its circumference scored or "milled."
It was cut into halves and quarters to make change.

trade in the eleventh century. Nevertheless, there were few coins with a value that was recognized other than locally. By 1300, the gold ducat of Venice and the gold florin of Florence had come to be accepted in Italy and also in the international markets of northern Europe. But no country could be said to have had a uniform monetary system. Nearly everywhere there was great confusion. Coins issued by kings circulated side by side with the money of foreign states. Moreover, the types of currency were modified frequently, and the coins themselves were often debased. A common method by which kings expanded their own personal revenues was to increase the proportion of cheaper metals in the coins they minted. But the growth of trade and industry in the Commercial Revolution accentuated the need for more stable and uniform monetary systems. The problem was solved by the adoption of a standard system of money by every important state to be used for all transactions within its borders. Much time elapsed, however, before the reform was complete. England began the construction of a uniform coinage during the reign of Queen Elizabeth, but the task was not finished until late in the seventeenth century. The French did not succeed in reducing their money to its modern standard of simplicity and convenience until the time of Napoleon. In spite of these long delays it appears safe to conclude that national currencies were really an achievement of the Commercial Revolution.

3. MERCANTILISM IN THEORY AND PRACTICE

*The meaning of
mercantilism*

The Commercial Revolution in its later stages was accompanied by the adoption of a new set of doctrines and practices known as mercantilism. In its broadest meaning, mercantilism may be defined as a system of government intervention to promote national prosperity and increase the power of the state. Though frequently considered as a program of economic policy exclusively, its objectives were quite largely political. The purpose of the intervention in economic affairs was not merely to expand the volume of manufacturing and trade, but also to bring more money into the treasury of the king, which would enable him to build fleets, equip armies, and make his government feared and respected throughout the world. Because of this close association with the ambitions of princes to increase their own power and the power of the states over which they ruled, mercantilism has sometimes been called *statism.* Certainly the system would never have come into existence had it not been for the growth of absolute monarchy in place of the weak, decentralized structure of feudalism. But kings alone did not create it. Naturally the new magnates of business lent support, since they would obviously derive great advantages from active encouragement of trade by the state. The heyday of mercantilism was the period between 1600 and 1700, but many of its features survived until the end of the eighteenth century.

If there was any one principle which held the central place in mercantilist theory, it was the doctrine of bullionism. This doctrine means that the prosperity of a nation is determined by the quantity of precious metals within its borders. The greater the amount of gold and silver a country contains, the more money the government can collect in taxes, and the richer and more powerful the state will become. But what of those countries that owned no bullion-producing colonies? How were *they* to achieve riches and power? For these questions the mercantilists had a ready answer. A nation without access to gold and silver directly should attempt to increase its trade with the rest of the world. If its government took steps to ensure that the value of exports would always exceed the value of imports, more gold and silver would come into the country than would have to be shipped out. This was called maintaining a "favorable balance of trade." To preserve this balance, three main devices would be necessary: first, high tariffs to reduce the general level of imports and to shut out some products entirely; second, bounties on exports; and third, extensive encouragement of manufactures in order that the nation might have as many goods to sell abroad as possible.

The theory of mercantilism also included certain elements of economic nationalism, paternalism, and imperialism. By the first is meant the ideal of a self-sufficient nation. The policy of fostering new industries was not intended merely as a device for increasing exports, but also as a means of making the nation independent of foreign supplies. In similar fashion, the mercantilists argued that the government should exercise the functions of a watchful guardian over the lives of its citizens. Relief should be provided for the poor, including free medical attention if they were unable to pay for it. These things were

Coining Money in the Sixteenth Century. These coins were not "milled" and therefore were easily "clipped," a process of scraping portions of the valuable metal from the edges of the coin.

to be done, however, not with any view to charity or justice, but mainly in order that the state might rest upon a secure economic foundation and have the support of a numerous and healthy citizenry in case of war. Finally, the mercantilists advocated the acquisition of colonies. Again, the primary purpose was not to benefit individual citizens of the mother country, but to make the nation strong and independent. The types of possessions most ardently desired were those that would enlarge the nation's hoard of bullion. If these could not be obtained, then colonies providing tropical products, naval stores, or any other commodities which the mother country could not produce would be acceptable. The theory which underlay this imperialism was the notion that colonies existed for the benefit of the state that owned them. For this reason they were not allowed to engage in manufacturing or shipping. Their function was to produce raw materials and to consume as large a proportion of manufactured products as possible. In this way they would infuse lifeblood into the industries of the mother country and thus give it an advantage in the struggle for world trade.

*The defenders of
mercantilism*

The majority of those who wrote on mercantilist theory were philosophers and men of action in the world of business. Among the former were such advocates of political absolutism as the Frenchman Jean Bodin (1530–1596) and the Englishman Thomas Hobbes (1588–1679), who were naturally disposed to favor any policy that would increase the wealth and power of the ruler. While most of the apologists for mercantilism were interested in it mainly as a device for promoting a favorable balance of trade, others conceived it as a species of paternalism for increasing prosperity within the country. Some, for example, advocated a policy somewhat similar to contemporary ideas of government spending, by recommending that the state should appropriate a huge fund for the relief of the poor and for the construction of public works as a means of stimulating business.

*Mercantilism in practice:
in Spain and in England*

Attempts to put various mercantilist doctrines into practice characterized the history of many of the nations of western Europe in the sixteenth and seventeenth centuries. The theories, however, were not universally applied. Spain, of course, had the initial advantage by reason of the flow of bullion from its American empire. And while the Spaniards did not need to resort to artificial devices in order to bring money into their country, their government nevertheless maintained a rigid control over commerce and industry. The policies of other nations were designed to make up for the lack of bullion-producing colonies by capturing a larger share of export trade. This naturally involved a program of bounties, tariffs, and extensive regulation of manufacturing and shipping. Mercantilist policies were largely adopted in England during the reign of Queen Elizabeth I and were continued by the Stuart monarchs and by Oliver Cromwell. Most of these rulers engaged in a furious scramble for colonies, bestowed monopolistic privileges upon trading companies, and sought in a wide variety of ways to control the economic activities of their citizens. The most interesting examples of mercantilist legislation in England were, first, the Elizabethan laws designed to eliminate idleness and stimulate production and, second, the Navigation Acts. By a series of laws enacted toward the end of the sixteenth century, Queen Elizabeth gave to the justices of the peace the authority to fix prices, regulate hours of labor, and compel every able-bodied citizen to work at some useful trade. The first of the Navigation Acts was passed in 1651 under Oliver Cromwell. With the aim of destroying Dutch predominance in the carrying trade, it required that all colonial exports to the mother country should be carried in English ships. A second Navigation Act was passed in 1660, which provided not merely that colonial exports should be shipped in British vessels but prohibited the sending of certain "enumerated articles," especially tobacco and sugar, directly to continental European ports. They were to be sent first of all to England, whence, after the payment of customs duties, they could be reshipped elsewhere. Both of these laws were based upon the principle that colonies should serve for the enrichment of the mother country.

The Germanic states during the Commercial Revolution were too completely occupied with internal problems to take an active part in the struggle for colonies and overseas trade. As a consequence, German mercantilism was concerned primarily with increasing the strength of the state from within. It partook of the dual character of economic nationalism and a program for a planned society. But, of course, the planning was done chiefly for the benefit of the government and only incidentally for that of the people as a whole. Because of their dominant purpose of increasing the revenues of the state, the German mercantilists are known as cameralists (from *Kammer,* a name given to the royal treasury). Most of them were lawyers and professors of finance. Cameralist ideas were put into practice by the Hohenzollern kings of Prussia, notably by Frederick William I (1713–1740) and Frederick the Great (1740–1786). The policies of these monarchs embraced a many-sided scheme of intervention and control in the economic sphere for the purpose of increasing taxable wealth and bolstering the power of the state. Marshes were drained, canals dug, new industries established with the aid of the government, and farmers instructed as to what crops they should plant. In order that the nation might become self-sufficient as soon as possible, exports of raw materials and imports of manufactured products were prohibited. The bulk of the revenues gained from these various policies went for military purposes. The standing army of Prussia was increased by Frederick the Great to 160,000 men.

The most thorough, if not the most deliberate, application of mercantilism was probably to be found in France during the reign of Louis XIV (1643–1715). This was due partly to the fact that the French

*Mercantilism in
Germany: the cameralists*

Jean Baptiste Colbert

French mercantilism under Colbert

state was the fullest incarnation of absolutism and partly to the policies of Jean Baptiste Colbert, chief minister under Louis from 1661 until his death in 1683. Colbert was no theorist but rather a practical politician, ambitious for personal power and intent upon magnifying the opportunities for wealth of the middle class, to which he belonged. He accepted mercantilism, not as an end in itself, but simply as a convenient means for increasing the wealth and power of the state and thereby gaining the approval of his sovereign. He firmly believed that France must acquire as large an amount of the precious metals as possible. To this end he prohibited the export of money, levied high tariffs on foreign manufactures, and gave liberal bounties to encourage French shipping. It was largely for this purpose also that Colbert fostered imperialism, hoping to increase the favorable balance of trade through the sale of manufactured goods to the colonies. Accordingly, he purchased islands in the West Indies, encouraged settlements in Canada and Louisiana, and established trading posts in India and Africa. Furthermore, he was as devoted to the ideal of self-sufficiency as any of the cameralists in Prussia. He gave subsidies to new enterprises, established a number of state-owned industries, and even had the government purchase goods which were not really needed in order to keep struggling companies on their feet. But he was determined to keep the manufacturing industry under strict control, so as to make sure that companies would buy their raw materials only from French or colonial sources and produce the commodities necessary for national greatness. Consequently, he clamped upon industry an elaborate set of regulations prescribing nearly every detail of the manufacturing process. Finally, it should be mentioned that Colbert took a number of steps to augment the political strength of the nation directly. He provided France with a navy of nearly 300 ships, drafting citizens from the maritime provinces and even criminals to man them. He sought to promote a rapid growth of population by discouraging young people from becoming monks or nuns and by exempting families with ten or more children from taxation.

4. THE RESULTS OF THE COMMERCIAL REVOLUTION

The foundation for modern capitalism

It goes without saying that the Commercial Revolution was one of the most significant developments in the history of the Western world. The whole pattern of modern economic life would have been impossible without it, for it changed the basis of commerce from the local and regional plane of the Middle Ages to the worldwide scale it has occupied ever since. Moreover, it exalted the power of money, inaugurated business for profit, sanctified the accumulation of wealth, and established competitive enterprise as the foundation of production and trade. In short, the Commercial Revolution was responsible for a large number of the elements that go to make up the capitalist regime.

But these were not the only results. The Commercial Revolution brought into being wide fluctuations of economic activity. What we now call booms and recessions alternated with startling rapidity. The inflow of precious metals, combined with a rise in population, led to rising prices and an unprecedented demand for goods. Businessmen were tempted to expand their enterprises too rapidly; bankers extended credit so liberally that their principal borrowers, especially nobles, often defaulted on loans. Spain and Italy were among the first to suffer setbacks. In both, failure of wages to keep pace with rising prices brought incredible hardships to the lower classes. Impoverishment was rife in the cities, and bandits flourished in the rural areas. In Spain, some ruined aristocrats were not too proud to join the throngs of vagrants who wandered from city to city. At the end of the fifteenth century the great Florentine bank of the Medici closed its doors. The middle of the century that followed saw numerous bankruptcies in Spain and the decline of the Fuggers in Germany. Meanwhile, England, Holland, and to some extent France, waxed prosperous. This prosperity was especially characteristic of the "age of silver," which lasted from about 1540 to 1620. In the seventeenth century decline set in once more after inflation had spent its force, and as a consequence of religious and international wars and civil strife.

The alternation of booms and recessions was followed by outbreaks of feverish speculation. These reached their climax early in the eighteenth century. The most notorious were the South Sea Bubble and the Mississippi Bubble. The former was the result of inflation of the stock of the South Sea Company in England. The promoters of this company agreed to take over a large part of the national debt and in return received from the English government an exclusive right to trade with South America and the Pacific islands. The prospects for profit seemed almost unlimited. The stock of the company rose rapidly in value until it was selling for more than ten times its original price. The higher it rose, the more gullible the public became. But gradually suspicion developed that the possibilities of the enterprise had been overrated. Buoyant hopes gave way to fears, and investors made frantic attempts to dispose of their shares for whatever they would bring. A crash which came in 1720 was the inevitable result.

During the years when the South Sea Bubble was being inflated in England, the French were going through a similar wave of speculative madness. In 1715 a Scotsman by the name of John Law, who had been compelled to flee from British soil for killing his rival in a love intrigue, settled in Paris, after various successful gambling adventures in other cities. He persuaded the regent of France to adopt his scheme for paying off the national debt through the issuance of paper money and to grant him the privilege of organizing the Mississippi Company for the colonization and exploitation of Louisiana. As the government loans were redeemed, the people who received the money were encouraged to buy stock in the company. Soon the shares began to soar, ultimately reaching a price forty times their original value. Nearly everyone who could scrape together a bit of surplus cash rushed forward to participate in the scramble for riches. Stories were told of butchers and tailors who were supposed to have become millionaires by buying a few shares and holding them for a rise in price. But as the realization grew that the company would never be able to pay more than a nominal dividend on the stock at its inflated value, the more cautious investors began selling their holdings. The alarm spread, and soon all were as anxious to sell as they had been to buy. In 1720 the Mississippi Bubble burst in a wild panic. Thousands of people who had sold good property to buy the shares at fantastic prices were ruined. The collapse of the South Sea and Mississippi companies gave a temporary chill to the public ardor for speculation. It was not long, however, until the appetite for speculative profits revived, and the stock-buying waves that followed in the wake of the Commercial Revolution were repeated many times over during the nineteenth and twentieth centuries.

*The rise of a new class
and the Europeanization
of the world*

Among other results of the Commercial Revolution were the rise of the middle class to economic power, the beginning of Europeanization of the world, and the revival of slavery. Each of these requires brief comment. By the end of the seventeenth century the middle class had become an influential group in nearly every country of western Europe. Its ranks included the merchants, the bankers, the shipowners, the principal investors, and the industrial entrepreneurs. Their rise to power was mainly the result of increasing wealth and their tendency to ally themselves with the king against the aristocracy. But as yet their power was purely economic. Not until the nineteenth century did middle-class supremacy in politics become a reality. By the Europeanization of the world is meant the transplanting of European manners and culture in other continents. As a result of the work of traders, missionaries, and colonists, North and South America were rapidly stamped with the character of appendages of Europe. No more than a beginning was made in the transformation of Asia, but enough was done to foreshadow the trend of later times when even Japanese and Chinese would adopt Western locomotives and shell-rimmed spectacles.

The most tragic, and humanly reprehensible, result of the Commercial Revolution was the revival of slavery—i.e., the buying and selling of human beings for forced labor and profit. Slavery had practically disappeared from European civilization around the year 1000. But the development of mining and plantation farming in the English, Spanish, and Portuguese colonies led to a tremendous demand for unskilled labor. At first the colonizers attempted to enslave Native Americans, but they usually proved too susceptible to European infectious diseases. The need was filled in the sixteenth century, and another "commodity" added to the system of colonial trade, by the importation of Africans. From then until the nineteenth century, slavery was an integral part of the European colonial system, especially in those regions producing tropical agricultural products: e.g., sugar cane, tobacco, and, after about 1780, cotton.

Finally, the Commercial Revolution was exceedingly important in preparing the way for the Industrial Revolution. This was true for a number of reasons. First, the Commercial Revolution created a class of capitalists who were constantly seeking new opportunities to invest their surplus profits. Second, the mercantilist policy, with its emphasis upon protection for infant industries and production of goods for export, gave a powerful stimulus to the growth of manufactures. Third, the founding of colonial empires flooded Europe with new raw materials and greatly increased the supply of certain products which had hitherto been luxuries. Most of these required fabrication before they were available for consumption. As a consequence, new industries sprang up wholly independent of any guild regulations that still survived. The outstanding example was the manufacture of cotton textiles, which, significantly enough, was one of the first of the industries to become mechanized. Last of all, the Commercial Revolution was marked by a trend toward the adoption of factory methods in certain lines of production, together with technological improvements, such as the discovery of more efficient processes of refining ores. Thus the Commercial Revolution led inevitably to the Industrial Revolution, as we shall see.

*Effects of the Commercial
Revolution in preparing
the way for the Industrial
Revolution*

5. REVOLUTIONARY DEVELOPMENTS IN AGRICULTURE

In the late seventeenth century and, above all, in the eighteenth century, sweeping changes occurred in European agriculture that may be regarded in part as effects of the Commercial Revolution. The rise in prices and increase in urban population brought about by commercial developments made agriculture an ever more profitable business and thus tended to stimulate agricultural improvements. In addition, one effect of overseas expansion was to familiarize Europeans with important new crops, above all, Indian corn and potatoes, which they could raise at home. But probably the most important influence of the Commercial Revolution on agricultural history was the triumph of the capitalist mentality. Landlords who had hitherto let peasants farm their lands inefficiently, now followed the model of businessmen in seeking a maximum of efficiency and profits. So long as these landlords were prepared to be ruthless, there were many revolutionary changes that they were able to bring about.

The countries that led the way in agricultural advance were Holland and England, no doubt largely because these countries had already

*Relations between the
Commercial Revolution
and changes in agriculture*

participated to the fullest in the Commercial Revolution. Since England was able to advance rapidly beyond Holland, owing to its greater size and natural resources, we may limit our remarks here to English developments. It will be recalled from Chapter 11 that the typical medieval agricultural regime was one in which groups of peasants collectively cultivated long and narrow unfenced strips of land. Of those, one-third would lie fallow in any given year in order to restore fertility. Other neighboring lands would be given over to pastures and meadows for the grazing of collectively owned peasant herds. Most often, the actual ownership of all these lands was ill-defined or almost randomly parceled out; usually, however, there would be a prominent landlord in each area who could lay claim to owning a large percentage of the land even though peasants farmed it for him. The same individual might also claim legal title to the pastures and meadows. In England most of these landlords decided to "enclose" their lands in order to make them more profitable.

The earliest "enclosures" in England took place in the fifteenth and sixteenth centuries and entailed the conversion of lands into fenced-off sheep meadows. Because of the great profits to be accrued from wool, some landlords decided to convert common pastures that hitherto had supported peasant livestock into their own preserves for sheep-raising. Sometimes they also succeeded in converting grain fields into sheep pastures by evicting peasants whose leaseholds were none too secure. This caused grave hardships for the peasants concerned. As Thomas More wrote in his *Utopia* (1516) "sheep that used to be so meek and eat so little now are becoming so greedy and wild that they devour men themselves . . . for they leave no land free for the plough." The humanitarian More, however, was exaggerating somewhat. In fact, no more than about 3 percent of arable land had been enclosed before 1525 and part of that was not for sheep pasturage.

The really dramatic enclosure movement in England took place between 1710 and 1810 and aimed not to free land for sheep but to increase the efficiency of crop-raising. In this period landlords became convinced of the necessity for "scientific farming." Above all, they realized that by introducing new crops and farming methods they could reduce the amount of fallow lands and bring in higher yields. Some of the important new crops with which they experimented were clover, alfalfa, and related varieties of leguminous plants. These reduced fertility much less than cereal grains and actually helped to improve the quality of the soil by gathering nitrogen and making the ground more porous. Another new crop that had a similar effect was the turnip. The greatest propagandist for the planting of this unattractive vegetable was Viscount Charles Townshend (1674–1738), a prominent aristocrat and politician, who toward the end of his life left the royal court to experiment with agriculture. In this he became a model for subsequent aristocratic interest in scientific farming. Townshend gained the nickname of "Turnip" Townshend because he was so dedicated to converting people to the use of the turnip in new crop rotation systems.

Clover, alfalfa, and turnips not only helped in doing away with the fallow but they provided excellent winter food for animals, thereby aiding the production of more and better livestock. And more livestock also meant more manure. Accordingly, intensive manuring became another way in which scientific farmers could eliminate the need for letting land lie fallow. Other improvements in farming methods introduced in the period were more intensive hoeing and weeding, and the use of the seed drill for planting grain. The latter eliminated the old wasteful method of sowing grain broadcast by hand, most of it remaining on top to be eaten by birds.

Scientific farming dictated the necessity of enclosures because the "improving" landlord needed flexibility to experiment as he wished. He simply could not try to plant one narrow open strip with turnips while peasants were continuing to rotate all the contiguous areas on the basis of the age-old three-field system. Instead, it was necessary for him to have fenced-off compact plots to leave no doubt as to which territory was his own, to maximize efficiency in experimentation, and to keep away stray grazing animals. It must also be added that when the enclosure movement gathered momentum, landlords were not above using the principle of reorganizing and enclosing territories to gain new lands from the peasantry that hitherto had in no way belonged to them. In all this they had the government on their side. Parliament stopped trying to prohibit enclosures in 1640 and actually started directing them in 1710. Thereafter, throughout the eighteenth century, parliamentary "acts of enclosure" provided that all the lands of a given village be completely redistributed into compact, fenced parcels, with the leading landlords of an area gaining far and away the most land. (Parliament did this because it was dominated by the landowning aristocracy.) The result was that many peasants were driven off the land but also that productivity soared. In eighteenth-century England wheat production, for example, increased by one-third, and the average weight of livestock doubled. All told, the increased abundance and concentration of wealth brought about by the agricultural revolution and enclosure movement was a necessary prerequisite for the Industrial Revolution that began in England around 1780.

On the continent of Europe, aside from the minor exception of Holland, there was nothing comparable to the English advance in scientific farming. In most parts of the Continent agricultural change transpired more slowly and the real breakthrough in scientific methods came only in the nineteenth, or in some places the twentieth century. But the eighteenth century was nonetheless an important epoch in continental agriculture from the point of view of the introduction of new crops. Most important was the cultivation of maize

A Ball-and-Chain Pump. Men walking in the treadmill at the left powered this mid–sixteenth-century irrigation device.

Consolidation of holdings

New Crops

Interior of a French Peasant's Cottage, Seventeenth Century. Virtually all activities centered about the hearth, the only source of heat for the entire dwelling.

(Indian corn) and the potato, both introduced from the New World. Since maize can only be grown in areas with substantial periods of sunny and dry weather, it was not planted in north Atlantic regions of Europe, but in the seventeenth and eighteenth centuries its cultivation spread through Italy and the southeastern part of the Continent. Its enormous attraction was that whereas an average ear of grain would yield only about four seeds for every one planted, an ear of maize would yield about seventy or eighty. That made it a "miracle" crop, filling granaries where they had been almost empty before. The potato was an equally miraculous innovation for the European north. Its great advantages were numerous: one was that potatoes could be grown on the poorest, sandiest, or wettest of lands where nothing else could be raised; another was that they could be fitted into the smallest of patches. Raising potatoes even on small patches was profitable because the yield of potatoes was extraordinarily abundant. Finally, the potato was an excellent food for the human diet: it is rich in calories, has many vitamins and minerals, and contains some protein as well. At first northern European peasants resisted growing potatoes because the plant is not mentioned in the Bible, but in the course of the eighteenth century they became accustomed to it, sometimes after considerable governmental pressure. Frederick the Great of Prussia at first practically forced potatoes down his peasants' throats, but soon the crop became a staple there and in the rest of northern Germany. By about 1800 the average northern German peasant family would be eating potatoes as a main course at least once a day. In the same period the potato was also introduced into Ireland and England: as late as the 1960s an English playwright could entitle his play about the lower classes *Chips* [i.e., fried potatoes] *with Everything*.

Probably the single most noteworthy fact about the economic history of the European continent in the eighteenth century was that poor people gradually stopped dying from famine. Until about 1700 about half of all European peasants could expect to see someone in their immediate family die from starvation about once every ten years. Often when periodic famines came whole families would be decimated. But the introduction of new crops like maize and the potato helped change all this. The result was that population began to soar as never before and that labor was ultimately freed for industrialization. At last, people in Europe were literally learning that they did not have to live by bread alone.

End of famine

6. THE NEW SOCIETY

Profound changes in the texture of society inevitably accompany economic revolutions. The society which was brought into being by the Commercial Revolution, though retaining characteristics of the Middle Ages, was markedly different in certain features. For one thing the population of Europe was becoming considerably larger. All told, the European population in 1500 is estimated to have numbered about 80 million; by 1800 it had more than doubled, to reach about 190 million. In 1378 London had a population of about 50,000; by 1600 the total had reached more than 200,000; and by 1800 more than 1 million! The reasons for these increases are closely related to the religious and economic developments of the time. In northern Protestant countries the overthrow of clerical celibacy and the encouragement of marriage were factors partly responsible. But far more important was the increase in means of subsistence brought about by the Commercial Rev-

Population growth

A Peasants' Meal by Louis Le Nain. This French painting of 1642 shows that the chief item of consumption was still bread and that grown men were often so poor that they had to go barefoot.

olution and agricultural improvements. Not only were new products, such as potatoes, maize, and tomatoes added to the food supply, but older commodities, especially sugar and rice, were now made available to Europeans in larger quantities.

As the figures for London suggest, Europe was becoming not just more populous but also more heavily urbanized. In 1500 there were only three cities in Europe—excluding Turkish Istanbul—with populations of more than 100,000; in 1800 there were twenty-two. Certainly the growth of new opportunities for earning a living in commerce and industry enabled most countries to support a larger population; it is significant that the bulk of these increases occurred in cities and towns. Nonetheless, the extent of urbanization before 1800 should not be exaggerated. In the seventeenth century 70 to 80 percent of all laborers were still agricultural workers; and most industrial labor remained handicraft labor. As one historian, R. S. Dunn, has observed, *"manufacture* still retained its Latin meaning: to make by hand." Even as late as 1800 most industries were centered around small shops, not mechanized factories. Although cities and towns had grown in size, only 3 percent of the European population lived in large cities of over 100,000 people. In short, the Industrial Revolution was only just beginning and the triumph of modern urbanism was yet to come.

Increased urbanization

Just as urbanism had not yet fully triumphed, neither had the social status of the middle class. Historians used to talk of an ever "rising" middle class, but they now realize that this trend is too easily exaggerated. Without doubt, throughout most of the period there were great opportunities for ambitious and talented merchants to pile up fortunes and thereby climb some of the higher rungs of the social ladder. Yet merchants were never as respected as aristocrats: the French playwright Molière (1622–1673) for example, ridiculed "the bourgeois gentleman"—a rich merchant who clumsily tried to ape the ways of his "betters." Some of the professions, it is true, gained more wealth and dignity than they had enjoyed in the Middle Ages. Specifically, the artist, the writer, the lawyer, the university professor, and the physician emerged into positions of importance roughly comparable to what they now hold in modern society. But in general the age was by no means one of economic or social leveling. Indeed the aristocracy, which gained most of its livelihood from land, was as much economically and socially entrenched towards the end of the period as it was at the beginning.

The middle class

The new egoism that characterized the middle and upper classes stood as a barrier to more generous treatment of the least fortunate human beings. Hearing a disturbance outside his quarters, the Emperor Charles V, in 1552, was reported to have asked who were causing the commotion. When told that they were poor soldiers, he said, "Let them die," and compared them to caterpillars, locusts, and june-

Lack of compassion

Slaves Being Ordered into the Hold of a Ship. Thousands of slaves died in the holds of ships during the long voyage to the Americas. Sympathetic but stylized illustrations such as this were designed to move the newspaper-reading public in the eighteenth century.

bugs that eat the good things of the earth. As a rule, the most pitiable fate was reserved for slaves and serfs. For the sake of big profits, blacks were hunted on the coast of Africa, captured and imprisoned in dungeons called "holding pens," and shipped to the American colonies. It may be of interest to note that one of the earliest Englishmen who engaged in this body-snatching business, Captain John Hawkins, called the ship in which he transported the victims the *Jesus.*

While black slaves were seldom employed in Europe proper, native Europeans were pitiably exploited as serfs. The institution of serfdom had died out in western Europe during the later Middle Ages, but after about 1600 it was revived and gained strength in those parts of Europe east of the Elbe river. There the desire for profit in agriculture and the collusion of the state with the aristocracy led to the growth of the "second serfdom"—a serf system much stronger than ever before. In East Prussia serfs often had to work from three to six days a week for their lord, and some had only late evening or night hours to cultivate their own lands. Worse, in Russia landlords had the power of life and death over their serfs and could sell them apart from the land and even apart from their families.

The second serfdom

Putting aside the plight of eastern European serfs, the eighteenth century did witness definite improvements in the living conditions of most Europeans. We have already seen that new items in the diet helped eliminate famine. Otherwise the poor stayed about as wretched as they had always been—the triumph over epidemic diseases like smallpox and malaria for the most part came about only in the nineteenth century—but there were improvements in the standard of living of the middle and upper classes. This is evidenced by the increasing per capita consumption of sugar, chocolate, coffee, and tea, which were not merely substituted for other foods and beverages but were additions to the average diet. The growing demand for linen and cot-

Changes in the standard of living

Effects of the coffee and
tobacco habits

ton cloth, and for such articles of luxury as mahogany furniture designed by such masters as Chippendale, Hepplewhite, and Sheraton, may be taken as a further indication of rising prosperity.

The widespread adoption of the tobacco and coffee habits in the seventeenth and eighteenth centuries had interesting social and perhaps physiological effects. Although the tobacco plant was brought into Europe by the Spaniards about fifty years after the discovery of America, another half-century passed before many Europeans adopted the practice of smoking. At first the plant was believed to possess miraculous healing powers and was referred to as "divine tobacco" and "our holy herb nicotian." (The word nicotine is derived from Jean Nicot, the French ambassador to Portugal who brought the tobacco plant into France.) The habit of smoking was popularized by English explorers, especially by Sir Walter Raleigh, who had learned it from the Indians of Virginia. It spread rapidly through all classes of European society despite the condemnation of the clergy and the "counterblaste" of James I against it. The enormous popularity of coffee-drinking in the seventeenth century had even more important social effects. Coffee houses or "cafés" sprang up all over Europe and rapidly evolved into leading institutions. They provided not merely an escape for the majority of men from a cribbed and monotonous home life, but they took others away from the excesses of the tavern and the gambling den. In addition, they fostered a sharpening of wits and promoted more polished manners, especially inasmuch as they became favorite meeting places for the literary lions of the time. If we can believe the testimony of English historians, there was scarcely a social or political enterprise which did not have its intimate connections with the establishments where coffee was sold.

The coexistence of genteel coffee houses with the rise of slavery reflects the fact that the Commercial Revolution was founded on the pursuit of self-interest and maintained by indifference to intense human suffering. Nonetheless, the economic advances achieved by the Commercial Revolution did bring great benefits to many and would lead to still greater economic advances in subsequent ages.

SELECTED READINGS

• *Items so designated are available in paperback editions.*
• Braudel, F., *Capitalism and Material Life, 1400–1800*, London, 1973. A fascinating review of evidence pertaining to the entire world by one of the greatest of living historians.
• ———, *The Mediterranean and the Mediterranean World in the Age of Philip II*, New York, 1972. One of the most important and brilliant history

books of our age. Treats life in the Mediterranean regions in the second half of the sixteenth century with particular emphasis on how geography determines the course of human history.

• Burke, Peter, *Popular Culture in Early Modern Europe,* London, 1978. Synthesizes the most recent work on the period between 1500 and 1800. Fascinating.

Chambers, J. D., and G. E. Mingay, *The Agricultural Revolution, 1750–1880,* London, 1966. Now the standard work.

• Cipolla, C. M., *Before the Industrial Revolution: European Society and Economy, 1000–1700,* 2nd ed. New York, 1980. Wide-ranging and full of deft observations.

• Davis, Natalie Z., *Society and Culture in Early Modern France,* Stanford, Calif. 1975. Eight scintillating essays by a pioneer in the use of anthropological methods for the study of early modern European history.

• Goubert, P., *The Ancien Régime: French Society, 1600–1750,* London, 1973. Particularly strong in its descriptions of rural life. Includes selections from illuminating documents.

• Hale, J. R., *Renaissance Exploration,* New York, 1968. A magnificent short introduction.

Heckscher, E., *Mercantilism,* rev. ed., London, 1955. The most influential, but controversial, work on the subject.

• Hill, Christopher, *Reformation to Industrial Revolution* (The Pelican Economic History of Britain, vol. 2), rev. ed., Baltimore, 1969. Comprehensive.

Hufton, O. W., *The Poor of Eighteenth-Century France,* New York, 1974.

Kamen, Henry, *The Iron Century: Social Change in Europe, 1550–1660,* New York, 1971. Supports the recent view that there was an economic crisis in this period that interrupted preceding and succeeding periods of prosperity.

• Laslett, Peter, *The World We Have Lost: England Before the Industrial Age,* 2nd ed., New York, 1971. A very readable introduction to preindustrial social history, but controversial in parts.

• Mandrou, R., *Introduction to Modern France, 1500–1640: An Essay in Historical Psychology,* London, 1975. Assumes some prior knowledge of French history and culture, but full of fascinating information about daily life.

Minchinton, W. E., ed., *Mercantilism: System or Expediency?* Lexington, Mass., 1969. A collection of readings that provides a valuable corrective to Heckscher.

• Morison, S. E., *Christopher Columbus, Mariner,* New York, 1955. A good shorter version of this master storyteller's definitive *Admiral of the Ocean Sea* (1942).

• Parry, J. H., *The Age of Reconnaissance,* London, 1963. The best history of the discoveries that emphasizes the details of shipbuilding and navigation.

• Penrose, B., *Travel and Discovery in the Renaissance,* Cambridge, Mass., 1952. Engrossing.

• de Roover, R., *The Rise and Decline of the Medici Bank, 1397–1494,* Cambridge, Mass., 1963. Authoritative, often very technical.

Rudé, George, *Hanoverian London, 1714–1808,* Berkeley, Calif. 1971.

SOURCE MATERIALS

Barnett, G. E., ed., *Two Tracts by Gregory King,* Baltimore, 1936. An introduction to the work of the modern world's first real statistician.

Mun, Thomas, *England's Treasure by Foreign Trade,* Oxford, 1928. (Reprint of the original edition of 1664.) A vigorous early argument in favor of the balance of trade.

Parry, J. H., *The European Reconnaissance: Selected Documents,* New York, 1968.

Young, Arthur, *Travels in France During the Years 1787, 1788, 1789,* London, 1912. Vivid observations by an English traveler.

Chapter 21

THE AGE OF ABSOLUTISM
(c. 1500–1789)

There are four essential characteristics or qualities of royal authority.
First, royal authority is sacred.
Second, it is paternal.
Third, it is absolute.
Fourth, it is subject to reason.

> —Jacques Bossuet, *Politics Drawn from the Very Words of Holy Scripture*

It now becomes necessary to go back and attempt to analyze the major political developments which accompanied the birth of modern civilization. During the fourteenth and fifteenth centuries the power of the medieval national monarchies had been gradually tested by the upheavals of the later Middle Ages. But, as we saw in Chapter 13, monarchical power was ultimately not found wanting. In the last quarter of the fifteenth century strong monarchs in the leading states of western Europe—England, France, and Spain—overcame threats of fragmentation and started to make royal power stronger than ever. Thereafter most of Europe experienced the fullest flowering of royal "absolutism," or untrammeled monarchy. The age of absolutism lasted in England until the middle of the seventeenth century, in France until 1789, and elsewhere on the European continent into the nineteenth century. There were several reasons why absolutism predominated in the period after 1500. One was that new wealth helped monarchs to pay for expanding bureaucracies and new departments of government, above all departments that directed military organization and the conduct of foreign policy. Another was that international warfare lasted throughout most of the period, and warfare tended to strengthen the power of the state because it allowed monarchs to maintain standing armies that could enforce peace at home as well as abroad. Finally, the Protestant Revolution contributed consid-

The age of absolutism

erably to the growth of royal omnipotence. It broke the unity of the Christian Church, abolished papal overlordship over secular rulers, fostered nationalism, revived the doctrine of the Apostle Paul that "the powers that be are ordained of God," and encouraged the rulers of northern Europe to extend their authority over religious as well as over civil affairs.

Character of absolute monarchy

Although government was certainly becoming stronger than ever, it is well not to confuse early modern western European absolutism with either despotism or totalitarianism. Western European kings were not really despots because no matter how strong they were they seldom ruled arbitrarily like Oriental pharaohs or caliphs. Owing to the strength of their aristocracies and merchant classes they could not whimsically issue decrees to be carried out by a few henchmen; instead they usually had to justify their policies to hundreds or even thousands before they could be implemented. Moreover, absolute monarchs usually respected due process of law and broke with traditions only in exceptional circumstances. Even less were the absolute monarchs similar to modern dictators. Quite obviously, before the nineteenth and twentieth centuries the state could not interfere very efficiently in the lives of its citizens; it lacked mechanized transportation and communications systems, as well as radio, film, and television for propaganda, and sophisticated instruments of terror. Throughout the period of royal absolutism there were hardly even any policemen. Today most of us fear that the state will become too strong—if it has not already—but between 1500 and 1789 in western Europe it was still only distantly shaping the lives of its subjects.

1. THE GROWTH AND DEFEAT OF ABSOLUTE MONARCHY IN ENGLAND

Reasons for defeat in England

England was the only European country in which absolutism was defeated before 1789. The reasons for this were political, economic, and religious. As we have seen, the principle of consent to royal decision-making was stronger in medieval England than elsewhere. Only in England did a body like Parliament emerge from the Middle Ages to stand as a potential barrier to absolutism. Throughout the sixteenth century, the English Crown knew how to use Parliament to serve its own interests, but in the seventeenth century royal personalities and policies began to provoke parliamentary resistance. When that happened, the economic strength of many members of the parliamentary opposition, which had been brought about by England's major participation in the Commercial Revolution, greatly aided them in fighting and finally defeating the monarchy. The major immediate cause of the revolt against royal absolutism was religious. Radical Protestants strongly objected to royal religious policy and ultimately made their objections a cause for civil war.

Before that happened, it might have seemed that England was moving toward absolutism in the same fashion as the states of the Continent. The Tudor dynasty, initiated by Henry VII in 1485, had gained remarkable success in regulating the consciences of its subjects and in binding the nation to its will. It should be added that the most celebrated Tudors, Henry VIII (1509–1547) and Elizabeth I (1558–1603), gained some of their power through shrewdly maintaining a semblance of popular government. When they desired to enact measures of doubtful popularity, they regularly went through the formality of obtaining parliamentary approval. Or when they wanted more money, they manipulated procedure in such a way as to make the appropriations appear to be voluntary grants by the representatives of the people. But the legislative branch of the government under these sovereigns was little more than a rubber stamp. They limited parliamentary sessions to only three or four months of the year; they interfered with elections and packed the two houses with their own favorites; and they cajoled, flattered, or bullied the members as the case might require in order to obtain their support.

In 1603 Elizabeth I, the last of the Tudors, died, leaving no direct descendants. Her nearest relative was her cousin, James VI of Scotland, who now became the sovereign of both England and Scotland under the name of James I. His accession marked the beginning of the troubled history of the Stuarts, the second and last of the absolute dynasties in England. A curious mixture of stubbornness, vanity, and

Queen Elizabeth I. Elizabeth, known to her admiring subjects as "Gloriana," is here depicted standing on a map of Britain.

James I. "The wisest fool in Christendom."

The high-handed policies of James I

Religious dissension during the reign of James I

erudition, James was appropriately called by Henry IV of France "the wisest fool in Christendom." Though he loved to have his courtiers flatter him as the English Solomon, he did not even have sense enough to emulate his Tudor predecessors in being satisfied with the substance of absolute power; he insisted upon the theory as well. From France he appropriated the doctrine of the divine right of kings, contending that "as it is atheism and blasphemy to dispute what God can do, so it is presumption and high contempt in a subject to dispute what a king can do." Although he himself was most undignified in appearance and behavior, in his speech to Parliament in 1609 he declared that "kings are justly called gods, for they exercise a manner of resemblance of divine power upon earth."

That such ridiculous pretensions to divine authority would arouse opposition among the English people was a result which even James himself should have been able to foresee, for England still had traditions of liberty which could not be ignored. The ideal of limited government expressed in Magna Carta had never been entirely destroyed. Moreover, the policies of the new king were of such a character as to antagonize even some of his most conservative subjects. He insisted upon supplementing his income by modes of taxation which had never been sanctioned by Parliament; and when the leaders of that body remonstrated, he angrily tore up their protests and dissolved the two houses. He interfered with the freedom of business by granting monopolies and extravagant privileges to favored companies. He conducted foreign relations in disregard for the economic interests of some of the most powerful citizens. Ever since the days of the Elizabethan sea captains Sir John Hawkins and Sir Francis Drake, English merchants had been ambitious to destroy the commercial empire of Spain. They openly desired a renewal of the war, begun during Elizabeth's reign, for that purpose. But James made peace with Spain and entered into negotiations for marriage alliances favorable to Catholic sovereigns.

It was not marriage alliances alone that involved James in religious troubles. The Elizabethan Compromise, which brought the Reformation in England to a close, had not been satisfactory to the more radical Protestants. They believed that it did not depart widely enough from the forms and doctrines of the Roman Church. During the reign of Queen Mary many of them had been in exile in France and had come under the influence of Calvinism. When Elizabeth's compromise policy took shape, they denounced it as representing too great a concession to Catholicism. Gradually they came to be called Puritans from their desire to "purify" the Anglican Church of all traces of "popish" ritual and observances. In addition, they preached an ascetic morality and condemned the episcopal system of church government. However, they did not form a united group. One faction believed that it could transform the Anglican Church by working within that organization. The other preferred to withdraw from the Anglican fold and

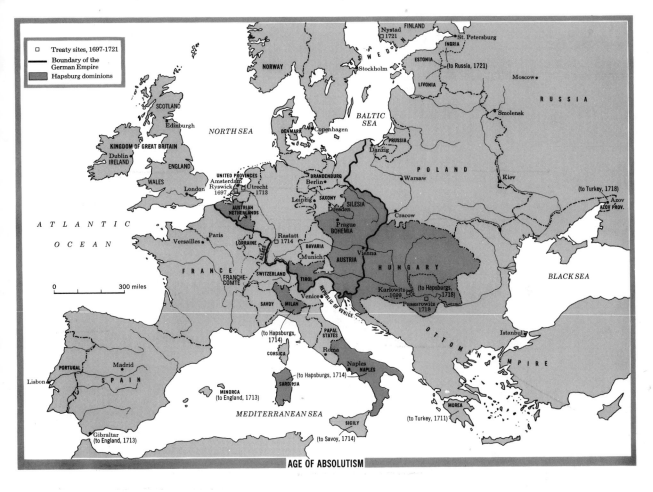

AGE OF ABSOLUTISM

establish separate congregations where they could worship as they pleased. The members of this latter group came to be designated Separatists. They achieved fame in American history as the so-called Pilgrims, who founded Plymouth Colony.

Any brand or faction of Puritans was anathema to King James because he distrusted any religion that did not fit in with his own ideas of relations between church and state. In his estimation the Puritans, by repudiating the episcopal system of church government, were threatening to pull down one of the chief pillars of monarchy itself. Refusal to submit to the authority of bishops appointed by the king was identical in his mind with disloyalty to the sovereign. For this reason he regarded the Puritans as the equivalent of traitors and threatened to "harry them out of the land." He showed little more wisdom in his dealings with the Catholics. For the most part, he favored them, though he could not resist the temptation to levy fines upon them from time to time for violating the severe code which came down from the Reformation. In 1605 a group of fanatical adherents of the Roman faith organized the Gunpowder Plot. They planned to blow

Relations with Puritans and Catholics

Sir Edward Coke

up the Parliament building while the king and the legislators were assembled in it, and, in the resulting confusion, seize control of the government. The plot was discovered, and Parliament enacted even more stringent laws against the Catholics. James, however, allowed the measures to go unenforced. Needless to say, his persistent leniency antagonized his Protestant subjects and made him more unpopular than ever.

From 1611 to 1621 James ruled virtually without Parliament. But this did not mean that his troubles were over. In 1613 the rights of the people found a new champion when Sir Edward Coke (pronounced Cook) was appointed chief justice. Coke was no democrat, but he did have a profound reverence for the common law and for the basic liberties inferred from Magna Carta. Moreover, he was a staunch defender of the privileged position of lawyers and judges. When the king insisted that he also had the faculty of reason and could interpret the law as well as the judges, Coke reminded him that he was not learned in the law, and that causes which concerned the lives and fortunes of his subjects were not to be decided by natural reason but only on the basis of long study and experience. Furthermore, the chief justice developed a rudimentary concept of judicial review. In the celebrated Dr. Bonham's case, he held that "when an act of Parliament is against common right and reason, or repugnant, or impossible to be performed, the common law will control it, and adjudge such act to be void." There is evidence that this opinion was highly regarded in colonial America, and that it was one of the factors which later gave rise to the idea that the Supreme Court of the United States has the authority to nullify laws of Congress which conflict with the Constitution.

The first of the Stuart kings died in 1625 and was succeeded by his son, Charles I (1625–1649). The new monarch was more regal in appearance than his father, but he held the same inflated notions of royal power. As a consequence, he was soon at odds with the Puritans and the leaders of the parliamentary opposition. As in the case of his father, religious tensions were exacerbated by questions of taxation. Soon after his accession to the throne Charles became involved in a war with France. His need for revenue was desperate. When Parliament refused to make more than the customary grants, he resorted to forced loans from his subjects, punishing those who failed to comply by quartering soldiers in their homes or throwing them into prison without a trial. The upshot of this tyranny was the Petition of Right, forced upon Charles by the leaders of Parliament in 1628. This document declared all taxes not voted by Parliament illegal. It condemned also the quartering of soldiers in private houses and prohibited arbitrary imprisonment and the establishment of martial law in time of peace.

But acceptance of the Petition of Right did not end the conflict. Charles soon resumed his old practices of raising money by various ir-

Charles I. This portrait by Van Dyck vividly captures the ill-fated monarch's arrogance.

regular means. He revived obsolete feudal laws and collected fines from all who violated them. He compelled rich burghers to apply for knighthood and then charged them high fees for their titles. He sold monopolies at exorbitant rates and admonished his judges to increase the fines in criminal cases. But the most unpopular of all his expedients for raising revenue was his collection of ship money. Under an ancient custom the English seaboard towns had been required to contribute ships for the royal navy. Since the needs of the fleet were now provided for in other ways, Charles maintained that the towns should contribute money; and he proceeded to apply the new tax not merely to the coastal cities but to the inland counties as well. The levies of ship money were particularly irritating to the merchant class and served to crystallize the opposition of that group to monarchical tyranny. Many refused to pay, and the king's attorney general finally decided to prosecute. A wealthy squire by the name of John Hampden was haled into court in a test case. When convicted by a vote of seven to five, he acquired a sort of martyrdom. For years he was venerated by many as a symbol of resistance to royal autocracy.

Like his blundering father before him, Charles also aroused the antagonism of the Calvinists. He appointed as archbishop of Canterbury a clergyman by the name of William Laud, whose sympathies were decidedly High Anglican. He outraged the Sabbatarianism of the Puritans by authorizing public games on Sunday. Worse still, he attempted to impose the episcopal system of church government upon the Scottish Presbyterians, who were radical Calvinists. The result was an armed rebellion by his northern subjects and the first step toward full-scale civil war.

In order to get money to punish the Scots for their resistance, Charles was finally compelled in 1640 to summon Parliament, after more than eleven years of autocratic rule. Knowing full well that the king was helpless without money, the leaders of the House of Commons determined to take the government of the country into their own hands. They abolished ship money and the special tribunals which had been used as agencies of tyranny. They impeached and sent to imprisonment in the Tower of London the king's chief subordinates, Archbishop Laud and the earl of Strafford. They enacted a law forbidding the monarch to dissolve Parliament and requiring sessions at least every three years. Charles replied to these acts by a show of force. He marched with his guard into the House of Commons and attempted to arrest five of its leaders. All of them escaped, but the issue was now sharply drawn between king and Parliament, and an open conflict could no longer be avoided. Both sides collected troops and prepared for an appeal to the sword.

These events ushered in a period of civil strife, which lasted from 1642 to 1649. It was a struggle at once political, economic, and religious. Arrayed on the side of the king were most of the chief nobles

Oliver Cromwell

The defeat and execution of the king

The Commonwealth and Protectorate

and landowners, the Catholics, and the staunch Anglicans. The followers of Parliament included, in general, the small landholders, tradesmen, and manufacturers. The majority were Puritans and Presbyterians. The members of the king's party were commonly known by the aristocratic name of Cavaliers. Their opponents, who cut their hair short in contempt for the fashionable custom of wearing curls, were called in derision Roundheads. At first the party of the royalists, having obvious advantages of military experience, won most of the victories. In 1644, however, the parliamentary army was reorganized, and soon afterward the fortune of battle shifted. The Cavalier forces were badly beaten, and in 1646 the king was compelled to surrender. The struggle would now have ended had not a quarrel developed within the parliamentary party. The majority of its members, who were now Presbyterians, were ready to restore Charles to the throne as a limited monarch under an arrangement whereby the Presbyterian faith would be imposed upon England as the state religion. But a radical minority of Puritans, made up principally of Separatists but now more commonly known as Independents, distrusted Charles and insisted upon religious toleration for themselves and all other Protestants. Their leader was Oliver Cromwell (1599–1658), who had risen to command of the Roundhead army. Taking advantage of the dissension within the ranks of his opponents, Charles renewed the war in 1648, but after a brief campaign was forced to concede that his cause was hopeless.

The second defeat of the king gave an indisputable mastery of the situation to the Independents. Cromwell and his friends now resolved to put an end to "that man of blood," the Stuart monarch, and remodel the political system in accordance with their own desires. They conducted a purge of the legislative body by military force, ejecting 143 Presbyterians from the House of Commons; and then with the "Rump Parliament" that remained—numbering about 60 members— they proceeded to eliminate the monarchy. An act was passed redefining treason so as to apply to the offenses of the king. Next, a special High Court of Justice was established, and Charles was brought to trial before it. His conviction was a mere matter of form. On January 30, 1649, he was beheaded in front of his palace of Whitehall. A short time later the House of Lords was abolished, and England became an oligarchic republic. The first stage in the so-called Puritan Revolution was now completed.

The work of organizing the new state, which was given the name of the Commonwealth, was entirely in the hands of the Independents. Since the Rump Parliament continued as the legislative body, the really fundamental change was in the nature of the executive. In place of the king there was set up a Council of State composed of forty-one members. Cromwell, with the army at his back, soon came to dominate both of these bodies. However, as time went on he became exas-

Cromwell Felling the Royal Oak of England. A Royalist print of 1656 which portrays Oliver Cromwell as a destructive villain.

perated by the attempts of the legislators to perpetuate themselves in power and to profit from confiscation of the wealth of their opponents. Accordingly, in 1653, he marched a detachment of troops into the Rump and ordered the members to disperse. This action was followed by the establishment of a virtual dictatorship under a constitution drafted by officers of the army. Called the Instrument of Government, it was the nearest approach to a written constitution Britain has ever had. Extensive powers were given to Cromwell as Lord Protector for life, and his office was made hereditary. At first a Parliament exercised limited authority in making laws and levying taxes, but in 1655 its members were abruptly dismissed by the Lord Protector. Thereafter the government was but a thinly disguised autocracy. Cromwell now wielded a sovereignty even more absolute than any the Stuart monarchs would have dared to claim. In declaring his authority to be from God he even revived what practically amounted to the divine right of kings.

That Cromwell's regime would have its difficulties was certainly to be expected, since it rested upon the support of only a few people. He was opposed not only by royalists and Anglicans but by various dissenters, including some more radical than he. Like all upheavals of a similar character, the Puritan Revolution tended to move farther and farther in an extremist direction. Some of the Puritans became Levelers, who derived their name from their advocacy of equal political rights and privileges for all classes. Expressly disclaiming any intention of equalizing property, they confined their radicalism to the political sphere. They insisted that sovereignty inheres in the people and that government should rest upon the consent of the governed. Long in advance of any other party, they demanded a written constitution,

Levelers and Diggers

Charles II

The Restoration

Causes of the Glorious
Revolution of 1688–1689

universal manhood suffrage, and the supremacy of Parliament. The Levelers were especially powerful in the army and through it exerted some influence upon the government. Still farther to the left were the Diggers, so called from their attempt to seize and cultivate unenclosed common land and distribute the produce to the poor. Though in common with the Levelers the Diggers appealed to the law of nature as a source of rights, they were more interested in economic than in political equality. They espoused a kind of primitive communism based upon the idea that the land is the "common treasury" of all. Every ablebodied man would be required to work at productive labor, and all persons would be permitted to draw from the common fund of wealth produced in proportion to their needs. The Church would be transformed into an educational institution and the clergy would become schoolmasters, giving instruction every seventh day in public affairs, history, and the arts and sciences.

In September 1658, the stout-hearted Lord Protector died. He was succeeded by his well-meaning but irresolute son Richard, who managed to hold office only until May of the following year. Perhaps even a man of much sterner fiber would also have failed eventually, for the country had grown tired of the austerities of Calvinist rule. Neither the Commonwealth nor the Protectorate had ever had the support of a majority of the English nation. Royalists regarded the Independents as usurpers. Republicans hated the disguised monarchy which Oliver Cromwell had set up. Catholics and Anglicans resented the branding of their acts of worship as criminal offenses. Even some members of the merchant class gradually came to suspect that Cromwell's war with Spain had done more harm than good by endangering English commerce with the West Indies. For these and similar reasons there was general rejoicing when in 1660 a newly elected Parliament proclaimed Charles I's exiled son king and invited him to return to England and occupy the throne of his father. The new king, Charles II, had gained a reputation for joyous living and easy morality, and his accession was hailed as a welcome relief from the somber rule of soldiers and zealots. Besides, he pledged himself not to reign as a despot, but to respect Parliament and to observe Magna Carta and the Petition of Right, for he admitted that he was not anxious to "resume his travels." England now entered upon a period known as the Restoration, covered by the reigns of Charles II (1660–1685) and his brother James II (1685–1688). Despite its auspicious beginning, many of the old problems had not really been solved but were simply concealed by the fond belief that the nation had regained its former stability.

Toward the end of the seventeenth century England went through a second political upheaval, the so-called Glorious Revolution of 1688–1689. Several of the causes were grounded in the policies of Charles II. That amiable sovereign was extravagant and carefree but determined on occasion to let the country know whose word was law.

His pro-Catholic attitude aroused the fears of patriotic Englishmen that their nation might once again be brought into subservience to Rome. Worse still, he showed a disposition, in spite of earlier pledges, to defy the authority of Parliament. In 1672 he suspended the laws against Catholics and Protestant Dissenters (i.e., all but Anglicans) and nine years later resolved to dispense with the legislative branch entirely. The policies of Charles II were continued in more extreme form by his brother, who succeeded him in 1685. James II was an avowed Catholic and seemed bent upon making that faith the established religion of England. He openly violated an act of Parliament requiring that all holders of public office should adhere to the Anglican church, and proceeded to fill important positions in the army and the civil service with his Romanist followers. He continued his brother's practice of exempting Catholics from the disabilities imposed upon them by Parliament, even going so far as to demand that the Anglican bishops should read his decrees for this purpose in their churches. As long as his opponents could expect that James II would be succeeded by one of his two Protestant daughters, they were inclined to tolerate his arbitrary rule, lest the country be plunged again into civil war. But when the king acquired a son by his second wife, who was a Catholic, the die of revolution was cast. It was feared that the young prince would be infected with his father's doctrines, and that, as a consequence, England would be fettered with the shackles of despotic and "papist"

Left: The Trial of Charles I (1649). Right: The Arrival of the First Course at James II's Coronation Dinner (1685). Both of these events took place at Westminster Hall: the first shows English royal power at its low point and the second at its apparent zenith. But James II was to be overthrown even more quickly than Charles I.

rule for an indefinite time to come. To forestall such a result it seemed necessary to depose the king.

The "Glorious Revolution" of 1688–1689 was an entirely bloodless affair. A group of politicians from the upper classes secretly invited Prince William of Orange and his wife Mary, the elder daughter of James II, to become joint rulers of England. William crossed over from Holland with an army and occupied London without firing a shot. Deserted even by those whom he had counted as loyal supporters, King James took refuge in France. The English throne was now declared vacant by Parliament and the crown presented to the new sovereigns. But their enthronement did not complete the revolution. Throughout the year 1689 Parliament passed numerous laws designed to safeguard the rights of Englishmen and to protect its own power from monarchical invasion. First came an act requiring that appropriations should be made for one year only. Next the Toleration Act was passed, granting religious liberty to all Christians except Catholics and Unitarians. Finally, on the sixteenth of December the famous Bill of Rights was enacted into law. It provided for trial by jury and affirmed the right of Englishmen to petition the government for a redress of grievances. It condemned excessive bail, cruel punishments, and exorbitant fines. And it forbade the king to suspend laws or to levy taxes without the consent of Parliament. More sweeping in its provisions than the Petition of Right of 1628, it was backed by a Parliament that now had the power to see that it was obeyed.

The significance of the revolution of 1688–1689 was very great. Since it marked the final triumph of Parliament over the king, it therefore spelled the doom of absolute monarchy in England. Never again was any crowned head in Britain able to defy the legislative branch of the government as the Stuart monarchs had done. The revolution also dealt a death blow to the theory of the divine right of kings. It would have been impossible for William and Mary to have denied the fact that they received their crowns from Parliament. And the authority of Parliament to determine who should be king was made more emphatic by the passage of the Act of Settlement in 1701. This law provided that upon the death of the heiress-presumptive Anne, younger sister of Mary, the crown should go to the Electress Sophia of Hanover or to the eldest of her heirs who might be Protestant. There were some forty men or women with better claim to the throne than Sophia, but all were eliminated by Parliament on the ground of their being Catholics. Finally, the Glorious Revolution contributed much to the American and French Revolutions at the end of the eighteenth century. The example of the English in overthrowing absolute rule was a powerful inspiration to the opponents of absolutism elsewhere. It was the British ideal of limited government which furnished the substance of the political theory of Voltaire, Jefferson, and Paine. And a considerable portion of the English Bill of Rights was incorporated in the French Declaration of the Rights of Man in 1789 and in the first ten amendments to the American Constitution.

In the eighteenth century English political life became far more stable. In 1714 the Electress Sophia's son succeeded Queen Anne as George I (1714–1727) and initiated the reign of the House of Hanover, which continued in England until 1901. Because George, who came to the throne at the age of fifty four, could speak no English and continued to spend much time in his German possession of Hanover, he was content to leave the real government of England to the leader of Parliament, Sir Robert Walpole (1676–1745). The latter deserves to be called the first English prime minister. During his supremacy Parliament became the real executive as well as legislative organ of England, and Walpole as parliamentary leader was the chief executive. Walpole ruled through a new system he devised, forever after called the cabinet system (originally because "cabinet" members met in a small room known as a cabinet). This meant that the leader of the parliamentary party in power (Walpole was a Whig, his opponents Tories) would work together with a group of like-minded parliamentary colleagues to push through legislation in Parliament and for practical purposes run the country. When the dominant party lost control, the opposition party would bring in a new prime minister and a new cabinet. The cabinet system continues in England until the present day.

Walpole, first prime minister

Walpole remained prime minister until 1742 by following a policy of cautious conservatism. Acting on his motto of *quieta non movere* ("let sleeping dogs lie") he kept England out of war for most of his supremacy and supported the financial interests of the upper classes.

George III

Sir Robert Walpole with Members of His Cabinet

New prime ministers continued to rule England more or less along the lines set down by Walpole throughout the rest of the reign of George II (1727–1760). They faced no interference from that monarch because, like his father, George II was really more German than English. But difficulties ensued at the beginning of the reign of George III (1760–1820). The latter was born in England and legend has it that his mother encouraged him to take an active role in English government by constantly saying "George, be king." Desiring to rule as well as reign, George III succeeded for a time in ensuring that only his favorites became prime ministers. But misrule followed. After England lost its American colonies and the king began to suffer from fits of insanity, Parliament regained the unimpeded initiative in governing the country which it has never lost since then.

2. ABSOLUTE MONARCHY IN FRANCE AND SPAIN

Contrasting conditions in England and France

The development of absolutism in France followed a course similar in some respects to early absolutism in England. Although France remained Catholic, its rulers had to contend with a Calvinist (Huguenot) opposition as formidable as that of the Puritans in England. Both nations had their staunch defenders of absolutism among lawyers and political philosophers. But there was one notable difference. England enjoyed an advantage of geographic isolation that sheltered it from foreign danger. It had not been invaded since the Norman Conquest in 1066. As a consequence, the English felt secure, and their rulers found it difficult to justify a huge professional army. They did, of course, maintain large fleets of war vessels, but a navy could not be used in the same manner as an army stationed in inland garrisons to overawe subjects or to stifle incipient revolutions. France, on the other hand, like most continental nations, faced almost constant threats of invasion. France's northeastern and eastern frontiers were poorly protected by geographic barriers and had been penetrated several times. As a result, it was easy for French kings to argue the need for massive armies of professional soldiers. And such troops could readily be utilized to nip domestic disturbances in the bud. It would doubtless be a mistake to give all of the credit to this difference in geographic position for the longer persistence of absolute government in France, but it was certainly a major factor.

The origins of absolutism in France

The growth of royal absolutism in France was the product of a gradual evolution. The most important antecedents were medieval. By 1300 the French kings were perfecting an efficient bureaucratic system of government. By 1450, largely owing to the results of the Hundred Years' War, they had introduced a standing army and had gained the right to collect national taxes. And by 1500 they had reduced regional separatism and the opposition of the provincial nobility. As royal power grew, the nobles were gradually reduced to the level of courtiers, dependent mainly upon the monarch for their titles and prestige. In the reign of Francis I (1515–1547) the crown became even stronger because it gained new control over ecclesiastics. By the Concordat of Bologna, an agreement struck with the papacy in 1516, the king gained the right to choose all French bishops and abbots. Although the pope was granted the first year's income from each new appointment, the agreement greatly favored the monarchy because it virtually conceded to it full political authority over the French Church.

The trend toward absolutism was interrupted during the sixteenth century when France was involved in a war with Spain and torn by a bloody struggle between Catholics and Huguenots at home. Ambitious nobles took advantage of the confusion to assert their power and contested the succession to the throne. Peace was restored to the exhausted kingdom in 1593 by Henry of Navarre (1589–1610), who four years before had proclaimed himself king as Henry IV. He was the founder of the Bourbon dynasty. Though at one time a leader of the Huguenot faction, Henry perceived that the nation would never accept him unless he renounced the Calvinist religion. Flippantly remarking that Paris was worth a Mass, he formally adopted the Catholic faith. In 1598 he issued the Edict of Nantes, guaranteeing freedom of conscience and political rights to all Protestants. With the grounds for religious controversy thus removed, Henry could turn his attention to rebuilding his kingdom. In this work, he had the able assistance of his chief minister, the duke of Sully. Grim, energetic, and penurious, Sully was a worthy forerunner of Colbert in the seventeenth century. For years the king and his faithful servant labored to repair the shattered fortunes of France. Sully devoted his efforts primarily to fiscal reform, so as to eliminate corruption and waste and bring more revenue into the royal treasury. He endeavored also to promote the prosperity of agriculture by draining swamps, improving devastated lands, subsidizing stock-raising, and opening up foreign markets for the products of the soil. The king gave most of his attention to fostering industry and commerce. He introduced the manufacture of silk into France, encouraged other industries by subsidies and monopolies, and made favorable commercial treaties with England and Spain. But Henry did not stop with economic reforms. He was deeply concerned with crushing the reborn power of the nobility, and so successful were his efforts in this direction that he restored the monarchy to the dominant position it had held under Francis I. He was active also in sponsoring the development of a colonial empire in America. During his reign the French acquired a foothold in Canada and began their exploration in the region of the Great Lakes and the Mississippi Valley. In short, his rule was intelligent and benevolent.

The reign of Henry IV was brought to an end by the dagger of a fa-

Francis I of France

*Henry IV and the duke
of Sully*

The Assassination of Henry IV. This contemporary engraving shows Ravaillac climbing on the wheel of Henry's carriage in order to stab the French ruler.

Cardinal Richelieu

natic in 1610. Since the new king, Louis XIII, was only nine years old, the country was ruled by his mother, Marie de'Medici, as regent. In 1624 Louis XIII, no longer under the regency, entrusted the management of his kingdom to a brilliant but domineering cleric, Cardinal Richelieu, whom he made his chief minister. Richelieu dedicated himself to two objectives: (1) to destroy all limitations upon the authority of the king; and (2) to make France the chief power in Europe. In the pursuit of these aims he allowed nothing to stand in his way. He ruthlessly suppressed the nobility, destroying its most dangerous members and rendering the others harmless by attaching them as pensioners to the royal court. Though he fostered education and patronized literature, he neglected the interests of commerce and allowed graft and extravagance to flourish in the government. His main constructive achievements were the creation of a postal service and the establishment of a system under which *intendants,* or agents of the king, took charge of local government. Both were conceived as devices for consolidating the nation under the control of the crown, thereby eradicating surviving traces of independent local authority.

Richelieu's foreign policy

Richelieu's ambitions were not limited to domestic affairs. To make France the most powerful nation in Europe it was necessary to pursue an aggressive diplomacy and eventually to enter into war. France was still surrounded by what Henry IV had referred to as a "Hapsburg ring." On its southern border was Spain, ruled since 1516 by a branch of the Hapsburg family. To the north, less than a hundred miles from Paris, were the Spanish Netherlands. Other centers of Hapsburg power included Luxemburg, the Franche-Comté, and Milan, and still farther to the east the great Austrian Empire itself (see map, p. 665 above). Cardinal Richelieu eagerly awaited an opportunity to break this ring. As we shall see, he finally found it in the Thirty Years' War. Though engaged in suppressing Protestants at home, he did not hesitate to ally himself with Gustavus Adolphus, king of Sweden and leader of a coalition of Protestant states. Long before his death in 1642 the great cardinal-statesman had forged to the front as the most powerful individual in Europe.

Absolute monarchy in France attained its zenith during the reigns of the last three Bourbon kings before the French Revolution. The first of the rulers of this series was Louis XIV (1643–1715), known as the "Grand Monarch," who epitomized the ideal of absolutism more completely than any other sovereign of his age. Proud, extravagant, and domineering, Louis entertained the most exalted notions of his position as king. Not only did he believe that he was commissioned by God to reign, but he also regarded the welfare of the state as intimately bound up with his own personality. The famous phrase imputed to him, *l'état c'est moi* (I am the state), may not represent his exact words, but it expresses very clearly the conception he held of his own authority. He chose the sun as his official emblem to indicate his belief that the nation derived its glory and sustenance from him as the planets do theirs from the actual sun. He gave personal supervision to every department and regarded his ministers as mere clerks with no duty but to obey his orders. In general, he followed the policies of Henry IV and Richelieu in consolidating national power at the expense of local officials and in trying to reduce the nobles to mere parasites of the court. But any possible good he may have done was completely overshadowed by his extravagant wars and his reactionary policy in religion. In 1685 he revoked the Edict of Nantes, which had granted freedom of conscience to the Huguenots. As a result, numbers of his most inventive and prosperous subjects fled the country.

Until the beginning of the revolution in 1789 the form of the French government remained essentially as Louis XIV had left it. His successors, Louis XV (1715–1774) and Louis XVI (1774–1792), also claimed to rule by divine right. But neither of these kings had the desire to emulate the Grand Monarch in his enthusiasm for work and his meticulous attention to the business of state. Louis XV was lazy and incompetent and allowed himself to be dominated by a succession of mistresses. Problems of government bored him, and when obliged to preside at the council table he "opened his mouth, said little, and thought not at all." His grandson, the ill-fated Louis XVI, was weak in character and mentally dull. Indifferent to politics, he amused himself by shooting deer from the palace window and playing at his hobbies of lock-making and masonry. On July 14, 1789 when mobs stormed the Bastille, he wrote in his diary "Nothing." Yet both of these monarchs maintained a government which was more arbitrary

Cardinal Richelieu

Louis XIV, the supreme incarnation of absolute rule

Louis XIV by Rigaud

Philip II of Spain. This painting by Coello shows the famous protruding chin and lower lip which were characteristic features of the Hapsburg family.

Absolutism in Spain

Philip II

than had ever been the case before. They permitted their ministers to imprison without a trial persons suspected of disloyalty; they suppressed the courts for refusing to approve their decrees; and they brought the country to the verge of bankruptcy by their costly wars and by their reckless extravagance for the benefit of their mistresses and favorites. If they had deliberately planned to provoke revolution, they could scarcely have succeeded better.

The growth of absolute monarchy in Spain was less interrupted than was true in France. As we have seen in Chapter 13, by 1500 Ferdinand and Isabella had united Spain and made it a very powerful kingdom. In 1516 the realm was inherited by their grandson Charles I, whose father had been a Hapsburg. Three years later Charles was elected Holy Roman Emperor as Charles V, thereby uniting Spain with central Europe and southern Italy. Charles was interested not merely in the destinies of Spain but in the welfare of the Church and in the politics of Europe as a whole. He dreamed that he might be the instrument of restoring the religious unity of Christendom, broken by the Protestant Revolution, and of making the empire over which he presided a worthy successor of imperial Rome. Though successful in holding his disjointed domain together and in fighting off attempts of the French to conquer his Italian possessions and of the Turks to overrun Europe, he failed in the achievement of his larger objectives. At the age of fifty-six, overcome with a sense of discouragement and futility, he abdicated and retired to a monastery. The German princes chose his brother, Ferdinand I, to succeed him as Holy Roman Emperor. His Spanish and Italian possessions, including the colonies overseas, passed to his son, who became king as Philip II (1556–1598).

Philip II came to the throne of Spain at the height of its glory. But he also witnessed, and to a considerable extent was responsible for, the beginning of its decline. His policies were mainly an intensification of those of his predecessors. He was narrow, despotic, and cruel. Determined to enforce a strict conformity in matters of religion upon all of his subjects, he is reputed to have boasted that he would gather faggots to burn his own son if the latter were guilty of heresy. Therefore, he encouraged the ruthlessness of the Spanish Inquisition and launched the war for suppression of the religious revolt in the Netherlands. Philip was equally shortsighted in his colonial policy. Indigenous peoples were butchered and their territories greedily despoiled of their gold and silver, which were dragged off to Spain in the mistaken belief that this was the surest means of increasing the nation's wealth. No thought was given to the development of new industries in either the colonies or the mother country. Instead, the gold and silver were largely squandered in furthering Philip's military and political ambitions. It can be said, however, in the king's defense that he was following the accepted theories of the time. Doubtless most other monarchs with a like opportunity would have imitated his example.

The Escorial. Built in the sixteenth century by Philip II of Spain, this palace originally served as his retreat.

Philip II's crowning mistake was his war against England. Angered by the attacks of English ships upon Spanish commerce and frustrated in his schemes to bring England back into the Catholic faith, he sent a great fleet in 1588, the "Invincible Armada," to destroy Queen Elizabeth's navy. But Philip had little knowledge of either the new techniques of naval warfare or of the robust patriotism of the English. A combination of fighting seamanship and disastrous storms (the "Protestant Wind") sent many of his 130 ships to the bottom of the Channel and the rest back home in disarray. Spain never recovered from the blow. Though a brilliant cultural afterglow, exemplified the work of great writers and artists like Cervantes and Velasquez, continued for some years, the greatness of Spain as a nation was approaching its end.

The Armada

3. ABSOLUTISM IN CENTRAL EUROPE

The chief countries in central Europe where absolutism flourished most were Prussia and Austria. The founder of absolute rule in Prussia (a state made up primarily of Brandenburg, in north-central Germany, and Prussia, far to the east, near Russia) was the Great Elector, Frederick William, who ruled from 1640 to 1688. He was the first member of the Hohenzollern family to acquire full sovereignty over Prussia and to introduce a standing army. In addition, he began to bring all his dominions under centralized rule. The work of the Great Elector was continued and extended by his grandson, known as Frederick William I (1713–1740), since he now had the title of *king* of Prussia. Frederick William's major concerns were to build up the Prussian bureaucracy and the Prussian army. His bureaucratic officials ran Prussia extremely efficiently and at such small expense that Prussia

Frederick William I of Prussia

Frederick William I

Frederick the Great

*Absolutism in Austria:
Maria Theresa and
Joseph II*

was the only continental state in the middle of the eighteenth century with a budgetary surplus, even though the country had very limited natural resources. But Frederick William's really consuming passion was his army. This he more than doubled in size and drilled to a machinelike efficiency. Since he could hardly count on volunteers, he introduced conscription and supplemented that by sending gangs of kidnappers to drag back forced recruits from neighboring German lands. Frederick William had a strange love for particularly tall soldiers: his own private regiment of "Potsdam Giants" was comprised exclusively of soldiers over six feet in height. The king traded musicians and prize stallions for such choice specimens and then spent the bulk of his time marching his "giants" around his palace grounds.

The style but not the substance of Frederick William's militarism was altered by his noted successor, Frederick II (1740–1786), commonly known as Frederick the Great. An earnest disciple of the reformist doctrines of the new rationalist philosophy, Frederick was the leading figure among the "enlightened despots" of the eighteenth century. Declaring himself not the master but merely the "first servant of the state," he wrote essays to prove that Machiavelli was wrong and rose at five in the morning to begin a Spartan routine of personal management of public affairs. He made Prussia in many ways the best-governed state in Europe, abolishing torture of accused criminals and bribery of judges, establishing elementary schools, and promoting the prosperity of industry and agriculture. He fostered scientific forestry and the cultivation of new crops such as the potato. He opened up new lands in Silesia and brought in thousands of immigrants to cultivate them. When wars ruined their farms, he supplied the peasants with new livestock and tools. As an admirer of the French philosopher Voltaire, whom he entertained for some time at his court, he tolerated all sorts of religious beliefs. He declared that he would build a mosque in Berlin if enough Muslims wished to locate there. Yet he was strongly anti-Semitic. He levied special taxes on the Jews and made efforts to close the professions and the civil service to them. Moreover, Frederick continued to invest heavily in his army, and such benevolence as he showed in internal affairs was not carried over into foreign relations. Frederick robbed Austria of Silesia, conspired with Catherine of Russia to dismember Poland, and contributed at least his full share to the bloody wars of the eighteenth century.

The full bloom of absolutism in Austria came during the reigns of Maria Theresa (1740–1780) and Joseph II (1780–1790). Maria Theresa was one of the most capable of all eighteenth-century monarchs. She played the role of a flighty woman when it suited her advantage, but actually ruled with great common sense and determination. During her reign a national army was established, the powers of the Church were curtailed in the interest of consolidated government, and elementary and higher education was greatly expanded. Unlike the rulers of most other countries, Maria Theresa was sincerely devoted to Christian morality. Though she participated in the dismemberment of Poland to make up for the loss of Silesia, she did so with grave misgivings—an attitude which prompted the scornful remark of Frederick the Great: "She weeps, but she takes her share." The reforms of Maria Theresa were extended, at least on paper, by her son Joseph II. Inspired by the teachings of French philosophers, Joseph determined to remake his empire in accordance with the highest ideals of justice and reason. Not only did he plan to reduce the powers of the Church by confiscating its lands and abolishing monasteries, but he aspired to humble the nobles and improve the condition of the masses. He decreed that serfs should become free and promised to relieve them of the obligations owed to their masters. He aimed to make education universal and to force the nobles to pay their proper share of taxes. But most of his magnificent plans ended in failure. He antagonized not merely the nobles and clergy but also the Hungarians, who were deprived of all rights of self-government. He alienated the sympathies of the peasants by making them liable to compulsory military service. He was scarcely any more willing than Louis XIV or Frederick the Great to sacrifice personal power and national glory even for the sake of his lofty ideals.

Maria Theresa of Austria

4. ABSOLUTISM IN RUSSIA

Russia at the beginning of the early modern age was a composite of European and Oriental characteristics. Much of its territory had been colonized by the Norsemen in the early Middle Ages. The Russian religion, calendar, and system of writing had been derived from Byzantium. Even the governing regime, with its boyars, or magnates, and serfs, was not greatly dissimilar to that of western Europe. On the other hand, much of Russia's culture, and many of its customs, were distinctly not European. Russian arts were limited almost entirely to icon painting and religious architecture, characterized by the onion dome. There was practically no literature in the Russian language, arithmetic was barely known, Arabic numerals were not used, and merchants made their calculations with the abacus. Nor were manners and customs comparable to those of the West. Women of the upper classes were veiled and secluded. Flowing beards and skirted garments were universal for men. Table manners were considered superfluous. Seasons of wild revelry alternated with periods of repentance and morbid atonement. It would be a mistake, however, to suppose that Russia was totally cut off from Europe. As early as the fourteenth century, German merchants of the Hanseatic League conducted some trade in Russian furs and amber. In the 1550s English merchants discovered the White Sea and made Archangel a port of entry through

Russia at the beginning of the modern age

which military supplies could be exchanged for a few Russian goods and even products from Persia and China. But with Archangel frozen most of the year, the volume of this trade was undoubtedly small.

As late as the thirteenth century Russia was a collection of small principalities. They were attacked from the west by Lithuanians, Poles, and the Teutonic Knights. The last were members of one of several religious and military organizations that sprang from the Crusades. Established originally for charitable purposes, their order developed into a military one which adopted as its mission the conversion and conquest of lands on Germany's eastern frontier. The operations of the Teutonic Knights were part of the famous *Drang nach Osten* (Drive to the East) which occupied such a prominent place in German history. From the east Russia was threatened by the Mongols (Tartars), who had established a great empire in central Asia, eventually including both northern India and China. In 1237 the Mongols began an invasion which led to their conquest of nearly all of Russia. Mongol rule was in several ways a disaster. It marked the development of a stronger Asiatic orientation. Henceforth Russia turned more and more away from Europe and looked beyond the Urals as the arena of its future development. Its inhabitants intermarried with Mongols and adopted some elements of their way of life.

Eventually, Mongol power declined. In 1380 a Russian army defeated the Mongols and thus initiated a movement to drive them back into Asia. The state which assumed the leadership of this movement was the Grand Duchy of Moscow. Under strong rulers it had been increasing its power for some time. Located near the sources of the great rivers flowing both north and south, it had geographic advantages surpassing those of the other states. Moreover, it had recently been made the headquarters of the Russian Church. The first of the princes of Moscow to put himself forward as tsar (caesar) of Russia was Ivan the Great (1462–1505). Taking as his bride the niece of the last of the Byzantine emperors, who had perished in the capture of Constantinople in 1453, he proclaimed himself his successor by the grace of God. He adopted as his insignia the Byzantine double-headed eagle and imported Italian architects to work on an enormous building complex, the Kremlin, in demonstration of Russia's new independence and greatness. Avowing his intention to recover the ancient lands that had been lost to foreign invaders, Ivan forced the prince of Lithuania to acknowledge him as sovereign of "all the Russias" and pushed the Tartars out of northern Russia and beyond the Urals.

The first of the tsars to attempt the Europeanization of Russia was Peter the Great (1682–1725). He stands out as the most powerful and probably the most intelligent autocrat yet to occupy the Russian throne. With a reckless disregard for ancient customs, Peter endeavored to force his subjects to change their ways of living. He forbade the Oriental seclusion of women and commanded both sexes to adopt European styles of dress. He made the use of tobacco compul-

Peter the Great. An eighteenth-century mosaic.

sory among the members of his court. He summoned the great nobles before him and clipped their flowing beards with his own hand. In order to make sure of his own absolute power, he abolished all traces of local self-government and established a system of national police. For the same reason, he annihilated the authority of the patriarch of the Orthodox church and placed all religious affairs under a Holy Synod subject to his own control. Deeply interested in Western technology, he made journeys to Holland and England to learn about shipbuilding and industry. He imitated the mercantilist policies of Western nations by improving agriculture and fostering manufactures and commerce. In order to get "windows to the west" he conquered territory along the Baltic shore and transferred his capital from Moscow to St. Petersburg, his new city at the mouth of the Neva river. But the good that he did was greatly outweighed by his extravagant wars and his fiendish cruelty. He put thousands to death for alleged conspiracies against him. He murdered his own son and heir because the latter boasted that when *he* became tsar he would return Russia to the ways of its fathers. To raise money for his expensive wars he debased the currency, sold valuable concessions to foreigners, established government monopolies on the production of salt, oil, caviar, and coffins, and imposed taxes on almost everything, from baths to beehives.

The significance of Peter the Great is not easy to evaluate. He did not singlehandedly transform Russia into a Western nation. Western influences had been seeping into the country as a consequence of trade contacts for many years. But Peter accelerated the process and gave it a more radical direction. Evidence abounds that he really did aim to

Peter the Great

Results of Peter's reign

Peter the Great's Execution of Conspirators. This contemporary print shows scores of corpses gibbeted outside the walls of the Kremlin. Peter kept the rotting bodies on display for months to discourage his subjects from opposing his efforts to westernize Russian society.

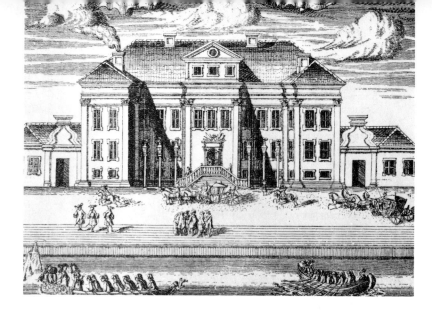

The Winter Palace. This contemporary engraving shows the palace built by Peter the Great in the town that bore his name, St. Petersburg.

remake the nation and to give it at least a veneer of cultivation. He sent many of his countrymen abroad to study. He simplified the ancient alphabet and established the first newspaper to be published in Russia. He ordered the publication of a book on polite behavior, teaching his subjects not to spit on the floor or to scratch themselves or gnaw bones at dinner. He encouraged exports, built a fleet on the Baltic, and fostered new industries such as textiles and mining. Though a reaction set in after Peter's death against many of his innovations, some of them survived for at least two centuries. The Church, for example, continued as essentially an arm of the stage, governed by a procurator of the Holy Synod appointed by the tsar himself. Serfdom continued in the extended forms required or authorized by Peter. No longer were serfs bound to the soil; they could be bought and sold at any time, even for work in factories and mines. Finally, the absolutism developed by Peter showed few signs of abating until the early twentieth century. It was an absolutism based upon force, with a secret police, an extensive bureaucracy, and a subordinated Church as instruments for imposing the autocrat's will.

Catherine the Great

The other most noted of the Russian monarchs in the age of absolutism was Catherine the Great (1762–1796), who before her marriage was a German princess. Frequently classified as one of the "enlightened despots," Catherine corresponded with French philosophers, founded hospitals and orphanages, and expressed the hope that someday the serfs might be liberated. Ambitious to gain for herself a place in intellectual history, she rose at five in the morning to engage in scholarship. She wrote plays, published a digest of Blackstone's *Commentaries on the Laws of England,* and even began a history of Russia. Her accomplishments as a reformer, however, had only a limited scope. She took steps toward a codification of the Russian laws, restricted the use of torture, and remodeled and consolidated local government. Any plans she may have had, however, for improving the lot of the peasants were abruptly canceled after a violent serf rebellion in 1773–1774. Landlords and priests were murdered and the ruling classes terrified as the revolt swept through the Urals and the valley of the Volga. Catherine responded with stern repression. The captured leader of the peasants was drawn and quartered, and, as a guaranty against future outbreaks, the nobles were given increased powers over their serfs. They were permitted to deal with them virtually as if they were chattel slaves. Catherine's chief significance lies in the fact that she continued the work of Peter the Great in introducing Russia to Western ideas and in making the country a formidable power in European affairs. She managed to extend the boundaries of her country to include not only eastern Poland but lands on the Black Sea.

Catherine the Great

5. THE WARS OF THE EARLY MODERN PERIOD

Between 1500 and 1789 the years of peace in Europe were outnumbered by the years of war. The earlier conflicts were largely religious in character and have already been dealt with in Chapter 15. The majority of the wars after 1600 partook of the nature of struggles for supremacy among the powerful autocrats of the principal countries. But religion was also a factor in some of them, and so was the greed of the commercial classes. In general, nationalistic motives were much less important than in the wars of the nineteenth and twentieth centuries. Peoples and territories were so many pawns to be moved back and forth in the game of dynastic aggrandizement.

Character of the wars in the age of absolutism for the despots

The major warfare of the seventeenth century revolved around a titanic duel between Hapsburgs and Bourbons. Originally the rulers of Austria, the Hapsburgs had gradually extended their power over Hungary and Bohemia as well. In addition, the head of the family enjoyed what was left of the distinction of being Holy Roman Emperor. Since the time of Charles V (1519–1556) branches of the Hapsburgs had ruled over Spain, the Netherlands, the Franche-Comté, Milan, and the Kingdom of the Two Sicilies. For many years this expansion of Hapsburg power had been a source of profound disturbance to the rulers of France. They regarded their country as encircled, and longed to break through the enclosing ring. But tensions were building up in other parts of Europe also. The princes of Germany looked with alarm upon the growing power of the Holy Roman Emperor and sought opportunities to restrict him in ways that would increase their own stature. The kings of Denmark and Sweden were also developing expansionist ambitions, which could hardly be realized except at the expense of the Hapsburg Empire. Finally, the seeds of religious conflict, sown by the Reformation, were about ready to germinate in a new crop of hostilities. In 1608–1609 two opposing alliances had been formed, based upon principles of religious antagonism. The existence of these mutually hostile leagues added to the tension in central Europe and

Underlying causes of conflict

The Thirty Years' War

contributed toward making an eventual explosion almost a certainty. The conflict that followed, known as the Thirty Years' War (1618–1648), was one of the most tragic in history.

The immediate cause of the Thirty Years' War was an attempt of the Holy Roman Emperor, Matthias, to consolidate his power in Bohemia. Though the Hapsburgs had been overlords of Bohemia for a century, the Czech inhabitants of the country had retained their own king. When the Bohemian throne became vacant in 1618, Matthias conspired to obtain the position for one of his relatives, Duke Ferdinand of Styria. By exerting pressure he induced the Bohemian Diet to elect Ferdinand king. The Czech leaders resented this, since both nationalist and Protestant traditions were strong in the country. The upshot was the invasion of the emperor's headquarters in Prague by Czech noblemen and the proclamation of Bohemia as an independent state with Frederick, the Calvinist Elector Palatine, as king. The war now began in earnest. The success of the Hapsburgs in suppressing the Bohemian revolt and in punishing Frederick by seizing his lands in the valley of the Rhine galvanized the Protestant rulers of northern Europe into action. Not only the German princes but King Christian IV of Denmark and Gustavus Adolphus of Sweden joined the war against Austrian aggression—with the additional purpose, of course, of expanding their own dominions. In 1630 the French intervened with donations of arms and money to the Protestant allies, and after 1632, when Gustavus Adolphus was killed in battle, France bore the brunt of the struggle. The war was no longer a religious conflict, but essentially a contest between the Bourbon and Hapsburg houses for domination of the continent of Europe. The immediate objectives of Cardinal Richelieu, who was directing affairs for Louis XIII, were to wrest parts of Germany from the Holy Roman Empire and to weaken

Two Artistic Broadsides from the Thirty Years' War. On the left the German peasantry is ridden by the soldiery; on the right is an allegorical representation of "the monstrous beast of war."

A Swearing of Oaths at the Peace of Westphalia, 1648

the hold of the Spanish Hapsburgs on the Netherlands. For a time the French armies suffered reverses, but the organizing genius of Richelieu and of Cardinal Mazarin, who succeeded him in 1648, ultimately brought victory to France and its allies. Peace was restored to a distracted Europe by the Treaty of Westphalia in 1648.

Most of the results of the Thirty Years' War were unmitigated evils. By the Treaty of Westphalia France was confirmed in the possession of formerly German territories in Lorraine and Alsace. Sweden also received territory in Germany; the independence of Holland and Switzerland was formally acknowledged, and the Holy Roman Empire was reduced to a complete fiction, since each of the German princes was now recognized as a sovereign ruler with power to make war and peace and to govern his state as he chose. But most of these changes merely laid the foundations for bitter international squabbles in the future. In addition, the war wrought terrible havoc in central Europe. Probably few military conflicts since the dawn of history had caused so much misery to the civilian population. It is estimated that fully one-third of the people in Germany and Bohemia lost their lives as a consequence of famine and disease and the marauding attacks of brutal soldiers. The armies of both sides pillaged, tortured, burned, and killed in such manner as to convert whole regions into veritable desert. In Saxony one-third of the land went out of cultivation, and packs of wolves roamed through areas where thriving villages once had stood. In the midst of such misery, intellectual achievement of every description was bound to decline, with the result that civilization in Germany was retarded by at least a century. Nonetheless, the settlement of 1648 put an end to religious warfare in Europe for all time and initiated a half-century of comparative peace.

In 1700 the French king saw what appeared to be a new opportunity for expanding Bourbon power. In that year Charles II, king of Spain,

Results of the Thirty Years' War

died with neither children nor brothers to succeed him, and willed his dominion to the grandson of Louis XIV. The Austrians denounced this settlement, and formed a new alliance with England, Holland, and Brandenburg. The War of the Spanish Succession, which broke out in 1702 when Louis attempted to enforce the claim of his grandson, was the last important stage in the struggle between Bourbons and Hapsburgs.[1] By the Peace of Utrecht (1713–1714) the grandson of Louis XIV was permitted to occupy the Spanish throne, on condition that France and Spain should never be united. Nova Scotia and Newfoundland were transferred to England from France, and Gibraltar from Spain. The Belgian Netherlands, the Kingdom of the Two Sicilies, and Milan were given to the Austrian Hapsburgs.

It would be difficult to exaggerate the significance of the War of the Spanish Succession. Since it involved most of the nations of Europe and also lands overseas, it was the first of what can be called "world wars." It was fought, however, not by mass armies but chiefly by professional soldiers. It was the prototype, therefore, of most of the wars of the eighteenth century. These were wars between kings, in which the masses of the people were involved only indirectly. Among large-scale conflicts the War of the Spanish Succession was the first in which religion played almost no part. Secular rivalries over commerce and sea power were the major bones of contention. The war put an end to the claims of the smaller states to rank equally with their larger neighbors. Brandenburg and Savoy were the only important exceptions. The first came to be called Prussia and the second, Sardinia. Aside from Sardinia, the rest of the Italian states dwindled into insignificance, and Prussia started to play an important role on the German scene. Holland suffered such a strain from the war that it ceased to be a prime factor in the competition for world power. With a Bourbon king on the throne, Spain was reduced to subservience to France. The Spanish Bourbon dynasty continued to rule, with brief interruptions, until the overthrow of Alphonso XIII in 1931, and the dynasty has returned to Spain since 1975. The War of the Spanish Succession left France and Great Britain as the two major powers in Europe. Of these, the latter was the principal victor. Not only did it acquire valuable possessions, but the British muscled their way into the Spanish commercial empire. By an agreement known as the Asiento, Britain gained the privilege of providing Spanish America with African slaves. This privilege opened the way to the smuggling of all kinds of goods into the Spanish colonies, and contributed toward making Great Britain the richest nation on earth.

The most important of the wars between the War of the Spanish

---

[1] The War of the Austrian Succession (1740–1748), in which France fought on the side of Prussia against Great Britain and Austria, also involved a struggle between Bourbons and Hapsburgs. But the results for France were indecisive: the war was mainly a duel between Prussia and Austria.

Succession and the French Revolution was the Seven Years' War (1756–1763), known in American history as the French and Indian War. The causes of this struggle were closely related to some of the earlier conflicts already discussed. A chief factor in several of these wars had been commercial rivalry between England and France. Each had been striving for supremacy in the development of overseas trade and colonial empires. The Seven Years' War was simply the climax of a struggle which had been going on for nearly a century. Hostilities began, appropriately enough, in America as the result of a dispute over possession of the Ohio valley. Soon the whole question of British or French domination of the North American continent was involved. Eventually, nearly every major country of Europe was drawn in on one side or the other. Louis XV of France enlisted the aid of his relative, the Bourbon king of Spain. A struggle begun in 1740 between Frederick the Great of Prussia and Maria Theresa of Austria over possession of Silesia was quickly merged with the larger contest. The Seven Years' War thus reached the proportions of what virtually amounted to another world conflict, with France, Spain, Austria, and Russia arrayed against Great Britain and Prussia in Europe, and with English and French colonial forces striving for mastery not only in America but also in India.

The Seven Years' War

The outcome of the Seven Years' War was exceedingly significant for the later history of Europe. Frederick the Great won a decisive victory over the Austrians and forced Maria Theresa to surrender all claims to Silesia. The acquisition of this territory increased the area of Prussia by more than a third, thereby raising the Hohenzollern kingdom to the status of a first-rank power. In the struggle for colonial supremacy, the British emerged with a sensational triumph. Of their once magnificent empire in America, the French lost all but two tiny islands off the coast of Newfoundland, Guadeloupe and a few other possessions in the West Indies, and a portion of Guiana in South America. All of the territory given up by the French was acquired by Great Britain, with the exception of Louisiana, which France turned over to Spain as a reward for its part in the war. France was allowed to retain its trading privileges in India, but was forbidden to build any forts or maintain any troops in that country. France's treasury was now depleted, its trade almost ruined, and its chances of dominance on the Continent badly shattered. These disasters, brought on by the stupid policies of the French kings, had much to do with preparing the ground for the revolution of 1789. By contrast, Britain was now riding the crest of the wave—in a literal as well as figurative sense, for its triumph in the Seven Years' War was a milestone in its struggle for supremacy on the seas. The wealth from its expanded trade enriched British merchants, thereby enhancing their prestige in political and social affairs. But perhaps most important of all, its victory in the struggle for colonies gave England an abundance of raw materials which enabled it to take the lead in the Industrial Revolution.

Results of the Seven Years' War

6. THE POLITICAL THEORY OF ABSOLUTISM

The influence of political philosophers in buttressing absolute rule

Jean Bodin

The autocratic behavior of the rulers of the sixteenth, seventeenth, and eighteenth centuries was sanctioned by the influence of political theory. Several of the Stuart and Bourbon kings, for example, derived justification for their policies from philosophers who expressed the prevailing ideas of their time in systematic and forceful writings.

One of the first of the philosophers to lend encouragement to the absolutist ambitions of monarchs was the Frenchman Jean Bodin (1530–1596). He agreed with the medieval philosophers that rulers were bound by the law of God, and he acknowledged that the prince had a moral duty to respect the treaties he had signed. But Bodin had no use for parliaments of any description. He emphatically denied the right of a legislative body to impose any limits upon royal power. And while he admitted that princes who violated the divine law or the law of nature were tyrants, he refused to concede that their subjects had any right of rebellion against them. The authority of the prince is from God, and the supreme obligation of the people is passive obedience. Revolution must be avoided at all costs, for it destroys that stability which is a necessary condition for progress. The main contribution of Bodin, if such it can be called, was his doctrine of sovereignty, which he defined as "supreme power over citizens and subjects, unrestrained by the laws." By this he meant that the prince, who is the only sovereign, is not bound by manmade laws. There is no *legal* restriction upon his authority whatever—nothing except obedience to the natural or moral law ordained by God.

The most noted of all the apostles of absolute government was Thomas Hobbes (1588–1679). Writing during and after the English Civil War and in close association with the royalists, Hobbes was disgusted with the turn which events had taken in England and longed for a revival of the monarchy. However, his materialism and his doctrine of the secular origin of the kingship made him none too popular with the Stuarts. For the title of his chief work Hobbes chose the name *Leviathan,* to indicate his conception of the state as an all-powerful monster. (In the Book of Job, Leviathan is the monster that ruled over the primeval chaos.) All associations within the state, he declared, are mere "worms in the entrails of Leviathan." The essence of Hobbes's political philosophy is directly related to his theory of the origin of government. He taught that in the beginning all human beings lived in a state of nature, subject to no law but brutal self-interest. Far from being a paradise of innocence and bliss, the state of nature was a condition of universal misery. As Hobbes said, "man is a wolf toward man." Life for the individual was "solitary, poor, nasty, brutish, and short." In order to escape from this war of each against all, people eventually united with one another to form a civil society. They drew

The Title Page of Hobbes's *Leviathan*

up a contract surrendering all of their rights to a sovereign, who would be strong enough to protect his subjects from violence. Thus the sovereign, while not a party to the contract, was made the recipient of absolute authority. The people gave up *everything* for the one great blessing of security. In contrast with Bodin, Hobbes did not recognize any law of nature or of God as a limitation upon the authority of the prince. Absolute government, he maintained, had been established by the people themselves, and therefore they would have no ground for complaint if their ruler became a tyrant. On the basis of pure deduction, without any appeal to religion or history, Hobbes arrived at the conclusion that the king is entitled to rule despotically—not because he has been appointed by God, but because the people have *given* him absolute power.

In a sense, the great Dutchman Hugo Grotius (1583–1645) may also be considered an exponent of absolutism; though with him the question of power within the state was more or less incidental to the larger question of relations among states. Living during the period of the revolt of the Netherlands and the Thirty Years' War, Grotius was impressed by the need for a body of rules that would reduce the dealings of governments with one another to a pattern of reason and order. He wrote his famous *Law of War and Peace* to prove that the principles of elemental justice and morality ought to prevail among nations. Some of these principles he derived from the Roman "law of peoples" and some from the medieval law of nature. So well did he present his case that he has been regarded ever since as one of the chief founders of international law. Grotius's revulsion against turbulence also inspired him to advocate absolutist government. He did not see how order could be preserved within the state unless the ruler possessed unlimited authority. He maintained that in the beginning the people had either surrendered to a ruler voluntarily or had been compelled to submit to superior force; but in either case, having once established a government, they were bound to obey it unquestioningly forever.

The theories just discussed were not simply those of a few isolated philosophers, but rather the widely accepted ideas of an age when order and security were considered more important than liberty. They reflected the desire of the commercial classes, especially, for the utmost degree of stability and protection in the interest of business. Mercantilism and the policies of rulers went hand in hand with the new theories of absolutism. The dictum, "I am the state," attributed to Louis XIV, was not just the brazen boast of a tyrant, but came close to expressing the prevailing conception of government in continental Europe. Those who had a stake in society really believed that the monarch *was* the state. They could hardly conceive of a government able to protect and assist their economic activities except in terms of centralized and unbridled authority. Their attitude was not so far dif-

*The significance of
philosophers' attempts to
justify absolutism*

ferent from that of some people today who believe that a dictatorship of one form or another is the only means for security and plenty.

7. SIGNIFICANCE OF THE AGE OF ABSOLUTISM

The age of absolutism was important not merely for the establishment of absolute monarchies. It bears even greater significance for its effects upon international relations. It was during this period that the modern state system came into existence. During the era of approximately a thousand years after the fall of Rome, states, in the sense in which we now understand the term, scarcely existed in Europe west of the Byzantine Empire. True, there were kings in England and France, but until almost the end of the Middle Ages, their relations with their subjects were essentially those of lords with their vassals. They had *dominium* but not sovereignty. In other words, they had the highest proprietary rights over the lands which constituted their fiefs; they did not necessarily possess supreme political authority over all the persons who lived on their lands. Only through extension of the taxing power, the judicial power, and the establishment of professional armies, did medieval rulers take steps toward becoming sovereigns in the modern sense.

Some historians consider the beginnings of the modern state system to date from the invasion of Italy in 1494 by King Charles VIII of France. Involved in this war for conquest of foreign territory were considerations of dynastic prestige, the balance of power, elaborate diplomacy, and alliances and counteralliances. It was in no sense a religious or ideological war but a struggle for power and territorial aggrandizement. Other historians conceive of the Reformation as the primary cause of the modern state system. The Protestant Revolution broke the unity of Western Christendom. It facilitated the determination of kings and princes to make their own power complete by repudiating the authority of a universal Church. As early as 1555 the Peace of Augsburg gave to each German prince the right to decide whether Lutheranism or Catholicism should be the faith of his people. It was probably the Treaty of Westphalia, however, that played the dominant role in making the modern state system a political reality. This treaty, which ended the Thirty Years' War in 1648, transferred territories from one rule to another with no regard for the nationality of their inhabitants. It recognized the independence of Holland and Switzerland and reduced the Holy Roman Empire to a fiction. Each of the German princes was acknowledged as a sovereign ruler with power to make war and peace and to govern his domain as he chose. Finally, the treaty introduced the principle that *all* states, regardless of their size or power, were equal under international law and endowed with full and complete control over their territories and inhabitants.

Beginnings of the modern state system

Causes of the rise of the state system

Whatever its origins, the modern state system may be considered to embody the following elements: (1) the legal equality and independence of all states; (2) the right of each state to pursue a foreign policy of its own making, to form alliances and counteralliances, and to wage war for its own advantage; (3) the use of diplomacy as a substitute for war, often involving intrigue and espionage to the extent necessary for political advantage; (4) the balance of power as a device for preventing war or for assuring the support of allies if war becomes necessary. Most of these elements of the state system have continued to the present day. Even the establishment of the League of Nations and the United Nations brought no substantial change, for both were founded upon the principle of the sovereign equality of independent states. Some observers believe that there will be no genuine prospect of world peace until the system of sovereign independent states is recognized as obsolete and is replaced by a world community of nations organized on a federal basis.

*Elements of the modern
state system*

SELECTED READINGS

• *Items so designated are available in paperback editions.*

Ashton, Robert, *The English Civil War: Conservatism and Revolution, 1603–1649,* New York, 1978.

• Birn, Raymond, *Crisis, Absolutism, Revolution: Europe, 1648–1789/91,* Hinsdale, Ill., 1977. A good college-level survey for the second half of the period covered in this chapter.

Carsten, F. L., *The Origins of Prussia,* London, 1954. Standard work, through the reign of the Great Elector.

Cherniavsky, M., *Tsar and People: Studies in Russian Myths,* 2nd ed., New York, 1969. Imaginative study of the symbolism of rulership.

Church, William F., *Louis XIV in Historical Thought,* New York, 1976.

Dorn, W., *The Competition for Empire, 1740–63,* New York, 1940. Excellent old-fashioned study of Europe in the mid–eighteenth century. Particularly strong on military affairs.

• Dunn, Richard S., *The Age of Religious Wars, 1559–1715,* 2nd ed., New York, 1979. The best college level text on this period. Extremely well written.

• Elliott, J. H., *Imperial Spain, 1469–1716,* London, 1963. A masterpiece of sophisticated synthesis.

Elton, G. R., *England under the Tudors,* 2nd ed., London, 1977. Engagingly written and authoritative.

Florinsky, M. T., *Russia: A History and an Interpretation,* Vol. I, New York, 1955. The best textbook on Russian history. Reviews divergent interpretations and emphasizes politics.

• Fraser, Lady Antonia, *Oliver Cromwell,* London, 1973. A popular biography.

Friedrich, Carl J., *The Age of the Baroque, 1610–1660,* New York, 1952.

• Goubert, P., *Louis XIV and Twenty Million Frenchmen,* New York, 1970.

Events of the reign seen against the background of economic and social conditions.

Hatton, Ragnhild, *Europe in the Age of Louis XIV*, London, 1969.

Holborn, H., *A History of Modern Germany: 1648–1840*, New York, 1964.

• Jones, J. R., *Britain and Europe in the Seventeenth Century*, New York, 1966.

———, *Country and Court: England, 1658–1714*, London, 1978. Now the best survey of the period surrounding the Glorious Revolution.

• ———, *The Revolution of 1688 in England*, New York, 1972.

• Mattingly, Garrett, *The Armada*, Boston, 1959. Fascinating narrative; thoroughly reliable but reads like a novel.

Nussbaum, F. L., *The Triumph of Science and Reason, 1660–1685*, New York, 1953.

• Pennington, D. H., *Seventeenth-Century Europe*, London, 1970.

• Rabb, T. K., *The Struggle for Stability in Early Modern Europe*, New York, 1975. A stimulating essay arguing for a shift from crisis to stability around 1650.

Roberts, Penfield, *The Quest for Security, 1715–1740*, New York, 1947.

• Roots, Ivan, ed., *Cromwell, A Profile*, New York, 1973. A collection of readings on problems in interpretation; complements Fraser.

• Rosenberg, Hans, *Bureaucracy, Aristocracy, and Autocracy: The Prussian Experience, 1660–1815*, Cambridge, Mass., 1958. Difficult but rewarding.

• Russell, Conrad, *The Crisis of Parliaments: English History, 1509–1660*, New York, 1971. The best survey covering this broad range of time.

Sabine, George H., *A History of Political Theory*, 3rd ed., New York, 1951. An older work, particularly good on thought of this age.

Smith, Lacey B., *Henry VIII: The Mask of Royalty*, Boston, 1971. A breathtaking interpretation of the last years of Henry VIII and the age in which he lived.

Speck, W. A., *Stability and Strife: England, 1714–1760*, Cambridge, Mass., 1977.

• Steinberg, S. H., *The Thirty Years' War and the Conflict for European Hegemony, 1600–1660*, New York, 1966. The best account.

• Stone, Lawrence, *The Causes of the English Revolution, 1529–1642*, New York, 1972.

• Sumner, B. H., *Peter the Great and the Emergence of Russia*, London, 1950. A good short introduction.

Wedgwood, C. V., *The Thirty Years' War*, London, 1938. More attention to narrative than Steinberg.

Wolf, John B., *The Emergence of the Great Powers, 1685–1715*, New York, 1951.

• ———, *Louis XIV*, New York, 1968. The standard biography in English.

SOURCE MATERIALS

Bodin, Jean, *Six Books Concerning the State*, Cambridge, 1962.

Grotius, Hugo, *The Law of War and Peace*, New York, 1963.

• Hobbes, Thomas, *Leviathan*. (Many editions.)

Chapter 22

THE INTELLECTUAL REVOLU-TION OF THE SEVENTEENTH AND EIGHTEENTH CENTURIES

We are to admit no more causes of natural things than such as are both true and sufficient to explain their appearances. To this purpose the philosophers say that nature does nothing in vain, and more is in vain when less will serve; for nature is pleased with simplicity, and affects not the pomp of superfluous cause.

—Isaac Newton, *The Mathematical Principles of Natural Philosophy*

The years which witnessed the rise of absolutism in Europe were witness, as well, to what can fairly be described as an intellectual revolution. Traditional ideas concerning God, human existence, and the universe were challenged and, to a large extent, either drastically modified or totally cast aside. In their place, philosophers and scientists constructed a new worldview, rational, mechanistic, and largely impersonal, yet at the same time humane, tolerant, and therefore understanding of both the foibles and aspirations of humanity. This intellectual revolution was rooted in the history of the Renaissance and the beginnings of the Commercial Revolution; it derived from the widened intellectual horizons and increased general prosperity that those movements had produced.

The nature of the revolution

The extraordinary galaxy of men and ideas that constitute the revolution make it worth examining in its own right. It must also be studied, however, in order to understand the origins of ideas, institutions, and movements still current today. The self-confidence that compelled men and women to examine their world critically, and the belief in progress that encouraged them to change that world—both characteristic attitudes of this revolution—in turn helped foster the French and Industrial Revolutions, and thus the modern world.

Reasons for examining the intellectual revolution

Engraved Title Page from Bacon's *Novum Organum*

René Descartes

1. THE PHILOSOPHICAL FOUNDATIONS OF THE INTELLECTUAL REVOLUTION

The progenitors of the intellectual revolution were four men: Francis Bacon, René Descartes, John Locke, and Isaac Newton. All four were willing to attack fundamental assumptions about the universe and the human mind; all four were able not only to demolish the old, but to construct new ideas and theories to replace those they had discarded. The son of an Elizabethan government official, Francis Bacon (1561–1626) was both a philosopher and an ambitious courtier, who, as lord chancellor, was sentenced to imprisonment on charges of bribery. Attention to his political career prevented his fully developing those ideas which were to be his intellectual legacy. Yet even granting their limitations, Bacon's conclusions were of immense influence in the history of modern thought. In his two most important works, *Novum Organum* (a treatise on the method of acquiring knowledge, published in 1620) and *The Advancement of Learning* (1623) he insisted upon the importance of doubting all received knowledge.

Bacon's most important contribution to philosophy was the glorification of the inductive method as the basis of accurate knowledge. He believed that all seekers of truth in the past were slaves of preconceived ideas or prisoners of Scholastic logic. He argued that the philosopher should turn to the direct observation of nature, to the accumulation of facts about things and the discovery of the laws that govern them. Induction alone, he believed, was the magic key that would unlock the secrets of knowledge. Authority, tradition, and syllogistic logic should be as sedulously avoided as the plague. Bacon also argued that the worth of any idea depended on its usefulness. The ideas generated and debated by medieval scholastics were, in his opinion, worthless, because they could be put to no real use. Scientific discoveries were a part of "true" knowledge only when they could be applied practically.

René Descartes (1596–1650), like Bacon, constructed a philosophy on the basis of a systematic questioning of received truths. Unlike Bacon, however, his system of belief was built by means of the mathematical instrument of pure deduction. In his famous *Discourse on Method* (1637), and in other scientific writings, he began with simple, self-evident truths or axioms, like those found in geometry, and reasoned from these to particular conclusions. Descartes believed that he had found such an axiom in his famous principle: "I think, therefore I am." From this he maintained that it is possible to deduce a sound body of universal knowledge—to prove, for example, that God exists, and that men and women are thinking animals. These "truths," he declared, are just as infallible as the truths of geometry, for they are products of the same unerring method.

But Descartes is important not only as the founder of the new rationalism. He was also partly responsible for introducing the conception of a mechanistic universe. He taught that the whole world of matter, organic and inorganic alike, could be defined in terms of extension and motion. "Give me extension and motion," he once declared, "and I will construct the universe." Every individual thing—a solar system, a star, the earth itself—is a self-operating machine propelled by a force arising from the original motion given to the universe by God. Descartes did not even exclude the bodies of animals and humans from this general mechanistic pattern. He declared that the whole world of physical nature is one, and that the behavior of animals and humans flow automatically from internal or external stimuli. Yet Descartes was unwilling to include the human mind as part of his mechanistic system. Mind was not a form of matter, but an entirely separate substance implanted in the body by God. The world was therefore *dualistic:* i.e., composed of mind and matter. As a corollary to this assumption, Descartes believed in the existence of innate ideas. He taught that self-evident truths having no relation to sensory experience must be inherent in the mind itself. They are not learned through the use of the senses, but are part of the human mind from birth.

The implications of the thought of Bacon and Descartes were of enormous significance. Those now living, they argued, not only possessed the right but were charged with a duty to reassess the past and, when warranted, to reject its assumptions. They must have the courage to experiment, in order to reveal and understand the mechanical nature of the universe. Such reasoning would have a practical end, since it would result in humanity's mastery of the world. "Understanding the forces and actions of fire, water, air, the stars and heavens," Descartes wrote in the *Discourse,* "we can use these forces . . . for all purposes for which they are appropriate, and so make ourselves masters and possessors of nature."

The principles of rationalism and mechanism were adopted in some form or other by the majority of the philosophers of the seventeenth century. The most noted of Descartes's intellectual successors were the Dutch Jew Benedict Spinoza and the Englishman Thomas Hobbes, whom we have already encountered as a political theorist. Benedict (or Baruch) Spinoza was born in Amsterdam in 1632 and died an outcast from his native community forty-five years later. His parents were members of a group of Jewish immigrants who had fled from persecution in Portugal and Spain and had taken refuge in the Netherlands. At an early age Spinoza came under the influence of a disciple of Descartes and as a result grew critical of some of the dogmas of the Hebrew faith. For this he was expelled from the synagogue and banished from the community of his people. From 1656 till his death he lived in various cities of Holland, eking out a meager existence by grinding lenses. During these years he developed a philoso-

A Diagram Illustrating Cartesian Dualism. The eyes perceive the arrow; the soul, in the pineal gland, transmits an impulse to the muscles, causing the finger to point to the arrow. From the 1677 edition of Descartes's *De Homine.*

phy which incorporated the rationalism and mechanism but not the dualism of Descartes. Spinoza maintained that there is only one essential substance in the universe, of which mind and matter are but different aspects. This single substance is God, who is identical with nature itself. Such a conception of the universe was pure pantheism; but it was grounded upon reason rather than upon faith, and it was intended to express the scientific notions of the unity of nature and the continuity of cause and effect.

Spinoza's ethics

Much more than Descartes, Spinoza was interested in ethical questions. Having come to the conclusion early in life that the things people prize most highly—wealth, pleasure, power, and fame—are empty and vain, he set out to inquire whether there was any perfect good which would give lasting and unmitigated happiness to all who attained it. By a process of geometric reasoning he attempted to prove that this perfect good consists in "love of God"—that is, in worship of the order and harmony of nature. If people would but realize that the universe is a beautiful machine, whose operation cannot be interrupted for the benefit of particular persons, they would gain that serenity of mind for which philosophers have yearned through the ages. We can only be delivered from impossible hopes and cringing fears by acknowledging to ourselves that the order of nature is unalterably fixed, and that human beings cannot change their fate. In other words, we gain true freedom by realizing that we are not free. But with all his determinism, Spinoza was an earnest apostle of tolerance, justice, and rational living. He wrote in defense of religious liberty and, in the face of cruel mistreatment, set a noble example in his personal life of kindliness, humanity, and freedom from vengeful passions.

Hobbes

Another of the great rationalists of the seventeenth century was Thomas Hobbes. Born before either Descartes or Spinoza, he outlived both. Hobbes agreed with his two contemporaries in the belief that geometry furnished the only proper method of discovering philosophic truth. But he denied the Cartesian doctrine of innate ideas, maintaining that the origin of all knowledge is in sense perception. He refused to accept either the dualism of Descartes or the pantheism of Spinoza. According to Hobbes, nothing exists except matter. Mind is simply motion in the brain or perhaps a subtle form of matter, but in no sense a distinct substance. God, also, if we can believe that He exists, must be assumed to have a physical body. There is nothing spiritual anywhere in the universe of which the mind can conceive. This was the most thoroughgoing materialism to make its appearance since the days of the Roman Lucretius. It was combined with mechanism, as materialism usually is. Hobbes contended that not only the universe but humanity as well can be explained mechanically. All that human beings do is determined by appetites or aversions, and these in turn are either inherited or acquired through experience. In similar fashion, Hobbes maintained that there are no absolute standards of good and evil. Good is merely that which gives pleasure; evil, that which brings pain.

Spinoza and Hobbes, though important as recruits in the army of intellectual revolutionaries, were not, like Bacon and Descartes, primary instigators of that revolution. John Locke (1632–1704), the English philosopher, was. Locke, in his *Treatise of Civil Government,* posited a political philosophy based upon natural law which was used to justify the Glorious Revolution of 1688, and, later, the American and French Revolutions of the eighteenth century. He was, as well, the author of an extremely influential new theory of knowledge. Rejecting Descartes's doctrine of innate ideas, Locke maintained that all knowledge originates from sense perception. This theory had already been asserted by Hobbes; but Locke systematized and enlarged it. In his *Essay Concerning Human Understanding* (1690), he insisted that the human mind at birth is a blank tablet, a *tabula rasa,* upon which absolutely nothing is inscribed. It does not contain the idea of God or any notions of right and wrong. Not until the newborn child begins to have experiences, to perceive the external world with its senses, is anything registered in its mind. But the simple ideas which result directly from sense perception are merely the foundations of knowledge; no human being could live intelligently on the basis of them alone. These simple ideas must be integrated and fused into complex ideas. This is the function of reason or understanding, which has the power to combine, coordinate, and organize the impressions received from the senses and thus to build a usable body of general truth. Sensation and reason are both indispensable—the one for furnishing the mind with the raw materials of knowledge, the other for working them into meaningful form.

Locke's theory of knowledge was as effective as were the ideas of Bacon and Descartes in freeing men and women from the restraints of received beliefs. If there was evil in the world, Locke's argument implied, it was not the result of some divine plan but rather of an environment and educational system that men and women had made and that men and women could change. Improve society, Locke was saying, and you will improve human behavior, since the latter takes its shape from the former. The optimism implicit in Locke grew explicit in the writings of other theorists as the eighteenth century progressed.

The fourth "founding father" of the intellectual revolution was the English scientist Isaac Newton (1642–1727). With the publication in 1687 of his *Mathematical Principles of Natural Philosophy,* Newton offered the world for the first time a single, coherent mechanical theory for the understanding of the universe. All measurable motion could be described by the same formulas. "Every particle of matter in the universe attracts every other particle with a force varying inversely as the square of the distance between them and directly proportional to the product of their masses." This force was gravity, which Newton dis-

John Locke

Locke

Locke's optimism

Newton

Sir Isaac Newton

covered, and the proposition defining that force he held to be valid not only on the earth but throughout the endless expanse of the solar system. Newton's discoveries were "true" knowledge, in the Baconian sense, since they had been arrived at through observation, and since they were useful in assisting men and women in mastering the world in which they lived. The measurement of tides; the locating of ships on the ocean; the predictability of a cannon ball's trajectory—all this and much more was the practical result of Newton's scientific achievement.

The implications of Newton's work were those of the entire philosophical and scientific revolution to which he himself contributed so signally: first, that it is the task of philosophers and scientists—and of all thoughtful people—to challenge the received opinions of the past, to think matters out for themselves anew; second, that nature is governed neither by mysterious divine intervention nor by caprice, but by rational, universal laws, which can be formulated as precisely as mathematical principles. From this latter conclusion it was but one further step to the assumption that there exists a set of natural laws governing the politics of the nations of the earth. Those laws were presumed to be reasonable in the freedoms they afforded legitimately constituted authority, yet stern in their prohibitions against arbitrary power that operated against their fixed principles. Third, men and women, though subject to all the laws governing the universe, could, by discovering the way those laws worked, put them to use to ensure the progress of the human race.

*Implications of Newton's
work*

2. THE PERSISTENCE OF SUPERSTITION

*The strength of
superstition*

Despite remarkable achievements in thought, the period of the intellectual revolution was by no means free from superstitions. Numerous quaint and pernicious delusions continued to be accepted as valid truths. The illiterate masses clung to their beliefs in goblins, satyrs, and wizards and to their fear of the devil, whose malevolence was assumed to be the cause of diseases, famine, storms, and insanity. But superstition was not harbored in the minds of the masses alone. The astronomer Kepler believed in astrology and depended upon the writing of almanacs, with predictions of the future according to signs and wonders in the heavens, as his chief source of income. Not only did Francis Bacon accept the current superstition of astrology, he also contributed his endorsement of the witchcraft delusion. Newton also lent his voice to superstition; for example, he searched the Bible for hidden references predicting the reign of Anti-Christ.

The worst of all the superstitions that flourished in this period was unquestionably the witchcraft delusion, under which women were tortured and burned as the assistants of Satan. Belief in witchcraft was by no means unknown in the Middle Ages or the Renaissance, but it never reached the proportions of a dangerous hysteria until after the beginning of the Protestant Revolution. The persecutions attained their most virulent form in the very countries where religious conflict raged the fiercest, that is, in Germany and France. The witchcraft superstition was a direct outgrowth of the belief in Satan which obsessed the minds of so many of the Reformers. In general, the tendency of each camp of theologians was to ascribe all the victories of their opponents to the uncanny powers of the Prince of Darkness. With such superstitions prevailing among religious leaders, it is not strange that the mass of their followers should have harbored bizarre and hideous notions. The belief grew that the devil was really more powerful than God, and that no one was safe from destruction. It was assumed that Satan not only tempted mortals to sin, but actually forced them to sin. This was the height of his malevolence, for it jeopardized chances of salvation.

The witchcraft delusion

According to the definition of the theologians, witchcraft consisted in selling one's soul to the devil in return for supernatural powers. It was believed that a woman who had concluded such a bargain was thereby enabled to work all manner of spiteful magic against her neighbors—to cause their cattle to sicken and die, their crops to fail, or their children to fall into the fire. But the most valuable gifts bestowed by Satan were the power to blind husbands to their wives' misconduct or to cause women to give birth to idiots or deformed infants. It is commonly assumed that the so-called witches were toothless old hags whose cranky habits and venomous tongues had made them objects of suspicion and dread to all who knew them. However, the writers on the Continent and in England generally imagined the witch to be a "fair and wicked young woman," and a large percentage of those put to death in Germany and France were adolescent girls and women not yet thirty.

The definition of witchcraft

The earliest persecutions for witchcraft were those initiated by Pope Innocent VIII in 1484, who instructed his inquisitors to use torture in procuring convictions. But it was not until after the beginning of the Protestant Revolution that witchcraft persecution became a mass hysteria. Luther himself provided some of the impetus by recommending that witches should be put to death with fewer considerations of mercy than were shown to ordinary criminals. Other Reformers quickly followed Luther's example. Under Calvin's administration in Geneva, twenty-one women first had their right hands cut off and were then burned for the alleged crime in 1545. From this time on the persecutions spread like a pestilence. Women, young girls, and even mere children were tortured by driving needles under their nails, roasting their feet in the fire, or crushing their legs under heavy weights until the marrow spurted from their bones, in order to force them to confess filthy orgies with demons. To what extent the persecutions were due to sheer sadism or to the greed of magistrates, who were sometimes permitted to confiscate the property of those con-

Witchcraft persecution

Burning of Witches at Dernberg in 1555. From a sixteenth-century German pamphlet denouncing witchcraft.

victed, is impossible to say. There were few people who did not believe that the burning of witches was justifiable. One of the most zealous defenders of the trials was the French political philosopher, Jean Bodin. The final number of victims will never be known. In the 1620s there was an average of 1,000 burnings a year in the German cities of Würzburg and Bamberg, and around the same time it was said the town square of Wolfenbüttel "looked like a little forest, so crowded were the stakes."

Decline of witchcraft

After about 1650 the mania gradually began to subside. The reasons for the decline are difficult to discern. Most likely the principal causes were the revival of reason and the influence of scientists and skeptical philosophers. At the very zenith of the witch-burning frenzy certain lawyers began to have doubts as to the value of the evidence admitted at the trials. In 1584 an English jurist by the name of Reginald Scot published a book condemning the belief in witchcraft as irrational and asserting that most of the lurid crimes confessed by accused women were mere figments of disordered minds. Such eminent scientists as Pierre Gassendi (1592–1655) and William Harvey also denounced the persecutions. The physician Harvey coolly dissected a toad that was alleged to be a witch's accomplice in order to show that it was just like any other and that there was no devil in it. Such appeals to scientific demonstration finally put the witch-hunting mania to an end.

3. THE ENLIGHTENMENT

Enlightenment concepts

The eighteenth-century cultural climate known as the Enlightenment was grounded on the rational, optimistic foundations laid by the seventeenth-century thinkers of the intellectual revolution. Enlightenment philosophy, as expressed in the writings of its leading exponents and popularizers, embodied among its principal tenets the following ideas and assertions:

The place of men and women within the universe: Men and women were no longer perceived as the explanation for the existence of the universe, as they had been in the theologically conceived worldview of the medieval period. Instead, they were considered only one link in a rationally ordered chain of being that included all living things. Yet their subjection to universal ordering by no means rendered them powerless or without purpose. Men and women, recognizing the extent to which their senses could ensnare them in acts of individual folly, were urged to exercise their reason as responsible beings in campaigns to eradicate folly from human society as a whole.

Attitudes toward God and organized religion: A rationally ordered universe, subject to invariable laws, precluded the existence of a capricious God, who could intervene through the agency of miracles to contradict those laws. If God did exist, as most Enlightenment philosophers believed, it was simply as a prime mover, as the force which had devised the laws, set them in motion, and ensured their continued functioning. Men and women who held to this view called themselves Deists. They attacked the biblical foundations of Christianity by subjecting the Bible to scholarly criticism and then arguing that it was no more than mythology. They joined a larger body of critics in denouncing institutionalized religions as instruments of exploitation, devised by rogues and scoundrels to enable them to prey upon the ignorant masses. They rejected the prayers and sacraments of organized Christianity as useless; God, they argued, cannot be persuaded to disregard natural law for the benefit of particular persons. They condemned the doctrine of original sin as pernicious. Men and women have the freedom and the rational ability to choose between good and evil; the notion that some are predestined for salvation and others for damnation denies humanity the dignity with which its reason has endowed it.

Classical civilization as exemplar: Enlightenment philosophers, having for the most part rejected the moral pronouncements of organized Christianity as an inspiration for right living, sought guidance instead in the history of the classical civilizations of Greece and Rome. By making the Greeks and Romans the arbiters of civilized behavior, Enlightenment thinkers were helping to deny to Christianity its claim as the central fact of human history. They rifled the vast store of ancient wisdom for precepts from writers as diverse as Socrates and Marcus Aurelius. They delighted in those passages where the Greeks and Romans attacked superstition and praised toleration; but they exercised extreme selectivity, ignoring the fact that classical civilization, taken as a whole, was more prey to irrationality and intolerance than was that of eighteenth-century Europe.

Emphasis upon the affairs and concerns of this world: The substitution of earthly for divine models of behavior was part of a broader movement, characteristic of the Enlightenment, which stressed the importance of thoroughly understanding the workings of this world, while dismissing as either unknowable or inconceivable the existence of some heavenly world-to-come. Travel to distant parts of the globe, which increased considerably during the eighteenth century, encouraged men and women to study other contemporary civilizations. As they observed the Chinese, the Persians, or the Tahitians, they began to argue the relative virtue of various ways of life, very often praising the attitudes of the supposedly inferior "natives"—toward sex and religion, for example—as superior to those characteristic of "civilized" western Europe. Concentration on the life of this world was a reflection of the attitudes expressed by Bacon when he defined "true" knowledge, and by Locke when he expounded his theory of knowledge. Truth was derived from the here-and-now, the practical concrete business of daily life. Knowledge came with the daily experiences imprinted upon the "blank tablet" of one's mind.

Humanitarianism: True understanding of the present world could lead, Enlightenment thinkers insisted, to an improved world in the future. A more perfect society could be realized once men and women applied reason to the task of banishing superstition and inhumanity. Happiness was perceived as a goal attainable on earth. As we shall see, this belief translated itself into practical programs of reform which went some way toward eliminating social evils and improving the general lot of humanity.

Although the Enlightenment derived much of its inspiration from the work of Englishmen, and although it was a general European phenomenon, it blossomed to its fullest glory in France, where its ideas were expressed in the writings of a group calling themselves *philosophes.* Without question, its leading exponent and propagandist in France was François Marie Arouet, a writer who signed himself Voltaire. Voltaire epitomized the Enlightenment as Luther did the Reformation or Michelangelo the Italian Renaissance. Voltaire was born in 1694 and, despite his delicate physique, lived until 1778, within eleven years of the outbreak of the French Revolution. He developed a taste for satiric writing early in his life and got himself into numerous scrapes by his ridicule of noblemen and pompous officials. As a consequence of one of his lampoons he was sent to prison and afterwards exiled to England. Here he remained for three years, acquiring a deep admiration for British institutions, and composing his first philosophic work, which he entitled *Letters on the English.* In this work he popularized the ideas of Newton and Locke, whom he had come to regard as two of the greatest geniuses who ever lived. Most of his later writings—the *Philosophical Dictionary, Candide,* his histories, and many of his poems and essays—were also concerned with exposition of the doctrine that the world is governed by natural laws, and that reason and concrete experience are the only dependable guides for men and women to follow. Voltaire had contempt for the smug optimism of some Enlightenment thinkers, who taught that the ills of

Voltaire by Houdon

THE INTELLECTUAL REVOLUTION
OF THE SEVENTEENTH AND EIGHTEENTH CENTURIES

• Birthplaces of scientists, artists, and writers
△ Scientific academies
—·—· Boundaries ca. 1740

England and Scotland Crowning Charles I, Rubens. This scene was part of a series painted in Whitehall Palace, London, to glorify the Stuart family. (Minneapolis Institute of Art)

The Last Judgment, Peter Paul Rubens (1577–1640). Vivid colors, voluptuous figures, and classical themes are typical of Rubens' work. (Alte Pinakothek, Munich)

Pope Innocent X, Velásquez. (Doria-Pamphili Collection)

The Marchessa Durazzo, Anthony Van Dyck (1599–1641). This portrait of a Genoese noblewoman suggests the Italian Renaissance sophistication admired by the Flemish burghers. (MMA)

The Night Watch, Rembrandt. (The Rijksmuseum)

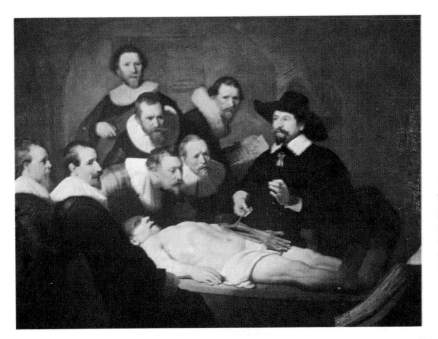

The Anatomy Lesson, Rembrandt van Rijn (1606–1669). Rembrandt scorned the classical themes of his contemporaries and turned to character analysis and the portrayal of life. (Mauritshuis, The Hague)

The Stonemason's Yard, Canaletto (1697–1768). A quiet scene of everyday life, in strong contrast to the portrait below. (National Gallery, London)

Marriage à la Mode, William Hogarth (1697–1764). A satirical look at the arranged marriage: the financial needs of the nobleman and the social aspirations of his middle class counterpart dominate the negotiations. (National Gallery, London)

Le Mezzetin, Antoine Watteau (1684–1721). Mezzetin was a popular character in Italian comedy who was much liked in France. Watteau enjoyed portraying the make-believe world of the court with its festivals and formalized elegance. (MMA)

The Blue Boy, Thomas Gainsborough (1727–1788). Though the costume suggests the romantic ideal of Prince Charming, the face is a penetrating study of the moodiness and uncertainty of adolescence. (Huntington Library)

Sarah Siddons as the Tragic Muse, Sir Joshua Reynolds (1723–1792). Mrs. Siddons, a famous actress of the XVIII cent., is here portrayed as the Queen of Tragedy, in accordance with Reynolds' habit of depicting wealthy patrons in impressive classical poses. (Huntington Library)

Madame de Pompadour, François Boucher (1703–1770). This portrait idealizes the favorite mistress of Louis XV. (The Wallace Collection, London)

Madame Recamier, Jacques Louis David (1748–1825). David was the exponent of a new classicism during and after the French Revolution. The couch, the lamp, and the costume are copied from Rome and Pompeii. (Louvre)

Execution of the Rioters, Francisco Goya (1746–1828). Unlike most artists of his time, Goya dealt unflinchingly with suffering, violence, fear, and death. Depicted here is the execution of Spanish rebels by Napoleon's soldiers in 1808. This harshness caused the rebellion to spread over the whole peninsula. (Prado)

The Raft of the Medusa, Théodore Géricault. Agony and suffering is vividly portrayed in Géricault's realistic figures. (Louvre)

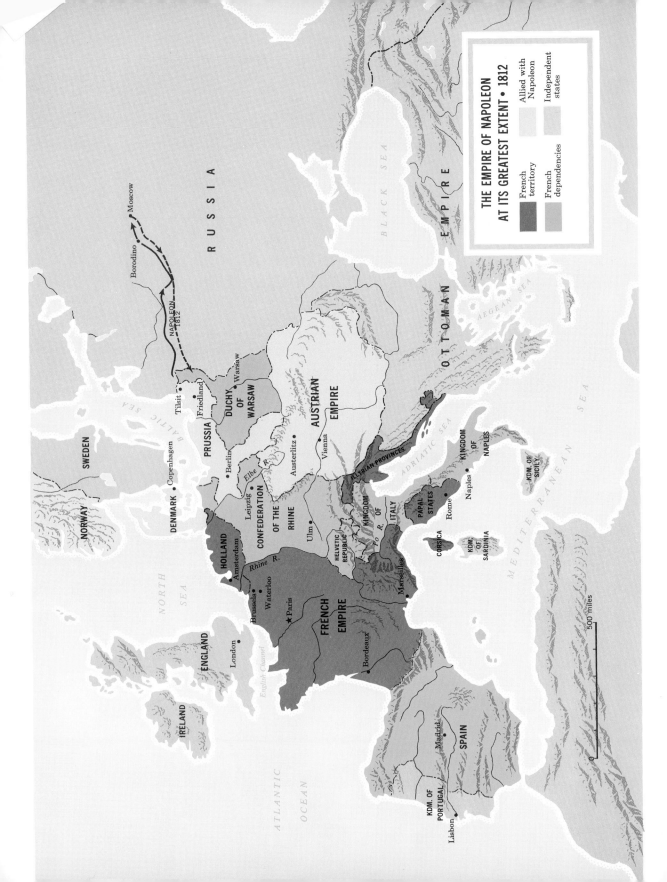

THE EMPIRE OF NAPOLEON
AT ITS GREATEST EXTENT • 1812

French
territory

French
dependencies

Allied with
Napoleon

Independent
states

RUSSIA

Moscow

Borodino

NAPOLEON
1812

Tilsit

Friedland

PRUSSIA

Warsaw

DUCHY
OF
WARSAW

AUSTRIAN
EMPIRE

Berlin

Elbe R.

Austerlitz

Vienna

Leipzig

CONFEDERATION

OF THE

RHINE

Ulm

HELVETIC
REPUBLIC

ILLYRIAN PROVINCES

ADRIATIC SEA

KINGDOM
OF
NAPLES

KINGDOM
OF
ITALY

PAPAL
STATES

Rome

Naples

KDM. OF
SICILY

CORSICA

KDM.
OF
SARDINIA

P. R. OF

HOLLAND

Amsterdam

Rhine R.

Brussels

Waterloo

★ Paris

FRENCH
EMPIRE

Marseilles

MEDITERRANEAN SEA

Bordeaux

Madrid

SPAIN

KDM. OF
PORTUGAL

Lisbon

NORWAY

SWEDEN

DENMARK

Copenhagen

BALTIC SEA

NORTH
SEA

ENGLAND

London

IRELAND

English Channel

ATLANTIC
OCEAN

OTTOMAN
EMPIRE

BLACK SEA

AEGEAN SEA

500 miles

each make up the good of all, and that everything is for the best in the best of all possible worlds. He saw, on the contrary, universal misery, hatred, strife, and oppression. Only in his utopia of El Dorado, which he described in his novel *Candide* and placed somewhere in South America, were freedom and peace conceivable. Here there were no priests, no lawsuits, and no prisons. The inhabitants dwelt together without malice or greed, worshiping God in accordance with the dictates of reason, and solving their problems by logic and science. But this idyllic life was made possible only by the fact that the land was cut off by impassable mountains from the "regimented assassins of Europe."

Voltaire is best known as a champion of individual freedom. He regarded all restrictions upon liberty of speech and opinion as barbarous. In a letter to one of his opponents he wrote what has often been quoted as the highest criterion of intellectual tolerance: "I do not agree with a word that you say, but I will defend to the death your right to say it." But if there was any one form of repression that Voltaire abhorred more than others, it was the tyranny of organized religion. He blasted the cruelty of the Church in torturing and burning those who dared to question its dogmas. With reference to the whole system of persecuting and privileged orthodoxy, he adopted as his slogan, "Crush the infamous thing." He was almost as unsparing in his attacks upon political tyranny, especially when it resulted in the slaughter of thousands to satisfy the ambitions of despots. "It is forbidden to kill," he sarcastically asserted, "therefore all murderers are punished unless they kill in large numbers and to the sound of trumpets."

Religious toleration

Among the other philosophers of the Enlightenment in France were Denis Diderot (1713–1784), Jean d'Alembert (1717–1783), and the marquis de Condorcet (1743–1794). Diderot and d'Alembert were the chief members of a group known as the Encyclopedists, so-called from their contributions to the *Encyclopedia*, which was intended to be a complete summation of the philosophic and scientific knowledge of the age. In general, both of them agreed with the rationalism and liberalism of Voltaire. Diderot, for example, maintained that "men will never be free till the last king is strangled with the entrails of the last priest." D'Alembert, while accepting the rationalist and individualist tendencies of the Enlightenment, differed from most of his associates in advocating a diffusion of the new doctrines among all the people. The general attitude of his contemporaries, notably Voltaire, was to despise the common people, to regard them as fools beyond redemption from ignorance and grossness. But for d'Alembert the only assurance of progress lay in universal enlightenment. Accordingly, he maintained that the truths of reason and science should be taught to the masses in the hope that eventually the whole world might be freed from darkness and tyranny. Condorcet, who committed suicide during the course of the French Revolution, was, like

Diderot, d'Alembert, and Condorcet

See color map facing page 704

The *Philosophes* at Supper. An imaginary convocation of some of the greatest of the French Enlightenment thinkers. The seated figures are Voltaire, with his left hand raised, and, moving to his left, Diderot, Père Adam, Condorcet, d'Alembert, Abbé Maury, and La Harpe.

d'Alembert, a devout believer in the theory of human progress. His book, *The Outline of the Progress of the Human Mind*, written while he was in hiding from revolutionary extremists, argued the possibility of general social improvement as a result of the application of reason to the problems of the world.[1]

Lessing Although the Enlightenment had much less influence in Germany than in France or England, it did give birth there to significant and progressive ideas. The most widely recognized of its German leaders was Gotthold Lessing (1729–1781), primarily a dramatist and critic but also a philosopher of humane and far-sighted views. The essence of his philosophy was tolerance, founded upon a sincere conviction that no one religion has a monopoly of truth. In his play, *Nathan the Wise*, he expounded the idea that nobility of character has no particular relation to theological creeds. Largely for this reason he condemned adherence to any one system of dogma and taught that the development of each of the world's great religions (Christianity included) was simply a step in the spiritual evolution of humanity.

Hume Two other philosophers commonly given a place in the Enlightenment—the Scotsman David Hume (1711–1776) and the Frenchman Jean-Jacques Rousseau (1712–1778)—were neither of them in full agreement with the majority of their contemporaries. Hume is noted above all for his skepticism. Like Hobbes, he taught that the mind is a bundle of impressions, derived exclusively from the senses and tied together by habits of association. That is, we learn from experience to associate warmth with fire and nourishment with bread. If we had

---

[1] The political and economic doctrines of the Enlightenment will be treated more fully in the following chapter on the French Revolution.

never actually experienced the sensation of warmth, no reasoning faculty in our minds would enable us to draw the conclusion that fire produces heat. But constant repetition of the fact that when we see a flame we generally experience warmth leads to the habit of associating the two in our minds. Impressions and associations are all that there is to knowing. Since every idea in the mind is nothing but a copy of a sense impression, it follows that we can know nothing of final causes, the nature of substance, or the origin of the universe. We cannot be sure of any of the conclusions of reason except those which, like the principles of mathematics, can be verified by actual experience. All others are likely to be the products of feelings and desires, of animal urges and fears. In his challenge to preconceived ideas, Hume was following Enlightenment practice. Yet in denying the competence of reason, Hume placed himself almost entirely outside the mainstream of contemporary thoughts.

In similar measure, Rousseau repudiated many of the basic assumptions which originated with Newton and Locke. An unhappy man, Rousseau failed in nearly every occupation he undertook. He preached lofty ideals of educational reform, but abandoned his own children to a foundling asylum. He quarreled with everybody and reveled in morbid self-disclosures. Undoubtedly it was these qualities of temperament which were largely responsible for his revolt against the coldly intellectual doctrines of his contemporaries. He maintained that to worship reason as the infallible guide to conduct and truth is to lean upon a broken reed. In the really vital problems of life it is much safer to rely upon feelings, to follow our instincts and emotions. These are the ways of nature and are therefore more conducive to happiness than the artificial lucubrations of the intellect. The "thinking man is a depraved animal." Yet notwithstanding his contempt for reason, Rousseau was in other ways thoroughly in agreement with the viewpoint of the Enlightenment. He extolled the life of primitive civilizations more fervently than did any of his associates. He shared the impatience of the Enlightenment with every sort of restriction upon individual freedom, though he was much more concerned about the liberty and equality of the masses than were the other reformers of his time. Rousseau's dogmas of equality and popular sovereignty, though frequently misinterpreted, became the rallying cries of late–eighteenth-century revolutionaries and of thousands of more moderate opponents of the existing regime. And, as the chapter on the French Revolution will show, it was Rousseau's political philosophy that provided the inspiration for the modern ideal of majority rule.

A movement as profoundly disturbing to Western society as the Enlightenment was bound to have its effects upon social customs and individual habits. Not all of the social progress of this time can be traced to intellectual influences; much of it derived from the prosperity induced by the expansion of trade in the Commercial Revolution.

Jean-Jacques Rousseau

Broader effects of the Enlightenment

Humanitarianism

Antislavery

Nevertheless, the progress of philosophy and science had more than incidental effects in clearing away ancient prejudice and in building a more humane society.

Mention has already been made of the influence of the Enlightenment in promoting the cause of social reform. A characteristic expression of this influence was agitation for revision of drastic criminal codes and for more liberal treatment of prisoners. With regard to both, the need for reform was urgent. Penalties even for minor offenses were exceedingly severe in practically all countries, death being the punishment for stealing a horse or a sheep or for the theft of as little as five shillings in money. During the first half of the eighteenth century no fewer than sixty crimes were added to the capital list in England. The treatment accorded to bankrupts and debtors was also extremely harsh. Beaten and starved by their jailers, they died by the thousands in filthy prisons. Conditions such as these eventually challenged the sympathies of several reformers. Foremost among them was Cesare Beccaria (1738–1794), a jurist of Milan, who had been deeply influenced by the writings of French rationalist philosophers. In 1764 he published his famed treatise *Crimes and Punishments,* in which he condemned the common theory that penalties should be made as severe as possible in order to deter potential offenders. Insisting that the purpose of criminal codes should be the prevention of crime and the reform of the wayward, rather than vengeance, he urged the abolition of torture as unworthy of civilized nations. He likewise condemned capital punishment as contrary to the natural rights of humans, since it cannot be revoked in case of error. Beccaria's book created a sensation. It was translated into a dozen languages, and stimulated efforts to improve conditions in many countries. By the end of the eighteenth century some progress had been made in reducing the severity of penalties, in relieving debtors from punishment, and in providing work and better food for prisoners.

The humanitarian spirit of the Enlightenment found an outlet also in other directions. Several of the scientists and philosophers denounced the evils of slavery. Many more condemned the slave trade. The efforts of intellectuals in this regard were warmly seconded by the leaders of certain religious groups, especially by prominent Quakers in America. Pacifism was another ideal of many of the Enlightenment thinkers. Voltaire's strictures on war were by no means the only example of such sentiments. Rousseau attacked as illogical attempts to draw a distinction between just and unjust wars. From the pens of other *philosophes* emanated various ingenious plans for insuring perpetual peace, including a scheme drafted by a Frenchman, the Abbé de Saint-Pierre (1658–1743), for a league of nations to take concerted action against aggressors.

Influential though the ideas of the Enlightenment were, they were not all-pervading, nor did everyone who encountered them find them persuasive. The intellectual revolution we have been describing occurred within a society the majority of whose members was illiterate and, as we have seen, deeply superstitious. When Halley's comet, named for the English astronomer Edmund Halley, made its appearance in 1682, popular imagination took it as an omen of impending cataclysm, much as it interpreted the devastating Lisbon earthquake of 1755 as a sign of divine displeasure. Men and women, literate or not, found it exceedingly difficult to surrender the reassuring idea that humankind and its activities were the center upon which the world was fixed. They continued to believe, despite what philosophers might tell them, that God was interested in their individual plight, and that their supplications would bring them the relief and support they sought. The ignorant still resorted to the full demonology and mythology of medieval folklore. The more thoughtful, dissatisfied with the theological and spiritual thinness of Deism or, indeed, of conventionally practiced orthodoxies, had recourse to an evangelicalism whose beliefs were the antithesis of Enlightenment rationalism. Quietists, whose greatest strength was in France, argued that God spoke directly to them of salvation. They denied the need for institutionalized religion, but for reasons far different from those of the Deists. The Jansenists, another French sect, revived a belief in predestination. And in England, John Wesley (1703–1791), the founder of Methodism, stirred mass meetings of thousands from mid-century on by preaching salvation through faith in God's love for sinful men and women.

*Rejection of the ideas of the
Enlightenment*

    Yet the impact of the Enlightenment, qualified though it must be, was nevertheless profound, both upon individuals and upon society as a whole. Those who read and accepted its doctrines and discoveries found their perceptions of themselves and their universe vastly altered. Its rationalism undoubtedly helped in some measure to improve the human condition. And its insistence upon a social order controlled by natural law and governed according to the practical experiences of this world was eventually instrumental in bringing an end to the remaining vestiges of feudalism and the monopolies of unearned privilege.

*The Enlightenment's
impact*

4. SCIENCE AND THE INTELLECTUAL REVOLUTION

The intellectual revolution celebrated the triumph not only of reason but of science as well. Prior to the seventeenth century, scientists had worked in isolation from one another and in opposition to a worldview which was inclined to regard their work as suspect, if not as outright blasphemy. From the mid–seventeenth century on, however, science became an international enterprise, encouraged by that willingness we have already noted to challenge accepted ideas, and supported by governments, as anxious as scientists themselves to put new

The prestige of science

An Illustration of a Laboratory from an Eighteenth-Century Edition of Diderot's *Encyclopedia*. The Enlightenment stressed the importance of scientific experiment.

discoveries to practical use. The Royal Society of London, founded in 1662 with King Charles II as its patron, and the French Academy of Sciences, founded four years later, stimulated the publication of scientific treatises and the exchange of scientific knowledge. Science was no longer seen as an esoteric field of inquiry, existing apart from the everyday business of the world. Instead it was welcomed for the very reason that its discoveries were proving to be of great value to humanity. Scientists themselves worked to apply their research to the needs of society. Newton, for example, devised a series of navigational tables, by which the changing positions of the moon among the stars could be accurately predicted. And he invented the sextant for measuring these positions and thereby determining latitude and longitude.

Some preliminary progress was made during this period in the understanding of electrical phenomena. At the beginning of the seventeenth century the Englishman William Gilbert (1540–1603), discovered the properties of lodestones and introduced the word "electricity" into the language.[2] Other scientists quickly became interested, and sensational results were anticipated from experiments with the marvelous "fluid." A learned Jesuit even suggested that two persons might communicate at a distance by means of magnetized needles which would point simultaneously to identical letters of the alphabet. Late in the eighteenth century Alessandro Volta (1745–1827) constructed the first battery. Still another important achievement in elec-

Electricity

---

[2] "Electric" comes from the Greek word for amber. Gilbert and others had observed that amber rubbed on fur will attract paper, hair, straw, and various other things.

trical physics was the invention in 1746 of the Leyden jar for the storage of electric energy. It was mainly as a result of this invention that the American Benjamin Franklin (1706–1790) was able to show that lightning and electricity are identical. In his celebrated kite experiment in 1752 he succeeded in charging a Leyden jar from a thunderstorm.

Almost as spectacular as the progress in physics was the development of chemistry. If any one scientist can be called the founder of modern chemistry, it is Robert Boyle (1627–1691). The son of an Irish nobleman, Boyle achieved distinction in 1661 with the publication of his *Sceptical Chymist, or Chymico-Physical Doubts and Paradoxes.* In this work he rejected the theories of the alchemists and thereby contributed toward the establishment of chemistry as a pure science. In addition, he distinguished between a mixture and a compound, learned a great deal about the nature of phosphorus, produced alcohol from wood, suggested the idea of chemical elements, and reviewed the atomic theory. No scientist before his time had foreshadowed so much of the knowledge of modern chemistry.

Chemistry: Boyle

Despite the work of Boyle, little further development of chemistry occurred for almost a hundred years. The reason lay partly in the wide acceptance of errors concerning such matters as heat, flame, air, and the phenomenon of combustion. The most common of these errors was the so-called phlogiston theory. The theory was based on the idea that phlogiston was the substance of fire—i.e., when an object burned, phlogiston was supposed to be given off. The remaining ash was said to be the "true" material. In the second half of the eighteenth century important discoveries were made which ultimately overthrew this theory and cleared the way for a real understanding of some of the most familiar chemical reactions. In 1766 the Englishman Henry Cavendish reported the discovery of a new kind of gas obtained by treating iron, zinc, and other metals with sulphuric acid. He showed that this gas, now known as hydrogen, would not of itself support combustion, and yet would be rapidly consumed by a fire with access to the air. In 1774 oxygen was discovered by another Englishman, the Unitarian minister Joseph Priestley. He found that a candle would burn with extraordinary vigor when placed in the new gas—a fact which indicated clearly that combustion was not caused by any mysterious principle or substance in the flame itself. A few years after this discovery, Cavendish demonstrated that air and water, long supposed to be elements, are actually a mixture and a compound, respectively, the first being composed principally of oxygen and nitrogen and the second of oxygen and hydrogen.

Cavendish and Priestley

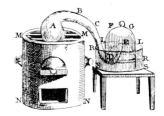

Lavoisier's Apparatus for the Decomposition of Air

The final blow to the phlogiston theory was administered by the Frenchman Antoine Lavoisier (1743–1794), one of the greatest of all scientists of the intellectual revolution, who later lost his life in the French Revolution. Lavoisier proved that both combustion and respiration involve oxidation, the one being rapid and the other slow. He

Lavoisier

provided the names for oxygen and hydrogen, demonstrated that the diamond is a form of carbon, and argued that life itself is essentially a chemical process. But undoubtedly his greatest accomplishment was his discovery of the law of the conservation of mass. He found evidence that "although matter may alter its state in a series of chemical actions, it does not change in amount; the quantity of matter is the same at the end as at the beginning of every operation, and can be traced by its weight." This "law" has, of course, been modified by later discoveries regarding the structure of the atom and the conversion of some forms of matter into energy. It is hardly too much to say, however, that as a result of Lavoisier's genius chemistry became a true science.

Although the physical sciences received the major attention in the intellectual revolution, the biological sciences were by no means neglected. One of the greatest of the early biologists was the Englishman Robert Hooke (1635–1703), the first to see and describe the cellular structure of plants. This achievement was soon followed by the work of Marcello Malpighi (1628–1694) in demonstrating the sexuality of plants and in comparing the breathing function of vegetable leaves with that of the lungs of animals. About the same time a Dutch businessman and amateur scientist, Anthony van Leeuwenhoek (1632–1723), discovered protozoa and bacteria and wrote the first description of human sperm. The seventeenth century also witnessed some progress in embryology. About 1670 the Dutch physician, Jan Swammerdam (1637–1680), carefully described the life history of certain insects from the caterpillar stage to maturity and compared the change of tadpole into frog with the development of the human embryo.

In many ways the end of the seventeenth century appeared to mark a decline of originality in the sciences that deal with living things. During the next hundred years biologists were inclined more and more to center their efforts upon description and classification of knowledge already in existence. The most brilliant classifier of biological knowledge was the Swedish scientist, Carl von Linné (1707–1778), more commonly known by his Latinized name of Linnaeus. In his *System of Nature* and in his *Botanical Philosophy* Linnaeus divided all natural objects into three kingdoms: stone, animal, and vegetable. Each of these kingdoms he subdivided into classes, genera, and species. He invented the system of biological nomenclature still in use, by which every plant and animal is designated by two scientific names, the first denoting the genus and the second the species. Thus he called humans *Homo sapiens*. Linnaeus's system of classification was widely adopted even in his own time.

The second great genius of descriptive biology in the eighteenth century was the Frenchman Georges Buffon (1707–1788). His *Natural History* in forty-four volumes, though intended as a general summa-

Biology

Linnaean classification

Buffon

tion of science, dealt mainly with humans and other vertebrates. While much of the material in this work was taken from the writings of other scientists and from the accounts of travelers, the author was able to reduce a vast body of knowledge to orderly arrangement and enliven it with his own interpretations. Buffon recognized the close relationship between humans and the higher animals. Though he could never quite bring himself to accept the full implications of a theory that linked human evolution directly to that of other animals, he was nonetheless strongly impressed by the striking resemblances among all of the higher species. He admitted the possibility that the entire range of organic forms had descended from a single species.

Despite the notable scientific advances of the seventeenth and eighteenth centuries, the development of physiology and medicine progressed rather slowly during the same period, and for several reasons. One was the inadequate preparation of physicians, many of whom had begun their professional careers with little more training than a kind of apprenticeship under an older practitioner. Another was the common disrepute in which surgery was held as a mere trade, like that of a barber or blacksmith. Perhaps the most serious of all was the prejudice against dissection of human bodies for use in anatomical study. As late as 1750 medical schools which engaged in this practice were in danger of destruction by irate mobs. Despite these obstacles some progress was still possible. About 1670 Malpighi and Leeuwenhoek confirmed the famous discovery of the Englishman William Harvey by observing the actual flow of blood through the network of capillaries connecting the arteries and veins. At approximately the same time an eminent physician of London, Thomas Sydenham, proposed a new theory of fever as a natural process by which diseased material is expelled from the system.

Medicine

Medical progress during the eighteenth century was somewhat more rapid. Among the noteworthy achievements were the discovery of blood pressure, the founding of histology or microscopic anatomy, the development of the autopsy as an aid to the study of disease, and the recognition of scarlet fever as a malady distinct from smallpox and measles. But the chief milestones of medical advancement in this period were the adoption of inoculation and the development of vaccination for smallpox. Knowledge of inoculation came originally from the Near East, where it had long been employed by the Muslims. Information concerning its use was relayed to England in 1717 through the letters of Lady Montagu, wife of the British ambassador to Turkey. The first systematic application of the practice in the Western world, however, was due to the efforts of the American Puritan leaders, Cotton and Increase Mather, who implored the physicians of Boston to inoculate their patients in the hope of curbing an epidemic of smallpox which had broken out in 1721. By the middle of the century inoculation was quite generally employed by physicians in Europe and in

Inoculation

America. In 1796 a milder method of vaccination was discovered by the Englishman Edward Jenner. It was now revealed that direct inoculation of human beings with the deadly virus of smallpox was unnecessary: a vaccine manufactured in the body of an animal would be just as effective and much less likely to have disastrous results. The vast possibilities thus opened up for the elimination of contagious diseases appeared to confirm the Enlightenment belief in the ability of men and women to make nature's laws work for the betterment of the human condition.

5. CLASSICISM IN ART AND LITERATURE

Classical models

The history of European art and literature during the seventeenth and eighteenth centuries reflects the respect for the classical world which we have noted as a particular characteristic of Enlightenment thought. Artists and writers strove to imitate classical models. They chose classical titles and themes for many of their works and embellished them wherever possible with allusions to antique mythology. Deploring the destruction of ancient civilization by "Christian barbarians," they were unable to see much value in the cultural achievements of later centuries. In particular, they despised what they termed the "Middle Ages" as a long night of barbaric darkness stretching between the classical period and their own. Most would have agreed with the dictum of Rousseau that the Gothic cathedrals were "a disgrace to those who had the patience to build them."

Left: *St. Peter's Cathedral, Rome.* The sweeping colonnades, designed by Bernini and begun in 1656, express the dramatic splendor that was characteristic of baroque architecture. Right: *St. Paul's Cathedral, London.* Designed by Christopher Wren, the boldness of the structure reflected the emergence of England as a world power.

The Chateau of Versailles. Dramatically expanded by Louis XIV in the 1660s from a hunting lodge to the principal royal residence and the seat of government, the chateau became the standard of secular baroque architecture and a monument to the international power and prestige of the Grand Monarch.

These attitudes were an inheritance from the Renaissance humanists. Yet the classicism of the seventeenth and eighteenth centuries was no mere copy of that espoused by earlier artists and writers. As adopted by architects, painters, and sculptors, classicism emerged in new forms as the baroque style. This style was initially developed as part of the Catholic Reformation of the late sixteenth century. Churches were built in a manner designed to inspire renewed reverence and respect for the Church of Rome. Classical elements such as columns, domes, and architectural sculpture were combined in such a way as to express both aggressive restlessness and extraordinary power. The results are clearly visible in a structure such as Giovanni Lorenzo Bernini's (1598–1680) colonnades at St. Peter's in Rome. The Englishman Christopher Wren (1632–1723), with Bernini among the most gifted of baroque architects, employed the same style in his design for St. Paul's Cathedral in Protestant London, an architectural statement whose grandeur challenged the authority claimed by Roman Catholicism.

The baroque style

The baroque style was soon adopted by the absolutist monarchs of seventeenth-century Europe to symbolize their power and magnificence. The palace of Louis XIV at Versailles is undoubtedly the supreme example of secular baroque architecture. Buildings and grounds together are a remarkable expression of the formality and hierarchy of the autocratic state, and of the power invested in the person of the monarch. Other European rulers commissioned royal residences in the style of Versailles: Peter the Great, for example, built the Peterhof at his capital of St. Petersburg; King William of England employed Wren to embellish the already standing palace of Hampton Court. None of these structures, however, could rival Versailles, ei-

Royal Baroque

Left: *The Petit Trianon, Versailles*. Added as a royal retreat in the gardens of Versailles by Louis XV, this structure expresses the refined elegance that characterized rococo architecture. Right: *The Interior of the Pilgrimage Church, Bavaria*. An example of the flamboyance of the late baroque architectural style.

ther in its grandeur or its total devotion to the harmony and proportion which characterized the baroque.

During the eighteenth century the baroque style gradually gave way to further adaptations of the classical. On the Continent, the baroque *Rococo* was succeeded by the rococo, a term perhaps derived from the French words for rock and shell (*rocaille* and *coquille*), two natural forms often employed in both exterior and interior rococo ornamentation. The rococo differed from the baroque in several ways: it was lighter, less majestic; it created an impression of grace and refinement. In place of a struggle for dynastic power and colonial empire, much of European society by now focused its attention on the dilletantism and elegance of the court of Louis XV, which set the standard for continental behavior among the ruling classes. The rococo both represented and reflected this change in focus. Well-known examples of the rococo are the Petit Trianon, a small palace built on the grounds of Versailles, which was designed as a royal retreat, and the palace of Sans Souci (literally, "Without Care") at Potsdam, built by Frederick the Great.

In England reaction to the baroque took the form of a return to the severer classicism of Renaissance architecture, adapted from the de-*Palladianism* signs of the Italian architect, Andrea Palladio (1508–1580) and from those of the seventeenth-century Englishman, Inigo Jones. Most of the imposing country houses built by the landed gentry in this period displayed a fidelity to the precise mathematical equations of neo-Palladianism. As such they reflected the general Enlightenment worship of reason and order.

To a certain extent the evolution of painting during the seventeenth and eighteenth centuries paralleled that of architecture. The greatest painters in the baroque tradition were the Flemish artists, Peter Paul Rubens (1577–1640) and Anthony Van Dyck (1599–1641), and the Spaniard, Diego Velásquez (1599–1660). Rubens was the outstanding genius among these three. In such works as *The Fates Spinning* and *Venus and Adonis,* he combined classical themes with sumptuous baroque color and richness pleasing to the affluent merchants and nobles of his day. The pink and rounded flesh of his full-blown nudes is thoroughly in keeping with the robust vitality of the age, Both Rubens and his gifted pupil, Anthony Van Dyck, are noted for their portraits of rulers and nobles, with full attention paid to the gorgeous details of elegant apparel and opulent furnishings in the background. Van Dyck's best-known portraits are those of the English kings, James I and Charles I, and their families. Velásquez, the third great artist of the baroque tradition, was the court painter to Philip IV of Spain. Much of his work consisted of royal portraits, suffused in soft and silvery light but fundamentally empty of meaning or emotional expression, a testimony, perhaps, to the waning power of the Spanish Empire.

Rubens's Portrait of His Son Nicolaus

See color plates following page 704

Venus and Adonis by Peter Paul Rubens. Rubens often painted classical themes, which he conceived on a grand scale and executed with sweeping vigor.

Self-Portrait by Rembrandt

All of the painters mentioned thus far were exponents in some degree of the classical influence. But there were others in both the seventeenth and eighteenth centuries who refused to be bound by the prevailing artistic conventions. Foremost among them was Rembrandt van Rijn (1606–1669), now universally considered one of the greatest painters of all time. The son of a well-to-do miller of Leyden, Rembrandt was allowed to begin his artistic education at an early age. Under a series of native masters he learned the technique of subtle coloring and a skillful depiction of natural phenomena. Famous by the time he was twenty-five, he fell upon evil days later in his life, mainly as a consequence of bad investments and the failure of critics to appreciate his more recondite works. In 1656 he was stripped by his creditors of all he possessed and driven from his house. Apparently these reverses served mainly to broaden and deepen his philosophy, for in this very same year he produced some of his greatest achievements. As a painter Rembrandt surpassed all the other members of the Dutch school and deserves to be ranked with the painters of the High Renaissance in Italy like Titian and Leonardo. No artist had a keener understanding of the problems and trials of human nature or a stronger perception of the mysteries of life. His portraits, including those of himself, are imbued with an introspective quality and with a suggestion that the half is not being told. Rembrandt departed from the subjects of classical mythology, preferring to portray solemn rabbis, tattered beggars, and scenes from the Old and New Testaments, rich in drama and in human interest. Some of his best-known works include *The Good Samaritan, The Woman Taken in Adultery, The Marriage of Samson,* and *The Night Watch.*

The history of literature in the seventeenth and eighteenth centuries exhibited tendencies quite similar to those of art. The most popular literary ideal was classicism, which generally meant not only a studied imitation of classical forms but also an earnest devotion to reason as a way of life. Although literary classicism was not confined to any one country, its principal center was France. The most noted member of the French group of poets and dramatists was Jean-Baptiste Poquelin (1622–1673), who is much better known by his adopted name of Molière. Less respectful of ancient formalism than any of his associates, Molière was the most original of French comedians. Few keener critics of human nature have ever lived. "The business of comedy," he once declared, "is to represent in general all the defects of men and especially of the men of our time." The mortal weakness he delighted most to ridicule was pretentiousness, as he did so brilliantly in plays such as *Tartuffe*. But with all of this penchant for satire, Molière had a measure of pity for the evil fortunes of humankind. In a number of his plays sympathy and even melancholy go hand in hand with clever wit and pungent scorn. His genius was probably broader in scope than that of any other dramatist since Shakespeare. Two French play-

Aristotle Contemplating the Bust of Homer by Rembrandt. A fine example of Rembrandt's obsession with the effects of light and shade as means of expression.

wrights whose work more directly mirrored the classical tradition were Pierre Corneille (1606–1684) and Jean Racine (1639–1699). Both took as their subjects the heroes and heroines of ancient literature and history—Medea, Pompey, and Phaedra, for example; and both chose as their literary models the poets and dramatists of classical Greece and Rome.

Seventeenth-century England also produced writers in the classical style. The greatest was the renowned Puritan poet, John Milton (1608–1674). The leading philosopher of Cromwell's Commonwealth, Milton wrote the official defense of the beheading of Charles I. Nearly all of his writings were phrased in the reasoned and formal expression of the classical tradition, while many of the lesser ones took their themes from Greek mythology. But Milton was as much a Puritan as he was a classicist. He could never escape from the idea that the essence of beauty is morality. Moreover, he was deeply interested in theological problems. His greatest work, *Paradise Lost,* is a synthesis of the religious beliefs of his age, a majestic epic of the Protestant faith. In spite of the fact that Milton was a Puritan, his views reflected ideas characteristic of the intellectual revolution. The principal themes of *Paradise Lost* are the moral responsibility of the individual and the importance of knowledge as an instrument of virtue. Paradise is lost repeatedly in human life to the extent that men and women allow passion to triumph over reason in determining the course of their actions.

Classicism in English literature reached its zenith in the eighteenth century with the poetry of Alexander Pope (1688–1744). Pope was a great exponent in verse of the mechanistic and Deist doctrines of the Enlightenment. In such poetic works as his *Essay on Man* and his *Essay on Criticism* he set forth the view that nature is governed by inflexible laws, and that men and women must study and follow nature if they

Milton

John Milton. From the First Edition of his poems, 1645.

Gin Lane by William Hogarth. Hogarth, like his friend Henry Fielding, believed in portraying human nature as he found it. In this famous engraving, he is preaching a sermon against the gin trade, one of the besetting evils of eighteenth-century London.

would bring any semblance of order into human affairs. Other English writers, however, turned from classical models to describe, castigate, and celebrate present-day eighteenth-century society. Jonathan Swift (1667–1745), Daniel Defoe (1660–1737), and Henry Fielding (1707–1754) all took as their subjects human nature as it manifested itself in the lives of their contemporaries. Swift, in *Gulliver's Travels*, ridiculed current human pretensions and political realities by contrasting them with the perceptions of a series of mythical races. Defoe, in *Robinson Crusoe,* the tale of one man's survival on a desert island, extolled practical ingenuity and defended the subjugation of indigenous peoples by Europeans. Fielding, in *Tom Jones,* the first modern novel, and one of the greatest, declared that men and women, if they are to be portrayed as they should be, must be depicted not as impossibly virtuous heroes and heroines, but simply as real people, responsible for their actions.

Literature in eighteenth-century England

6. MUSIC IN THE SEVENTEENTH AND EIGHTEENTH CENTURIES

The seventeenth century witnessed a dramatic change in the form of musical structure and composition, one which reflected shifts occurring elsewhere in the intellectual world. As we have previously observed, the end of the sixteenth century had marked the culmination of a long era of choral, polyphonic music. Almost immediately, however, a reaction set in, so powerful that the polyphonic style became obsolete within twenty-five years of the death of its most gifted and

Italian opera

advanced practitioner, Palestrina, in 1594. A new ideal, that of primary voice accompanied by one of several musical instruments, swept Italy in a remarkably short time, and became known as monody. One of the major reasons for this change was a growing and characteristically baroque insistence upon the dramatic, and a realization on the part of Italian composers that the intense feelings of an individual cannot be adequately expressed by a many-voiced chorus. The same impulses that produced the architecture of Bernini and the paintings of Rubens led to the creation of opera, which reached its first powerful manifestation in *Orfeo* (1607) by the Italian Claudio Monteverdi (1567–1643), the dominating musical personality in the first half of the new century. Within a generation operas were performed in most important cities in Italy; by 1736 Venice boasted an opera house for every parish. Opera, staged within magnificent settings, and calling upon the talents of singers, musicians, artists, dramatists, and as master of the grand design—the conductor—expressed as clearly as any art form the dedication of the baroque to grandeur, complexity, and display.

During this same period, the instrumental tradition of the Renaissance began to produce works for organ, harpsichord, and the various string and wind instruments. In the last third of the century instrumental music created the concerto, along with opera one of the greatest original stylistic accomplishments of the Italian baroque. Both opera and concerto soon spread beyond the Alps. Though the seventeenth century was preoccupied with musical experiments, it created an impressive synthesis upon which the first half of the eighteenth century could build the final great achievements of late baroque music.

The concerto

The late baroque culminated in two towering composers: Johann Sebastian Bach (1685–1750) and George Frederick Handel (1685–1759). Though both were born in Saxony, Bach became the epitome of German musical genius, while Handel, who lived for almost half a century in London and became a British subject, embodied an English national style. Bach combined an unbounded imagination and a capacious intellect with heroic powers of discipline and an unquenchable zeal for work. By lifelong study he made himself the master of most existing types and styles of music, from little dance pieces for the clavichord to gigantic choral works. As a church musician, Bach's duty was to provide new music for elaborate Sunday and holy day services. Therefore the bulk of his work is made up of cantatas (over 200 preserved), oratorios, Passions, and Masses. His settings of the Gospels according to St. John and St. Matthew represent the unsurpassable peak of this genre. Fundamentally, though, Bach was an instrumental composer, the creator of tremendous works for organ and harpsichord, and of spacious concertos and sonatas for various combinations of instruments, and suites for orchestra. Bach was steeped in German Protestantism in a way that makes him, in one sense, uncharacteristic of the generally antireligious Enlightenment.

Johann Sebastian Bach

"The Charming Brute." A contemporary caricature of Handel, engraved by Joseph Groupy, 1754.

Classical music

Mozart

Yet no one who has heard Bach's music or studied his scores can deny the extent to which they reflect the attention to rational order and mathematical harmony that lay at the heart of the intellectual revolution.

Handel was the absolute antithesis of his great fellow-Saxon. After four years spent in Italy he completely absorbed Italian techniques and modes of composition, subsequently settling in England, where for years he ran an opera company that produced nothing but Italian operas, mostly his own. Italian opera did not suit the English middle class public, however, and after decades spent in composing and producing dozens of operas, Handel realized that he must turn to something more acceptable to the English taste. This he found in the "oratorio," a musical drama intended for performance in concert form. With the exception of *Messiah,* the most famous of his oratios, these works were not religious music, although their themes came from the Old Testament. Undoubtedly one reason for Handel's success in his adopted country was the fact that his virile and heroic oratorios could be said to symbolize the English people, their pride in their institutions and their attainment of national greatness.

After the mid–eighteenth century, the center of the musical world shifted to Vienna, where a group of highly gifted composers achieved a remarkable stylistic synthesis by reconciling baroque weightiness, rococo charm, and preromantic excitement into the form that has been labeled classical. Christoph Willibald von Gluck (1714–1787) reformed the declining "serious" opera into a noble drama that recalls the tone of classical antiquity. The appeal of the mischievous, Italian comic opera, the *opera buffa,* forced a fusion with serious opera which reached its greatest height in the operas of Wolfgang Amadeus Mozart (1756–1791), while chamber and orchestral music achieved a new formal and expressive level under the leadership of Joseph Haydn (1732–1809).

The eighteenth century was full of music, but its social organization severely hampered the creative artist. Handel, who ran his own business and left behind a respectable estate, was an exception to the general rule. In most instances, if a composer or musician was not employed by a court, noble house, church, or municipality, or if he was not an internationally acclaimed virtuoso or a renowned teacher, he ran the risk of being ground down in an effort to make a living. Mozart was among the first to shed the security of a position as "musical lackey" and to try the free artistic economy of the metropolis. While a child prodigy he was adored and admired, but when he left the employ of the archbishop of Salzburg to take up the career of a freelance artist in Vienna, he could support himself only with the greatest difficulty. Although the remaining ten years of his life were spent in bountiful productivity, he had to live from hand to mouth.

Mozart, at the Age of Six, Plays Before Empress Maria Theresa. This contemporary illustration suggests the importance of royal patronage and the often demeaning relationship between artists and patrons in this era.

Financial troubles pursued him until his death at the age of thirty-five.

When appraising the music of the classical era we must realize that in spite of its magnificent sonatas and symphonies, the stylistic core of the era was still in the dramatic music of the opera. Mozart used the operatic form to shape the characters, fates, and conflicts of human beings in a way that other forms too became permanent. Each great Mozart opera—*The Marriage of Figaro, Don Giovanni, The Magic Flute*—provides a center from which the form of piano sonatas, quartets, quintets, concertos, and symphonies were subsequently derived by his successors.

Mozart's operas

Haydn was carved from sterner timber than Mozart; his peasant background made him tenacious and stubborn. If Mozart embodied the aristocratic spirit, Haydn did that of the liberated plebeian. It was because of their diametrically opposed personalities that the two musicians got along so well; they complemented each other, learned from each other, and, in fact, were friends. Haydn had a sharp intellect and acquired his extensive knowledge of music through incessant study and experimentation. His art conveys the impressions of the village and the countryside, but also the elegance of the princely Austrian household that patronized him for many years. Haydn's compositions are so numerous that a complete edition of them has never been made. They include many operas and Masses, oratorios, concertos, over eighty string quartets, and more than 100 symphonies. It was Haydn who firmly established the technical and stylistic principles of symphonic construction, creating, with Mozart, the pattern of the symphony orchestra which remained the basis for all future musical developments.

The careers of Mozart and Haydn suggest both the achievements

Joseph Haydn

and limitations of the revolution we have traced. Their compositional innovations were a part of that broad series of intellectual changes that assisted in carrying Europe forward into the modern world. Yet Haydn's dependence upon aristocratic patronage, and Mozart's inability to live apart from it, make clear the extent to which the world of the Enlightenment remained a world bound together by rank and privilege. Only at the very end of the eighteenth century, with the coming of the French and Industrial Revolutions, did the ideas of the intellectual revolution begin to play an active role in altering, in any major way, the structure of the social and political institutions of the West.

SELECTED READINGS

• *Items so designated are available in paperback editions.*
• Carl Becker, *The Heavenly City of the Eighteenth-Century Philosophers,* New Haven, Conn., 1932. Relates the Enlightenment to its medieval origins.
• Burford, W. H., *Germany in the Eighteenth Century: The Social Background of the Literary Revival,* London, 1935. A combination of social and intellectual history, this work remains the best introduction in English to the German Enlightenment.
  Cassirer, Ernst, *The Philosophy of the Enlightenment,* Princeton, N.Y., 1951. Emphasizes the role of critical thinking on the part of the *philosophes* and the nature of reason in the Enlightenment.
  Cobban, Alfred, *In Search of Humanity: The Role of the Enlightenment in Modern History,* London, 1960.
• Gay, Peter, *The Enlightenment: An Interpretation;* Vol. I, *The Rise of Modern Paganism;* Vol. II, *The Science of Freedom,* New York, 1966–69. A brilliant work by the leading authority on the eighteenth-century intellectual world. Argues that the Enlightenment represented a complete break with the medieval past and the first stage of the modern world. Contains superb bibliographies.
  Gillespie, C. C., *The Edge of Objectivity: An Essay in the History of Scientific Ideas,* Princeton, N.J., 1960.
• Grimsley, Ronald, *Jean-Jacques Rousseau: A Study in Self-Awareness,* Cardiff, 1961. An excellent biography concerned with Rousseau's psychological development.
  Haldane, E. S., *Descartes, His Life and Times,* London, 1905. An old but thorough biography.
• Hall, A. R., *The Scientific Revolution, 1500–1800: The Formation of the Modern Scientific Attitude,* rev. ed., New York, 1966.
• Hampshire, Stuart, *Spinoza,* London, 1952.
  Havens, George R., *The Age of Ideas: From Reaction to Revolution in Eighteenth-Century France,* New York, 1955. Short biographies of the major French *philosophes*.

Humphreys, A. R., *The Augustan World: Society, Thought, and Letters in Eighteenth-Century England,* London, 1954.

Manuel, Frank E., *A Portrait of Isaac Newton,* Cambridge, Mass., 1968. A psychoanalytic interpretation.

Mellone, S. H., *The Dawn of Modern Thought: Descartes, Spinoza, Leibniz,* London, 1930. Explains the Cartesian system and its influence.

Monter, E. W., ed., *European Witchcraft,* New York, 1969. Selected readings with fine introductions by one of the world's leading experts.

More, L. T., *Isaac Newton: A Biography,* New York, 1934. The standard biography.

Ornstein, Martha, *The Role of Scientific Societies in the Seventeenth Century,* rev. ed., Hamden, Conn., 1963.

Palmer, R. R., *Catholics and Unbelievers in Eighteenth-Century France,* New York, 1939. Argues that Catholic thinkers were as enlightened as the *philosophes,* and that, ironically, their very tolerance contributed to the anticlericalism of the age.

• Phillipson, Coleman, *Three Criminal Law Reformers: Beccaria, Bentham, Romilly,* rev. ed., London, 1970.

Shackleton, Robert, *Montesquieu: A Critical Biography* London, 1961. The man and his thought.

Shryock, Richard H., *The Development of Modern Medicine: An Interpretation of the Social and Scientific Factors Involved,* London, 1948.

• Thomas, Keith, *Religion and the Decline of Magic,* London, 1971. A marvelously insightful study of popular belief in England.

SOURCE MATERIALS

Beccaria, Cesare, *An Essay on Crimes and Punishments, with a Commentary by M. de Voltaire,* Stanford, 1953. A reprint of the 1767 edition. Beccaria advocates a rational approach to punishment, with the good of the state outweighing motives for revenge. Voltaire's Commentary contains some interesting remarks on witchcraft.

• Boswell, James, *Life of Johnson,* London, 1970. The classic biography of the English man of letters, Samuel Johnson, written by his protégé; contains a superb portrait of eighteenth-century London.

Gibbon, Edward, *Autobiography,* London, 1961.

• ———, *The Decline and Fall of the Roman Empire,* 3 vols., New York, 1960. Published in 1776, this classic work exemplifies the skeptical, anticlerical nature of much of Enlightenment thought of the eighteenth century, especially Chapters 15 and 16 of Volume I.

• Kors, Alan C., and E. Peters, eds., *Witchcraft in Europe, 1100–1700: A Documentary History,* Philadelphia, 1972.

• Kramer, Heinrich, and James Sprenger, *The Malleus Maleficarum,* New York, 1971. An extraordinary work, the *Malleus* ("The Hammer of Witches") was the handbook of the witchcraft prosecutors of the Inquisition.

• Locke, John, *Two Treatises of Government,* ed. by Peter Laslett, London,

1960. Locke's celebrated tracts invoking the concept of the contractual nature of government and the sanctity of private property. An excellent introductory essay by Laslett.

• Voltaire, *Candide,* New York, 1956. Voltaire's satirical critique of the contemporary philosophy that "this is the best of all possible worlds," traced through a series of disasters experienced by his protagonist. First published in 1759.

Chapter 23

INDIA, THE FAR EAST, AND AFRICA DURING THE EARLY MODERN ERA (c. 1500-1800)

Fuji-ichi was a clever man, and his substantial fortune was amassed in his own lifetime. . . . He noted down the market ratio of copper and gold; he inquired about the current quotations of the rice brokers; he sought information from druggists' and haberdashers' assistants on the state of the market at Nagasaki; for the latest news on the prices of ginned cotton, salt, and saké, he noted the various days on which the Kyoto dealers received dispatches from the Edo branch shops. Every day a thousand things were entered in his book, and people came to Fuji-ichi if they were ever in doubt. He became a valuable asset to the citizens of Kyoto.

—I. Saikaku, *The Tycoon of All Tenants* (1688)

Between the sixteenth and the nineteenth centuries a reinvigorated Indian empire headed by a new dynasty attained the rank of a major power; China, under the last of a long series of imperial dynasties, waxed even stronger, becoming the largest and most populous country in the world; and Japan adapted her feudal institutions to the requirements of a despotic government. In both India and China, and to a lesser degree in Japan, splendor and magnificence reflected the tastes of wealthy societies and mighty rulers, as was also true in much of Europe during this same period. In the long run, however, the great Asian states found themselves at a disadvantage because they played a passive rather than an active role in the Commercial Revolution. As western European nations turned to empire building and expanded their naval forces, they established direct contacts with the coastal regions of Asia, took over the bulk of the trade between East and West, and frequently threatened the independence of non-European peoples. For several centuries the principal Eastern states were strong enough to protect themselves against the threat of aggression from the West. Faced with rigid trade restrictions in China and almost totally excluded from Japan, the seafaring Europeans

Impact of the West upon the East

turned to other quarters. In the 1570s the Spanish occupied the Philippines, subduing the native tribes and the communities of Chinese colonists in the Islands. A few years later the Dutch, through their East India Company, laid the foundations of a rich empire in Indonesia, dislodging the Portuguese who had preceded them by almost a century. The British and French somewhat belatedly turned their attention to the mainland of India, where they secured valuable trading posts in the course of the seventeenth century. During this same period the Portuguese, the British, and the Dutch established commercial enclaves on the coast of Africa.

I. INDIA UNDER THE MOGUL DYNASTY

In the sixteenth century a new invasion of India by Muslim forces from the north produced very different results from those that had accompanied the Turkish inroads and the institution of the Delhi Sultanate. It led to the establishment of the dynasty known as the Mogul—a Persian variant of the word "Mongol"—which created an efficient and, on the whole, successful pattern of government and, most significant, demonstrated the possibility of an integration of the Indian people regardless of religious profession. Actually, the ruling family and the administrative officers were far from pure-blooded Mongols. Babur ("the Tiger"), the founder of the dynasty, was descended on his father's side from Timur (of Turkish stock) and on his mother's side from the Mongol conqueror Genghis Khan. His own descendants were of mixed parentage, including Turkish, Persian, and Indian strains. Babur, like many another conqueror, began his career as the head of a small state in Turkestan. By advancing into Afghanistan he secured control of the frontier mountain passes commanding the route to the Punjab. Within the space of five years (ended by his death in 1530) he conquered the greater part of Hindustan, while retaining his territories in Afghanistan and southern Turkestan. His conquest was facilitated by the fact that he possessed artillery and match-fired muskets of European manufacture, although these guns were very primitive. The empire which Babur had begun to mark out was fully established and also given its most distinctive character by his grandson, Akbar.

Akbar, the Great Mogul

Akbar, deservedly termed "the Great Mogul," was truly remarkable both as a personality and as a sovereign. He is generally considered India's greatest ruler, although he evidently fell short of the noble idealism exemplified by Asoka some 1,800 years earlier. Perhaps the scarcity of records for Asoka's reign makes a comparison unfair. At any rate, enough data are available for Akbar's period to show that he was unquestionably one of the world's outstanding political figures in the sixteenth century. His reign was a long one—from 1556 to 1605

Babur "the Tiger"

(the dates almost coincide with the reign of Elizabeth I of England). Much of it was devoted to schemes of conquest, unsuccessfully in the Deccan but resulting in the extension of Mogul authority over all northern India and the neighboring portion of Afghanistan. Far more important was Akbar's determination to conciliate and secure the support of the Hindu population, a decision to which he adhered inflexibly throughout his reign. For his large harem (said to number over 5,000) he chose wives of several different nationalities, partly with an eye toward political expediency. By contracting marriage alliances with the proud Rajput clans, whose spirit had never been broken by the Turks, he hoped to win their allegiance. (Akbar's favorite wife and the mother of his successor to the throne was a Rajput princess.) Early in his reign he took the important step of abolishing the special taxes on non-Muslims, and he appointed Hindus—especially Rajputs—to civil and military office. A Hindu raja served in the highly responsible post of minister of finance. Akbar abandoned entirely all attempts to win converts to Islam by coercion and introduced a policy of religious toleration, although he tried to discourage those Hindu practices which he considered reprehensible, such as animal sacrifice, child marriage, and suttee.

Akbar's administration was bureaucratic and relatively efficient. At the head of each of the provinces and districts into which he divided

The Court of the Emperor Babur "the Tiger," Founder of the Mogul Dynasty

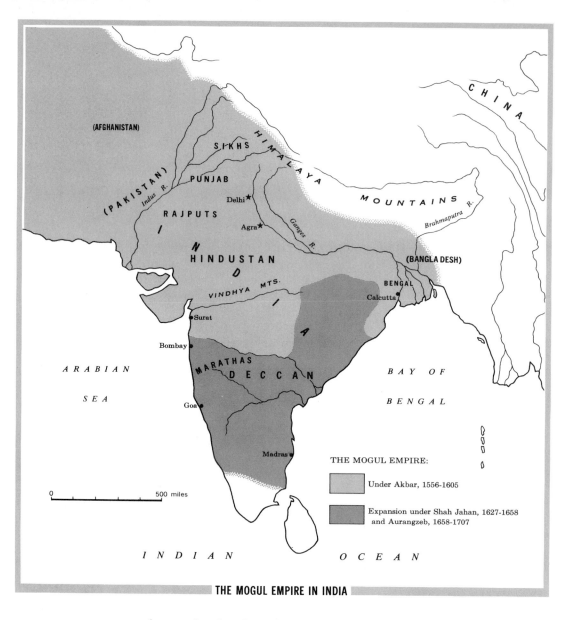

Map labels:

CHINA

(AFGHANISTAN)

H I M A L A Y A

SIKHS

PUNJAB

M O U N T A I N S

(PAKISTAN)

Indus R.

Delhi ★

RAJPUTS

Brahmaputra R.

Agra ★

Ganges R.

I N D I A

HINDUSTAN

(BANGLA DESH)

VINDHYA MTS.

BENGAL

Calcutta

●Surat

Bombay ●

MARATHAS

D E C C A N

A R A B I A N

B A Y   O F

S E A

Goa ●

B E N G A L

Madras ●

THE MOGUL EMPIRE:

0   500 miles

☐ Under Akbar, 1556-1605

☐ Expansion under Shah Jahan, 1627-1658
and Aurangzeb, 1658-1707

I N D I A N   O C E A N

THE MOGUL EMPIRE IN INDIA

Akbar's administrative methods

the state he placed a military governor who was paid a generous salary but was required to maintain a prescribed number of troops and was held to a strict accountability for his actions. Thus the government was not feudal in basis, although there was a nobility of various grades (including some Hindus and Indian Muslims as well as Moguls). While Akbar was unable to keep an adequate check on every part of his large dominions, he made a sincere effort to enforce justice among his mixed population, and he severely punished officials whose corruption was detected. The criminal code was a savage one, but not more barbarous than in most European countries of that day. Civil law was based largely upon Islamic tradition and the Koran. Akbar's chief source of revenue was a land tax, assessed upon the fields actually under cultivation and amounting to one-third of the annual value of the crop, based on the average yield over a ten-year period. This assessment, though heavy enough to provide a huge income to the state, was actually less than that exacted by other rulers both before and after Akbar; also it was applied uniformly and with safeguards against the cupidity of local officials.

The latter part of Akbar's long reign was generally peaceful, and, in spite of the invasions and the murderous strife of preceding centuries, a high level of prosperity seems to have been reached in India. Akbar maintained a sound currency, typified by gold coins of extraordinary fineness. Commerce throve, cities expanded, and a substantial middle class of traders and skilled artisans flourished. Common laborers, however, were far from prosperous, and many were slaves. The country villagers also, who made up the majority of the population, apparently subsisted on a very low standard of living. Great wealth and lavish display were confined to large landowners and officials and were most conspicuous in the court of the emperor. It is estimated that Akbar's total revenue from all sources was equal to more than $200,000,000 a year. Of a total population approximating 100 million, country villagers made up the majority, as they have down to the present day. Although their standard of living was pitifully low, it was probably higher than in modern times.

Prosperity for the rich, hardships for the poor

Akbar's unusual personality and rare combination of interests left their mark upon all aspects of his reign. Endowed with a superb physique, he loved feats of strength and dangerous exploits, sometimes risking his life in the most reckless fashion by attacking a lion single-handed or by riding wild elephants. In a fit of temper he could be pitilessly cruel, but he was generally fair in judgment and frequently generous to a defeated opponent. This high-strung emperor was endowed with lively intellectual curiosity and a capacious mind. He is credited with several inventions, chiefly in connection with the improvement of artillery. Although he stubbornly refused to learn to read or write, he was fond of literature and metaphysical speculation and collected a huge library. A gifted musician, he not only acquired skill as a performer (especially on a type of kettle drum) but also became versed in the highly intricate theory of Hindu vocalization. The promotion of art and architecture was another of his ardent pursuits.

Akbar's personality and his cultural interests

The Mogul rulers did not lack heirs, but each reign usually ended with princes revolting against their father and joining in fratricidal strife with one another. Nevertheless, the administrative system and policies of Akbar were retained substantially for half a century after his death. The most renowned of his successors was Shah Jahan, whose reign extended from 1627 to 1658. Shah Jahan devoted much of his resources to the erection of costly buildings to gratify a sumptuous but exquisite taste. He established his chief royal residence at

Shah Jahan

Top: *Mumtaz Mahal ("Ornament of the Palace")*. The favorite wife of Shah Jahan, who died in childbirth in 1631 at the age of 39. Bottom: *Shah Jahan (1627–1658)*. The Mogul emperor was famous for his luxurious court and his magnificent buildings.

The Sikhs

Delhi, where he laid out a new city and named it after himself. Both Delhi and Agra in the seventeenth century were among the world's greatest cities in respect to number of inhabitants and impressive public buildings. Agra, with a population of 600,000, was divided into separate sections for the different types of merchants and artisans and contained 70 great mosques and 800 public baths. The new Delhi was protected by walls rising 60 feet above the river. Here was constructed a huge royal palace that beggars description. It housed the famous Peacock Throne, inlaid with precious metals and jewels, the value of which has been estimated as in excess of $5,000,000. His extravagant tastes and luxurious court, coupled with fruitless military expeditions against Persia and into Central Asia, so depleted the royal treasury that the emperor raised the land tax to one-half of the annual crop value, putting a crushing burden upon the poorer peasants. Shah Jahan's most celebrated monument is the Taj Mahal, located at Agra and designed as a mausoleum and memorial to his favorite wife (who died while bearing her fourteenth child to the emperor). The Taj engaged the labor of 20,000 workmen and was some twenty years in construction. The building is a unique blend of Persian and Indian architectural elements, executed with meticulous craftsmanship. Its charm is enhanced by its setting, amid shaded walks, lakes, and gardens.

Before the Moguls had completed their cycle of power, they were confronted with a hostile Hindu confederacy known as the Marathas, located in the hilly region of the western Deccan. The Maratha tribesmen, reputedly of the lowest (*sudra*) caste, were a sturdy people who, under the leadership of their wily and resourceful king Sivaji, became a scourge to the Moguls' supremacy. Masters of guerrilla tactics, the Marathas could not be crushed, even though their strongholds were taken and the "Mountain Rat" was himself held captive for a time. The confederacy became a state within the state, collecting taxes and governing a large section of the Deccan, apparently with greater satisfaction to the inhabitants than under the Mogul administration.

Another native faction which acquired an undying hatred for the Moguls was the Sikhs of the Punjab. In origin the Sikhs were a religious group with progressive and idealist convictions. The sect had been founded in the fifteenth century by Nanak, a philanthropic and spiritually minded preacher whose teachings and influence have been the subject of conflicting interpretation. Recent scholars question the claim of some admirers that Nanak sought to establish a common bond between Hindus and Muslims by combining the best elements of each of the two faiths. Undoubtedly he drew much of his inspiration from contemporary Hindu beliefs and traditions, but he was a genuinely original thinker. The essence of his teaching was the brotherhood of man, the oneness of God, and the duty of acts of charity:

The Taj Mahal at Agra. Built by Shah Jahan in memory of Mumtaz Mahal, it is considered one of the finest examples of Indian Muslim architecture.

Make love thy mosque; sincerity thy prayer-carpet; justice thy Koran;
Modesty thy circumcision; courtesy thy Kaaba; truth thy Guru; charity thy
    creed and prayer;
The will of God thy rosary, and God will preserve thine honor, O Nanak.[1]

Nanak rejected formal scriptures and mechanical rites, and because he repudiated caste he gained many adherents from among the depressed classes of Hindus. Although his religion contained doctrines common to Islam and Hinduism (and Christianity), the Sikhs ("disciples") became a distinctive community rather than a branch of Hinduism. Akbar had treated the Sikhs kindly and made a grant of land to their Guru (spiritual teacher), but the hostility of later Moguls goaded them to fury. The sect which had begun as a peaceful reformist movement was gradually transformed into a military order. Its members were initiated by a rite called "Baptism of the Sword," and many of them adopted the surname Singh, meaning "Lion." While they retained an antipathy toward caste and subscribed to a strict code of personal discipline, they lost much of the generous idealism of their early leaders. Appearing sometimes as no better than brigands, they showed particular relish for slaughtering Muslims. Thus at the opening of the eighteenth century the Mogul power was menaced not only by the usual court intrigues but also by the spirited defiance of powerful Indian groups—Rajputs, Marathas, and Sikhs.

The evolution of the sect

The long and calamitous reign of Shah Jahan's son Aurangzeb (1658–1707) pushed the empire to its farthest territorial limits but drained it of much of its strength. A man of tremendous energy, sobriety, and fanatical piety, Aurangzeb sacrificed almost every prin-

Aurangzeb

[1] Quoted in H. G. Rawlinson, *India, a Short Cultural History,* p. 378.

ciple of prudent statesmanship in a futile attempt to establish religious conformity and orthodoxy. He demolished Hindu temples and revived the hated poll tax on non-Muslims which Akbar had wisely rescinded. He waged wars not only against Hindu princes but also against heretical Muslim states in the Deccan. Although he devoted some 25 years to military campaigns and won many victories, he created enemies faster than he could subdue them and he left the Marathas—whom he had tried to destroy—more firmly united than ever.

One further catastrophe robbed the Mogul Dynasty of most of its remaining vitality, although the Moguls were accorded the formal dignity of ruling sovereigns until long after the British had entrenched themselves in India. In 1739 a usurper to the throne of Persia, Nadir Shah, invaded India and sacked Delhi with terrific carnage. He carried off an enormous quantity of booty, including the Peacock Throne, and left much of the city in ruins.

The Mogul period in India was one of considerable activity in intellectual and artistic fields. The emperors were generally cosmopolitan in outlook and welcomed both commercial and cultural intercourse with foreign states. A fusion of Indian, Turkish, Arabic, and Persian elements took place as manifested in literature, the arts, and the general tone of society. As might be expected, architecture illustrates most perfectly the interaction of Hindu and Islamic motifs. Muslim builders introduced the minaret or spire, the pointed arch, and the bulbous dome; Hindu and Jain traditions emphasized horizontal lines and elaborate ornamentation. Because Indian stonemasons and architects were frequently employed even on Muslim religious edifices, there was bound to be a fruitful interchange of ideas, and this culminated in the sixteenth and seventeenth centuries in the production of a distinctive Indo-Muslim architectural style. Some of Akbar's constructions at Agra, of durable red sandstone, are still standing; and so is most of an entire city which he conceived and had completed at a

The Great Mosque in Lahore, Pakistan. Built under the Mogul emperor Aurangzeb, this mosque of red sandstone with marble-covered domes shows Persian influence.

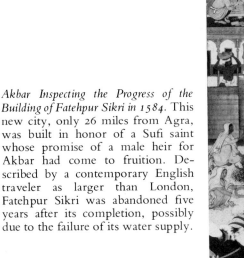

Akbar Inspecting the Progress of the Building of Fatehpur Sikri in 1584. This new city, only 26 miles from Agra, was built in honor of a Sufi saint whose promise of a male heir for Akbar had come to fruition. Described by a contemporary English traveler as larger than London, Fatehpur Sikri was abandoned five years after its completion, possibly due to the failure of its water supply.

site a few miles west of Agra and then abandoned only five years later. But Akbar's forts and government halls lacked the choice materials, the refinement, and the sensuous beauty of the buildings executed for Shah Jahan a half-century later. In place of sandstone, these employed the finest marbles, agate, turquoise, and other semiprecious stones, and were frequently decorated with inlays of gold and silver. Shah Jahan's dazzling structures, contrasting markedly with the robustness of Akbar's work, betray an excessive elegance bordering on decadence.

The Islamic taboos against pictorial representation were almost totally disregarded by the Mogul rulers, who were enthusiastic collectors and connoisseurs of painting. Reflecting the influence of contemporary Persian art, the most typical examples of painting were miniatures, including landscapes and especially portraits, executed with realism and meticulous detail. Calligraphy also enjoyed the status of a fine art, and many manuscripts were illuminated with pictures as in medieval Europe. Texts from the Koran were employed as decorative devices on screens and the façades of buildings, in keeping with a general practice in Muslim countries.

Painting and calligraphy

Probably the most significant expression of Indian creative talent during the Mogul period was literature, which was stimulated by royal patronage and also by the fact that several languages could be drawn upon. Both Turkish and Persian were spoken in court circles; familiarity with Arabic, the language of the Koran, was a necessity for educated Muslims, and a knowledge of the native dialects of northern India was essential for administrators. A permanent result of the intermingling between Turko-Persian and Indian cultures was the rise of

Languages and the foundations of literature

a variety of speech known as Urdu ("the camp language"). While Urdu in its vocabulary includes many Persian and Arabic words and is written in Arabic script, its grammatical structure is basically the same as that of Hindi, the most prevalent Aryan vernacular of northern India. Both Urdu and Hindi came to be standard mediums of communication throughout northern India. (Urdu is now confined chiefly to Pakistan.)

Hindu literature

While the Mogul rulers fostered a cosmopolitan atmosphere at court, attracting thither many Persian scholars and poets, the literary works of most enduring value were produced by Hindus, especially during the tolerant regime of Akbar. This emperor showed great interest in India's literary treasures as well as in her art and music, and he had Persian translations made from the *Vedas* and the Epics. Tulsi Das, one of India's greatest poets, lived during Akbar's reign. His principal work was an idealized and highly spiritual version of the ancient epic, the *Ramayana*. This poem, which combines fine craftsmanship with a warm and fervent moral earnestness, was written in the vernacular tongue rather than in Sanskrit, although its author was a Brahman.

Cultural decline

The reigns of Akbar's later successors, so disastrous to the political fortunes of the Mogul state, were also marked by social unrest and cultural decline. The fanatical Aurangzeb frowned upon art as idolatrous and discouraged literature on the ground that it exalted human vanity. He banished music from his court and, in his extreme mania for orthodoxy, even replaced the Persian solar calendar with the clumsier lunar calendar because the latter had been used by Muhammad. Mogul culture at its best, however, had always been largely a phenomenon of the court and nobility, with few roots among the mass of the populace. Consequently its decline, which was rapid in the eighteenth century, had little effect upon the great body of Hindu society. In many parts of India skillful craftsmanship and exacting artistic standards were carried on much as they had been before the Muslim invasions. Particularly notable was the so-called Rajput school of painting, which was fostered at the courts of native princes in Rajputana and which was more vigorous and less sensuous than the Mogul school.

The coming of Europeans

One aspect of the Mogul period which was bound to have tremendous consequences for the future was the coming of Europeans to India. Although the trading settlements which they established at various points on the coast were small and seemingly insignificant, they denoted the awakening of Europeans to the commercial possibilities of the Far East. The maritime enterprise so highly developed by the Indian states in earlier times had fallen into decay; and even the Mogul empire, for all its splendor, did not long maintain an effective navy. The rise of powerful western European states ended the control of Eastern waters by Arab navigators and brought direct pressure to bear on Indian territory.

Portuguese Goa. A map from Pedro Barreto de Resende's revised edition of Antinio Bocarto's *Curo do Estado da India Oriental, 1646.* Wrested from the Deccan state of Bijapur in 1510, Goa remained under Portuguese control for 451 years.

In the early sixteenth century the Portuguese acquired and fortified several ports on the Indian coast and in Ceylon. Although they lost most of these to more powerful European rivals, they managed to retain Goa, Damão, and Diu until forcibly dispossessed by the government of independent India in December 1961. More significant for the future was the activity of the British East India Company, which was chartered in 1600 and a few years later acquired a port at Surat, north of Bombay on the western coast. This was the fruit of patient negotiation carried on with officials of the Mogul emperor, for whose power the British agents necessarily felt a healthy respect. The Moguls were reluctant to offend the Portuguese as long as the latter commanded the sea routes which Muslim pilgrims used in traveling to Mecca; consequently, only minor concessions were granted to the English in the beginning. William Hawkins, a swashbuckling adventurer, and the more sedate Sir Thomas Roe served successively as English representatives at the court of the Mogul Jahangir, and each wrote a lively account of this eccentric and self-indulgent emperor, who showered hospitality upon his foreign visitors but shrewdly avoided committing himself to a formal treaty. Sir Thomas Roe, while resolutely upholding the dignity of his station before the Mogul courtiers, at the same time warned his own countrymen not to repeat the Portuguese policy of seizing territory and attempting to found

The Portuguese and British footholds

colonies in India. The English, he urged, should seek profit "at sea and in quiet trade," remembering that "war and traffic are incompatible." This advice was little heeded in the subsequent history of the East India Company. Before the close of the seventeenth century the company had secured three locations, of strategic as well as commercial importance, in widely separated regions of India: the island of Bombay off the western coast (given by Portugal in 1661 when the English king, Charles II, married a Portuguese princess), Madras on the soueastern coast, and Fort William (Calcutta) at the mouth of the Ganges.

2. CHINA UNDER THE MANCHU (CH'ING) DYNASTY

*Establishment of Manchu
rule*

With the disintegration of the Ming Dynasty it was China's fate to succumb, for the second time in her history, to conquest by a foreign invader. By the early seventeenth century a strong military organization had been formed in the Amur River region by the Manchus, kinsmen of the Juchên who had divided China with the Sung emperors 500 years before. Taking advantage of China's weakness and factional strife, the Manchu forces pushed southward through Manchuria and occupied Peking in 1644. A few years previously their chieftain had exchanged his tribal title of khan for that of emperor and assumed a Chinese dynastic name—Ch'ing, meaning "Clear" or "Pure." While the Manchu (or Ch'ing) Dynasty, which lasted until the revolution of 1911, is dated from 1644, it was not firmly established until considerably later. Northern China was occupied with little opposition, but many campaigns were required to subdue the stubbornly resisting southern Chinese. Near the end of the seventeenth century a rebellion led by Chinese generals was so nearly successful that it threatened to detach southern China from Manchu rule entirely, but it was finally crushed in 1681 by the young Manchu emperor. Not until 1683 was the last anti-Manchu regime overthrown in Formosa (Taiwan), which was then incorporated into the Chinese empire. The Manchu rulers took steps to make revolt more difficult in the future. They strengthened the control of the central government at Peking over the provinces and distributed the authority in each province among several officials so that each could exercise a check upon the others. Also they won the support of the influential gentry of the Yangtze valley by promising them security in their land holdings. Instead of uprooting Chinese political institutions, the Manchu conquerors adapted them to the requirements of a uniform and centralized administrative system and laid the foundations for a long period of internal peace.

*The dimensions of the
Manchu empire*

From the material standpoint the Manchu Dynasty, which proved to be the last of China's imperial ruling houses, was one of the most successful of all. The state was larger than at any other time in its history except for the brief period in the thirteenth century when

China was part of the pan-Asian Mongol empire. It included Manchuria, Mongolia, Sinkiang, and Formosa, while Tibet was a protectorate, and Korea, Burma, Nepal, and parts of Indochina were tributary dependencies. The government was also remarkably efficient during the first century and a half of the dynasty's history, partly because most of this period was covered by the reigns of two very able and long-lived emperors. One, who while still a youth had broken the rebellion in south China and whose role period is called K'ang Hsi, reigned for sixty-one years (1661–1722). He was therefore a contemporary of King Louis XIV of France, but he was far more of a statesman than the celebrated "Sun King." Under his grandson, who ruled for another sixty years (1736–1796, known as Ch'ien Lung), the dynasty reached the climax of its prestige and effectiveness. Thus, while Europe was in a condition of turbulence and shaken by the wars of rival despots, China enjoyed the advantages of unity and peace under a government which was stable if not entirely benevolent. That Chinese society was generally prosperous is indicated by a phenomenally rapid growth in population under the Manchus. But while China in the eighteenth century was one of the best-governed and most civilized states in the world, its society was highly inequitable and, under a double standard of morals, women were more oppressed than ever before. While prostitution and concubinage flourished, widows were expected to remain in permanent mourning or even prove their fidelity to a departed husband by committing suicide. The cruel and crippling custom of female foot-binding, which was supposed to make a woman more attractive to a man and effectively ensure her remaining dependent upon him, grew in popularity in spite of the efforts of several emperors to stamp it out. Not until the twentieth century was the practice of foot-binding completely abandoned.

Obviously, the Manchu Dynasty was by no means a repetition of the Mongol, even though it was founded by northern invaders of nomadic origin. From the outset the Manchu emperors attempted to identify themselves with the culture and institutions of their Chinese subjects and to rule in accordance with accepted traditions. As a safeguard against rebellion they stationed garrisons in various parts of the country, composed of Chinese and Mongol troops as well as Manchu. They required Chinese men to braid their hair in a queue after the Manchu fashion and to adopt the Manchu style of dress as a token of submission. At the same time they preserved the ancient administrative framework, continued the civil-service examinations, and exalted the state cult of Confucius by requiring temples to be maintained in every district and by elevating the spirit of the ancient sage to the highest rank of official deities. In appointments to office the Manchus showed partiality to their own national group, but nothing like the extreme discrimination which had characterized the Mongol rule. More than 80 percent of the lower governmental offices were filled by Chinese. The top administrative posts were divided about equally

Ch'ien Lung (1736–1796). The great Manchu emperor under whom the Ch'ing Dynasty reached its climax. (Painting on silk by a nineteenth-century artist.)

Manchu administrative policies

between Manchus and Chinese, with half of the Chinese quota going to northerners and half to southerners. Unfortunately, this seemingly equitable arrangement was somewhat unfair to southern China because this region was the more heavily populated.

The substantial material progress that took place during the Manchu period was not an unmixed benefit to the entire nation. Nothing equivalent to an industrial revolution occurred, but there were sufficient social and economic changes to create serious problems for the future. While Chinese society remained basically unaltered in organization and structure between the tenth and the nineteenth centuries, it experienced a great increase in numbers. From time to time the imperial government had taken a census of the population, and the returns—though probably incomplete and inaccurate—indicate an upward trend, especially during the period of Manchu rule. By the early twelfth century, under the Sung, the number of Chinese people had grown to about 100 million. Following the Mongol conquest there was an appreciable decline, but this was only temporary. During the first two centuries of the Manchu Dynasty the population seems to have increased nearly fourfold. It is estimated that by the middle of the nineteenth century the empire included approximately 400 million inhabitants. The causes of this rapid growth are not entirely clear, but it is certain that before the end of the Manchu Dynasty, China was feeling acute distress from the pressure of population upon food supply. The lack of sufficient arable land to support such large numbers led to the clearing and cropping of areas in the upper river valleys which had hitherto been left to nature. Soil erosion subsequently increased the danger of floods and droughts, thus aggravating China's agrarian problem in the modern era.

Although the Chinese were basically one people in their fundamental institutions and cultural heritage, significant sectional differences, which augured trouble for the Manchu regime, had developed between the northern and the southern portions of the country. The sectional contrasts were largely the result of geographic and climatic differences between north and south, but they were intensified by historic factors. The Yangtze valley and the southeastern coastal region were by far the most productive agricultural areas and also contained the largest cities which had long been centers of international commerce. The inhabitants of these areas were characterized by a breadth and diversity of interests and frequently by an independence of spirit which stemmed not so much from an extreme individualism as from a strong sense of family solidarity. Southern Chinese resented the fact that they paid the greater share of taxation, and yet the government seemed to spend most of its money for the benefit of the Peking region. They also felt that they were discriminated against in the competitive examinations, so that the leadership they might have supplied was denied adequate recognition. In spite of their efforts toward conciliation, the Manchu emperors were never able to repose complete confidence in the loyalty of the southern Chinese, and the revolution which finally overthrew the dynasty had its origin in the south.

Not the least among the problems with which the Manchu regime ultimately had to contend was that caused by the penetration of Europeans into the Far East, although as long as the dynasty remained vigorous it experienced little difficulty in holding the foreigners within bounds. The overseas expansion of the Western nations during the Commercial Revolution affected China as well as India and other Eastern lands. By the early sixteenth century the Portuguese had occupied Malacca, and one of their trading vessels reached Canton in 1516. The Chinese authorities, long accustomed to peaceful commercial intercourse with Arabs and other foreigners, at first had been disposed to grant the normal privileges to the newcomers. Portuguese adventurers, however, pillaged Chinese ships engaged in trade with the Indies and raided coastal cities, looting and massacring the inhabitants. Such actions convinced the Chinese that Europeans were no better than pirates; nor was their opinion favorably revised with the arrival, a little later, of the Dutch and the English. The wanton depredations perpetrated by these early Western seafarers were responsible for the unflattering name which the Chinese came to apply to Europeans—"Ocean Devils." The government finally determined to exclude Europeans from the coastal cities but allowed the Portuguese to maintain a trading center and settlement at Macao in the far south. Established in 1557, this post has been retained by the Portuguese to the present day. As a security measure, the local officials constructed a wall blocking off the Portuguese settlement on the island of Macao and imposed rigid restrictions upon the activities of the foreigners. The trade was too profitable for the Chinese to want to abolish it altogether, and the Portuguese were soon extended the privilege of docking at Canton at prescribed times and under strict supervision.

Thus, before the Manchu conquest of China, precedents had already been set for dealing with Western traders. When the Manchus attacked the Ming empire, the Portuguese assisted the Ming court, supplying artillery and some military personnel. This intervention was a portent of things to come, suggesting the ominous possibilities of European interference in Chinese affairs; but its immediate effect was to implant in the Manchu rulers a prejudice against the meddling "Ocean Devils" at the very time when the new regime was being inaugurated. Nevertheless, as the Manchu emperors succeeded in strengthening their position, they were willing to allow European trade to continue, though restricting it chiefly to Canton. Meanwhile, the suspicion attaching to Europeans had been partially dispelled through contacts with Christian missionaries, especially the Jesuits, who had been active in the Far East since the sixteenth century. Many of these Catholic missionaries impressed the Chinese with their breadth of scholarship, their respect for Chinese culture, and their sincere interest in the people among whom they had come to work.

Father Adam Schall with His Astronomical Instruments. Director of the Imperial Board of Astronomy, he wears the "mandarin square" of a Manchu civilian official.

Father Matteo Ricci of Macerata, the First Jesuit Missionary to Work in China, and His Chief Convert, Hsü Kuang-ch'i Pao-lu of Shanghai

Consequently they were permitted to win converts to Christianity and were welcomed into intellectual circles. The early Manchu emperors were generally cordial to Christian missionaries, particularly the French Jesuits, whom they employed at court in such various capacities as instructors in science, mathematics, and cartography.

Encroachments of the
Russians

While the maritime expansion of Western nations was bringing Portuguese, Spanish, French, and others into the Far East, China came into more direct contact with another European power as Russia extended the frontier of her empire overland toward the Pacific. By the latter seventeenth century the Russians were encroaching on the Manchurian border. The success of the Manchus in meeting this threat from the north illustrates the strength of the state at this time, in decided contrast to the weakness which it exhibited before the great Western powers a century and a half later. In 1689 a treaty negotiated with Russian officials defined the boundary between the two countries, provided for a limited commercial intercourse, and arranged for the reciprocal extradition of criminals. This treaty (and subsequent ones negotiated during the eighteenth century) in no way impaired the sovereignty or prestige of China. Her day of humiliation under the impact of Western imperialism was yet to come.

Cultural conservatism

In cultural fields the Manchu period was one of abundant productivity but little originality. It is probably correct to say that the overall trend was toward sterility or even decadence. Chinese culture was still of high level and even brilliant, but it was largely an echo of the genius of earlier centuries. This does not mean that the Chinese had deteriorated in vitality or innate capacity. The decline was partly due to the rigidity of their social institutions and to the fact that they had developed an extreme veneration for ancient authorities, which fostered an attitude of stiff conservatism. More directly it was the result of the government's policy of encouraging docility among the people and frowning upon all innovation. Under the Manchu emperors more than under any native Chinese dynasty the accumulated dogmas of orthodox Confucianism (the Neo-Confucianism of Chu Hsi) were upheld inflexibly and perpetuated in the civil-service examinations through which officials were recruited. Inevitably, as the bureaucracy grew ever more conventional and inelastic in its thinking, it was ill prepared to cope with new problems as they arose. The exalting of orthodoxy above every other virtue led slowly but surely to a state of intellectual stagnation.

Vitality in philosophy

Examples can be found, however, of vigorous and independent thinkers among the Chinese of this period, even in the field of philosophy. Valuable contributions were made by a school of critical scholars who pioneered in the objective and scientific study of ancient classics. The prime objective of this school was to purge Chinese philosophy of the Buddhist and Taoist influences which had encrusted it during the Sung period. Hence, in spite of their perceptiveness and their defiance of conventions, the "Han Learning" scholars were attempting to rehabilitate the distant past rather than to deal directly with the needs of the present. While they were unable to dislodge the narrow conservatism that prevailed in high quarters, the movement was not devoid of results. That such was the case is indicated by the decline of Buddhism as an intellectual force in China even though it remained a popular religion.

If freshness and originality were lacking in most fields of expression, a notable exception was provided by the novel, which continued to be a successful literary medium and reached an even higher state of excellence than it had under the Ming. The best Chinese novels of this period readily bear comparison with significant prose works of other nations, Eastern or Western. As under the Ming, the novel was sometimes a vehicle for satire or trenchant criticism of governmental policies. One early nineteenth-century novel embodied an attack upon the subjection of women and advocated sweeping social and educational reforms.

During the early Manchu period Chinese culture—retrogressive as it may have been—created a more distinct impression upon the civilized nations of the West than had ever been true before. In the eighteenth century especially, Chinese-style gardens, pagodas, and pavilions became fashionable among the wealthy classes of western Europe. Other items borrowed from China included sedan chairs, lacquer, and incense, while the craze for Chinese porcelain reached such proportions that it had the unfortunate effect of lowering the quality of the product. In addition, largely through translations and commentaries prepared by the Jesuits, European intellectuals were introduced to Chinese thought and literature. European acquaintance with these subjects was, of course, limited and superficial, but it was sufficient to arouse curiosity and admiration. Spokesmen of the Enlightenment upheld the somewhat mythical "Chinese sage" as an example of how man could be guided by reason, and fragments of Confucian texts were cited in support of deism.

The Manchu rulers had demonstrated their ability to adapt themselves to the institutions and traditions of their subjects. At the same time, they proved their inability to escape the enfeebling influences that tended to undermine every successful Chinese dynasty. By the nineteenth century their leadership had degenerated seriously, control was slipping into the hands of palace eunuchs, and the court was becoming the scene of soft living and intrigue. As the rulers grew less effectual, they were inclined to compensate for their own deficiencies by appearing more stern and arrogant than their predecessors. Occasionally they instigated persecution of the Christians, and they displayed a haughty and overbearing attitude toward the few European delegations which sought an audience with the emperor. Meanwhile, domestic discontent was manifest in rebellions—both incipient and overt—in various parts of China. Secret societies, hostile to the Manchu government, were organized. The dynasty was probably doomed

Chinese Porcelain. Decorated with "famille verte," a vivid green enamel typical of the K'ang Hsi period (1661–1722).

even before friction with the Western powers later in the nineteenth century created new and distressing problems.

3. JAPAN UNDER THE TOKUGAWA SHOGUNATE

The end of feudalism

The most turbulent period of Japanese feudalism was ended rather abruptly at the close of the sixteenth century when a series of military campaigns forced the daimyo (great lords) to acknowledge the authority of a single ruler. The rise of the daimyo[2] had led to the establishment of fairly effective government within their individual domains, some of which were large enough to include several of the ancient provinces. Hence, when the great lords were brought under a common central authority, the way was open for a genuine unification of the country, and Japan entered upon an era of comparative peace and stability extending to the threshold of modern times.

Nobunaga

The establishment of a stable central government after the ravages of 100 years of feudal warfare was achieved in the space of one generation by three military heroes whose careers were marked with bloodshed, treachery, and pitiless cruelty, but whose work endured. Nobunaga, a small provincial lord who dared to challenge the great daimyo fought his way to control of the imperial city of Kyoto, where he rebuilt palaces and took the Shogun under his protection. When this official proved troublesome, Nobunaga expelled him, thus ending the Ashikaga Shogunate (1573). He moved swiftly to break the power of the great Buddhist monasteries, storming their strongholds and massacring thousands of monks, women, and children. Before his death in battle (1582) he had conquered about half of Japan's provinces.

Hideyoshi

The work of consolidation was carried forward by Nobunaga's ablest general, Hideyoshi, who is commonly regarded as the greatest man in Japanese history. Hideyoshi was a brilliant commander, highly intelligent, and usually sound in judgment, but his fame rests equally on the fact that he is the only figure in Japan's history to rise from the lowest rank (he was a peasant's son) to ruler of the nation. By 1590 he had broken all resistance in Japan and nourished still larger ambitions. He sent an army into Korea, insulted envoys from the Ming imperial court, and launched a second ill-fated expedition with the avowed intention of conquering China.

Tokugawa Ieyasu

The third member of the triumvirate of heroes was Tokugawa Ieyasu. Once a vassal of Nobunaga, he had become the most powerful of the daimyo by the time of Hideyoshi's death in 1598. Following a decisive military victory over rebellious rivals, Ieyasu had himself appointed Shogun in 1603 (the title had been in abeyance for thirty years) and took steps to ensure that this office would remain hence-

---

[2] See above, p. 541.

forth in his family, the Tokugawa. Reaping the fruits of the labors of his two predecessors, Tokugawa Ieyasu made the Shogunate a much more efficient instrument of government than it had ever been before.

Under the Tokugawa Shogunate (1603–1867), Japan's feudal institutions remained intact, but they were systematized and made to serve the interests of a strong central government. Ieyasu founded his capital at Edo (now Tokyo), where he built a great castle surrounded with moats and an elaborate series of outer defenses. The great domains of central and eastern Japan were held by members of the Tokugawa or by men who had helped Ieyasu in his campaigns. These trusted supporters of the regime were known as "hereditary daimyo," while the lords who had acknowledged Ieyasu's supremacy only when forced to do so were called "outer daimyo." The members of both groups were hereditary vassals of the Shogun and were kept under careful surveillance lest they should try to assert their independence. The Shogun employed a corps of secret police to report any signs of disaffection throughout the country. As a special precaution he required all daimyo to maintain residences in Edo and reside there every other year, and also to leave their wives and children as hostages when they returned to their own estates. The system Ieyasu devised was so well organized and thorough that it did not depend on the personal ability of the Shogun for its operation. For the first time Japan had a durable political framework, which remained undisturbed in the hands of the

Five-storied Pagoda at Nikko, in Central Japan. It was built in 1636 and dedicated to the Tokugawa Ieyasu, founder of the Tokugawa Shogunate. The structure (about 100 feet high) is ornately carved, painted, and lacquered, but is given a magnificent natural setting by the surrounding forest.

Tokugawa for two and a half centuries. While the Shogunate was essentially a feudal power structure, it developed for administrative purposes a large bureaucracy of carefully recruited and competent officials.

*Persistence of dual
government*

It should be noted that the Japanese government was still dual in form. The imperial family and a decorative court nobility continued to reside at Kyoto, while the real power was lodged in the Bakufu, the military hierarchy headed by the Shogun at Edo. The Tokugawa Shoguns cultivated the fiction that they were carrying out the will of a divine emperor. By emphasizing the emperor's sanctity they added an aura of invulnerability to their own position, and by keeping him in seclusion they rendered him harmless. The shadow government at Kyoto was now entirely dependent upon the Shogun even for its financial support, but it was carefully and respectfully preserved as a link with Japan's hallowed past.

Relations with Europeans

The most serious problem of the early Tokugawa period concerned relations with Europeans. Before the close of the sixteenth century both the Portuguese and the Spanish were carrying on considerable trade in Japan, and the Dutch and the British secured trading posts early in the following century. Europeans had been accorded a favorable reception by the Japanese, who seemed eager to learn from them. Firearms, acquired from the Portuguese, came into use for the first time in Japan and played a part in the feudal battles of the late sixteenth century. The introduction of gunpowder had the effect temporarily of stimulating the construction of heavy stone castles by the daimyo, a practice which was carefully regulated by the Tokugawa after they had seized the Shogunate.

*The growth and
suppression of Christianity*

Along with the Western traders came missionaries, who at first encountered little hostility. Vigorous proselyting by Portuguese Jesuits and Spanish Franciscans met with remarkable success in winning converts to the Catholic faith among all classes of the population, including some of the feudal nobles. By the early seventeenth century there were close to 300,000 Christian converts in Japan, chiefly in the south and west where the European trading centers were located. Eventually, however, the Shoguns decided that Christianity should be proscribed, not because they objected to the religion as such but because they were afraid it would divide the country and weaken their authority. They were annoyed by the bickering between rival European groups and also feared that their subjects were being enticed into allegiance to a foreign potentate, the pope. The first persecutions were mild and were directed against Japanese Christians rather than against the Europeans; but when the missionaries refused to halt their work they were severely dealt with, and many were executed. Finally, in 1637, when a peasant revolt against oppressive taxation developed into a Christian rebellion, the Shogun's forces conducted a real war against the Christian strongholds in southwestern Japan and, in spite of the most heroic resistance, wiped out the Christian communities and exterminated the religion almost completely.

Following this bloody purge, the Shoguns adopted a policy of excluding all Europeans from Japanese settlement. That they were able to enforce it shows how strong their government had become. Reluctant to cut off Western trade entirely, they made a slight exception in the case of the Dutch, who seemed to be the least dangerous politically. The Dutch were permitted to unload one ship each year at the port of Nagasaki in the extreme western corner of Japan, but only under the strictest supervision. Going even further along the line of reaction, the Shogun next forbade his Japanese subjects to visit foreign lands on pain for forfeiting all their rights and commanded that no ship should be built large enough to travel beyond the coastal waters of the island empire. Although traffic with China was continued, the Shoguns forced upon their country a policy of almost complete isolationism, thus reversing the course which had been followed advantageously during many centuries preceding.

The Tokugawa era gave Japan a long period of peace and orderly government and promoted the ideal of a perpetually hierarchical society. Theoretically, the social structure was arranged in accordance with the classes of China, which ranked, in order of importance: (1) scholar-officials, (2) farmers, (3) artisans, (4) merchants, and (5) soldiers, bandits, and beggars. In Japan, however, the realities of a feudalized society produced a peculiar distortion of the ideal arrangement, which was somewhat fanciful even in China. The warrior (*samurai*), who had enjoyed a position of leadership for centuries, was elevated from the lowest category to the highest. In return for the place of honor assigned to him he was expected to exhibit the qualities of the scholar also, and to a considerable extent he did. The daimyo and the samurai were no longer the uncouth, lawless ruffians of early feudal days but refined aristocrats, who cultivated literature and the arts and took pride in the rigorous discipline to which they were bred. Still, their pre-eminence had been won in the first instance by force, and their position was regarded as a hereditary right, not to be challenged by men of superior ability who had been born to a lower class.

The artificiality and formal rigidity of the Tokugawa regime did not stifle economic progress. By the early eighteenth century Japan's population had reached a total of 30 million; thenceforth it increased but slightly for a century and a half. This slow rate of population growth apparently was more the result of voluntary family planning than of a scarcity of resources, although occasional famines did occur. The country as a whole was prosperous; industry and internal trade continually expanded even though foreign commerce had been curtailed. Communication was relatively easy through all parts of Japan, both by waterways and by improved highways. A brisk exchange of agricultural and manufactured goods promoted the growth of a capitalist economy. Rice merchants occupied a strategic position in the world of finance and their establishments, offering commercial credit and daily price quotations, bore some resemblance to a modern stock exchange. Cities grew in size, especially in the central area of the

Japanese Bronze, Eighteenth Century. The figure depicted is Kuan Ti, Chinese "God of War"—actually a deified military hero of the early third century A.D. Regarded as the patron of military officials, he was particularly revered in China during the late Ch'ing (Manchu) period.

Expansion of agricultural productivity

country. By the late eighteenth century Edo had attained a population of one million and was probably the largest city in the world at that time.

Economic progress, coupled with a rigid and inherently authoritarian political regime, produced severe strains within society. The position of the samurai became more and more anomalous. While they possessed a monopoly of the profession of arms, they found little opportunity to practice it because the Shogun discouraged feudal quarrels, and there were no foreign wars. Thus the samurai became, by and large, a group of respectable parasites, although many of them displayed both talent and energy. They were often employed in administrative functions by the daimyo, and sometimes took over the management of a great domain so completely that the daimyo was reduced to little more than a figurehead. On the other hand the merchants, who were ranked at the bottom of the social pyramid, steadily accumulated wealth, formed their own trade associations to replace the older and more restrictive guilds, and exerted a potent influence over the whole national economy. Inevitably they imparted a bourgeois tone to society in the bustling cities.

Until recently historians commonly assumed that the peasants' lot under the Tokugawa was a miserable one, but research in Japanese sources has discredited this assumption. It is true that peasant labor supported the upper classes of daimyo and samurai as well as the Shogun and his bureaucracy. It is also true that peasants endured privation and sometimes cruel treatment at the hands of their social superiors, who dismissed them contemptuously as seeds to be pressed or cattle to be driven. The outbreak of riots and actual local rebellions—in a society as disciplined as the Tokugawa—indicates the reality and the depth of popular discontent. But the evidence is undeniable that Japanese farmers and tenants not only contributed to but also shared in the country's rising prosperity. Forbidden to bear arms, they were relieved from the burden of military service, and they benefited from the two and a half centuries of almost uninterrupted peace that followed the accession of Tokugawa Ieyasu.

Japanese agriculture was vastly more progressive than in earlier times. The amount of land under cultivation doubled, new crops were introduced, intensive fertilization and better tools, including a mechanical thresher, came into use, and irrigation was extended through the cooperative efforts of farm villages. A steady expansion in productivity, together with regional specialization keyed to market demands, enabled the majority of peasants to sustain a rising standard of living in spite of tax increases during the eighteenth century. But while agriculture enjoyed a flourishing condition, its rewards were not evenly distributed. A trend away from large family combinations to smaller units that could be run more efficiently widened the spread between prosperous and indigent peasants, and there was an increase in tenantry as opposed to individual farm ownership. At the same

Woman Weaving Cloth

time the emergence of a mobile class of wage earners stimulated growth of village industries—processing silk, cotton, salt, tobacco, saké, and sugar cane—and provided a reserve labor force which eventually contributed to the rapid industrialization of Japan in the post-Tokugawa period.

During the Tokugawa era Japanese culture, being largely cut off from outside contacts, acquired a distinctive national character. This is not negated by the fact that intellectual circles manifested a heightened interest in Chinese philosophy. A number of Chinese scholars had fled to Japan when the Ming Dynasty was overthrown by the Manchus and, more importantly, the Shoguns encouraged study of the Confucian classics, particularly among the aristocracy, because they thought it would help to inculcate habits of discipline in their subjects. These writings, of course, had long been honored in Japan, but now they were diligently examined for the purpose of developing a native school of philosophers who, through their example and through their position as administrators, could inculcate the principles of virtue—especially obedience—among all classes of the population.

The growing interest in Chinese philosophy

The most significant social and cultural changes were those related to the growth of large cities, such as Edo, Osaka, and Kyoto, where men of wealth were creating an atmosphere of comfort and gaiety in contrast to the restrained decorum of the feudal nobility. In these populous commercial and industrial centers the trend in art and literature and especially in the field of entertainment was toward a distinctly middle-class culture, which was sometimes gaudy but appealing in its exuberance and spontaneity. In the pleasure quarters of the cities an important figure was the geisha girl, who combined the qualities of a

Life and customs in the large cities

The Art of Tile Making. A wood block by Hokusai (1760–1849), an artist famous for landscapes.

Woman Playing the Flute. The flutist is by Harunobu (1724–1770), earliest master of the multicolored-print technique.

modern beauty queen with the talents of a nightclub entertainer. Trained in the art of conversation as well as in song and dance, she provided the sparkling companionship which men too often missed in their own homes because of the habits of docility and self-effacement that they instilled into their wives and daughters. Prostitution, also, was prevalent on a large scale in the towns, in spite of attempts by the authorities to curtail the evil. Inherently sordid as was the practice, it took on a specious refinement under the patronage of the well-do-do, and some courtesans acquired an enviable standing in the loose but highly sophisticated society which flouted established conventions. Not only merchants and businessmen but even samurai and daimyo were attracted by the gay diversions of city life, and surreptitiously exchanged the boredom of their routine existence for the delights of a "floating world" of pleasure and uninhibited self-expression.

The dissolute society of the Tokugawa cities was by no means utterly degenerate. Some of the best creative talents in Japan catered to bourgeois appetites, just as they did in Italy during the Renaissance. Racy novels, satirizing contemporary figures and piquant with gossip, innuendo, and scandal, came into vogue. Previously art had been chiefly aristocratic and religious except for the exquisitely designed articles of ordinary household use produced by the various handicrafts. Now a type of folk art was appearing that mirrored society realistically and also was enlivened with humor and caricature. Its chief medium was the wood-block color print, which could be produced cheaply enough to reach a wide public and which has ever since been a popular art form. Another proof of the influence that urban tastes were exerting in the aesthetic sphere is seen in the evolution of the Kabuki drama. In contrast to the No, the highly stylized and austere dance-drama that had been perfected a few centuries earlier under the patronage of the aristocracy, the Kabuki offered entertainment appealing to the middle and lower classes of the towns. Although it owed something to traditional dance forms, the Kabuki drama was derived more immediately from the puppet theater and, unlike the No, it was almost entirely secular in spirit. As developed in the seventeenth and eighteenth centuries, the Kabuki drama attained a high degree of realism, with exciting plots, lively action, and effective stage devices. In the opinion of some theatrical experts, it deserves to rank as the greatest drama any civilization has ever produced.

Various forces at work in Japan tended to undermine the foundations of Tokugawa institutions in spite of their apparent durability. The partial transformation of Japan's economy from an agrarian to a mercantile basis enhanced the importance of men engaged in manufacture, trade, and transport. As a result feudalism was rendered obsolete, and the feudal classes began to feel the pinch of adversity. Although money had been in circulation for many centuries, the incomes of daimyo and of their samurai retainers were still computed in measures of rice, the chief agricultural staple. The merchants who provisioned such great cities as Edo and Osaka controlled the market-

Economic changes

Kabuki Theater. Left: Kabuki actor (Matsumoto Koshiro) portrayed here as a fishmonger by Sharaku, a wood-block artist noted for his caricatures of actors (1794 or 1795). Right: Famous actor Mitsugoro Bando portraying the aged warrior Ikyu in the play *Sukeroku.*

ing of a large proportion of the rice crop; hence they were able to foresee fluctuations in price and sometimes even to induce fluctuations for their own benefit. Naturally, the daimyo and samurai were at a disadvantage in a period of unstable prices, because their incomes were from land rents, and because their necessities were increasingly supplied by articles that had to be purchased in the cities. Often the price of rice was considerably below the general price level; and even when it was high, the middleman appropriated most of the profit. The landed aristocrats found their real incomes diminishing while low-born traders and brokers grew richer and richer.

The disruption of classes

Inevitably, class lines began to break down, just as they did in western Europe under similar conditions during the period of the Commercial Revolution. Wealthy Japanese merchants purchased samurai rank and title, while nobles adopted children of bourgeois families or contracted marriage alliances with this class in an effort to recoup their fortunes. Feeling honor-bound to maintain their accustomed style of living—at least in appearances—the aristocrats borrowed recklessly. As early as 1700 the indebtedness of the daimyo class was reputed to have reached a figure one hundred times greater than the total amount of money in Japan. Impoverished samurai pawned their ceremonial robes and even the swords which were their badge of rank. While townspeople in large numbers were entering the lower grades of samurai, samurai and farmers were flocking to the towns, where the more successful ones merged into the bourgeois class.

Cultural trends generate unrest

The unrest generated by economic dislocation was further augmented by cultural trends in the later Tokugawa period. As a national spirit developed, it was accompanied by a renewal of interest in Japan's past. Shintoism, the ancient cult over which the imperial family presided, had been largely eclipsed by Buddhism. Gradually its popularity revived, and several new Shinto sects obtained an enthusiastic following. The study of ancient records (historical and mythological) stimulated reflection on the unique character of Japan—"founded by a heavenly ancestry, country of the gods"—and on the alleged origins of the imperial office. It directed attention to the fact that the Shogunate was a comparatively recent innovation or actually a usurpation, not an authentic part of the ancient political structure. At the same time, familiarity with China's political heritage—fostered by the vogue of Confucian scholarship which the Shoguns themselves had promoted—raised doubts among Japanese intellectuals as to the merits of a dual administrative system and of feudal institutions. Moreover, Western books and ideas were seeping into Japan through the port of Nagasaki where the Dutch were permitted a very limited trade. Even before Japan was "opened" in the nineteenth century, considerable interest had been aroused in Western guns, ships, watches, glassware, and scientific instruments. Thus Japan's insulation from the outside world was beginning to develop cracks at the same time that internal discontent had reached a dangerous point. By the opening of the nineteenth century the Shogun's position was precarious, unlikely to withstand the shock of a severe crisis, especially since other powerful families were eagerly watching for any sign of weakness on the part of the Tokugawa.

The sweeping and revolutionary changes in Japan since the abolition of the Shogunate in 1867 have made it difficult to view the Tokugawa period with an undistorted perspective. Inward-looking, conservative, and devoted to hierarchy as it was, the Tokugawa regime went far toward unifying the nation, instilled habits of discipline, and provided a long period of security. Class structure was not so rigid as to prevent the realization of a fairly homogeneous society, especially as urban centers grew and communication improved. Education advanced significantly; by the end of the Tokugawa period about 45 percent of the male population was literate (only 15 percent of the female), a record unmatched in the rest of Asia and better than that of many countries today. Although Japan was still a predominantly agrarian society, capital techniques had been developed and applied to agriculture as well as to commerce and manufacture. Seemingly, although certainly unintentionally, the Tokugawa Shoguns had laid the foundation for Japan's transformation into a modern state.

*Contributions of the
Tokugawa period*

Recently a group of Japanese historians—disillusioned with the effects of modernization and proponents of what they call "people's history"—have depicted the Tokugawa period as a kind of golden age. They claim that it contained the seeds of a freer society and even of democracy, evidenced by the growth of village cooperatives which stimulated social initiative and active participation among the peasants. They indict the imperial restoration as a "failed vision," a regretable step toward state worship, and they argue that the Tokugawa era could have provided the base for a structure different from and better than a duplication of Western industrialized society.[3]

*An unconventional
interpretation*

4. AFRICA UNDER DIVINE RULERS AND RITUAL CHIEFS

The period 1500 to 1800 marked the beginning of Africa's incorporation into the capitalist world economy. From about 1500, western Europe transformed Africa into a satellite of its own burgeoning capitalistic system. The network of international trade established by the Arabs by the thirteenth century was seized and extended by the Europeans from the opening of the sixteenth century. This maritime contact ended Africa's long isolation from the West and brought all coasts of the continent into the European commercial orbit.

*Africa as Europe's
Economic Satellite*

[3] Carol Gluck, "The People in History: Recent Trends in Japanese Historiography," *Journal of Asian Studies,* November 1978, pp. 25–50.

*European presence on the
coast forces a reorientation
of trade*

This period also witnessed the arrival of European traders and adventurers on Africa's sub-Saharan shores. A revolution in maritime and military technology enabled Europeans to navigate beyond sight of land and to conduct an efficient ocean-borne trade with swift, well-armed ships. For West Africans this necessitated a reorientation of trade from their ancient North African markets across the Sahara to western Europe and the Americas via the Atlantic. A voluminous and highly profitable Atlantic traffic ensued with explosive force and required a concentration of territorial power in the hands of a few rulers. Instability generated by the introduction of arms trafficking and slave raiding forced weaker communities either to coalesce in self-defense or to seek the protection of larger, better organized societies in neighboring areas. First coastal kingdoms, then empires, emerged in the tall forests after the 1650s in response to increasing opportunities for trade in guns, gunpowder, and exotic luxury items.

*Pre-European trading
networks*

Long-distance trading networks from coast to interior and coast-wise by canoe from the Niger Delta to the Ivory Coast antedated European contact. Indeed, small, independent fishing communities had dotted the palm-studded coast at least since 1300. Fisherfolk exchanged ocean salt and dried fish with forest farmers for yams, goats, and cattle. Later, such local industries as fishing, weaving, and brewing were weakened when communities turned to the less expensive though often inferior European substitutes. Ultimately, European traders fostered economic rivalries and precipitated civil wars between African communities to prevent indigenous traders and chiefs from uniting. Such unity could inflate prices and weaken the European trade advantage. Nevertheless, on an individual basis, African traders sometimes proved superior to Europeans in the art of bargaining.

*European traders restricted
to the coast*

Between about 1730 and 1800 the less accessible interior states sought to extend their authority to the sea in order to trade directly with the Europeans. Seldom, however, were foreign traders permitted to operate beyond the coast. In Benin, Dahomey, and Oyo they were restricted to designated seaports and could only lease the land upon which they constructed their warehouses, fortresses, and slave markets.

Some states, like Oyo, Benin, and Asante, prospered and became territorial empires. Others, particularly Kongo, Ngola, and Mwenemutapa, failed to keep the Europeans at arm's length or to comprehend fully their true motives. Their history was punctured by foreign intrigue, political instability, and eventual collapse. Numerous African governments became so dependent on European trade that a shift in pattern spelled economic doom.

*Divine kings and
territorial aggrandizement*

During this era, kings, claiming divine attributes, aggrandized their authority through military force. Often, neighbors were reduced to tributary status. Royal subordinates, dispatched to the conquered areas, guarded against conspiracies and assimilated the vanquished.

Folkways and authority patterns, if strong, were usually left intact, while prisoners of war and dissidents were sold into slavery in order to replenish supplies of gunpowder. Africa's human losses were America's gains in this vicious circle initiated by amoral white traffickers and facilitated by selfish black collaborators.

Like the divine emperors of Japan, the Obas of Benin, Asantehenes of Asante, Manikongos of Kongo, Alafins of Oyo, and other African monarchs shrouded themselves in mystery and appeared only on ceremonial occasions. Much of their time was devoted to state rituals and sacrifices to ancestral heroes. They evolved rigid codes of court etiquette and communicated with commoners only through intermediaries. Some wore finely crafted, oversized sandals to shield their feet from direct contact with the sacred earth. All of them fostered a hieratic art, aimed as exalting the sanctity of the state. To achieve this, guild artists were supported by the monarchy and forced to remain within the palace confines so that their talents would not pass to others.

These kings, their paramount chiefs, and lesser titled hereditary officials devised ingenious systems of checks and balances to prevent a concentration of power in any single office. In the Oyo empire (in western Nigeria) the Alafin served as hereditary secular leader. Yet his power had to be shared with a royally appointed nobility, which organized itself into a kind of electoral college and administrative watchdog called the Oyo *Mesi*. Its leading member, the *Bashorun,* acted as prime minister and as spokesman for most of the powerful national cults or religious orders. As a counterforce to the Oyo *Mesi,* the Alafin appointed trusted slaves, called *Ilari*. They were responsible for collecting tribute and overseeing local government. At the same time, every important town was headed by a hereditary mayor or *Oba*. Though the *Oba*'s authority derived from ancestral mandate and tradition, his powers were limited by the Ogboni Society. This organization of influential and prosperous townsfolk linked the masses of peasants, traders, and artisans to royal authority. Everyone in the Oyo empire, from the Alafin down to the poorest peasant, swore allegiance to the Oni of Ifé. Ifé was the founding city-state of the Oyo empire, the fount of Yoruba civilization; and the ancient office of Oni served as the supreme authority over spiritual matters. Power was therefore diffused throughout society. From at least the fifteenth to the late eighteenth century the Yoruba peoples of Oyo were well served by this unwritten constitution.

In the 1790s, the authority and prestige of the Alafin's office, so vital to national solidarity, was severely diminished when its holder challenged the spiritual supremacy of the Oni of Ifé. The time-honored rules of the game eroded further when the *Bashorun,* or prime minister, tested his own strength against the Alafin's. Preoccupation with such power struggles weakened central authority and enabled the tributary states to secede. Civil war erupted, and in the mid-nine-

Royal Dignitary. Bronze plaque fragment. Bini tribe, Benin.

Political organization

Weakening of the central authority

Yoruba civilization

Belt Mask. Ivory. Bini Tribe, Benin.

*Afro-European relations
poisoned by the demands
of the slave trade*

teenth century the crumbling empire fell prey to European intrigue from the south and Muslim Fulani challenges from the north.

Even though the Oyo empire disintegrated, its artistic and musical traditions continued to thrive. In both Oyo and neighboring Benin, guilds of Yoruba craftsmen turned out a rich variety of sculpture in brass, bronze, ivory, and wood. Metal commemorative busts and plaques, some antedating European contact by centuries, were delicate, strikingly naturalistic, and secular in intent. Companies of professional acrobats, dancers, and musicians traveled about the countryside giving performances which were sometimes critical of government practices, royal behavior, and social convention. In many ways, their programs were like an editorial column of a modern newspaper.

Many forest states could boast of magnificent capital cities, holding sprawling palaces and temples with sunken atriums surrounded by columns. Benin city was one of the world's few urban centers to be laid out on a gridiron pattern, with broad tree-lined avenues intersecting streets at near right angles. Kumasi, the capital of Asante, was described by foreigners as Africa's garden city because of its lush flowering undergrowth set against tidy compounds with multicolored stylized facades.

It is significant that most West African forest civilizations had emerged, and in some cases reached their zenith, before European involvement. The Obaship in Benin was well established before Portuguese explorers arrived at Benin's major seaport of Gwato in 1472. Likewise, the Manikongo of Kongo ruled over an expansive domain with almost unchallenged authority before Portuguese contact a decade later. And Ifé was already recognized by the Yoruba as their major religious and cultural center.

Many African leaders received the Portuguese initially with great enthusiasm, hoping to taste the fruits of new techniques in agriculture, industry, and warfare. Before 1505 Benin and Kongo dispatched ambassadors and young intellectuals to Lisbon and the Vatican. But when America's vast resources were discovered by European explorers, it became obvious that the wealth could best be exploited by cheap labor in massive quantities. Only nearby Africa seemed to possess that necessary commodity. Thus, after about 1505, traders, missionaries, and other European visitors to Africa had different intentions from their predecessors. They came not as skilled technicians but as "advisers" who would gradually infiltrate African governments in order to better organize them for the slave trade. Thus, even though the political unification of Portugal and Spain in 1580 sacrificed African involvement to other interests, it in no way spelled an end to the Atlantic trade in humans.

Portuguese initiative in nautical science had already passed to the English, Dutch, and French—all of whom had begun to establish their own colonies of exploitation and settlement in the New World.

View of Benin City before the British Conquest. Note the gridiron street pattern.

Between 1637 and 1642 the Portuguese lost almost all their enclaves in West Africa to the Dutch. The Hollanders, unable to buy enough slaves on the West African coast, soon looked to the Ngola kingdom farther south. Only there did the Portuguese mount a successful resistance.

European rivalries for the African trade

In the course of the seventeenth century, royally chartered companies from many European states formed monopoly enterprises and constructed warehouses and strings of stone fortresses along the West African coast. In 1672 the Royal African Company received a charter from the English crown and soon became the most active buyer of West African gold and slaves. Still, fierce competition with the Dutch in arms and munitions sales to Africans quickly led to a proliferation of deadly weapons among certain forest societies. To many African chiefs, slave raiding and trading became a painful necessity. If they refused to engage in it, the Europeans would supply arms to rivals who might in turn use them to sell their people into captivity. Dahomey and the Kongo, initially opposed to the slave trade, soon found it necessary either to play the European game or face possible economic and political ruin. Benin was one of the few African states that successfully controlled slave trading. It remained an independent political entity until the British invasion of 1897.

A number of small states were born in the seventeenth century in

Demoralizing effects of the slave and arms trade

Dutch Ambassador Welcomed by King Alvaro II of the Kongo. Early in the seventeenth century the Dutch began to rival the Portuguese for control of the kingdoms near the mouth of the Congo River.

Asante civilization

the Akan forest behind the Gold Coast. They were known to have supplied by that time more than 20 percent of Europe's gold reserves. Under the stimulus of the Royal African Company, this trade increased and led in the late seventeenth century to the rise of the Asante empire. The Akan peoples of Asante grew extremely powerful and wealthy by taxing trade passing through their territory en route to the coast. Between 1721 and 1750 Asante civilization reached its zenith. Asante artisans crafted earrings, anklets, pendants, and armbands from gold and bronze. On horizontal stip looms they wove polychromed togas of varied designs. Each pattern had a name and conveyed a symbolic meaning.

Dahomey: example of extreme centralization

The Atlantic slave trade received a great boost after 1713 when England secured the Spanish *Asiento,* or license, to supply slaves to Spanish New World possessions. In response, the Yoruba state of Oyo expanded into a territorial empire, serving as middleman in the slave trade between the Hausaland interior and the coast. Other states exhibited a similar pattern. Immediately west of Oyo appeared the highly centralized kingdom of Dahomey. Between 1724 and 1729 Dahomey swept into the coastal Aja states and assimilated them.

Unable to foster other sorts of trade with the Europeans, the Daho-means became both suppliers and brokers in the slave trade. Oyo, fearful of this competition, diverted traffic to its own ports in 1750. To survive the consequent economic dislocation, the Dahomean government developed a state-controlled totalitarian economic and political system unparalleled in the eighteenth century. All state officials were appointed by the king, who ruled as a dictator, and a secret police was established to enforce his will. No system of checks and balances existed; only precedent and ancestral sanction guided his rule. Acting as high priest, the king dominated the major cults. He also controlled the craft guilds which produced pictorial tapestries and graceful statues to glorify royal power. A national military draft of men and women was instituted as well as a census bureau to administer it. Slave-worked plantations were established and placed under the close supervision of a minister of agriculture. Dahomey's economy was tightly regulated with central control over taxation and currency. Prices and wages, on the other hand, were set by producers' organizations. Culturally, westernization was actively discouraged by recourse to an aggressive policy of conquest and enforced assimilation into the traditional Fon way of life. Dahomey outlived the destructive effects of the slave trade and was able to safeguard its dynamic cultural institutions until French guns disrupted them in 1894.

Kongo and Ngola, in the savanna zone of West Central Africa, did not fare as well. After 1482 the Kongolese monarch, anxious to learn the secrets of European technology, assumed a Christian name and converted to Catholicism. But within two decades, Catholic missionaries had driven a wedge between the king and the nobility, who wished to follow the time-honored indigenous traditions. In 1556 rivalries among Portuguese advisers in the Kongo and Ngola dragged these two kingdoms into a destructive war against each other. Ngola won, but the real beneficiaries were European and mulatto slavers who reaped huge profits selling the war prisoners and refugees. Escalating demands for miners in Portuguese Brazil finally led to the total destruction of Kongo and Ngola (called Angola by the Portuguese) in 1665 and 1671 respectively. Their governments collapsed, although the Kongolese tradition of fine raffia cloth weaving remained vigorous. Slave trading persisted and resulted in a further moral and ethical deterioration among certain segments of the population. Successor African Lunda and Luba kingdoms arose deep in the interior, safely beyond direct Portuguese interference. Some of these highly centralized kingdoms survived into the twentieth century, but only to lose their independence to a new wave of Europeans, in search not of slaves but of copper

Portuguese involvement on the East African coast was equally destructive, even though it had little to do with the slave trade. In 1498 Vasco Da Gama rounded the Cape and sailed northward along

*Kongo and Ngola become
major sources for slaves
and fail to survive
European intrusions*

the Swahili coast in search of the East Indies. He was astounded to discover a series of prosperous and highly civilized city-states with strong commercial and cultural links to Arabia, the Persian Gulf, and India. But it was distressing to him that their Sultans were fervent practitioners of Islam. It is no wonder that Da Gama had battles in three of the four city-states he visited. At Milandi his reception was cordial, only because Da Gama had sacked Malindi's commercial rival, Mombasa.

The Portuguese were impressed by the gold and copper flowing out of Central Africa and by the extensive Indian Ocean trading network which carried the ore to distant ports. They hoped to use the Swahili city-states as a springboard to the Indies and as a source of gold for financing commercial operations in India and the Spice Islands. By 1505, after several Portuguese voyages of plunder and bombardment, the city-states were reduced to tributary status.

The Portuguese did not intend to govern the Swahili city-states. Rather, they attempted, with only limited success, to monopolize the Indian Ocean trade through their Viceroy at Goa on the western coast of India. After troubles with Turkish pirates and pillaging Zimba tribesmen, the Portuguese in 1593 constructed a massive stone citadel, called Fort Jesus, at Mombasa, and the malleable Sultan of Malindi was appointed to govern on their behalf. In 1622 the Portuguese were driven out of Ormuz, their strategic stronghold in the Persian Gulf, by a powerful Persian fleet. The fragility of Porguguese rule soon

Islam in East Africa. Mombassa Mosque with minaret. Sixteenth century.

Portuguese in East Africa. Fort Jesus was built in 1593 at Mombassa by the Portuguese. It served as their major foothold in East Africa until 1728, when they were driven out under a combined Afro-Arab siege.

became evident to others. From the 1630s they had to suppress costly revolts in numerous Swahili towns. After Muscat, the gateway to the Persian Gulf, fell in 1650, the Omani Arabs emerged as a formidable naval power. In 1698 they drove the Portuguese out of Mombasa, their major port of call en route to India, and Portuguese supremacy north of Mozambique crumbled like a house of cards. In its wake lay the ruins of a once magnificent Swahili civilization. The Omani came to East Africa as liberators, but stayed on as conquerors, practicing a kind of benign neglect which led to further cultural and economic deterioration.

The Portuguese also failed in their attempts to control the gold and copper mines of the Rhodesian and Katangan plateaus. After one hundred eighty years of interference in the political and religious institutions of the Mwenemutapa empire, they were forced to retreat to the Mozambique coast. Their traders and soldiers were simply no match against the more determined and better organized Shona armies. African resistance was clearly stronger than the Portuguese will to conquer. In 1798 the Portuguese attempted to link their colony in Angola with Mozambique in the hope of forging a transcontinental African empire. But malaria and the unwillingness of the crown to administer such a vast area were responsible for its failure.

Portuguese repelled

Africans gained little from the Europeans in their first three centuries of contact. The exchange of guns, powder, alcoholic beverages, and cheap manufactured textiles for humans, gold, ivory, pepper, and palm oil stimulated the centralization of African authority in some areas and contributed to the growth of empires. But it added little to the advance of African civilizations. The south Atlantic trade system also led to the introduction into tropical Africa of new food crops from the Americas, particularly manioc, maize, bananas, cassava, and peanuts. These crops enabled certain regions of the continent to sustain much higher population densities which in turn contributed to

Europeans contribute little to the advance of African civilization

the tendency to state formation. However, disease remained an important determinant in African history. The growth of long-distance trade increased intercommunication among regions in Africa and thus facilitated the transmission of disease among population groups. On the other hand, yellow fever and malaria, so fatal to Europeans, kept white mortality rates high and discouraged extensive direct commercial penetration and colonization in all but the temperate coasts of North and South Africa. Christianity, introduced by force and often for ulterior motives, did not take firm hold. On the other hand, Islam, having suffered a severe setback in the western Sudan after the Moroccan invasion of Songhay in 1591, flourished in the Hausa city-states in northern Nigeria. After 1725 Islamic Sufi orders had begun to declare *jihads,* or holy wars, in the Senegal region and to establish theocratic states based on strict adherence to Islamic practices. Yet Islam remained an unknown factor until the nineteenth century for the vast majority of sub-Saharan Africans.

The nature of trade with Europe

Unlike Japan, Africa's real economic growth was slowed by the exploitative, nonproductive nature of the European trade. Europeans exported items which could not be used in the production of other goods. In West Africa, guns and gunpowder by the eighteenth century had become the most important foreign trade commodity. Between 1796 and 1805 more than 1.6 million guns were sent to West Africa from England alone. A strong connection developed between firearms and the acquisition of slaves. The weapons were used mainly for interethnic raids and wars connected with the gathering of people for the slave markets. Wars which created many slaves for the Atlantic markets were particularly stimulated by competition among Africans for control of trade routes to the coast. Some African ethnic groups sold slaves to obtain guns to ensure their own political survival against

Reconstruction of a Kabaka's Reed in Kampala, Uganda. These structures, once common to Buganda royalty, have disappeared.

African Craftsmen. Dye pits in Kano (northern Nigeria) were and still are owned by traditional craft guilds.

internal rivals. In other words, slave exports were sometimes the result of politically motivated warfare rather than of pure economic incentive.

African contact with the Euro-American capitalist system contributed to the evolution of state formation. However, in the long run it generated political instability, bred by struggles for power and status between the old elites and the emerging military and commercial entrepreneurs. The existing bases of political and social differentiation were challenged. Greater popular involvement in warfare and in the trade in gold, slaves, and forest agricultural products enabled clever and ambitious commoners to generate independent wealth. In Asante, Oyo, Dahomey, and elsewhere the traditional royal lineages were forced to alter the hereditary political structures by incorporating ability and meritocracy into them. The rulers who failed to accommodate themselves to the changing order were faced with destructive civil wars and chronic political instability which ultimately rendered them more susceptible to European imperialist conquest in the late nineteenth century.

Political and social change

Yet, in spite of these disruptive influences, these three centuries witnessed steady artistic advancement. Royal families in the centralized states became wealthy and commissioned artisans to fashion rings, pendants, bracelets, and hairpins from gold, copper, ivory, and exotic woods. Impressive mud or reed palaces were constructed with galleries and courtyards adorned with polychromed woven, batik, or tied-and-dyed tapestries. Basic ideals of beauty were expressed through distinct symbols stamped onto cloth, molded in high relief on the façades of buildings, or shaped into fine wood or metal sculpture. Forms such as the circle, rectangle, oval, and square were brilliantly

Artistic advances

translated into artistic symbols and given deep philosophical and religious meaning. And complex notions of God and the universe were expressed in the verbal symbolism of proverbs and epic poems or in the intricate designs of royal thrones, scepters, swords, and craftsmen's tools. Over the course of these three centuries, the forest civilizations, with their unlimited supplies of timber, used a wide variety of wood as the primary art medium for sculpturing. They achieved a brilliant artistic synthesis of surrealist and expressionist, abstract and naturalistic elements. The cubist tradition itself was born not in western Europe in the early twentieth century but among artistic circles in the West African forest societies centuries before. Although Europeans robbed Africans of much of their physical and human resources, they did not succeed in weakening their artistic vitality. Indeed, the trauma of European contact seemed to propel Africans toward even greater cultural achievements.

Stool with Caryatid. Wood. Luba, Congo.

SELECTED READINGS

- *Items so designated are available in paperback editions.*
- Binyon, Laurence, *The Spirit of Man in Asian Art,* New York, 1935.
- Nakamura, Hajime, *Ways of Thinking of Eastern Peoples: India, China, Tibet, Japan,* Honolulu, 1964.

INDIA

Archer, J. C., *The Sikhs,* Princeton, 1946.
- Cole, W. O., and P. S. Sambhi, *The Sihks: Their Religious Beliefs and Practices,* Boston, 1978. Based on recent scholarship.
Garratt, G. T., ed., *The Legacy of India,* Oxford, 1937.
Ikram, Mohamad, *Muslim Civilization in India,* ed. A. T. Embree, New York, 1964.
Kabir, Humayun, *The Indian Heritage,* New York, 1955.
Moreland, W. H., and A. C. Chatterjee, *A Short History of India,* 4th ed., London, 1957.
Prawdin, Michael, *The Builders of the Mogul Empire,* New York, 1965.
Rawlinson, H. G., *A Concise History of the Indian People,* 2d ed., New York, 1950.
- ———, *India, a Short Cultural History,* New York, 1952. An excellent interpretive study.
Smith, V. A., *Akbar the Great Mogul,* Oxford, 1917.
Spear, Percival, *India: A Modern History,* 2d ed., Ann Arbor, 1972. An excellent survey.
- ———, *The Oxford History of Indian, 1740–1975,* 2d ed., New York, 1979.
- Wolpert, Stanley, *A New History of India,* New York, 1977. An admirable survey, informative and well written.

- Eberhard, Wolfram, *A History of China,* 4th ed., Berkeley, 1977.
- Elvin, Mark, *The Pattern of the Chinese Past,* Stanford, 1975.

  Fairbank, J. K., E. O. Reischauer, and A. M. Craig, *East Asia: Tradition and Transformation,* rev. ed., Boston, 1978. A shortened edition of a major text.
- Fitzgerald, C. P., *China, a Short Cultural History,* 3d ed., New York, 1961. Unconventional in viewpoint.

  Honour, Hugh, *Chinoiserie: The Vision of Cathay,* New York, 1962. An account of the rise of European interest in the arts and crafts of the Orient.

  Hucker, C. O., *China's Imperial Past: An Introduction to Chinese History and Culture,* Stanford, 1975. Remarkably clear, comprehensive, and readable.
- Hudson, G. F., *Europe and China: A Survey of Their Relations from the Earliest Times to 1800,* London, 1930.

  Michael, Franz, *The Origin of Manchu Rule in China,* Baltimore, 1942.
- Moore, C. A., ed., *The Chinese Mind: Essentials of Chinese Philosophy and Culture,* Honolulu, 1967.

  Ronan, C. A., ed., *The Shorter Science and Civilization in China,* New York, 1978. Abridgement of the first two volumes of a monumental study by Joseph Needham.

  Rowbotham, `A. H., *Missionary and Mandarin: The Jesuits at the Court of China,* Berkeley, 1942.

  Scott, A. C., *The Classical Theater of China,* New York, 1957.

  Shryock, J. K., *The Origin and Development of the State Cult of Confucius,* New York, 1932.

  Sickman, L., and A. Soper, *The Art and Architecture of China,* Baltimore, 1956. Reliable, richly illustrated.
- Sullivan, Michael, *A Short History of Chinese Art,* rev. ed., Berkeley, 1970.

  Tuan Yi-fu, *China,* Chicago, 1970. An excellent cultural geography.

JAPAN

  Boxer, C. R., *The Christian Century in Japan, 1549–1650,* Berkeley, 1951.
- Brandon, J. R., W. P. Malm, and D. H. Shively, *Studies in Kabuki: Its Acting, Music, and Historical Context,* Honolulu, 1978.

  Cole, Wendell, *Kyoto in the Momoyama Period,* Norman, Okla., 1967.

  Dore, R. P., *Education in Tokugawa, Japan,* Berkeley, 1965.
- Duus, Peter, *Feudalism in Japan,* 2d ed. New York, 1975. A concise account of political developments through the nineteenth century.

  Eliot, Charles, *Japanese Buddhism,* New York, 1959. A standard text.

  Embree, J. F., *The Japanese Nation,* New York, 1945. A brilliant and well-balanced study by an anthropologist.
- Hall, J. W., *Japan: From Prehistory to Modern Times,* New York, 1971.
- Keene, Donald, *Japanese Literature: An Introduction for Western Readers,* New York, 1955.

  Langer, P. F., *Japan, Yesterday and Today,* New York, 1966. An excellent summary.

• Moore, C. A., ed., *The Japanese Mind: Essentials of Japanese Philosophy and Culture,* Honolulu, 1967.

• Munsterberg, Hugo, *The Arts of Japan: An Illustrated History,* Rutland, Vt., 1957.

• Reischauer, E. O., *Japan: The Story of a Nation,* 5th ed., New York, 1974. Lucid and well organized.

Sadler, A. L., *The Maker of Modern Japan: The Life of Tokugawa Ieyasu,* London, 1937.

Sansom, G. B., *Japan, a Short Cultural History,* rev. ed., New York, 1952. A substantial but highly readable work by an eminent British scholar.

———, *The Western World and Japan,* New York, 1950.

• Smith, T. C., *The Agrarian Origins of Modern Japan,* Stanford, 1959.

• Warner, Langdon, *The Enduring Art of Japan,* Cambridge, Mass., 1952.

Yukio, Y., *Two Thousand Years of Japanese Art,* New York, 1958.

AFRICA

Curtin, Philip D., ed., *Horizon History of Africa,* New York, 1972.

• Davidson, Basil, *The African Genius,* Boston, 1969.

Egharevba, Jacob, *A Short History of Benin,* Ibadan, 1960.

Gailey, H. A., *History of Africa: From Earliest Times to 1800,* New York, 1970.

Gray, Richard, ed., *The Cambridge History of Africa,* Vol. 4: *c. 1600 to c. 1790,* Cambridge, 1975.

Hallett, Robin, *Africa to 1875,* Ann Arbor, 1970.

Hull, Richard W., *Munyakare: African Civilization before the Batuuree,* New York, 1972.

Roberts, A., ed., *Tanzania before 1900,* Nairobi, 1968.

Smith, Robert S., *Kingdoms of the Yoruba,* London, 1969.

SOURCE MATERIALS

Davenport, T. R. H., and K. S. Hunt, eds., *The Right to the Land: Documents on Southern African History,* Capetown, 1974.

• de Bary, W. T., ed., *Sources of Chinese Tradition,* Chaps. XXII, XXIII, New York, 1960.

• ———, ed., *Sources of Indian Tradition,* "Islam in Medieval India"; "Sikhism," New York, 1958.

• ———, ed., *Sources of Japanese Tradition,* "The Tokugawa Period," New York, 1958.

Gallagher, L. J. tr., *China in the Sixteenth Century. The Journals of Matthew Ricci: 1583–1610,* Milwaukee, 1942.

• Hibbett, Howard, *The Floating World in Japanese Fiction,* New York, 1959.

• Keene, Donald ed., *Anthology of Japanese Literature,* New York, 1960

Lu, David, ed., *Sources of Japanese History,* Vol. 1, New York, 1973.

Markham, C. R., ed., *The Hawkins' Voyages,* London, 1878.

Morse, H. B., ed., *The Chronicles of the East India Company Trading to China,* 5 vols., Cambridge, Mass., 1926–1929.

Oliver, Roland, ed., *The Middle Age of African History,* New York, 1967.

Smith, V. A., ed., *F. Bernier: Travels in the Mogul Empire* A.D. *1656–1668,* London, 1914.

Vansina, Jan, *Kingdoms of the Savanna,* Madison, Wis., 1966.

Wang, C. C., tr., *Dream of the Red Chamber,* New York, 1929.

Whiteley, W. H., compiler, *A Selection of African Prose: Traditional Oral Texts,* Oxford, 1964.

Part Five

THE FRENCH AND INDUSTRIAL REVOLUTIONS AND THEIR CONSEQUENCES

No two events more profoundly altered the shape of Western civilization than the French and Industrial Revolutions. "Modern" history begins with their occurrence. The major happenings of the nineteenth and early twentieth centuries—the spread of middle-class liberalism and economic success; the decline of the old, landed aristocracies; the growth of class consciousness among urban workers—all had their roots in these two revolutions.

The French and Industrial Revolutions took place at about the same time and affected many of the same people—though in different ways and to varying degrees. Together they resulted in the overthrow of absolutism, mercantilism, and the last vestiges of manorialism. Together they produced the theory and practice of economic individualism and political liberalism. And together they ensured the growth of class consciousness, and the culmination of those tensions between the middle and working classes that imparted new vitality to European history after 1800.

Each revolution, of course, produced results peculiarly its own. The French Revolution encouraged the growth of nationalism and its unattractive step-child, authoritarianism. The Industrial Revolution compelled the design of a new, urban social order. Yet despite their unique contributions, the two revolutions must be studied together and understood as the joint progenitors of Western history in the nineteenth and early twentieth centuries.

The French and Industrial Revolutions and Their Consequences

POLITICS	SCIENCE & INDUSTRY

1770

James Watt's steam engine, 1763
Spinning jenny patented, 1770

American War of Independence, 1775–1783

Beginning of factory system, 1780s

French Revolution begins, 1789

Lavoisier discovers the indestructibility of matter, 1789

France declared a republic, 1792
Declaration of Pillnitz, 1792
Reign of Terror, 1793–1794

Cotton gin invented, 1793
Edward Jenner develops smallpox vaccine, 1796

Treaty of Campo Formio, 1797

1800
Napoleon, first consul of France, 1799
Treaty of Lunéville, 1801
Napoleon declared first consul for life, 1802
Napoleon crowns himself emperor of the French, 1804
Continental System established, 1806

Reforms of Hardenberg and Stein, Prussia, 1808

Napoleon's invasion of Russia, 1812
Congress of Vienna, 1814–1815

Battle of Waterloo, 1815

"Peterloo Massacre," England, 1819
Congress of Verona, 1822
Monroe Doctrine, 1823

Louis Pasteur, 1822–1895

1825
"Decembrist" Revolt, Russia, 1825
Greek Independence, 1829
Revolution in France, 1830
"Young Italy," 1831
Reform Bill of 1832, England
Slavery abolished, British colonies, 1833
Poor Law reform, England, 1834
Chartist movement, England, 1838–1848

First railway, England, 1825

Corn Laws repealed, England, 1846
Revolutions in Europe, 1848
Karl Marx, *Communist Manifesto,* 1848
Second Republic, France, 1848
Frankfurt Assembly, Germany, 1848–1849
Reign of Louis Napoleon, 1851–1870

Great Exhibition, London, 1851
Invention of the sewing machine, 1850s

ECONOMICS & SOCIETY	ARTS & LETTERS	
		1770
Jean-Jacques Rousseau, *The Social Contract,* 1762		
	Ludwig van Beethoven, 1770–1827	
Adam Smith, *Wealth of Nations,* 1776		
	Immanuel Kant, *Critique of Pure Reason,* 1781	
Jeremy Bentham, *The Principles of Morals and Legislation,* 1789		
Utilitarianism, 1790–1870	Johann von Goethe, *Faust,* 1790–1808	
	Romantic movement, 1790–1850	
Tom Paine, *The Rights of Man,* 1791–1792		
Thomas Malthus, *An Essay on the Principle of Population,* 1798	William Wordsworth, *Lyrical Ballads,* 1798	
		1800
	G. W. Hegel, *Phenomenology of the Spirit,* 1807	
Louis Blanc, 1811–1882	I. G. Fichte, *Addresses to the German Nation,* 1808	
	Francisco Goya, *The Executions of the Third of May,* 1814	
Founding of Prussian Zollverein, 1818		
		1825
	Honoré de Balzac, *The Human Comedy,* 1829–1841	
	Eugène Delacroix, *Liberty Leading the People,* 1830	
	Realism in literature and art, 1840–1870	
Friedrich Engels, *The Condition of the Working Class,* 1844		
John Stuart Mill, *Principles of Political Economy,* 1848	Pre-Raphaelite Brotherhood formed, 1848	

POLITICS	SCIENCE & INDUSTRY

1850

Crimean War, 1854–1856

Invention of the Bessemer process, 1856

Unification of Italy, 1858–1866

Charles Darwin, *Origin of Species,* 1859

Civil War, United States, 1861–1865
Otto von Bismarck's accession to power, 1862
First International, 1864

Parliamentary Reform Bill, England, 1867

Suez Canal opened, 1869
Union Pacific railroad, United States, 1869

Franco-Prussian War, 1870

ECONOMICS & SOCIETY	ARTS & LETTERS	
	Giuseppe Verdi, *Il Trovatore*, 1853	**1850**
	Richard Wagner, *The Ring of the Nibelung*, 1854–1874	
	Charles Dickens, *Hard Times*, 1854	
	Gustave Flaubert, *Madame Bovary*, 1857	
Emancipation of the serfs, Russia, 1861		
	Leo Tolstoy, *War and Peace*, 1866–1869	
Karl Marx, *Capital*, 1867		
	Pope Pius IX, *Syllabus of Errors*, 1869	

Chapter 24

THE FRENCH REVOLUTION

Men are born, and always continue, free and equal in respect of their rights. Civil distinctions, therefore, can be founded only on public utility.

The nation is essentially the source of all sovereignty; nor can any individual, or any body of men, be entitled to any authority which is not expressly derived from it.

—*The Declaration of the Rights of Man and of the Citizen, 1789*

I n 1789, one European out of every five lived in France. And most Europeans, French or not, who thought beyond the boundaries of their own immediate concerns, perceived of France as the center of European civilization. It followed, therefore, that a revolution in France would immediately command the attention of Europe, and would from the first assume far more than mere national significance. Yet the French Revolution attracted and disturbed men and women for reasons other than the fact that it was French. Both its philosophical ideals and its political realities mirrored attitudes, concerns, and conflicts that had occupied the minds of Europeans for several decades. When the revolutionaries pronounced in favor of liberty, they spoke not only with the voice of the eighteenth-century *philosophes,* but with those of the English aristocracy in 1688 and the American revolutionaries of 1776. Absolutism was the bane of continental noblemen, jealous to preserve their ancient freedoms from monarchical inroads; it was also the bane of continental merchants, chafing under the constraints of mercantilist authority. Across Europe, monarch, nobility, and middle class confronted each other in uneasy hostilities that varied in intensity, but reflected common mistrust and uncertainty.

The era of revolution

Louis XVI

Governmental structure

Financial problems

1. THE BACKGROUND OF THE FRENCH REVOLUTION

To understand why revolution came to France, we must first understand the major components of French society in the late eighteenth century and the manner in which they stood in opposition to each other. At the head of society stood the king, Louis XVI. Neither the most talented nor the most incompetent of the Bourbons, Louis XVI was attempting to rule France as he believed he should rule: absolutely in theory, yet in practice in consort with the most capable advisors willing to serve under him. He was hampered in his attempts to rule effectively by two major factors.

First, the governmental structure of France was both illogical and unsystematic. Confusion reigned in nearly every department, the product of a long and somewhat irregular growth extending back into the Middle Ages. New agencies had been established from time to time to meet some particular condition, often with a total disregard for those already in existence. As a result there was much overlapping of functions, and numerous useless officials drew salaries from the public purse. Conflicts of jurisdiction between rival departments frequently delayed action on vital problems for months at a stretch. In financial matters there was no more regularity than in other branches of public policy. The collection of public revenues was exceedingly haphazard. Instead of appointing official collectors, the king employed the old Roman system of farming out the collection of taxes to private corporations and individuals, permitting them to retain as profit all that they could obtain from the people in excess of a stipulated amount. Similar disorganized conditions prevailed in the realm of law and judicial procedure. Nearly every province of France had its special code based upon local custom. As a consequence, an act punishable as a crime in southern France might be no concern of the law in a central or northern province.

Louis XVI's second major difficulty was financial. England and France had been in conflict for most of the eighteenth century. In all but one of the wars between them, France had emerged the loser and had paid for those losses with surrendered colonies. Ironically, it was the war which the French had helped to win—the American War of Independence—that was now causing them the most immediate problems. The expense of maintaining fleets and armies in the Western Hemisphere had been particularly heavy and had demanded extensive borrowing. The result was a national debt which the inefficient and overly bureaucratic French government found it could not sustain, although it was no greater than that left by Louis XIV in 1714, and no more than half that incurred by the British. Louis pressed his advisors to devise new methods of retrenchment and taxation to keep the government afloat. Yet these men, and Louis with them, recognized that they could make no headway unless by some miracle they could induce the clergy and nobility to surrender the ancient privileges which allowed them to escape payment of an equitable share of the nation's taxes.

The likelihood of this surrender was remote. The system of privilege was one the nobility and the church, the first two of the three "estates" of the realm, were loath to alter. This remained the case despite the clamor of the third estate, the commoners, that they do so. Although many parish priests were as poor as their humble parishoners, the monsignors, bishops, archbishops, and cardinals of the Roman Catholic Church in France enjoyed large incomes, as did the institution of the Church itself. The Church rulers claimed the medieval right to evade taxes on their properties by the payment of a periodic "free gift" to the state, invariably far less than might have been obtained from direct taxation of church property.

The nobility was also protected by custom from the payment of anything like its proportionate share of taxes. Taxes in France, long before 1789, had come to consist of two main types, direct and indirect. The direct taxes included the *taille,* or tax on real and personal property; the poll tax; and the tax on incomes, originally at the rate of 5 percent, but in the eighteenth century more commonly at 10 or 11 percent. The indirect taxes, or taxes added to the price of commodities and paid by the ultimate consumer, embraced mainly the tariffs on articles imported from foreign countries and the tolls levied on goods shipped from one province of France to another. In addition, the *gabelle,* or tax on salt, was a form of indirect tax. For some time the production of salt had been a state monopoly in France; every individual inhabitant was required to buy at least seven pounds a year from the government works. To the cost of production was added a heavy tax, with the result that the price to the consumer was often as much as fifty or sixty times the actual value of the salt.

While exceedingly burdensome, the indirect taxes were not as a rule unfair distributed. It was difficult for anyone, regardless of social status, to avoid paying them. The case of most of the direct taxes, however, was far otherwise. The clergy escaped payment of both the *taille* and the income tax. The nobles, especially those of higher rank, made use of their influence with the king to obtain exemption from practically all direct levies. As a result, the main task of providing funds for the government fell upon the common people, or members of the third estate. And since few of the artisans and laborers had much that could be taxed, the chief burden had to be borne by the peasants and the middle class.

Not all the nobles opposed the king's plan to abolish their customary exemptions. Many of the most ardent reformers were the *nobles of the robe,* men who had acquired judicial office (hence the "robe") which conferred a title of nobility, as well as an opportunity to ac-

Le Hameau. This rustic villa was constructed in the gardens of Versailles to allow the French court to experiment with the "return to nature" advocated by some of the *philosophes.*

cumulate a substantial fortune in land and other property. Included in this group were such talented and concerned men as the philosopher the baron de Montesquieu, the lawyer the comte de Mirabeau, and the statesman the marquis de Lafayette, who had come to the aid of the American colonies. Among the nobles of the robe were men who would play prominent roles in the revolution itself. In contrast—and often in opposition—to this group stood the *nobles of the sword,* those whose titles extended back to the feudal lords of the Middle Ages. Many of these aristocrats looked with disdain upon their brethren of the robe. Though in general not nearly so widely representative a group as the nobles of the robe, those of the sword nevertheless held many of the leading positions in the government, delegating their work to subordinates. The nobles of the sword owned large estates, upon which they seldom resided, living instead at the court of Versailles, relying upon bailiffs and stewards to extract all they could from the peasants who lived under their jurisdiction at home. Theirs was an expensive, if not particularly purposeful, existence. Their polished, artificial style of life required increasingly large sums of money. Hence their natural unwillingness to surrender tax exemptions, no matter how hard pressed the government.

To reinforce their political intransigence and economic independence, the nobles had insisted on a greater share in both central and local administration. They asserted their claim by making increased use of three governmental institutions—parliaments, provincial estates, and intendencies. The thirteen French parliaments were regional courts of appeal, but the nobility used them to play an increasingly po-

Nobles of robe and nobles of the sword

Aristocratic demands

litical role. The provincial estates, also under the control of the nobility, claimed not only judicial but legislative power. Both parliaments and estates insisted, specifically, upon the right to consent to taxation. Both argued that they were exercising this right to protect the population from the never-ceasing demands of a greedy state treasury. In fact, the nobility used these bodies with increasing frequency to do no more than protect its own privileges. Finally, the nobility had entrenched itself in many of the intendencies, those offices from which the thirty-four generalities, or districts, of the country were administered. During the reign of Louis XIV, intendents had, for the most part, been commoners, whose assignment it was to keep the nobility in line. Now many were nobles themselves, less likely to come to the king's aid than to oppose his will.

Within the third estate the peasants, upon whom the nobility depended for much of their income, had come to resent their increasingly intolerable economic situation. A major source of the peasants' discontent were the customary duties that had survived the end of manorialism. True, a vast majority of peasants were free; a considerable proportion owned the lands they cultivated. Others were tenants or hired laborers; the largest percentage appear to have been sharecroppers, farming the lands of the nobles for a portion of the harvest, generally ranging from a third to a half. Even those peasants who were entirely free, however, were required to perform obligations inherited from the later Middle Ages. One of the most odious of these was the payment of an annual rental to the lord who had formerly controlled the land. Another was the donation to the local noble of a share of the price received whenever a tract of land was sold. In addition, the peasants were still required to contribute *banalités,* or fees for the use of various facilities owned by the noble. During the Middle Ages *banalités* had been paid for the use of the lord's flour mill, his wine press, and his bake oven. In spite of the fact that by the eighteenth century many of the peasants owned such equipment themselves and no longer benefited by the services provided by the noble, the *banalités* were still collected in the original amounts.

Probably the most exasperating of all the relics of manorialism were the *corvée* and the hunting privileges of the nobility. The *corvée,* formerly a requirement of labor on the lord's demesne and in the building of roads and bridges on the manorial estate, had become an obligation to the government. For several weeks each year the peasant was forced to put his own work aside and devote his labor to maintaining the public highways. No other class of the population was required to perform this service. Even greater inconvenience was suffered as a result of the hunting privileges of the nobles. From time immemorial the right to indulge in the diversions of the chase had been regarded as a distinctive badge of aristocracy. The property rights of the peasants were not allowed to stand in the way of this gentlemanly pastime. In some parts of France the peasants were forbidden to weed or mow in

The third estate: the peasants

The relics of manorial custom

breeding time lest they disturb the nests of partridges. Rabbits, crows, and foxes could not be killed regardless of how much damage they did to the crops or to domestic fowl and young animals. Furthermore, the peasant was expected to resign himself to having his fields trampled at any time by the horses of a thoughtless crew of noble hunters.

Not only did the peasants suffer under the vestiges of manorial custom. During the eighteenth century they also came under pressure as a result of the increasingly frequent enclosure of what had been common land. Fields allowed to lie fallow, together with those tilled only infrequently, were considered "common," land on which all persons might graze their livestock. These common lands, particularly extensive in the west of France, were an important resource for the peasants. In addition to the above-mentioned right to pasturage, they enjoyed that of gathering wood and of gleaning cultivated fields following a harvest. Now the king's economic advisors—Charles Calonne, Étienne Loménie de Brienne, the Swiss banker Jacques Necker—declared these collective rights to be obstacles in the path of agricultural improvement. Anxious to increase their income by increasing the efficiency of their estates, the landlords agreed. The result was authorization, by the crown, of the breakup of common lands and their enclosure as private property.

Here, then, were peasants pressed on the one side to acknowledge the duties of an outmoded manorial system and on the other to acquiesce in the exactions of modern agricultural capitalism, all the while paying taxes from which their aristocratic neighbors were exempt.

The frustrations of the peasants mirrored those of the most dynamic element within French eighteenth-century society, the middle class. This group was by no means homogeneous; there were within it

Enclosure of common land

A Gentleman of the Third Estate with His Family. A contemporary engraving which illustrates the respectability the Third Estate wished to see translated into political power.

many ranks, graded according to both occupation and income. At the top stood financiers and wholesale traders. Many of these men were also shareholders in various enterprises and in the government bonds which had been issued throughout the eighteenth century. (Noblemen invested in business as well; the economic line between the second and third estate was not as heavily drawn as was the social.) Professionals ranged throughout the ranks of the middle class: doctors and lawyers, many of the latter to play roles central to the revolution. Industry remained subordinate to trade: although a few factories existed in France prior to 1789, most manufacturing took place in homes, and most consumers were supplied by local craftsmen. For every capitalist entrepreneur, there were scores of small-scale masters, lodged somewhere in the lower reaches of the middle class, at home in the workshop yet removed by virtue of their ownership of that shop from the ranks of the laboring classes below them.

The third estate: the middle class

While these men acknowledged the gradations that separated them from each other, they resented the privileges that excluded them from any consequential participation in the affairs of state. No matter how much money a merchant, manufacturer, banker, or lawyer might acquire, he was still excluded from political privileges. He had almost no influence at the court; he could not share in the highest honors; and, except in the choice of a few petty local officers, he could not even vote. He was looked down upon as an inferior by the nobility. As the middle class rose in affluence and in consciousness of its own importance, its members were bound to resent such social discrimination. Above all, it was the demand of the commercial, financial, and industrial leaders for political power commensurate with their economic position that turned members of the middle class into revolutionaries.

Lack of political power

A demand for political power was not the only consequence of the growing prosperity of the middle class; there was also an increasing clamor for the abandonment of mercantilist policies. In earlier times mercantilism had been welcomed by merchants and manufacturers because of its effects in procuring new markets and fostering trade. But those times occurred at the beginning of the Commercial Revolution, when business was still nascent. As commerce and industry flourished through succeeding centuries, the middle class became increasingly confident of its ability to stand on its own feet. The result was a growing tendency to look upon the regulations of mercantilism as oppressive restrictions. Merchants disliked the special monopolies granted to favored companies and the interference with their freedom to buy in foreign markets. Manufacturers chafed under the laws controlling wages, fixing prices, and restricting the purchase of raw materials outside of France and its colonies. These were only a few of the more annoying regulations enforced by a government operating under the twin objectives of paternalism and economic self-sufficiency.

Antimercantilism

Like the peasantry, the middle class saw itself bearing a major portion of the state's financial burdens. Unlike the peasants, however, the middle class—at any rate its upper echelons—represented an economic force that was compelling change in a new and untried direction. The peasants, opposing enclosure, wanted to return to what had been. The prosperous financiers, the frustrated lawyers, the emerging entrepreneurs wanted to play leading roles in encouraging an expansion of international trade and in moving France ahead in its commercial competition with Britain.

Peasants vs. middle class

France on the eve of revolution was thus a country divided against itself. Monarchy struggled to exact money from an aristocracy increasingly determined not to pay and increasingly anxious in turn to exact what it could from a sullen peasantry. The middle classes resented a government that appeared at best an anachronism and at worst a tyranny, frustrated and furious that a country as prosperous as France should find it impossible to pay its debts. France did not fall to revolution because it was poor. It succumbed because those who knew best how rich it was were dissatisfied with the slow rate of its commercial progress.

France divided

No event as all-encompassing as the French Revolution occurs in a cultural vacuum. Although ideas may not have "caused" the revolution, they played a most important role in giving shape and substance to the discontent experienced by so many, particularly among the middle class. These ideas derived from the thought of the Enlightenment. Two theories, in particular, expressed the concerns and aspirations of the revolutionaries. The first was the *liberal* theory of such writers as Locke, Voltaire, and Montesquieu; and the second was the *democratic* theory of Rousseau. While the two were fundamentally opposed, they nevertheless had elements in common. Both were predicated upon the assumption that the state is a necessary evil and that government rests upon a contractual basis. Each had its doctrine of popular sovereignty, although with contrasting interpretations. Both upheld in some measure the fundamental rights of the individual. And both contained elements appealing to those who, for various reasons, were dissatisfied with things as they were.

Intellectual background

The father of the liberal theory of the seventeenth and eighteenth centuries was John Locke. His philosophy of education, as we have seen, was intrinsic to the development of Enlightenment thinking. His political beliefs are contained chiefly in his *Second Treatise of Civil Government*, published in 1690. In this book he developed a theory of limited government, which was used to justify the new system of parliamentary rule set up in England as a result of the Glorious Revolution. He maintained that originally all humans had lived in a theoretical state of nature in which absolute freedom and equality prevailed, and in which there was no government of any kind. The only law was the law of nature, which each individual enforced for himself in order to protect his natural rights to life, liberty, and property. It was not long, however, until men began to perceive that the inconveniences of the

The liberal political theory of John Locke

state of nature greatly outweighed its advantages. With individuals attempting to enforce their own rights, confusion and insecurity were the unavoidable results. Accordingly, the people agreed among themselves to establish a civil society, to set up a government, and to surrender certain powers to it. But they did not make that government absolute. The only power they conferred upon it was the executive power of the law of nature. Since the state is nothing but the joint power of all the members of society, its authority "can be no more than those persons had in a state of nature before they entered into society, and gave it up to the community."[1] All powers not expressly surrendered are reserved to the people themselves. If the government exceeds or abuses the authority explicitly granted in the political contract, it becomes tyrannical; and the people then have the right to dissolve it or to rebel against it and overthrow it.

Locke condemned absolutism in every form. He denounced despotic monarchy, but he was no less severe in his strictures against the absolute sovereignty of parliaments. Though he defended the supremacy of the law-making branch, with the executive primarily an agent of the legislature, he nevertheless refused to concede to the representatives of the people an unlimited power. Arguing that government was instituted among people for the preservation of property (which he generally defined in the inclusive sense of life, liberty, and estate), he denied the authority of any political agency to invade the natural rights of a single individual. The law of nature, which embodies these rights, is an automatic limitation upon every branch of the government. Regardless of how large a majority of the people's representatives should demand the restriction of freedom of speech or the confiscation and redistribution of property, no such action could legally be taken. If taken illegally it would justify effective measures of resistance on the part of the majority of citizens. Locke was much more concerned with protecting individual liberty than he was with promoting stability or social progress. If forced to make a choice, he would have preferred the evils of anarchy to those of despotism in any form.

*Locke's condemnation of
absolutism*

The appeal of Locke's ideas to the French middle class can be readily understood. His doctrines of natural rights, limited government, and the right of resistance to tyranny, as well as his stout defense of property, reflected the values of that element in French society. Like their American counterparts, who a decade earlier had incorporated Locke's theories into the Declaration of Independence, these middle-class Frenchmen opened their minds to Lockean suppositions and explanations.

Locke's appeal

In France the foremost exponents of the liberal political theory were Voltaire and Montesquieu (1689–1755). As was indicated earlier, Voltaire considered orthodox Christianity to be the worst of the enemies

---

[1] *Second Treatise of Civil Government* (Everyman Library ed.), p. 184.

*The liberal political
theory of Voltaire*

of humanity; he reserved contempt for tyrannical government as well. During his exile in England he had studied the writings of Locke and had been deeply impressed by their vigorous assertions of individual freedom. In common with Locke he conceived of government as a necessary evil, with powers which ought to be limited to the enforcement of natural rights. He maintained that all are endowed by nature with equal rights to liberty, property, and the protection of the laws. But Voltaire was no democrat. He was inclined to think of the ideal form of government as either an enlightened monarchy or a republic dominated by the middle class.

A more systematic political thinker than Voltaire was his older contemporary, Montesquieu. Though, like Voltaire, a student of Locke and an ardent admirer of British institutions, Montesquieu was a unique figure among the political philosophers of the eighteenth century. In his celebrated *Spirit of Laws* he brought new methods and new conceptions to the theory of the state. Instead of attempting to found a science of government by pure deduction, he followed the Aristotelian method of studying actual political systems as they were supposed to have operated in the past. He denied that there is any one perfect form of government suitable for all peoples under all conditions. He maintained, on the contrary, that political institutions in order to be successful must harmonize with the physical conditions and the level of social advancement of the nations they are intended to serve. Thus he declared that despotism is best suited to countries of vast domain; limited monarchy to those of moderate size; and republican government to those of small extent. For his own country, France, he was disposed to think that a limited monarchy would be the most appropriate form, since he regarded the nation as too large to be made into a republic unless on some kind of federal plan.

Montesquieu

*The separation of powers;
checks and balances*

Montesquieu is especially famous for his theory of the separation of powers. He avowed that it is a natural human tendency to abuse any power, and that consequently every government, regardless of its form, is liable to degenerate into despotism. To prevent such a result he argued that the authority of government should be broken up into its three natural divisions of legislative, executive, and judicial. Whenever any two or more of these are allowed to remain united in the same hands, liberty, he declared, is at an end. The only effective way to avoid tyranny is to enable each branch of the government to act as a check upon the other two. For example, the executive should have the power by means of the veto to curb the encroachments of the lawmaking branch. The legislature, in turn, should have the authority of impeachment in order to restrain the executive. And, finally, there should be an independent judiciary vested with power to protect individual rights against arbitrary acts of either the legislature or the executive. This favorite scheme of Montesquieu was not intended, of course, to facilitate democracy. Its purpose was largely the opposite: to prevent the absolute supremacy of the majority, expressed as it normally would be through the people's representatives in a legislature. Montesquieu's ideas thus appealed to both nobility and middle class. The nobility read his writings as a defense of their ancient privileges—elevated by Montesquieu into "liberties." The provincial estates, where noblemen exercised considerable political power, were the constituted bodies which would provide a check to royal power. The middle class welcomed further theoretical support to substantiate its preference for something other than the monarchical absolutism and centralized mercantilism of eighteenth-century France.

Additional arguments in favor of governmental nonintervention was provided by another group of libertarians—theoreticians who were redefining the study of economics.

In the second half of the eighteenth century a number of writers began attacking traditional assumptions with regard to public control over production and trade. Their special target of criticism was mercantilist policy. To a large extent the new economics was founded upon the basic conceptions of the Enlightenment, particularly the idea of a mechanistic universe governed by inflexible laws. The economists argued that the sphere of the production and distribution of wealth was subject to laws just as irresistible as those of physics and astronomy. The new economic theory was a counterpart of political liberalism. The cardinal aims of the two doctrines were quite similar: to reduce the powers of government to the lowest minimum consistent with safety and to preserve for the individual the largest possible measure of freedom in the pursuit of his own devices.

The new economists

The greatest of all the economists of the age of the Enlightenment and one of the most brilliant of all time was Adam Smith (1723–1790). A native of Scotland, Smith began his career as a lecturer on English literature at the University of Edinburgh. From this position he was soon advanced to a professorship of logic at Glasgow College. In 1776 he published his *Inquiry into the Nature and Causes of the Wealth of Nations*. In this work he maintained that labor, rather than agriculture or the bounty of nature, is the real source of wealth. While in general he accepted the principle of laissez faire, avowing that the prosperity of all can best be promoted by allowing all individuals to pursue their own interests, he nevertheless recognized the necessity for certain forms of governmental interference. The state should intervene for the prevention of injustice and oppression, for the advancement of education and the protection of public health, and for the maintenance of necessary enterprises which would never be established by private capital. Notwithstanding these rather broad limitations upon the principle of laissez faire, Smith's *Wealth of Nations* was adopted as holy writ by the economic individualists of the eighteenth and nineteenth centuries. Its influence in causing the French

The economics of Adam Smith

Democratic political theory

Rousseau's political theory

Rousseau's conception of popular sovereignty

Revolution was indirect but nonetheless profound. It furnished the final answer to mercantilist argument and thereby strengthened the ambition of the middle class to have done with a political system which continued to block the path to economic freedom.

The second of the great political ideals which occupied an important place in the intellectual background of the French Revolution was the ideal of democracy. In contrast with liberalism, democracy, in its original meaning, was much less concerned with the defense of individual rights than with the enforcement of popular rule. What the majority of the citizens wills is the supreme law of the land, for the voice of the people is the voice of God.

The foremost theoretician of democracy in eighteenth-century Europe was Jean-Jacques Rousseau (1712–1778). The most significant of his writings on political theory were his *Social Contract* and his *Discourse on the Origin of Inequality*. In both of these he upheld the popular thesis that humans had originally existed in a state of nature. But in contrast with Locke he regarded this state of nature as a veritable paradise. People suffered no inconvenience from maintaining their own rights against others. Indeed, there were very few chances of conflict of any sort; for private property did not exist for a long time, and every person was the equal of every other. Eventually, however, evils arose, due primarily to the fact that some staked off plots of land and said to themselves, "This is mine." It was in such manner that various degrees of inequality developed; and, as a consequence, "cheating trickery," "insolent pomp," and "insatiable ambition" soon came to dominate the relations among men.[2] The only hope of security was now to establish a civil society and to surrender all rights to the community. This was accomplished by means of a social contract, in which each individual agreed with the whole body of individuals to submit to the will of the majority. Thus the state was brought into existence.

Rousseau developed an altogether different conception of sovereignty from that of the liberals. Whereas Locke and his followers had taught that only a portion of sovereign power is surrendered to the state, the rest being retained by the people themselves, Rousseau contended that sovereignty is indivisible, and that all of it became vested in the community when civil society was formed. He insisted further that each individual in becoming a party to the social contract gave up all rights to the people collectively and agreed to submit absolutely to the general will. It follows that the sovereign power of the state is subject to no limitations whatever. When Rousseau referred to the state he did not mean the government. He regarded the state as the politically organized community, which has the sovereign function of expressing the general will. The authority of the state cannot be repre-

[2] *Discourse on the Origin of Inequality* (Everyman Library ed.), p. 207.

sented, but must be expressed directly through the enactment of fundamental laws by the people themselves. The government, on the other hand, is simply the executive agent of the state. Its function is not to formulate the general will but merely to carry it out. Moreover, the community can set the government up or pull it down "whenever it likes."[3]

Rousseau's influence was great. His appeal, however, was not so much to those members of the middle class whose thoughts and actions dominated the first stage of the revolution. Although they might have agreed with Rousseau's opposition to hereditary privilege, they were, as convinced individualists, unmoved by arguments in favor of surrender to a "general will." Rousseau's influence upon the revolution was greatest during its second stage, when a more democratic and radical coterie emerged to lead events, first in the direction of democracy and then along a course toward an absolutism that nevertheless accorded with Rousseau's notions of the sovereign state.

Rousseau's appeal

2. THE DESTRUCTION OF THE ANCIEN RÉGIME

The French Revolution occurred when it did because of the government's inability to resolve its financial crisis. When the king's principal ministers Calonne and Loménie de Brienne attempted in 1787 and 1788 to institute a series of financial reforms in order to stave off bankruptcy, they encountered not just opposition but entrenched aristocratic determination to extract further governmental concessions from the king. To meet the mounting deficit, the ministers proposed new taxes, notably a stamp duty and a direct tax on the annual produce of the soil. The king summoned an assembly of notables from among the aristocracy, in the hope of persuading the nobles to agree to his demands. Far from acquiescing, however, the nobles insisted that to institute a general tax such as the stamp duty the king would first have to call together the Estates General, representative of the three estates of the realm.

The crisis of the monarchy

The summoning of this body, which had not met for over a century and a half. seemed to many the only solution to France's deepening problems. No doubt most of those aristocrats who argued for its calling did so from short-sighted and selfish motives. Yet the politically conscious population as a whole agreed with the idea in an unreasonable and desperate hope that this unusual event might, because of its very strangeness, work a miracle and save the country from ruin. During the period before the rise of monarchical absolutism, when the Estates General was convened more or less regularly, the representatives of each estate had met and voted as a body. Generally this meant that the first and second estates combined against the third.

The Estates General

[3] *The Social Contract* (Everyman Library ed.), p. 88.

FRANCE IN 1789 • THE "GOVERNMENTS"

By the late eighteenth century the third estate had attained such importance that it was not willing to tolerate such an arrangement. Consequently its leaders demanded that the three orders should sit together and vote as individuals. More important, it insisted that the representatives of the third estate should be double the number of the first and second. Leaving this issue unresolved, Louis XVI, in the summer of 1788, yielded to popular clamor and summoned the Estates General to meet in May of the following year.

In the intervening months, the question of "doubling the third" was fiercely debated. When the king pronounced against the idea, he lost support he might otherwise have obtained from the middle class, and virtually preordained the outcome of the convocation. Shortly after

The new political role of the third estate

the opening of the Estates General at Versailles, in May 1789, the representatives of the third estate took the revolutionary step of leaving the body and declaring themselves the National Assembly. "What is the third estate?" asked the Abbé Sieyès, one of the most articulate spokesmen for a new order, in his famous pamphlet of January 1789. The answer he gave then—"everything"—was the answer the third estate itself gave when it constituted itself the National Assembly of France. Sieyès, unlike most other revolutionaries at this point, derived his argument from Rousseau, and claimed that the third estate was the nation and that as the nation it was its own sovereign. Now the middle-class lawyers and businessmen of the third estate acted on that claim. Locked out of their meeting hall on June 20, the commoners and a handful of sympathetic nobles and clergymen moved to a nearby indoor tennis court.

Here, under the leadership of Mirabeau and the Abbé Sieyès, they bound themselves by a solemn oath not to separate until they had drafted a constitution for France. This Oath of the Tennis Court, on June 20, 1789, was the real beginning of the French Revolution. By claiming the authority to remake the government in the name of the people, the Estates General was not merely protesting against the rule of Louis XVI but asserting its right to act as the highest sovereign power in the nation. On June 27 the king virtually conceded this right by ordering the remaining delegates of the privileged classes to meet with the third estate as members of the National Assembly.

The course of the French Revolution was marked by three stages, the first of which extended from June 1789 to August 1792. During most of this period the destinies of France were in the hands of the Na-

Abbé Sieyès

The Tennis Court Oath

The Opening of the Estates General in Versailles, May 5, 1789

The Tennis Court Oath by David. In the hall where royalty played a game known as *jeu de paume* (similar to tennis) leaders of the revolution swore to draft a constitution. In the center of this painting, with his arm extended, is Jean Bailly, president of the National Assembly. Seated at the table below him is Abbé Sieyès. Somewhat to the right of Sieyès, with both hands on his chest, is Robespierre. Mirabeau, with a hat in his left hand and wearing a black coat, stands somewhat farther to the right.

The first stage of the revolution

Fall of the Bastille

tional Assembly. In the main, this stage was moderate, its actions dominated by the leadership of liberal nobles and equally liberal men of the third estate. Yet three events in the summer and fall of 1789 furnished evidence that the revolution was to penetrate to the very heart of French society, ultimately touching both the urban populace and the rural peasants.

News of the events of late spring 1789 had spread quickly across France. From the very onset of debates on the nature of the political crisis, public attention was high. It was roused not merely by abstract interest in matters of political reform, however. Prices had risen to a point where the cost of bread alone consumed more than 50 percent of a poor family's income in August 1788, and 80 percent in February and July 1789. Belief was widespread that the aristocracy and king were together conspiring to punish an upstart third estate by encouraging scarcity and high prices. Rumors circulated in Paris during the latter days of June 1789. At their clubs and in their shops, those men and women who would come to be called the sans-culottes[4]—workshop masters, craftspeople, shopkeepers, petty tradespeople—worried about their fate. Determined to obtain arms to defend themselves from the threat of counterrevolution, they successfully stormed the ancient fortress of the Bastille on July 14, thereby establishing the fact of the king's impotence within his own capital. Built in the Middle Ages as a stronghold, the Bastille was no longer much used; but it symbolized royal authority to the masses. When crowds demanded

[4] So-called because the men did not wear upper-class breeches.

arms from its governor, he refused and opened fire. The crowd took revenge, not only by capturing the fortress but by murdering the governor.

The fall of the Bastille was the first of those events which were to demonstrate the commitment of the common people to revolutionary change. The second occurred in the countryside, where the peasants were suffering the direct effects of economic privation. They, too, feared a monarchical and aristocratic counterrevolution. Eager for news from Versailles, their anticipation turned to fear when they began to understand that a middle-class revolution might not address itself to their problems. Frightened and uncertain, peasants in many areas of France panicked in July and August, setting fire to manor houses and the records they contained, destroying monasteries and the residences of bishops, and murdering some of the nobles who offered resistance.

The "Great Fear"

The third instance of popular uprising, in October 1789, was also brought on by economic crisis. This time women, angered by the price of bread and fired by rumors of the king's continuing unwillingness to cooperate with the assembly, marched to Versailles on October 5 and demanded to be heard. Not satisfied with its reception by the assembly, the crowd broke through the gates to the palace, calling for the king to return to Paris. On the afternoon of the following day the king yielded. The National Guard, sympathetic to the agitators, led the crowd back to Paris, the procession headed by a soldier holding aloft a loaf of bread on his bayonet.

The "October Days"

In each case, these three popular uprisings produced a decided effect on the course of political events as they were unfolding at Versailles. The storming of the Bastille helped persuade the king and nobles to treat the National Assembly as the legislative body of the nation. The "Great Fear" inspired an equally great consternation among the debaters in the assembly. On August 4, with one sweep, the remnants of manorialism were largely obliterated. Ecclesiastical tithes and the *corvée* were formally abolished. Serfdom was eliminated. The hunting privileges of the nobles were declared at an end. Exemption from tax-

Achievements of the first stage: (1) the destruction of feudal privilege

The Departure of the Women of Paris for Versailles, October 1789. Note that the contemporary caption refers to the "heroines of Paris." An early example of revolutionary propaganda.

ation and monopolies of all kinds were sacrificed as contrary to natural equality. While the nobles did not surrender all of their rights, the ultimate effect of these reforms of the "August Days" was to annihilate distinctions of rank and class and to make all French citizens of an equal status in the eyes of the law.

(2) the Declaration of the Rights of Man

Following the destruction of privilege the assembly turned its attention to preparing a charter of liberties. The result was the Declaration of the Rights of Man and of the Citizen, issued in September 1789. Property was declared to be a natural right as well as liberty, security, and "resistance to oppression." Freedom of speech, religious toleration, and liberty of the press were held to be inviolable. All citizens were declared to be entitled to equality of treatment in the courts. No one was to be imprisoned or otherwise punished except in accordance with due process of law. Sovereignty was affirmed to reside in the people, and officers of the government were made subject to deposition if they abused the powers conferred upon them.

(3) secularization of the Church

The king's return to Paris during the October Days confirmed the reforms already underway and guaranteed further liberalization along lines decreed by the middle-class majority in the assembly. In November 1789, the National Assembly resolved to confiscate the lands of the Church and to use them as collateral for the issue of *assignats,* or paper money, which, it was hoped, would resolve the country's inflationary economic crisis. In July of the following year the Civil Constitution of the Clergy was enacted, providing that all bishops and priests should be elected by the people and should be subject to the authority of the state. Their salaries were to be paid out of the public treasury, and they were required to swear allegiance to the new legislation. The secularization of the Church also involved a partial separation from Rome. The aim of the assembly was to make the Catholic Church of France a truly national institution with no more than a nominal subjection to the papacy.

An Assignat

(4) constitution of 1791

Not until 1791 did the National Assembly manage to complete its primary task of drafting a new constitution for the nation. The constitution as it finally emerged gave eloquent testimony to the dominant position now held by the middle class. The government was converted into a limited monarchy, with the supreme power virtually a monopoly of the well-to-do. Although all citizens possessed the same civil rights, the vote was allowed only to those who paid a certain amount in taxes. About half the adult males in France made up this latter category of "active" citizen. Yet even their political power was curtailed, for they were to vote for electors, whose property ownership qualified them for that position. Those electors, in turn, chose department officials and delegates to the National—or, as it was now called, Constituent—Assembly. The king was deprived of the control he had formerly exercised over the army and local governments. His ministers were forbidden to sit in the assembly, and he was shorn of all power over the legislative process except a suspensive veto, which in fact could be overridden by the issuance of proclamations.

The economic and governmental changes the Constituent Assembly adopted were as much a reflection of Enlightenment liberalism as were its constitutional reforms. To raise money, it sold off Church lands, but in such large blocks that peasants seldom benefited by the sales as they had expected to. In opposition to the interests of the peasantry, the assembly proceeded with the enclosure of common lands in order to facilitate the development of capitalist agriculture. To encourage the growth of unfettered economic enterprise, guilds and trade unions were abolished. To rid the country of authoritarian centralization and of aristocratic domination, local governments were completely restructured. France was divided into eighty-three equal departments. All towns henceforth enjoyed the same form of municipal organization. All local officials were locally elected. This reorganization and decentralization expressed a liberal belief in the necessity of individual liberty and freedom from ancient privilege. As such these measures proclaimed, as did all the work of the assembly, that the "winners" of this first stage of the revolution were the men and women of the middle class.

(5) economic and governmental changes

3. A NEW STAGE: RADICAL REVOLUTION

Their triumph did not go unchallenged, however. In the summer of 1792, the revolution entered a second stage, which saw the downfall of moderate middle-class leaders and their replacement by radical republicans claiming to rule on behalf of the common people. Two major reasons accounted for this abrupt and drastic alteration in the course of events. First, the politically literate lower classes grew disillusioned as they perceived that the revolution was not benefiting them. The uncontrolled free-enterprise economy of the government resulted in constantly fluctuating and generally rising prices. These increases particularly exasperated those elements of the Parisian population that had agitated for change in preceding years. Rioting urban mobs demanded bread at prerevolutionary prices, while their spokesmen called for governmental control of the ever-growing inflation. Their leaders articulated as well the frustrations of a mass of men and women who felt cheated by the constitution. Despite their major role in the creation of a new regime, they found themselves deprived of any effective voice in its operation.

The second stage: (1) disappointment of the common people

The second major reason for the dramatic turn of events was the fact that France now found itself at war with much of the rest of Europe. From the outset of the revolution, men and women across Europe had been compelled, by the very intensity of events in France, to take sides in the conflict. What we have called the first revolution

(2) the revolution abroad

A Contemporary Engraving of the September Massacres in Paris, 1792

won the support of a wide range of thoughtful intellectuals, politicians, businessmen, and artisans. Strikes and revolts broke out in Germany and Belgium. In England, philosophical radicals such as Joseph Priestley, the scientist, and Richard Price, a Unitarian minister, joined with businessmen such as James Watt and Matthew Boulton to welcome the overthrow of privilege and absolutism. Others opposed the course of the revolution from the start. Edmund Burke, in his famous pamphlet, *Reflections on the Revolution in France,* denounced the egalitarian actions of the revolutionaries. The monarchs of Europe responded with at least passive sympathy to the distressed clamorings of Louis XVI, Marie Antoinette, his impetuous, ultra-conservative queen, and the émigré nobles who soon fled to the courts of German principalities in pursuit of assistance for their doomed cause.

It is questionable, however, whether that sympathy would have turned to active opposition, had not the French soon appeared as a threat to international stability and the individual ambitions of the great powers. It was that threat which led to war in 1792, and which kept the Continent in arms for a generation.

This state of war had a most important impact on the formation of political and social attitudes during this period in Europe. Once a country declared war with France, its citizens could no longer espouse sympathy with the revolution without paying severe consequences. Those who continued to support the revolution, as did a good many among the artisan and small tradespeople class, were persecuted and punished for their beliefs. To be found in Britain, for example, possessing a copy of Tom Paine's revolutionary tract, *The Rights of Man* (1791–1792), a prorevolutionary response to Burke's *Reflections,* was enough to warrant imprisonment. As the moderate nature of the early revolution turned to violent extension, entrepreneurs and business-

The impact of international war

men eagerly sought to live down their radical sentiments of a few years past. The wars against revolutionary France came to be perceived as a matter of national survival; to ensure internal security, it seemed, particularly to the English, that patriotism demanded not only a condemnation of the French but of French ideas as well.

The first European states to express public concern about events in revolutionary France were Austria and Prussia. They were not anxious to declare war; their interests at the time centered upon the division of Poland between themselves. Nevertheless, they jointly issued the Declaration of Pillnitz in August 1791, in which they avowed that the restoration of order and of the rights of the monarch of France was a matter of "common interest to all sovereigns of Europe." The leaders of the French government at this time were the moderate Girondists, many of whom came from the mercantile Girondist department. The Girondists drew their support largely from regions outside Paris, and were inclined to mistrust urban radicals. Afraid of losing political support in France, they pronounced the Declaration of Pillnitz a threat to national security, hoping that enthusiasm for a war would unite the French and result also in enthusiasm for their continued rule. They were aided in their scheme by the activities of monarchists, both within and outside France, whose plottings and pronouncements could be made to appear an additional threat, though to a greater extent than they actually were. On April 20, 1792, the assembly declared war against Austria and Prussia.

Although the Girondist faction expected that military success would solidify the loyalty of the people to the regime, many anti-Girondist radicals were clamoring for war in the secret hope that the armies of France would suffer defeat, and that the monarchy would thereby be discredited. A republic could then be set up, and the heroic soldiers of the people would turn defeat into victory and carry the blessings of freedom to all the oppressed of Europe. As the radicals had hoped, the forces of the French met serious reverses. By August 1792 the allied armies of Austria and Prussia had crossed the frontier and were threatening the capture of Paris. A fury of rage and despair seized the capital. The belief prevailed that the military disasters had been the result of treasonable dealings with the enemy on the part of the king and his conservative followers. As a consequence, a vigorous demand arose from the radicals for drastic action against all who were suspected of disloyalty to the revolution. It was this situation more than anything else which brought the extremists to the fore and enabled them to gain control of the assembly and to put an end to the monarchy.

From this point, the country's leadership passed into the hands of an equalitarian-minded "middle" middle class. These new leaders called themselves Jacobins, after the Parisian political club to which they belonged. The hallmarks of the Jacobin, or second, stage of the French Revolution were its radical republicanism and its "Reign of Terror."

Edmund Burke

Declaration of Pillnitz

The course of war

Thomas Paine

The government during the second stage: the national convention

One of the Jacobins' first actions was to ask all Frenchmen to vote for delegates to a national convention, to draft a new and more republican constitution. This convention, which assembled in September 1792, became the effective governing body of the country for the next three years. It was composed entirely of republicans; 486 of its 749 members were men who had not sat in the old assembly. On September 21, the convention abolished the monarchy and declared France a republic. In December, the convention placed the former king, Louis XVI, on trial; in January he was, by one vote, condemned to death. He and his queen suffered death on the guillotine, the frightful mechanical headsman that was one of the most famous and feared instruments of revolutionary fervor.

Domestic reforms

Meanwhile, the convention turned its attention to the enactment of further domestic reforms. Among its most significant accomplishments over the next three years were the abolition of slavery in French colonies; the prohibition of imprisonment for debt; the establishment of the metric system of weights and measures; and the repeal of primogeniture, so that property might not be inherited exclusively by the oldest son, but be divided in substantially equal portions among all immediate heirs. The convention also attempted to supplement the decrees of the assembly in abolishing the remnants of manorialism and in providing for greater freedom of economic opportunity for the commoner. The property of enemies of the revolution was confiscated for the benefit of the government and the lower classes. Great estates were broken up and offered for sale to poorer citizens on easy terms. The indemnities hitherto promised to the nobles for the loss of their privileges were abruptly canceled. To curb the rise in the cost of living, maximum prices for grain and other necessities were fixed by

The Execution of Louis XVI. A revolutionary displays the king's head moments after it had been severed by the guillotine in January 1793.

law, and merchants who profiteered at the expense of the poor were threatened with the guillotine. Still other measures of reform were those in the sphere of religion. At one time during the period, an effort was made to abolish Christianity and to substitute the worship of Reason in its place. In accordance with this purpose a new calendar was adopted, dating the year from the birth of the republic (September 22, 1792) and dividing the months in such a way as to eliminate the Christian Sunday. Later, this cult of Reason was replaced by a Deistic religion dedicated to the worship of a Supreme Being and to a belief in the immortality of the soul. Finally, in 1794, the convention decreed simply that religion was a private matter, that Church and State would therefore be separated, and that all beliefs not actually hostile to the government would be tolerated.

While effecting this political revolution in France, the convention's leadership at the same time accomplished an astonishingly successful reorganization of its armies. By February 1793, Britain, Holland, Spain, and Austria were in the field against the French. Britain's entrance into the war was dictated by both strategic and economic reasons. The English feared French penetration into the Low Countries directly across the Channel; they were also concerned that French expansion might pose a serious threat to Britain's own growing mercantile hegemony around the globe. The allied coalition ranged against France, though united only in its desire to somehow contain this puzzling, fearsome revolutionary phenomenon, was nevertheless a formidable force. To counter it, the French organized an army that was able to win engagement after engagement during these years. In August 1793, the revolutionary government imposed a levy on the entire male population capable of bearing arms. Fourteen hastily drafted armies were flung into battle under the leadership of young and inexperienced officers. What they lacked in training and discipline, they made up for in improvised organization, mobility, flexibility, courage, and morale. (In the navy, however, where skill was of paramount importance, the revolutionary French never succeeded in matching the performance of the British.) In 1793–1794, the French armies preserved their homeland. In 1794–1795, they occupied the Low Countries, the Rhineland, parts of Spain, Switzerland, and Savoy. In 1796, they invaded and occupied key parts of Italy and broke the coalition that had arrayed itself against them.

These achievements were not without their price, however. To insure their accomplishment, the rulers of France resorted to a bloody authoritarianism that has come to be known as the Reign of Terror. Although the convention succeeded in 1793 in drafting a new democratic constitution, based upon manhood suffrage, it deferred its introduction because of wartime emergency. Instead, the convention prolonged its own life year by year, and increasingly delegated its responsibilities to a group of twelve leaders known as the Committee of Public Safety. By this time the moderate, upper middle-class Giron-

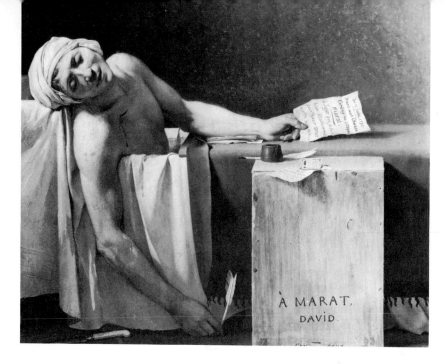

The Death of Marat. This painting by the French artist David immortalized Marat. The bloody towel, the box, and the tub were venerated as relics of the revolution.

Marat and Danton

Danton

dists had lost all influence within the convention. Complete power had passed to the Jacobins, who, though themselves from the middle class, were ardent disciples of Rousseau and champions of the urban workers.

Foremost among the leaders of the extremist faction and members of the Committee of Public Safety, were Marat, Danton, and Robespierre. Jean Paul Marat (1743–1793) was educated as a physician, and, by 1789, had already earned enough distinction in that profession to be awarded an honorary degree by St. Andrews University in Scotland. Almost from the beginning of the revolution he stood as a champion of the common people. He opposed nearly all of the dogmatic assumptions of his middle-class colleagues in the assembly, including the idea that France should pattern its government after that of Great Britain, which he recognized to be oligarchic in form. He was soon made a victim of persecution and was forced to find refuge in sewers and dungeons, but this did not stop him from his efforts to rouse the people to a defense of their rights. In 1793 he was stabbed through the heart by Charlotte Corday, a young woman who was fanatically devoted to the Girondists. In contrast with Marat, Georges Jacques Danton (1759–1794) did not come into prominence until the revolution was three years old; but, like Marat, he directed his activities toward goading the masses into rebellion. Elected a member of the Committee of Public Safety in 1793, he had much to do with organizing the Reign of Terror. As time went on he appears to have wearied of ruthlessness and displayed a tendency to compromise. This gave his opponents in the convention their opportunity, and in April 1794, he was sent to the guillotine. Upon mounting the scaffold he is reported to have said: "Show my head to the people; they do not see the like every day."

The most famous and perhaps the greatest of all the extremist leaders was Maximilien Robespierre (1758–1794). Born of a family reputed to be of Irish descent, Robespierre was trained for the law and speedily achieved a modest success as an advocate. In 1782 he was appointed a criminal judge, but soon resigned because he could not bear to impose a sentence of death. Of a nervous and timid disposition, he was never able to display much executive ability, but he made up for this lack of talent by fanatical devotion to principle. He had adopted the belief that the philosophy of Rousseau held the one great hope of salvation for all mankind. To put this philosophy into practice he was ready to employ any means that would bring results, regardless of the cost to himself or to others. This passionate loyalty to a gospel that exalted the masses eventually won him a following. Indeed, he was so lionized by the public that he was allowed to wear the knee breeches, silk stockings, and powdered hair of the old society until the end of his life. In 1791 he was accepted as the oracle of the Jacobin Club, now purged of all but its most radical elements. Later he became president of the National Convention and a member of the Committee of Public Safety. Though he had little or nothing to do with originating the Reign of Terror, he was nevertheless responsible for enlarging its scope. He actually came to justify ruthlessness as a necessary and therefore laudable means to revolutionary progress. In the last six weeks of his virtual dictatorship, no fewer than 1,285 heads rolled from the scaffold in Paris.

Robespierre

The years of the Reign of Terror were years of ruthless dictatorship in France. Pressed by foreign enemies from without, the committee faced sabotage from both the political Right and Left at home. In 1793, a large band of peasants, opposed to military conscription and encouraged by British and royalist agents, revolted in the western area of the Vendée. Girondist fugitives helped fuel rebellions in the great provincial cities of Lyon, Bordeaux, and Marseilles. This harvest of the decentralizing policies of the National Assembly was bitter fruit to the committee. At the same time they met with the scornful criticism of revolutionaries even more radical than themselves. This latter group, known as the *enragés,* was led by the journalist Jacques Hébert, and threatened to topple not only the government but the country itself by its extremist crusades. Determined to stabilize France, whatever the necessary cost, the committee dispatched commissioners into the countryside to suppress the enemies of the state. During the period of the Terror, from September 1793 to July 1794, the most reliable estimates place the number of executions at approximately twenty thousand in France as a whole. A law of September 17, 1793, made every person who had been identified in any way with the Bourbon government or with the Girondists an object of suspicion; and no one who was a suspect or who was suspected of being a suspect was entirely

Jacobins. Contemporary drawings by Heuriot.

A Meeting of the Revolutionary Committee During the Reign of Terror

safe from persecution. When some time later the Abbé Sieyès was asked what he had done to distinguish himself during the Terror, he responded dryly, "I lived."

Three points need to be made with regard to the Committee of Public Safety. First, it dramatically reversed the trend toward decentralization, which had characterized the reforms of the assembly. In addition to dispatching its own commissioners from Paris to quell provincial insurrection, the committee published a *Bulletin des loix*, to inform all citizens what laws were to be enforced and obeyed. And it replaced local officials, some of them still royalist in sympathy, with its own loyal "national agents." Second, by fostering, as it did, the interests of the lower middle class the committee significantly retarded the pace of industrial transformation in France. Through policies which assisted the peasant, the small craftsman, and the shopkeeper to acquire property, the government during this "second" revolution encouraged the entrenchment of a class at once devoted to the principle of republicanism while unalterably opposed to a large-scale capitalist transformation of the economy of France. Third, the ruthless Terror of the committee undoubtedly achieved its end, by saving France from defeat at the hands of the coalition of European states. Whether the human price extracted in return for that salvation was worth the paying is a matter historians—and indeed all thoughtful human beings—may well never finally resolve.

The Committee of Public Safety, though able to save France, could not save itself. It failed to put a stop to inflation, thereby losing the support of those commoners whose dissatisfactions had helped bring the convention to power. The long string of military victories convinced growing numbers that the committee's demands for continuing self-sacrifice, as well as its insistence upon the necessity of the Ter-

The achievements of the committee

The Thermidorian reaction: stage three

ror, were no longer justified. By July 1794, the committee was virtually without allies. On July 27 (9 Thermidor, according to the new calendar) the convention "outlawed" Robespierre; on the following day he was executed. The only remaining leaders in the convention were men of moderate sympathies, who, as time went on, inclined toward increasing conservatism. Gradually, the revolution came once more to reflect the interests of the upper middle class. Much of the extremist work of the radicals was now undone. The law of maximum prices and the law against "suspects" were both repealed. Political prisoners were freed, the Jacobins driven into hiding, and the Committee of Public Safety shorn of its absolute powers. The new situation made possible the return of priests, royalists, and other émigrés from abroad to add the weight of their influence to the conservative trend.

In 1795 the National Convention adopted a new constitution, which lent the stamp of official approval to the victory of the prosperous classes. The constitution granted suffrage to all adult male citizens who could read and write. They were permitted to vote for electors, who in turn would choose the members of the legislative body. In order to be an elector, one had to be the proprietor of a farm or other establishment with an annual income equivalent to at least one hundred days of labor. The drafters of the constitution thus ensured that the authority of the government would actually be derived from citizens of considerable wealth. Since it was not practicable to restore the monarchy, lest the old aristocracy also come back into power, executive authority was vested in a board of five men known as the Directory, chosen by the legislative body. The new constitution included not only a bill of rights but also a declaration of the *duties* of the citizen. Conspicuous among the latter was the obligation to bear in

The 1795 constitution

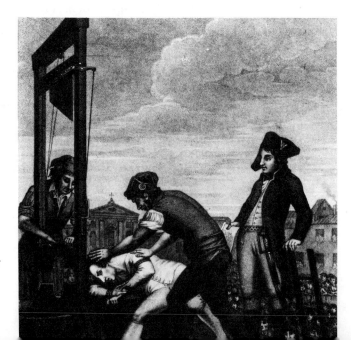

The Death of Robespierre

mind that "it is upon the maintenance of property . . . that the whole social order rests."

The reign of the Directory has not enjoyed a good historical press. The collection of *nouveau riche* speculators and profiteers who rose to prominence as they labored to make a good thing for themselves out of the war were not a particularly attractive crew. They were lampooned as ostentatious and vulgar *"merveilleuses"*—outrageously overdressed men and underdressed women. But however anxious they were to live down the self-denying excesses of the past several years by self-indulgent excesses of their own, they were in no mood to see the major accomplishments of the revolution undone. They had no difficulty in disposing of threats from the Left, despite their failure to resolve that bugbear of all revolutionary governments, inflation and rising living costs. When in 1796 the radical "Gracchus" Babeuf[5] launched a campaign to abolish private property and parliamentary government, his followers were arrested, executed, and deported.

To dispatch threats from the Right was not so easy. Elections in March 1797—the first free elections held in France as a republic—returned a large number of constitutional monarchists to the councils of government. Leading politicians, among them some who had voted for the execution of Louis XVI, took alarm. So too did the Directory's brilliant young general, Napoleon Bonaparte (1769–1821). His plans for permanent French expansion in Belgium and Italy were threatened by a promonarchist "peace" party that was urging an end to war, even if it meant the surrender of recent French conquests. Desperate to save republican France—and themselves—from the monarchists, the directors called for Napoleon's assistance. He sent a general to their aid. With the support of the army thus assured, the Directory in September 1797 annulled most of the election results of the previous

---

[5] Called "Gracchus" after the Roman tribune Gaius Gracchus, a hero of the people.

The Eighteenth Brumaire. A detail from a painting by Bronchet depicting Napoleon as the man of the hour.

spring. Its bold coup did little, however, to end the nation's political irresolution. Two years later, after a series of further abortive uprisings and purges, and with the country still plagued by severe inflation, Bonaparte seized his opportunity to fill the vacuum of French leadership. Leaving his army as it attempted to free itself from British naval domination in Egypt, Bonaparte appeared in France. Appealing to the desperate Directory, he descended upon them as the answer to their prayers: a strong popular leader who was not a king. Abbé Sieyès, who had once declared for revolution in the name of the third estate, now declared for counterrevolution in the name of virtual dictatorship: "Confidence from below, authority from above." With those words Sieyès foreshadowed the end of the revolutionary period.

4. NAPOLEON AND EUROPE

Few men in Western history have compelled the attention of the world as Napoleon Bonaparte did during the fifteen years of his absolutist rule in France. And few men have succeeded as he has in continuing to live on as myth in the consciousness, not just of his own country, but of all Europe. Without doubt, part of the success of the Napoleonic myth can be credited to the fact that Napoleon never attempted to disguise his less-than-gentlemanly background. Although born in Corsica into a family that held a title of nobility from the Republic of Genoa, he cultivated the rude manners of an *arriviste,* losing his temper, cheating at cards, taking what he could get without regard to the conventions of polite society. As such, he appealed to the new citizens of a triumphantly middle-class Europe. In the minds of his admirers he would remain the "little corporal" who, without the privileges of the aristocrat, had made it to the top on his own.

The character of Napoleon Bonaparte

Yet the myth was also grounded in the important fact of Bonaparte's undoubted abilities. Schooled in France and at the military academy in Paris, he possessed a mind congenial to the ideas of the Enlightenment—creative, imaginative, and ready to perceive things anew. His primary interests were history, law, and mathematics. His particular strengths as a leader lay in his ability to conceive of financial, legal, or military plans and then to master their every detail; his capacity for inspiring others, even those initially oppsed to him; and his belief in himself as the destined savior of the French. That last conviction eventually became the obsession that led to Napoleon's undoing. But supreme self-confidence was just what the French government had lacked since the first days of the revolution. Napoleon believed both in himself and in France. That latter belief was the tonic France now needed, and Napoleon proceeded to administer it in liberally revivifying doses.

His abilities

During the years from 1799 to 1804, Napoleon ruled under the title of first consul, but in reality as a dictator. Once again, France was

Napoleon. A famous unfinished portrait by David.

(2) education and law

(3) reconciliation

given a new constitution. Though the document spoke of universal male suffrage, political power was retained, by the now familiar means of indirect election, in the hands of middle-class entrepreneurs and professionals. Recognizing, however, that his regime would derive additional substance if it could be made to appear the government of the people of France, Bonaparte instituted what has since become a common authoritarian device: the plebiscite. The voters were asked to approve the new constitution and did so by the loudly proclaimed vote of 3,011,107 in favor, 1,567 opposed.

Although the constitution provided for a legislative body, that body could neither initiate nor discuss legislation. The first consul made use of a Council of State to draft his laws; but in fact the government depended on the authority of one man. Bonaparte had no desire to undo the major egalitarian reforms of the revolution. He reconfirmed the abolition of estates, privileges, and local liberties, thereby reconfirming as well the notion of a meritocracy, of "careers open to talent," dear to the hearts of the middle class. Through centralization of the administrative departments, he achieved what no recent French regime had yet achieved, an orderly and generally fair system of taxation. His plan, by prohibiting the type of exemptions formerly granted the nobility and clergy, and by centralizing collection, enabled him to budget rationally for expenditures and consequent indebtedness. In this way he reduced the inflationary spiral that had entangled so many past governments.

Napoleon's most significant accomplishment was his completion of the educational and legal reforms begun during the revolutionary period. He ordered the establishment of *lycées* (high schools) in every major town and a school in Paris for the training of teachers. To supplement these changes, Napoleon brought the military and technical schools under state control and founded a national university to exercise supervision over the entire system. Like almost all his reforms, this one proved of particular benefit to the middle class; so did the new legal code promulgated in 1810. The Code Napoleon, as the new body of laws was called, reflected two principles which had threaded their way through all the constitutional changes since 1789: uniformity and individualism. The code made French law uniform, declaring past customs and privileges forever abolished. By underscoring in various ways a private individual's right to property, by authorizing new methods for the drafting of contracts, leases, and stock companies, and by once again prohibiting trade unions, the code worked to the benefit of individually minded entrepreneurs and businessmen.

To accomplish these reforms Napoleon called upon the most talented men available to him, regardless of their past political affiliations. He admitted back into the country émigrés of all political stripes. His two fellow consuls—joint executives, but in name only—were a regicide of the Terror and bureaucrat of the Old Regime. His minister of police had been an extreme radical republi-

Coronation of Napoleon and Josephine by David. Napoleon crowned himself and his wife and assumed the title of Napoleon I, emperor of the French.

can; his minister of foreign affairs was the opportunist aristocrat Talleyrand. The work of political reconciliation was assisted by Napoleon's 1801 concordat with the pope, which reunited Church and State. Though the action disturbed former anti-Church Jacobins, Napoleon, ever the pragmatist, believed the reconciliation of Church and State necessary for reasons both of domestic harmony and of international solidarity. According to the terms of the concordat, the pope received the right to depose French bishops and to discipline the French clergy. At the same time, the Vatican agreed to lay to rest any claims against the expropriation of former Church lands. Hereafter, that property would remain unchallenged in the hands of its new middle-class rural and urban proprietors. In return, the clergy was guaranteed an income from the state. The concordat did nothing to revoke the principle of religious freedom established by the revolution. Although the Roman Catholic clergy received state money, so did Protestant clergy.

Napoleon's agreement won him the support of those conservatives who had feared for France's future as a Godless state. To prove to the old Jacobins, in turn, that he remained a child of their revolution, he invaded the independent state of Baden in 1804 to arrest and then execute the duke of Enghien, a relative of the Bourbons, whom Napoleon falsely accused of a plot against his life. (Three years before he had deported over one hundred Jacobins on a similar charge, but with no permanent political repercussions.) The balancing act only served to increase Napoleon's general popularity. By 1802 the people of France were prepared to accept him as "consul for life." In 1804, they rejoiced when, in the cathedral of Notre Dame, in Paris, he crowned himself Emperor Napoleon I.

Across the boundaries of France, the nations of Europe had watched, some in admiration, others in horror, all in astonishment, at

Napoleon crowned emperor

the phenomenon that was Napoleon. They had fought France since 1792 in hopes of maintaining European stability. Now they faced the greatest threat to that stability yet to arise. The detailed history of the wars fought to contain the French is complex, and of little direct relevance to the patterns of ideas, institutions, and societies we are tracing. Suffice it to say that from 1792 until 1795 France had been at war with a coalition of European powers—principally Austria, Prussia, and Britain. In 1795, Prussia retired from the fray, financially exhausted and at odds with Austria. In 1797, the Austrians, defeated by Bonaparte in northern Italy, withdrew as well, signing the Treaty of Campo Formio, which ceded to France territories in Belgium, recognized the Cisalpine Republic which Bonaparte had established in Italy, and agreed to France's occupation of the left bank of the Rhine.

By the following year, Britain was left to fight the French alone. In 1798 it formed a second coalition against the French, this one with Russia and Austria. The results did not differ significantly from those of the first allied attempt to contain France. Russia and Austria had no success in driving the French from Italy; the French likewise failed to break Britain's advantage at sea. By 1801, the coalition was in tatters, Russia having withdrawn two years previously. The Treaty of Lunéville, signed by France and Austria, confirmed the provisions of Campo Formio; in addition the so-called Batavian, Helvetian, Cisalpine, and Ligurian republics—established by Napoleon from territories in the Low Countries, Switzerland, Italy, and Piedmont—were legitimized. The Austrians also acquiesced to a general redrawing of the map of Germany, which resulted eventually in an amalgamation of semi-independent states under French domination into the Confederation of the Rhine. The following year Britain, no longer able to fight alone, settled with the French as well, returning all the territories it had captured in overseas colonial engagements except Trinidad and Ceylon.

Under Napoleon's reign, the territories of central Europe underwent a revolution. This revolution was a thorough governmental reorganization, one which imposed the major egalitarian reforms of the French Revolution upon lands outside the borders of France, while building a French empire. Most affected were territories in Italy (the "Kingdom of Italy" as it was now called); Germany (the Confederation of the Rhine, including the newly formed Kingdom of Westphalia); Dalmatia (the Illyrian provinces); and Holland. (Belgium had been integrated directly into the empire.) Into all these territories Napoleon introduced a carefully organized, deliberate system of administration, based upon the notion of careers open to talent, equality before the law, and the abolition of ancient customs and privileges. The Napoleonic program of reform in the empire represented an application of the principles that had already transformed postrevolutionary France. Manorial courts were liquidated, and Church courts abolished. Provinces were joined into an enormous bureaucratic network that reached directly back to Paris. Laws were codified, the tax system modernized, and everywhere individuals were freed to work at whatever trade they chose. The one freedom denied throughout this new grand hegemony was that of self-government: i.e., all governmental direction emanated from Paris, and therefore from Napoleon. Despite that fact, middle-class business and professional men, who had chafed against restrictions imposed upon them by petty despotic traditions, welcomed this chance to exercise their talents to a fuller degree than they had ever before enjoyed.

Napoleon's motives in introducing these various radical changes were by no means altruistic. He understood that the defense of his enormous domain depended on efficient administration and the rational collection and expenditure of funds for his armies. His boldest attempt at consolidation, however, a policy forbidding the importation into the Continent of British goods, proved a failure. This "Continental System," established in 1806, was designed as a strategic measure in Napoleon's continuing economic war against Britain. Its purpose was to destroy Britain's commerce and credit—to starve it economically into surrender. The system failed for several reasons. Foremost was the fact that throughout the war Britain retained control of the seas. The British naval blockade of the Continent, implemented in 1807, served, therefore, as an effective counter to Napoleon's system. While the empire labored to transport goods and raw materials overland to avoid the British blockade, the British worked with success to develop a lively trade with South America. Internal tariffs were a second reason for the failure of the system. Napoleon was unable to persuade individual territories to join a tariff-free customs union. As a result Europe remained divided into economic camps, fortified against each other by tariffs, and at odds with each other as they attempted to subsist on nothing more than what the Continent could produce and manufacture. The final reason for the system's collapse was the stark fact that the Continent had more to lose than Britain. Trade stagnated; ports and manufacturing centers grumbled as unemployment rose.

5. THE END OF THE REVOLUTIONARY ERA

The Continental System was Napoleon's first serious mistake. As such it was one of the causes of his ultimate downfall. A second cause of Napoleon's decline was his constantly growing ambition and increasing sense of self-importance. Napoleon's goal was a united Europe modeled after the Roman Empire. The symbols of his empire—reflected in painting, architecture, and the design of furniture and clothing—were deliberately Roman in origin. But Napoleon's Rome was without question imperial, dynastic Rome. The triumphal

The Empress Josephine

Reasons for Napoleon's fall

columns and arches he had erected to commemorate his victories recalled the ostentatious monuments of the Roman emperors. He made his brothers and sisters the monarchs of his newly created kingdoms, which Napoleon controlled from Paris. He divorced his first wife, the Empress Josephine, alleging her childlessness, and insured himself a successor of royal blood by marrying into the house of Hapsburg. Even his admirers began to question if Napoleon's empire was not simply a larger, more efficient, and, therefore, ultimately more dangerous despotism than the monarchies of the eighteenth century. War again broke out in 1805, with the Russians, Prussians, and Austrians joining the British in an attempt to contain France. But to no avail; Napoleon's military superiority led to defeats, in turn, of all three continental allies. Ultimately only the emperor's own unwillingness to recognize that his supply of men, materiel, and good fortune was not limitless brought military defeat upon him.

Invasion of Spain

In 1808, Napoleon invaded Spain on the pretext of guarding its coasts against the British, but with the intention of establishing his brother Joseph as king. Scarcely had the new monarch been crowned than the Spanish people rose in revolt. Though Napoleon sent an army against them, he was never able to crush the rebellion entirely. With encouragement and assistance from the British, the Spaniards kept up a series of guerilla attacks which caused no end of expense and annoyance to the great warlord of France. Further, the courage of Spain in resisting the invader promoted a spirit of defiance elsewhere, with the result that Napoleon could no longer count upon the docility of any of his victims.

See color map facing page 705

A more fateful stage in the downfall of the Corsican adventurer was

The Retreat from Russia. In this painting by Charlet the horrors of the Russian winter can be seen.

the disruption of his alliance with Russia. As a purely agricultural country, Russia had suffered a severe economic crisis when it was no longer able, as a result of the Continental System, to exchange its surplus grain for British manufactures. The consequence was that Tsar Alexander began to wink at trade with Britain and to ignore or evade the protests from Paris. By 1811 Napoleon decided that he could endure this flouting of the Continental System no longer. Accordingly, he collected an army of 600,000 men and set out in the spring of 1812 to punish the tsar. The project ended in disaster. The Russians refused to make a stand, thereby leading the French farther and farther into the heart of their country. They finally permitted Napoleon to occupy their ancient capital of Moscow. But on the very night of his entry, a fire of suspicious origin broke out in the city. When the flames subsided, little but the blackened walls of the Kremlin palaces remained to shelter the invading troops. Hoping that the tsar would eventually surrender, Napoleon lingered amid the ruins for more than a month, finally deciding on October 22 to begin the homeward march. The delay was a fatal blunder. Long before he had reached the border, the terrible Russian winter was upon his troops. Swollen streams, mountainous drifts of snow, and bottomless mud slowed the retreat almost to a halt. To add to the miseries of bitter cold, disease, and starvation, mounted Cossacks rode out of the blizzard to harry the exhausted army. Each morning the miserable remnant that pushed on left behind circles of corpses around the campfires of the night before. On December 13 a few thousand broken soldiers crossed the frontier into Germany—a miserable fraction of what had once been proudly styled the *Grande Armée*. The lives of nearly 300,000 men had been sacrificed in Napoleon's Russian adventure.

EXTRAIT DU MONITEUR.

ACTE
D'ABDICATION
DE
L'EMPEREUR NAPOLÉON.

Napoleon's Abdication Proclamation, 1814

The allies now took advantage of Napoleon's depleted forces to engineer victory. By March of 1814 their armies were in Paris and Napoleon prepared for surrender. Exiled to the island of Elba, in the Mediterranean, he plotted return, while his successor Louis XVIII, brother of Louis XVI and the choice of the allies, attempted to fill a space far too great for his mediocre talents. In the spring of 1815, Napoleon returned to France, where he was received enthusiastically. But the rekindled loyalties could not outlast his final defeat at the Battle of Waterloo, in Belgium, on June 18, 1815. This time the allies exiled him to the tiny island of St. Helena, in the south Atlantic, where he died in 1821.

The Russian campaign

The Battle of Waterloo

To appreciate the impact of this era of revolution upon Western civilization, one must trace the ideas and institutions it fostered as they work their way into the history of nineteenth- and twentieth-century Europe and America. Liberty—the right to act within the world with responsibility to no one but oneself—was a notion dear to those who made the French Revolution, and one which remained embodied in the reforms it produced. So was equality—the notion of rational laws

The era of revolution: liberty, equality, nationality

applied even-handedly to all, regardless of birth or position. National pride, the era's third legacy, was bred in the hearts of the French people as they watched their citizen armies repel attacks against their newly won freedoms. It was instilled, as well, into those whose opposition to the French made them more conscious of their own national identity. The three concepts—liberty, equality, and nationality—were now no longer merely ideas; as laws and as a new way of addressing life, they rested at the center of European reality. They were together one of the two elements upon which a new ruling class—the middle class—now rose to power. The other element—economic success—is the subject of the next chapter.

SELECTED READINGS

* *Items so designated are available in paperback editions.*
* Arendt, Hannah, *On Revolution*, New York, 1963. An analysis of the American and French Revolutions and their meaning for modern man.

Bosher, J. F., *French Finances, 1770–1795: From Business to Bureaucracy*, Cambridge, 1970. An impressive study concerned with the financial apparatus of Old Regime and revolutionary France.

* Breunig, C., *The Age of Revolution and Reaction, 1789–1850*, 2nd ed., New York, 1978.

* Brinton, Crane, *Anatomy of Revolution*, rev. ed., New York, 1961. Attempts to create a general model of revolutions by comparing the English, American, French and Russian Revolutions.

* ———, *A Decade of Revolution, 1789–1799*, New York, 1934. An excellent European survey.

* Bruun, Geoffrey, *Europe and the French Imperium, 1799–1814*, New York, 1938. Describes the impact of Napoleon upon Europe.

Cobban, Alfred, *The Social Interpretation of the French Revolution*, Cambridge, 1964. A penetrating critique of the radical interpretation of the revolution, more important for its questions than its conclusions.

Cone, Carl B., *The English Jacobins: Reformers in Late 18th-Century England*, New York, 1968.

Dansette, Adrien, *A Religious History of Modern France*, Vol. I, New York, 1961. Traces the position of the Catholic Church during the revolutionary and Napoleonic periods.

Ford, Franklin, *Robe and Sword: The Regrouping of the French Aristocracy after Louis XIV*, Cambridge, Mass., 1953. An important social study of the nobility of the robe and its striving for political dominance prior to the revolution.

* Gershoy, Leo, *The French Revolution and Napoleon*, rev. ed., New York, 1964. A good survey with annotated bibliography.

———, *From Despotism to Revolution, 1763–1789*, New York, 1944. Valuable for background on the revolution.

Geyl, Pieter, *Napoleon: For and Against*, rev. ed., New Haven, Conn., 1964. The ways in which Napoleon has been interpreted by French historians and political figures.

Gooch, G. P., *Germany and the French Revolution*, New York, 1920. An old but still valuable account of the German political and intellectual response to the French Revolution.

Goodwin, Albert, *The French Revolution*, rev. ed., London, 1958. A good introduction to the years 1789–1794.

Greer, Donald, *The Incidence of the Terror During the French Revolution: A Statistical Interpretation*, Cambridge, Mass., 1935. An important study which reveals that the lower classes suffered most during the Terror, rather than the nobility or the clergy.

• Hampson, Norman, *A Social History of the French Revolution*, London, 1963.

Herold, J. Christopher, *The Age of Napoleon*, New York, 1963.

• Lefebvre, Georges, *The Coming of the French Revolution*, Princeton, N.J., 1947. An excellent study of the causes and early events of the revolution.

———, *The French Revolution*, 2 vols., New York, 1963–64. An impressive synthesis by the greatest modern scholar of the revolution.

———, *Napoleon*, New York, 1969.

———, *The Thermidorians and the Directory*, New York, 1964.

McManners, John, *The French Revolution and the Church*, New York, 1969. Describes the impact of revolutionary anticlericalism upon the French Church.

Mathiez, Albert, *The French Revolution*, New York, 1928. Sympathetic to Robespierre.

• Palmer, R. R., *The Age of the Democratic Revolution: A Political History of Europe and America, 1760–1800*, 2 vols., Princeton, N.J., 1964. Impressive for its scope; places the French Revolution in the large context of a worldwide revolutionary movement.

———, *Twelve Who Ruled*, Princeton, 1958. Excellent biographical studies of the members of the Committee of Public Safety. Demonstrates that Robespierre's role has been exaggerated.

• Rudé, George, *The Crowd in the French Revolution*, Oxford, 1959. An important monograph which analyzes the composition of the crowds which participated in the great uprisings of the revolution.

Schapiro, J. S., *Condorcet and the Rise of Liberalism in France*, New York, 1934. A splendid study of revolutionary idealism.

Soboul, Albert, *The Sans-Culottes: The Popular Movement and Revolutionary Government, 1793–1794*, Garden City, N.Y., 1972. An outstanding example of "history from below"; analyzes the pressures upon the Convention in the year of the Terror.

Thompson, J. M., *Napoleon Bonaparte: His Rise and Fall*, Oxford, 1958. The standard work.

• ———, *Robespierre and the French Revolution*, London, 1953. An excellent short biography.

• Tilly, Charles, *The Vendée: A Sociological Analysis of the Counter-Revolution of 1793*, Cambridge, Mass., 1964. An important economic and social analysis of the factors that led to reaction in the Vendée.

• Tocqueville, Alexis de, *The Old Regime and French Revolution*. Originally written in 1856, this remains a classic analysis of the causes of the French Revolution.

• Williams, Gwyn A., *Artisans and Sans-Culottes*, New York, 1969.

SOURCE MATERIALS

• Burke, Edmund, *Reflections on the Revolution in France,* London, 1790. The great conservative statement against the revolution and its principles.
• Montesquieu, Baron de, *The Spirit of the Laws,* New York, 1945. See especially Books I, II, III, XI.
• Paine, Thomas, *The Rights of Man,* 1791. (Many editions.) Paine's eloquent response to Burke's *Reflections* resulted in his conviction for treason and banishment from England.
• Rousseau, Jean-Jacques, *Discourse on the Origin of Inequality,* 1754. (Many editions.)
——, *The Social Contract,* 1762, (Many editions.) Rousseau's *Social Contract* provided a philosophical justification for both the American and French Revolutions.
Sieyès, Abbé, *What Is the Third Estate?* 1789. The most important political pamphlet in the decisive year 1789.
Stewart, John Hall, *A Documentary Survey of the French Revolution,* New York, 1951.
Thompson, J. M., *French Revolution Documents, 1789–1794,* Oxford, 1948.
Young, Arthur, *Travels in France during the Years 1787, 1788, 1789,* London, 1912. France on the eve of revolution, as seen by a perceptive English observer.

Chapter 25

THE INDUSTRIAL REVOLUTION

Providence has assigned to man the glorious function of vastly improving the productions of nature by judicious culture, of working them up into objects of comfort and elegance with the least possible expenditure of human labor—an undeniable position which forms the basis of our Factory System.

—Andrew Ure, *The Philosophy of Manufactures*

There have been many revolutions in industry during the history of Western civilization, and there will undoubtedly be many more. Periods of rapid technological change are often called revolutions, and justifiably so, But, historically, there is but one Industrial Revolution. Occurring during the one hundred years after 1780, it witnessed the first breakthrough from a rural, handicraft economy to one dominated by urban, machine-driven manufactuting.

The fact that it was a European revolution was not accidental. Although Europe was, in the mid–eighteenth century, a continent still predominantly agricultural, although the majority of its people remained illiterate and destined to live out impoverished lives within sight of the place they were born—despite these conditions, which in our eyes might make Europe appear "underdeveloped," it was of course no such thing. European merchants and men of commerce were established as the world's foremost manufacturers and traders. Rulers relied upon this class of men to provide them with the wherewithal to maintain the economy of their states, both in terms of flourishing commercial activity and of victorious armies and navies. Those men, in turn, had for the most part extracted from their rulers the understanding that the property they possessed, whether invested in land, or commerce, or both, was theirs outright. That understanding, substantiated by the written contracts that were replacing unwritten, long-acknowledged custom, helped persuade merchants, bankers, traders, and entrepreneurs that they lived in a world that was

A European revolution: the commercial class

stable, rational, and predictable. Believing the world was so, they moved out into it with self-confidence and in hopes of prospering. Only in Europe does one find these presuppositions and this class of men in the eighteenth century; only through the activities of such a class could the Industrial Revolution have taken place.

Increasing markets

These capitalists could not have prospered without an expanding market for their goods. The existence of this market explains further why it was in Europe that the Industrial Revolution took place. Ever since the beginning of the seventeenth century, overseas commercial exploration and development had been opening new territories to European trade. India, Africa, North and South America—all had been woven into the pattern of European economic expansion. The colonies and commercial dependencies took economic shape at Europe's behest. Even the new United States had not been able to declare its economic independence. Whatever new design Europe might devise, all would be compelled to accomodate themselves to Europe's demands.

Population growth

A third factor helping to insure that the revolution would occur in Europe was the continuing growth of its population. In England, the population increased from about 4 million in 1600 to about 6 million in 1700, to 9 million in 1800. The population of France grew from 17 million in 1700 to 26 million a century later. Population growth on this scale provided, as did overseas expansion, an ever-increasing market for manufactured goods. It furnished, as well, an adequate pool— eventually a surplus—of laboring men, women, and children to work in the manufacture of those goods either at home or in factories.

Yet these factors—a thriving commercial class, growing markets, and an increasing population—while helping to explain why the Industrial Revolution took place in eighteenth-century Europe, fail to tell us enough about its origins. For that understanding, we must focus our attention from Europe as a whole to its most prosperous state, England.

1. THE INDUSTRIAL REVOLUTION IN ENGLAND

Why in England? (1) an economy of abundance

It was in England that the Industrial Revolution first took hold. England's economy had progressed further than that of any other country in the direction of abundance. In simplest terms: fewer people were engaged in the crude struggle to do no more than remain alive; more people were in a position to sell a surplus of the goods they produced to an increasingly expanding market; and more people had money enough to purchase the goods that market offered. English laborers, though poorly enough paid, enjoyed a higher standard of living than their continental counterparts. They ate white bread, not brown, and meat with some regularity. Because a smaller portion of their income was spent on food, they might occasionally have some to spare for articles which were bought rather than homemade.

Further evidence of this increasing abundance was the number of bills for the enclosure of agricultural land passed by an English Parliament sympathetic to capitalism during the last half of the eighteenth century. The enclosure of fields, pasture, and waste lands into large fenced tracts of land under the private ownership and individual management of capitalist landlords, although it deprived local agricultural laborers of the right to share in the use of common lands as they had in past times, meant an increased food supply to feed an increasing and increasingly urban population. Yet another sign of England's abundance was its growing supply of surplus capital, derived from investment in land or commerce, and available for further employment to finance new economic enterprises. Thus English capitalists had enough money on hand to underwrite and sustain an industrial revolution.

But the revolution required more than money. It required habits of mind that would encourage investments in enterprises at once risky, but with an enormous potential for gain. In England, far more than on the Continent, the pursuit of wealth was perceived to be a worthy end in life. The aristocracy of Europe had, from the period of the Renaissance, cultivated the notion of "gentlemanly" conduct, in part to hold the line against social encroachments from below. The English aristocrats, whose privileges were meager when compared with those of continental nobles, had never ceased to respect men who made money; nor had they disdained to make whatever they could for themselves. They invested and speculated. Their scramble to enclose their lands reflected this sympathy with aggressive capitalism. Below the aristocracy, there was even less of a barrier separating the world of urban commerce from that of the rural "gentry." Most of the men who pioneered as entrepreneurs in the early years of the Industrial Revolution sprang from the minor gentry or yeoman farmer class. To a degree unknown on the Continent, men from this sort of background felt themselves free to rise as high as their abilities might carry them on the social and economic ladder.

Eighteenth-century England was not by any means free of social snobbery, however: lords looked down upon bankers, as bankers looked down upon artisans. But a lord's disdain might well be tempered by the fact of his own grandfather's origins in the counting-house. And the banker would gladly lend money to the artisan if convinced that the artisan's invention might make them both a fortune. The English, as a nation, were not afraid of business. They respected the sensible, the practical, and the financially successful. Robinson Crusoe, that desert island entrepreneur, was one of their models. In the novel (1719) by Daniel Defoe, the hero had used his wits to master nature and become lord of a thriving economy. His triumph was not diminished because it was a worldly triumph; far from it. "It is our vanity which urges us on," the economist Adam Smith, defender of laissez faire capitalism, declared. And thank God, Smith implied, for our blessed vanity! An individual's desire to show himself a success worked to produce prosperity for the country as a whole.

(3) increasing markets

England's eighteenth-century prosperity was based upon an expanding market for whatever goods it manufactured. Its small size and the fact that it was an island encouraged the development of a nationwide domestic market. The absence of a system of internal tolls and tariffs, such as existed on the Continent, meant that goods could be moved freely to the place where they could fetch the best price. This freedom of movement was assisted by a constantly improving transportation system. Parliament in the years just before the Industrial Revolution passed acts to finance turnpike building at the rate of forty per year; the same period saw the construction of canals and the further opening up of harbors and navigable streams. Unlike the government of France, whose cumbrous mercantilist adventures as often as not thwarted economic growth, the English Parliament believed that the most effective way in which it could help businessmen was to assist them in helping themselves.

Overseas expansion

Parliament's members had every reason to promote England's economic fortunes. Some were businessmen themselves; others had invested heavily in commerce. Hence their eagerness to encourage by statute the construction of canals, the establishment of banks, and the enclosure of common lands. And hence their insistence, throughout the eighteenth century, that England's foreign policy respond to its commercial needs. At the end of every major eighteenth-century war, England wrested overseas territories from its enemies. At the same time, England was penetrating hitherto unexploited ports and territories, such as India and South America, in search of further potential markets and resources. The English possessed a merchant marine capable of transporting goods across the world, and a navy practiced in the art of protecting its commercial fleets. London, already a leading center for the world's trade, served as a headquarters for the transfer of raw material, capital, and manufactured products. By 1780 England's markets, together with its fleet and its established position at the center of world trade, combined to produce a potential for expansion so great as to compel the Industrial Revolution.

The cotton industry

English entrepreneurs and technicians responded to the compulsion by revolutionizing the production of cotton textile goods. Although far less cotton goods were made in eighteenth-century England than wool, the extent of their manufacture by 1760 was such as to make cotton more than an infant industry. Tariffs prohibiting the importation of East Indian cottons, imposed by Parliament to stimulate the sale of woolen goods, had instead served to spur the manufacture of domestic cotton goods. Thus the revolution, when it did occur, took place in an already well-established industry. Yet without the inven-

The Spinning Jenny. Invented by James Hargreaves in 1767

tion of some sort of machinery which would improve the quality and at the same time dramatically increase the quantity of spun cotton thread, the necessary breakthrough would not have come. The invention of the fly-shuttle, which greatly speeded up the process of weaving, only made the bottleneck in the prior process of spinning the more apparent. The problem was solved by the invention of a series of comparatively simple mechanical devices, the most important of which was the spinning jenny, invented by James Hargreaves, a carpenter and hand-loom weaver, in 1767 (patented 1770). The spinning jenny, named after the inventor's wife, was a compound spinning wheel, capable of producing sixteen threads at once. The threads it spun were not strong enough, however, to be used for the longitudinal fibers, or warp, of cotton cloth. It was not until the invention of the water frame by Richard Arkwright, a barber, in 1769, that quantity production of both warp and woof (latitudinal fibers) became possible. This invention, along with that of the spinning mule, conceived of by Samuel Crompton in 1779, and combining the features of both the jenny and the frame, solved the problems that had heretofore curtailed the output of cotton textiles. They increased the mechanical advantage over the spinning wheel enormously. From six to twenty-four times the amount of yarn could be spun on a jenny as on the wheel; by the end of the century two to three hundred times as much on the mule. Just as important, the quality of the thread improved not only in terms of strength but also of fineness.

Once these machines came into general use, the revolution proceeded apace. Cotton suited the mule and the jenny because it was a tougher thread than wool—fiber which could withstand the rough

Eli Whitney

Growth of factories

The extent of the cotton trade

treatment it received at the mechanical hands of the crude early machines. In addition, the supply of cotton was expandable in a way that the supply of wool was not. The cotton gin, invented by the American Eli Whitney in 1793, separated seeds from fiber, thereby making cotton available at a lower price. The invention kept America's slave plantations profitable, and meant that supply would be available to meet increased demand.

The first machinery was cheap enough to allow spinners to continue to work their own machines at home. But as the machinery increased in size, it was more and more frequently housed not in the cottages of individual spinners, but in workshops or mills located near water which could be used to power the machines. Eventually, with the further development of steam-driven equipment, the mills could be built wherever it might suit the entrepreneur—frequently in towns and cities in the north of England.

The transition from home to factory industry was of course not accomplished overnight. Cotton yarn continued to be spun at home at the same time that it was being produced in mills. Eventually, however, the low cost of building and operating a large plant, plus the efficiency realized by bringing workers together under one roof, meant that larger mills more and more frequently replaced smaller workshops. By 1851, three-fifths of those employed in cotton manufacture worked in medium- to large-sized mills. Weaving remained a home industry until the invention of a cheap, practical power loom convinced entrepreneurs that they could save money by moving the process from home to mill. Hand-loom weavers were probably the most obvious victims of the Industrial Revolution in England. Their unwillingness to surrender their livelihood to machinery meant that they continued to work for less and less—by 1830, no more than a pitiful six shillings a week. In 1815 they numbered about 250,000; by 1850, there remained only 40,000; by 1860, only 3,000.

English cotton textiles flooded the world market from the 1780s. Here was a light material, suitable for the climates of Africa, India, and the more temperate zones of North America. Here was a material cheap enough to make it possible for millions who had never before enjoyed the comfort of washable body clothes to do so. And here was material fine enough to tempt the rich to experiment with muslins and calicos in a way they had not done before. Figures speak eloquently of the revolutionary change wrought by the expanding industry. In 1760, England exported less than £250,000 worth of cotton goods; by 1800 it was exporting over £5 million worth. In 1760, England imported 2.5 million pounds of raw cotton; in 1787, 22 million pounds; in 1837, 366 million pounds. By 1800, cotton accounted for about 5 percent of the national income of the country; by 1812, from 7 to 8 percent. By 1815, the export of cotton textiles amounted to 40 percent of the value of all domestic goods exported from Great Britain. Although the price of manufactured cotton goods fell dramatically, the market expanded so rapidly that profits continued to increase.

Unlike the changes in the textile industry, those occurring in the manufacture of iron were not great enough to warrant their being labeled revolutionary. Yet they were most significant. Britain's abundant supply of coal, combined with its advanced transportation network, allowed the English, from the middle of the eighteenth century, to substitute coal for wood in the heating of molten metal. A series of discoveries made fuel savings possible, along with a higher quality of iron, and the manufacture of a greater variety of iron products. Demand rose sharply during the war years at the end of the century. It remained high as a result of calls for plant machinery, agricultural implements, and hardware; it rose dramatically with the coming of railways in the 1830s and 1840s. Britain was exporting 571,000 tons of iron in 1814; in 1852, it exported 1,036,000 tons out of a total of almost 2,000,000—more iron than was made by all the rest of the world combined.

The iron industry

The need for more coal required the mining of deeper and deeper veins. In 1712, Thomas Newcomen had devised a crude but effective steam engine for pumping water from mines. Though of value to the coal industry, it was of less use in other industries, since it was wasteful of both fuel and power. In 1763, James Watt, a maker of scientific instruments at the University of Glasgow, was asked to repair a model of the Newcomen engine. While engaged in this task he conceived the idea that the machine would be greatly improved if a separate chamber were added to condense the steam, so as to eliminate the necessity of cooling the cylinder. He patented his first engine incorporating this device in 1769. Unfortunately, Watt's genius as an inventor was not matched by his business ability. He admitted that he would "rather face a loaded cannon than settle a disputed account or make a bargain." As a consequence, he fell into debt in attempting to place his

The steam engine

James Watt Working on a Model of Thomas Newcomen's Steam Engine

The Staffordshire Collieries. In the building to the right is a whimsey, or coal-powered steam engine, used to lift loads of coal from the mines.

machines on the market. He was rescued by Matthew Boulton, a wealthy hardware manufacturer of Birmingham. The two men formed a partnership, with Boulton providing the capital. By 1800 the firm had sold 289 engines for use in factories and mines. One must not exaggerate the speed with which the steam engine replaced water as the principle motive force in industry. In 1850 more than a third of the power used in woolen manufacture and an eighth of that used in cotton was still produced by water. Despite those facts, there is no question that without the steam engine there could have been no expansion in those or other industries on the scale that we have described.

Other industries experienced profound changes during the hundred years of the Industrial Revolution. Many of those changes came in response to the growth of textile manufacture. The chemical industry, for example, developed new methods of dyeing and bleaching, as well as improved methods of production in the fields of soap and glass-making. Production of goods increased across the board, as profits from the boom in manufacturing increased the demand for new and more sophisticated articles. Pottery, metalware—these and other trades expanded to meet demands, in the process adopting methods that in most instances reduced cost and speeded manufacture.

To understand fully the nature of the Industrial Revolution in England one must not lose sight of two important factors: the first is that dramatic as the revolution was, it happened over a period of two or three generations, at varying paces in different industries. Some men and women continued to work at home, much as their grandfathers

Other advances

*The limits of the
Industrial Revolution*

and grandmothers had. Old tools and old methods were not immediately replaced by new ones, any more than populations fled the countryside overnight for the city. Second, the revolution was accomplished from a very limited technological and theoretical base. Except in the chemical industry, change was not the result of pure scientific research. It was the product of empirical experimentation—in some cases, of little more than creative tinkering. To say this is not to disparage the work of men such as Arkwright, Hargreaves, Watt, and their like. It is to suggest, however, the reason why England, without a national system of education on any level, was nonetheless able to accomplish the revolution it did. Nor are these remarks designed to belittle the magnitude of the change. What occurred in England was a revolution because of the way in which it reshaped the lives, not just of the English, but of people across the globe. By responding as it did to the demands of its apparently insatiable markets, England made a revolution every bit as profound and long-lasting as that which occurred simultaneously in France.

2. THE INDUSTRIAL REVOLUTION ON THE CONTINENT

The Industrial Revolution came in time to the Continent, but not to any important degree before about 1830. Manufacturing in eighteenth-century France and Germany clustered in regions whose proximity to raw materials, access to markets, and traditional attachment to particular skills had resulted in their development as industrial centers. Flanders and Normandy in France, and Saxony in Germany were centers for the manufacture of woolen cloth; Switzerland, southern Germany, and Normandy, of cottons; Wallonia (the area around Liège in Belgium), the Marne valley, and Silesia in Germany, of iron. Yet for a variety of reasons, these areas failed to experience the late-eighteenth-century breakthrough that occurred in Britain. Nor were they capable at first of imitating Britain's success, once they began to perceive the great economic advantages that its pronounced lead was bringing it. There were a number of reasons for the delay of continental industrialization, most of them opposite to those reasons which had brought the Industrial Revolution first to England. Whereas England's transportation system was highly developed, those of France and Germany were not. France was far bigger than England, its rivers were not as easily navigable, its seaports further apart. Central Europe was so divided into tiny principalities, each with its own set of tolls and tariffs, as to make the transportation of raw materials or manufactured goods over any considerable distance most impractical. Nor was France itself free of the sorts of regulations that thwarted easy shipments. In addition, the Continent was not as blessed with an abundance of raw materials as England. France, the Low Countries, and

Reasons for delay: (1) lack of transport and raw materials

Germany had to import wool. Europe, though richer than England in timber, lacked an abundant supply of the fuel that was the new source of industrial energy; few major coal deposits had as yet been discovered.

Distances and distinctions between social and economic ranks were far greater on the Continent than in England. Money was not the social solvent in France and Germany that it was across the Channel. Before the French Revolution, continental aristocrats were unwilling to invest in commercial enterprises they believed would damage their social standing. More important, after the revolution middle-class Frenchmen, though free in theory to rise as high on the social and economic ladder as they might aspire, appear largely to have remained content to make only enough money to sustain a modest-sized business. Those revolutionary constitutional changes which had favored the lower middle class by encouraging its acquisition of property, prevented the growth of industry by dispersing capital into the hands of innumerable small-scale enterprises. The entrepreneurial spirit that compelled Englishmen to drive competitors to the wall was not as highly developed in France and Germany in the years after 1815. Exhausted by the competitiveness of war, and fearful of the disruptions that war brought in its train, continental businessmen remained far more willing than the English to keep on manufacturing and selling on the same scale they always had.[1]

(2) lack of entrepreneurial spirit

The Continent did not simply stand idle as England assumed its industrial lead. The pace of mechanization was increasing in the 1780s. But the French Revolution and the wars which followed disrupted the growth which might have otherwise taken place. Battles fought on French, German, and Italian soil destroyed factories and machinery. Although ironmaking increased to meet the demands of the wars, techniques remained what they had been. Commerce was badly hurt both by British destruction of French merchant shipping and by Napoleon's Continental System. Probably the revolutionary change most beneficial to industrial advance in Europe was the removal of previous restraints on the movement of capital and labor; for example, the abolition of trade guilds, and the reduction in the number of tariff barriers across the Continent. On balance, however, the revolutionary and Napoleonic wars clearly thwarted industrial development on the Continent, while at the same time intensifying it in England.

(3) effect of wars

A number of factors combined to produce a climate more generally conductive to industrialization on the Continent after 1815. Population continued to increase, not only throughout Europe, but in those areas now more and more dependent upon the importation of manufactured goods—Latin America, for example. These increases, which doubled the populations of most European countries between 1800 and 1850, meant that the Continent would be supplied with a growing

Increases after 1815: (1) population rise

---

[1]On this point, see David S. Landes, *The Unbound Prometheus*, pp. 132–33.

A Swedish Mining Town, 1790

number of producers and consumers. More people did not necessarily mean further industrialization. In Ireland, for example, where other necessary factors were absent, more people meant less food. But in those countries with an already well-established commercial and industrial base—France and Germany, for example—increased population did encourage the adoption of the technologies and methods of production that had transformed Britain.

Transportation improved in the West both during and following the Napoleonic wars. The Austrian Empire added over 30,000 miles of roads between 1830 and 1847; Belgium almost doubled its road network in the same period; France built, in addition to roads, 2,000 miles of canals. In the United States, where industrialization was occurring at an increasingly rapid rate after 1830, road mileage jumped from 21,000 miles in 1800 to 170,000 in 1856. When these improvements were combined with the introduction of rail transport in the 1840s, the resulting increase in markets available to all Western countries encouraged them to introduce methods of manufacturing that would help meet new demands.

In this endeavor, governments played a more direct role on the Continent than in Britain. Napoleon's rationalization of French and imperial institutions had introduced Europe to the practice of state intervention. His legal code, which guaranteed freedom of contract and facilitated the establishment of joint-stock enterprises, encouraged other rulers to provide a similar framework for commercial expansion. In Prussia, lack of private capital necessitated state operation of a large proportion of that country's mines. In no European country but Britain would railways be built without the financial assistance of the state. In the private sector, as well, more attention was given on the Continent than in England to the need for artificial stimulation to

(2) improved transportation

(3) centralization

produce industrial change. It was in Belgium that the first joint-stock investment bank—the Société Générale—was founded, an institution designed to facilitate the accumulation of ready capital for investment in industry and commerce. Europeans were also willing for the state to establish educational systems whose aim, among others, was to produce a well-trained elite capable of assisting in the development of industrial technology. What Britain had produced almost by chance, the Europeans began to reproduce by design.

(4) the lack of technicians

Until the Continent produced its own technicians it was compelled to rely on British expertise. And another reason why the pace of continental, and also American, industrialization, even after 1815, remained far slower than in Britain was Britain's natural reluctance to see its methods of production pirated by others. Until 1825, British artisans were forbidden to emigrate; until 1842, much innovative machinery could not be exported. Laws did not, however, prevent the movement of creative technician-entrepreneurs and their particular skills; many Englishmen, during the first part of the nineteenth century, made fortunes as they taught others in Europe and America to do what they had taught themselves. But an initial shortage of home-grown experts undoubtedly hampered rapid industrial expansion on the Continent.

Textiles

The growth of the textile industry in Europe was patterned by the circumstances of the Napoleonic wars. The supply of cotton to the Continent had been interrupted, thanks to the British blockade, but the military's greater demand for woolen cloth meant that expansion occurred more rapidly in the latter than in the former industry. By 1820, the spinning of wool by machine was the common practice on the Continent; weaving, however, was still accomplished largely by hand. Centers for the production of wool were located at Rheims and in Alsace, in France; in what is now Belgium; and, in Germany, in

Silk Weavers of Lyon, 1850. The first significant working-class uprisings in nineteenth-century France occurred here in 1831 and 1834. Note the domestic character of the working conditions.

A German Textile Factory, 1848. This is an unusually large manufacturing facility for this period on the Continent.

Saxony and Silesia. Mechanization was retarded by the fact that hand labor was cheap, and by the important fact that since Britain's market was so large, continental profits too often depended upon the manufacture of some particular specialty not made in England, and therefore without broad commercial appeal. Cotton manufacture was curtailed by the same circumstances. In France, as a result, mechanization occurred first in the silk industry and those sections of the cotton industry which produced finer specialty materials—lace, for example. A tradition of prestige associated with the production of luxury goods, dating back to the reign of Louis XIV, encouraged entrepreneurs to invest in this branch of the textile industry. They were willing to forego mass markets in the hope that their products would not meet with British competition. France nevertheless remained the largest continental producer of cotton goods, followed, again, by Belgium, the German territories of the Rhine valley, Saxony, Silesia, and Bavaria.

In the area of heavy industry on the Continent, the picture was much the same as in textiles: i.e., gradual advances in the adoption of technological innovation against a background of more general resistance to change. Here, however, because change came later than in Britain, it coincided with an increased demand for various goods that had come into being as a result of industrialization and urbanization: iron pipe, much in use by 1830 in cities for gas, water, and drainage; metal machinery, now replacing earlier wooden prototypes. Con-

Heavy industry

sequently, the iron industry took the lead over textiles on the Continent, accompanied by an increase, where possible, in the production of coal. Coal was scarce, however; in the Rhineland wood was still used to manufacture iron. The result was an unwillingness on the part of entrepreneurs to make as extensive use of the steam engine as they might have otherwise; it used too much fuel. In France, as late as 1844, hydraulic (i.e., water-driven) engines were employed far more often for the manufacture of iron than were steam engines. One further problem hampered the development of continental heavy industry during the first half of the nineteenth century. British competition forced continental machine construction firms to scramble for whatever orders they could get. This need to respond to a variety of requests meant that it was difficult for firms to specialize in a single product. The result was a lack of standardization, and continued production to order, when rationalization and specialization would have resulted in an increased volume of production.

3. THE COMING OF RAILWAYS

Railways as a stimulus to the European and American economies

By about 1840, then, European countries, and to some degree, as well, the United States, were moving gradually along the course of industrialization traced by Britain, producing far more than they had, yet nothing like as much as their spectacular pace-setter. Within the next ten years, the coming of the railways was to alter that situation. Though Britain by no means lost its lead, the stimulus provided generally to Western economies by the introduction of railway systems throughout much of the world carried Europe and America far enough and fast enough to allow them to become genuine competitors with the British.

Railways as goods carriers

Railways came into being in answer to two needs. The first was the obvious desire on the part of entrepreneurs to transport their goods as quickly and cheaply as possible across long distances. Despite already mentioned improvements in transportation during the years before 1830, the movement of heavy materials, particularly coal, remained a problem. It is significant that the first modern railway was built in England in 1825 from the Durham coal field of Stockton to Darlington, near the coast. "Tramways"—parallel tracks along which coal carts were pulled by horses—had long been in use at pitheads to haul coal short distances. The Stockton-to-Darlington railway was a logical extension of this device, designed to answer the transportation needs produced by constantly expanding industrialization. The man primarily responsible for the design of the first steam railway was George Stephenson, a self-made engineer who had not learned to read until he was seventeen. He talked a group of North-of-England investors into the merits of steam traction and was given full liberty to carry out his plans. The locomotives on the Stockton-Darlington line traveled at fifteen miles per hour, the fastest rate at which human beings had yet moved overland.

Railways were also built in response to other than purely industrial needs: specifically, the need for capitalists to invest their money. Englishmen such as those who had made sizable fortunes in textiles, once they had paid out workers' wages and plowed back substantial capital in their factories, retained a surplus profit for which they wanted a decent yet reliable return. Railways provided them with the solution to their problem. Though by no means as reliable as had been hoped, railway investment proved capable of more than satisfying the capitalists' demands. No sooner did the first combined passenger and goods service open in 1830, on the Liverpool to Manchester line, than plans were formulated and money pledged to extend rail systems throughout Europe, the Americas, and beyond. In 1830, there were no more than a few dozen miles of railway in the world. By 1840, there were over 4,500 miles; by 1850, over 23,000. The English contractor, Thomas Brassey, the most famous, but by no means the only one of his kind, built railways in Italy, Canada, Argentina, India, and Australia.

The railway boom was a boom to industrialization generally. Not only did it increase enormously the demand for coal and for a variety of heavy manufactured goods—rails, locomotives, carriages, signals, switches; by enabling goods to move faster from factory to salesroom, railways decreased the time it took to sell those goods. Quicker sales meant, in turn, a quicker return on capital investment, money which could then be reinvested in the manufacture of more goods. Finally, by opening up the world market as it had never been before, the railway boom stimulated the production of such a quantity of material goods as to insure the rapid completion of the West's industrialization.

Thomas Brassey

Railways as stimulus to industry

The New Railway Age. Left: Stephenson's "Rocket." A reconstruction of the railway engine built by George Stephenson in 1829. Right: "The Railway Juggernaut of 1845." A cartoon from the English humor magazine *Punch* satirizing speculation—often financially disastrous—in railway stocks.

The building of a railway line was an undertaking on a scale infinitely greater than the building of a factory. Railway construction required capital investment beyond the capacity of any single individual. In Britain, a factory might be worth anything from £20,000 to £200,000. The average cost of twenty-seven of the more important railway lines constructed between 1830 and 1853 was £2 million. The average labor force of a factory ranged from 50 to 300. The average labor force of a railway, after construction, was 2,500. Because a railway crossed the property of a large number of individual landowners, each of whom would naturally demand as much remuneration as he thought he could get, the planning of an efficient and economical route was a tricky and time-consuming business. The entrepreneur and contractor had to concern themselves not only with the purchase of right-of-way. They also contended with problems raised by the destruction of sizable portions of already existing urban areas, to make room for stations and switching yards. And they had to select a route that would be as free as possible of the hills and valleys that would necessitate the construction of expensive tunnels, cuts, and embankments. Railway-builders ran tremendous risks. Portions of most lines were subcontracted at fixed bids to contractors of limited experience. A spate of bad weather might delay construction to the point where builders would be lucky to bring in the finished job within 25 percent of their original bid. Of the thirty major contractors on the London-to-Birmingham line, ten failed completely.

If the business of a contractor was marked by uncertainty, that of the construction worker was characterized by back-breaking labor. The English "navvies," who built railways not only throughout Britain but around the world, were a remarkable breed. Their name derived from "navigator," a term applied to the construction workers on England's eighteenth-century canals. The work that they accomplished was prodigious. Because there is little friction between a train's wheels and its tracks, it can transport heavy loads easily. But

Construction of the London to Birmingham Railway, London, 1838. This drawing of the building of retaining walls in a new railway cut evokes the chaos created by railway construction within urban areas.

Railway Navvies. Without the aid of machinery, the burden of building Britain's railways fell on the backs of men such as these.

lack of friction ceases to be an advantage when a train has to climb or descend a grade, thereby running the risk of slippage. Hence the need for comparatively level roadbeds; and hence the need for laborers to construct those tunnels, cuts, and embankments that would keep the roadbeds level. In England and in much of the rest of the world, mid-nineteenth-century railways were constructed almost entirely without the aid of machinery. An assistant engineer on the London-to-Birmingham line, in calculating the magnitude of that particular construction, determined that the labor involved was the equivalent of lifting 25 billion cubic feet of earth and stone one foot high. This he compared with the feat of building the Great Pyramid, a task he estimated had involved the hoisting of some 16 billion tons. But whereas the building of the pyramid had required over 200,000 men and had taken twenty years, the construction of the London-to-Birmingham railway was accomplished by 20,000 men in less than five years. Translated into individual terms, a navvy was expected to move an average of twenty tons of earth per day. Railways were laid upon an almost infinite base of human muscle and sweat.

4. INDUSTRIALIZATION AFTER 1850

In the years between 1850 and 1870, Britain remained very much the industrial giant of the West. But France, Germany, Belgium, and the United States assumed the position of challengers. In the iron industry, Britain's rate of growth during these years was not as great as that of either France or Germany (5.2 percent for Britain, as against 6.7 percent for France and 10.2 percent for Germany). But in 1870 Britain

Britain still the leader

The Early Industrial Landscape. Stockport, England, in the 1840s.

was still producing half the world's pig iron; 3.5 times as much as the United States, more than 4 times as much as Germany, and more than 5 times as much as France. Although the number of cotton spindles increased from 5.5 to 11.5 million in the United States between 1852 and 1861, and by significant but not as spectacular percentages in European countries, England in 1861 had 31 million spindles at work in comparison with France's 5.5 million, Germany's 2 million, Switzerland's 1.3 million, and Austria's 1.8 million.

Most of the gains experienced in Europe came as a result of continuing changes in those areas we have come to recognize as important for sustained industrial growth. The improved transportation systems that resulted from the spread of railways helped encourage an increase in the free movement of goods. International monetary unions were established, and restrictions removed on international waterways such as the Danube. The Prussian *Zollverein,* or tariff union, an organization designed to facilitate internal free trade, was established in 1818 and was extended over the next twenty years to include most of the German principalities outside Austria. Free trade went hand in hand with further removal of barriers to the freedom to enter trades and to practice business unhampered by restrictive regulation. Control of guilds and corporations over artisan production was abolished in Austria in 1859 and in most of Germany by the mid-1860s. Laws against usury, most of which had ceased to be enforced, were officially abandoned in Britain, Holland, Belgium, and in many parts of Germany. Governmental regulation of the operation of mines was surrendered by the Prussian state in the 1850s, freeing entrepreneurs to develop resources as they saw fit. The formation of investment banks proceeded apace, encouraged by an important increase in the money supply and therefore an easing of credit, following the opening of the California gold fields in 1849.

Continuing European advance

See color map facing page 960

A further reason for increased European production was the growing trade in raw materials. Wool and hides imported from Australia helped diminish the consequences of the cotton shortage suffered after the outbreak of the United States Civil War and the Union blockade of the American South. Other importations—guano from the Pacific, vegetable oils from Africa, pyrites (sulphides) from Spain—stimulated the scale of food production and both altered and increased the manufacture of soap, candles, and finished textiles. Finally, discoveries of new sources of coal, particularly in the Pas-de-Calais region of France and in the Ruhr valley in Germany, had dramatic repercussions. Production of coal in France rose from 4.4 million to 13.3 million tons between 1850 and 1869; during the same years, German production increased from 4.2 million to 23.7 million tons.

By 1870 Europe had by no means turned its back on agriculture. Fifty percent of France's labor force remained on farms. Agricultural laborers were the single largest occupational category in Britain during the 1860s. Great stretches of the Continent—Spain, southern Italy, eastern Europe—were almost untouched by the Industrial Revolution. And in the industrialized countries, much work was still accomplished in tiny workshops or at home. Yet if Europe was by no means wholly industrial, it was far and away the most industrially advanced portion of the globe—and not by accident. In order to maintain its position of producer to the world, Europe, and Britain particularly, made certain that no other areas stood a chance to compete. Europe used its economic and, when necessary, its military strength to insure that the world remained divided between the producers of manufactured goods—Europe itself—and suppliers of the necessary raw materials—everyone else. Often this arrangement suited those in other parts of the world who made their money by providing the raw materials that fueled the European economy. Cotton-growers in the southern United States, sugar-growers in the Caribbean, wheat-growers in the Ukraine—all remained content with arrangements as dictated by the industrialized West. Those countries which expressed their discontent—Egypt, for example, which in the 1830s attempted to establish its own cotton textile industry—were soon put in their place by a show of force. Western Europeans, believing in their right to industrial leadership in the world, saw nothing wrong with employing soldiers, if they had to, to make others understand their destiny.

SELECTED READINGS

• Items so designated are available in paperback editions.
• Ashton, T. S., *The Industrial Revolution, 1760–1830,* London, 1948. An excellent short introduction.
  Checkland, S. G., *The Rise of Industrial Society in England, 1815–1885,* New York, 1965. Emphasizes the economic organization of England.

• Deane, Phyllis, *The First Industrial Revolution*, Cambridge, 1965.

Henderson, W. O., *The Industrialization of Europe, 1780–1914*, New York, 1969.

————, *The State and the Industrial Revolution in Prussia, 1740–1870*, Liverpool, 1958. A biographical approach. Good on technical education.

• Hobsbawm, Eric, *Industry and Empire: 1750 to the Present Day*, New York, 1968. A general survey of industrialization in Britain.

Hoffman, Walther, *British Industry, 1700–1950*, Oxford 1955. A good source for statistics.

• Landes, David S., *The Unbound Prometheus*, London, 1969. An excellent treatment of the technological innovations and economic results of the Industrial Revolution.

McManners, John, *European History: Men, Machines and Freedom*, New York, 1967.

Mantoux, Paul, *The Industrial Revolution in the Eighteenth Century*, rev. ed., New York, 1961. The beginnings of the modern factory system in England.

• Rostow, Walt W., *The Stages of Economic Growth*, rev. ed., Cambridge, 1971. A synthesis by the exponent of the "take-off" theory of economic development.

• Taylor, George Rogers, *The Transportation Revolution, 1815–1860*, New York, 1968.

Usher, A. P., *A History of Mechanical Invention*, Cambridge, Mass., 1954.

SOURCE MATERIALS

Dodd, George, *Days at the Factories; or the Manufacturing Industry of Great Britain Described, and Illustrated by Numerous Engravings of Machines and Processes*, Totawa, N.J., 1975. A reprint of the 1850 edition.

Mitchell, Brian R., and Phyllis Deane, *Abstract of British Historical Statistics*, Cambridge, 1962. The single best source for statistics on population, trade, manufacturing, etc.

• Smith, Adam, *An Inquiry into the Nature and Causes of the Wealth of Nations*, Chicago, 1977. Written in 1776, this revolutionary work called for the end of mercantilism and the enshrinement of laissez faire.

Ward, J. T., *The Factory System, 1830–1855*, New York, 1970. Excerpts from contemporary documents describing, defending, and criticizing the factory system and industrialization.

Chapter 26

CONSEQUENCES OF INDUSTRIAL-IZATION: URBANIZATION AND CLASS CONSCIOUSNESS (1800–1850)

What Art was to the ancient world, Science is to the modern: The distinctive faculty. In the minds of men the useful has succeeded the beautiful. Yet rightly understood, Manchester is as great a human exploit as Athens.

—Benjamin Disraeli, *Coningsby*

The Industrial Revolution was more than an important event in the economic and technological history of the West. It helped to reshape the patterns of life for men and women, first in Britain, then in Europe and America, and eventually throughout much of the world. By increasing the scale of production, the Industrial Revolution brought about the factory system, which in turn compelled the migration of millions from the countryside and small towns into cities. Once in those cities, men and women had to learn a new way of life, and learn it quickly: how to discipline themselves to the factory whistle and survive in a slum, if they were first-generation urban workers; how to manage a work-force and achieve respectable prominence for themselves in the community, if they were businessmen and their wives. One particular lesson that industrialization and urbanization taught was that of class consciousness. Men and women, to a far greater degree than heretofore, began to perceive themselves as part of a class with interests of its own, and in opposition to the interests of men and women in other classes.

We shall examine this range of social and cultural changes as they occurred during the first fifty years or so of the nineteenth century, after looking briefly first at the condition of the bulk of the popula-

Consequences of the Industrial Revolution

tion, which, despite industrialization, remained on the land. Since the Industrial Revolution came first to Britain, our focus will be on that country. Yet the pattern set by the British was one that was repeated to a great extent in other European countries, as industrialization came to them in time.

1. PEOPLE ON THE LAND

Population increase

The dramatic story of the growth of industrialization and urbanization must not be allowed to obscure the fact that, in 1850, the population of Europe was still overwhelmingly a peasant population. Demographic pressures which helped produce chaos in the cities, likewise caused severe hardship in the countryside. The population increase which took place throughout Europe during this period appears to have been caused by two factors. The first was the occurrence of earlier and more frequent marriages. The second, from which the first followed, was the availability of cheaper food, the result of increased production, improved agricultural technology, and, in many places, the introduction of the potato. Coupled with these factors was a gradually decreasing deathrate. The populations of countries that were predominantly agricultural lept forward with those that were industrializing. The population of Ireland, despite famine, grew from 5.5 to 8 million, Russia's population from 39 to 60 million, in the years from 1800 to 1850.

Wretched rural conditions

Although conditions allowed a population increase, they were not such as to make the life of the poorer inhabitants of Europe anything other than bleak. Overpopulation brought underemployment, and hence poverty, in its train. Conditions in rural areas deteriorated sharply whenever there was a bad harvest, as there was with continuing regularity. Hunger, typhus, and near-starvation were not uncommon. The result was a standard of living—if one can dignify the condition with that name—that for many rural inhabitants of many areas in Europe declined in the first half of the nineteenth century, although not enough to reverse general population growth. Governments in some countries attempted to solve the related problems of population pressure and impoverishment by passing laws raising the age of marriage. In some of the states of southern and western Germany, as well as in Austria, men were forbidden to marry before the age of thirty, and were also required to prove their ability to support a family.

Agricultural capitalism

Even had such laws acted as an effective curb on population growth—which, in the main, they did not—they would nevertheless have failed to prevent the rural stresses that resulted from the continuing spread of agricultural capitalism. The pace of this change varied across Europe; it was furthest advanced in England and Prussia. Wherever landed proprietors determined to meet increased demand

Interior of an English Farm Laborer's Cottage, 1846. Note the wooden crate used as an infant's cradle.

for food by farming large areas as a capital investment, they imposed a series of transformations that were bound to affect the lives of agricultural laborers. First, land must be made a negotiable commodity. It must not, therefore, be tied to ancient customs which clouded its title—as was the case, for example, with common land, to which the poor within a community might have some right of access or cultivation. Second, land must be in the hands of those with capital enough to improve it, in order to make of it a profitable investment. It must be "enclosed"—"regulated" was the term in Prussia—so that it could be properly fertilized and drained, or, if it was grazing land, so that breeds might be scientifically improved without fear of mongrelization. Finally, a mobile force of agricultural laborers must be available to work at the capitalists' behest. They must not be "tied" to a particular piece of land, either through systems of customary rights or bondage. They must be free to go where they were told to go, to work whatever land would bring most profit to its owners.

These requirements, as they were imposed, produced dislocation and hardship. In Scotland, workers were cleared from land which they had farmed as tenants, in order to provide pasturage for the more profitable sheep. In Germany, those serfs emancipated by a reform-minded government in 1807 were compelled to forfeit somewhere between a third to a half of their land in return for their freedom; those who were able to retain small holdings were in most cases pressured to sell out to larger landholders. Not all landlords were ruthless. "Model" improvers among the wealthiest of the English landowners adjusted to capitalist competition without entirely forswearing traditional responsibilities. They built houses for tenants and laborers, and provided them with schools and churches. In eastern Europe there were among the Prussian landlords (Junkers) pietists who acknowledged obligations to their tenants as well as to the market.

Its results

The speed with which agricultural change occurred in various parts of Europe depended upon the nature of particular governments. Those more sympathetic to new capitalist impulses facilitated the transfer and reorganization of land by means of enabling legislation. They encouraged the elimination of small farms and an increase in larger, more efficient units of production. In England, over half the total area of the country, excluding waste land, was composed of estates of a thousand acres or more. In Spain, the fortunes of agricultural capitalism fluctuated with the political tenor of successive regimes: with the coming of a liberal party to power in 1820, came a law encouraging the free transfer of land; with the restoration of absolutism in 1823, came a repeal of the law. Russia was one of the countries least affected by agricultural change in the first half of the nineteenth century. There land was worked in vast blocks; some of the largest landowners possessed over half a million acres. But the institution of manorial serfdom, which bound hundreds of thousands of men, women, and children to particular estates for generations, prohibited the use of land as a negotiable commodity and therefore prevented the development of agricultural entrepreneurship. In France, despite the fact that manorialism had been abolished by the revolution, there was no rapid movement toward large-scale capitalist farming. An army of peasant proprietors, direct beneficiaries of the Jacobins' democratic constitution, continued to work the small farms they owned. The fact that France suffered far less agricultural distress, even in the 1840s, than did other European countries, and the fact that there was less migration in France from the country to the city and overseas than there was in Germany and England, are marks of the general success of this rural lower middle class in sustaining itself on the land. Its members were content to farm in the old way, opposed agricultural innovation, and, indeed, innovation generally. Despite their veneration of the revolution, they were among the most conservative elements in European society.

2. URBANIZATION AND THE STANDARD OF LIVING

If the countryside continued to hold the bulk of Europe's population in the years between 1800 and 1850, the growth of cities nevertheless remains one of the most important facts in the social history of that period. Cities grew in size and number once the steam engine made it practical to bring together large concentrations of men, women, and children to work in factories. Previously, workshops had been located throughout the countryside, close to the water power that provided the primary means of operating machinery. Steam engines freed entrepreneurs from their dependence on water power and allowed them to consolidate production in large cities. In cities, transportation was more accessible than in the countryside. Hence it was less costly to import raw materials and ship out finished goods. Workers were more readily available in cities, as well, attracted as they were in large numbers in the hope—often false—of finding steady work at higher wages than those paid agricultural laborers. Industrialization was not the only reason for the growth of cities in the early nineteenth century, however. General population growth combined with industrialization forced cities to expand at an alarming rate.

In the ten years between 1831 and 1841 London's population grew by 130,000, Manchester's by 70,000. Paris increased by 120,000 between 1841 and 1846. Vienna grew by 125,000 from 1827 to 1847, into a city of 400,000. Berlin had as large a population by 1848, having increased by 180,000 since 1815. The primary result in these and other fast-growing centers was dreadful overcrowding. Construction lagged far behind population growth. In Vienna, though population rose 42 percent during the twenty years before 1847, the increase in housing was only 11.5 percent. In many of the larger cities, old and new, working men and women lived in lodging houses, apart from families left behind in the country. The poorest workers in almost all European cities dwelt in wretched basement rooms, often without any light or drainage. Governments did their best to encourage emigration to ease the overcrowding, the majority of emigrants relocating in the Americas. Emigration from England rose from 57,000 in 1830, to 90,000 in 1840, to 280,000 in 1850. Ireland, in the early years of the nineteenth century, witnessed the departure of over 1.5 million before the great potato famine of 1846, which increased the flow to a flood. In that year, approximately three out of every four acres of potatoes were blighted. Over 1 million died between 1846 to 1851, either from starvation, or as a result of their weakened physical condition which left them prey to disease.

With cities as overcrowded as they were, it is no wonder that they were a menace to the health of those who lived within them. The middle classes moved as far as possible from disease and factory smoke, leaving the poorest members of the community isolated and a prey to the sickness which ravaged working-class sections. Cholera, typhus, and tuberculosis were natural predators in areas without adequate sewerage facilities and fresh water, and over which smoke from factories, railroads, and domestic chimneys hung heavily. Measures were gradually adopted by successive governments in an attempt to cure the worst of these ills, if only to prevent the spread of catastrophic epidemics. Legislation was designed to rid cities of their worst slums by tearing them down, and to improve sanitary conditions by supplying both water and drainage. Yet by 1850, these projects had only just begun. Paris, perhaps better supplied with water than any European city, had enough for no more than two baths per capita per year; in London, human waste remained uncollected in 250,000 do-

Wentworth Street by Gustav Doré. The artist was much concerned with the overcrowding squalor which resulted from early industrialization in London.

mestic cesspools; in Manchester, no more than a third of the dwellings were equipped with toilets of any sort.

The standard of living debate

Conditions such as these are important evidence in a debate which has occupied historians for the past several decades. The question is: Did the standard of living rise or fall in Europe during the first half-century of the Industrial Revolution? One school, the "optimists," argues that workers shared in the more general increase in living standards which occurred throughout Europe from 1800 onward. It is true, certainly, that some skilled workers within the new factories, along with some artisans in older trades as yet unaffected by industrialization, did benefit by a slight rise in wages and a decline in living costs. But regional variables, along with a constantly fluctuating demand for labor in all countries, have led most commentators to temper their conclusions.

Instability and unemployment

There is no evidence to suggest that the more lowly paid, unskilled worker, whether in England or on the Continent, led anything more than a precarious existence. Textile workers in England, if guaranteed something like full employment, could theoretically earn enough to support a family. Such was not the case in Switzerland, however, where similar work paid only half what was necessary, or in Saxony, where a large portion of the population was apparently dependent upon either poor relief or charity. One of the most depressing features of working-class life in these years was its instability. Economic depressions were common occurrences; when they happened, workers were laid off for weeks at a time, with no system of unemployment insurance to sustain them. Half the working population of England's industrial cities were out of work in the early 1840s. In Paris, 85,000 went on relief in 1840. One particularly hard-pressed district of Silesia reported 30,000 out of 40,000 citizens in need of relief in 1844. Nor must one overlook the plight of those whose skills had been replaced by machinery—the hand-loom weavers being the most notable examples. In the English manufacturing town of Bolton, a hand-loom weaver could earn no more than about three shillings per week in 1842, at a time when experts estimated it took at least twenty shillings a week to keep a family of five above the poverty line. On that kind of pay, workers were fortunate if they did not starve to death. Forced to spend something like 65 percent of their income on food, the per capita meat consumption of the average worker declined to about forty pounds per year in the early nineteenth century.

Such figures make the optimists' generalizations hard to countenance. Figures of whatever sort fail to take into account the stress that urban factory life extracted from the workers. Even workers making thirty shillings a week might well wonder if they were "better off," forced as they were to come to terms with the factory disciplines and living conditions imposed upon them. Though most of those who moved into factory towns migrated but a short distance from their place of birth, the psychological distance they traveled was tremendous. These qualitative factors, admittedly difficult to assess, must be weighed along with more easily quantifiable evidence before reaching any conclusion as to the increased standard of living in early–nineteenth-century cities. Whether or not life in cities was pleasant or ghastly, however, it was, for rapidly increasing numbers, a fact of life. Once we examine that life we will better understand the full impact of industrialization and urbanization upon those who first experienced it.

The quality of life

Soup Kitchen Run by Quakers, Manchester, England, 1862. Enterprises of this sort, which doled out charity "indiscriminately"—that is, without investigating the recipient's character — were condemned by many members of the middle class as encouraging the "worst" elements — idlers and loafers — among the poor.

3. THE LIFE OF THE URBAN MIDDLE CLASS

The urban middle class which emerged during this period was by no means one homogeneous unit, in terms of occupation or income. In a general category that includes merchant princes and humble shopkeepers, subdivisions are important. The middle class included families of industrialists, such as the Peels (cotton) in England and, at a later period, the Krupps (iron) in Germany. It included financiers like the internationally famed Rothschilds, and, on a descending scale of wealth and power, bankers and capitalists throughout the major money markets of Europe: London, Brussels, Paris, Berlin. It included entrepreneurs like Thomas Brassey, the British railway magnate, and technicians, like the engineer Isambard Kingdom Brunel, designer of the steamship *The Great Western*. It included bureaucrats, in growing demand when governments began to regulate the pace and direction of industrialization, and to ameliorate its harshest social and economic results. It included those in the already established professions—in law particularly, as lawyers put their expertise to the service of industrialists. It included the armies of managers and clerks necessary to the continuing momentum of industrial and financial expansion, and the equally large army of merchants and shopkeepers necessary to supply the wants of an increasingly affluent urban middle-class population. Finally, it included the families of all those who lived their lives in the various subcategories we have listed.

Movement within these ranks was often possible, in the course of one or two generations. Movement from the working class into the middle class, however, was far less common. Most middle-class successes originated within the middle class—the children of farmers, skilled artisans, or professionals. Upward mobility was almost impossible without education; education was an expensive, if not unattainable luxury for the children of a laborer. Careers open to talents, that goal achieved by the French Revolution, frequently meant middle-class jobs for middle-class young men who could pass exams. The examination system was an important path for ascendancy within governmental bureaucracies. If passage from working class to middle class was not common, neither was the equally difficult social journey from middle class to aristocratic, landed society. This was particularly the case on the Continent, where the division between nobility and commoner had traditionally been most pronounced. In Britain, mobility of this sort was easier. Children from wealthy upper middle-class families, if they were sent, as occasionally they were, to elite schools and universities, and if they left the commercial or industrial world for a career in politics, might effect the change. William Gladstone, son of a Liverpool merchant, attended Eton and Oxford, exclusive educational preserves, married a connection of the aristocratic Grenville family, and became prime minister of England. Yet Gladstone was an

Isambard Kingdom Brunel. Behind him are lengths of anchor chain from the steamship *The Great Western.*

Social mobility

Young Gentlemen, 1834. It was to models such as these that the young men of the middle class aspired.

exception to the norm in Britain, and Britain was an exception to the Continent. Movement, when it occurred, did so in less spectacular degrees.

Nevertheless, the European middle class helped sustain itself with the belief that it was possible to get ahead by means of intelligence, pluck, and serious devotion to work. The Englishman Samuel Smiles, in his extraordinarily successful how-to-succeed book *Self Help*, preached a gospel dear to the middle class. Although the gospel declared that anyone willing to exert himself could rise to a position of responsibility and personal profit, however, and although some men actually did so, the notion remained no more than myth for the great majority.

Self-help

Seriousness of purpose was reflected in the middle-class devotion to the ideal of family and home. A practical importance attached to the institution of the family in those areas in England, France, and Germany where sons, sons-in-law, nephews, and cousins were expected to assume responsibility in family firms when it came their turn. Yet the worship of family ignored those practical considerations and assumed the proportions of a sacred belief. Away from the business and confusion of the world, sheltered behind solid masonry and amid the solid comfort of their ornate furnishings, middle-class fathers retired each evening to enjoy the fruits of their daily labors. Inside the home, life was enclosed in a hierarchical and ritualistic system under which the husband and father was absolute master. His wife was called his help-mate but was unquestionably his servant as well. Her task was to keep the household functioning smoothly and harmoniously. She maintained the accounts and directed the activities of the servants—

Family and home

Left: *A Salon in Vienna, 1830s.* A representation of middle-class home life on the Continent. Right: *A Victorian Family at Tea, 1860s*

usually two or three women. Because of the extent of her duties as overseer, she was excused from the everyday drudgeries of washing and cleaning. Called in Victorian England the "Angel in the House," the middle-class woman was responsible for the moral education of her children. Yet she probably spent no more than two or three hours a day at most with her offspring. Until sent to school, they were placed in the custody of a nursemaid or governess. Much of a middle-class woman's day was spent in the company of other women from similar households. An elaborate set of social customs involving "calls" and "at homes" was established in European middle-class society. Women were not expected to improve their minds. They were not expected to be the intellectual companions of their husbands. Rather, they were encouraged to be dabblers, education for them usually consisting of little more beyond reading and writing, a smattering of arithmetic, geography, history, and a foreign language, embellished with lessons in drawing, painting in watercolor, singing, or piano-playing.

Sexuality Middle-class wives were indoctrinated to believe that they were superior to their husbands in one area only. A wife was "the better half" of a middle-class marriage because she was deemed pure—the untainted Vestal of the hearth, unsullied by cares of the world outside her home, and certainly untouched by those sexual desires which marked her husband, her natural moral inferior. A wife's charge was to encourage her husband's "higher nature." She must never respond to his sexual advances with equal passion; passion was, for her, a presumed impossibility. Instead she must persuade him to seek, through love of home and family, a substitute for the baser instincts with which nature had unhappily endowed the male. Should she fail—and the numberless prostitutes and courtesans in the streets and clandestine boudoirs of nineteenth-century cities suggest that she often did fail—she must accept the fact of her "failure" as she was bound to accept the rest of her life: uncomplainingly. Should she herself succumb to "unwomanly desires" and be discovered to have done so, she could expect nothing less than complete social banishment. The law tolerated a husband's infidelity and at all times respected a husband's rights both to his wife's person and to her property. It made quick work of an "unfaithful" wife, granting to her husband whatever he might desire in terms of divorce, property, and custody, to make him amends for the personal wrongs and embarrassments he had suffered at the hands of his "unnatural" spouse.

Middle-class family rituals helped to sustain this hierarchy. Daily meals, with the father at the head of the table, were cooked and brought to each place by servants, who were a constant reminder of the family's social position. Family vacations were a particularly nineteenth-century middle-class invention. Thanks to the advent of the railways, excursions of one or two weeks to the mountains or to the seashore were available to families of even moderate means. Entrepreneurs built large, ornate hotels, adorned with imposing names—Palace, Beau Rivage, Excelsior—and attracted middle-class customers by offering them on a grander scale exactly the same sort of comfortable and sheltered existence they enjoyed at home.

Domestic rituals

The Middle Class at Leisure. The "morning lounge" at Biarritz, a French resort on the Atlantic coast.

Houses

The houses and furnishings of the middle class were an expression of the material security the middle class valued. Solidly built, heavily decorated, they proclaimed the financial worth and social respectability of those who dwelt within. In provincial cities they were often free-standing "villas." In London, Paris, Berlin, or Vienna, they might be rows of five- or six-story townhouses, or large apartments. Whatever particular shape they took, they were built to last a long time. The rooms were certain to be crowded with furniture, art objects, carpets, and wall hangings. Chairs, tables, cabinets, and sofas might be of any or all periods; no matter, so long as they were adorned with their proper compliment of fringe, gilt, or other ornamentation. The size of the rooms, the elegance of the furniture, the number of servants, all depended, of course, on the extent of one's income. A bank clerk did not live as elegantly as a bank director. Yet in all likelihood both lived in obedience to the same set of standards and aspirations. And that obedience helped bind them, despite the differences in their material way of life, to the same class.

Cities and the middle class

The European middle class had no desire to confront the unpleasant urban by-products of its own success. Members of the middle class saw to it that they lived apart from the unpleasant sights and smells of industrialization. Their residential areas, usually built to the west of the cities, out of the path of the prevailing breeze, and therefore of industrial pollution, were havens from the congestion for which they were primarily responsible. When the members of the middle class rode into the urban centers they took care to do so over avenues lined with respectable shops, or across railway embankments that lifted them above monotonous working-class streets en route to their destination. Yet the middle class, though it turned its face from what it did not want to see, did not turn from the city. Middle-class men and women celebrated the city as their particular creation and the source of their profits. They even praised its smoke—as a sign of prosperity—so

The Paris Opera. An exterior view of the Opera. Designed by Charles Garnier, it was constructed between 1861 and 1875. This grandiose display of wealth and luxury epitomized the taste of the new industrial middle class.

long as they did not have to breathe it night and day. For the most part, it was they who managed their city's affairs. And it was they who provided new industrial cities with their proud architectural landmarks: city halls, stock exchanges, opera houses. These were the new cathedrals of the industrial age, proclamations of a triumphant middle class.

4. THE LIFE OF THE URBAN WORKING CLASS

Like the middle class, the working class was divided into various subgroups and categories, determined in this case by skill, wages, and workplace. The working class included skilled workers in crafts that were centuries old—glassblowing and cabinetmaking, for example. It included as well mechanics equally skilled in new industrial technology. It included the men who built textile machinery and the women and children who tended it. It included the men, women, and children who together worked in mines and quarries. And it included the countless millions who labored at unskilled jobs—railway navvies, coal porters, cleaning women, and the like. The nature of workers' experiences naturally varied, depending upon where they worked, where they lived, and, above all, how much they earned. A skilled textile worker lived a life far different from that of an unskilled dock laborer, the former able to afford the food, shelter, and clothing necessary for a decent existence, the latter so busy trying to keep himself and his family alive that he would have little time to think about anything but the source of their next meal.

Ranks within the working class

Some movement from the ranks of the unskilled to the skilled was possible, if children were provided, or provided themselves, with at least a rudimentary education. Yet education was considered by many parents a luxury, especially since children could be put to work at an early age to supplement a family's meager earnings. There was movement from skilled to unskilled also, as technological change—the introduction of the power loom, for example—drove highly paid workers into the ranks of the unskilled and destitute. Further variations within the working class were the result of the fact that though more men, women, and children were every year working in factories, the majority still labored either in workshops or at home. These variations mean that we cannot speak of a common European working-class experience during the years from 1800–1850. The life we shall be describing was most typical of English workers, during the first half-century of their exposure to industrialization. Only in the years 1850–1900 did continental workers undergo to anything like the same extent, this harsh process of urban acclimatization.

Social mobility

Life in industrial cities was, for almost all workers, uncomfortable at best and unbearably squalid at worst. Workers and their families

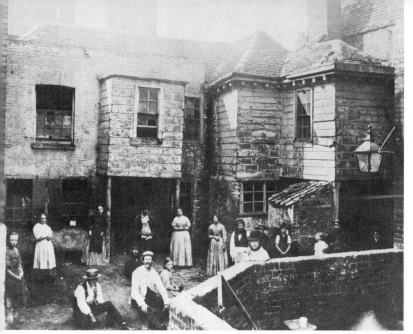

Left: *An Urban Courtyard in London*. Right: *A Working-Class Tenement in Glasgow, Scotland*. Courtyards such as these were frequently the only available dumping grounds for household sewage and garbage.

Housing

lived in housing that failed to answer the needs of its inhabitants. In older cities single-family dwellings were broken up into apartments of often no more than one room per family. In new manufacturing centers, rows of tiny houses, located close by smoking factories, were built back-to-back, thereby eliminating any cross-ventilation or space for gardens. Whether housing was old or new, it was generally poorly built. Old buildings were allowed by landlords to fall into disrepair; new houses, constructed of cheap material, decayed quickly. Water often came from an outdoor tap, shared by several houses and adjacent to an outdoor toilet. Crowding was commonplace. Families of as many as eight lived in two or, at the most, three rooms. Housewives could not rely, as in the country, on their own gardens to help supply them with food. Instead, they went to markets that catered to their needs with cheap goods, often stale or nearly rotten, or dangerously adulterated (formaldehyde was added to milk, for example) to prevent further spoilage.

The role of women

The life of working-class wives and mothers was hard. Lack of cheap contraceptive devices and a belief that these devices were immoral helped to keep women pregnant through most of their child-bearing years, thus endangering their general health and adding to the burden of their lives. Wives were usually handed a portion of the weekly wage packet by their husbands, and were expected to house, feed, and clothe the family on the very little they were given. Their daily life was a constant round of cooking, cleaning, shopping, and washing—in a tiny space and without enough money. Their problems were compounded, of course, when they themselves had to work, and therefore had far less time to accomplish the household tasks they were still expected to perform.

Since many working-class families had only recently migrated from the country into the city, life there could be a lonely experience for them. If possible, they would live near relatives who had already made the transition and who could assist the newcomers in adjusting to their very different existence. In many cities working-class families lived in districts inhabited primarily by others working at the same trade—weavers in one place, miners in another—and in this way achieved some sense of commonality.

Adjustment to the demands of the factory was every bit as difficult for workers as was acceptance of urban living patterns. Factory hours were long, before 1850 usually twelve to fourteen hours a day. Conditions were dirty and dangerous. Textile mills remained unventilated, so that bits of material lodged in workers' lungs. Machines were unfenced and were a particular danger to child workers, often hired, because of their supposed agility, to clean under and around the moving parts. Manufacturing processes were unhealthy. The use of poison lead in the making of glazed pottery, for example, was a constant hazard to men and women workers in that industry.

As upsetting as the physical working conditions in factories was the psychological readjustment demanded of the first-generation workers in them. Preindustrial laborers had had to work long hours and for very little monetary reward. Yet, at least to some degree, they were free to set their own hours and structure their own activities, to move from their home workshops to their small garden plots and back again as they wished. In a factory, all "hands" learned the discipline of the whistle. To function efficiently, a factory demanded that all employees begin and end work at the same time. Most workers could not tell time; fewer possessed clocks. None were accustomed to the relent-

847

The Life of the Urban Working Class

Loneliness

Factory life

Daily routine

A Laundress and Her Children. Note the cramped and cluttered living quarters.

less pace of the machine. In order to increase production, the factory system encouraged the breaking down of the manufacturing process into specialized steps, each with its own assigned time, an innovation that upset workers accustomed to completing a task at their own pace. The employment of women and children was a further disturbing innovation. In preindustrial communities, women and children had worked, as well as men, but more often than not, all together and at home. In factory towns women and children were frequently hired instead of men: they could be paid less and were declared to be easier to manage. When this happened, the pattern of family life was severely disrupted, and a further break with tradition had to be endured.

Escape

Faced with a drastic reordering of their lives, working-class men and women reacted in various ways. Some sought "the shortest way out of Manchester" by taking to drink (there were 1,200 public houses in that city in 1850). Some women turned to prostitution to supplement their meager wages. Many more men and women struggled to make some sort of community out of the street where they lived or the factory where they worked. It was a long and discouraging process. Yet by mid-century their experiences were beginning to make them conscious of themselves as different from and in opposition to the middle class that was imposing a new way of life on them.

5. THE MIDDLE-CLASS WORLDVIEW

The middle class was not unaware of the many social problems it was generating as it created an industrial society. Despite its general con-

"Capital and Labour." In its earliest years, *Punch,* though primarily a humorous weekly, manifested a strong social conscience. In this 1843 cartoon, the capitalists are seen revelling in the rewards of their investments while the workers—men, women, and children—who toiled in the mines under cruel and dangerous conditions are found crippled and starving.

The Interior of the Crystal Palace. This building of iron and glass was constructed to house exhibits sent to the Exhibition of the Works of Industry of All Nations, held in London in 1851. The exhibition celebrated the triumph of middle-class industrialization.

fidence that the world was progressing—and at its own behest—the middle class was beset by uncertainties. Its belief in its own undoubted abilities was shadowed by concern as to whether its particular talents might ultimately prove irrelevant to the preservation of prosperity. Self-assurance could dissolve in the face of bankruptcy and prosperity vanish in the abyss of economic catastrophe. Those who had risen by their own exertions might fall victim to someone else's ambitions. Nor was it always a simple matter for the middle class to reconcile its own affluence with the poverty of the thousands of workers exploited under its aegis. The middle class was responsible for having wrenched European society out of old patterns of living and thrust it into new ones. To those willing to acknowledge that responsibility, the realization was enough to temper confidence with apprehension. As a result, the middle class worked hard to rationalize its own prosperity, and to make legitimate its ascendancy over both the old society of the land and the urban working poor.

Uncertainty and the need for reassurance

To assist themselves in constructing this congenial worldview, the members of the new industrial middle class made use of the theories of a number of political economists. It is important to recognize that a factory-owner or a banker was not likely to have read the works of these theorists. He might, however, have encountered popular journalistic condensations of their ideas, or have participated in discussions at which the conclusions, if not the reasoned arguments, of the economists were aired. Because those conclusions supported his own inter-

Political economics and the worldview

Classical economics

ests, he grew familiar with them, until, in time, he could talk of the ideas of these men as if they were his own.

We have noted already the manner in which the writings of the economist Adam Smith sustained middle-class respect for individual enterprise. The writings of another group, the classical, or liberal, economists—particularly the Englishmen Thomas Malthus (1766–1834) and David Ricardo (1772–1823)—embodied principles appealing to businessmen who desired a free hand to remake the economies of their countries. The chief elements in the theories as formulated by liberal economists were:

(1) Economic individualism. Individuals are entitled to use for their own best interests the property they have inherited or acquired by any legitimate method. People must be allowed to do what they like so long as they do not trespass upon the equal right of others to do the same.

(2) Laissez faire. The functions of the state should be reduced to the lowest minimum consistent with public safety. The government should shrink itself into the role of a modest policeman, preserving order and protecting property, but never interfering with the operation of economic processes.

(3) Obedience to natural law. There are immutable laws operating in the realm of economics as in every sphere of the universe. Examples are the law of supply and demand, the law of diminishing returns, and so on. These laws must be recognized and respected; failure to do so is disastrous.

(4) Freedom of contract. Individuals should be free to negotiate the best kind of contract they can obtain from any other individual. In particular, the liberty of workers and employers to bargain with each other as to wages and hours should not be hampered by laws or by the collective power of labor unions.

(5) Free competition and free trade. Competition serves to keep prices down, to eliminate inefficient producers, and to ensure the maximum production in accordance with public demand. Therefore, no monopolies should be tolerated, nor any price-fixing laws for the benefit of incompetent enterprisers. Further, in order to force each country to engage in the production of those things it is best fitted to produce, all protective tariffs should be abolished. Free international trade will also help to keep prices down.

Businessmen naturally warmed to theories so congenial to their own desires and intentions. But Malthus and Ricardo made further contributions to the middle-class worldview, based upon their perceptions of conflicting interests within society. Malthus, in his well-known *Essay on Population,* first published in 1798, argued that nature has set stubborn limits to the progress of mankind in happiness and wealth. Because of the voracity of the sexual appetite there is a natural tendency for population to increase more rapidly than the supply of

Thomas Malthus

food. To be sure, there are powerful checks, such as war, famine, disease, and vice; but these, when they operate effectively, further augment the burden of human misery. It follows that poverty and pain are inescapable. Even if laws were passed distributing all wealth equally, the condition of the poor would be only temporarily improved; in a very short time they would begin to raise larger families, with the result that the last state of their class would be as bad as the first. In the second edition of his work, Malthus advocated postponement of marriage as a means of relief, but he continued to stress the danger that population would outrun any possible increase in the means of subsistence.

Malthus on population

Malthus's arguments allowed the middle class to acquiesce in the destruction of an older society which had made some attempt to care for its poor. In England, for example, officials in rural parishes had instituted a system of doles and subsidized wages to help sustain laborers and their families when unemployed. The attempt failed to prevent distress and was met with increasing resistance by taxpayers. Now Malthus told taxpayers that schemes designed to help the poor damaged both rich and poor alike. Poor relief took money, and therefore food, from the mouths of the more productive members of society and put it into the mouths of the least productive. Malthus helped shift the responsibility for poverty from society to the individual, a shift appealing to the middle class, which wished to be freed from the burden of supporting the urban unemployed.

The application of Malthusian doctrine

Malthusian assumptions played a large role in the development of the theories of the Scottish economist Ricardo. According to Ricardo, wages seek a level which is just sufficient to enable workers "to subsist and perpetuate their race, without either increase or diminution." This Ricardo held to be an iron law, from which there is no escape. If wages should rise temporarily above the subsistence standard, the population would increase, and the ensuing competition for jobs would quickly force the rate of pay down to its former level. Ricardo devised a law of rent as well as a law of wages. He maintained that rent is determined by the cost of production on the poorest land that must be brought under cultivation, and that, consequently, as a country fills up with people an ever-increasing proportion of the social income is taken by the landlords.

Ricardo on wages and rent

Here again, a theorist provided arguments useful to the middle class in its attempt to define and defend itself within a new social order. The law of wages gave employers a useful weapon to protect themselves from their workers' petitions for higher pay. The law of rent justified middle-class opposition to the continuing power of landed interests: a class which derived its income not from hard work but simply from its role as rent-collector was profiting unfairly at the expense of the rest of society and deserved to have its profit-making curtailed.

The uses of Ricardo's laws

As soon as the middle class began to argue in this fashion, however,

Jeremy Bentham

Benthamite utilitarianism

Utilitarianism's appeal to the middle class

it betrayed its devotion to the doctrine of laissez faire. Businessmen and entrepreneurs vehemently opposed to government intervention which might deny them the chance to make as much money as they could, were nevertheless prepared to see the government step in and prevent profiteering landlords from making what *they* could from their property. How could this apparent inconsistency be justified? The answer lay in the theories of the Englishman Jeremy Bentham (1748–1832), without doubt the mainstay of middle-class apologists. Bentham, whose major work, *The Principles of Morals and Legislation,* was published in 1789, argued against the eighteenth-century notion that a satisfactory theory of social order could be grounded in a belief in the natural harmony of human interests. Men and women were basically selfish beings. To suppose that a stable and beneficent society could emerge unassisted from a company of self-interested egos was, Bentham believed, to suppose the impossible. Society, if it was to function properly, needed an organizing principle that would both acknowledge humanity's basic selfishness and at the same time compel people to sacrifice at least a portion of their own interests for the good of the majority. That principle, called utilitarianism, stated that every institution, every law, must be measured according to its social usefulness. And a socially useful law was one which produced the greatest happiness of the greatest number. If a law passed this test, it could remain on the books; if it failed, it should be abandoned forthwith, no matter how venerable. A selfish man would accept this social yardstick, realizing that in the long run he would do himself serious harm by clinging to laws that might benefit him, but produce such general unhappiness as to result in disruptions detrimental to his own interests as well as to those of others.

In what ways did this philosophy particularly appeal to the industrial middle classes? First, it acknowledged the importance of the individual. The interests of the community were nothing more than the sum of the interests of those selfish egos who lived within it. Each individual best understood his or her own interests, and was therefore best left free, whenever possible, to pursue those interests as he or she saw fit. Only when they conflicted with the interests—the happiness—of the greatest number were they to be curtailed. Entrepreneurs could understand this doctrine as a license to proceed with the business of industrialization, since, they argued, industrialization was so clearly producing happiness for the majority of the world's population. At the same time, Bentham's doctrines could be used to justify those changes necessary to bring an industrial world into being. Was the greatest happiness produced, English factory-owners might ask, by an antiquated electoral system which denied representation to growing industrial cities? Obviously not. Let Parliament reform itself so that the weight of the manufacturing interests could be felt in the drafting of legislation.

Utilitarianism was thus a doctrine that could be used to cut two ways—in favor of laissez faire; in favor of governmental intervention. And the middle class proceeded to cut both ways at once. Benthamite utilitarianism provided the theoretical basis for many of the middle-class interventionist reforms, such as a revised poor law in Britain and an expanded educational system in France, achieved between 1815 and 1848.[1] At the same time utilitarianism, combined with the theories of Malthus and Ricardo, fortified the position of those businessmen who believed that unfettered individualism had produced the triumphs of the Industrial Revolution. To restrain that individualism was to jeopardize the further progress of industrialization and hence the greatest happiness of the greatest number.

Individualism and intervention

In arguing as it did, the middle class relied upon the conviction that industrialization and the factory system were together showering benefits on all—not just themselves. As we shall see, there were those who disagreed, who pressed, for example, for regulation of factory wages and hours. But the capitalists claimed intervention would inhibit the distribution of those benefits, and hence the proliferation of general happiness. In their support they could cite the English economist Nassau Senior, who claimed that the net profit of any industrial enterprise was derived solely from its last hour of daily operation. Reduce working hours, said Senior, and you eliminate profits, thereby compelling factories to close and workers to starve. The middle class believed Senior because it was clearly in its interest to do so. The middle class also believed him because the enterprise upon which it was embarked was so new and so uncharted that it was hard to prove him wrong. Their uncertainty led them to believe those theories which provided them with the most reassurance and encouraged them to think that what they were doing was of benefit to their fellow men.

Belief in improvement

Political economists and philosophers in France as well as in England helped provide the new middle class with a congenial worldview. Count Claude de Saint-Simon (1760–1825), while a proponent of utopian schemes for social reorganization, nevertheless preached the gospel of "industrialism" and "industrialists" (two words which he coined). Disciples of Saint-Simon were among the leading proponents in France of industrial entrepreneurship and a standardized and centralized financial system.

Far more generally influential was the Positivist philosophy of Auguste Comte (1798–1857). Comte's philosophy, like utilitarianism, insisted that all truth is derived from experience or observation of the physical world. Comte rejected metaphysics as utterly futile; no one can discover the hidden essences of things—why events happen as they do, or what is the ultimate meaning and goal of existence. All one can really know is how things happen, the laws which control their

Auguste Comte

[1] These and other similar reforms will be discussed in the following chapter.

The Positivism of Comte

occurrence, and the relations existing between them. Positivism derived its name from the assertion that the only knowledge of any current value was "positive," or scientific, knowledge. Comte argued that humankind's ability to analyze society scientifically and to predict its future had reached a point which would soon enable Europe to achieve a "positive" society, organized not in terms of belief but in terms of facts. Such an achievement would not be a simple matter, however; "positive" attitudes and institutions could not replace those of the "metaphysical" stage through which Europe had just passed without a struggle. By dividing the history of the world into progressive stages (a "religious" stage had preceded the "metaphysical"), and by declaring that the achievement of the highest stage was not possible without the turmoil of industrialization, Comte assured the middle class of its leading role in the better world that was to be.

6. EARLY CRITICS OF THE MIDDLE-CLASS WORLDVIEW

Honoré de Balzac

Gustave Flaubert

The middle-class worldview did not go unchallenged. Many writers deplored the social disintegration and moral hypocrisy they saw as the legacy of the Industrial Revolution. The Scot Thomas Carlyle (1795–1881), though a defender of the French Revolution and a believer in the need for a new aristocracy of industrialists ("captains of industry"), had nothing but contempt for the theories of the utilitarians. In Carlyle's view, they did no more than excuse the greed and acquisitiveness of the new middle class. Equally scathing in his attacks on the middle class was the English novelist Charles Dickens (1812–1870). In such novels as *Oliver Twist, Hard Times,* and *Dombey and Son,* he wrote with sympathy of the tyrannization of industrial workers by the new rich. In France, the Abbé Félicité Lamennais (1782–1854), though preaching respect for private property, nevertheless attacked self-interest. He argued, in his *Book of the People,* that the "little people" of the world enjoyed far too small a share in the direction of their lives. Honoré de Balzac (1799–1850) wrote *The Human Comedy* to expose the stupidity, greed, and baseness of the middle class. Gustave Flaubert (1821–1880) in his foremost novel *Madame Bovary,* depicted the banal, and literally fatal, nature of bourgeois existence for women.

One of the most trenchant critics of early industrialization was the English philosopher and economist John Stuart Mill (1806–1873). Though Mill as an economist is often considered a member of the classical school, he actually repudiated a number of its most sacred premises. First, he rejected the universality of economic laws. Though he admitted that there are unchangeable laws governing the field of production, he insisted that the distribution of wealth can be regulated by society for the benefit of the majority of its members. Second, he advocated more radical departures from laissez faire than any recommended by his forerunners. He favored legislation, under certain conditions, for shortening the working day, and he believed that the state might properly take preliminary steps toward the redistribution of wealth by taxing inheritances and by appropriating the unearned increment of land. In the fourth book of his *Principles of Political Economy* he urged the abolition of the wage system and looked forward to a society of producers' cooperatives in which the workers would own the factories and elect the managers to run them. On the other hand, Mill was no socialist. He distrusted the state, and his real reason for advocating producers' cooperatives was not to exalt the power of the workers but to give them the fruits of their labor.

Artists, too, attacked the values of industrial society in their painting and sculpture. The art preferred by the European middle class in the nineteenth century was that which in some way either told a story or, better still, preached a message. Beauty was surface decoration, which could be admired for its intrinsic richness and for what it therefore declared about its owner's wealth. Or beauty was a moralism, easily understood and, if possible, reassuring. When the Great Exhibition of the Works of Industry in All Nations was held at the Crystal Palace in London in 1851 to celebrate the triumph of industrialism, one of the most popular exhibits was *The Greek Slave,* a statue by the American sculptor Hiram Powers. Depicting a young Christian stripped bare and standing, according to the catalogue, before the gaze of an Eastern potentate, the work allowed its Victorian male admirers a chance to relish its salaciousness, while at the same time profiting from its depiction of the woman's righteous disdain for her captor.

Some of the artists most critical of the middle class, while repudiating the artificial and decorative, nevertheless reflected the middle-class obsession with art as morality. The self-designated Pre-Raphaelite Brotherhood of English painters was a group of men and women, led by the painter-poet Dante Gabriel Rossetti (1828–1882), determined to express its disdain for contemporary values. They called themselves Pre-Raphaelites as a way of announcing their admiration for the techniques of early Renaissance artists, untainted, supposedly, by corrupted artistic taste. Yet the works of the leading members of the Brotherhood exuded a degree of sentimentality that compromised their rebel nature and rendered them conventionally pietistic and ultimately innocuous as social protest. The same can be said, to a lesser degree, of the work of the Frenchman Jean François Millet (1814–1875). His *Man with the Hoe* is a stark, bitter statement about peasant life; his *The Angelus* softens the statement to sentiment. In both England and France, however, some of the most talented painters seriously questioned many of the values the middle class revered. Gustave Courbet (1819–1877) and Honoré Daumier (1808–1879)

John Stuart Mill

Middle-class art and its critics

The Pre-Raphaelites; Courbet and Daumier

See color plates following page 960

The Angelus by Jean-François Millet. The artist's peasants accept their humble lot in this sentimental portrayal.

both expressed sympathy toward the plight of the French working class, contrasting scenes of rural and urban misfortune with unflattering caricatures of the bourgeoisie. Daumier, in particular, was a powerful satirist of social and political evils, ridiculing the corruption of petty officials and the hypocritical piety of the rich. There was a harsh bite to most of the work of Daumier and Courbet that proscribed sentimentalizing.

Past or present? These writers and artists, while critical of the Industrial Revolution and middle-class values, proposed nothing very tangible in the way of radical reform. If they opposed the triumph of a materialistic middle class, they opposed, as well, the idea of complete democracy. Carlyle, in particular, criticized the present by comparing it with a rosy past that had never been. In this he was like one of the doughtiest critics of the new middle-class society, the Englishman William Cobbett (1763–1835). Cobbett, in his newspaper the *Political Register,* argued against industrialization itself as well as its effects. His propaganda mirrored the dilemma most critics had to face: Granted industrialization has brought great social and economic hardship in its train; does this mean that we should try to return to the life of preindustrial society, also often harsh, and always confining, though probably more secure?

Utopians For some time, a small band of thinkers had been answering that question with a resounding "no." They argued that there could be no return to old times and old ways, but that society could be at the same time both industrial and humane. These radical thinkers were often explicitly utopian. Two of the most persuasive were the Englishman

Robert Owen (1771–1858) and the Frenchman Charles Fourier (1772–1837). Though both writers are correctly seen as utopian, with all the practical limitations that label carries with it, in their day many of their followers believed in the possibility of instituting the programs Fourier and Owen propounded. Owen, himself the proprietor of a large cotton factory at New Lanark in Scotland, argued against the middle-class belief that the profit motive should be allowed to shape social and economic organization. Having reorganized his own mills to provide free schooling and a system of social security for his workers, he proceeded to advocate a general reorganization of society on the basis of cooperation, with communities rewarding workers solely on the basis of their actual labor. Fourier urged an even more far-reaching reconstitution, including the abolition of the wage system and the complete equality of the sexes. Followers of Owen and Fourier sought escape from the confusions of the contemporary world in idealist communities founded according to the principles of their leaders. All these attempts failed after a time, victims of faulty leadership and, in the case of Fourierist communities in France, of charges of moral turpitude resulting from Fourier's revolutionary sexual doctrines.

Less utopian radical theories were proposed during the 1840s, years which witnessed recurring economic depressions and their horrifying consequences. The French politician and journalist Louis Blanc (1811–1882), stood, like many contemporary critics, against the competitiveness of the new industrial society and particularly opposed the exploitation of the working class. His solution was to campaign for universal male suffrage, which would give working-class men control of the state. Following their triumph, these workers would make the state the "banker of the poor" and institute "Associations of Production"—actually a system of workshops governed by workers—which would guarantee jobs and security for all. Once these associations became established, private enterprise would wither through competition, and with it the state, for which there would no longer be any need. As we shall see, these workshops were briefly instituted in Paris during the Revolution of 1848. Another Frenchman, Pierre Proudhon (1809–1865), condemned the profits accruing to employers at the expense of their employees. He, too, proposed new institutions, which he argued could be made to produce goods at a price fairer to the worker, a price based solely on the amount of labor devoted to the manufacture of any particular product.

The ideas contained in the works of Blanc and Proudhon and other radical writers received their clearest and most forceful expression by the German theorists Karl Marx (1818–1883) and Friedrich Engels (1820–1895). Both Marx and Engels were sons of wealthy middle class parents. Marx studied philosophy at the University of Berlin. Determined to play an active role in the transformation of a society he was growing to despise, he took a job as editor of the *Rhineland Gazette* in

Louis Blanc

Blanc and Proudhon

Marx and Engels

1842. His radical policies soon put him at odds with his publishers. In 1843, he moved to Paris to devote further thought to the process and possibility of revolutionary change. From there he migrated to Brussels, where he was instrumental in founding the Communist League, a body whose declared aim was the overthrow of the middle class—or to use Marx's terminology, the bourgeoisie. While in Paris, Marx had renewed a former friendship with Engels, who had been living in Manchester where his family owned a cotton mill. While there, Engels wrote a devastating description of the effect of early industrialization upon the workers of England: *The Condition of the Working Class in England in 1844*. Together, Marx and Engels worked to produce a theory that would both explain how society had come to its present state and propose the means whereby it might be altered to benefit all. The theory was published by Marx at the request of the league in 1848, at the height of revolutionary agitation on the Continent, as *The Communist Manifesto*.

The Communist Manifesto

In the *Manifesto* Marx outlined a theory of history which owed a good deal to the German philosopher Georg Wilhelm Hegel (see below, p.892). Hegel had argued that ideas, the motive force of history, were in constant conflict with each other, and that this antithetical relationship between ideas in turn would produce an eventual synthesis, representing an advance in the history of the human race. Marx adopted this particular progressive notion of history to his own uses. Whereas Hegel perceived conflict and resolution (a dialectic) in terms of ideas, Marx saw them in terms of economic forces. Society, he argued, was at any time no more than the reflection of a hierarchy dictated by those who own the means of production and control the distribution of its material goods. As history has progressed, so have the means changed. Feudalism and manorialism were vanquished by capitalism. And capitalism, Marx declared, would be vanquished in turn by communism. That process, however, will first involve the concentration of capitalist economic power into fewer and fewer hands, and the consequent opposition of an ever-increasing and ever-debased working class (the proletariat). Once the proletariat overthrows the bourgeoisie by revolution, as it is bound to do eventually, society as a whole will be emancipated. An interim period in which a "dictatorship of the proletariat" rids the world of the last vestiges of bourgeois society will be followed by an end of the dialectical process and the emergence of a truly classless civilization.

Marx insisted that the *Manifesto* was not just another theory. His declaration that the proletariat together could consciously participate in the revolutionary process he described—could actually advance history through its own efforts—helps explain the document's appeal. The writings of Marx and Engels did not bring about an immediate proletarian revolution. Though the *Manifesto,* in its famous declaration, called upon the workers of the world to unite, Marx and Eng-

Karl Marx

els realized that this goal would not be achieved quickly. Marx and Engels, however, more than any other political thinkers of the 1830s and 1840s, provided workers with a potential sense of their worth as human beings and of their vital role in the historical process of the world. Engels made workers understand what factory work and urban living was doing to them: turning them from men and women into machines, alienated (a Marxian term) from themselves as human beings because they were alienated from the work over which they had no control. Marx gave workers the sense that those sufferings Engels described had an ultimate purpose, that they represented the workers' own particular contribution to the eventual and inevitable triumph of their class.

The theories of Marx and Engels spread throughout Europe after 1850. Like the theories of those other writers whom we have been considering—both the defenders and the opponents of the middle-class industrial world—they are historically important for two reasons. First, the ideas helped men and women better understand the new social order which had sprung up following the French and Industrial Revolutions, and the part they might play, as members of a class, in that new order. Second, the ideas themselves helped inspire the concrete political, social, and economic changes and events which are the subject of the next two chapters.

Friedrich Engels

SELECTED READINGS

• *Items so designated are available in paperback editions.*
• Berlin, Isaiah, *Karl Marx: His Life and Environment,* New York, 1948. The best short account.

  Briggs, Asa, *The Age of Improvement,* New York, 1959.
• ———, *Victorian People,* London, 1954.
• Burn, W. L., *The Age of Equipoise,* London, 1964. A charming account of the mid-Victorian years.

  Chevalier, Louis, *Laboring Classes and Dangerous Classes,* New York, 1973. An intriguing though controversial study of the quality of life in Paris between 1815 and 1848 which concludes that social mobility was downward and that the fear of crime dominated social consciousness.

  Gide, Charles, and Charles Rist, *A History of Economic Doctrines,* rev. ed., Boston, 1948. A good summary.

  Halevy, Elie, *The Growth of Philosophical Radicalism,* rev. ed., London, 1949. The best introduction to the thought of Malthus, Ricardo, Bentham, and their philosophical heirs.

  ———, *England in 1815,* London, 1949. The classic work by the greatest historian of nineteenth-century England.
• Hammond, J. L., and Barbara Hammond, *The Town Labourer, 1760–1832,* London, 1917. An impassioned account of the economic changes which affected the quality of life of the English worker.

Hobsbawm, Eric, *The Age of Capital, 1848–1875*, London, 1975. A perceptive world survey which traces the global triumph of capitalism and its impact upon the working classes.

• ———, *Labouring Men: Studies in the History of Labour*, London, 1964. A series of essays on workers and the working class in England.

• Langer, William L., *Political and Social Upheaval, 1832–1852*, New York, 1969. Comprehensive survey of European history, with excellent analytical chapters and thorough bibliographies.

Manuel, Frank E., *The Prophets of Paris*, Cambridge, Mass., 1962. An entertaining introduction to the philosophers of progress, from Turgot to Comte.

• Mehring, Franz, *Karl Marx: The Story of His Life*, New York, 1976.

• Rudé, George, *The Crowd in History*, New York, 1964.

• Thompson, E. P., *The Making of the English Working Class*, London, 1963. Argues that the coincidence of the French and Industrial Revolutions fostered the growth of working-class consciousness. A brilliant and important work.

Walker, Mack, *German Home Towns: Community, State, and General Estate, 1648–1871*, Ithaca, N.Y., 1971. Attempts to explain the absence of a strong middle class in Germany.

Zeldin, Theodore, *France, 1848–1951*, 2 vols., Oxford, 1973–77. A highly individualistic synthesis of French history, remarkable for its scope and insight.

SOURCE MATERIALS

• Engels, Friedrich, *The Condition of the Working Class in England*, New York, 1958. A much criticized, but reliable firsthand account by the later collaborator of Marx, written in 1844. Presents a devastating portrait of living and working conditions, especially in Manchester.

• Malthus, Thomas R., *An Essay on Population*, London, 1798 and 1803. Malthus's famous essay relating population growth and food production.

• Marx, Karl, *The Communist Manifesto*, 1848. Written under the spell of European revolutions, this was the young Marx's call for a revolution by the working class.

• Marx, Karl, and Friedrich Engels, *The Marx-Engels Reader*, 2nd ed., ed. by R. C. Tucker, New York, 1978.

• Mayhew, Henry, *London Labor and the London Poor*, New York, 1968. A reprint of the 1851 edition, provides a fascinating view of the population and trades of London. A good factual companion to Dickens.

Owen, Robert, *A New View of Society*, London, 1813. A proposed utopian society based upon cooperative villages by the founder of British socialism.

Chapter 27

THE RISE OF LIBERALISM
(1815–1870)

The general thought, the hope of France, has been order and liberty reuniting under constitutional monarchy.

—François Guizot, "Speech on the State of the Nation," 1831

The history of nineteenth-century Europe was to a great extent shaped by the interplay of the forces of liberalism and nationalism. The middle classes of France and England, where liberalism was strongest, espoused a set of doctrines reflecting their concerns and interests. Liberalism to them meant (1) an efficient government prepared to acknowledge the value of commercial and industrial development; (2) a government in which their interests would be protected by their direct representation in the legislature—in all probability, a constitutional monarchy, and most certainly not a democracy; (3) a foreign policy of peace and free trade; and (4) a belief in individualism and the doctrines of the classical economists.

The components of liberalism

Many middle-class men and women in other European countries shared these beliefs and assumptions, and worked diligently and with some success to carry through specific liberal reforms. But for them, an equally important and often more immediate objective was the achievement of some form of national unity. The middle classes in Germany, Italy, Poland, and the Austrian Empire, however dedicated they were to liberalism, believed that their chances of achieving liberal goals would be greatly enhanced if they could unify the patchwork of principalities that surrounded them into a vigorous, "modern" nation-state. In this chapter, we shall examine the phenomenon of liberalism, primarily as it affected the fortunes of England and France. In the following chapter, we shall describe the way in which liberalism combined with nationalism to reshape the history of central Europe.

The compulsion of nationalism

Congress of Vienna

I. CONSERVATIVE REACTION, 1815–1830

The growth of liberalism occurred, in part, as a reaction to the conservative policies adopted by frightened governments anxious to restore domestic and international order following the Napoleonic wars. For a period of about fifteen years after 1815 the rulers of most European countries did their best to stem the advance of middle-class liberalism. In most instances, however, their repressive policies only made liberals more determined than ever to succeed. The primary concern of governments was to ensure that Europe would never again fall prey to the sort of revolutionary upheavals which it had experienced during the preceding quarter-century. To that end, when representatives of the European powers had met at the <u>Congress of Vienna</u> in 1814 to <u>draw up a permanent peace settlement for Europe</u>, they labored to produce an agreement that would as nearly as possible guarantee international tranquility. At the same time, however, they were by no means unwilling to advance the claims of their own countries to new territories, though such claims threatened conflict, or even war. Although the principle decisions of the congress were made by representatives of the major powers, it was attended by an array of dignitaries from almost all the principalities of Europe. No fewer than six monarchs attended: the tsar of Russia, the emperor of Austria, and the kings of Prussia, Denmark, Bavaria, and Württemberg. Great Britain was represented by Lord Castlereagh and the duke of Wellington. From France came the subtle intriguer Talleyrand, who had served as a bishop under Louis XVI, as foreign minister at the court of Napoleon, and who now stood ready to espouse the cause of reaction.

Alexander I

The dominant roles at the Congress of Vienna were played by <u>Alexander I (1801–1825)</u> and <u>Metternich (1773–1859)</u>. The dynamic tsar is one of the most baffling figures in history. Reared at the court of Catherine the Great, he imbibed the doctrines of Rousseau from a French Jacobin tutor. In 1801 he succeeded his murdered father, Paul, as

The Congress of Vienna. The figure to the left of center is Metternich. Seated at the right, with his arms on the table, is Talleyrand.

tsar and for the next two decades disturbed the dreams of his fellow sovereigns by becoming the most liberal monarch in Europe. After the defeat of Napoleon in the Russian campaign, Alexander's mind turned more and more to mystical channels. He conceived of a mission to convert the rulers of all countries to the Christian ideals of justice and peace. But the chief effect of his voluble expressions of devotion to "liberty" and "enlightenment" was to frighten conservatives into suspecting a plot to extend his power over all of Europe. He was accused of intriguing with Jacobins everywhere to substitute an all-powerful Russia for an all-powerful France.

Tsar Alexander I

The most commanding figure at the congress was Klemens von Metternich, born at Coblenz in the Rhine valley, where his father was Austrian ambassador at the courts of three small German states. As a student at the University of Strassburg the young Metternich witnessed some excesses of mob violence connected with the outbreak of the French Revolution, and to these he attributed his life-long hatred of political innovation. After completing his education, he entered the field of diplomacy and served for nearly forty years as minister of foreign affairs. He was active in fomenting discord between Napoleon and Tsar Alexander, after the two became allies in 1807, and he played some part in arranging the marriage of Napoleon to the Austrian archduchess, Marie Louise. In 1813 he was made a hereditary prince of the Austrian Empire. At the Congress of Vienna Metternich distinguished himself for charm of manner and skillful intrigue. His two great obsessions were hatred of political and social change and fear of Russia. Actually the two were related. It was not simply that he feared revolutions as such; he feared, even more, revolutions inspired by the tsar for the sake of establishing Russian supremacy in Europe. For this reason he favored moderate terms for France in its hour of defeat, and was ready at one time to sponsor the restoration of Napoleon as emperor of the French under the protection and overlordship of the Hapsburg monarchy.

Metternich

The basic idea that guided the work of the Congress of Vienna was the principle of *legitimacy*. This principle was invented by Talleyrand as a device for protecting France against drastic punishment by its conquerors, but it was ultimately adopted by Metternich as a convenient expression of the general policy of reaction. Legitimacy meant that the dynasties of Europe that had reigned in prerevolutionary days should be restored to their thrones, and that each country should regain essentially the same territories it had held in 1789. In accordance with this principle Louis XVIII, brother of Louis XVI,[1] was recognized as the "legitimate" sovereign of France, and the restoration of Bourbon rulers in Spain and the Two Sicilies was also confirmed. France was compelled to pay an indemnity of 700 million francs to the victorious

Klemens von Metternich

---

[1] Louis XVII, the young son of the executed king and queen, had died under mysterious circumstances in the hands of revolutionary captors in 1795.

Barriers to French expansion

The German settlement

allies, but its boundaries were to remain essentially the same as in 1789.

To ensure that the French would not soon again overrun their boundaries, however, a strong barrier was erected to contain them. The Dutch Republic, conquered by the French in 1795, was restored as the Kingdom of the Netherlands, with the house of Orange as its hereditary monarchy. To its territory was added that of Belgium, formerly the Austrian Netherlands, with the hope that this now substantial power would serve to discourage any future notions of French expansion. For the same reason the German left bank of the Rhine was ceded to Prussia, and Austria was established as a major power in northern Italy.

The principle of legitimacy was not extended to the German principalities, however. There, despite pleas from rulers of the sovereign bits and pieces that had existed before 1789, the great powers agreed to retain the boundaries as redrawn by Napoleon. Fear of an aggressive Russia led the other European nations to support the maintenance—as an anti-Russian bulwark—of the Napoleonic kingdoms of Bavaria, Würtemberg, and Saxony. At the same time, however, Tsar Alexander was demanding that Poland, partitioned into virtual extinction by Russia, Austria, and Prussia in the 1790s, be reconstituted a kingdom with himself as its constitutional monarch. Prussia was prepared to agree with this scheme, provided that it be allowed to swallow Saxony. National avarice for territorial expansion rapidly eclipsed legitimacy as a guiding principle in these negotiations. Metternich, horrified at the double threat thus presented to Austria by Prussia and Russia, allied himself with Talleyrand and Castlereagh, both of whom secretly agreed to go to war against Russia and Prussia, if necessary, in order to prevent them from consumating their Polish-Saxon deal. A compromise was eventually reached, allowing to Russia the major part of Poland and to Prussia a part of Saxony. Britain, no less anxious

"Dividing the Cake." A contemporary cartoonist's impression of the work of the congress diplomats.

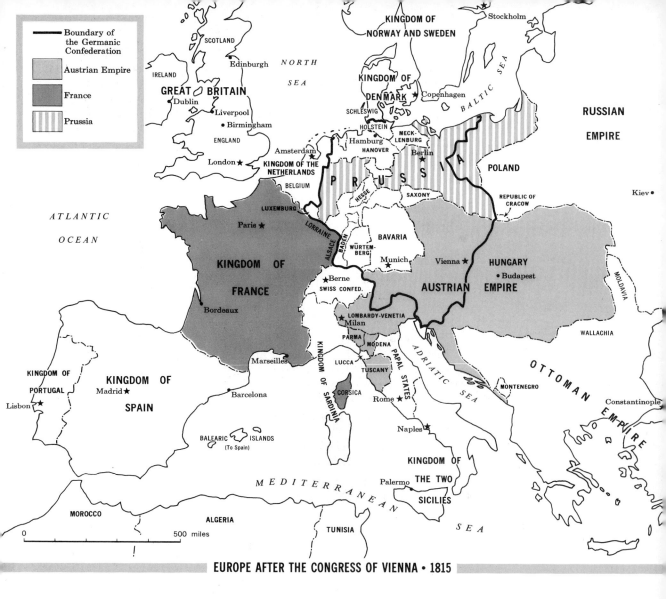

EUROPE AFTER THE CONGRESS OF VIENNA · 1815

Legend:
— Boundary of the Germanic Confederation
Austrian Empire
France
Prussia

than the other victorious powers to gain compensation for its long years at war, received territories principally under French dominion in South Africa and South America and the island of Ceylon, thus adding further to its commercial empire.

Following Napoleon's final defeat at Waterloo in 1815, the major powers reconfirmed the Vienna settlement in the hope that their efforts might result in a permanently stable "Concert of Europe." To further ensure an end to revolutionary disturbances, they formed the Quadruple Alliance—Britain, Austria, Prussia, and Russia; when France was admitted as a fifth member in 1818 it became the Quintuple Alliance. Its members pledged to cooperate in the suppression of any disturbances which might arise from attempts to overthrow legitimate governments or to alter international boundaries. At the same

The system of alliances

time, Tsar Alexander, his mystic nature now in the ascendant, persuaded the allies to join him in the declaration of another alliance—a "Holy Alliance"—dedicated to the precepts of justice, Christian charity, and peace. The only result of this second league was to confuse Europe's leaders as to Alexander's intentions. Was he a liberal—a Jacobin even, as Metternich feared—or a reliable conservative? The confusion was cleared away, as in one country after another, liberal uprisings were stifled by stern reactionary policies of the allied governments, Alexander's among them.

Suppression of liberal uprisings

Attacks against reactionary governments in Naples and in Spain brought the allies scurrying to a conference at Troppau in Austria in 1820. Secret brotherhoods of young liberals, many of them army officers, had spearheaded these revolts. These organizations, which originated in Italy, called themselves *Carbonari.* They were an active counterreactionary force, whose influence spread throughout Europe in the early 1820s. In both Naples and Spain, they succeeded in forcing the kings to take oaths to establish constitutions modeled on the liberal French constitution of 1789–1791. At Troppau, Austria, Prussia, and Russia reacted to these threats to international order and absolutism by pledging to come to each other's aid to suppress revolution. France and Britain declined to endorse the pledge, not so much because they opposed repression, but because they did not wish to curtail their freedom of action by binding themselves to detailed international treaties. Metternich nevertheless proceeded, with Russian and Prussian concurrence, in a repression of the *Carbonari* rebels through imprisonment or exile.

Defying the congress system

Two years later, in 1822, another congress was convened at Verona, this one to deal with the continuing liberal threat to stability in Spain, with the series of revolutions occurring in Spanish colonies in South America, and with an insurrection in the Near East. To resolve the Spanish problem, the French dispatched an army of 200,000 men to the Iberian peninsula in 1823. Without much difficulty, this force put an end to the Spanish liberals, who opposed King Ferdinand VII's attempt to undermine representative government. The French assisted Ferdinand in restoring his authority to rule as he pleased. Contrary to their experience in Spain, the defenders of the status quo were unable to succeed in stemming the move to independence and liberalism in the colonies. In 1823 President James Monroe of the United States issued the "Monroe Doctrine," which declared that attempts by European powers to intervene in the affairs of the New World would be looked upon as an unfriendly act by his government. Without British maritime support, the doctrine would have remained a dead letter. Britain was ready to recognize the independence of the South American republics, however, since as new countries they were prepared to trade with Britain instead of Spain. The British therefore used their navy to keep Spain from intervening to protect its vanishing empire.

In the Near East, a Greek soldier, Alexander Ypsilanti, was attempting to encourage the formation of a Greek "empire," to be constructed on vaguely liberal principles. In doing so, he had engaged his band of armed followers in battles against the Turks who ruled over Greece. Though Ypsilanti was soon defeated, his movement lived on. Five years later its aims had been narrowed to the more accessible goal of an independent Greece. Supported for reasons of Mediterranean naval strategy by a joint Anglo-French-Russian naval intervention, and by a Russian invasion of the Balkans, the rebels this time succeeded. Their success signaled the extent of changes that had occurred since the Congress of Verona. No longer could Metternich and other reactionaries build alliances on the assumption that, for the powers of Europe, preservation of the status quo was, before everything else, the major goal. Britain, in particular, could not be relied upon. There, by the late 1820s, the liberal movement was gaining momentum fast.

Rebellion in Greece

2. LIBERAL GAINS IN WESTERN EUROPE, 1815–1830

Liberal gains in Britain came after an era of reaction that paralleled that which occurred on the Continent. There the conservative Tory party had enjoyed almost unbroken political supremacy since the younger William Pitt had become first minister in 1783. Though Pitt had begun his career as something of a reformer, the French Revolution had turned him, along with his fellow-Tories, into a staunch defender of the status quo. The Tories' political opponents, the Whigs, had throughout the long years of the revolutionary and Napoleonic conflicts, remained to some degree conciliatory to the French. But Whigs were as unsympathetic as Tories to democratic notions and as defensive of their rights to the full fruits of their property.

British politics

Hence when rioting broke out in England after 1815 as a result of depression and consequent unemployment, there was general support among the well-to-do for the repressive measures adopted by the British government. Spies were hired to ferret out evidence against popular agitators. In the industrial north, where conditions were particularly severe, radical members of the middle and working classes capitalized on the general unrest to press their demands for increased representation in Parliament. At Manchester a crowd of 80,000, demonstrating for political reform in St. Peter's Fields, was fired upon by soldiers. Eleven persons were killed and over 400 injured, including 113 women. The massacre was thereafter called "Peterloo" by British radicals: i.e., a domestic Waterloo. It was the first of several repressive measures taken by the government to stifle reform. Another was the legislation known as the Six Acts, which was passed by Parliament in 1819, and outlawed "seditious and blasphemous" literature; levied a stamp tax on newspapers; allowed the searching of houses for arms; and restricted the rights of public meeting.

"Peterloo" and the Six
Acts

Yet within a surprisingly short time British political leaders re-

The Peterloo Massacre, 1819. A contemporary rendering of the shootings which condemned the "wanton and furious attack by that brutal armed force The Manchester & Cheshire Yeomanry Cavalry."

The liberalizing Tories

versed their opposition to everything new. Instead, they displayed an ability to compromise which kept their country free from revolution. George Canning, the foreign minister, and Robert Peel, the home secretary, son of a rich cotton manufacturer, were both sensitive to the interests of Britain's liberal-minded capitalist entrepreneurs. Under their direction, the government retreated from its commitment to the intransigent Quintuple Alliance; it was Canning who took the lead in recognizing the new South American republics. At home, these same politicians began to make order of the inefficient tangle of British laws; for example, they abolished capital punishment for about a hundred different offenses. And Canning liberalized, though he did not abolish, the Corn Laws. These laws levied a tariff on the importation of cheap foreign grain. As such, they benefited English landlords, but hurt manufacturers, who had to pay higher factory wages to enable their workers to purchase more expensive bread. These "liberalizers" among the still essentially conservative Tories even succeeded in abolishing the laws which had kept both dissenting Protestants (members of Protestant sects—Baptist, Congregationalist, Methodist—other than Anglican) and Roman Catholics from full participation in public political life.

Parliamentary reform

What the conservatives would not do was reform the system of representation in the House of Commons, heavily weighted on the side of the landed interests. Here the Tories, the majority party in Parliament, drew the line and showed themselves still basically committed to the status quo. Yet members of the liberal middle class argued that such a reform was absolutely necessary before they could themselves play a constant and active role in shaping British policy to comply with their own interests. "Interest" was, indeed, the key word in the debate over parliamentary reform. For centuries Parliament had represented the interests of landowners, the major propertied class in England. About two-thirds of the members of the House of Commons were either directly nominated by or indirectly owed their election to the patronage of the richest landowners in the country. Many of the parliamentary electoral districts, or boroughs, which returned members to the House of Commons, were controlled by landowners who used the pressure of their local economic power—or, in many cases, outright bribery—to return candidates sympathetic to their interests. These were the "rotten" or "pocket" boroughs, so-called because they were said to be in the pockets of those men who controlled them. Those who favored the system as it was argued that it mattered little that electoral politics were corrupt, that electoral districts represented unequal numbers, or that very, very few (about one in a hundred) were enfranchised. What did matter, they claimed, was that the interests of the nation at large, which they perceived to coincide with the interests of landed property, were well looked after by a Parliament elected in this fashion.

Of course the new industrial middle class did not agree with the arguments of the landowners. They insisted, for example, that the Corn Laws did not coincide with the nation's best interest. (If they were followers of the theories of Jeremy Bentham, they might argue that the Corn Laws did not produce "the greatest happiness of the greatest number.") Rather, the Corn Laws worked only for the benefit of landlords, by keeping the price of grain high; and they worked to the disinterest of everyone else. Therefore, said members of the middle class, Parliament must be reformed to represent not only landlords but the interests of industrial England. It is important to note that the liberal middle class was *not* arguing in favor of reform on the basis of a belief in democracy. Some leaders within the emerging working class did make this argument—and, as we shall see, continued to make it after a reform bill was passed in 1832. Most of those who spoke in favor of reform, however, declared that the middle class was capable of representing the interests of the working class, as well as of itself, in Parliament. Reformers took this position either because they believed it; or because they were afraid of working-class representatives; or because they realized that to favor direct representation for the working class would frighten the more timid reformers and hence defeat their whole campaign.

The middle class and reform

Spurred by the example of liberal reformers on the Continent (see below, p. 681) and by the oratory and organizational abilities of middle-class and artisan radicals at home, the movement for reform intensified after 1830. It was strong enough to topple the Tories and to embolden the Whigs, under the leadership of Lord Grey, to bring in a bill to reform the electorate. The government was clearly frightened. Revolution, if it were ever to come in England, would come as a result of the alliance now threatening between middle-class industrialists and the artisan/tradesman leadership of the new working class. In Bir-

A working-class alliance

mingham, a middle-class banker, Thomas Attwood, organized a "Political Union of the Lower and Middle Classes of the People." By July 1830, there were similar organizations in Glasgow, Manchester, Liverpool, Sheffield, Newcastle, and Coventry. The king, William IV, wrote worriedly to Lord Grey that "miners, manufacturers, colliers, and labourers" appeared ready for some sort of open rebellion.[2] Sensing the grave danger of a possible union of the working and middle classes, the governing class once more accommodated to change, as it had in the 1820s.

The Reform Bill of 1832

The Reform Bill of 1832, however, was not a retreat from the notion of representation by interest. No attempt was made to create equal electoral districts. The franchise, though increased, was defined in terms of the amount of property owned and the length of time one had owned it. In the counties, for example, a man could vote if he paid at least ten pounds annual rental for land held on a long-term sixty-year lease. In other words, the vote was granted to the middle class, but to very few of the working class. Probably more significant than its extension of the franchise, was the bill's scheme for a redistribution of seats. One hundred and forty-three seats were reallocated, most of them from the rural south to the industrial north, thereby increasing representation in and around cities such as Manchester, Leeds, and Birmingham; and thereby increasing, in turn, the political power of the industrial middle classes. Though the bill was the product of change and itself brought change in its wake, it was understood as a conservative measure. It by no means destroyed the political strength of landed aristocratic interests, though it reduced that strength somewhat. And it preserved the notion of representation by interest. The liberal, industrial middle classes had been admitted into junior partnership with the landed oligarchy that had for centuries ruled Britain and was to rule it for at least one more generation.

Liberalism in other parts of the West

Efforts to introduce liberal political reforms were not limited to Britain during this period. In the United States, the rule of eastern landed and commercial interests was superseded by the antiprivilege Democratic party, led by the hero of the War of 1812, General Andrew Jackson. Across the world, in Russia, a group of army officers revolted, following the death of Tsar Alexander in 1825, in hopes of persuading his liberally minded brother, Constantine, to assume the throne and guarantee a constitution. In this case, however, the attempt at reform failed. Constantine was unwilling to usurp power from the rightful heir, a third brother, Nicholas. The officers, called Decembrists (because of the month of their rebellion), were harshly punished; Nicholas continued to rule in the severely autocratic ways Alexander had adopted toward the end of his life, creating the Third Section, a political police force, to prevent further domestic disorder.

Meanwhile autocracy also threatened the liberal revolutionary and

[2] Asa Briggs, *The Age of Improvement*, New York, 1959, p. 248.

Napoleonic heritage in France. The upper middle class in France had remained generally content with the domestic settlement agreed upon by the major powers in 1814 and confirmed at the Congress of Vienna the following year. Louis XVIII had issued a "constitutional charter" upon his succession to the French throne. While refusing to deny himself absolute power in theory, in practice Louis XVIII had willingly enough agreed to support those principles most desired by French middle-class liberals: legal equality; careers open to talent; and a two-chamber parliamentary government, with the vote confined to property-holders.

In 1824, Louis died and was succeeded by his reactionary brother Charles X. By his policies Charles immediately declared himself a foe of liberalism, modernization, and the general legacies of the revolutionary and Napoleonic eras. At his direction the French assembly voted indemnities to those aristocratic émigrés whose land had been confiscated by the state. The Church was allowed to reassert its traditionally exclusive right to teach in French classrooms. The upper middle class, strengthened by its role within the country's growing industrial economy, reacted by heading a rebellion against Charles's reactionary policies. In March 1830, members of the Chamber of Deputies, led by bankers, passed a vote of no confidence in the government. Charles dissolved the chamber, as he was constitutionally empowered to do, and called new elections for deputies. When those elections went against his candidates, Charles further retaliated by a series of ordinances, issued on his own authority, which (1) again dissolved the newly elected chamber before it had even met; (2) imposed strict censorship on the press; (3) further restricted suffrage so as to exclude the upper middle class almost completely; and (4) called for new elections.

What Charles got in return for these measures was revolution. Led by republicans—workers, artisans, students, writers, and the like—Parisians took to the streets. For three days, behind hastily constructed barricades, they defied the army and the police, neither of which was anxious to fire into the crowds. Sensing the futility of further resistance, Charles abdicated. Those who had manned the barricades pressed for a genuine republic. But those with the power—bankers, merchants, and industrialists—wanted none of that. Instead they brought the duke of Orleans to the throne as King Louis-Philippe (1830–1848), after extracting a promise from him to abide by the constitution of 1814 which had so suited their particular liberal needs. The franchise was extended, from about 100,000 to 200,000 males. But the right to vote was still based upon property ownership. The major beneficiaries of the change were members of the middle class, those whose interests the Revolution of 1830 primarily served.

Other countries in Europe caught the revolutionary fever in the summer of 1830. As we have already noted, middle- and working-class radicals in England were inspired by the French to press their

The July Revolution of 1830 in Paris. Workers construct street barricades to ward off government troops.

Liberal revolts elsewhere

own case for liberal reform. In Belgium, an insurrection which combined elements of liberal and national sentiment put an end to the union of that country with the Dutch, instituted by the Congress of Vienna. The European powers strengthened Belgium's political structure, and hence its independence, by agreeing to the accession of Leopold of Saxe-Coburg, uncle of the future Queen Victoria of England, as king. Once again, a middle class had succeeded in establishing a constitutional monarchy to its liking, congenial to its liberal and entrepreneurial goals. No such fate awaited the liberal nationalists in Poland, who moved at this time to depose their ruler, the Russian Tsar Nicholas, whose hegemony extended to Poland as a result of the Vienna settlement of 1815. Western Europe did not intervene; Russian troops crushed the Polish liberal rebels, and Poland was merged into the tsarist empire.

Spain

Liberal forces in Spain enjoyed a greater success. There middle-class liberalism was linked to the attempts of Queen Maria Christina, widow of King Ferdinand, to secure the throne for her daughter, Isabella. Though no liberal herself, the queen was prepared to court the favor of urban middle-class elites to win her struggle against her late husband's brother, Don Carlos. During the so-called Carlist Wars, which lasted from 1834 to 1840, liberals extracted from Isabella a constitution which ensured them a strong voice in the legislature, while restricting the franchise in such a way as to keep the more radical lower middle and artisan classes at bay. By mid-century, however, fear of these radicals led the middle class to acquiesce in a government that was nothing more or less than an authoritarian dictatorship, but that did not threaten directly their own economic interests.

3. LIBERALISM IN BRITAIN AND FRANCE, 1830–1848

The Revolution of 1830 in France and the Parliamentary Reform Bill of 1832 in England represented a setback for aristocratic power in both countries. Aristocrats and their supporters did not cease overnight to play an active role in politics, however. Lord Palmerston, for example, was one of England's most influential prime ministers at mid-century and one of Europe's most authoritative arbiters. But no longer would it be possible for the legislatures of France and England to ignore the particular interests of the middle class. Henceforth representatives would include members from that class in sufficient numbers to press successfully for programs which accorded with liberal beliefs.

*Decline of aristocratic
power*

One of the major accomplishments of the first British Parliament elected after 1832 was passage of a new law governing the treatment of paupers. In accordance with the law passed in 1602 under Elizabeth I, each parish in England had been declared responsible for the maintenance of its own poor, either through accommodation in poorhouses, or through a system of doles, coupled with local public employment programs. This system, although it by no means eliminated the debilitating effects of poverty, did provide a kind of guarantee against actual starvation. But by 1830 it had broken down. Population growth and economic depressions had produced a far larger number of underemployed men and women in Britain than had ever before existed, placing tremendous strain upon those funds, levied as taxes, which each parish used to provide relief. Industrialization also demanded that families move in search of employment from one part of the country to another; yet the old poor law provided assistance only to those who applied in the parish of their birth. The old law did not accord with liberal notions of efficiency; the new Parliament set about to amend it. The result, drafted by Jeremy Bentham's former private secretary,

*Liberal legislation in
Britain: the new poor law*

An English Workhouse for the Able-Bodied Poor. This workhouse in the county of Devon was built in the late 1830s.

Edwin Chadwick, and passed almost without dissent, clearly reflected the liberal, middle-class notion of how to achieve "the greatest happiness of the greatest number." Doles were to cease forthwith. Those who could not support themselves were to be confined in workhouses. Here conditions were to be made so severe as to all but compel inmates to depart and accept either whatever work they might find outside, no matter how poorly paid, or whatever charity their friends and relatives might be able to provide them. Parishes were to be grouped together into more efficient unions; the law was to be administered by a central board of commissioners in London. Inspiring this new legislation were the liberal belief that poverty was a person's own fault and the liberal assumption that capitalism, though unregulated, was capable of providing enough jobs for all who genuinely wanted them. Economic depressions in the early 1840s proved that latter assumption false, and wrecked the tidy schemes of the poor-law administrators. Doles were once more instituted, taxes once more increased. Yet the law's failure did not shake the liberal conviction that poverty was, in the end, an individual and not an institutional problem.

Repeal of the Corn Laws

Even more symbolic of the political power of Britain's middle class than the new poor law was the repeal of the Corn Laws in 1846. The laws, even after their modification in the 1820s, continued to keep the price of bread artificially high, forcing employers, in turn, to pay wages high enough to allow workers to keep food on their tables. More than that, the Corn Laws symbolized to the middle classes the unwarranted privileges of an ancient and, to their minds, generally useless order: the landed aristocracy. The campaign to accomplish repeal was superbly orchestrated and relentless. The Anti–Corn Law League, an organization of middle-class industrialists and their supporters, held large meetings throughout the north of England, lobbied members of Parliament, and, in the end, managed to persuade Sir Robert Peel, now prime minister, of the inevitability of their goal. They were aided, as well, by the potato famine in Ireland, whose existence argued in favor of ending restrictions against the importation of cheap foodstuffs. That Peel was willing to split the Tory—or as it was now coming to be called, Conservative—party to introduce repeal suggests the power of the middle class and its belief in the gospel of free trade.

Legislation during this period reflected other middle-class concerns, and in some cases, directly conflicted with the liberal doctrine of nonintervention. Many members of the urban middle class professed devotion to the tenets of Christianity, particularly that doctrine which argued that all human beings have within themselves a soul which they must work to preserve from sin for their eternal salvation. This belief in the ability of an individual to achieve salvation, which contradicted the older Calvinist doctrine of a predestined "elect," accorded

Robert Peel

well with more general middle-class notions about the importance of individualism and the responsibility of the individual for his or her own well-being. It produced legislation such as the abolition of the slave trade in British colonies (1833), and the series of Factory Acts which, in 1847, culminated in the curtailment of the workday in some trades to ten hours. Evangelicals such as William Wilberforce, who was throughout his life an eloquent spokesman for enslaved blacks, and Lord Shaftesbury, who campaigned to end the employment of women and children in mines, maintained that individual souls could not find God when imprisoned in the overworked bodies of plantation slaves or factory operatives. They were joined by others who argued, simply, that to keep people tied to their work for as long as twelve or fourteen hours a day was both inhuman and unnecessary. Middle-class liberals found the arguments confusing. The laws of classical economics pulled them in one direction; the ethics of Christianity in another. Their uncertainty mirrored the extent to which no one could discern a right course in this world of new difficulties and fresh options.

   The years of Louis Philippe's reign in France were not so marked as those in England with significant reforms. In the first place, France was not confronted with anything like the same degree of rapid industrialization that was compelling legislative activity on a number of fronts in England. France had nothing to compare with the problems generated by the growth of urban manufacturing centers in the north of England. Though the Chamber of Deputies contained representatives from the upper middle class, they tended to be bankers and merchants, not industrialists. Some were willing to espouse the notion of free trade, though not with the general enthusiasm of their British counterparts, whose unrivaled position as the world's leading manufacturers gave them a vested interest in that cause. Under the succession of governments dominated by France's leading politician of the period, François Guizot (1787–1874), the French expanded their educational system, thereby further underwriting their belief in the liberal doctrine of a meritocracy, or careers open to talent. A French law of 1833 provided for the establishment of elementary schools in every village. Children of indigent parents were to receive a free education; all others would pay a modest fee. In addition, larger towns were to provide training schools for trade and industry, and departments, schools for teacher training. As a result, the number of pupils in France increased from about 2 million, in 1831, to about 3.25 million in 1846. Little else of lasting importance was accomplished during the liberal regime of Louis Philippe. Guizot became more and more an apologist for the status quo. Everyone was free, he argued, to rise to the upper middle class and thus to a position of political and economic power. His advice to those who criticized his complacency was: "enrich yourselves." Politicians followed his advice, finding in

Louis Philippe

schemes for the modernization of Paris and the expansion of the railway system ample opportunities for graft. Louis Philippe did little to counteract the lifelessness and corruption that characterized his regime. Although he had played a minor part in the first stage of the revolution of 1789, he was no revolutionary. He did not have the dash and glamor of a Napoleon. He was a paunchy, fussy, and undistinguished person, easily caricatured by his enemies and without the talent necessary to rise above his stodgy public image.

Growing dissatisfaction of radicals

Meanwhile radical members of the French and British lower middle and working classes who had assisted—if not propelled—the forces of liberalism to victory in 1830 and 1832 grew increasingly dissatisfied with the results of their efforts. In Britain they soon realized that the Reform Bill had done little to increase their chances for political participation. For a time they devoted their energies to the cause of trade unionism, believing that industrial, rather than political, action might bring them relief from the economic hardships they were suffering.

Trade unionism

Trade union organization had been a goal of militant workers since the beginning of the century. Among the first workers' campaigns in the nineteenth century were those often riotous revolts organized both in England and, later, on the Continent against the introduction of machinery. In some instances, factories were attacked by workers and machines smashed, in the belief that machines, by replacing skilled workers, were producing widespread unemployment. In England, the rioters were called Luddites, after "Ned Ludd," who was the mythical leader of the movement. In other instances, the hostility of trade unionists was not directed so much toward machinery as toward those workers who refused to join in unions against their masters. Yet nowhere in Europe were trade unions able to organize themselves into effective bargaining agents before 1850. They came closest in England. There, artisans and skilled workers had banded together in the mid-1820s to form both Friendly Societies, really mutual aid and insurance organizations, and cooperatives, communal stores which cut prices by eliminating the middleman between producer and consumer. By 1831, there were about 500 cooperative societies in England, with a membership of something like 20,000. These organizations encouraged the parallel growth of trade unions, which, in the early 1830s, reached the peak of their early power and effectiveness. The National Association for the Protection of Labour comprised about 150 separate local unions in the textile and mining industries of the north; the Operative Builder's Union about 30,000 workers throughout the country. In 1834, a new and potentially far more radical organization, the Grand National Consolidated Trades Union of Great Britain and Ireland, was organized by a group of London artisans. Its leadership declared that only by bringing the country to a standstill with a general strike could workers compel the governing class to grant them a decent life. At that point, the governing class realized a serious threat to its existence and decided to put an end to

The Chartist Procession to the Houses of Parliament, April 1848

unions. Six organizers for the Grand National were convicted of administering secret oaths (unions were not themselves illegal) and sentenced to transportation (forced emigration to penal colonies in Australia). Subsequently employers demanded that their workers sign a document pledging their refusal to join a union, thereby stifling opportunities for further organization.

After the defeat of the Grand National, the efforts of radical democratic reformers in England turned back from trade union to political activity, centering on attempts to force further political reform upon the uninterested government through the device of the "People's Charter." This document, circulated across the country by committees of Chartists, as they were known, and signed by millions, contained six demands: universal manhood suffrage; institution of the secret ballot; abolition of property qualifications for membership in the House of Commons; annual parliamentary elections; payment of salaries to members of the House of Commons; and equal electoral districts.

Chartism

The fortunes of the Chartist movement waxed and waned. In some areas its strength depended upon economic conditions: Chartism spread with unemployment and depression. There were arguments among its leaders as to both ends and means: Did Chartism imply a reorganization of industry or, instead, a return to preindustrial society? Were its goals to be accomplished by petition only, or by more violent means if necessary? The Chartist William Lovett, a cabinet-maker, for example, was as fervent a believer in self-improvement as any member of the middle class. He advocated a union of educated workers to acquire their fair share of the nation's increasing industrial bounty. The Chartist Feargus O'Connor, on the other hand, appealed to the more impoverished and desperate class of workers. He urged a rejection of industrialization, and the resettlement of the poor on agri-

Varieties of Chartism

cultural allotments. These polarities and disagreements regarding the aims of the movement suggest the extent of the confusion within the working class, whose consciousness as a separate political force was only just beginning to develop. Events answered most of the Chartists' questions for them. In 1848, revolutionary outbreaks across the Continent inspired Chartist leaders to plan a major demonstration and show of force in London. A procession of 500,000 workers was called, to bear to Parliament a petition containing 6,000,000 signatures demanding the six points. Special constables and contingents of the regular army were marshaled under the now aged duke of Wellington to resist this threat to order. Less than 50,000 made the march to Parliament, however. Rain, poor management, and unwillingness on the part of many to do battle with the well-armed constabulary put an end to the Chartists' campaign, if not their cause.

In France, radical agitation produced very different results. There, as well, those who had manned the barricades in 1830 soon grew disgusted with the liberalism for which they had risked their lives. In their minds they carried memories or myths of the years of the first French Republic—its domestic accomplishments, its foreign victories, if not its Reign of Terror. They were opposed to constitutional monarchy, and only mildly enthusiastic about parliamentary government. They were prepared, if necessary, to use force in order to achieve their ends. Centered in Paris, they were for the most part either writers, students, or working-class leaders. They met in secret, studied the works of the radical theorist, Gracchus Babeuf (see above, p. 802), whose socialist *Conspiracy of Equals,* written during the French Revolution, became their Bible, and succeeded in making constant trouble for the liberal, middle-class governments of Louis Philippe. Their leading spokesman was the socialist Auguste Blanqui (1805–1881). He argued the victimization of the workers by the middle class, and helped organize secret societies which were to become the instruments of eventual insurrection. Radicals waged some of their most successful campaigns in the press. Honoré Daumier's savage caricatures of Louis

A Caricature of Louis Philippe by Daumier. The inscription reads "Louis Philippe, the Last King of France." It reflects a popular sentiment of the time.

Rue Transnomain. A drawing by Daumier to commemorate the victims of government repression in 1834.

The Revolution of 1848 in France. A contemporary broadside celebrating the triumph of the people.

Philippe landed him in prison more than once. But radical campaigning took to the streets as well. In retaliation, the government in 1834 declared radical political organizations illegal. Rioting broke out in Lyon and Paris in protest, where for two days government troops massacred hundreds of insurgents, and arrested some 2,000 republican leaders. In 1835, following an attempt to assassinate Louis Philippe, the government passed a censorship law, which forbade the publication of articles attempting to inspire contempt for the king and which prohibited the printing of any drawing or emblem without prior governmental approval.

French republicans and socialists

These repressive measures served only to increase dissatisfaction with the regime. Guizot was advised by more progressive members of the legislature to extend the franchise to professionals whose lack of wealth now denied them the vote, but whose general adherence to the doctrines of liberalism was unquestioned. Guizot unwisely refused, thereby driving these moderates into the camp of the more radical republicans. By 1847, various elements within the opposition were disaffected enough to instigate a general campaign of agitation throughout France. At political banquets, republicans such as the poet Alphonse de Lamartine (1790–1869) and socialist republicans such as Louis Blanc (see above, p. 857) preached drastic reform, though not outright revolution. Contrary to the expressed wishes of the king, a giant protest meeting was announced for February 22, 1848. The day before, the government forbade the meeting. Rioting and barricading during the following two days ended in the abdication of Louis Philippe and increased demands for a republic.

The origins of the Revolution of 1848 in France

4. THE REVOLUTION OF 1848 IN FRANCE

The February revolution in France was a catalyst which, as we shall see, helped to produce uprisings in the succeeding months throughout much of Europe. Meanwhile, in Paris, a provisional government was

A National Workshop. When few could read, newspapers were heard rather than scanned. Under government auspices, these workshops achieved a good deal less than Louis Blanc had envisioned.

Republican-socialist split: Blanc's workshops

established consisting of ten men, seven of whom, including Lamartine, were middle-of-the-road republicans; three of whom, including Blanc, were socialists. The tensions between middle-class republicans and radical socialists, which had been masked by a common disgust with the government of Louis Philippe, now emerged to shape the political events of the ensuing months in several specific ways. Blanc insisted upon the establishment of national workshops, institutions he had championed as a writer, which were to be organized by trades as producers' cooperatives, where men and women workers would be trained if necessary, put to work, and paid two francs a day when employed and a smaller stipend when unemployed. Instead, the government established what it called workshops, but what amounted to nothing more than a program of public works in and around Paris, where economic conditions had resulted in widespread unemployment. Initially, plans had called for the employment of no more than ten or twelve thousand in projects throughout the city. But with unemployment running as high as 65 percent in construction trades and 51 percent in textiles and clothing, workers began to flood into the government's so-called workshops, as many as 66,000 by April, and 120,000 by June.

Continuing agitation

Paris meanwhile attracted numbers of radical writers, organizers, and agitators. The provisional government had removed all restrictions upon the formation of political clubs and the dissemination of political literature. As a result, 170 new journals and more than 200 clubs formed within weeks; the club headed by the socialist Auguste Blanqui claimed a membership of some 3,000. Delegations claiming to represent the oppressed of all European countries—Chartists, Hungarians, Poles—moved freely about the city, attracting attention, if not devoted followings, and contributing to tension which was convincing more and more members of the middle class that stern measures were needed to forestall further insurrectionary outbreaks. The middle-class side was strengthened as a result of elections held at the end of April. The provisional government had been pressured by Parisian radicals into decreeing universal manhood suffrage. Yet the election returned only a small proportion of radical socialists. The largest blocs consisted of "true," or moderate republicans and monarchists—this latter group was divided, however, between supporters of the Bourbon dynasty and the Orleanist Louis Philippe. The generally conservative tenor of the newly elected assembly strengthened the hand of those who pressed for the repression of the socialists. It also, naturally, convinced the socialists that once again, as in the 1790s, a potentially radical revolution had been betrayed by the timid, self-serving middle class.

By late spring, a majority of the assembly believed that the workshop system represented both an unbearable financial drain and a serious threat to social order. At the end of May, the workshops were closed to new enrollment as a first step toward barring membership to all who had resided for less than six months in Paris and sending all members between the ages of eighteen and twenty-five to the army. Thousands of workers lost their state-financed jobs, and with them their best chance for survival. Desperate, they and their supporters once more threw up barricades across Paris. From June 23–26, they defended themselves in an ultimately hopeless military battle against armed forces recruited, in part, from willing provincials eager enough to assist in the repression of the urban working class. Whether or not the Parisian insurrectionists were fighting as members of a beleaguered class, or simply as men and women on the brink of starvation, is a matter that historians continue to debate. That they were taken seriously as a revolutionary threat can be seen by the ferocity with which they were hunted out once the street fighting had ceased. About 3,000 were killed and 12,000 more arrested, the majority of whom were deported to Algerian labor camps.

The "June Days"

In the aftermath of the "June Days," the French government moved quickly to bring order to the country. The assembly, faced with the task of drafting a republican constitution, contained a large number of men to whom the idea of a republic was anathema. Assembly members therefore arranged for the immediate election of a president. Their hope was that a strong leader might assist in bringing dissidents to heel. Four candidates stood: Lamartine, the moderate republican; General Eugene Cavaignac, who had commanded the troops in June; Alexander Ledru-Rollin, a socialist; and Louis Napoleon Bonaparte, nephew of the emperor, who polled more than twice as many votes as the other three candidates combined.

The imposition of order

The astonishing upstart Louis Napoleon had spent most of his life in exile. Returning to France after the Revolution of 1830, he was imprisoned a few years later for attempting to provoke a local uprising. But in 1846 he escaped to England, where he was supplied with funds by

*The rise of Louis
Napoleon*

A second emperor

*Napoleon III's Decree Dissolving
the National Assembly*

both British and French reactionaries. By the summer of 1848 the situation in France was such that he knew it was safe to return. In fact, he was welcomed with open arms by members of all classes. Conservatives were looking for a savior to protect their property against the onslaughts of the radicals. Workers were beguiled by his glittering schemes for prosperity in his book, *The Extinction of Pauperism,* and by the fact that he had corresponded with Louis Blanc and with Pierre Proudhon, the anarchist. In between these two classes was a multitude of patriots and hero-worshipers to whom the very name Napoleon was a matchless symbol of glory and greatness. It was chiefly to this multitude that the nephew of the Corsican owed his astounding triumph. As one old peasant expressed it: "How could I help voting for this gentleman—I whose nose was frozen at Moscow?"

With grandiose dreams of emulating his uncle, Louis Napoleon was not long content to be merely president of France. Almost from the first he used his position to pave the way for a higher calling. He enlisted the support of the Catholics by permitting them to regain control over the schools and by sending an expedition to Rome to restore the pope to his temporal power. He courted the workers and the middle class by introducing old-age insurance and laws for the encouragement of business. In 1851, alleging the need for extraordinary measures to protect the rights of the masses, he proclaimed a temporary dictatorship and invited the people to grant him the power to draw up a new constitution. In the plebiscite held on December 21, 1851, he was authorized by an overwhelming majority (7,500,000 to 640,000) to proceed as he liked. The new constitution, which he put into effect in January 1852, made the president an actual dictator. After exactly one year Louis Napoleon Bonaparte ordered another plebiscite and, with the approval of over 95 percent of the voters, assumed the title of Napoleon III, emperor of the French.

What is the significance of the French Revolution of 1848 and its political aftermath in the history of middle-class liberalism, which is our subject? Two points need particular emphasis. First, we must recognize the pivotal role of the liberal middle class. Under Louis Philippe, it increasingly perceived itself and its particular interests as neglected. Denied a direct political voice because of a severely limited franchise, it swung to the left, allying itself with radicals who, by themselves, would probably have stood no chance of permanent success. Yet no sooner had Louis Philippe abdicated than the liberal middle class began to wonder if "success" was not about to bring disaster upon its heels. And so it swung again, this time to the right, where it found itself confronting the mysterious and yet not entirely unattractive prospect of Louis Napoleon. He, in turn, was clever enough to understand this first lesson of 1848, that in France no government could survive that did not cater to the interests of the middle class. By assisting it to achieve its liberal economic goals, the emperor helped it forget just how heavily he was trampling on its political liberties.

Yet 1848 proved that there was now in France another element—class consciousness may, at this point, not yet be the correct term—that governments ignored at their peril. If mid–nineteenth-century Europe saw the middle class closer than ever to the center of power, it saw the workers moving rapidly in from the edge. Their barricades could, if necessary, be destroyed, and their demands ignored, but only at an increasingly grave risk to the fabric of the state. Middle-class liberalism, if it was to thrive, would not only have to pay lip service to working-class demands, but in some measure accommodate to them as well.

Napoleon III

5. LIBERALISM IN FRANCE AND BRITAIN AFTER 1850

Napoleon III recognized the vital role that public opinion had now assumed in the management of affairs of state. He labored hard and successfully to sell his empire to the people of France. He argued that legislative assemblies only served to divide a nation along class lines. With power residing in him, he would unite the country as it had not been for generations. The French, who craved order following their recent political misadventures, bought the program he was selling willingly enough. Napoleon III modeled his constitution upon that of his uncle. An assembly, elected by universal manhood suffrage, in fact possessed almost no power. It could do no more than approve legislation drafted at the emperor's direction by a Council of State. Elections were manipulated by the government to insure the return of politically docile representatives. Control of finance, the army, and foreign affairs rested exclusively with the emperor. France was a democracy only in the sense that its people were periodically afforded a chance, through elections, to express their approval of Napoleon's regime.

Napoleon III's
constitution

In return for the gift of almost absolute power, Napoleon III gave the French what they appeared to want. For the middle class, he provided a chance to make a great deal of money. The device of the *Crédit Mobilier,* an investment banking institution, facilitated the expansion of industry by selling its shares to the public and using its income to underwrite various entrepreneurial schemes. In 1863 a limited liability law encouraged further investment by guaranteeing that stockholders could lose no more than the par value of their stock no matter how indebted the company in which they had invested. Railways, owned by the state, spread across the country, and spurred further industrial expansion. So prosperous did the French economy appear that Napoleon was prepared to follow Britain's lead in pressing for tariff-free trade between the two countries. A treaty was signed in 1860; though funds were set aside to compensate French industries for any loss they might suffer, they were never completely expended, suggesting that French manufacturers were now well enough established to meet the threat of British competition. The apparent satisfaction of the middle class with

Napoleon III and the
middle class

Paris Under the Second Empire. The Avenue de l'Imperatrice was designed for the enjoyment of the middle class.

Empress Eugénie

Napoleon III and the workers

Napoleon's regime provides a measure with which to assess the state of liberalism in France after 1850. The fact that the country no longer enjoyed a free press, that universities were politically controlled, and that political opposition was repressed seemed to matter very little to most. Liberalism, if it existed at all, existed as the freedom to have one's own economic way.

Napoleon III, though he catered to the middle class, did not fail to court the favor of the workers as well. He encouraged the establishment of hospitals and instituted a program of free medical assistance. More important, he permitted, if he did nothing to encourage, the existence of trade unions and in 1864 introduced legislation to legalize strikes. Ultimately, he appealed to the workers much as he appealed to the middle class, as a glamorous, if not heroic symbol of his country's reemergence as a leading world power. The activities of his court, and of his glamorous empress, Eugenie, were well publicized. The reconstruction of Paris into a city of broad boulevards and grand open spaces was calculated to provide appropriate scenery for the theatre of empire—as well as to lessen the chances for successful proletarian barricade-building across narrow streets.

Grandeur, however, appeared to Napoleon III to demand an aggressive foreign policy. Although early in his regime he declared himself in favor of that central liberal tenet—international peace—he was soon at war: first against Russia in the Crimea; then in Italy; then in Mexico, where he attempted to assist in the establishment of another empire; and finally and disastrously with Prussia. The details of these adventures are part of the subject of the following chapter. It is enough at this point to remark that Napoleon III's foreign policy reflects clearly how far he—and the rest of France with him—had subordinated the liberal heritage of the first French Revolution to that of another of its legacies: national glory.

What, meanwhile, of the liberal tradition in Britain? There the course of liberalism was altered by changes occurring within the working class. Industrialization had, by this time, begun to foster and sustain a growing stratum of labor "aristocrats," men whose particular skills, and the increasing demand for them, allowed them to demand wages high enough to insure them a fairly comfortable standard of living. These workers—concentrated for the most part within the building, engineering, and textile industries—turned from the tradition of militant radicalism that had characterized the so-called hungry forties. Having succeeded within the liberal economic system imposed upon Britain by the middle class, they were now prepared to accept many liberal, middle-class principles as their own. They believed in self-help, achieved by means of cooperative societies or through trade unions, whose major function was the accumulation of funds to be used as insurance against old age and unemployment. They believed in education as a tool for advancement, and patronized the Mechanics Institutes and other similar institutions either founded by them or on their behalf.

Yet the labor aristocracy, as it came to appreciate its ability to achieve a decent life for itself within the capitalist system, grew all the more dissatisfied with a political system which excluded it from any direct participation in the governmental process. Although some pressed for extension of the franchise as democrats, as many argued for it on the same grounds the middle class had used in 1832. They were responsible workers, whose loyalty to the state could not be questioned. As such, they were a bona fide "interest," as worthy of the vote and of direct representation as the middle class. They were joined in their campaign by many middle-class reformers who continued to chafe at the privileged position of national institutions which they associated with the landed society and the old order. Many middle-class men and women, for example, were dissenters from the Church of England; yet they were forced to pay taxes to support a church which was staffed, in the main, by sons of the gentry. Their sons were denied the facilities of the nation's ancient universities, Oxford and Cambridge, unless those sons subscribed to the articles of faith of the Anglican Church.

Together with working-class leaders, these middle-class dissidents organized a Reform League to campaign across the country for a new reform bill and a House of Commons responsive to their interests. Though by no means revolutionary, the reformers made it clear by their actions that they were determined to press their case to the utmost. Politicians in Britain in the 1860s were confronted by a situation not unlike that which had faced Guizot in France in 1848: middle class, lower middle class, and skilled workers discontented and demanding reform. Unlike Guizot, however, the leaders of both British political parties, Conservative (formerly Tory) and Liberal (formerly Whig), were prepared to concede what they recognized it would be dangerous to withhold. In fact, it was a Conservative government, with the future prime minister Benjamin Disraeli as its leader in the House of Commons, that enacted the second Reform Bill in 1867. The bill doubled the franchise by extending the vote to any males who paid poor rates or rent of ten pounds or more a year in urban areas (this would mean, in general, the skilled workers), and to tenants paying rent of twelve pounds or more in the counties. Seats were again redistributed as in 1832, with large northern cities gaining representation at the expense of the rural south. The "responsible" working class had been deemed worthy to participate in the affairs of state. For the next twenty years it showed its appreciation by accepting its apprentice position without demur, and by following the lead prescribed by the middle class.

The Triumph of British liberalism

The decade or so following the passage of the Reform Bill of 1867 marked the high point of British liberalism. The labor aristocracy was accommodated with the Education Act, virtually guaranteeing a primary education to all, with legalization of trade unions, and with a series of measures designed to improve living conditions in the great cities; yet it was the middle class that set the governmental tone. Under Disraeli and his Liberal counterpart William Gladstone, and with the cooperation of the newly enfranchised skilled workers, Britain celebrated the triumph of the liberal principles of free trade, representative—but not democratic—government, and general prosperity.

SELECTED READINGS

• *Items so designated are available in paperback editions.*

Anderson, R. D., *Education in France, 1848–1870*, New York, 1975. Covers every level of formal education and its practical and theoretical relationship to state and society.

• Artz, Frederick B., *Reaction and Revolution, 1814–1832*, New York, 1934. A European survey, dated but still useful.

• Binkley, Robert C., *Realism and Nationalism, 1852–1871*, New York, 1935.

Blake, Robert, *Disraeli*, London, 1966. A masterful biography.

Duveau, Georges, *1848: The Making of a Revolution*, New York, 1967. Focuses on the working class during the revolution in Paris: their unity at the outset, their division in the "June Days."

Finer, Samuel E., *The Life and Times of Edwin Chadwick*, London, 1952. An excellent biography of the great English Benthamite reformer.

Halèvy, Elie, *A History of the English People*, Vols. II–IV, London, 1949–52. The best survey of nineteenth-century England, comprehensive and analytical.

Harrison, Royden, *Before the Socialists: Studies in Labour and Politics, 1861–1881*, London, 1965. Examines the social and political background of franchise extension in Britain.

- Hobsbawm, E. and Rudé G., *Captain Swing: A Social History of the Great English Agricultural Uprising of 1830*, New York, 1975.
- Houghton, Walter, *The Victorian Frame of Mind, 1830–1870*, New Haven, Conn., 1957. An outstanding attempt to synthesize the Victorian middle-class mentality.
- Kissinger, Henry, *A World Restored: Metternich, Castlereagh, and the Problem of Peace, 1812–1822*, Boston, 1957. By an admirer of Metternich.
- Langer, William L., *Political and Social Upheaval, 1832–1852*, New York, 1969. (Several chapters have been published separately under the title *The Revolutions of 1848*.)
- McCord, Norman, *The Anti–Corn Law League,* London, 1955.
  Magnus, Philip, *Gladstone: A Biography,* London, 1955.
  Merriman, John M., ed., *1830 in France*, New York, 1975. Recent scholarship emphasizing the nature of revolution and examining events outside of Paris.
- Nicolson, Harold, *The Congress of Vienna, a Study in Allied Unity,* New York, 1946.
- Pinkney, David, *Napoleon III and the Rebuilding of Paris*, Princeton, N.J., 1958. An interesting account of the creation of modern Paris during the Second Empire.
  ———, *The French Revolution of 1830,* Princeton, N.J., 1972. A reinterpretation, now the best history of the revolution.
  Roberts, David, *Victorian Origins of the British Welfare State*, New Haven, Conn., 1960. Examines various nineteenth-century reforms in England.
- Robertson, Priscilla, *The Revolutions of 1848: A Social History,* Princeton, N.J., 1952.
  de Sauvigny, G. de Bertier, *The Bourbon Restoration*, New York, 1967. An outstanding work. The best history of a neglected period.
- Stearns, Peter N., *1848: The Revolutionary Tide in Europe,* New York, 1974.
  Thompson, J. M., *Louis Napoleon and the Second Empire,* Oxford, 1954. A good biography. Presents Louis Napoleon as a modern Hamlet.
  Woodward, E. L., *The Age of Reform,* Oxford, 1962. An excellent survey from the Oxford History of England series.
- Zeldin, Theodore, *The Political System of Napoleon III*, New York, 1958. Examines the processes by which Napoleon maintained power as the first modern dictator.
  ———, *France, 1848–1951,* 2 vols., Oxford, 1973–77.

SOURCE MATERIALS

- Flaubert, Gustave, *L'Education Sentimentale*, London, 1961. Contains an unsympathetic but memorable portrait of the Revolution of 1848 and of the bourgeois style of life that contributed to its outbreak.
- Greville, Charles Fulke, *Memoirs,* ed. by Roger Fulford, New York, 1963. Originally published in seven volumes in 1875, these comprise the diaries of the secretary to the Privy Council for the years 1821–1861. An excellent source for the court and politics of the period.

- Mill, John Stuart, *Autobiography,* London, 1873. The life of one of the germinal minds of the century. Serves as an excellent social history of the period.
- ———, *On Liberty,* ed. by P. Appleman, New York, 1975. The classic statement of liberalism first published in 1859.
- Price, Roger, ed., *1848 in France,* Ithaca, N.Y., 1975. An excellent collection of eyewitness accounts, annotated.

  Stewart, John Hall, *The Restoration Era in France, 1814–1830,* Princeton, N.J., 1968. A brief narrative and a good collection of documents.

Chapter 28

NATIONALISM AND NATION-BUILDING (1815–1870)

The present problem, the first task . . . is simply to preserve the existence
and continuance of what is German.

> —Johann Fichte, *Addresses to the German Nation*

The great questions of the day will not be decided by speeches or by majority decisions—that was the mistake of 1848 and 1849—but by blood
and iron.

> —Otto von Bismarck, speech, 1862

I f the history of nineteenth-century Britain and France can be studied against a general background of middle-class liberalism, that of much of the rest of Europe during the same period must be understood in terms of a more complex combination of the forces of liberalism, nationalism, and nation-building. We shall define nationalism as a sentiment rooted in broad historical, geographical, linguistic, or cultural circumstances. It is characterized by a consciousness of belonging, in a group, to a tradition derived from those circumstances, which differs from the traditions of other groups. Nation-building is the political implementation of nationalism, the translation of sentiment into power.

Nationalism and nation-building defined

Men and women in Britain and France during the nineteenth century entertained national as well as liberal sentiments. When Britain's prime minister, Lord Palmerston, declared in 1850 that any British citizen, in any part of the world, had but to proclaim, like a citizen of the Roman Empire, "civis Romanus sum" ("I am a citizen of Rome") to summon up whatever force might be necessary to protect him from foreign depradations, he was echoing his countrymen's pride in the powers of their nationhood. When the French rejoiced in 1840 at the return of the Emperor Napoleon's remains from St. Helena to an elaborate shrine in Paris, they were reliving triumphs that had become

Nationalism in Britain and France

part of their nation's heritage. Palmerston's boast and Napoleon's bones were both artifacts of national traditions and sentiments bound up in the life of the English and the French.

Nineteenth-century nationalism in other areas of Europe was to be a more assertive phenomenon than it was in Britain and France, which had for centuries existed as particular geographical, cultural, and political entities. Elsewhere, common traditions and assumptions were less clearly articulated, because the political unity that might have helped define them did not exist. East Prussians or Venetians had no difficulty in perceiving of themselves as such; history had provided them with those identities. But history had not provided them, except in the most general way, with identities as Germans or Italians. They had to make a deliberate effort to think of themselves in those terms before the terms could have any political reality.

Neither nationalism nor nation-building stood in necessary opposition to liberalism. Indeed, to the extent that nationalism celebrated the achievements of a particular common people over those of a cosmopolitan aristocratic elite, it reflected liberalism's abhorrence of traditional privilege. Yet to liberalism's readiness to accept the new, nationalism responded with an appreciation, if not veneration, of the past. And to the liberals' insistence upon the value and importance of individualism, nation-builders replied that their vital task might require the sacrifice of some measure of each citizen's freedom. The success of nation-building rested upon the foundation of a general balance of international power, achieved by the European states during the half-century after 1815. The emergence of new nations—a unified Italy and Germany—would require readjustments to that balance. But accommodation remained possible, with only minor skirmishes marring the stability of the settlement achieved at the Congress of Vienna.

1. ROMANTICISM AND NATIONALISM

As we noted in the preceding chapter, nationalism was in part a child of the French Revolution. It was closely related, as well, to the intellectual movement that has been called "romanticism." Romanticism was so broad and so varied that it all but defies definition, if not analysis. Perhaps as much as anything, romanticism represented a reaction against the rationalism of the eighteenth-century Enlightenment. Where the eighteenth century relied on reason, the romantics put their faith in emotion. The eighteenth century understood the mind as a blank tablet, which received knowledge from impressions imprinted upon it through the senses by the external world. Romantics also believed in the importance of sense experience. But they insisted that innate sensibility—that which constituted a person's own particular personality—was inherited, and therefore present in the mind from birth. Knowledge, then, for the romantic, was the product of both innate feelings *and* external perceptions. Romanticism thus stressed individualism, and the individual creativity that resulted from the interaction of unique personality with external experience. At the same time, by stressing the inheritance of attitudes, it also celebrated the past. And that celebration was its link with nationalism.

Johann von Herder

Romanticism and nationalism were connected by their common belief that the past should be made to function as a means of understanding the present and planning for the future. It was in Germany that this notion received its fullest airing and most enthusiastic reception. One of the earliest and most influential German romantics was Johann von Herder (1744–1803). A Protestant pastor and theologian, his interest in past cultures led him, in the 1780s, to set out his reflections in a lengthy and detailed treatise, *Ideas for a Philosophy of Human History*. Herder traced what he perceived to be the progressive development of European society from the time of the Greeks through the Renaissance. He believed that civilization was not the product of an artificial, international elite—a criticism of Enlightenment thinking—but of the genuine culture of the common people, the *Volk*. No civilization could be considered sound which did not continue to express its own unique historical character, its *Volksgeist*. Herder did not argue that one *Volksgeist* was either better or worse than any other. He insisted only that each nation must be true to its own particular heritage. He broke dramatically with the Enlightenment idea that human beings could be expected to respond to human situations in more or less the same fashion, and with the assumption that the value of history was simply to teach by example.

Herder's intellectual heirs, men like the conservative German romantics Friedrich Schlegel (1772–1829) and Friedrich von Savigny (1779–1861) condemned the implantation of democratic and liberal ideas—"foreign" to Germany—in German cultural soil. History, they argued, taught that institutions must evolve organically—a favorite word of the political romantics, and that proper laws were the product of historical growth, not simply deductions from universal first principles. This idea was not peculiar to German romantics. The English romantic poet and philosopher Samuel Taylor Coleridge (1772–1834) argued against the utilitarian state and in favor of giving that ancient institution, the national church, a larger role in the shaping of society. The French conservative Chateaubriand (1768–1848) made much the same case in his treatise, *The Genius of Christianity*, published in 1802. The past is woven into the present, he declared. It cannot be unwoven without destroying the fabric of a nation's society. Religion, both as individual experience and as an expression of national heritage, played a large role in romantic thinking.

The role of history and religion

The theory of the organic evolution of society and the state received its fullest exposition in the writings of the German metaphysician

Georg Wilhelm Hegel

Fichte

Georg Wilhelm Hegel (1770–1831). Professor of philosophy at the University of Berlin, he attracted many adherents. Hegel wrote of history as development: Social and political institutions grew to maturity, achieved their purposes, and then gave way to others. Yet the new never entirely replaced the old, for the pattern of change was "dialectic." When new institutions challenged established ones, there was a clash of "thesis" and "antithesis" producing a "synthesis," a reordering of society that retained elements from the past while adapting to the present. Hegel expected, for example, that the present disunity among the German states (thesis), which generated the idea of unity (antithesis), would inevitably result in the creation of a nation-state (synthesis). Hegel had no use for the theory of a state of nature, so popular with philosophers like Rousseau and Hobbes. Men and women have always lived within some society or other, Hegel argued. The institution of the state was itself a natural historic organism; only within that institution, protected by its laws and customs from personal depradations, could men and women enjoy freedom, which Hegel defined not as the absence of restraint but as the absence of social disorder.

These theories of history and of historical development articulated by the romantics relate directly to the idea of nationalism formulated during the same period. The French Revolution provided an example of what a nation could achieve. Nationhood had encouraged the French to raise themselves to the level of citizenship; it had also allowed them to sustain attacks from the rest of Europe. Applying the historical lessons of the French Revolution and the theories of romantics, Germans, in particular, were roused to a sense of their own historical destiny. The works of the philosopher J. G. Fichte (1762–1814) are an example of this reawakening. As a young professor at the University of Jena, Fichte had at first advanced a belief in the importance of an individual's inner spirit, the creator of its own moral universe. Devoid of national feeling, he welcomed the French Revolution as an emancipator of the human spirit. Yet when France conquered much of Germany, Fichte's attitude changed dramatically. He adopted Herder's notion of a *Volksgeist;* what mattered was no longer the individual spirit, but the spirit of a whole people, expressed in its customs, traditions, and history. In 1808, Fichte delivered a series of *Addresses to the German Nation,* in which he declared the existence of a German spirit, not just one among many such spirits, but superior to the rest. The world had not yet heard from that spirit; he predicted it soon would. Although the French military commander in Berlin, where Fichte spoke, believed the addresses too academic to warrant censorship, they expressed a sentiment that aided the Prussians in their conscious attempt to rally themselves, and, as a political *Volk,* to drive out the French.

Nationalism, derived from romantic notions of historical development and destiny, manifested itself in a variety of ways. The brothers Grimm, editors of *Grimm's Fairy Tales* (1812) traveled across Germany to study native dialects, and collected folktales that were published as part of a national heritage. The poet Friedrich Schiller's (1759–1805) drama of *William Tell,* the Swiss hero (1804), became a rallying cry for German national consciousness. In Britain, Sir Walter Scott (1771–1832) retold in many of his novels the popular history of Scotland, while the poet William Wordsworth (1770–1850) consciously strove to express the simplicity and virtue of the English people in collections such as his *Lyrical Ballads (1798).* Throughout Europe, countries assiduously catalogued the relics of their historical past as in the society for publishing the *Monumenta Germaniae Historica* (Monuments of German History), founded in 1819; the French École des Chartes (1821); and the English Public Records Office (1838). In France, the neoclassical style, typified by the paintings of David, and used by Napoleon to exalt his image, gave way to the turbulent romanticism of painters like Eugène Delacroix, whose painting *Liberty Leading the People (1830)* was a proclamation not only of liberty, but of the courage of the French nation. Music, too, reflected national themes, though not until a generation or so after 1815. Many of Guiseppe Verdi's (1813–1901) operas, for example, *Don Carlo,* contained musical declarations of faith in the possibility of an Italian *risorgimento: a resurrection of the Italian spirit.* The operas of Richard Wagner (1813–1883)—in particular, those based on the German epic, *Song of the Nibelung*—managed to raise veneration for the myths of Nordic gods and goddesses to the level of pious exaltation. Architects, though they found it difficult to escape entirely from the neoclassicism of the eighteenth century, often tried to resurrect a "national" style in their designs. Sir Charles Barry, assigned the task of redesigning the British Houses of Parliament following their destruction by fire in 1836, managed to mask a

Giuseppe Verdi

Romanticism, nationalism, and the arts

See color plates following page 960

Houses of Parliament, London. Redesigned by Sir Charles Barry with a Gothic facade after the earlier structure was destroyed by fire.

*A William Blake Etching for a
Children's Book Written by Mary
Wollstonecraft*

George Sand

straightforward and symmetrical classical plan behind a Gothic screen, intended to acknowledge the country's debt to its own past. All this creative activity was the spontaneous result of artists' and writers' enthusiastic response to the romantic movement. Yet politicians soon perceived how historical romanticism might serve their nationalist ends. They understood how an individual work of art, whether a painting, a song, a drama, or a building, could translate into a national symbol. And they did not hesitate to assist in that translation when they deemed it useful.

Though romanticism and nationalism shared a common devotion to the past, romantics were not necessarily nationalists. Indeed, romanticism was explicitly international in its celebration of nature, and above all, of individual creativity. The romantics declared that nature was best perceived not by reason, but by the senses. And they respected those elements of nature which appeared the product of chance, not rational order. Whether as a single flower or a mountain range, nature was welcomed as it impressed itself directly on the senses. Men and women were declared free to interpret nature—and life as well—in terms of their individual reactions to it, not simply as it might reflect a set of general rational precepts. The English poet Percy Shelley (1792–1822), the German poet Heinrich Heine (1797–1856), the French novelist Victor Hugo (1802–1885), the Spanish painter Franciso Goya (1746–1828)—all characteristic figures of the romantic movement—expressed in their works romanticism's concern for the experiences of human individuals, a concern that transcended national boundaries. Human experience, romantics believed, was not linked to any one national tradition or *Volksgeist,* but rather to transcendant nature. The paintings of the Englishmen William Blake (1757–1827) and J. M. W. Turner (1775–1851), although they often reflect "Englishness," transcend nationalism by recording a communion with the fundamental elements of nature.

Romantics were internationalists because they enjoyed freedom from the confinement of any boundary—metaphysical or political—which tended to restrict a person's ability to realize his or her potential. In this way romanticism encouraged women to make themselves heard. The Englishwoman Mary Wollstonecraft (1759–1797), author of *A Vindication of the Rights of Woman;* Madame de Staël (1766–1817), an emigré from France to Germany during the revolutionary period, whose essay *De l'Allemagne* (On Germany) was steeped in romanticism; George Sand (1804–1876), whose novels, and whose life, proclaimed allegiance to the standards of radical individualism—these women exemplify romanticism's readiness to break with the past, and its assumptions and stereotypes, if they stood in the path of individual expression.

Romantics, as worshipers of individuality, worshiped "genius." The genius was possessed of a spirit which could not be analyzed and must be allowed to make its own rules. (It was the particular genius of an entire people, of course, that Herder extolled as the *Volksgeist.*) And the human spirit must never allow itself to be fettered by national prescriptions, any more than by social conventions, in such a way as to prevent enjoyment of its most precious possession, its freedom.

Freedom and the problem of self-recognition were major themes in the work of two of the giants of the romantic movement, the composer Ludwig van Beethoven (1770–1827) and the writer Johann Wolfgang von Goethe (1749–1832). The most remarkable quality about Beethoven's compositions is their uniqueness and individuality. In the Fifth Symphony Beethoven reaches the summit of symphonic logic, the Sixth is a glorification of nature, the Seventh a Dionysian revelry, the Eighth a genial conjuring up of the spirit of the eighteenth-century symphony. Then Beethoven, in his later years suffering from deafness, embarks on his last artistic journey: Five piano sonatas, five string quartets, the Ninth Symphony, and the great Mass, *Missa Solemnis,* constitute his final legacy. They fill the listener with awe not so much because of their unusual form or their vast proportions, but because they express boundless individual will and power.

Beethoven

Goethe's dedication to the idea of individual freedom was, in part, the product of his having been born and raised in the free imperial city of Frankfurt. Frankfurt was an international center, a trading place open to intellectual winds from all quarters. Goethe was, in terms of his environment, free from the particularist, nationalist influences which directed the work of other German romantics. Goethe's own "genius" drove him first to the study of law, then medicine, then the fine arts and natural sciences. In 1775 he took up residence at the court

Goethe

Left: *A Page from the Score of Beethoven's Piano Sonata Opus 109 in E Major.* Right: *Ludwig van Beethoven*

An Illustration from Goethe's
Sorrows of Werther

Immanuel Kant

of the young duke of Weimar. Weimar was a tiny German principality with a population of no more than half a million, another cosmopolitan community and in this respect not unlike Frankfurt. Influenced by Herder, Goethe had already published various romantically inclined works, including the immensely popular *Sorrows of Werther,* a novel expressive of Goethe's early restlessness and emotionalism. The almost excessive sensitivity characteristic of Goethe's earlier writings gave way, in his middle years, to the search for a new spirit, equally free and yet more ordered. This mode derived from his experiences in Italy and from his study of the ancient Romans and Greeks. In 1790 Goethe published the first part of his masterpiece, *Faust,* a drama in verse, which he completed a year before his death in 1831. The play, in its retelling of the German legend of the man who sold his soul to the devil in return for universal knowledge, reflects the romantic unwillingness to restrain the spirit; it also expresses Goethe's own recognition of the magnitude of humanity's daring in its desire for unlimited knowledge and its own fulfillment.

The theme of self-realization as humanity's ultimate goal, so characteristic of so much of romantic thinking, contrasted with the notions of those other romantics we have discussed, who, like Herder, insisted upon the subordination of one human spirit to the spirit of a whole people. Immanuel Kant (1724–1804), Goethe's only rival as a thinker during this period, expressed himself as opposed to the idea that unbounded individual freedom was the highest good. Kant, a retiring scholar who lived his life out in the city of Königsberg, where he was born, argued that there were limits to human knowledge, that beyond the world of appearances there lay an unknowable realm of what he called "things in themselves." This thesis, first expounded in his *Critique of Pure Reason* (1781), was further developed in his *Critique of Practical Reason* (1790), in which he attempted to establish proper criteria for personal behavior. If pure reason could neither prove nor disprove the existence of God, Kant argued, practical reason tells us that in the idea of God there exists an idea of moral perfection toward which all people must strive. They must live consistent with what Kant called the "categorical imperative": to act as if one's actions were to become a universal law of nature. Kant argued that only by living according to his categorical imperative could men and women enjoy true freedom. Freedom he defined in terms of self-imposed duty, rather than the absence of restraint or—as in Goethe's case—the compulsion to achieve self-fulfillment.

Whether or not Kant was a romantic is a question that historians have continued to debate. His devotion to reason has often led scholars to consider him a late Enlightenment figure. In one respect, however, Kant certainly thought with the romantics. His insistence that "things in themselves" were ultimately unknowable, reflected the romantics' willingness to surrender to the mysterious. "There is nothing beautiful, pleasing, or grand in life, but that which is more or less mysterious," Chateaubriand wrote, in his defense of Christianity. While Kant was not an explicit defender of Christianity, his philosophy helped perpetuate religious belief, and was thus one in its effect with romanticism. Certainly Kant was not a romantic nationalist, although nationalists used his arguments to support their claim that men and women had a duty to an authority higher than themselves. Kant himself, however, in his treatise *On Perpetual Peace,* published at the height of the revolutionary wars in 1795, argued vehemently against national aggrandizement and in favor of a kind of European federal union.

Kant as a romantic

Romanticism and nationalism bear much the same relationship to each other in the history of nineteenth-century Europe as they do in the thought of the men and women we have just surveyed. At some points, as in England, they appear to run separate courses. At others they join together, as they did in Germany, whose own history lies at the center of the history of both romanticism and nationalism.

*The relationship between
romanticism and
nationalism*

2. NATIONALISM AND NATION-BUILDING: 1800–1848

The humiliating French occupation of Prussia, combined with the growing sense of national destiny exemplified in Fichte's *Addresses,* resulted in a drive on the part of Prussian intellectuals and political reformers to bring their country once more to its former position among European powers. Prussia's crushing defeat by the French in 1806 had been the logical outcome of the inertia that had gripped the country during the half-century or so since the aggressive achievements of Frederick the Great. Unlike the rest of the German states, however, allied directly with France in the Confederation of the Rhine, the separate kingdom of Prussia consciously avoided French "contamination," participating unwillingly in the Continental System, and otherwise holding itself aloof.

*Nationalism and reform in
Prussia, 1806–1815*

Its major task was to rebuild its armies, since only by that means could Prussia reassert itself against Napoleon. To that end, two generals, Gerhard von Scharnhorst and August Gneisenau, instituted changes based on an essential lesson in nation-building they had learned from the French Revolution: that men were far more effective fighters if they believed themselves to have some direct stake in the wars they fought. A reconstituted national army, eventually based upon a system of universal military service, involved the country as a whole in its own defense and grew to become a far more consciously "Prussian" force than it had been heretofore. Officers were recruited and promoted on the basis of merit, not birth, although the large majority continued to come from the Junker (gentry) class. This breach with tradition encouraged the Prussian middle class to take a more ac-

Military reforms

Baron Heinrich vom Stein

*Stein's governmental
reforms*

Economic nationalism

tive and enthusiastic interest in its country's affairs. Old or inefficient officers, despite their social standing, were removed from positions of command; training at the royal cadet school in Berlin was modernized.

These reforms, which illustrate the way in which a liberal desire for modernization might combine with nationalism, paralleled similar changes instituted during the same period under the direction of Prussia's principal minister, Baron Heinrich vom Stein(1757–1831), and his successor, Karl von Hardenberg (1750–1822). Stein was not himself a Prussian; he was initially less interested in achieving a Prussian nation-state than in uniting by some means or other all the various principalities of Germany. Only after the disasters wrought upon the Germans by Napoleon did Stein turn to Prussia as a last resort. He had read Kant and Fichte, and was convinced by them that a state must somehow make its citizens aware of their obligations to the national interest. A sense of duty to the state could hardly be kindled, however, without first convincing men and women that loyalty meant reward as well as obligation. Stein therefore labored to dismantle the caste system which had until that time characterized Prussia, in order to permit individuals to rise within society. Stein's Municipal Ordinance of 1808 was a conscious attempt to increase the middle-class Germans' sense of themselves as citizens—again, a goal shared by both liberals and nationalists. All cities and towns were henceforth required to elect their councilmen, while local justice and security continued to be administered by the central government in Berlin; all other matters, including finance, were left to individual communities. Education played a vital role in nation-building. Schools were ideal agencies for the dissemination of the doctrines of national duty. Recognizing this fact, the Prussian reformers expanded facilities for both primary and secondary education. The University of Berlin, founded in 1808, numbered among its faculty such ardent nationalists as Fichte and Savigny, and was the institutional embodiment of the new spirit that contributed to Prussia's eventual victory over the French.

The history of Prussia between 1815 and 1850 can most easily be understood in terms of its continuing struggle to establish itself as an independent national power within Germany and in opposition to Austria. The most important Prussian victory in this respect was the establishment of the *Zollverein,* or customs union. By the 1840s, the union included almost all of Germany except German Austria. Meanwhile Prussia had produced in the work of the economist Friedrich List (1789–1846), a nationalist response to the internationalism of the liberal free-trade economists. List wrote that while free trade might suit the British, it did not suit Prussia. Economics, he argued, far from being an abstract science equally applicable everywhere, was a discipline which must be grounded in the particular national experience of individual countries. Germany's, and therefore Prussia's, experience demanded <u>not free trade but high tariffs.</u> Only when sheltered behind a protectionist system could Prussia build the factories and manufacture the goods that would guarantee its economic health.

The events which had altered the political shape of Britain and France in the early 1830s—revolution in the latter and liberal reforms in both—did not have lasting counterparts in Germany. A revolutionary movement of sorts, spawned in the universities and youthful secret societies, did result in temporary changes in a few German principalities. But Metternich, still in control of Austrian policy and determined to thwart Prussia's attempts to assert its nationality, used the occasion of those outbreaks to encourage a general antiliberal reaction throughout the German states by playing on the fears of the propertied classes. The diet of the German Confederation, the loose organization of sovereign powers that had replaced the finally defunct "Holy Roman Empire" after 1815, coordinated the repression. Prussia avoided revolution as a result of the reforms instituted a generation before by Stein and Hardenberg. In 1840 <u>Frederick William IV</u> succeeded to the Prussian throne. Apparently devoted to liberal principles, he relaxed censorship laws and encouraged participation in the central government by provincial diets. It soon became apparent, however, that the king was no liberal, but some sort of romantic-nationalist, and an authoritarian as well. He declared himself opposed to constitutionalism, that central doctrine in the liberal canon of beliefs. When middle-class Prussian liberals pressed, in 1847, for control over legislative and budgetary matters in the recently convened assembly of diets (<u>the *Landtag*</u>), the king saw to it that their request was denied. Frederick William then turned his attention to a scheme whereby Prussia might play a far larger role in the confederation. But before his plan could receive a hearing, it was overtaken by the revolutionary movement of 1848, which, as we shall see, engulfed central Europe as it had western Europe, though with different results.

National sentiment, the spirit which served to unite the Prussians, was at the same time <u>operating to divide</u> the heterogeneous elements within the <u>Austrian Empire</u>. Its people, who lived within three major geographical areas—Austria, Bohemia, and Hungary—were composed of a considerable number of different ethnic and language groups: Germans, Czechs, Magyars, Poles, Slovaks, Serbs, and Italians, to name the most prominent. In some parts of the empire, these people lived in isolation; elsewhere they dwelt in direct proximity, if not much harmony, with others. The Austrian Empire attempted to unite these groups by means of a reigning house, the Hapsburgs, and a supposedly benevolent bureaucracy. These devices failed increasingly to satisfy the various groups, in whom a spirit of cultural, if not political, nationalism grew persistently stronger in the years after 1815. In the Polish territories of the empire, where the gentry had for generations been conscious of themselves as Poles, the imperial government

*The failure of liberalism
in Germany*

*Nationalism in the
Austrian Empire*

succeeded in stifling the sentiment by playing off the serfs against their masters, encouraging a class war as a means of preventing an ethnic one. Elsewhere within the empire they were less adroit. In Hungary, nationalism expressed itself in both cultural and political forms. In 1827, a Hungarian national theatre was established at Budapest. The year before, Magyar was substituted for Latin as the official language of government. A political movement, whose most formidable leader was the radical nationalist Louis Kossuth (1802–1894), was at the same time seeking independence and a parliamentary government for Hungary.

Pan-Slavism

The most widespread of the eastern European cultural nationalist movements was Pan-Slavism, at this period just beginning. Slavs included Russians, Poles, Czechs, Slovaks, Slovenes, Croats, Serbs, and Bulgars. Before 1848 Pan-Slavism was an almost exclusively cultural movement, united by a generalized anti-Western sentiment, yet divided by a tendency to quarrel as to the primacy of this or that particular language or tradition. These divisions did not substantially lessen the effect of Pan-Slavism as a further problem of the Austrian Empire. The literature of the movement—for example, the historian Francis Palacky's (1836–1867) *History of the Bohemian People* and the poetry of the revolutionary Pole Adam Mickiewiez (1798–1855), fed the desires of those who wished to rid themselves of what they considered a foreign yoke. In Russia, slavophilism had been held in check by the Western-looking Alexander I. After his death, however, the notion that the Russian people possessed its particular *Volksgeist* increased in general popularity.

Nationalism in Italy

Two other national movements were growing beyond infancy during the years before 1848: one in Italy, the other in Ireland. Among the organizations formed in the confused period at the end of the Napoleonic wars, none was louder in its nationalist proclamations than the Italian *Carbonari*. One member of that group, Joseph Mazzini (1805–1872) founded a society of his own in 1831, Young Italy, which was dedicated to the cause of uniting the peninsula. In 1834, from Switzerland, Mazzini launched a totally unsuccessful verbal assault against the Kingdom of Sardinia, in the hope that the rest of Italy would join with him. Mazzini subsequently contented himself with propagandizing for the cause of Italian nationalism and republicanism, attracting a devoted following, particularly among British liberals. Liberals in Italy, however, mistrusted him. Although they too wished to see Italy one nation, they were dismayed, as "good" liberals, and members of the middle class, by Mazzini's insistence upon a republic, hoping instead to merge existing principalities together into some sort of constitutional monarchy.

Nationalism in Ireland

If Italian nationalism was primarily a middle-class liberal phenomenon at this time, the same was not true of the Irish movement to repeal the union with England. Headed by Daniel O'Connell (1775–1847), it derived its strength from the support of Irish peasants. O'Connell's remarkably successful appeal was based on the hatred all Irish felt for the English, because of the centuries of oppression Irish Catholics had suffered under English Protestant rule. Both before and after the official union of 1801, the English had imposed on the Irish a foreign rule that had brought with it little but poverty and persecution. O'Connell's campaign for the repeal of the union was grounded in the hope that he would be able to negotiate some sort of moderate agreement with the English ruling class. The desires of his followers exceeded him in being far more radical in nature. Neither the separatist hopes of O'Connell, called by the Irish the "Liberator," nor the more genuinely nationalist hopes of his followers, however, were to achieve realization. Unlike the nationalist movements of central Europe, nationalism in Ireland faced a powerful and determined adversary—England—who would for a century deny it victory.

Joseph Mazzini

3. NATIONALISM, LIBERALISM, AND REVOLUTION, 1848

The history of the revolutions of 1848 in central Europe can most easily be understood in terms of two major themes: the first, the struggle of various nationalities, particularly within the Austrian Empire, to assert their own autonomy; the second, the contention between the forces of liberalism and nationalism in Germany.

News of the February revolution in France traveled quickly eastward. By the end of March the Austrian Empire was split apart. Hungary, with Kossuth in the lead, severed all but the most tenuous of links with the House of Hapsburg and prepared to draft its own constitution. In Vienna, workers and students imitated their counter-

The "March Days" in Austria

The March Days in Vienna, 1848

Counternationalism as an
aid to restoration

Civil war in Hungary

parts in Paris, erecting barricades and invading the imperial palace. A measure of the political chaos was the fact that Metternich, veteran of a score of threats to the precarious stability he had crafted, found the pressure this time too great, and fled in disguise to Britain. Deserted by that tower of reactionary strength, the Hapsburg emperor, Ferdinand, yielded to nationalist demands from Bohemia and granted that kingdom its own constitution as well. To the south, Italians launched attacks against the Austrian-held territories in Milan, Naples, Venetia, and Lombardy, where the forces of the Sardinian ruler, King Charles Albert, routed the Austrians.

Yet the forces of national sentiment which had brought Austria to its knees then succeeded in allowing the empire to recoup its fortunes. The paradox of nationalism, as it manifested itself in central Europe, was that as soon as a cultural majority had declared itself an independent or semi-independent state, other cultural minorities within that new state complained bitterly about their newly institutionalized inferiority. This is precisely what happened in Bohemia. There the anti-German Czech majority refused to send delegates to an all-German assembly, meeting at Frankfurt to draft a German constitution. Instead, they summoned a confederation of Slavs to Prague. The delegates, most of them from within the boundaries of the old Austrian Empire, immediately recognized that the idea of a united Germany represented a far greater threat to their political and cultural autonomy than the fact of the empire ever had. The German minority in Bohemia, however, was naturally anxious to participate in discussions which might result in closer union with their ethnic counterparts. They resented the Bohemian government's refusal to do so. The resulting animosities made it all the easier for the Austrians to take advantage of a May 1848 insurrection in Prague, subdue the city, send the Slav congress packing, and reassert control in Bohemia. Although the Austrian government was at this time a liberal one, the product of the March revolution in Vienna, it was no less determined than its predecessor had been to prevent the total dismemberment of the empire. For this reason it was quick to restore Lombardy and Venetia to its realm when quarrels among the heretofore united Italian allies had sufficiently weakened their common stand against the Austrians.

Nationalism and counternationalism in Hungary set the stage for the final act of the restoration of Austrian hegemony. Kossuth's radical party was, above all, a Magyar nationalist party. Once in power, in early 1849 it moved the capital from Pressburg, near the Austrian border, to Budapest, and again proclaimed Magyar as the country's official language. These actions offended national minorities within Hungary, particularly the Croats, who prior to the revolution had enjoyed certain liberties under Austrian rule. The Croatians raised an insurgent army and launched a civil war. The Emperor Ferdinand, once more encouraging division along nationalist lines, named the Croatian rebel Josef von Jellachich his military commander against the

Maygars. By this time the Viennese liberals began to recognize—too late—that their turn might come next. They were right. Despite a second uprising in Vienna in October, the revolution was spent. Forces loyal to the emperor descended upon Vienna from Bohemia. On October 31, the liberal government capitulated.

Once the imperial government had reasserted itself, it labored to suppress nationalist impulses as thoroughly as possible. Austria's ministers recognized that, though tactically advantageous at times, nationalist movements operated generally to the detriment of imperial unity. The emperor's chief minister, Prince Felix von Schwarzenberg, and the minister of the interior, Alexander Bach, both nation-builders, together centralized the state within one united political system. Hungary and Bohemia no longer enjoyed separate rights. Peasants of all ethnic groups, liberated from serfdom as part of the general reform movement, were permitted to retain their freedom, on the grounds of their loyalty to the empire. The law was reformed, again to achieve uniformity, and railways and roads were constructed to link the empire. Tariff walls were erected around imperial boundaries to exclude foreign manufactures, while a free trade area within the empire encouraged home industries. Having done all it could to eradicate separatist movements, the Austrian government thus moved to secure its advantage by engaging in a vigorous campaign of nation-building.

Imperial nation-building

In Prussia, revolution ran a similar course. In March, King Frederick William found himself compelled to yield to demands for a popularly elected legislative assembly. When it met, the body proved particularly sympathetic to the plight of the Polish minority within Prussia, and antagonistic toward the Russians, whom radical legislators saw as the major threat to the spread of enlightened political ideas in central Europe. When the assembly's sympathy with Polish nationalism extended to the granting of self-government to Prussian Poland, however, it generated the same feelings among the German minority there that we have seen arousing minorities within the Austrian Empire. In so doing, it precipitated the same eventual results. Germans in Posen, the major city of Prussian Poland, revolted against the newly established Polish government; not surprisingly, Prussian army units on duty sided with the Germans and helped them crush the new government. Power, it now became clear, lay with the army, professionalized since the days of Gneisenau and Scharnhorst, yet still dominated by the Junkers. Against the armed authority of the military, the radical legislators of Berlin were no match; revolution ended in Prussia as quickly as it had begun.

*The failure of revolution
in Prussia*

Meanwhile, at Frankfurt, Germans engaged in the debate that provides the history of central Europe in these revolutionary years with its second theme: liberalism vs. nationalism. Delegates had been chosen from across Germany and Austria to attend the Frankfurt Assembly. They were largely from the professional classes—professors, lawyers, administrators—and generally devoted to the cause of

The Frankfurt Assembly

Procession of the German National Assembly to Its Opening Session at St. Paul's Church, Frankfurt, May 1848

middle-class liberalism. Many had assumed that their task would resemble that of the assembly which had met in 1789 to draft a constitution for the French: i.e., they would draft a constitution for a liberal, unified Germany. That former convocation, however, had been grounded in the simple but all-important fact that a French nation-state already existed. The French assembly had been elected to give the nation a new shape and new direction. But a centralized sovereign power was there to reshape; there was an authority that could be either commandeered or, if necessary, usurped. The Frankfurt Assembly, in contrast, was grounded upon nothing but its own words. It was a collection of thoughtful, well-intentioned middle-class liberals, committed to a belief that a liberal-national German state could somehow be constituted out of abstract principles. These men, from the start of their deliberations, ruled out the use of violence to achieve their ends. At the same time, they failed to ally themselves with the urban workers. If by 1848 the workers were not yet a self-conscious and articulate class, they were nevertheless a force no reformer or revolutionary could reckon without. Yet the Frankfurt debaters by and large ignored them, and thus denied themselves the one source of power they might otherwise have called to their aid.

Almost from the start, the assembly found itself tangled in the problems of nationality. Who, they asked, were the Germans? A majority of the delegates argued that they were all those who, by language, culture, or geography, felt themselves bound to the enterprise now underway at Frankfurt. The German nation that was to be constituted must include as many of those "Germans" as possible. This point of view came to be known as the "Great German" position. Great Germans found themselves stymied, however, by the unwillingness of other nationalities to be included in their fold. The Czechs in Bohemia, as we have seen, wanted no part of Great Germany. In the end the Great Germans settled that the nation for which they were drafting a constitution should include, among other territories, all Austrian lands except Hungary. This decision meant that the crown of their new country might most logically be offered to the Hapsburg emperor. At this point the voice of the "Little Germans" began to be heard. Prussian nationalism took precedence over German nationalism; a minority argued that Austria should be excluded altogether and the crown instead offered to King Frederick William of Prussia.

Great Germans vs. Little Germans

The liberalism of the assembly was put to the test by events in Austria and Poland in the fall of 1848. When the imperial forces crushed the Czech and Hungarian rebellions, when the Prussian Junkers put an end to Polish self-government, liberals found themselves forced to cheer. They were compelled to support the suppression of minority nationalities; otherwise there would be no new Germany. But their cheers were for the forces not only of German nationalism but of antiliberal authoritarianism. The assembly's most embarrassing moment occurred when it found itself compelled to take shelter behind the Prussian army. Riots broke out in Frankfurt protesting the assembly's willingness to withdraw from a confrontation with the Danes over the future of Germans in Schleswig, a Danish province. That particular area, which many considered to be part of Germany, had been annexed by the Danes in March 1848. The Frankfurters had been unable to do more than ask the Prussians to win Schleswig back for them; and the Prussians had refused. Hence the riots; hence a second request, this time heeded, for Prussian assistance.

Liberalism vs. nationalism

Reduced to the status of dependents, the Frankfurt delegates nevertheless, in the spring of 1849, produced a constitution. By this time Austria, fearing its Prussian rival, had decided to have no more to do with Frankfurt. The Little Germans thus won by default and offered their constitutional monarchy to Frederick William of Prussia. Though tempted, he turned them down, arguing that their constitution was too liberal, embodying as it did the revolutionary notion that a crown could be offered to a monarch. Frederick wanted the crown; but on his own terms. The delegates went home, disillusioned by their experience, many of them convinced that their dual goal of liberalism and nationalism was an impossible one. Some, who refused to surrender that goal, emigrated to the United States, where they believed the goal had already been achieved. Many of those who stayed behind convinced themselves that half the goal was better than none, and sacrificed their liberalism to nationalism.

The end of the assembly

4. NATION-BUILDING, 1850–1870

The twenty years between 1850 and 1870 were years of intense nation-building in the Western world. Of the master-builders, none was more accomplished than the man who brought Germany under Prussian rule, <u>Otto von Bismarck (1815–1898)</u>. He was born into the Junker class. During the revolutionary period of 1848 and 1849, Bismarck had served in the Prussian parliament as a defender of the monarchy. Bismarck was really neither a liberal nor a nationalist; he was a Prussian. When he instituted domestic reforms, he did so not because he favored the "rights" of this or that particular group, but because he thought that his policies would result in a more united, and hence more powerful, Prussia. When he maneuvered to bring other German states under Prussian domination, he did so not in conformity with a grand Germanic design but because he believed that some sort of union was almost inevitable and, if so, that it must come about at Prussia's behest. He prided himself on being a <u>realist;</u> and he became a first-rate practitioner of what has come to be called <u>*Realpolitik*</u>—the politics, not of idealism, but of hard-headed reality.

When Bismarck came to power as minister-president of Prussia in 1862, he was confronted by a liberal parliamentary majority which, since 1859, had opposed a campaign to increase military expenditures despite pressure from the king. This majority had been produced by an electoral system that was part of the constitution granted by Frederick William to Prussia in 1850, following the collapse of the assembly. The parliament was divided into two houses, the lower one elected by universal male suffrage. Votes were apportioned according to one's ability to pay taxes, however; those few who together paid one-third of the country's taxes elected one-third of the legislators. A large landowner or industrialist exercised about a hundred times the voting power of a poor man. Contrary to the king's expectations, however, under this constitution a liberal majority was succeeding in thwarting the plans of the sovereign and his advisors. It was to break this deadlock that King William I, who succeeded his brother Frederick William in 1861, summoned Bismarck. In Bismarck the liberals more than met their match. When they refused to levy taxes, he collected them anyway, claiming that the constitution, whatever its purposes, had not been designed to subvert the state. When liberals argued that Prussia was setting a poor example for the rest of Germany, Bismarck replied that Prussia was admired not for its liberalism but its power.

Whether or not the Germans—or the rest of Europe—admired Prussia's power, they soon found themselves confronted by it. Bismarck proceeded to build a nation that in the short space of eight years came into being as the German Empire. Bismarck was assisted in his task by his readiness to take advantage of international situations as

British Encampment Near Sebastopol, 1854–1855. Photograph taken by Roger Fenton. The Crimean War was the first to be reported to the world by photograph as well as by news dispatch.

they presented themselves, without concerning himself particularly with the ideological or moral implications of his actions. He was aided as well by developments over which he had no initial control but which he was able to turn to his advantage. The first of these, the Crimean War, had occurred in 1854–1856, prior to his taking office. Russia and Turkey, perennial European squabblers, had precipitated the hostilities. Russia invaded the territories of Moldavia and Wallachia (later Rumania) in an attempt to take advantage of the continuing political rot that made the Ottoman Empire an easy prey. In 1854 France and then Britain came to the aid of the Turks by invading Russia's Crimean peninsula. These allies were soon joined by Austria and Sardinia. The quarrel had by this time enlarged to include the question of who was to protect the Christians in Jerusalem from the Turks; it was fueled from the start as well by Britain's continuing determination to prohibit a strong Russian presence in the Near East. The allies' eventual victory was the result primarily of a British blockade of Russia. The peace settlement was a severe setback for Russia, whose influence in the Balkans was drastically curbed. Moldavia and Wallachia were united as Rumania, which, along with Serbia, was granted power as a self-governing principality. Austria, though it had sided with the victor, lost more than it gained from the war. Austrian military resources were severely taxed during the invasion and occupation of Moldavia and Wallachia. It was the subsequent weakness of both Russia and Austria, the result of the Crimean War, that Bismarck used to his advantage in the 1860s.

The Crimean War

In consolidating the German states into a union controlled by Prussia, Bismarck first moved to eliminate Austria from its commanding position in the Germanic Confederation. As a means to this end he inflamed the long-smoldering dispute with Denmark over the possession of Schleswig and Holstein. Inhabited largely by Germans, these two provinces had an anomalous status. Since 1815 Holstein had been

Steps to German unification: (1) weakening of Austria

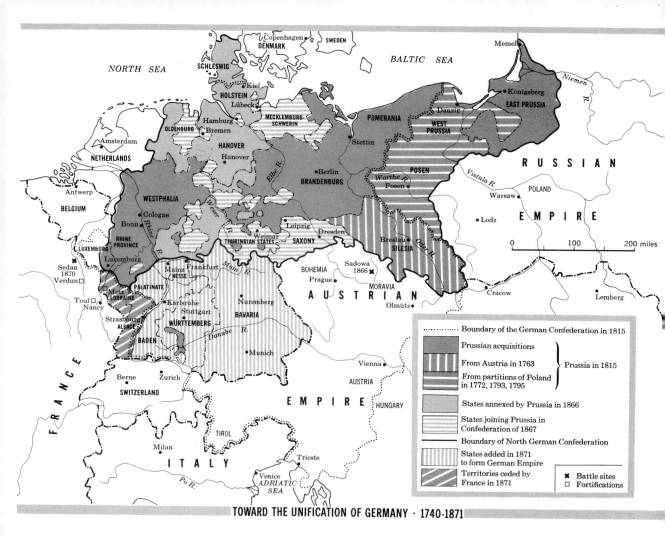

TOWARD THE UNIFICATION OF GERMANY · 1740-1871

included in the Germanic Confederation, but both were subject to the personal overlordship of the king of Denmark. When, in 1864, the Danish king attempted to annex them, Bismarck invited Austria to participate in a war against Denmark. A brief struggle followed, at the end of which the Danish ruler was compelled to renounce all his claims to Schleswig and Holstein in favor of Austria and Prussia. Then the very sequel occurred for which Bismarck ardently hoped: a quarrel between the victors over division of the spoils. The conflict which followed in 1866, known as the Seven Weeks' War, ended in an easy triumph for Prussia. Austria was forced to give up all claims to Schleswig and Holstein, to surrender Venetia, and to acquiesce in the dissolution of the Germanic Confederation. Immediately following the war Bismarck proceeded to unite all of the German states north of the Main River into the North German Confederation.

To achieve the confederation Bismarck willingly turned himself into a democrat. He saw that if he was to attain his end, which was a strong union with Prussia at its head, he would need to cultivate a constituency hitherto untapped by any German politicians: the masses. He appreciated the manner by which Napoleon III had reinforced his regime through plebiscites. And Bismarck understood that the majority of Germans were not particularly enthusiastic supporters of capitalist liberals, of the bureaucracies of their own small states, or of the Austrian Hapsburgs. The constitution he devised for his confederation provided for two chambers: the upper chamber represented the individual states within the union, though not equally; the lower chamber was elected by universal manhood suffrage. The liberal middle class, to say nothing of the Junkerdom, was astonished and dismayed, as well they might be. Bismarck's intention was to use popular support to strengthen the hand of the central government against the interests of both landlords and capitalists. To this end, he struck a bargain with German socialists, who agreed to exchange support for the confederation for universal suffrage.

(2) *courting the masses*

Bismarck's final step in the completion of German unity was the Franco-Prussian War of 1870–1871. He hoped that a conflict with France would kindle the spirit of German nationalism in Bavaria, Würtemberg, and other southern states still outside the confederation. Taking advantage of a diplomatic tempest concerning the right of the Hohenzollerns (Prussia's ruling family) to occupy the Spanish throne, Bismarck worked hard to force a Franco-German misunderstanding. King William agreed to meet with the French ambassador at the resort spa of Ems in Prussia to discuss the Spanish succession. When William telegraphed Bismarck that the demands of the French for perpetual exclusion of the Hohenzollern family from the Spanish throne had been refused, Bismarck released portions of the message to the press so as to make it appear that King William had insulted the ambassador—which he had not done. When the garbled report of what happened at Ems was received in France, the nation reacted with a call for war. The call was echoed in Prussia, where Bismarck published evidence which he claimed proved French designs upon the Rhineland. Once war had been declared the south German states rallied to Prussia's side in the belief that it was the victim of aggression. The war was quickly fought. The French were no match for Prussia's professionally trained and superbly equipped forces. Nor did other European powers come to France's assistance. Austria, the most likely candidate, remained weakened by its recent war with Prussia. The Magyars, who at this time had assumed positions of influence within the Austrian government, were quite prepared to welcome a strengthened Prussia; Prussia's growing strength in Germany would further increase Austria's weakness there. And the weaker Austria was as a German power, the stronger would be the claims of the Magyars to predominance. Once more one nationalist consciousness was grinding against another. The war began in July; it ended in September with the defeat of the French and the capture of Napoleon III himself at Sedan in France.

(3) *the Franco-Prussian War*

Following the collapse of the French imperial government, insurrectionary forces in Paris continued to hold out against the Germans until the winter of 1871. Bismarck meanwhile proceeded to consummate the German union toward which he had worked so assiduously. On January 18, 1871, in the great Hall of Mirrors at Versailles the German Empire was proclaimed. All those states, except Austria, which had not already been absorbed into Prussia declared their allegiance to William I, henceforth emperor or kaiser. Four months later, at Frankfurt, a treaty between the French and Germans ceded the border region of Alsace to the new empire, condemned the French to an indemnity of five billion francs, and thereby broadcast to the world the remarkable success of Bismarck's nation-building.

Events in Italy ran a course almost parallel to that which had led to the unification of Germany. Italy before 1848, it should be remembered, was a patchwork of petty states. The most important of those possessing independence were the Kingdom of Sardinia in the north, the Papal States in the central region, and the Kingdom of the Two Sicilies in the south. The former republics of Lombardy and Venetia were held by Austria, while Hapsburg dependents ruled in Tuscany, Parma, and Modena. As the revolutionary fervor of 1848 swept across the peninsula, one ruler after another granted democratic reforms. Charles Albert of Sardinia outdistanced all the others by providing for civil liberties and a parliamentary form of government. But it soon became evident that the Italians were as interested in nationalism as in liberalism. For some years romantic patriots had been dreaming of the *Risorgimento,* which would restore the nation to the position of glorious leadership it had held in Roman times and during the Renaissance. To achieve this, it was universally agreed that Italy must be welded into a single state. But opinions differed as to the form the new government should take. Young idealists followed the leadership of Mazzini. Religious-minded patriots believed that the most practicable solution would be to federate the state of Italy under the presidency of

Meeting to Arrange Peace Terms at the End of the Franco-Prussian War. On the left is Otto von Bismarck, chancellor of the new German Empire. In the center is Jules Favre and to his right Louis-Adolphe Thiers, both representing the provisional government set up after the overthrow of Napoleon III.

the pope. The majority of the more moderate nationalists advocated a constitutional monarchy built upon the foundations of the Kingdom of Sardinia. The aims of this third group gradually crystallized under the leadership of a shrewd Sardinian nobleman, Count Camillo di Cavour (1810–1861). In 1850 he was appointed minister of commerce and agriculture of his native state and in 1852 prime minister.

The campaign for unification of the Italian peninsula began with efforts to expel the Austrians. In 1848 revolts were organized in the territories under Hapsburg domination, and an army of liberation marched from Sardinia to aid the rebels; but the movement ended in failure. It was then that Cavour, as the new leader of the campaign, turned to less heroic but more practical methods. In 1855, to attract the favorable attention of Great Britain and France, he had entered the Crimean War on their side, despite the fact that he had no quarrel with Russia. In 1858 he held a secret meeting with Napoleon III and prepared the stage for an Italian War of Liberation. Napoleon agreed to cooperate in driving the Austrians from Italy for the price of the cession of Savoy and Nice by Sardinia to France. A war with Austria was duly provoked in 1859, and for a time all went well for the Franco-Italian allies. But after the conquest of Lombardy, Napoleon III suddenly withdrew, fearful of ultimate defeat and afraid of antagonizing the Catholics in his own country by aiding the avowedly anticlerical government of Cavour. Thus deserted by its ally, Sardinia was unable to expel the Austrians from Venetia. Nevertheless, extensive gains were made; Sardinia annexed Lombardy, and acquired by various means the duchies of Tuscany, Parma, and Modena, and the northern portion of the Papal States. Sardinia was now more than twice its original size and by far the most powerful state in Italy.

The second step in consolidating the unity of Italy was the conquest of the Kingdom of the Two Sicilies. This kingdom was ruled by a Bourbon, Francis II, who was thoroughly hated by his Italian subjects. In May 1860 a romantic adventurer, Giuseppe Garibaldi, set out with a regiment of one thousand "red shirts" to rescue his fellow Italians from oppression. Within three months he had conquered the island of Sicily and had then marched to the deliverance of Naples, where the people were already in revolt. By November the whole kingdom of Francis II had fallen to Garibaldi. He at first intended to convert the territory into an independent republic but was finally persuaded to surrender it to the Kingdom of Sardinia. With most of the peninsula now united under a single rule, Victor Emmanuel II, king of Sardinia, assumed the title of king of Italy (March 17, 1861). Venetia was still in the hands of the Austrians, but in 1866, following their defeat in the Seven Weeks' War, they were forced by the Prussians to cede it to Italy. All that remained to complete the unification of Italy was the annexation of Rome. The Eternal City had resisted conquest thus far, largely because of the military protection accorded the pope by Napoleon III. But in 1870 the outbreak of the Franco–Prussian War

Camillo di Cavour

Giuseppe Garibaldi

Garibaldi

SWITZERLAND

AUSTRIA

The Kingdom of Sardinia at the time
of the Congress of Vienna, 1815

Territories acquired, 1859–1860

Territories acquired, 1860–1870

SAVOY
(To France in 1860)

**KINGDOM OF
SARDINIA**

LOMBARDY

•Milan

VENETIA

•Venice

PIEDMONT

Po R.

•Turin

FRANCE

PARMA

MODENA

Genoa•

ROMAGNA

•Bologna

LUCCA

Florence•

Arno R.

P A P A L

TUSCANY

UMBRIA

S T A T E S

Tiber R.

Rome ★

CORSICA
(To France)

A D R I A T I C

S E A

KINGDOM

★ Naples

OF

**KINGDOM
OF
SARDINIA**

T Y R R H E N I A N

THE

S E A

TWO

0   200 miles

SICILIES

Palermo•

•Messina

M E D I T E R R A N E A N

SICILY

S E A

THE UNIFICATION OF ITALY

Italy and the Papal States

compelled Napoleon to withdraw his troops. In September 1870 Italian soldiers occupied Rome, and in July of the following year it was made the capital of the by now united kingdom.

The occupation of Rome brought the kingdom of Italy into conflict with the papacy. Indeed, the whole movement for unification had been characterized by hostility to the Church. Such was inevitably the case, with the pope ruling in the manner of a secular prince over the Papal States and opposing those who would rob him of his domain for the sake of a united Italy. Following the occupation of Rome in 1870, an attempt was made to solve the problem of relations between the state and the papacy. In 1871 the Italian parliament enacted the Law of

Papal Guaranties, purporting to define the status of the pope as a reigning sovereign. This law the reigning pontiff, Pius IX, promptly denounced on the ground that issues affecting the pope could be settled only by an international treaty to which he himself was a party. Whereupon he shut himself up in the Vatican and refused to have anything to do with a government which had so shamefully treated Christ's vicar on earth. His successors continued this practice of voluntary imprisonment until 1929, when a series of agreements between the Italian government and Pius XI effected settlement of the dispute.

Nation-building was the preoccupation of another major country in the first half of the nineteenth century: the United States. The history of the expansion and consolidation of this newly born country into a nation of remarkable economic potential in little over half a century can best be understood in terms of several major factors. The first is the growth of political democracy.

Nation-building in the U.S.: (1) the growth of democracy

The United States did not begin its history as a democracy. Although a few early leaders professed democratic ideals, these were not the doctrines of the most prominent. The authors of the Constitution were not interested in the rule of the masses. The primary aim of the founders of the United States was to establish a *republic* that would promote stability and protect the rights of private property against the leveling tendencies of majorities. For this reason they adopted checks and balances, devised the Electoral College for choosing the president, created a powerful judiciary, and entrusted the selection of senators to the legislatures of the several states.

Following the establishment of a new government under the Constitution of 1789, democratic ideals began to win acceptance in the United States. Until 1801 the Federalist party held the reins of power, representing big landowners, big money, and the conservatives generally. In the latter year the Democratic-Republicans gained control as a result of the election of Thomas Jefferson (1743–1826) to the presidency. This event is often referred to as the Jeffersonian Revolution, on the supposition that Jefferson was the champion of the masses and of the political power of the underprivileged. There is danger in carrying this interpretation too far. In several respects Jefferson's ideas were far removed from democracy in its historic meaning. He strenuously opposed the unlimited sovereignty of the majority. His conception of an ideal political system was an aristocracy of "virtue and talent," in which respect for personal liberty would be the guiding principle.

Thomas Jefferson by Gilbert Stuart

Yet the Jeffersonian movement had a number of democratic objectives of cardinal importance. Its leaders were vigorous opponents of special privilege, whether of birth or of wealth. They worked for the abolition of established churches. They led the campaign for the addition of a Bill of Rights to the Constitution and were almost exclusively responsible for its success. Although professing devotion to the principle of the separation of powers, they actually believed in the supremacy of the representatives of the people and viewed with abhor-

Jeffersonian principles

rence the attempts of the executive and judicial branches to increase their power.

By 1820, these notions were being expressed in more direct and forceful terms. Urban populations grew increasingly conscious of their political importance and demanded attention to their interests. The predominance of the agricultural Old South (the South of the original thirteen colonies) had declined. As a result of the Louisiana Purchase (a vast tract bought from the French in 1803) and of increased settlement in the area known as the Northwest Territory (western New York State and Ohio), a new frontier had come into existence. Life there was characterized by a rugged freedom that left little room for class distinctions. In the struggle to survive, hard work and sharp wits counted for more than birth and education. As a consequence a new democratic spirit, which eventually found its leader in Andrew Jackson (1767–1845), took shape around the principle of equality. The Jacksonian Democrats transformed the doctrines of liberalism into a more radical creed. They pronounced all (excluding slaves, American Indians, and women) politically equal, not merely in rights but in privileges. They were devoted adherents to the causes of suffrage for all white males; the election, rather than appointment, of all governmental office-holders; and the frequent rotation of men in positions of political power—a doctrine that served to put more Democratic politicians into federal office. These democratic beliefs helped encourage a spirit of unity within the United States during a period of rapid territorial expansion.

As the United States continued to acquire more territories in the West (the most notable addition resulting from the conquest of lands

"Meal Time." Between the decks on an immigrant ship to the United States in the mid–nineteenth century.

in the southwest from Mexico in 1846), it not only faced the task of binding those areas and their settlers into the nation. There was, as well, the problem of assimilating the thousands of immigrants who came to America from Europe in the first half of the century. Many were Scottish and English; for them the difficulties of adjusting to a new life in a new country were generally not difficult, since they spoke a common language with their fellow-citizens. For others the problems were far greater. For the Irish, who immigrated in great numbers, particularly during the 1840s, there was the fact of their alien religion, Roman Catholicism. For Germans and others from the Continent, there was the language barrier. The United States's policy towards its immigrants was directed against the creation of any foreign nationalist enclaves apart from the main body of its citizenry. Although foreign-language newspapers were tolerated, and immigrants were free to attend churches and social gatherings as they chose, English remained the language of the public schools, the police, the law courts, and the government. To hold a job, a person was almost always forced to learn at least some English. In this way, the United States encouraged immigrants to shed their "foreign" ways and to commit themselves to their adopted nation.

(2) immigration

If there were enclaves in the United States, they existed in the South, where the institution of slavery and the economic dependence of the planters upon England produced two distinct minorities, neither of which was to be assimilated without resort to war. During the nineteenth century, slavery had been abolished throughout much of the Western world, for both economic and humanitarian reasons. Southern planters continued to insist that without the slave system they would go bankrupt. To humanitarians they responded with arguments based upon theories of racial inferiority and upon their self-professed reputation as benevolent masters. The position of these southern spokesmen grew increasingly distasteful and unconvincing to the North. As the country opened to the west, North and South engaged in a protracted tug-of-war as to which new states were to be "free" and which "slave." Northerners were motivated by more than concern for the well-being of southern blacks. The North was industrializing fast. Capitalists there were demanding protective tariffs to assist them in their enterprises. Southerners favored free trade, since they wished to import British goods in return for the cotton they sold to the manufacturers of Lancashire.

(3) slavery and the South

The American Civil War, when it came in 1861, was a war not about the issue of slavery so much as it was about preserving the union of American states and territories. President Abraham Lincoln undertook the war to defend the unity of the United States. European governments, while never recognizing the Confederacy officially, nevertheless remained sympathetic to its cause. They hoped that the fragmentation of the United States would result in the opening up of markets for their manufactured goods, much as the dissolution of the

The Civil War

Spanish Empire had proved a boon to European commercial interests. The victory of the North in 1865, however, insured the continued growth of the United States as a nation. The Fourteenth Amendment to the Constitution stated specifically that all were citizens of the United States, and not of an individual state or territory. In declaring that no citizen was to be deprived of life, liberty, or property without due process of law, it established that "due process" was to be defined by the national, and not the state or territorial governments.

The years following the American Civil War witnessed the binding together of the nation economically under the direction of northern private enterprise. The symbol of the North's triumph as nation-builder came with the driving of the final spike of the transcontinental Union Pacific railroad in 1869. Nation-building in Europe and the United States helped insure the continuing expansion of capitalism. Liberalism had provided a general climate of opinion and a set of attitudes toward government that encouraged industrialization. Nation-building, in its turn, produced the necessary economic units: large enough to generate the wherewithal to sustain economic growth; confident enough to enter into competition with the British Goliath.

SELECTED READINGS

• *Items so designated are available in paperback editions.*

Artz, Frederick B., *France under the Bourbon Restoration, 1814–1830,* New York, 1963. A basic survey with a good treatment of romanticism.

• Binkley, Robert C., *Realism and Nationalism, 1852–1871,* New York, 1935. An excellent synthesis.

Brunschwig, Henri, *Enlightenment and Romanticism in Eighteenth-Century Prussia,* rev. ed., Chicago, 1974.

• Craig, Gordon, *The Politics of the Prussian Army,* Oxford, 1955. Much more than the title implies. An excellent analysis of Prussian social structure and the role of the army in social reform and unification.

Deutsch, Karl W., and W. J. Folz, eds., *Nation-Building,* New York, 1963.

• Eyck, Erich, *Bismarck and the German Empire,* London, 1958. The best one-volume study of Bismarck.

Eyck, Frank, *The Frankfurt Parliament, 1848–49,* New York, 1968. A detailed study of its composition and procedure.

Ford, Guy Stanton, *Stein and the Era of Reform in Prussia, 1807–1815,* New York, 1922. An old but still valuable work on a leading Prussian reformer.

Gewehr, W. M., *The Rise of Nationalism in the Balkans, 1800–1930,* New York, 1931.

• Gleckner, R. F., and G. E. Ersco, eds., *Romanticism,* Englewood Cliffs, N.J., 1962.

Gooch, G. P., *Germany and the French Revolution,* New York, 1920. Examines the origins of reform in Germany in the aftermath of the French Revolution.

Griffith, G. O., *Mazzini: Prophet of Modern Europe*, London, 1931. The standard biography.

• Hamerow, Theodore, *Restoration, Revolution, Reaction*, Princeton, N.J., 1958. An excellent social and economic history of Germany between 1815 and 1871.

• ———, *The Social Foundations of German Unification, 1858–1871*, 2 vols., Princeton, N.J., 1969. Concentrates on economic factors which determined the solution to the unification question. An impressive synthesis.

Hayes, C. J. H., *The Historical Evolution of Modern Nationalism*, rev. ed., New York, 1968.

Holborn, Hajo, *History of Modern Germany*, Vols. II, III, New York, 1964. The best survey of German history in English.

• Kohn, Hans, *The Idea of Nationalism*, New York, 1944. A perceptive analysis.

———, *Panslavism: In History and Ideology*, South Bend, Ind., 1953.

• Langer, William L., *Political and Social Upheaval, 1832–1852*, New York, 1969.

Mack Smith, Dennis, *Garibaldi: A Great Life in Brief*, New York, 1956.

Namier, Lewis B., *1848: The Revolution of the Intellectuals*, London, 1947. A controversial analysis, highly critical of the Frankfurt Assembly.

Noyes, P. H., *Organization and Revolution: Working-Class Associations in the German Revolutions of 1848–49*, Princeton, N.J., 1966. An important monograph.

• Pflanze, Otto, *Bismarck and the Development of Germany, 1815–1871*, Princeton, N.J., 1963. An impressive analysis of Bismarck's aims and policies.

• Robertson, Priscilla, *The Revolutions of 1848: A Social History*, Princeton, N.J., 1952.

• Rosenberg, Hans, *Bureaucracy, Aristocracy, and Autocracy: The Prussian Experience, 1660–1815*, Cambridge, Mass., 1958. A difficult but valuable book explaining the forces that molded the modern Prussian state.

• Stearns, Peter N., *1848: The Revolutionary Tide in Europe*, New York, 1974.

• Taylor, A. J. P., *The Hapsburg Monarchy, 1809–1918*, rev. ed., London, 1960. An idiosyncratic account by an eminent historian.

SOURCE MATERIALS

Bismarck, Otto von, *Bismarck, the Man and the Statesman, Written and Dictated by Himself*, London, 1899. Bismarck's memoirs, written after his fall from power.

• Clausewitz, Karl von, *On War*, London, 1968. Published posthumously in 1831, this work, in reality a philosophy of war, was perceived by the Prussian military bureaucracy as a mandate for total war—for the subjugation of all interests of the state to war.

Fichte, Johann Gottlieb, *Addresses to the German Nation*, New York, 1968. Presented in 1808 while French armies occupied Prussia, these lectures helped stir a German nationalist spirit.

Schurz, Carl, *The Reminiscences of Carl Schurz*, 3 vols., New York, 1907–8. Especially valuable is Vol. I. A young German liberal in 1848 and a delegate to the Frankfurt Assembly, Schurz spent the rest of his life as an exile in the United States.

Part Six

THE WEST AT THE WORLD'S CENTER

The years between 1870 and 1945 found the West at the center of global affairs. The industrial supremacy of western Europe and the United States gave them a combined power greater than that possessed by any nation or empire in previous times. Yet world domination was by no means accompanied by any sense of general world order. The economic might of the Western nations, while it resulted in their ability to dominate the less developed quarters of the globe, resulted, as well, in their concern lest one of their number overpower the others. The old system of the balance of power, designed to preserve peace by insuring that no one country achieved overwhelming predominance at the expense of its neighbors, was strained to the breaking point by economic rivalries that stretched around the world. Meanwhile, tensions mounted within each nation, as landed and middle classes, threatened by the possibility of social turmoil, tried to balance the mounting clamor for political concessions against their desire to retain power in their own hands. Twice during the period, in 1914 and 1939, international and domestic pressures exploded into global wars. Those wars and their results, generated by the rivalries and miscalculations of the Western nations, so sapped the strength of those nations as to depose them thereafter as the sole arbiters of the world's destinies. The Nations of the Far East, subjected to the high tide of Western expansionism, reacted in different ways.

China, under a decrepit dynasty and exhausted by rebellion, was reduced for several decades to a condition of economic dependence, while Japan displayed new vigor when forced out of isolation. Both nations adapted elements of Western civilization to their own basic culture patterns. The great lords of Japan, in drawing up a constitution in 1889, saw fit to establish the forms of cabinet government. The leader of the Chinese Revolution of 1911 made "democracy" one of his shibboleths. But the most powerful current reaching its climax between 1870 and 1945 was undoubtedly nationalism. New states multiplied especially in Europe and in Latin America, and the peoples of the Middle and Far East struck out boldly for control of their own destinies. The peoples of Africa were condemned to a longer struggle for independence. Although the notorious slave trade was gradually ended, the political and technological advantages accruing to the leading Western nations were utilized by them to strengthen their hold on the resources of disunited Africa.

THE FAR EAST	AFRICA	
	British occupation of Cape Colony, 1795	
	House-Canoe system in Niger Delta, c. 1800	**1800**
	Expansion of East African trade, 1800–1875	
	Sultan Sayyid, Zanzibar, 1805–1856	
	Sierra Leone founded, 1808	
	Liberia founded, 1821	
		1825
	British consulates in coastal states, 1830–1860	
	Exploration of interior of continent, 1830–1875	
Anglo-Chinese War (Opium War), 1839–1842		
	Decline of slave trade, 1840–1863	
		1850
Taiping Rebellion, 1851–1864		
Opening of Japan, 1854		
Sun Yat-sen, 1866–1925		
Meiji Restoration in Japan, 1867–1868	Opening of Suez Canal, 1869	
End of feudalism in Japan, 1871		
		1875
	Destruction of Zulu empire, 1879	
	British invasion of Egypt, 1882	
Adoption of constitution in Japan, 1889	Berlin West African Conference, 1884	
Sino-Japanese War, 1894–1895	European Settlement of Rhodesia, 1890	
	Boer War, 1899–1902	
Boxer Uprising, 1900		**1900**
Russo-Japanese War, 1904–1905		
Revolution in China, 1911		

POLITICS	SCIENCE & INDUSTRY

1870

First commercially practical electrical generator, 1870

Gilcrist-Thomas steel process, 1870s

Paris Commune, 1871
Kulturkampf, Germany, 1872
League of Three Emperors, 1873
Constitution for Third French Republic, 1875
End of First International, 1876
Congress of Berlin, 1878

Germ theory of disease, 1875
Invention of telephone, 1876

Triple Alliance, 1882
Berlin conference on imperialism, 1885
Second International formed, 1889
Pan-Slavism, 1890–1914

Dreyfus affair, 1894–1899

Discovery of the X-ray, 1895
Marie Curie, discovery of radium, 1898

Spanish-American War, 1898

Boer War, 1899–1902

Invention of wireless telegraph, 1899

1900

V. Lenin, *What Is to Be Done?,* 1902

First airplane flight, 1903
Ivan Pavlov, Nobel Prize for physiology, 1904
Albert Einstein, development of relativity theory, 1905–1910

Russo-Japanese War, 1904–1905
Revolution in Russia, 1905

Triple Entente, 1907
Bosnian Crisis, 1908
Revolt of the Young Turks, 1908

Model T Ford, 1908

Balkan Wars, 1912–1913

First World War, 1914–1918
Russian Revolution, 1917

Treaty of Versailles, 1919
Socialist revolution, Germany, 1919
League of Nations, 1920–1946

1920

NEP, Russia, 1921

Mussolini's March on Rome, 1922

Hitler's beer-hall putsch, 1923
New constitution, Soviet Union, 1924
Locarno agreements, 1925

Discovery of viruses, sulfa drugs, and penicillin, 1930s

Hitler, chancellor of Germany, 1933
New Deal, United States, 1933–1940

World economic conference, 1933

ECONOMICS & SOCIETY	ARTS & LETTERS	
	Impressionism in art, 1870–1900	**1870**
Growth of finance capitalism, 1880s
Social welfare legislation, Germany, 1882–1884		
	Émile Zola, *Germinal,* 1885	
Sherman Anti-Trust Act, United States, 1890	Henrik Ibsen, *Hedda Gabler,* 1890
Paul Cézanne, *The Card Players,* 1890–1892	
Meline tariff, 1892		
	George Bernard Shaw, *Plays Pleasant* and *Unpleasant,* 1898	
Women's suffrage movement, England, 1900–1914	Sigmund Freud, *The Interpretation of Dreams,* 1900	**1900**
Social welfare legislation, France, 1904; 1910	Cubism in art 1905–1930	
Social welfare legislation, England, 1906–1912		
	Marcel Proust, *Remembrance of Things Past,* 1913–1918	
	Oswald Spengler, *The Decline of the West,* 1918
Bauhaus established, 1919	
German inflation, 1920s	Writers of the "Lost Generation," 1920–1930
Surrealism and Dadaism, 1920s
Ludwig Wittgenstein, *Tractatus Logico-philosophicus,* 1921
T. S. Eliot, *The Waste Land,* 1922
James Joyce, *Ulysses,* 1922	**1920**
Great Depression, 1929–1940	Neo-realism in art, 1930s	

POLITICS	SCIENCE & INDUSTRY
Italy conquers Ethiopia, 1935–1936	National rearmament programs, 1935
Rome-Berlin Axis, 1936	
Spanish Civil War, 1936–1939	
Germany annexes Austria, 1938	
Munich conference, 1938	
Nazi-Soviet pact, 1939	Discovery of atomic fission, 1939
Second World War, 1939–1941	
United States enters war, 1941	
Allied invasion of Normandy, 1944	
Bombing of Hiroshima and Nagasaki, 1945	First atomic bomb test, 1945
United Nations founded, 1946	

1940

ECONOMICS & SOCIETY   ARTS & LETTERS

J. M. Keynes, *General Theory of Employment, Interest,*
and Money, 1936

Jean-Paul Sartre, *Being and Nothingness,* 1943

1940

Chapter 29

THE PROGRESS OF INDUSTRIALIZATION (1870–1914)

We have conquered for ourselves a place in the sun. It will now be my task to see to it that this place in the sun shall remain our undisputed possession . . .

— Kaiser William II, speech, **1901**

I f most historians now speak of a second industrial revolution occurring during the years after 1870, they are quick to qualify the term. Whatever the changes in technique and in scope—and they were significant—they do not compare to those which characterized the first revolution—*the* Industrial Revolution. There is, however, good reason to distinguish a second period of industrial development and advance from the first. Successful nation-building meant that the years 1870–1914 would be characterized by sharply increased international economic rivalries, culminating in a scramble after imperial territories in Africa and Asia. Britain, if it did not actually surrender its industrial lead during this period, failed to counter with any real success the energetic and determined challenges from Germany and the United States to its constantly decreasing lead. New technology, particularly in the fields of metals, chemicals, and electricity, resulted in new products. Improving standards of living produced greater demand, which, in turn, increased the volume of production. And the need for increased production called forth significant reorganization to provide a freer supply of capital and to ensure a more efficient labor force. It is these changes that distinguish the second stage of industrialization from the first, and therefore warrant its separate treatment. Yet they must be perceived as stemming not only from those economic conditions which were the result of the first stage, but also from the more general political, social, and cultural climate whose history we have been tracing.

A second industrial revolution

In analyzing the progress of industrialization, we shall deal with changes in three major areas: in technology; in scope and scale of production; and in the reorganization of the capitalist system. Finally we shall examine the phenomenon of late–nineteenth-century imperialism, and consider the extent to which that phenomenon can be attributed to increasing economic and industrial rivalries.

1. NEW TECHNOLOGIES

Technology in steel

A most important technological change in this period resulted in the mass production of steel. The advantages of steel over iron—a result of steel's lower carbon content—are its hardness, its malleability, and its strength. Steel can keep its cutting edge, where iron cannot; it can be worked more easily than iron, which is brittle and which, if it is to be used industrially, must almost always be cast (that is, poured into molds). And steel, because of its strength in proportion to its weight and volume, makes a particularly adaptable construction material. These advantages had been recognized by craftsmen for centuries. Until steel could be produced both cheaply and in mass, however, the advantages remained more theoretical than real. Two inventions, during the earlier years of the Industrial Revolution, had reduced the price and increased the output of steel to some degree. The crucible technique, discovered in the eighteenth century in England, called for the heating of relatively small amounts of iron ore to a point at which foreign matter could be removed by skimming, the carbon content reduced, and a proper proportion of carbon distributed evenly throughout the finished product. Although individual crucibles were not large, holding on the average no more than forty-five to sixty pounds, they could be poured together to produce steel ingots of several tons. A century later, in the early 1840s, two Germans adapted the puddling process, used in the production of iron, to the manufacture of steel. While it did not produce steel as hard as that made in crucibles, it reduced its price considerably.

Bessemer, Siemens-Martin, and Gilchrist-Thomas systems

Not until the invention of the Bessemer and Siemens-Martin processes, however, could steel begin to compete with iron. In the 1850s, an Englishman, Henry Bessemer, discovered that by blowing air into and through the molten metal he could achieve a more exact degree of decarbonization in much shorter time, and with far larger quantities of ore, than was possible with either the crucible or puddling methods. Bessemer soon found, however, that his "converters" were incapable of burning off sufficient quantities of phosphorous; and phosphorous in anything but the smallest quantities made the metal unworkable. A partial solution was achieved with the introduction of non-phosphoric hematite ores. Yet this was of little long-term use in most European countries, where supplies of hematite ore were not

The Manufacture of Steel by the Bessemer Process. An 1875 engraving.

abundant. This same problem plagued the German inventors Frederick and William Siemens, whose furnace made use of waste gases to increase heat. Not until Pierre Martin, a Frenchman, discovered that the introduction of scrap iron into the mix would induce proper decarbonization, could the Siemens furnace be used to make steel commercially. And not until the late 1870s was the problem of phosphoresence solved for both the Bessemer and the Siemens-Martin processes. The solution was a simple one, discovered by two Englishmen, a clerk and a chemist: Sidney Gilchrist Thomas and his cousin Sidney Gilchrist. They introduced limestone into the molten iron to combine with the phosphorous, which was then siphoned from the mix. And they lined the converter in such a way that the slag was prevented from eating away the walls and releasing phosphorous back into the molten metal.

Together, these three processes revolutionized the production of steel. Although the use of iron did not end overnight, steel soon moved into the lead. In the British shipbuilding industry, for example, steel had overtaken iron by 1890. In part because Siemens-Martin was particularly suited to the manufacture of steel plates used in shipbuilding, that process dominated the manufacture of steel in Britain, where shipbuilding was a major industry. Bessemer steel, which could be manufactured more cheaply and in larger plants, was more commonly produced on the Continent and in America. The result was a particular increase in the production of German steel: by 1901, German converters were capable of pouring an average of 34,000 tons, compared to Britain's 21,750. By 1914 Germany was producing twice as much steel as Britain, and the United States twice as much as Germany.

Increased steel production

A second and equally important technological development resulted in the availability of electric power for industrial, commercial, and domestic use. Electricity's particular advantages result from the fact that it can be easily transmitted as energy over long distances, and from the fact that it can be converted into other forms of energy—heat and light, for example. Although electricity had, of course, been discovered prior to the first Industrial Revolution, its advantages could not have been put to general use without a series of inventions which occurred during the nineteenth century. Of these, some of the most important were the invention of the chemical battery by the Italian Alessandro Volta in 1800; of electromagnetic induction by the Englishman Michael Faraday in 1831; of the electromagnetic generator in 1866; of the first commercially practical generator of direct current in 1870; and of alternators and transformers capable of producing high-voltage alternating current in the 1880s. These inventions meant that by the end of the century it was possible to send electric current from large power stations over comparatively long distances. Electric power could be manufactured by water—hence cheaply—and delivered from its source to the place where it was needed.

Once it had been delivered to its destination, the power was converted and put to use in myriad ways. Households quickly became one of the major users of electrical power. The invention by Thomas Edison of the incandescent filament lamp—or light bulb—was crucial in this regard. As individual houses were electrified to receive the power that was to be transformed into light, consumer demand for electricity resulted in further expansion of the electrical industry. Demand for electrical power was increasing in the industrial sector as well. Electric motors soon began to power subways, tramways, and, eventually, long-distance railways. Electricity made possible the development of new techniques in the chemical and metallurgical industries. Most important, electricity helped to transform the work patterns of the factory. Heavy steam engines had made equipment and machinery stationery; electric motors meant that comparatively lightweight power tools could be moved—often by hand—to the site of a particular piece of work. The result was far greater flexibility in terms of factory organization. Smaller workshop industries benefited as well; they could accommodate themselves to electrically powered motors and tools in a way they could not to steam.

An Early Dynamo Used for Lighting

Steel and electricity were only two of the most important areas where technological changes were taking place. The chemical industry was significantly advanced by developments in the manufacture of alkali and organic compounds. Demand for alkali had increased with the demand for soaps and textiles, and with the changes in the manufacturing process of paper, which required large amounts of bleach. An older, more expensive and wasteful technique used extensively by the British was superseded after 1880 by a new process perfected by the Belgian Ernest Solvay. The result was, again, a rapid overtaking of the British by the Germans in the production not only of alkalis but of sulphuric acid, a by-product recoverable in the Solvay process, and used in the manufacture of fertilizers, petroleum refining, iron, steel, and textiles. In the field of organic compounds, the impetus for further discovery came as a result of demand for synthetic dyes. Although the British and French were the first successful pioneers in this area, the Germans once more moved ahead to a commanding lead by 1900. At the turn of the century German firms controlled about 90 percent of the world market.

The need for more and more power to meet increasing industrial demands resulted not only in developments in the field of electricity, already noted, but in the improved design and expanded capacity of steam engines. The most noteworthy invention in this area was the steam turbine, which permitted steam engines to run at speeds heretofore unobtainable. Internal combustion engines made their appearance during this period as well. Their major advantage lay in their efficiency; i.e., they could be powered automatically, and did not need to be stoked by hand like steam engines. Once liquid fuels—petroleum and distilled gasoline—became available, as they did increasingly with the discovery of oil fields in Russia, Borneo, and Texas about 1900, the internal combustion engine took hold as a serious competitor to steam. By 1914 most navies had converted from coal to oil, as had domestic steamship companies. The automobile and the airplane, both still in their infancies, made little impact upon the industrial world, however, before 1914.

Improved engines

2. CHANGES IN SCOPE AND SCALE

These technological changes must be understood as occurring against a background of—indeed in part as a result of—a generally increased standard of living for the majority of men and women in the Western

The First Successful Airplane Flight

The Interior of a Berlin Department Store, 1882

world. There were, of course, still a great many very poor people, both in cities and in the country: casual laborers, the unemployed, those in declining industries and trades. Those skilled workers and their families whose real incomes did rise as a result of deflation and higher wage rates did not experience anything like the rate of increase enjoyed by most of the middle class. Nor could they expect to avoid altogether the stretches of unemployment that made life so chaotic for so many of their unskilled co-workers. Yet despite these qualifications, it is fair to say that more people enjoyed a higher standard of living than ever before. And a higher standard of living produced the demand for an increase in consumer goods.

Increased consumption of manufactured goods was by no means uniform; it was higher in urban and industrialized areas than in the country. But even in the country, traditional thrift was challenged as farmers and their wives journeyed by train into the cities, saw what they had not imagined they could have, and then decided they must spend their savings to have it. To accommodate the new and largely middle-class consumers, department stores and chain stores designed their products and their advertising to make shopping as easy and inviting as possible. Behind large plate-glass windows goods were displayed attractively and temptingly; periodic sales encouraged householders to purchase "bargains"; catalogues and charge accounts made it easy for customers to spend money without leaving home. The result was an enormous increase in the volume of manufactured consumer goods produced for this rapidly expanding consumer market. Bicycles, clocks, appliances, furnishings—these and a great many other things were now being made in large quantities, and with new materials (cheap steel) and new techniques (electrical power). Many of these products were designed according to the correct assumption that women were more and more responsible for household purchases. Therefore, goods were fashioned to appeal directly to women, or to the children for whom women were responsible. The foot-powered sewing machine was a particular case in point—the first domestic appliance. Isaac Singer, the American responsible for the development of the treadle and straight needle in the 1850s, was as much an entrepreneur as an inventor. He was a pioneer in the field of advertising and promotion, encouraging purchase on the installment plan and providing courses for would-be domestic seamstresses.

Sewing machines changed far more than the sewing habits of housewives, however. They were cheap, lightweight tools, easily installed and easily operated. Workshop masters could set up several, employ a handful of young women at very low wages, and make a profit turning out cheap ready-made clothing in response to increasing markets. Here is just one of the ways in which the scale of manufacturing altered during the latter part of the nineteenth century, both demand and technology conspiring to produce the change. In metal-working, hard-edged steel allowed for the rapid cutting of patterns, which reduced price, which, in turn, encouraged the manufacture of a variety of inexpensive metal goods—kitchenware, for example. The sewing machine led to the development of other new tools that helped cut costs in the clothing industry: button-holers, lace-makers, leather-stitchers. Whereas it took one cobbler ten hours to make a pair of shoes in 1850 by hand, by the end of the century it took a team of cobblers but a few hours to produce ten pairs using machinery. In

The web of industrial change

Advertisement for a German Sewing Machine. The company proclaims the machine's versatility: unsurpassed for use in the home as well as in the workshop or factory.

textiles, improved engines doubled the pace of mules and looms. In heavy industry, steam hammers performed the work of many men more precisely and with greater speed than before. New equipment of this sort was expensive. As a result, in heavy industry, it was the larger companies that prospered, and in the course of their prosperity, they grew even larger.

In all the countries of Europe, and in the United States, the pattern is one of expansion and consolidation. This was especially the case in Germany, where in the iron and steel industry nearly 75 percent of those employed worked in factories of a thousand or more, and where over 90 percent of the electrical equipment manufactured was made in factories with over fifty employees. Machinery was thus altering the scale of manufacturing in two directions at once. In the clothing industry, entrepreneurs could use inexpensive machines to make small workshops turn a profit. In steel foundries, the cost of new equipment forced small competitors to the wall, with the result that the foundries grew very much bigger.

The increase in the scale of manufacturing had important and often disturbing consequences for workers. The most obvious was the need for men and women to relearn their trades. They were compelled to adapt their older skills to the new machines. Very often this adaptation resulted in a loss of either pay or prestige, or both. Most machine work was not skilled work. A trainee could "pick up" a trade in a week or so. Workers who had prided themselves on a particular skill and had been paid according to their ability to perform it, had to face the fact that industrial change was not only forcing them to relearn, but was compelling them to tell themselves that their new "skills"—if they could be called that—did not amount to very much. For example, when the machine itself could cut metal with infinitesimal accuracy, there was far less need than there had been previously for the skills of a human "fitter." Even if workers were not forced to relearn in these ways in order to accommodate to increased scale, they often had at least to accommodate to factory reorganization and rationalization. In workplaces where the hand-carrying of materials had been a major factor in their final cost, mechanization to reduce that cost would produce a bewildering series of changes. Electric cranes, used together with huge magnets in the iron and steel industries, increased the speed with which goods could be moved, and demanded that workers defer to whatever changes their introduction might entail.

A second—and even more important—effect of the change in scale was the constant demand for further efficiency. The greater the scale of the operation, the more important it became to eliminate waste. One minute lost in the production of every ten pairs of shoes might not make much difference if only fifty pairs were produced in a day. But if hundreds were being made, it became crucial, in the eyes of management, to see that those minutes were no longer lost. In facto-

Technological Change and Production Speed-Up. An early assembly line of the Ford Motor Company, United States, 1913. Car bodies slid down the ramp and were attached to the chassis as they passed through the line below. One thousand cars were produced each day.

ries where capital had been spent on new machinery, the owners, conscious of the cost of their investment, increased output in order to realize a profit on their recent investment. In factories where older machinery was still in use, owners believed that the only way they could remain competitive with modernized operations was by extracting all they could from their less productive equipment. In both cases, workers were pressed to produce more and more. One result of this drive for efficiency was a restructuring of wage scales. Prior to this period, although there had been serious wage disputes, both management and labor appeared content to bargain from the traditional notion of "a fair day's wage for a fair day's work." Definitions of what was fair naturally varied. But the level of individual performance was generally set by custom. What workers produced in the course of a day continued to determine what they were expected to produce. From about 1870 onward, however, expectations and procedures began to change. Periodic economic depressions in the last quarter of the nineteenth century saw profits fall before wages. This pattern caused employers to insist on greater individual productivity from their employees. It was no longer enough to work at a job with customary speed. Workers were now asked to produce as much as the owners thought they were potentially capable of producing.

But who was to determine that potential? That question plagued industrial relations during these years. Employers, who were adopting precision tools in order to increase production, grew more and more convinced that worker output could be gauged with a like precision as well. The foremost theoretician of worker efficiency and what was called scientific management of labor was the American Frederick W.

Scientific management

Taylor (1865–1915). Taylor devised a three-step system whereby a worker's output could be "scientifically" measured, a system which, he argued, would provide a precise method for the determination of wage scales. First, he observed, timed, and analyzed workers' movements on the job, in order to determine how long a particular task should take. Second, he figured the labor costs of these movements. Third, he produced "norms," or general standards, which all workers were expected to maintain. These norms were invariably higher than those which had prevailed under traditional conditions.

Piece rates

In order to encourage workers to accept these increased standards, Taylor urged all factory-owners to adopt piece rates (i.e., payment to workers according to the specific amount produced) rather than hourly or daily wages. Payment by piece rate was already a growing practice in many European and American factories. In theory, at least, workers were not opposed to this method of payment; they reasoned that their only hope for a share in increasing output lay in their chance to be paid directly for what they made. But when they were told that their pay would not increase unless they measured up to predetermined—and, to their mind, unrealistic—norms, they rebelled. They argued that rates were set according to the performance of the speediest workers. Even though workers might earn more money if they agreed to the new rates, they resented the intrusion of management upon the pace of their working lives. Despite this opposition, scientific management spread throughout the industrialized West. In England, the United States, and on the Continent, particularly in the engineering trades, factory after factory subscribed to the new gospel. Where it could not entirely succeed in introducing "efficiency" on the shop floor, management proceeded to rationalize its own procedures. Accounting departments were expanded, and encouraged to attend closely to the problem of cost control in all areas of production and distribution. These reforms were no more than a reflection of the general move in the direction of greater efficiency. They were brought on by the vastly increased scale of production, the need to reduce waste wherever possible, and the desire to derive maximum profits from the elimination of unnecessary motions and unproductive habits.

3. THE NEW CAPITALISM

The growth of incorporation

Responding to the increased scope of production and to the consequent pressures for further efficiency, the institutions of capitalism began to reorganize toward the end of the nineteenth century. Hitherto, most firms had been small or at most middle-sized; now, as firms grew and their need for capital increased, they began to incorporate. Limited liability laws, enacted by most countries in the course of the century, worked to encourage this incorporation. "Limited liability" meant that an individual owning stock in a particular corporation could be held liable only for the amount of his or her shares, should that corporation bankrupt itself. Once insured in this way, many thousands of middle-class men and women considered corporate investment a safe and financially promising way of making money for themselves. A stockholding, "rentier" class emerged, brought into existence by the willingness of governments to encourage capitalism through friendly legislation, and by the desire of capitalist businessmen to expand their industrial undertakings to meet increased demands. More and more companies incorporated. In doing so, their management tended to be removed from the direct control of family founders or of company-based boards of directors. The influence of bankers and financiers, often situated in cities far removed from the factories they invested in, grew accordingly. These men were not investing their own money but the money of their clients; their power to stimulate or to discourage the growth of particular industries and enterprises encouraged a kind of impersonal "finance" capital.

Corporate organization on a large scale facilitated the spread of industrial unification. Some industries—steel, for example—combined vertically. Steel companies, to ensure uninterrupted production, acquired their own coal and iron mines. By doing so, they could guarantee themselves a supply of raw materials at attractive prices. Often the same steel companies would obtain control of companies whose products were made of steel: for example, shipyards or railway factories. Now they would not only possess a ready stock of raw materials but an equally ready market for their manufactured products—steel plates, steel rails, whatever they might be. Such vertical integration was only

Vertical organization

The New York Stock Exchange, 1893

*Horizontal organization:
cartels and trusts*

possible as a result of the money available for investment through the institutions of finance capital.

A second form of corporate organization was a horizontal formation: the cartel. These were combinations of individual companies producing the same kind of goods, joined for the purpose of controlling, if not eliminating, competition. Since their products were identical, an identical price could be charged. Companies involved in the production of coal and steel were especially suited to the organization of cartels because of the costs of initial capitalization. It is very expensive to build, equip, and man a steel foundry; thus there were relatively few of them. And because there were few, they were the more easily organized into a combine. Cartels were particularly strong in Germany; less so in France, where there was not as much heavy industry, where the tradition of the small family firm was particularly entrenched, and where there was long-standing opposition to competition in the form of price-cutting and general intra-industrial warfare. In Britain, though some cartels were formed, continuing subscription to the policy of free trade meant that companies would find it difficult to maintain fixed prices. How could they do so if they could not exclude, by means of a tariff, foreign competitors who wanted to undersell them? Germany had abandoned the policy of free trade in 1879; the United States, where cartels were known as trusts, did the same after the Civil War, though not all at once. Britain, however, clung to free trade until well into the twentieth century.

*Opposition to cartels and
trusts*

Defenders of the cartel argued that the elimination of competition brought more stable prices and more continuous employment. They pointed out as well that cartels almost always reduced the cost of production. Opponents questioned, however, whether those reduced costs were reflected in lower prices, or, as they charged, in higher stockholder profits. Critics of cartels were vocal in the United States, where the so-called captains of industry, most prominently the financier J. P. Morgan (1837–1913), were attacked as a new breed of feudal barons. The Sherman Anti-Trust Act was passed by Congress in 1890 to curb the practice of industrial combination. It had little effect in retarding the process, however, until the trust-busting presidency of Theodore Roosevelt (1901–1906). Elsewhere in the West, corporate cartels and combines of various sorts were either encouraged or at least tolerated as a natural stage in the growth of a capitalist system that, it was argued, was showering benefits on all classes of society.

4. INTERNATIONAL COMPETITION: BRITAIN VS. GERMANY

Throughout the period we have been examining, Britain and Germany were locked in industrial competition. By 1914, both the United States and Germany were outproducing Britain in a number of

J. P. Morgan

areas. Yet the German challenge was, for the British, the more significant. Industrial competition with Germany helped reshape international political alliances at the end of the century. Britain, moving to align itself with its ancient enemy France against the Germans, found itself engaged in a contest of naval superiority with the latter, determined that in that field the British would not lose their age-old advantage to the upstart challenger.

To what degree did the Germans succeed in overtaking the British? By 1914, Britain's industrial-commercial day was by no means over. The volume of German trade at the turn of the century was no more than 60 percent as great. Britain, more mature industrially than Germany, was shifting resources to the service sector of the economy, into areas such as the wider distribution of goods. If Britain's output of manufactured goods did no more than double between 1870 and 1913, as compared to Germany's sixfold increase, it was in part for this reason. Nor should one suppose that all areas of German industry were functioning as efficient, modernized, and technologically advanced units. For every up-to-date chemical plant, for every thriving steel mill, there were many smaller workshops where manufacturing took place on little more than a domestic scale. Having said this, however, the fact remains that the Germans *were* a powerful threat to the British. Even before 1870, Germany had ceased to provide a ready market for British manufactures; the Germans were supplying their own needs. After 1870, Germany began to export to the rest of the world. Moving into markets that the British had considered exclusively their own, German salesmen promoted German goods in Australia, South America, China, and in Britain itself. In fields such as the manufacture of organic chemicals and electrical equipment, Germany outsold Britain across the globe.

The extent of Germany's achievement

How can Germany's success and, perhaps more important, Britain's inability to counter it be explained? To attempt an answer to the latter question first: Britain was handicapped because it had been the first nation to industrialize. Because of the capital they had invested in older factories and equipment, the British were reluctant to enter new fields or to exploit new methods. For example, because the British had constructed plants to manufacture alkali by an earlier, less efficient process, they found themselves trapped into continuing to produce in that way after the Solvay process had been discovered. Rather than make the expensive switch, British manufacturers attempted to make their alkali more competitive by cutting costs and improving worker efficiency. But when further refinements were introduced in the 1890s, British output not only failed to keep pace with German and also American increases, but actually decreased. The same difficulties arose with steel. Here again Britain was hampered by the problem of priority. Because the British were the first to industrialize, their manufacturing centers took shape in accordance with the scale of early- and mid–nineteenth-century production. Now there was need for

*Reasons for Britain's lag:
(1) the problem of priority*

Interior of a Krupp Steel Mill, Essen, Germany

large tracts of land, close to transportation, to accommodate steel mills. Because of the cramped layout of Britain's industrial cities, it could not build mills as large as those in Germany or the United States. The result was that by 1900 the largest British steel mills were no bigger than the average-sized mills in Germany. Even new plants built for other manufacturing purposes in Britain were only a third as large as those constructed by its major rival. Because German plants were big, and because, therefore, they represented a large investment of capital, those who managed them did all they could to ensure their efficient operation. They rationalized design and standardized parts to an extent the British, with their smaller plants, continued to believe unnecessary. Smaller firms tended to receive smaller and more specialized orders which did not encourage standardization. Although standardization was accomplished by 1914 in Britain in some industries—notably iron and steel—in many others it remained more the exception than the rule.

(2) *attitudes*   Britain's industrial lead, which froze its urban areas into obsolete patterns and thus prevented growth, froze British attitudes as well. Because they had come so far so fast, the British had grown complacent. Nowhere is this fact more clearly reflected than in the British attitude toward education. If the achievements of the first Industrial Revolution—for example, the steam engine, the spinning jenny—were the result of what might be called creative tinkering, those of the second revolution were the product of a close and fruitful union of pure science with technology. Achievement now depended on a generally literate work-force, a trained body of mechanics, a scientifically grounded body of technicians, and a corps of highly trained, creative scientists. Germany was producing these cadres; Britain was not.

Only in 1870 was a system of public elementary education instituted in Britain, and not until ten years later was it made compulsory. In Germany, compulsory education dated from the eighteenth century. The British governing class believed the primary purpose of education was social control: teaching a boy or girl not only how to read and write, but to accept his or her particular place within the social structure. Though German elementary education was authoritarian in many respects as well, the fact that it had begun earlier and was directly joined to systems of secondary education encouraged the development of abilities; it was in this respect far less wasteful than the British. As Britain lagged in the area of elementary education, it lagged in the development of scientific and technological laboratories and training centers. In Germany, the state established an elaborate network of such technical institutions; in Britain there were almost none before the First World War.

Complacency was the major reason for this lack. The British tended to believe, wrongly, that practical experience and on-the-job training would produce the skills necessary to keep abreast of change. In addition, the British upper middle class convinced itself that the goal of education was not the production of creative technologists but of "gentlemen." Fathers who had made their fortunes as entrepreneurs during the first Industrial Revolution sent their sons to private boarding schools and to the ancient universities of Oxford and Cambridge to receive a "gentleman's" education—training in Greek and Latin, primarily. Those sons, whose creative talents might otherwise have been channeled into science and technology, chose careers in politics, or in the imperial or domestic bureaucracies instead. The result was a severe narrowing of the pool of creative technologists and dynamic entrepreneurs. There were fewer men than in either Germany or the United States interested in organizing the increasingly large amounts of capital necessary to engage in industrial expansion. It was easier to invest money overseas than to undertake the revitalization of various enterprises at home. A suspicion of what was new, encouraged by the British tendency to rely upon practical experience of the past, prevented Britain from rising in more than a fitful way to the German challenge.

Complacency

5. INTERNATIONAL COMPETITION: IMPERIALISM

The rivalry between Britain and Germany was only the most intense aspect of international competitiveness during the last decades of the nineteenth century. As nations proceeded with the business of industrialization, their search for markets brought them into direct opposition with one another. One result was that the dogma of free trade was abandoned by all save Britain. As we have seen, the Germans

A global economy

rejected the policy of low tariffs in 1879. Austria and Russia had already done so. Spain instituted new scales of import duties in 1877 and again in 1891. In France, two decades of gradual abandonment were climaxed by the passage of the Méline Tariff in 1892. Although individual nations attempted to isolate themselves from each other in this way, developments in international economics mandated the continuing growth and development of an interlocking, worldwide system of manufacturing, trade, and finance. For example, the general adoption by western Europe and the United States of the gold standard meant that the currencies of the so-called civilized world could be readily exchanged with each other against the measure of a common standard—the international price of gold. Hence countries needing to import from the United States, for example, did not have to sell goods directly to that country. They could sell to South America, exchange the money they received for gold, and then buy from America.

"Invisible" exports

Almost all European countries, dependent on vast supplies of raw materials to sustain their rate of industrial production, imported more than they exported. To avoid the mounting deficits that would otherwise have resulted from this practice, they relied upon "invisible" exports: i.e., shipping, insurance, and interest on money lent or invested. The extent of Britain's exportations in these areas was far greater than that of any other country. London was the money market of the world, to which would-be borrowers looked for assistance before turning elsewhere. By 1914, Britain had $20 billion invested overseas, compared with the $8.7 of the French and the $6 billion of the Germans. The insurance firm of Lloyds of London serviced clients around the world. The British merchant fleet transported the manufactured goods and raw materials of every trading nation. It was the volume of its "invisible" exports that permitted Britain to remain faithful to the doctrine of free trade while other European nations were forced to institute tariffs.

Effects on Africa and Asia

The competition between the principal economic powers of this worldwide marketplace affected not only their relationships with each other but also with those less developed areas upon which they were increasingly dependent for both raw materials and markets. Some of those areas, such as India and China, were the seats of ancient empires. Others, such as central Africa, sheltered less complex tribal soicieities. No matter what the nature of the indigenous civilization, the intrusion upon it of modern science and technology, systematic wage labor, financial and legal institutions caused enormous disruption. Though drawn into the world economy, these areas did not draw from it the benefits that the West did. Native industries such as Indian textile spinning and weaving stood no chance in competition with the factory-made products of Manchester. African herdsmen and hunters endured the disruption of their living habits by the activities of European ranchers and miners. Men who had made their living as boatmen and carters lost their livelihood to the railways constructed by Western nations. New jobs there might be; but they were jobs worked according to a Western style, dictated by Western economic demands, and threatened by Western economic disorders. In great measure the workers of this emerging world were assuming the role of a global unskilled working class under the hegemony of Western capitalism.

With this global background before us it is easier to understand the patterns of late–nineteenth-century imperialism. Imperialism we shall define simply as the domination of one people by another. So defined, imperialism had existed throughout the nineteenth century. The French had penetrated Algeria and the British, India. In other parts of the world, where Western powers did not govern directly, they often exercised an indirect influence so powerful as to preclude "native" defiance. When the West "opened" China beginning in 1834, it left the Chinese in nominal charge of their state. But it insured that affairs would be conducted to its advantage and within its "sphere of influence." Britain added to its "informal" empire in this way in South America, Africa, and south and east Asia.

Imperialism defined

As time passed, and rivalries increased, European powers moved with greater frequency and determination to control both the government and the economy of underdeveloped nations and territories. Although the primary reasons for the new imperialism were political and economic, support for imperial policy was motivated by a variety of sentiments. Some argued that it was Europe's duty to civilize—or to Christianize—the "barbaric" and "heathen" quarters of the globe. To combat slave-trading, famine, filth, and illiteracy seemed to many legitimate reason for invading the heart of Africa and the jungles of Asia. Hundreds of Europeans gave up comfortable middle-class lives to participate in what was without question a selfless mission. Others supported imperialism because the policy allowed them to celebrate their country's power. Men, women, and children took pleasure in pointing to those remote areas on the map colored with their particular hue. It was somehow reassuring to know that the sun never set on the British Empire.

Reasons for the new imperialism

Those in charge of the imperial building process, however, although they welcomed support from whatever quarter and for whatever reason, decided policy in response to a combination of political and economic considerations, and as a corollary to the process of nation-building. National security and the preservation of a general balance of power were issues never far from the forefront of politicians' thinking and planning. Britain's domination of Egypt in the 1880s was the result, in large measure, of its fear of what might occur in the Near East should large portions of the decaying Ottoman Empire fall into Russian hands. Britain had purchased 44 percent of the shares in the Suez Canal Company in 1875, and considered the waterway a strategic lifeline to the east. The canal had been built by the French under the direction of the engineer Ferdinand de Lesseps. Begun in 1859 and completed in 1869, it was expected to assist France in its bid for com-

The politics of imperialism

mercial expansion to the East. Britain obtained its shares from the spendthrift khedive (viceroy) of Egypt at a time when he was threatened with bankruptcy. When, in 1882, nationalist rebels protested continuing British intervention in the internal affairs of Egypt, the British claimed they had no choice but to bombard the port of Alexandria and place the Egyptian ruler under their protection. A continuing British presence in Egypt, and the willingness of the British government to support Egyptian claims to the Upper Nile, worried the French, who were growing to fear Britain's political domination of the entire African continent. Moving to correct what they perceived as a severe political imbalance, the French challenged the British and at Fashoda, in the Sudan, came close to war in 1898. The British called the French bluff, however, and war was averted. The power struggle over the Suez, Egypt, and the Sudan provides an excellent example of the manner in which international politics was directly related to the advancement of imperialism.

The economics of imperialism

Equally important as an explanation for imperialism are the facts of late–nineteenth-century world economics. There are those who have argued that imperialism was the result of the need for industrial Europe to invest surplus capital. This argument makes some sense when applied to Britain, about half of whose total of $20 billion in foreign investments was at work within its empire. But it fails to explain the imperial ambitions of the Germans and the French, who had much less capital to invest, and who invested that which they had in non-imperial enterprises. Only a very small portion of German capital was invested in German colonies by 1914; about one-fifth of French capital was so invested. The French had more capital in Russia, hoping to stabilize that ally against the Germans, than in all their colonial possessions.

A more important economic reason for imperial expansion lay in Europe's continuing need for imports. Demand for raw materials, far

Dredges and Elevators at Work on the Construction of the Suez Canal, 1869

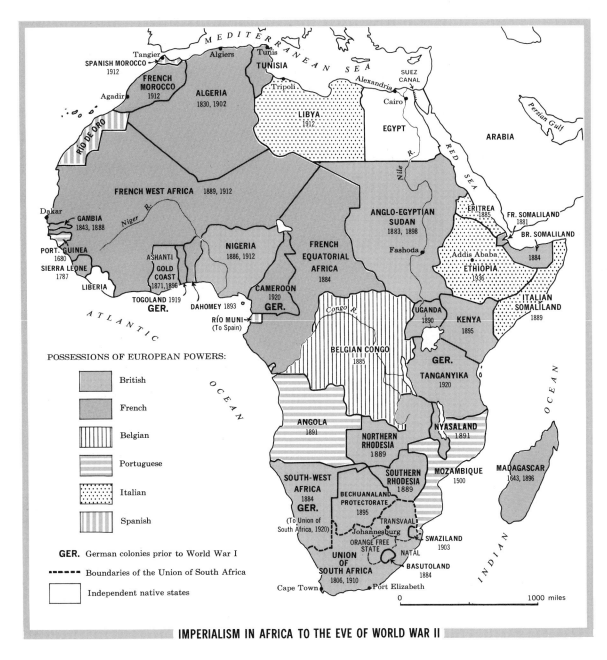

POSSESSIONS OF EUROPEAN POWERS:

British

French

Belgian

Portuguese

Italian

Spanish

GER. German colonies prior to World War I

- - - - - Boundaries of the Union of South Africa

Independent native states

IMPERIALISM IN AFRICA TO THE EVE OF WORLD WAR II

more than the need to spend surplus capital, <u>made colonies a necessary investment and imperialism,</u> therefore, <u>a worthwhile policy</u>. Certainly Europe, and particularly Britain, continued to need more and more markets for manufactured goods. Yet those areas into which the imperially minded nations penetrated after 1870, though they afforded their colonial masters an opportunity to increase exports to some degree, were generally too poor to answer fully the market needs of Europe's manufacturers. In 1914, despite imperialism, the industrial

The need for imports

countries remained their own best customers. Economics, although an important explanation for the rise of imperialism, is by no means the only one.

Imperial competition centered in Africa. Germans pressed inward from the east; Frenchmen from the west. The Portuguese schemed to connect the ancient colonies of Angola, on the west, with Mozambique, on the east. Most active among the European powers during this initial period of late–nineteenth-century colonization was a privately financed group of Belgians under the leadership of that country's king, Leopold II. In association with H. M. Stanley, an American newspaperman and explorer, Leopold and a group of financiers founded the International Congo Association in 1878, which negotiated treaties with chieftains that opened the Congo River basin to commercial exploitation. A conference, called in Berlin in 1885 and attended by most European nations and the United States, attempted to establish certain ground rules for the game of imperial acquisition. The Congo was declared a Free State, under the trusteeship of Leopold (the first example of this later familiar device of protecting "backward" peoples). A European nation with holdings on the African coast was declared to have first rights to territory in the interior behind those coastal regions. Those rights, however, could be sustained only by what was termed "real" occupation—that is, the presence on the ground of either administrators or troops. The scramble was on! Occupation was accompanied by the exploitation of native labor. Agreements reached with local chieftains, whom the Europeans courted, authorized the employment of men and women as laborers under conditions little better than slavery. Often forced to live in compounds apart from their families, Africans were victimized by a system which rooted out prevailing custom without attempting to establish anything like a new civilization in its place.

The division of the geographical spoils proceeded apace. The Portuguese increased their hold in Angola and Mozambique. The Italians invaded Somaliland and Eritrea. They attempted to extend their controls to Ethiopia, but were repulsed by an army of 80,000 Ethiopians, the first instance of a major victory by native Africans over whites. Germany came relatively late to the game. Bismarck was reluctant to engage in an enterprise which, he believed, would do little to profit the empire either politically or economically. Eventually concluding, however, that they could not afford to let other powers divide the continent between them, the Germans established colonies in German East Africa, in the Cameroons and Togo on the west coast, and in the desertlike and economically valueless territory of South West Africa. The French controlled large areas in West Africa and, in the Red Sea, the port of Obok. It was to further their plan for an east-west link that the French had risked challenging the British at Fashoda. That scheme, however, fell afoul of Britain's need to dominate Egypt, and

"The Rhodes Colossus." The ambitions of Cecil Rhodes, the driving force behind British imperialism in South Africa, is satirized in this cartoon, which appeared in *Punch*.

of its plans for a north-south connection through the African continent.

Cecil Rhodes, the English entrepreneur and imperial visionary, promoted the notion of a Capetown-to-Cairo railway both before and after his assumption of the prime-ministership of the Cape Colony in 1890. His plans were thwarted in the south, however, by the presence of two independent neighboring republics, the Transvaal and the Orange Free State, both inhabited by descendents of the original Dutch settlers in South Africa. These Boers—the Dutch word for "farmers"—had fled from the British in the Cape Colony and established themselves in their agricultural states in defiant opposition to the freebooting and exploitationist spirit of the British economic adventurers who had driven them from the Cape. When diamonds and gold were discovered in the Transvaal in 1886, the tension between the British and the Boers grew. As British prospectors and entrepreneurs moved in, the Boers refused to pass laws permitting the exploitation of their resources by foreign firms. They also taxed the interlopers heavily. Rhodes retaliated by attempting to force a war with the republics. His first try, the dispatching of a force of irregular volunteers under the command of Dr. L. S. Jameson in 1895, failed to

The Boer War

Boer Commandos Under Louis Botha. Botha became the first prime minister of the Union of South Africa following the Boer War.

provoke a conflict, but precipitated general censure on the British for harassing a peaceful neighbor. Rhodes was forced to resign as prime minister of the Cape Colony in 1896. War broke out in 1899. Its course, however, did not run according to British plans. The Boers proved tough fighters. It took three years to secure an armistice; it took further long months and resort to brutal policies such as detention camps and farm-burning to bring the resilient republicans to heel. The major consequence of the Boer War was to reduce Britain's stature in the eyes of its own citizens and in the eyes of the world.

Britain in India   Britain's imperial record in India was more distinguished than it was in Africa. The "informal" rule of the commercially motivated East India Company had proved ineffective in 1857, when native Indian troops and a large number of other disaffected elements within the subcontinent rebelled in what the British chose to call "The Indian Mutiny," but which was in fact a far more serious and deep-seated challenge to foreign control. Henceforth the British determined to rule directly. But at the same time, they decided to rule through the Indian upper classes, and not, as in the past, in opposition to them. Although instruction in British-sponsored schools continued in English, Indian customs were tolerated as they had not been before, and princes and their bureaucracies were incorporated as protectorates into the general scheme of government. A class of westernized, and yet devotedly Indian, civil servants and businessmen thus emerged by the end of the nineteenth century, trained by the British yet burdened by no sense of obligation to their tutors. This group provided the leader-

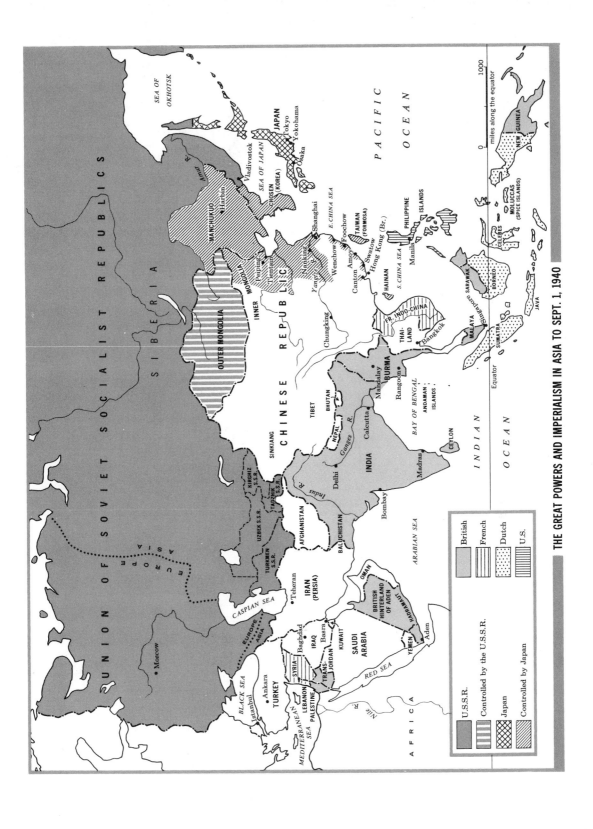

THE GREAT POWERS AND IMPERIALISM IN ASIA TO SEPT. 1, 1940

Imperialism. Left: Germans traveling in East Africa, 1907. Right: A British officer in India, c. 1900.

ship for the nationalist movement that was to challenge British rule in India in the mid–twentieth century.

Imperialism elsewhere

Elsewhere in the world, Western nations hastened to plant their colors upon those territories that promised rewards, either economic or strategic. Britain, France, Germany, and the Netherlands all staked claims in the East Indies, the Dutch achieving an overall hegemony there by 1900. China allowed itself to be victimized by a series of commercial treaties; among the predators was China's neighbor Japan, the only non-Western nation able to modernize in the nineteenth century. The United States played a double game. It acted as champion of the underdeveloped countries in the Western Hemisphere when they were threatened from Europe. Yet the Americans were willing, whenever it suited them, to prey on their neighbors, either "informally" or formally. When, at the end of the century, Spain's feeble hold on its Caribbean and Pacific colonies encouraged talk of rebellion, the United States stepped in to protect its investments and guarantee its maritime security. It declared and won a war against Spain in 1898 on trumped-up grounds. In the same year, the United States annexed Puerto Rico and the Philippines, and established a "protectorate" over Cuba. When Colombia's colony, Panama, threatened to rebel in 1903, the Americans quickly backed the rebels, recognized Panama as a republic, and then proceeded to grant it protection while Americans built the Panama Canal on land leased from the new government. Intervention in Santo Domingo and in Hawaii proved that the United States was no less an imperial power than the nations of western Europe. Together, by the end of the century, those countries had succeeded in binding the world together as it had never been before. The military and economic power with which they had accomplished that achievement meant that, for the time being at any rate, they would be the world's masters.

SELECTED READINGS

• *Items so designated are available in paperback editions.*

• Ashworth, W., *A Short History of the International Economy since 1850,* rev. ed., London, 1975.

Barkin, Kenneth D., *The Controversy Over German Industrialization, 1890–1902,* Chicago, 1970. The political and social struggles between agricultural and industrial interests. An important monograph.

Betts, Raymond F., *Europe Overseas: Phases of Imperialism,* New York, 1968.

Branschwig, H., *French Colonialism, 1871–1914,* New York, 1966.

Cameron, Rondo E., *France and the Economic Development of Europe, 1800–1914,* Princeton, N.J., 1961. Emphasizes the export of French capital and skill in the economic growth of Europe.

Clapham, John, *The Bank of England: A History,* Cambridge, 1944. The best history of this important institution.

Cooke, James J., *The New French Imperialism, 1880–1910; The Third Republic and Colonial Expansion,* Hamden, Conn., 1973.

• Fieldhouse, D. K., *The Colonial Empires,* London, 1966. A general survey from the eighteenth to the twentieth centuries.

• Gollwitzer, Heinz, *Europe in the Age of Imperialism, 1880–1914,* London, 1969.

Henderson, W. O., *Studies in German Colonial History,* Chicago, 1962.

• Hobsbawm, Eric, *Industry and Empire: The Making of Modern English Society, 1750 to the Present Day,* New York, 1968.

• Hodgart, Alan, *The Economics of European Imperialism,* New York, 1978.

• Kindleberger, C. P., *Economic Growth in France and Britain, 1851–1950,* Cambridge, Mass., 1963. A technical account.

• Landes, David S., *The Unbound Prometheus,* London, 1969. Particularly good on the Anglo-German rivalry.

Langer, William L., *The Diplomacy of Imperialism, 1890–1902,* New York, 1960.

Louis, William Roger, ed., *Imperialism: The Robinson and Gallagher Controversy,* New York, 1976. The best introduction to recent debate over the nature and causes of imperialism.

May, E. R., *American Imperialism,* New York, 1968.

Milward, Alan S., and S. B. Saul, *The Development of the Economies of Continental Europe, 1850–1914,* Cambridge, Mass., 1977. An excellent, comprehensive text, particularly good on the smaller European nations.

Platt, D. C. M., *Finance, Trade, and Politics in British Foreign Policy, 1815–1914,* Oxford, 1968.

Price, Roger, *The Economic Modernization of France,* New York, 1975. Rejects conventional periodizations; stresses the advent of railroads which transformed the market structure of France.

Robinson, Ronald, and J. Gallagher, *Africa and the Victorians: The Official Mind of Imperialism,* London, 1961. Contains their famous thesis that imperialism was not deliberately pursued as a policy of state, but rather was a response to events in colonial areas. The modern debate over imperialism begins with this work.

• Shannon, Richard, *The Crisis of Imperialism, 1865–1915,* St. Albans, Eng., 1976. An excellent survey of the transformation of British society in the wake of modern industrialization.

Stolper, Gustav, et al., *The German Economy, 1870 to the Present,* New York, 1967. A good introduction.

Thornton, A. P., *Doctrines of Imperialism,* New York, 1965.

SOURCE MATERIALS

Court, W. H. B., *British Economic History, 1870–1914: Commentary and Documents,* Cambridge, 1965. An excellent collection of documents.

Lenin, Vladimir, *Imperialism: The Highest Stage of Capitalism,* 1916. (Many English editions.) Lenin's most significant contribution to Marxist ideology. He saw the essence of imperialism as the export of capital rather than goods which led to worldwide competition, of which World War I was an inevitable result.

• ———, *The Lenin Anthology,* ed. by R. C. Tucker, New York, 1975.

Reitz, Deneys, *Commando: A Boer Journal of the Boer War,* London, 1929. A superb memoir of the Boer War.

Chapter 30

THE MIDDLE CLASS CHALLENGED

The time of surprise attacks, of revolutions carried through by small conscious minorities at the head of unconscious masses, is past. Where it is a question of a complete transformation of the social organization, the masses themselves must also be in it, must themselves already have grasped what is at stake, what they are going in for, with body and soul.
—Friedrich Engels, *The Class Struggles in France, 1848–50*

Capitalism's <u>continuing expansion</u> encouraged middle-class men and women at the end of the nineteenth century to believe themselves the necessary key to the progress of the human race. At the same time, however, that belief was being challenged from several directions. In each case, the challenges called into question assumptions close to the core of middle-class consciousness. Socialist doctrine, which was for the first time receiving a widespread hearing, pronounced capitalism a threat, rather than a boon, to society. New scientific theories—particularly the theory of evolution—declared that the key to progress was not the well-laid schemes of humanity, but chance. <u>Psychologists</u> discovered the irrationality of human beings and <u>philosophers their ultimate helplessness</u>. Paintings, poetry, and music proclaimed an artists' revolution on behalf of the idea of <u>art for its own sake,</u> not for the edification of a middle-class public. Together, these various intellectual and cultural currents threatened the notion that society would most successfully advance under middle-class auspices, setting its course in accordance with middle-class moral and economic precepts, and placing its faith in a belief in the importance and inevitability of <u>continued material progress</u>.

The dimensions of the challenge

1. THE CHALLENGE OF SOCIALISM

Marx in England

The history of socialism in the latter half of nineteenth century is, to a great degree, the biography of its most famous propagandist and theoretician, Karl Marx (1818–1883). Marx was both a social thinker and a political leader. At certain times theory dictated his actions; at others, political events led him to alter doctrine. But always he was at the center of the socialist movement, his moral passion, as much as his scholarly research, shaping the course of its events. The fact of his continuing influence is particularly remarkable for two reasons. First, although a German, he lived from 1849 until his death in London, an exile from the mainstream of continental socialism, in a country whose toleration of socialists was a mark of its comparative immunity from their doctrines. Second, Marx was not a leader who readily took others into his confidence. His antisocial nature was due, in part, to the poverty in which he was forced to live. He and his family were kept alive by gifts of money from his faithful friend and collaborator, Friedrich Engels, who had gone to work for his father's Manchester textile firm, and by occasional stints as a political journalist—for a time Marx was a correspondent for the *New York Tribune*.

Capital

During the 1850s and 1860s Marx labored to produce his definitive analysis of capitalist economics, *Capital*, the first volume of which was published in 1867. In it Marx elaborated upon the theories first enunciated in his earlier economic tracts. He described in detail the processes of production, exchange, and distribution as they operated within the capitalist system. He argued that under capitalism, workers were denied their rightful share of profits. The value of any manufactured item, Marx claimed, was determined by the amount of labor necessary to produce it. Yet workers were hired at wages whose value was far less than the value of the goods they produced. The difference between the value of workers' wages and the value of their work as sold was pocketed by members of the capitalist class, who, according to Marx, made off with far more than a justifiable portion of the sale price. This so-called labor theory of value, borrowed from a somewhat similar doctrine held by Ricardo and other classical economists, was the basis for Marx's claim that the working class was compelled to suffer under the capitalist system. Because workers were forced to sell their labor they became nothing more than commodities in the economic market.

So long as capitalists refused to pay wages more nearly equal to the labor value of their employees' work, those employees would remain exploited. Marx preached that the only class which, under capitalism, produced more wealth than it enjoyed was the working class, the proletariat. The bourgeoisie, which owned the means of production and was therefore able to appropriate that which was rightfully the work-

Karl Marx

ers', had a vested interest in maintaining the status quo; hence its willingness to make use of political, social, religious, and legal institutions to keep the proletariat in its place.

Marx predicted that capitalism would eventually do itself in. He argued that as time passed, market competition would compel the formation of ever-larger industrial and financial combinations. As the smaller enterpreneurial class—the petty bourgeoisie—was squeezed out by more powerful combines, its members would join with the proletariat, until society resembled a vast pyramid, with a much-enlarged proletariat at its base and an opposing force of a few powerful capitalists at its tip. At this point, Marx declared, the proletariat would rise in revolution against what was left of the bourgeoisie.

Marx as prophet

After capitalism had received its death blow at the hands of the workers, it would be followed by a stage of socialism. This would have three characteristics: the dictatorship of the proletariat; payment in accordance with work performed; and ownership and operation by the state of all means of production, distribution, and exchange. But socialism was intended to be merely a transition to something higher. In time it would be succeeded by communism, the goal of historical evolution. Communism would mean, first of all, the classless society. No one would live by owning, but solely by working. The state would now disappear, relegated to the museum of antiquities, "along with the bronze ax and the spinning wheel." Nothing would replace it except voluntary associations to operate the means of production and provide for social necessities. The *essence* of communism was payment in accordance with needs. The wage system would be completely abolished, and citizens would be expected to work in accordance with their faculties, entitled to receive from the total fund of wealth produced an amount in proportion to their needs.

The advent of communism

In the ten years after its publication, *Capital* was translated into English (Marx had written it in German), French, Russian, and Italian. It became the theoretical rallying point for a growing band of socialists who stood opposed to the world the middle class had made. For a time it breathed life into an organization of continental and British workers that had been founded in London in 1864: the International Workingmen's Association, usually referred to as the International. This body had been formed with the declared purpose of forging an international working-class alliance to overthrow capitalism and abolish private property. Marx delivered its inaugural address, in which he preached that workers must win political power for themselves if they were ever to escape their industrial bondage. Various difficulties had prevented the formation of a radically oriented workers' organization prior to this time. There was, first of all, fear of official reprisal. Second, the irregular pace of industrialization across Europe meant that workers in one country could have little understanding of the particular plight of their fellow-workers elsewhere. Finally, the period after

The First International

1850 had witnessed an increase in general prosperity which encouraged the more highly skilled—and more politically conscious—workers to forsake revolutionary goals and to pursue the more immediate end of accommodation with middle-class politicians. The German socialists' dealings with Bismarck (see below, p. 789), were a case in point. Meanwhile, however, the determination of a small band of dedicated radical socialists temporarily surmounted the problems to permit the formation of the first international workers' association.

Marx immediately assumed the direction of the International. He labored to exclude moderates from its councils and denounced the German socialists, and their leader Ferdinand Lassalle (1825–1864), for

striking bargains with Bismarck. The duty of socialists, Marx argued, was not partnership with the state, but rather its overthrow. At the same time Marx battled the doctrines of the Russian anarchist Michael Bakunin (1814–1876), who opposed the socialist notion that social evil was the product of capitalism. Bakunin argued that the state was the ultimate villain, and preached its immediate destruction through isolated acts of terrorism. He also opposed centralization within the International, urging instead a kind of federal autonomy for each national workers' group. To Marx, these individualist notions represented nothing more than reversion to a kind of primitive rebellion, heroic but ultimately fruitless. He succeeded in having Bakunin banished from the International in 1872. The International prospered for a time during the 1860s. Individual trade unions in various countries were persuaded to join in this united campaign which preached revolution and, through the application of pressure both at the ballot box and in the factory, seemed to promise at least higher wages and shorter hours. Under Marx's direction the International was a highly organized and tightly controlled body, far more effective in this respect than any previous socialist organization.

Yet by 1876 it had faded from existence. Despite Marx's abilities as an authoritarian chief of staff, the International throughout its existence had to battle those same circumstances which delayed its foundation. In addition, Marx's insistence upon control from the center

thwarted a growing desire on the part of individual socialist organizations to pursue programs of immediate benefit to themselves. These factors weakened the International. What probably brought about its demise was its association with events occurring in Paris after the defeat of France by Germany in 1870 in the Franco–Prussian War.

Following the collapse of Napoleon III, a new republic, generally conservative in tone, had been established by the French. In March

1871, the government attempted to disarm the Paris National Guard, a volunteer citizen army with radical political sympathies. The guard refused to surrender, declared its autonomy, deposed officials of the new government, and proclaimed a revolutionary committee—the Commune—as the true government of France. Though this move-

The Aftermath of the Paris Commune. A view of Champs Élysées showing damage resulting from the 1871 uprising. The Arc de Triomphe may be seen in the distance.

ment is commonly described as a rebellion of dangerous radicals intent upon the destruction of law and order, most of its members resembled the Jacobins of the first French Revolution and belonged largely to the lower middle class. They did not advocate the abolition of private property but rather its wider distribution. The movement was precipitated by bitterness over the defeat of Napoleon III and exhaustion by the long siege of Paris that followed. Added to these factors were fears that the central government would be dominated by the rural population to the disadvantage of the urban masses in the capital. After several weeks of frustrating disputation, the conflict turned into a bloody civil war. The Communards killed about sixty hostages, including the archbishop of Paris. The government numbered its victims by the thousands. The courts-martial which were set up executed twenty-six. Thousands of others were sentenced to imprisonment or banishment in New Caledonia, in the South Pacific.

While middle-class Europe reacted in horror at what it perceived as a second Reign of Terror, Marx, in the name of the International, extolled the courage of the Communards, who, he wrote, had fought the first pitched battle in the class war he had predicted. In a pamphlet entitled *The Civil War in France* (1871), Marx claimed that the Commune was an example of the transitional form of government through which the working class would have to pass on its way to emancipation. But many of the less radical members of the International were frightened and disturbed not only by the events of the Commune itself, but by the possibility of reprisals against members of an organization that openly praised men and women who were considered by the middle class to be little more than murderers. In 1872 Marx acknowl-

The Commune and the International

The Assassination of Hostages by the Communards in Paris, 1871

edged defeat by moving the seat of the International's council to the United States, a country far removed from the organization's affairs and from the criticisms that had begun to be heaped upon Marx for his misdirection. In 1876, the First International expired.

The spread of socialism

Although the International collapsed, socialism continued to gain ground as both a theory and a program. The German Social Democratic party was founded in 1875; a Belgian Socialist party in 1879; and in France, despite the disasters of the Commune, a Socialist party was established in 1905. In England, although socialism was much debated and discussed, no party proclaiming itself socialist emerged. When the Labour party came into being in 1901, however, various socialist societies were represented on its executive council, along with less radical, nonsocialist trade union groups. On the periphery of Europe—in Spain, Italy, and Russia—socialism made less headway. There the absence of widespread industrialization and the educational backwardness of large elements within the population retarded the development of a working-class consciousness, and of socialism as its political expression.

"Purists" vs. "revisionists"

During the years before the First World War, socialists continuously and often bitterly debated the course they should follow as they attempted to achieve their goal of radical change. One group, led by Marx himself until his death, urged socialists to avoid collaboration with other parties to achieve such immediate ends as higher wages, shorter working hours, unemployment insurance, etc. These reforms, the "purists" declared, were the means by which the bourgeoisie could buy off the proletariat and hence indefinitely postpone revolution. On the other hand, "revisionist" socialists urged their followers to take advantage of the fact that many of them now could vote for socialist candidates in elections. They argued that those candidates, if elected, could help them obtain a better life in the immediate future. Socialist theory might proclaim a worldwide struggle of the proletariat against the bourgeoisie; but was this any reason to turn one's back on a chance to make real headway through the ballot box in achieving reforms that would put a better life within reach of workers and their families?

Revisionism spread despite efforts of the "purists" to put a stop to it. In Germany the pattern had been established by Lassalle, whose opportunism had led him to bargain with Bismarck. Following his death, his place as theorist was taken by Eduard Bernstein, a Social Democrat and member of the German parliament, the Reichstag. Bernstein argued that capitalism could be gradually transformed to benefit the working class, and that revolution might not be necessary to achieve this end. Bernstein's most outspoken opponent in Germany was his fellow socialist Karl Kautsky, an orthodox Marxist who warned that collaboration would end in the total corruption and demoralization of the proletariat. In France, the same battle was waged by the "purist" Jules Guesde, who preached that the Socialist party's primary goal should be the development of proletarian class consciousness, and Jean Jaurès, socialist leader in the Chamber of Deputies, who advocated a revisionist course. In both Germany and France, revisionists outnumbered purists by a wide margin. This was, to an even greater degree, the case in Britain. There, Fabian socialists—so named from their policy of delay, in imitation of the tactics of Fabius, a Roman general—preached what they called "the inevitability of gradualism." They believed their country would evolve towards socialism by means of parliamentary democracy. Prominent among the Fabians were the social investigators Sidney and Beatrice Webb, the novelist H. G. Wells, and the playwright George Bernard Shaw.

The continued success of revisionism led its opponents to sharpen their attack and to advocate increasingly violent means to achieve their ends. Their campaigns, though they never managed to convince a majority of the working class, nevertheless attracted an increasing number of adherents. Some who had originally supported the revisionists grew disappointed when reforms did not come as quickly as expected. At the same time, in much of Europe, the cost of living began to rise for many workers. The comparative prosperity that some members of the working class had experienced vanished in the face of price rises that were not matched by wage increases. The result was a frustration which encouraged the adoption of a more militant stance. Germans rallied to the side of the radical socialists Rosa Luxemburg and Karl Liebknecht, while in France a new revolutionary socialist party disowned the reformist leader Alexandre Millerand, after he agreed to serve as cabinet member in a nonsocialist government.

Jean Jaurès

*Anarchism and
syndicalism*

The Second International, which had been founded in 1889, demanded at a conference in 1906 that affiliated parties declare their goal to be the destruction of the bourgeois order and the state which served its interests.

This militant mood encouraged acceptance of the doctrines of anarchists and syndicalists. Anarchists preached the overthrow of capitalism by violence. They differed from socialists, however, in their hatred of the machinery of the state or any government based upon coercion. Socialists argued that until the communist millennium promised by Marx, the state would remain a necessary means to the achievement of that eventual end. Anarchists worked to see the immediate abolition of a state bureaucracy which, no matter who controlled it, they believed would result in tyranny. Bakunin, whom Marx had succeeded in expelling from the First International, was anarchism's most popular propagandist. Syndicalism, like anarchism, demanded the abolition of both capitalism and the state. It resembled socialism in its demand that workers share in the ownership of the means of production. Instead of making the state the owner and operator of the means of production, however, the syndicalist would delegate these functions to syndicates of producers. Thus all the steel mills would be owned and operated by the workers in the steel industry, the coal mines by the workers in the coal industry, and so on. These associations would take the place of the state, each one governing its own members in all of their activities as producers. In all other matters workers would be free from interference.

Sorel

Syndicalism received its most sympathetic hearing in France, where a General Confederation of Labour, after 1902, resolved to seek solutions to economic problems outside the legally constituted framework of French politics. The most effective spokesman for syndicalism was the Frenchman Georges Sorel (1847–1922). Sorel, in his *Reflections on Violence,* published in 1908, argued that workers should be made to believe in the possibility of a general strike by the proletariat which would result in the end of bourgeois civilization. The general strike might be nothing more than myth, Sorel acknowledged. Yet, as myth, it remained a powerful weapon in the hands of those whose goal was the destruction of society and who must not shy from the employment of violent means to achieve that end.

Socialism before the First World War, then, was not a unified force. It was divided by quarrels between purists and revisionists, and challenged by the even more radical proposals of anarchists and syndicalists. Socialists, intent on their goal of international solidarity among working classes, ignored the appeal that nationalism and imperialism might make to workers in France, Germany, and Britain. Yet despite its divisions and weaknesses, socialism appeared to the middle classes of Europe as a real threat to their continued prosperity. Capitalism had provided the machinery by which the bourgeoisie had

Georges Sorel

THE INDUSTRIAL REVOLUTION

Percent of population living in cities
of 100,000 or more

5% or less

6-10%

20% or more

Iron ore deposits

Coal and lignite deposits

Centers of industry

Railroads in 1850

0   300 miles

RUSSIAN EMPIRE

St. Petersburg

Moscow

SWEDEN

Uppsala
Stockholm

NORWAY

DENMARK

BALTIC SEA

NORTH SEA

GERMAN EMPIRE

Warsaw

Lodz

Posen

Berlin

Hamburg

Bremen

Amsterdam

Rotterdam

NETHERLANDS

Brussels

BELGIUM

Lille

Liège

RUHR

Essen

Cologne

SAAR

Strasbourg

Frankfurt

Karlsruhe

Stuttgart

Mulhouse

Basel

SWITZERLAND

Zurich

Leipzig

Dresden

SILESIA

Breslau

Prague

Pilsen

Chemnitz

Zwickau

Eisenach

Kassel

Nuremberg

Munich

Steyr

Vienna

Cracow

Lemberg

AUSTRIAN EMPIRE

Budapest

KINGDOM OF GREAT BRITAIN

Glasgow

Dublin

Darlington

Leeds

Sheffield

Liverpool

Manchester

Birmingham

Cardiff

London

ATLANTIC OCEAN

Le Havre

Amiens

Paris

Orleans

Nantes

Tours

Limoges

FRANCE

Lyons

Avignon

Marseilles

Milan

Turin

Livorno

Florence

ITALY

Rome

Naples

Barcelona

SPAIN

Madrid

Bilbao

Santander

Gijon

Oviedo

Seville

Jerez

Granada

MEDITERRANEAN SEA

BLACK SEA

OTTOMAN EMPIRE

The Massacre of Chios, Eugène Delacroix (1798–1863). During the Greek war for independence, Turks slaughtered more than 20,000 Greeks in 1822, depicted in this famous painting. (Louvre)

Liberty Leading the People, Eugène Delacroix (1798–1863). Delacroix was a colorful painter of dramatic and emotional themes, as exemplified by this imaginary scene from the Revolution of 1830. (Louvre)

The Last of England, Ford Madox Brown (1821–1893). A haunting scene of a couple emigrating from England by one of the most noted pre-Raphaelites. (The City Museum and Art Gallery, Birmingham, England)

Valley of Aosta—Snowstorm, Avalanche, and Thunderstorm, Joseph M. W. Turner (1775–1851). Turner's complete absorption in light, color, and atmosphere helped to prepare the way for the French impressionists. (MMA)

Portrait of a Gentleman, Jean Auguste Ingres (1780–1867). A student of David, Ingres was a devoted admirer of classical antiquities. But he was also influenced by romanticism. (MMA)

A Woman Reading, Camille Corot (1796–1875). Corot was predominantly a naturalist, a painter of lifelike scenes of innocence and simplicity. He shared the romanticists' sentimental worship of woods and fields. (MMA)

The Port of La Rochelle, Corot. (Louvre)

Beatrice and Dante, William Blake (1757–1827). This painting is from Blake's series for *The Divine Comedy*. (The Tate Gallery, London)

The Gleaners, Jean François Millet (1814–1875). Sensuous colors and love of natural settings typifies Millet's work. (Louvre)

Above: *The Guitarist*, Édouard Manet (1832–1883). Right: *Émile Zola*, Manet. Though Manet is called the "father of impressionism," he was also a rebel against the traditions of sweetness and artificiality that dominated the XIX cent. He liberated painting, as his friend Zola emancipated literature. (MMA) (Louvre)

Village Girls, Gustave Courbet (1819–1877). One of the first of the realists, Courbet often portrayed life in a bitter and disparaging light. He eschewed imagination and painted only what he saw. (MMA)

The Third-Class Carriage, Honoré Daumier (1808–1879). Though Daumier was noted for his realistic caricatures and satires, his attitude toward common folk was one of sympathy and understanding. (MMA)

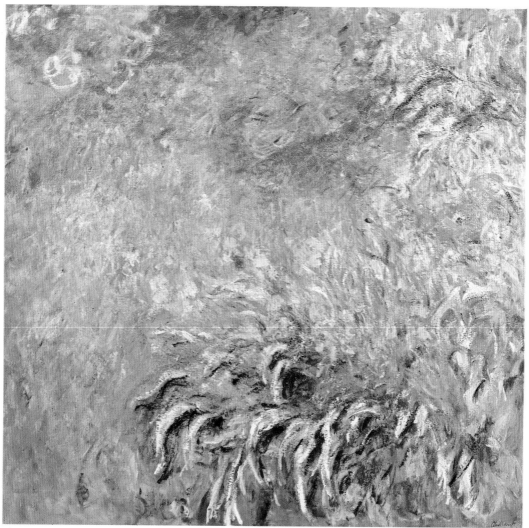

Iris beside a Pond, Claude Monet (1840–1926). Monet called some of his paintings Impressions, and the name soon came to designate a school. (Art Institute of Chicago)

Pink and Green, Edgar Degas (1834–1917). Degas was an impressionist to the extent of his interest in fleeting motion. But as an admirer of the classicist Ingres, he emphasized line and careful composition. (MMA)

Still Life, Cézanne. It has been said that when the impressionists painted a haystack, there was light, but there was no haystack. When Cézanne painted an apple, there was the play of light; there was also the apple. (MMA)

Montagne Sainte-Victoire with Aqueduct, Paul Cézanne (1839–1906). This landscape has been a source of inspiration for many of the tendencies of so-called "modern" art. The composition is as structurally balanced and proportioned as a Greek temple. (MMA)

The Japanese Divan, Henri de Toulouse-Lautrec (1864–1901). Toulouse-Lautrec found his chief source of inspiration in the night life of Paris. *Divan Japonais* was a noted Paris café. (MMA)

The Card Players, Cézanne. Here are exemplified Cézanne's skill in composition, his discriminating sense of color, and the sculptured qualities of solidity and depth he gave to his figures. (Stephen C. Clark)

Portrait of the Artist, Vincent van Gogh (1853–1890). This self-portrait shows a deep seriousness and intense concentration. (V. W. van Gogh)

Ia Orana Maria, Paul Gauguin (1848–1903). Gauguin revolted not only against the complexity and artificiality of European life, but against civilization itself. He finally fled to Tahiti to paint the lush, colorful life of an uncorrupted society. (MMA)

The Starry Night, van Gogh. This painting gives vivid expression to van Gogh's bold conceptions. (Museum of Modern Art)

Sunflowers in a Vase, van Gogh. The feverish technique seems to have endowed the flowers with rhythmic motion. (V. W. van Gogh)

A Young Woman in the Sun, Auguste Renoir (1841–1919). Though Renoir used impressionist techniques, the results sometimes bore little resemblance to the work of other impressionists. He believed that "a picture ought to be a lovable thing, joyous and pretty." (Jeu de Paume)

Balzac, Auguste Rodin (1840–1917). Rodin was the great realist of XIX-cent. sculpture. He concentrated most of his attention upon facial detail, no matter how unflattering the result might be. (MMA)

Luncheon of the Boating Party, Renoir. (Phillips Memorial Gallery)

The Piano Lesson, Henri Matisse (1869–1954). Matisse conveyed a freshness of approach and a vitality of line and color. (Museum of Modern Art)

Portrait of Gertrude Stein, Pablo Picasso (1881–1973). Picasso seems to have given this portrait of the great experimenter in poetry some elements of the distortion of form characteristic of the work of both. (Museum of Modern Art)

Three Musicians, Pablo Picasso. This painting, regarded by many as the masterpiece of cubism, sums up the final stage of the movement. (Museum of Modern Art)

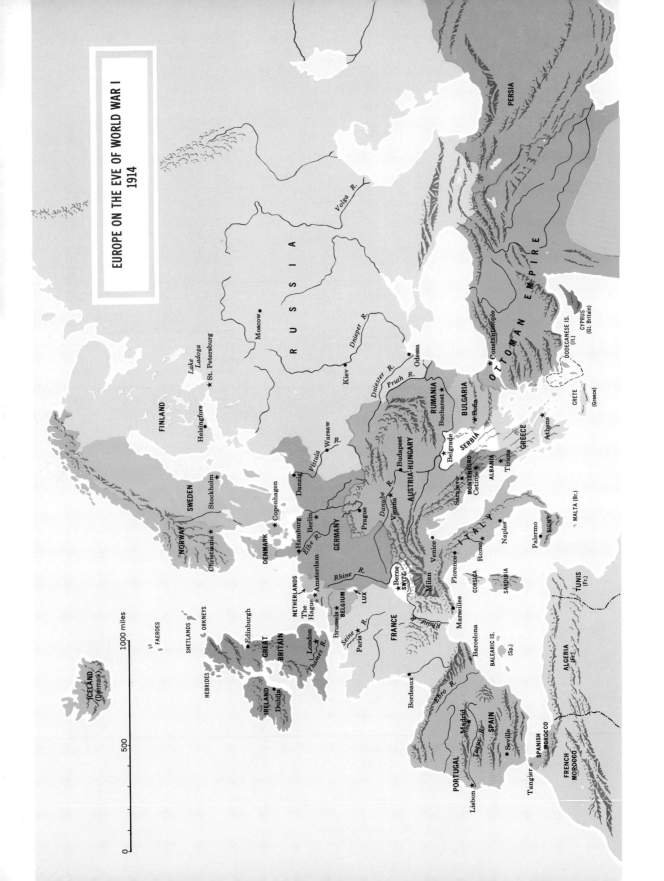

EUROPE ON THE EVE OF WORLD WAR I
1914

ICELAND
(Denmark)

FAEROES

SHETLANDS
ORKNEYS

HEBRIDES

IRELAND
• Dublin

GREAT
BRITAIN
• Edinburgh

London ★
Thames R.

FINLAND

NORWAY
Christiania ★

SWEDEN
Stockholm ★

DENMARK
Copenhagen ★

Helsingfors •

Lake
Ladoga
★ St. Petersburg

Moscow •

R U S S I A

Volga R.

Dnieper R.

Kiev •

Odessa •

Dniester R.

Pruth R.

NETHERLANDS
The Hague ★
Amsterdam •
Brussels ★
BELGIUM
LUX.

Danzig •

Vistula

Warsaw •
R.

GERMANY
Hamburg •
Berlin ★
Elbe R.

Prague ★
Vienna ★

Budapest ★

AUSTRIA-HUNGARY

Danube R.

RUMANIA
Bucharest ★

BULGARIA
Sofia ★

Belgrade ★
SERBIA

Sarajevo •
MONTENEGRO
Cetinje ★
ALBANIA
Tirana ★

GREECE
Athens ★

OTTOMAN EMPIRE

★ Constantinople

PERSIA

DODECANESE IS.
(It.)

CYPRUS
(Gt. Britain)

CRETE
(Greece)

Rhine R.

★ Berne
SWITZ.

FRANCE

Seine R.

Paris ★

Bordeaux •

Milan •
Venice •
ITALY
Florence •
Rome ★

CORSICA

SARDINIA

Naples •

Palermo •
SICILY

MALTA (Br.)

Marseilles •

Rhone R.

Barcelona •

Ebro R.

SPAIN
Madrid ★
Seville •

Tagus R.

PORTUGAL
Lisbon •

Tangier •
SPANISH
MOROCCO

FRENCH
MOROCCO

ALGERIA
(Fr.)

TUNIS
(Fr.)

BALEARIC IS.
(Sp.)

1000 miles

500

0

The Haymarket Riots, Chicago, 1886. A comtemporary illustration depicting the results of attempts to unionize workers at the McCormick Harvester works.

achieved power. Socialism attacked capitalism and hence those who were its direct beneficiaries. Although most socialists disapproved of violence, violent acts were attributed by middle-class men and women to an amorphous, anticapitalist body easily labeled "socialist." Riots by trade unionists in Chicago's Haymarket Square in 1886 and in London's Trafalgar Square in 1887; the assassinations of President Sadi Carnot of France in 1894, of King Humbert of Italy in 1900, and of President William McKinley of the United States in 1901; strikes which grew in number and violence throughout Europe and America after 1900—all these events were perceived by members of the middle class as part of a larger movement whose professed goal was to tear from them their economic, political, and social security.

Socialism as a threat to the middle class

2. THE CHALLENGE OF SCIENCE AND PHILOSOPHY

While socialism challenged middle-class self-confidence from one quarter, science and philosophy threatened from another. The fact that science might undermine, rather than sustain, certainty was all the more difficult to comprehend, given the manner in which science and technology had together assisted in the birth and continued development of industrialization. This is not to say that science abandoned its role as an instrument for the solving of human problems and as a vital aid to continuing progress. There were striking improvements in the field of medicine, for example. The Frenchman Louis Pasteur (1822–1895) proved that all forms of life, no matter how small, are reproduced only by living beings. Hitherto, according to the theory of spontaneous generation, it had commonly been supposed that bacte-

Science and progress

Louis Pasteur

Marie Curie

Darwin

ria and other microscopic organisms originated from water or from other decaying vegetable and animal matter. By locating the source of bacteria, Pasteur's discovery opened the way for major improvements in the areas of public sanitation and health, among others, the process of ridding food of objectionable bacteria by sterilization—pasteurization—that was named for him. Pasteur, along with the German Robert Koch (1843–1910), also proved conclusively that germs were not, as was commonly supposed, the result but rather the cause of disease. The discovery of the X-ray by the German Wilhelm von Röntgen in 1895 and of radium by the Polish scientist Marie Curie in 1898 not only altered perceptions as to the nature of energy, but suggested ways in which energy could be put to use for medical purposes. These discoveries—along with similarly important ones in the areas of cell theory, anesthetics, and antiseptics—worked to convince the educated public that science was a friend of humanity, and that it was also predictable, operating in accordance with laws which had only to be discovered in order to be put to use. Isaac Newton's law of gravitation continued to reign supreme, arguing that the universe was orderly, and essentially timeless, and that the passage of time brought with it no fundamental change.

Against this psychologically reassuring fortress of a harmonious universe, biological scientists hurled the bomb of evolutionary theory. We have seen that this theory was at least as old as Anaximander in the sixth century B.C., and that it was accepted by many of the great minds of antiquity. We have learned also that it was revived in the eighteenth century by the scientists Buffon and Linnaeus. But neither of these men offered much proof or explained how the process of evolution works. The first to develop a systematic hypothesis of evolution was the French biologist, Jean Lamarck (1744–1829). The essential principle in Lamarck's hypothesis, published in 1809, was the inheritance of acquired characteristics. He maintained that an animal, subjected to a change in environment, acquired new habits, which in turn were reflected in structural changes. These acquired characteristics of body structure, he believed, were transmissible to the offspring, with the result that after a series of generations a new species of animal was eventually produced. Lamarck's successors found little evidence to confirm this hypothesis, but it dominated biological thought for nearly fifty years.

A much more convincing hypothesis of organic evolution was that of the English naturalist Charles Darwin (1809–1882), published in 1859. The son of a small-town physician, Darwin began the study of medicine at the University of Edinburgh, but soon withdrew and entered Cambridge to prepare for the ministry. Here he gave most of his time to natural history. In 1831 Darwin obtained an appointment as naturalist without pay on H.M.S. *Beagle,* which had been chartered for a scientific expedition around the world. The voyage lasted nearly five years and gave Darwin an unparalleled opportunity to become acquainted at first hand with the manifold variations of animal life. He noted the differences between animals inhabiting islands and related species on nearby continents, and observed the resemblances between living animals and the fossilized remains of extinct species in the same locality. It was a magnificent preparation for his life's work. Upon returning from the voyage he read Malthus's essay on population, and was struck by the author's contention that throughout the world of nature many more individuals are born than can ever survive, and that consequently the weaker ones must perish in the struggle for food. Finally, after twenty more years of careful and extensive research, he issued his *Origin of Species* (1859).

Darwin's hypothesis was that of natural selection. He argued that it is nature, or the environment, which selects those variants among offspring that are to survive and reproduce. Darwin pointed out, first of all, that the parents of every species beget more offspring than can possibly survive. He maintained that, consequently, a struggle takes place among these offspring for food, shelter, warmth, and other conditions necessary for life. In this struggle for existence certain individuals have the advantage because of the factor of *variation,* which means that no two of the offspring are exactly alike. Some are born strong, others weak; some have longer horns or sharper claws than their brothers and sisters or perhaps a body coloration which enables them better to blend with their surroundings and thus to evade their enemies. It is these favored members of the species that win out in the struggle for existence and survive as the "fittest" of their generation; the others are eliminated generally before they have lived long enough to reproduce. Darwin regarded variation and natural selection as the primary factors in the origin of new species. In other words, he taught that individuals with favorable characteristics would transmit their inherited qualities to their descendants through countless generations, and that successive eliminations of the least fit would eventually produce a new species. Darwin applied his concept of evolution not only to plant and animal species but also to humans. In his second great work, *The Descent of Man* (1871), he attempted to show that the human race originally sprang from some apelike ancestor, long since extinct, but probably a common forebear of the existing anthropoid apes and humans.

The Darwinian hypothesis was elaborated and improved by several later biologists. The German August Weismann (1834–1914) flatly rejected the idea that acquired characteristics could be inherited. He conducted experiments to show that body cells and reproductive cells are entirely distinct, and that there is no way in which changes in the former can effect the latter. He concluded, therefore, that the only qualities transmissible to the offspring are those which have always been present in the reproductive cells of the parents. In 1901 the Dutch botanist Hugo De Vries (1848–1935) published his celebrated mutation hypothesis, based upon Darwin's original hypothesis and, in

Charles Darwin

Illustrations from Darwin's First Edition of *The Descent of Man.* The drawings were used to point up the similarities between a human embryo *(top)* and that of a dog *(bottom).*

large part, upon laws of heredity discovered by the Austrian monk Gregor Mendel (1822–1884). De Vries asserted that evolution results not from minor variations, as Darwin had assumed, but from radical differences or mutations, which appear in more or less definite ratio among the offspring. When any of these mutations are favorable to survival in a given environment, the individuals possessing them naturally emerge triumphant in the struggle for existence. Not only do their descendants inherit these qualities, but from time to time new mutants appear, some of which are even better adapted for survival than their parents. Thus in a limited number of generations a new species may be brought into existence. The mutation theory of De Vries corrected one of the chief weaknesses in the Darwinian hypothesis. The variations which Darwin assumed to be the source of evolutionary changes are so small that an incredibly long time would be necessary to produce a new species. De Vries made it possible to conceive of evolution as proceeding by sudden leaps.

Evolution and chance

Clearly, the implications of this new theory were deeply disturbing for those who had until now believed in an orderly universe, or had taken as literal the words of the Bible. For the latter the task of reconciling Darwin's account of creation with the first chapter of Genesis, though troublesome, was often not insuperable. Outside fundamentalist sects, the Bible was, at this time, perceived by growing numbers as containing a combination of myths, legends, history, and profoundly important moral truths. The work of the German theologian David Friedrich Strauss (1808–1874) and of the French historian Ernest Renan (1832–1892) had cast doubt on the historical accuracy of the Bible, and dealt with its inconsistencies. These writers had defended the intentions of the Bible's various authors, while firmly insisting upon their human fallibilities. Their searching yet nevertheless sensitive critiques helped people understand that they need not abandon their Christian faith simply because Darwin insisted that the world and all that lived within it had been created over millions of years and not in six days. Far more difficult to deal with was the notion, explicit in Darwin, that nature was not a changeless harmony, but instead a constant and apparently undirected struggle. Chance, and not order, ruled the universe. Nothing was fixed, nothing perfect, all was in a state of flux. Good and bad were defined only in terms of an ability to survive. The "best" of a species were those that triumphed over their weaker rivals. All of a sudden, the universe had become a harsh and uncompromising place, deprived of pre-Darwinian certainties; belief in a benevolent God was now much harder to sustain.

Thomas Henry Huxley

Darwin's most vigorous defender, the philosopher Thomas Henry Huxley (1825–1895), was one of those who could no longer reconcile science with a belief in God. While he did not reject the possibility of a supernatural power, Huxley averred that "there is no evidence of the existence of such a being as the God of the theologians." He pronounced Christianity to be "a compound of some of the best and some of the worst elements of Paganism and Judaism, moulded in practice by the innate character of certain people of the Western World."[1] Huxley coined the word *agnosticism* to express his contempt for the attitude of dogmatic certainty symbolized by the beliefs of the ancient Gnostics.[2] As propounded by Huxley, agnosticism is the doctrine that neither the existence nor the nature of God nor the ultimate character of the universe is knowable.

The most uncompromising of the evolutionist philosophers was Ernst Heinrich Haeckel (1834–1919). Originally a physician, later a professor of biology, Haeckel was the first outstanding scientist on the Continent to subscribe wholeheartedly to Darwinism. At the age of sixty-five he summarized his conclusions in a book entitled *The Riddle of the Universe.* The philosophy of Haeckel comprised three main doctrines: atheism, materialism, and mechanism. He would have nothing to do with Huxley's agnosticism; on the contrary, he dogmatically affirmed that nothing spiritual exists. The universe, he maintained, was composed of matter alone, in a process of constant change from one form into another. Life, Haeckel stated, originated from the spontaneous combination of the essential elements of protoplasm. From these earliest forms of protoplasm all the complex species of the present gradually evolved through the process of natural selection. Haeckel regarded the mind of humans as just as much a product of evolution as the body. The human mind differs only in degree from the minds of the lower animals. Memory, imagination, perception, and thinking are mere functions of matter; psychology should be considered a branch of physiology. Such was the compact philosophy of materialism and determinism which appeared to Haeckel and his followers to be a logical deduction from the new biology.

The middle classes of western Europe and the United States, disoriented by the antireligious implications of evolutionary theory, received some comfort from the writings of those who adapted Darwinian thought to the analysis of society—the so-called Social Darwinists. These thinkers argued that the apparent "success" of Western civilization was the result of its special fitness. The white race, they boasted, had proved itself superior to the black; non-Jews superior to Jews; rich superior to poor; the British Empire superior to the subject territories it controlled. If nature was a matter of competition, so was society, with the victory going to that race or nation which could demonstrate its fitness to survive by subduing others.

Though he never expressed his ideas that crudely, the English philosopher Herbert Spencer (1820–1903) extolled the virtues of competition in a way that made it easier for others to do so. Spencer grounded

[1]T. H. Huxley, *Collected Essays,* V (London, 1902), 142.
[2]See above, p. 72.

Herbert Spencer

Anthropology

Friedrich Nietzsche

his philosophy upon evolutionary theory. His keynote was his idea of evolution as a universal law. He was deeply impressed by Darwin's *Origin of Species* and enriched the hypothesis of natural selection with a phrase that has clung to it ever since—"the survival of the fittest." He contended that not only species and individuals are subject to evolutionary change, but also planets, solar systems, customs, institutions, and religious and ethical ideas. Everything in the universe completes a cycle of origin, development, decay, and extinction. When the end of the cycle has been reached, the process begins once more and is repeated eternally. As a political philosopher, Spencer was a vigorous champion of individualism. He condemned collectivism as a relic of primitive society, as a feature of the earliest stage of social evolution. Any so-called assistance individuals might receive from the state, Spencer argued, would result not only in their own degeneration, but in that of society as well.

If Social Darwinists could reassure some by implying the biological right of Western civilization to survive as the "fittest" within the contemporary world, anthropologists—pioneers in what was essentially a new scientific discipline—argued, on the contrary, that no culture could be perceived as "better" than any other. All societies were adaptations to a particular environment. Each society produced its own customs, which could not be declared "good" or "bad," but only successful or unsuccessful, according to the degree to which they helped that society survive. This notion of cultural "relativism" was a theme in the influential work of the English anthropologist Sir James Frazer (1854–1941). In his masterpiece, *The Golden Bough*, he demonstrated the relationship of Christianity to primitive practices and magical rites. Christianity was nothing more or less than one society's response to the craving for an explanation of the apparently inexplicable.

Christianity was challenged far more directly in the writings of the German philosopher Friedrich Nietzsche (1844–1900). Nietzsche was not a scientist, nor was he interested in the nature of matter or in the problem of religious truth. He was essentially a romantic poet glorifying the struggle for existence to compensate for his own life of weakness and misery. Born in 1844, the son of a Lutheran minister, he was educated in the classics at Leipzig and Bonn and at the age of twenty-five was made a professor of philology at the University of Basel. Ten years later repeated and severe attacks of nerves forced his retirement. He spent the next decade of his life in agony, wandering from one resort to another in a fruitless quest for relief. If we can believe his own statement, each year was made up of two hundred days of pain. In 1888 he lapsed into hopeless insanity, which continued until his death in 1900.

Nietzsche's philosophy is contained in such works as *Thus Spake Zarathustra, A Genealogy of Morals,* and *The Will to Power*. His cardinal idea was the notion that natural selection should be permitted to operate unhindered in the case of human beings as it does with plants and animals. He believed that such a constant weeding out of the unfit would eventually produce a race of supermen—not merely a race of physical giants but men distinguished above all for their moral courage, for their strength of character. Those who should be allowed to perish in the struggle were the moral weaklings, who had neither the strength nor the courage to battle nobly for a place in the sun. Before any such process of natural selection could operate, however, religious obstacles would have to be removed. Nietzsche therefore demanded that the moral supremacy of Christianity and Judaism be overthrown. Both of these religions, he alleged, glorified the virtues of the downtrodden. They exalted into virtues qualities which ought to be considered vices—humility, nonresistance, mortification of the flesh, and pity for the weak and incompetent. The enthronement of these qualities prevented the elimination of the unift and preserved them to pour their degenerate blood into the veins of the race.

His philosophy

Scientists and philosophers, as they continued to explore the various and sometimes contradictory implications of evolutionary theory, helped to undermine the comforting notion of humankind's essential superiority to the rest of the animal kingdom. The work of the Russian psychologist Ivan Pavlov (1849–1936) resulted in the discovery of the conditioned reflex. Although Pavlov experimented with animals, he insisted that his conclusions applied equally to human beings. The conditioned reflex is a form of behavior in which natural reactions are produced by an artificial stimulus. Pavlov showed that if dogs were fed immediately following the ringing of a bell, they would eventually respond to the sound of the bell alone and secrete saliva exactly as if confronted by the sight and smell of the food. This discovery suggested the conclusion that the conditioned reflex is an important element in human behavior and encouraged psychologists to center their attention upon physiological experiment as a key to understanding the mind.

Pavlov

Pavlovians inaugurated a type of physiological psychology known as behaviorism. Behaviorism is an attempt to study the human being as a purely physiological organism—to reduce all human behavior to a series of physical responses. Such concepts as *mind* and *consciousness* are relegated to the scrap heap as vague and meaningless terms. For the behaviorist nothing is important except the reactions of muscles, nerves, glands, and visceral organs. There is no such thing as an independent psychic behavior; all that humans do is physical. Thinking is essentially a form of talking to oneself. Every complex emotion and idea is simply a group of physiological responses produced by some stimulus in the environment. Such was the extremely mechanistic interpretation of human actions offered by followers of Pavlov.

Behaviorism

The other important school of psychology to make its appearance

Sigmund Freud

after the turn of the century was psychoanalysis, founded by Sigmund Freud (1856–1939), an Austrian physician. Psychoanalysis interprets human behavior mainly in terms of the unconscious mind. Freud admitted the existence of the conscious mind (the ego), but he avowed that the unconscious (the id) is much more important in determining the actions of the individual. He considered humans as egoistic creatures propelled by basic urges of power, self-preservation, and sex. These urges are much too strong to be overcome; but inasmuch as society (the superego) has branded their unrestrained fulfillment as sinful, they are commonly driven into the unconscious, where they linger indefinitely as suppressed desires. Yet they are seldom completely submerged; they rise to the surface in dreams, or they manifest themselves in lapses of memory, in fears and obsessions, and in various forms of abnormal behavior. Freud believed that most cases of mental and nervous disorders result from violent conflicts between natural instincts and the restraints imposed by an unfortunate environment. Freud hoped that by elucidating his theory of the unconscious he could impose predictable patterns upon the irrationality that seemed to characterize so much human activity. His search for order, however, resembled that of the behaviorists by continuing to stress the extent to which men and women, like animals, were prey to drives, impulses, and reflexes over which they could exercise at best only minimal control.

Under the impact of these various scientific and philosophical challenges, the institutions responsible for the maintenance of traditional faith found themselves hard pressed. Protestantism had based its revolt against Roman Catholic orthodoxy upon the belief that men and women should seek to understand God with the aid of not much more than the Bible and a willing conscience. In consequence, Protestants had little in the way of authoritarian doctrine to support them when their faith was challenged. Some—the fundamentalists—chose to ignore the implications of scientific and philosophical inquiry altogether, and continued to believe in the literal truth of the Bible. Some were willing to agree with the school of American philosophers known as Pragmatists (Charles Pierce, William James), that if belief in a personal God produced mental peace or spiritual satisfaction, that belief must therefore be true. Truth, for the Pragmatists, was whatever provided useful, practical results. Other Protestants sought solace from religious doubt in religious activity, founding missions, and laboring among the poor. Many adherents to this "Social Gospel" were also "Modernists," determined to accept the ethical teachings of Christianity while discarding belief in miracles and the doctrines of original sin and the Incarnation.

The Roman Catholic Church was compelled by its tradition of dogmatic assertion to assist its followers in their response to the modern world. In 1864 Pope Pius IX issued a *Syllabus of Errors* condemning what he regarded as the principal religious and philosophical "errors" of the time. Among them were materialism, free thought, and "indifferentism," or the idea that one religion is as good as another. Though the *Syllabus* was generally accepted by the Church, it was condemned by some critics as a "crusade against civilization." While heated discussions continued over the *Syllabus of Errors* Pope Pius convoked a Church council in 1869, the first to be summoned since the Catholic Reformation. The most noted pronouncement of the Vatican Council was the dogma of papal infallibility. In the language of this dogma the pope, when he speaks *ex cathedra*—that is in his capacity "as pastor and doctor of all Christians"—is infallible in regard to all matters of faith and morals. Though generally accepted by pious Catholics, the dogma of papal infallibility evoked a storm of protest in many circles. Governments of several Catholic countries denounced it, including France, Spain, and Italy. The death of Pius IX in 1878 and the accession of Pope Leo XIII brought a more accomodating climate to the Church. The new pope was ready to concede that there was "good" as well as "evil" in modern civilization. He added a scientific staff to the Vatican and opened archives and observatories. However, he made no concessions to "liberalism" or "anticlericalism" in the political sphere. He would go no farther than to urge capitalists and employers to be more generous in recognizing the rights of organized labor.

The effect of various scientific and philosophical challenges upon the men and women who lived at the end of the nineteenth century cannot be measured in any exact way. Millions undoubtedly went about the business of life untroubled by the implications of evolutionary theory, content to believe as they had believed. Certainly, for most members of the middle class, the challenge of socialism was understood as "real" in a way that the challenge of science and philosophy probably was not. Socialism was a threat to livelihood. Darwinism, relativism, materialism, and behaviorism, though "in the air" and troublesome to those who breathed that air, did not impinge upon consciousness to the same degree. Men and women can postpone thoughts about their origins and ultimate destiny in a way that they cannot postpone thoughts about their daily bread. And yet the impact of the changes we have been discussing was eventually profound. Darwin's theory was not so complicated as to prevent its popularization. If educated men and women had neither the time nor inclination to read the *Origin of Species,* they read magazines and newspapers which spelled out for them its implications. Those implications induced an uncertainty that tempered the optimism of capitalist expansion.

Men and women who had never read the German philosopher Arthur Schopenhauer (1788–1860) might well have agreed with his assessment of this world as one condemned to witness the devouring of the weak by the strong. Yet their commitment to the ways of the

Pope Pius IX

Pope Leo XIII

world prevented their acceptance of Schopenhauer's particular remedy: an escape into a life of personal asceticism and self-denial. Like the English poet and essayist Matthew Arnold, sensitive men and women might feel themselves trapped in a world resembling no more than "a darkling plain," where there was "neither joy, nor love, nor light, nor certitude, nor peace, nor help for pain."

3. THE CHALLENGE OF LITERATURE AND THE ARTS

The revolt against art as morality

Literature and the arts in the late nineteenth century continued to challenge the middle-class worldview by drawing attention to the shortcomings as well as the achievements of industrial society. By 1900, however, many artists and writers were working according to a precept even more disturbing in its implications to the educated public than a critique of social values and realities. They agreed with the writers who were protesting middle-class values that the purpose of art was not to pander or to sentimentalize. They disagreed with them, however, by declaring that art had no business preaching morality—attempting to "improve" by example. This generation of artists and writers argued that one did not look at a painting or read a poem to be instructed in the difference between good and evil, but to understand what was eternally true and beautiful—to appreciate art for its own sake. They were not so much interested in reaching a wider audience, whose standards of taste they generally deplored, as they were in addressing each other. This self-conscious desire not only to live apart but to think apart from society was reflected in their work. In 1850, educated men and women could read a Dickens novel or examine a Daumier print and understand it, even if they did not admire it or agree with its message. In 1900, men and women found it much harder to understand, let alone admire, a painting by Paul Cézanne or a poem by Paul Valéry. Artists and public were ceasing to speak the same language, a fact which contributed, as did the ideas of Darwin and Nietzsche, Pavlov and Freud, to the further confusion and fragmentation of Western culture.

Realism

These new perceptions of the artist's relationship to society did not surface to any measurable degree before the very end of the century. Until that time, the arts were dominated by what has come to be called *realism*. Realists were predominantly critics of contemporary society. Swayed by a fervor for social reform, they depicted the inequities of the human condition against the sordid background of industrial society. Like the romantics, the realists affirmed the possibility of human freedom, although realists emphasized more than romantics the obstacles that prevented its achievement. Realists differed most markedly from romantics in their disdain of sentiment and emotional extravagance. Adopting from natural science the idea of life as a struggle for survival, they tried to portray human existence in accordance with hard facts, often insisting that their characters were the irresponsible victims of heredity, environment, or their own animal passions.

Realism as a literary movement made its initial appearance in France. Its leading exponents included the novelists Honoré de Balzac and Gustave Flaubert,[3] whose work, as we have already noted, contained a stinging assessment of the dullness and greed of modern life. Émile Zola (1840–1902), another Frenchman, is often called a naturalist rather than a realist, to convey the idea that he was interested in an exact, scientific presentation of the facts of nature without the intrusion of personal philosophy. Naturalism was expected to dismiss moral values in a way that realism was not. Zola did have a definite moral viewpoint, however. His early years of wretched poverty imbued him with a deep sympathy for the common people and with a passion for social justice. Though he portrayed human nature as weak and prone to vice and crime, he was not without hope that a decided improvement might come from the creation of a better society. Many of his novels dealt with such social problems as alcoholism, poverty, and disease.

Realism in the writings of the Englishman Charles Dickens was overlaid with layers of sentimentality. Dickens was a master at depicting the evils of industrial society, but the invariable happy endings of his novels testify to his determined—and unrealistic—unwillingness to allow wrong to triumph over right. No such ambivalence marked the works of the later English novelist Thomas Hardy (1840–1928), however. In such well-known narratives as *The Return of the Native, Jude the Obscure,* and *Tess of the D'Urbervilles,* he expressed his conception that humans are the playthings of an inexorable fate. The universe, though beautiful, was depicted as in no sense friendly, and the struggle of individuals with nature was a pitiable battle against almost impossible odds. If any such being as God existed, he watched with indifference while the helpless denizens of the human ant-heap crawled toward suffering and death. Hardy pitied his fellow creatures, regarding them not as depraved animals but as specks of dust caught in the wheels of a cosmic machine.

Pity for humanity was a central theme in the work of the German Gerhard Hauptmann (1862–1946). Calling himself a naturalist, Hauptmann nevertheless reflected the realists' concern for suffering. His plays show the influence of Darwin in their emphasis upon determinism and environment. *The Weavers,* which depicts the suffering of Silesian weavers in the 1840s, is probably his most outstanding work. Doubtless the most eminent playwright among realists and naturalists was the Norwegian Henrik Ibsen (1828–1906). Ibsen's early dramas were not favorably received, and while still a young man he decided to abandon his native country. Residing first in Italy and then in Ger-

[3] See above, p. 854.

many, he did not return permanently to Norway until 1891. His writings were characterized most of all by bitter rebellion against the tyranny and ignorance of society. In such plays as *The Wild Duck, A Doll's House, Hedda Gabler,* and *An Enemy of the People,* he mercilessly satirized the conventions and institutions of respectable life, and showed, with great insight, how these oppressed women in particular. Along with his scorn for hypocrisy and social tyranny went a profound distrust of majority rule. Ibsen despised democracy as the enthronement of unprincipled leaders who would do anything for the sake of votes to perpetuate themselves in power. As one of his characters in *An Enemy of the People* says: "A minority may be right—a majority is always wrong."

Russian literature: Turgenev and Dostoevsky

The literature of the Russians, while it came into its own during the period of realism, includes within it themes that are both romantic and idealist as well. Russia's three most outstanding novelists of this period were Ivan Turgenev (1818–1883), Feodor Dostoevsky (1821–1881), and Leo Tolstoy (1828–1910). Turgenev, who spent much of his life in France, was the first of the Russian novelists to become known to western Europe. His chief work, *Fathers and Sons,* describes in brooding terms the struggle between the older and younger generations. The hero is a nihilist (a term first used by Turgenev), who is convinced that the whole social order has nothing in it worth preserving. Dostoevsky was almost as tragic a figure as any he projected in his novels. Condemned at the age of twenty-eight on a charge of revolutionary activity, he was exiled to Siberia, where he endured four horrible years. His later life was harrowed by poverty, family troubles, and epileptic fits. As a novelist, he chose to explore the anguish of people driven to shameful deeds by their raw, animal emotions and by the intolerable meanness of their lives. He was a master of psychological analysis, probing into the motives of distorted minds with an intensity that was almost morbid. At the same time he filled his novels with a broad sympathy and with a mystic conviction that humanity can be purified only through suffering. His best-known works are *Crime and Punishment* and *The Brothers Karamazov.*

Henrik Ibsen

Tolstoy

It is generally conceded that the honor of being Russia's greatest novelist must be divided between Dostoevsky and Tolstoy. As an earnest champion of the simple life of the peasant, Tolstoy was somewhat less deterministic than the author of *Crime and Punishment.* Yet in his *War and Peace,* a majestic epic of Russian conditions during the period of the Napoleonic invasion, he expounds the theme that individuals are at the mercy of fate when powerful elemental forces are unleashed. His other most celebrated novel, *Anna Karenina,* is a study of the tragedy which lurks in the pursuit of individual desire. The hero, Levin, is really Tolstoy himself, who eventually finds refuge from doubt and from the vanities of worldly existence in a mystic love

Leo Tolstoy in His Study Dictating to His Secretary

of humanity. As Tolstoy grew older he became more and more an evangelist preaching a social gospel. In such novels as *The Kreutzer Sonata* and *Resurrection* he condemned most of the institutions of civilized society and called upon men and women to renounce selfishness and greed, to earn their living by manual toil, and to cultivate the virtues of poverty, meekness, and nonresistance. His last years were devoted mainly to attacks upon such evils as war and capital punishment and to the defense of victims of persecution.

The works of all these realists and naturalists, whatever their individual differences, shared two things in common: they contained vigorous moral criticism of present-day middle-class society, and they were written in direct and forceful language that the middle class could understand, if it chose to read or listen. The same can be said of realist painters such as Courbet and Daumier, discussed previously, and of the sculptor Auguste Rodin (1840–1917), whose style and message were neither difficult to comprehend nor easy to ignore. Realist artists were still anxious to address the public, if only to attack its members for their shallowness and insensitivity. The advent of the *impressionist* movement in painting in the 1870s marks the first significant break in this tradition. It is at this point that artists began to turn away from the public and toward each other. The movement started in France, among a group of young artists whose work had been refused a place in the annual exhibitions of the traditionally minded French Royal Academy. They had been labeled "impressionists" in derision by critics who took them to task for painting not an object itself, but only their impression of that object. The name in fact suited the personal, private nature of their work. They were painting only to please themselves, to realize their own potential as artists.

In a sense, impressionists were realists, for they were determined to paint only what they saw, and they were vitally interested in the

Realism in art

scientific interpretation of nature. But impressionist technique was different from that of the older realist painters. Scenes from the world around them were not depicted as if the results of careful study. On the contrary, the works of impressionists sought to reveal immediate sense impressions, leaving it to the mind of the observer to fill in additional details. This often resulted in a type of work appearing at first glance to be nonnaturalistic. Figures were commonly distorted; a few significant details were made to represent an entire object; and dabs of primary color were placed side by side without a trace of blending. Convinced that light is the principal factor in determining the appearance of objects, the impressionists fled from the studio to the woods and fields in an attempt to capture the fleeting alterations of a natural scene with each transitory shift of sunlight and shadow. From science they had learned that light is composed of a fusion of primary colors visible in the spectrum. Accordingly, they decided to use these colors almost exclusively. They chose, for example, to achieve the effect of the green in nature by placing daubs of pure blue and yellow side by side, allowing the eye to mix them.

Impressionism differed from realism in one other very important respect. In these new paintings artists remained detached from their subject. They did not paint to evoke pity, or to teach a lesson. They painted to proclaim the value and importance of painting *as painting*. In doing so, the artist was not deliberately setting out to exclude the viewers. It was clear, however, that the viewer must not expect to understand a painting except on the artist's terms. Probably the greatest of the impressionists were the Frenchmen Claude Monet (1840–1926) and Auguste Renoir (1841–1919). Monet was perhaps the leading exponent of the new mode of interpreting landscapes. His paintings have no structure or design in the conventional sense; they suggest, rather than depict, the outlines of cliffs, trees, mountains, and fields. Intensely interested in the problem of light, Monet would go out at sunrise with an armful of canvases in order to paint the same subject in a dozen momentary appearances. It has been said of one of his masterpieces that "light is the only important person in the picture." Renoir's subjects include not only landscapes but portraits and scenes from contemporary life. He is famous most of all for his pink and ivory nudes, which, as expressions of frank sexuality, represented a threat to middle-class sensibilities.

The freedom explicit in the work of the impressionists encouraged other painters to pursue fresh techniques and to define different goals. The *expressionists* turned upon the impressionists, objecting to their preoccupation with the momentary aspects of nature and their indifference to meaning. Expressionists were not arguing a return to meaning in the sense of "message." They were instead insisting that a painting must represent the artist's particular intellect. Here again, they were making art a private matter, removing it yet another step from

Impressionism

Monet and Renoir

See color plates following page 960

Expressionism: Cézanne

the public. The artist who laid the foundations of expressionism was Paul Cézanne (1839–1906), now recognized as one of the greatest painters who ever lived. A native of southern France, Cézanne labored to express a sense of order in nature that he believed the impressionists had ignored. To achieve this end, he painted objects as a series of planes, each plane expressed in terms of a color change. While Cézanne was in this way equating form with color, he also began to reduce natural forms to their geometrical equivalents, hoping thereby to express the basic shapes of existence itself. He distorted form into geometrical regularity until abstraction became reality. In all this Cézanne was declaring the painter's right to recreate nature in such a way as to express an intensely personal vision.

Art as personal expression was the hallmark of two other painters in the so-called post-impressionist period, the Frenchman Paul Gauguin (1848–1903) and the Dutchman Vincent Van Gogh (1853–1890). Both, by their life as well as their art, declared war on traditional nineteenth-century values. Dismayed by the artificiality and complexity of civilization, Gauguin fled to the South Sea Islands and spent the last decade of his life painting the hot and luscious colors of an unspoiled, primitive society. Van Gogh, whose passionate sympathy for the sufferings of his fellow humans led him to attempt the life of a minister to poor mining families and undoubtedly contributed to his eventual insanity and ultimate suicide, poured out the full intensity of his feelings in paintings such as *The Starry Night,* which seem to swirl off the canvas.

In the years between 1900 and the First World War, art underwent still further revolutionary development. Henri Matisse (1869–1954) greatly extended Cézanne's use of distortion, thereby declaring once again the painter's right to create according to an individual definition of aesthetic merit. This declaration was given its most ringing prewar endorsement by Pablo Picasso (1881–1973). Picasso, a Catalan Spaniard who came to Paris in 1903, developed a style, *cubism,* that takes its name from an attempt to carry Cézanne's fascination with geometrical form to its logical conclusion. Influenced both by the work of Cézanne and by African sculpture, cubism results not only in distortion but in some cases in actual dismemberment. The artist may separate the various parts of a figure and rearrange them in other than their natural pattern. The purpose is partly to symbolize the chaos of modern life but also to express defiance of traditional notions of form—to repudiate once and for all the conception of art as representational prettiness.

The artistic declaration of independence from middle-class society was enunciated most dramatically by painters, but was heard also in the realms of literature and music. In France, the work of a group calling itself the symbolists, and centered upon the poetry of Paul Verlaine, Arthur Rimbaud, Stéphane Mallarmé, and Paul Valéry at-

Self-Portrait by Paul Gauguin

Cubism: Picasso

See color plates following page 960

New directions in literature and music

Girl Before a Mirror by Pablo Picasso

tempted to intensify the personal while transcending reality in a way reminiscent of the impressionists, expressionists, and cubists. In music, as well, there was a break from the romantic tradition that dominated the nineteenth century and was expressed in the works of composers such as Robert Schumann (1810–1856), Felix Mendelssohn (1809–1847), and Franz Liszt (1811–1886). Already the late romantic operas of Richard Wagner had taken vast liberties with harmony and departed from stereotypical melodic patterns, producing music that was not subject to the tyranny of form but sensitive to personal expression.

Self-imposed isolation

Whether in painting, in literature, or in music, artists sought to escape to a position from which they could learn and then express what was closest to their own consciousness. Their direct, calculated dismissal of conventional form and content declared their fundamental disdain for—more important, their complete lack of interest in—the problems of the world at large. Their self-imposed isolation served only to increase the general sense of a fragmented world that, despite its material prosperity, was at war with itself.

SELECTED READINGS

• *Items so designated are available in paperback editions.*

SOCIALISM

• Avineri, S., *The Social and Political Thought of Karl Marx,* London, 1968.
• Cole, G. D. H., *A History of Socialist Thought,* Vols. I–III, London, 1953–56.
  A comprehensive treatment of the period 1789–1914.

Gay, Peter, *The Dilemma of Democratic Socialism: Eduard Bernstein's Challenge to Marx,* New York, 1952.

Goldberg, Harvey, *A Life of Jean Jaurès,* Madison, Wisc., 1962. A good biography of the eminent French socialist.

Joll, James, *The Anarchists,* London, 1964.

Landauer, C., and E. Valkenier, *European Socialism,* Berkeley, Calif., 1959.

Lichtheim, G., *A Short History of Socialism,* New York, 1970.

• McBriar, A. M., *Fabian Socialism and English Politics, 1884–1918,* Cambridge, 1966. An extensive study of this important circle: their composition, their ideology, their methods.

Noland, Aaron, *The Founding of the French Socialist Party, 1893–1905,* Cambridge, Mass., 1956. Primarily a narrative account of the translation of ideology into political reality.

Schorske, Carl E., *German Social Democracy, 1905–1917,* Cambridge, Mass., 1955. A magnificent study of the problems of the Social Democrats in a time of imperialism and war.

SCIENTIFIC THOUGHT

• Butterfield, Herbert B., *The Origins of Modern Science,* rev. ed., New York, 1957.

Eiseley, Loren C., *Darwin's Century: Evolution and the Men Who Discovered It,* New York, 1961.

Fothergill, P., *Historical Aspects of Organic Evolution,* London, 1952.

Gillespie, C. C., *The Edge of Objectivity,* Princeton, N.J., 1960. A history of scientific ideas.

• Hughes, H. Stuart, *Consciousness and Society,* New York, 1958. Examines the reaction to Positivism and the growing interest in the irrational by considering the work of Freud, Max Weber, and others.

• Jones, Ernest, *The Life and Work of Freud,* 3 vols., New York, 1953–57. The official biography, by a close collaborator and eminent psychoanalyst.

• McKenzie, A. E. E., *The Major Achievements of Science,* Cambridge, 1960.

Singer, Charles, and A. E. Underwood, *A Short History of Medicine,* rev. ed., New York, 1962.

Wightman, W. P. D., *The Growth of Scientific Ideas,* Edinburgh, 1951.

THE ARTS

Barzun, Jacques, *Darwin, Marx, and Wagner,* Boston, 1941. Argues that these men were not so much originators of new ideas, as founders of systems which are mechanistic and pseudoscientific and therefore threatening to the human cultural heritage.

Kaufmann, Walter A., *Nietzsche: Philosopher, Psychologist, Anti-Christ,* Princeton, N.J., 1974.

Lang, Paul, *Music in Western Civilization,* New York, 1941.

Mosse, G. L., *The Culture of Western Europe: The Nineteenth and Twentieth Centuries,* Chicago, 1961.

Shattuck, Roger, *The Banquet Years: The Arts in France, 1885–1918,* New York, 1958. The emergence of modernism in French art, literature, and music.

SOURCE MATERIALS

- Arnold, Matthew, *Culture and Anarchy,* New York, 1971. Originally published in 1867. A perceptive criticism of English society and a call for an authoritarian principle in an increasingly democratic society.
- Darwin, Charles, *The Descent of Man,* Cambridge, Mass., 1964. See especially Chapter XXI.
- ———, *Origin of Species,* Cambridge, Mass., 1964. See especially Chapters IV, XV.

  Edwards, Stewart, ed., *The Communards of Paris, 1871,* New York, 1976. Annotated eyewitness reports, documents, and accounts of the Paris Commune.
- Gosse, Edmund, *Father and Son,* New York, 1963. A moving autobiography by a distinguished Victorian literary critic, this work reveals the conflict between the religious fundamentalism of the father and the skepticism of the son in the wake of Darwinian theory.

  Kohn, Hans, *The Mind of Modern Russia,* New Brunswick, N.J., 1955. An edited collection of historical, literary, and philosophical works of nineteenth- and twentieth-century Russian authors, designed to reveal the conflict between traditional and Western thought in Russia.
- Marx, Karl, *Capital,* intro. by G. D. H. Cole, New York, 1974.

  Webb, Beatrice, *My Apprenticeship,* London, 1926. Beatrice Webb was one of the leading Fabian Socialists, and in this first volume of her autobiography she explains how she, as a member of one of England's wealthier families, was converted to a socialist creed.

  Zola, Émile, *L'Assommoir,* London, 1970. Written in 1877 and set in the Paris of the 1860s, this bitterly realistic novel portrays the brutalization of the French working class by the forces of industrial change, poverty, and alcohol.

Chapter 31

THE SEARCH FOR STABILITY
(1870–1914)

Ah! What a seething there has been, . . . customs worthy of the inquisition and despotism, the pleasure of a few gold-braided individuals setting
their heels on the nation, and stifling its cry for truth and justice, under the
mendacious and sacrilegious pretext of the interest of the State!

—Émile Zola, "J'accuse"

B etween 1870 and 1914, the major powers of Europe worked to
maintain both domestic and international stability. Accomplishment of this goal was facilitated by continuing industrialization. Despite periodic trade depressions, general prosperity increased for almost all classes of society at least until 1900. And
prosperity, in its turn, helped to produce stability, allowing for the establishment in many countries of social welfare systems designed to
benefit workers and their families, and thus to gain their political
allegiance. At the same time, various factors operated to make the
achievement of a generally stable Western world difficult, and ultimately impossible. First, the process of nation-building, which had resulted in the dramatic creation of a modern Germany and Italy, left
potential conflict in its wake. Second, although the majority of citizens
in most western European countries participated at least indirectly in
the governance of their country and enjoyed certain guaranteed rights,
heated debate continued as to the political usefulness of such arrangements. In France, monarchists threatened the republic; in Germany,
democrats battled imperial and bureaucratic oligarchy; in Russia, liberals rose against tsarist autocracy. And across Europe, socialists contended against the political strength of the middle classes. Finally, the
international rivalries that we have seen growing between nations as
they reached out to build empires became more heated with the coming of the new century. Nations grouped into alliances, hoping that a

The roots of instability

balance between power blocs might continue to provide the international stability that Europe had enjoyed since 1815, and that had prevented general war. Instead, the alliances produced only further tensions, and ultimately general world conflict.

1. GERMANY: THE SEARCH FOR IMPERIAL UNITY

During the years immediately following the foundation of the German Empire, Bismarck was particularly anxious to achieve imperial unity under Prussian domination. In this he was aided by the economic and military predominance of the Prussian state, and by the organizational framework upon which the empire had been constructed. All powers not granted to the central government were reserved to the individual states. Each had control over its own form of government, public education, highways, police, and other local agencies. Even the enforcement of the laws was left primarily in the hands of the state governments, since the empire had no machinery for applying its laws against individuals. Despite their apparent autonomy, however, the states were in fact subordinate to the empire, and to the emperor himself, the Prussian William I. President A. Laurence Lowell of Harvard once accurately described the German imperial units as comprised of "a lion, a half-dozen foxes, and a score of mice." The Prussian "lion" exercised authority through the person of the emperor and his chancellor. The empire was not governed by a cabinet system, in which ministers of state were responsible to a popularly elected legislature. Instead, the chancellor and other ministers were responsible solely to the emperor. And William was no mere figurehead; he was vested with extensive authority over the army and navy, over foreign relations, and over the general enactment and execution of imperial laws. He had the authority to declare war if the coasts or territory of the empire were attacked. And as king of Prussia, he controlled that country's block of one-third of the votes in the generally conservative upper house, or Bundesrat, of the imperial parliament.

The parliament was by no means a mere rubber stamp, however. All treaties had to be approved by the Bundesrat. Money for the imperial treasury had to be voted by the lower house, the Reichstag, which was elected by universal manhood suffrage and whose membership was primarily middle class. Yet these powers were essentially negative. Although the parliament could veto proposals of the kaiser (emperor) and his ministers, it could not initiate legislation on its own. Hence, although Bismarck often found himself temporarily stymied by the activities of an unsympathetic legislature, he could expect, in the end, to have his way. That way was directed toward the goal of a unified Germany under Prussian domination: essentially conservative; antisocialist, though not necessarily opposed to social welfare schemes; protectionist, and thus sympathetic to the interests of Ger-

William I of Germany

man industrialists; and, in foreign affairs, anti-French, standing firm against any threat from that longtime antagonist.

Bismarck's first campaign on behalf of imperial unity was launched against the Roman Catholic Church. Called the *Kulturkampf,* or "struggle for civilization," the attack was initiated, with some help from intellectual liberals, in 1872. Bismarck's motives were almost exclusively nationalistic. He perceived in some Catholic activities a threat to the power and stability of the empire he had just created. He resented, first of all, the support Catholic priests continued to give to the states'-rights movement in southern Germany and to the grievances of Alsatians and Poles. He was alarmed also by recent assertions of the authority of the pope to intervene in secular matters and by the promulgation in 1870 of the dogma of papal infallibility. For these reasons he resolved to deal such a blow to Catholic influence in Germany that it would never again be a factor in national or local politics. His weapons were a series of laws and decrees issued between 1872 and 1875. First, he induced the Reichstag to expel all the Jesuits from the country. Next, he forced through the so-called May Laws, which placed theological seminaries under state control and permitted the government to regulate the appointment of bishops and priests. No one was allowed to be appointed to any position in the Church unless a German citizen, and then only after a state examination. At the same time civil marriage was made compulsory, even though a religious ceremony had already been performed. In the enforcement of these measures, six of the ten Catholic bishops in Prussia were imprisoned, and hundreds of priests were driven from the country.

The Kulturkampf

Although Bismarck won some of the chief battles of the *Kulturkampf,* he lost the war. The Catholic or Center party appealed so effectively on behalf of the persecuted clergy, and adopted so enlightened an economic program, that it grew into the largest political party in Germany. In the elections of 1874 it captured nearly a fourth of the seats in the Reichstag. Recognizing that he needed this party to support other elements of his program, Bismarck gradually relaxed his persecution of the Catholics. Between 1878 and 1886 nearly all of the obnoxious legislation was repealed, and the Catholic Church restored practically to its former position in Germany.

The failure of the Kulturkampf

By the late 1870s Bismarck had declared war on German socialism, now perceived by him as a far more immediate threat to the empire than Catholicism. The Social Democratic party, under the reformist leadership of the politician Wilhelm Liebknecht (1829–1900), successor to Ferdinand Lassalle, was building a substantial following. Bismarck, his memory of the Paris Commune (see above, pp. 957) still fresh, feared socialism as anarchy, and therefore as a direct challenge to the stability and unity he was attempting to achieve within the empire. Forgetting for the moment the manner in which he had courted the socialists when he needed their support in the 1860s, Bismarck now appeared determined to extinguish them. His attack was motivated

Bismarck's antisocialism

not only by his personal perception of the socialist threat; he was by now anxious to continue to court the favor of industrialists whom he had won to his side by his policy of protective tariffs. In 1878, two separate attempts were made by unbalanced zealots on the life of the emperor. Although neither would-be assassin had anything but the most tenuous connection with the socialists, Bismarck used their actions as an excuse to secure legislation abolishing workers' rights to meet and to publish. The legislature also agreed to a law which gave the government the right to expel socialists from major cities, as was later done in Berlin, Breslau, and Leipzig.

Social welfare legislation

Bismarck was too clever a politician to suppose that he could abolish socialism solely by means of repression. He was prepared to steal at least a portion of the socialists' thunder by adopting parts of their legislative program as his own. In a speech in the Reichstag he frankly avowed his purpose of insuring the worker against sickness and old age so that "these gentlemen [the Social Democrats] will sound their bird call in vain." In addition, he had military purposes in mind. He was desirous of making the German worker a loyal soldier by safeguarding his health in some measure from the debilitating effects of factory labor. Bismarck's program of social legislation was initiated in 1883–1884 with the adoption of laws insuring workers against sickness and accidents. These acts were soon followed by others providing for rigid factory inspection, limiting the employment of women and children, fixing maximum hours of labor, establishing public employment agencies, and insuring workers against incapacity on account of old age. By 1890, when Bismarck was dismissed by the young Emperor William II, Germany had adopted nearly all the elements, with the exception of unemployment insurance, in the pattern of social legislation that later became familiar in the majority of Western nations.

Continuing spread of German socialism

Neither Bismarck's repressive nor his progressive legislation succeeded in killing German socialism, however. The Social Democratic party continued to grow. Bismarck's dismissal came in part over William's insistence that the antisocialist legislation was achieving nothing. The disagreement between the two men extended beyond the question of socialism, however. William II was determined to be his own master. Unity and stability would be the result of his personal initiative, not that of his chancellor. In this, William was expressing his belief in the divinely ordained prerogatives of the Hohenzollerns, the royal house of Prussia. He was asserting claims that—though they sat well enough with the federated princes, the large landowners, the military, and the big industrialists—were increasingly anathema to the democratic forces of the lower middle and working classes. Social Democrats and Progressives were demanding a new constitution guaranteeing control over the chancellor by the majority party in the Reichstag. To these demands the intransigent emperor remained deaf,

Bismarck and William II of Germany

further threatening the fragile stability which Bismarck's policies had attempted to encourage. In the election of 1912 the Social Democrats polled 4,250,000 votes and elected 110 members—the largest single bloc—to the Reichstag. National unity was on a collision course with class conflict. Germany was spared a domestic constitutional crisis only by the infinitely more profound international crisis of the First World War.

2. FRANCE: THE EMBATTLED THIRD REPUBLIC

Although France, in 1870, was not a newly constructed nation, like the German Empire, it was a nation sorely in need of reunification and dedication to a common set of political purposes. Its history for the past century had left it torn between various factions. Monarchists were divided between supporters of the Bourbon and Orleanist dynasties, their allegiance sustained by loyalties either to the descendents of Louis XVIII or of Louis Philippe. Bonapartists looked for political salvation to Napoleon III's son and heir Louis Napoleon. Republicans recalled the short-lived triumphs of their revolutionary ancestors. Socialists called down plagues on all political houses but their own. The result of this deep division was that not until 1875 did France have a constitution under which it could function.

Politically divided France

Following the collapse of Napoleon III's empire a provisional government was organized to rule the country until a new constitution could be drafted. Elections held in 1871 for a national constituent assembly resulted in the choice of some 500 monarchists and only about

200 republicans. Conservative political sentiment was further reinforced by the events of the Paris Commune, which occurred during the period immediately following the elections. But the apparent winners, the monarchists, could not agree among themselves as to whether their king should be a Bourbon or an Orleanist. This stalemate led to the eventual passage in 1875—by one vote—of a series of constitutive laws which made France a republic. These laws established a parliament with a lower house elected by universal manhood suffrage (the Chamber of Deputies) and an upper house elected indirectly (the Senate); a cabinet of ministers presided over by a premier; and a president. Although at first the relative powers of president and premier were not clearly established, within two years the nation had declared itself in favor of a premier at the head of a government answerable to the Chamber of Deputies. An early president, Marshal MacMahon, attempted in 1877 to dismiss a premier with whom he disagreed but who was supported by a majority in the chamber. When new elections were held, MacMahon's policy was repudiated. Henceforth, premiers of the Third Republic were answerable to the chamber and not to the president, who became a figurehead. Yet the resolution of this constitutional question failed to produce political stability, since the premier had no authority to dissolve the legislature. This meant that members of the chamber could vote a premier and his fellow ministers out of office at will, with no risk of being forced to stand for reelection. If defeated on a vote, the premier and his colleagues had no alternative but to resign. The result was no fewer than fifty ministries in the years between 1870 and 1914. The Third Republic, for all its constitutional shortcomings, nevertheless managed to last until 1940—far longer than any system of French government since 1789. Its longevity was due, as much as anything, to the stability of other French institutions—the family, the law courts, and the police, for example.

In the years after 1875, the republicans, who had been feared at first as dangerous radicals, proved themselves to be generally moderate. It was the discontented monarchists and authoritarian sympathizers within the army, the Roman Catholic Church, and among the families of the aristocracy who took to plotting the overthrow of duly constituted governmental authority. Much of the time of successive republican governments was taken up defending the country from these reactionary radicals. In the late 1880s, a general, Georges Boulanger, gathered about him a following not only of Bonapartists, monarchists, and aristocrats, but of workingmen who were generally disgruntled with their lot and who believed, with Boulanger, that a war of revenge against Germany would put an end to all their troubles. Thanks to the general's own indecisiveness, the threatened coup d'état came to nothing. But Boulanger was a symptom of deep discontents; he appealed, like Napoleon III, to disparate groups of disenchanted citizens, promising quick, dramatic solutions to tedious problems.

One further symptom of the divisions which plagued the republic during the later years of the nineteenth century was the campaign of anti-Semitism which the reactionaries adopted to advance their aims. The fact that certain Jewish bankers were involved in scandalous dealings with politicians lent color to the monarchist insistence that the government was shot through with corruption and that Jews were largely to blame. In the face of those charges it is not strange that anti-Semitism should have flared into a violent outbreak. In 1894 a Jewish captain of artillery, Alfred Dreyfus, was accused by a clique of monarchist officers of selling military secrets to Germany. Tried by court-martial, he was convicted and sentenced for life to Devil's Island, a ghastly prison camp in the Caribbean. At first the verdict was accepted as the merited punishment of a traitor; but in 1897 Colonel Picquart, a new head of the Intelligence Division, announced his conclusion that the documents upon which Dreyfus had been convicted were forgeries. A movement was launched for a new trial, which the War Department promptly refused. Soon the whole nation was divided into friends and opponents of Dreyfus. On his side were the radical republicans, socialists, people of liberal and humanitarian sympathies, and such prominent literary figures as Émile Zola and Anatole France. The anti-Dreyfusards included monarchists, clerics, anti-Semites, militarists, and a considerable number of conservative workingmen. Dreyfus was finally set free by executive order in 1899, and six years later was cleared of all guilt by the Supreme Court and restored to the army. He was immediately promoted to the rank of major and decorated with the emblem of the Legion of Honor.

The history of the Dreyfus affair gave the republicans the solid ground they had lacked in order to end the plottings of the radical reactionaries once and for all. The leaders of the republic chose to attack their enemies by effectively destroying the political power of the Roman Catholic Church in France. The anticlericalism expressed in

The Dreyfus affair

Anticlericalism

Alfred Dreyfus Leaving His Court-Martial

this campaign was probably in part the product of a materialistic age, and of a long-standing mistrust by French republicans of the institution of the Church. Its main source, however, was the nationalism which we have already seen fueling Bismarck's *Kulturkampf.*

Anticlericalism in France reached its peak between 1875 and 1914. The great majority of the leaders of the Third Republic were hostile to the Church; and naturally so, for the Catholic hierarchy was aiding the monarchists at every turn. Clerics had conspired with monarchists, militarists, and anti-Semites in attempting to discredit the republic during the Dreyfus affair. But in the end they had overreached themselves. In 1901 the government passed a series of acts prohibiting the existence of religious orders not authorized by the state, forbidding members of religious orders to teach in either public or private schools, and finally, in 1905, dissolving the union of Church and State. For the first time since 1801 the adherents of all creeds were placed on an equal basis. No longer were the Catholic clergy to receive their salaries from the public purse. Although some of these measures were modified in later years, the Church remained in the minds of most Frenchmen under a heavy cloud of suspicion.

The republic was, during these years, pressed from the Left as well as the Right. Socialism was a political force in France, as it was in Germany. Yet the response of republicans in France to socialist pressure differed markedly from that of Bismarck. There was no antisocialist legislation. Indeed, a law was passed in 1881 abolishing "crimes of opinion," thereby extending the freedom of the press considerably. In the same year, another law authorized public meetings without prior official approval. But if there was no attempt at repression, there was little positive social reform. The largest single party in the republic, the Radicals or Radical Socialists, was really a party representing small shopkeepers and lesser propertied interests. The Radicals were willing to found and maintain a democratic compulsory educational system, but they were reluctant to respond to demands for labor legislation such as had been granted to German workers. Those laws which were passed—establishing a ten-hour workday in 1904 and old-age pensions in 1910—were passed grudgingly and only after socialist pressure. The result was a growing belief among socialists and other workers that parliamentary democracy was worthless, that progress, if it was to be made, would be made only as a result of direct industrial action: the strike. A wave of strikes swept the country for several years before 1914, including one by postal workers in 1909 and by teachers and railwaymen in 1910. The government suppressed these actions by ruthless intervention. By 1914, the republic, though hardly on the brink of revolution, remained divided and uncertain. If the threat from the radical Right had been quelled, the challenge from the Left was only just being faced.

3. GREAT BRITAIN: FROM MODERATION TO MILITANCE

During the half-century before 1914, the British prided themselves on what they believed to be a reasonable, orderly, and workable system of government. Following the passage of the Second Reform Bill in 1867, which extended suffrage to over a third of the nation's adult males, the two major political parties, Liberal and Conservative, vied with each other in adopting legislation designed to provide an increasingly larger proportion of the population the chance to lead fuller and healthier lives. Laws which recognized the legality of trade unions, allowed male religious dissenters to participate fully in the life of the ancient universities of Oxford and Cambridge, provided elementary education for the first time to all children, and facilitated the clearance and rebuilding of large urban areas, were among those placed on the books during the administrations of the two leading politicians of the period, the Conservative Benjamin Disraeli (1804–1881) and the Liberal, William Gladstone (1809–1898). In 1884, suffrage was once more widened, to include over three-fourths of the adult males, and to allow rural workingmen the chance to vote for the first time. Coupled with a previous act which instituted the secret ballot, this electoral reform bill brought Britain nearer to representative democracy.

Benjamin Disraeli

Yet Britain continued to be governed almost exclusively by a small ruling class of men drawn either from landed society or from the upper reaches of the middle class. As members of successive governmental cabinets they recognized their responsibility to Parliament and, in particular, to its lower House of Commons. It was their task, as cabinet ministers, to impose a legislative program upon the Commons. And if the House refused to agree to that program, they recognized, as well, their obligation either to resign forthwith—to make way for a cabinet of opposing party members—or to "go to the country," that is, to dissolve Parliament and order a new election to test the opinion of the voters. This system of "ministerial responsibility" meant that the cabinet retained full responsibility for the management of public affairs, subject, however, to the will of the people as represented by the House of Commons. It produced a generally stable government: Although ministries had to answer to Parliament, Parliament would think twice before voting a ministry out of office when it knew that the ministry might well appeal to the voters for support in a general election. (The lack of this particular feature was what had condemned the French Third Republic to its succession of short-lived governments.) Political stability was insured by more than the device of ministerial responsibility, however. Since both the Conservative and Liberal political leadership was drawn in large part from similar social and economic strata, there was little chance for violent change during these years. One party might espouse a particular cause—the

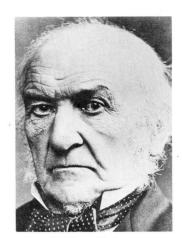

William Gladstone

*"Ministerial
responsibility"*

*Liberal reforms,
1906–1914*

Lloyd George's budget

Conservatives imperialism, the Liberals more self-government for Ireland, for example. But both parties generally agreed upon a course steered by men whose similar background and temperament promised programs that were neither radical nor reactionary. This moderation suited the electorate, which was content to defer to politicians whose leadership was secured by the undoubted fact of Britain's general prosperity.

By 1914, however, that leadership was being seriously challenged. Prosperity, though widespread enough, did not extend to the un-skilled: dock workers, transport workers, and the like. These groups formed trade unions to press their claims. Their determination encouraged other unions to assume a more militant and demanding stance. In the 1890s this activity produced a reaction in the form of anti–trade union employers' associations and a series of legal decisions limiting the right of unions to strike. Workers, in turn, reacted by associating with middle-class socialist societies to form an independent Labour party, which was born in 1901 and five years later managed to send twenty-nine members to the House of Commons. Sensitive to this pressure from the Left, the Liberals, during their ministry which began in 1906, passed a series of reforms they hoped would insure a minimum standard of living for those who had heretofore known little security. Sickness, accident, old-age, and unemployment insurance schemes were adopted. A minimum wage was decreed in certain industries. Labor exchanges, designed to help unemployed men and women find new jobs, were established. Restrictions on strikes and on the right of trade unions to raise money for political purposes were relaxed.

Much of this legislation was the work of David Lloyd George (1863–1945), chancellor of the exchequer (finance minister) in the Liberal cabinet of Prime Minister Herbert Asquith. Together with another young Liberal, Winston Churchill (1874–1965), Lloyd George had hammered together legislation that was both a reflection of his own political philosophy and a practical response to the growing political power of the working class. To pay for these programs—and for a larger navy to counter a German build-up—Lloyd George proposed a budget in 1909 that included progressive income and inheritance taxes, designed to make wealthier taxpayers pay at higher rates. His proposals so enraged the aristocratic members of the House of Lords that they declared themselves prepared to throw out the budget, an action contrary to constitutional precedent. Asquith countered with a threat to create enough new peers (titled noblemen) sympathetic to the budget to insure its passage.[1] The House of Lords eventu-

---

[1] In Britain the monarch had the authority to elevate an unlimited number of men to the peerage. But since the crown acts only on the advice of the prime minister, it is this official who has the actual power to create new members of the House of Lords. If necessary, he could use this power to pack the upper house with his own followers.

Lloyd George and Winston Churchill on Their Way to the House of Commons on Budget Day, 1910

ally surrendered; the result of the crisis was an act of Parliament which provided that the House of Lords could not veto legislation passed by the House of Commons.

The rancor aroused by this constitutional conflict was intense. Self-proclaimed defenders of the House of Lords screamed threats in a chamber unused to anything but gentlemanly debate. Angry threats were by no means confined to the Houses of Parliament during these years, however. Throughout Britain, men and women threw moderation to the winds as they disputed issues in an atmosphere little short of anarchic. The reasons for this continued agitation were various. A decline in real wages after 1900 kept the working class in a militant mood, despite Liberal reforms, and produced an unusually severe series of strikes in 1911 and 1912. A liberal plan to grant Home Rule (self-government) to Ireland produced not only panic in the Protestant minority counties of the north (Ulster) but arming and drilling of private militias with an intensity that seemed to forecast civil war.

Perhaps the most alarming—because the most unexpected—of the militant revolts that seized Britain in the years before 1914 was the campaign for women's suffrage. The middle-class women who engaged in this struggle enjoyed more freedom of opportunity than their mothers had known. Laws had been passed easing the process of divorce and permitting married women control of their own property. Some universities had started to grant degrees to women. Contraceptive devices—and feminist propaganda defending their use—had begun to result in changed attitudes toward sexuality within the middle class. Perhaps because of these gains, many women felt their lack

Increased militance

Suffragettes

London Dock Strike, 1911. Police move to clear demonstrators from shops where they have taken refuge after having been fired upon.

of the vote all the more acutely. Although the movement began among middle-class women, it soon included some female members of the working class and the aristocracy. Agitation reached a peak after 1900, when militant suffragettes—under the leadership of Emmeline Pankhurst, her daughters Christabel and Sylvia, and others—resorted to violence in order to impress upon the nation the seriousness of their commitment. Women chained themselves to the visitors' gallery in the House of Commons; slashed paintings in museums; invaded that male sanctum, the golf course, and inscribed VOTES FOR WOMEN in acid on the greens; disrupted political meetings; burned politicians' houses; and smashed department store windows. The government countered violence with repression. When women, arrested for their disruptive activities, went on hunger strikes in prisons, wardens proceeded to feed them forcibly, tying them down, holding their mouths open with wooden and metal clamps, and running tubes down their throats. When hunger strikes threatened to produce deaths and thus martyrs for the cause, the government passed the constitutionally dubious Cat and Mouse Act, which sanctioned the freeing of prisoners to halt their starvation and then, once they had regained their health, authorized their rearrest. The movement was not to see the achievement of its goal until after World War I, when reform came largely because of women's contributions to the war effort.

Instability   Whether Britain's militant mood might have led to some sort of general conflict had not the war begun in 1914, is a question historians continue to debate. Suffice it to say that national sentiment in the last few years before the outbreak of general hostilities was a far different

Violent Suffragette Protest. Emily Davison was killed when she threw herself in front of the king's racehorse at the Epsom Derby, June 4, 1913. Her purpose was to call attention to the suffragette cause.

one from that of the 1870s. Britain, so confident of itself and of its moderation, was proving no less a prey to instability than other European nations.

4. RUSSIA: THE ROAD TO REVOLUTION

In only one European country, Russia, did conditions pass from instability to insurrection during these prewar years. The Russian revolutionary movement had numerous forerunners. Waves of discontent broke out several times during the nineteenth century. Threatened uprisings between 1850–1860 persuaded Tsar Alexander II to grant local self-government, to reform the judicial system, and, most important of all, to liberate the serfs. Yet his government failed to sustain all these reforms; a wave of reaction followed. Radicalism revived and the number of revolutionary sects increased. Allied with them were the nihilists, who tended to condemn the whole political and social system. Although nihilism originated about 1860 as a movement to solve Russian problems by spreading enlightenment among the peasants, its failure to win general support by propagandist methods turned its leadership more and more to terrorism. The culmination of this terrorism was the assassination of the tsar in 1881.

The years that followed the death of Alexander II marked the floodtide of reaction against the entire policy of reform. The new tsar, Alexander III (1881–1894), governed under the theory that Russia had nothing in common with western Europe, that its people had been

Reform and reaction in nineteenth century Russia

nurtured on despotism and mystical piety for centuries and would be utterly lost without them. Such Western ideals as rationalism and individualism would undermine the childlike faith of the Russian masses and would plunge the nation into the dark abyss of anarchy and crime. In like manner, Western institutions of trial by jury, parliamentary government, and free education could never bear fruit if planted in Russian soil. With such doctrines as his guiding principles, Alexander III enforced a regime of stern and vengeful repression. He curtailed in every way possible the powers of the local assemblies, increased the authority of the secret police, and subjected villages to government by wealthy nobles selected by the state. These policies were continued, though in somewhat less rigorous form, by his son, Nicholas II (1894–1918), a much less effective ruler. Both tsars were ardent proponents of Russification and used it with a vengeance to strengthen their power. Russification was simply the more ruthless counterpart of similar nationalistic movements in various countries. Its purpose was to extend the language, religion, and culture of Great Russia, or Russia proper, over all of the subjects of the tsar and thereby to simplify the problem of governing them. It was aimed primarily at the Poles, Finns, and Jews, since these were the nationalities considered most dangerous. Inevitably it resulted in oppression. The Finns were deprived of their constitution; the Poles were compelled to study their own literature in Russian translations; and high officials in the tsar's government connived at *pogroms,* i.e., wholesale massacres, against the Jews.

Despite these attempts to turn Russia's back to the West, however, the nation was being drawn more closely than it had ever been before into the general European orbit. Russia was industrializing, and making use of European capital to do so. Economic policies during the

A Railroad Yard in Eastern Russia, 1896

1890s, when Count Sergei Witte was the tsar's leading minister, resulted in the adoption of the gold standard, which made Russian currency easily convertible. Railways and telegraph lines were constructed; exports and imports multiplied by factors of seven and five respectively from 1880 to 1913. In addition, Russian writers and musicians contributed in a major way to the enriching of Western culture. We have already noted the singular contributions of Tolstoy, Turgenev, and Dostoevsky. The musical works of Peter Tchaikovsky (1840–1893) and Nikolai Rimsky-Korsakov (1844–1908), while expressing a peculiarly Russian temperament and tradition, were recognized as important additions to the general body of first-rate contemporary composition.

With Westernization came the growth of both the business and wage-earning classes. And with an increase in class consciousness new political parties emerged. Middle-class businessmen and professionals combined with enterprising landowners in 1903 to form a Constitutional Democratic party, whose program included the creation of a nationally elected parliament or Duma to determine and carry out policies which would further the twin goals of liberalization and Westernization. Meanwhile, two essentially working-class parties, the Social Revolutionaries and the Social Democrats, began to agitate for far more radical solutions to the problems of Russian autocracy. The Social Revolutionaries concerned themselves with the continued plight of the peasants, who, when serfdom was abolished, were compelled to purchase their land, and who were burdened with high taxes. The Social Revolutionaries wanted to equalize the landholdings of peasants within their local agricultural communes or *mirs,* and to increase the power of the *mirs* in their continuing competition with large landowners. The Social Democrats were Marxists, who saw themselves as westerners and as part of the international working-class movement. In 1903 the leadership of the Social Democratic party split in an important disagreement over revolutionary strategy. The Mensheviks, who took their name from the Russian word for minority, argued unsuccessfully for a broadly based party which, while remaining revolutionary, would nonetheless accept assistance from progressives and democrats. The Bolsheviks—the majority of the Social Democrats—favored a strongly centralized party controlled by a committee whose "party line" would be accepted at all organizational levels. The Bolsheviks reorganized the Social Democrats under the leadership of the young, dynamic, and dedicated revolutionary Vladimir Ulanov (1870–1924), who wrote under the pseudonym of N. Lenin.

Lenin was a member of the middle class, his father having served as an inspector of schools and minor political functionary. He had been expelled from the University of Kazan for engaging in radical activity, following the execution of his elder brother for his involvement in a

The Young Lenin, 1897

plot to assassinate Alexander III. Lenin spent three years as a political prisoner in Siberia; from 1900 until 1917 he lived as a political exile in western Europe. His zeal and abilities as both a theoretician and a political activist are evidenced by the fact that he retained leadership of the Social Democrats even while residing abroad. Lenin continued to preach the gospel of Marxism and of a relentless class struggle. His treatise *What Is to Be Done?* was a stinging response to revisionists who were urging collaboration with less radical parties. Revolution was what was to be done, Lenin argued, revolution "made" as soon as possible by an elitist group of agitators working through the agency of a disciplined party. Lenin and his followers, by merging the tradition of Russian revolutionism with Western Marxism, and by endowing the result with a sense of immediate possibility, fused the Russian situation in such a way as to make eventual explosion almost inevitable.

The Russo-Japanese War

The revolution that came in 1905, however, took even the Bolsheviks by surprise. Its unexpected occurrence was the result of a war between Russia and Japan, which broke out in 1904, and in which the Russians were soundly beaten. Both countries had conflicting interests in Manchuria and Korea; this fact was the immediate cause of the conflict. On land and sea the Japanese proved themselves the military superiors of the Russians. As dispatches continued to report the defeats of the tsar's army and navy, the Russian people were presented with dramatic evidence of the inefficiency of autocracy.

The Revolution of 1905

Members of the middle class who had hitherto refrained from association with the revolutionists, now joined in the clamor for change. Radical workingmen organized strikes and held demonstrations in every important city. Led by a priest, Father Gapon, a group of 200,000 workers and their families went to demonstrate their grievances at the tsar's winter palace in St. Petersburg on January 22, 1905—ever after known as Bloody Sunday. The demonstrators were met by guard troops and many of them were shot dead. By the autumn of 1905 nearly the entire urban population had enlisted in a strike of protest. Merchants closed their stores, factory-owners shut down their plants, lawyers refused to plead cases in court, and even valets and cooks deserted their wealthy employers. It was soon evident to Tsar Nicholas that the government would have to yield. On October 30, he issued his October Manifesto, pledging guarantees of individual liberties, promising a moderately liberal franchise for the election of a Duma, and affirming that henceforth no law would be valid unless it had the Duma's approval. This was the high-water mark of the revolutionary movement. During the next two years Nicholas issued a series of sweeping decrees which negated most of the promises made in the October Manifesto. He deprived the Duma of many of its powers, and decreed that it be elected indirectly on a class basis by a number of electoral colleges. Thereafter the legislative body contained a majority of obedient followers of the tsar.

Bloody Sunday. Demonstrating workers who sought to bring their grievances to the attention of the tsar are met and gunned down by government troops, January 1905.

The reasons for this setback to the revolutionary movement are not hard to discover. In the first place, the army remained loyal to its commander-in-chief. Consequently, after the termination of the war with Japan in 1905, the tsar had a large body of troops that could be counted upon if necessary to decimate the ranks of the revolutionists. An even more important reason was the split in the ranks of the revolutionists themselves. After the issuance of the October Manifesto, large numbers of the bourgeoisie became frightened at threats of the radicals and declared their conviction that the revolution had gone far enough. Withdrawing their support altogether, they became known henceforth as Octobrists. The more radical merchants and professional men, organized into the Constitutional Democratic party, maintained that opposition should continue until the tsar had been forced to establish a government modeled after that of Great Britain. This fatal division rendered the middle class politically impotent. Finally, disaffection appeared within the ranks of the workers. Further attempts to employ the general strike as a weapon against the government ended in disaster.

The reasons for setback

But the Russian revolutionary movement of 1905 was not a total failure. The cruel vengeance taken by the tsar convinced many people that their government was not a benevolent autocracy, as they had been led to believe, but a stubborn and brutal tyranny. The uprising revealed to the masses their principal mistakes and taught them what sources of strength they should rely upon for success in the future. Moreover, some of the concessions actually obtained were not completely wiped out. The Duma was not abolished. It continued to serve

Gains from the revolutionary movement

as a means by which at least scattered opponents of reaction could make themselves heard. In addition, the revolt of 1905 persuaded some of the more sagacious advisors of the tsar that last-ditch conservatism was none too safe. The result was the enactment of a number of reforms designed to conciliate the troublesome classes. Among the most significant were the agrarian reforms sponsored by the government's leading minister, Peter Stolypin, between 1906 and 1911. These included: (1) the transfer of 5 million acres of royal land to the peasants for a price; (2) permission for the peasant to withdraw from the *mir* and set up as an independent farmer; and (3) cancellation of the remaining installments owed by the peasants for their land. Nor were the working classes altogether forgotten. Decrees were issued permitting the formation of labor unions, providing for a reduction of the working day (to not more than ten hours in most cases), and establishing sickness and accident insurance. Yet the hopes of some liberals that Russia was on the way to becoming a progressive nation on the Western model proved illusory. The tsar remained stubbornly autocratic. Few peasants had enough money to buy the lands offered for purchase. In view of the rising cost of living, the factory workers considered their modest gains insufficient. A new revolutionary outbreak merely awaited a convenient spark.

5. THE SEARCH FOR STABILITY ELSEWHERE IN THE WEST

Reforms in Italy

Other European countries generally found it just as difficult to attain internal tranquility in the late nineteenth century as did those whose history we have surveyed. Italy was plagued by squabbles among its political leaders, aggravated by the festering quarrel with the papacy over the seizure of ecclesiastical territories. Illiteracy and poverty, particular problems in the agrarian south, contributed to unrest, as did working-class radicalism in the industrial cities of the north. Attempts were made to relieve distress by the passage of social welfare legislation, including provision for nationalized life insurance. In 1912 a law tripled the electorate, instituting something approximating universal manhood suffrage. Relatively few of the newly enfranchised exercised their right to vote, choosing to register their discontent by more direct means such as strikes.

Nationalism in Austria-Hungary

Nationalist aspirations continued to be a major problem in eastern Europe. In 1867 an attempt had been made to resolve national differences in Austria by dividing the empire in two—an Austrian empire west of the river Leith, and a kingdom of Hungary to its east. Each of the two components in this so-called Dual Monarchy was to be the equal of the other, though the two were joined by the same Hapsburg monarch, by several common ministries, and by a kind of super-parliament. This solution failed to put an end to nationalist divisions, however. Czechs and other Slav minorities in both of the new terri-

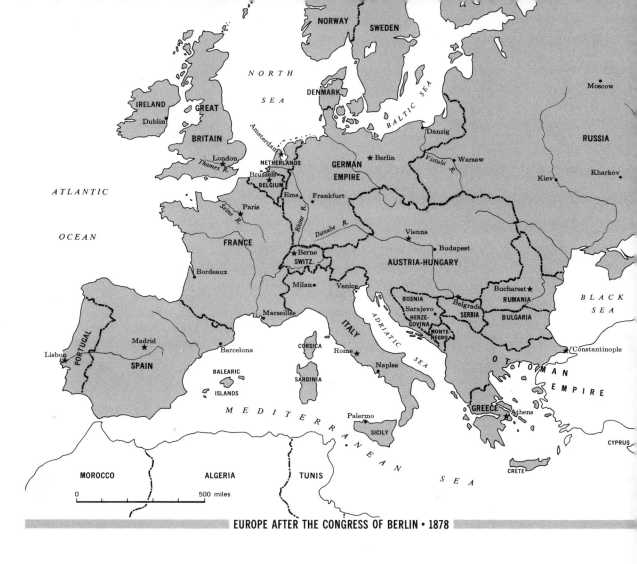

EUROPE AFTER THE CONGRESS OF BERLIN · 1878

tories nursed resentment against what they perceived as domination by alien German or Magyar culture. Despite the division of responsibilities between Austria and Hungary, the government remained centralized under the rule of the Emperor-King Francis Joseph. Social agitation was countered, as in Germany, by repression coupled with welfare measures. Universal male suffrage was introduced into Austria in 1907; in Hungary it was opposed by the Magyar majority which saw it as a device whereby the Slavic minority might increase its power.

In southeastern Europe nationalist agitation continued to rend the ever-disintegrating Ottoman Empire. Before 1829 the entire Balkan peninsula—bounded by the Aegean, Black, and Adriatic Seas—was controlled by the Turks. But during the next eighty-five years a gradual dismemberment of the Turkish Empire occurred. In some instances the slicing away of territories had been perpetrated by rival European powers, especially by Russia and Austria; but generally it

The Ottoman Empire

was the result of nationalist revolts by the sultan's Christian subjects. In 1829, at the conclusion of a war between Russia and Turkey, the Ottoman Empire was compelled to acknowledge the independence of Greece and to grant autonomy to Serbia and to the provinces which later became Rumania. As the years passed, resentment against Ottoman rule spread through other Balkan territories. In 1875–1876 there were uprisings in Bosnia, Herzegovina, and Bulgaria, which the sultan suppressed with murderous vengeance. Reports of atrocities against Christians gave Russia an excuse for renewal of its age-long struggle for domination of the Balkans. In this second Russo-Turkish War (1877–1878) the armies of the tsar won a smashing victory. The Treaty of San Stefano, which terminated the conflict, provided that the sultan surrender nearly all of his territory in Europe, except for a remnant around Constantinople. But at this juncture the great powers intervened. Austria and Great Britain, especially, were opposed to letting Russia assume jurisdiction over so large a portion of the Near East. In 1878 a congress of the great powers, meeting in Berlin, transferred Bessarabia to Russia, Thessaly to Greece, and Bosnia and Herzegovina to the control of Austria. Seven years later the Bulgars, who had been granted some degree of autonomy by the Congress of Berlin, seized the province of Eastern Rumelia from Turkey and in 1908 established the independent Kingdom of Bulgaria.

*The Young Turk
revolution*

In the very year when this last dismemberment occurred, Turkey itself was engulfed by the tidal wave of nationalism. For some time the more enlightened Turkish citizens had been growing increasingly disgusted with the weakness and incompetence of the sultan's government. In particular, those who had been educated in European universities were growing more and more convinced that their country should be rejuvenated by the introduction of Western ideas of science, patriotism, and democracy. Organizing themselves into a society known as the Young Turks, they forced the sultan in 1908 to establish constitutional government. The following year, when a reactionary movement set in, they deposed the reigning sultan, Abdul Hamid II, and placed on the throne his brother, Mohammed V, as a titular sovereign. The real powers of government were now entrusted to a grand vizier and ministers responsible to an elected parliament. This revolution did not mean increased liberty for the non-Turkish inhabitants of the empire. Instead, the Young Turks launched a vigorous movement to Ottomanize all of the Christian subjects of the sultan. At the same time the disturbances preceding and accompanying the revolution opened the way for still further dismemberment. In 1908 Austria annexed the provinces of Bosnia and Herzegovina, which the Treaty of Berlin had allowed it merely to administer, and in 1911–1912 Italy entered into war with Turkey for the conquest of Tripoli.

Of all the major nations of the West, the United States probably underwent the least domestic turmoil during the several decades before

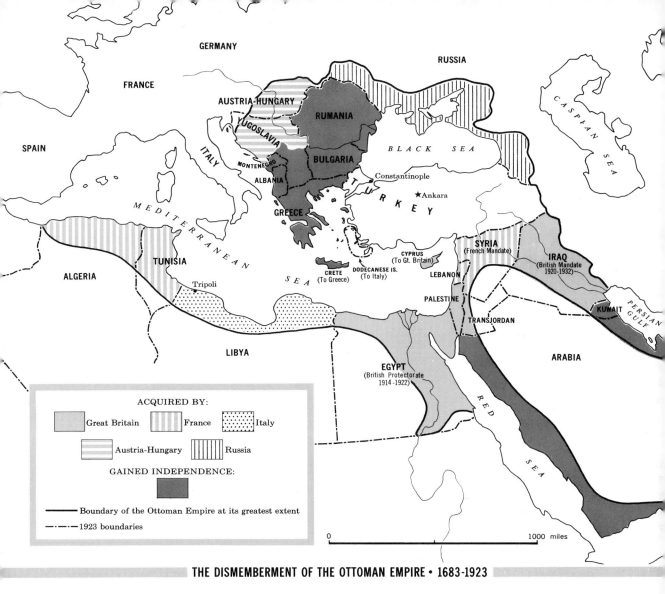

THE DISMEMBERMENT OF THE OTTOMAN EMPIRE · 1683-1923

Map labels:

GERMANY

FRANCE

RUSSIA

SPAIN

AUSTRIA-HUNGARY

YUGOSLAVIA

ITALY

MONTENEGRO

ALBANIA

RUMANIA

BULGARIA

BLACK SEA

CASPIAN SEA

Constantinople

GREECE

TURKEY

★Ankara

CRETE (To Greece)

DODECANESE IS. (To Italy)

CYPRUS (To Gt. Britain)

SYRIA (French Mandate)

LEBANON

IRAQ (British Mandate 1920-1932)

KUWAIT

PERSIAN GULF

MEDITERRANEAN SEA

TUNISIA

ALGERIA

Tripoli

PALESTINE

TRANSJORDAN

ARABIA

LIBYA

EGYPT (British Protectorate 1914-1922)

RED SEA

ACQUIRED BY:

Great Britain   France   Italy

Austria-Hungary   Russia

GAINED INDEPENDENCE:

——— Boundary of the Ottoman Empire at its greatest extent

—·—·— 1923 boundaries

0   1000 miles

1914. The Civil War had exhausted the country; until the end of the century the ever-expanding frontier provided an alternative for those discontented with their present lot. Yet the United States also felt, to some degree, the pressures that made stability so hard to sustain in Europe. Though the Civil War had ended, the complex moral problem of racism remained to block all attempts to truly heal the nation. Severe economic crises, particularly an economic depression in the 1890s, accompanied by the collapse of agricultural prices and the closing of factories, caused great suffering and aroused anger at capitalist adventurers who seemed to be profiting at the expense of the country as a whole. Many grew convinced that a restricted money supply had produced the depression. Demand for the issuance of paper money

Unrest in the United States

Eugene Debs

and the increased coinage of silver were at the heart of the programs of the Greenback and the Populist parties, which attracted large followings, and which campaigned as well for an income tax and government ownership of railways, and telephone and telegraph lines. Socialism of a reformist brand was espoused by Eugene V. Debs (1855–1926), leader of a mildly Marxist Socialist party. It failed to appeal to the generally un–class-conscious American worker, who continued to have faith in the dream of economic mobility. More radical was the membership of the Industrial Workers of the World, a general union whose goal was to organize the unskilled and immigrant worker. Perceived as a device of foreign agitators, the IWW was repressed both by the government and by industrial management. Characteristic of the generally moderate tone of American reformism was the Progressive movement, which captured both the imagination and votes of a vocal minority of middle-class Americans whose hostility over the accumulation of private economic power and the political corruption of urban "bosses" was balanced by their belief in the democratic process and in the possibility of continuing human progress. The movement, many of whose ideas were embodied in the programs of Presidents Theodore Roosevelt and Woodrow Wilson, was halted by the First World War, which fostered an environment hostile to the democratic process.

6. INTERNATIONAL RIVALRIES: THE ROAD TO THE FIRST WORLD WAR

The end of a century of peace

Despite the domestic instabilities and uncertainties that characterized the Western world in the years before 1914, a great many men and women retained a faith in the notion of peaceful progress. There had been an absence of multinational armed conflict—with the exception of the Crimean War—for a century. European countries—even autocratic Russia—had been moving gradually towards what most agreed was the worthy goal of democracy. Indeed, instability could be understood as the result of either an overzealous or an overdelayed movement in that direction. Above all, industrialization seemed to be providing a better standard of living for all—or at least all within the Western world. There is little wonder, therefore, that men and women reacted with disbelief as they saw their world crumbling during the days of frantic diplomatic maneuvering just prior to the outbreak of war in August 1914.

The balance of power

The key to an understanding of the coming of World War I lies in an understanding of international diplomacy during the years after 1870. Europe had prided itself on the establishment of a balance of power, which had kept any one nation from assuming a position so powerful as to threaten the general peace. During his years as chancellor, Bismarck played a diplomatic variation upon this general theme, in order to ensure that France would not engage in a war of revenge against the German victors of 1870. There was little prospect that the French would attempt war singlehanded. Therefore, Bismarck determined to isolate France by attaching all of its potential allies to Germany. In 1873 he managed to form an alliance with both Austria and Russia, the so-called League of the Three Emperors, a precarious combination that soon went on the rocks. With the League of the Three Emperors defunct, Bismarck cemented a new and much stronger alliance with Austria. In 1882 this partnership was expanded into the celebrated Triple Alliance when Italy was added as a member. The Italians did not join out of love for either Germany or Austria but from motives of anger and fear. They resented the French occupation of Tunisia (1881), a territory which they regarded as properly theirs. Moreover, Italian politicians were still at odds with the Church, and they feared that supporters of the papacy in France might gain the upper hand and send a French army to defend the pope. In the meantime, the Three Emperors' League had been revived. Though it lasted for only six years (1881–1887), Germany managed to hold the friendship of Russia until 1890.

Thus after little more than a decade of diplomatic maneuvering, Bismarck had achieved his ambition. By 1882 France was cut off from nearly every possibility of obtaining aid from powerful friends. Austria and Italy were united with Germany in the Triple Alliance, and Russia after a three-year lapse was back once more in the Bismarckian

Bismarck's diplomatic success

Grand Palace, Paris Exposition, 1900. European nations continued to promote exhibitions of this sort, patterned after the Crystal Palace exhibition of 1851. Designed to celebrate the growth of Western industrialism, they also served to promote international rivalry.

camp. The only conceivable quarter from which help might come was Great Britain; but, with respect to continental affairs, the British were maintaining a policy of "splendid isolation." Therefore, so far as the danger of a war of revenge was concerned, Germany had little to fear. Bismarck's complicated structure of alliances appeared to answer the purpose for which he claimed it had been built—to keep the peace. But the alliance system was a weapon that could cut two ways. In Bismarck's hands, it kept the peace. In hands less diplomatically capable, it might become less an asset than a liability, as was the case after 1890.

During the years between 1890 and 1907, European nations, competing against each other across the globe for trade and territory, became more suspicious of the intentions of each other. This general international insecurity produced a diplomatic revolution that obliterated Bismarck's handiwork, and resulted in a new alignment which threatened the Germans. To be sure, the Germans had Austria still on their side; but they lost the friendship of both Russia and Italy, while Britain abandoned its isolation to enter into agreements with Russia and France. This shift in the balance of power had fateful results. It convinced the Germans that they were surrounded by a ring of enemies, and that consequently they must do everything in their power to retain the loyalty of Austria-Hungary—even to the extent of supporting that country's foreign adventures.

A diplomatic revolution

The first of the major results of this diplomatic revolution was the formation of the Triple Entente. In 1890 Russia and France began a political flirtation which gradually turned into a binding alliance. The secret military convention signed by the two countries in 1894 provided that each should come to the aid of the other in case of an attack by Germany, or by Austria or Italy supported by Germany. This Dual Alliance of Russia and France was followed by an Entente Cordiale between France and Great Britain. During the last two decades of the nineteenth century, the British and the French had frequently been involved in sharp altercations over colonies and trade, as in the Sudan. By 1904, however, France, fearing Germany, had buried its differences with Britain and in that year signed the Entente Cordiale. This was not a formal alliance but a friendly agreement, covering a variety of subjects. The final step in the formation of the Triple Entente was the conclusion of a mutual understanding between Great Britain and Russia. Again there was no formal alliance. The two powers simply came to an agreement in 1907 concerning their ambitions in Asia.

The Triple Entente

Thus by 1907 the great powers of Europe had come to be arrayed in two opposing combinations, the Triple Alliance of Germany, Italy, and Austria-Hungary, and the Triple Entente of Britain, France, and Russia. Had these combinations remained stable and more or less evenly matched, they might well have promoted the cause of peace. But no such condition prevailed. Each grew weaker and less stable with the passage of time. And it was this instability, rather than the al-

Two opposing camps

The Baghdad Railroad. German and Turkish officials celebrate the launching of the enterprise.

liance system itself, which was perhaps the most important contributing factor leading to the outbreak of war.

The tensions within the new alliances become more comprehensible if one considers the national aims of each of the principal European states. By 1900 six great powers in Europe—Germany, France, Russia, Italy, Austria-Hungary, and Great Britain—were competing for power, security, and economic advantage. Each had specific objectives, the fulfillment of which it regarded as essential to its national interest. Germany built its ambitions around eastward expansion. After 1890 German capitalists and imperialists dreamed of a *Drang nach Osten* (drive to the east) and planned the construction of a railway from Berlin to Baghdad to facilitate economic control of the Ottoman Empire. Austria also looked to the east, but to the Balkans rather than to any part of western Asia. Austria's hold on Trieste and other portions of the Adriatic coast was precarious, since much of this territory was inhabited by Italians. If it could carve a highway through the Balkans to the Aegean, its access to the sea would be more secure.

Aims of the great powers: Germany and Austria-Hungary

To a large degree the objectives of France were dictated by a desire to curb or counterbalance the growing might of Germany. France hoped to recover Alsace and Lorraine. But recovery of these lost provinces was not the only French objective. The French were also determined to add Morocco to their African empire regardless of the interests of other powers. The motives of the French were both economic and political. Morocco contained rich mineral deposits, and would be also valuable for strategic reasons and as a reservoir from which troops might be drawn.

Ambitions of France

A paramount ambition of Russia was to gain control of the Bosporus and the Dardanelles. Achievement of this long-desired goal would prevent the Russian fleet from being bottled up in the Black Sea in the event of war. Besides, it would give unquestioned access to the Mediterranean and probably possession of Constantin-

Ambitions of Russia

ople. Turkey would be eliminated from Europe, and Russia would fall heir to the Balkans. In addition, if the tsar's agents could get to Constantinople before the Germans, they could turn the Berlin-to-Baghdad railway into an empty dream. But the Russians had other ambitions. They coveted access to the Persian Gulf and Indian Ocean and tried for years to make Persia a Russian protectorate. They also strove for better outlets to the Pacific and attempted to extend their control over Manchuria. That each of these ambitions constituted a threat to the status quo scarcely needs emphasis.

*Ambitions of Great
Britain and Italy*

The power policies of Great Britain and Italy were somewhat less closely related to the specific actions of other countries. The policy of Britain, in fact, was directed against almost everyone. It was no less suspicious of the Russian ambitions at Constantinople than it was of the German. Until after the beginning of the twentieth century the British distrusted France. Their cardinal aims were (1) to maintain the lifelines of their empire; (2) to keep open the sea lanes to their sources of imports and foreign markets; and (3) to preserve a balance among the nations on the Continent so that no one of them would ever become strong enough to attack Great Britain. If the actions of any other country threatened to interfere with these cardinal aims (as they often did), the hostility of Britain would instantly be aroused. The offending nation would be put in its place by diplomatic pressure, by forming an alliance against it, or by going to war, as the British finally did against Germany in 1914. Italian policy was mainly based on hopes of aggrandizement at the expense of Austria and Turkey. Austria continued to hold territories which the Italians regarded as rightfully theirs—the so-called *Italia Irredenta* (unredeemed Italy) as late as 1915—while Turkey blocked Italy's acquisition of Tripoli and other territories in North Africa.

Resulting conflicts

These often conflicting ambitions naturally placed strains on the alliances between the great powers. The Triple Alliance declined in strength because of a growing coolness between Italy and Austria. Moreover, Italian nationalists coveted territory in North Africa, notably Tripoli, which they believed they could obtain only by supporting French ambitions in Morocco. Meanwhile, the Triple Entente was threatened by discord between Britain and Russia. Because their lifeline to the East might be imperiled, the British could not view with equanimity the cardinal aim of Russia to gain control of the Bosporus and the Dardanelles and thus of Constantinople. Disharmony in the Triple Entente also increased when Britain and France refused to support Russia in its dispute with Austria over the latter's annexation of Bosnia and Herzegovina. In short, conflicts were so numerous that the members of neither alliance could be quite sure where their opposite numbers might stand in case of a real threat of a European war.

If diplomatic instability was the major cause of the war, two others must nevertheless be emphasized as well. Nationalism, particularly in eastern Europe, played an important role in heightening international conflict. Since the beginning of the twentieth century, Serbia wanted to extend its jurisdiction over all the peoples alleged to be similar to its own citizens in race and in culture. Some of these peoples inhabited what were then the two Turkish provinces of Bosnia and Herzegovina. Others included Croatians and Slovenes in the southern provinces of Austria-Hungary. After 1908, when Austria suddenly annexed Bosnia and Herzegovina, the Serbian scheme was directed exclusively against the Hapsburg Empire. It took the form of agitation to provoke discontent among the Slav subjects of Austria, in the hope of drawing them away and uniting the territories they inhabited with Serbia. It resulted in a series of dangerous plots against the peace and integrity of the Dual Monarchy.

Other causes: nationalism

In many of their activities the Serbian nationalists were aided and abetted by the Pan-Slavists in Russia. The Pan-Slav movement was founded upon the theory that all of the Slavs of eastern Europe constituted one great family. Therefore, it was argued that Russia as the most powerful Slavic state should act as the guide and protector of the smaller Slavic nations of the Balkans. Pan-Slavism was not merely the wishful sentiment of a few ardent nationalists, but was a part of the official policy of the Russian government. It went far toward explaining Russia's aggressive stand in every quarrel that arose between Serbia and Austria.

Pan-Slavism

One further expression of the growth of international instability, and hence one further cause of war, was the spread of militarism. Uncertainty as to the reliability of alliances encouraged the belief that national security depended upon the extent of military and naval preparedness. War scares produced a compulsion to build larger armies and navies. After 1870, every major European power, with the exception of Britain, had adopted conscription and universal military training. Germany and Britain strained their resources either to achieve or to maintain naval superiority. Accompanying this arms race was a growing willingness to acknowledge the place of international aggression in the conduct of world affairs. The American President Theodore Roosevelt had argued that training for war was necessary to preserve the "manly and adventurous qualities" in a nation. The German Field Marshal von Moltke and historian Heinrich von Treitschke saw in military conflict one of the divine elements of the universe and a "terrible medicine" for the human race. The French philosopher Ernest Renan justified war as a condition of progress, "the sting which prevents a country from going to sleep."

Militarism

All these factors—diplomatic instability, nationalism, and militarism—combined to produce a series of crises between 1905 and 1913. They were not so much causes as they were symptoms of international animosity. Yet each left a heritage of suspicion and bitterness that made war all the more probable. In some cases hostilities were

Field Marshal von Moltke

averted only because one of the parties was too weak at the time to offer resistance. The result was a sense of humiliation, a smoldering resentment that was almost bound to burst into flame in the future. Two of the crises were generated by disputes over Morocco. Both Germany and France wanted to control Morocco; and in 1905 and 1911 the two powers stood on the brink of war. Each time the dispute was smoothed over, but not without the usual legacy of suspicion.

Moroccan crises

In addition to the clash over Morocco, two crises occurred in the Near East. The first was the Bosnian crisis of 1908. At the Congress of Berlin in 1878 the two Turkish provinces of Bosnia and Herzegovina had been placed under the administrative control of Austria, though actual sovereignty was still to be vested in the Ottoman Empire. Serbia also coveted the territories, since they would double its kingdom and place it within striking distance of the Adriatic. Suddenly, in October 1908, Austria annexed the two provinces, in flat violation of the Treaty of Berlin. The Serbs were furious and appealed to Russia. The tsar's government threatened war, until Germany addressed a sharp note to St. Petersburg announcing its firm intention to back Austria. Since Russia had not yet fully recovered from its war with Japan and was plagued by internal troubles, Russian intervention was postponed.

Serbian crisis

Still more bad blood between the nations of eastern Europe was created by the Balkan Wars. In 1912 Serbia, Bulgaria, Montenegro, and Greece, with encouragement from Russia, joined in a Balkan alliance for the conquest of the Turkish province of Macedonia. The war started in October 1912, and in less than two months the resistance of the Turks was shattered. Then came the problem of dividing the spoils. In secret treaties negotiated before hostilities began, Serbia had been promised Albania, in addition to a generous slice of Macedonia. But now Austria, fearful as always of any increase in Serbian power, intervened at the peace conference and obtained the establishment of Albania as an independent state. For the Serbs this was the last straw. It seemed that at every turn their path to western expansion was certain to be blocked by the Hapsburg government. From this time on, anti-Austrian agitation in Serbia and in the neighboring province of Bosnia became ever more venomous.

Balkan Wars

It was the assassination of the Austrian Archduke Francis Ferdinand by a Serbian sympathizer on June 28, 1914, that ignited the conflict. The four-year war that ensued altered the Western world immeasurably. Yet many changes which came either during or after World War I were the result, not of the war itself, but of pressures and forces we have seen at work during the prewar years. Then European power, at its height, was challenged by forces which that power had unleashed and which it proved unable to contain.

A world at war

SELECTED READINGS

• *Items so designated are available in paperback editions.*

• Berghahn, Victor, *Germany and the Approach of War in 1914,* New York, 1973. Examines the domestic background of German foreign policy, especially the naval program.

Brogan, D. W., *France under the Republic, 1870–1930,* New York, 1940. An excellent survey, comprehensive and analytical.

• Dangerfield, George, *The Damnable Question: One Hundred and Twenty Years of Anglo-Irish Conflict,* Boston, 1976. A sensitive and judicious assessment of the Irish question.

• ———, *The Strange Death of Liberal England,* New York, 1935. Examines England's three major crises of the prewar period: women's suffrage, labor unrest, and Irish home rule.

Dansette, Adrien, *A Religious History of Modern France,* Vol. II, New York, 1961. Covers the period 1870–1940.

Ensor, R. C. K., *England, 1870–1914,* Oxford, 1949. From the Oxford History of England series.

• Eyck, Erich, *Bismarck and the German Empire,* New York, 1968.

• Haimson, L., *The Russian Marxists and the Origins of Bolshevism,* Cambridge, Mass., 1955.

Halèvy, Elie, *A History of the English People,* Vols. IV–VI, London, 1949–52. The best survey of the period.

Hoffman, Ross, *Great Britain and the German Trade Rivalry, 1875–1914,* Philadelphia, 1933. A perceptive account.

Jenks, William A., *Austria under the Iron Ring, 1879–1893,* Charlottesville, Va., 1965. An examination of Austria's attempts at political and social reform, set in the context of a struggle for autonomy from German domination.

Johnson, Douglas, *France and the Dreyfus Affair,* London, 1966.

• Jones, Gareth Stedman, *Outcast London,* Oxford, 1971. A remarkable book which examines the breakdown in the relationship between classes in London during the latter half of the nineteenth century.

Mack Smith, Dennis, *Italy: A Modern History,* rev. ed., Ann Arbor, Mich. 1969. An excellent survey.

• McManners, John, *Church and State in France, 1870–1914,* New York, 1972. Particularly good on the question of education and the final separation of Church and State.

• May, Arthur J., *The Hapsburg Monarchy, 1867–1914,* Cambridge, Mass., 1951.

• Mosse, W. E., *Alexander II and the Modernization of Russia,* New York, 1958.

Nichols, John Alden, *Germany After Bismarck,* New York, 1959.

Rémond, Rene, *The Right Wing in France from 1815 to De Gaulle,* Philadelphia, 1969. Traces the survival of royalism and Bonapartism in French thought and politics.

Seton-Watson, Hugh, *The Russian Empire, 1801–1917,* Oxford, 1967.

• Simon, Walter M., ed., *Germany in the Age of Bismarck,* New York, 1968.

- Taylor, A. J. P., *The Struggle for Mastery in Europe, 1848–1918*, Oxford, 1954. An excellent diplomatic history.

  Thompson, Paul R., *The Edwardians: The Remaking of British Society*, Bloomington, Ind., 1975. Examines social change in England at the turn of the century and the instruments of that change.

- Thomson, David, *Democracy in France since 1870*, rev. ed., New York, 1969.

  Weber, Eugen, *Peasants into Frenchmen: The Modernization of France, 1870–1914*, Stanford, Calif., 1977. Argues that the great achievement of the Third Republic was the consolidation of France, accomplished by bringing rural areas into the mainstream of modern life.

- Williams, Roger L., *The French Revolution of 1870–1871*, New York, 1969. A good narrative account.

SOURCE MATERIALS

  Booth, Charles, ed., *Life and Labour of the People in London*, 9 vols., London, 1892–97. A remarkable document for its time. A street-by-street survey of London's labor and poverty. One of the most comprehensive social surveys ever.

  Childers, Erskine, *The Riddle of the Sands*, New York, 1978. A best-seller in England in 1903, this novel concerns a future war between England and Germany. Its reception gives evidence of the rise of anti-German sentiment prior to World War I.

- Hamerow, Theodore S., ed., *The Age of Bismarck: Documents and Interpretations*, New York, 1973.

- Lenin, Vladimir, *What Is to Be Done?* London, 1918. Written in 1902, this is Lenin's most famous pamphlet. In it he called for the proletarian revolution to be led by elite cadres of bourgeois intellectuals, like himself.

- Mackenzie, Midge, ed., *Shoulder to Shoulder*, New York, 1975. A richly illustrated documentary history of the British movement for women's suffrage.

- Pankhurst, Emmeline, *My Own Story*, New York, 1914. The memoirs of one of the leaders of England's militant suffragettes.

- Turgenev, Ivan, *Fathers and Sons*, New York, 1966. Turgenev's greatest novel is set in Russia in the 1860s and portrays the ideological conflict between generations at the time of the emancipation of the serfs and the rise of nihilism.

- Zola, Émile, *Germinal*, New York, 1964. Zola's realistic novel describes class conflict in France's coal mining region.

Chapter 32

CHINA, JAPAN, AND AFRICA UNDER THE IMPACT OF THE WEST (1800-1914)

The virtue and prestige of the Celestial Dynasty having spread far and wide, the kings of the myriad nations come by land and sea with all sorts of precious things. Consequently there is nothing we lack, as your principal envoy and others have themselves observed. We have never set much store on strange or ingenious objects, nor do we need any more of your country's manufactures.

—Edict of the Ch'ien Lung Manchu emperor to King George III of England, 1793

During the nineteenth century, for the first time in history the most advanced western states, through the dynamic effects of the Industrial Revolution, became strong enough to alter the destinies of Far Eastern and African nations by direct intervention. Consequently, the chief problems affecting these Eastern and African nations in this period revolved around the readjustments necessitated by Western expansion. Cultural phenomena were subordinated to political objectives, and international relations became of crucial importance. Because China, Japan, and the African states responded quite differently to the changing world conditions that confronted them, the contrasts among these countries became greater than ever before.

Increased Western intervention

1. IMPERIALISM AND REVOLUTION IN CHINA

The nineteenth century, which witnessed tremendous economic, political, and intellectual progress in the Western world, was a period of trouble for China. The central factor in China's distress was the decadence of the Manchu Dynasty and the incompetence of its admin-

*The misfortunes of China
under the impact of
imperialism*

istration, but all her problems were aggravated by the pressure that Western powers were now exerting in the Far East. As in the case of India the objectives of the Westerners at the outset were almost exclusively commercial, and in China as in India the British played the leading role. Although China escaped complete subjugation, her institutions were greatly altered under the Western impact; she suffered the humiliation of seeing her territory and sovereignty infringed upon by Europeans; and for the first time in history Japan displaced China as the leading Asian state.

It was unfortunate that increasing interest in the China trade on the part of Western nations came at a time when the imperial government was almost moribund, undermined by corruption, and lacking in imaginative leadership. During many earlier periods of their history the Chinese had shown themselves to be not only enterprising traders but also capable of profiting from the stimulation offered by contacts with the outside world. By the nineteenth century the eyes of officials were closed to the desirability of any change and to the danger of having unwelcome changes forced upon them. Both the Manchu aristocracy and the Chinese class of scholar-officials that supported it were schooled in the tradition that trade was a contemptible business, unworthy of a gentleman's attention. The Westerners who came to China specifically for purposes of trade were looked down upon as a low order of humanity, and the power they were able to exert in enforcing their demands was slow to be recognized. The policy of the Manchu government was to avoid contamination from the Western hucksters by keeping them at a safe distance and requiring them to have relations only with Chinese merchants, not with government officials. At the same time the government expected to derive profit from levying taxes on whatever trade was permitted, and members of the bureaucracy from top to bottom also exacted commissions for extending privileges to merchants.

At the opening of the nineteenth century, although Western trade had reached fairly large proportions, it was still carried on under cumbersome restrictions which in many ways were disadvantageous to the Chinese as well as to foreigners. Aside from the Portuguese settlement at Macao, the only authorized port of exchange was Canton (by an imperial edict of 1757), at the opposite extremity of the empire from Peking, the seat of government. Silk and tea, the leading Chinese exports, had to be carried overland a distance of at least 500 miles to Canton; their transportation by boat along the coast was not permitted for fear that payment of the excise tax might be evaded. The trade at Canton was under the general supervision of a Manchu official known to foreigners as the "Hoppo" and was handled through a guild of Chinese merchants called the Co-hong. While the Co-hong merchants enjoyed a monopoly of foreign trade, they were taxed and "squeezed" by numerous officials and also were held personally

River View of Canton in the Early Twentieth Century. Canton was the only authorized port of exchange, other than Macao, where the Portuguese had special privileges, until the mid-nineteenth century.

responsible for the conduct of the foreigners with whom they dealt. Beginning about the middle of the eighteenth century a system of "security merchants" had been instituted, whereby every incoming foreign vessel was assigned to the supervision of a particular member of the Chinese guild during its entire stay in port. Foreign merchants were permitted to come to Canton only during the designated trading season (the winter months) and their activities were highly circumscribed. They were forbidden to bring their women or families with them, to ride in sedan chairs, or to employ Chinese servants. They were, theoretically at least, confined to the special area set aside for the "factories," and they could make no request to a government officer except through a Co-hong merchant as intermediary.

That the Canton trade was profitable both to the Chinese and to the foreigners is evidenced by the fact that it continued to grow in spite of the annoying regulations surrounding it and in spite of fluctuations in the assessments upon it. Foreigners were often kept in ignorance of the schedule of duties fixed by the Peking government. The Co-hong merchants—under pressure from the Hoppo, who in turn had to satisfy various other greedy bureaucrats and recover the expenses he had incurred in getting himself appointed to office—were inclined to charge what the traffic would bear. The foreign traders, if fleeced unduly, could of course threaten to break off intercourse altogether.

Methods of trade

"Factories" of the Foreign Powers in Canton, c. 1800. Chinese painting on glass. Western merchants were obliged to confine their activities to this prescribed area of the city. The "factories" were actually trading centers.

The development of friction between Chinese and Westerners

Actually, remarkably stable relations were established between Chinese and foreign merchants at Canton. Large transactions were handled, sometimes on a credit basis, with only oral agreements between the two parties, and by communication through a vernacular known as "pidgin English." [1]

As the volume of Western trade increased, however, friction was bound to arise. Two fundamentally different civilizations were coming into contact with each other. There were wide gaps between the Western and the Chinese concepts of justice and legal procedure. Westerners regarded as barbarous the Chinese view of group, rather than individual, responsibility for misbehavior and the use of torture in obtaining confessions. Consequently, misunderstandings occurred over the apprehension and punishment of criminals. Perhaps even more serious was the fact that the character of the trade began to change in a direction that was disadvantageous to China. In early days Chinese exports—tea, silk, and cotton cloth in lesser quantities—had far exceeded the value of imports into China; and the difference was made up in silver payments to Chinese merchants. Western traders would have preferred to make the exchange in goods, but they had difficulty in discovering any appreciable Chinese demand for commodities which they could supply. The Chinese attitude, as expressed by the Ch'ien Lung emperor to the British in 1793, was: "The Celestial Empire possesses all things in prolific abundance and lacks no product within its borders. There is therefore no need to import the

[1] Some large fortunes were accumulated in the process. In 1834, one member of the Co-hong estimated his personal estate at $26,000,000. H. B. Morse and H. F. MacNair, *Far Eastern International Relations,* p. 68.

manufacturers of outside barbarians in exchange for our own products."[2]

Eventually, a means of altering the balance of trade was supplied by the increase of opium consumption in China. Opium had long been used in China as a medicine and as a drug, and the practice of smoking it was introduced along with tobacco-smoking in the seventeenth century. In spite of imperial edicts against it, traffic in the drug grew steadily, with the bulk of the shipments coming from India. So ineffective was an imperial order of 1800 prohibiting this trade that by 1839 more than 4 million pounds of opium were being shipped in annually. Thoroughly aroused to the gravity of the situation, the imperial government resolved to take stronger measures, both for moral and for economic reasons. The traffic was draining specie out of China and, because it was illegal, it brought no revenue to the state while lining the pockets of smugglers and conniving officials.

Although traders of various nationalities, including Americans, participated in the China trade, the greater share had been in the hands of the British East India Company. When, in 1834, the company was divested entirely of its trading functions and the traffic was thrown open to all comers,[3] the situation in China became more critical than ever. As British mercantile interests in the Far East continued to expand, the demand arose in England for the establishment of regular diplomatic relations with the Chinese government. In 1834 Lord Napier was sent as chief superintendent for British trade, under instructions to announce his arrival directly to the viceroy, the highest Chinese functionary at Canton. Napier was unable to carry out his instructions because the viceroy refused to see him on the ground that the "barbarian headman" must conduct his business through the Cohong merchants, in keeping with law and custom. According to the

[2] C. P. Fitzgerald, *China, a Short Cultural History,* 3d ed., pp. 557–558.
[3] See p. 1209.

Chinese Silk Factory, c. 1800. (Illustration from a French treatise on the silk industry.)

*The Opium War of
1839–1842 and the
"unequal treaties"*

viceroy: "The petty affairs of commerce are to be directed by the merchants themselves. The officials are not concerned with such matters. . . . To sum up the whole matter: the nation has its laws; it is so everywhere. Even England has its laws; how much more the Celestial Empire!"

The vigorous attempts of a special Chinese commissioner to enforce the prohibitions against the opium traffic created a series of incidents which culminated in the Anglo-Chinese War of 1839–1842. This conflict, which was confined to the coastal regions near Canton and the lower Yangtze ports, is known as the Opium War because of the dispute that precipitated it. Actually the British objectives were broader and more ambitious than this title suggests. The real importance of the war is that it served as an entering wedge for the expansion of commercial intercourse and marked the beginning of the subjection of China to conditions imposed by the Western powers. By the treaty of Nanking in 1842 (supplemented the following year) the Chinese government ceded the island of Hong Kong to the British, promised an indemnity and compensation for the opium chests which had been confiscated, and agreed to treat Britain as a most favored nation in any future concessions that might be made. Four ports besides Canton were opened to trade, the Co-hong monopoly was abolished, and the right of residence was granted to foreigners in the treaty ports. Other nations, which had followed the course of the war with interest, were quick to follow the example of Britain in demanding similar privileges, confirmed in separate treaties. A significant feature of the treaty negotiated by the American minister, Caleb Cushing, was that it specifically included the principle of extraterritoriality, which conceded to foreigners accused of crime the right to be tried in their own national courts rather than by Chinese tribunals. These initial treaties omitted reference to the opium traffic but provided that the Chinese tariff on exports and imports should be "uniform and moderate," a

The Emperor Tao Kuang Reviewing His Guard inside the Forbidden City of Peking at the Time of the Opium War. From a painting by Thomas Allom.

The Signing of the Treaty of Tientsin. The treaties of Tientsin and Peking (1858, 1860) formalized the Chinese government's acceptance of the demands of the Western powers trading with China.

phrase interpreted as denying the Chinese government the right to raise the tariff without consent of the Western commercial powers. Thus by 1844 China was saddled with "unequal treaties," depriving her of control over her tariffs and limiting the powers of her courts over foreigners.

The results of the first Anglo-Chinese war were to intensify friction instead of removing it. Much of the fault lay with the foreigners, who took advantage of the weakness and corruption in the Chinese administration to enlarge their own interests. The privilege of extraterritoriality was abused, being extended to cover Chinese servants in the employ of foreigners, and inadequate punishment was given by the foreign powers to their own nationals who were convicted of crime. Portuguese vessels, and some others, engaged in "convoying," nominally to protect coastal shipping against piracy but actually to extort tribute from legitimate traders. Another reprehensible practice, carried on by Europeans and Americans during the middle of the century, was the recruiting of Chinese contract labor for export to plantations in the New World under conditions reminiscent of the old African slave trade. On the other hand, Westerners complained that the Chinese were evading both the spirit and the letter of the treaties. The attempt to establish foreign settlements at Canton led to rioting, because the Cantonese interpreted the treaties as granting foreigners the right of residence only outside the city walls. Less trouble was encountered in the new trading ports, where local sentiment was eager to attract commerce away from Canton now that Canton's monopoly had been broken. In Shanghai, the influx of foreigners resulted in the creating of an "International Settlement"—controlled jointly by British and Americans—and a separate French Settlement in the same city.

In all disputes with China the Western powers had the advantage of superior force, which they did not hesitate to use upon occasion. For

Results of the war and the treaties

a time, pressure was applied only locally, in the particular district where an untoward incident had occured. In 1858, however, the British and French cooperated in large-scale hostilities against the Peking government. After negotiations at Tientsin (the port of Peking), a misunderstanding arose as to the route for the foreign representatives to follow en route to Peking, whereupon the British and French forced their way up the river to the capital, drove the emperor in flight into Manchuria, and burned the beautiful summer palace of the Manchus. This war of 1858–1860 opened China more widely than ever before to Western penetration. The treaties of Tientsin and Peking added eleven ports to the list of authorized trading centers, legalized and imposed a tax upon the opium traffic, granted foreigners the right to travel in all parts of China, and promised that diplomatic representatives of the Western nations would be received in Peking. Largely because of the interest of the French in missionary activity, the Chinese government, compelled to acknowledge that "the Christian religion inculcates the practice of virtue," undertook to protect missionaries and their property.

Although by 1860 the ineffectiveness of China as a sovereign state had been clearly demonstrated, the Manchu government showed no inclination to take a realistic view of the situation or to profit from its own mistakes. The heavily staffed bureaucracy numbered some men of genuine ability among its ranks, but it was practically paralyzed by its own inertia. Local officials had acquired the habit of minimizing or concealing problems rather than attacking them, and the top authorities provided no incentive for the drastic renovation that was needed to make the country strong enough to stop the intrusion of European powers. Unwilling to contemplate the necessity or the desirability of change, they tended to regard the Western pressure as a temporary affliction that would disappear in the course of time, as had other calamities in the past. Unable any longer to repel the ocean-borne "barbarians" the government nevertheless indulged in annoying and dilatory tactics, exhausting the patience of Westerners (not a very difficult task) without gaining any real advantage in return. The Manchu rulers were reluctant to give up the illusion that foreign emissaries were merely tribute-bearers from vassal states who should perform the *kowtow* (ceremonial prostration) before the throne. In spite of the pledges given in 1860, no imperial audience was granted to the foreign diplomatic corps at Peking before 1873, and not until twenty years later was it conducted in a manner acceptable to the Western ministers. Oddly enough, while the Manchu rulers persisted in an attitude of irresponsible and haughty superiority toward the Western nations, they were coming to rely upon these nations to carry out some of the normal functions of government within the Chinese empire and even to protect their regime when it was menaced by rebellion.

While the Western powers were tightening their grip on China's commerce and installing their agents in her coastal cities, internal upheavals created havoc and threatened to overthrow the dynasty. The most famous example, although actually only one of a number of contemporary revolts, was the movement known as the Taiping Rebellion, which began in 1851 and was not suppressed until more than a decade later. Its originator and leader, Hung Hsiu-ch'üan, was a native of the region near Canton in Kwangtung province who had shown promise as a scholar but had thrice failed in the provincial civil-service examinations. Frustrated in office-seeking, he nourished a bitter grudge against the Manchu government (which, with some justice, was suspected of discriminating against southern Chinese), and gradually his resentment became fused with a conviction that he had a divine mission to perform. He had received instruction for a short period from a Baptist missionary in Canton and, after an illness and a series of visions which he interpreted as revelations from God Almighty, he undertook to win his countrymen to the true faith. Hung's religion was largely Christian in ideology but with peculiar variations. He recognized God the Father as supreme deity, revered Christ as Elder Brother, and described himself as "Heavenly King and Younger Brother of Jesus." He also identified God with the ancient deity Shang Ti whom the Chinese had worshipped in pre-Chou times, and therefore believed that in propagating his version of Christianity he was actually urging the Chinese to return to their own original faith. Taoism, Buddhism, and ancestor worship he regarded as idolatry, and his followers first attracted the attention of authorities by their zeal in desecrating temples. Eventually Hung conceived his destiny to be to lead the "Association for Worshiping God" in a movement to overthrow the Manchus and inaugurate the "Heavenly Kingdom of Great Peace." Thus the Taiping Rebellion was both an antidynastic revolt and a religious crusade.

Originating in the extreme south, the rebellion spread northward and in 1853 the Taiping leaders captured Nanking, which they retained as their capital for eleven years, entirely cutting off the rich Yangtze valley from the control of the Peking government. Fighting occurred in fourteen out of China's eighteen provinces, and in 1853 rebel troops came within twelve miles of Tientsin. That the Taiping regime ultimately collapsed in spite of the inability of the Manchus to suppress it was due partly to inherent limitations in the movement and partly to the attitude of the great powers. Fundamentally a peasant uprising, the rebellion failed to win the support of the Chinese intelligentsia and actually antagonized this class by repudiating not only popular religions but the whole Confucian tradition as well. In addition, the Chinese gentry realized that the Taipings would institute radical economic changes, jeopardizing private property rights. Some foreign residents, especially Protestants, were at first inclined to view the revolt with sympathy because of its association with Christian

RUSSIAN EMPIRE

Amur R.

KURILE
ISLANDS

SAKHALIN I.

MARITIME
PROVINCE

MONGOLIA

MANCHURIA

Mukden

SEA OF
JAPAN

JAPAN

Tokyo
(Edo)

LIAOTUNG
PENIN.

CHINESE TURKESTAN
(SINKIANG)

Peking

(Rus.)

Tientsin

(Brit.)

(Ger.)

SHANTUNG
PROVINCE

KOREA

Seoul

Kyoto

Tokyo
Bay

Shimonoseki

M A N C H U   E M P I R E

INNER
TIBET

Yellow R.

YELLOW
SEA

Nagasaki

CHINA

Nanking

Shanghai

EAST CHINA
SEA

TIBET

Hankow

Yangtze R.

RYUKYU ISLANDS

PACIFIC

OCEAN

NEPAL

BHUTAN

FUKIEN
PROVINCE

INDIA

YUNNAN
PROVINCE

KWANGTUNG
PROVINCE

FORMOSA
(To Japan, 1895)

Canton

Hong Kong
(Brit.)

PESCADORES IS.

BURMA

Macao

(Fr.)

0   1000 miles

INDO-CHINA

SOUTH CHINA

PHILIPPINE

○ Areas leased by
European powers, 1898

SIAM

SEA

ISLANDS

INDIAN   OCEAN

CHINA AND JAPAN IN THE NINETEENTH CENTURY

teaching, but they soon became aware that a triumph of the Taipings would not serve the interests of Christian missionaries. Hung evidently believed that all Christians in China should accept his authority because his revelations were more recent than any described in the Bible, and the rebel leaders became increasingly fanatical. Undoubtedly also, a factor influencing the decision of the Western powers not to support the Taiping movement was that these powers had already successfully pressed demands upon the imperial government and preferred a weak but compliant regime to an aggressive one founded upon revolution.

Without formal intervention in the Taiping wars, the Western powers assisted the Manchus in suppressing the rebellion—even while the British and French were conducting their own war against the Peking authorities in 1858–1860. In view of the confused state of Chinese affairs, perhaps it is not strange that one of the military heroes in the imperial service was Frederick T. Ward, a sea captain from Salem, Massachusetts, who raised a volunteer corps for the protection of Shanghai contrary to the wishes of his own government and over the protest of British naval authorities. General Ward adopted Chinese citizenship, and, in gratitude for the exploits of his "Ever-Victorious Army," the emperor commanded that altars should be erected and perpetual sacrifices offered to his spirit. Ward's most distinguished successor was an Englishman, Major Charles ("Chinese") Gordon. Meanwhile several able Chinese, from the civilian gentry rather than from the professional military clique, had come to the rescue of the hapless Manchus and earned the major credit for suppressing the rebellion. In 1864, the combined Chinese, French, and British forces captured Nanking, the last Taiping stronghold.

The liquidation of Hung's "Heavenly Peace" movement did not bring peace even of an earthly variety to China. Muslim rebellions in the southwest and the northwest remained unsubdued until considerably later. During the thirteen years of Taiping intransigence two-thirds of the provinces had been devastated, the whole country impoverished, and probably no less than 20 million people killed by battle, massacre, and famine. The Manchu Dynasty had been saved only through the efforts of its Chinese subjects and by grace of the foreign powers. Furthermore, the injury to China's intellectual heritage through the destruction of libraries and academies in the Yangtze valley was incalculable. In reaction against Taiping fanaticism the bureaucracy became more uncompromisingly conservative than ever.

The story of China from 1869 to 1911 is the depressing tale of a discredited dynasty clinging to its prerogatives while its people were oppressed and the nation's independence was being gradually whittled away. A little color was added by the career of the famous Empress Dowager, T'zu Hsi, a Manchu woman of great cunning and strong will, who dominated the Peking administration through her control of puppet emperors during much of the period between 1861 and her death in 1908. The "old Buddha," as she was nicknamed, in spite of her irregular and unscrupulous methods, somewhat recouped the prestige of the ruling house, but she neither understood nor contributed to the solution of China's basic problems. Out of the chaos of the Taiping era came a reorganization and centralization of the Chinese maritime customs service. A temporary arrangement, whereby foreigners had collected tariff duties at Shanghai while the authority of the Peking government was paralyzed, was perpetuated and extended to all the treaty ports. The higher personnel of the customs service was composed of foreigners, nominated by their consuls but appointed by Peking, with the understanding that so long as the English predominated in China's foreign trade the inspector general would always be a British subject. Thus the customs administration, while foreign-staffed, was an agency of the Chinese government, maintained its headquarters at Peking, and operated as a unit regardless of provincial divisions. The fact that the foreign inspectorate functioned efficiently emphasized all the more glaringly the general decrepitude of the Manchu administration.

Dividing the Chinese melon

In the last quarter of the nineteenth century China's weakness was further revealed in the loss of some of its outlying possessions. By 1860 it had renounced to Russia all claims to territory beyond the Amur and the Ussuri rivers, thus allowing Russia to surround Manchuria and to control the entire Asiatic seacoast north of Korea. Through a combination of diplomatic and military pressure, culminating in a small-scale war (1884–1885), France acquired a protectorate over virtually all of Indochina except the independent state of Siam. The murder of a British explorer in China's southwestern province of Yunnan led the British to demand, and China to yield, sovereignty over Upper Burma (1886). The Japanese government enforced a claim to suzerainty over the Ryukyu Islands (1881). Not to be outdone, the Portuguese, who had occupied Macao for 300 years, obtained its formal cession in 1887. The full measure of China's humiliation, however, followed the Sino-Japanese War of 1894–1895. Japan, only recently emerged from feudalism and isolation, gave the world a startling demonstration of China's impotence by defeating the Celestial Empire in the short space of eight months. Shortly afterward five great powers—Russia, Great Britain, France, Germany, and Japan—participated in a "battle for concessions," through which the major part of China proper was partitioned into "spheres of interest." The spheres of interest, somewhat vaguely defined and usually radiating from a leased port, theoretically did not impair China's sovereignty; but the concessions as a whole made the country an economic dependency of the great powers.

The "Hundred Days of Reform"

Before the close of the nineteenth century, conditions in China provoked a growing spirit of resentment against both the incompetence of the government and the foreign elements that had taken advantage of it. A group of educated Chinese who were sincerely interested in their country's welfare and also appreciative of Western institutions began to agitate for reform. As might be expected, the reformers were mostly from southern China, especially Kwangtung province. Their first outstanding leader was K'ang Yu-wei, who had been influenced by the Han Learning scholars and wished to utilize Confucian principles in reconstructing the government. On social questions K'ang adopted some decidedly radical views, even contemplating the abolition of the family; but he was not impetuous and set as his immediate goal the attainment of constitutional monarchy for China. For a brief period, known as the "Hundred Days of Reform" (June to September 1898), it looked as if the ideas of K'ang would bear fruit as the young emperor, under K'ang's guidance, issued a series of edicts that indicated a break with the past. The movement came to an unhappy end, however, when the Empress Dowager T'zu Hsi executed a *coup d'état* and forced the emperor into retirement. K'ang Yu-wei escaped arrest and decapitation by fleeing the country.

Having rebuffed the liberal reformers, the Manchu court next gave its blessing to extreme reactionaries. The Empress Dowager shrewdly directed the fulminations of various secret societies—which were potentially a threat to the dynasty—into the channel of antiforeignism. The climax came in 1900 when the so-called Boxers ("Society of Harmonious Fists") unleashed a violent attack upon Christians and foreigners in Shantung and the adjacent northeastern provinces. In view of the fact that the movement was secretly encouraged by the Empress Dowager and was based on extreme anti-Western fanaticism, the number of lives lost was not tremendous even in the critical areas. In other parts of China the provincial authorities, disregarding T'zu Hsi's instructions, generally tried to maintain order and protect the resident foreigners. Thus the Boxer movement was neither a revolution nor

The Boxer uprising

Boxer Uprising. German troops march into the Forbidden City of Peking after the rebels have been driven from the city.

an actual war against the West; but the Western powers cooperated to stifle it with promptness and vigor, allowing their troops to indulge in wanton looting in Tientsin and in Peking, where far more damage was inflicted after the allied forces occupied the capital than while it had been held by the Boxers. Instead of abolishing the Manchu Dynasty as they might easily have done, however, the Western governments decided to shore it up, extracting certain guaranties of good behavior for the future. By the terms of settlement (the Boxer Protocol of 1901) the imperial government was required to pay heavy indemnities and to mete out punishments to certain of its own officials; the civil-service examinations and the importation of arms were suspended temporarily; and the Western powers were granted permission to maintain military units in the Peking area.

Efforts to shore up the old regime

In a final attempt to save the dynasty and partly in response to foreign pressure, the Manchu rulers during the period 1901–1911 projected a series of reforms, which emphasized railroad construction, modernization of the military services, public education, and liberalization of the political structure. These measures, beneficial as they appeared to be, were poorly planned and carried out only half-heartedly, and the reform program actually speeded the coming of revolution. In 1905 the ancient civil-service examinations were formally abolished, preparatory to erecting a modern educational system. But the initiative in implementing the program was left to the provincial governors, most of whom did little about it. Many ambitious Chinese youths went abroad to study, particularly to Japan, where instruction of a very superficial character was supplied to meet the sudden desire for "Western learning." A youth movement began to manifest itself in China, characterized by impatience with the old order but inadequately prepared for leadership in the creation of anything better. The government announced plans for a gradual transition to a constitutional regime with an elected parliament and, as a first step in this direction, established provincial assemblies in 1909. Although these assemblies were not democratically elected and were intended to be only debating societies, they vociferated so loudly that the government deemed it expedient to summon a National Assembly the following year. The National Assembly of 1910 was devised as a bulwark of conservatism, with half its members directly appointed by the emperor. Nevertheless, it proceeded to criticize the government and pressed the demand for more rapid reform.

The Revolution of 1911

Meanwhile resentment was mounting against the policy of the government in regard to railroad construction. The original plan had been to build a unified network of roads by letting the provincial authorities assume responsibility for specific sections, raising the necessary funds by stock subscriptions among the wealthy citizens of each province. It was hoped thus to stimulate national interest in the project and also to avoid recourse to foreign loans. In 1909, however, the Peking government took the whole program into its own hands, partly because it feared that decentralization was dangerous to the imperial authority and partly because mismanagement and graft in the provinces were eating up the funds. The government's decision made it necessary to borrow from foreign capitalists and offended provincial interests. Investors were angered when they learned that their stock would not be redeemed at face value, and in the fall of 1911 outbreaks of violence occurred. The railroad controversy was only one among many factors which brought antidynastic feeling to the point of open rebellion. A bomb explosion in Hankow, on October 10, touched off a general uprising in the Yangtze valley cities, during which Li Yüan-hung, commander of a rebellious imperial garrison, cast in his lot with the revolutionaries.

The revolutionary elements in China, which moved into the foreground with the impromptu insurrections of 1911, were by no means in agreement as to program or tactics. A number of liberal leaders, headed by K'ang Yu-wei, clung to the ideal of a limited monarchy. They would accept the continuation of the dynasty if it was willing to renounce absolutism and promote progress. A more radical group wished to abolish the monarchy altogether and convert China into a republic. The prime figure among the radicals was Dr. Sun Yat-sen (1866–1925), born of a peasant family near Canton, in the province which had produced the leader of the Taipings and countless other opponents of the Manchu regime. At the invitation and expense of an elder brother, Sun had gone to Hawaii to obtain a Western education and had been converted to Christianity. After returning to China he studied medicine, chiefly with Protestant missionary physicians, and received a medical diploma at Hong Kong. He participated in an abortive revolt against the government in 1895, from which he barely escaped with his life. Thereafter Dr. Sun traveled widely, residing in the United States and visiting both England and Continental Europe. During these years he had studied Western institutions, which he became convinced could be successfully adopted in China, and dedicated his energies to stirring up opposition to the Manchus among Chinese at home and abroad. In China his work was carried forward by a secret "Alliance Society," which attracted various disaffected elements in the period preceding the 1911 outbreak.

Lack of coordination among reformist and revolutionary groups, the distracted and impoverished state of the country, and the persistence of strong sectional loyalties made it impossible for the revolution to follow a clear-cut pattern. Events of the next few years were confused and somewhat paradoxical. Yüan Shih-k'ai, a conservative bureaucrat who had reorganized the army in northern China, was ordered by the Manchu court to suppress the rebellion. Probably because he realized that the dynasty's days were numbered, he avoided decisive engagements with the southern insurgents, even though his

"Father of the Chinese Republic." Dr. Sun Yat-sen and his second wife, Soong Ching-ling (sister of Mme. Chiang Kai-shek).

Yüan Shih-k'ai and the Revolution

Yüan Shih-k'ai. Yüan, chosen provisional president of the Republic of China, ruled as dictator from 1912 until his death in 1916.

The dictatorship of Yüan Shih-k'ai

army was superior to theirs. The National Assembly at Peking, while demanding immediate constitutional reforms and amnesty for the rebels, at the same time nominated Yüan Shih-k'ai—the Manchu's last hope—as prime minister. There was even more confusion in the south than in the north, although a united front was presented against the imperial government by an assembly at Nanking in which central Chinese and Cantonese cooperated. The Nanking assembly elected as president Dr. Sun, who had only recently arrived in China, and declared for a republic. Instead of puncturing this radical trial balloon with one stroke, Yüan arranged with the representatives of Nanking a settlement which embodied a compromise between the northern and southern groups. As a concession to the southern (and radical) factions, China was to be designated a republic with Li Yüan-hung as vice-president and with Nanking as the capital. But to promote harmony, Dr. Sun stepped out of the limelight and recommended that Yüan Shih-k'ai, who was supported by the northern armies, be made provisional president of the republic. Although the Manchu emperor was required to abdicate, Yüan secured an extremely generous settlement for the royal family.

Thus, with comparatively little bloodshed or social upheaval and without interference by the great powers, both the Manchu Dynasty and the institution of monarchy had been overthrown. However, these events proved to be only the beginning of China's revolution; and they were a prelude to one of the most severe periods of distress in China's long history. Obviously, any regime that succeeded the Manchus was confronted with the staggering problems of administrative corruption, economic stagnation, and general demoralization which were the fruits of Manchu misrule. Furthermore, the unequal treaties and foreign spheres of interest that had been imposed upon the country made the attainment of a unified modern state doubly difficult. Progress was bound to be slow at best, but the men who attained power during this stage of the revolution seemed more bent on advancing their own interests than those of the country. Yüan Shih-k'ai, who had not the least sympathy with republican principles, maneuvered himself into the position of a dictator. He refused to transfer the seat of government to the south, and when a parliament met at Peking in 1913 to draw up a constitution he intimidated, tricked, and bribed the delegates. Dr. Sun's Alliance Society had reorganized as the Kuomintang ("Chinese Nationalist Party"), and Kuomintang elements were dominant in the parliament which was attempting to prepare a frame of government. The constitution as drafted placed limits on the executive power; but so successful was Yüan in corrupting the members of parliament that they elected him to the presidency. Yüan then contemptuously dissolved the assembly, outlawed the Kuomintang, and promulgated a "Constitutional Compact" of his own devising, retaining himself as president. From 1914 until his death two years later Yüan Shih-k'ai ruled as a military dictator, backed by the northern army which he had organized for the imperial service. The Western governments, whose attitude toward the Chinese revolution had been remarkably apathetic, were on the whole favorably disposed toward Yüan and extended loans to him through an international banking group. The powers were willing to support a "strong man" in China—so long as China itself remained weak. Russian intrigue combined with Mongol nationalist sentiment to secure autonomy for Outer Mongolia; rebellion in Tibet enabled the British to extend their influence in that dependency; and the Japanese were beginning to cast covetous eyes on the Shantung Peninsula.

Although reactionary, Yüan Shih-k'ai's dictatorship at least demonstrated the fact that monarchy was thoroughly discredited in China. When Yüan committed the mistake of trying to perpetuate the power of his family by ascending the Dragon Throne as the founder of a new dynasty, he met with unexpected opposition. The great powers, particularly Japan, disapproved of his scheme, and fresh rebellions broke out in the southern provinces. The sudden death of the frustrated dictator in the summer of 1916 theoretically restored the republic under its "permanent" constitution. But a clique at Peking carried on Yüan's highhanded methods, while various provincial governors and military commanders were rendering themselves independent of any central authority. China, it seemed, had gotten rid of the Manchus only to fall prey to greedy and unprincipled war lords.

The death of Yüan Shih-k'ai and the rise of the warlords

2. THE TRANSFORMATION OF JAPAN INTO A MODERN STATE

Japan's policy of isolation, carefully maintained since the early seventeenth century by the Tokugawa Shoguns, was bound to give way when Western nations expanded their trading activities in the Far East. Before the middle of the nineteenth century several attempts, all unsuccessful, had been made by European powers to open Japan to trade. That the United States government finally took the initiative in forcing the issue was due partly to the fact that the British were busily engaged in China. It was also an indication that America's Far Eastern commerce had attained considerable proportions. Since about 1800, United States whaling and clipper ships had passed through Japanese waterways en route to China, and with the rise of steam navigation the need for stations where ships could be refueled and provisioned became more imperative.

The end of Japanese isolation

When Commodore Perry's "black ships" steamed into Tokyo Bay in July 1853, Perry was under instructions from Washington to secure from the Japanese government the promise of protection for shipwrecked United States seamen, permission for merchant ships to

The Arrival of Commodore Perry's Squadron off Uraga, July 8, 1853. This Japanese woodcut was published in 1876.

Commodore Perry and Townsend Harris

obtain repairs and fuel, and the right to trade. Perry's gunboats were sufficiently impressive to induce the Shogun to give a favorable reply when the commodore returned to Edo early the following year. However, the significance of the change in Japan's position was not apparent until a United States consul-general, Townsend Harris, after many vicissitudes negotiated a commercial treaty with the Shogun in 1858. Harris had no gunboats to back his arguments, but he skillfully used the object lesson of European aggression in China to convince the Japanese that they would be better off to yield peaceably to American demands. The Harris Treaty provided for the opening of several ports to traders and for the establishment of diplomatic intercourse, placed limitations on the Japanese tariff, and recognized the principle of extraterritoriality. Following the United States lead, other Western powers secured treaties granting them similar privileges, and it seemed that the pattern that was unfolding in China might be duplicated in Japan. But, as events turned out, Japan's reaction to the Western impact produced results almost the opposite of contemporary developments in China. The reason for this contrast is that the Japanese, after recovering from their initial shock, turned enthusiastically to the task of assimilating Western culture and techniques for the purpose of strengthening their state and winning equal recognition among other nations.

The first important effect of the opening of Japan was that it led to the abolition of the Shogunate, making possible a reorganization of the government along modern lines. The "outer daimyo"—especially the heads of four great domains: Choshu, Satsuma, Hizen, and Tosa—

had long been awaiting an opportunity to displace the Tokugawa family from its dominant position. The action of the Shogun in yielding to the Western powers provided just such an opportunity. Before signing the treaties the Shogun had taken the unprecedented step of going to Kyoto to consult the emperor. The domain lords subsequently demanded that the emperor should be restored to his rightful position as ruler, denounced the Shogun for his weakness in submitting to the foreigners, and raised the cry that the "barbarians" must be expelled. The antiforeignism of the great daimyo was broken by direct action on the part of the "barbarians." In 1863, after an Englishman had been slain by people of the Satsuma daimyo, British vessels bombarded the domain capital. Duly impressed, the Satsuma leaders immediately voiced the desire to acquire a navy like that of Britain. The feudal lords of Choshu were similarly chastened and reoriented in their thinking in 1864 when British, French, Dutch and United States men-of-war unleashed a joint action upon Shimonoseki. In a remarkably short time the key men of the great feudal estates dropped their attitude of uncompromising hostility to the foreigners, meanwhile becoming more determined than ever to end the outmoded dual system of government.

In 1867 the Shogun was prevailed upon to surrender his prerogatives to the emperor. He had expected to be retained as generalissimo, and when he was ordered to lay down his military command also, he resisted. However, the principal clans, acting in concert and in the name of the emperor, quickly defeated the ex-Shogun's forces and relegated the Tokugawa family not to obscurity but to private station. Upon the abolition of the Shogunate, which had existed for almost 700 years, the imperial residence was moved from Kyoto to Edo, renamed Tokyo ("Eastern Capital"), and the old castle of the Shogun was converted into an imperial palace. This series of events constituted what is known as the Meiji Restoration.

It so happened that Emperor Mutsuhito, a lad of fifteen at the time of the Restoration, proved to be an extremely capable person who helped materially in the task of reorganizing Japanese institutions. The years of his reign, known as the Meiji or "Enlightened" era (1868–1912), witnessed the emergence of Japan as a modern and powerful state. Nevertheless, it would be a mistake to attribute Japan's transformation to the initiative of the emperor. As in previous periods of the country's history, effective leadership was supplied by less exalted figures, who used the throne as a symbol to promote a sentiment of national solidarity and to give the sanction of authority to their program. Quite understandably, the leaders in the political field were recruited chiefly from the ranks of feudal society, although they included some members of the old court nobility. In spite of their aristocratic backgrounds, however, the leaders were quick to perceive the necessity of breaking with the past if genuine progress along West-

The abolition of the Shogunate

The Meiji Restoration (1867–1868)

The emergence of Japan as a modern state

ern lines was to be achieved. Some of the daimyo voluntarily liquidated feudal institutions within their own jurisdiction, urging others to follow their example, and in 1871 the emperor formally abolished the whole feudal system. The hereditary fiefs reverted to the state and by authority of the emperor were divided into prefectures for administrative purposes; the peasants were made, in theory, free landowners, paying taxes instead of feudal rents. The daimyo and their samurai retainers were granted pensions (later converted into lump-sum payments) amounting to less than the revenues they had formerly claimed.

The last gasp of feudalism

It may seem strange that a feudal nobility would so readily surrender its privileges. The explanation lies partly in the genuine desire of foreward-looking members of the aristocracy to strengthen Japan and partly in the fact that feudal institutions were no longer very profitable and had been largely undermined by the growth of a mercantile economy. Furthermore, able members of the samurai class, who had been the real managers of great domains in Tokugawa times, saw the advantages in establishing a regime in which their talents could be more fully utilized and more adequately recognized. This class did in fact supply many of the leading statesmen during Japan's period of transition. Nevertheless, the abolition of feudalism exacted a real sacrifice of the samurai as a whole. The daimyo received a fairly generous financial settlement and were assigned ranks in a newly created order of nobility. But the samurai found themselves deprived of their incomes while, at the same time, the government forbade them to wear any longer the traditional two swords and ordered them to merge into the ranks of the commonalty. Smoldering discontent among the samurai broke out into open revolt in 1877, presenting the government with a test of strength which it met with complete success. The newly organized concript army, composed of peasants with modern weapons, quickly defeated the proud samurai, and the rebellion of 1877 proved to be "the last gasp of a fast dying feudal society."

The revolution from above

The sweeping political, social, economic, and intellectual changes which took place in Japan during the Meiji era were sufficient to constitute a revolution. However, they were not the result of a mass movement or of any tumultuous upheaval from the bottom of society. The revolution was one directed and carefully controlled from above. The fact that the Tokugawa regime had already unified the country and through its discipline had instilled habits of docility in the population facilitated the work of the Restoration leaders. The majority of the population played only a passive role in the transformation, even though they were profoundly affected by it.

The Constitution of 1889

In carrying out their carefully channeled revolution, Japan's leaders made a painstaking study of the institutions of all the major Western nations and copied, with adaptations, what seemed to be the best features of each. In the political sphere, they reached the conclusion that the principles of constitutional monarchy should be introduced. A bold but somewhat ambiguous statement of policy, known as the Emperor's Charter Oath (1868), had hinted at the establishment of a deliberative assembly; but when plans for the drafting of a constitution were announced, it was made clear that any concessions would be in the nature of a gift from the throne rather than in recognition of inherent popular rights. A hand-picked commission drafted a constitution which, promulgated by the emperor in 1889, was patterned somewhat after the model of the German Imperial Constitution of 1871. It provided for a bicameral parliament or Diet, with a House of Peers (including some representatives of the wealthy taxpayers) and a House of Representatives chosen by an electorate of property owners. The Diet was assigned the normal legislative powers, except that its control over finance was limited, and the constitution included a bill of rights. In spite of some liberal features, the conservative character of the new government was unmistakable. So high was the property qualification for voting that only about 1 percent of the population was enfranchised. The position of the emperor was declared to be inviolable; he retained supreme command of the army and navy, directed foreign affairs, and could veto bills passed by the Diet. Notably lacking was the principle of parliamentary control over the executive; ministers were responsible not to the Diet but to the emperor. Furthermore, although there was a Cabinet of Ministers as well as a Privy Council, both these bodies were created *before* the Constitution went into effect. A peculiarity of the Japanese Cabinet (aside from the fact that it was not responsible to the Diet) was that the Army and

The Opening of the First Japanese Parliament, in November 1890. From a Japanese engraving. Note the Western-style Diet chamber, lighting, decor, and costumes.

Navy ministers could consult with the emperor directly, without the mediation of the premier.

While the Japanese constitution incorporated several important features and much of the nomenclature of Western political institutions, the government remained close to Japanese traditions in its spirit and functioning. These traditions (which had more in common with Confucianism than with Western political concepts) included such fundamental ideas as that men are by nature unequal and the inferior person should be subject to the superior, that society is more important than the individual, that government by man is better than government by law, and that the patriarchal family is the ideal pattern for the state.[4] Political reforms were considered only a means to an end, which was not necessarily to produce the greatest happiness of the greatest number but to promote the efficiency, strength, and prestige of the state. The men who, in consultation with the emperor, introduced the constitution of 1889 had no notion of relinquishing their command at the instigation of parliamentary cliques or under the pressure of public opinion. The guiding personalities were a fairly large group, numbering perhaps a hundred men, chiefly ex-daimyo and ex-samurai, who together composed a sort of oligarchy. Young men at the time of the Restoration, they retained their influence throughout the Meiji period and beyond, and eventually were referred to as the "elder statesmen" (*Genro*). Acting quietly behind the scenes, they frequently made important decisions of policy. Fortunately for Japan, these "elder statesmen" were as a whole realistic in outlook, moderate in judgment, and highminded.

In spite of the absence of democratic traditions and in spite of the authoritarian character of the Restoration government, the granting of a constitution led, almost from the outset, to a desire for further political reforms. Members of the Diet at least had the right to criticize the ministers, and voices were raised in favor of the extension of parliamentary control over the ministry. Political parties were organized, leading to a struggle in the Diet between the defenders of bureaucratic government and the advocates of the cabinet system. The germination of political parties actually antedated the constitution. The "Liberal" party, which appeared in 1881, was primarily an outgrowth of an "association for the study of political science" founded several years earlier by Itagaki, a samurai of the Tosa domain. In 1882, Count Okuma of Hizen launched his "Progressive" party. These two "radical" aristocrats were doubtless motivated partly by resentment against the fact that their own affiliates had secured relatively few posts in the bureaucracy, most of which were filled by Choshu or Satsuma men. Nevertheless, the introduction of political parties helped to strengthen the movement for the establishment of representative government.

After the constitution went into effect, the character and the activi-

[4]For an illuminating discussion of these concepts, see R. K. Reischauer, *Japan: Government-Politics*, chapter I.

ties of political parties in Japan were peculiar and not entirely healthy. Emphasizing personalities rather than specific programs, parties came and went, fusing into one another, or changing their names in a bewildering fashion. Their effectiveness was lessened by their lack of a broad popular base, by the government's censorship of press and speech, and by the fact that when party spokesmen became too troublesome they could usually be quieted by offering them patronage or admitting them to the lower ranks of the bureaucracy. But, with all their faults, the parties provided opportunities for acquiring political experience and also forced the bureaucrats to explain and defend their policies to the public. The campaign to achieve party government—that is, to make the Cabinet responsible to the Diet—gained considerable headway on the eve of World War I and was resumed vigorously during the 1920s.

Experiments with constitutional government were only one aspect of Japan's political transformation. A modern and efficient military establishment was a prime objective that was rapidly attained, with a navy modeled after Great Britain's and an army copied from that of Germany, largely because the superiority of the latter had been strikingly demonstrated in the Franco-Prussian War. The principle of universal military service, introduced in 1873, was not a Japanese invention (although conscript peasant armies had been known to both China and Japan in ancient times and had played a part in Japan's feudal wars of the sixteenth century), but was based upon the example of modern European states. The administrative system was revised, and new judiciary and legal codes were adopted which compared favorably with those of Western countries and enabled the Japanese to claim successfully that they were not behind the West in the administration of justice. In 1894 Great Britain voluntarily surrendered extraterritorial rights in Japan, and by 1899 all the other powers had taken the same step. The abrogation of external control over the customs duties required a longer period of negotiation, but tariff autonomy was achieved in 1911. Henceforth Japan was entirely free from the humiliation of "unequal treaties."

*Militarism and the
abolition of foreign
privileges*

The economic changes of the Meiji era were perhaps even more significant than the political. In Tokugawa feudal days Japan was far from being a purely agrarian nation, and before the Restoration of 1867 an urban economy, chiefly mercantile and capitalistic, had come into being. When the new regime undertook to strengthen the state and secure the benefits of Westernization, it launched an ambitious program for the development of industry and a modern system of communications. Because private capital was not available in sufficient quantities to do the job quickly and because of the fear that extensive borrowing from foreign investors would endanger Japan's economic independence, the government assumed the initiative in constructing railroads, telegraph and telephone lines, docks, shipyards, and even manufacturing plants, while it also aided private industry by loans and subsidies. There was no tradition of laissez faire in Japan to stand in the way of government participation in the economic sphere, and public officials were anxious to move ahead as rapidly as possible. However, many enterprises which had been fostered by the state were eventually transferred to private hands, although the state retained control of railways and communications for strategic and security reasons. Hence, in Japan, economic progress led to the growth of a capitalist class, but one which did not correspond exactly with similar classes in the Western industrial nations. The members of the new capitalist class, like the prominent political figures, were drawn largely from the old aristocracy, while not excluding men of bourgeois origin—money-lenders and rice merchants of the Tokugawa era. Daimyo now found a profitable field of investment for the funds they had received upon surrendering their feudal privileges, and the more nimble-witted of the samurai also participated in industrial development.

Mitsui and Mitsubishi

The history of the famous house of Mitsui, which grew to be the largest combination of mercantile, financial, and industrial interests in Japan, illustrates the remarkable success of a samurai family that was shrewd enough to anticipate future developments. In early Tokugawa times the Mistui, defying the prejudices of their class, had abandoned fighting in favor of the more solid rewards of commerce. They opened a store in Kyoto and in its management apparently anticipated the techniques of modern scientific salesmanship, displaying advertising posters and on rainy days giving away to customers paper umbrellas printed with the Mitsui trademark. Before the close of the seventeenth century, the family had established a banking house in Edo. The Mitsui heartily welcomed the opening of Japan to foreign trade, and so confident were they of the success of the Restoration that they lent large sums of money to the emperor and his entourage while the new government was in the process of formation. The Mitsui family also formed a connection with the great Choshu domain whose members filled important government posts, and thus were enabled to participate in various aspects of the economic program.[5] The Mitsubishi group of interests, which was the greatest rival of the Mitsui and, like them, developed under samurai leadership, effected a similar connection with the Satsuma group. In spite of the rapid industrialization of Japan, capitalists were relatively few, and they were generally affiliated with clan bureaucrats who dominated the government.

*Peculiarities of Japanese
capitalism*

Industrial developments in Japan in the late nineteenth and early twentieth centuries differed in several respects from the typical pattern of economic change in the West. In the first place, they were so rapid that in one generation the country was producing a surplus of manufactured goods, and foreign markets had become essential to the

[5] O. D. Russell, *The House of Mitsui.*

national economy. Second, the Industrial Revolution was transported to Japan after it had already reached an advanced stage in the Western nations, and consequently characteristics of the early and late Industrial Revolutions were intermingled. The employment of women in industry at low wages, the lack of organization among the laborers or of legal safeguards to protect them, and the working conditions in factories and mines were parallel to the early stages of the Industrial Revolution in the West. On the other hand, the projection of the government into the business sphere and the appearance of finance capitalism were phenomena that were only beginning to manifest themselves in western Europe and the United States. To a considerable extent in Japan, finance capitalism preceded industrial capitalism, because there had not been time for financial reserves to accumulate from the savings effected by a gradual mechanization of industry. The wealth of the aristocracy and of merchant and banking houses—essentially unproductive classes—was drawn upon to expedite industrial progress, and the fortunate members of these groups were in a position to dominate the productive enterprises of mining, manufacturing, and distribution as these grew to maturity.

Another peculiarity of Japan's industrial development was the fact that, while total production increased rapidly and some large plants were built for heavy industries, the majority of the factories remained small. Even in the 1930s, when Japan's industrial laborers numbered 6 million, almost three-fourths of them worked in small establishments employing fewer than a hundred workers and about one-half of them toiled in plants employing not more than five. The small factories, however, were usually not independent but were controlled by the great financial houses, which resembled trusts in their structure and obtained monopolies of whole fields of production. Workers in the cotton and silk textile mills, for example, might be likened to

The Japanese trusts

Japanese Buddhists Expiate Their Sins. Japanese Buddhists, seen copying sutras in Zojoji Temple in Tokyo, reflect one of the traditional religious means of coping with the stress of modernization.

workers under the domestic system in early modern Europe, even though they tended machines instead of using hand tools. The supplying of raw materials and the distribution and sale of finished products—especially in the export trades—were handled by a few centralized organizations from which a network of controls extended over hundreds of tiny workshops scattered throughout the country. Naturally this system placed the worker at a great disadvantage, and his bargaining position was further weakened by the prevalence of an oversupply of cheap labor. In spite of the growth of huge cities, the larger part of the population remained on the land, which was insufficient in resources to support the peasant families. Hence these families were glad to supplement a meager income by letting some of their members, especially daughters, work in the shops for such wages as they could get. Between the depressed class of small farmers and laborers and the wealthy capitalists, the gulf was as great as that which had separated the upper and lower strata of the old feudal hierarchy.

Extensive social and cultural changes also accompanied the transformation of Japan's economic and political institutions. Some of these changes were brought about deliberately by government action; others were unintended or even unwelcome. To carry out a program of Westernization a system of public education was clearly necessary. A Ministry of Education was established in 1871, careful studies were made of the procedures of Western countries, and schools were built rapidly at state expense. Japan was the first Asian nation to introduce compulsory education and did it so successfully that illiteracy almost disappeared, even among the poorest classes of society. There was also notable progress in instructional facilities at the higher level, providing boys with opportunities for technical and professional as well as academic training, and offering separate and more limited instruction for girls. The program was extremely ambitious and the curricula of the middle and higher schools were exacting. The study of Chinese classics and Confucian philosophy was retained, and to these were added—besides Japanese language, literature, and history—Western scientific and technical subjects as well as foreign languages. Notably lacking, however, was the encouragement of original thought. The system was devised to serve the ends of the government and aimed to produce a nation of loyal, efficient, and disciplined conformists. To that end, all students were required to take so-called "morals classes," which stressed patriotism. Western science and technology were appropriated without the liberal and humanistic traditions which had engendered them; and investigation of the social sciences was almost entirely neglected. Thus, the emphasis was not upon the fullest development of the individual but upon enabling him to fit into a firmly fixed pattern of society without questioning it. The Ministry of Education exercised strict surveillance over teachers and texts, making the schools a powerful agency for indoctrination.

Japanese Agriculture. Left: Transplanting rice in a paddy field early in June. Right: Harvesting rice in a farm village. In the background is Mount Fuji.

The creation of a wide reading public stimulated literary production, some of which was intended for mass circulation. Although Japanese writers were greatly influenced by contemporary Western literature, as reflected in their tendency toward realism, they were by no means mere imitators and produced literary work of great merit. Journalism became a flourishing occupation, and some newspapers of high caliber appeared. The Japanese press, however, labored under disadvantages, the most serious being the arbitrary and often erratic governmental censorship. Editors who dared to criticize officials, or who were merely unlucky enough to publish news which officials desired to keep from the public, were likely to be fined and imprisoned or to have their offices closed. It is significant that a considerable number of journalists, in spite of the risks involved, persisted in giving expression to independent and critical opinion.

Literary production

In passing successfully through the difficult years of the Restoration period, the Japanese gave abundant evidence of vitality, courage, and versatility. In many fields they had come abreast of the Western nations, while they had also retained their own distinctive cultural heritage. At the same time, the accomplishments were not an unmixed good, and social problems had arisen which could not be easily solved. The most dubious aspect of Japan's condition, in spite of its mounting industrial strength, was in the economic sphere. Scientific knowledge, improved sanitation and medical facilities, and especially the impact of the Industrial Revolution induced a terrific increase in a population that had remained almost stationary for over

New social problems

a century. Between 1867 and 1913, the population grew from about 30 million to more than 50 million, and from this time on the rate of growth was still more rapid. There was hardly enough arable land in Japan to produce food for such large numbers, even under the most efficient methods of cultivation. While a brisk foreign trade could correct the deficiency, not only was a sufficient volume of trade difficult to maintain but the profits from manufacturing and commerce were concentrated in the hands of a small group. The standard of living of the farmers—the great majority of the population—remained almost at a standstill while the total national income was rising. With the abolition of feudalism, the peasants had become free landed proprietors, but their economic condition was not greatly improved thereby. Taxation bore far too heavily upon them; they had to compete in a cash market dominated by large landlords and industrialists; and their individual holdings were often insufficient to support a family. Many farmers had to supplement their small plots by renting additional holdings. Tenant farming in place of independent proprietorship became a striking characteristic of Japanese agriculture. The urban laborers were even worse off than the poor farmers; and Japan lacked a strong middle class to redress the balance of society. The revolutions of the Meiji era, unlike their counterparts in the Western world, were not essentially middle-class movements and had not broken the ascendancy of leaders whose ideals and outlook had been shaped in a feudal atmosphere.

Factors contributing to an authoritarian trend

The fundamental attitudes and loyalties of the old Japan passed into the new, even though they wore a somewhat different guise and were associated with more effective implements. It was not difficult for the creed of unswerving loyalty to a feudal superior to be converted into an intense patriotism, for which the emperor served as a symbol of national unity and object of common devotion. Ancient legends and

Japanese Religious Festival. The participants are dressed in costumes of different epochs. Spectacles of this sort served to remind the people of their national heritage and consolidated their devotion to the state.

A Gate of the Toshogu Shrine, Nikko National Park. Although the Japanese have adopted Western architectural styles for their public buildings, for their religious edifices they retain the native style, with its curved roofs and lavish ornamentation.

the Shinto cults were refurbished to stimulate patriotic sentiments and to inspire confidence in Japan's unique destiny. As already suggested, an efficient and in many ways progressive educational system was utilized for this same end. The army, also, became an educational agency of a very potent kind. It was made up largely of literate but unsophisticated peasants, who found membership in the military establishment more rewarding financially and more gratifying to the ego than a life of grubbing on a tiny farm. The provincialism, prejudices, and legitimate resentments of the peasant rendered him susceptible to indoctrination by fanatics who preached the superiority of Japan over other nations, the infallibility of the divine emperor, and the subordination of civilians to the military. However, the influences promoting an authoritarian or militaristic regime were never unopposed. Continuous and broadening contacts with the outside world and a gradual reaction to the disturbing consequences of rapid economic change introduced a train of liberal thought, which threatened to collide with the forces of conservatism.

Japan's external relations during the Meiji era were directly related to, and appreciably affected by, internal developments. It is not strange that Japan, in the process of becoming a modern state, adopted a policy of imperialism, in view of its agility in assimilating the tech-

Moderates vs. *extremists*

niques of Western nations and also in view of the stresses created by the industrialization of the country. As time went on, however, differences of opinion appeared among Japanese statesmen, business and financial leaders, and intellectuals as to the proper course to pursue in advancing the interests of the state. Some bureaucrats were conservative or even reactionary, generally unsympathetic to parliamentary institutions, and inclined to favor an aggressive foreign policy. Others were primarily interested in building up Japan's economic and financial strength, securing foreign markets by peaceful penetration, and creating a prosperous and stable society at home. While not genuinely democratic, they at least accepted the implications of constitutional government and were anxious to win an honorable position for their country within the family of nations. Fortunately for Japan, the moderate expansionists were fairly successful during this period in holding the militant faction in check, although not without making some concessions to them.

Adventures in imperialism

Japanese expansion in Eastern Asia would almost inevitably be at the expense of the decadent Chinese Empire. In 1876, the Japanese government took direct steps to end the isolation of Korea, a "hermit nation" which had been as tightly sealed against outside influences as Japan under the Tokugawa Shogunate. Copying a page from the Western book, the Japanese negotiated a treaty with the Seoul government which accorded them extraterritoriality and other rights, as well as opening Korea to commercial intercourse. The treaty also recognized Korea as an independent state, in total disregard of the fact that the Peking government considered the peninsula a tributary dependency of the Manchu Empire. Actually the Manchu officials had neglected to enforce their claims, and their belated attempt to recover their position by counterintrigue against the Japanese was almost certain to provoke a clash with Japan. Korea, at this time, was an ideal breeding ground for war. In spite of brilliant episodes in its past, the kingdom had degenerated into one of the most backward regions of Asia. The administration was corrupt and predatory, the peasants ignorant and wretched, and conditions in general thoroughly belied the country's poetic name—Chosen ("Land of the Morning Calm"). Japan's interest in Korea was both economic and strategic, the latter because Russia had acquired the Maritime Province on the Pacific coast directly north of the Korean border and had already attempted to intervene in Korea's troubled affairs. After a local rebellion had furnished the excuse for both China and Japan to rush troops into Korea, the Sino-Japanese War was precipitated.

Wars with China and Russia

It could be—and has been—argued that, beginning with its swift victory over China in 1895, Japan's policy in Asia was one of territorial aggression. In the treaty of Shimonoseki, Japan required from China not only recognition of Korean independence and the payment of an indemnity but also the cession of Formosa, the Pescadores

Islands, and the southern projection of Manchuria—the Liaotung Peninsula. Japan joined in the scramble for concessions in China, acquiring a sphere of interest in Fukien province opposite Formosa. When harassed by the advance of Russian imperialism in Korea, Japan attacked Russia in 1904 and, after defeating its forces on land and sea, annexed the southern half of Sakhalin Island and obtained economic concessions in Manchuria. These facts, however, are only part of the story, which in its entirety indicates that the Japanese were adept in mastering the object lessons of European diplomacy and power politics. Following the Sino-Japanese War, under pressure from Russia, France, and Germany, Japan had been forced to relinquish its claim to the Liaotung Peninsula, on the ground that occupation of this region by a foreign power would threaten the safety of the Peking government. Almost immediately afterward, Russia, by a treaty of alliance with China, secured control of the very region it had denied to Japan and converted practically all Manchuria into a Russian sphere of interest. Several attempts on the part of the Japanese government to reach an accommodation with Russia in regard to Korea and Manchuria were frustrated by the recklessness and duplicity of the Tsar's agents. Nevertheless, some influential Japanese considered war with Russia too dangerous an undertaking, and the government would probably not have dared to attack Russia except for the fact that the Anglo-Japanese Alliance of 1902 assured Japan of the friendly backing

The Sino-Japanese War. Japanese troops attack Chinese forces defending Pyongyang in Korea, September 15, 1894.

NAVAL SEE-SAW.—LI HUNG CHANG GETS A JOLT.

JAPANESE NAVY RESCUING COREA FROM THE CHINESE DRAGON.

The Sino-Japanese Struggle over Korea, as Seen by a Japanese Cartoonist (1894)

CHINA AND JAPAN WRESTLING OVER THE MAP OF COREA.

A PAGE OF CARTOONS BY A JAPANESE ARTIST.

of the world's greatest naval power. The British welcomed Japan's accession to a position of strength as a means of checking Russian expansion in the Far East. During the Russo-Japanese War, sentiment in both Great Britain and the United States was prevailingly in favor of Japan, largely because of the devious and bullying tactics that the Russians had been pursuing. President Theodore Roosevelt's sympathy for Japan helped in terminating the hostilities, and the peace treaty was negotiated at Portsmouth, New Hampshire.

A temporary balance of power in East Asia

Japan's victory over Russia seemed for a time to restore a balance of power in the Far East. Russia, shaken by the Revolution of 1905, and Japan, its financial reserves drained by the war, quickly agreed on apportioning their respective spheres in Manchuria—publicly affirming, of course, that they had no intention of violating China's territorial integrity. But the balance of power proved to be unstable. The outbreak of the European war in 1914, necessitating a "retreat of the West" from Asia, provided Japan with a golden opportunity to consolidate and extend her position.

3. AFRICA DURING THE CENTURY OF EUROPEAN IMPERIALIST EXPANSION

Free trade, abolitionist sentiment grows

By the opening of the nineteenth century, the cause for the abolition of the slave trade was winning a growing number of converts among governing circles in Denmark, England, France, and the United States. Humanitarian abolitionist sentiment was strongest among the Quakers, particularly in Great Britian. And in the economic realm, a growing chorus of British merchants and industrialists questioned mercantilism and championed the doctrines of laissez faire and free trade. There was an increasing belief among plantation owners that free, paid labor was more efficient than slave labor. At the same time, sons of the Industrial Revolution were convinced that greater profits could be made from trade in tropical raw materials, especially mineral resources, needed to supply European industries. Moreover, British attitudes toward the establishment and maintenance of colonies had become increasingly negative since the fiasco of the American Revolution. In the first decade of the nineteenth century these sentiments prompted the abolition of the slave trade. Denmark took the lead in 1805, followed by Britain in 1807 and the United States shortly afterward. Henceforth, British naval squadrons in West African waters would protect legitimate traders and attempt to suppress the seaborne trade in slaves.

In West Africa the slave trade had contributed to the growth of autocratic, militaristic institutions in those societies that had profited from it. In some forest states, power had shifted from the elders, priests, and traditional chiefs to kings and their warrior bands. From an economic point of view, the productive capacities of Africans had been severely retarded by the slave trade. Therefore, it was now incumbent upon the Europeans to encourage farming, mining, and legitimate trading, and to stimulate the cultivation of cotton, tobacco, cocoa, and other cash crops which might contribute to an improvement in African living standards while also serving as a resource for European industries. Freed slaves from the ships of illegal slavers would be Westernized, Christianized, and returned to the "Dark Continent." Africa was still considered the "white man's graveyard," and humanitarians confidently assumed that repatriated blacks were better equipped to spread the fruits of Western civilization to their benighted brothers in the bush. All these assumptions, while perhaps well meaning, were deeply rooted in a cultural chauvinism dating back to the heyday of the slave trade. Yet in response to such sentiments, colonies for freed blacks were established by the British in Sierra Leone in 1808, by the Americans in Liberia in 1821, and by the French at Libreville in Gabon in 1849.

Ironically, the outlawing of the slave trade contributed to an inflation in the price of slaves and a consequent growth in volume of the traffic. Furthermore, Eli Whitney's cotton gin, invented in 1795, created new demands for slaves on the plantations of the southern United States. The growth in illicit trade led to more stringent attempts at suppression after 1820. United States participation in the antislave-trade naval squadrons propelled American legitimate merchants to Africa's shores in large numbers. Between 1850 and 1862, United States merchants, mainly from Salem, Massachusetts, dominated West African transatlantic commerce. From the mid-1840s the Atlantic slave trade declined steadily, and President Lincoln's Emancipation Proclamation of 1863 nearly brought it to an end.

The slave trade and the concomitant traffic in European arms contributed to the emergence of a new class of African and mulatto mer-

A shift in the locus of power

U.S. participation in antislave trade squadrons

Middlemen in the African Slave Trade. The nineteenth-century residence of a mulatto merchant who was active in the slave trade. Elmina, Gold Coast.

chants in West African seaports. In their societies, power rested on personality and ability, not birth. A few of these merchants became extremely wealthy capitalists.

The House-Canoe system

The Atlantic trade after 1800 triggered unprecedented political and economic expansion in the palm-oil-rich Niger Delta. Local chiefs and affluent nonroyal entrepreneurs organized a remarkably democratic House-Canoe institution of governance, which acted as a cooperative trading unit and as an institution of local government. The old hierarchical forest empires of Benin and Oyo, unable to adjust to the challenges of legitimate trade and to the rise of this dynamic merchant class, were gradually eclipsed. Asante and Dahomey, on the other hand, survived by culturally assimilating their slaves and organizing them to perform large-scale labor in Asante gold mines or on expansive plantations in Dahomey.

African and European responses to the abolition of the slave trade

Former European slaving nations also had to make painful economic readjustments to the termination of the slave trade. After 1843 it was clear to the British that chartered companies lacked the financial resources to maintain the old coastal fortresses and warehouses. Reluctantly, the Crown assumed these responsibilities. The Dutch and the Danes failed to make the adjustment to the changing nature of trade and transferred their coastal installations to the British in 1850 and 1872 respectively. British treaties with African potentates, aimed initially at restricting the slave trade, gave way in the 1830s to treaties calling for the protection of European commercial interests through the establishment of consulates. British consuls would be responsible for ensuring the free flow of goods from the interior to European warehouses in coastal ports. Because the British treasury, bending to popular opinion at home, refused to undertake the costs of maintaining such enclaves, the consuls had to finance them by levying duties. Beginning in the 1860s, ambitious consuls, on their own initiative, did not hesitate to dispatch military expeditions to inland kingdoms to punish chiefs if they hindered the free flow of trade.

Such interference in the affairs of African governments created a vicious cycle of political disintegration. Recalcitrant chiefs, humiliated and intimidated by the superior firepower of European weapons, lost their ability to hold distant provinces together. In Oyo in the 1860s and in Asante after 1874, this condition released centrifugal tendencies and contributed to a breakdown of law, order, and security. Oyo's economy, crippled from the decline of the slave trade, was further weakened by the rise of a coastal trade in palm oil. As inland states, Benin and Oyo found it impossible to compete effectively with African trading houses located among the oil-rich estuaries of the Niger Delta. From 1821 to 1893 the Oyo empire in particular was torn first by a breakdown in the constitution, then by a destructive Fulani invasion that left its magnificent capital in ruins, and finally by civil war. By 1865 refugees from the countryside had begun to stream into stockaded villages like Ibadan, which swelled into sprawling cities. The Yoruba became an urbanized people almost overnight, and leadership passed into the hands of professional military men who could offer protection.

Political disintegration

Once the British had thrown their weight onto the balance of African rivalries, it became a matter of prestige and commitment for them to remain in Africa. In the Niger Delta in 1854 they exiled the powerful African trader king, Dappa Pepple, for cornering the lucrative palm-oil trade to the detriment of British nationals. In 1861 they established a consulate at Lagos, thus opening a hundred-year chapter of direct interference in Nigerian trade and politics. In 1874 they bombarded the capital of Asante in order to punish the king for closing trade routes to the coast. And after 1874 they squelched an experiment by the Fante people in nation building along Western democratic lines by declaring their territory a "Gold Coast Colony." Likewise, ambitious French governors in Senegal had, since 1854, become involved in the internal affairs of inland Muslim states.

*British interference in
Nigerian trade and politics*

Significantly, these militant gestures were usually initiated not by home governments but rather by men in the field—governors, consuls, and sometimes traders. Before 1875, European powers rarely manifested an impulse to territorial empire in Africa. Nor had any of them formulated a coherent or consistent colonial African policy. The tide of public opinion, especially in Great Britain, ran against imperialist ventures, largely because they were so costly. Other than officials and entrepreneurs, those who came to Africa were usually scientists, privately financed and interested in resolving botanical, ethnographic or geographical questions; or they were missionaries and physicians

*Local initiatives and anti-
imperialist sentiment in
Europe*

like David Livingstone, who sought to root out domestic slavery and the slave trade, introduce modern medical practice, and further Christian proselytization.

By 1875 the major geographical mysteries had been solved: the course of the Niger River (1830), the source of the Nile (1862), Mounts Kilimanjaro and Kenya (1848 and 1849, respectively) and the vast river system of the upper Congo Basin (1860s). European explorers had also made direct contact with the major inland empires: Asante (1817), Sokoto Caliphate (1824), Bunyoro (1872). In 1854 quinine proved to be an effective drug for mitigating the effects of the hitherto deadly malaria. European probes into the interior now became more frequent and less costly in human lives. Fear of malaria had previously discouraged the white man from penetrating the tropical rain forest.

Unlike West Africa, East Africa during the first three quarters of the nineteenth century witnessed a dramatic revival of trade, particularly in slaves, cloves, and ivory. By 1800 Africans in what are today Kenya and Tanzania had begun to organize long-distance caravans and trading networks. Previously, items passed haphazardly from community to community before reaching their destination. Criteria for leadership among these small-scale societies now changed from skills in hunting and expertise in rain making to ability in organizing trade, negotiating business deals, and accumulating European manufactured weapons.

The Omani Arabs, preoccupied with internal strife in southern Arabia for a century, were reunited by 1805 and determined to reassert their authority over the East African coastal towns. Under the cunning leadership of Sultan Sayyid Said, Omani hegemony was restored and the capital was transferred from Muscat in Oman to the fertile and picturesque island of Zanzibar, some twenty miles off the East African coast. On Zanzibar, Sultan Said stimulated the growth of a vast plantation economy, built upon the cultivation of cloves and coconuts and worked by African slaves imported from the mainland. Indians were attracted to the island to serve as financial advisers and moneylenders to Arab and Swahili caravan operators.

Slaves were readily available in the 1840s because of a severe social and demographic upheaval in what are known today as Tanzania, Malawi, and northern Mozambique. Thousands of warrior bands of Ngoni streamed into the region from South Africa. They descended upon the local populations, which had no tradition of fighting and were therefore defenseless. Entire communities were often sold into bondage to Arab, Swahili, and other African slavers.

East Africa by mid-century had become the world's most important source of ivory and the major area for illicit slaving. Dispossessed captives were forced to carry huge quantities of elephant and rhinoceros tusks to the coast. The ivory was shipped to Britain and India while the slaves were sold either to Arab plantation owners on Zan-

Indian Financiers in Zanzibar. An Indian merchant's house in Zanzibar.

zibar, to French planters on the nearby sugar-producing islands of Mauritius and Réunion, or to sheikhs in Arabia.

By the 1870s numerous East African individuals and communities had established their own trading networks and armed themselves to protect their economic spheres. The He-he, taking advantage of an unprecedented growth in the European arms traffic after the Franco-Prussian War, became highly organized warriors. Entrepreneurs like Tippu Tip and Mirambo forged their own extensive trading operations and successfully competed with the Arabs for inland resources. However, the Arabs enjoyed the financial backing of Zanzibar as well as commercial connections with Indian and Arabian overseas markets.

In 1843 Arab traders were received at the court of the king of Buganda on the northwest shore of Lake Victoria. Within another decade they extended their operations west of Lakes Victoria and Tanganyika. They were not interested in the propagation of Islam nor in territorial conquest; their sole concern was for trade. And for that reason they often found a warm reception among East African chiefs, who sought arms and imported luxury items in order to boost their own prestige.

Arab penetration

While the East African interior sank into a condition of almost complete social disintegration, Sayyid Said continued to build a vast commercial empire in the western Indian Ocean. Nearly every important coastal town from Mombasa in Kenya to the Mozambique border fell under Said's commercial sway. Not since the fifteenth century had the Swahili city-states enjoyed such prosperity. But it was a false wealth, based on exploitation of the interior. Fortunes were made in Zanzibar on slaves, cloves, and ivory; and the economic stability and security provided by Sultan Said attracted seafarers from Britain, Germany,

Growing British influence over the Zanzibar Sultanate

Panorama of the Island Town of Zanzibar. Zanzibar, one of the oldest Swahili city-states, may have been flourishing as early as the first century A.D. In the fifteenth century it was minting its own coinage and trading actively with

France, and the United States. While these nations established consulates at Zanzibar, only the British one survived beyond 1850. Indeed, after the opening of the Suez Canal in 1869, the western Indian Ocean, particularly Zanzibar, became strategically more important to British interests in India than it had ever been before.

Since 1822, the British had forced on Sultan Said a series of ordinances restricting his slave-trading activities. In return, the British navy would protect the Sultan's legitimate trade and government from foreign interference. Sayyid Said struck an excellent bargain and kept it until his death in 1856, after more than half a century in power. After his demise, the British quickly split his domain into two parts, Muscat and Zanzibar, with separate sultans over each. Henceforth, ambitious British consuls in Zanzibar used the pretense of slave-trade suppression as a cloak for the expansion of their own control over the Sultanate.

In the 1870s Zanzibar became a springboard for European missionary activity on the mainland. British, German, and French mission-

Zanzibar: springboard for missionary activity in East Africa

cities of the Persian Gulf and beyond. By the nineteenth century there was a significant Western presence. Note that the Sultan's palace, arsenal, and battery are flanked by European and American consulates.

aries, Catholic and Protestant, followed the trails blazed only decades earlier by the caravan drivers. They found the interior of Tanzania in social and political chaos. The fabric of civilization had been almost totally destroyed. Yet along the western shores of Lake Victoria, the highly centralized kingdom of Buganda had begun to emerge as the most powerful state in East Africa. Its king, or *kabaka,* was both respected and feared by Europeans and Africans alike. Buganda itself had recently passed from a feudal to a bureaucratic stage of development and was in the process of undertaking an imperialistic policy of territorial expansion.

Buganda's ascendancy

   The nineteenth century in South Africa opened with a change of European rule at the Cape from the Dutch East India Company to the British Crown. The Dutch East India Company had established a refreshment station at Table Bay in 1652 for their ships sailing between the Netherlands and Java. By 1750 it had swelled into a large company colony, consisting not only of Dutch settlers and company employees but also of French Huguenots and Germans. Some merged

South Africa and the Dutch East India Company

into the indigenous African population to form a distinct racial group called the "Cape Colored." However, the majority of these predominantly Calvinistic settlers remained racially aloof and clung dogmatically to a fundamentalist interpretation of the Bible. Their religion became a justification for racial separation. Far removed from the European Enlightenment and liberal currents, they remained intensely provincial in outlook. The majority were illiterate farmers and cattlemen whose only socially cohesive force was the Dutch Reformed Church and its preachers, or predikants. As strong individualists, these frontiersmen resented the authority of company rule, emanating from distant Cape Town.

In 1795 the British temporarily occupied the Cape to prevent it from falling into the hands of Napoleon's navy. The Netherlands had already been overrun by the French and were in no position to assume responsibilities for the nearly bankrupt Dutch East India Company. British occupation became permanent after 1806. Following the Napoleonic wars, Britain enjoyed mastery of the world's major sea lanes. The Cape Colony was thus taken primarily for its strategic importance in relation to India. Table Bay, at the foot of the African continent, offered one of the finest harbors en route to the Orient.

Britain's attempt to Anglicize the Cape Colony met with fierce resistance from the predominantly Dutch settlers. The settlers hated the liberal, cosmopolitan, nonracial attitudes of these newcomers, many of whom were Anglican missionaries. They also resented the substitution of English for Afrikaans as the official language and the introduction of British-staffed circuit courts, with judges who allowed slaves to testify against their masters. In 1834 the institution of slavery was abolished and Africans were henceforth equal to Europeans before the law.

The following year, several thousand Dutch settlers, called Boers, reacted to these ordinances by migrating en masse across the Orange River onto the high grassy plains known as the veld. This "Great Trek" culminated in the establishment of a series of autonomous racist republics. However, the so-called Promised Land had been inhabited by politically segmented but culturally related Bantu societies for nearly six hundred years. Their small, defenseless communities were no match for well-armed, determined foreigners. The Boers, however, were not the only group in search of new pastures. Both the savanna people and the Boers had to contend with an expanding Zulu empire moving up from the southern coast. Tragically, the savanna dwellers became caught in this destructive Boer-Zulu vise.

British policy toward the Boers and Bantu had always been one of vacillation. In 1848 the British crushed the new Boer republics, only to restore their independence less than a decade later. Their policy regarding the Bantu swung from noninterference and racial separation to paternalistic cooperation and integration. The only constant ele-

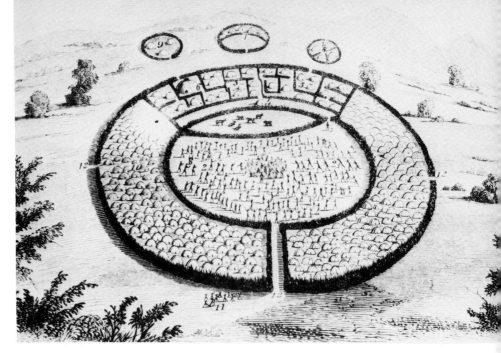

The Zulu City of Umgungundhlovu. All Zulu royal cities followed a consistent elliptical design. These were essentially predatory cities, which thrived not on market or craft activity, but on pillage of the surrounding countryside. At its zenith, Umgungundhlovu contained over 1,700 dwellings, capable of accommodating twenty soldiers in each. This city was burned to the ground by Boer commandos in 1838.

ments in their policy were the prevention of Boer access to the sea and the minimization of Bantu-Boer conflicts.

Clashes between Zulu and Boer east of the Orange River brought havoc to the local Sotho, Nguni, and Ndebele populations and forced them to disperse in all directions. Some refugees coalesced and organized centralized kingdoms in parts of what are today Lesotho, Swaziland, Botswana, Zambia, and Zimbabwe. Others, like the Nguni, became warriors in self-defense against Zulu imperialism and moved northward across the Zambezi River into Tanzania. There these roving bands of Ngoni (as they were called in East Africa) caused the same kind of social disruption that had been inflicted upon them by the Zulu and Boers only decades earlier in their former South African homelands. In 1879, in a gesture of conciliation to the Boers, the British defeated the highly disciplined though ill-equipped Zulu and shattered their proud empire into thirteen weak chieftaincies. The Zulu empire ceased to exist, but Zulu nationalism and culture continued to flourish.

The African diaspora

Of the hundreds of African states, only Ethiopia and Liberia succeeded in withstanding the European imperialist conquest. Ethiopia survived largely because of its modernization programs. Since the 1850s it had begun to emerge from nearly four centuries of isolation. By 1855 a young warrior from the Shoa kingdom had gained control over the nearly independent kingdoms of Gondar, Gojjam, and Tigre, and in so doing had reunited them into an Ethiopian empire. Taking the title of Emperor Theodore II, he laid the foundations of a modern state through administrative reforms and through the creation of a modern national army. For the first time, an effort was made to bring

The new Ethiopian empire

the clergy's extensive feudal estates under government control and to weaken the provincial nobility by establishing districts under Theodore's own appointed governors.

Ethiopian expansion and modernization

Theodore's work was extended under Emperor Menelik II (1889–1913), who with Italian firearms launched an era of imperial expansion. By the turn of the century, he had through war and diplomacy conquered the Galla in the north, the Gurage and Kaffa in the south, the Muslim state of Harar and Somali-occupied Ogaden in the east, and Wallage in the west. At the Battle of Adowa in 1896 Menelik's 100,000-strong army defeated the invading Italians and saved Ethiopia from European conquest. From his new capital of Addis Ababa in the Abyssinian highlands, he employed European technocrats to construct highways and bridges, hospitals and schools, a postal and telegraphic network, a modern banking system, and a more efficient civil service.

Liberian dependence on the United States

Liberia, independent since 1847, also attempted to modernize, using the United States as a model. But faced with chronic economic stagnation, soaring debts, and gradual frontier encroachments by the British and French, the Liberians turned for survival to the United States in 1912. Though the nation became an economic dependency of American corporate and financial institutions, it was able to maintain its political sovereignty. This was largely due to solidarity among the Americo-Liberian ruling elites, whose ancestors had returned to Africa from America.

SELECTED READINGS

• *Items so designated are available in paperback editions.*

GENERAL

Clyde, P. H., and B. F. Beers, *The Far East,* 4th ed., Englewood Cliffs, N.J., 1966.

• Griswold, A. W., *The Far Eastern Policy of the United States,* New York, 1938.

Peffer, Nathaniel, *The Far East: A Modern History,* Ann Arbor, 1958.

Romein, Jan, *The Asian Century: A History of Modern Nationalism in Asia,* Berkeley, 1962.

Vinacke, H. M., *A History of the Far East in Modern Times,* 6th ed., New York, 1959.

CHINA (*See also Readings for Chapter 23*)

Bays, D. H., *China Enters the Twentieth Century: Chang Chih-tung and the Issues of a New Age, 1895–1909,* Ann Arbor, 1978.

Bland, J. O. P., and E. T. Backhouse, *China under the Empress Dowager,* Philadelphia, 1910.

Chang Chung-li, *The Chinese Gentry,* Seattle, 1955.

Ch'ên, Jerome, *Yuan Shih-k'ai,* 2d ed., Stanford, 1972

- Chesneaux, Jean, *Peasant Revolts in China: 1840–1949*, New York, 1973.

  Collis, Maurice, *Foreign Mud*, London, 1964. An account of life among the English merchants at Canton.

- Fairbank, J. K., *The United States and China*, 4th ed., Cambridge, Mass., 1979. Brief but perceptive.

  Fleming, Peter, *The Siege at Peking*, New York, 1959. The Boxer uprising and its suppression.

- Franke, Wolfgang, *A Century of Chinese Revolution 1851–1949*, New York, 1971.

  Gaster, Michael, *Chinese Intellectuals and the Revolution of 1911*, Seattle, 1969.

  Hsü, C. Y., *The Rise of Modern China* 2d ed., New York, 1975. Especially good on the nineteenh century.

- Levenson, J. R., *Confucian China and Its Modern Fate: A Trilogy*, Berkeley, 1968.

- Michael, Franz, *The Taiping Rebellion: History*, Seattle, 1972.

- Schiffrin, H. Z., *Sun Yat-sen and the Origins of the Chinese Revolution*, Berkeley, 1968.

- Tan, C. C., *The Boxer Catastrophe*, New York, 1955.

  Yeng, S. Y., *The Taiping Rebellion and the Western Powers*, New York, 1971. Comprehensive and informative.

JAPAN (*See also Readings for Chapter 23*)

Allen, G. C., *A Short Economic History of Modern Japan, 1867–1937*, rev. ed., New York, 1963.

Barr, Pat, *The Coming of the Barbarians: The Opening of Japan to the West, 1853–1870*, New York, 1967.

Beckmann, G. M., *The Making of the Meiji Constitution: The Oligarchs and the Constitutional Development of Japan, 1868–1891*, Lawrence, Kan., 1957.

Borton, Hugh, *Japan's Modern Century*, 2d ed., New York, 1970.

Brown, D. M., *Nationalism in Japan: An Introductory Historical Analysis*, Berkeley, 1955.

Craig, A. M., *Chōshū in the Meiji Restoration*, Cambridge, Mass., 1961.

Jansen, M. B., *Sakamoto Ryōma and the Meiji Restoration*, Princeton, 1961. A penetrating study of the conflict and confusion in Japanese politics at the end of the Tokugawa period.

- Lockwood, W. W., *The Economic Development of Japan, 1868–1938*, Princeton, 1954.

Reischauer, R. K., *Japan: Government-Politics*, New York, 1939.

Roberts, J. G., *Mitsui: Three Centuries of Japanese Business*, New York, 1974. Carries the story through the American occupation.

Russell, O. D., *The House of Mitsui*, Boston, 1939.

Scalapino, R. A., *Democracy and the Party Movement in Prewar Japan*, Berkeley, 1953.

- Storry, Richard, *A History of Modern Japan*, Baltimore, 1960.

  Walworth, Arthur, *Black Ships off Japan*, New York, 1946.

  Yanaga Chitoshi, *Japan since Perry*, New York, 1949.

AFRICA

Anstey, Roger, *The Atlantic Slave Trade and British Abolition, 1760–1810*, London, 1975.

Boahen, Adu, *Topics in West African History,* New York, 1968.

Carter, Gwendolen, and Patrick O'Meara, eds., *Southern Africa in Crisis,* Bloomington, 1977.

Curtin, Philip D., *The Image of Africa,* Madison, Wis., 1964.

• Davidson, Basil, *The African Slave Trade,* Boston, 1961.

Duignan, Peter, and L. H. Gann, eds., *Colonialism in Africa, 1860–1960,* London, 1975.

• Fage, J. D., *A History of West Africa,* New York, 1969.

Flint, John, ed., *The Cambridge History of Africa,* Vol. 5, *c. 1790 to c. 1870,* Cambridge, 1976.

Forde, D., and P. M. Kaberry, eds., *West African Kingdoms in the Nineteenth Century,* New York, 1967.

Gailey, H. A., *A History of Africa 1800 to the Present,* New York, 1972.

Konczacki, Z. A., and J. M. Konczacki, eds., *The Economic History of Tropical Africa,* Vol. 1, *The Pre-Colonial Period,* London, 1977.

Miers, Suzanne, *Britain and the Ending of the Slave Trade,* London, 1975.

Miers, Suzanne, and Igor Kopytoff, eds., *Slavery in Africa: Historical and Anthropological Perspectives,* Madison, Wis., 1977.

Munro, J. Forbes, *Africa and the International Economy, 1800–1960,* London, 1976.

Ogot, B. A., and J. A. Kieran, eds., *Zamani: A Survey of East African History,* New York, 1969.

Penrose, E. F., ed., *European Imperialism and the Partition of Africa,* London, 1975.

Pope-Hennessy, John, *A Study of the Atlantic Slave Traders: Sins of the Fathers,* New York, 1969.

Wilson, Henry S., *The Imperial Experience in Sub-Saharan Africa since 1870,* London, 1977.

SOURCE MATERIALS

Crowder, M., and J. F. Ade Ajayi, eds., *History of West Africa,* Vol. I, New York, 1972.

Curtin, Philip D., ed., *Africa Remembered,* Madison, 1967.

• de Bary, W. T., ed., *Sources of Chinese Tradition,* Chaps. XXIV, XXV, XXVI, New York, 1960.

• ———, ed., *Sources of Japanese Tradition,* Chaps. XXIV, XXV, New York, 1958.

• Michael, Franz, *The Taiping Rebellion: Its Sources, Interpretations, and Influences.*

Emerson, Joyce, tr., *The Lotus Pool,* London, 1961. Autobiographical account of struggle against restrictions of the patriarchal family.

The Complete Journal of Townsend Harris, New York, 1930.

• Teng Ssu-yu, and J. K. Fairbank, *China's Response to the West: A Documentary Survey,* 2 vols., Cambridge, Mass., 1954.

Toson, S., *The Broken Commandment,* tr. K. Strong, Tokyo, 1974. A major novel of the Meiji period.

Waley, Arthur, tr., *The Opium War through Chinese Eyes,* London, 1958.

Chapter 33

WORLD WAR I

Nevertheless, except you share
With them in hell the sorrowful dark of hell,
Whose world is but the trembling of a flare,
And heaven but as the highway for a shell,

You shall not hear their mirth:
You shall not think them well content
By any jest of mine. These men are worth
Your tears. You are not worth their merriment.

—Wilfred Owen, "Apologia Pro Poemate Meo"

The war that broke out in 1914 was one of the most extraordinary in history. Though it was not really the "first world war," since such conflicts as the Seven Years' War and the Napoleonic wars had also been global in extent, it had an impact far exceeding either of those. It quickly became a "people's war," in which civilians as well as soldiers in the trenches participated in violent demands for extermination of the enemy. It bore fruit in an epidemic of revolutions and sowed the dragon's teeth of new and even more venomous conflicts in the future. In such ways it set the pattern for an age of violence that has continued through most of the twentieth century.

A world at war

Historians who have studied the evidence are generally of the opinion that no one nation was solely responsible for the outbreak of war. Perhaps none of the combatants really wanted war; they would have preferred to achieve their aims by other means. But in pursuing these aims they followed policies that made war virtually inevitable. The most dangerous of national objectives were probably those of Germany. This was true not because they were more self-serving than those of other Western powers, but because they posed a more serious threat to the balance of power in Europe. As the war progressed it appeared that Germany was attempting to achieve on the Continent objectives that Britain and France had succeeded in attaining in Asia and Africa. From the beginning of the war, Germany's rulers were think-

Responsibility for war

ing in terms of a vastly enlarged German empire that would include as satellite states Poland, Belgium, Holland, the Balkans, and Turkey, establishing a great sphere of influence comparable to that of the United States in the Western Hemisphere and of Russia in the heartland of Eurasia. Fears of what this German scheme would do to the European balance of power frightened diplomats in other European capitals.

1. THE ROAD TO ARMAGEDDON

The assassination of Francis Ferdinand

It has been generally held that the assassination of the Austrian archduke was the immediate cause of World War I. Francis Ferdinand was soon to become emperor of Austria-Hungary. The reigning monarch, Francis Joseph, had reached his eighty-fourth year, and his death was expected momentarily. The murder of the heir to the throne was therefore considered in a very real sense as an attack upon the state.

Motives of the assassins

The actual murderer of Francis Ferdinand was a Bosnian student by the name of Gavrilo Princip, the tool of Serbian nationalists. The murder, though committed in Sarajevo, the capital of Bosnia, was the result of a plot hatched in Belgrade, the Serbian capital. The conspirators were members of a secret society officially known as Union or Death, but commonly called the Black Hand. What were the motives of the conspirators? If there is any one answer, it would seem to lie in the plan which Francis Ferdinand was known to be developing for the reorganization of the Hapsburg Empire. This plan, designated as *trialism,* involved a proposal for changing the Dual Monarchy into a triple monarchy. In addition to German Austria and Magyar Hungary, already practically autonomous, there was to be a third semi-independent unit composed of the Slavs. This plan was exactly what the Serb nationalists did not want. They feared that if it were put into effect, their Slovene and Croatian kinsmen would be content to remain under

The Archduke Francis Ferdinand. He and his wife are leaving the Senate House in Sarajevo shortly before the assassination, June 28, 1914.

Hapsburg rule. They therefore determined to get Francis Ferdinand out of the way before he could become emperor.

In the weeks immediately following the assassination, Austrian officials conducted an investigation which confirmed their suspicions that the plot was of Serbian origin. Consequently, on July 23, they dispatched to the Serbian government a severe ultimatum consisting of eleven demands: among them Serbia was to suppress anti-Austrian newspapers; to crush secret patriotic societies; to eliminate from the government and from the army all persons guilty of anti-Austrian propaganda; and to accept the collaboration of Austrian officials in stamping out the subversive movement against the Hapsburg Empire. On July 25, in accordance with the time limit of forty-eight hours, the Serbian government transmitted its reply. Of the total of eleven demands, only one was emphatically refused, and five were accepted without reservations. The German chancellor regarded it as almost a capitulation, and Emperor William II declared that now all reason for war had dissipated. The Austrians, however, pronounced the Serbian reply unsatisfactory, severed diplomatic relations, and mobilized parts of their army. The Serbs themselves had been under no illusions about pleasing Austria, since, three hours before transmitting their reply, they had issued an order to mobilize the troops.

Austrian ultimatum to Serbia

The Austrian intransigence vis-à-vis the Serbian response was actually the culmination of a belligerence which had been growing among European nations prior to the events which followed the assassination. As early as July 18 Sergei Sazonov, the Russian foreign minister, warned Austria that Russia would not tolerate any effort to humiliate Serbia. On July 24 Sazonov informed the German ambassador: "I do not hate Austria; I despise her. Austria is seeking a pretext to gobble up Serbia; but in that case Russia will make war on Austria."[1] In the adoption of this attitude, Russia had the support of France. About the twentieth of July, Raymond Poincaré, president of France, paid a visit to St. Petersburg. He kept urging Sazonov to "be firm" and to avoid any compromise which might result in a loss of prestige for the Triple Entente. He warned the Austrian ambassador that "Serbia has very warm friends in the Russian people. And Russia has an ally, France."[2]

Russia and France

The attitude of Germany in these critical days was ambiguous. Although the kaiser was shocked and infuriated by the assassination, his government did not make any threats until after the actions of Russia gave cause for alarm. Yet both William II and the chancellor, Theobald von Bethmann-Hollweg, adopted the premise that stern punishment must be meted out to Serbia without delay. They hoped in this way to confront the other powers with an accomplished fact. The kaiser declared on June 30: "Now or never! Matters must be cleared up with the Serbs, *and that soon.*" On July 6 Bethmann-Hollweg gave

The attitude of Germany

---

[1] S. B. Fay, *The Origins of the World War*, II, 300.
[2] *Ibid.*, II, 281.

Nicholas II and Raymond Poincaré, the President of the French Republic, in St. Petersburg on July 23, 1914

a commitment to the Austrian foreign minister which was interpreted by the latter as a blank check. The Austrian government was informed that the kaiser would "stand true by Austria's side in accordance with his treaty obligations and old friendship." In giving this pledge Bethmann and his imperial master were gambling on the hope that Russia would not intervene for the protection of Serbia, and that therefore the quarrel would remain a mere local squabble.

Russian mobilization

Austria declared war against Serbia on July 28, 1914. For a fleeting, anxious moment there was a possibility that the conflict might be contained. But it was quickly transformed into a war of larger scope by the action of Russia. On July 29 Sazonov and a prowar military clique persuaded Tsar Nicholas II to issue an order mobilizing all troops, not only against Austria but against Germany as well. Their argument was a logical one. Such a vast country as Russia would require considerable time to get its military machine into operation. But before the order could be put into effect, Nicholas changed his mind, having just received an urgent appeal from the kaiser to help preserve the peace.

See color map facing page 961

On July 30 Sazonov and the Russian chief of staff went to work to induce the tsar to change his mind again. For more than an hour they sought to convince the reluctant autocrat that the entire military system should be set in motion. In the end, Nicholas signed an order for immediate mobilization.

There was now no drawing back from the abyss. The Germans were alarmed over Russian preparations for war. The latest action of the tsar's government made the situation far more critical, since in German military circles, and also in French and Russian, general mobilization meant war. Upon learning that the tsar's decree had gone into effect, William II's government sent an ultimatum to St. Petersburg demanding that mobilization cease within twelve hours. On the afternoon of August 1, the German ambassador requested an interview with the Russian foreign minister. He appealed to Sazonov for a favorable answer to the German ultimatum. Sazonov replied that mobilization could not be halted, but that Russia was willing to continue negotiations. The ambassador repeated his question a second and a third time, emphasizing the terrible consequences of a negative answer. Sazonov finally replied: "I have no other answer to give you." The ambassador then handed the foreign minister a declaration of war and, bursting into tears, left the room. In the meantime, the kaiser's ministers had also dispatched an ultimatum to France demanding that its leaders make known their intentions. Premier René Viviani replied on August 1 that France would act "in accordance with her interests," and immediately ordered a general mobilization of the army. On August 3 Germany declared war upon France.

All eyes now turned in the direction of Britain. What would happen, now that the other two members of the Triple Entente had rushed headlong into war? For some time after the situation on the Continent had become critical, Britain vacillated. It is difficult to believe that the British would have long remained out of the war, even if the neutrality of Belgium had never been violated. In fact, as early as July 29, Sir Edward Grey, Britain's foreign secretary, had given the German ambassador in London a warning that if France were drawn into the war, Great Britain would enter also. Nevertheless, it was the invasion of Belgian territory which provided the immediate cause of

The German ultimatums to Russia and France

Britain enters the war

August 1, 1914. A German officer reads the declaration of war in the streets of Berlin.

Britain's entry. In 1839, along with the other great powers, Britain had signed a treaty guaranteeing the neutrality of Belgium. Moreover, it had been British policy for a century or more to try to prevent domination of the Low Countries, lying directly across the Channel, by any powerful continental nation. The Germans planned to attack France through Belgium. Accordingly, they demanded of the Belgian government permission to send troops across its territory, promising to respect the independence of the nation and to pay for any damage to property. When Belgium refused, the kaiser's legions began pouring across the frontier. The British foreign secretary immediately went before Parliament and urged that his country should rally to the defense of international law and to the protection of small nations. He argued that peace under the circumstances would be a moral crime, and declared that if Britain should fail to uphold its obligations of honor in this matter it would forfeit the respect of the civilized world. The next day, August 4, the cabinet sent an ultimatum to Berlin demanding that Germany respect Belgian neutrality, and that the Germans give a satisfactory reply by midnight. The kaiser's ministers offered no answer save military necessity, arguing that it was a matter of life and death for Germany that its soldiers should reach France by the quickest and easiest way. As the clock struck twelve, Great Britain and Germany were at war.

The conflagration spreads

Other nations were quickly drawn into the terrible vortex. On August 7 the Montenegrins joined with their kinsmen, the Serbs, in fighting Austria. Two weeks later the Japanese declared war upon Germany, partly because of their alliance with Great Britain, but mainly for the purpose of conquering German possessions in the Far East. On August 1 Turkey negotiated an alliance with Germany, and in October began the bombardment of Russian ports on the Black Sea. Thus most of the nations definitely bound by alliances entered the conflict in its early stages on one side or the other. Italy, however, though still technically a member of the Triple Alliance, proclaimed neutrality. The Italians insisted that the Germans were not fighting a defensive war, and that consequently they were not bound to go to their aid. Italy remained neutral until May 1915, when Britain and France bribed its leaders with secret promises of Austrian and Turkish territory to engage in the war on the side of the Triple Entente.

2. THE ORDEAL OF BATTLE

The "holy war" of the principal powers

In the Book of Revelation it is related that the forces of good and evil shall be gathered together on "the great day of God" to do battle at Armageddon. The author might almost have been thinking of the titanic conflict which engulfed the nations of Europe in 1914. For World War I was seldom admitted to be a struggle between rival imperialist powers or a product of nationalist jealousy. Instead, it was represented by spokesmen for both sides as a crusade against the forces of evil. No sooner had war begun than social and political leaders in England and France pronounced it a gallant effort to safeguard the rights of the weak and to preserve the supremacy of international law and morality. Prime Minister Asquith on August 6, 1914, declared that Britain had entered the conflict to vindicate "the principle that smaller nationalities are not to be crushed by the arbitrary will of a strong and overmastering Power." Across the Channel, President Poincaré was assuring his fellow citizens that France had no other purpose than to stand "before the universe for Liberty, Justice and Reason." Socialists who had, in the past, proclaimed their international solidarity and their opposition to the wars of capitalism, now in almost all cases declared themselves national patriots. Later, as a consequence of the preaching of such writers and orators as H. G. Wells, Gilbert Murray, and the American president, Woodrow Wilson, the crusade of the Entente powers became a war to redeem mankind from the curse of militarism. In the opposing camp, the subordinates of the kaiser were doing all in their power to justify Germany's military efforts. The struggle against the Entente powers was represented to the German people as a crusade on behalf of a superior *Kultur* and as a battle to protect the fatherland against the wicked encirclement policy of the Entente nations. German socialist politicians were persuaded to vote for the war on the grounds that a German war with Russia would help liberate the Russian people from the tsarist yoke.

World War I fooled military experts who believed it would end quickly. Open warfare soon disappeared from the Western Front—the battle line that stretched across France from Switzerland to the North Sea, where the fighting was concentrated for four years. Following

War of attrition

Modern Warfare. After the first few battles, the war on the Western Front settled into static or position warfare. During the four-year period, veritable cities of mud, stone, and timber sprang up behind the trenches.

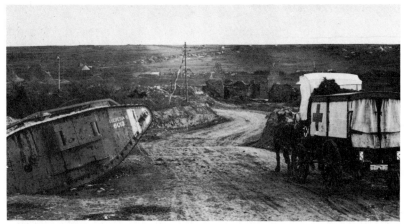

Left: British armored trucks move toward the front. Above: *A British tank and field ambulance.*

Germany's initial advance into France, the opposing armies settled down in a vast network of trenches, from which attacks to dislodge the enemy were launched, usually in the murky hours just before dawn. These attacks always failed to achieve more than very limited gains. Protected by barbed wire and machine-guns—both making their first major appearance in a European war—defenders had the advantage. The one weapon with the potential to break the stalemate, the tank, was not introduced into battle until 1916, and then with such reluctance by tradition-bound commanders that its half-hearted employment made almost no difference. Airplanes were used almost exclusively for reconnaissance, though occasional "dog-fights" did occur between German and Allied pilots. The Germans sent Zeppelins to raid London, but they did little significant damage. Commanding officers continued to believe that the war would have to be won on the ground. Only by battering their enemies first with artillery and then with thousands of men armed with rifles, grenades, and bayonets, did they believe they could achieve the always elusive "breakthrough." On more than one occasion those in charge of the war attempted to end the stalemate by opening military fronts in other areas of the world. In 1915, Britain and France attempted a landing at Gallipoli, in Asia Minor, in the hope of driving Turkey from the war. The campaign was a disaster for the Entente powers, however, failing, as did others, to refocus the fighting or to free it from the immobility of the trenches.

Life for the common soldier on the Western Front alternated between the daily boredom and extreme unpleasantness of weeks spent *The toll* in muddy and vermin-ridden trench communities, and the occasional and horrifying experience of battle, a nightmare not only of artillery, machine-guns, and barbed wire, but of exploding bullets, liquid fire, and poison gas. Battles that accomplished almost nothing devoured

Wartime Leaders. Left: Haig, Joffre, and Lloyd George discuss strategy. Right: Reviewing a map are Hindenburg, William II, and Ludendorff, members of the German high command.

the men who fought them. Over 600,000 soldiers were killed and wounded when the Germans unsuccessfully besieged the French stronghold of Verdun, near France's eastern border, for six months in the spring of 1916. In the battle along the Somme River, which lasted from July to October 1916, and which gained the British and French no more than a few miles, the Germans lost 500,000 men, the British 400,000, and the French 200,000. Although the war, because of its stationary nature, took a relatively light civilian toll, the total numbers of dead and wounded were staggering: out of an estimated 65 million men who fought under the flags of the various belligerents, 10 million were killed and another 20 million wounded. The struggle was an endurance contest. The victory of the Entente powers came as a result of their continued control of the seas and of their ability to obtain almost unlimited supplies of money, food, and munitions from allies and neutral countries around the world.

As the conflict dragged on, more and more nations entered the war on one side or the other. Italy postponed its entry until the spring of 1915. Bulgaria joined Germany and its allies, known as the Central Powers, in September 1915, and Rumania entered on the opposite side about a year later. The event which helped greatly to tip the scales in favor of an Entente victory was the declaration of war against Germany by the United States on April 6, 1917. The United States entered the war for a variety of reasons. All sorts of moral arguments were avowed by President Wilson and other high officials of the government—to "make the world safe for democracy," to banish autocracy and militarism, and to establish a league or society of nations in place of the old diplomatic maneuvering. Undoubtedly, the primary reason, though, was the concern of the American government to maintain the balance of power in Europe. For years it had been a cardinal doctrine in the State Department and among military and naval

World War I Posters Held Back Little in Their Appeal to Emotions

The Lusitania *Leaving New York Harbor.* In February 1915 the *Lusitania* was torpedoed and sunk by a German U-boat. Among the 1,200 people drowned were 119 Americans. The disaster was one step in the chain of events which led to the entry of the United States into the war on the side of Britain and France.

officers that the security of the United States depended upon a balance of forces in the Old World. No one power must be allowed to establish its supremacy over all of Europe. So long as Great Britain was strong enough to prevent that supremacy, the United States was safe. Some authorities believe that American officials had grown so accustomed to thinking of the British navy as the shield of American security that they could hardly tolerate the thought of any different situation. Germany, however, presented not merely a challenge to British naval supremacy, but threatened to starve the British nation into surrender and to establish a hegemony over all of Europe.

Submarine warfare

The direct cause of United States participation in World War I was the U-boat, or submarine, warfare of the Germans. Once it became clear that the war would be one of attrition, the Germans recognized that unless they could break the Entente's stranglehold on their shipping, they would be defeated. The result was a campaign of submarine warfare. In February 1915, the kaiser's government announced that neutral vessels headed for British ports would be torpedoed without warning. President Wilson replied by declaring that the United States would hold Germany to a "strict accountability" if any harm should come to American lives or property. The warning had little effect. The Germans were convinced that the U-boat was one of their most valuable weapons, and they considered themselves justified in using it against the British blockade. They also believed, correctly, that the British were receiving war materiel clandestinely shipped aboard passenger ships from the United States, and continued to sink them, thus appearing to violate United States neutrality. When the kaiser's ministers announced that, on February 1, 1917, they would launch a campaign of unrestricted submarine warfare, Wilson cut off diplomatic relations with the Berlin government. On April 2 he went before a joint session of the two houses of Congress and requested and received a declaration of war.

3. REVOLUTION IN THE MIDST OF WAR

In the midst of world war came revolution. Russia, already severely weakened by internal conflicts before 1914, found itself unable to sustain the additional burden of continuous warfare. In a nation ruled as autocratically as was Russia, a successful war effort depended greatly on the determination and talents of its ruler, the tsar. Nicholas II was, by nature, irresolute and weak. His limited capabilities were further undermined by the irrationality of his wife, Alexandra, a religious fanatic, and of her spiritual mentor, the monk Rasputin. The latter had gained the tsarina's sympathy by his ability to alleviate the sufferings of her hemophiliac son, and used his influence over her to shape policy to his own self-aggrandizing ends. The tsar's incompetent direction meant that Russia's armies could not win battles, and suffered a series of humiliating defeats by the Germans. In some instances soldiers were sent to the front without rifles; their clothing supplies were also inadequate. Medical facilities were scarce. The railway system broke down, producing a shortage of food not only in the army but in the cities as well. By the end of 1916, Russia's power to resist had practically collapsed.

Incompetence of the tsar

The revolution in Russia followed a succession of stages somewhat similar to those of the French Revolution of 1789. The first of these began in March 1917 with the forced abdication of the tsar. For this the immediate cause was disgust with the conduct of the war. But there were many other factors—inflation and consequent high prices, and scarcity of food and coal in urban areas. With the overthrow of the

The March 1917 revolution

Tsar Nicholas II and His Family on the Eve of the Revolution

tsar, the authority of the government passed into the hands of a provisional ministry organized by leaders in the Duma in conjunction with representatives of workers in Petrograd, calling themselves a *soviet*, or government council. (The city had abandoned the supposedly Germanic name of St. Petersburg at the beginning of the war.) With the exception of Alexander Kerensky (1881–1970), who was a member of the rurally based Social Revolutionary party, nearly all of the ministers were bourgeois liberals. Their hope was to transform the Russian autocracy into a constitutional monarchy modeled after that of Great Britain. In accordance with this aim, they issued a proclamation of civil liberties, released thousands of prisoners, and made plans for the election of a constituent assembly.

The provisional government

The provisional government proved itself inadequate to deal with the problems it faced. Its leaders did not seem to understand the new conditions created by the war, or even some of those arising in the prewar period. Among these were overcrowding in the cities, the emergence of an urban working class, and the inevitable harshness of the class conflict in the initial stages of industrialization. Further, the heads of this provisional government made the mistake of attempting to continue the war on the basis of previous imperialist aims. They hoped to obtain Constantinople and everything else that had been promised to Russia in its secret treaties. But the masses of the Russian people were desperately weary of the years of hardship and struggle. What they wanted was peace and a chance to return to a normal life. Consequently, in May, when the leaders renewed their pledge of support for the Entente powers, opposition was so strong that they were forced to resign. A new government was organized which managed to stay in power until September. Led by Kerensky, it consisted

Scenes from the Russian Revolution. Left: Street Fighting in Petrograd, 1917. Right: Russian soldiers join the Bolsheviks in front of the Winter Palace.

Strife in Ireland, 1916. British troops raiding the office of a Dublin printer who supported the rebellion.

primarily of moderate socialists. The ultimate failure of this regime may be ascribed chiefly to the insignificant role played by the middle class in Russia at the time. In no sense can it be compared as a revolutionary force with the bourgeoisie in France in 1789. It was much smaller in size and lacked the prestige and wealth of the elements that destroyed the absolute monarchy of Louis XVI. Moreover, it had little support from the mass of the Russian people.

The downfall of Kerensky's regime marked the end of the first stage of the Russian Revolution. The second began immediately after, with the accession of the Bolsheviks to power under the leadership of Lenin on November 7, 1917. Soon after the overthrow of the tsar the Bolsheviks had begun to plan for a socialist revolution. They worked their way into the Petrograd Soviet, the Council of Workers' and Soldiers' Deputies, and quickly gained control of it from the Mensheviks and Social Revolutionaries. They organized an armed Red Guard and took possession of strategic points throughout the city. By November 7 everything was ready for a coup d'état. Red Guards occupied nearly all the public buildings and finally arrested the members of the government, though Kerensky himself escaped. Thus the Bolsheviks climbed to power with scarcely a struggle. Their slogan of "Peace, Land, and Bread" made them heroes to the soldiers disgusted with the war, to the peasants hungry for land, and to the urban population suffering from various shortages. As soon as possible, the Bolsheviks sued for peace with the Germans, accepting terms that included the surrender of Poland, the Ukraine, and Finland. The treaty was signed at Brest-Litovsk in March 1918.

Triumph of the Bolsheviks

Yet another outbreak of revolution in this period was the so-called Easter Rebellion in Ireland. At the beginning of World War I, Irish nationalists, who resented the rule of their country by the British, were ripe for revolt. They had been promised self-rule on the eve of the war, but the British later reneged on the ground that a national

The Easter Rebellion in Ireland

emergency must take preeminence over everything else. This greatly angered the Roman Catholic majority of southern Ireland. They scheduled Easter Monday, 1916, as a day for revolt. British forces quelled the uprising, but not until after a hundred people had been killed. Sporadic outbreaks kept the island in turmoil for years thereafter, but were finally brought to a temporary end by an agreement constituting southern Ireland as a free republic. The northern counties, or the province of Ulster, were to continue subject to the British crown.

4. ARMISTICE AND PEACE

Peace proposals

While fighting on the several fronts raged through four horrible years, various attempts were made to bring about the negotiation of peace. In the spring of 1917, Dutch and Scandinavian socialists decided to summon an international socialist conference to meet at Stockholm in the hope of drafting plans for ending the fighting which would be acceptable to all the belligerents. The Petrograd Soviet embraced the idea and on May 15 issued an appeal to socialists of all nations to send delegates to the conference and to induce their governments to agree to a peace "without annexations and indemnities, on the basis of the self-determination of peoples." The socialist parties in all the principal countries on both sides of the war accepted this formula and were eager to send delegates to the conference, but when the British and French governments refused to permit any of their subjects to attend, the project was abandoned. That the rulers of the Entente states were not afraid of these proposals merely because they emanated from socialists is indicated by the fact that a similar formula suggested by the pope was just as emphatically rejected. Nowhere was there a disposition to take peace proposals seriously. Woodrow Wilson, as spokesman for the Allies, declared that negotiation of peace under any conditions was impossible so long as Germany was ruled by the kaiser. The Central Powers professed to regard with favor the general import of the papal suggestions, but they refused to commit themselves on indemnities and restorations, especially the restoration of Belgium.

The Fourteen Points

The best-known of all the peace proposals was President Wilson's program of Fourteen Points, which he incorporated in an address to Congress on January 8, 1918. Summarized as briefly as possible, this program included: (1) "open covenants openly arrived at," i.e., the abolition of secret diplomacy; (2) freedom of the seas; (3) removal of economic barriers between nations; (4) reduction of national armaments "to the lowest point consistent with safety"; (5) impartial adjustment of colonial claims, with consideration for the interests of the peoples involved; (6) evacuation of Russia by foreign armies; (7) restoration of the independence of Belgium; (8) restoration of Alsace and Lorraine to France; (9) a readjustment of Italian frontiers "along clearly recognizable lines of nationality"; (10) autonomous development for the peoples of Austria-Hungary; (11) restoration of Rumania, Serbia, and Montenegro, with access to the sea for Serbia; (12) autonomous development for the peoples of Turkey, with the straits from the Black Sea to the Mediterranean "permanently opened"; (13) an independent Poland, "inhabited by indisputably Polish populations," and with access to the sea; (14) establishment of a League of Nations. On several other occasions throughout 1918 Wilson reiterated in public addresses that this program would be the basis of the peace for which he would work. Thousands of copies of the Fourteen Points were scattered by Allied planes over the German trenches and behind the lines, in an effort to convince both soldiers and civilians that the Entente nations were striving for a just and durable peace.

By the close of the summer of 1918 the long nightmare of bloodshed was approaching its end. A great offensive launched by the British, French, and United States forces in July dealt one shattering blow after another to the German battalions and forced them back almost to the Belgian frontier. By the end of September the cause of the Central Powers was hopeless. Bulgaria withdrew from the war on September 30. Early in October the new chancellor of Germany, the liberal Prince Max of Baden, appealed to President Wilson for a negotiated peace on the basis of the Fourteen Points. But the fighting went on, for Wilson had returned to his original demand that Germany must agree to depose the kaiser. Germany's remaining allies tottered on the verge of collapse. Turkey surrendered at the end of October. The Hapsburg Empire was cracked open by rebellions on the part of the empire's subject nationalities. Moreover, an Austrian offensive against Italy had not only failed but had incited the Italians to a counteroffensive, with the consequent loss to Austria of the city of Trieste and 300,000 prisoners. On November 3 the Emperor Charles, who had succeeded Francis Joseph in 1916, signed an armistice which took Austria out of the war.

Germany was now left with the impossible task of carrying on the struggle alone. The morale of its troops was rapidly breaking. The

The collapse of the Central Powers

German Supplies Moving toward the Somme During the Last German Offensive in 1918

blockade was causing such a shortage of food that there was real danger of starvation. The revolutionary tremors that had been felt for some time swelled into a mighty earthquake. On November 8 a republic was proclaimed in Bavaria. The next day nearly all of Germany was in the throes of revolution. A decree was published in Berlin announcing the kaiser's abdication, and early the next morning he was moved across the frontier into Holland. In the meantime. the government of the nation had passed into the hands of a provisional council headed by Friedrich Ebert, leader of the socialists in the Reichstag. Ebert and his colleagues immediately took steps to conclude negotiations for an armistice. The terms as now laid down by the Entente powers provided for acceptance of the Fourteen Points with three amendments. First, the item on freedom of the seas was to be stricken (in accordance with the request of the British). Second, restoration of invaded areas was to be interpreted in such a way as to include reparations, that is, payment to the victors to compensate them for their losses. Third, the demand for autonomy for the subject peoples of Austria-Hungary was to be changed to a demand for independence. In addition, troops of the Entente nations were to occupy cities in the Rhine valley; the blockade was to be continued in force; and Germany was to hand over 5,000 locomotives, 150,000 railway cars, and 5,000 trucks, all in good condition. There was nothing that the Germans could do but accept these terms. At five o'clock in the morning of November 11, two delegates of the defeated nation met with the commander of the Entente armies, Marshal Foch, in the dark Compiègne forest and signed the papers officially ending the war. Six hours later the order, "cease fire," was given to the troops. That night thousands of people danced through the streets of London, Paris, and Rome in the same delirium of excitement with which they had greeted the declarations of war.

The peace concluded at the various conferences in 1919 and 1920 more closely resembled a sentence from a court than a negotiated settlement. Propaganda had encouraged victorious soldiers and civilians to suppose that their sacrifices to the war effort would be compensated for by payments extracted from the "wicked" Germans. The British prime minister, David Lloyd George, campaigned during the election of 1918 on the slogan, "Hang the Kaiser!", while one of his partisans demanded "Squeeze the German lemon until the pips squeak!". In all the Allied countries nationalism and democracy combined to make compromise impossible and to reassert the claim that the war was a crusade of good against evil. The peace settlement drafted by the victors inevitably reflected these feelings.

The conference convoked in Paris[3] to draft a peace with Germany

---

[3] The conference did most of its work in Paris. The treaty of peace with Germany, however, takes its name from Versailles, the suburb of Paris in which it was signed.

The Council of Four. Meeting to draft a peace treaty in Paris were Orlando of Italy, Lloyd George of Britain, Clemenceau of France, and Wilson of the United States.

was technically in session from January until June of 1919, but only six plenary meetings were ever held. All of the important business of the conference was transacted by small committees. At first there was the Council of Ten, made up of the president and secretary of state of the United States, and the premiers and foreign ministers of Great Britain, France, Italy, and Japan. By the middle of March this body had been found too unwieldy and was reduced to the Council of Four, consisting of the American president and the English, Italian, and French premiers. A month later the Council of Four became the Council of Three when Premier Vittorio Orlando withdrew from the conference in a huff because Wilson refused to give Italy all it demanded.

The Paris Conference

The final character of the Treaty of Versailles was determined almost entirely by the so-called Big Three—Wilson, Lloyd George, and Clemenceau. These men were about as different in personality as any three rulers who could ever have been brought together for a common purpose. Wilson was an inflexible idealist, accustomed to dictating to subordinates and convinced that the hosts of righteousness were on his side. When confronted with unpleasant realities, such as the secret treaties among the Entente governments for division of the spoils, he had a habit of dismissing them as unimportant and eventually forgetting that he had ever heard of them. Though he knew little of the devious maneuvers of European diplomacy, his unbending temperament made it difficult for him to take advice or to adjust his views to those of his colleagues. Lloyd George, the canny Welshman who had succeeded Asquith as prime minister of Britain in 1916, possessed a cleverness and Celtic humor that enabled him to succeed, on occasions, where Wilson failed; but he was above all a politician—shifty and not particularly sympathetic to particular European problems such as nationalism.

The Big Three: Wilson and Lloyd George

The third member of the great triumvirate was the aged and cynical

French premier, Georges Clemenceau. Born in 1841, Clemenceau had been a journalist in the United States just after the Civil War. Later he had won his nickname of "the Tiger" as a relentless foe of clericals and monarchists. He had fought for the republic during the stormy days of the Boulangist episode, the Dreyfus affair, and the struggle for separation of Church and State. Twice in his lifetime he had seen France invaded and its existence gravely imperiled. Now the tables were turned, and the French, he believed, should take full advantage of their opportunity. Only by keeping a strict control over a prostrate Germany could the security of France be preserved.

From the beginning a number of embarrassing problems confronted the chief architects of the Versailles treaty. The most important was what to do about the Fourteen Points. There could be no doubt that they had been the basis of the German surrender on November 11. It was beyond question also that Wilson had represented them as the Entente program for a permanent peace. Consequently there was every reason for the peoples of the world to expect that the Fourteen Points would be the model for the Versailles settlement—subject only to the three amendments made before the armistice was signed. In actuality, however, no one among the highest dignitaries at the conference, with the exception of Wilson himself, gave more than lip service to the Fourteen Points. In the end, the American president was able to salvage, in unmodified form, only four of the parts of his famous program; point seven, requiring the restoration of Belgium; point eight, demanding the return of Alsace and Lorraine to France; point ten, providing for independence for the peoples of Austria-Hungary; and the final provision calling for a League of Nations. The others were ignored or modified to such an extent as to change their original meanings.

By the end of April 1919 the terms of the Versailles treaty were ready for submission to the enemy, and Germany was ordered to send delegates to receive them. On April 29, a delegation headed by Count von Brockdorff-Rantzau, foreign minister of the provisional republic, arrived in Versailles. A week later the members of the delegation were commanded to appear before the Allied representatives to receive the sentence of their nation. When Brockdorff-Rantzau protested that the terms were too harsh, he was informed by Clemenceau that Germany would have exactly three weeks to decide whether or not to sign. Eventually the time had to be extended, for the heads of the German government resigned their positions rather than accept the treaty. Their attitude was summed up by Chancellor Philip Scheidemann in the pointed statement: "What hand would not wither that sought to lay itself and us in those chains?" The Big Three now made a few minor adjustments, mainly at the insistence of Lloyd George, and Germany was notified that seven o'clock on the evening of June 23 would bring either acceptance or invasion. Shortly after five a new government of the provisional republic announced that it would yield to "overwhelming force" and accede to the victors' terms. On June 28, the fifth anniversary of the murder of the Austrian archduke, representatives of the German and Allied governments assembled in the Hall of Mirrors at Versailles and affixed their signatures to the treaty.

The provisions of the Treaty of Versailles can be outlined briefly. Germany was required to surrender Alsace and Lorraine to France, northern Schleswig to Denmark, and most of Posen and West Prussia to Poland. The coal mines of the Saar Basin were to be ceded to France, to be exploited by the French for fifteen years. At the end of this time the German government would be permitted to buy them back. The Saar territory itself was to be administered by the League of Nations until 1935, when a plebiscite would be held to determine whether it should remain under the league, be returned to Germany, or be awarded to France. Germany's province of East Prussia was cut off from the rest of its territory, and the port of Danzig, almost wholly German, was subjected to the political control of the League of Nations and the the economic domination of Poland. Germany was disarmed, surrendering all its submarines and navy of surface vessels, with the exception of six small battleships, six light cruisers, six destroyers, and twelve torpedo boats. The Germans were forbidden to have any airplanes, either military or naval, and their army was limited to 100,000 officers and men, to be recruited by voluntary enlistment. To make sure that Germany would not launch any new attack upon France or Belgium, it was forbidden to keep soldiers or maintain fortifications in the Rhine valley. Lastly, Germany and its allies were held responsible for all the loss and damage suffered by the Entente governments and their citizens, "as a consequence of the war imposed upon them by the aggression of Germany and her allies." This was the so-called war-guilt provision of the treaty (Article 231), but it was also the basis for German reparations. The exact amount that Germany should pay was left to a Reparations Commission. In 1921 the total was set at 33 billion dollars.

The main provisions of the Treaty of Versailles

For the most part, the Treaty of Versailles applied only to Germany. Separate pacts were drawn up to settle accounts with Germany's allies—Austria-Hungary, Bulgaria, and Turkey. The final form of these treaties was determined primarily by a Council of Five, composed of Clemenceau as chairman and one delegate from the United States, Great Britain, France, and Italy. The treaties reflected a desire on the part of their drafters to recognize the principle of national self-determination. The experience of the prewar years convinced diplomats that they must draw national boundaries to conform as closely as possible to the ethnic, linguistic, and historical traditions of the people they were to contain. Yet practical, political difficulties made such divisions impossible.

The goal of self-determination

The settlement with Austria, completed in September 1919, is

ICELAND
(Denmark)

FAEROES
(Denmark)

SHETLANDS

ORKNEYS

HEBRIDES

SCOTLAND

*NORTH
SEA*

NORWAY   SWEDEN

GULF OF BOTHNIA

FINLAND

Helsingfors

Leningrad

Christiania ★   Stockholm ★   *G. of Finland*

★ Tallinn

ESTONIA

★ Riga

LATVIA

GOTLAND

ÖLAND

Skagerrak   *Kattegat*

BALTIC   *SEA*

LITHUANIA

★ Kaunas

GREAT   BRITAIN

IRELAND   Dublin

ENGLAND

London ★

ATLANTIC

OCEAN

English Channel

DENMARK

Copenhagen ★

Danzig

E. PRUSSIA
(Germany)

NETHERLANDS

Amsterdam ★

Brussels ★   *Rhine*

BELG.

LUXEMBURG

R.

Berlin ★

GERMANY

Warsaw ★

Brest-Litovsk

POLAND

Paris ★

Prague ★

CZECHOSLOVAKIA

Danube   R.

Vienna ★

AUSTRIA

LORRAINE

ALSACE

Berne ★
SWITZ.

BAY OF
BISCAY

FRANCE

★ Budapest

HUNGARY

RUMANIA

ITALY

ADRIATIC

SEA

Belgrade ★

YUGOSLAVIA

SERBIA

Bucharest ★

Sofia ★   BUL-

MONTENEGRO

Tirana ★

ALBANIA

PORTUGAL ★

Lisbon ★

Madrid ★

SPAIN

BALEARIC IS.
(Spain)

CORSICA
(France)

Rome ★

SARDINIA
(Italy)

GREECE

Aegean

Athens ★

*Strait of
Gibraltar*

Tangier

SP. MOROCCO

Algiers

Tunis

MEDITERRANEAN

SICILY
(Italy)

MALTA
(Gt. Britain)

CRETE
(Greece)

Rabat

MOROCCO

ALGERIA

TUNISIA

Tripoli

0   1000 miles

LIBYA

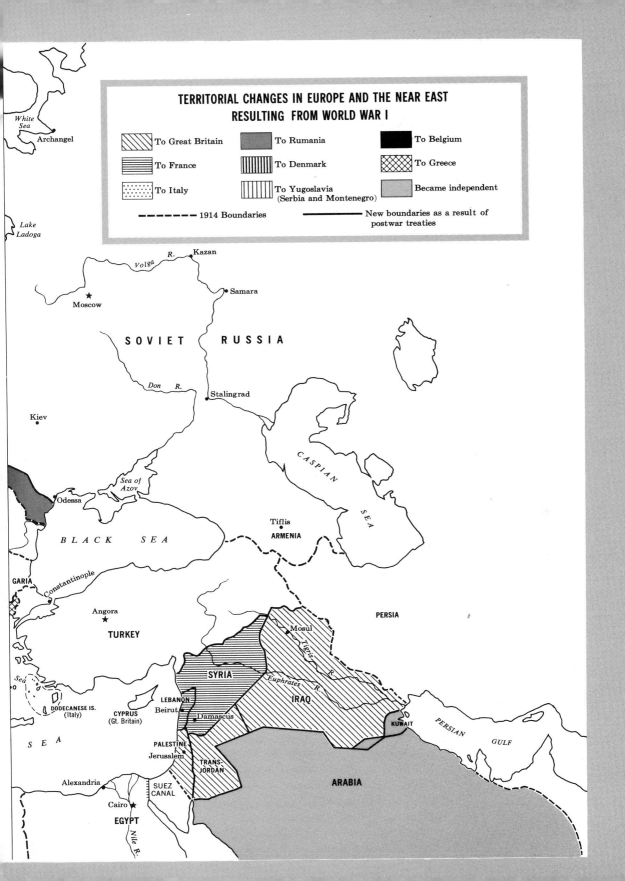

TERRITORIAL CHANGES IN EUROPE AND THE NEAR EAST
RESULTING FROM WORLD WAR I

*The treaty with Austria:
The compromising of
national self-determination*

*The treaties with
Bulgaria and Hungary*

*The Treaties of Sèvres
and Lausanne with
Turkey*

known as the Treaty of St. Germain. Austria was required to recognize the independence of Hungary, Czechoslovakia, Yugoslavia, and Poland and to cede to them large portions of its territory. In addition, Austria had to surrender Trieste, the south Tyrol, and the Istrian peninsula to Italy. Altogether the Austrian portion of the Dual Monarchy was deprived of three-fourths of its area and three-fourths of its people. Contrary to the principles of self-determination, in several of the territories surrendered the inhabitants were largely German-speaking—for example, in the Tyrol, and the region of the Sudeten mountains awarded to Czechoslovakia. The Austrian nation itself was reduced to a small, land-locked state, with nearly one-third of its population concentrated in the city of Vienna.

The second of the treaties with lesser belligerents was that with Bulgaria, which was signed in November 1919 and called the Treaty of Neuilly. Bulgaria was forced to give up nearly all of the territory it had gained since the First Balkan War. Land was ceded to Rumania, to the new kingdom of Yugoslavia, and to Greece. Here again, self-determination was compromised. All of these regions were inhabited by large Bulgarian minorities. Since Hungary was now an independent state, it was necessary that a separate treaty be imposed upon it. This was the Treaty of the Trianon Palace, signed in June 1920. It required that Slovakia should be ceded to Czechoslovakia, Transylvania to Rumania, and Croatia-Slovenia to Yugoslavia. In few cases was the principle of self-determination of peoples more flagrantly violated. Numerous sections of Transylvania had populations that were more than half Hungarian. Included in the region of Slovakia were not only Slovaks but almost a million Magyars and about 500,000 Ruthenians. As a consequence, a fanatical irredentist movement flourished in Hungary after the war, directed toward the recovery of these lost provinces. The Treaty of the Trianon Palace slashed the area of Hungary from 125,000 square miles to 35,000, and its population from 22 million to 8 million.

The settlement with Turkey was a product of unusual circumstances. The secret treaties had contemplated the transfer of Constantinople and Armenia to Russia and the division of most of the remainder of Turkey between Britain and France. But Russia's withdrawal from the war after the Bolshevik Revolution, together with insistence by Italy and Greece upon fulfillment of promises made to them, necessitated considerable revision of the original scheme. Finally, in August 1920, a treaty was signed at Sèvres, near Paris, and submitted to the government of the sultan. It provided that Armenia be organized as a Christian republic; that most of Turkey in Europe be given to Greece; that Palestine and Mesopotamia become British "mandates," i.e., to remain under League of Nations control but to be administered by Britain; that Syria become a mandate of France; and that southern Anatolia be set apart as a sphere of influence for Italy. About all that would be left of the Ottoman Empire would be the city of Constantinople and the northern and central portions of Asia Minor. The decrepit government of the sultan, overawed by Allied military forces, agreed to accept this treaty. But a revolutionary government of Turkish nationalists, which had been organized at Ankara under the leadership of Mustapha Kemal (later called Atatürk), determined to prevent the settlement of Sèvres from being put into effect. The forces of Kemal obliterated the republic of Armenia, frightened the Italians into withdrawing from Anatolia, and conquered most of the territory in Europe which had been given to Greece. At last, in November 1922, they occupied Constantinople, deposed the sultan, and proclaimed Turkey a republic. The Allies now consented to a revision of the peace. A new treaty was concluded at Lausanne in Switzerland in 1923, which permitted the Turks to retain practically all of the territory they had conquered. Though much reduced in size compared with the old Ottoman Empire, the Turkish republic still had an area of about 300,000 square miles and a population of 13 million.

Incorporated in each of the five treaties which liquidated the war with the Central Powers was the Covenant of the League of Nations. The establishment of a league in which the states of the world, both great and small, would cooperate for the preservation of peace had long been the cherished dream of President Wilson. Indeed, that had been one of his chief reasons for taking the United States into the war. He believed that the defeat of Germany would mean the deathblow of militarism, and that the road would thenceforth be clear for setting up the control of international relations by a community of power instead of by the cumbersome and ineffective balance of power. But in order to get the league accepted at all, he felt himself compelled to make numerous compromises. He permitted his original idea of providing for a reduction of armaments "to the lowest point consistent with domestic safety" to be changed into the altogether different phrasing of "consistent with national safety." To induce the Japanese to accept the league he allowed them to keep the former German concessions in China. To please the French, he sanctioned the exclusion of both Germany and Russia from his proposed federation, despite his long insistence that it should be a combination of all the nations. These handicaps were serious enough. But the league received an even more deadly blow when it was repudiated by the very nation whose president had proposed it.

Established under such unfavorable auspices, the league never succeeded in achieving the aims of its founder. In only a few cases did it succeed in allaying the specter of war, and in each of these the parties to the dispute were small nations. But in every dispute involving one or more major powers, the league failed. It did nothing about the seizure of Vilna by Poland in 1920, because Lithuania, the victimized nation, was friendless, while Poland had the powerful backing of France. When, in 1923, war threatened between Italy and Greece, the

Kemal Atatürk

The League of Nations

Successes and failures of the league

League of Nations Buildings, Geneva, Switzerland

Italians refused to submit to the intervention of the league, and the dispute had to be settled by direct mediation of Great Britain and France. Thereafter, in every great crisis the league was either defied or ignored. Its authority was flouted by Japan in seizing Manchuria in 1931 and by Italy in conquering Ethiopia in 1936. By September 1938, when the Czechoslovakian crisis arose, the prestige of the league had sunk so low that scarcely anyone thought of appealing to it. On the other hand, the point must be made that Wilson's great project justified its existence in other, less spectacular, ways. It reduced the international opium traffic and aided poor and backward countries in controlling the spread of disease. Its agencies collected invaluable statistics on labor and business conditions throughout the world. It conducted plebiscites in disputed areas, supervised the administration of internationalized cities, helped in finding homes for racial and political refugees, and made a notable beginning in codifying international law. Such achievements may well be regarded as providing a substantial groundwork for a later effort at international organization, the United Nations, formed after World War II.

A war of waste

The league, with all its failings, was seen as the one promising result of the war that many soon recognized as a hideously wasteful carnage. The price would have been enormous even if all the results which were supposed to flow from an Entente victory had really been achieved. But few indeed were the permanent gains. In fact, the war which was to "end all wars" sowed the seeds of a new and more terrible conflict in the future. The autocracy of the kaiser was indeed destroyed, but the ground was prepared for new despotisms. World War I did nothing to abate either militarism or nationalism. Twenty years after the fighting had ended, there were nearly twice as many men under arms as in 1913; and national and ethnic rivalries and hatreds were as deeply ingrained as ever.

If the war failed to make the world less of an armed camp, it nevertheless altered it drastically in other ways. In the first place, it strengthened a belief in the efficacy of central planning and coordination. To sustain the war effort, the governments of all the major belligerents were forced to manage their economies by regulating industrial output, exercising a close control over imports and exports, and making the most effective use of manpower—both civilian and military. Second, the war upset the world trade balance. With few manufactured goods coming from Europe, Japanese, Indian, and South American capitalists were free to develop industries in their own countries. When the war was over, Europe found it had lost many of its previously guaranteed markets. Third, while war was altering the patterns of world trade, it was also producing worldwide inflation. To finance their fighting, governments resorted to policies of deficit financing (spending above their income) and increased paper money which, with the shortage of goods, inflated their price. Inflation hit hardest at the middle class, those men and women who had lived on their income from invested money, and now saw that money worth far less than it once had been. Fourth, the war, while it brought hardships to most, brought freedom to many. Women were emancipated by their governments' need for them in factories and on farms. The contribution of women to the war effort undoubtedly explains the granting of female suffrage in both Great Britain and the United States in 1918 and 1920. Finally, despite this legacy of liberation, the war's most permanent contribution to the spirit of the postwar years was

Changes brought by the war

Women at Work in a German Gun Factory. Because of the manpower shortage at home women played a greater role in industry.

disillusion—particularly within the middle classes. A generation of men had been sacrificed—"lost"—to no apparent end. Many of those left alive were sickened by the useless slaughter, to which they knew they had contributed and for which they believed they must share at least part of the guilt. They were disgusted by the greedy abandonment of principles by the politicians at Versailles. Hatred and mistrust of the "old men" who had dragged the world into an unnecessary conflict, who had then mismanaged its direction with such ghastly results, and who had betrayed the cause of international peace for national gain soured the minds of many younger men and women in the postwar period. The British poet Edmund Blunden expressed this profound disillusionment when he took as the title for a poem, written to celebrate New Year's Day 1921, the Biblical verse: "The dog is turned to his own vomit again, and the sow that was washed to her wallowing in the mire."

SELECTED READINGS

• *Items so designated are available in paperback editions.*

THE WORLD WAR AND THE PEACE SETTLEMENT

• Falls, Cyril, *The Great War,* New York, 1959. A military history.
• Fay, Sidney B., *The Origins of the World War,* 2 vols., New York, 1928–30. Comprehensive.
  Feldman, Gerald D., *Army, Industry, and Labor in Germany, 1914–1918,* Princeton, N.J., 1966.
• Fischer, Fritz, *Germany's Aims in the First World War,* New York, 1967. One of the most significant historical works of the twentieth century. Thoroughly documents Germany's goal of world domination in World War I and reopens the question of war guilt.
• ———, *World Power or Decline,* New York, 1974.
• Fussell, Paul, *The Great War and Modern Memory,* New York, 1975. A brilliant examination of British intellectuals' attitudes toward the war.
  Gatzke, Hans, *Germany's Drive to the West,* Baltimore, 1950.
  Guinn, Paul, *British Strategy and Politics, 1914–1918,* Oxford, 1965.
  Hardach, Gerd, *The First World War, 1914–1918,* Berkeley, Calif., 1977. An excellent economic history of the war.
  Horne, Alastair, *The Price of Glory: Verdun, 1916,* New York, 1963.
• Lafore, Laurence D., *The Long Fuse: An Interpretation of the Origins of World War I,* Philadelphia, 1971. Argues that the war was the result of obsolete institutions and ideas.
  Lacqueur, Walter, and G. L. Mosse, eds., *1914: The Coming of the First World War,* New York, 1969. An excellent series of essays by modern scholars.
  Liddell Hart, B. H., *The War in Outline,* London, 1936. A good introduction to the military history of World War I.
  Mayer, Arno, *Political Origins of the New Diplomacy, 1917–1918,* New York,

1969. An important work which examines the advent of Wilson and Lenin into world diplomacy.

————, *Politics and Diplomacy of Peacemaking: Containment and Counter-revolution at Versailles, 1918–1919,* New York, 1967.

Moorehead, Alan, *Gallipoli,* London, 1956. A study of the British campaign.

Nicolson, Harold, *Peacemaking, 1919,* Boston, 1933. Written by a participant, provides a good account of the atmosphere of Versailles.

• Steiner, Zara S., *Britain and the Origins of the First World War,* New York, 1977. Argues that external rather than internal strains brought Britain into the war.

• Taylor, A. J. P., *English History, 1914–1945,* New York, 1965. An excellent treatment of the war and its impact on British society.

• Turner, L. C. F., *Origins of the First World War,* New York, 1970.

• Tuchman, Barbara, *The Guns of August,* New York, 1962. A popular account of the outbreak of war.

• Wheeler-Bennett, J. W., *The Forgotten Peace: Brest-Litovsk, March 1918,* London, 1939. An excellent study of personalities involved in the Russo-German peace treaty.

Zeeman, Z. A. B., *The Break-up of the Hapsburg Empire, 1914–1918,* New York, 1961.

THE RUSSIAN REVOLUTION

Carr, E. H., *A History of Soviet Russia,* Vols. I–III, London, 1950 ff. A comprehensive treatment of the Russian Revolution from 1917–1923.

• Deutscher, Isaac, *The Prophet Armed,* New York, 1954. The first volume of a magnificent biography of Trotsky; covers the years 1879–1921.

Fischer, Louis, *The Life of Lenin,* New York, 1964. A lengthy, somewhat popularized biography by a journalist who was present during the revolution.

Keep, John L. H., *The Russian Revolution,* New York, 1977.

• Pares, Bernard, *A History of Russia,* rev. ed., New York, 1953.

• Rabinowitch, Alexander, *The Bolsheviks Come to Power,* New York, 1976.

• Tucker, Robert C., *Stalin as Revolutionary,* New York, 1973. Stalin's life to 1929; a psychobiography.

• Ulam, Adam, *The Bolsheviks: The Intellectual and Political History of the Triumph of Communism in Russia,* New York, 1965.

• Von Laue, T. H., *Why Lenin? Why Stalin? A Reappraisal of the Russian Revolution, 1900–1930,* Philadelphia, 1964.

• Wolfe, Bertram D., *Three Who Made a Revolution,* rev. ed., New York, 1964. A study of Lenin, Trotsky, and Stalin.

SOURCE MATERIALS

Carnegie Foundation, Endowment for International Peace, *The Treaties of Peace, 1919–1923,* 2 vols., New York, 1924.

Gooch, G. P., and H. Temperley, eds., *British Documents on the Origins of the War, 1898–1914,* London.

Keynes, John Maynard, *The Economic Consequences of the Peace,* London, 1919. A contemporary attack upon the peace settlement, particularly the reparations agreements, by the brilliant economist who served on the British delegation to the peace conference.

Trotsky, Leon, *History of the Russian Revolution,* 3 vols., Ann Arbor, Mich., 1957.

Chapter 34

THE WEST BETWEEN THE WARS

Democracy of the West today is the forerunner of Marxism, which would
be inconceivable without it. It is democracy alone which furnishes this
universal plague with the soil in which it spreads. In parliamentarianism,
its outward form of expression, democracy created a monstrosity of filth
and fire . . .

—Adolf Hitler, *Mein Kampf*

The First World War had been waged in hopes of making the
world "safe for democracy." And for a short time after 1918,
despite the shortcomings of the Versailles settlement, it
seemed as if that elusive goal might stand a chance of success. Germany began the postwar era as a republic. Most of the new states
created by the Treaty of Versailles attempted to function under representative governments. Yet by 1939 only three of the chief powers—
Great Britain, France, and the United States—remained on the list of
democratic countries. Among the lesser states democracy survived in
Switzerland, the Netherlands, Belgium, the Scandinavian countries, a
few republics of Latin America, and the self-governing dominions of
the British Commonwealth. Nearly all of the rest of the world had
succumbed to despotism of one form or another. Italy, Germany, and
Spain were fascist; Hungary was dominated by a landowning oligarchy; Poland, Turkey, China, and Japan were essentially under military
rule. Russia, although professing to be a communist utopia, was in
fact a dictatorship.

Decline of democracy

The reasons for the decline of democracy in the West varied according to particular national circumstances. Generally, however, democracy's failure can be attributed to several major causes. First, class
conflict increased in many countries during the interwar years. The
real issue in most parts of continental Europe was whether control of
the government and economic system would continue in the possession of aristocracies, industrialists, and financiers, or some combina-

Reasons for its decline

tion of these elements. None of them were willing to surrender more than a fraction of their considerable power to the less privileged majorities which, at great sacrifice, had made major contributions to the war effort. The common people expected and had been promised that those contributions would be rewarded by greater attention to their political rights and economic needs. When they were ignored, they were naturally embittered, and hence prey to the blandishments of political extremists. Second, economic conditions worked against the establishment of stable democracies. The creation of new nations encouraged debilitating economic rivalries. War had disoriented the world's economy, leaving in its wake first inflation and then depression. Finally, nationalist sentiment encouraged discontent among minorities in the newly established states of central Europe. Countries weakened by conflicts between national minorities were an unlikely proving ground for democracy, a political system which functions best in an atmosphere of unified national purpose. Instead they turned, along with others, to totalitarianism, a system which holds out the promise of efficiency and strength of purpose, achieved by centralized authority in return for the surrender of individual liberties.

1. TOTALITARIANISM IN COMMUNIST RUSSIA

Lenin

Soon after the November 1917 revolution Russia began to succumb to totalitarian rule. The country's desperate plight—the result of wartime devastation and governmental corruption and mismanagement—compelled the Bolshevik leaders to centralize power in the hands of a few. During this transformation, Lenin assumed ultimate control of the government. He had all of the qualities necessary for success as a revolutionary figure. He was an able politician and an exceedingly effective orator. Absolutely convinced of the righteousness of his cause, he could strike down his opponents with the zeal and savagery of a Robespierre. On the other hand, he cared nothing for the luxuries of wealth or personal glory. He lived in two rooms in the Kremlin and dressed little better than an ordinary workman.

Trotsky

The most prominent of Lenin's lieutenants was the brilliant but erratic Leon Trotsky (1879–1940). Originally named Lev Bronstein, Trotsky was born of middle-class Jewish parents in the Ukraine. He was a stormy petrel of revolutionary politics during most of his life. Before the revolution he refused to identify himself with any particular faction, preferring to remain an independent Marxist. For his part in the revolutionary movement of 1905 he was exiled to Siberia; but he escaped, and for some years led a roving existence in various European capitals. He was expelled from Paris in 1916 for pacifist activity and took refuge in the United States. Upon learning of the overthrow of the tsar, he attempted to return to Russia. Captured by British

Lenin Speaking to Crowds in Moscow. To the right of the platform, in uniform, is Trotsky.

agents at Halifax, Nova Scotia, he was eventually released through the intervention of Kerensky. He arrived in Russia in April 1917 and immediately began plotting for the overthrow of the provisional government and later of Kerensky himself. He became minister of foreign affairs in the government headed by Lenin, and later, commissar for war.

No sooner had the Bolsheviks come to power than they proceeded to effect drastic alterations in the political and economic system. On November 8, 1917, Lenin decreed nationalization of the land and gave the peasants the exclusive right to use it. On November 29 control of the factories was transferred to the workers, and a month later it was announced that all except the smallest industrial establishments would be taken over by the government. Banks also were nationalized soon after the Bolshevik victory. Scarcely had the Bolsheviks concluded the war with the Central Powers, than they were confronted with a desperate civil war at home. Landlords and capitalists did not take kindly to the loss of their property. The result was a prolonged and bloody combat between the Reds, or Bolsheviks, and the Whites, including not only reactionary tsarists but also disaffected liberals, Social Revolutionaries, Mensheviks, and some peasants. The Whites were assisted for a time by expeditionary forces of British, French, and Japanese troops—hoping to defeat the Bolsheviks in order to bring Russia back into the war against Germany—and later by the armies of the newly created republic of Poland. Under the direction of Trotsky, who appealed to the Russian people both in the name of revolution and the fatherland, the Red army was mobilized to a degree that allowed it to withstand both the foreign invaders and the Russian insurgents. By 1922, the Bolsheviks had managed to stabilize their boundaries, although to do so they were forced to cede former Russian territory to the Finns, to the Baltic states of Latvia and Estonia, to Poland, and to Rumania. Internally, the Bolsheviks responded to the White counter-

The civil war

See color map following page 1088

The Red Army, 1919. This scene near the southern front was the celebration of the victory over the counter-revolutionary forces.

revolution by instituting a "Terror" far more extensive than the repression that had earned that name during the French Revolution. A secret police force shot thousands as suspects or merely as hostages. The tsar and tsarina and their children were executed by local Bolsheviks in July 1918 as White forces advanced on the town of Ekaterinburg, where the family was held prisoner. That same year, a Social Revolutionary attempted to assassinate Lenin; what followed in Petrograd can only be described as a massacre. The Terror abated when the regime had satisfied itself that it had destroyed its internal opposition.

Economic and constitutional changes

The civil war was accompanied by an appalling economic breakdown. In 1920 the total industrial production was only 13 percent of what it had been in 1913. To make up for the shortage of goods, the government abolished the payment of wages and distributed supplies among the workers in the cities in proportion to their need. All private trade was prohibited, and everything produced by the peasants above what they required to keep from starving was requisitioned by the state. This system was an expedient to crush the bourgeoisie and to obtain as much food as possible for the army in the field. It was soon abandoned after the war had ended. In 1921 it was superseded by the New Economic Policy (NEP), which Lenin described as "one step backward in order to take two steps forward." The NEP authorized private manufacturing and private trade on a small scale, reintroduced the payment of wages, and permitted peasants to sell their grain in the open market. In 1924 a constitution was adopted, replacing imperial Russia with the Union of Soviet Socialist Republics. The union represented an attempt to unite the various nationalities and territories that had constituted the old empire. Each separate republic was, in theory, granted certain autonomous rights. In fact, government remained centralized in the hands of a few leaders. Further, central authority was maintained by means of the one legal political party—the Communist party—whose Central Committee was the directing force behind both politics and government, and whose organizational apparatus reached out into all areas of the vast country.

The philosophy of Bolshevism, now more popularly known as communism, was developed primarily by Lenin during these years. It was proclaimed, not as a new body of thought, but as a strict interpretation of Marx's writings. Nevertheless, from the beginning there were various departures from Marx's teachings. These changes were the necessary result of the fact that Marx had expected revolution to occur first in highly industrialized countries, whereas it had in fact broken out and succeeded in one of the least industralized nations in Europe. Marx had assumed that a capitalist stage must prepare the way for socialism; Lenin denied that this was necessary and insisted that Russia could leap directly from a manorial to a socialist economy. In the second place, Lenin emphasized the revolutionary character of socialism much more than did its original founder. Marx did believe that in most cases revolution would be necessary, but he was inclined to deplore the fact rather than to welcome it. Further, he had stated that "there are certain countries such as England and the United States in which the workers may hope to secure their ends by peaceful means." Last of all, Bolshevism differed from Marxism in its conception of proletarian rule. There is nothing to indicate that Marx ever envisaged a totalitarian state. True, he did speak of the "dictatorship of the proletariat," but he meant by this a dictatorship of the whole working class over the remnants of the bourgeoisie. Within the ranks of this class, democratic forms would prevail. Lenin, however, set up the ideal of the dictatorship of an elite, a select minority, wielding supremacy not only over the bourgeoisie but over the bulk of the proletarians themselves. In Russia this elite has remained the Communist party, whose membership has varied from 1,500,000 to 15,700,000.

The tenets of communism

The death of Lenin in January 1924 precipitated a titanic struggle between two of his lieutenants to inherit his mantle of power. Outside of Russia it was generally assumed that Trotsky would be the man to succeed the fallen leader. But the fiery commander of the Red army had a formidable rival in the tough and mysterious Joseph Stalin (1879–1953). The son of a peasant shoemaker in the province of Georgia, Stalin received part of his education in a theological seminary. Expelled at the age of seventeen for "lack of religious vocation," he thereafter dedicated his career to revolutionary activity. In 1917 he became secretary-general of the Communist party, a position through which he was able to build up a political machine. The battle between Stalin and Trotsky was not simply a struggle for personal power; fundamental issues of political policy were also involved. Trotsky maintained that socialism in Russia could never be entirely successful until capitalism was overthrown in surrounding countries. Therefore, he in-

The struggles between Trotsky and Stalin

Left: *Lenin's Casket Is Carried Through the Streets of Moscow.* It was not known with certainty until 1956 that, prior to his death, Lenin had discredited Stalin. Right: *Lenin and Stalin.* Under Stalin this picture was used to show his close relationship with Lenin. In fact, the photograph has been doctored.

sisted upon a continuous crusade for world revolution. Stalin was willing to abandon the program of world revolution, for the time being, in order to concentrate on building socialism in Russia itself. His strategy for the immediate future was essentially nationalist. The outcome of the duel was a complete triumph for Stalin. In 1927 Trotsky was expelled from the Communist party, and two years later he was driven from the country. In 1940 he was murdered in Mexico City by Stalinist agents. Lenin did not hold either Stalin or Trotsky in lofty esteem. In a "testament" written shortly before his death, he criticized Trotsky for "far-reaching self-confidence" and for being too much preoccupied with administrative detail. But he dealt far less gently with Stalin, condemning him as "too rough" and "capricious" and urging that the comrades "find a way" to remove him from his position at the head of the party.

In his struggle with Trotsky, Stalin had insisted that Russia's first priority was economic well-being. In line with this doctrine, one of Stalin's first major reforms was the introduction of the so-called Five-Year Plan. Based upon the conviction that the Soviet Union had to take drastic steps to industrialize and thereby achieve economic parity among the nations of the world, the plan instituted an elaborate system of national priorities. It decreed how much of each major industrial and agricultural commodity the nation should produce, the amount of wages workers should receive, and the prices that should be charged for all that was sold at home and abroad. The first plan, instituted in 1928, was succeeded by others during the 1930s. In some areas goals were met, in a few they were exceeded, in some they fell

Five-Year Plan

short. One of the major results of the Five-Year Plans was the creation of an extensive state bureaucracy, charged with the task of organization and supervision at all levels.

Included in the first plan was a program for agricultural collectivization. The scheme was designed to bring rural farms together into larger units of several thousand acres, under the communal proprietorship of peasants. Only with this sort of reorganization, Russia's rulers declared, could the new and expensive processes of mechanization be introduced, and the country's agricultural yield thereby increased. Not surprisingly, the argument failed to win the support of the more prosperous farmers—the kulaks—who had been allowed to retain ownership of their land despite the revolution. Their opposition led to another Terror, made all the more deadly by a famine which occurred in southeast Russia in 1932. The kulaks were liquidated, either killed or transported to distant labor camps—i.e., the rural bourgeoisie was eliminated, to be replaced by a rural proletariat. Collectivization was an accomplished fact by 1939. It represented to a vast number of Russians a revolution far more immediate than that of 1917. Twenty million people were moved off the land, which, once it had been reorganized into larger units, and production mechanized, required fewer laborers. They were sent to cities, where most went to work in factories. Agricultural output did not increase during the early years of collectivization. But the scheme was nevertheless of benefit to the government. By controlling production, the central bureaucracy was able to regulate the distribution of agricultural products, allocating them for export, where necessary, to pay for the importation of much-needed industrial machinery.

Collectivization

As part of Stalin's campaign to put the interests of Russia ahead of those of international communism, the Bolshevik regime adopted a new and more conservative foreign policy during the 1930s. Its international goals contradicted the militant socialist internationalism of the 1920s. Lenin had supported revolutionary leftist movements in Europe, sending money and lending moral support to the radical German Marxists Karl Liebknecht and Rosa Luxemburg in 1919, and to the short-lived Soviet regime of the Bolshevik Béla Kun in Hungary in the same year. Shortly thereafter, the Third International—later called the Comintern—was formed. It declared its allegiance to international communism; its policy was to oppose cooperation or collaboration with the capitalist governments of the West and to work for their overthrow.

The Third International

With Stalin's suppression of the internationalism advocated by Lenin and Trotsky, however, came a change in tactics and a revival of militarism, or nationalism, and of an interest in playing the game of power politics. The Russian army was more than doubled in size and was reorganized in accordance with the western European model. Patriotism, which the older strict Marxists despised as a form of capital-

Stalinist conservatism

ist propaganda, was exalted into a Soviet virtue. When Germany once again appeared to threaten Russian security, as it did in the 1930s, the rulers of the Kremlin decided that Russia needed friends. Along with their efforts to build up a great army and to make their own country self-sufficient, they adopted a policy of cooperation with the western European powers. In 1934 they entered the League of Nations, and in 1934 they ratified a military alliance with France.

Constitution of 1936

In 1936, the rulers of Communist Russia drafted a new constitution. It was adopted by popular vote and went into effect January 1, 1938. It continued to provide for a union of eleven (later fifteen) republics, each supposedly autonomous and free to secede if it chose. The constitution established universal suffrage for all citizens eighteen years of age and over. They were to vote not only for the local soviets but for members of a national parliament. The highest organ of state power was declared to be the Supreme Soviet of the USSR, composed of two chambers, both given equal legislative powers. To represent it when it was not meeting, the Supreme Soviet was to elect a committee of thirty-seven members known as the Presidium. This body was also empowered to issue decrees, to declare war, and to annul the acts of administrative officials which did not conform to law. The highest executive and administrative agency was to be the Council of Ministers, likewise elected by the Supreme Soviet. The constitution contained a bill of rights. Citizens were guaranteed the right to employment, the right to leisure, the right to maintenance in case of old age or disability, and even the traditional privileges of freedom of speech, of the press, of assemblage, and of religion. The constitution of 1936 was, and still is, more of a sham than a reality. Its provisions for universal suffrage, for the secret ballot, and for a bill of rights had little meaning. The explanation lies in the fact that the real power in the Soviet Union rests with the Communist party, the only party allowed to exist. The organs of the government are little more than the vocal mechanisms through which the party expresses its will.

The purges

It is noteworthy that the very period in which the constitution was being put into effect witnessed an eruption of mass arrests and executions of persons alleged to be "Trotskyists, spies, and wreckers." Collectivization and industrialization had not been achieved without bitter disagreement among Russia's political leadership. Critics on the Left and Right were disturbed by both the ends and means of Stalin's programs, and by his obvious craving for personal power. Before his critics could strike at him, Stalin struck at them. Between 1936 and 1938 more than a score of prominent Old Bolsheviks were tried, confessed publicly to having plotted against the state, were condemned either as Trotskyites or bourgeois collaborators, and put to death. Their confessions, which surprised the world at the time, were obtained, it was later learned, by means of physical and psychological torture. Some 9 million further victims of these purges were arrested, impri-

Panel (3), Wassily Kandinsky (1866–1944). The Expressionist painters carried their explorations of the psychological properties of color and line to the point where subject matter was deemed unnecessary and even undesirable. (Museum of Modern Art)

Nude Descending a Staircase, Marcel Duchamp (1887–1968). An example of the impact of film on painting. The effect is that of a series of closely spaced photographs coalescing to create motion. (Philadelphia Museum of Art)

The Table, Georges Braque (1881–1963). An example of later cubism showing the predominance of curvilinear form and line instead of geometric structure. (Museum of Modern Art)

I and the Village, Marc Chagall (1889–   ). The subject refers to the artist's childhood and youth in Vitebsk, Russia. The profile on the right is probably that of the artist himself. (Museum of Modern Art)

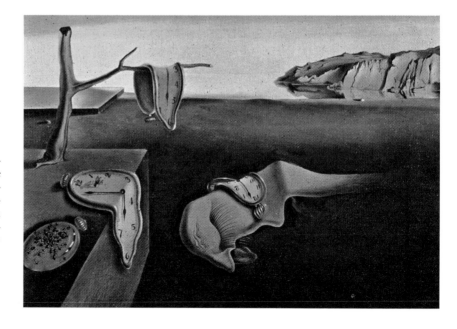

The Persistence of Memory, Salvador Dali (1904–   ). The Spaniard Dali is the outstanding representative of the surrealist school. Many objects in his paintings are Freudian images. (Museum of Modern Art)

Barricade, José Clemente Orozco (1883–1949). The Mexican muralist Orozco was one of the most celebrated of contemporary painters with a social message. His themes were revolutionary fervor, satire of aristocracy and the Church, and deification of the common man. (Museum of Modern Art)

Sea and Gulls, John Marin (1870–1953). A native of New Jersey, Marin was a gifted abstract painter. His objects are sometimes recognizable, sometimes not. He painted not the likeness of nature, but *about* nature. (Museum of Modern Art)

Around the Fish, Paul Klee (1879–1940). Klee is recognized as the most subtle humorist of XX-cent. art. The central motif of a fish on a platter suggests a banquet, but many of the surrounding objects appear to be products of fantasy. (Museum of Modern Art)

Above: *Little Big Painting*, Roy Lichtenstein (born 1923). Oil on canvas. (The Whitney Museum of American Art). In the 1960's and early 1970's, American artists dominated the new movements, particularly "Pop," "Op," and "the New Realism." The works on this and the following page are by some of the best-known contemporary artists.

Left: *Summer Rental No. 2*, Robert Rauschenberg (born 1925). Oil on canvas. (Collection Whitney Museum of American Art). Gift of the Friends of the Whitney Museum of American Art.

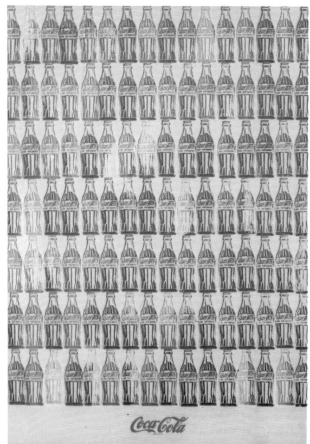

Top Left: *Girl in Doorway*, George Segal (born 1924). A life-size construction in plaster, wood, glass, and aluminum paint. (Collection Whitney Museum of American Art). Top Right: *Green Coca Cola Bottles*, Andy Warhol (born 1931). Oil on canvas. (Collection Whitney Museum of American Art). Gift of the Friends of the Whitney Museum of American Art. Left: *Gran Cairo*, Frank Stella (born 1936). Synthetic polymer paint on canvas. (Collection Whitney Museum of American Art). Gift of the Friends of the Whitney Museum of American Art.

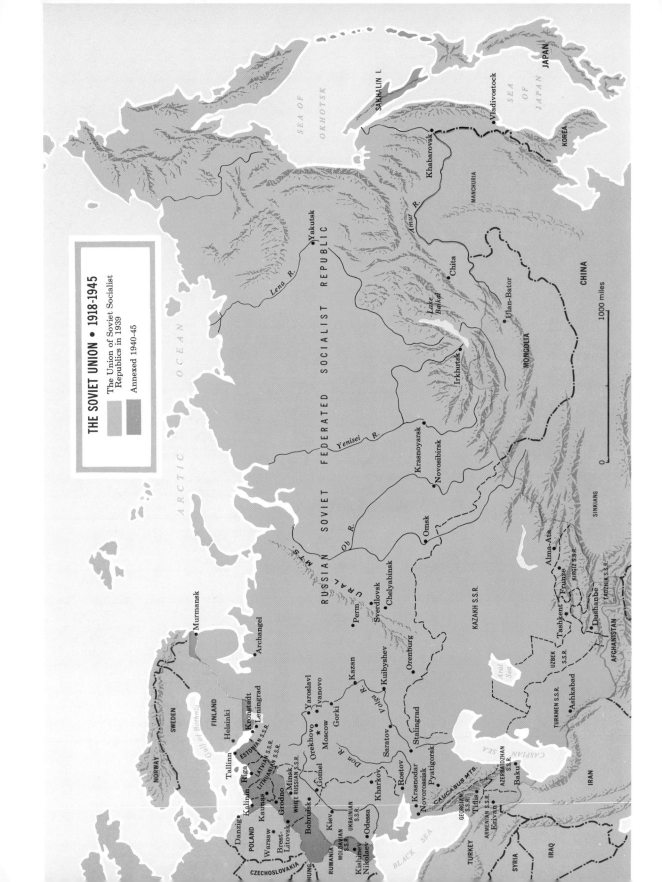

THE SOVIET UNION • 1918-1945

The Union of Soviet Socialist Republics in 1939

Annexed 1940-45

SEA OF OKHOTSK

SAKHALIN I.

JAPAN

Vladivostock

SEA OF JAPAN

KOREA

Khabarovsk

MANCHURIA

Amur R.

Chita

Yakutsk

Lena R.

RUSSIAN SOVIET FEDERATED SOCIALIST REPUBLIC

Lake Baikal

Irkhutsk

Ulan-Bator

MONGOLIA

CHINA

1000 miles

ARCTIC OCEAN

Yenisei R.

Krasnoyarsk

Novosibirsk

Omsk

Ob R.

KAZAKH S.S.R.

SINKIANG

Alma-Ata

Frunze

KIRGIZ S.S.R.

Tashkent

Dushanbe

TADZHIK S.S.R.

UZBEK S.S.R.

AFGHANISTAN

Ashkabad

TURKMEN S.S.R.

URAL MTS.

Perm

Sverdlovsk

Chelyabinsk

Orenburg

Kazan

Kuibyshev

Kama R.

Aral Sea

Murmansk

Archangel

FINLAND

Helsinki

Kronstadt

Leningrad

SWEDEN

Gulf of Bothnia

NORWAY

Tallinn

ESTONIAN S.S.R.

Riga

LATVIAN S.S.R.

Kalinin

LITHUANIAN S.S.R.

Kaunas

Grodno

Minsk

WHITE RUSSIAN S.S.R.

Danzig

POLAND

Warsaw

Brest-Litovsk

Bobruisk

Gomel

Kiev

UKRAINIAN S.S.R.

Kishinev

MOLDAVIAN S.S.R.

Nikolaev

Odessa

RUMANIA

CZECHOSLOVAKIA

HUNG.

Yaroslavl

Ivanovo

Orekhovo

Moscow

Gorki

Volga R.

Saratov

Don R.

Stalingrad

Kharkov

Rostov

Krasnodar

Novorossisk

Pyatigorsk

CAUCASUS MTS.

BLACK SEA

CASPIAN SEA

Baku

AZERBAIDZHAN S.S.R.

GEORGIAN S.S.R.

Tiflis

ARMENIAN S.S.R.

Erivan

TURKEY

IRAN

IRAQ

SYRIA

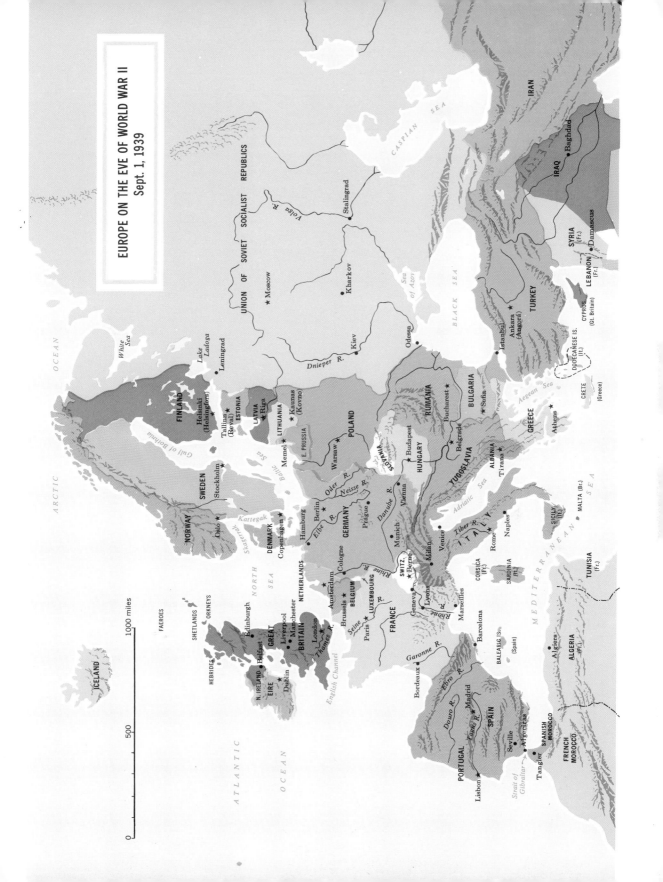

EUROPE ON THE EVE OF WORLD WAR II
Sept. 1, 1939

ARCTIC OCEAN

ICELAND

FAEROES

SHETLANDS

ORKNEYS

HEBRIDES

N. IRELAND
EIRE
Belfast
Dublin

GREAT
BRITAIN
Edinburgh
Liverpool
Manchester
London
Thames R.

ATLANTIC OCEAN

English Channel

NORTH SEA

NETHERLANDS
Amsterdam
BELGIUM
Brussels
LUXEMBOURG

FRANCE
Paris
Seine R.
Bordeaux
Garonne R.
Lyons
Marseilles
Rhône R.

Cologne
Rhine R.
SWITZ.
Berne
Geneva

PORTUGAL
Lisbon
Douro R.
Tagus R.

SPAIN
Madrid
Seville
Ebro R.
Barcelona
BALEARIC IS.
(Spain)

Strait of Gibraltar
Algeciras
Tangier
SPANISH MOROCCO
FRENCH MOROCCO
Algiers
ALGERIA (Fr.)

MEDITERRANEAN SEA

TUNISIA (Fr.)

MALTA (Br.)

SARDINIA (It.)
CORSICA (Fr.)

I T A L Y
Rome
Naples
Tiber R.
Venice
Milan
SICILY (It.)

NORWAY
Oslo
Stockholm
SWEDEN
Kattegat
Skagerrak

DENMARK
Copenhagen

Hamburg
Elbe R.
Berlin
GERMANY
Prague
Munich
Oder R.
Neisse R.
Danube R.
Vienna
E. PRUSSIA
Memel

BALTIC SEA

Gulf of Bothnia

FINLAND
Helsinki (Helsingfors)
Tallinn (Reval)
ESTONIA
Riga
LATVIA
Kaunas (Kovno)
LITHUANIA

White Sea

Lake Ladoga
Leningrad

UNION OF SOVIET SOCIALIST REPUBLICS

Moscow

Volga R.

Stalingrad

Kharkov

Kiev
Dnieper R.
Odessa

Sea of Azov

CASPIAN SEA

BLACK SEA

POLAND
Warsaw

SLOVAKIA
HUNGARY
Budapest

RUMANIA
Bucharest

YUGOSLAVIA
Belgrade

BULGARIA
Sofia

ALBANIA
Tirana

Adriatic Sea

GREECE
Athens

Aegean Sea

CRETE (Greece)

DODECANESE IS. (It.)

TURKEY
Istanbul
Ankara (Angora)

CYPRUS (Gt. Britain)

SYRIA (Fr.)
Damascus
LEBANON (Fr.)

IRAQ
Baghdad

IRAN

1000 miles

500

0

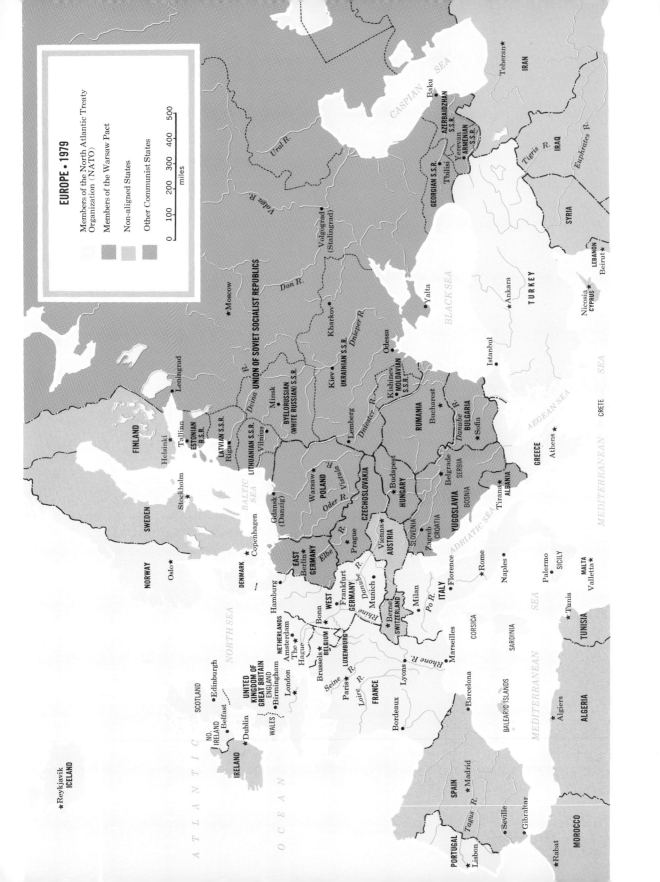

Members of the North Atlantic Treaty
Organization (NATO)

Members of the Warsaw Pact

Non-aligned States

Other Communist States

miles

0 100 200 300 400 500

★ Reykjavik
ICELAND

ATLANTIC

OCEAN

IRELAND
★ Dublin
NO.
IRELAND
• Belfast

SCOTLAND
• Edinburgh

UNITED
KINGDOM OF
GREAT BRITAIN
ENGLAND
•Birmingham
London •

WALES

NORTH SEA

NORWAY

Oslo ★

SWEDEN

Stockholm
★

FINLAND

Helsinki
★

Leningrad •

Tallinn •
ESTONIAN
R.S.R.

Riga •
LATVIAN S.S.R.

LITHUANIAN S.S.R.
Vilnius •

BALTIC
SEA

Copenhagen •
DENMARK

Hamburg •

NETHERLANDS
Amsterdam •
The
Hague
BELGIUM
Brussels •
LUXEMBURG

Gdansk
(Danzig) •

EAST
Berlin • GERMANY

WEST
GERMANY
Frankfurt •
Bonn •

Elbe R.

Oder R.

POLAND
Warsaw •

Vistula R.

Prague •
CZECHOSLOVAKIA

Minsk •

BYELORUSSIAN
(WHITE RUSSIAN) S.S.R.

Dvina R.
UNION OF SOVIET SOCIALIST REPUBLICS

Ural R.

Moscow ★

Volga R.

Don R.

Volgograd
(Stalingrad) •

CASPIAN
SEA

Baku •
AZERBAIDZHAN
S.S.R.

GEORGIAN S.S.R.
Tbilisi •
Yerevan •
ARMENIAN
S.S.R.

Teheran ★
IRAN

Tigris R.
IRAQ

Euphrates R.

SYRIA

LEBANON
Beirut •

UKRAINIAN S.S.R.
Kiev •
Kharkov •

Dnieper R.

Lemberg •

Dniester R.

Kishinev •
MOLDAVIAN
S.S.R.

Odessa •

Yalta •

BLACK SEA

Istanbul •

Ankara •
TURKEY

Nicosia
CYPRUS

AEGEAN SEA

CRETE

MEDITERRANEAN SEA

RUMANIA
Bucharest •

Danube R.

BULGARIA
Sofia ★

Budapest •
HUNGARY

Vienna •
AUSTRIA

Berne ★
SWITZERLAND

Munich •

Danube R.

Rhine R.

FRANCE
Paris ★

Seine R.

Loire R.

Bordeaux •

Lyons •
Rhône R.

Marseilles •

Milan •
Po R.

ITALY
Florence •

Rome ★

Naples •

CORSICA

SARDINIA

Belgrade •
SERBIA
YUGOSLAVIA
BOSNIA
Zagreb •
CROATIA
SLOVENIA

Tirana •
ALBANIA

ADRIATIC SEA

GREECE
Athens •

Zagreb •

Palermo •
SICILY

MALTA
Valletta ★

Tunis ★
TUNISIA

Algiers •
ALGERIA

MOROCCO
★ Rabat

SPAIN
Madrid ★

Barcelona •

BALEARIC ISLANDS

MEDITERRANEAN SEA

Tagus R.

Seville •

Gibraltar •

PORTUGAL
Lisbon ★

soned, or sent to Siberia. By ridding the country of his opposition Stalin forestalled further revolution—not an unlikely possibility, given discontent with his policies—and solidified his position as virtual dictator of Russia.

The Soviet revolution achieved profound results. By 1939 private manufacturing and private trade had been almost entirely abolished. Factories, mines, railroads, and public utilities were exclusively owned by the state. Stores were either government enterprises or cooperatives in which consumers owned shares. Agriculture also had been almost completely socialized. No less revolutionary were the developments in the social sphere. Religion as a factor in the lives of the people declined to a place of small importance. Christianity was still tolerated, but churches were reduced in number, and were not permitted to engage in any charitable or educational activities. Furthermore, members of the Communist party were required to be atheists. Postrevolutionary communism not only renounced all belief in the supernatural but attempted to cultivate a new ethics. The cardinal virtues in this positive morality are industry, respect for public property, willingness to sacrifice individual interests for the good of society, and loyalty to the Soviet fatherland and to the socialist ideal.

Results of the Soviet upheaval

By the outbreak of World War II the Soviet regime had undeniable accomplishments to its credit. Among the principal ones were: (1) the reduction of illiteracy from at least 50 percent to less than 20 percent; (2) a notable expansion of industrialization; (3) the establishment of a planned economy, which operated successfully enough to prevent unemployment; (4) the opening of educational and cultural opportunities to larger numbers of the common people; and (5) the establishment of a system of government assistance for working mothers and their infants and free medical care and hospitalization for most citizens.

Accomplishments of the Bolshevik regime

But these accomplishments were purchased at a very high price. The program of socialization and industrialization was pushed at so frantic a pace that the good of individual citizens was overlooked. The Stalinist regime fastened upon Russia a tyranny as extreme as that of the tsar. Indeed, the number of its victims sentenced to slave-labor camps—estimated to be as high as 20 million—probably exceeded the number consigned by the tsars to exile in Siberia.

The price of revolution

2. THE EMERGENCE OF FASCISM IN ITALY

That Italy turned to totalitarianism may seem strange in view of the fact that the Italians emerged from World War I on the winning side. Italy had been the victim of frustrated nationalism for many years. Its aspirations for power and for empire had been shattered. The effect was to produce a sense of humiliation and shame, especially in the minds of the younger generation, and to foster an attitude of contempt

Frustrated nationalism in Italy

for the existing political regime. Members of the old ruling class were held up to scorn as cynical, vacillating, defeatist, and corrupt. Even before World War I there was talk of revolution, of the need for a drastic housecleaning that would deliver the country from its incompetent rulers.

But the establishment of a dictatorship in Italy would never have been possible without the demoralizing and humiliating effects of World War I. The chief business of the Italian armies had been to keep the Austrians occupied on the Southern Front while the British, French, and Americans hammered Germany into submission along the battle lines on the Western Front. To accomplish its purpose Italy had to mobilize more than 5,500,000 men; of these nearly 700,000 were killed. The direct financial cost of Italian participation in the struggle was over 15 billion dollars. These sacrifices were no greater than those made by the British and the French, but Italy was a poor country. Moreover, in the division of the spoils after the fighting was over, the Italians got less than they expected. While Italy did receive most of the Austrian territories promised in the secret treaties, the Italians maintained that these were inadequate rewards for their sacrifices and for their valuable contribution to an Entente victory. At first the nationalists vented their spleen for the "humiliation of Versailles" upon President Wilson, but after a short time they returned to their old habit of castigating Italy's rulers. They alleged that such men as Premier Orlando had been so cravenly weak and inept that they had allowed their own country to be cheated.

The war contributed to the revolution in a multitude of other ways. It resulted in inflation of the currency, with consequent high prices, speculation, and profiteering. Normally wages would have risen also, but the labor market was glutted on account of the return to civilian life of millions of soldiers. Furthermore, business was demoralized, owing to extensive and frequent strikes and to the closing of foreign markets. Perhaps the most serious consequence of the war, to the upper and middle classes at least, was the growth of socialism. As hardship and chaos increased, the Italian socialists embraced a philosophy akin to Bolshevism. They voted as a party to join the Third International. In the elections of November 1919, they won about a third of the seats in the Chamber of Deputies. During the following winter socialist workers took over about a hundred factories and attempted to run them for the benefit of the workers. Radicalism also spread through the rural areas, where so-called Red Leagues were organized to break up large estates and to force landlords to reduce their rents. The landowning classes were badly frightened and were therefore ready to accept Fascist totalitarianism as a less dangerous form of radicalism that might save at least part of their property from confiscation.

How much the Fascist movement depended for its success upon the leadership of Benito Mussolini is impossible to say. Mussolini was born in 1883, the son of a socialist blacksmith. His mother was a schoolteacher, and in deference to her wishes he eventually became a teacher. But he was restless and dissatisfied and soon left Italy for further study in Switzerland. Here he gave part of his time to his books and the rest of it to writing articles for socialist newspapers. He was finally expelled from the country for fomenting strikes in factories. Upon returning to Italy he took up journalism as a definite career and eventually became editor of *Avanti,* the leading socialist daily. His ideas in the years before the war were a mixture of contradictory forms of radicalism. He professed to be a Marxist socialist, but he mingled his socialism with doctrines of corporatism, adapted from the French syndicalists.

Mussolini in fact believed in no particular set of doctrines. No man with a definite philosophy could have reversed himself so often. When war broke out in August 1914, Mussolini insisted that Italy should remain neutral. But he had scarcely adopted this position when he began urging participation on the Entente side. Deprived of his position as editor of *Avanti,* he founded a new paper, *Il Popolo d'Italia,* and dedicated its columns to arousing enthusiasm for war. He regarded the decision of the government the following spring to go in on the side of the Entente allies as a personal victory.

The word *fascism* derives from the Latin *fasces,* the ax surrounded by a bundle of sticks representing the authority of the Roman state; the Italian *fascio,* means group or band. *Fasci* were organized as early as October 1914, as units of agitation to swing Italy over to the Entente cause. Their membership was made up of young idealists, fanatical nationalists, and bored white-collar workers. The original platform of the Fascist movement was drafted by Mussolini in 1919. It was a surprisingly radical document, which demanded, among other things, universal suffrage; abolition of the conservative Senate; the establishment by law of an eight-hour day; a heavy capital levy; a heavy tax on inheritances; confiscation of 85 percent of war profits; acceptance of the League of Nations; and "opposition to all imperialisms." This platform was accepted more or less officially by the movement until May 1920, when it was supplanted by another of a more conservative character. Indeed, the new program omitted all reference to economic reform. On neither of these platforms did the Fascists achieve much political success.

The Fascists made up for their initial lack of numbers by disciplined aggressiveness and strong determination. As the old regime crumbled, they prepared to take over the government. In September 1922, Mussolini began to talk openly of revolution and raised the cry, "On to Rome." On October 28 an army of about 50,000 Fascist militia, in blackshirted uniforms, occupied the capital. The premier resigned, and the following day the king, Victor Emmanuel III, invited Mussolini to form a cabinet. Thus, without firing a shot the blackshirts had

Left: *"On to Rome."* Mussolini (wearing a suit) and uniformed Fascists march into Rome in October 1922. Right: *Mussolini Addressing a Crowd of His Followers from the Balcony of the Palazzo Venezia in Rome*

gained control of the Italian government. The explanation is to be found not in the strength of fascism, but in the chaos created by the war and in the weakness and irresolution of the old ruling classes. By the end of the next three years Mussolini's revolution was virtually complete. He had abolished the cabinet system, made the political system a one-party system, and reduced the functions of the parliament to ratifying decrees.

The leading doctrines of Italian fascism may be summarized as follows:

Major doctrines of fascism

(1) Totalitarianism. The state incorporates every interest and every loyalty of its members. There must be "nothing above the state, nothing outside the state, nothing against the state."

(2) Nationalism. The nation is the highest form of society ever evolved by the human race. It has a life and a soul of its own apart from the lives and souls of the individuals who compose it. There can never be a real harmony of interests between two or more distinct peoples. Internationalism is therefore a perversion of human progress.

(3) Militarism. Strife is the origin of all things. Nations which do not expand eventually wither and die. War exalts and ennobles man and regenerates sluggish and decadent peoples.

Declaring his allegiance to these principles, Mussolini began to build what he called the corporatist state. The Italian economy was

Corporatism

placed under the management of twenty-two corporations, each responsible for a major industrial enterprise. In each corporation were representatives of trade unions, whose members were organized by the Fascist party, the employers, and the government. Together, the members of these corporations were given the task of determining working conditions, wages, and prices. In fact, however, the decisions of these bodies were closely managed by the government. In 1938 the last vestiges of democratic control were removed in Italy. The Chamber of Deputies was replaced by the Chamber of Fasces and Corporations, whose members were appointed by the government.

Corporatism did little to lessen Italy's plight during the years of worldwide depression which occurred in the 1930s. Although he managed to make his country appear more efficient—his admirers often bragged that he had at last "made the trains run on time"— Mussolini failed to solve its major problems, particularly those of the peasantry, whose standard of living remained desperately low. Mussolini's fascism was little more than illusion. It is a measure of the Italians' disgust with their past leaders that they were so ready to be taken in.

Its failure

3. THE RISE OF NAZI GERMANY

Germany succumbed to totalitarianism later than Italy. For a brief period following World War I, events seemed to be moving the country to the Left. Most of the leading politicians in the immediate postarmistice government were socialists, members of the Social Democratic party. Their reformist policies, which had seemed radical enough to many prior to the war, now appeared too mild to a group of extreme Marxists who had been encouraged by the revolution in Russia. Calling themselves Spartacists,[1] and led by the able Rosa Luxemburg and Karl Liebknecht, they attempted an uprising in 1919 designed to bring the proletarian revolution to Germany. Despite assistance from the Russian Bolsheviks, the rebellion was crushed; Liebknecht and Luxemburg were killed by soldiers while being taken to prison. In engineering the Spartacists' defeat, the German government had recourse to private vigilante groups headed by disillusioned former army officers, men whose true sympathies lay no more with democratic socialism than with Russian communism, and whose discontent would soon focus on the government they had helped to salvage.

Germany: the Spartacists

With the Spartacist revolt only just behind them, the leaders of a coalition of socialists, Catholic Centrists, and liberal democrats in 1919 drafted a constitution for the new German republic reflecting a generally progressive political and social philosophy. It provided for universal suffrage, for women as well as men; the cabinet system of government; and for a bill of rights, guaranteeing not only civil liberties but the right of the citizen to employment, to an education, and to protection against the hazards of an industrial society. But the republic set up under this constitution was beset with troubles from the start.

The Weimar Republic

---

[1] After the Roman, Spartacus, who led a slave revolt.

Karl Liebknecht (center) *and Rosa Luxemburg*

Reactionaries and other extremists plotted against it. Moreover, the German people had had little experience with democratic government. The Weimar Republic (named for the city where its constitution was drafted) did not spring from the desires of a majority of the nation. It was born of change forced upon Germany in its hour of defeat. Its instability made it a likely victim of the forces it was desperately attempting to tame.

Causes of German totalitarianism: (1) defeat in war

The factors which led to the eventual triumph of German totalitarianism were many and various. First was the sense of humiliation arising from defeat in the war. Between 1871 and 1914 Germany had risen to lofty heights of political and cultural prestige. German universities, science, philosophy, and music were known and admired all over the world. The country had likewise attained a remarkable prosperity, by 1914 surpassing Britain and the United States in several fields of industrial production. Then came the crushing blow of 1918. Germany was toppled from its pinnacle and left at the mercy of its powerful enemies. It was too much for the German people to understand. They could not believe that their invincible armies had really been worsted in battle. Quickly the legend grew that the nation had been "stabbed in the back" by socialists and Jews in the government. Though there was no truth in this charge, it helped to salve the wounded pride of German patriots. Those in search of a scapegoat also blamed the laxity and irresponsibility that appeared to distinguish the republican regime. It was alleged that Berlin had displaced Paris as the most frivolous and decadent city of Europe. What the country seemed to need was authoritative leadership to spearhead a campaign to regain the world's respect.

Another major reason for the appeal of totalitarianism was the inflation that Germany suffered in the 1920s. When the country began to experience severe unemployment, the government increased the supply of paper money—eventually to a flood—in order to finance programs of unemployment insurance and to try to provide its citizenry with the economic wherewithal to stay alive. The result was a period of wild inflation, particularly demoralizing to the middle class. Salaries could not keep up with the vast increase in the cost of living. Those who existed on fixed incomes—pensioners, stockholders—saw their security vanish. As they lost their faith in the ability of the government to come to their aid, these men and women began, as well, to lose whatever faith they may have had in the republic. Germany recovered from inflation in the late 1920s, thanks, largely, to the scaling down of reparations payments and to foreign loans and investments. But the middle class, traumatized by its experience of inflation, continued its search for a government that promised attention to its needs and sympathy with its problems. That search intensified with the advent of the Great Depression of 1929. As we shall see, the depression was a major disaster for most of the world. In few countries, however, were its effects more keenly felt than in Germany. Farmers were angered by the collapse of agricultural prices and by their burden of debts and taxes. University students saw little prospect of gaining a place in already overcrowded professions. Six million workers were unemployed. Once again the middle class saw its savings vanish.

(2) economics

One political result was a swing on the part of many workers to the German Communist party. The Spartacist failure had, for a time, quelled middle-class fears of a leftist takeover. But in the presidential election of 1932, the Communist party polled about 6 million votes, or over one-seventh of the total. As had happened in Italy, a number of capitalists and property-owners were alarmed at what they regarded as a growing danger of Bolshevik revolution and lent their support to a different sort of totalitarianism as the lesser of two evils.

(3) fear of Bolshevism

The origins of German totalitarianism go back to 1919 when a group of seven men met in Munich and founded the National Socialist

Depression in Germany. Following the defeat in World War I, inflation was rampant and food in short supply. Here a fallen horse is torn to shreds by hungry citizens.

*The founding of the Nazi
party; the early career of
Hitler*

German Workers' party.[2] Presently the most obscure of the seven emerged as their leader. He was Adolf Hitler, born in 1889, the son of a petty customs official in the Austrian civil service. Hitler's early life was unhappy and maladjusted. Rebellious and undisciplined from childhood, he seems always to have been burdened with a sense of frustration. He was a failure in school and decided that he would become an artist. With this purpose in view he went to Vienna in 1909, hoping to enter the Academy. But he failed the required examinations; for the next four years he was compelled to eke out a dismal existence as a casual laborer and a painter of little sketches and watercolors. Meanwhile he developed some violent political prejudices. He became an ardent admirer of certain vociferously anti-Semitic politicians in Vienna; and since he associated Judaism with Marxism, he hated that philosophy also. When World War I broke out, Hitler was living in Munich, and though an Austrian citizen, he immediately enlisted in the German army. Following the war, he joined with other disaffected Germans to denounce the Weimar Republic. In 1923, Hitler led an attempt in Munich by the Nazis' private army, the Brownshirts, to stage a "putsch," or sudden overthrow of the government. The revolution was proclaimed in a beer hall, with Hitler firing a revolver into the ceiling. The Brownshirts were quickly dispersed, and Hitler sentenced to a term in prison, where he composed a declaration of his beliefs, *Mein Kampf* (My Struggle). In this rambling treatise he expressed his hatred of Jews and communists, his sense of Germany's betrayal by its World War I enemies, and his belief that only with strong leadership could the country regain its rightful place within the European concert of nations.

Hitler's message appealed to an ever-growing number of his disillusioned and economically threatened countrymen and women. In the election of 1928 the Nazis won 12 seats in the Reichstag. In 1930, they won 107 seats, their popular vote increasing from 800,000 to 6,500,000. During the summer of 1932 the parliamentary system broke down. No chancellor could retain a majority in the Reichstag, for the Nazis declined to support any cabinet not headed by Hitler, and the communists refused to collaborate with the socialists. In January 1933, a group of reactionaries—industrialists, bankers, and Junkers—prevailed upon President Paul von Hindenburg to designate Hitler as chancellor, evidently in the belief that they could control him. It was arranged that there should be only three Nazis in the cabinet, and that Franz von Papen, a Catholic aristocrat, should hold the position of vice-chancellor. But the sponsors of this plan failed to appreciate the tremendous resurgence of mass feeling behind the Nazi movement. Hitler was not slow in making the most of his new opportunity. He persuaded von Hindenburg to dissolve the Reichstag and to

---

[2] The name of the party was soon abbreviated in popular usage to Nazi.

One Step Away from Power. President von Hindenburg followed by Hitler, Göring on the extreme right, and other Nazi party members.

order a new election on March 5. When the new Reichstag assembled, it voted to confer upon Hitler practically unlimited powers. Soon afterward the flag of the Weimar Republic was hauled down and replaced by the swastika banner of the National Socialists. The new Germany was proclaimed to be the Third Reich, the successor of the Hohenstaufen Empire of the Middle Ages and of the Hohenzollern Empire of the kaisers.

Within a few months, other and more sweeping changes occurred. Germany was converted into a highly centralized state with the destruction of the federal principle that had been a feature of Bismarck's imperial scheme. All political parties except the Nazi party were declared illegal. Totalitarian control was extended over the press, over education, the theater, the cinema, radio, and many branches of production and trade. Drastic penalties were imposed upon the Jews: they were eliminated from government positions, deprived of citizenship, and practically excluded from the universities. With the passing of the years, the entire regime seemed to shift more and more in a radical direction. The new tendency approached its climax in 1938 with the extension of party control over the army and with the institution of a fanatical crusade against the Jews to expel them from the Reich or to annihilate them entirely.

Consolidation of Nazi rule

So far as its ideology was concerned, German totalitarianism resembled the Italian variety in a great many of its essentials. Both were collectivistic, authoritarian, nationalistic, militaristic, and anti-intellectual. Yet there were some outstanding differences. Italian fascism never had a racial basis. True, after the formation of the Rome-Berlin Axis, an alliance made in 1936, Mussolini issued anti-Jewish decrees.

Nazi racism

But race was not a central theoretical pillar of Italian fascism as it was of German National Socialism. The Nazis argued that the so-called Aryan race, which was supposed to include the Nordics as its most perfect specimens, was the only one ever to have made any notable contributions to human progress. They contended further that the accomplishments and mental qualities of a people were determined by blood. Thus the achievements of the Jew forever remained Jewish, or Oriental, no matter how long he or she might live in a Western country. It followed that no Jewish science or Jewish literature or Jewish music could ever truly represent the German nation. Obviously, most of this racial doctrine was mere rationalization. The Nazis persecuted the Jews because Hitler was himself rabidly anti-Semitic and because they needed a scapegoat upon whom they could place the blame for their nation's troubles. Before this extremism had run its course, millions of Jews had been rounded up, tortured, and murdered in concentration camps. Other representatives of "imperfect" racial and social groups—homosexuals, gypsies, and anti-Nazi intellectuals—met a similar fate. The extremism of Hitler's anti-Semitic campaigns underscores the fact that National Socialism was more fanatical than Italian fascism. It was comparable to a new religion, not only in its dogmatism and its ritual, but in its fierce intolerance and its zeal for expansion.

Despite the fact that Germany was one of the most highly industrialized countries in the world, National Socialism had a peculiar *Dissimilarities with Italian fascism* peasant flavor which Italian fascism did not possess. The key to Nazi theory was contained in the phrase *Blut und Boden* (blood and soil). The word *soil* typified not only a deep reverence for the homeland but an abiding affection for the peasants, who were considered to embody the finest qualities of the German race. No class of the population was more generously treated by the Nazi government. This high regard for country folk came partly no doubt from the circumstance that they had the highest birthrate of the nation's citizens and therefore were

A Nazi Party Rally. Hitler at the height of his power, followed by other Nazi party officials.

most valuable for military reasons. It was explainable also by the reaction of the Nazi leaders against everything that the city stood for—not only intellectualism and radicalism but high finance and the complicated problems of industrial society. In its attempt to control all aspects of national life, Nazism resembled not only Italian fascism but all totalitarian regimes. Trade unions were replaced by the government-controlled National Labor Front. Public works programs—including reforestation and housing and highway construction—were begun. A policy of rearmament led to further industrial organization, and helped reduce unemployment.

The significance of German and Italian totalitarianism is still a subject of controversy among students of modern history. Some argue that it was simply the enthronement of force by big capitalists in an effort to save their dying system from destruction. It is true that the success of both movements in gaining control of the government depended in some measure upon support from great landowners and captains of industry. A second interpretation would explain German and Italian totalitarianism as a reaction of debtors against creditors, of farmers against bankers and manufacturers, and of small businessmen against high finance and monopolistic practices. Still other students of the movement interpret it as a revolt against communism, a reversion to primitivism, a result of the despair of the masses, a protest against the weaknesses of democracy, or a supreme manifestation of nationalism. Undoubtedly it was all of these things combined. An increasingly popular view in recent years holds that fascism and Nazism were extreme expressions of tendencies prevalent in all industrialized countries. If official policies in most Western countries in the 1930s took on more and more of an authoritarian semblance—a tightly controlled economy, limitation of production to maintain prices, and expansion of armaments to promote prosperity—it was because nearly all nations in that period were beset with similar problems.

The complex significance of German and Italian totalitarianism

4. THE DEMOCRACIES BETWEEN THE WARS

The histories of the three Western democracies—Great Britain, France, and the United States—run roughly parallel during the years after the First World War. In all three countries there was an attempt by governments to trust to policies and assumptions that had prevailed before the war. The French, not surprisingly, continued to fear Germany and to take whatever steps they could to keep their traditional enemy as weak as possible. Under the leadership of the moderate conservative, Raymond Poincaré, who held office from 1922 to 1924, and again from 1926 to 1929, the French pursued a policy of deflation, which attempted to keep the price of manufactured goods low, by restraining wages. This policy pleased businessmen, but was hard on the working class. Edouard Herriot, a Radical Socialist who

Class conflict in France

served as premier from 1924 to 1926 was, despite his party's name, a spokesman for the small businessman, farmer, and lower middle class. Herriot declared himself in favor of social reform, but he refused to raise taxes in order to pay for it. Class conflict lay close to the surface of French national affairs throughout the 1920s. While industries prospered, employers rejected trade unionists' demands to bargain collectively. A period of major strikes immediately after the war was followed by a sharp decline in union activity. Workers remained dissatisfied, even after the government passed a modified social insurance program in 1930, insuring against sickness, old age, and death.

Britain's economic difficulties

Class conflict flared in Britain as well. Anxious to regain its now irretrievably lost position as the major industrial and financial power in the world, Britain, like France, pursued a policy of deflation, designed to lower the price of manufactured goods and thus make them more attractive on the world market. The result was a reduction in wages which undermined the standard of living of many British workers. Their resentment helped to elect a Labour party government in 1924 and 1929. But its minority position in Parliament left it little chance to accomplish much of consequence, even had its leader, Prime Minister J. Ramsay MacDonald, been a more adventurous socialist than he was. In 1926 British trade unions grew increasingly militant because of the particularly distressing wage levels in the coal mining industry, and because the Conservative government, returned to power under Prime Minister Stanley Baldwin in 1925, refused to be deflected from its deflationary stance. The unions staged a nationwide general strike which, though it failed as an industrial strategy, turned the middle class more than ever against the workers.

Conservatism in the U.S.

The United States was undoubtedly the most impregnable fortress of conservative power among the democracies. The presidents elected during the 1920s—Warren G. Harding, Calvin Coolidge, and Herbert Hoover—upheld a social philosophy formulated by the barons of big business in the nineteenth century, and the Supreme Court used its power of judicial review to nullify progressive legislation enacted by state governments and occasionally by Congress.

Labor Troubles in Britain. Mounted police escorting delivery wagons through a mob of angry strikers during the general strike of 1926.

The Stock Market Crash, October 24, 1929. Crowds milling outside the New York Stock Exchange on the day of the big crash.

The course of Western history was dramatically altered by the advent of worldwide depression in 1929. We have already mentioned this event as it contributed to the rise of Nazism. But all countries were forced to come to terms with the economic and social devastation it produced. The Great Depression had its roots in a general agricultural slump in the 1920s, the result of increased postwar production which drove down the price of grain and other commodities to the point of bankrupting farmers, though not far enough to benefit the urban poor. To chronic agricultural distress was added the financial crisis that began with the collapse of prices on the New York stock exchange in 1929. With a drop in the value of stocks, banks found themselves short of capital and forced to close. International investors called in their debts. Industries, unable to sell, stopped manufacturing and started laying off workers. Unemployment further contracted markets—fewer people had money with which to buy goods or services—and that contraction led to more unemployment.

The Great Depression

The results of the depression took varied forms throughout the West. In 1931 Great Britain abandoned the gold standard, and the government of the United States followed suit in 1933. By no longer pegging their currencies to the price of gold, these countries hoped to make money cheaper, and thus more available for programs of public and private economic recovery. This action was the forerunner of a broad program of currency management, which became an important element in a general policy of economic nationalism. By way of illustration, President Franklin D. Roosevelt informed the London Economic Conference of 1933 that "the sound internal economic system of a nation is a greater factor in its well-being than the price of its currency in changing terms of the currencies of other nations." As early as 1932 Great Britain abandoned its time-honored policy of free trade. Protective tariffs were raised in some instances as high as 100 percent.

Results of depression: economic nationalism

Léon Blum

Domestic policies

The New Deal

Its achievements

Domestically, Britain moved cautiously to alleviate the effects of the depression. A national government, which came to power in 1931 with a ministry composed of members from the Conservative, Liberal, and Labour parties, was reluctant to spend beyond its income, as it would have to in order to underwrite effective programs of public assistance. Of the European democracies, France adopted the most advanced set of policies to combat the inequalities and distress that followed in the wake of the depression. In 1936, responding to a threat from ultraconservatives to overthrow the republic, a Popular Front government, under the leadership of the socialist Léon Blum (1872–1950), was formed by the Radical, Radical Socialist, and Communist parties, and lasted for two years. The Popular Front nationalized the munitions industry and reorganized the Bank of France so as to deprive the 200 largest stockholders of their monopolistic control over credit. In addition, it decreed a forty-hour week for all urban workers and initiated a program of public works. For the benefit of the farmers it established a wheat office to fix the price and regulate the distribution of grain. Although the threat from the political Right had for a time been quelled by the Popular Front, conservatives were generally uncooperative and unimpressed by its attempts to ameliorate the conditions of the French working class. The anti-Semitism that had surfaced at the time of the Dreyfus affair resurfaced; Blum was both a socialist and a Jew. Businessmen saw him as the forerunner of a French Lenin, and were heard to opine, "better Hitler than Blum." They got their wish before the decade was out.

The most dramatic changes in policy after the depression occurred, not in Europe, but in the United States. The explanation was twofold. The United States had clung longer to the economic philosophy of the nineteenth century. Prior to the depression the business classes had adhered firmly to the dogma of freedom of contract and insisted upon their right to form monopolies and to use the government as their agent in frustrating the demands of both workers and consumers. The depression in the United States was also more severe than in the European democracies. Industrial production shrank by about two-thirds. The structure of agricultural prices and of common stocks collapsed. Thousands of banks were forced to close their doors. Unemployment rose to 15 million, or to approximately 33 percent of the total labor force. An attempt to alleviate distress was contained in a program of reform and reconstruction known as the New Deal. The chief architect and motivator of this program was Franklin D. Roosevelt (1882–1945), who succeeded Herbert Hoover in the presidency on March 4, 1933.

The aim of the New Deal was to preserve the capitalist system, by managing the economy and undertaking programs of relief and public works to increase mass purchasing power. Although the New Deal did assist in the recovery both of individual citizens and of the country, through programs of currency management and social security, it left the crucial problem of unemployment unsolved. In 1939, after six years of the New Deal, the United States still had more than 9 million jobless workers—a figure which exceeded the combined unemployment of the rest of the world. Ironically, only the outbreak of a new world war could provide the full recovery that the New Deal had failed to assure, by directing millions from the labor market into the army and by creating jobs in the countless factories that turned to the manufacture of war materiel.

5. INTELLECTUAL AND CULTURAL TRENDS IN THE INTERWAR YEARS

The First World War, which proved so disillusioning to so many, and the generally dispiriting political events which followed in its train, made it difficult to hold fast to any notion of a purposeful universe. Philosophers, to a greater degree than their predecessors, declared that there was little point in attempting to discover answers to questions about the nature of ultimate reality. These antimetaphysicians discarded the search for God or for the "meaning" of life as a hopeless and therefore pointless task. Probably the most influential of these thinkers was the Viennese Ludwig Wittgenstein (1889–1951), founder, with the Englishman Bertrand Russell (1872–1970), of the school of Logical Positivism. Developed further by the so-called Vienna Circle, whose leader was Rudolf Carnap, Logical Positivism emerged as an uncompromisingly scientific philosophy. It is not concerned with values or ideals except to the extent that they may be demonstrable by mathematics or physics. In general, the Logical Positivists reject as "meaningless" everything that cannot be reduced to a "one-to-one correspondence" with something in the physical universe. In other words, they reduce philosophy to a mere instrument for the discovery of truth in harmony with the facts of the physical environment. They divest it almost entirely of its traditional content and use it as a medium for answering questions and solving problems. They are concerned especially with political theory, regarding that subject as particularly burdened with unproved assumptions and questionable dogmas.

Sociologists reinforced philosophers in denying the value of metaphysics. One of the most important was the German Max Weber (1864–1920), who, in his book *The Protestant Ethic and the Spirit of Capitalism* (1905), argued that religion must be understood as a cultural force, in this case assisting directly in the spread of capitalism. By making work a cardinal virtue and idleness a supreme vice, Protestantism had encouraged the work ethic, which, in turn, had fueled the energies of early capitalist entrepreneurs. When he turned to a study of

Bertrand Russell

the contemporary world, Weber concluded that societies would inevitably fall more and more under the sway of ever-expanding and potentially totalitarian bureaucracies. Recognizing the extent to which such a development might threaten human freedom, Weber posited the notion of "charismatic" leadership as a means of escaping the deadening tyranny of state control. A term derived from the Greek word for gift, "charisma" was, according to Weber, an almost magic quality which could induce hero worship and which, if properly directed by its possessor, might produce an authority to challenge bureaucracy. Weber himself recognized the dangers as well as the attractions of charismatic authority, dangers which the careers of Hitler and Mussolini soon made all too apparent. Another thinker who treated religion as a powerful social and psychological force, rather than as a branch of metaphysics, was the Swiss psychologist Carl Jung (1875–1961). Originally a student and disciple of Freud, Jung broke with his intellectual mentor by proclaiming the existence of a force behind individual id, ego, and superego: the "collective unconscious." Jung's literary background and his personal penchant for mysticism helped persuade him of the enduring psychological and therapeutic value of myth and religion, something Freud refused to acknowledge.

Antirationalist and antidemocratic philosophies

The writings of some philosophers during the interwar years not only reflected a sense of crisis and despair but, because of the influence of those works, contributed to it as well. Foremost among these were the Italian Vilfredo Pareto (1848–1923) and the German Oswald Spengler (1880–1936), who agreed in their contempt for the masses, in their belief that democracy was impossible, in their anti-intellectual viewpoint, and in their admiration for strong and aggressive leaders. Spengler was, in many respects, more extreme than Pareto. Although he completed in about 1918 an erudite and in some respects brilliant philosophy of history, which he entitled *The Decline of the West,* his later writings reflected totalitarian prejudices. In his *Hour of Decision,* published in 1933, he fulminated against democracy, pacifism, internationalism, the lower classes, and nonwhite peoples. He sang the praises of those "who feel themselves born and called to be masters," of "healthy instincts, race, the will to possession and power." Spengler despised the old, analytical reasoning of urban intellectuals and called upon men to admire the "deep wisdom of old peasant families." Human beings, he maintained, are "beasts of prey," and those who deny this conclusion are simply "beasts of prey with broken teeth."

Literary disillusion

Literary movements during the interwar period showed tendencies similar to those in philosophy. The major novelists, poets, and dramatists were deeply concerned about social and political problems and about the hope and destiny of humanity. Like the philosophers, they were disillusioned by the brute facts of World War I and by the failure of victory to fulfill its promises. Many were profoundly affected also by revolutionary developments in science and especially by the probings of the new science of psychoanalysis into the hidden secrets of the mind. Much of the literature of the interwar period expressed themes of frustration, cynicism, and disenchantment. It was an era dominated by those whose ideals had been shattered by the events of their time. Its mood was set by the early novels of the American Ernest Hemingway (1899–1961), by the poetry of the Anglo-American T. S. Eliot (1888–1965), and by the plays of the German Bertolt Brecht (1898–1956). In *The Sun Also Rises,* Hemingway gave the public a powerful description of the essential tragedy of the so-called lost generation and set a pattern which other writers, like the American F. Scott Fitzgerald, were soon to follow. In his poem *The Waste Land* (1922), T. S. Eliot presented a philosophy that was close to despair. Once you are born, he seemed to be saying, life is a living death, to be ground out in boredom and frustration. The German, Brecht, in plays written to be performed before the proletarian patrons of cabarets, proclaimed the corruption of the bourgeois state and the pointlessness of war.

The works of many writers in the interwar period reflected to an increasing extent the isolation of self-conscious intellectuals and the constricting of their audience that, as we have seen, characterized the years before the First World War. While Brecht carried his revolutionary messages into the streets of Berlin, other writers wrote primarily for each other or for the small elite group who could understand what they were saying. Eliot crammed his poetry with esoteric allusions. The Irishman James Joyce (1882–1941), whose ability to enter his characters' minds and to reproduce their "stream-of-consciousness" on paper made him a writer of the very first order, nevertheless wrote with a complexity that only few could appreciate. The same was true, though to a lesser extent, of the novels of the Frenchman Marcel Proust (1871–1922) and the Englishwoman Virginia Woolf (1882–1941). In her novels and essays, Woolf was an eloquent and biting critic of the ruling class of Britain, focusing in part on the enforced oppression of women even in that class.

The Great Depression of the 1930s forced a reexamination of the methods and purposes of literature. In the midst of economic stagnation and threats of totalitarianism and war, the theory evolved that literature must have a political purpose, that it should indict meanness, cruelty, and barbarism, and point the way to a more just society. It should also be a literature addressed not to fellow intellectuals, but to common men and women. The new trend was reflected in the works of a diversity of writers. The American John Steinbeck (1902–1968), in *The Grapes of Wrath,* depicted the sorry plight of impoverished farmers fleeing from the "dust bowl" to California only to find that all the land had been monopolized by companies that exploited their workers. Pervading the novels of the Frenchman André Malraux

T. S. Eliot

Intellectual isolation

Virginia Woolf

Influence of the depression

Jean-Paul Sartre

Existentialism

George Orwell

John Maynard Keynes

(1901–   ) was the strong suggestion that the human struggle against tyranny and injustice is that which gives meaning and value to life. Young British writers such as W. H. Auden, Stephen Spender, and Christopher Isherwood declared, as communist sympathizers, that artists had an obligation to politicize their art for the benefit of the revolution. They rejected the pessimism of their immediate literary forebears for the optimism of political commitment to a common cause.

In this they differed radically from their French contemporary, Jean-Paul Sartre (1905–1980), whose pessimistic philosophy of Existentialism was receiving its first hearing at this time. Sartre was a teacher of philosophy in a Paris *lycée* and subsequently a leader of the French resistance movement against the Germans. His philosophy takes its name from its doctrine that the *existence* of human beings as free individuals is the fundamental fact of life. But this freedom is of no help to humanity; instead it is a source of anguish and terror. Realizing, however vaguely, that they are free agents, morally responsible for all their acts, individuals feel themselves strangers in an alien world. They can have no confidence in a benevolent God or in a universe guided by purpose, for, according to Sartre, all such ideas have been reduced to fictions by modern science. The only way of escape from despair is the path of "involvement," or active participation in human affairs. It should be noted that in addition to the atheistic Existentialism of Sartre, there was also a prior Christian version, which had its origin in the teachings of Søren Kierkegaard (1813–1855), a Danish theologian of the mid–nineteenth century. Like its atheistic counterpart, Christian Existentialism also teaches that the chief cause of human agony and terror is freedom, but it finds the source of this freedom in original sin.

Another writer who refused to allow himself the luxury of political optimism was the Englishman George Orwell (1903–1950). Although sympathetic to the cause of international socialism, Orwell continued to insist that all political movements were to some degree corrupted. He urged writers to recognize a duty to write only on the basis of what they had themselves experienced. Above all, writers should never simply parrot party propaganda. Orwell's last two novels, *Animal Farm* and *1984*, written during and immediately after the Second World War, are powerful expressions of his mistrust of political regimes—whether of the Left or the Right—that profess democracy but in fact destroy human freedom.

Optimism during the 1930s was generally the property of those writers who were prepared to advocate a violent change in the social order, most notably men and women sympathetic to the doctrines of communism and the achievements of Soviet Russia. An exception to this rule was the British economist John Maynard Keynes (1883–1946), who argued that capitalism could be made to work if governments would play a part in its management, and whose theories helped shape the economic policies of the New Deal. Keynes had served as an economic adviser to the British government during the 1919 treaty-making at Paris. He was disgusted with the harsh terms imposed upon the Germans, recognizing that they would serve only to keep alive the hatreds and uncertainties that breed war. His dismay did not induce him to turn his back on the world and its problems, however. Keynes was very much a man of the world, among other things a successful financial speculator in his own right. Keynes believed that capitalism with its inner faults corrected could provide all the justice and efficiency reasonable people could expect. Capitalism, though, would require a "face-lifting" that some of its more conservative defenders would consider drastic. First, the idea of a perpetually balanced budget would need to be abandoned. Keynes never advocated continuous deficit financing. He would have the government deliberately operate in the red whenever private investment was too scanty to provide for the needs of the country. But when depression gave way to recovery, private financing could take the place for most purposes of deficit spending. He favored the accumulation and investment of large amounts of venture capital, which he declared to be the only socially productive form of capital. Finally, Keynes recommended monetary control as a means of promoting prosperity and full employment. He would establish what is commonly called a "managed currency," regulating its value by a process of contraction or expansion in accordance with the needs of the economy. Prosperity would thus be assured in terms of the condition of the home market, and no nation would be tempted to "beggar its neighbor" in the foolish pursuit of a favorable balance of trade.

John Maynard Keynes

Trends in art tended to parallel those in literature. For much of the period, visual artists continued to explore aesthetic frontiers far re-

Big Julie by Fernand Léger. Note the artist's fascination with industrial shapes and images.

Mountain, Table, Anchors, Navel
by Jean Arp

Trends in art

See color plates following
page 1088

Art and the depression

moved from the conventional taste of average men and women. Picasso followed his particular genius as it led him further into cubist variations and inventions. So did others, such as the Frenchman Fernand Léger (1881–1955), who combined devotion to cubist principles and a fascination with the artifacts of industrial civilization. A group more advanced, perhaps, than the cubists, the expressionists argued that since color and line express inherent psychological qualities which can be represented without reference to subject matter, a painting need not have a "subject" at all. The Russian Wassily Kandinsky (1866–1944) carried the logic of this position to its conclusion by calling his untitled paintings "improvisations," and insisting that they meant nothing. A second group of expressionists rejected intellectuality for what they called "objectivity," by which they meant a candid appraisal of the state of the human mind. Their analysis took the form of an attack upon the greed and decadence of postwar Europe. Chief among this group was the German George Grosz (1893–1959), whose cruel, satiric line has been likened to a "razor lancing a carbuncle." Another school expressed its disgust with the world by declaring that there was in fact no such thing as aesthetic principle, since aesthetic principle was based on reason and the world had conclusively proved by fighting itself to death that reason did not exist. Calling themselves dada-ists (after a name picked at random, allegedly, from the dictionary) these artists, led by the Frenchman Marcel Duchamp (1887–1968), the German Max Ernst (1891–   ), and the Alsatian Jean Hans Arp (1887–1966), concocted "fabrications" from cut-outs and juxtapositions of wood, glass, and metal, and gave them bizarre names: *The Bride stripped bare by her Bachelors, even* (Duchamp), for example. These works were declared by critics, however, to belie their professed meaninglessness, to be, in fact, expressions of the subconscious. Such certainly were the paintings of the surrealists, artists such as the Italian Giorgio de Chirico (1888–1978) and the Spaniard Salvador Dali (1904–   ), whose explorations of the interior of the mind produced irrational, fantastic, and generally melancholy images.

For a time in the 1930s artists, like writers, responded to the sense of international crisis by painting to express their pain and outrage directly to a mass audience. Among the chief representatives of the new movement were the Mexicans Diego Rivera and Jose Clemente Orozco, and the Americans Thomas Hart Benton, Reginald Marsh, Edward Hopper, and Grant Wood. The fundamental aim of these artists was to depict the social conditions of the modern world and to present in graphic detail the hopes and struggles of peasants and workers. While they scarcely adhered to any of the conventions of the past, there was nothing unintelligible about their work; it was intended to be art that anyone could understand. Much of it bore the sting or thrust of social satire. Orozco, in particular, delighted in pillorying the hypocrisy of the Church and the greed and cruelty of plutocrats and plunderers.

Mural of Kansas City, Missouri by Thomas Hart Benton. The mural protests the corruption of American politics and the depression misery and degradation of farm workers and industrial laborers. The man in the armchair is the political boss of Kansas City in the 1930s, Tom Pendergast.

It was inevitable that music should reflect the spirit of disillusionment that reached a climax following World War I. The more original developments were closely parallel to those in painting. Most fundamental of all was the revolt against the romantic tradition, especially as it had culminated in Wagner. Many, although by no means all, composers went so far as to repudiate the aesthetic ideal entirely, relying upon complexity and novelty of structure or on a sheer display of energy to supply interest to their works.

The chief trends in contemporary music

Deviations from the classical and romantic formulas have been generally of two types, designated broadly as impressionism and expressionism. The former seeks to exploit the qualities of musical sound to suggest feelings or images. The latter is concerned more with form than with sensuous effects and tends toward abstraction. The most perfect exponent of impressionism was Claude Debussy (1862–1918), its originator. Even in France impressionism did not prove to be an enduring school. With Maurice Ravel (1875–1937), most celebrated of the composers who reflected Debussy's influence, it became less poetic and picturesque and acquired a degree of cold impassivity together with greater firmness of texture.

Musical impressionism

Expressionism, more radical and more influential than impressionism, comprises two main schools: atonality, founded by the Viennese Arnold Schoenberg (1874–1951), and polytonality, best typified by the Russian Igor Stravinsky (1882–1971). Atonality abolishes key. In this type of music, dissonances are the rule rather than the excep-

Musical expressionism: atonality

Igor Stravinsky

Development of functional architecture

tion, and the melodic line commonly alternates between chromatic manipulation and strange unsingable leaps. In short, the ordinary principles of composition are reversed. The atonalists attempt, with some success, to let musical sound become a vehicle for expressing the inner meaning and elemental structure of things.

Polytonality, of which Stravinsky is the most famous exponent, is essentially a radical kind of counterpoint, deriving its inspiration partly from baroque practices of counterpoint that were placed in the service of new ideas. However, it does not simply interweave independent melodies which together form concord, but undertakes to combine separate keys and unrelated harmonic systems, with results that are highly discordant. While the atonalists have retained elements of romanticism, the polytonalists have tried to resurrect the architectural qualities of pure form, movement, and rhythm, stripping away all sentimentality and sensuous connotations.

Architects during this period were also intent upon denying sentimentality. Between 1880 and 1890 certain architects in Europe and America awoke to the fact that the prevailing styles of building construction were far out of harmony with the facts of modern civilization. The result was the launching of a new architectural movement known as functionalism. Its chief pioneers were Otto Wagner (1841–1918) in Germany and Louis Sullivan (1856–1924) and Frank Lloyd Wright (1869–1959) in the United States. The basic principle of functionalism is the idea that the appearance of a building shall proclaim its actual use and purpose. There must be no addition of friezes, columns, tracery, or battlements merely because some people consider such ornaments beautiful. True beauty consists in sincerity, in an honest adaptation of materials to the purpose they are intended to serve. Functionalism also includes the idea that architecture shall express either directly or symbolically the distinguishing features of contemporary culture. Ornamentation must therefore be restricted to such elements as will reflect an age of science and machines. Modern men and women do not believe in the Greek ideas of harmony, bal-

Taliesin East by Frank Lloyd Wright. A famous example of the functional style, with the pattern of the house conforming to the natural surroundings.

Contrasting Architectural Styles in Germany Between the Wars. Left: The Bauhaus by Walter Gropius. This school in Dessau, Germany, is a starkly functional prototype of the interwar "international style." Right: The Chancellery in Berlin by Albert Speer. Note the massive qualities of the Nazi state style.

ance, and restraint or in the medieval virtues of piety and chivalry, but in power, efficiency, speed, and comfort. These are the ideals which should find a place in architecture.

The functional style of building construction is one of the most significant architectural developments since the Renaissance. Among all of the styles which have been adopted during the last 300 years, it is the only one that is really original. Known also as modern architecture or the international style, it is the best approach that has yet been made to an efficient use of the tremendous mechanical and scientific resources of the contemporary world. It permits an honest application of new materials—chromium, glass, steel, concrete—and tempts the builder's ingenuity in devising others. One of the pioneer practitioners of the functional or international style was the German Walter Gropius (1883–1969), who, in 1919, established a school—the *Bauhaus*—to serve as a center for the theory and practice of modern architecture. Gropius and his followers declared, as good functionalists, that the aesthetic content of a building can only be expressed legitimately in terms of its purpose.

Gropius was one of the multitude of German intellectuals—both Jewish and non-Jewish—to leave their country after Hitler's rise to

The significance of functional architecture

power. Nazism had its own cultural aesthetic, which it imposed upon Germany. Functionalism, which celebrated the qualities of material, line, and proportion, had no place in a totalitarian regime, where the arts were obliged to advertise the virtues of the state, its tradition, and the aspirations of its people. Instead of Gropius, Hitler had Albert Speer, an architect of unimpressive talents, who produced for him grandiose designs whose vacuous pretentiousness was an unconscious parody of Nazi ideology. Atonality in music was banished along with functionalism in architecture, to be replaced by the mystical and heroic nationalism of Wagner.

Art was an important part of the new and cultural arm of totalitarianism: propaganda. Never before had so many of the world's people been able to read. Nineteenth- and twentieth-century governments had encouraged literacy, fearing an ignorant working class as a revolutionary threat. Now totalitarian regimes used education unashamedly as a means of indoctrination. Books critical of the state were banned, their places on school and library shelves taken by others specifically written to glorify the present leadership. Youth programs instructed children in the virtues of discipline and loyalty to the state. Mass gymnastic displays suggested the ease with which well-trained bodies could be made to respond to the military needs of the nation. Propagandizing was made more effective by the advent of mass-circulation publishing, the radio, and the motion picture. Newspapers which printed only what the state wanted printed reached a wider audience than ever before. Party political broadcasts, beamed into homes or blared through loudspeakers in town squares, by their constant repetitiveness made people begin to accept—if not believe—what they knew to be untrue. Films could transform German youths into Aryan gods and goddesses, as they could Russian collective farms into a worker's paradise. Sergei Eisenstein (1898–1948) the Russian director, rewrote Russian history on film to serve the ends of the Soviet state. Hitler commissioned the filmmaker Leni Riefenstahl to record a political rally staged by herself and Speer. The film, entitled *Triumph of the Will,* was a visual hymn to the Nordic race and the Nazi regime. (And the comedian Charlie Chaplin riposted in his celebrated lampoon, *The Great Dictator,* an enormously successful parody of totalitarian pomposities.)

In Western democracies, although the media were not manipulated by the state as they were elsewhere, their effectiveness as propagandizers was nevertheless recognized and exploited. Advertising became an industry when manufacturers realized the mass markets that newspapers, magazines, and radio represented. Much that was printed and aired was trivialized by writers and editors who feared that serious or difficult material would antagonize the readers or listeners upon whom they depended for their livelihood. This is not to say that the new media were uniformly banal, or that artists and per-

A Scene from John Ford's film of
Steinbeck's *The Grapes of Wrath*

formers were unable to use them to make thoughtful protests. The
film version of Steinbeck's *Grapes of Wrath,* directed by John Ford,
though an exception to the normal run of escapist Hollywood comedies and adventures, was perhaps as stinging an indictment of capitalism as the novel, and it reached far more people. During these years
popular culture, whatever else it was, remained a powerful and alarming new fact of life: powerful in terms of its vast audience; alarming
because of its particular applicability as a means of controlling the
minds of men and women.

SELECTED READINGS

• *Items so designated are available in paperback editions.*

GENERAL

Galbraith, John Kenneth, *The Great Crash, 1929,* Boston, 1955. An enter-
taining and informative account by the celebrated economist.
• Hamilton, George Heard, *Painting and Sculpture in Europe, 1880–1940,* Bal-
timore, 1967. An excellent survey.
Hughes, H. Stuart. *Contemporary Europe: A History,* Englewood Cliffs,
N.J., 1971. A good general text.
Laqueur, W., and G. L. Mosse, eds., *The Left-Wing Intellectuals between the
Wars, 1919–1939,* New York, 1966. Recent essays by modern historians.

• Passmore, John A., *A Hundred Years of Philosophy*, New York, 1968.
• Rothschild, Joseph, *East Central Europe between the Two World Wars*, Seattle, 1975. An authoritative survey; does not include Austria.
  Shapiro, Theda, *Painters and Politics: The European Avant-Garde and Society, 1900–1925*, New York, 1976. An analysis of the political and social attitudes of a revolutionary generation in the arts.

THE SOVIET UNION

  Carr, E. H., *A History of Soviet Russia*, Vols. IV–VII, London, 1950 ff. Comprehensive analysis of the period 1923–26.
• Daniels, Robert U., *The Conscience of the Revolution*, Cambridge, Mass., 1960. Discusses the opposition to Bolshevism in the 1920s.
• Deutscher, Isaac, *The Prophet Unarmed*, London, 1959. Trotsky, 1921–1929.
• ———, *The Prophet Outcast*, London, 1963. Trotsky in exile, 1929–1940.
  ———, *Stalin: A Political Biography*, New York, 1949.
  Fainsod, Merle, *How Russia Is Ruled*, Cambridge, Mass., 1967.
  Nettl, J. P., *The Soviet Achievement*, New York, 1967.

FASCISM

• Bracher, Karl Dietrich, *The German Dictatorship: The Origins, Structure, and Effects of National Socialism*, New York, 1970. A penetrating and exhaustive study of the Nazi state by a political scientist.
• Bullock, Alan, *Hitler: A Study in Tyranny*, rev. ed., New York, 1962. The standard biography.
  Conway, John S., *The Nazi Persecution of the Churches*, London, 1968. A thorough and judicious account.
• Dahrendorf, R., *Society and Democracy in Germany*, Garden City, N.Y., 1967.
  Delzell, Charles F., *Mussolini's Enemies: The Italian Anti-Fascist Resistance*, Princeton, N.J., 1961.
• Eyck, Erich, *History of the Weimar Republic*, 2 vols., Cambridge, Mass., 1962. A sympathetic account by a prominent German liberal.
• Gatzke, Hans, *Stresemann and the Rearmament of Germany*, Baltimore, 1954. Details German rearmament in violation of the Treaty of Versailles and secret agreements between Weimar Germany and Soviet Russia in the 1920s.
  Gay, Peter, *Weimar Culture: The Outsider as Insider*, New York, 1968. Examines the failure of commitment to the Weimar Republic by German intellectuals.
  Kirkpatrick, Ivone, *Mussolini: A Study in Power*, New York, 1964. The standard biography.
• Mosse, G. L., ed., *Nazi Culture*, New York, 1966.
• Nolte, Ernst, *The Three Faces of Facism*, New York, 1966. A difficult but rewarding study of Germany, Italy, and France, from a philosophical perspective.
• Schoenbaum, David, *Hitler's Social Revolution: Class and Status in Nazi Germany, 1933–39*, Garden City, N.Y., 1966.
• Waite, R. G. L., *The Psychopathic God*, New York, 1977. An intriguing if not always successful attempt to explain Hitler's character and actions with the aid of psychoanalytic theory.

- ———, *Vanguard of Nazism: The Free Corps Movement in Postwar Germany, 1918–1923,* New York, 1952. An important monograph which describes the mentality of violence within elements of German society.
- Weiss, John, *The Fascist Tradition: Radical Right-Wing Extremism in Modern Europe,* New York, 1967.
- Wiskemann, Elizabeth, *Fascism in Italy: Its Development and Influence,* New York, 1969.
- Zeman, Z. A. B., *Nazi Propaganda,* New York, 1973. Examines an important bulwark of the authoritarian state.

THE DEMOCRACIES

Bullock, Alan, *The Life and Times of Ernest Bevin: Trade Union Leader, 1881–1940,* London, 1960. An excellent study of the British trade unionist and the political and social history of Britain between the wars.
- Burns, James M., *Roosevelt: The Lion and the Fox,* New York, 1956.
Curtis, Michael, *Three Against the Third Republic: Sorel, Barres, and Maurras,* Princeton, N.J., 1959. The attack from the French Right.
- Graves, Robert, and Alan Hodge, *The Long Week-End: A Social History of Great Britain, 1918–1939,* London, 1940. A striking portrait of England in the interwar years.
- Greene, N., *From Versailles to Vichy: The Third Republic, 1919–1940,* New York, 1970.
Harrod, R. F., *The Life of John Maynard Keynes,* New York, 1951.
Hughes, H. Stuart, *The Obstructed Path: French Social Thought in the Years of Desperation, 1930–1960,* New York, 1968.
Joll, J., *Intellectuals in Politics: Three Biographical Essays,* London, 1960. Léon Blum, Walther Rathenau, and Filippo Marinetti.
- Leuchtenburg, W. E., *Franklin Roosevelt and the New Deal, 1932–1940,* New York, 1964. A good introduction.
Lorwin, V. R., *The French Labor Movement,* Cambridge, Mass., 1954.
Lyman, Richard W., *The First Labour Government,* London, 1957.
- Mitchell, Broadus, *Depression Decade: From New Era through New Deal, 1929 to 1941,* New York, 1947.
Mowat, Charles L., *Britain between the Wars, 1918–1940,* Chicago, 1955. A detailed political and social history, especially valuable for its extensive biographical footnotes.
- Schlesinger, Arthur M., Jr., *The Age of Roosevelt,* 3 vols., Boston, 1957–1964. An extensive biography by an admirer of Roosevelt.
- Taylor, A. J. P., *English History, 1914–1945,* New York, 1965. The best survey of the period. Witty, provocative, insightful.
- Thomson, David, *Democracy in France since 1870,* rev. ed., New York, 1969.
- Weber, Eugen, *Action Française: Royalism and Reaction in Twentieth-Century France,* Stamford, Conn., 1962. The best study of this protofascist movement.

SOURCE MATERIALS

Cole, G. D. H., and M. I. Cole, *The Condition of Britain,* London, 1937. A contemporary analysis by English socialists.

Greene, Nathanael, comp., *European Socialism Since World War I,* Chicago, 1971. A collection of contemporary accounts.

Hitler, Adolf, *Mein Kampf,* New York, 1962. Hitler's autobiography, written in 1925. Contains his version of history and his vision for the future. Especially important for his insight into the nature of the masses and the use of propaganda.

Noakes, Jeremy, and Geoffrey Pridham, *Documents on Nazism, 1919–1945,* New York, 1975. An excellent sourcebook. Comprehensive and annotated.

• Speer, Albert, *Inside the Third Reich,* New York, 1964. The self-serving but informative memoirs of one of the leaders of Nazi Germany.

Tucker, Robert C., ed., *The Great Purge Trial,* New York, 1965. An annotated edition of the transcript of one of the Soviet ''show-trials'' that so puzzled Western observers.

• Woolf, Virginia, *Three Guineas,* New York, 1938. The brilliant analytical work in which Woolf takes apart both the motivation for war and the oppression of women in modern society.

Chapter 35

WORLD WAR II

The President [Roosevelt] and the Prime Minister [Churchill], after a complete survey of the world situation, are more than ever determined that peace can come to the world only by a total elimination of German and Japanese war power. This involves the simple formula of placing the objective of this war in terms of an unconditional surrender by Germany, Italy, and Japan.

—Franklin D. Roosevelt, Casablanca, January 24, 1943

In September 1939, Europe plunged again into war. The peace of 1919–1920 turned out to be no more than an armistice; once more millions of people were locked in a conflict that surpassed any that had occurred heretofore. As had happened in 1914–1918, the new struggle soon became worldwide. Although World War II was not merely a continuation of, or a sequel to, World War I, the similarity in causes and characteristics was more than superficial. Both were precipitated by threats to the balance of power, and both were conflicts between peoples, entire nations, rather than between governments. On the other hand, there were notable differences. The methods of warfare in World War II had little in common with those of the earlier conflict. Trench warfare was largely superseded by bombing and by sudden aerial (Blitzkrieg) attacks, with highly mobile armies, on both civilian populations and military installations. Because so many were now vulnerable to the ravages of warfare, it seems safe to say that the distinction between soldiers and civilians was more completely obliterated in the second conflict than it had been in the first.

A comparison of the two world wars

1. THE CAUSES OF THE WAR

The causes of World War II were related to the failure of the peace terms of 1919–1920. Those terms, while understandable in view of the passions and hatreds engendered by the First World War, created almost as many problems as they solved. By yielding to the demands of the victors for annexation of territory and the creation of satellite states, the peacemakers sowed new seeds of bitterness and conflict. By proclaiming the principle of self-determination while acquiescing in the distribution of national minorities behind alien frontiers, the treaties raised expectations while at the same time frustrating them. Perhaps most important, by imposing harsh terms on Germany, the treaty-makers gave the Germans what seemed to many to be legitimate grievances, by depriving them of their rightful share of international power and saddling them with the entire burden of war "guilt."

The role of power politics in causing World War II is undeniable. Although Woodrow Wilson and other sponsors of the League of Nations had acclaimed the league as a means of eliminating power struggles, it did nothing of the sort. It merely substituted a new and more precarious balance for the old. The signatures on the peace treaties had scarcely dried when the victors began the construction of new alliances to maintain their supremacy. A neutralized zone consisting of the Baltic states, Poland, and Rumania was created as a buffer against Soviet Russia. A Little Entente composed of Czechoslovakia, Yugoslavia, and Rumania was established to prevent a revival of Austrian power. These combinations, together with a Franco-Belgian alliance and a Franco-Polish alliance, would also serve to isolate Germany. Thus the old system of power politics was reconstituted along essentially the same lines it had had before World War I. Even the league itself was fundamentally an alliance of the victors against the vanquished. That there would be fears and anxieties over a disturbance of the new power arrangement could hardly be unexpected. The first sign of such a disturbance appeared in 1922 when Germany and Russia negotiated the Treaty of Rapallo. Though disguised as a mere trade agreement, it opened the way for political and, according to some accounts, even military collaboration between the two states.

Diplomats made various attempts to preserve or restore international amity during the 1920s and 1930s. Some saw in disarmament the most promising means of achieving their purpose. Accordingly, a succession of conferences was called in the hope of limiting at least the competition in armaments. The results were negligible. In 1925 representatives of the chief European powers met at Locarno and acted on the suggestion of the German foreign minister, Gustav Stresemann, that Germany and France pledge themselves to respect the Rhine frontiers as established in the Versailles treaty. They agreed also that they would never go to war against each other except in "legitimate defense." More widely celebrated than the Locarno Agreements was the Pact of Paris, or Kellogg-Briand Pact of 1928. Its purpose was to outlaw war as an international crime. Eventually, nearly all the nations of the world signed an agreement renouncing war as "an instrument

Members of the Council of the League of Nations. In the front row, from the right, are Chamberlain of Britain, Vandervelde of Belgium, Stresemann of Germany, and Briand of France

of national policy" and providing that the settlement of international disputes "of whatever nature or of whatever origin" should never be sought "except by peaceful means." Neither the Locarno Agreements nor the Pact of Paris was much more than a pious gesture. The signatory nations adopted them with so many reservations and exceptions in favor of "vital interests" that they could never be effective instruments for preserving peace. Had the League of Nations they set up been better organized, it might have relieved some of the tensions and prevented clashes between nations still unwilling to relinquish their absolute sovereignty. It was not a league of all nations, however. Both Germany and Russia were excluded, at least for a time, thereby pushing them into the role of outsiders.

Economic conditions were a third important cause of the outbreak of war. The huge reparations imposed upon the Germans, and the French occupation of much of Germany's industrial heartland, helped, as we have seen, to retard Germany's economic recovery and bring on the debilitating inflation of the 1920s. The depression of the 1930s contributed to the coming of the war in several ways. It intensified economic nationalism. Baffled by problems of unemployment and business stagnation, governments resorted to high tariffs in an attempt to preserve the home market for their own producers. The depression was also responsible for a marked increase in armaments production, which was seen as a means of reducing unemployment. Despite the misgivings of some within the governments of Britain and France, Germany was allowed to rearm. Armaments expansion, on a large scale, was first undertaken by Germany about 1935. The results in a few years were such as to dazzle the rest of the world. Unemployment disappeared and business boomed. It would have been too much to expect that other dissatisfied nations would not copy the German example. Similarly, the depression resulted in a new wave of militant expansionism directed toward the conquest of neighboring territories as

Economic conditions

The Krupp Shipworks in Germany. Seen here are German submarines in the final stages of assembly.

a means of solving economic problems. Japan took the lead in 1931 with the invasion of Manchuria. The decline of Japanese exports of raw silk and cotton cloth meant that the nation as a consequence was unable to pay for needed imports of coal, iron, and other minerals. Japanese militarists were thus furnished with a convenient pretext for seizing Manchuria, where supplies of these commodities could then be purchased for Japanese currency. Mussolini, in part to distract the Italians from the domestic problems brought on by economic depression, invaded and annexed Ethiopia in 1936. Finally, the depression was primarily responsible for the triumph of Nazism, whose expansionist policies contributed directly to the outbreak of war.

Nationalism

Nationalism was a further cause of the general discontent that helped increase the chances for world war. In eastern Europe, national and ethnic minorities remained alienated from the sovereign states into which the treaty-makers had placed them. This was particularly the case of the Sudetenland Germans, who had been included in the newly created state of Czechoslovakia. That country could in fact boast no national majority, including as it did Czechs, Slovaks, Poles, Ruthenians, and Hungarians, as well as Germans. Although it possessed an enlightened policy of minority self-government, the patchwork state of Czechoslovakia remained unstable. And its instability was to prove a key factor as the tensions mounted in the late 1930s.

Appeasement

A final cause of war was the policy of "appeasement" which was pursued by the Western democracies in the face of German, Italian, and Japanese aggression. The appeasers' strategy was grounded in three commonly held assumptions. The first was that the outbreak of another war was unthinkable. With the memory of the slaughter of 1918 fresh in their minds, many in the West embraced pacifism, or at any rate adopted an attitude that kept them from realistically addressing the implications of Nazi and fascist policies and programs. Secondly, many in Britain and the United States argued, as the years passed, that Germany had been mistreated in the Versailles treaty, that the Germans had legitimate grievances which should be acknowledged and resolved. Finally, the appeasers were, for the most part, staunch anticommunists. They believed that by assisting Germany to regain its former military and economic power, they were constructing a bulwark to halt the westward advance of Soviet communism. When Japan invaded Manchuria, the West refused to impose sanctions against the Japanese through the League of Nations, arguing that Japan, too, could serve as a counterweight to Russia.

Hitler took advantage of this generally tolerant attitude to advance the expansionist ambitions of Germany. As the country rearmed, Hitler played upon his people's sense of shame and betrayal, proclaiming their right to regain their former power within the world. In 1933, he removed Germany from the League of Nations—and thus from any obligation to adhere to its declarations. In 1935 Hitler tore up the disarmament provisions of the Treaty of Versailles, announcing the revival of conscription and the return to universal military training. In 1936 he repudiated the Locarno Agreements and invaded the Rhineland. Britain and France did nothing to stop him, as they had done nothing to prevent Mussolini's invasion and conquest of Ethiopia the previous year. *Hitler's aggressive moves*

In 1936 civil war broke out in Spain; a series of weak republican governments had proved unable to prevent the country's political disintegration. Although they had signed a pact of nonintervention with the other Western powers, Hitler and Mussolini both sent troops and equipment to assist the forces of the rebel fascist commander, Francisco Franco. Russia countered with aid to the communist troops serving under the banner of the Spanish republic. Again, Britain and France did nothing. The Spanish Civil War lasted three years, with the forces of the fascists finally victorious over those of the republicans. The conflict engaged the commitment of many young European and American leftists and intellectuals, who saw it as a test of the West's determination to resist totalitarianism. The fighting was brutal; aerial bombardment of civilians and troops was employed for the first time on a large scale. Hence the Spanish war has often been seen as a "dress rehearsal" for the much larger struggle that was shortly to follow. *The Spanish Civil War*

In March of 1938, Hitler annexed Austria, declaring it his intention to bring all Germans into his Reich. Once more, there was no official reaction from the West. Hitler's next target was the Sudetenland in Czechoslovakia. With Austria now a part of Germany, Czechoslovakia was almost entirely surrounded by its hostile and rapacious neighbor. Hitler declared that the Sudetenland was a natural part of the Reich and that he intended to occupy it. The British prime minister, Neville Chamberlain, determined to negotiate, but on Hitler's terms. On September 28, Hitler agreed to meet with Chamberlain, Premier Édouard Daladier of France, and Mussolini in a four-power *Munich and after*

The Munich Conference, 1938. Left: Prime Minister Chamberlain of Britain and Hitler during the Munich conference. Right: Chamberlain addressing a crowd on his return from the Munich conference. In his speech, September 30, 1938, he proclaimed that "peace in our time" would result from the agreement.

conference in Munich. The result was another capitulation by France and Britain. During the next few months Hitler not only annexed the Sudetenland (as the Munich agreement had permitted him to do), but he annihilated the entire Czech republic. This action intensified the crisis. The Soviet government was convinced that the Munich settlement was a plot by Britain and France to save their own skins by diverting Nazi expansion eastward. In August 1939, Stalin and his colleagues, having failed to persuade Britain and France to ally with them on their terms, entered into a pact of their own with the Nazi government. Its effect was to give Hitler the green light for an attack on Poland. There was an understanding that the two dictators would divide Poland between them. In going to Munich, Britain and France had thought of their own interests; Russia would now look after its own.

See color map following page 1088

2. THE OUTBREAK OF HOSTILITIES

Beginning of the war

Following the extinction of Czechoslovakia, Hitler demanded the abolition of the Polish Corridor, a narrow strip of territory connecting Poland with the Baltic Sea. The corridor contained a large German population, which Hitler declared must be reunited with the Fatherland. Convinced finally that Hitler's appetite for power was insatiable, Chamberlain announced that Britain would give Poland armed assistance. Soon afterward he declared that his government would come to the aid of any country that felt itself menaced by Hitler's ambitions. In the weeks that followed, both Britain and France gave definite guarantees not only to Poland but to Greece, Rumania, and Turkey. Hitler, judging Britain and France by past performance, believed these pledges were worthless. With the Soviets drawn into his camp, he expected that Poland would quickly capitulate, and that the Western allies would back down once more as they had done at Munich. When Poland stood firm, Hitler decided to attack. On September 1, 1939, a long column of German tanks crossed the Polish border. Upon learning of the attack, Britain and France sent a joint warning to Germany to cease its aggression. To this there was no reply. September 3 brought a radio announcement by Neville Chamberlain that Britain was at war with Germany. He spoke of the "bitter blow" it was to him that his "long struggle for peace" had failed. He asserted that it was evil the British nation would be fighting against—"brute force, bad faith, injustice, oppression, and persecution." Later the same day France also entered the war.

The conflict with Poland proved to be a brief encounter. In less than three weeks the Polish armies had been routed, Warsaw had been captured, and the chiefs of the Polish government had fled to Rumania. For some months after that the war resolved itself into a kind of siege, a "phony war" or "sitzkrieg," as it was sometimes called. Such fighting as did occur was largely confined to submarine warfare, aerial raids on naval bases, and occasional battles between naval vessels. In the spring of 1940 the sitzkrieg was suddenly transformed into a Blitzkrieg, or "lightning war." The Germans struck blows at Norway, Denmark, Belgium, the Netherlands, and France, conquering them one after another. In France a puppet government loyal to the Germans was established at Vichy under the leadership of the aged World War I hero, Marshal Henri-Philippe Petain.

The "phony war"

Following these conquests the war entered a new stage, the so-called Battle of Britain. Before launching an invasion across the Channel, the Nazis decided to attempt the reduction of Britain's military strength and civilian will by air raids. From August 1940 to June 1941

The Battle of Britain

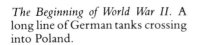

The Beginning of World War II. A long line of German tanks crossing into Poland.

A German V-2 Rocket. Used in the later years of the war, it was the forerunner of the early space launch vehicles.

thousands of planes smashed at British ports, industrial centers, and air defenses throughout the country. Despite the fact that whole sections of cities were laid in ruins and more than 40,000 civilians killed, the British held firm. Winston Churchill had by this time succeeded Neville Chamberlain as prime minister of Britain. A maverick Conservative, who had served in Britain's World War I government as a Liberal, Churchill was not trusted by his party's leadership, particularly since he had been one of the few who had spoken out in favor of British rearmament during the years of appeasement. Now that his warnings had proved true, he was given direction of the war as head of a national government composed of ministers from the Conservative, Liberal, and Labour parties. Churchill, an exceedingly compelling orator, used the radio to persuade his countrymen and women—and the rest of the free world—that Britain must not, and would not, surrender to the Nazis. His friendship with President Roosevelt, and the latter's conviction that the United States must come to Britain's aid, resulted in the shipment of military equipment and ships to the British under the so-called Lend-Lease Act passed by the U.S. Congress in 1941.

Meanwhile, Germany moved eastward into the Balkans, subduing the Rumanians, Hungarians, Bulgarians, and Yugoslavs. The Italians, less successful in their campaigns in Greece and North Africa, required German assistance to accomplish their missions. Scornful of Mussolini's military inadequacies, Churchill called him Hitler's "jackal." Frustrated in his attempt to subjugate Britain, Hitler broke with his erstwhile ally Russia, and turned eastward, on June 22, 1941, with a massive invasion. Before the end of the year his armies had smashed

Left: *London During the Blitz.* This picture conveys a vivid impression of the agony which the British capital suffered during the Battle of Britain, which lasted from August 1940 to June 1941. Behind the tumbling ruins brought down by firebombs is St. Paul's Cathedral. Right: *French Refugees Driven from Their Homes During the Early Years of the Nazi Occupation.*

Pearl Harbor, December 7, 1941. This photo shows American battleships sunk at their moorings, following the Japanese raid on what President Franklin D. Roosevelt declared was "the day that will live in infamy."

their way to the gates of Moscow but never actually succeeded in capturing it.

The war was converted into a global conflict when Japan struck a deadly blow at Pearl Harbor on December 7 of the same year. The Japanese had been involved in a costly war with China since 1937. To wage it successfully they needed the oil, rubber, and extensive food resources of the Netherlands Indies, the Malay Peninsula, and Southeast Asia. They had allied with Germany in 1940. Now, before attacking south, they considered it necessary to lock the back door by crushing American naval and air power on the base of Pearl Harbor. The next day the United States Congress recognized a state of war with Japan, and on December 11 Germany and its allies declared war upon the United States. *Pearl Harbor*

The course of the war was marked by several turning points. The first was the stubborn defense of Moscow by Stalin's armies in November and December 1941. The second was the defeat of the Germans under General Erwin Rommel in North Africa in 1942, which opened the way for the Allied invasion of Italy and the overthrow of Mussolini in the following year. The third was the Battle of Stalingrad in 1943, when the Germans failed in their attempt to cut northern Russia off from the food-producing region of the Ukraine and from the oil resources north and south of the Caucasus. The turning points in the Pacific war came during the spring of 1942 with the defeat by the United States Navy of Japanese forces in the battles of the Coral Sea and of Midway. These defeats spelled the doom of Japanese attempts to capture Australia and the Hawaiian Islands and thereby deprive the United States of advance bases for a counteroffensive against Japan. *The war's turning points*

By the winter of 1944–1945 World War II was nearing its end. On June 6, 1944 (D-Day), Allied forces had crossed the English Channel and landed successfully in northern France. On August 25 Paris was liberated. In September advance detachments drove to the Rhine, and

Left: *D-Day.* Cargo ships are seen pouring supplies ashore during the invasion of France. Balloon barrages float overhead to protect the ships from low-flying enemy planes. Right: *Signing the German Surrender, May 7, 1945.*

End of the war in Europe

eventually whole armies penetrated to the heart of Germany, an advance necessitated by Hitler's refusal to surrender unconditionally. At the same time, Soviet troops were approaching from the east. On April 21, 1945, they hammered their way into the suburbs of Berlin. During the next ten days a savage battle raged amid the ruins and heaps of rubble. On May 2 the heart of the city was captured, and the Soviet red banner flew from the Brandenburg Gate. A few hours earlier Adolf Hitler killed himself in the bomb-proof shelter of the Chancellery. On May 8 representatives of the German High Command signed a document of unconditional surrender. Peace had come at last to an exhausted Europe after five years and eight months of slaughter.

The concentration camps

It was only then that the world began to learn the extent of German tyranny. When Allied armies opened the concentration camps in Germany and elsewhere in what had been German-occupied Europe, they found the starved, diseased, and brutalized remnants of a total of six million prisoners, those who had been able to survive the ghastly experience of Nazi persecutions. Most of the men, women, and children who had been imprisoned, tortured, and killed, were Jews, although Poles, Russians, gypsies, homosexuals, and other "traitors" to the Reich had been incarcerated, used for forced labor, and executed also.

The atomic bomb; Japan's surrender

The end of the war in the Pacific was delayed for another four months. Victory over the Japanese Empire had to be achieved by savage naval battles and by bloody assaults upon almost impregnable islands. In June 1945, Okinawa was taken, after eighty-two days of desperate fighting. The Americans now had footholds less than 500 miles from the Japanese homeland. The government in Tokyo was nervously anticipating an invasion and calling upon the citizens for supreme endeavors to meet the crisis. On July 26 the heads of the United States, British, and Chinese governments issued a joint proclamation calling upon Japan to surrender or be destroyed. In the absence of a reply the highest officials of the United States government resolved to make use of a new and revolutionary weapon to end the war quickly. This weapon was the atomic bomb, recently developed in secrecy by Allied scientists. Many high military and naval officers contended that use of the bomb was not necessary, on the assumption that Japan was already beaten. Harry Truman, who had succeeded Roosevelt following the latter's death in April 1945, decided otherwise. On August 6, a single atomic bomb was dropped on Hiroshima, completely obliterating about 60 percent of the city. Three days later a second bomb was dropped, this time on Nagasaki. These actions, like the fire-bombing of Dresden and Tokyo, insured that the Allies would share the responsibility for the carnage of the war, and that, unlike the First World War, this one would take a heavy toll of civilian lives. President Truman warned that the United States would continue to use the atom bomb as long as might be necessary to bring Japan to its knees. On August 14, Tokyo transmitted to Washington an unconditional acceptance of Allied demands.

3. THE PEACE SETTLEMENT

The war was over. To fight it, governments had been compelled, to an even greater degree than during the First World War, to mobilize their entire populations. Both sides used mass propaganda techniques to maintain popular commitment to their cause. As Wilson had spoken of a war "to end wars," so the Western leaders promised a peace that would rid the world of conflict. The first statement of Allied objectives in the event of victory was the Atlantic Charter,

The Atlantic Charter and the United Nations declaration

Victims of the Nazi Concentration Camp at Belsen, Germany. Photographed in 1945.

View of Hiroshima After the First Atom Bomb Was Dropped, August 6, 1945. This photo, taken one month later, shows the utter devastation of the city. Only a few steel and concrete buildings remained intact.

issued by Roosevelt and Churchill on August 14, 1941. Its essential principles were as follows: (1) no territorial changes that do not accord with the wishes of the people concerned; (2) the right of all peoples to choose the form of government under which they will live; (3) all states to enjoy access, on equal terms, to the trade and raw materials of the world; (4) freedom to traverse the seas without hindrance; (5) disarmament of all nations that threaten aggression. The Atlantic Charter acquired a broad significance when it was reaffirmed by the United Nations declaration on January 2, 1942. Twenty-six nations signed this declaration, including Great Britain, the United States, the Soviet Union, and the Republic of China. Subsequently about fourteen others added their signatures. The declaration resembled Wilson's Fourteen Points: both were ringing affirmations of international peace and freedom; both were designed to bolster Allied morale; and both fell victim to the realities of power politics.

The Cairo Declaration

As the war progressed, high officials of the leading United Nations met in various conferences for the purpose of determining the conditions of peace. The first of outstanding importance was the conference that met in Cairo in November 1943, to discuss the fate of the Japanese Empire. The participants were Roosevelt, Churchill, and the Chinese leader, Generalissimo Chiang Kai-Shek. They agreed that all of the territories taken by Japan from China, with the exception of Korea, were to be restored to the Chinese Republic. Korea was to become free and independent. They agreed, further, that Japan was to be stripped of all the islands in the Pacific which it had seized or occupied since 1914 and of "all other territories which she had taken by violence or greed." What disposition was to be made of these islands and territories was not specified.

The second important conference to determine the conditions of peace met at Yalta, in the Crimea, in February 1945. This time the chief participants were Roosevelt, Churchill, and Stalin. A formal report issued at the close of the conference declared that the Big Three had agreed upon plans for the unconditional surrender of Germany, upon methods of controlling Germany and its allies after the war, and upon the establishment of a United Nations Organization to keep the peace. In addition, it was announced that Poland would surrender its eastern provinces to Russia and be compensated by "substantial accessions of territory" in the north and west—to be taken, of course, from Germany. The existing government of Poland, set up under Soviet auspices, was to be reorganized with the inclusion of democratic leaders from among the Poles. The government of Yugoslavia was also to be broadened in similar fashion. Regarding the Far East, it was agreed that Russia should enter the war against Japan and receive as its reward all the territories taken from it by Japan in the Russo-Japanese war of 1904–1905.

The Yalta agreement reflected the idealism of the Atlantic Charter in its provision for a United Nations. It also foreshadowed the tension between East and West which in a few years, would take the shape of a "cold war" between Russia and its political satellites, on the one side, and the Western powers, on the other. Stalin, a determined power politician, was anxious to protect Russian interests. Hence his insistence on a Polish settlement that would insure a strong, pro-Soviet bulwark against Germany. Although Stalin promised free elections there, he refused to agree to an international commission to supervise them.

The surrender of Germany required yet another conference of the victorious powers. On July 17, 1945, Stalin, Churchill, and Truman, met in Potsdam, a suburb of Berlin. Before the Potsdam Conference had finished its work, Churchill had been replaced by Clement Attlee,

The Yalta agreement

The implications of the Yalta agreement

The Yalta Conference. Churchill, Molotov, Secretary of State Stettinius, at the left, and Stalin, in the center, with glasses raised in a toast. Roosevelt is also to Stalin's left.

The Potsdam Conference. Churchill, a cigar in his mouth, is seated in the back to the left; Stalin is at the right; Truman is seated with his back to the camera.

The Potsdam agreement

the new Labour prime minister of Great Britain. The most important provisions of the formal declaration, issued on August 2, were as follows: (1) the territory formerly known as East Prussia was to be divided into two parts, the northern part to go to the Soviet Union, and the southern part to be assigned to Poland; (2) Poland was to receive the former free city of Danzig; (3) all German territory east of the Oder and Neisse rivers would be administered by Poland, pending a final settlement; (4) the military power of Germany would be totally destroyed; and (5) Germany would be divided into four occupation zones, to be governed, respectively, by the Soviet Union, Great Britain, the United States, and France. In November 1945, a trial of major Nazi leaders, conducted by an inter-Allied tribunal, began in Nuremberg, Germany. In September of the following year, eighteen of the twenty-two defendants were found guilty of "war crimes," receiving sentences ranging from ten-years' imprisonment to death.

The peace treaties

After the end of the war the victorious states drafted peace treaties with Japan and with Germany's satellites. The treaty with Japan deprived the Japanese of all the territory they had acquired since 1854—in other words, their entire overseas empire. They gave up the southern half of Sakhalin Island and the Kuril Islands to Soviet Russia, and the Bonins and Ryukyus to control by the United States. They also renounced all rights to Formosa, which was left in a status still undefined. They yielded to the United States the right to continue maintaining military installations in Japan until the latter was able to defend itself. The treaty went into effect in April 1952, against the opposition of the Russians, who had hoped that Japan would be crippled by more drastic punishments and thereby left an easy convert to communism.

As in the case of the Versailles treaty one of the most significant elements in the World War II settlement was its provision for an international organization. The old League of Nations had failed to avert the outbreak of war in 1939, and in April 1946 it was formally dissolved. Allied statesmen had long recognized the need for a new organization. In February 1945, they agreed at Yalta that a conference to implement that need should be convoked for April 25 in San Francisco. Despite the sudden death of Roosevelt two weeks earlier, the conference met as scheduled. A charter was adopted on June 26, providing for a world organization to be known as the United Nations and to be founded upon the principle of "the sovereign equality of all peace-loving states." Its important agencies were to be (1) a General Assembly composed of representatives of all the member states; (2) a Security Council composed of representatives of the United States, Great Britain, the Soviet Union, the Republic of China, and France, with permanent seats, and of six other states chosen by the General Assembly to fill the nonpermanent seats; (3) a Secretariat consisting of a secretary-general and a staff of subordinates; (4) an Economic and Social Council composed of eighteen members chosen by the General Assembly; (5) a Trusteeship Council; and (6) an International Court of Justice.

Establishment of the United Nations

Although the United Nations has failed to live up to the hopes of its founders, it continues to function as the world's longest-lived international assembly of nations. By far the most important functions of the new organization were assigned by the charter to the Security Council. This agency has the "primary responsibility for the maintenance of international peace and security." It has authority to investigate any dispute between nations, to recommend methods for settlement, and, if necessary to preserve the peace, to employ diplomatic or economic measures against an aggressor. If, in its judgment, these have proved, or are likely to prove, inadequate, it may "take such action by air, naval, or land forces" as may be required to maintain or restore international order. The member states are required by the charter to make available to the Security Council, on its call, armed forces for the maintenance of peace.

The Security Council

The Security Council was so organized as to give almost a monopoly of authority to its permanent members. It was the belief of the Big Three who assembled at Yalta, and of President Roosevelt especially, that the peace of the world depended upon harmony among the states primarily responsible for winning the war. Accordingly, they agreed that when the Security Council should be set up, no action of any kind could be taken without the unanimous consent of Great Britain, France, the United States, the Republic of China, the Soviet Union, and two other members besides. This absolute veto given to each of

The veto power of the Big Five

the principal states had none of the hoped-for effects. Instead of bolstering the peace of the world, its chief result was to cripple the council and to render it helpless in the face of emergencies. The primary cause of this was the growth of distrust between Soviet Russia and the West.

Other agencies of the U.N.

The remaining agencies of the U.N. were given a wide variety of functions. The Secretariat, composed of a secretary-general and a numerous staff, is chiefly an administrative authority. Its duties, though, are by no means routine, for the secretary-general may bring to the attention of the Security Council any matter which, in his opinion, may threaten international peace. The functions of the Economic and Social Council are the most varied of all. Composed of eighteen members elected by the General Assembly, it has authority to initiate studies and make recommendations with respect to international social, economic, health, educational, cultural, and related matters, and may perform services within such fields at the request of U.N. members. Under its jurisdiction are such specialized agencies as the World Health Organization (WHO), which works to control epidemics and to assist underdeveloped nations in stamping out cholera, typhus, and veneral disease, and in raising standards of health and sanitation; and the Food and Agriculture Organization (FAO), which seeks to promote increases in food production by finding remedies for agricultural depressions, for plant and animal diseases and insect pests, and by projecting plans for mechanizing small farms and for the more efficient distribution of food.

Failures of the U.N.

During the first three decades the work of these agencies helped the U.N. achieve a modestly impressive record of accomplishment. But against its successes must be recorded major failures as well. The U.N. failed in its efforts to establish control of nuclear weapons. And it was powerless in the face of any determined effort by a major power to have its own way, as in the case of the Soviet suppression of a revolt in Hungary in 1956; or the massive intervention by the United States in Vietnam. If the United Nations acted upon occasion to defuse potentially explosive world situations, it failed to achieve the lofty peace-making and peace-keeping goals set for it by its ambitious and idealistic founders.

SELECTED READINGS

• *Items so designated are available in paperback editions.*
  Aron, Raymond, *The Century of Total War,* New York, 1954.
  Carr, E. H., *The Twenty-Years Crisis,* London, 1942. Stimulating, though somewhat dogmatic.
• Carr, Raymond, *The Spanish Tragedy: The Civil War in Perspective,* London, 1977. A thoughtful introduction to the Spanish Civil War and the evolution of Franco's Spain.

- Churchill, Winston S., *The Second World War*, 6 vols., London, 1948–1954. His history and apologia. Particularly useful is Volume I, *The Gathering Storm*.
- Divine, Robert A., *Roosevelt and World War II*, Baltimore, 1969. A diplomatic history.
- Feis, Herbert, *Churchill-Roosevelt-Stalin: The War They Waged and the Peace They Sought*, Princeton, N.J., 1957.

 Géraud, André, *The Gravediggers of France*, Garden City, N.Y., 1944. A critical and impassioned account of the fall of France.

 Gilbert, Martin, and R. Gott, *The Appeasers*, Boston, 1963.
- Hersey, John, *Hiroshima*, New York, 1946.

 Hilberg, Raul, *The Destruction of the European Jews*, Chicago, 1961. Exhaustive.

 Holborn, Hajo, *The Political Collapse of Europe*, New York, 1951. Examines Europe's position in light of the rise of Russia and the United States as superpowers.
- Jackson, Gabriel, *The Spanish Republic and the Civil War, 1931–1939*, Princeton, N.J., 1965.
- Lafore, Laurence D., *The End of Glory: An Interpretation of the Origins of World War II*, New York, 1970.

 Milward, Alan S., *War, Economy, and Society, 1939–1945*, Berkeley, Calif., 1977. Analyzes the impact of the war on the world economy and the ways in which economic resources of the belligerents determined strategies.

 Neumann, W. L., *After Victory: Churchill, Roosevelt, Stalin, and the Making of the Peace*, New York, 1967.
- Paxton, Robert D., *Vichy France: Old Guard and New Order*, New York, 1972.. A bitter account.
- Payne, Stanley, *The Spanish Revolution*, New York, 1970.
- Reitlinger, G., *The Final Solution: The Attempt to Exterminate the Jews of Europe, 1939–1945*, New York, 1968.

 Snell, J. L., *Illusion and Necessity: The Diplomacy of Global War, 1939–1945*, Boston, 1963.
- Taylor, A. J. P., *The Origins of the Second World War*, New York, 1962. A controversial but provocative attempt to prove that Hitler did not want a world war.
- Wright, Gordon, *The Ordeal of Total War, 1939–1945*, New York, 1968. Particularly good on the domestic response to war and the mobilization of the resources of the modern state.

SOURCE MATERIALS

- Bloch, Marc, *Strange Defeat: A Statement of Evidence Written in 1940*, London, 1949. An analysis of the fall of France, written by one of France's greatest historians, who later died fighting for the resistance.
- Churchill, Winston, *Churchill in His Own Words: Years of Greatness; The Memorable Wartime Speeches of the Man of the Century*, New York, 1966.
- De Gaulle, Charles, *The Complete War Memoirs*, New York, 1964.

 Noakes, Jeremy, and Geoffrey Pridham, *Documents on Nazism, 1919–1945*, New York, 1975.

Part Seven

THE EMERGENCE OF
WORLD CIVILIZATION

*Western civilization, as we have described and analyzed it, no longer
exists today. Instead, we speak in terms of a world civilization, one that
owes much of its history and many of its most perplexing problems to the
West, but one which is no longer shaped by those few nations that for so
many centuries dominated the globe.*

*The great powers of the nineteenth century—Britain, France, and Ger-
many—are powers now only insofar as they have agreed to pool their interests in an all-European Common Market. The mid–twentieth century
superpowers, the United States and the Soviet Union, after two decades of
confrontation, have begun to understand the limitations of their power and
to adjust their expectations accordingly. Power, and with it the attention of
the world, is shifting from the West to the emerging nations of Africa, the
Middle East, Asia, and Latin America. Their vast natural resources are
affording many of them the chance to play the old Western game of power politics, and in a world arena wider than ever before. The equally vast dimensions
of their internal problems—economic, racial, nutritional, and political—suggest that their solution will have to be worldwide as well. We are all,
as the American designer Buckminster Fuller has said, partners for better or
worse on "spaceship earth."*

The Emergence of World Civilization

THE AMERICAS	INDIA AND THE MIDDLE EAST

1800

Latin American wars of independence, 1808–1826
Independence of Argentina, 1816
Independence of Brazil, 1822
Independence of Mexico, 1822
U.S. Monroe Doctrine, 1823

1850

Great Indian Mutiny, 1857–1858

Empire of Maximilian, 1862–1867
Dominion of Canada established, 1867

Mahatma Gandhi, 1869–1948

Republic of Brazil, 1889

Organization of Indian National Congress, 1885
Jawaharlal Nehru, 1889–1964

1900

Organization of Australian Commonwealth, 1901

Madero Revolution in Mexico, 1911

New Constitution in Mexico, 1917

Amritsar Massacre (India), 1919
Intensification of Indian nationalism, 1919–1947
Republic of Turkey proclaimed, 1923
Mustafa Kemal Atatürk, president of Turkey, 1922–1938

Perón regime in Argentina, 1946–1955

Independence of India and Pakistan, 1947
State of Israel proclaimed, 1948

1950

Egypt becomes a republic, 1952–1953
Suez crisis, 1956

Establishment of Castro regime in Cuba, 1959
Military dictatorship in Brazil, 1964–

Second Turkish Republic, 1961

Indira Gandhi prime minister of India, 1966–1977; 1980–

Separatist movement in Quebec, 1967–

Six-Day War, 1967
ASEAN, 1967

Military dictatorship in Chile, 1973–

India-Pakistan war, 1971
Republic of Bangladesh, 1972
"Yom Kippur War," 1973

Panama Canal treaties, 1977
Revolutions in Nicaragua and El Salvador, 1979

Egyptian-Israeli peace treaty, 1979
Revolution in Iran, deposing the Shah, 1979
Soviet military intervention in Afghanistan, 1979–

1980

THE FAR EAST	AFRICA	
	Expansion of East African trade, 1800–1875	**1800**
	Sierra Leone founded, 1808	
	Liberia founded, 1821	
	British consulates in coastal states, 1830–1860	
	Exploration of interior of continent, 1830–1875	
Anglo-Chinese War (Opium War), 1839–1842	Decline of slave trade, 1840–1863	
		1850
Taiping Rebellion, 1852–1864		
Opening of Japan, 1854		
Sun Yat-sen, 1866–1925		
Meiji Restoration in Japan, 1867–1868	Opening of Suez Canal, 1869	
	Destruction of Zulu empire, 1879	
Adoption of constitution in Japan, 1889		
Sino-Japanese War, 1894–1895		
Boxer Uprising, 1900	Boer War, 1899–1902	**1900**
Russo-Japanese War, 1904–1905	Union of South Africa, 1909	
Revolution in China, 1911		
Dictatorship of Yüan Shih-k'ai, 1914–1916		
Era of warlords in China, 1916–1928		
Nationalist regime in China, 1928–1949		
Triumph of militarists in Japan, 1936		
War in Far East, 1937–1945		
Vietnam War, French phase, 1947–1954	Apartheid policy in South Africa, 1948–	
Communist regime in China, 1949–	Independence of Libya, 1949	
Independence of Indonesia, 1949		
Korean War, 1950–1953	Mau Mau revolts in Kenya, 1952–1958	**1950**
Bandung Conference, 1955	Algerian war of independence, 1954–1962	
	Conflict in the Congo, 1960	
Vietnam War, American phase, 1963–1973	Organization of African Unity, 1963–	
Great Proletarian Cultural Revolution in China, 1966–1969	Civil war in Nigeria, 1967–1970	
	Guerrilla war in Rhodesia, 1972–1980	
Vietnam-Cambodia war, 1978–1979		
Chinese invasion of Vietnam, 1979		
	Rhodesia becomes independent state of Zimbabwe, 1980	**1980**

The Emergence of World Civilization—Europe and the Superpowers

	POLITICS	SCIENCE & INDUSTRY
1945		
	Truman Doctrine, 1947 Communist regimes established in eastern Europe, 1947–1948 Marshall Plan, 1948 Division of Germany, 1949 NATO, 1949 Korean war, 1950–1953	
	Death of Stalin, 1953	Hydrogen bomb, 1952 Discovery of polio vaccine, 1953 Discovery of DNA, 1953
	Hungarian revolt, 1956 Suez crisis, 1956	
		Sputnik launched, 1957
1960		
	Berlin wall, 1961	
	Cuban missile crisis, 1962 Assassination of John F. Kennedy, 1963 War in Vietnam, 1964–1975 (U.S. phase) Assassination of Malcolm X, 1965	
	Assassination of Martin Luther King, Jr., 1968	Manned U.S. spacecraft lands on moon, 1969
1970		Advent of automation, 1970s
	First SALT agreements signed, 1972	

ECONOMICS & SOCIETY   ARTS & LETTERS

Abstract expressionism in art, mid-1940s
Albert Camus, *The Plague*, 1947

Simone de Beauvoir, *The Second Sex*, 1949–1950

Samuel Beckett, *Waiting for Godot*, 1952

European Common Market established, 1958

Lorraine Hansberry, *A Raisin in the Sun*, 1959
Black civil rights movement, United States,   "Pop" art, 1960s
   1960–1968
Frantz Fanon, *Wretched of the Earth*, 1961
Youth "revolution," 1960s
Women's liberation movement, 1960s–1970s

Arthur Penn, *Bonnie and Clyde*, 1972
Alexsandr Solzhenitsyn, *The Gulag Archipelago*,
   1973

1945

1960

1970

Chapter 36

THE EMERGENCE OF
LATIN AMERICA

What is the oligarchy? It consists of the great landowners—the *"latifun-distas"*—their political and military henchmen, and their financial allies (the bankers and the capitalists, in the old sense of the word). . . . The oligarchs form a true caste, with aristocratic impulses, racist attitudes, and a profound contempt for their own countries.

—Victor Alba, *Alliance without Allies: The Mythology of Progress in Latin America*

The Hemisphere is coming apart. The Monroe Doctrine is dead, and the era of American paternalism is ended.

—O. Edmund Clubb

I. CONQUISTADORES AND COLONISTS OF LATIN AMERICA

By far the oldest civilization in the Western Hemisphere is that of Latin America. Here the first settlements were made by the Spanish and Portuguese explorers and conquerors who followed in the path of Columbus. But centuries before any white men set foot on American soil, Indians in Guatemala, Mexico, and the Andean Highland had developed superior cultures which bore almost all the characteristics of civilizations. Had they not been conquered, they might well have provided the basis for a native cultural growth in Central and South America equal to that of any of the other continents. The reasons for this superiority appear to lie almost exclusively in geographic conditions favorable to the progress of agriculture. The lush fertility and benign climate of the valleys of Central America and the northwest portion of South America made possible the production of surplus food. As a result, population increased rapidly, a diversification of trade and industry occurred, cities and towns multiplied, and

Native civilizations of Latin America

The Public Entry of Cortés into the Aztec Capital. Hernando Cortés arrived in Mexico in 1519 and within four years had overrun the entire area of high culture in central Mexico.

a priestly class came into existence devoted to the cultivation of sacred lore. Such developments facilitated the growth of science and other branches of learning and the invention of new crafts and skills. By contrast, the Indians of the greater part of the United States and Canada were forced to continue their existence as nomads and hunters. Their homelands were either so densely forested or so arid as to make agriculture discouraging and profitless.

The principal discoverers of Latin America—Christopher Columbus, Amerigo Vespucci, Juan de Solis, and Vasco de Balboa—were quickly followed by a horde of conquerors. Best known among them were Hernando Cortés and Francisco Pizarro. Restless, greedy, and zealous for adventure, they endured incredible hardships, dragging their men through jungles and swamps and over snow-capped mountains in quest of plunder. The former won fame of a sort as the subjugator of Mexico and the latter as the conqueror of Peru. At the time they made their conquests both countries were occupied by various peoples in advanced stages of cultural development. Mexico was inhabited by the Aztecs and Mayas, while Peru was the home of the Incas. The Aztecs were relative newcomers on the scene of civilization. They established themselves in central Mexico about the thirteenth century A.D. and founded their capital, Tenochtitlán (Mexico City), a short time later. Their achievements included a system of pictographic writing, some knowledge of astronomy and engineering, an elaborate architecture, and the building of roads and aqueducts. Their capital city had a population of some 200,000. Its streets were paved with stone and were kept scrupulously clean by an efficient public-works department. The ruler of the country was a hereditary monarch whose powers were limited to those of commander of the army and chief justice. Aztec religion can only be described as a maze of superstitions and cruel practices. Its distinguishing feature

Civilized Indians in Latin America: (1) the Aztecs

was the sacrifice of war captives and, on occasions, of Aztecs themselves on the altars of the gods. Pouring out the blood of human beings was believed to be especially effective in winning the divine favor.

Representing higher stages of cultural achievement were the Mayas and Incas. The former originated in Guatemala and Honduras and reached the climax of their progress in the eighth and ninth centuries A.D. About 1000 A.D. most of them migrated to Yucatán and were concentrated there when conquered by the Spaniards. Mayan culture seems to have been developed primarily by a leisure class of nobles and priests. It revealed a high level of progress in many fields. A system of writing, in which some of the symbols apparently had phonetic value, was extensively used for religious purposes. Writing materials included stone, deer skin, and a kind of paper made from the maguey plant. A calendar, with a year of 365 days, enabled the priests to determine lucky and unlucky days and the appropriate periods for planting and harvesting crops. Mathematical calculations were refined to the extent of having a vigesimal system (with twenty instead of ten as the basic unit) and a conception of zero as a device for giving different values to the same number. Notable also was progress in the arts. The Mayas excelled in making gold and silver ornaments and in the erection of truncated pyramids with temples on top. Tastes in personal adornment included the curious practice of filing and chipping teeth to give them sharp points and sometimes inlaying them with precious stones. Beards were removed by a scorching process instead of by shaving. Religion was no more highly developed than that of the Aztecs and included the same barbarities of human sacrifice.

(2) the Mayas

Of more recent origin than the culture of the Mayas was that of the Incas, who were at the zenith of their progress when conquered by the Spaniards. Extending into Ecuador, Bolivia, northern Chile, and

Detail of an Aztec Pyramid in Central Mexico. The serpent was an object of worship for the Aztecs.

Machu Picchu. The "Lost City of the Incas" is located in the Andes Mountains, Peru.

(3) the Incas

northwestern Argentina, the Inca empire had its center in southeastern Peru. It was organized on the basis of collectivist paternalism. All the land belonged to the emperor, to the priests, or to the tribe, and was cultivated by males of the common classes between the ages of twenty-five and fifty. In good years the surplus production was stored by the emperor to provide for his subjects in time of famine. From the produce on its lands the tribe took care of the young and the aged, the disabled and the sick. It was a paradise of security but with little freedom. In intellectual achievements the Incas did not equal the Mayas. They had no system of writing but used knotted strings of many colors to record numbers and sets of facts. On the other hand, they had an extensive knowledge of medicine and surgery and built excellent roads and suspension bridges. They understood also the principles of fertilization and irrigation and knew how to terrace hillsides to prevent erosion.

Division of Latin America between Spain and Portugal

During the sixteenth and seventeenth centuries the entire area of Mexico and Central and South America passed under the domination of Spain and Portugal. Three-fifths of it was taken by Spain, and the remainder probably would have been also, had not the pope intervened in an attempt to give an equal recognition to the claims of both countries. In 1493 he issued a Bull of Demarcation, drawing a line from north to south 100 leagues west of the Azores. All territory that might be discovered east of the line was to belong to Portugal, and everything west of the line to Spain. In 1494 the two countries signed a treaty relocating the line 370 leagues west of the Cape Verde Islands. Portugal thereby acquired a foothold on the eastern bulge of South America, which was later expanded into Brazil.

The methods of colonization and colonial administration followed by both Spain and Portugal were of such a character as to influence profoundly the entire history of Latin America. This was particularly true of Spain, which also set the pattern for her neighboring state since both were united under a common sovereign between 1580 and 1640. The cardinal elements in Spanish colonial policy were despotism and paternalism. The highest authorities in the empire were the viceroys, who ruled as the personal representatives of the Spanish king. At first there were two, one in New Spain, including Mexico and Central America, and the other in Peru. In the eighteenth century two additional viceroyalties were created: New Granada (Panama, Colombia, Venezuela, Ecuador) and La Plata, or Buenos Aires. The viceroys were paid magnificent salaries, amounting at one time to the equivalent of $200,000 a year. The purpose behind such generosity was to prevent corruption, an objective by no means universally attained. At the same time their royal master took precautions to prevent the viceroys from becoming too powerful. The authority they exercised was to be that of the Spanish crown, not their own. For this reason they had to tolerate the existence of an advisory council, or *audiencia,* which also served as a court of appeal against their decisions. Members of the *audiencia* had the right to communicate with the king regarding the acts of the viceroy without the latter's knowledge. At the end of his term, and occasionally during it, the viceroy must submit to a searching inquiry or investigation in which a royal judge heard the complaints of all and sundry as to official misconduct.

As an adjunct to despotic rule in the colonies, the Spanish kings made use of the Church. The priests gave valuable help in teaching the population to obey the king and his agents and in opposing new ideas and expressions of discontent. In almost any emergency the hierarchy could be counted upon to give loyal support to the govern-

Spanish colonial policy

The Church as an arm of the government

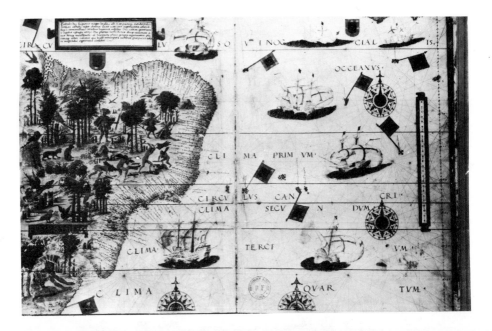

Portuguese Chart of the South Atlantic. Miller Atlas, 1519.

ment. By the middle of the sixteenth century the Inquisition had been extended to Latin America as an instrument for maintaining absolute rule. Headquarters were established in Mexico City and Lima from which inquisitors were sent out to all parts of the continent to discover and punish unorthodox belief. Public executions were occasionally staged in the principal cities to provide object lessons of the fearful punishment in store for any who might waver in the faith. To such exhibitions the public was regularly invited in the hope that the deterrent effect would be complete. That the penalties of the Inquisition were sometimes invoked for political and personal reasons goes almost without saying.

Paternalism and mercantilism

The keynote of economic administration in the colonies was paternalism. Actually, nothing else could have been expected, since, according to the theory, the land of the Americas was the personal possession of the king. It was his private estate which he could dispose of as he saw fit. But economic administration in the Spanish colonies was also shaped to a large extent by the theory of mercantilism, which was beginning to dominate the thinking of all Western nations. Mercantilism demanded that colonies should exist for the benefit of the mother country; they should bring bullion into her treasury and contribute in every way possible toward making her rich and powerful. It followed that the government of the mother country had the right to regulate and control the economic activities of the colonies in her

Brazilian Colonial Church in the Portuguese Baroque Style. Baroque workmanship in colonial Latin America is thought by some authorities to be finer than that in Spain and Portugal.

Silver Mining at Potosi. By an unknown artist, about 1584. The discovery of silver at Potosi in the Bolivian highlands in 1545 marked the beginning of a greatly accelerated flow of bullion from the New World to Spain.

own interest—to dictate what they should produce and from whom they should buy and to whom they should sell. In substance this meant a monopoly of colonial trade for the merchants of the mother country and a strict prohibition of manufactures.

The economic policies described had unfortunate effects upon both the Spanish colonies and the homeland. The resources of the former were poorly developed, and some lay unused or undiscovered for centuries. With attention focused upon gold and silver and with manufacturing prohibited, there was little incentive to exploit the deposits of copper, manganese, and other minerals which might well have supported a considerable industry. Some branches of agriculture were also discouraged in order that the colonies might produce vast quantities of sugar, cotton, and tobacco which would help the mother country in maintaining a favorable balance of trade, since these products would not have to be purchased for gold outside the empire. The whole system of restrictive policies was stupid and vicious and retarded the development not only of the colonies but of the country that owned them. As late as the end of the sixteenth century Spain was an economically backward nation, with a large portion of her

Effects of economic policies

wealth concentrated in cattle and sheep, with no powerful commercial or industrial class, and with manual labor frowned upon as unworthy of a good Spaniard.

Early in the eighteenth century the Hapsburg dynasty in Spain was supplanted by Bourbon rulers. Recognizing the corruptions and inefficiency of the system of colonial administration, the Bourbon kings initiated reforms. They were no more interested in the welfare of the colonies than their predecessors had been, but they did perceive the danger that a disgruntled colonial population might become a prey to foreign conquest. They hoped, moreover, to increase the flow of revenue into the royal treasury. With these ends in view they modified trade restrictions, encouraged industry and a more varied agriculture, and even granted commercial concessions to foreigners. The most noted of these was the *asiento* of 1701, which conferred upon France the privilege of supplying the Spanish colonies with Negro slaves. In 1713, at the end of the War of the Spanish Succession, it was transferred to Britain. By the close of the eighteenth century the Spanish-American trade as a whole was the richest in the world, and had more than tripled in fifty years.

2. REVOLUTIONS FOR INDEPENDENCE

Between 1808 and 1826 Latin America was engulfed by a tidal wave of revolutions. The underlying causes did not differ greatly from the factors which had produced the North American Revolution of 1775. Pre-eminent among them was dissatisfaction with the mercantilist policies of the home government. Despite the reforms of the Bourbons, many relics of oppression and discrimination survived. A rigid censorship was imposed. Books of European and North American radicals could be obtained only by smuggling. As late as 1773 a Colombian scientist was condemned for giving lectures on the Copernican system. Taxes were numerous and excessive, and monopoly and favoritism flourished. Prosperous Creoles, or colonial whites, resented their exclusion from the highest and most lucrative positions in the government and the Church, which were reserved for Spanish-born aristocrats. The former were not starving, any more than were the members of the bourgeoisie in France on the eve of that country's revolution. What rankled in their breasts was being deprived of privileges that they believed should rightly belong to them on the basis of their wealth and intelligence.

It is possible that the discontent of Spain's colonies would never have reached revolutionary proportions had it not been for the examples already set by the revolutions in France and in North America. The colonists' grievances had abated rather than increased and probably would have lessened still further. But revolutions are contagious.

An outbreak in one country is almost certain to spread to other countries where similar conditions exist even if in much smaller degree. This is especially true when a philosophy of discontent is propagated on an international scale. During the latter half of the eighteenth century hundreds of Creoles had adopted revolutionary doctrines from the writings of Voltaire, Rousseau, Jefferson, and Paine. Some had been educated or had traveled in Europe or in the United States. The discovery that intellectual leaders in other countries were boldly attacking despotic government and superstitious religion made a profound impression and led Spanish colonials to ask themselves why such things should be tolerated in their own lands.

Influence of the French and North American revolutions

Just as in North America a period of indifference and "salutary neglect" by the British government fostered a spirit of independence in the colonies, so in Latin America a similar period weakened the ties between Spain and her possessions. Between 1803 and 1808 Spain as a satellite of France took part in the wars of Napoleon to make himself master of Europe. In 1805 the British defeated Napoleon's fleet at Trafalgar and virtually destroyed the sea power of France and her allies. Spain, in particular, experienced great difficulty in maintaining communications with her empire. As a result her colonies in Latin America acquired habits of self-reliance. More and more they depended upon their own efforts in solving political and economic problems. So great was their isolation from Spain that they cultivated a profitable trade with the British. For the mother country to have forced them back under the yoke of mercantilist restrictions would have been difficult indeed.

Spain's neglect of her colonies during the wars of Napoleon

The spark that ignited colonial unrest into actual revolution burst forth in 1808. A quarrel had developed between the weak Bourbon king of Spain, Charles IV, and his son Ferdinand. Napoleon forced

Spanish Colonial Patio. Examples of the cultural heritage of old Spain have been adapted by the wealthier citizens of Latin America.

LATIN AMERICA ON THE EVE OF INDEPENDENCE ca. 1800

both to abdicate and gave the Spanish crown to his brother Joseph. When news of these highhanded proceedings reached the colonies, there was general indignation. At first the colonies vented their wrath against the French, but gradually they came to realize that here was an opportunity to get rid of all foreign oppressors. Agitation took an anti-Spanish turn and was ultimately followed by declarations of independence and revolutionary wars. Wealthy Creoles took the lead, especially in Caracas, Buenos Aires, Quito, Bogotá, and Santiago.

Immediate cause of the revolutions

The first of the larger Spanish colonies to proclaim its independence was Venezuela. Here a revolutionary pattern had been developing for a number of years. In 1806 the impetuous Creole, Francisco de Miranda, attempted with the help of foreigners to land expeditions in his native country and wrest control of it from Spain. He obtained aid from English and American sources but failed to gain more than a temporary foothold on the territory of Venezuela. Five years later representatives from a nubmer of provinces met in a revolutionary assembly and declared Venezuela an independent republic. Learning of the revolutionists' activities, Miranda sailed from England to enlist in the cause. Appointed commander-in-chief of the patriot armies, he launched a campaign to conquer the remainder of the country. Misfortune stalked his efforts. Reverses suffered by his armies were turned into disaster when an earthquake shook the provinces controlled by the revolutionists and snuffed out the lives of 20,000. Equal to the occasion, the Spanish government sent priests with instructions to tell the people that the catastrophe was a divine punishment for their sin of rebellion. The patriot armies disintegrated, and their commander was seized and thrown into the dungeon.

The revolt in Venezuela

With the defeat of Miranda, the revolution in Venezuela was left to be completed by his erstwhile friend, Simón Bolívar. A wealthy Creole rancher, Bolívar had finally turned against Miranda, accusing him of deserting the revolution, and had been partly responsible for his capture by the Spaniards. Concluding thereafter that the revolutionary cause in Venezuela was hopeless, he went to Colombia and joined the patriot forces there. He returned to Venezuela in 1813 and captured Caracas. In January 1814, the Second Venezuelan Republic was proclaimed with Bolívar as its head with the title of "Liberator." In six months the new government had been crushed by the Spaniards, and its founder fled to Jamaica. He did not return for three years. In 1817 he began the rebuilding of a stronger patriot force in Venezuela, and two years later, with the help of 4,000 soldiers of fortune from Great Britain, completed a spectacular foray into Colombia. Inflicting a decisive defeat upon the Spaniards and their collaborators, he proclaimed the Republic of Colombia on August 10, 1819. Three months later a constitution was issued for the United States of Colombia, including Venezuela, with Bolívar as president. Thereafter the great Liberator devoted his efforts to freeing the remainder of the northern

Equestrian Statue of Simón Bolívar (1783–1830), Soldier, Statesman, and Revolutionary Leader. On Plaza Bolívar, Caracas, Venezuela.

portion of the continent from Spanish rule. By 1821 he had liquidated the royalist forces in Venezuela. Meanwhile, his able lieutenant Antonio José de Sucre, had begun the liberation of Ecuador, and in 1822 won a brilliant victory against the Spaniards, which assured the independence of the country. Soon afterward Bolívar arrived in Quito and persuaded the Ecuadorean revolutionists to unite with Colombia and Venezuela in a republic of Gran Colombia.

Concurrently with these events in the northern areas, an independence movement was growing apace in the south. As early as 1790 businessmen in the port of Buenos Aires had developed a profitable trade with Spain and an even more profitable one with Great Britain. They longed for relief of these ventures from monopolistic restrictions imposed by the Spanish government. During the Napoleonic Wars their demands were encouraged by the British government. In 1810 a band of Creoles in Buenos Aires overthrew the vice-regal government of Joseph Bonaparte and appointed a supreme governing council to rule in the name of Ferdinand VII. While the urban Creoles were debating how far they should go in the direction of complete independence, and what form of government would best suit their needs, delegates from the outlying provinces assembled at Tucumán in 1816 and declared absolute independence from the mother country. Thenceforth rivalry between the capital and the rural provinces impeded the progress of the revolution.

At least one native of Argentina perceived that internal squabbles would lead to nothing but ultimate defeat. This man was José San Martín, who had served in the Spanish army from the age of eleven and had fought the French invaders in the Peninsular campaign. With Spain under the heel of Napoleon, he had returned to his native country. Ignoring local quarrels, he determined to give positive direction to the Argentine revolution by attacking the royalists in Peru, their principal stronghold on the continent. He obtained an appointment as governor of the province of Cuyo, on the eastern slope of the Andes, where he planned to organize and equip an army for an incursion into Chile, which would then be used as a base for operations against Peru. In his preparations he was assisted by Bernardo O'Higgins, a Chilean revolutionary of Irish descent. By 1817 everything was ready for the daring expedition. Scrambling over the rocky slopes of the continental divide, the invaders came down into Chile, fell upon the royalists near Santiago, and won a spectacular triumph. The grateful Chileans offered San Martín a dictatorship, which he declined, insisting that it be conferred upon his Chilean collaborator, O'Higgins. San Martín then turned his attention to completing plans for the attack on Peru. The expedition got under way in September 1820. Less than a year later the redoubtable patriot entered Lima, issued a declaration of independence from Spain, and was vested with the title of "Protector" of the new Peruvian government. Although a dictator in theory, he exercised little power. He seemed to feel that his mission as a revolutionist was now fulfilled. Moreover, he was unable to agree with Bolívar as to the form of government to be established when the time should come to unite the countries they had liberated from Spanish rule. In 1822 he left Peru, sojourned briefly in Chile and Argentina, and then left for France, where he died in 1850.

The struggle for independence in Brazil followed a less violent course than that in most other South American countries. Revolutionary feeling was not strong, perhaps for the reason that Brazil was more backward than most of her neighbors. Two-thirds of her population were slaves. There was no large middle class, and there were no cities worthy of the name. Schools were few, and scarcely more than a tenth of the people could read and write. Even more than in the Spanish colonies, the impetus for revolution in Brazil came from the Napoleonic Wars. When Napoleon's troops drove the Portuguese rulers from Lisbon in 1807, they sailed to Brazil, arriving in Rio de Janeiro in March 1808. The Regent, Prince John, was chagrined to find his colony so backward and launched an immediate program of reform and improvement. He established schools, a bank, hospitals, and a library. He reorganized the administration of the colony, sponsored new methods of agriculture, and abolished the restrictions on colonial manufacturing. He raised the status of the colony to that of a kingdom on a par with Portugal itself. But upon becoming king of both countries after the death of his deranged mother in 1816, he surrounded himself with a royal court in Brazil and gave a virtual monopoly of high offices in Church and state to his Portuguese favorites. The effect was to antagonize many of his Creole subjects. Although the majority confined the expression of their discontent to grumbling, a group in the north attempted unsuccessfully to establish an independent republic (1817).

Portuguese rule in Brazil

In 1820 a liberal revolution broke out in Portugal. King John sailed for Lisbon and left his young son Pedro as Regent in Brazil. Scarcely had the new government gained power in Portugal than it turned to a reactionary policy, particularly with regard to the empire. Brazil was reduced once more to a mere colony, and Pedro was ordered to return to Portugal to "complete his political education." The Brazilians implored him to remain as their ruler, and he agreed to do so. When all attempts to compromise with the Portuguese failed, a revolt broke out in Brazil. In 1822 Pedro was raised to the status of emperor, and within a year the Portuguese troops had been driven from the country.

The Brazilian revolution

By 1826 all the South American countries had thrown off the yoke of European rule. Uruguay remained a province of Brazil, however, until 1828, and Argentina was unable to solve the problem of unity between Buenos Aires and her rural provinces until 1861. Meanwhile another section of Latin America was striving for the goal of indepen-

The revolution in Haiti

dence. This was the viceroyalty of New Spain, which included Mexico, Central America, portions of the West Indies, and the Spanish territory within the present limits of the United States. The island of Haiti was the first to raise the standard of revolt. During the eighteenth century it had become a colony of France—her most lucrative, by the way. It was a seething volcano of discontent, however. Its population had a three-class structure. At the top were a few thousand whites, mostly French planters and officials. At the bottom were 500,000 miserably exploited Negro slaves. A middle layer comprised the mulattoes, torn into mutually hostile factions and despised by both blacks and whites. In 1791 Toussaint L'Ouverture, a slave but the grandson of an African king, emerged as the leader of the Negroes. Under the influence of the French Revolutionary policy of abolishing slavery in the colonies, he led the Negroes in a prolonged revolt against their masters. With some accuracy he can be regarded as a forerunner of twentieth-century guerrilla leaders. His followers were a straggling force of irregulars, poorly armed and equipped, who followed a tactic of strike and run. In ten years they gained control of the entire island. Toussaint issued a constitution and assumed dictatorial powers.

When Napoleon had established himself as master of France, he resolved to put an end to the rule of the upstart rebel. Avowing that he would never "leave an epaulette on the shoulder of a Negro," he sent a huge expedition under the command of his brother-in-law, General Le Clerc, to overthrow Toussaint's government. Nearly two years and an act of treachery were required to accomplish the task. Informing Toussaint that he would "not find a more sincere friend than myself," Le Clerc invited the Negro to his quarters for negotiations. He then seized him and shipped him off in chains to a prison in France. Angered by this treachery, the slaves again rose in rebellion and with new and equally capable leaders soon forced the French to withdraw. In 1803 Haiti was proclaimed an independent kingdom. Curiously, the precedent set by the Haitians seemed to exert little influence upon the other principal islands of the West Indies. Cuba and Puerto Rico, for example, remained under Spanish rule until 1898.

Scarcely anywhere in Latin America did the revolution present a more discouraging aspect than in Mexico. Here the Creoles did not constitute so powerful a middle class as in some parts of South America. Moreover, the antagonism of the Indians and the poorer *mestizos,* or half-breeds, against the whites hindered combined action to oust the Spaniards. A revolt was finally launched in 1810, however, in the rural provinces. Its leader was a Creole priest, Father Hidalgo. The son of a poor farmer, he had obtained a good education and had become rector of the Colegio de San Nicolàs. But he was an ardent admirer of Rousseau and was reputed to have questioned the Virgin

Birth and the authority of the pope. His original plan was to lead the Indians in a rebellion against the Spanish-born aristocrats, but when his scheme was exposed he turned upon the government itself. He captured the important towns of Guanajuato and Guadalajara and then advanced with 80,000 men upon Mexico City. Ultimately defeated, he was captured, condemned by the Inquisition, and shot. One of his followers, José Morelos, continued the revolution for four more years and attempted to set up an independent government. But like Hidalgo, he eventually fell into the hands of the royalists and was condemned to death. The destinies of the revolution then passed into the hands of a crafty adventurer, Agustín de Iturbide. A soldier by profession, who had hitherto fought on the side of the royalists, Iturbide saw a chance to further his ambitions by joining the patriots. Openly espousing independence and racial equality, he attracted formidable support and, in September 1821, entered Mexico City in triumph. The following year he proclaimed himself emperor of an independent Mexican empire. But since the basic economic and social problems remained unsolved, the future of the nation continued to be fraught with anxiety and turmoil.

3. PROBLEMS OF GROWTH AND DEVELOPMENT

Following their achievement of independence, the Latin American states went through a long struggle for national maturity. It could scarcely be said that many of them attained this goal before the end of the nineteenth century. A score of difficulties beset them on every hand. To begin with, the population was heterogeneous. The former Spanish colonies were composed of 45 percent Indians, 30 percent *mestizos* or half-breeds, 20 percent whites, and 5 percent Negroes. In Brazil half the people were Negroes, a fourth were whites, and the remainder Indians and half-breeds. Over the continent as a whole the nonwhites outnumbered the Caucasians 4 to 1; yet the latter fought tooth and nail to maintain a dominant position. The success achieved in this struggle was purchased at the price of class hatred and the perpetuation of social and economic backwardness.

*Obstacles to national
maturity: (1)
heterogeneous population*

A second obstacle, related to the first, was the wide disparity of economic condition among the classes. At the top was a tiny minority of rich Spaniards and prosperous Creoles. At the bottom was a vast multitude of half-starved peasants, eking out a precarious livelihood on lands no one wanted or compelled to become laborers on the estates of the rich. The inevitable consequence was periodic revolts of the masses to force a redistribution of the land. Since land comprised the bulk of the wealth, capital accumulated slowly. In the main, the deficiency was made up by foreign investors, who frequently demanded political concessions and were eager to fish in troubled

*(2) the gulf between rich
and poor*

(3) political inexperience

Contrasts between North America and Latin America

Contrasting conditions of Indian populations

Differences between the founding empires

waters for their own advantage. Few causes contributed more toward encouraging unscrupulous adventurers to overturn governments at the behest of their foreign sponsors.

Still a third difficulty was the political inexperience of the Latin American peoples. More than 90 percent, of course, were uneducated, and consequently both ignorant and indifferent with respect to political problems. But even many of the educated ones were ill prepared to assume the tasks of governing. Their knowledge of politics came not from experience but from reading the books of theorists. Enthusiasm for this or that form of government burned with white-hot intensity, and factions vied with each other to put their ideas into effect overnight, frequently by revolutionary action. Worse yet, as a result of the long and sanguinary struggles for independence, a military tradition was firmly implanted in most of the states, and swaggering generals overshadowed civilian leaders.

Although Latin Americans are often reproached with their failure to achieve political maturity and stability as soon as did the English-speaking inhabitants of North America, such comparisons have little validity. They leave out of reckoning the fact that the United States went through a long period of sectional conflict, culminating in civil war, before its people could decide whether they were one nation or a confederation of nations. But aside from this, the circumstances affecting Latin America were so different from those obtaining in Canada and the United States that any conception of the two regions as parallel entities is bound to be inaccurate.

Perhaps the most important difference resided in the fact that Canada and the United States comprised millions of acres of practically unoccupied land. The native peoples were so few in numbers and so widely scattered that they could easily be pushed aside or exterminated. In Latin America the Indians were more numerous, in many cases more highly civilized, and therefore more successful in resisting the encroachments of the whites. The policy of the Spaniards, moreover, was to convert the natives to Christianity, not to exterminate them. It did not seem inconsistent with this that they should also be exploited and oppressed. As a consequence, there quickly developed a class system based upon race, with a prosperous minority of Spaniards and Creoles monopolizing the good things of life and a subject population composed of Indians and half-breeds living in squalor and toiling for the barest subsistence.

As a second difference, the Spanish colonies were founded by one of the most unprogressive nations in Europe. The economic system of Spain was outmoded. Her government was despotic and corrupt. Spanish Catholicism reeked with intolerance and superstition. The Church was used by the government as an instrument of repression, and the fanaticism of the Spanish Inquisition was notorious. On the eve of the discovery of America the most enterprising of Spain's inhabitants—the Moors and the Jews—had been driven from the country. England had the advantage of not beginning her colonization of the New World until the seventeenth century. By that time the power of her middle class was well consolidated and able to set up obstacles to despotic government. Instead of one church having a monopoly of religious authority, the Christians of England were divided into competing sects, and no one of them was strong enough to impose its will upon the others. The country, moreover, had been a haven of refuge for persecuted religionists from other nations, for the Huguenots in particular. Many of these were enterprising merchants and artisans who brought their initiative and skills with them, adding no small amount to the intellectual wealth of England. Long before the end of the seventeenth century, the "tight little island" was the most progressive nation in Europe. And while the Spanish colonists brought with them the customs and institutions of the Middle Ages, those who went out from England carried the ideas of the modern world. They believed in education, in equality of opportunity, and in the application of ambition and intelligence to the solution of human problems. These viewpoints helped immensely in promoting a free and dynamic society in North America in contrast with the static, semifeudal society of Central and South America.

The last three quarters of the nineteenth century unfolded a record of developments in Latin America similar in some respects to that in the United States. There was the same feverish activity in railroad building and in the construction of telegraph and telephone lines. There was the same rapid growth of population, owing largely to the influx of immigrants from Europe. The population of Argentina, for example, grew from 2 million in 1870 to about 4 million in 1900; and more than half of this increase was the result of immigration from Italy, Spain, France, Germany, and the British Isles. In Latin America as in the United States there were bitter struggles over centralization versus states' rights. There was sharp rivalry also between liberals and conservatives over extension of the suffrage and over economic reform for the benefit of the lower classes.

*Growth and development
during the nineteenth century*

But the differences were quite as significant. Nearly every country of Latin America was torn by revolutions, many of them resulting in the enthronement of military dictators. The history of Colombia was almost unique in that only twice during the century following independence was her government overthrown by violence. In neighboring Venezuela revolutions occurred with such frequency as to reduce economic development virtually to a standstill. Only the accession in 1909 of a man on horseback, Juan Vicente Gómez, who ruled for twenty-six years, brought a semblance of stability to the country. In many states of both Central and South America, religion complicated the struggle between factions. The conservatives, made up of the landholding and aristocratic elements, invariably supported the

Political instability

Emperor Pedro II of Brazil

Church. The liberals, who drew their following mainly from the business classes, were anticlerical. On occasion the latter allied themselves with the landless peasants in attacks upon the extensive holdings of the clergy.

The major difference, however, consists in the numerous wars fought by the Latin American states against each other. The longest was the struggle between Uruguay and Argentina, which lasted for fourteen years (1838–1852). The most famous was the War of the Pacific (1879–1883), in which Chile, Peru, and Bolivia fought over the desert region of Atacama. The bloodiest was the war of 1865–1870, in which the dictator of Paraguay (Francisco López) resisted the combined onslaughts of Brazil, Uruguay, and Argentina for five years. The Paraguayans fought almost literally to the last man. Only a handful of adult males survived, and more than half of the total population was wiped out. The only element of justice in the outcome was the fact that López himself was numbered among those killed. It was this dictator's imperialist ambitions which had precipitated the conflict in the first place.

Two states of Latin America went through experiences during the nineteenth century in a number of respects distinctive. One was Brazil and the other was Mexico. The former was almost unique in its political stability. A constitution drafted by a commission under Emperor Pedro I in 1824 remained in effect for sixty-five years. It was a moderately liberal document, guaranteeing freedom of speech, of the press, and of religion, and providing for a legislative assembly, but it left the emperor above the law and exempt from responsibility for the acts of his ministers. Disaffection against the monarchy mounted under Pedro II and culminated in revolution after his government enacted a measure emancipating all the slaves without compensation to their owners. An armed uprising forced the emperor to abdicate in 1889, and a republic was proclaimed under a provisional government headed by the victorious general. A constitution drafted in 1891 by a committee of lawyers for the Republic of Brazil continued in effect, with few changes, until the suspension of constitutional government by the Vargas dictatorship in 1937.

The history of Mexico in the nineteenth century resembled the history of Brazil in that both countries wavered between monarchy and republicanism and had similar conflicts over church and state. But Mexico was one of the few Latin American countries in which the *mestizos* and Indians (the former especially) played an active part in determining the course of political developments. Her first ruler after independence, Iturbide, who became Emperor Agustín I, was of mixed white and Indian parentage. As a statesman he was a failure and in little more than a year was driven from the throne and forced into exile. In 1824 a republic was set up with a constitution similar to that of the United States, except that the Roman Catholic faith was made the established religion. Between 1833 and 1855 Mexico was ruled most of the time by the redoubtable Antonio López de Santa Anna, famous as the opponent of the United States in the dispute over Texas and in the war that followed. Although holding the title of president, he governed as a dictator with the support of a clerico-military oligarchy. Cruel, treacherous, and greedy for power, he exemplified that *personalismo* which has been the curse of so many Latin-American countries. His downfall was achieved by a coalition of radicals and liberals led by two full-blooded Indians, Juan Álvarez and Benito Juárez, and a Creole, Ignacio Comonfort. Although Comonfort became president, the real leader of the coalition was Juárez. He and his followers inaugurated a program aimed at the destruction of clerical and military privilege, the suppression of the Church, and the distribution of Church lands to the people. These reforms were eventually incorporated in a new constitution adopted in 1857.

Antonio López de Santa Anna

The clericals and conservatives did not take kindly to the Constitution of 1857. The consequence was civil war, the so-called War of the Reform, from 1858 to 1861. It ended in a complete victory for Juárez and his followers, with the result that more drastic anticlerical laws were enacted to supplement the provisions of the constitution. Religious orders were suppressed, Church property was nationalized, and civil marriage was established. But the triumph of the liberals did not obliterate the nation's troubles. The government was so desperate for money that it sold some of the confiscated Church lands to secular landlords. The peasants were merely transferred from one exploiter to another. The war disrupted economic conditions to such an extent that payments on foreign debts were suspended. This gave the wily Napoleon III an excuse to intervene. In 1862 he sent a French army to Vera Cruz, which finally battered its way to Mexico City and took possession of the government. Meanwhile an assembly of Mexican conservatives went through the sham of "offering" the Mexican throne to Archduke Maximilian of Austria, who had already been selected by Napoleon III as his puppet ruler.

*The War of the Reform
and the overthrow of the
republic*

As emperor of Mexico, Maximilian was worse than a failure. Although he was kindly, idealistic, and sympathetic with the plight of most of his new subjects, he was amateurish and dominated by an overly ambitious wife. Moreover, he antagonized the conservatives by his acid criticisms of corruption and indifference in the Church and in the army. The followers of Juárez had distrusted him from the beginning. The primary cause of his downfall, however, was a shift in the power struggle in Europe. The Austro-Prussian War of 1866 put Napoleon in a position where he could no longer afford to give military support to Maximilian. As a result of her victory in that war Prussia now loomed as a dangerous rival of France. Soon afterward, therefore, the French emperor withdrew his troops. He was impelled to take this action partly, of course, by vigorous protests from the

Maximilian, Emperor of Mexico

government of the United States against French violation of the Monroe Doctrine. But even without these protests, his decision could not have been long delayed.

In the absence of French military support, Maximilian's empire in Mexico speedily collapsed. The liberal forces of Juárez closed in upon him, and he was captured, court-martialed, and executed by a firing squad. Juárez was quickly elected president and re-elected in 1871, but death overtook him the following year. He had time to accomplish only a few of his aims for making Mexico a modern, progressive state. He drastically reduced the size of the army, eliminated waste and extravagance in the government, and initiated steps for a wide extension of public education. But the troubles of the nation were far from ended. It was impossible to repair overnight the damage caused by twenty years of civil strife. The national debt continued to increase, economic activity had shrunk, and the country seemed almost on the verge of exhaustion. In 1877 the government of Juárez's successor was overthrown, and a dictatorship was established that was destined to remain in power for more than thirty years. The new ruler was Porfirio Díaz, the son of a Creole father and an Indian mother. Originally a pupil and follower of Juárez, he repudiated his master when the latter was re-elected president in 1871. Thereafter he pursued his own ambitions and strove with an iron will to mold his country in accordance with his cherished schemes.

The regime of Díaz brought Mexico prosperity but nothing that resembled democracy. For the most part he ruled benevolently but always with an eye to the perpetuation of his own power. He soon controlled the electoral machinery and used government funds to buy off potential opponents. Those who couldn't be bought he dealt with in more summary fashion. For disposing of suspected revolutionaries his general order to the army and the public was: "When caught in the act, kill in cold blood." Yet under his rule the nation made rapid progress, and the business classes at least luxuriated in dividends and profits. Foreign trade multiplied six times over, and railroad mileage increased from 400 to 16,000. Mines were brought up to unprecedented levels of production, smuggling was eliminated, the national budget was balanced, and interstate tariffs were abolished to the substantial benefit of industry and commerce. Many of these improvements were made possible, however, by the importation of foreign capital. The suppliers of these funds frequently drove unscrupulous bargains as part of the terms of the investment. They exacted concessions to buy land at ridiculous prices, including full title to all minerals beneath the surface. Prosperity at the price of so large a part of the nation's heritage eventually proved to be too much for the middle classes to endure. By 1900 the reputation of Díaz had lost its luster. By 1911 when his government collapsed and the aged dictator sailed for France, the Mexican republic was ripe for revolution to undo the evils of three decades.

Porfirio Díaz. The Díaz rule in Mexico from 1877 to 1911 was characterized by political dictatorship and economic development.

It would scarcely be an exaggeration to say that Latin America witnessed more social and political changes from 1900 to 1980 than in the previous four centuries of her history. Two significant developments distinguish the record of the twentieth century thus far. The first is a phenomenal increase in population. Around 1800, Central and South America had a population of about 17 million; by 1900 this had grown to about 70 million and by 1979 to 350 million. The population of Brazil more than trebled between 1900 and 1960. Argentina surpassed even this ratio, with a growth in numbers from 4,200,000 in 1900 to 20 million sixty years later. The number of Mexicans rose from 20 million in 1940 to 47 million in 1968 and 67 million by the later 1970s. With an average annual growth rate of about 3 percent, the Latin American countries seem destined to more than double their present population before the year 2000 when, according to predictions, it would total 650 million. Nearly everywhere population was beginning to exert terrific pressure upon available resources. Since 1950 there has been a steady migration of people from rural districts to the cities, but the expansion of industry and commerce has been too limited to absorb them into profitable employment.

Closely related to the growth of population was the increasing tension inherent in a sharply polarized society. A small elite controlled both the economy and the political structure, while the great majority remained impoverished and unprivileged, and a genuine middle class failed to develop. At the turn of the century, 90 percent of Latin Americans lived a hand-to-mouth existence of squalor and wretchedness. Most of them were peons, or laborers on large estates, doomed to a kind of slavery by debts they could never repay. Their families were crowded together in one-room shacks with no stove or fireplace, no running water, and no sanitary facilities. Wages received for a day's toil scarcely equaled the hourly pay for comparable work in the United States. As the twentieth century approached, the picture was very much the same, in spite of political rhetoric and promises of reform. The progress of industrialization, though significant, had done little to relieve the inequities in society; in some ways it had intensified them. Most of the fertile lands were still owned by a few wealthy families who ruled their great estates, or *haciendas,* in semifeudal fashion. Though less than 10 percent of the population, this powerful landlord class, together with its allies in banking and industry, monopolized the professions, government positions, and the officer ranks in the army.

The country which seemed most likely to move forward along the path of social progress was the Republic of Mexico. A revolt in 1911, which overthrew the dictatorship of Porfirio Díaz, inspired hope for reform. But the years ahead were filled with domestic turmoil and troubled by unfriendly relations with the United States. The great

CANADA

UNITED STATES
OF AMERICA

A T L A N T I C

O C E A N

*GULF OF
MEXICO*

**MEXICO
(1821)**

★ Mexico City

Havana

Nassau

**BAHAMAS
(Brit.)**

**CUBA
(1898)**

HAITI (1804)

DOMINICAN REP. (1844)

San Juan

PUERTO RICO (U.S.)

**JAMAICA
(1962)**

Port au Prince

Santo
Domingo

SEE INSET
BELOW →

CARIBBEAN SEA

BARBADOS (1967)

**TRINIDAD AND
TOBAGO (1962)**

Caracas ★

Port of Spain

**VENEZUELA
(1811)**

Orinoco R.

Georgetown
Paramaribo

GUYANA (1966)

SURINAM (Du.)

FRENCH GUIANA

Cayenne

Bogotá ★

**COLOMBIA
(1821)**

Equator

R.

Quito ★

ECUADOR (1822)

Amazon

P A C I F I C

GALAPAGOS IS.
(Ecuador)

O C E A N

**PERU
(1821)**

Lima ★

ANDES MTS.

**BOLIVIA
(1825)**

★ La Paz

Sucre ★

BRAZIL (1822)

★ Brasília

**PARAGUAY
(1811)**

★ Asunción

Rio de Janeiro

0   1000   2000 miles

**CHILE
(1818)**

ANDES MOUNTAINS

URUGUAY (1828)

Santiago ★

Buenos Aires ★

★ Montevideo

La Plata R.

**ARGENTINA
(1816)**

FALKLAND ISLANDS
(Br.)

*CAPE
HORN*

Dates indicate year
of independence

CENTRAL AMERICA

**JAMAICA
(1962)**

★ Belize

BRITISH HONDURAS

Kingston

**GUATEMALA
(1821)**

HONDURAS (1821)

Tegucigalpa ★

*CARIBBEAN
SEA*

Guatemala ★

Salvador ★

**EL SALVADOR
(1821)**

**NICARAGUA
(1821)**

Managua ★

**PANAMA
CANAL**

Panama

San José ★

**COSTA RICA
(1821)**

PANAMA (1903)

P A C I F I C   O C E A N

LATIN AMERICA TODAY

neighbor to the north had annexed about half of Mexico's territory following the war of 1846–1848 and in the early twentieth century appeared quite willing to intervene in behalf of North American interests. In 1916 the United States government sent an expeditionary force across the border in pursuit of the revolutionary general Pancho Villa and backed Villa's rival, Carranza, for the presidency. Under President Carranza a constitutional convention in 1917 drafted a new constitution which went into effect in May of that year.

The Constitution of 1917 had several objectives in line with the revolutionary ideals of those who had been struggling to remake the country ever since the end of the Díaz regime: (1) to democratize the government; (2) to reduce the influence of the Church; and (3) to give to the nation control over its economic resources and to provide for the masses a more equitable share of the wealth they produced. In pursuance of the first, the Constitution bestowed the suffrage upon all male citizens twenty-one years of age and over and subjected the powers of the president to a measure of control by Congress. In keeping with the second, freedom of religion was guaranteed, the Church was forbidden to conduct primary schools, and the state legislatures were empowered to limit the number of priests in each district. But the most significant provisions of the Constitution were probably those dealing with economic reform. Peonage was abolished. An eight-hour day with one day's rest in seven was proclaimed the standard for industrial workers. The right to strike was recognized, and the government was given the authority to provide for social insurance. Mineral resources were declared to be the property of the nation. No foreigners were to be granted concessions to develop them unless they agreed to be treated as Mexican citizens. Private property of any kind might be expropriated by the government after the payment of just compensation.

*The Mexican
Constitution of 1917*

Pancho Villa (Center) and General John J. Pershing of the United States Army. In 1916 Pershing commanded the United States expeditionary force sent to Mexico to apprehend Villa.

In spite of its liberal constitution and success in avoiding military dictatorships, Mexico has not yet fulfilled the promise of an equitable and democratic society. The failure is partly due to problems which have grown to such proportions that they frustrate efforts to resolve them. Several presidents strove earnestly to complete the revolutionary aims of the Constitution of 1917. They expropriated millions of acres of land and redistributed them to the peasants. They instituted teacher-training programs, built new schools, and made primary education free and compulsory. Legislation was enacted guaranteeing old-age pensions and providing insurance for illness, accidents, and unemployment. Mexico became the first country in the world to nationalize its oil industry (in 1938, with compensation to the former owners). Nevertheless, changes have been more in form than in substance, and they have not eliminated the sources of social unrest.

For the past fifty years the government of Mexico has been dominated by a single political party, the Institutional Revolutionary Party (PRI). The PRI chooses the presidential candidate, the legislature, the state governors, and most of the judges. The president in turn exercises practically unlimited authority over all branches of government. This system has bred complacency, inefficiency, and corruption. Although Mexico achieved a high economic growth rate, industrial progress did not benefit those most in need of help. Agrarian reform, the core of the revolutionary program, has been limited and sporadic. With only 12 percent of the land under cultivation or grazing, rapid population increase forced a migration of unemployed peasants into the towns, with the consequent creation of large urban slums. Mexico City has been called the "largest poor city" in the world. The rural areas, lacking adequate schools and medical care, remain neglected and exploited. In 1968 only 175,000 students were enrolled in public universities—out of a population of close to 50 million. Repressive policies provoked a student insurrection at the University of Mexico in 1968, which was brutally suppressed by President ·Díaz Ordaz's special troops. Although officially denied, the jails hold many political prisoners, some of whom have been tortured.

Luis Echeverría Alvarez, president from 1970 to 1976, promised the people social justice and a more equitable distribution of wealth. A flamboyant figure who courted popularity with Third World nations and brashly offered to settle the Middle East crisis, he put forward a program of "shared growth," increasing both industrial production and social services and expropriating more than a million acres for distribution to landless peasants. His reforms, though not radical, antagonized large property owners and business interests, and were also expensive. The government deficit mounted alarmingly, the consumer price index rose 90 percent within five years, and when the peso was devalued in 1976 it suffered a 50 percent decline.

Echeverría's successor, José López Portillo, political scientist, novelist, and former finance minister, reverted to a more conservative course and attempted to regain the confidence of influential groups his predecessor had alienated, including foreign investors. By a stroke of good fortune the beginning of his term of office coincided with the discovery of enormous oil and gas reserves along and off the western shore of the Gulf of Mexico. As recently as 1973 Mexico had been an oil importing country, and suffered severely in that year when the price of oil quadrupled. Recent surveys indicate that Mexico's petroleum reserves are among the world's largest. It remained to be seen whether this potential source of prosperity would merely speed the growth of capitalist enterprise or be devoted to fulfilling the long postponed promise of the Mexican Revolution. Seventy percent of the nation's wealth was controlled by 20 percent of its people; unemployment or underemployment victimized half of the population; three-fifths of the adult population was still illiterate. To an increasing extent oil exports had to be drawn upon to offset the country's deficiency in the production of foodstuffs. At the same time, Mexico's newly discovered mineral resources had given it an improved bargaining position with the United States and the means for pursuing an independent foreign policy. President López Portillo declared his government's intention to assist struggling revolutionary regimes in Central America and the Caribbean.

Brazil—the largest Latin American country, with a land area greater than that of the forty-eight continental United States—made only limited advances toward democracy, and these were halted in the 1930s. Constitutional changes adopted in 1934 provided for the secret ballot and the enfranchisement of both men and women, though a literacy qualification debarred many from voting. Three years later President Getulio Vargas, using economic depression and the growth of communism as an excuse, made himself dictator and issued a new constitution which gave him practically absolute authority. Forced to resign by a bloodless revolution in 1945, he was again chosen president in 1950 but was ousted by the military four years later. For several years a bitter struggle raged between Vargas's followers and their opponents.

In spite of factional wrangling, the later 1950s showed stirrings of progress in Brazil. President Juscelino Kubitschek planned an ambitious program of economic development, but because he avoided tax increases, his policy of government spending was highly inflationary. At the same time, volunteer reformers, supported by trade unions, political radicals, a Catholic Action Movement, and even some bishops of the Church hierarchy, brought help to the depressed rural area of northeastern Brazil, organizing peasant cooperatives, starting schools and health clinics, and offering technical assistance. Such radical activity at the grass roots, added to the mild reformism of the government, was too much for the oligarchy that controlled most of the land and the army. Kubitschek's successors had been no more successful than he in stabilizing the economy, and in April 1964 Pres-

President López Portillo of Mexico

Progress in the 1950s

President Getulio Vargas of Brazil

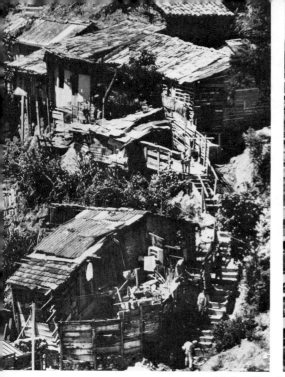

Modern Brazil. Left: A slum on the outskirts of Rio de Janeiro contrasts sharply with Brasília, Brazil's capital, on the right.

*Specious prosperity under
a military dictatorship*

ident João Goulart, a leader of the Labor party, was overthrown by a coup d'état. A military dictatorship has held Brazil in its grip ever since.

In the 1960s the country seemed to be caught in the surge of an economic boom. A resplendent new capital, Brasília, was constructed deep in the interior, and São Paulo on the coast grew from a sleepy provincial town to become the largest industrial city in the Southern Hemisphere. Proponents of a trans-Amazonian highway boasted that the gigantic project would be visible to the naked eye from the moon, although ecologists warned that destruction of the Amazon rain forests would endanger the oxygen supply and lead to soil exhaustion. Industry expanded and diversified, to free the economy from dependence upon its single staple, coffee. Manufactures—including shipbuilding, automobiles, steel products, and precision instruments—increased sufficiently to contribute 20 percent of Brazil's exports. By 1971 the overall annual growth rate approached 11 percent. Prosperity, however, was somewhat fictitious and was obtained at the risk of eventual disaster. The increasingly industrialized economy depended precariously on outside support—chiefly from the United States, Canada, Japan, and West Germany—for 40 percent of capital investment and 60 percent of foreign trade. During the mid-1970s the growth rate slumped to below 5 percent, and there were signs that the "economic miracle" was coming to an end. Because imports supplied 80 percent of its oil, Brazil was badly jolted by the sharp rise in the price of this commodity. By 1978 the national debt had reached $40 billion, and inflation was running at an annual rate of over 40 percent. While the value of agricultural exports—chiefly coffee and sugar—declined, the government attempted to improve industrial output by offering generous concessions to multinational corporations. It also invested heavily in arms production and succeeded in making Brazil one of the world's leading exporters of armaments. While national income rose substantially between 1964 and 1969 and the earnings of university graduates went up by 50 percent, real wages for the great body of workers declined in about the same proportion and, a decade later, more than one-fifth of them were unemployed. Brazil's prosperity has done little to improve health care and social services; the infant mortality rate is one of the highest in Latin America.

The military junta that has governed Brazil for the past fifteen years suppressed not only the democratic process but every vestige of civil liberty, imposing tight censorship, incarcerating citizens without trial, and torturing suspected opponents of the regime. President Ernesto Geisel, who described his government as a "relative democracy," partially relaxed the censorship and granted limited responsibility to a Congress chosen by general election in November 1978. General João Baptista Figueiredo, handpicked by Geisel to succeed him as president in March 1979, declared: "I intend to open this country up to democracy. And anyone who is against that, I will jail, I will crush." Disdainful of opposition from within or without, recent presidents have displayed an independent stance in foreign relations. President Geisel abruptly terminated a military-aid agreement with the United States and, defying remonstrances from Washington, signed a pact with West Germany for the purchase of nuclear reactors and uranium enrichment technology. Proclaiming that Brazil was no longer an emerging nation but a full-fledged power, the ruling generals appeared ready to disclaim the "special relationship" with the United States on which they had previously relied.

The recent history of Chile adds a somber chapter to the story of the misfortunes and frustrations enveloping the countries of Latin America. From the time of independence in 1818, Chile had been remarkably free from internal upheavals. As in most other parts of the continent the economy was dominated by large landowners and foreign investors, while peasants and industrial workers—together constituting 70 percent of the population—lived in poverty. Yet the political structure seemed relatively stable, committed to democratic principles, and—with a few brief interruptions—controlled by civilians. Following the authoritarian presidency of Carlos Ibañez in the early 1930s, constitutional rule continued unbroken for four decades. In 1973 it was destroyed in a blood bath precipitated by a combination of domestic traitors, fascist-minded generals, and international conspirators.

In 1964 Eduardo Frei, a lawyer of German extraction, was chosen

El Teniente Copper Mine, Chile. El Teniente Mining Company had been jointly owned by the Kennecott Copper Corporation and the Chilean government until the Allende government expropriated it in 1971. Chile ranks third in world copper production, after the United States and Zambia.

Allende's Popular Unity coalition and its opponents

president. His party, the Christian Democrats, advocated social welfare measures and his administration accomplished some reforms, including agreements for a gradual transfer of the copper mines from foreign to national ownership. It made little progress, however, with the basic problem of land ownership and distribution. The presidential election of 1970, with 86 percent of the registered voters participating, brought Salvador Allende into office at the head of a Popular Unity coalition of Socialists, Communists, and other leftists. A long-time member of the Chilean Socialist party, Allende sought radical changes but was determined to achieve them by democratic methods. His government broke the control of monopolies, enacted a substantial program of agrarian reform, improved health care sufficiently to cut the infant mortality rate in half, and brought relief to the workers by reducing unemployment. His determination to pursue a "Chilean way to socialism"—democratic and nonviolent—aroused the fears of both native and foreign business interests, who resolved to fight him with all the resources they could command. Economic crises, aggravated by a simultaneous rise in food costs and a drop in the price of copper, Chile's main export, plagued Allende's government. What was not generally known at the time is that an economic breakdown—attributed by critics to Allende's ineptitude and Marxist ideology—was deliberately engineered by Chilean far-right elements, with the support of multinational corporations and the United States government. The CIA, at the urging of the International Telephone and Telegraph Company, had tried to prevent Allende's installation as president in

1970. Failing in this the CIA, with the approval of President Nixon and Henry Kissinger's "Forty Committee" of the National Security Council, secretly spent some $8 million in an attempt to "destabilize" the Chilean government. A black market disrupted trade, acts of sabotage and strikes instigated by agents provacateurs crippled key industries, and an avalanche of propaganda attempted to convince all classes that Allende was violating the constitution while he was wrecking the economy.

In spite of a well-financed scare-and-smear campaign, the congressional elections of March 1973 gave Allende's Popular Unity coalition almost 44 percent of the vote, actually increasing its representation in the legislature although not to the point of holding a majority. Infuriated by this popular vote of confidence in the president, his opponents resorted to extreme measures. After several abortive attempts to incite a popular uprising against the government, the military high command mobilized a force of 100,000 men and on September 11, 1973, launched attacks on key centers throughout the country. The operation was less a coup d'état than an undeclared civil war, though such an uneven contest that there could be little doubt as to the outcome. Although disorganized and poorly armed, civilian resistance proved much stiffer than had been expected. A small band led by Allende defended the Presidential Palace for five hours against tanks and aerial bombardment. Allende was machine-gunned by his captors (who announced his death as suicide) and the slaughter continued for weeks. Some 15,000 civilians were killed outright; thousands more were imprisoned, tortured, or exiled.

The overthrow of one of the few constitutional democracies in Latin America transferred power to a four-man junta headed by General Augusto Pinochet Ugarte, an unappealing figure who liked to compare himself to Spain's Generalissimo Franco and who vowed to replace discredited "liberal democracy" with something more suitable to the times. His methods evoked memories of the horrendous days of Hitler and Stalin. Secret police, the DINA, caused people to "disappear" without a trace and abused prisoners in torture chambers bearing such sardonic titles as "Discothèque" and "Palace of Laughter." An International Commission of Jurists has estimated that during the first eighteen months after the military takeover 95,000 persons—about 1 percent of the population—were arrested for at least a twenty-four-hour period. Unrelenting repression and terror failed to break all internal resistance, while reports of violations of human rights pushed Chile toward a position of international isolation. The United States Congress ended military aid in 1976, but private banks continued to provide financial assistance to the junta. Uneasy relations between Santiago and Washington were severely strained when Orlando Letelier, formerly Allende's ambassador to the United States and an outspoken critic of the junta, was murdered on the streets of Washington, D.C., by DINA agents in September 1976. President

Forceful overthrow of democratic government in Chile

Salvadore Allende, President of Chile, 1970–1973

Rule of the junta

Pinochet made a few cosmetic changes intended to mollify his critics. In 1977 he dissolved the dreaded DINA, but it immediately reappeared under a new name—National Information Center (CNI). The following year he granted permission for a May Day demonstration, following which his police only mildly abused the 500 dissidents they rounded up. Going further, the general tentatively scheduled parliamentary elections for the mid-1980s, while warning that there could be no relaxation of military rule and no presidential election before 1991.

Internal opposition

General Pinochet described Chile under his regime as an island of peace in a troubled world and boasted that he had laid a sound economic base for future development, but there was reason to doubt the durability of his "new democracy." Chile's productive enterprises were heavily mortgaged to foreign corporations, while small industrial concerns faced the prospect of bankruptcy. Eduardo Frei's Christian Democrats, who had helped overthrow Allende only to be outlawed along with other political parties, were having second thoughts. Divisions within the armed forces threatened to erode the power base. Workers were daring not only to grumble but to revive union activity, including resort to strikes and boycotts. They had ample ground for dissatisfaction. In 1977 Chile's industrial production was lower than in 1970, construction had fallen off 20 percent in the same period, real wages were down by more than 18 percent, and the incidence of unemployment was as high as Brazil's.

Obstacles to democracy in Argentina

Amply endowed with agricultural and pastoral resources, though weak in oil and minerals, Argentina is potentially the richest of Latin American countries, but it has made little progress toward either political or economic democracy. Universal manhood suffrage and the secret ballot were adopted in 1912, but voting has typically been manipulated by powerful cliques for their own advantage. Argentina's political history is marked not only by addiction to authoritarian gov-

Agriculture in Argentina. A harvesting scene at the end of the nineteenth century. The nation's booming wheat industry contributed substantially to its prosperity early in the twentieth century.

ernment but also by extraordinary instability. Since 1930 only one president has completed his mandated term of office. Seemingly, the ingredients for a homogeneous society are present. The Indian minority has always been small, and a liberal immigration policy has given the nation a predominantly European character. Argentina is the most urbanized Latin American country, and its people are among the best educated. Yet deep-seated animosities persist which jeopardize democratic progress and political stability. They can be traced in part to rapid industrialization and to the fierce antagonism between urban and rural classes. More than 50 percent of the population is employed in industry, and a wide gulf separates the interests and attitudes of Buenos Aires—where a third of the population is concentrated—from those of the outlying provinces. A second and related source of conflict has been the role of the trade unions. Originating under the leadership of Spanish and Italian immigrants tinged with syndicalist ideology, they developed a strong sense of labor solidarity and militancy. A national confederation of organized workers (CGT), eventually encompassing half of the labor force, became a power within the state, alternately supporting and combating the recurring military dictatorships. Still another factor tending to foster autocratic government has been an intense national pride. Argentinians believe their country should be the leader of Latin America and particularly resent interference by the United States in the affairs of the southern continent.

Much of Argentine political history in the twentieth century has revolved around a small number of dominating personalities. One such was Hipólita Irigoyen, who inspired fanatical loyalty among his followers and was elected president in 1916 for a six-year term and again in 1928. His popularity stemmed partly from the fact that he managed to keep Argentina neutral during World War I and later gained for her a place of recognition in world affairs. But he ruled as an autocrat, enforcing a vicious antistrike policy against labor, and, during his second term, permitting widespread corruption. He was overthrown by a bloodless revolution in 1930 engineered by conservatives and high-ranking officers of the armed forces. For several years conservatives and bourgeois liberals alternated in the possession of power. With the outbreak of World War II a sinister fascist movement began to develop in Argentina. Sympathy with the Axis, based in part upon fear of communism, was widely prevalent. Large numbers of the business classes were of German or Italian extraction, and many army officers were German trained. The nation was already in the throes of economic crises, the government was almost bankrupt, and inflation and overcrowding in the cities inflicted cruel hardships on people with meager resources. The official policy of paying low wages as a means of boosting exports created a surly, rebellious class of workers ready to follow any demagogue who promised to better their condition. The man who stepped into this role was Juan D.

*The road to fascism: Juan
Perón*

Juan Perón, President of Argentina

Perón. Leader of a movement to force the resignation of the incumbent president, he ran for the office himself in 1946. By promising wage increases, rent controls, and partitioning of great estates, he won enough support among the *descamisados* ("shirtless ones") in addition to that of the military and business elements to ensure his election. By recruiting peasants he enlarged the trade unions and made them his power base, using them to intimidate the industrial oligarchy and to hold the military in check. His colorful personality and bold, unscrupulous actions attracted a devoted mass following, but his methods of governing resembled the familiar pattern of fascist dictatorship—censorship, saber rattling, antiforeignism, and economic nationalism.

Perón antagonized the Catholics by legalizing divorce and by attempting the separation of church and state. And while he did little for the peasants, he incurred the enmity of the middle class by conferring expensive benefits upon his followers in the General Confederation of Labor and by expanding the national debt. Though a revolt which broke out in June 1955 was suppressed, it flared up again in September. The rebels won the support of the navy and finally threatened to bombard the city of Buenos Aires if Perón did not surrender. A military junta persuaded him to relinquish his rule and go into exile. He fled to Paraguay and later found refuge in Madrid. In May 1956 the constitution was restored and the great liberal newspaper *La Prensa* was given back to its rightful owners.

The persistence of the Peronist heritage

The restoration of constitutional government proved to be short-lived and did not end the threat to democracy in Argentina. It was impossible to eradicate overnight the influence of 2 million *peronistas* who longed for a revival of the dictatorship that had conferred favors upon the working classes. It was also impossible to suppress the ambitions of the generals and colonels, who demanded strong government until Peronism and communism could be completely eliminated as effective instruments of class legislation. In 1962 and again in 1966 the army removed an elected president from office. Meanwhile economic ills remained, dating from the depression of the 1930s as well as from the Perón regime—a foreign-trade deficit, chronic unemployment, a mountain of public debt, and a steadily advancing cost of living. The military junta that seized power in 1966 dissolved all political parties, purged the universities, and tightened control over the trade unions, but it was unable to resolve the economic crises. Three army generals ruled successively, the third of whom was Alejandro Lanusse, chosen by the joint chiefs of staff as head of the nation in March 1971. Abler than his predecessors, Lanusse also showed himself to be more conciliatory. He legalized political parties, restored some confiscated property, and announced his intention of holding elections for the office of president within two years. This seemed a bold plan in view of the dissensions within the country. Lanusse faced two military uprisings against him and opposition from both the right and the left, including labor unions, middle-class terrorists, and even a revolutionary faction of the Catholic clergy. Though he had himself once been imprisoned by Perón, Lanusse invited the exiled dictator to return for a month's visit, and unregenerate *peronistas* nominated their aging hero as the presidential candidate of their Justicialist Liberation Front. Perón chose not to run, but when the elections were held as scheduled in March 1973, his stand-in, Dr. Héctor Cámpora, a sixty-four-year-old former dentist, outdistanced his closest rival by better than two to one. Accepting the unexpected verdict, Lanusse relinquished the presidential office in May. But Cámpora's inauguration as the first civilian president in seven years did not halt the bloody violence and terrorism that racked the country, and in July Cámpora stepped down in favor of Perón. Upon the death of the ex-dictator the following summer, his widow Isabel, a former cabaret dancer, attempted to fill the post of chief executive. Her disastrous administration of twenty months witnessed the spread of corruption throughout the bureaucracy, black marketing, debasement of the currency, and the world's highest rate of inflation, bringing the government to the brink of ruin. She was deposed by a smoothly executed coup in March 1976, and a three-man junta, headed by General Jorge Videla, acceded to power.

The military junta that has ruled Argentina since the overthrow of Señora Perón retrieved the economy from chaos, but at the expense of every trace of civil liberty. The trade deficit was erased and the rate of inflation reduced—from over 500 percent in 1976 to about 100 percent in 1978. While not abolishing trade unions, the junta seized control of the powerful CGT and froze wages, but not prices. The unions represent a potential threat to the regime and have ventured to call strikes. The generals vowed to exterminate the guerrilla terrorist bands that had shaken the country over a period of many years. Determined to suppress even subversive thoughts, the government unleashed a terror of its own, employing more than a dozen different agencies to stifle dissidents by fright, torture, and execution. Domestic violence increased significantly after the coup of March 1976. Two years later Amnesty International estimated that 15,000 persons had disappeared, between 8,000 and 10,000 more were held in official prisons, while unnumbered victims were suffering in secret detention camps.

The Argentine military junta

Nearly 60 percent of the people of Latin America live under direct military rule or under governments responsible to the military. These regimes are notoriously unstable. Bolivia, an extreme example, has had more than 200 coups during the past century and a half, three of them since 1978. A civilian administration, elected in 1979 after ten years of army rule, lasted less than three months. Democratic prospects brightened that fall when, following the expulsion of a coup leader, the presidency was entrusted to Lydia Gueiler, an elderly

Prevalence of military governments: Bolivia an extreme example

grandmother, who kept the generals in their barracks until she had carried out plans for a free general election, held in June 1980. But when the voters chose as president an elder statesman who had enacted popular reforms during his tenure of office in the 1950s, the military, led by General Luis Garcia Meza, struck swiftly, arresting Gueiler and her cabinet and preventing the newly elected president from taking office. The coup was encouraged and actively assisted by General Videla, dictator of Argentina, who declared that an elected government in Bolivia posed "a high degree of risk."

Peru, an exceptional case

Most of the Latin American military governments are both repressive and reactionary, depleting resources through excessive defense budgets and employing specially trained counterinsurgency forces to quell any opposition within their own countries. They are generally allied with local oligarchs and assisted by foreign capital. An exception to the norm is Peru, where in 1968 the army installed a regime that was both authoritarian and progressive. Under the leadership of General Juan Velásco Alvarado some 8 million acres of land were redistributed, workers' cooperatives set up, educational opportunities extended for both men and women, and large foreign properties nationalized. These reforms for the benefit of the poor antagonized the rich, while a depressed economy and steadily increasing cost of living aroused general discontent, leading in the mid-1970s to riots, which the government forcefully suppressed. When Velásco was overthrown by another officer in 1975, his successor promised a return to civilian rule. A general election in May 1975 resulted in a clear victory for ex-President Fernando Belaúnde Terry, an architect, city planner, and political moderate.

The rise and fall of democracy in Uruguay

Uruguay, smallest of the South American republics with a population of less than 3 million, had a better record of educational and political progress than most of its neighbors for many years. A constitution, modeled upon that of Switzerland, provided for equal suffrage, the secret ballot, and minority representation. José Batlle y Ordóñez, an outstanding statesman, president from 1903 to 1907 and from 1911 to 1915, created a type of welfare state. His reforms, which included the eight-hour day and minimum wages, old-age pensions and social insurance, benefited city workers but, unfortunately, did less for the peasants because they left the monopolistic land system unchanged. After several decades of relative prosperity and a rising standard of living, since mid-century the country has suffered economic decline, attributable partly to falling prices for its exports of wool, meat, and hides, but partly to such internal factors as a narrow concentration of wealth, inefficiency in both agriculture and industry, and bureaucratic waste in government. Demoralized by a runaway inflation, Uruguay was torn by strikes and riots and terrorized by bands of desperate guerrillas. Yielding to pressure from the army, President Juan Bordaberry, in June 1973, dissolved Congress and announced that he would govern by decree. His coup was accompanied by harsh repression and the wholesale arrest of trade union leaders. Subsequently, the constitution was suspended, parliament replaced by a National Security Council, political parties and trade unions suppressed, and censorship imposed. The military dictatorship, following the gruesome pattern of intimidation and torture, set a new record for political imprisonment. By the end of 1975, 2 percent of the population was under detention. Uruguay—a state once hailed as the "Switzerland of South America" and a model of democracy—had become one of the worst offenders against human rights.

Most of the small banana and sugar republics of Central America and the West Indies have been denied the advantages of democratic government. Guatemala, for instance, has been the victim of foreign intervention and dictatorship. When President Jacobo Arbenz of Guatemala attempted to expropriate idle lands and transfer them to landless peasants in 1954, the oligarchy of large estate owners overthrew his government by an armed invasion, staged in neighboring Honduras with the support of the United Fruit Company and the CIA. Internal violence, endemic in Guatemala since the 1954 coup, has cost the lives of at least 40,000 people. Despite acceptable constitutions, the Dominican and Haitian republics passed under personal dictatorships tempered by assassination or the threat thereof. The Dominican Republic suffered under the misrule of General Rafael L. Trujillo for nearly thirty years until he was blotted out by assassins' bullets in 1961. Graft, nepotism, and police terrorism had been the instruments of his power. Elections held in 1962 resulted in the choice of Juan Bosch, a liberal intellectual, as president. After less than a year he was overthrown, and a military clique assumed power. In 1965 Bosch and his followers, including some Communists, launched a counterrevolt. Bloody strife ensued followed by prompt United States intervention. President Johnson professed an obligation to protect American lives and to save the island from communism. Eventually, upon pleas from Washington, the Organization of American States sent a joint expedition to maintain order in the Dominican Republic, but unrest continued. The inauguration in August 1978 of Antonio Guzmán as president marked the first peaceful transfer of power between constitutionally elected governments in the nation's history.

*Political turbulence in
Central America and the
West Indies*

Similar troubles beset the republic of Haiti. Beginning in 1945 a series of revolutions alternating with chaos culminated in 1957 in the dictatorship of François Duvalier. Though he ruled with the title of president, his power rested upon the armed forces. In 1964 he was made president for life. Relying on repression as harsh as that of General Trujillo, he faced the constant possibility of revolution, for Haiti is poorer and culturally more backward than the Dominican Republic. It has the highest rate of illiteracy, the deepest poverty, and the most primitive economic development of all the countries of Latin America. Nevertheless, its government had one advantage over the governments of some neighboring states: it enjoyed the support of

*The Duvalier dictatorship
in Haiti*

Washington. The State Department evidently considered Duvalier the least of a number of possible evils. When "Papa Doc" died in 1971, his twenty-year-old playboy son, Jean-Claude Duvalier, succeeded him as president for life. Although "Baby Doc" freed a few political prisoners and gave the appearance of relaxing the terror, he only made it less open; conditions remained the same as before. Farmers, comprising 80 percent of the population, barely subsist on soil depleted in fertility and impaired by erosion. Three-fourths of Haiti's children suffer from malnutrition; the infant mortality rate is more than ten times that of the United States. Factory workers, for near-starvation wages, produce underwear, wigs, stuffed toys, and baseballs for export to American markets. One proof of the desperate plight of these people of the "Fourth World" is that thousands of them have attempted to escape by boat, hoping to be granted political asylum in the United States. Upon reaching Miami, many have been jailed for illegal entry or forced to return to Haiti.

The Cuban revolution

Among the smaller Latin American nations, Cuba occupies a unique position because of the transformation it has undergone and because of the controversy it has aroused. Freed from Spanish rule in 1898, Cuba became nominally independent but actually a semicolony of the United States. By treaty and by a clause inserted in the Cuban Constitution of 1901, the United States was given the right to intervene in the internal affairs of the new republic, and did so several times before the so-called Platt Amendment was revoked in 1934 under President Franklin Roosevelt's "good neighbor" policy. The United States, however, retained a naval base at Guantánamo Bay. A rising spirit of nationalism, resentment against a narrow concentration of wealth, and the weakness of a two-crop economy left the country a prey to disorder. Events reached a crisis during the world depression of the 1930s. In 1936 a ruthless army sergeant, Fulgencio Batista, with aid from the United States and the support of the army, gained control of the government. In 1940 he was elected president. With the titular as well as the actual authority in his hands, he maintained a dictatorial rule until 1959. In that year he was overthrown by a coterie of young revolutionists under the leadership of Fidel Castro. Castro's program was essentially a patchwork and his followers a motley assortment. Some were anti-Communists, some were democratic socialists, and several had definite commitments to communism. Calling their bid for power the Twenty-sixth of July Movement because it had been launched on July 26, 1953, Castro and his comrades eventually demanded a complete revolution in Cuba. They would obliterate all traces of United States imperialism, expropriating American owners of banks, industries, and hotels. They would nationalize these properties and some others in order to provide jobs for the unemployed. They proposed also an extensive land reform for the benefit of the peasants. As the movement extended its power over the country and

Fidel Castro

gained full control in 1959, it took on a more radical character. In 1961 Castro announced himself "a Marxist-Leninist."

Following their dramatic victory in 1959 the revolutionaries faced difficult years as they attempted to transform Cuba's social and economic base while struggling to survive and to win international recognition. Alarmed at the prospect of profit losses to investors if foreign holdings were nationalized, the United States severed relations with Cuba in 1961, later persuaded the Organization of American States to expel Cuba from membership, and imposed a trade embargo. Unable to isolate the wayward island republic completely, the Washington government in April 1961 planned and assisted an invasion of Cuba by embittered Cuban exiles. An attempted landing at the Bay of Pigs was a total failure. Stung by this rebuff the Kennedy administration permitted anti-Castro saboteurs and terrorists to operate out of Miami and urged the CIA to "get rid of" Castro. A Senate investigating committee later reported that between 1961 and 1963 eight separate assassination plots against the Cuban prime minister had been considered. The threat of invasion or subversion from the Colossus of the North helped to unify the islanders behind their revolutionary leaders. It also forced Castro to seek allies outside the Western Hemisphere and, ultimately, to become dependent on the Soviet Union for financial, military, and diplomatic support. Although the U.S.S.R. has kept Cuba in line by absorbing half of its sugar crop and providing free military assistance, the relationship has been an uneasy one. The discovery by United States intelligence agencies that the Soviets had stationed bombers and established missile bases in Cuba led to a critical confrontation between the two superpowers in October 1962. After exchanges with President Kennedy, Premier Khrushchev agreed to remove the missiles and dismantle the bases, but Cubans resented the fact that they had not been consulted during the crisis, even though the nuclear war so narrowly averted would have begun on their soil. Castro's government has sought, with growing success in recent years, to establish ties with other Latin American countries and with distant nations of the Third World. It has sent technicians, military instructors, and troops to several fledgling African states, not always with the blessing of the Soviet Union.

Years of crisis

The Cuba of Fidel Castro's revolution presents strange contradictions. The revolution has accomplished needed reforms and, in spite of erratic changes in government policy, has bettered living conditions for classes that had always been impoverished. It has lifted the country out of the stagnation that paralyzes most Latin American societies. Improved sanitation, hygiene, medical and hospital facilities raised the level of public health, as evidenced by a decline in deaths from tuberculosis, malaria, typhoid, and polio. The infant mortality rate is the lowest in Latin America, as is illiteracy, now down to about 4 percent of the population. Women, given legal equality with men, have

*The contradictions of
Castro's Cuba*

advanced in all the professions; 52 percent of the doctors are women. Beaches and resorts have been opened to the public, and the administration of justice—except for political offenders—is evenhanded. Economically, Cuba has remained dependent on a few exports, such as nickel and especially sugar, and the price of these declined sharply in the 1970s. There are shortages of many commodities; even necessities are rationed. Belying Castro's boast that by 1980 every family would own a house or an apartment and that every farmer would have an air-conditioned tractor, plans for industrial development have been drastically curtailed. But Cuba possesses fertile farmlands and with more efficient management could become a prosperous agricultural country. Aside from serious blunders in economic planning, the picture is shadowed by the suppression of personal freedom, censorship, and constant indoctrination—"government by oratory." By 1960 Castro was holding more political prisoners than had been jailed by Batista. Over 700,000 Cubans have left the country and other hundreds of thousands undoubtedly would do so if they could. The strong and weak points of the regime reflect the complex personality of its ruler, a man of tremendous charisma, courage, and drive but essentially an improviser, who drifted ideologically from constitutional democrat and anti-Communist "humanist" to "socialist" and then to "Marxist-Leninist" and Communist. Conceivably, with changing circumstances he might shift again. In 1978 he initiated a dialogue with leaders of his exiled countrymen, promised to free political prisoners and permit emigration, and welcomed foreign visitors to Havana. Having proved that a small country on the United States' doorstep could make itself independent of its mighty neighbor, he seemed eager to mend broken ties.

The "boatlift" of 1979–1980

Cuban efforts to improve relations with the United States have generally been rebuffed, and American animosity was reinforced when, beginning in the spring of 1979, a flood of Cuban emigrants crowded into vessels of every description and descended upon the Florida coast. Castro's motive for permitting this exodus was partly a desire to embarrass the United States government, which had failed to act upon an agreement negotiated in 1965 to admit to the United States 130,000 Cuban residents holding dual citizenship. Castro also saw an opportunity to get rid of undesirable elements, including mental patients and criminals, although these were a small minority of the more than 125,000 who came to American shores in 1979–1980. The "boatlift" operation was abetted by the 800,000-strong community of Cuban exiles living in the Miami area, and the sudden influx into southern Florida put a severe strain upon communities already overcrowded and afflicted by racial tensions.

Major changes in Latin America are needed before its people can approach the degree of well-being enjoyed by developed nations of the Western Hemisphere. Significant changes began during the 1970s. A step toward regional federation was taken in 1969 with the forma-

The Cuban "Boatlift." Between 800 and 900 Cuban refugees crammed on board the ocean-going tug *Dr. Daniels* on this day in early 1980 for the perilous trip from Cuba to Key West, Florida. Thousands of Cubans seized the opportunity to leave Cuba on any boat that would take them to the United States. The Cuban government sought to use this embarrassing situation to rid itself of individuals it identified as "undesirables."

tion of an Andean Pact comprising Bolivia, Chile, Colombia, Ecuador, and Peru, and joined by Venezuela in 1973. Chile, however, withdrew three years later; Bolivia's brutal July 1980 coup alienated other pact members; and the association has made little headway toward its goal of creating a common market. For an indefinite future Latin America will require financial and technical assistance, but the effectiveness of outside help depends upon the type of aid and the terms under which it is granted. Multinational corporations with large Latin American investments have used local capital for development projects while displacing local management and siphoning off most of the profits. United States corporations control upward of 75 percent of Latin America's raw materials and approximately half of its modern industry, banking, and foreign trade. President Kennedy's Alliance for Progress, initiated in 1961, disbursed aid chiefly in the form of loans, tied to United States exports and primarily benefiting the groups that already had a stranglehold on the Latin American economies. Designed to usher in a "Development Decade," the Alliance for Progress actually widened the gap between rich and poor and kept governments dependent upon foreign investors. The desire for economic independence has sparked a demand for restructuring the Organization of American States (OAS). A call for revision of the OAS, with exclusion of the United States, came from Venezuela, a country whose large petroleum reserves gave its economy the highest growth rate on the continent by the mid-1970s and upon which the United States relied for one-third of their crude oil imports. A seemingly minor but by no means negligible challenge to Washington's hegemony appeared in tiny Puerto Rico, a colony that had advanced

Problems and prospects

The Panama Canal under Construction. The Miraflores Lower Locks, November 12, 1912.

in 1952 to a partially self-governing commonwealth, but which after a period of rapid economic development was nearing financial collapse. While disagreeing on the solution for their problems, the islanders were nearly unanimous in desiring a change in the status quo.

The effects of Carter's human rights policy

The human-rights policy enunciated by President Jimmy Carter produced slight but potentially significant changes in the relationship between the United States and Latin America. Soon after taking office in 1977 President Carter pledged support to "political systems that allow their people to participate freely and democratically in the decisions that affect their lives." His administration cut off or reduced military aid to such flagrantly oppressive Latin American regimes as Argentina, Chile, and Bolivia; welcomed democratic tendencies discernible in Ecuador, Honduras, Peru, and even Brazil; and actually prevented a military coup in the Dominican Republic in 1978. After pressuring the Dominican president Joaquin Balaguer to honor his pledge to hold free elections, Washington, with the backing of the Organization of American States, warned Balaguer that serious consequences would follow any interference with the electoral process. The result was a victory for a popular coalition, the peaceful accession to office of a civilian president, Antonio Guzmán, and a softening of the traditional image of "Yankee imperialism."

The Panama Canal treaties

A notable departure in United States policy, marking perhaps the beginning of a new era in interhemisphere relations, was the settling, through patient negotiation, of a long and bitter dispute over the Panama Canal. Under United States control since 1903, the canal had declined in both economic and strategic importance. The surrounding zone, however, held fourteen military bases, used by the U.S. South-

ern Command and by the School of the Americas which trained counterinsurgency forces for Latin American military governments. In
September 1977 President Jimmy Carter and General Omar Torrijos
of Panama signed treaties providing for United States withdrawal
from the zone, the gradual phasing out of the military bases, and the
transfer of canal operation to Panama by the end of the century. In
their first free election in nearly a decade, Panamanians ratified the
treaties by plebiscite in October 1977.

Solid and lasting progress for Latin America requires transformation of the political and economic structure. In El Salvador, fiefdom
of a coffee oligarchy, 2 percent of the population owns 60 percent of
the land; illiteracy in the rural areas runs as high as 67 percent. Ecuador
is owned by a Spanish landed aristocracy constituting 5 percent of the
population, and by foreign corporations—Pepsi Cola, General Electric, Texaco, and United Fruit. Native Indians have been driven from
their lands or reduced to a state of serfdom; 70 percent of Ecuador's
children die before the age of three. More than half of Guatemala's
arable land is owned by 2 percent of the farmers. Bolivia has the tin,
silver, gold, and natural gas resources to make it a prosperous country, but a majority of its 5.5 million people—two thirds of them Indians—exist at or below the poverty level. While these illustrations are
extreme cases, they are not too far from the norm. If reform does not
come, revolution inevitably will. This fact was convincingly demonstrated in 1979 when a ragged band of guerrillas toppled Nicaragua's
Anastasio Somoza, one of the most notorious dictators in Latin America. Somoza's father, commanding a national guard trained by United
States Marines, had made himself president of Nicaragua in 1937, and
his family henceforth treated the country as its private possession,
acquiring ownership of practically the whole economy while forcibly

*The Nicaraguan
revolution*

The Nicaraguan Revolution. San-
danista commandos and elated
citizens celebrate the fall of the
Somoza government by top-
pling a huge statue of Anastasio
Somoza Garcia, the father of the
ousted president, in Managua,
the nation's capital.

stifling opposition. Somoza's corruption and insatiable greed eventually lost him support of the business community, but effective resistance awaited the rise of the Sandinista National Liberation Front (named after a guerrilla leader who had been treacherously murdered by the elder Somoza) from the ranks of the dispossessed. In August 1978 twenty-five Sandinista commandos stormed the national palace, seized 1,500 hostages, and held them for ransom. By the following July the rebels had enlisted support throughout the country and, after forcing Somoza to flee to Miami, they set up a National Reconstruction Government, representing a wide spectrum of political opinion and including several Catholic priests. The junta undertook the staggering task of rebuilding a shattered economy, of wiping out illiteracy (within two years reducing it from 50 percent to 12 percent), and of developing democratic institutions. Although the revolutionary government nationalized the Somoza family's holdings, it adopted the goal of a mixed capitalist-socialist economy in which private enterprise would retain an important role. Affirming its commitment to human rights, the ruling group abolished the death penalty. It also pursued an independent foreign policy, attempting to cultivate friendly relations with Nicaragua's neighbors and with the United States.

The bloody struggle in El Salvador

The successful Nicaraguan revolution sent tremors through neighboring Honduras, Guatemala, and El Salvador, all under harsh military regimes. The woefully undeveloped country of Honduras was returned to civilian rule with the election of a constituent assembly in April 1980. In October 1979 a coup led by younger army officers ousted the hard-line dictator of El Salvador. A joint military-civilian junta that came to power with the coup enunciated a far-reaching reform program, including nationalization of banks and land redistribution. Opposition from large landowners and conservative business interests crippled the reform process and infuriated the radical left, resulting in rapidly escalating outbreaks of violence. The ruling junta allied itself more and more closely with the extreme right, tolerating right-wing death squads that kidnaped, tortured, and executed their opponents. Battle lines were drawn between the National Guard and the Democratic Revolutionary Front, which had been formed by representatives of some 150 organizations. In 1980 the death toll exceeded 10,000 and an equal number of families fled from their homes. In March Archbishop Oscar Romero, who had protested the shipment of U.S. arms to El Salvador, was assassinated. The following December four American missionary women were murdered in the countryside. In January 1981 two more Americans, including the head of El Salvador's Agrarian Reform Institute, were killed. Although evidence pointed to the National Guard's complicity in these outrages, the United States government early in 1981 decided to increase military aid to the junta. As U.S. intervention was countered by Cuban help to the guerrillas by way of Nicaragua, the tiny country faced the prospect of a long and devastating civil war.

Revolutionary movements in Latin America have won substantial support from segments of the Catholic church and from Protestant denominations. Beginning in the 1960s, groups of young priests became outspoken advocates of social justice and sought to relieve mass poverty by direct action, a stand that brought them increasingly into conflict with their governments. Some 850 bishops, priests, and nuns have been murdered, arrested, or tortured during the past ten years; church publications have been seized and presses destroyed. In El Salvador Jesuits were denounced as "agents of international communism." In light of the church's historic role as ally and staunch support of dominant Latin American oligarchies, the shift during the last two decades is truly dramatic.

SELECTED READINGS

• *Items so designated are available in paperback editions.*
Alexander, R. J., *The Perón Era,* New York, 1951.
———, *Prophets of the Revolution: Profiles of Latin American Leaders,* New York, 1962.
———, The Tragedy of Chile, Westport, Conn., 1978. A detached political narrative.
Arciniegas, Germán, *Latin America: A Cultural History,* New York, 1967.
Bailey, Helen, and A. P. Nasatir, *Latin America: The Development of Its Civilization,* 2d ed., Englewood Cliffs, N.J., 1968.
• Boorstein, Edward, *Allende's Chile: An Inside View,* New York, 1977. By Allende's economic adviser.
Burnell, Elaine, ed., *One Spark from Holocaust: The Crisis in Latin America,* Santa Barbara, 1972. A valuable and provocative symposium.
• Cardoso, F. H., and E. Faletto, *Dependency and Development in Latin America,* tr. M. M. Urquidi, Berkeley, 1979.
• Cline, H. F., *The United States and Mexico,* Cambridge, Mass., 1953.
Crawford, W. Rex, *A Century of Latin American Thought,* Cambridge, Mass., 1944.
• Cumberland, C. C., *The Meaning of the Mexican Revolution,* New York, 1967.
DeVylder, Stefan, *Allende's Chile: The Political Economy of the Rise and Fall of the Unidad Popular,* New York, 1976.
• Dobyns, H. F., and P. L. Doughty, *Peru: A Cultural History,* New York, 1977.
Draper, Theodore, *Castroism, Theory and Practice,* New York, 1965. Highly critical.
Fagg, J. E., *Latin America, a General History,* 3d ed., New York, 1977.
Fiechter, G. A., *Brazil since 1964: Modernization under a Military Regime,* tr. Alan Braley, New York, 1975. A judicious account by a Swiss author.
• González Casanova, Pablo, *Democracy in Mexico,* 2d ed., tr. Danielle Salti, New York, 1972. A brief study by a distinguished Mexican scholar.

Gordon, W. C., *The Political Economy of Latin America,* New York, 1965.

• Halperin, Maurice, *The Rise and Decline of Fidel Castro,* Berkeley, 1972. A critical account of the years 1959–1964.

Hanke, Lewis, *Latin America, a Historical Reader,* Boston, 1974.

• Hellman, J. A., *Mexico in Crisis,* New York, 1978. Assesses developments since the 1910 Revolution.

Hemming, John *Red Gold: The Conquest of the Brazilian Indians,* Cambridge, Mass., 1978. Depicts the tragic results of European expansionism.

LaFeber, Walter, *The Panama Canal: The Crisis in Historical Perspective,* New York, 1978. An informative study of U.S.–Panamanian relations.

Lambert, Jacques, *Latin America: Social Structure and Political Institutions,* tr. Helen Katel, Berkeley, 1967.

Llerena, Mario, *The Unsuspected Revolution: The Birth and Rise of Castroism,* Ithaca, 1978.

• Loveman, Brian, *Chile: The Legacy of Hispanic Capitalism,* New York, 1979. A social and economic history to the overthrow of Allende.

• Lynch, John, *The Spanish American Revolutions, 1808–1826,* New York, 1973.

MacEoin, Gary, *Revolution Next Door: Latin America in the 1970s,* New York, 1971. A profoundly disturbing view of Latin American realities.

• Picón-Salas, Mariano, *A Cultural History of Spanish America: From Conquest to Independence,* tr. I. A. Leonard, Berkeley, 1962.

• Pike, Frederick B., *Spanish America 1900–1970: Traditional and Social Innovation,* New York, 1973.

• Poppino, R. E., *Brazil: The Land and People,* 2d ed., New York, 1973.

Rotberg, R. I., with C. K. Clague, *Haiti: The Politics of Squalor,* Boston, 1971.

Sandford, R. R., *The Murder of Allende and the End of the Chilean Way to Socialism,* tr. Andrée Conrad, New York, 1975. A harrowing narrative by a Chilean political journalist.

• Skidmore, T. E., *Politics in Brazil, 1930–1964: An Experiment in Democracy,* New York, 1969.

• Smith, P. H., *Labyrinths of Power: Political Recruitment in Twentieth-Century Mexico,* Princeton, 1979. A careful analysis of the Mexican political power structure.

Steenland, Kyle, *Agrarian Reform under Allende: Peasant Revolt in the South,* Albuquerque, 1978.

Thomas, Hugh, *Cuba: The Pursuit of Freedom,* New York, 1971. A monumental, well-documented history of Cuba from 1762 to 1970.

• Waddell, D. A. G., *The West Indies and the Guianas,* Englewood Cliffs, N.J., 1967.

Weaver, Muriel, *The Aztecs, Maya, and Their Predecessors: Archaeology of Mesoamerica,* New York, 1972.

Weinstein, Martin, *Uruguay: The Politics of Failure,* Westport, Conn., 1975. A compact, informative analysis.

Wilgus, A. C., ed., *South American Dictators during the First Century of Independence,* Washington, 1937.

Chapter 37

THE COMMONWEALTH OF NATIONS

We are fortunate to witness the emergence of the Republic of India and our successors may well envy us this day, but fortune is a hostage which has to be zealously guarded by our own good work and which has a tendency to slip away if we slacken in our efforts or if we look in wrong directions.

—Jawaharlal Nehru, 1951

Millions of our countrymen filled the jails again and again to attain freedom, but after twenty-seven years of that freedom the people are groaning. Hunger, soaring prices and corruption stalk everywhere. The people are being crushed under all sorts of injustice.

—Jayaprakash Narayan, 1974

One of the most significant developments in the history of democracy in the modern world has been the evolution of the Commonwealth of Nations. Originally called the British Commonwealth of Nations, it now includes a number of states which repudiate any suggestion of allegiance to Britain. All members of the Commonwealth are self-governing, but many of them recognize the British monarch, represented by a governor-general, as their head of state. This group includes—in addition to the United Kingdom—the large Dominions of Canada, Australia, and New Zealand, and such small ones as Barbados, Jamaica, Malta, Mauritius, Sierra Leone, and Trinidad and Tobago. Political changes within the last few years have resulted in the creation within the Commonwealth of many republics, with no ties to the British Crown. The most conspicuous example is India, but the Commonwealth embraces more than a dozen republics, ranging in size from medium to tiny: Bangladesh, Botswana, Cyprus, Sri Lanka (Ceylon), Fiji, Gambia, Ghana, Guyana, Kenya, Malawi, Malaysia, Nigeria, Singapore, Tanzania, Uganda, and Zambia. The little African state of Lesotho (an enclave within the Republic of South Africa) has the distinction of being a separate kingdom within the

The Commonwealth defined

Commonwealth, under the headship of its Paramount Chief. Evidently the only requisite for membership in the Commonwealth is the desire to belong. Because members may secede at any time and new states may join, the Commonwealth is an evolving organization. Ireland withdrew in 1949 and South Africa in 1961. Pakistan—shaken by a disastrous war with India and angered by the recognition accorded to Bangladesh—terminated its membership in the Commonwealth in 1972. The newly independent Republic of Bangladesh joined the next year. The status of Rhodesia was in dispute for fifteen years following a declaration of independence in 1965 by Ian Smith, leader of Rhodesia's white minority. Britain is no longer the focal point of the Commonwealth, whose membership is spread around the globe. Since 1965 the organization has had its own Secretariat headed by a secretary-general. In recent years the area of most active political change has been the Caribbean, where all of Britain's former colonies are preparing for, or have already achieved, independence. The dozen or so ministates resulting from this movement seek economic aid outside the Commonwealth and also wish to establish closer ties with their non-English-speaking neighbors. Dominica, a tiny island of the Lesser Antilles, which progressed from an "associated state" to an independent republic in 1978, elected to remain in the Commonwealth but also planned to join the Organization of American States and other international organizations. Jamaica (which retains as nominal head of state a governor-general appointed by the British Crown rather than an elected president), under Prime Minister Michael Manley (1972–1980), experimented with close ties to Castro's Cuba.

The history of the United Kingdom and of the principal African states is discussed elsewhere. The purpose of this chapter is to give an account of the major Asian republics that arose within the Commonwealth and of the self-governing dominions settled primarily by emigrants from Britain.[1]

The Commonwealth of Nations as an association of independent or virtually independent states has a history of about seven decades. At

The growth of the Commonwealth

an Imperial Conference in 1887, attended by prime ministers of the principal British possessions, suggestions were made that the colonies furthest advanced ought to have the right to participate in the government of the Empire. The idea was revived at subsequent Imperial Conferences, in 1897, in 1902, and in 1907. It was not, however, until World War I that the proposal gave much promise of becoming a reality. The free and liberal assistance given to the mother country by the dominions in that struggle fortified their claims not only to a direct

[1] The Commonwealth of Nations must be distinguished clearly from the British Empire. The latter consists of two parts: the independent empire and the dependent empire. The independent empire includes those members of the Commonwealth of Nations which still render some tenuous allegiance to Great Britain. The dependent empire comprises a diminishing number of colonies ruled directly from London.

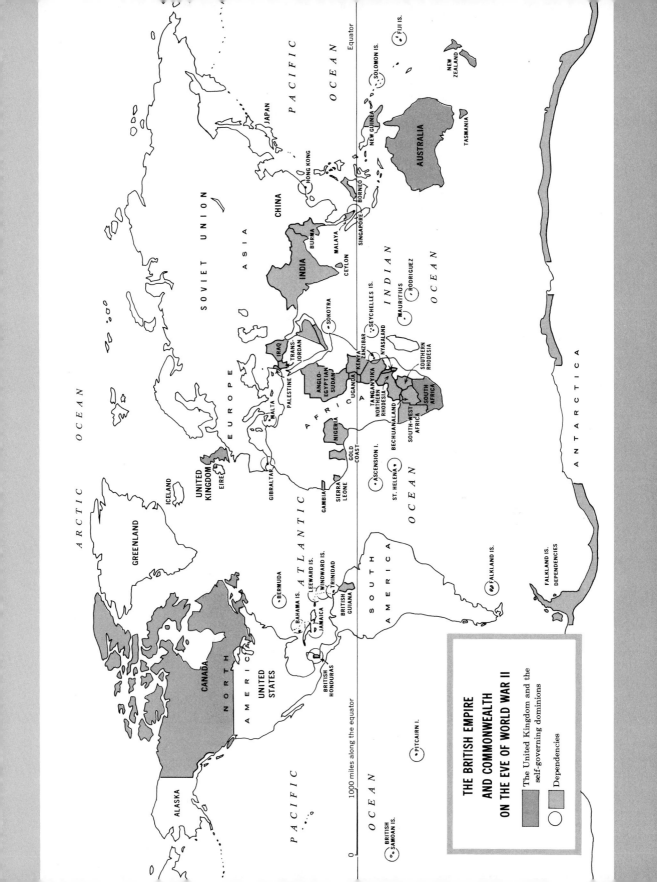

THE BRITISH EMPIRE
AND COMMONWEALTH
ON THE EVE OF WORLD WAR II

The United Kingdom and the
self-governing dominions

○ Dependencies

voice in imperial affairs but to a more definite recognition of their own independence. The Imperial Conference of 1921 agreed that the events of the war had clearly established the right of the self-governing dominions to be considered coequals with the mother country in foreign affairs. The Conference of 1926 adopted a report prepared by Arthur James Balfour, former prime minister of Great Britain. The report described the self-governing areas under the British flag (including the United Kingdom) as "autonomous communities within the British Empire, equal in status, in no way subordinate one to another in any aspect of their domestic or external affairs, though united by a common allegiance to the crown, and freely associated as members of the British Commonwealth of Nations." In 1931 the substance of the Balfour Report was enacted by Parliament in a memorable law known as the Statute of Westminster.

Since the enactment of the Statute of Westminster the several states of the Commonwealth of Nations have functioned as practically independent republics. No longer may any law passed by a dominion parliament be disallowed by the Parliament in London or vetoed by the British Cabinet, and no law of the British Parliament may be applied to any dominion unless its government specifically requests that this be done. The prime minister of each dominion has an equal right with the prime minister of Britain to "advise" the king directly. The king himself serves as a mere symbol of the unity of the Commonwealth. Although he is represented in each dominion (but not in the Republics) by a governor-general, the latter has no real authority. His primary function is to receive the resignation of an outgoing prime minister and to designate the leader of the opposition party as his successor. This involves no more freedom of choice than is exercised by the monarch himself when the head of the British Cabinet loses the support of the majority in the House of Commons and gives way to the leader of His (Her) Majesty's Loyal Opposition.

The Commonwealth is no longer the boon to Great Britain that it formerly was. Even those members that acknowledge allegiance to the British monarch have shown an increasing spirit of economic independence and indifference to the welfare of the United Kingdom. It has been said that most of the Old World members are about as beneficial to the former mother country as "poor relations on pay day." Though they continue to look for generous contributions of British aid, they show little disposition to confer any benefits in return. Ghana, for example, grants no preference to British goods. While Australian industrial products enter New Zealand duty free, British goods are subject to tariffs. Air India not only competes with British Airways, but equips its fleet with commercial airliners purchased from the United States. In 1965 Britain had a total trade deficit with the Commonwealth nations of over $1 billion.

The recorded history of Canada dates from 1608 when Samuel Champlain, a French naval officer with an interest in the fur trade, founded a settlement at Quebec. For thirty years thereafter he continued his activities in the St. Lawrence valley, staking claims for the French king as far west as Lake Huron. Later in the seventeenth century the French government granted monopolies to trading companies to colonize and develop "New France." Although the companies ultimately failed, they did establish a few forts and trading posts and brought over a few thousand of their countrymen as permanent settlers. Finally, Jesuit missionaries contributed their part toward opening up the country and enlarging knowledge of its resources and attractions. By the middle of the eighteenth century the population of Canada included about 60,000 Frenchmen.

The founding of Canada

France lost Canada to Great Britain in the French and Indian War, but for some years thereafter the British continued to assume that their newly acquired possession would remain French. When the British Parliament passed the Quebec Act in 1774 to correct certain defects in the organization of the Empire, Canada was not given a representative assembly, since it was taken for granted that the people could neither understand nor be loyal to British institutions. But after the American War for Independence so many Loyalist refugees from the United States, together with immigrants from Great Britain, settled in Ontario that William Pitt thought it advisable to have Parliament enact a law in 1791 separating Upper Canada (Ontario), which was almost entirely British, from Lower Canada (Quebec), which was overwhelmingly French, and providing for an elective assembly in each of the two provinces. The scheme ended in failure. The French and British distrusted each other, and conflicts soon arose between the elective assemblies and the royal governors sent out from London. In 1837 the antagonism flared into an open rebellion. Although quickly suppressed, it called attention to Canada's grievances and impressed upon the British government the necessity of doing something about them. The result was the appointment of a High Commissioner, Lord Durham, with authority to investigate conditions and to institute reforms. When he proceeded to act in too arbitrary a fashion, the government in London withdrew its support and revoked some of his decrees. Durham resigned in anger and returned to England, but subsequently published a report which was destined to become famous in the history of dominion government.

Troubles between French and British Canada

The Durham Report enunciated two principles, which may be regarded as the cornerstone of the dominion system. First, its author declared that colonies already possessing representative institutions should be granted "responsible government." This meant that they

The beginning of responsible government

should be permitted to manage their local affairs through cabinets or ministries responsible to their own legislatures. In the second place, Lord Durham urged the principle that similar colonies in the same geographic area should be federated into one large unit. Applying this to Canada, he pleaded for the unification of the British and French portions into a single dominion. In accordance with this recommendation Upper and Lower Canada were presently united. In 1847 Lord Durham's son-in-law, Lord Elgin, became governor of Canada and put into effect the principle of choosing his cabinet from the party that controlled a majority of seats in the assembly. He allowed it to be inferred that the cabinet would remain in office only so long as it received the support of the majority party. In addition he signed bills sponsored by the cabinet, despite the fact that they conflicted with the interests of the mother country. By these means he conferred upon Canada for all practical purposes a system of responsible government similar to that of Great Britain.

Establishment of the Dominion of Canada

But the dominion government as we now know it dates only from 1867. In that year the hitherto separate colonies of New Brunswick and Nova Scotia united with Quebec and Ontario to form a confederation under the name of the Dominion of Canada. A frame of government was provided for them by the British North America Act passed by the London Parliament in the same year. This act embodied a constitution which the Canadians themselves had adopted in 1864. It established a federal system with a division of powers between the central government and the governments of the provinces. All powers not delegated to the governments of the provinces were declared to be reserved to the central government, with its capital at Ottawa in Ontario Province. This departure from the federal pattern in the United States was inspired in part by the fact that the claims of the seceding southern states to full sovereignty had helped to bring on the American War between the States.

The British North America Act

The British North America Act confirmed the principle of responsible government. A governor-general, appointed technically by the king but actually by the British Cabinet, was made the nominal head of the Dominion. The real power over local affairs was placed in the hands of a Dominion cabinet, nominally appointed by the governor-general but actually responsible to the lower house of the legislature for its official acts and its tenure of office. Legislative power was vested in a Parliament of two houses, a Senate appointed by the governor-general for life, and a House of Commons elected by the people. Except for the fact that cabinet responsibility was to be enforced by the House of Commons exclusively and that money bills must originate therein, both houses were given equal powers. In practice, however, the Senate has retired into a kind of dignified obsolescence, performing no functions except those of an unambitious revising chamber. The Canadian constitution also provided for responsible government in the provinces. The nominal head of each province is a

The Fathers of Confederation. Painting by R. Harris. The constitution that established the confederation was based on the British system of parliamentary government. The British system had to be adapted to satisfy the need for a federal rather than a unitary structure and the framers of the constitution and the confederation inevitably looked to the Constitution of the United States for guidance. The result was a uniquely Canadian achievement designed to address Canada's particular requirements.

lieutenant-governor appointed by the Dominion cabinet. The effective authority is exercised by a cabinet responsible to the provincial legislature. Except in Quebec the legislative bodies in the provinces have only one house.

Since 1867 the growth of Canada has roughly paralleled that of the United States. When the British North America Act was passed, Canada had a population of 3 ½ million. By 1966 it had grown to 20 million. During the same period the population of the United States increased from 38 million to 196 million. The growth in area of the Dominion of Canada was equally phenomenal. In 1869 the province of Manitoba was carved out of territory purchased from the Hudson's Bay Company. In 1871–1873 British Columbia and Prince Edward Island were added to the Dominion. By 1905 the completion of the Canadian Pacific Railway made possible the creation of two new prairie provinces, Alberta and Saskatchewan. But the growth of Canada cannot be measured in terms of area and population alone. The latter half of the nineteenth century and the early years of the twentieth witnessed the establishment of a sound banking and currency system, a civil service, and a protective tariff for the benefit of Canadian industry. Marked progress occurred also in the exploitation of mineral and forest resources. Canada became the chief supplier of nickel, asbestos, cobalt, and wood pulp to the United States.

Growth of the Dominion

But the Dominion had not yet attained national maturity. It could not amend its own constitution, which in form was an act of the British Parliament, and it was dependent upon the mother country for the conduct of its foreign relations. Perhaps more significant, its population was not being welded into homogeneity. With the opening up of the West, thousands of Ruthenians, Russians, Poles, Scandinavians, and Germans flooded the prairie provinces. Between 1903 and 1914 nearly 2,700,000 such immigrants made their way into Canada. As late as 1941 more than 40 percent of the population of the prairie provinces was of Central or East European origin. But by far the largest minority population was to be found in Quebec. It comprised the French Canadians, whose settlement in the country went back to the earliest beginnings. Fearful of domination by the English-speaking majority and unable to exert much influence on the policies of the central government, they fortified their independent spirit by an increase in numbers—the "revenge of the nursery." Until well into the twentieth century French Canadians had one of the highest birth rates in the world, and today they constitute more than 25 percent of Canada's total population of 23 million. Since 1954, however, their birth rate has been declining, and Quebec now has the lowest rate of population increase in the Dominion. A growing disadvantage in numbers strengthened the French Canadians' determination to resist assimilation.

*Effects of the World Wars
in welding Canada into a
nation*

It is generally asserted that Canada achieved maturity as a nation during World War I. Although interested but little in the tortuous diplomacy leading up to the conflict, the Ottawa government accepted Britain's declaration as an automatic commitment for the whole Empire. The Dominion pledged itself to unlimited support and made sacrifices proportionately equal to those of the mother country itself. Out of a population of only 9 million at the time, 600,000 joined the armed forces, and more than 50,000 gave up their lives on the fighting front. Proud of their efforts in what was generally regarded as a noble cause, Canadians lost their sense of colonial inferiority and came forth as leading champions of Western ideals of democracy and peace. After 1917 the Canadian prime minister sat in the Imperial War Cabinet as an equal of the prime minister of Great Britain in formulating policy. When the war ended, Canada demanded and received a seat at the Peace Conference and subsequently was admitted to the League of Nations. In the years that followed, the Dominion asserted its independence in foreign policy by refusing to accept commitments under treaties negotiated by the British without Canadian participation. Nevertheless, when World War II broke out, Canada plunged into the fray with hardly a moment's hesitation. The threat to the survival of Britain was almost universally regarded as a threat to the interests of Canada. Although the Dominion might legally have remained neutral, it pledged its wealth and the lives of its youth in the same unstinted measure as had characterized its action in World War I.

By the end of World War II Canada, with a greatly strengthened economy, had won a prominent place in world affairs. The Dominion made loans to Great Britain and played a significant role in the development of the United Nations and in the establishment of NATO. At the same time, many old problems remained unsolved. As a nation Canada was still underpopulated. With an area almost equal to that of Europe, it had fewer inhabitants than New York State. Forty-five percent of its people dwelt in the St. Lawrence valley in an area covering but 2 percent of the country. The Yukon and Northwest territories, equal in size to half of the United States, contained only 14,000 inhabitants. At least 50 percent of the land of the Dominion remained unsuitable for agriculture or for almost any other occupation except fur trading and mining. Worse still, the population was sharply divided on the basis of sectional and ethnic interests. Ontario was dominated by industrial and financial ambitions, which gave to the province a conservative outlook in economic affairs and at the same time a determination to achieve independence from British and American influences. The prairie provinces, inhabited largely by immigrants from the United States and from Continental European countries, were the stronghold of agrarian collectivism and of radical innovations for currency inflation and cheap credit. French Canada, embraced by the province of Quebec, continued its devotion to the culture and religion of its ancestors and its resistance to domination from Ottawa.

Old problems remaining unsolved

The geographic position of Canada was also a source of uneasiness. It had the misfortune to lie directly athwart the air routes between Russia and the United States. As the Cold War between these two giants waxed in intensity, Canada had reason to fear that the United States might attempt to dictate an increasing number of its military and economic policies. Many Canadian businessmen disliked the influx of capital investment from the United States, the control of branch factories by foreign head offices, and the excess of imports from the United States over Canadian exports purchased by the States. So strong was the ill feeling that President Eisenhower paid a visit to Ottawa in 1958 and arranged for the setting up of a joint governmental committee to promote cooperation and a better understanding between the two countries. Any results the committee may have achieved were nullified by sharp criticism by the United States government, early in 1963, of Canada's unwillingness to equip its armed forces with nuclear weapons. In the ensuing controversy the Conservative prime minister, John Diefenbaker, lost the support of a majority in the House of Commons and yielded his office to Lester Pearson, leader of the Liberal party. In 1968 Pearson resigned on account of ill health and was succeeded by Pierre Trudeau.

Canada's crucial position

Prime Minister Pierre Trudeau of Canada

The eleven-year ministry of Canada's Liberal party under Pierre Trudeau was a colorful but hardly a tranquil period. Endowed with a lively intellect and considerable personal charm, Trudeau, even with a substantial following, was unable to solve Canada's basic problems. In spite of economic growth and the stimulus of profitable grain exports during the 1970s, nearly 8 percent of the work force was unemployed, and the Canadian dollar slumped below the exchange value of the United States dollar, which was also declining. Confidence in Trudeau's leadership was weakened by his wife's erratic conduct and also by the revelation of surreptitious activities carried on by the Royal Canadian Mounted Police. This revered police force, it was discovered, had for many years secretly opened mail, committed burglaries, and falsified records in combating suspected subversives. Like President Nixon when confronted with Watergate, Trudeau attempted—but failed—to block a judicial investigation of the affair, invoking the claim of "national security." An even deeper source of dissatisfaction lay in the opposition of Canada's provinces to the tightened control exercised by the central government ever since World War II. In Quebec, discontent threatened to disrupt the Dominion.

The French-speaking Québecois, comprising five-sixths of the province's 6 million inhabitants, had long-standing economic and ciate of Frank Lloyd Wright. In 1927 the seat of government of the Commonwealth was formally transferred to the new federal city. resented being conscripted to fight wars they regarded as English and imperialist. They wanted their own educational system to preserve their language and culture. In 1967 René Lévesque organized the *Parti Québecois,* which set as its goal the separation of Quebec from the Canadian federation. Steadily gathering support, the separatist party won a sizable majority of the provincial legislature in the election of 1976 and Lévesque became Quebec's premier. The Parti Québecois's victory made the question of separation a foremost national issue, and tralia policy has been motivated both by feelings of race superiority a French-speaking mother, Trudeau in 1969 had secured passage of the Official Languages Act, making the nation bilingual in public announcements and throughout the civil service. On the other hand, he had used extreme repression after the murder of a Quebec cabinet minister in 1970, and he was adamantly committed to maintaining the unity of Canada.

The Parti Québecois *and separatism*

The May 1979 general election toppled Trudeau's government but produced no clear mandate fot the Progressive Conservative party which took office without a majority in the House of Commons. The returns revealed the indifference of the majority of Canadians to the problem of Quebec. Curiously, the antiseparatist Trudeau carried Quebec while losing heavily throughout English-speaking Canada. The election also reflected the discontent of the western provinces. Joe Clark, the new prime minister and the youngest in Canadian history, was a native of the plains of Alberta. Canadians soon wearied of

A short-lived Conservative ministry

Clark, especially when he proposed an austerity program of steep tax increases and curtailed government spending, and his ministry was overthrown by an adverse vote on budgetary measures. In a special election in February 1980 the Liberal party won a clear majority, and the resilient Trudeau again became prime minister. Among the still unresolved problems confronting his government was the issue of Quebec separatism, which Trudeau, in common with the Conservative opposition, continued to oppose. It seemed doubtful that an independent Quebec could survive even if permitted to secede. Its industry has depended on access to a protected market within Canada. The province receives more in federal aid than it pays in taxes to the central government, yet it has a sizable budgetary deficit. A referendum that Lévesque held in the spring of 1980 indicated that two thirds of Quebec's voters opposed separation from the Canadian federation.

Serious disputes persisted between Ottawa and the sparsely inhabited but richly endowed and rapidly developing western provinces of Manitoba, Saskatchewan, Alberta, and British Columbia, toward which the balance of political power was shifting. Westerners complained that their interests were subordinated to those of populous Ontario and the Atlantic provinces. Trudeau resolved to replace the British North America Act of 1867 with a new constitution that would not only eliminate any hint of dependence on Great Britain, but would also give the central government greater control over natural resources and enable it to redress the inequitable distribution of wealth among the provinces. A conference of provincial premiers in the fall of 1980 failed to agree on constitutional changes. Western oil producers demanded the right to raise the price of oil, which had been kept at about half the current world price, and bridled at suggestions that the oil and gas industries might be nationalized.

Growing discontent of the Western provinces

Relations between Canada and the United States have long been close though sometimes strained. With investments of some $35 billion, by 1970 United States capital controlled the greater part of Canada's rubber and petroleum industries and about 45 percent of total manufacturing and mining capacity. The United States absorbed two-thirds of the Dominion's exports and supplied even more of its imports. Although Ottawa in 1976 established a contractual link with the European Common Market and entered into trade negotiations with Japan, trade between Canada and the United States increased even further. The two countries are each other's most important trade partner and seem likely to remain so. Beginning in 1968 the balance of trade shifted in Canada's favor, and Canada now has heavy capital investments in the United States. In the fall of 1980 the Canadian government took a number of controversial steps designed to reduce foreign control of its mineral and energy resources.

Relations with the United States

With full allowance for Canada's difficulties, there is little doubt that its future holds bright promise. Canada is one of the world's most richly endowed countries in natural resources. With a population hardly more than one-tenth that of the United States, the Dominion's foreign trade is almost one-third as large. Canada leads the world in the production of asbestos, nickel, platinum, zinc, and wood pulp. The nation ranks second in the production of aluminum, cobalt, and uranium, third in the production of gold and titanium, and fourth in the production of wheat. Extensive deposits of iron ore have been discovered in Labrador. Rich deposits of natural gas and oil (some of it under Arctic ice) are a particularly valuable asset when the world's energy sources are shrinking.

2. THE COMMONWEALTH OF AUSTRALIA

The second largest island[2] in the world and the smallest of the continents, Australia began its recorded history under inauspicious circumstances. Discovered by the Dutch in the seventeenth century and rediscovered and claimed for England by Captain James Cook in 1770, it was too remote from the homeland to offer attractions for settlement. When the American Revolution eliminated the thirteen colonies in the Western Hemisphere as dumping grounds for British convicts, the government in London turned to Australia. The first convict ship sailed for the island continent in 1787, and Australia remained a penal colony for fifty years. It should be noted, however, that not all the prisoners transported were burglars and cutthroats. The criminal laws of England at that time provided drastic penalties for trivial offenses, such as petty larceny or hunting partridges on

[2] Australia has an area of 2,967,000 square miles. Antarctica, also an island and a continent, has an estimated area of 6,000,000 square miles.

The Landing of Captain Cook at Botany Bay, 1770. This painting, by E. Phillips Fox, depicts the first landing by Englishmen on the east coast of the Australian continent.

Commissioner Hardy Collecting License Fees in the Victoria Gold Fields in the 1850s. Diggers scatter in order to evade paying the fees.

some noble's estate. We can reasonably assume, therefore, that many of the original colonists in Australia were far from being what we would now call hardened ciminals.

The first settlers were convicts exclusively, except for 200 soldiers sent to guard them. This continued to be the case for some time. Gradually a few adventurous free citizens learned of the possibilities of sheep raising and filtered into the colony to establish ranches or "stations." Convicts were released to them as shepherds, with the provision that after the expiration of their terms of sentence they would continue to live in Australia. By 1830 the wool industry had become the backbone of the Australian economy. Ten years later the number of free settlers had grown sufficiently large to justify a decision by the British government to abandon the practice of dumping prisoners in most parts of the continent.

Convicts and settlers

In 1848 the trend of Australian development was abruptly changed by the discovery of gold in New South Wales and Victoria. Fortune hunters and adventurers from all over the world followed the magic lure of the yellow metal. Between 1850 and 1860 the population of the continent almost trebled. Inevitably more people came than could find a livelihood in prospecting and mining. When the excitement died away, and the hills and streams no longer yielded gold in easy abundance, the problem arose of what to do with the surplus population. The logical solution seemed to be to encourage them to become farmers. Efforts to establish themselves in this occupation involved a desperate struggle. Scanty rainfall, inadequate transportation facilities, and refusal of the wool growers to "unlock" their vast estates dogged the footsteps of all but the most fortunate farmers with disaster. Not

The discovery of gold

until the building of railways to the ports, the perfection of dry-farming techniques, the development of suitable strains of wheat, and the improvement of chemical fertilizers was agriculture in Australia placed on a sound foundation.

A considerable number of the basic political and social policies of Australia as a nation can be traced to the gold rushes of the 1850s and their aftermath. First was the White Australia policy, designed to exclude black, brown, and yellow races from settlement on the continent. This policy was an outgrowth of conflicts between Chinese and Caucasian miners in the gold fields. A second was the attempt to build up a manufacturing industry through the use of protective tariffs. Originally adopted by the colony of Victoria in the 1860s, tariffs were later extended to the Commonwealth as a whole. Their use was motivated in part at least by the need for domestic industry to absorb the surplus miners. A third policy was the adoption of heavy governmental borrowing for the construction of public works. Obviously, the need for publicworks construction could be justified for many reasons: to provide irrigation projects for the benefit of farmers in arid regions; to speed up the development of transportation facilities; to furnish employment opportunities for the influx of immigrants brought in by the discovery of gold.

The Australian Commonwealth as an organized state did not come into existence until 1901. Prior to that time the continent was divided into separate colonies, most of which had split off from the original colony of New South Wales. Movements to federate them made slow progress, mainly because the weak feared domination by the strong and prosperous. But such fears did not prevent a rapid growth of local democracy. By 1850 each of the colonies had its legislative council as a check upon the governor, and had obtained the right to alter its own constitution. Soon afterward the eastern colonies achieved responsible government. Universal manhood suffrage was introduced in South Australia in 1855, in Victoria in 1857, and in New South Wales a year later. About the same time the secret ballot was adopted in Victoria, South Australia, New South Wales, and Queensland. Before 1900 two colonies had begun payment of salaries to members of their legislatures, and several had given women the privilege of voting.

The stage was eventually reached where the arguments for federation outweighed the objections. Foremost among them was the need for a common defense against the militant imperialism of the Great Powers. Important also was the growing inconvenience of tariffs levied by the various colonies against each other. The first step for a union of the continent was taken in 1885 with the establishment of the Australasian Federal Council. Possessing only legislative power with no executive or financial authority, this agency was reduced to impotence by the noncooperation of New South Wales. Its chief significance lay in the renewed impetus it gave to the demand for effective

Establishment of the Seat of Government at Canberra. The Duke and Duchess of York in the Senate at the official opening of the Federal Parliament House in Canberra on May 9, 1927. The Duke reads King George V's commission for the establishment of the seat of government at Canberra.

union. In 1897–1898 a series of conferences resulted in the drafting of a plan of federation which in 1901 was approved by the British Parliament and became the Constitution of the Commonwealth of Australia. The Commonwealth was organized as a federal union comprising the six states of New South Wales, Victoria, Queensland, South Australia, Western Australia, and Tasmania. The capital was temporarily established at Melbourne, but the Constitution contained a provision that a permanent capital should be built in the state of New South Wales, not less than 100 miles from Sydney. In the course of a decade the government invited city planners from all over the world to submit blueprints for a garden municipality to be known as Canberra. The award was given to W. B. Griffin of Chicago, an associate of Frank Lloyd Wright. In 1927 the seat of government of the Commonwealth was formally transferred to the new federal city.

The government of Australia bears a closer resemblance to that of the United States than does the government of Canada. Such a development was rendered inevitable by the spirit of independence existing within the states of Australia and by their distrust of each other. Consequently, when the division of powers was made by the Constitution, it was logical that the government of the Commonwealth should be given only specified powers, and that all powers not thus delegated should be reserved to the states. In some other respects also the Australian system resembles, superficially at least, the American. The Australian Parliament consists of two houses, a Senate and a House of Representatives. The former is composed of six members from each state, elected directly by the people for six years. Membership in the House is proportionate to population. Like several other members of the Commonwealth, Australia has a governor-general representing

The government of Australia

*Factors contributing to
social and economic
planning: (1) scanty
rainfall*

the British Crown, but his powers are insignificant. As in all of the dominions, executive authority as well as the primary control over legislation is vested in the cabinet headed by the prime minister.

One of the most interesting facts of Australian history is the extent to which the country has pursued a policy of social and economic planning. Even during the nineteenth century when the mother country was worshiping the slogans of free competition and free trade, Australia was steadily enlarging the sphere of governmental action to promote social cohesion and maintain a high standard of living. The reasons for this policy are numerous and varied. Geography alone provides a large part of the explanation. One-third of the continent has an average annual rainfall of less than 10 inches, and most of the remainder has less than 20. But even these averages do not reflect the poor distribution of the rain that does fall. In many areas the precipitation may be concentrated within a short period of the year, with months or years of subsequent drought. As a result, only about 8 percent of the total area can be utilized for farming or orchard purposes. About 40 percent is waste, and 50 percent is used for pasture. Under such conditions, it has been impossible for Australia to develop into a nation of independent proprietors cultivating small plots as family farms. In the pasture areas rainfall is so scanty or unreliable that sheep and cattle must be grazed over thousands of acres. This has necessitated the development of vast estates or pastoral "stations" established by owners with considerable capital. They provide employment for what is essentially an agricultural proletariat: shepherds, shearers, and "boundary riders," who have no hope of ever becoming proprietors. Conscious of their grievances, they have been drawn since the later nineteenth century into militant trade unions to struggle for old-age pensions, unemployment insurance, and minimum wages. They have been among the most consistent supporters of government intervention in economic affairs.

A second factor contributing to governmental control and regulation was the gold rushes of the 1850s. As previously noted, these produced a surplus of prospectors and miners who had to be channeled into new occupations. The result was positive action by the colonial governments to promote the development of industry and to extend agriculture into all parts of the limited area where rainfall would permit. The discovery of gold also gave rise to racial problems. In the 1850s thousands of Chinese poured into Victoria and New South Wales and threatened the wage scales and living standards of the white miners. Rapidly the Australians became obsessed with the idea that their country was a "white island in a vast colored ocean." Having already expropriated and partially exterminated the native black population, they pointed to the hundreds of millions of dark-skinned inhabitants of India, the Netherlands Indies, China, and Japan as a flood tide which would overwhelm them unless they built dikes in the form of rigid exclusion laws. Even the tropical regions of northern Australia were to be kept uncontaminated by Oriental labor. Queensland, for example, has taken pride in recent years in the ability of its white inhabitants to cultivate its sugar plantations without being defeated by the moral and physical diseases that have commonly wreaked such havoc upon Caucasians in the tropics.[3] The White Australia policy has been motivated both by feelings of race superiority and by fear of economic competition. Some of its sponsors argue that it is essential to democracy. Racial divisions, they say, would create tensions and conflicts and destroy the spirit of compromise which can exist only in a community of equals. After World War II immigration policy was modified somewhat. Yet as late as 1960 only 5 percent of Australians were of non-British origin. A few of these were Asians, but most had migrated from European countries other than Britain.

One of the earliest forms of government intervention in Australia was control of international trade. The methods employed have included tariffs, bounties, quotas, and marketing restrictions. From the middle of the nineteenth century the several Australian colonies imposed protective tariffs on intercolonial trade. They did so not merely for the benefit of the business classes but to provide employment and to maintain as high a standard of living as possible for farmers and workers. When the Commonwealth was established in 1901, the tariff policy was continued, and the rates have been steadily increased. Sentiment in favor of protection is almost universal. Labor as well as capital insists upon the importance of controlling economic forces for the general welfare. Neither has any respect for the laissez-faire philosophy or is willing to trust the fate of Australia to the shifting trends of the international market.

Protectionism

A second form of government intervention for which Australia has been particularly noted is public ownership of a wide variety of economic enterprises. Ventures brought under government ownership include railways, shipping lines, power plants, hotels, banks, insurance companies, lumber mills, and coal mines. Because of the federal structure of the government, most of such enterprises are conducted by the states rather than by the Commonwealth. Government ownership in Australia is the result in part of the strong influence which labor wields in both state and national politics. Owing to a rigid control of immigration, the supply of labor has been kept from exceeding the demand. This has fostered the growth of a unionism surpassing in strength that of most other countries. In Australia at the present time about 40 percent of all wage earners are enrolled in labor unions, compared with little more than 25 percent in the United States. But orga-

Government ownership

---

[3] It is an ironical fact, however, that in the nineteenth century thousands of Melanesians and Polynesians were brought in from the Pacific islands and shamelessly exploited. They were deported in 1906.

Australia's Nuclear Power Project. A 350-megawatt turbo-generator was commissioned in August 1973 at Yallourn, 90 miles east of Melbourne. The Yallourn complex is the main source of power for the highly industrialized state of Victoria. The plant, built by a Japanese firm, is dominated by the two giant cooling towers. In the background are the old Yallourn power station and an open cut coal field.

nized labor has not been the only force supporting state ownership. The geography of Australia has impelled many capitalists and landowners to look with favor upon government operation of railways and public utilities, at least. Scanty rainfall over most of the continent has limited the growth of cities and towns in the hinterland. But the construction of railroads to bring out the grain, wool, meat, and minerals has been none the less important. With few private corporations bold enough to incur the risks involved, there was no alternative but for governments to shoulder the burden. As a consequence, in these and in some other lines, public ownership of economic ventures has been welcomed as an aid and support of private business.

Other forms of collectivism

In social-welfare legislation Australian achievements have been little more distinctive than those of most other democracies. In a number of cases Australia (together with New Zealand) pioneered in this type of regulation. Other cases merely duplicated the pattern of Great Britain. Old-age pensions, widows' allowances, unemployment and health insurance, slum clearance, and child subsidies stand out as the principal examples. A bonus is paid for every infant born in Australia, and an endowment is provided for every child under sixteen. A National Health System furnishes free drugs, subsidizes hospital and medical expenses, and provides pensions for the blind and victims of tuberculosis. One other element of Australian collectivism, however, has had no counterpart in the mother country. This is a system of compulsory arbitration and wage fixing, designed to maintain industrial peace and safeguard standards of living for industrial workers. In sharp contrast with the attitude of organized labor in most countries, Australian workers have accepted, and for the most part actually welcomed, compulsory arbitration. They regard it as a means to security and as a source of strength for the labor movement, since it tends to bring more members into the union. Moreover, the political strength of the workers is so great that they look upon the government as an agency they can hope to control. Therefore, they do not fear compulsory arbitration as a device which antilabor elements might use against them.

During the past three decades, except for a brief interlude in 1972–1975, Australian politics have been dominated by a coalition of two parties, the Liberal party and the Country party, each of which is actually conservative. A split in the ranks of the Labor party and apprenhension over national security, aggravated by the Cold War, helped give the conservatives their long tenure of power. During this era the government generally followed the lead of the United States in foreign affairs. It sent troops to fight in Korea and in Vietnam, and permitted the United States to install defense bases and electronic communications stations on Australian soil. Growing dissatisfaction with these commitments, together with inflation and the threat of rising unemployment, undermined the popularity of the conservative administration of Prime Minister William McMahon. The national election of December 1972 returned the Labor party to office with a majority in the House of Representatives, and the new prime minister, Gough Whitlam, embarked on an active policy in both domestic and external affairs. He introduced new social-welfare measures, including free university education and the promise—long overdue—of humane treatment of the black aborigines who had been oppressed, neglected, and forced to live in the desolate "Outback" or in city slums. While not repudiating the tripartite security treaty which bound Australia and New Zealand to the United States, Whitlam sought a more independent role for his country. He withdrew Australian troops from the Vietnam War, of which he had long been a critic, ended the military draft, and normalized relations with North Vietnam, North Korea, and the People's Republic of China.

The Labor government under Whitlam's innovative leadership lasted only three years. The high cost of his welfare measures aroused resentment, particularly in business circles, and his display of independence in foreign policy displeased Washington. In October 1975 the Australian Senate, for the first time in the Commonwealth's history, refused to pass the government's budget bill, and the governor-general took the unprecedented step of dismissing the prime minister. Whitlam denounced the governor-general's action as unconstitutional, and Labor demonstrated support for its ousted leader by staging strikes and mass rallies, but in the national election of December 1975 the conservative coalition of Liberal and Country parties won by a landslide. The new prime minister, Malcolm Fraser, a wealthy farmer, promised to combat inflation, cut welfare spending, and restore business confidence.

Australia's defense and intelligence systems are heavily dependent

The Labor Ministry of Gough Whitlam

E. Gough Whitlam, Prime Minister of Australia (1972–1975)

Return of the Conservative Coalition

upon the United States, which country is also an important trading partner. The Commonwealth's economic relationships, however, have shifted considerably during the past twenty years and probably will continue to change. In 1960 Australia sent Great Britain 27 percent of its exports and received in return 36 percent of its imports. A decade later its chief market was Japan. By 1971 30 percent of Australia's exports went to Japan and more than 60 percent of its mineral exports. For coking coal the figure was close to 100 percent. And while Australians had become Japan's chief supplier of raw materials other than oil, they might also expect to develop eventually a profitable market in China, especially for their wheat.

3. THE DOMINION OF NEW ZEALAND

Located about 1,100 miles southeast of Australia, New Zealand was also discovered by the Dutch but explored and claimed for the British by Captain James Cook. At the time of discovery (1769) it was inhabited exclusively by Maoris, an intelligent but warlike people of Polynesian stock. For three-quarters of a century thereafter the only white settlers were missionaries, who labored with modest success to convert the Maoris to Christianity. In 1840 the first boatload of British colonists entered the harbor of what is now Wellington. They had been sent out by the New Zealand Company, founded by Edward Gibbon Wakefield, leader of the new British school of systematic colonizers. While completing a prison term for abducting a schoolgirl heiress, Wakefield came to the conclusion that Britain would be engulfed by civil war unless new economic opportunities could be found for the distressed population of its industrial cities. Caught in the maelstrom of depression and unemployment, workers by the thousands were turning to Chartism and sundry varieties of socialism. A conflict with the privileged classes was inevitable. Eventually Wakefield hit upon the idea that colonization would banish the specter of civil war. The company he founded would transport selected colonists to New Zealand. They would be provided with land at prices sufficiently high to discourage easy accumulation. Only the more prosperous and enterprising colonists would attain the status of owners. The others would have to content themselves for years with jobs as farm laborers. In time they too would buy land, and the proceeds from the sale would be used to finance further immigration.[4]

Wakefield's scheme attracted so much attention that the British government decided to take action. A governor was appointed, and

---

[4] The scheme had already been tried in South Australia, but with limited success. Wakefield subsequently turned to New Zealand in the hope that his theories would be vindicated.

the islands were formally annexed to the British Empire. The announced purpose was to protect the Maoris against unscrupulous white settlers. A week after the first colonists landed at Wellington the newly appointed governor arrived. He proceeded to negotiate a treaty with the native chiefs recognizing the sovereignty of the British Crown over all New Zealand. In return the British guaranteed to the Maoris full possession of their lands, "except as the Crown might wish to purchase them," and granted to the natives the rights and privileges of British subjects. Perhaps it was well that the government acted as it did, for a broadening stream of colonists continued to flow to the islands. By 1856 New Zealand had a white population of 45,000.

In 1852 the British government endowed New Zealand with a constitution. It conferred the executive power upon a governor-general representing the king, and acting with the advice of an Executive Council. Legislative authority was vested in a House of Representatives elected by the people and a Legislative Council appointed by the governor-general. In 1856 the Executive Council was formally recognized as a cabinet, exercising its functions under the principle of responsible government, and in 1951 the appointive upper house was abolished. Other steps in the direction of political democracy came easily. In 1879 universal manhood suffrage was adopted, and a few years later plural voting was abolished. In 1893 New Zealand led the Commonwealth of Nations in bestowing the suffrage upon women in national elections.

Economic reform followed in the wake of political democracy. When the Liberals came into power in 1891 they dedicated their efforts to making New Zealand a nation of small, independent farmers and herdsmen. Measures were adopted to break up large holdings, the formation of which had previously been encouraged by the sale of Maori lands to wealthy individuals. To combat the power of the big landowners required the support not only of landless agriculturists but also of workers in the cities. The Liberals therefore espoused a program of combined agrarian and labor reform which won the allegiance of both classes. The agrarian measures took the form primarily of special taxes on land held for speculative purposes and limitation of the size of holdings in the future. For the benefit of the workers the Liberals provided old-age pensions, factory inspection, regulation of working hours, and compulsory arbitration of industrial disputes. The accession of the Labor party to power in 1935 brought an extension of these measures, with increased benefits to the urban workers.

New Zealand has followed policies of collectivization quite similar to those of Australia. The reasons also have been similar. Lacking the capital to take advantage of new inventions, especially the railroad and the telegraph, the Dominion turned to foreign sources. Money proved to be more easily obtainable when the government itself was the borrower. Moreover, there was a deeply rooted fear among the colonists themselves of private monopoly. The beginning of collectivism occurred about 1870, when the Dominion government entered the London capital market for funds to construct roads, trunk railways, and telegraph lines. About the same time a state life-insurance system was established, and later state fire and accident insurance. A few coal mines also were added to the list of public enterprises, and finally a Bank of New Zealand. Important as a principle of collectivization has been the use of state-owned enterprises for "yardstick" purposes. Government purchase of coal mines, for example, was dictated by the theory that private companies needed the restraint of state competition to keep them from charging excessive prices.

Comparison of New Zealand and Australia

It is not an exaggeration to say that New Zealand enjoys all the advantages for future progress possessed by Australia with none of Australia's disadvantages. The two dominions have homogeneous populations overwhelmingly British in origin. In Australia 99.2 percent of the people are of European extraction, and 97 percent of these are of British ancestry. In New Zealand the percentages are 93 and 96, respectively. In both dominions systematic efforts have been made to preserve perpetually the British character of the nation. The early emigrants to New Zealand brought with them not merely the social customs and political institutions but the flowers, trees, birds, and even animal pests of their native England. New Zealand, like Australia, was populated in considerable measure by people of liberal and even radical tendencies. Both dominions received inundations of immigrants attracted thither by the discovery of gold. Coming from the landless and unemployed elements of Britain, many were infected with Chartism and even traces of socialism. As a consequence, they developed in the colonies institutions of political and economic democracy surpassing those of the mother country.

Upper Takaka Valley, Nelson, New Zealand. New Zealand enjoys the advantages of beautiful scenery, an ideal climate, and an abundance of space for its population.

Geographically, New Zealand has a wide margin of superiority over Australia. Although a mountainous region, with peaks that rise to 12,000 feet, extends the entire length of the southern island, there are no deserts and few areas unsuited to agriculture or grazing. Almost everywhere rainfall is adequate and permits an intensive use of the land. North Island, which contains over 60 percent of the population, has an average of about 50 inches of rain annually. Throughout the Dominion temperatures fluctuate within a comparatively narrow range. Extremes of over 100 degrees or below zero have never been recorded, and in both islands 75 degrees is considered unpleasantly high and 40 degrees uncomfortably low. Such favorable geographic conditions have given to New Zealand a character quite different from that of Australia. For one thing, the distribution of population is much more even. Instead of a few large cities along the seacoast and an almost unoccupied hinterland, there are hundreds of towns of moderate size and not a single city exceeding 400,000. The mean density of population is slightly over 15 persons per square mile compared with 2 for Australia. Geography, more than anything else, has made New Zealand a democracy of small, independent agrarians.

New Zealand has remained more closely connected with its British antecedents than has Australia. For one reason, the British and New Zealand economies are complementary rather than competitive. New Zealand is predominantly agricultural. Two-thirds of its land is suitable for farming and grazing. Its only important manufactures are meat and dairy products, fertilizer, pulp and paper. Two-thirds of New Zealand's exports are sold to Great Britain, and half of its imports come from British sources. However, with the recent British trend toward withdrawal from responsibilities east of Suez, New Zealand's ties with Great Britain appear to be loosening. Also Britain's entry into the European Common Market in 1973—ending the protected market in the mother country for the Dominion's butter, cheese, and lamb—affected New Zealand more seriously than it did Australia.

4. INDIA UNDER COMPANY AND CROWN

In securing outposts in India, the British were motivated solely by an interest in trade and had no intention either of colonizing or of ruling territories. Gradually and quite unsystematically, their trading posts were transformed into centers of political administration. The absorption or conquest of native states, even though it ultimately involved large-scale military operations, was carried out not by the British government but by the British East India Company—a privately owned joint-stock corporation, chartered by the Crown and increasingly subjected to control by Parliament. When finally, in 1858, the company was dissolved and the British government assumed full responsibility for Indian affairs, the administrative and financial system developed by the company was continued in essential features. Another distinctive aspect of the British position in India was the fact that the country was never conquered in its entirety. The British seized strategic regions until their possessions formed a ring around the whole subcontinent (and included substantial portions of the interior as well), but they left hundreds of native states nominally independent. Nevertheless, although Britain's control over India was acquired piecemeal and indirectly, it became as thorough as if it had been imposed by a conquering horde capable of beating down all resistance.

The British East India Company as sovereign

As the trading posts of the East India Company expanded, they gradually took on the nature of colonies. This process had begun even before the close of the seventeenth century and increased rapidly during the eighteenth century. The assumption by the company of sovereign power over various territories created a need for efficient administration, a need which was not met promptly or adequately. In the early days company agents had been selected without regard to their knowledge of Indian affairs (proficiency in Latin and Greek literature was considered much more important), and most of the agents did not remain in India long enough to become well acquainted with the country or its people. There was little integration between the administration of the separate British holdings, although the acquisition of the great province of Bengal (by Robert Clive, in 1757) made Calcutta eventually the company's most important center of administration. Furthermore, the governing body of the company, the court of directors in London, was so far away that its members could not be adequately informed as to what was going on in India. The governors, sent out as servants of the company, in practice often modified

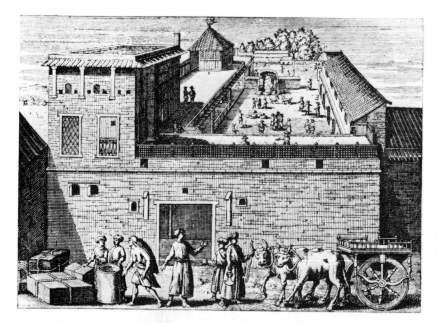

The Modest Beginning of British Rule in India. An early "factory" or trading station, with a walled enclosure containing a warehouse, promenade area, and church. From a copper engraving.

Tipu's Tiger. Wooden model of a tiger mauling a British East India Company officer. This monstrosity (fitted inside with a bellows and miniature organ pipes to simulate groans) was made for Sultan Tipu, ruler of Mysore. Tipu was defeated and killed by Governor Wellesley's troops in 1799.

or even formulated its policies. They negotiated treaties with native rulers, fought wars, and annexed territories.

An act of Parliament in 1814, which renewed the company's charter for twenty years, threw open the commerce of India to all British subjects but allowed the company to retain its monopoly in China and the Far East. By 1834 free-trade sentiment had become so influential in England that the Charter Act of that year deprived the company of all its trading privileges, in China as well as in India. Since it had originally been founded for the purpose of engaging in trade and had now lost that function altogether, the British East India Company might logically have expired in 1834. Instead of doing so, it was permitted to continue administering patronage in the British portions of India, serving as a governmental agency although ultimately subject to parliamentary check. Furthermore, to satisfy the English stockholders, dividends of the company were fixed by law at 10½ percent annually, to be derived no longer from the profits of commerce but levied as a permanent charge upon the revenues of India.

Changes in the status of the company

British territorial expansion inevitably led to conflicts with states beyond the Indian borders. Two Burmese wars made possible the annexation of Lower Burma (1852) and gave the British control of the Bay of Bengal. Less fortunate in sequel was an intervention in the independent state of Afghanistan in 1838–1839, a project unjustified in the first place and so thoroughly bungled that out of an invading force of 16,000 troops only one man escaped death or capture. The fiasco of the Afghan war, however, was a prelude to one of the boldest strokes in the history of British imperialism—the conquest and annexation of Sind. In violation of a signed treaty, the British, during the Afghan war, marched their troops through this independent and neu-

Expansion and conquest

Indian Mutineers Surprised by the Ninth Lancers Unit. A drawing from the book *Campaign in India, 1857–1858.*

tral state and used the country as a military base. Shortly afterward the British government sent Sir Charles Napier with an army into Sind to impose new demands upon the ruling princes. Without even a declaration of war Napier razed a fortress, exiled the rulers, and transferred their sovereignty to the company (1843). Apparently Sir Charles, whose share of the plunder was £70,000, believed that the benefits of British rule outweighed any irregularities in the methods used to establish it. He referred to his own conduct in Sind as "a very advantageous, useful, humane piece of rascality."[5] After two wars against the Sikhs in the Punjab, the governor-general, acting on his own responsibility, annexed the Punjab in 1849. Thus, by the middle of the century, most of the sovereign units in India capable of offering a serious military threat to the British position had been neutralized or brought under the jurisdiction of the company.

The Great Mutiny of 1857

In 1857 an armed uprising, known as the Great Mutiny, produced a crisis in Anglo-Indian relations and necessitated significant changes in British policy. Although the revolt was technically a mutiny because it originated among the native troops (sepoys) employed by the British, it received some popular support and it reflected the political aspirations both of Muslim and of Hindu elements. The underlying causes of the Mutiny lay in general discontent and in suspicions which British policies had aroused. The immediate cause can be attributed to carelessness and gross errors of judgment on the part of

[5] P. E. Roberts, *History of British India*, p. 330.

the military commanders. The British officials were caught quite unprepared for the revolt, which began near Delhi in May 1857, raged intensively for a few months in parts of northern and central India, and was not entirely suppressed until the following year. Many Europeans were slaughtered indiscriminately by the rebel troops, and sickening atrocities were committed on both sides, but the uprising never assumed the character of a mass movement or a genuine revolution. Its leaders were divided in purpose from the beginning. While Muslims dreamed of rehabilitating the Mogul Empire, the Marathas hoped to recover their ascendancy as a powerful Hindu state. The great majority of native princes remained aloof from the rebellion, probably because they recognized the superiority of British military resources.

The most important political result of the Mutiny was the termination of the East India Company and the transfer of full responsibility for the government of India to the British Crown and Parliament.[6] The Government of India Act of 1858 created a secretary of state for India with an advisory council to assist him and bestowed upon the governor-general the title of viceroy. There was no immediate change in the details of the administrative system, but a royal proclamation issued by Queen Victoria offered conciliatory assurances in regard to religious toleration, material improvements, and the admission of native Indians to government service.

The termination of the East India Company

After 1858, in contrast to the earlier period, the policy of the British government in India was one of caution and conservatism. To minimize the danger of rebellion in the future, the bulk of the people were disarmed and the army was reorganized. The recruited troops were carefully trained, instilled with pride in the service, and grouped in accordance with sectarian, tribal, or local divisions so that there would be little feeling of common interest among the different units. Although Europeans formed a minority of the military personnel, they monopolized the ranks of commissioned officers and retained possession of the heavy artillery. At the same time the government sought to avoid antagonizing any powerful element or prejudice within the population. Notably, the British authorities refrained from further territorial aggression. By treaties with the remaining native princes, the British government guaranteed to these rulers their hereditary rights and possessions but required them to relinquish all control over external affairs. Henceforth a clear division was maintained between the five or six hundred native states and the British provinces. The states ranged in size from Hyderabad—with an area almost equal to that of Great Britain—to tiny principalities, and included altogether about 40 percent of the land area of India. A few of the rulers were more progressive than the British, but most of them were

The government's policy of conservatism and caution

---

[6] The company stockholders were still treated with tender consideration. The guaranteed annual dividends of 10½ percent continued to be paid until 1874, at which time the stock was redeemed by a government purchase in the amount of £12,000,000.

The Indian civil service

uninspiring survivals from an age of despotism, quite content to enjoy the protection of the "paramount" power, Great Britain.

The several changes introduced into the government of British India between 1858 and 1919 were more in form than in substance. While the governor-general retained full authority, the door was gradually opened for Indian participation in the administrative machinery by the development of the Indian civil service. From the 1880s on, Indians were allowed to compete in examinations for the selection of civil servants, and they eventually came to supply most of the personnel for the lower and intermediate positions. The Indian civil service grew to be one of the most remarkable institutions of its kind in the world and a source of great pride to the British because of the integrity, efficiency, and loyalty of its members. It exhibited, however, the typical faults of a bureaucracy—inflexibility, conservatism, and lack of imagination. Because there was always an oversupply of educated Indians seeking government posts, and the lucky ones who obtained appointments found their modest salaries considerably above the average income of their countrymen, the civil servants usually developed an attitude of subservience to their superiors. In spite of its beneficent aspects, the Indian civil service became—like the native states—a bulwark of English supremacy and of the status quo.

Benefits of British rule

Widely divergent views have been expressed concerning the overall effects which British administration had upon India and her people, particularly in the nineteenth century. Indisputably, a number of material benefits resulted from British rule. English authorities were generally effective in checking the more violent types of crime, suppressing organized bands of marauders, reducing the hazards of travel, and protecting property. They also attempted to eliminate such cruel customs as suttee, which was outlawed in 1829, and infanticide. Under British rule the population of India expanded greatly, rising from 150 million in 1850 to 250 million in 1881. By 1921 it exceeded 300 million, and another 100 million was added by 1945. This impressive increase is attributable largely to the curbing of internal warfare and to improvements in sanitation and medical facilities under British auspices. Irrigation works were constructed sufficient to provide for 30 million acres of land. Modern communications were introduced, including an extensive network of railroads totaling eventually more than 40,000 miles, a figure far in excess of the railroad mileage of any other Asian country.

The darker side of the picture

Almost all the improvements, however, had their darker side. The rapid increase in population depressed the living conditions of large numbers of the people, and the problem of an adequate food supply was never solved. Severe famines had been known in India long before the British arrived, but some of the worst occurred during the period of British control. Ironically, the proclamation of Queen Victoria as empress of India in 1877 coincided with the greatest famine in

India's history, which took a toll of 5 million lives. It is estimated that between 1877 and 1900 no fewer than 15 million people died of famine. A basic cause of these disasters was the fact that a majority of the population lived close to the starvation level even in normal times and had no savings and no reserves of physical stamina to carry them through an emergency.

Although British rule did not introduce poverty into India, it did little to alleviate it and in some areas intensified it. The taxation system contributed heavily to the poverty of India's population. The principle generally followed by the government was to demand one-half the rental value of the land. British officials pointed to the fact that the tax schedules were somewhat less extortionate than those of earlier autocratic regimes. An important difference, however, was that the British assessments were not theoretical; they were actually collected. Also, in contrast to the situation under earlier empires, much of the revenue raised was drained out of India—in salaries to the higher administrative officials and to European army officers, in dividends to the East India Company stockholders, and in interest on the public debt, most of which was held by Englishmen. Not only did taxation bear too heavily upon the poorest classes but only a small fraction of the government's budget was allotted to relief, social welfare, or education. The major portion was expended on the police, the courts, and especially the Indian army, a professional body which was sometimes used in imperial wars outside of India—in Afghanistan, Burma, or China. In spite of the introduction of sanitation measures, the Indian death rate remained appallingly high, augmented by such diseases as cholera, malaria, and bubonic plague, which can be controlled by modern medical science and have been almost eliminated in Western countries.

Inequities in the system of taxation

Probably the aspect of British rule in India most open to criticism was its economic policy. In the early days of the East India Company there had been a great demand for Indian handmade goods of superior quality, especially silks, cottons, and muslins, which were generally paid for in specie. With the coming of the Industrial Revolution in England, the character of Far Eastern commerce changed. The British became interested in India as a source of raw materials and, even more, as a market for manufactured goods. The Indians were forced to accept "free trade" as applied to British manufactures but were effectively denied the right to export their own manufactures either to England or other countries. An inevitable result of this policy was the decline of village handicrafts which had for centuries constituted a vital element in the whole Indian economy. During the period of British rule, in spite of the growth of some large cities, the proportion of India's population dependent on the land for sustenance actually increased, until by the opening of the twentieth century it constituted more than 80 percent of the total. Excessive ruralization, small tenant holdings, oppressive taxes, and the unchecked extortions of money-

Other evils of economic policy

lenders go far to explain why India remained a land of poverty and famine. The introduction of factory industries in the late nineteenth century offered a new source of employment, but only for a tiny fraction of the population. An oversupply of labor kept wages extremely low, and the sordid conditions of English mill towns during the early Industrial Revolution were repeated and far exceeded in India.

Social and cultural effects of British rule

Somewhat more difficult to assess are the effects of the British occupation upon Indian society, culture, and mentality. Quite early the English rulers recognized an obligation to promote educational facilities. Several European scholars became intensely interested in the study of Sanskrit and the related ancient languages and advocated the promotion of a fuller knowledge of India's intellectual heritage. The printing press, introduced by missionaries, was utilized for works in the vernacular. The first newspaper, published in the Bengali dialect, appeared in 1818. A fundamental change in English educational policy in India came in 1833 with the decision to devote all educational funds henceforth to instruction solely in the English language. Lord Macaulay, the famous essayist and historian, who was a member of the governor's council at this time and was primarily responsible for the decision, regarded Hindu literature as nothing but "false history, false astronomy, false metaphysics, false religion."[7] As a matter of fact, the government did very little to carry out the educational plans which had been announced, and it is probable that, with the economic and political decline of the formerly autonomous villages, instructional facilities in India actually deteriorated. Some village schools were still flourishing in the early nineteenth century, but with the decay of village life education gradually fell into neglect and illiteracy increased accordingly. Nevertheless, the official emphasis upon Western studies familiarized Indian intellectuals with nineteenth-century liberal traditions and in the long run intensified their desire for self-government.

Indian National Congress

Toward the close of the nineteenth century the growth of an Indian nationalist sentiment manifested itself in various ways. The event of greatest import for the future was the formation of the Indian National Congress in 1885 under the initiative of educated Hindus and English sympathizers. The objectives of the organization were ambitious if somewhat vague, and embodied the hope that it would "form the germ of a Native Parliament and . . . constitute in a few years an unanswerable reply to the assertion that India is still wholly unfit for any form of representative institutions." The Congress was never exclusively a Hindu body. It attracted a number of Muslims, and during the first thirty years of its existence five Englishmen were elected to its presidency.

Government officials had at first looked upon the Indian National Congress with benevolence, regarding it as a harmless debating soci-

[7]H. G. Rawlinson, *India, a Short Cultural History,* p. 409.

ety or as a safety valve for upper-class discontent. However, as the Congress—which met every December in a different Indian city—pressed more insistently for reform measures, the official attitude became cool or hostile. The result was that the nationalist movement entered a more radical phase about the turn of the century. A contributing factor to this trend was the shattering of the myth of European invincibility by the Italian defeat in Ethiopia in 1896, by the difficulty which Britain encountered in subduing the small Boer states of South Africa, and by Japan's dramatic victory over the great Russian empire in 1905. Incensed by the dictatorial policy of the viceroy, Lord Curzon, some Indian patriots began to demand *swaraj* (independence) and also launched a *swadeshi* campaign, which was an attempt to injure Britain economically by boycotting the sale of British goods and reviving native industries. Outbreaks of violence in western Bengal and in the Punjab merely strengthened the determination of the government to stand firm. The vernacular press was muzzled; agitators were arrested and some of them were deported.

The growth of a militant opposition to British rule led to dissension within the Indian National Congress and to a cleavage between the moderates and the extremists. The 1907 meeting of the Indian Congress was disrupted by rioting, but the moderate faction succeeded in retaining control of the organization. The nationalist movement, hampered by disagreement among the Hindu leaders, was also weakened somewhat by the establishment of a Muslim organization which stood in rivalry to the Indian National Congress. The Muslim League, founded in 1905, was inspired partly by the fear of the Muslim minority that they might be subjected to Hindu domination if popular government was established in India—a fear heightened by the truculence and the appeal to religious prejudice which some radical Hindu nationalists had displayed. The league also reflected an attempt to reawaken interest in the whole community of Islam, which seemed to be jeopardized by the decline of the Ottoman Empire. In contrast to the Indian Congress the Muslim League was a communal (sectarian) organization; further, it was founded under conservative rather than liberal auspices.

During World War I only minor disturbances occurred in India. Representatives of all important organizations expressed their sympathy for the British cause and offered assistance. Indian contributions in behalf of Britain and its allies were tremendous. Indian troops fought on the Western front, in East Africa, in the Middle East, and in the Far East; and the country furnished vast supplies of raw materials, foodstuffs, and even manufactures, as cotton, jute, and steel production was intensified. The cooperative attitude of the Indian people during the war was induced by the belief that a victory for Britain and its allies would bring benefits to the world's colonial areas. Woodrow Wilson's utterances on war aims and peace objectives aroused enthusiasm in India as elsewhere, and from the beginning of the war British spokesmen had intimated that generous reforms would be forthcoming in recognition of Indian loyalty. In 1917 Edwin Montagu, secretary of state for India, announced in the House of Commons that England's policy toward India was "the increasing association of Indians in every branch of the administration and the gradual development of self-governing institutions with a view to . . . responsible government as an integral part of the British Empire."

The bitter fruit of disillusionment

Although the close of the war found India in a state of high expectancy, the prevailing mood quickly changed to disappointment for several reasons. First, the period was one of widespread suffering, caused by inflated prices, a severe famine, and the ravages of disease, including an influenza epidemic that wiped out 13 million people in 1918–1919. Second, the political reforms embodied in the Government of India Act of 1919 fell far short of responsible government. The franchise was still restricted to a tiny minority of property owners numbering about 3 percent of the population of British India. In addition, the electorate was split up into communal groups, with separate constituencies for Hindus, Muslims, Sikhs, landholders, and other special interests. To Indian nationalists, the constitution of 1919 appeared to be a breach of promise on England's part.

British repression; the Amritsar massacre

Probably an even greater factor than the Act of 1919 in arousing resentment was the repressive policy which the British government of India adopted at the close of the war. Punitive measures against rioting led to angry protests and to open violence, climaxed by one of the most shocking affairs in the annals of British rule in India—the Amritsar massacre of 1919. To check a series of outrages in the Punjab, the government had sent troops into the province under the command of Brigadier-General Dyer. At Amritsar on April 13, learning that a large crowd of people was assembling for a public demonstration, General Dyer took a detachment of soldiers to the meeting place and immediately ordered his men to open fire. The crowd, which was listening to speeches and was unarmed, had gathered in an enclosed space, of which Dyer blocked the exit. After ten minutes of steady rifle fire, almost 400 people were killed and more than a thousand wounded. News of this cold-blooded butchery—perpetrated in the name of upholding the "rule of law"—inflamed public indignation throughout India and elsewhere. General Dyer was deprived of his commission but received no other punishment, and English admirers raised a purse in his behalf. The Amritsar massacre, and the indulgent attitude of the government toward those responsible for it, antagonized many Indian leaders who had previously been consistent defenders of Britain. The great poet and educator, Rabindranath Tagore, returned the commission of knighthood with which he had been honored. Another Hindu and friend of Tagore who now became the enemy of British rule and threw himself into the nationalist cause was Mohandas K. Gandhi.

The man who was destined to make the greatest single contribution to the movement for Indian independence gave little evidence in his early life that such would be his role. Gandhi was born in 1869 in a small native state on the western coast of India. He came from a middle-class family which had supplied prime ministers to the prince, and his mother, a pious Hindu, endeavored to instill in him fidelity to the traditions of their caste. His family sent him to England to study law, and after his return home he was offered a position with an Indian firm in South Africa, where he spent some twenty years and had a successful legal practice. His chief interest in South Africa, however, became a deep concern for the unfair treatment to which his countrymen were subjected in that color-conscious region. At the risk of his life and in disregard of insults and humiliation, he campaigned continually against economic and social discrimination, encouraging the timid Indian laborers to organize and calling upon the government to remove flagrant injustices. In this campaign he eventually met with considerable success, but even more important to his later career was his discovery of a technique of mass action that could be effectively employed in defending a moral principle against superior physical force. Gandhi called this technique *satyagraha,* which is loosely translated as "nonviolent resistance" but which means literally "soul force" or "the power of truth." With a keen sensitivity to social injustice, he also became convinced that social and political evils could never be eliminated through violence. He believed these evils should be fought against, but with such weapons as refusal to cooperate with oppressors, no matter what the price; attempting to change the evildoer by force of example; and, above all, developing in oneself the attitudes and the disciplines which are essential to an improved social order. While arriving at these ideas by the route of religion, Gandhi also applied them to the political sphere.

Returning to India in 1914, Gandhi warmly endorsed the cause of Britain in the war against the Central Powers, even putting aside his pacifist principles to urge people to enlist, so confident was he that the struggle was against autocracy and militarism. But disillusioned by the government's behavior and shocked by the Amritsar massacre, he repudiated the new Indian constitution of 1919 and persuaded the Indian National Congress to adopt a program of noncooperation with the government. In 1922, he launched his first mass campaign of nonviolent resistance or "civil disobedience," but suspended the movement after a few weeks when he found that it was being used by terrorists to injure life and property. The program of the Indian National Congress and of the associated Gandhian movement already had begun to attract wide support and cut across sectarian lines. The Muslim League supported it for a while, and Gandhi was unswerving in his insistence upon Hindu–Muslim cooperation.

During the 1920s, as the nationalist movement acquired momen-

Nehru

tum, a number of new personalities came to the fore, of whom the most prominent was Jawaharlal Nehru. The Nehrus were a distinguished Brahman family, wealthy and influential. They had everything to lose, from the purely material standpoint, by casting their lot with a revolutionary movement; but such was the choice they made. Both father and son, and other members of the family, became admirers of Gandhi and joined the National Congress. The father adhered generally to the moderate faction, while his son, who was elected president of the Congress several times, became a leader of the militant and radical wing. The son, Jawaharlal (1889–1964), was educated at the best English schools, taking a B.A. degree at Cambridge University, and became thoroughly Westernized in his tastes and personal interests. Unlike Gandhi, he was by temperament rational and scientific and approached India's problems from a secular standpoint, welcoming industrial development and material progress. While he revered India's cultural heritage, he was emancipated from the dogmas and taboos of traditional Hinduism and—like most of the educated nationalist reformers—opposed the institution of caste. Nehru also became intensely concerned with the need for social reform. He did not embrace Marxism, but he advocated government intervention to alleviate poverty, rehabilitate the peasants, and protect industrial workers. Under Nehru's influence a substantial segment of the National Congress adopted as its two major objectives the winning of complete independence for India and the establishment of a democratic and moderately socialistic regime.

Civil disobedience

The Indian National Congress at its 1928 session had adopted a resolution demanding that Britain grant dominion status within one year. At a lively and unusually large conclave of the Congress in December 1929, the dynamic triumvirate of Gandhi and the two Nehrus persuaded members to take the pledge of *Purna Swaraj* ("Complete Independence"). They announced that January 26 would be celebrated

Leaders of Indian Nationalism—Nehru and Gandhi. Gandhi was assassinated in 1948. Nehru served as Prime Minister of India from 1947 to his death in 1964.

as "Independence Day," reinforced by the threat of civil disobedience. Accordingly, Gandhi's second mass campaign of civil disobedience was launched in the spring of 1930. Indians resigned from public office, stopped buying foreign goods, picketed shops and courts, and even refused to pay taxes. The most dramatic event was Gandhi's famous "march to the sea," in which he led a large body of followers on foot through village after village until they reached the coast. There they filled pans with sea water and let it evaporate to make salt, breaking the law by evading the salt tax and defying a government monopoly. In the salt episode as in the boycotting of state liquor shops, Gandhi shrewdly combined a political issue with a moral principle, thus putting his opponents in an embarrassing position. Widespread arrests accompanied the disobedience campaign. Gandhi was imprisoned in May, and the total number of Congress members jailed at this time has been estimated as high as 60,000.

Modifying his strategy but not his objectives, Gandhi next attempted to reach an understanding with the British authorities. Released from prison early in 1931, he obtained a series of interviews with the viceroy, Lord Irwin (much to the disgust of Winston Churchill, who was "nauseated" at the thought of "a seditious fakir striding half-naked up the steps of the Viceregal Palace"), and he agreed to participate in a round table conference in London, which proved unproductive.

At the close of the civil-disobedience campaign of 1931–1934, Gandhi retired temporarily from politics. He had proved to be the most powerful political figure in the Congress; he was a factor to reckon with at Whitehall and Westminster as well as at Delhi, and he had thousands of followers who would carry out his will almost blindly. Furthermore, he had developed, in the technique of nonviolent resistance, an instrument of mass action of immeasurable potency. In stepping out of the political arena Gandhi was not unaware of the effectiveness of the political weapons he had forged. He recognized, however, the dangers in any form of mass action, and he believed that the Indian people, including himself, needed to perfect their self-control. He said openly that he would prefer for India to remain subject to Britain than for her to attain freedom through a violent revolution. At the opposite pole from Machiavelli, Lenin, and many others, Gandhi denied that the end justifies the means. He believed instead that the means largely determine what the end will be.

Another factor which influenced Gandhi to disassociate himself from the Congress temporarily was that he did not consider himself primarily as a political leader. He disavowed the title of Mahatma ("Great Soul") by which he was known and strenuously discouraged the tendency of ignorant admirers to deify him. Still, he was essentially a religious figure in his personal convictions and in his world

Gandhi en Route to Meetings with Viceroy Lord Irwin in March 1931. Gandhi had recently been released from prison, where he had been interned after his dramatic "march to the sea" in 1930.

The religious motivation of Gandhi's philosophy

The Round Table Conference on the Indian Constitution in Session in London, 1931. Gandhi, the sole delegate from the Indian National Congress, sits at the chairman's left.

view. His beliefs were derived partly from the *Bhagavad-Gita* (which he first read in London in an English translation), partly from the writings of Tolstoi and Ruskin, and partly from the New Testament. He considered himself a Hindu and retained many traditional notions, but he embraced much of the spirit of Christianity, and his real interest lay in the development of religious and ethical values in human society. He had no faith in any political or economic formula and believed that the only real hope for India—or for the world—lay in the cultivation of spiritual resources.

Gandhi's constructive program

Finally, Gandhi wished to devote the remaining years of his life to helping the downtrodden peasants. He established his *ashram* (disciplined community) in one of the poorest regions of Central India and attempted to educate the villagers in better methods of cultivation and sanitation and in the use of subsidiary industries, especially home spinning and weaving, to improve their living standards. He gave impetus to a widespread movement to rehabilitate the ancient village economy which had long been in decay. He hoped to inaugurate a nonviolent agrarian revolution, carried out by the Indian people without benefit of capital or government, to create a society free from misery while retaining simplicity and closeness to nature. Gandhi became the special champion of the Untouchables, whom he called *Harijan,* or "children of God." His campaign on their behalf illustrates his ability to relate an ideal goal to immediate and practical objectives. Full social acceptance of Untouchables was a necessary act of justice. But Gandhi also perceived that only by breaking the taboo against handling dirt and filth—traditionally the exclusive responsibility of the despised lowest class—could hygienic habits be instilled among the general population. The comprehensive "Constructive Program," to which Gandhi dedicated years of effort, was largely forgotten after India achieved political independence.

A new constitution embodied in the Government of India Act of 1935 disappointed Indian nationalists, both radicals and moderates. It made provincial ministries responsible to elected assemblies which could discuss and act upon any matter not reserved to the central authority. But the provincial governor retained "special responsibilities" and "discretionary powers," which raised doubts as to whether the new system would be much different from the old. The franchise was considerably extended to include about 30 million voters, roughly one-fourth of the adult population of British India, but the device of communal electorates was carried to an excess. Not only religious groups but also special economic classes were given separate representation, and the constitution seemed to be weighted in favor of religious minorities and the propertied interests. The act also provided for letting the native states enter a federation with the central government under terms which would have given the states (most of which were autocracies) an excessive representation.

Disappointment with the Government of India Act of 1935

The Indian National Congress strongly condemned the new constitution, but decided to run candidates in elections, first with the intention of obstructing the processes of government, and later, as the Congress party gained sweeping victories at the polls, with the idea of forming ministries and enacting legislation. By 1937, the Indian Congress had working majorities in seven of the eleven provinces of British India, and during the next two years these provinces enjoyed a taste of responsible parliamentary government. Most remarkable was the novel sight of English civil servants dutifully executing the policies of Indian ministers.

The ascendancy of the Congress party

In spite of the good omen of Anglo-Indian cooperation, there were signs of trouble in the offing. A cleavage was growing between the moderate and radical wings of the National Congress, and even more serious was the increased friction between the Congress and the Muslim League. The Hindu-Muslim tension was caused partly by occasional outbreaks of violence incited by religious fanatics; partly by a fear among Muslims that if India became self-governing they would be at a disadvantage as a minority group; and partly by the fact that the Muslim League had come under the aggressive leadership of Mohammed Ali Jinnah and began to revive as a definite political force.

Muhammad Ali Jinnah, President of the Muslim League

That M. A. Jinnah (1876–1948) should become the guiding figure of a militant sectarian organization was somewhat ironic. Jinnah, a successful lawyer, had received a Western education and was decidedly secular in temperament. He did not observe the code of pious Muslims, and he had married a Parsee. Jinnah joined the Indian National Congress, in which he took an active part, but he resigned when Gandhi began to come into ascendancy. After withdrawing from political activity for a while, Jinnah undertook to vitalize the Muslim League and succeeded in making it, for the first time, the mouthpiece of the majority of Indian Muslims and a political party which would have to be bargained with in the future. Jinnah insisted that special guaranties were necessary to protect the Muslim minority, and finally, by 1940, went so far as to claim that the Indian Muslims were not merely a minority or a religious community but a distinct nation. The claim was dubious. Most Muslims in India were the descendants of natives who had been converted to Islam (Jinnah's family belonged to a group of recent converts) and were as truly Indian as the Hindus. If religious affiliation were to be made the basis of nationhood, then India would have to be split into many fragments and a united state would be impossible. The championing by the Muslim League of the interests of the Islamic community finally culminated in the demand for a separate state—Pakistan—an idea not original with Jinnah but which he at last adopted.

India and World War II

The outbreak of World War II brought matters to a critical juncture in India. The Congress took the blunt position that India would fight only as a free nation and demanded self-government with permission to draw up a new constitution. The viceroy could only promise that the 1935 Constitution would be reconsidered after the war and that, for the time being, he would welcome greater "consultation" with representative groups. In October 1940, the Congress authorized the Mahatma to inaugurate a nonviolent civil-disobedience campaign, which began at once. It was not a mass movement, though, and took the form of having individuals make speeches against the war. In each instance the authorities were duly notified in advance, the speaker was arrested quietly, and the jails began to swell again. There was no active interference with the civil or military administration. Actually, Indian contributions to the war against the Axis were enormous—far greater than in World War I—because Indian manufactures had now become important. Two million men were recruited for the Indian army and many Indian officers were commissioned.

The Cripps Offer

With the Japanese invasion of Malaya and Burma, the British government determined on a new effort to rally Indian public opinion to its support and sent Sir Stafford Cripps to India in March 1942 to present an offer of full dominion status under a constitution to be drafted by Indians, including representatives of the native states. The plan called for a federation rather than a unitary state and would have allowed any province that so desired to remain outside the union and retain a separate connection with Britain. It was to become effective only after the war ended, and it made no provision for immediate transfer of responsibility to Indians in the viceroy's council. For these reasons, combined with distrust of the Churchill government, the proposal was rejected by practically all articulate Indian groups.

The failure of the Cripps Offer of 1942 revealed that Indian nation-

Indian Railway Workshop Producing Munitions during World War II

alist sentiment had reached such a degree of agitation that it could no longer be smoothed over. Events moved rapidly when the Churchill government was replaced by a Labor cabinet under Clement Attlee. In March 1946 Attlee announced that the choice of a new constitution would be India's alone and that, while he hoped the Indian people would remain within the Commonwealth, this must be by their own free will. A Cabinet Mission accordingly was sent to India to work with Indian leaders in arranging the transfer of authority.

Now that the British government was prepared to grant independence, the chief stumbling block was found to lie in the Hindu-Muslim controversy, which had grown to large proportions as a political issue only during the preceding decade. For a while it looked as if the partition of India could be avoided. The Cabinet Mission drafted a scheme for a federal union with safeguards to protect minorities and with provisions for considerable regional autonomy. Both the Congress and the League at first accepted this general plan, but in July 1946 Jinnah, reversing his earlier position, rejected the mission proposal, demanded a separate Muslim state, and summoned his followers to engage in "direct action." The consequence was bloody communal rioting in which about 12,000 lives were lost. When a constituent assembly met in December to draft a constitution, the Muslim League sent no representatives, nor could it be persuaded to do so. Although Jinnah's intransigence was evident, some of the blame must rest with Congress members, who made it clear that they would not be bound by any pledges emanating from the British Cabinet Mission. So much ill will had been aroused on both sides that compromise was very difficult. A few extreme Hindu nationalists viewed the prospect of partition with indifference, rashly assuming that a separate Muslim state would sooner or later have to seek reunion with India on India's terms. The British government's determination to relinquish its responsibilities as quickly as possible—in striking contrast to the cau-

The Hindu-Muslim controversy and the decision for partition

Riot in Calcutta, 1946. A dead Hindu surrounded by Muslims armed with lathis. Such scenes were not uncommon on the eve of Indian independence, when extreme tension developed between Hindu and Muslim segments of the population.

The end of British Raj

tious and dilatory policy of the preceding 90 years—doubtless also lessened the chances of resolving the deadlock between the Hindu and Muslim communities. Attlee had served notice that England would leave India by June of 1948. Seeing no other alternative, the new viceroy (Lord Mountbatten) prepared to transfer British authority to two governments instead of one, a delicate and difficult operation. Not only were the Hindu and Muslim provinces separated, but three provinces—Bengal, the Punjab, and Assam—had to be split in order to prevent large Hindu minorities from being assigned to Pakistan. Although Pakistan did not include all the areas demanded by the Muslim League, the division was accepted by both sides in the controversy. Indian independence was formally granted by act of Parliament in July 1947, and in August all authority was surrendered to the two new dominions.

5. INDEPENDENT INDIA, PAKISTAN, AND BANGLADESH

It was a tragic circumstance that the Indian struggle for independence, characterized more by patience than by slaughter, should conclude with the country divided and in an atmosphere of hostility. The partition of India, from the standpoints of geography and economics, was highly artificial. Pakistan included the areas producing jute, cotton, and rice. India, with an insufficient food supply, had the factories needed to process Pakistan's raw materials. Important canals and river systems were bisected by the political boundaries. Nor did partition solve the minority problem. Approximately 15 percent of Pakistan's inhabitants are non-Muslims, chiefly Hindus. The Republic of India has a Muslim minority of approximately 11 percent. Even before partition was completed, refugees began to stream across the borders— Hindus and Sikhs fleeing from Muslim domination and Muslims fearing Hindu persecution. More than 10 million people were involved in the mass exodus during the latter part of 1947, and their suffering was indescribable. The governments of India and Pakistan could not prevent the outrages committed by frenzied fanatics on both sides. It was in connection with this religious strife that Gandhi, a frail old man in his late seventies, performed his last service to India. By appealing to the Hindus and by threatening to fast, he stopped riots in Calcutta. Early in 1948 he went to Delhi and began a fast which ended when the key spokesmen for the Congress pledged protection for the lives and property of Muslims. On January 30, on his way to evening prayers, Gandhi was shot to death by a member of a chauvinistic Hindu society. He was mourned all over India and in Pakistan, and the shock of his assassination had at least a temporarily sobering effect upon the public temper.

The tragic division of India; the assassination of Gandhi

A prime source of controversy between India and Pakistan was the disposition of the native states. Since the states were no longer protected by the British Raj, it was assumed that they would voluntarily join either India or Pakistan. Most of them did so, the greater number of course going to India, but in a few instances there was trouble. Hyderabad in the Deccan, the largest state in India, had a Hindu population ruled over by a Muslim prince, the Nizam. The Indian government refused to let the Nizam remain independent, as he apparently planned to do. It dispatched an army into Hyderabad and quickly took over the administration (September 1948). In this instance the Indian government claimed to be acting on behalf of the Nizam's Hindu subjects, but it had already taken a somewhat different position in the Kashmir dispute. In this northern state a Hindu prince ruled over subjects who were predominantly Muslims. In 1947 the New Delhi government announced that Kashmir had acceded to the Indian Union at the request of the Maharaja, who, it was argued, had the legal right to transfer his sovereignty. The Maharaja, faced with an invasion of Muslim tribesmen, had appealed to India for military support, and the Indian government had insisted upon the accession of Kashmir to India as a prior condition to granting his request. Fighting between Indian and Pakistani troops was halted in 1949 by a cease-

The native states; the Kashmir conflict

The Republic of India

fire agreement arranged through a United Nations commission. The cease-fire, however, proved to be only a truce and left Kashmir divided into two parts, occupied respectively by Pakistan and India, with the larger portion under Indian control.

India retained the status of a dominion only until 1950, when a new constitution made it an independent republic, replacing the governor-general by an elected president and severing all ties with the British Crown. Nevertheless, India voluntarily remained within the Commonwealth of Nations (with the term "British" deleted) and thus became the first completely independent republic to hold membership in the association. The Constitution provides for an independent judiciary and a president chosen by an electoral college, but follows the English system of parliamentary government, with the chief power vested in a prime minister responsible to the lower house of the central legislature. The subordinate states, with unicameral legislatures, have the same type of ministerial government. Both the state and national legislative bodies are elected by universal adult suffrage for five-year terms. The Constitution includes a comprehensive bill of rights, outlawing untouchability and discrimination based on caste, and providing for legal equality of the sexes. Although federal in structure, the government has been handicapped by a distribution of power between the center and the states which is both rigid and ambiguous. The Constitution gives the president power to suspend a state government in an emergency, but some very critical areas of jurisdiction are reposed in the states, including education, agriculture, and taxes on land.

Many difficulties confronted the Republic of India from the very beginning. The absorption of more than 500 princely states into the new political structure, a formidable task in itself, was handled with relative dispatch. Some of the dethroned rajas were retained as governors for a time, but by 1957 all of them were removed from office.

Obstacles to Indian unity: linguistic differences

Republic of India Declared. Prime Minister Jawaharlal Nehru moves the resolution for an independent sovereign republic before the constituent assembly in New Delhi in 1950.

They were compensated for their loss of power by the award of generous pensions which continued until 1971, when a constitutional amendment reduced the maharajas to the rank of commoners. Other problems proved more obstinate, revealing dangerous sectional and social cleavages. One of them had to do with linguistic rivalries. In the interest of promoting national unity, the government announced that Hindi, the principal tongue of northern India but spoken by only about one-third of the total population, was to become the official language of the country by 1965. Resistance on the part of other regional linguistic groups proved so strong, however, that on the date when the change was to go into effect, in January 1965, bloody riots broke out in the south, two cabinet ministers resigned, and the government felt constrained to announce that English would remain an "associate official language." as long as non-Hindi-speaking Indians desired.

The independent states of India and Pakistan were bequeathed many things of value by the British: the rudiments of parliamentary government, trained civil servants, an excellent network of railroads, the nuclei of effective military forces, and an educated elite versed in Western institutions and practices. The new states also inherited the unsolved problems of the era of colonial rule, chief of which is the backwardness and crushing poverty of most of the population. Steady and substantial economic progress is necessary if India and Pakistan are to make their way as successful modern states—or even to survive as political entities. The Indian government, committed to material progress, created a Planning Commission and launched a series of Five-Year Plans, beginning in 1951. In many fields impressive results were achieved. Food production has grown by almost 90 percent; power generation increased sevenfold in less than a decade, while irrigation facilities doubled. By 1970 India was exporting heavy machinery and manufacturing 85,000 motor vehicles a year. Two nuclear power plants were in operation by August 1972, but in 1979 they still had only a 640 megawatt capacity. Even in the vital area of agriculture, improvements did not suffice to offset an inexorable growth in the numbers of people. Widely publicized campaigns in support of birth control failed to check the rate of increase, which has doubled since independence. By 1970 India's population of about 550 million was receiving an increment of 13 million each year and was expected to approach 695 million within the next decade. Consequently, per capita annual income has remained at a level of about $100. Social services are lacking for the bulk of the population, 75 percent of whom are still illiterate.

Nature has not condemned India to be a land of poverty forever. The country holds extensive resources—the world's largest iron-ore reserves, estimated at nearly 22 billion tons, manganese and other valuable minerals, substantial deposits of coal and probably of oil, and

Prime Minister Nehru with His Daughter, Mrs. Indira Gandhi, in 1956

Economic problems; the Five- Year Plans

INDIA TODAY

*India's great but
unrealized potential*

great potential for hydroelectric development. Under effective leadership India could doubtless support a prosperous, industrialized, and educated society. The Five-Year Plans fell short of their objectives for a variety of reasons. An overgrown and inept bureaucracy mangled well-intentioned projects, but considerable blame must be placed on the Congress party and its leader Nehru for failure to press vigorously for necessary changes. Long on rhetoric but short on performance, they continually postponed action or compromised with vested interests.

While India is predominantly a country of landowners and cultivators, the poor peasants at the bottom have not shared in agricultural progress as have the upper strata of large landowners who control the farm cooperatives and wield a disproportionate influence over the state and national legislatures. This fortunate minority, possessing considerable capital, has almost entirely escaped taxation. Consequently the government has lacked funds to implement its ambitious development and welfare programs. Even scientifically designed projects for the modernization of agriculture through mechanization, intensive fertilization, and diversified cropping have thus far proved disappointing. The widely acclaimed "green revolution," launched in the late 1960s with the help of international experts, brought a spectacular increase in the per-acre yield of grains, particularly wheat. But the benefits accrued to relatively prosperous landowners, rather than to small farmers, tenants, and laborers unable to afford the new techniques. With 5 percent of rural householders possessing 35 percent of the cultivable land and about half of all agricultural families owning no land at all, the basic need is for a thorough reorganization of land ownership, something the government has never undertaken in spite of its promises.

Within the framework of democratic institutions India, during its first thirty years of independence, operated under what was in effect a one-party system. The Congress party, instead of dissolving as Gandhi had recommended, dominated all branches of the government, and Jawaharlal Nehru served continuously as prime minister until his death in May 1964. This long tenure of power was not an unmixed blessing either for the party or for the country. Once the focal point of an indomitable struggle for freedom, the Congress developed into an Establishment, entrenched behind its monopoly of patronage and the administrative services (vastly larger than the old British Indian civil service), and its vigor and integrity became corroded. Even the

*Preponderance of the
Congress party under
Nehru*

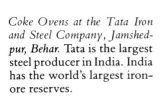

*Coke Ovens at the Tata Iron
and Steel Company, Jamshed-
pur, Behar.* Tata is the largest
steel producer in India. India
has the world's largest iron-
ore reserves.

luster of Nehru—generally revered as a revolutionary hero and Gandhi's heir—dimmed in later years. Endowed with qualities of mind and heart that entitle him to high rank among popular leaders of this century, Nehru was not entirely successful as a statesman. His own idealism was unquestionable but fuzzy in application, his policies vacillating and impulsive. As an avowed enemy of colonialism, in 1961 he authorized the forcible occupation of Goa, Diu, and Damão, the last remnants of Portugal's empire on the subcontinent; but the next year he blundered into a border clash with Communist China with humiliating results. In the long controversy with Pakistan over Kashmir he was both unyielding and inconsistent. Although publicly admitting the right of the Kashmiris to determine their own destiny, he deposed and imprisoned without trial Sheikh Muhammad Abdullah, the premier of Kashmir, when Abdullah advocated independence for the country. In 1957 he announced the formal annexation of Kashmir to India and subsequently took the position that Kashmir was a domestic issue not subject to mediation by any outside agency.[8] Nehru appeared blind to the corruption and incompetence of his trusted associates, and he neglected to press for the reform program that he himself recognized as essential to India's welfare. His chief asset as a leader was his personality, which combined intellectual faculties of a high order with a charisma that won and held the allegiance even of the unlettered masses.

Nehru's death left the party with no leader of sufficient stature to hold its dissident factions together; rivalries broke out into the open, while India's internal condition deteriorated. In 1966 the party chiefs picked as prime minister Nehru's daughter, Mrs. Indira Gandhi, hoping that the prestige of the family name would restore public confidence. Disenchantment with the administration was amply demonstrated in India's fourth general election (February 1967), the first one to be marred by tumult and violence. Although the Congress party retained a slim majority in the central parliament, it lost control in half of the state governments. Threatened by opposition from elements of both the extreme right and the extreme left, the Congress party in 1969 split into two factions, and a struggle for power ensued between established leaders of the "old Congress" and Mrs. Gandhi's "new Congress party." Squarely accepting the challenge, Nehru's daughter exhibited a tenacity equal to her father's and a superior talent for practical politics. She took the bold step of calling for general elections in March 1971—a year ahead of schedule—and she campaigned throughout the country, sometimes making fourteen speeches in a single day. The result was a personal triumph for Indira

Difficulties following Nehru's death; Indira Gandhi's new Congress party

---

[8] Sheikh Abdullah, after being twice imprisoned for championing self-determination for Kashmir, accepted union with India as a political and economic necessity and resumed the prime ministership in February 1975. This helped relax tension between India and Pakistan but did not end Kashmiri discontent.

Gandhi and a sweeping victory for her party, which won a two-thirds majority in the national legislature (Lok Sabha).

In the light of Mrs. Gandhi's campaign promises, the 1971 election was a mandate for social reform—to abolish poverty and promote "the fullest internal democracy." In reality it was the beginning of a period of personal rule culminating in dictatorship. Emboldened by the popular enthusiasm she had aroused—the "Indira wave," which reached its apogee with India's smashing defeat of Pakistan in the brief December war—Mrs. Gandhi became increasingly arbitrary and inflexible. She blamed her political opponents for the failure of the economy to improve, while her own administration was, like its predecessors, inefficient and tainted with corruption. In 1974 she used troops to break a strike of railway workers and arrested union leaders. As discontent grew she attempted to quiet it by spectacular diversions. In May 1974 her government announced it had exploded a 10-kiloton nuclear device—proof of technological progress but alarming to neighboring countries despite assurances of "purely peaceful" intent. A year later she annexed the tiny protectorate of Sikkim after Indian troops, on the pretext of quelling a rebellion, arrested the monarch.

A crisis in the summer of 1975 led to a coup—not against the government, but by Mrs. Gandhi against the Constitution and the political opposition. On June 12 a state court pronounced her guilty of illegal campaign practices. Instead of resigning the prime ministership, she ordered wholesale arrests of political opponents of all shades of opinion, including members of her own party. The nature of her crackdown was dramatized by the night arrest of "the People's Hero," ailing seventy-two-year-old Jayaprakash Narayan, one of the few remaining uncompromising disciples of Mahatma Gandhi. On June 26 Mrs. Gandhi had the president of India proclaim a state of national emergency. Then she induced a compliant parliament to amend the Constitution to free the executive from any restraint by the judiciary, suspended civil liberties, and imposed a rigid censorship. Indira Gandhi's "emergency" rule—which lasted twenty-one months—was far more repressive than any the British had fastened upon the country. By 1976 the number of arrests and detentions was in the neighborhood of 100,000.

Mrs. Gandhi justified her extreme measures as necessary to contain a widespread conspiracy that threatened to subvert law and order. Many observers inside and outside India questioned whether turning the "world's largest democracy" into a dictatorship (which she called "disciplined democracy") was not too high a price to pay for suppressing a conspiracy, even if one had been proven to exist. In the long run, Mrs. Gandhi's methods defeated her objectives, however laudable, and failed to bring the benefits she had promised. She cleared out slums in Delhi, reduced smuggling, prodded the industrial sector to a burst of productivity, and halted inflation temporarily. Food

Slums in Bombay. The Indian government has struggled to provide better housing for the poor, but frequently the net effect is to supplement old slums with new slums.

prices dropped in 1975–1976, thanks to a bumper crop in that year which brought a surplus of grain. Meanwhile a land distribution program failed to change the structure of rural society, which was still dominated by a minority of wealthy peasants and commercial farmers. Rural unemployment continued to rise; city workers, forbidden to strike, benefitted little if any from the slight increase in industrial production.

End of the emergency government

Resentment against the emergency government was intensified by a sterilization campaign carried out with such zealous insensitivity that it created a strong backlash. Mrs. Gandhi's son Sanjay, who subjected 7 million men to vasectomies with or without their consent, became a special object of hatred. With no official position in either the Congress party or the government, Sanjay attained the prominence of an heir apparent, and he symbolized the favoritism and corruption that infected the regime. India's sixth general election, after being postponed for a year, was held in March 1977. To the surprise of many, and to Mrs. Gandhi's credit, she accepted the verdict of a free election, which repudiated her authoritarian rule, and she stepped down from office. The decisive factor in her defeat was her alienation of the Muslim community and the Untouchables, two important minorities which had originally been the core of her support.

With Mrs. Gandhi ousted and the Congress party fragmented, political responsibility in 1977 passed to the recently formed Janata party, a shaky coalition of diverse groups, including Muslims, Untouchables, and some elements of the Hindu extreme right. Recruited from competing factions, lacking a positive program, and led by quarreling old men, the Janata party could accomplish little. Although Mrs. Gandhi's defeat in 1977 had been celebrated as a day of national liberation, the ineffectiveness of her successors was so apparent that her star soon began to rise. She regained a seat in parliament in November 1978. Fourteen months later, backed by a two-thirds majority in the Lok Sabha, she became prime minister for the second time. The enthusiasm that greeted her return to power did not remove the stubborn problems confronting the nation. Hindu-Muslim conflicts erupted into violence, strikes and rioting in Assam disrupted oil production, industrial productivity declined while inflation mounted. Mrs. Gandhi suffered a severe personal blow in June 1980 when her son Sanjay, on whom she had relied increasingly for distribution of patronage and party management, was killed in an airplane crash. The following September her government enacted a National Security Ordinance giving police officers extraordinary powers and reminiscent of the repressive measures of the Emergency Rule of 1975–1977. In campaigning for office Indira Gandhi had deplored the plight of the "backward masses," and the evils of "casteism, capitalism, and communalism." Whatever her ability to conquer these evils, there was no doubt that they existed. Belying its liberal constitution and democratic electoral process, India's society has remained undemocratic. Caste is still a potent factor, intensifying regional and linguistic jealousies, class conflicts, and political divisions. The outlawing of untouchability has not improved the lot of the Harijans, who suffer from discrimination, segregation, and even physical abuse. And—Indira Gandhi's dazzling career notwithstanding—women are subjected to the traditional restrictions of a male-dominated society.

Under Jawaharlal Nehru's guidance India's foreign policy initially was one of nonalignment, stemming from a distaste for military alliances and from a desire to cultivate a spirit of friendship with other Asian countries, including the Communist. Sino-Indian relations, which had been marked by expressions of cordiality on both sides, suffered a rude shock following China's provocative action in Tibet. The New Delhi government gave asylum to the Dalai Lama, who escaped from his country while Chinese troops were suppressing a Tibetan rebellion in 1959. A brief border war between India and China in 1962, although accompanied by acrimonious debate, apparently stemmed more from the absence of clearly defined geographical boundaries in the snow-capped Himalayas than from planned aggression by either party. The abrupt rout of ill-equipped Indian troops

Failure of the Janata party; Mrs. Gandhi's political comeback

Indira Gandhi Campaigning on the Eve of Her Return to Power in Early 1980

Indian foreign policy

induced the government to upgrade and expand its military forces, which proved more effective in a three weeks' war against Pakistan in 1965. These summer hostilities, provoked by friction over Kashmir, accomplished nothing except to aggravate bad feelings between the two nations and to draw India away from the United States and into the orbit of the Soviet Union, with whom the Delhi government signed a twenty-year treaty of friendship and cooperation in August 1971. India relied on Moscow's backing during a two weeks' war with Pakistan the following December, when both China and the United States supported Pakistan and refused to denounce the brutalities committed by Pakistani troops in East Bengal. If the conflict over Bangladesh was something less than the "holy war for democracy and human rights" acclaimed by a Calcutta journalist, India's smashing victory at least heightened national self-confidence. India had attained an identity—not as the exemplar of nonviolence that Gandhi envisioned—but as a military power.

The problems confronting Pakistan have been similar to India's and even more acute. Pakistan began not as a nation but as a collection of heterogeneous racial and linguistic communities dominated by the Urdu-speaking Punjabis. The country's West and East wings—separated geographically by 1,000 miles—were equally far apart in terms of economics, language, and cultural traditions, with religion serving as the only common bond. Separatist movements within a state which was itself the fruit of separatism threatened to disrupt it and finally succeeded, with the secession of East Pakistan in 1971.

Political democracy has been almost nonexistent in Pakistan, where the creation of any kind of viable government proved an arduous task. Against a background of dissension and without effective leadership (M. A. Jinnah died in 1948 and the Muslim League gradually disintegrated), two successive constituent assemblies struggled with the drafting of a constitution, which was declared in effect in March 1956. Pakistan, while remaining a member of the Commonwealth, was defined as an "Islamic Republic" under a president who was required to be a Muslim. Elections were never held under this constitution. The ensuing period was one of unbridled political bickering, racketeering, and corruption, terminated only when General Muhammad Ayub Khan in October 1958 seized control of the government and imposed martial law. Although Ayub had acted at the instigation of the president, he soon removed him from office along with other prominent party officials, offering them a choice between jail sentences or retirement from politics (most of them chose the latter). Ayub's avowed purpose was to "clean up the mess," and in this he temporarily succeeded, by direct and peremptory measures.

Ayub Khan's military rule brought some improvement over the conditions prevalent during the politicians' paradise of the preceding decade. Inflation was halted, a few modest reforms were enacted, and

General Muhammad Ayub Khan, Pakistan's Head of State, 1958–1969

a new capital, Islamabad, was built near the Northwest Frontier. Most impressive was the economic development of West Pakistan, whose economy during the 1960s seemed to be booming. Agricultural expansion exceeded the rise in population, and manufactures showed one of the highest growth rates in the world. But rapid industrialization, producing a prosperity more apparent than real, was accompanied by questionable and potentially damaging policies. It depended on heavy doses of foreign aid, both economic and military, from the United States. To a large extent it was accomplished at the expense of the peasants. Wages and food prices were kept low while the profits from manufacture soared, creating capital to provide a high rate of reinvestment for further growth but widening the gap between the upper and lower segments of society. Most of the wealth remained concentrated in a plutocracy of "twenty-two families," which controlled 65 percent of Pakistan's industry and 80 percent of its banking assets, as well as the best farmland. Finally, the progress of West Pakistan rested on the exploitation of the eastern wing, which the government treated like a colony. East Pakistan (formerly East Bengal and now Bangladesh) with only one-sixth of the nation's area contained more than half of the population. Its jute industry earned most of Pakistan's foreign exchange, but the larger share of this was diverted to development in the West, and the disparity in per capita income between the two sections increased steadily. Economic oppression—coupled with political discrimination, social neglect, and undisguised contempt for Bengalis—prepared the ground for revolt in East Pakistan.

Although President Ayub gave the country the appearance of stability, public confidence in his rule deteriorated, especially after his futile war with India in 1965. Widespread poverty and the government's suppression of civil rights fostered opposition. Ayub had introduced a new constitution in 1962 incorporating what he called "Basic Democracy," but its operation was strictly authoritarian. The regime that had justified its seizure of power in 1958 as an attack on corruption became itself riddled with corruption from top to bottom. Demonstrations by workers and students erupted into bloody riots, and when the army refused any longer to support him, Ayub resigned in March 1969. His successor was another general, Yahya Khan, who proclaimed martial law, rooted out corruption, and restored order, filling much the same role as had his ousted predecessor a decade earlier. But he was no more able than Ayub to resolve the country's troubles, which centered more and more insistently in the rebellious mood of the East Pakistanis. Seemingly inclined to a policy of reconciliation, President Yahya Khan agreed to hold general elections for a national assembly to draft a new constitution as a step toward parliamentary government resting on universal suffrage. The elections, held in December 1970, brought a resounding victory in East Pakistan to

Sheikh Mujibur Rahman and his Awami League, a party demanding regional autonomy. Even with no support in the West, Mujibur had won the largest representation in the national assembly and was acknowledged by President Yahya as "the next prime minister of Pakistan." But the hard-liner Zulfikar Ali Bhutto, whose Pakistan People's party had gained a majority of West Pakistan's seats, obstructed attempts to work out a settlement. President Yahya postponed the opening of the assembly; yet he agreed to negotiate with Sheikh Mujibur and, accompanied by Bhutto, went to Dacca in March 1971. Apparently the talks served to screen more drastic action. Yahya's troops, with reinforcements secretly flown in, suddenly struck in Bengal, and Mujibur was imprisoned.

The India-Pakistan war of 1971

The murderous events in East Bengal from March to December 1971, resulting in a full-scale war between India and Pakistan, were among the most horrible in a century of unprecedented horrors. Atrocities may have been initiated by the Bengalis, and were perpetrated by them on the Bihari minority after the war had ended; but the most revolting excesses were committed by government troops. West Pakistani soldiers, who began their attack by shooting helpless university students, raped some 200,000 women and slaughtered whole communities of civilians. Their program of genocide was apparently aimed at exterminating every potential leader among the population they despised as rebels and racial inferiors. The government of India admitted 10 million refugees into West Bengal, assisted East Pakistani guerrillas, and early in December entered the war as an active belligerent. The brief combat, conducted on western and eastern fronts, demonstrated India's decisive military superiority over its rival, whose forces surrendered on December 16.

Sheik Mujibur Rahman, Prime Minister of Bangladesh, 1971–1975

Bangladesh ("Bengal Nation") was born from the ashes of victory as an independent state, but whether its 80 million people could survive as a political entity—or survive at all—was a difficult question to determine. With a population density of 1,400 per square mile, it is a land of poverty, and one frequently subject to disastrous storms and floods. To the normal level of misery was now added the problems of repairing the ravages of war, finding food and shelter for returning refugees, disarming guerrilla bands that still roamed the countryside, and creating a government out of chaos. Sheikh Mujibur Rahman, given a hero's welcome when he entered Dacca in January 1972 after nine months in West Pakistani jails, set up a provisional government with himself as prime minister and vowed that Bangladesh would be "a secular, democratic socialist state."

The downfall of Sheikh Mujibur

Although he was able to attract $3 billion in foreign aid, Sheikh Mujib failed completely to achieve his objectives for Bangladesh. The hostility of his countrymen to the idea of a secular state—added to friction between the Muslim majority and minority groups, especially the 10 million Hindus—made the attainment of democracy seemingly

Victims of the Indian-Pakistani War of 1971. Left: Refugees from East Bengal seeking sanctuary in India. Right: Prime Minister Indira Gandhi of India visiting a refugee camp in West Bengal, offering reassurance to homeless East Bengalis.

impossible. As a step toward socialism the jute industry, banks, and major corporations were nationalized, but they were run for the benefit of a clique of Awami League bureaucrats. Mujib's regime became increasingly corrupt and increasingly autocratic until, discarding even the forms of democracy, he dissolved parliament and imposed presidential rule. In August 1975 the discredited hero of Bangladesh's struggle for independence was overthrown and brutally murdered in a coup led by young military officers. A year later the army chief of staff, Ziaur Rahman, assumed the position of martial-law administrator and imposed strict measures to check disorder, including press censorship and thousands of arrests. After taking over the office of president in 1977, General Ziaur amended the constitution to bring it into conformity with the religion of Islam. "Re-elected" president in June 1978, he relaxed the press censorship and lifted martial law. In a parliamentary election of February 1979 his Nationalist party won a comfortable majority of the elected representatives. General Ziaur's accession to power strained the already deteriorating relations with Bangladesh's erstwhile ally, India, but it improved prospects for obtaining financial assistance from other quarters, including the United States. In 1976 Bangladesh restored diplomatic ties with Pakistan, where it found a market for exports of tea and jute. However, any appearance of stability in Bangladesh was jeopardized by the assassination of General Ziaur in May 1981.

Pakistan, reduced in territory and resources, was left with 60 million people, mostly illiterate and increasing their numbers at the alarming rate of 3 percent a year. Humiliated by defeat, the mood of the nation was resentment against the leaders responsible for a policy of disaster. Yahya Khan resigned the presidency in December 1971, and for the first time in thirteen years Pakistan had a civilian head of state when Zulfikar Ali Bhutto took the oath as president and immediately assumed most of the other important cabinet posts as well. A graduate of the University of California and of Oxford, Bhutto was a colorful figure, with a talent for arousing mass enthusiasm. He chose as motto for his Pakistan People's party, "Islam is our faith, democracy is our policy, socialism is our economy, all power to the people." His six-year rule did little credit to these ideals. It followed the familiar path of corruption and tyranny, marked by arrests, kidnaping, and torture of opponents. Elections held in March 1977 were so obviously rigged in Bhutto's favor that they provoked widespread rioting, and the country seemed on the brink of civil war. In July the army removed Bhutto in a coup led by the chief of staff, General Muhammad Zia ul-Haq, who imposed a second era of military rule upon Pakistan. In response to popular clamor, Zia ul-Haq had the deposed president brought to trial. Convicted of conspiracy to commit murder, he was sentenced to death and hanged in April 1979. To his dedicated followers, who hailed him as a "Martyr King," Bhutto's grave became a shrine. Although Zia had promised to hold elections within three months of his accession to power, he repeatedly postponed them and governed by martial law. Furthermore, he took steps intended to transform Pakistan into a fundamentalist Islamic society, rewriting the legal code and giving judicial and political authority to a body of religious scholars known as the *ulema*. A devout Sunnite Muslim, Zia apparently believed that Pakistan, where Western-style democracy had fared so badly, could survive only under a firm leader capable of enforcing religious orthodoxy and a program of austerity. The government's sanction of an Islamic code that legalized such punishments as flogging and hanging aroused discontent, which was aggravated by economic stagnation and rising prices. In spite of opposition from the Pakistan People's party, revived by Bhutto's energetic daughter Benazir, and from the Shiite Muslim minority, by the fall of 1980 an improved economy and the loyalty of his troops made Zia's position appear secure.

*Changes in Pakistan's
foreign policy*

Pakistan's international position has been materially affected by a disillusioning experience with alliances. While India was pursuing the path of neutralism, Pakistan became a member both of SEATO and of CENTO, thus identifying itself with the Western power bloc. Under a military-aid pact of 1954, the United States agreed to provide supersonic aircraft and other modern weapons, and in turn received permission to use Pakistan territory for strategic intelligence activities.

This military partnership intensified India's mistrust and hostility but did nothing to mitigate Pakistan's disastrous defeat in the Bangladesh war. In 1972 President Bhutto announced his country's withdrawal from the Commonwealth of Nations and also from SEATO. A factor contributing further to Pakistan's isolation was the discovery that its government had for some time been secretly developing atomic weapons—the "Islamic bomb"—to offset India's nuclear capacity. The international situation was altered suddenly when Russian troops invaded Afghanistan in December 1979 to install a Soviet puppet in Kabul. Western powers—and China—turned hopefully to Islamabad as a possible buffer against Russian expansion. The United States offered Zia military aid and sent advisers to plan the upgrading of his forces. General Zia, however, avoided any binding alliance. Possibly a greater threat to the stability of his regime than the presence of Russian troops on his doorstep was posed by the Baluch and Pushtun peoples who inhabited both sides of the Pakistan-Afghanistan border. Their common ethnic and linguistic ties and their solidarity in opposing the Communist military occupation of Afghanistan proved very helpful to Afghan guerrilla fighters and very troublesome to the Russian invaders. Conceivably though, an active role by such minority groups, with loyalties extending beyond Pakistan's artificial frontiers, could hasten the state's dismemberment. In the Northwest Frontier and in Baluchistan—where Bhutto fought a four-year war against insurgents—the demand for autonomy or independence has been a recurrent theme.

Pakistan's international position

SELECTED READINGS

• *Items so designated are available in paperback editions.*

THE COMMONWEALTH

Belshaw, Horace, *New Zealand,* Berkeley, 1947.

Brady, Alexander, *Democracy in the Dominions,* Toronto, 1958.

Cameron, Roderick, *Australia: History and Horizons,* New York, 1971.

Creighton, Donald G., *Dominion of the North, a History of Canada,* Boston, 1944.

Dawson, R. M., *The Government of Canada,* Toronto, 1963.

Fitzpatrick, Brian, *The Australian People, 1788–1945,* Melbourne, 1946. An analytical and revealing account.

Grattan, C. H., *Australia,* Berkeley, 1947.

Lipson, Leslie, *The Politics of Equality: New Zealand's Adventures in Democracy,* Chicago, 1948.

MacInnes, Colin, *Australia and New Zealand,* New York, 1966.

McInnis, E. W., *Canada: A Political and Social History,* New York, 1959.

McIntyre, W. D., *The Commonwealth of Nations: Origins and Impact, 1869–1971*, Minneapolis, 1977.

Millar, T. B., *Australia in Peace and War: External Relations, 1788–1977*, New York, 1978. Emphasizes the recent period.

Shaw, A. G. L., *Convicts and the Colonies*, New York, 1966.

• Siegfried, André, *The Race Question in Canada*, New York, 1907. A perceptive study.

Wade, Mason, *The French Canadians*, New York, 1955.

INDIA, PAKISTAN, AND BANGLADESH (*See also Readings for Chapter 23*)

Bhatia, Krishan, *Indira: A Biography of Prime Minister Gandhi*, New York, 1974.

———., *The Ordeal of Nationhood: A Social Study of India since Independence, 1947–1970*, New York, 1971. Informed and objective account of India's problems.

Bonarjee, N. B., *Under Two Masters*, New York, 1970. By a former civil servant; highly critical.

• Bondurant, Joan, *Conquest of Violence: The Gandhian Philosophy of Conflict*, rev. ed., Berkeley, 1965.

Brecher, Michael, *Nehru: A Political Biography*, New York, 1959.

• Brown, D. M., *The Nationalist Movement: Indian Political Thought from Ranade to Bhave*, Berkeley, 1961.

Brown, W. N., *The United States and India, Pakistan, Bangladesh*, 3d ed., Cambridge, Mass., 1972.

Edwardes, Michael, *Nehru: A Political Biography*, New York, 1972.

Embree, A. T., *India's Search for National Identity*, New York, 1972. An analysis of Indian nationalism to 1947.

• Erikson, E. H., *Gandhi's Truth: On the Origins of Militant Nonviolence*, New York, 1969.

Fischer, Louis, *The Life of Mahatma Gandhi*, New York, 1950. An admirable biography.

Frankel, Francine, *India's Green Revolution: Economic Gains and Political Costs*, Princeton, 1971. A significant and challenging study.

• ———, *India's Political Economy, 1947–1977: The Gradual Revolution*, Princeton, 1979.

Hardgrave, R. L., Jr., *India: Government and Politics in a Developing Nation*, New York, 1970. Well balanced and clear.

Heimsath, C. H., *Indian Nationalism and Hindu Social Reform*, Princeton, 1964.

Hodson, H. V., *The Great Divide: India-Britain-Pakistan*, New York, 1971. An examination of events leading to Partition.

Ikram, S., and P. Spear, eds., *The Cultural Heritage of Pakistan*, London, 1956.

• Iyer, R. N., *The Moral and Political Thought of Mahatma Gandhi*, New York, 1973. A stimulating analysis.

Kothari, Rajni, *Politics in India*, Boston, 1970. Throws light on relationship between caste and politics.

Malik, Hafeez, *Moslem Nationalism in India and Pakistan,* Washington, 1963.

• Maxwell, Neville, *India's China War,* Garden City, N.Y., 1972. Scathingly critical of India's role in the 1962 clash.

Mehta, Ved, *Mahatma Gandhi and His Apostles,* New York, 1977. Emphasizes India's failure to realize Gandhi's ideals.

Menon, V. P., *The Transfer of Power in India,* Princeton, 1957.

Metcalf, T. R., *The Aftermath of Revolt: India, 1857–1870,* Princeton, 1964.

Moore, R. J., *Churchill, Cripps, and India 1939–1945,* New York, 1979. Attributes the partition of India to the failure of the Cripps mission of 1942.

• Morris-Jones, W. H., *The Government and Politics of India,* London, 1964.

• Nehru, Jawaharlal, *The Discovery of India,* New York, 1946.

• Palmer, N. D., *The Indian Political System,* Boston, 1961.

Roberts, P. E., *History of British India under the Company and the Crown,* 3d ed., New York, 1952. An excellent political text.

Sayeed, K. B., *Pakistan: The Formative Phase, 1857–1948,* 2d ed., New York, 1968.

• Sen Gupta, Bhabani, *Communism in Indian Politics,* New York, 1972.

Siddiqui, Kalim, *Conflict, Crisis, and War in Pakistan,* New York, 1972. An indictment of Pakistan's civilian and military elites.

• Srinivas, M. N., *Social Change in Modern India,* Berkeley, 1966.

von Vorys, Karl, *Political Development in Pakistan,* Princeton, 1965. Pessimistic.

Weekes, R. V., *Pakistan: Birth and Growth of a Muslim Nation,* Princeton, 1964.

• Woodruff, Philip, *The Men Who Ruled India,* 2 vols., New York, 1954.

Ziring, Lawrence, *The Ayub Khan Era: Politics in Pakistan 1958–1969,* Syracuse, N.Y., 1971. Generally favorable to Ayub.

SOURCE MATERIALS

Birla, G. D., *In the Shadow of the Mahatma: A Personal Memoir,* Bombay, 1953. Selections from Gandhi's correspondence, interviews and conversations.

Chakravarty, A., ed., *A Tagore Reader,* New York, 1961.

• Gandhi, M. K., *The Story of My Experiments with Truth,* Boston, 1957. Autobiography.

• Jack, H. A., ed., *The Gandhi Reader: A Source Book of His Life and Writings,* Bloomington, Ind., 1956.

McLane, J. R., ed., *The Political Awakening in India,* Englewood Cliffs, N.J., 1970.

Narayan, Jayaprakash, *Prison Diary,* ed. A. B. Shah, Seattle, 1978. Secret diary of Mrs. Gandhi's most famous prisoner.

• Nehru, Jawaharlal, *Toward Freedom,* New York 1951. Autobiography.

———, *Independence and After* (speeches, 1946–1949), New York, 1950.

———, *Jawaharlal Nehru's Speeches, 1949–1953,* Delhi, 1954.

Philips, C. H., *The Evolution of India and Pakistan, 1858 to 1947: Select Documents,* New York, 1962.

Russell, W. H., *My India Mutiny Diary,* London, 1957. Contemporary account by the London *Times* correspondent.

Tagore, Rabindranath, *My Reminiscences,* New York, 1917.

Chapter 38

THE MIDDLE EAST AND AFRICA

All secular power, no matter what form it takes, is the work of Satan. It is our duty to stop it in its tracks and to combat its effects. . . . It is not only our duty in Iran, but it is also the duty of all the Muslims of the world, to carry the revolutionary Islamic policy to its final victory.

—Ayatollah Ruholla Khomeini, *Islamic Government*

I. THE MIDDLE EAST

Few areas of the earth have witnessed more turbulence and rapidity of change than have the countries of the Middle East in recent times. The pattern of their history has been much the same. Before World War I most of them stagnated and slumbered under the rule of the Ottoman Turks. With the breakup of the Ottoman Empire they saw visions of independence and a chance to throw off all traces of foreign domination. Nationalist movements sprang up to prod governments into vigorous action. In many instances they gained control of governments, often in defiance of the religious authorities. They proceeded then with attempts to launch programs of modernization, for building highways, railroads, and schools, subsidizing industries, and sponsoring scientific agriculture and land reform. The problems they encountered, however, in the form of ignorance, corruption, vested interests, and foreign meddling were often too great to be overcome. To this day illiteracy, disease, and high death rates persist in many parts of the Middle East, and poverty is all but universal.

The pattern of Middle Eastern history

A survey of the Middle East may properly begin with Turkey, since it ranks first in population and since nearly the whole region at one time was subject to Turkish rule. We have already seen that the dismemberment of the Turkish Empire began as early as 1829 when the Sultan's government was forced to acknowledge the independence of Greece. Thenceforth one after another of the European provinces

Establishment of the Turkish republic

broke away. By 1914 Turkey in Europe had been reduced to nothing but Istanbul (Constantinople) and a corner of eastern Thrace. But Turkey in Asia still included a vast area from the western border of Persia to the Mediterranean Sea. At the end of World War I, the Turkish government, which had fought on the losing side, accepted a treaty depriving the empire of virtually everything except Istanbul and the northern and central portions of Asia Minor. But before this treaty could be put into effect a group of nationalists, under the leadership of Mustafa Kemal, reconquered much of the lost territory. In 1922 they marched on Istanbul, deposed the Sultan, and in 1923 proclaimed Turkey a republic. The Allies, in the meantime, consented to the making of a new treaty at Lausanne, Switzerland, which permitted the Turks to retain practically all the lands they had reconquered. The new state included Anatolia, Armenia, and eastern Thrace, but none of the outlying territories of Mesopotamia, Arabia, Palestine, or Syria.

Mustafa Kemal: political and educational reforms

For two decades the history of the Turkish republic was almost synonymous with the personal history of Mustafa Kemal. It was his imagination and determination that made the country over from a corrupt and somnolent Oriental despotism into a modern, progressive state with most of the forms if not the substance of democratic government. He began by abolishing the Caliphate and secularizing the state. Under the Sultan religion and the state were intertwined. The Sultan himself was the Caliph, or "Successor of the Prophet," and therefore the spiritual ruler of all Muslims. The law was religious law, and the only officially recognized schools were those attached to the mosques. Kemal's decree abolishing the Caliphate declared that the antiquated religious courts and codes must be replaced by "modern scientific civil codes," and that the schools of the mosques must give way to government schools, which all children between the ages of six and sixteen would be required to attend. But before much progress could be made in educational reform, it was necessary to take one further step, and that was to adopt a new system of writing. The Turkish language was still written in Arabic script, which Kemal regarded as an impossible medium for the expression of Western ideas. In 1928 he had a commission prepare an alphabet using the Roman letters, and this was done so successfully that modern Turkish spelling is consistently phonetic. When he had taught himself the new alphabet, Kemal proceeded to teach others, traveling throughout the country with his blackboard, lecturing audiences on how the characters should be formed. Soon he issued a decree forbidding the holding of public office by anyone who was not adept in the new writing.

Social and economic reforms

The achievements of Kemal also included a social and economic revolution. He issued decrees abolishing the fez, discouraging polygamy, and encouraging women to appear unveiled and both sexes to wear Western clothes. He established schools for girls and made women eligible for business careers and for the professions. In 1929 he gave women the suffrage in local elections and five years later in national elections. The initiative shown by Turkish women under the Republic, not only in entering occupations and professions previously reserved for men but in rising to positions of leadership, makes Turkey unique among Muslim countries and an example for others as well. Equally significant were Kemal's economic reforms. He endowed agricultural colleges, established model farms, and founded banks to lend money to farmers. He freed the peasant from the tithe and set up agencies to distribute seed and farm machinery to almost anyone who could offer a guaranty to use them effectively. Although he undoubtedly had the power to do so, he refrained from instituting measures of forced collectivization such as those of the Russians. He chose rather to adhere to the tradition of Muhammad in encouraging small holdings, in helping the farmer to buy his land, and in teaching him to work it profitably. At the same time he recognized the importance of promoting industrialization. Agriculture alone could not provide the people with a high standard of living or enable the country to make the best use of all its resources. He therefore built thousands of miles of railways and established state monopolies for the manufacture of tobacco, matches, munitions, salt, alcohol, and sugar. Despite the fact that Turkey has abundant resources of coal, iron, copper, and petroleum, and is the world's largest producer of chrome, three-fourths of its nearly 40 million inhabitants still derive their living from agriculture.

Mustafa Kemal Atatürk

Mustafa Kemal (later called Kemal Atatürk) ruled over Turkey from 1922 until his death in 1938. Whether he was simply another twentieth-century dictator, somewhat more benevolent than his compeers, is a question for debate. Legally, his position was that of an elective president, chosen by the Assembly for a four-year term and indefinitely re-eligible. But he himself was president of the Assembly, and, except for a brief period in 1930, he permitted no opposition party to exist. On the other hand, he always described his regime as temporary and transitional. After ten years he still maintained that the people were not yet ready for self-government. He must continue to rule for another decade or so until the citizens grew in wisdom and a sense of responsibility and liberated themselves from the habits and prejudices of the past. To his credit it can be said that he did not involve his country in war and that he never sought the extermination of racial minorities. Although he suppressed a revolt of the Kurds in 1930 with merciless severity, executing twenty-nine of the leaders, he never maintained a Gestapo or Cheka or any similar agency of irresponsible tyranny.

Under Kemal Atatürk's successors, Ismet Inönü and Celal Bayar, Turkey took steps toward supplanting its benevolent dictatorship with a democratic republic. But after World War II, severe economic difficulties, resulting mainly from extravagant spending and inflation, led the government of Premier Adnan Menderes to impose restric-

Revolution of 1960; The Second Turkish Republic

tions. Freedom of the press was abolished, and members of Parliament opposing the government were arrested. Successive student demonstrations against these repressive measures triggered a revolt in 1960 by army officers, who seized control and established a provisional government. Nearly 600 members of the previous regime were tried on charges of corruption and subversion of the Constitution. Of those convicted by the court, three were executed, including the deposed prime minister Adnan Menderes. In 1961 a new constitution was adopted proclaiming the Second Turkish Republic. It provided for a president elected by a Grand National Assembly (parliament) for a seven-year term and ineligible for re-election, and for a prime minister designated by the president on the basis of party representation in the parliament. It included also guaranties of civil liberties, clauses for the protection of workers' rights, and safeguards against abuse of executive power. When elections were held in October 1961, no party gained a majority. A coalition government was formed with the seventy-seven-year-old Ismet Inönü as prime minister. Faced with vexing difficulties and lacking adequate support in the National Assembly, he resigned in 1965.

Economic progress and social unrest

During the 1960s Turkey made considerable economic progress, accompanied by political instability and ominous social unrest. Although inflation continued at a galloping rate, industry expanded steadily and Turkish oil production almost kept pace with domestic demand. A huge dam constructed on the Euphrates promised electric power to transform the primitive rural area of eastern Anatolia. But while foundations were being laid for a modern industrialized society, both the economy and democratic institutions were threatened by bitter factional strife among opposing political extremists and among rival religious groups. Strikes and riots, violent clashes, and political assassinations produced hundreds of deaths and an atmosphere of terror. In March 1971 the military forces imposed martial law for the second time in the history of the republic. Whereas in the 1960 revolution the army had intervened on the liberal side, in 1971 it backed an ultraconservative and repressive "government of national union," which ruled for twenty-nine months. When parliamentary government was resumed, no party could win a majority, and the prime ministership alternated between Bülent Ecevit, leader of the Republican People's party (custodian of Atatürk's reforms but now divided) and Süleyman Demirel, head of the conservative Justice party. Ecevit garnered popularity as champion of the Turkish minority in Cyprus. But when, during the crisis of 1974, he sent an invading army to occupy the whole northern half of the island, he aroused resentment abroad. Both Demirel and Ecevit found it necessary to woo the Islamic-oriented National Salvation party, which controlled 15 percent of the popular vote.

Because of the economic and strategic importance of the Middle

East, unrelaxed tensions in that volatile region made the role of Turkey a matter of concern to neighboring states and to the superpowers as well. The United States operated military bases and electronic listening posts within Anatolia and regarded the Turks, with their army of half a million men, as a key NATO partner. The Turkish invasion of Cyprus in 1974—which so angered the Athens government that it withdrew Greece from NATO—strained relations with the United States. Although Washington had exerted little or no pressure to restrain Ankara's belligerency during the crisis, the United States subsequently suspended arms sales to Turkey. In retaliation the Turks closed twenty-six United States bases within their country. A few years later, after revolution in Iran and Russian-inspired coups in Afghanistan created fears that Western influence in the Middle East might completely collapse, the United States lifted its arms embargo and negotiated for reopening the bases, over which the Turkish government now insisted it should share control.

Turkey's international position

With a strong secular tradition and Western orientation but desirous of maintaining friendship with neighboring Muslim peoples, Turkey has found its position increasingly difficult. Hoping to keep a United States connection without antagonizing the Soviet Union—whose proffered financial aid they sorely need—the Turks seem determined not to become political pawns in the game of the superpowers. But the nation's desperate internal condition makes its future extremely uncertain. By 1979 there were shortages of most basic commodities, including foodstuffs. Industry was operating at about half its capacity, 20 percent of the labor force was unemployed, the annual inflation rate had reached almost 100 percent, and one-third of the country was under martial law. Rival Muslim factions were feuding, and the Kurdish minority in eastern Anatolia adjacent to Iraq and Iran showed signs of unrest. In September 1980 the army high command, after admonishing politicians to unite to fight "anarchy, terrorism, and separatism," executed an almost bloodless but decisive coup, suspending the constitution and arresting more than one hundred persons, including not only party leaders, but also the heads of labor unions. While enforcing martial law, the generals pledged that after the drafting of a new constitution designed to curb social disorder, they would honor the republic's tradition of a return to civilian rule.

Uncertainty as to the future

Second in population—and fast on its way to becoming first in that category among nations of the Middle East—is the Arab Republic of Egypt. Although technically a part of the Ottoman Empire until 1914, Egypt was for all practical purposes a dependency of Great Britain after 1882. The British kept up the pretense of acknowledging the sovereignty of the Khedive and his overlord the Sultan, but when Turkey joined the Central Powers in 1914 the London government issued a proclamation that Egypt would henceforth constitute a protectorate of the British Empire. When the war ended, the London

The beginning of nationalism in Egypt; the rise of the Wafd

authorities refused to allow Egypt to send a delegation to Paris to lay its case before the peace conference. The upshot was the emergence of an Egyptian nationalist movement known as the *Wafd*. The name means literally "delegation," and the movement had been organized originally to present Egypt's demands and grievances at the peace conference. When the British attempted suppression and deported its leader to Malta, the *Wafd* came forth with an insistence upon nothing less than complete independence.

Abolition of the British protectorate

Following a campaign of sabotage and terrorism waged by the *Wafd,* the British decided to abolish the protectorate and in 1922 proclaimed Egypt an independent and sovereign state. But "independence" was made subject to four reservations, to be left absolutely to the discretion of the British pending adjustment by mutual agreement. The first was the protection of the Suez Canal and other vital links in the lifeline of the British Empire. The second was the defense of Egypt itself against foreign encroachments or interference. The third was the protection of foreign interests and minorities in Egypt. The fourth was the maintenance of the dependent status of the Sudan under the joint rule of Britain and Egypt. For the next three decades the history of Egypt was largely occupied by controversy and conflict over these four points or reservations.

The revival of nationalism after World War II

Although the majority of Egyptians resented the attempts of the British to keep the country in a state of vassalage, they were alarmed by Mussolini's invasion of Ethiopia in 1935, and in 1936 accepted an Anglo-Egyptian Treaty of Friendship and Alliance. Egypt agreed to coordinate its foreign policy with that of Britain in return for British assistance in gaining admission to the League of Nations. Before all the terms of the Anglo-Egyptian Treaty could be put into effect, World War II broke out. The British were reluctant to take any steps that might threaten their communications with the East, and the Egyptians did not press the issue of the removal of British troops from

Suez Canal at the Onset of World War I. Britain's concern for the Suez Canal as a lifeline to the Empire was one of the primary factors behind the establishment of a protectorate over Egypt in 1914 and the "reservations" linked to the proclamation of independence in 1922.

their soil. But when the war ended, the flames of nationalist aspirations were kindled anew. The Egyptians now demanded that the British withdraw entirely from both the Suez Canal area and the Sudan. In 1951 the Egyptian government announced that it was abrogating the Treaty of 1936 and also the condominium or joint rule in the Sudan. In July 1954 Britain agreed to the removal of all British troops from Egyptian territory.

Gamal Abdul Nasser, Dynamic Arab Nationalist and President of Egypt, 1956–1970

In July 1952, Major General Muhammad Naguib seized control of the Egyptian government and the army. The pleasure-loving King Farouk I, alleged to be subservient to the British, was deposed. A year later Egypt was proclaimed a republic, with General Naguib as its first president and premier. The new ruler announced a program of sweeping economic and social reforms, but before it could be fully effected, conflict developed within the military junta that had overthrown the monarchy. Naguib's rival, Lieutenant-Colonel Gamal Abdul Nasser, secured the office of premier, and in June 1956, in a carefully managed election in which he was the only candidate, Nasser was chosen president. In the same election the Egyptian voters adopted a new constitution proclaiming the country an Islamic-Arab state with a democratic form of government.

The Suez crisis; Arab-Israeli wars

Nasser resolved to continue and enlarge the program of economic and social reform. In particular, he was determined to relieve the condition of the impoverished masses. He proceeded with plans to distribute 750,000 acres of land, giving farms to 250,000 landless peasants. He soon realized, however, that on account of Egypt's rapid growth in population, more productive land must be made available. To accomplish this purpose he decided upon the construction of the Aswan High Dam, a gigantic reservoir to back up the waters of the Upper Nile and provide irrigation for 2 million acres of arable land. Since the cost ($1.3 billion) would be more than Egypt could stand, he hoped to borrow large sums of money from the World Bank and from the United States and British governments. Alarmed by the Egyptian purchases of arms from Czechoslovakia (a Communist source), the United States suddenly withdrew its offer of a loan to Nasser, and Great Britain did likewise soon after. Nasser retaliated by expropriating the owners of the Suez Canal, who were chiefly British and French, and declared that he would use the revenues of the canal to build the dam. After months of fruitless negotiation, the British and French encouraged an invasion of Egyptian territory by the Republic of Israel. The Israelis had plenty of grievances, since they had been the victims of border raids from the Sinai Peninsula for many years. The invasion began on October 29, 1956, and the British and French intervened soon afterward. The affair precipitated a crisis which threatened for a time to engulf the world. The Soviet rulers warned Israel that its very existence was in danger and darkly hinted their intention of joining forces with Egypt. The United Nations finally arranged a cease-fire, and in March 1957 the Nasser government reopened the canal, under its own terms of national ownership, to all users except Israel. Nasser formed alliances with Jordan and Syria and vowed that Israel must be wiped from the map. In 1967, when he closed Aqaba, Israel's only direct outlet to the Red Sea, the Israelis responded with a lightning war against Egypt and its Arab allies. The Egyptian and Syrian forces were routed in six days, and the Syrians accepted a cease-fire a short time later, leaving Israel in occupation of the Sinai peninsula and the West Bank of the Jordan River. Violence erupted again in October 1973 when Egypt and Syria launched a surprise offensive in the Sinai and Golan Heights areas respectively. After seventeen days of fierce fighting a cease-fire was established under pressure from the United States and the U.S.S.R.

Peace negotiations between Egypt and Israel

Following Nasser's death in 1970, Anwar Sadat, a relatively obscure member of the group that had overthrown the monarchy in 1952, became president of Egypt. Confronted with problems at home and abroad, he attempted to continue Nasser's policies while moderating their harshness. A new constitution enacted in 1971 contained democratic features, but political power remained with the one and only legal party, the Arab Socialist Union, which had become bureaucratic and unprogressive. Sadat's most distinctive contribution was the reversal of his predecessor's foreign policy. At the risk of sacrificing leadership of the Arab world, he resolved to end the state of war with Israel which exacted a tremendous economic price and continually posed the threat of a general conflagration. Piecemeal agreements, negotiated with the help of United States Secretary of State Henry Kissinger in 1974 and 1975, provided for mutual disengagement in the Suez Canal area and the return of Sinai oilfields to Egyptian control. In June 1975 the canal—closed since 1967—was reopened to merchant

Aswan High Dam. The dam was designed to serve a twofold purpose: to facilitate the irrgation of vast areas of arid land and to generate electrical power.

Israeli Tanks Move into Jerusalem. A scene during the second Arab-Israeli War, June 1967.

ships of all nations, including Israel. Seizing an even bolder initiative, President Sadat—after requesting an invitation—in November 1977 became the first Arab leader to pay an official visit to the state of Israel, where he met an enthusiastic reception in Tel Aviv and Jerusalem. This surprisingly auspicious weekend visit resolved none of the difficulties between the two states but it opened the door to improved relations. In his speech before the Israeli parliament (Knesset) Sadat affirmed Israel's right to exist, but at the same time he called unequivocally for withdrawal from all occupied Arab lands, for Arab access to the holy city of Jerusalem, and for the creation of an independent Palestinian state. Not until March 1979, after many months of negotiation, was an Egyptian-Israeli peace treaty signed, and it left important issues unresolved, particularly the exact nature of the "full autonomy" promised to the Palestinians, and the status of the city of Jerusalem—sacred to the adherents of three religions but which the Israelis had vowed to retain as their nation's capital.

The movement toward accommodation with Israel brought radical changes in Egypt's international position. In 1972 President Sadat expelled his Soviet advisers, thus rebuffing the country that had been Egypt's chief source of economic and military aid. However, his overtures to Israel, which began shortly after the 1973 war and were strongly encouraged by the United States, won for him access to the world's leading arms emporium. United States diplomatic support was also welcome at a time when Egypt was facing isolation in the Arab and Islamic international community. Following the peace treaty with Israel, sixteen Arab states, the Palestinian Liberation Organization, and Iran severed diplomatic relations with Cairo. Sadat continued to be at odds with Arab leaders and Islamic fundamentalists until he was assassinated in October 1981.

President Anwar Sadat of Egypt Addressing the Israeli Knesset in 1977

Egypt's economic performance failed to match its stellar role in the field of diplomacy. With an annual per capita income of $280, the nation is among the world's poorest. Egypt is the most urbanized of the Arab countries and its population of 39 million is growing so rapidly, especially in the cities, that overcrowding and shortages are inevitable. Cairo, with 2 million inhabitants in 1952, had 9 million twenty-five years later. Housing was so scarce that as many as ten people slept in a single room, and squatters improvised living quarters in Cairo's cemeteries. In one of mankind's oldest agricultural regions, farming methods are still primitive. Yet the economic picture is not utterly bleak. Within two years of the reopening of the Suez Canal in 1975 its annual revenue had reached $500,000. Plans were announced to enlarge the waterway to accommodate 200,000-ton supertankers, and the increase in traffic was stimulating rapid urban growth along the canal route. The Aswan Dam, though it has not produced the economic miracle hoped for on its completion in 1970, could provide water for desert reclamation in the Sinai peninsula. Egypt has appreciable reserves of petroleum and in 1977 began to produce some for export.

When World War I ended, the country now known as Israel was a province of Turkey. Its population was about 70 percent Arab and 30 percent Jewish and Christian. By the defeat of Turkey in 1918, it was made a mandate of the League of Nations under the guardianship of Great Britain. In the meantime, Zionists in Britain and the United States worked zealously to convert Palestine into a national home for the Jewish people. In return for their labors the British government issued the famous Balfour Declaration promising to view with favor the establishment in Palestine of a national home for Jewish people. At the same time provision would be made for safeguarding the rights of non-Jewish communities in Palestine.

On the basis of the Balfour Declaration, Britain accepted the mandate for Palestine, promising not merely to establish a Jewish national home, but "to secure the preservation of an Arab National Home and to apprentice the people of Palestine as a whole in the art of self-government." It was an optimistic ambition, but at the time optimism seemed justified. In fact, for ten years there was every reason to expect that the undertaking would be successful. Palestine prospered as never before in its history. Factories were built, land was reclaimed, irrigation works were constructed, the Jordan River was harnessed for electric power, and unemployment disappeared from the face of the land. Except for rioting in Jaffa in 1921, no incident of violence occurred to disturb the general tranquillity. The aspect of the country was so peaceful that in 1926 the British reduced their armed forces to a single RAF squadron and two companies with armored cars.

By 1929, however, evidences of disharmony had begun to appear in the land that was holy to three great religions. The Jews were too prosperous and well educated and were arousing the envy and fears of the Arabs by their high standard of living and their more strenuous competition. Their purchases of land, in many cases from absentee owners, had resulted in the displacement of thousands of Arab cultivators and had thrown them into the cities at a time when the Great Depression was beginning to make unemployment a serious problem. But the major cause of Arab foreboding was the steady increase in the Jewish population. The opportunity to emigrate to Palestine had offered a greater temptation than the Arabs had expected. As a consequence, some of them foresaw a relentless advance and expansion of Europeans and Americans, backed by foreign capital and flaunting a culture that was alien to the ways of the Arab majority. In 1929, 1930, and 1931 armed attacks were waged upon Jewish settlements followed by terrorist murders.

But these episodes paled into insignificance when compared with the bloody violence that followed. When the mandate was established, no one could have foreseen the desperate plight that was to overtake the European Jews with the accession of the Nazis to power in Germany. As news of the persecutions spread, it was inevitable that pressure should be brought upon the British government to relax the barriers against immigration into Palestine. During the period 1933–1935 the admission of more than 130,000 Jewish immigrants was authorized, and uncounted thousands more came in illicitly. From this time on Palestine was a seething caldron of violence and warfare. The Arabs rose in open rebellion against the mandate. Organized terrorism swept the country. Guerrilla attacks in the rural areas and looting, burning, and sabotage in the towns and cities kept the whole population in turmoil. By 1938 Britain had 20,000 troops in Palestine, and even these were unable to maintain order.

The early years of World War II were characterized by relative quiet in Palestine, but trouble broke out anew when a conference of American Zionists at the Biltmore Hotel in New York, in May 1942,

The development of conflicts between Jews and Arabs

Rebellion of the Arabs against the mandate

Immigration to Palestine. Left: British soldiers guard the shore as a ship loaded with unauthorized refugees attempts to land in 1947. Right: A view of the unbearably crowded conditions aboard ships bringing refugees to Palestine.

adopted the so-called Biltmore Program, demanding the establishment of a Jewish state and a Jewish army in Palestine. Soon afterward both Jews and Arabs prepared for war to the hilt. Fanatical Zionists, as well as Arabs, resorted to the use of terrorist methods. Illegal military organizations sprang up on both sides and devoted their energies to raiding, burning, and assassination.

Termination of the mandate and establishment of the State of Israel

In April 1947 the British government referred the Palestine problem to the United Nations and announced that a year later it would terminate the mandate and withdraw all its troops from the country. On May 15, 1948, the British mandate came to an end, and on the same day a Jewish provisional government proclaimed the establishment of an independent State of Israel. Elections were held for a Constituent Assembly, which met in February of the following year and adopted a temporary constitution for a democratic republic. Its chief features were a weak president, a strong cabinet, and a powerful parliament. The constitution also provided for proportional representation, a unicameral parliament, and universal suffrage for Jews and Arabs alike. A unique element in the system was the close association of religion with the state. Marriage and divorce were placed under the exclusive jurisdiction of religious courts—Jewish, Christian, or Muslim as the affiliation of the parties might require.

The Arab-Israeli wars

Meanwhile, from the day of proclaimed independence until the spring of 1949, Israel and its Arab neighbor countries were at war. United Nations efforts brought about truces several times; Israel and Egypt signed a general armistice agreement in February 1949; Jordan and Syria also signed armistices in April. The status at the cease-fire was regarded as a victory for Israel and a defeat for the Arab powers; neither, however, accepted it as final. Violent incidents continued to occur, including retaliatory massacres.

Agricultural development

Despite troubles with the Arabs, Israel strengthened its economy, and many new industries were created. Large sums of money flowed into the country as a result of West German restitution for the outrages of Nazism. Agriculture advanced to a stage sufficient to supply the needs of the home market while export crops such as olives, melons, and citrus fruits were rapidly developed. Land under cultivation more than doubled between 1955 and 1967. The index of industrial production increased from 100 in 1963 to 185 in 1969. The nation had seven universities, two with more than 10,000 students each. Total enrollment in all state schools had increased from 130,000 in 1948 to approximately 800,000 in 1970.

The heavy burden of defense

Yet the fate of Israel was not a happy one. The state was born in strife and during the first twenty-five years of its existence fought four wars with its Arab neighbor states. In the face of adversity Israel managed not only to endure but to grow in strength—a testimony to the resourcefulness and determination of its citizens but also owing to massive economic and military aid from the United States (currently

On the Path to Peace in the Middle East. From left to right, Egyptian President Anwar Sadat, U.S. President Jimmy Carter, and Israeli Prime Minister Menachem Begin shake hands at the announcement of the Camp David accord which laid the groundwork for a peace treaty between Egypt and Israel.

nearly $2 billion a year). Obsession with the problem of security has exacted a heavy economic and psychological toll. Between 1967 and 1975 defense spending rose to become the highest in the world in proportion to population ($1,040 per capita), consuming half the national budget and 32 percent of the gross national product. Armed to the teeth, Israel became an exporter of arms to some fifty other countries; yet peace seemed as elusive as ever.

The Labor party, after thirty years in office, was defeated in the elections of May 1977 and replaced by the Likud bloc, which drew much of its support from extreme nationalists opposed to any compromise with Israel's enemies. Menachem Begin, the new prime minister, was a veteran of the struggle for independence and known as a hard-liner. Nevertheless, he agreed to exploratory talks with President Sadat of Egypt and accepted the invitation to a summit meeting at Camp David, Maryland, where President Carter's patience and persistence bore fruit in the signing of a basic agreement. The Camp David Accords of September 1978 bound Sadat and Begin to take positive steps toward peace in the Middle East. But the formidable difficulties remaining were scarcely lessened by the Egyptian-Israeli treaty signed the following March. While Arab spokesmen denounced Sadat as a traitor to their cause, the Arab populations of Israeli-occupied lands accused Israel of planning to keep them in permanent subjection. The Israeli government refused to treat with the Palestine Liberation Organization, even though the PLO had won wide recognition as the most articulate champion of the cause of the Palestinian refugees. Since 1967 the Israelis had planted more than sixty new Jewish settlements in the West Bank, the Gaza Strip, and the Golan Heights, and a fervent Zionist faction was demanding permanent

The Camp David Accords

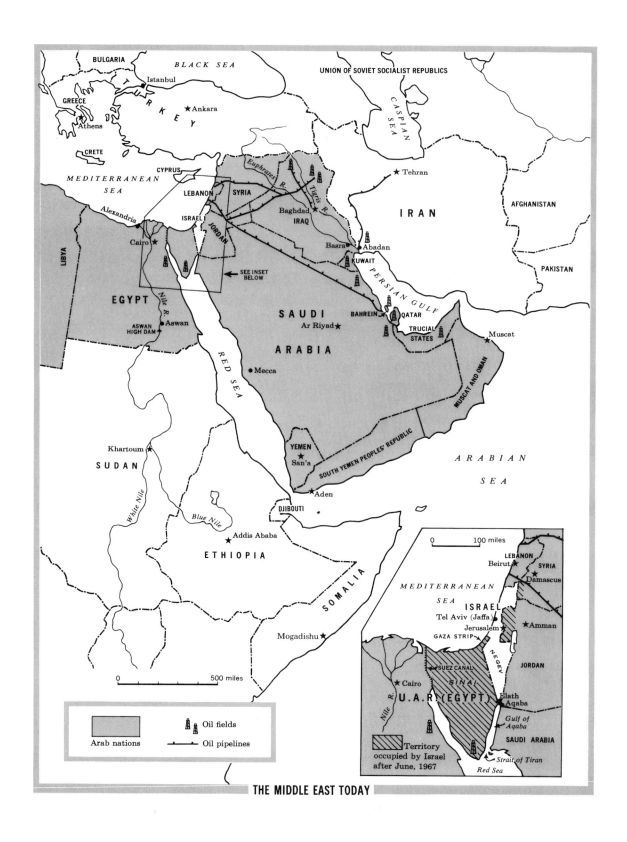

THE MIDDLE EAST TODAY

retention of these territories. Meanwhile, the need for a peace agreement became more imperative, not only because of the constant danger that a major war might break out but for the sake of ensuring Israel's survival. Arab populations were increasing much more rapidly than was Israel's, and Arab armies were improving in military effectiveness, as shown in the October 1973 ("Yom Kippur") war. Also, following that conflict, international support for the Israeli position weakened, partly in reaction to the oil embargo imposed by Arab producers. Recognition of these factors prompted a demand within Israel for a policy of accommodation and compromise. In October 1979 Moshe Dayan, hero of the 1967 war, resigned his post as foreign minister in Begin's government because he disapproved of its adamant stand on the Palestinian issue. Further defections from the cabinet followed, and by January 1981 Begin has lost his majority in the Knesset.

The ethnic problem

During the first thirty years of Israel's existence as a state, the character of the nation changed considerably. Many early Zionists had visualized Israel as a haven for small farmers or a community of agricultural cooperatives. By the mid-1970s it had become a land of teeming cities, with a society 80 percent urban. Rapid industrial growth was paced by rampant inflation, which by 1980 had reached an annual rate in excess of 100 percent. A potential internal problem centered on the Israeli citizens of Arab descent, who were subjected to the strain of conflicting loyalties in times of controversy between Israel and Arab states. Theoretically equal under the law, Israeli Arabs were discriminated against in practice, and most of them lived in exclusively Arab villages in northern Israel. With the world's highest birth rate, their numbers had tripled since 1948, reaching a figure of half a million and constituting about 15 percent of the total population of Israel. Another factor affecting the character of society was a change in the pattern of immigration—a decline in the influx of Western Jews and an increase in those coming from Arabic and North African countries. By 1977 the Sephardic or "Oriental" elements outnumbered those of Western European or American origin (called Ashkenazi), but they suffered some of the same disadvantages as the Israeli Arabs. The combination of internal pressures and external threats created an identity crisis for Israeli citizens. A prominent intellectual, formerly president of the World Zionist Organization, urged Israel to seek security by fulfilling its destiny as a unique spiritual center rather than striving to be "a state like all other states." He recommended Israel's neutralization—returned to its pre-1967 borders but with independence and sovereignty guaranteed by the two superpowers—and a gradual demilitarization of the states of the Middle East.[1]

Until recently, the most barren and backward of the countries formerly included in the Ottoman Empire was that which is now called

[1] Nahum Goldmann, "True Neutrality for Israel," *Foreign Policy*, Winter 1979–80, pp. 113–41.

A Meeting of the Arab Kings. In the wake of a war on the Nejd-Iraq border, King Faisal of Iraq (seated fourth from the left) and King Abdul Ibn Saud of Saudi Arabia (seated fifth from the left) negotiated a lasting peace under British auspices in 1930.

The formation of Saudi Arabia

Saudi Arabia. Covering an area more than one-fourth that of the United States, Arabia is almost 100 percent desert. Not a single river or lake exists to relieve the monotonous aridity. Inhabited to this day by only 9½ million people, the country did not become a united state until 1927. Prior to that time it was divided into the two main areas of the Hejaz and Nejd. The king of the Hejaz was Sherif Hussein, Protector of the Holy Cities of Mecca and Medina and, after 1924, self-appointed Caliph of Islam. Hussein was driven from his kingdom by the ruler of Nejd, Abdul ibn Saud (1880–1953), who in January 1926 had himself proclaimed King of the Hejaz in the Great Mosque of Mecca. Soon afterward he united his two kingdoms of Hejaz and Nejd into a theocratic state which he named Saudi Arabia.

Saudi oil and ARAMCO

Ibn Saud was shrewd enough to realize that the Muslim world could not hold its own against Western encroachments without adopting Western improvements. Accordingly, he allowed a few railways to be built and imported motor vehicles for his own court and for the transportation of pilgrims to the Holy Cities, and he instituted plans for free education. By far the greatest impetus was the discovery, in the 1930s, that eastern Arabia contained undreamed of riches in the form of petroleum deposits, amounting to the world's largest known reserves. King ibn Saud granted concessions for the exploitation of this wealth to the Arabian-American Oil Company (Aramco), owned jointly by Texaco and the Standard Oil Company of California. Royalties paid by Aramco provided the funds for electrification of cities and the construction of highways, railroads, and airports, to say nothing of aid to agriculture, education, and public health.

Abdul ibn Saud's son and heir, a wildly reckless spendthrift, was deposed by the royal family in 1964 and replaced by his half brother Faisal. King Faisal, who also retained the prime ministership, proved to be an enlightened and able statesman. He abolished slavery in his kingdom, opened public schools for girls, and won wide respect. His success owed much to the loyal service of Sheikh Ahmed Zaki Yamani. Western-educated (New York University, Columbia, Harvard), brilliant, and level-headed, Yamani had been appointed minister of petroleum and mineral resources in 1962, before Faisal's accession to the throne. Sheikh Yamani negotiated agreements with Aramco providing for the gradual transfer of ownership to Saudi Arabia, directed similar negotiations with Western oil companies for other Arab states, and initiated the formation of the Organization of Petroleum Exporting Countries (OPEC). In April 1978 King Faisal was assassinated by a member of his own family. His brother Khalid, who succeeded to the throne, was conservative, puritanical, and too infirm physically to play an active role, but Khalid's designated successor, Crown Prince Fahd, entertained ambitious plans for modernization and industrial development.

Yamani and OPEC

Saudi Arabia affords a striking illustration of how the impact of advanced technology and an expanding market can telescope centuries and divergent cultures. The government is an absolute monarchy, with power exercised by the king but residing in about 3,000 princes of the Saudi royal household. Abject poverty is still prevalent outside the few rapidly modernizing cities. Society for the most part is bound by the rigid restrictions of Muslim traditionalism, seen typically in the banning of alcoholic beverages and in the seclusion of women. But the citizens, with no elections and no parliament to represent them, nevertheless enjoy welfare benefits that might be envied by socialist democracies: free medical service, free education through the university level, subsidies to farmers, and loans to homeowners. The wealth accruing to Saudi Arabia as the world's largest oil-exporting country has enabled it to finance ambitious domestic projects and also to con-

Modernization

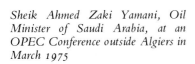
Sheik Ahmed Zaki Yamani, Oil Minister of Saudi Arabia, at an OPEC Conference outside Algiers in March 1975

tribute subsidies to Egypt, Jordan, Syria, and the PLO. Since the possession of oil has become not only an economic prize but a potent political weapon as well, Saudi Arabia has acquired a key strategic international position. This was illustrated in 1973–1974 when an Arab oil embargo—instituted by King Faisal against the Western powers—sent shock waves around the globe.

Petrodollars

Saudi Arabia's foreign policy has been anti-Israel, but at the same time anti-Communist and generally aligned with that of the United States. The United States depends on Saudi Arabia for about 20 percent of its oil imports and provides technology and managerial skill in exchange. Through oil royalties the Riyadh government accumulated a huge dollar reserve, amounting by 1975 to more than $70 billion. The investment of the bulk of these "petrodollars" in United States bonds, stocks, and banks provided critical support for the dollar at a time when it was being eroded by the United States' large foreign trade deficit.

The triumph of Iranian nationalism under Riza Khan

The only country of the Middle East which was not under the rule of Turkey at one time or another before 1918 was Persia. But this did not mean freedom from foreign domination. Remote, steeped in languor, and rich in resources, Persia was a constant temptation to ambitious imperialists. In 1907 Great Britain and Russia signed an agreement providing for the division of the country into spheres of influence. The northern sphere was assigned to Russia and the southern to Great Britain. A middle zone was to be left, temporarily at least, under the control of the native Shah. The overthrow of the tsar in 1917 filled the minds of British imperialists with hopes that all Persia might be theirs. By 1919 Lord Curzon had extorted from the Shah

A Saudi Arabian Oil Refinery and Storage Tanks. The Saudis have been producing 10.5 million barrels of oil per day (at least 1 million barrels per day more than they have produced in recent years) in order to make up the shortfall created by the Iranian-Iraqi war that began in the fall of 1980 and to force the OPEC nations to devise a unified policy for the first time in eight years.

an agreement transferring to Great Britain political and military control of the entire country. But the plans of the British were frustrated by Riza Khan, a young army officer who forced the Shah to appoint him minister of war and commander-in-chief of the army. In 1923 he became premier and two years later Shah with the title Riza Pahlavi. In 1932 he canceled the concession of the powerful Anglo-Persian Oil Company and obtained a new contract with terms more advantageous to his own government. In 1935 he changed the name of his country from Persia to Iran, or land of the Aryans.

World War II brought almost as much turmoil and anguish to Iran as if it had been one of the belligerents. Accused of Nazi sympathies, Riza Shah in 1941 was forced to abdicate and was succeeded on the throne by his son Muhammad Riza Pahlavi. Because of its strategic importance, Iran's territory was occupied by the British, Russians, and Americans under pledges to respect its sovereignty and independence and to render economic assistance during and after the war. Despite these pledges, unrest and inflation plagued the country. An internal political conflict led to the temporary expulsion of the Shah. Premier Muhammad Mossadegh, a nationalist leader, precipitated an international crisis in 1951 when he secured authorization from parliament to nationalize the petroleum industry. Western opposition to any assertion of economic independence by an underdeveloped semi-colonial country was complicated by Anglo-American rivalry. Averse to prolonged negotiation, the United States government cut off aid to Teheran and persuaded the British to join in enforcing a boycott which denied Iran access to oil tankers and oil markets. The consequent shutdown of the huge Anglo-Iranian refinery at Abadan brought the Iranian government to the point of bankruptcy. In August 1953 a CIA-directed coup overthrew the government, replacing Mossadegh with a former Nazi collaborator and restoring the Shah to his throne. Under a new agreement, 40 percent of Iran's petroleum industry was allotted to five American companies.

Expulsion and restoration of the Shah

Muhammad Riza Pahlavi's reign, spanning nearly four decades, brought his country considerable material progress, an overblown military establishment, brutal repression, and finally a revolution that shook society to its roots. During the 1960s Iran achieved an annual economic growth rate of 9 percent and doubled the gross national product. Revenues from oil, the chief natural resource, made possible highway construction, power-generating dams, and the beginnings of a system of public education. In 1963 The Shah launched what he called a "White Revolution," dedicated to raising living standards of his subjects. However, in spite of the state's ample revenues, "the Shah-People Revolution" produced meager results. A highly touted program of land redistribution reduced the number of tenants but left the majority of farmers on tiny plots, while great landlords retained large estates and the most profitable holdings. In 1979 three out of five

Material progress, but meager social benefits

rural families owned either no land or practically none, and millions of uprooted agricultural workers had drifted to the cities in search of work. One-tenth of the population controlled half of the wealth. Social services were inadequate and inferior. In a population of 35 million, 60 percent of adults were illiterate.

While indulging in the trappings of absolute monarchy—exemplified by five palaces maintained for the royal family, and by a multi-million-dollar extravaganza at Persepolis in 1971 to celebrate the 2,500th anniversary of Persian monarchy—the Shah hoped to modernize the nation. Seemingly equating modernization with militarization, between 1959 and 1978 he spent $36 billion on arms, about half of them purchased from the United States. In order to pay for sophisticated planes, missiles, and supporting equipment, he raised the price of oil—contributing to the upward surge that quadrupled oil prices in 1974. Expansion of land, air, and naval forces made Iran the strongest military power in the Persian Gulf area.

Muhammad Riza Pahlavi, Shah of Iran

An Iranian constitution, dating from 1906 and modeled on that of Belgium, provided for the separation of powers and guaranteed basic rights to the citizens. The Shah, however, suppressed all political parties except one of his own invention and forbade any opposition to his rule. Commander-in-chief of the armed forces, he bolstered his position by keeping an imperial guard and, especially, through the notorious SAVAK, a secret police force trained by the CIA and under the Shah's personal control. SAVAK agents, systematically employing terror and various forms of torture, made the Shah's regime one of the most brutal among the many dictatorships afflicting contemporary civilization. And while repression did not prevent eventual revolution, it eliminated much of the potential leadership needed for reconstruction after the advent of revolution.

Extreme repression

Revolution: expulsion of the Shah

Latent opposition to the Shah's rule had long rankled among Muslim religious leaders, the *mullahs,* both because their influence had been curtailed and because some aspects of modernization were repugnant to them. Intellectuals were alienated by government repression and corruption. Disaffection spread throughout the Iranian population in the late 1970s when an economic slump halted industrial projects and rising unemployment was accompanied by a 50-percent rate of inflation. January 1978 inaugurated a year of riots and bloody clashes. Crowds of millions demonstrated in the streets; some 8,000 people were killed as the police cracked down on protesters. In September the Shah imposed martial law and appointed a military governor, confident that, with the army behind him, he could weather the storm. But strikes in the oil fields and violent eruptions led by university students paralyzed the government and brought the economy to a standstill. When it became evident that the army was not without sympathy for the revolutionaries and might refuse orders to fight against the people, the Shah was forced to vacate his throne. On

January 16, 1979, he left Iran by plane "on a vacation," and a Revolutionary Council was installed in his place. Revolutionary courts sentenced and executed hundreds of the Shah's former supporters, including nearly a third of the military high command.

The Shah's abrupt capitulation left the country in a divided and chaotic state. Western governments had been strangely blind to flaws in Iran's economy and to the nearly universal hatred which Iranians bore toward their ruler. Having praised the Shah as a staunch ally, commanding "an island of stability in one of the most troubled areas of the world," American officials were unprepared to deal effectively with his successors. According to the U.S. ambassador in Teheran, sharp disagreements within the Washington bureaucracy prevented the establishment of links with revolutionary leaders that might have salvaged some United States influence and smoothed the process of transition.[2]

Washington's failure to anticipate the revolution

Beyond expulsion of the Shah, the objectives of the popular revolution that swept Iran were not entirely clear. The key revolutionary figure and temporary wielder of power was a seventy-eight-year-old Islamic theologian, Ayatollah Ruholla Khomeini. A life-long enemy of the Pahlavi dynasty, Khomeini had been exiled in 1964, sought refuge in Iraq and later in Paris, and in the French capital gathered around him the nucleus of a revolutionary government. A man of great energy and passionate convictions, Khomeini was idolized upon his re-entry into Iran on February 1 and, with the assistance of a Revolutionary Council, issued decrees for the nation. The Ayatollah's political precepts were derived from theological studies and from his devout Shiite faith, tempered somewhat by the idealism of Plato's *Republic*. Within a few months he drafted a new constitution for Iran, providing for a popularly elected president but making Islamic law binding upon all citizens, and secular officials subject to supervision and removal by the religious authorities. Staggering internal problems confronted the new regime: a crippled economy; tension between religious conservatives and proponents of modernization and secularism; nationalist aspirations among minorities, especially the Kurds of Kurdistan in western Iran. External relations also presented problems. Khomeini, a fervent Islamic nationalist, was not only anti-U.S.A. and anti-Israel but also anti-Communist and anti-Soviet. Iranian resentment toward the United States for its close ties with the Shah's government was aggravated when the ailing exiled monarch was admitted to an American hospital for treatment. In reprisal a group of militants seized the United States embassy in Teheran in November 1979 and held fifty-two hostages captive for 444 days. Their release was

Ayatollah Ruholla Khomeini of Iran

Problems confronting the revolutionary government

[2] William H. Sullivan, "The Road Not Taken," *Foreign Policy,* Fall 1980. pp. 175–86. Sullivan alleges that National Security Adviser Zbigniew Brzezinski tried to promote an army coup in support of the Shah.

*Persistent sources of
conflict*

obtained only after long, repeatedly stalemated, and humiliating negotiations.

A formidable addition to the troubles afflicting Khomeini's regime was the outbreak of war with Iraq, a neighbor with whom Iran had long-standing disputes. The Iraqis' motives in launching their attack in September 1980 were partly territorial. Repudiating a 1975 agreement made with the Shah, they hoped to gain control of the Shatt al-Arab—the 100-mile-long terminus of the great Tigris-Euphrates river system emptying into the Persian Gulf. The Baghdad government also feared the spread of Islamic fundamentalism and revolutionary fervor which, if it reached beyond Iran's borders, might disaffect Iraq's predominantly Shiite population. Although Iraqi troops were able to penetrate Iran's territory, Iranian defenses proved stronger than anticipated, and Iranian planes bombed Baghdad. Each side claimed to be fighting a holy war (Khomeini added the charge that Iraq was acting at the behest of the "Satan" United States). The conflict imperiled the source of 40 percent of the industrialized West's oil requirements and threatened to ruin the economies of both belligerents.

The ferment agitating the Middle East ever since World War II seemed to reach a critical stage as the 1970s ended. Lands that had nurtured ancient empires and cradled Western civilization were subjected to more rapid change than ever before in their long history. Scarcely anywhere could the assurance of stability be found. Competing pressures from without intensified domestic and regional problems that were already perplexing enough. The most obvious and persistent source of conflict was that between Israel and surrounding Arab peoples, exacerbated by the presence of more than a million Palestinian refugees—bereft of a homeland ever since the Arabic-Jewish war of 1948—and by the disaffection of Arab populations in lands occupied by Israel since the 1967 war. But other rivalries of comparable bitterness divided the region. The "Arab World" was by no means a solid entity. An Arab League, formed in 1945 with Egypt, Saudi Arabia, Jordan, Iraq, Syria, Lebanon, and Yemen as the original members, failed to resolve the differences between conservatives and radicals; nor could it keep its members from being drawn into the power struggle between the United States and the Soviet Union. Egypt, the league's military right arm, was expelled in 1979 in retaliation for Sadat's rapprochement with Israel, and became temporarily a pariah in the eyes of fellow Arabs. A ruinous civil war which racked the tiny state of Lebanon for nineteen months during 1975–1976, pitting Lebanese Christians against Muslims, was symptomatic of the struggle for leadership among Arab states as well as a manifestation of the Israeli-Palestinian conflict. Fighting in Lebanon was halted by the joint intervention of Israel and Israel's official enemy, Syria. President Hafez Assad of Syria was anxious to prevent the complete dismem-

Iranian Demonstrators Outside the U.S. Embassy in Teheran, November 25, 1979. Militants, bearing portraits of Ayatollah Khomeini and cardboard effigies of President Jimmy Carter, protested the American role in Iranian affairs during the previous 26 years while 52 American hostages were held in the embassy.

berment of Lebanon, which he hoped to use as a base for expanding his own influence, and to this end he did not scruple to use force against the Palestinians.

As Egypt's influence waned, Iraq, with a population of only 12 million, appeared a likely candidate for primacy among Muslim countries of the Middle East. Once regarded as highly volatile and unstable, Iraq during the last decade moved rapidly to change its image. In 1968 the Baath Socialist party seized control and established a military dictatorship which was repressive but also introduced positive economic reforms. Huge oil reserves—largest among the Arab states excepting Saudi Arabia, and carefully managed—gave Iraq an advantageous position in foreign trade and its people a relatively high standard of living. Saddam Hussein, leader of the Baath party and, since 1979, president of Iraq, in June 1980 permitted the election of a 250-member assembly to share legislative power with the dominant Revolutionary Council. In the 1970s Hussein loosened ties with Moscow, in spite of a fifteen-year friendship treaty signed in 1972. He repudiated the Iraqi Communist party and dismissed its representatives from his cabinet. Steadily increasing Iraq's armaments, Hussein intended his country to displace Iran as the strongest military power in the Persian Gulf. The exhausting war with Iran put his ambition to a severe test.

Iraq's growing strength

Explosive forces in the Middle East include the nationalist ambitions of ethnic minorities: the Baluchi of Iran, Afghanistan, and Pakistan; the Kurds of Iran, Iraq, and Turkey. Mistrust between the Shiite and Sunnite divisions of Islam is another factor, as is the struggle between advocates and opponents of progressive change. The inherent danger in conflict springing from these issues is multiplied beyond

Dangers inherent in policies of the superpowers

measure by the fact that Middle Eastern nations are heavily armed. For this, responsibility rests mainly with the two superpowers, who sought both profits from arms sales and at the same time the acquisition of client states. They are discovering, however, that client states, sufficiently armed, cannot only bully their neighbors but also turn against their supposed benefactors.

The strategic position of OPEC

Until recently the Middle East was a region of abject poverty. Among great numbers of the population it still is, but the tapping of its enormous stores of petroleum—totaling two-thirds of the world's proven reserves—has brought wealth and clout to those in control of this natural resource. The result has been to make the Middle East not only the scene of confrontation between the superpower blocs but also a focal point in the growing tension between advanced industrial nations and undeveloped countries of the Third World. The embargo on oil shipments imposed by the Arab states in 1973 demonstrated their ability to regulate supply and manipulate price. By 1980 the Organization of Petroleum Exporting Countries—with the ready compliance of Western oil conglomerates—had raised the price of oil to nine times what it was in October 1973. The revolution in oil prices has brought a parallel revolution in trade relationships. Industrialized nations like the United States face mounting trade deficits, while desert monarchies and Gulf sheikhdoms pile up surpluses of "petrodollars." Whether to devote this accumulating surplus to raising living standards in the desperately poor countries of Africa and Asia or use it to bolster the economies of the industrial states—highly developed but increasingly dependent upon imports for vital raw materials—is a crucial question confronting the OPEC governments. The leverage which they can exert in either direction is evident.

President Paul Kruger of the Transvaal

2. THE REPUBLIC OF SOUTH AFRICA

Perhaps in no other African state have the problems of nation building, tribalism, and racial cooperation proved more difficult than in the Republic of South Africa. Conflicts between Boer, Bantu, and Briton have punctuated the history of South Africa for generations. Each group almost fanatically adheres to its own traditions and conceptions of how society should be organized.

The discovery of diamonds and gold

Before the 1870s Great Britain had followed a colonial policy of benign neglect toward South Africa. The interior, long considered barren in natural resources, was of little importance to the British. Indeed, their prime concern lay in protecting the vital sea route to India by controlling the strategically important harbors along the South African coast. But in 1870 diamonds were discovered at Kimberley, and fifteen years later the fabulous gold fields of the Witwatersrand became a mecca for prospectors and adventurers from all over the world. Between 1872 and 1902 the white population of South Africa quadrupled. Congested cities such as Johannesburg and Bloemfontein mushroomed on the veldt. The simple pastoral economy of the old-fashioned Boers had come to an end.

The discovery of diamonds and gold multiplied the political difficulties of the Boer republics. British and other foreigners swarmed in in such numbers that they threatened to overwhelm the white Afrikaner settlers. The latter retaliated by branding the immigrants as outlanders and denying them political privileges except under the most rigorous conditions. The suffrage was refused, the press censored, and public meetings practically forbidden. In desperation the British organized a conspiracy to overthrow the most obstinate of the Boer governments, that of Paul Kruger, president of the Transvaal. Ammunition was collected, with the connivance of Cecil Rhodes, prime minister of the Cape Colony; and on December 29, 1895, 600 Britons and their armed retainers, under the leadership of Rhodes's friend, Dr. Leander Jameson, raided the Transvaal. The invaders were quickly surrounded and captured, but their act greatly magnified the tension between British and Boers. The Afrikaner governments increased the restrictions against foreigners and accumulated arms in preparation for a showdown. In October 1899, war broke out between these republics and the colonies predominantly British.

Prime Minister Cecil Rhodes of the Cape Colony

The Boer War dragged its length through three bloody years. Not until Britain sent sizable reinforcements under the leadership of its best generals was it able to snatch victory from the jaws of defeat. Finally, outnumbered seven to one, the Boers yielded and signed the Treaty of Vereeniging. In return for submitting to British rule, they were exempted from indemnities, promised representative institutions at an early date, and permitted to retain their own language in the courts and schools. The British government provided $15,000,000 to accelerate the process of reconstruction. It was one of the most generous peace settlements in history. At this time the victorious British were in the position to impose on South Africa a universal, nonracial franchise. Tragically, the plight of the African majority was ignored. The question of racial justice was avoided in the name of Boer-British reconciliation.

The Boer War (1899–1902)

In 1909 Cape Colony, Natal, the Orange Free State, and the Transvaal were merged into the Union of South Africa. The National Convention that drafted the Constitution provided for a unitary instead of a federal state. The reasons were several. The need for railway construction and for solving the problems of a large black population seemed to demand unification. More important was the fact that the two white nationalities did not occupy separate provinces as in Canada. In most states the rural population was Afrikaner or Boer, the urban population British. In some additional respects also the government of South Africa differed from that of the other dominions. The

The Union of South Africa

General James B. M. Hertzog, Leader of the Afrikaner National-ist Party

Growth of the nationalist movement

Cabinet did not stand or fall as a unit, but, theoretically at least, disagreements were permitted among the members. Its control over the upper house of Parliament was more effective. In case of a conflict between the Cabinet and the Assembly, or lower house, both houses might be dissolved and their members compelled to stand for re-election. South Africa had a much more conservative attitude toward the suffrage than did the other dominions. Universal manhood suffrage for whites was not adopted until 1930. Woman suffrage was also adopted in the same year, but in the face of stiff opposition. The minister of justice, for example, declared that the female franchise conflicted "with the intentions that the Creator had for women." As for the Africans, who constituted more than 75 percent of the population, all were disfranchised except in the southernmost Cape Province, where Negro and Asian citizens voted under limited conditions.

The sharpest controversies in South African politics since the formation of the Union have been those relating to nationality and race. Although the British made repeated efforts at reconciliation following the Boer War, the old hatreds died hard. In 1912 a faction of extremist Boers broke away from their kinsmen and formed the Nationalist party. Under the leadership of General Hertzog, they strove to preserve the cultural independence of the Afrikaners and to tolerate no fusion with the British. They resented British aggressiveness and regarded it as synonymous with an imperialism which threatened to obliterate the customs and institutions of their revered ancestors. They eventually came to advocate the severance of all ties with the British and the transformation of the Dominion into an Afrikaner republic. Anti-Semitism also emerged as a cardinal policy in the minds of the most fanatical. The finance capitalists who controlled the gold and diamond mines of the Rand[3] were alleged to be mostly Jews who were lightly taxed by the British-dominated government. By 1938 the Nationalists seemed almost as greatly disturbed by the "Jewish Menace" as they were by the "Black Peril" and were demanding the exclusion of all Jewish immigrants.

The two world wars of 1914 and 1939 contributed to the strength of the Nationalist movement. The followers of General Hertzog were determined that South Africa should not be dragged into war at the behest of the London government. The right to remain neutral they considered an indispensable badge of their nation's sovereignty. In 1914 some of them organized a rebellion as an armed protest against enslavement to British objectives. But the policy of their opponent, General Jan Christiaan Smuts, prevailed, and South Africa contributed its share toward winning the war. Eight years after the Armistice the Nationalists, supported by Labor, gained control of the government, but with a watered-down program that did not demand complete

[3] The Rand, or Witwatersrand, is a sixty-mile ridge which constitutes a watershed between the Vaal and Limpopo Rivers.

independence. When Britain again went to war in 1939, the South African government split. Six Cabinet ministers supported the war, five opposed. In the Assembly the vote was 80 in favor of the war to 67 against. It was obvious that the termination of hostilities would leave the country torn asunder and that the difficulties and tensions growing out of the war would widen the cleavage still further. Military production brought thousands of Africans into the towns and created fears of Communist uprisings or some other form of social revolution. In the official census of 1946, blacks for the first time in history outnumbered whites in the urban areas. Following this, the government-appointed Fagan Commission held that the incorporation of blacks in the nation's economic system is an irrevocable reality and that the Africans' progressive integration into the whites' political system should be accepted as a logical consequence.

As an Afrikaner party of the extreme right, the Nationalists played upon the fears engendered by the Fagan Commission and in the 1948 elections they gained control of parliament. The Nationalists not only espoused the idea of an independent republic purged of British influence but demanded a policy of apartheid, or strict legal separation of the races. South Africa would be a republic founded upon the ideals of Paul Kruger, not upon those of Cecil Rhodes or Jan Smuts.

General Jan Christiaan Smuts, Spokesman of South African Moderates

In the decade ahead, the Nationalist-dominated parliament passed a long series of segregationist legislation, affecting every aspect of life. The Prohibition of Mixed Marriages Act (1949) made interracial marriages illegal. In 1950, the Population Registration Act provided for the classification of the population into whites, coloreds (people of mixed race and Indians), and Bantu. The Group Areas Act, passed in the same year, called for the division of the nation into separate areas according to race and tribe. Apartheid in the realm of land ownership was already enshrined in the Native Land Act of 1913, which was aimed at regulating the purchase, ownership, and occupation of land outside urban areas on a racial basis. Only 13 percent of South Africa's total land area was reserved for Africans, even though they made up more than 80 percent of the population. Attempts to control the movement of Africans from place to place, particularly from rural to urban areas, date back to 1760 with the first pass law. Civil and political rights have always been withheld from urban Africans on the pretext that they are "temporary sojourners" with a permanent residence in some far-off tribal reserve.

The Reservation of Separate Amenities Act (1953) provided for the segregation of public amenities, including parks and transportation terminals. In the same year, the Native Labour Act redefined the term "employee" to exclude all blacks, thereby disenfranchising their unions and forbidding strikes. African trade unions, while not prohibited, were denied recognition and severely circumscribed. The Industrial Conciliation Act of 1956 and subsequent amendments banned

Apartheid in South Africa. Among the restrictions imposed upon blacks is the requirement that they carry passports. Here a policeman and an interpreter check the papers of an African bound for Johannesburg to work in the mines.

racially mixed labor unions and provided that certain jobs or occupations be reserved for whites only.

Apartheid laws: education and the franchise

A series of Bantu Education Acts brought schools under central government control and extended segregation to university education. Moreover, a constitutional amendment disenfranchised coloreds, who had veen voting in Cape province since the 1850s. Africans had been taken off the voter rolls in 1936. Opposition to these and the plethora of other apartheid laws was stifled through the Suppression of Communism Act (1950), an omnibus law which empowered the government to ban any organization or person suspected of "communism" or of endangering the security of the state.

Policy of divide and rule

In an attempt to control the rising tide of African nationalism by fostering tribalism at the expense of pan-Africanism, the government passed the Promotion of Bantu Self-Government Act (1959). In classical divide-and-rule fashion, it envisioned the consolidation of the 260 scattered native reserves into a series of "independent" Bantu states, or Bantustans, each with its own tribal identity.

The polarization of politics

African reaction to these and the many other segregationist laws, including the pass laws, was manifested in a number of futile passive-resistance and defiance campaigns between 1952 and 1956. Their failure led to a rift within the African National Congress (founded in 1912); and in 1959 a radical group split off under the leadership of Robert Sobukwe and took the name of Pan-Africanist Congress. The white political spectrum had also become more polarized. The United party, mainly English-speaking, over the years had steadily lost ground in parliament to the Afrikaner-dominated Nationalists. In 1959 a small group of antiapartheid white liberals broke from the

United party and formed the Progressive party. Over the next decade and a half they held a single seat in the Assembly.

In 1960 African resistance to apartheid culminated in a passive demonstration at Sharpeville. The South African police panicked in the face of the large, angry gathering and killed sixty-seven peaceful black demonstrators. Following the Sharpeville massacre a state of emergency was declared, the African National Congress and the Pan-Africanist Congress was banned, and their leaders who escaped arrest either fled the country or went underground to engage in terrorist activity. Whites, growing ever more fearful of the "black menace," responded in the 1960s with legislation further eroding the personal liberties of nonwhites. The General Law Amendment Act of 1963 empowered police to arrest and detain people indefinitely without trial or access to legal counsel. A Publications Control Board, created in the same year, imposed censorship over literature and films. Throughout the 1960s police raids resulted in the arrest and imprisonment of militants.

In 1961 Prime Minister Hendrik Verwoerd took steps toward implementing these ideals when he ordered the withdrawal of South Africa from the Commonwealth of Nations and proclaimed the country an independent republic. For the time being there would be two capitals, Cape Town and Pretoria, and two languages, English and Afrikaans. It was clear, however, that the ultimate objective was an Afrikaner nation thoroughly purged of British influences.

Verwoerd was assassinated in 1966 and was succeeded by John B. Vorster. In the following year, a severe Terrorism Act was passed, presuming the guilt of everyone accused of terrorism until proven innocent. Two years later, the Bureau of State Security (BOSS) was created to suppress radical movements.

South Africa's economy boomed in the early 1970s, benefiting most racial and ethnic groups. White feelings of security were sufficiently restored for the Vorster government to embark on a futile policy of rapprochement with black African nations to the north. It also moved quickly to devolve more autonomy on the newly created Bantu states within South Africa. In late 1976, the Transkei became the first Bantu homeland to receive its independence.

Economic prosperity led to a shortage of white skilled labor, and as a consequence the job reservation act was eased to enable blacks to move into positions formerly reserved for whites. These moves failed to assuage African nationalism. In 1972 the moderate Black Peoples' Convention was formed, along with the black South African Students' Movement. This reawakening of black consciousness, led by a new and more militant generation of youths, was further stimulated by the articulate speeches of Gatsha Buthelezi, chief of the KwaZulu homeland.

Among white Afrikaners, two schools of thought emerged: the

enlightened, or verlighte, and the narrow-minded, or the verkrampte. The verlightes demanded an easing of the rigid apartheid laws, especially in the areas of sports and culture. But they were not prepared to grant the principle of "one man one vote."

This state of political and social ferment in South Africa subsided almost as quickly as it had begun. In 1975 Portugal, in a surprising about-face, gave independence to Mozambique and Angola, two close neighbors of South Africa. This rekindled the revolution of rising political expectations among South Africa's blacks, coloreds, and Asians. Moreover, in the same year, the nation began to slide into an economic recession, after enjoying a steady annual growth rate of more than 5 percent since 1933. Whites again became fearful of a loss of status; and this fear was exacerbated by the installation of Marxist, militantly anti–South African governments in Mozambique and Angola. South African military intervention in the Angolan civil war in 1975–1976 drew world-wide condemnation and killed Vorster's détente program with black Africa. African student militancy, inspired by such intellectuals as Steve Biko, grew rapidly after a 1974 pro-Mozambique student rally. Feelings exploded in violent riots in June 1976 in Soweto, a sprawling ghetto of nearly 3 million Africans not far from downtown Johannesburg. More than a thousand black youths were killed by the South African police and many more were imprisoned. An intensification of the suppression and liquidation of black opposition came to world attention in September 1977 with the police killing of the jailed Steve Biko, president of the Black Peoples' Convention. Racial tension was mounting and the major African newspaper, the *World,* was banned and its editor detained.

Police Action in Johannesburg. In downtown Johannesburg the authorities disperse a group of black and white demonstrators who were protesting police actions in the huge Soweto ghetto. Over 1,000 blacks were killed by police in Soweto in June 1976.

As world opinion turned against South Africa, the white pendulum swung further to the right. English-speaking and Afrikaans-speaking whites began to close political ranks. The opposition United party disintegrated, with most of its members joining the Nationalist party but a few joining with the Progressives to form the Progressive Federal party. In the November 1977 elections the Nationalist party gained vast new strength, winning 134 of 165 seats in the all-white National Assembly. South Africa was moving toward a one-party state.

October 1978 witnessed the retirement of John Vorster, who became titular president, and the appointment of the Defense Minister Pieter W. Botha as new prime minister. In early 1979, racial and ethnic relations continued their steady deterioration among the 4.3 million whites, 2.4 million coloreds, 765,000 Asians, and 19 million blacks. The South African government became increasingly isolated from the world community of nations.

3. THE UPSURGE OF AFRICA

Modern African nationalism and pan-African sentiment are not post–World War II phenomena. Their roots go back to 1847 with the establishment of the independent Republic of Liberia. Liberia was the first independent state in Africa to support Western-style institutions and to prove that black men were capable of governing themselves along so-called modern lines. Edward Blyden, a leading Liberian intellectual (born in the West Indies), called in the 1860s for racial integrity and solidarity and coined the phrase "Africa for Africans." He exhorted black men to preserve the African essence of their civilizations and to resist Westernization at the hands of European imperialists. Native-born, Western-educated intellectuals on the Gold Coast (now Ghana) and Nigeria were to take up this call in the two decades prior to the first World War. Nevertheless, these protonationalists represented but a thin veneer and were predominantly drawn from among second sons of wealthy traditional nobility. Many of them were torn between their rich African heritage and that of Western civilization and found it difficult to identify with their peasant brethren in the bush. They were willing to work within the colonial framework and to pursue a moderate, gradualist course. After World War II, these early elites were eclipsed by impatient youthful nonaristocratic intellectuals who returned to Africa after many years abroad. Armed with the techniques of political party organization, they reached out to the masses, particularly the urban unemployed.

The 1950s and 1960s witnessed a groundswell of colonial revolts in northern and central Africa. For the most part, they were directed against Great Britain and France, though Belgium, Italy, and Portugal

The war in Algeria

were also involved. The first of the former colonies to gain independence was Libya. Taken by Italy from Turkey in 1912, Libya passed under the control of the United Nations at the end of World War II. In 1949 the U.N. recognized the Libyan demand for freedom, and two years later independence was formally proclaimed.

The most violent of the colonial revolts in northern Africa occurred in Algeria. Algeria had been a part of the French Empire since the middle years of the nineteenth century. The French poured millions of dollars of capital into their colony, and thousands of French nationals came there to settle. Many people of other nationalities, especially Spaniards, also emigrated to Algeria, with the result that by 1960 the European inhabitants numbered about 1 million in a total population of 10,300,000. These Europeans, inaccurately referred to as the "French" population, monopolized not only the government positions but also the best economic opportunities in industry, agriculture, trade, and finance. The Arab and Berber inhabitants were chiefly peasants and laborers, though some, of course, maintained their own shops in the *casbah,* or native quarter, of each of the large cities. In 1954 Arab and Berber (Muslim) nationalists rose in revolt when their demand for equal status with the European population was denied by the French government. The revolt continued its bloody course for seven years. It was complicated by the fact that many of the European settlers (*colons*) hated the government in Paris almost as much as they did the Algerian nationalists. They were determined to keep Algeria "French" and feared a sell-out by President Charles de Gaulle that would make the former colony independent and subject the *colons* to the rule of the Arab and Berber majority. In April 1961, the announcement of a plan by de Gaulle to negotiate a settlement in Algeria that would pave the way for eventual independence led to a revolt in the

Algeria, 1962. After nearly eight years of strife and terror, Algeria was on the threshold of independence.

territory by four French generals. They seized government buildings, arrested loyal French officials, and threatened to invade France. De Gaulle proclaimed a state of emergency and ordered a total blockade of Algeria. In the face of such determined opposition the revolt collapsed. The war of the nationalists, however, continued for another year. On a promise of immediate self-government and eventual independence the nationalists laid down their arms in March 1962. Three months later Algeria entered the ranks of independent states and was admitted to the United Nations. The war had cost the lives of about 40,000 soldiers and civilians and had left a heritage of bitterness that would probably linger for years.

If any one country could be considered the leader of the African colonial revolt, it was Ghana, formerly called the Gold Coast, a colony of Great Britain. In 1954 Britain granted self-government, independence in 1957, and in 1960 Ghana became a republic. Leadership of the Ghana independence movement was at that time supplied by Kwame Nkrumah. The son of an illiterate goldsmith, he obtained an education in the United States and in England. He returned to his homeland in 1948 and became a nationalist agitator. Though he classified himself as a Marxist, he denied being a Communist. Yet he admired Lenin and generally looked to Moscow for support of his policies rather than to London or Washington. Apparently the key to his thinking was opposition to imperialism. He considered it preposterous that the Africans of Central Africa, with their proud traditions of an ancient culture, should be ruled by Europeans. He regaled his followers with stories of a Golden Age in Africa, whose cultural center was in Timbuktu, with a great university manned by distinguished scholars. For a time Nkrumah ruled benevolently even after converting the nation into a one-party state. He established hospitals and schools and raised the literacy standards. Accused of extravagance and corruption, he was deposed by a revolt of army officer in 1966. He was driven from his homeland and forced to take refuge in Guinea where he died in 1972. Nevertheless, Nkrumah's writings on neocolonialism and his pan-African ideas are still widely read by African intellectuals.

Kwame Nkrumah (Center, Seated) and Members of His Government in Ghana

The most violent of the revolts in Central Africa occurred in the Congo, where there was not simply one previous colony but two. The smaller is now the People's Republic of the Congo. Though granted nominal independence in 1960, it is still under the influence of France and the People's Republic of China. Conditions in the larger Congo, now called Zaire, which was at one time a colony of Belgium, have been more serious. Fearing an outbreak of violence among its disaffected colonial subjects, Belgium, in 1960, granted them independence. This was the signal for the beginning of a series of rebellions and assassinations that raged for more than five years. A chief cause of the flaming disorders centered in the southeastern province of

The revolt in the Congo

THE NEW AFRICA • 1981

Katanga. Here were located rich copper resources controlled by Belgian capitalists. At one time the copper mines of Katanga had produced revenues sufficient to defray one-half the costs of the colonial government. In July 1960, Katanga seceded and attempted to gain control of the entire country. In the revolt several former premiers and other high officers were murdered. The U.N. Security Council sent a contingent to guard against revival of civil war. Strong-man rule was revived by President Mobutu, and a degree of stability was ultimately restored.

In most other sections of Central and Eastern Africa there was at least the illusion of tranquillity. Such countries as Nigeria and Kenya seemed like good examples. Both were former British colonies. Some authorities held that British and French colonial administrations were wiser than that of most other European empires. Whereas the Portuguese and Belgians withheld self-government as long as they could, and then granted it suddenly, the British and French brought their colonies to independence more gradually. Many local leaders were trained in administration and knew how to deal with intricate problems before they actually arose. Yet even in Nigeria the familiar charges of corruption and inefficiency led to the murder of the premier and the overthrow of the government in 1966. After more assassinations a military government seized control. Within a year the Eastern Region seceded and proclaimed itself the Republic of Biafra. Civil war followed and harassed the country for three years. The total of casualties was enormous. More than 1 million people lost their lives. Thousands were killed in battle, but many more died of starvation. The rebels capitulated in 1970. From every standpoint the war was a tragedy. Nigeria is one of the most richly endowed of African countries. Its natural resources include oil and natural gas, coal, and the world's greatest abundance of columbium (used in steel manufacturing).

Civil War in Nigeria

Also hovering on the verge of tragedy has been the recent history of Kenya, a country of East Africa lying athwart the equator. Unlike Nigeria, Kenya is a poor country. The whole northern three-fifths of the territory is barren and almost waterless. Sections can be found in which there is no rainfall whatever for years at a time. The only well-watered sections are in the south and along the coast. It follows that agricultural resources are limited. The staple crops include coffee, sisal, tea, and wheat. Sugar cane, maize, tobacco, and cotton are also grown. Most of the farms are small. The construction of the railroad from the Kenya coast to Uganda at the turn of the century brought in thousands of Indian settlers. They did not become farmers or artisans, but settled in the cities and towns as petty traders. Despite their low standard of living and their meager profits they encouraged the Africans to substitute a money economy for the age-old system of barter. Nevertheless, many Indians in Uganda and Kenya remained aloof, choosing not to become citizens or to allow Africans to enter their trades. This caused serious friction between the two races, and in 1972 led to the mass expulsion of Indians from Uganda.

Conditions in Kenya

The population of Kenya has never been closely unified. Ethnic jealousies are rampant and sometimes break into open conflict. These jealousies seem not to be based on economic competition or greed. They appear rather to spring from ancient differences rooted in cultural characteristics and hatreds from the past. The most serious of these conflicts broke into the open in 1952 when the Mau Mau rebellion occurred. The Mau Mau were an offshoot of the Kikuyu tribe, who had been forcibly removed from their ancestral lands by European settlers at the turn of the century. By the close of the Second World War, the Kikuyu were experiencing a population explosion and sought to regain their lost territory. They instituted a reign of terror in some parts of the colony against the white settlers and all their kinsmen who sympathized with the colonial government. By 1958 the revolt was suppressed, and five years later the country obtained independence. Basically, Mau Mau was a Kikuyu-inspired nationalist movement aimed at achieving African self-determination over questions of land and governance.

The leader who had done most to promote the growth and progress of Kenya was Jomo Kenyatta, president of his country from 1963 until his death in August 1978, when he was succeeded by his vice president, Daniel Arap Moi. However, his own people, the Kikuyu, continued to dominate the nation's political and economic institutions, despite growing challenges from the large Luo ethnic group. In 1951 he was thrown into prison for seven years, accused as a Mau Mau leader and a dangerous enemy of the state. His imprisonment seems to have done more to educate him in the realities of politics than to imbue him with hatred of his captors. While in prison he developed his philosophy of African socialism. Although for a time Kenyatta had studied at Moscow University, he adopted almost none of the trappings of Soviet communism. Instead his socialism bore a closer resemblance to that of the British or the Scandinavian countries. He urged his followers to forget the wrongs of the past and to concentrate on building a better world for the future. This future would be found in avoiding affiliations with either the East or the West. The African way has little in common with either capitalism or communism. The sharp antagonisms of class that exist in Europe and America have not been conspicuous elements in the African tradition. African socialism, according to Kenyatta, cannot be based on a dictatorship of the proletariat or any other form of class rule. Rather, its aim should be to prevent the seizure of power by individuals or groups armed with economic power. Its aim should be to enable every mature citizen to participate fully and equally in political affairs. Such is the essence of democracy and also of African socialism, according to Kenyatta's conception.

One of the most successful experiments in African nation building has occurred in Tanzania under its president, Julius Nyerere. Unlike neighboring Kenya, Tanzania is not plagued by tribalism. There are not two or three major tribes maneuvering for power. Rather, Tan-

Jomo Kenyatta Addressing an All-Africa Congress in London.

President Julius Nyerere of Tanzania. Nyerere, accompanied by a group of Chinese officials, lays the foundation stone of the New Chinese-Tanzanian Friendship Textile Mill in Dar es Salaam.

zania embraces a multitude of small tribes none of which is strong enough to dominate the political system. Tanzania itself is the result of the merging of two British-administered colonial units: the United Nations Trust Territory of Tanganyika and the Protectorate of Zanzibar. Since their union in 1964, Nyerere has gradually decreased his dependence on British trade and is relying more heavily on foreign assistance from the Communist world, particularly the People's Republic of China, which is completing a rail link between landlocked, copper-rich Zambia and Tanzania's port of Dar es Salaam on the Indian Ocean. Nevertheless, under Nyerere's able and democratic leadership, Tanzania is pursuing a policy of nonalignment. Nyerere, a noted Third World political theorist, has developed a unique brand of African socialism called *Ujamaa* ("familyhood" in Swahili) which is rooted in the traditional communalistic, extended family form of social organization. Yet it also draws heavily upon the experimental Chinese communes and the Israeli kibbutzim. The accent of Nyerere's socialism is upon the dignity of work and national self-reliance. While Nyerere, a practicing Catholic, claims to be a socialist, he is opposed to Marxist doctrinaire socialism. According to Nyerere, modern African socialism "can draw from its traditional heritage the recognition of 'society' as an extension of the basic family unit." While it is

Tanzania and experiments in African socialism

*Kenneth D. Kaunda, President of
the Republic of Zambia*

still too early to predict the success of Tanzania's model Ujamaa villages, Nyerere's influence is strongly felt throughout Africa south of the Sahara.

Since independence, African systems of government have succumbed to personal rule rather than to sweeping institutional reform. In other words, authority became personalized, not institutionalized. Most notable of the charismatic heads of state were Sese Seko Mobutu of Zaire, Dr. Kamuzu Banda of Malawi, Seko Touré of Guinea, Leopold Senghor of Senegal, Felix Houphouet-Boigny of Ivory Coast, Julius Nyerere of Tanzania, Jomo Kenyatta of Kenya, Seretse Khama of Botswana, Kenneth Kaunda of Zambia, Samora Machel of Mozambique, and Kwame Nkrumah of Ghana. The trend toward personalization was first evident during the struggle for independence. It reached a high in 1977 when Jean-Bedel Bokassa suspended all democratic institutions and crowned himself emperor of the Central African Empire. In some respects, this trend is simply a return to the precolonial situation in which some rulers governed by divine and ancestral right and in which little differentiation existed between executive, judicial, and legislative powers.

Since the eve of independence, the old traditional political elites have been gradually edged out of leadership positions in the central governments. Some countries have abolished chieftaincy altogether. The new, Western-educated and modernizing elites have sought to follow two often contradictory paths: the formation of a national belief system or ethos based on a return to authentic African values, and the fostering of pan-Africanist ideology. Internally, ethnic conflicts continue to impede the process of nation building. And the realization of the pan-African dream, a united states of Africa, is blocked by the colonial legacy. International disputes persist over artificial boundaries drawn during the European scramble for African territory in the late nineteenth century. African diplomacy is hindered by the diversity of European languages, and regional economic integration is made difficult by continuing patterns of dependency on the economic ties to former colonial masters. In many states today, particularly in French-speaking Africa, European technocrats and capitalists continue to play important roles in the political and economic sectors. Some political scientists have called this situation "neocolonialistic." The Organization of African Unity (OAU), established in 1963, has had a dismal record in resolving inter-African disputes and in preventing external Great Power interference.

While the influence of popularly elected legislative bodies has steadily diminished, local government remains remarkably dynamic and responsive to the masses. Nevertheless, the process of government centralization continues in most countries. Corruption and nepotism in many African nations, particularly in Kenya, Nigeria, and Zaire, by 1979 had become major corrosive forces in national life. The contrast of great affluence among bureaucrats and extravagant public spending on the one hand and persistent poverty among the broad masses on the other has bred popular political apathy and cynicism. In an attempt to stem this tide, Presidents Nyerere and Kaunda of Tanzania and Zambia, respectively, have developed strict codes of behavior for their civil servants. Generally, African leaders are less bound by public opinion today than they were in the early years of independence. Nearly everywhere, opposition parties have been suppressed and a large majority of Africans remain outside the decision-making process. Only Nigeria, Gambia, Botswana, and Senegal actively encourage multiparty activity.

Political repression and falling food production in some African nations have created a serious refugee problem. By 1977, nearly one in every two hundred Africans was a refugee. Indeed, Africa suffered the highest ratio of refugees to total population in the world, with more than 2 million displaced persons.

The refugee problem

Military coups have been a major factor in African politics since the mid-1960s. The first military coup in independent Africa occurred in 1952 in Egypt. By 1976, twenty out of forty-one African states were ruled by military elements or by military/civilian coalitions. Between 1965 and 1978 Africa experienced thirty-three military coups, eight in Dahomey (now Benin) alone. By 1979, most African nations had armed forces and military budgets far in excess of their defense needs. This growing militarism has contributed to an escalating incidence of inter-African warfare and internal instability. In 1978 alone, Tanzania and Uganda were at war with each other; Soviet-supplied Ethiopia fought a civil war against the secessionist Eritrean province and a war with Somalia over the Ogaden. Morocco and Mauretania battled in the western Sahara against an Algerian-backed liberation force. In

Militarism

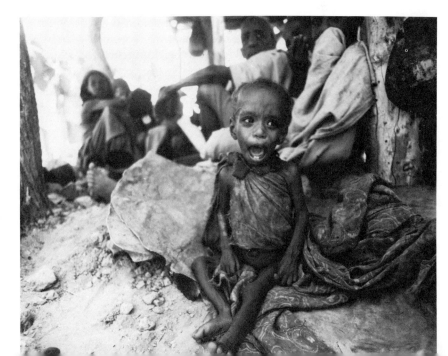

The Refugee Problem. A starving child crying at a feeding center in a village in southern Ethiopia. Due to overpopulation, a number of African nations are facing serious problems which manifest themselves in the form of food shortages, inadequate housing, poor health and educational services, and high unemployment rates.

Central Africa, Zaire was assisted by French- and American-equipped Morocco in repelling an Angolan-based invasion of its copper- and cobalt-rich Shaba province. Southward, Soviet- and Chinese-supplied guerrillas struggled against the white-dominated and South African–equipped Rhodesian army.

Growing public disenchantment with military governance led in 1979 to the restoration of free elections and civilian rule in Ghana and Nigeria. Impatience with corruption and nepotism brought down the fascist dictatorships of Presidents for Life Macias Nguema in Equatorial Guinea and Idi Amin in Uganda and Emperor Jean-Bedel Bokassa of the Central African Empire. In a bloodless coup, Bokassa was replaced by David Dacko, who restored the republic and who was himself overthrown in 1966. In neighboring Chad, the Christian-dominated government of President Felix Malloum was toppled, opening the way for a civil war between Christians and Muslims.

Early in 1980, a military coup in Liberia ended the nepotistic regime and the life of President William R. Tolbert, Jr. In the same year, Great Britain ended nearly two centuries of colonial rule in Africa by transforming the Crown colony of Rhodesia into the independent nation of Zimbabwe, under Robert Mugabe, a Marxist and former guerrilla leader.

By mid-1980, only the Republic of South Africa and Namibia remained under white political control. Black majority rule had been achieved everywhere else. Many of these nations are richly endowed with minerals, essential to industrial development in Africa as well as in western Europe, North America, and Japan. Nigeria, a major member of the Organization of Petroleum Exporting Countries (OPEC), had become the United States' second largest source of imported oil. Western Europe depended on Zaire for most of its copper, uranium, and cobalt, and on South Africa for its gold, chrome, and industrial diamonds.

Africa, in turn, continued to rely on the West for advanced technology and development loans. With global inflation and soaring oil prices, many of the developing nations found themselves terribly in debt to Western creditors, especially to the International Monetary Fund. In some respects, these near-bankrupt nations had to surrender a considerable degree of fiscal autonomy to the IMF in order to be eligible for debt rescheduling. These interdependencies will undoubtedly grow in the decades ahead. A few African nations hold great promise for economic growth through the twenty-first century, particularly those endowed with mineral resources. However, most others will suffer from chronic underdevelopment. The challenge of Africa lies in its ability to bargain on a more equitable basis with both the East and West.

Prime Minister Robert Mugabe of Zimbabwe

• *Items so designated are available in paperback editions.*

THE MIDDLE EAST

Ahmed, J. M., *The Intellectual Origins of Egyptian Nationalism,* New York, 1960. Informative and well-documented account.

Bose, T. C., *The Superpowers and the Middle East,* New York, 1972.

• Chaliand, Gérard, *The Palestinian Resistance,* Baltimore, 1972.

Halpern, Manfred, *The Politics of Social Change in the Middle East and North Africa,* Princeton, 1967.

• Hitti, Philip K., *History of the Arabs,* New York, 1940.

Hoskins, H. L., *The Middle East,* New York, 1954. A careful, judicious study.

Issawi, Charles, *Egypt in Revolution: An Economic Analysis,* New York, 1963.

Karpat, Kemal, *Turkey's Politics: The Transition to a Multi-Party System,* Princeton, 1959. Sophisticated account by a Turkish political scientist.

Khouri, Fred J., *The Arab-Israeli Dilemma,* Syracuse, N.Y., 1968.

• Kirk, George E., *A Short History of the Middle East,* London, 1948.

• Laqueur, Jacques, *The Struggle for the Middle East,* Baltimore, 1972.

Lenczowski, George, *The Middle East in World Affairs,* 3d ed., Ithaca, 1962.

———, *Oil and State in the Middle East,* Ithaca, 1960.

• Lewis, Bernard, *The Emergence of Modern Turkey,* 2d ed., New York, 1968.

Lewis, Geoffrey, *Turkey,* 3d ed., London, 1965.

• Prittie, Terence, *Israel: Miracle in the Desert,* rev. ed., Baltimore, 1968.

Quandt, W. B., F. Jabber, and A. M. Lesch, *The Politics of Palestinian Nationalism,* Berkeley, 1973.

• Rodinson, Maxime, *Israel and the Arabs,* Baltimore, 1970.

Segre, V. D., *Israel: A Society in Transition,* New York, 1971.

Stone, I. F., *Underground to Palestine,* New York, 1979. Account of a secret voyage through the British blockade in 1946.

Twitchell, K. S., *Saudi Arabia,* Princeton, 1958.

• Wilber, D. N., *Iran Past and Present,* 7th ed., Princeton, 1975.

AFRICA

Bartlett, Vernon, *Struggle for Africa,* New York, 1953.

Carter, G. M., *The Politics of Inequality,* New York 1958. A penetrating study of South Africa.

Clark, M. K., *Algeria in Turmoil,* New York, 1959.

• Davenport, T. R. H., *South Africa: A Modern History,* London, 1977.

Decalo, Samuel, *Coups and Army Rule in Africa,* New Haven, 1976.

Fasholé-Luke, Edward, and Richard Gray, eds., *Christianity in Independent Africa,* Bloomington, 1977.

• Geiss, Immanuel, *The Pan-African Movement,* New York, 1974.

• Gutkind, Peter C. W., and Immanuel Wallerstein, eds., *The Political Economy of Contemporary Africa,* Beverly Hills, 1976.

Hartwig, Gerald W., and K. David Patterson, eds., *Disease in African History,* Durham, 1978.

Low, D. A., and Alison Smith, eds., *History of East Africa,* Vol. III, London, 1976.

• Macmillan, W. M., *Africa Emergent,* 1949.

• Marquard, L., *The Peoples and Policies of South Africa,* New York, 1952.

Nyerere, Julius, *Ujamaa: Essays on Socialism,* New York, 1971.

• Oliver, Roland, and Anthony Atmore, *Africa since 1800,* New York, 1967.

Owen, Roger, and Robert Sutcliffe, eds., *Studies in the Theory of Imperialism,* London, 1975.

Pannikkar, K. M., *The Afro-Asian States and Their Problems,* New York, 1959. Brief but discerning.

Ranger, T. O., ed., *Aspects of Central African History,* London, 1969.

Thompson, L. M., *Politics in the Republic of South Africa,* Boston, 1966.

Wilson, M., and L. M. Thompson, eds., *The Oxford History of South Africa,* 2 vols., New York, 1971.

SOURCE MATERIALS

Apartheid: Its Effects on Education, Science, Culture and Information (UNESCO).

Ben-Gurion, David. *Israel: A Personal History,* New York, 1971.

Berkes, Niyazi, *Turkish Nationalism and Western Civilization,* tr. Z. Gökalp, London, 1959.

Brookes, Edgar H., *Apartheid: A Documentary Study,* London, 1968.

Edib, Halide, *Memoirs,* London, 1926.

Hobart Houghton, D., and Jennifer Dagut, eds., *Source Material on the South African Economy: 1860–1970,* London, 1972.

Horrell, Muriel, comp., *A Survey of Race Relations in South Africa, 1977,* Johannesburg, 1978.

Meir, Golda, *My Life,* New York, 1975.

Weizmann, Chaim, *Trial and Error,* New York, 1949.

Chapter 39

ERUPTION IN THE FAR EAST

Countries want independence, nations want liberation, and people want
revolution.

—Premier Chou En-lai

The current international situation is excellent; there is great disorder
under heaven.

—Chairman Mao Tse-tung

The contemporary era of the Far Eastern countries began under
the stimulation provided by the impact of Western explorers
and merchants. By the middle of the twentieth century profound changes had taken place not only within the Eastern countries
but also in their relationship to the West. No longer merely peripheral
to the main fields of interest of the Western nations, they had become
in some measure the pivotal center of world affairs. Japan seized upon
a large empire in Asia and the Pacific, which she retained until
defeated in a long struggle against the most powerful of the Western
states. China, after almost disintegrating and after passing through a
cycle of revolution, emerged with radically altered institutions but,
once again, as one of the strongest states of Asia. Moreover, China
for the first time in her history was in a position to assume a major
role in world politics.

The new Far East

I. NATIONALISM AND COMMUNISM IN CHINA

The overthrow of the Manchu Dynasty, accomplished with comparatively little effort in 1911, marked the beginning in China of a long
period of instability and disorder that has witnessed a wide displacement of China's traditional institutions and culture. Perhaps never
before in the country's history has there occurred such a transforma-

*Stages of the Chinese
Revolution*

tion as during its modern revolutionary era. The Chinese Revolution falls roughly into four overlapping stages: (1) the pseudo-republic of Yüan Shih-k'ai, 1912–1916; (2) the rule of warlords and the weakening of the central government, 1916–1928; (3) the Nationalist revolution, 1923–1949; and (4) the Communist revolution, which gained momentum in the 1930s and, after a military triumph in 1949, brought fundamental external and internal changes to China. The second period, almost purely negative, was the natural result of the decadence that had preceded the downfall of the Manchu Dynasty. The third and fourth stages had some objectives in common and were combined for a time, although they finally came to be directly opposed to each other.

The rise of the warlords

Yüan Shih-k'ai, the first president of the Republic, who tried unsuccessfully to restore the monarchy, maintained at least a semblance of unity in the state. After his death in 1916, much of China passed under the rule of independent military commanders, although a group at Peking preserved the fiction of a republican government. Some of these militarists had been officials under the Manchus; others were ex-soldiers or ex-bandits who had collected an army and taken over the administration of one or more provinces. Most of them were extortionate, and the common people of China suffered deplorably from their tyranny. China's participation in World War I at a time when the central government was unable even to put its own house in order was a factor contributing to internal confusion. At the urging of the Allied powers, the Peking government declared war on Germany in 1917, hoping to gain advantages at the peace settlement. During the war, however, Japan seized the opportunity to "assist" her weak ally, selling war materials and extending loans to China and securing economic concessions within the country. At the Paris Peace Conference the requests of the Chinese delegation were almost completely disregarded, and Japan refused to restore the Shantung Peninsula, which she had taken over from Germany.

The Kuomintang

The third stage of the Revolution is associated with the personality and program of Sun Yat-sen. Dr. Sun's part in the inauguration of the Republic in 1912 had been a brief one, but after returning to Canton, where his following was strongest, he directed a barrage of criticism against the Peking military government. The rise of warlords was not confined to the north, and Sun actually was dependent for support upon militarists in control of the Kwangtung-Kwangsi area. His party, the Kuomintang, was a small faction, and its professed principles of parliamentary democracy seemed utterly unrealistic in a "phantom Republic" ravaged by irresponsible military bands. But with remarkable swiftness the Kuomintang changed into a dynamic organization capable of making a bid for control of the state. The initiative and organizing skill for accomplishing this transformation were largely supplied from outside China, by agents of the revolutionary Communist regime in Russia.

Understandably, the Bolshevik leaders, faced with the task of consolidating their power in Russia and confronted by the hostility of the Great Powers, were eager to win support in revolutionary China. Rebuffed by the Peking government, they turned to Dr. Sun in Canton. The Third (Communist) International had organized a Far Eastern division and established at Moscow a university named after Sun Yat-sen to train Chinese revolutionaries, some of whom joined the Communist party. Although Dr. Sun rejected communism, he had hoped for the support of Western nations and welcomed the offer of Russian cooperation. In 1923 Sun and the Russian emissaries arrived at a working agreement which provided for Russian assistance and for the admission of Chinese Communists to the Kuomintang but left Sun the undisputed head of the Kuomintang party. Acknowledging that China's immediate task was to achieve national unity and free itself from the yoke of foreign imperialism, the Soviet government sent military and political advisers to Canton.

During the Moscow-Canton entente of 1923–1927, the Chinese nationalist movement acquired a disciplined leadership, clear-cut objectives, and considerable popular support. A general dissatisfaction with the dreary and corrupt rule of the military cliques, the humiliation of China at the Paris Peace Conference, and the entrenched position of the Great Powers in their spheres of interest all helped to intensify nationalist sentiment. Disillusionment following the war stimulated a spirit of revolt among young intellectuals and among the lower classes, as evidenced by the growth of labor unions in the Yangtze valley industrial cities, peasant movements, youth movements, and movements for the emancipation of women. The various dissident elements needed only effective leadership to be enlisted in a campaign for the regeneration and strengthening of China under a truly national government. Soviet advisers taught Sun Yat-sen and his associates how to supply this leadership. Under the direction of Michael Borodin, a seasoned revolutionary who had worked as an agitator in Turkey and Mexico, the Kuomintang was revamped on the model of the Russian Communist party. On the propaganda front, posters, pictures, and slogans dramatized the Kuomintang program, which was to unseat the warlords, introduce honest and democratic government, stamp out the opium habit, and promote other reforms.

By 1925 Canton had become the center of a small but effective government, which collected taxes, regulated commerce, and was developing its own "new model" army, officered by men trained at the Whampoa Academy (near Canton) under supervision of European military experts, and indoctrinated with loyalty to Sun Yat-sen and to his party. This Canton government was actually a Soviet regime without being Communist. Controlled by the high command of the Kuomintang, it provided the first example of a party dictatorship in China. Although the Canton government showed vigor, it was not recognized by foreign powers, not even by Soviet Russia. Russia

Russian aid to the Kuomintang under Dr. Sun

Consolidation of power by the Kuomintang at Canton

Character of the Canton government

Dr. Sun Yat-sen Surrounded by His Military Staff

maintained correct relations with the Peking government, and restored some Russian concessions to its jurisdiction after Peking recognized the Soviet Union in 1924. At the same time, Russian agents were assisting Sun Yat-sen's group in preparations to overthrow the Peking regime.

The doctrines of Sun Yat-sen

Dr. Sun did not live to see the phenomenal success of the organization that he had founded, but he left a body of doctrines as a heritage of the Kuomintang party. His most important writings were put together rather hastily during the period of Communist-Kuomintang collaboration and partly at the urging of Borodin, who recognized their value for propaganda purposes. The gist of Sun's program and political philosophy is contained in the famous *San Min Chu I* ("Three Principles of the People"), which became a sort of Bible for the Kuomintang. The Three Principles, usually translated as "Nationalism," "Democracy," and "Livelihood," have been likened to Abraham Lincoln's "government of the people, by the people, and for the people"; but there is considerable difference between the American and the Chinese interpretations of the terms. By nationalism Sun meant, first, the freeing of China from foreign interference and, second, the development of loyalty among the people to the state instead of to the family or the province. In his second principle, Sun was concerned with popular sovereignty and the ideal of representative government. Recognizing that people are unequal in capacity, he believed that the chief political problem, in both China and the West, was to discover how popular sovereignty could be combined with direction by experts. The principle of livelihood referred to the necessity for material progress and also to social reform, rejecting Marxism but failing to outline any specific program. Sun's ideas as a whole were neither very original nor very radical nor even very clear. Democracy apppeared in his conception as a rather remote goal, to be attained at the end of the revolutionary struggle. The three stages of revolution, according to Sun, would be (1) the military stage, necessary to establish order; (2) the "tutelage" stage, devoted to training the people and with power restricted to the revolutionary leaders (the Kuomintang party); and (3) the constitutional stage, embodying representative popular government.

In view of Dr. Sun's limitations both as a leader and as a thinker, it is remarkable that he came to be revered as the Father of the Revolution. His life ended, characteristically, on a note of futility. He had gone north in the latter part of 1924 to arrange an alliance with two of the war lords against a third, but arrived in Peking to find that a settlement had been made without his knowledge. Already in poor health, he died the following March. But when finally removed from the scene, Sun became a legendary figure to his followers, and "Sun-yatsenism" proved to be a far more potent force than Dr. Sun had ever been. He left behind him a legacy of hope, and he had stirred the imagination of Chinese all over the world with the vision of a strong and free China under a republican constitution which would combine the best thought of ancient sages with modern scientific techniques. By the Kuomintang his writings and speeches were treasured as unalloyed wisdom, while their vagueness made it possible to invoke the master's authority for contradictory policies.

By 1926, when the Canton government had become strong enough to challenge the northern militarists, the Nationalist revolution entered its active phase. Kuomintang forces under command of the young general Chiang Kai-shek (1888–1975) swept rapidly northward into the Yangtze valley and in less than six months overran half the provinces of China. The success of this "punitive expedition," however, brought to the surface a dissension that had been stirring for some time within the party. A conservative faction distrusted the Communist connection and wanted to oust Communists entirely. The radical wing, hoping to base the organization upon the support of the peasant and working classes, stressed the desirability of a concrete reform program and of continued association with the Russian advisers. Temporarily the radicals seemed to have won. Chiang Kai-shek, whose sympathies were conservative and who had suppressed radical demonstrations at Shanghai and executed Communists and suspected Communists when Kuomintang troops occupied this important city, was temporarily deprived of his command. But by midsummer of 1927 the picture had completely changed. Borodin and the other Russian advisers were dismissed; trade unionists and radicals were disciplined or driven out of the party, and some party members went into voluntary exile in Russia.

Although the reversal of direction in 1927 was startling and deci-

Dr. Sun Yat-sen (Seated) and Chiang Kai-shek

The temporary defeat of the Communists

sive, actually there had been little likelihood that the radicals could maintain their ascendancy. The Chinese Communists at this time numbered only about 50,000. While there were plenty of discontented peasants and a Chinese Federation of Labor claimed two and a half million members, these groups were not capable of carrying to successful conclusion the fight against the northern militarists. And the Kuomintang army was far from being a radical body. Kuomintang leaders had welcomed and benefited from Russian assistance, but now that they felt strong enough to stand alone they had no desire to serve the interests of a foreign power. There were grounds for suspecting that the Russians intended to convert the Chinese revolution into an outpost of Soviet Communism, and the discovery of a Soviet plot at Peking prompted the northern government to break off relations with Russia. In supporting the Moscow-Canton entente of 1923–1927, the Soviet leaders, hoping for the speedy coming of world revolution, had gambled and lost. But they had provided the spark without which the Kuomintang might never have been fired into action.

Capture of Peking (Pei-p'ing) by Kuomintang forces

After the purge of the radical wing, the Kuomintang leaders proceeded rapidly with their plan to extend their authority throughout the country. From this time forward the dominant figure of the party was Chiang Kai-shek, whose return to a position of influence was automatic with the triumph of the conservatives. In addition to his repute as a military commander, Chiang enjoyed the prestige of belonging to the "ruling family" of the Revolution, through his marriage to the American-educated Soong Mei-ling, a sister of Madame Sun Yat-sen. Kuomintang forces pushed on, without too much difficulty, through the territories of discredited military governors, and occupied Peking in 1928. The Nationalists renamed the city Pei-p'ing ("Northern Peace") and moved their capital to Nanking, in keeping with pledges made in the early period of the Revolution.

Chiang Kai-shek's Nationalist regime at Nanking

The task of national reconstruction confronting the Kuomintang leaders was a far more difficult undertaking than the seizure of power had been. Even the maintenance of power was not easy, as remnants of the war-lord regimes lingered on in various parts of China. Although Kuomintang supremacy still depended upon military support, the party claimed that it had completed the first, or military, stage of Dr. Sun's formula of revolution and had inaugurated the second stage—that of political "tutelage." In spite of its anti-Communist orientation, the structure both of the Kuomintang and of the government which it set up at Nanking followed closely the Soviet pattern. The party was a hierarchy, reaching from the smallest units, or cells, through district and provincial bodies up to the Central Executive Committee at the top. The president of the National Government and the members of his Council of State were selected by the Central Executive Committee of the Kuomintang, of which the key member was Chiang Kai-shek. At the central, provincial, and local levels the government embodied, not democracy, but a party dictatorship.

A number of important accomplishments can be credited to the Nationalist regime at Nanking. The portions of China which were brought under its jurisdiction became more unified than at any time since the eighteenth century, and China's prestige in the eyes of the world was enhanced. The Nationalists promptly secured diplomatic recognition and financial assistance from abroad. Following the lead of the United States, the Great Powers agreed to relinquish their control over customs duties, granting tariff autonomy to China by 1929. It was more difficult to persuade them to surrender their privileges of extraterritoriality, a step not taken by the United States and Great Britain until 1943.

Accomplishments of the Nationalist regime

While progress undeniably occurred during the era of Nationalist rule, the defects of the regime became more and more serious. Radical elements had been expelled before the triumph of the Kuomintang, and even moderate liberals were given scant encouragement. Originating as a party of revolution, the Kuomintang when in power neglected to carry out the social reforms that were necessary to win the allegiance of the common people. Very little was done to improve the condition of poor tenants and farm laborers, even though Sun Yat-sen had specified assistance to these classes as a primary objective of the "Principle of Livelihood." In command of a one-party government and eager to perpetuate its own authority, the Kuomintang employed coercive measures against those who opposed it. It maintained secret police, disguised under the title of "Bureau of Investigation and Statistics." To indoctrinate potential party members it organized a tightly disciplined Youth Corps (ironically named the *San Min Chu I* after Sun's "Three Principles"). The Nationalist regime seemed to be preparing the Chinese people less for constitutional democracy than for a permanent condition of tutelage.

Defects of the Nationalist regime

The downfall of the Kuomintang in China after a rule of twenty years was caused by three factors: (1) failure of the Kuomintang regime to solve the problems of Chinese society; (2) unrelenting opposition from the Chinese Communists, who ultimately set up a rival government; and (3) the long war beginning with the Japanese invasion of 1937, which drained the country's resources, demoralized the people, and promoted the chaotic conditions so favorable to the spread of communism. The struggle against the Communists began almost as soon as the Kuomintang had established its government at Nanking and was a continuous process even during the most successful years of the Nationalist period. Following the rupture with the Kuomintang in 1927, the Communist party had been driven underground but extended its activities in both rural and urban areas of central and southern China, and in Kiangsi province it organized a rival government in the form of a Soviet Republic. Almost annihilated by Kuomintang forces in a series of military campaigns, the Communist leaders turned the desperate struggle to their advantage by inciting revolutionary aspirations among the depressed peasantry and

Causes of the Kuomintang's failure

*Mao Tse-tung's strategy
of revolution*

by developing the technique of guerrilla warfare into a fine art. Mao Tse-tung was the key personality behind both of these policies.

The son of a relatively well-to-do peasant, Mao Tse-tung as a youth had rebelled against landlordism and the tyranny of parental authority. One of a dozen men who founded the Chinese Communist party in 1921, he became a deputy member of the Central Executive Committee of the Kuomintang and was entrusted by the Communists with the task of peasant organization. A report prepared for the Chinese Communist party in 1927 on peasant revolutionary activity in Hunan (south central China) provides the clue to Mao's strategy of revolution and is prophetic of his ultimate program for China. Already he was instigating direct action among the lowliest tenants: (1) forming village co-operative associations; (2) smashing temples and burning the wooden idols for fuel; (3) intimidating and assaulting "bad gentry." "A revolution is not the same as inviting people to dinner," he wrote. "A rural revolution is a revolution by which the peasantry overthrows the authority of the feudal landlord class. . . . several hundred million peasants will rise like a tornado or tempest, a force so extraordinarily swift and violent that no power, however great, will be able to suppress it." In sharp disagreement with both the Chinese and Russian party leaders, Mao was convinced that whoever won the peasants would win China.

*The "Long March" to
Yenan*

Threatened with extinction by Chiang's superior troops, Mao Tse-tung conceived and executed the famous "Long March" of October 1934 to October 1935—a mass migration across 6,000 miles of difficult terrain and one of the most amazing exploits in military history. Of the 90,000 men who slipped through Chiang's lines in southwestern China, not more than 20,000 reached Yenan, in northern Shensi Province, which was to be the Communists' headquarters until their

Chinese Civilians on the Szechuan Road. Chinese residents of Shanghai pour into the International Settlement upon hearing rumors that a Japanese attack on the city was imminent. December 2, 1935.

final victory in the civil war. Shattering as the experience had been, it served to weld the survivors into a solid group of tested loyalty and toughness, relying upon their own ingenuity rather than upon directives from Moscow, and it established Mao Tse-tung as undisputed leader of the party. He had demonstrated his tactics of "retreat in order to advance" and his ability to sustain and renew his forces directly from the countryside while the cities and economic apparatus of the state were in the hands of his enemies. Gradually the Communist region of the northwest acquired the attributes of a separate state, with a fluid political structure and well-organized military units. In expanding the area of their influence, the Communists' chief asset was their introduction of reforms which the Nanking government had promised but never fulfilled. They tackled the land problem directly, breaking up great estates, forcing rent reductions, establishing land banks and cooperative societies, building irrigation works, and educating ignorant peasants in better methods of cultivation and crop control. Their immediate and practical assistance to farmers who had been oppressed by high rents and high taxes and their success in eliminating graft in the region under their administration enabled them to compete successfully with the Kuomintang regime for popular favor. The Communists also strengthened their position by calling for national resistance against Japanese aggression, to which Chiang Kai-shek, intent upon crushing Communism, had offered only half-hearted opposition.

When, in line with the Soviet strategy of fostering antifascist "popular fronts," the Chinese Communists appeared cooperative, pressure within the Kuomintang induced Chiang Kai-shek to enter into an alliance with them to halt the common enemy, Japan. But this had the unfortunate effect of encouraging the Japanese militarists to make

War with Japan

Japanese Troops Enter Peking in July 1937 at the Beginning of the Eight-Year War with China

Chinese Communist Artillery Units in Action near Peking

war. Faced with the prospect of a united China, they goaded their government into launching an attack in the Pei-p'ing area (July 7, 1937). This was the beginning of a fateful conflict which soon expanded into World War II.

The course of the war revealed that China was a far stronger nation than it had been forty years earlier. Even though the mighty Japanese military machine eventually occupied the coastal cities and almost all of eastern China and forced the Nationalist government to move its capital far inland to Chungking, it was never able to conquer the entire country. Actually, after the United States entered the war against Japan and began to supply China with substantial military aid, the Nationalist government contributed little to the war effort. Chiang Kai-shek, unsure of the loyalty of his own staff and determined to hoard his military resources, ignored the American advisers who tried to prod him into action. While doing little against the Japanese, he kept an army of half a million men in the northwest to isolate the Communist "Border Region" government at Yenan. American negotiations attempting to bring the Yenan and Chungking regimes into a coalition government failed because Chiang insisted that the Communists give up their separate command and put all military forces at his disposal, a condition they regarded as equivalent to a death sentence. Without the advantage of foreign aid or help from Chungking, Communist guerrillas successfully penetrated Japanese lines and gradually secured control of much of northern China. At the close of the war when the Nationalists, assisted by an American airlift, occupied the principal cities, Communist units held the countryside, and they seized stores of Japanese arms and ammunition that Russian troops withdrawing from Manchuria had conveniently left behind. After the Japanese surrender, China's international conflict gradually turned into a civil war.

China in World War II; prelude to civil war

The Nationalists had formulated plans for reform and promised to replace the party dictatorship with a democratic representative government. They drafted a constitution and early in 1947 conducted elections for a National Assembly, which dutifully chose Chiang Kai-shek as president of the Republic. But while the Nationalists were inaugurating a democratic constitution for China, they were rapidly being dispossessed from the country by the advance of Communist

"Support for the People's Very Own Army." This woodcut, dating from the 1940s, illustrates the close ties that existed between the peasantry and the Communist army. Such illustrations may have overstated the case, but they did highlight a striking contrast between the Communists and the Nationalists.

armies. So low had the prestige of the Kuomintang party fallen that it could summon very little assistance in its hour of peril. In 1949 the southerly retreat of Nationalist forces turned into a rout that ended with all the mainland in the hands of the Communists. By 1950 the jurisdiction of President Chiang's government was confined to the island of Taiwan (Formosa).

The People's Republic of China; the Constitution of 1954

After their victory over the Nationalists, the Communist leaders moved rapidly to secure their hold upon the vast territory of China. In October 1949 they proclaimed the People's Republic of China with its capital in Peking. In 1954 they enacted a Constitution for the People's Republic, which, like the constitution of Soviet Russia, combines the language and forms of parliamentary democracy with the principle of domination by the Communist party. Nominally, supreme authority is vested in an All-China People's Congress, charged with enacting laws and electing major officials. The Constitution contains a Bill of Rights which covers the whole field of individual liberties, recognizes equality of the sexes, declares all persons over eighteen years of age eligible to vote and to hold office, and even guarantees the ownership of private property. However, it leaves the application of these rights very tentative by giving the government power to punish "traitors, counterrevolutionaries, and bureaucratic capitalists."

Unique features of the Communist revolution

The accession of the Chinese Communists to power was followed by sweeping economic, social, and cultural changes which transformed the country and its people in fundamental ways. The Chinese Revolution, one of the most far-reaching in history and in some ways unique, was stamped by the dominating personality of Party Chairman Mao Tse-tung, who adapted theoretical Marxism to immediate problems and blended it with elements of China's traditional culture pattern. Combining fixity of purpose with flexibility in tactics, Mao was pragmatic and innovative in both thought and action. His oversimplified but stimulating interpretation of history bore a strong flavor of nationalism. Invoking reverence for China's "splendid

Mao Tse-tung at a Desk in His Cave Headquarters during the Communist Advances in 1948

historical heritage" and "glorious revolutionary tradition," he paid tribute to some pre-Communist reformers and to Sun Yat-sen, whose widow—Chaing Kai-shek's sister-in-law—became a vice-chairman of the People's Republic. Although he accepted the Marxist dogma of class struggle, Mao identified it with recurring unsuccessful peasant uprisings, including the nineteenth-century Taiping rebellion. Mao's was the first large-scale and successful revolution anywhere in the world that was founded on peasant support and directed by a leader from the peasant class. In this respect it contrasts with the revolution of Lenin and Stalin, which entailed expropriation and forcible suppression of the peasants. No less than the Soviet revolution, it aimed at creating a new society, but, again in contrast with the Russian example, this radical objective was pursued for nearly thirty years—until Mao's death in 1976.

The Communist regime in China claimed to have achieved a coalition of classes, namely peasants, workers, petty bourgeoisie, and "national bourgeoisie." The inclusion of the last two classes marked a departure from orthodox Marxism and an attempt to win the support of financial and industrial elements whose cooperation was essential to bolstering the economy. Businessmen who qualified as "Communist" or "national" capitalists by being willing to work with the new government were allowed to retain their properties temporarily, but found their affairs subjected to rigid control, and in 1956 the national bourgeoisie were formally expropriated. The Central Committee of the Communist party or Chairman Mao himself determined public policies, the permissible limits of debate, and the operation of organs of government, in keeping with the principles of a "People's Democratic Dictatorship."

The "Democratic Dictatorship"

The economic transformation of China since 1949 is an impressive aspect of the Communist revolution, all the more remarkable when viewed against the previous retarded condition of the country. As in India, industrialization was given high priority and—in contrast to India—the government possessed sufficient coercive power to effect rapid change. Geological surveys have revealed mineral resources far in excess of previous estimates. Oil reserves, including offshore deposits, are enormous. By 1977 China's oil production equaled that of Indonesia. In coal deposits China ranks third among the world's countries and also has large known reserves of natural gas as well as adequate supplies of manganese, tungsten, antimony, tin, copper, and aluminum. In recent years the Chinese have supplemented their energy sources by building 7 million small biogas plants which, at low cost, convert animal and vegetable waste into methane gas and fertilizer. By 1960 China's furnaces were producing almost as much steel as was made in France, and the output of electric power had been increased ten times. The acreage of irrigated land more than doubled between 1949 and 1960, and the same period witnessed an extensive forestation program highly significant for soil and water conservation.

Economic objectives and prospects

Blast Furnaces at Anshan. The major steel-producing center in southern Machuria, it is a testament to China's growing industrial strength.

A complex system of dams and reservoirs in the Yellow River valley, designed to end the danger of flooding in this region and to provide a larger and surer crop yield, has not yet been completed. Railroad mileage has doubled but is still far from adequate, especially since the objective is a wide dispersion of industry hitherto concentrated in Manchuria and the eastern seaboard. With Soviet technical assistance the Chinese trained their own engineers capable of designing precision tools. Their manufactures include such items as cars, trucks, and jet planes; also electronic, surgical, and scientific instruments.

The agrarian revolution and the "Great Leap Forward"

More profound than the changes in the scope and tempo of industrialization has been the agrarian revolution. The character of agriculture and of the society engaged in it has been altered radically, through successive stages. The first phase of land reform was simply expropriation of the landlords, many of whom were killed. Then, the newly created peasant proprietors were urged to form cooperatives, pooling the resources of one or more villages. The next step was a drive for collective farms, communally owned and directed by party members or supporters. This was accomplished with remarkable swiftness between 1955 and 1957, by which time more than 90 percent of the family holdings had been collectivized. Although Chinese farmers undoubtedly "volunteered" to join cooperatives because they were given little choice, the government relied primarily upon psychological and social pressure, employing what Mao has described as "persuasive reasoning," and there was no liquidation of resisting peasants. But Mao attempted to make material and institutional changes serve as instruments for molding the psychology of the masses. More than once his dogged pursuit of ideological goals threatened to jeopardize the positive gains of the revolution. The first example was a program announced as the "Great Leap Forward," launched in 1959. It called for the merging of rural co-operatives and collective farms into large communes, which, it was claimed, embodied the principle of ownership by the whole people rather than by a single community. The purpose of the communes was to provide a mobile labor force to implement an overly ambitious program of rapid industrialization and to increase food production. For a variety of reasons—including the callousness and ineptitude of local directors and a prolonged drought in the Yellow River valley that brought poor harvests in 1959 and 1960—the Great Leap Forward turned out to be a disaster. Food shortages necessitated the importation of grain, and the demoralization of labor and the drainage of capital resources caused a severe industrial depression. Forced to revise its tactics drastically, the government in 1962 announced its intention to give agriculture top priority for the immediate future. While the communes were retained and their number increased (now totaling 190), they were reduced in size, a degree of ownership and management was restored to local production teams, and farmers were permitted to cultivate small private plots and sell on the open market.

The failure of the Great Leap Forward temporarily weakened Mao's position. In 1959 he relinquished the office of state chairman and, continuing as head of the party, worked quietly to consolidate his support within the party and within the army. When he felt his base to be strong enough he made a second major attempt to radicalize the revolution and, at the same time, immobilize his opponents. More ambitious and more effective than the 1958 Leap Forward, this second thrust was embodied in the celebrated Great Proletarian Cultural Revolution, which kept China in turmoil from 1966 to 1969 and was not formally laid to rest until August 1977.

The background and objectives of the Proletarian Cultural Revolution are complex. To some extent it was a power struggle between "moderates," represented by Chief of State Liu Shao-ch'i (Liu Shao-qi), and "radicals," led by Chairman Mao and Defense Minister Lin

Preparation for a second attempt at radical change

A People's Court in Session. The establishment of local community courts such as this served as a self-liberating exercise for the peasantry.

Piao (Lin Biao). It also reflected disagreement concerning China's response to escalation of the Vietnam War by the United States. Liu Shao-ch'i, viewing the United States' massive military intervention as a prelude to an attack on China, called for a united front of all socialist countries in defense of North Vietnam. Mao Tse-tung, backed by Lin Piao, insisted that China should not be drawn into a "people's war of liberation" unless directly attacked. He argued that China, by concentrating on its own internal development, could "bypass the Soviet Union on its way to Communism." By August 1966 the Mao-Lin faction dominated the Central Committee of the party, although it by no means controlled the entire party hierarchy or all units of the army.

Undoubtedly the overriding factor in precipitating the Cultural Revolution was ideological. Mao resolved at all costs to prevent his revolution from subsiding until it had produced an equalitarian society. He chastised Soviet leaders for stopping short of this goal and denounced as "revisionists" all those within his own party who showed signs of succumbing to the fleshpots of capitalism. He feared that the prospect of material success had brought a relaxation of effort, which China could ill afford in view of its unrealized potential and weak military posture. He viewed with misgivings the tendency of a bureaucracy to grow rigid and complacent, producing a managerial class more "expert" than "red." In his determination to reform the party both in personnel and structure he temporarily disrupted it completely.

Before 1965 the Communist movement in China had presented the outward appearance of remarkable harmony. But with the onset of the Cultural Revolution scores of officials were arrested, demoted, or forced to make public confession of such crimes as "hedonism," "revisionism," "antiparty activity," or "taking the road to capitalism." The purge numbered high personnel among its targets, includ-

A Red Guard Demonstration in Peking. Middle-school students display their solidarity with the Cultural Revolution by waving copies of the book of quotations from Chairman Mao. The slogan painted on the wall proclaims: "We are not only able to destroy the old world, we are able to build a new world instead—Mao Tse-tung."

ing Liu Shao-ch'i, president of the Republic since 1959 and long regarded as Mao's heir apparent. As the stepped-up purification campaign met with stubborn resistance, Mao turned to the nation's youth, exhorting them to undertake their own Long March and to "learn revolution-making by making revolution." He closed the schools and urged students to organize themselves into units of Red Guards (formally inaugurated at Peking in August 1966) and devote their energies to ferreting out enemies of the revolution. China was treated to the unprecedented spectacle of mobs of teenage youths denouncing their elders, smashing ancient monuments, invading private homes, and noisily demanding unswerving devotion to the thought of Mao Tsetung. Mao encouraged the formation of Revolutionary Committees combining party and nonparty members, and put them in charge of factories, local and provincial governments, and even important departments of the central government. He hoped to replace the Soviet-style dual system of state and party structures that was developing in China with a flexible but unified system.

The attempt to achieve such radical goals generated a condition of chaos bordering on anarchy. Strikes in major industrial centers, disruption of the transport system, and widespread disorders in rural areas placed China's economic gains in jeopardy. At the same time the Chinese found themselves isolated diplomatically, even in the Communist world. Excesses committed by Red Guards and bands of "Revolutionary Rebels," leading to the outbreak of civil war in some provinces in 1968, made it imperative for Mao and Chou En-lai to stem the revolutionary tide. They called on the People's Liberation Army to restore order, and the party line shifted to a denunciation of extremists. Lin Piao, a prime instrument of the Cultural Revolution and named as Mao's successor in a new party constitution of 1960, fell into disgrace. Reportedly he was killed in an airplane crash while attempting to defect to Russia in September 1971.

Undoubtedly the Cultural Revolution of 1966–1969 exacted a heavy price. It left a residue of suspicion and fear and set a precedent for youthful violence, reflected, perhaps, in recent years in the rampages of hoodlum gangs in several cities. Still, in spite of its ugly aspects, its toll of lives and property, the Cultural Revolution was not the total catastrophe envisioned by some foreign critics. Testifying to rapid economic recovery was a record high output of food grains in 1970–1972 and an annual industrial growth rate of about 10 percent. In the midst of its domestic crisis China managed to produce a hydrogen bomb (June 1967), far earlier than Western experts had thought possible. Also Mao had succeeded in inspiring and energizing his massive following, even though his ideal of permanent revolution seemed unlikely to outlive him.

Chinese society—for centuries one of the most stable in the world—has been profoundly affected by the Communist revolution. A fore-

Chairman Mao Tse-tung. Shown here with his then "closest comrade" Marshal Lin Piao (Defense Minister and Vice Chairman of the Republic who was purged in 1971). Premier Chou En-lai stands behind them.

Effects of the Cultural Revolution

Left: *The Cultural Revolution at the Grass Roots*. Agricultural workers have erected red painted signs with quotations from Chairman Mao and carry copies of his "Quotations" into the fields with them. Right: *A Reservoir and Irrigation Project in Chekiang Province, Eastern China*. Labor-saving machinery is still in short supply.

Changes in society; restrictions on urban growth

most problem, inherited from the past, was how to nourish a large and continually expanding population, especially with an economy disrupted by civil war. Vigorous campaigns were conducted to restrict the birth rate—by providing contraceptives and family-planning courses, by encouraging late marriages, and by offering economic incentives for couples to limit the number of their children to one or two. The result has been a dramatic drop in the rate of increase, with the likelihood that China's population, now in the neighborhood of 900 million, will be stabilized by the end of the century. Although less than 15 percent of China's land area is cultivated, more than 80 percent of its people are rural dwellers. The government has restricted the growth of cities (Shanghai with nearly 11 million is the largest) and has tried to establish a symbiotic relationship between each urban center and the surrounding farm area. Not only has immigration from country to town been controlled, but also some 12 million city-educated youths have been resettled in rural areas since the Cultural Revolution. Economic planning has emphasized decentralization and has allowed considerable autonomy to regional units in development programs. To some extent efficiency has been subordinated to the goals of widely dispersed industry, interdependence between industry and agriculture, and regional "self-reliance."

China is still poor in comparison with developed Western countries or Japan. Annual per capita income—about $340—does not greatly exceed that of India, but a significant difference is that instead of being concentrated at the top, it is fairly evenly distributed. No doubt the majority of the Chinese people are better off in basic material necessities than they have been for many centuries. Improved standards of hygiene and sanitation, expanded medical facilities, and intense educational campaigns succeeded in stamping out opium addiction, curtailing prostitution, and raising the level of public health. By supplementing a scarce supply of skilled professionals with semiskilled trainees, the Chinese have been able to make generally available such social services as child day-care centers, hospitals, and mobile clinics employing both up-to-date Western and traditional Chinese medicines and techniques. Although wages and farm incomes are low, the individual has the benefit of low rents, free medical service, and disability and retirement pensions.

A significant aspect of social change is the demise of the centuries-old patriarchal family structure and the emancipation—at least in theory—of women. A marriage law of 1950 gave women equal rights with men in respect to choice of spouse, conjugal privileges and obligations, and divorce. Legal equality between the sexes led to enhanced status of the single-unit monogamous family. It is still common for working couples to house their retired elders (and housing space is at a premium), but the tyrannical authority formerly wielded by a clan matriarch over daughters-in-law has been broken, and progress toward bridging the proverbial generation gap has occurred. Women have entered the labor force in large numbers and have been admitted to occupations and professions that formerly were man's preserve. In China as elsewhere women are a decided minority in levels of highest responsibility, and at lower levels it is usually the husband rather than the wife whose job determines a couple's place of residence. But if Chinese women are not yet fully liberated, they are far freer from exploitation by male kindred than they were or than are the women of many other lands.

Changes in the family and the position of women

Some cultural changes promoted by the Communists had their beginnings during the Nationalist era. A "literary revolution" of the 1920s had made vernacular speech an accepted vehicle for modern authors in place of the difficult, archaic language of Chinese literary classics. Linguistic reform under the Communists involved simplification of written characters and adoption of an allegedly more nearly phonetic system of transliteration into languages using the Roman alphabet (*pinyin,* in place of the older "Wade-Giles" system). As in other totalitarian regimes, the Communists undertook to define cultural standards and to make art the handmaiden of ideology, a policy which during the height of the Proletarian Revolution reduced it to a level of mediocrity. Education inevitably was buffeted by shifting revolutionary currents. Mao Tse-tung repudiated completely the classical Chinese tradition of a scholarly elite drawn from the gentry. He stressed the need to combine theory with practice, instituted "half-

Cultural and educational trends

study, half-work" programs, and sent youths from city classrooms out into the fields to work with and learn from the peasants. The regular schools, closed during the Cultural Revolution, were not restored to normal operation until after Mao's death. In spite of vicissitudes one educational objective has been largely met—about 90 percent of the population has become literate.

Attempts to remake human nature

The dark side of the picture of China's changing society is the high price that has been paid for rapid material progress. The party chiefs used ruthless means to seize power and to keep it. Although violence and terror have not been the typical weapons either of party discipline or of popular coercion and there has been no general liquidation of "kulaks" or of bourgeoisie, psychological pressure, "thought control," and "reform through labor" have been employed regularly in the effort to remold recalcitrants. The whole citizen body is constantly exposed to political indoctrination through the communication media, entirely controlled by the government. Paradoxically, although Mao restricted intellectual freedom and resorted to coercion, his view of human nature was neither cynical nor pessimistic. Rejecting the historical determinism of orthodox Marxism, he insisted that ideas and human will and resolution can play an important part in shaping events. He believed it possible not only to reform institutions but to remake human nature, producing a "new man" who would instinctively put the interests of society foremost. The very chaos of the Cultural Revolution he hoped would further his purpose of creating a direct and permanent working relationship between the party's leaders and the masses, eliminating as far as possible the middle levels of authority. This radically utopian concept did not prevent the rise of a bureaucratic managerial class; actually it served to legitimatize the authority of the managers. To some observers the contemporary Chinese Communist regime bears more than a superficial resemblance to the classical imperial tradition of a benevolent government wielding

Workers' School. Railway workers in northern China attend classes as part of the state's attempt to extend education.

absolute power over an obedient and disciplined population. It follows that as long as the rulers enjoy the "mandate of Heaven," their position will not be seriously challenged.

The rapid unification of China under a totalitarian regime has drastically altered the power relationships in Asia and the Far East. With a powerful army at their disposal, the Communists re-established Chinese jurisdiction over important areas that had been lost during the decline of the Manchu Dynasty. They took possession of Manchuria, retained Sinkiang in the far west, and installed their forces in Tibet. And while augmenting China's national prestige they posed as the champions of Asian peoples against Western imperialism, assisting revolutionary movements against the British in Malaya and against the French in Indochina.

China's internal developments and policies have been affected by her relations with other countries. At the outset the greatest threat to the Communist regime seemed to lie with the United States, which had supported Chiang Kai-shek throughout the war, continued its alliance with him, and financed his military establishment of 600,000 troops on the island of Taiwan—within 100 miles of the mainland. Stung by charges that liberals in the State Department had "lost" China for the United States, successive Washington administrations clung to an unrealistic and contradictory policy of regarding the People's Republic, on the one hand, as a bungling incompetent unworthy of notice and, on the other, as a dangerous and demonic power bent on world conquest. The United States withheld diplomatic recognition from Peking, blocked its admission to the United Nations, embargoed American trade with the mainland, and installed a ring of military bases around East Asia. Through its "containment" policy, implemented by a network of defensive alliances, the United States sought to isolate China, and effectively isolated its own citizens from contact with an important area of the world.

The simultaneous isolation of China and Russia—as the Cold War alienated the U.S.S.R. from her erstwhile Western allies—at first strengthened the fraternal and ideological bonds between the two large Communist states. In 1950 their representatives signed a thirty-year treaty of "friendship, alliance, and mutual assistance," which invalidated the 1945 treaty between the U.S.S.R. and the Chinese Nationalists. The preamble of China's 1954 Constitution reaffirmed "indestructible friendship" with the Soviet Union. China relied heavily upon Russia for technical assistance in economic development. Between 1950 and 1955 China's exchange with the Soviet-bloc countries increased from 26 percent to 75 percent of her total foreign trade. The late 1950s, however, evidenced disaffection between the two Communist giants. Differences led swiftly to deterioration in both diplomatic and economic relations. The Sino-Soviet rift is attributable to a number of causes. The Chinese resented the Russian's failure to

China's foreign relations

Hostility of the United States; the "containment" policy

The Sino-Soviet rift and its significance

May Day Parade in Peking. Processions such as this commemorate the success of the revolutionary struggle and serve to reinforce the popular commitment to revolutionary values and to a strong state.

fulfill their aid agreements, including the promise of help in developing atomic weapons. Other factors were the inevitable rivalries of great-power politics and conflicting national territorial ambitions. The Chinese hinted at the eventual rectification of their frontiers at Russia's expense, and both China and the Soviet Union deployed large numbers of troops along their 5,000-mile common border from Central Asia to Manchuria. In 1969 violent clashes occurred between Russian and Chinese troops in Sinkiang in the far west and along the Ussuri River in the northeast. The most fundamental source of disagreement between the two countries was ideological. Peking accused the Russians of abandoning the cause of world revolution against imperialism and condemned Khrushchev's policy of peaceful coexistence. The breach between Peking and Moscow reflected the differences in outlook between the heirs of an old revolution and the directors of one still comparatively young. In Mao Tse-tung's view Soviet Russia, now a have nation, had succumbed to revisionism and was taking the primrose path to accommodation with the capitalist powers for the sake of security and the grantification of consumer demands.

While breaking with much of the past, Mao Tse-tung and his comrades retained the ancient concept of China as a unique and indestructible community, proudly self-sustaining. They strove to avoid close dependence on any other state, Communist or not. (Russian assistance during the 1950s was chiefly in the form of loans and these were repaid.) For many years China was forced into isolation by the hostility of Western nations. The break with the Soviets in the early 1960s and the internal turmoil that followed a few years later made the country's isolation almost complete. But the return to more moderate policies brought decided changes in foreign relations. The Peking government restored diplomatic relations ruptured during the Cultural Revolution and proceeded to win recognition from a rapidly growing number of states. The end of China's isolation was dramatically illustrated in 1971 by rapprochement with the United States and by China's admission to the United Nations and the transfer of a permanent seat in the Security Council from the Chinese Nationalists to the People's Republic.

Ironically, the American president who renewed ties with China had built a political career on strident anti-Communism. President Nixon's decision to cultivate cordial relations with his inveterate ideological enemies was prompted partly by the promise of new trade opportunities and partly by the hope of gaining an advantage in dealing with the Soviets by drawing closer to their repudiated ally. In any case it was no longer possible to ignore the People's Republic, which had become a military power equipped with nuclear bombs and missiles. Summit meetings in 1972 did not produce formal diplomatic recognition of the Peking government by Washington, but a joint communiqué issued at Shanghai on February 28 pledged the two countries to work toward the normalization of relations and the relaxation of tensions in Asia, including Indochina. One crucial question remained unresolved: the Chinese stipulated that "the liberation of Taiwan is China's internal affair"; the Americans affirmed "interest in a peaceful settlement of the Taiwan question by the Chinese themselves," and the "ultimate objective of the withdrawal of all United States forces and military installations from Taiwan."

The subject of Taiwan is a story in itself, which cannot be detailed here. Ever since 1949 when Chiang Kai-shek and his defeated forces retreated to the island, it had been a thorn in the side of the Peking government and the chief source of friction with the United States. The United States retained its alliance with Chiang Kai-shek, recognized his government at Taipei as the "Republic of China," supplied him with arms and money, and threatened to "unleash" his forces to reconquer the mainland. On one point the Communists and the Nationalists agreed—that Taiwan was an integral part of China. They disagreed as to whether it was a severed head or a severed foot. In an atmosphere of international tension, Taiwan's economy thrived. The Nationalists had imposed themselves upon the Taiwanese by force; their rule was an extension of the party dictatorship they had devel-

Generalissimo Chiang Kai-shek

The U.S. break with Taiwan and restoration of diplomatic relations with China

Death of Mao Tse-tung and conservative reaction

oped at Nanking. But while Chiang Kai-shek had botched the governance of China, he scored a major success in Taiwan. Helped by United States investments and by World Bank credits, the Nationalists' republic sustained a high rate of economic growth. Between 1952 and 1978 the gross national product increased nearly twenty-fold and per capita annual income rose from $148 to $1,304, bringing Taiwan to third rank in that category (after Japan and Singapore) among Far Eastern countries. While the native Taiwanese—about 85 percent of the island's 17 million inhabitants—were given very limited political rights and held under martial law, they shared in the material progress of both agriculture and industry. Wealth is fairly evenly distributed and, while women have achieved none of the freedoms enjoyed by their sisters in the People's Republic, the Taiwanese are far better off in material goods than are the mainland Chinese. With sizable military forces as well as a bustling and technologically advanced economy, Taiwan has many characteristics of an independent middle-class power. Yet political independence (which native Taiwanese might prefer) is out of the question because of the fixed policies of both the Taipei and Peking governments.

In December 1978 President Carter abruptly announced his intention to break diplomatic relations and abrogate the 1954 mutual defense treaty with the Taiwan regime, and the following March he restored normal diplomatic relations with Peking. The initial shock of this policy reversal was softened somewhat when Congress passed the Taiwan Relations Act in April 1979. The act stipulated that the United States would regard any attempt to determine the future of Taiwan by other than peaceful means as "of grave concern to the United States." The diplomatic break had no adverse effect on the island's economy. During the first four months of 1979 Taiwan's foreign trade rose 36 percent over the same period of the preceding year, and trade with the United States increased by more than 20 percent. At an annual figure of close to $10 billion, United States trade with Taiwan was ten times as great as with the mainland. Chiang Ching-kuo, who succeeded to the presidency after the death of his father Chiang Kai-shek in 1975, held fast to the claim that his was the only legitimate Chinese government. Peking's present leaders have indicated that they would accept an arrangement allowing full autonomy to Taiwan under its present government, in turn for acknowledgment of China's formal sovereignty.

The death in September 1976 of Mao Tse-tung—the most influential Chinese personality since Confucius—marked the end of an era. In the years following the Cultural Revolution, with the aging chairman's health declining, intraparty strife persisted between the "radicals," who stressed revolutionary ideology, and the "moderates," who desired stability and rapid material progress. Premier Chou En-lai's death in January 1976 removed a steadying influence that had repeatedly been effective in bridging the gap between opposing factions. Despite some ominous disturbances, following Mao's death his hand-picked successor to the premiership, Hua Kuo-feng (Hua Guo-feng), was named party chairman (October 1976). But that the political pendulum was swinging to the right was reflected in the increasingly prominent role of a Chou En-lai protégé, Vice-Premier Teng Hsiao-ping (Deng Xiaoping), who had been purged during the Cultural Revolution and purged again as late as April 1976. Hua Kuo-feng gradually receded into the background (he resigned the premiership in September 1980), while the ascendant Teng faction not only undertook to purge the party of radicals, but also repudiated the Cultural Revolution almost completely—villifying its heroes and rehabilitating its victims (a posthumous award in some cases). Though still honoring Mao Tse-tung's memory, the new leaders hinted that even the "Great Helmsman" had made mistakes.

In a sensational sixty-seven-day public trial ending on January 25, 1981, ten defendants were accused of having killed 34,000 people during the Cultural Revolution, of torturing or persecuting hundreds of thousands, and of plotting to poison Chou and eliminate Mao. Pilloried as the archvillain was none other than the widow of Mao Tse-tung, the feared and hated Chiang Ch'ing (Jiang Qing), acknowledged leader of the notorious "gang of four," which had become a scapegoat for the excesses and failures of the Cultural Revolution. Chiang's scornful and defiant outbursts against her accusers and judges injected a note of excitement into an otherwise dismal, and apparently well-coached, performance. She was given a suspended death sentence, subject to commutation to life imprisonment after a two-year probationary term at hard labor.

Vice-Premier Teng Hsiao-ping

More than a reaction against the radicalism of the Cultural Revolution, the policies of China's post-Mao leadership seemed to herald the end of the revolutionary process that had kept the country in ferment throughout a generation. Teng and his associates set as their goals internal order, efficient management, and rapid economic development. Eager to modernize China, they declared that "the proletariat can and must learn from the bourgeoisie," and they called upon industrial nations for technological help, opened their country to tourists, and began cautiously to accept foreign investments and credits. But while condemning the terror tactics of their predecessors and while offering greater material incentives to the populace, the new leaders evidenced a determination to maintain authoritarian control. They tightened discipline in the Communist party, purging about a third of its trained personnel, clamped down on the display of unauthorized wall posters which had become a popular vehicle for airing grievances, and emphasized the goal of political stability, to be achieved through "democratic centralism." To speed technological progress, they were willing to sanction the profit motive and to risk dependence on foreign capital—steps that Mao had steadfastly avoided. These concessions to capitalist ideology suggested that China's "moderni-

Changing goals—toward "modernization"

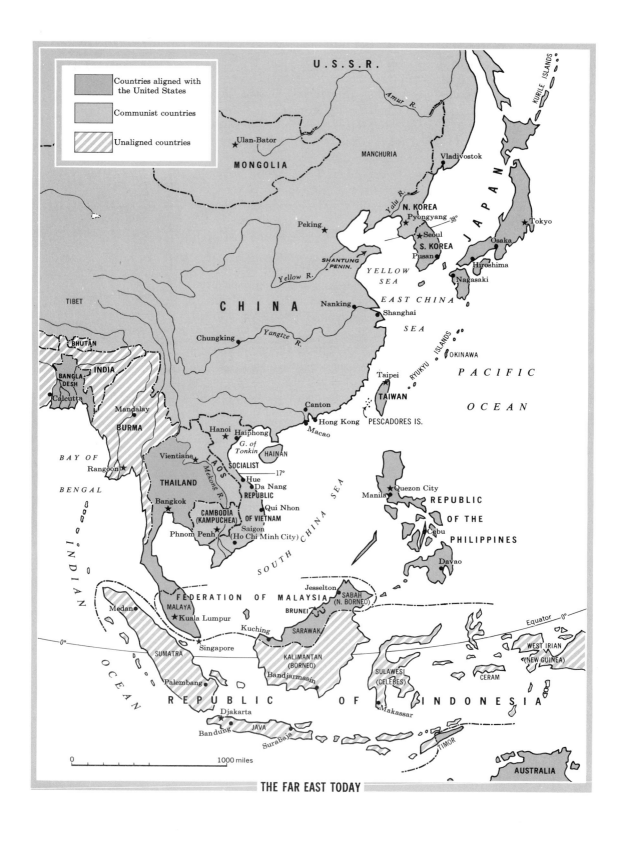

THE FAR EAST TODAY

zation" might reverse the movement toward an equalitarian society and create a new elite class. The dismissal or sidetracking of Mao's revolutionary dream was by no means universally approved. It would be rash to assume that the dominance of a conservative faction has been fixed for an indefinite future, or that the pendulum—which has swung over such a wide arc—will never swing again.

New departures in foreign relations

Changes in foreign relations demonstrated most clearly China's departure from the prescriptions of Mao. According to the "Three-World Thesis"—attributed to Mao but in reality one of Chou's contributions—the two superpowers constituted the first "world," other advanced industrial nations of West and East formed the second, and underdeveloped ex-colonial nations represented the third. While the Chinese claimed affiliation with the last group, they began avidly to cultivate relations with the second, for the twin purposes of speeding their own economic development and of enlisting support against the U.S.S.R., which they had come to regard as the "principal enemy." Along with their predilection for rapid economic growth, the successors of Mao showed themselves much less concerned with ideological purity than with raising China's stakes in the game of power politics. That ideologies come and go while human nature and politics remain much the same could hardly be better illustrated than it was by the sight of a Communist government—one that had for years castigated American "imperialism"—now advocating a stronger NATO and the retention of United States military bases in Japan and the Philippines. Pressing the advantage of cooling relations between Japan and the Soviets, the Chinese, after four years of negotiation, secured a formal peace treaty with Japan, signed in Peking in August 1978. By this time Japan had become China's largest trading partner, contributing one-fourth of the total foreign trade of the People's Republic.

2. THE CLIMAX OF IMPERIALISM AND THE BEGINNING OF A NEW ERA IN JAPAN

The ascendancy of Japan by 1914

In the early twentieth century, while China was in the throes of revolutionary struggle, Japan was enjoying relative stability and increasing prosperity. The transformations which characterized the Meiji Restoration had been accomplished without seriously disturbing the structure of Japanese society. Before 1914 Japan had enlarged its territories, acquired the basis for a strong industrial economy, and finally found itself in a position to seek hegemony in the Far East.

Results of participation in World War I

The Japanese government entered the war against Germany in 1914, nominally out of regard for the Anglo-Japanese alliance but actually from a desire to secure Kiaochow Bay and the German concessions in the Shantung Peninsula. The Japanese also seized the German outposts in the Pacific north of the equator—the Marshall, Caroline, and Mar-

*Japan's victories and
defeats at the Peace
Conference*

iana Islands. Japan showed little interest in the Western phases of the war, but utilized to the utmost the opportunities presented by China's weakness and by the involvement of the Western powers in the titanic struggle in Europe.

The success of Japan's policy of exerting diplomatic and economic pressure was demonstrated at the Peace Conference of 1919. The Chinese delegation naturally demanded the restoration of Shantung, a request entirely consonant with Wilsonian principles. The Japanese refused to comply, and Wilson did not press the matter vigorously, partly because another Japanese objective of a less questionable character had been defeated. The Japanese had asked for a declaration endorsing the principle of "the equality of nations and the just treatment of their nationals." The fear that such a declaration would conflict with the policy of limiting Oriental immigration led the Americans and British to oppose it when the matter was put to a vote in the League of Nations Commission. At the same time they yielded to Japan on the Shantung question and also allowed Japan to retain, as mandates under the League of Nations, the North Pacific islands taken from Germany.

In spite of having plucked the fruits of imperialism, Japan after World War I seemed to be moving in a liberal direction, both in domestic affairs and in her international relations. The antiwar sentiment prevalent for a short time in much of the Western world was manifest, to a lesser degree, in Japan and provoked a revulsion against military leadership. Japan had been associated with the foremost Western democracies during the war, was one of the "Big Five" at the Paris Peace Conference, and—in contrast to Wilson's own United States—signed the Versailles Treaty and joined the League of Nations. Twice before in their history the Japanese had revealed a capacity for adopting what seemed to be the most effective and up-to-date institutions in the world as they knew it, and many of their leaders were persuaded that democracy was essential for progress in the twentieth century. Japanese statesmen were impressed by the fact that autocratic and militaristic Germany had been defeated and autocratic Russia had collapsed in revolution, while the apparently weaker democratic nations had been victorious. And, although few of these statesmen were convinced democrats in the full sense of the term, they were at least desirous of retaining the good will of the democratic powers which seemed to be in command of the world's destiny at the moment.

During much of the 1920s Japan's international policy was on the whole conciliatory, as illustrated by the Washington Conference of 1921–1922, which produced a Naval Arms Limitation Agreement, a Nine-Power "Open Door" Treaty concerning China, and a Four-Power Pacific Pact. The Japanese accepted a limitation of Japan's battleship tonnage to a figure three-fifths that of the United States and of Britain, and agreed to terminate their alliance of twenty years' standing with Great Britain. The Four-Power Pact which replaced the alliance was based on nothing more substantial than the promise of friendly consultation on problems of the Pacific and pledges to maintain the status quo in regard to fortifications in this area. The Nine-Power Treaty, affirming the principle of the Open Door, actually restored nothing to China, but the Japanese delegates, in private conferences with the Chinese, promised that their government would withdraw its troops from Shantung and return the administration of the province to China, leaving Japanese interests represented only in the form of private capital investments. This action was carried out as promised before the close of 1922. Many Japanese businessmen were convinced that the cultivation of friendly relations with the sprawling mainland state would pay far bigger dividends than would the seizure of territory by force and at the risk of inviting a boycott of Japanese trade.

Promising as the liberal-democratic trends in Japan were, they did not become vigorous enough to extinguish deeply entrenched reactionary forces which eventually led the country to disaster. The failure of the liberal elements must be attributed in part to external factors. The disillusionment and cynicism that became general in the postwar years throughout the West had their counterpart in Japan. The trends of international politics did not indicate a substantial gain for democratic processes. The rise of fascism in Europe demonstrated a powerful movement in the opposite direction. Almost everywhere, virulent nationalism seemed to be in the ascendancy, obscuring the hope of a cooperative world order. With democracy on the defensive or in retreat in the countries of the West, where it was indigenous, it could scarcely be expected to triumph easily in such a nation as Japan, where it was a recent innovation with no cultural or institutional roots.

The counterinfluence of nationalism

The sensibilities of the Japanese were irritated by the discrimination they encountered in the form of tariffs against their goods and immigration laws against their citizens. In 1924 the United States Congress passed an Oriental Exclusion law, placing Asians in a category inferior to that of the most backward Europeans. The United States was not alone in such a policy, and many Japanese began to feel that the great white nations were determined never to treat them as equals. The high tariff policies of the United States and other Western powers were another disturbing factor, producing psychological as well as economic repercussions. By 1930 the larger share of Japan's foreign trade, both export and import, was with the United States, with a trade balance decidedly favorable to the latter country. Protectionists in the United States alleged that American standards were threatened by competition from "cheap" Japanese labor. Yet the chief Japanese import was raw cotton and Japan's leading export to the United States was raw silk, an item hardly competitive with American industry.

Discriminatory polices of Western nations

In the last analysis, the defeat of liberal forces was due to deficiencies in the structure of Japanese society and in the economic system. The fundamental problem of creating a stable economy and satisfactory living standards for the majority of the people was never solved, and the problem became steadily more acute as the population continued to increase at the rate of 1 million a year. In spite of the expansion of commerce and manufacture, Japan's per capita income by 1928 was equal only to about one-eighth of that of the United States. Japan's prosperity, such as it was, depended upon participation in a world market that was subjected to more and more intense competition. Foreign trade received a severe blow when the price of silk, her leading article of export, declined about 75 percent between 1925 and 1934. To compensate for the collapse of the silk market, Japanese manufacturers stepped up the production of cotton cloth, but in this field they were bucking old and strongly established competitors. The Great Depression struck Japan just when the country seemed to be pulling out of a slump. Between 1929 and 1931 Japan's foreign commerce fell off by one-half, while rural and industrial indebtedness swelled to a figure in excess of the national income.

The highly inequitable distribution of wealth within Japan made for an artificial stratification of classes and interests that was unfavorable to the development of a democratic society. The middle class was too small and insecure to be a very effective liberal force. The great body of farmers and laborers had been ushered out of the discipline of Tokugawa feudalism into the discipline of an efficient centralized bureaucracy, without ever being emancipated from their traditions of docility and the acceptance of direction from above. Aspects of a feudal mentality persisted within the nation after feudalism had been replaced by a modern capitalist order. Industry, commerce, and finance were concentrated in the hands of a few huge trusts, known collectively as the Zaibatsu, each controlled by a closely integrated family group and almost beyond the reach of public supervision. The Zaibatsu not only dominated the economic picture but also were affiliated with bureaucrats in the government and deeply influenced political parties.

The flimsy foundations of Japanese liberalism are revealed in the history and character of political parties during the 1920s and early 1930s, by which time two competing parties had risen to prominence. The Seiyukai was a descendant of the old Liberal party of Itagaki, but it exemplified a metamorphosis of liberalism into something almost its opposite. Itagaki's party, largely agrarian from the beginning, had passed under the domination of great landlords in place of the small tenants. To this conservative agrarian element was added the leading representative of big business, the house of Mitsui. Thus the Seiyukai constituted an alliance of landlords, monopoly capitalists, and bureaucrats, and it had connections also with the armed services. While the party favored constitutional methods, it was extremely conservative on domestic issues and rabidly expansionist on foreign policy, advocating forceful measures to improve Japan's economic position.

In 1927 an opposition party to the Seiyukai was formed, incorporating remnants of the old Progressive party of Count Okuma. This new party, the Minseito, was backed primarily by industrial rather than agrarian interests, and favored policies conducive to the health of the business community, including social-welfare measures to relieve working-class discontent. But while it was progressive in comparison with the Seiyukai, it could hardly be considered truly liberal in composition or principles. It was supported by one of the great Zaibatsu houses (the Mitsubishi) and was as intensely nationalistic as the Seiyukai, differing from the latter chiefly on the question of which methods would best advance the country's interests.

A hopeful interlude, of brief duration, began when a Minseito cabinet came into office in 1929 and attempted to reverse the "strong" policy of the previous ministry, which had thrown troops into Shantung province as the Chinese Nationalist forces advanced toward Peking. The impact of the world depression upon Japan's economy, however, jeopardized the position of the moderate Minseito cabinet, and the assassination of the premier by a fanatic not only weakened the cabinet but also gave ominous warning of the length to which intransigent nationalist groups would go in promoting their own cause. Then, in September 1931, the Japanese army stationed in Manchuria took matters into its own hands by attacking Chinese troops. By the following February, Manchuria had become the "independent" state of Manchukuo under Japanese auspices, and in 1933 Japan, branded publicly as an aggressor, defiantly withdrew from the League of Nations.

Throughout the 1930s liberal elements in Japan never entirely abandoned their struggle to hold back the tide of militant nationalism. But when the issues became international, as in the struggle over Manchuria and, later, in the war against China, patriotic sentiments blunted the edge of popular opposition. The only groups strong enough to challenge the militarists were the financial and business interests, and these were easily seduced by the promise of profits in the offing. Most of the business leaders had come to regard expansion as essential to Japan's economy. They hoped it could be carried out peacefully and painlessly, but they had helped to build, and had profited from building, a war machine that would be extremely difficult to hold within bounds.

Of course, the primary center of aggressive truculence lay in the military services themselves, particularly the army. As previously pointed out, the Japanese army was composed largely of peasants, an unfortunate class, whose legitimate discontents were, under skillful direction, sublimated into an unreasoned and frenzied patriotism. After the Meiji period the army officers also were drawn chiefly from small towns and rural communities, and they lacked the temperate and relatively broad-minded attitude that had distinguished the samurai leaders. Gradually a "young officer" group developed an ideology of its own, which began to permeate the rank and file. Idealists in the worst sense of the term, these soldier fanatics preached absolute loyalty to the emperor and affirmed that Japan, of divine origin and superior to other nations, had the right to extend its rule over other parts of the world. At the same time, reflecting their peasant affinities, they demanded agrarian reforms or even nationalization of the land and castigated both capitalists and politicians as selfish and corrupt. Their program, a medley of radical and reactionary principles, aimed to make Japan an invincible state, solidly unified under the imperial will, which they claimed to represent most faithfully. Although it has been likened to fascism, the "Imperial Way" proclaimed by the ultranationalists undoubtedly had more in common with the ancient Japanese concepts of the state as a patriarchal society and of the superiority of government by men to government by law.

The conquest of Manchuria as a prelude to war against China

The creation of the puppet state of Manchukuo in 1932 and its development under Japanese management did not yield the substantial benefits to Japan's economy that had been anticipated. To exploit the coal, iron, and oil resources of Manchuria required an extensive outlay of capital, and Japanese capital was not readily forthcoming, partly because of the fear that industry in Manchukuo would compete with Japan's and partly because of the rigid governmental controls imposed upon capital and industry in the puppet state. As plans matured for making Manchuria not simply a source of raw materials for Japan but a center of heavy industry for Asia, it became apparent that the assurance of access to a wide market area was imperative. Hence, Japanese expansionists attempted to convert China's northeastern provinces into an "autonomous" region, linked economically with Manchukuo. Finally they enlarged their objectives to encompass the creation of a "Greater East Asia Co-Prosperity Sphere." Instead of alleviating Japan's economy, this aggressive imperialistic policy saddled it with

Japanese Troops in the Walled City of Mukden, Manchukuo (Manchuria)

The Beginning of the Occupation in Japan. American troops entering Tokyo September 8, 1945. The devastating effects of the bombing raids are plainly evident.

additional burdens, entailing larger and large expenditures for armaments in support of a program that had no foreseeable limits and was bound to meet with resistance at every point.

The role of Japan in World War II, into which its conflict with China was merged, is discussed elsewhere in this volume. Japan's surrender in 1945 was the prelude to a new phase of history, in many ways different from anything experienced in the past. Never before had the Japanese nation been defeated in war and never before had the country been occupied by a foreign power. The occupation of a conquered country was also a new experience for the United States. At the very least it can be said that both the Japanese and the Americans conducted themselves in such a way as to produce a minimum of friction in relationships which were necessarily difficult.

For six and a half years, authority in Japan was nominally held by the Far Eastern Commission in Washington and the advisory Allied Council for Japan in Tokyo. Actually it was held by General Douglas MacArthur as Supreme Commander for the Allied Powers (SCAP) under orders from Washington. From beginning to end the Japanese Occupation was an undertaking and a responsibility of the United States. Military rule was indirect, however, and was exercised through the regular Japanese government, which had not disintegrated with Japan's military defeat. The emperor accepted the surrender terms, called upon his subjects to cooperate with the occupying forces, and served as the connecting link between the old order and the new. In spite of the relative unimportance of the emperor politically in modern times, his role was of great value psychologically in

The defeat of Japan in World War II

The American Occupation

providing a symbol of continuity when so much of the past seemed to have been destroyed forever.

Japan's military defeat and subsequent occupation by the conqueror's troops marked the third time in the country's history that it was subjected to strong doses of foreign influence. Unlike the earlier occasions, the Japanese were not acting voluntarily. But although forced to accept changes, they again succeeded to a remarkable degree in adapting these to their own social and cultural traditions and in using them to promote renewed growth and fresh achievements.

One of the first major tasks of the Occupation authorities was to furnish Japan with a new constitution grounded in democratic principles. A draft prepared by a group of Japanese consultants was replaced by an American document, which was approved by the emperor and formally promulgated by him in the Diet in November 1946. It went into effect in May of the following year. Breaking cleanly with tradition and with the Constitution of 1889, it declared that sovereignty lay with the Japanese people and left the emperor with only formal powers like those of the British monarch. The new Constitution contained an elaborate Bill of Rights, in which to the normal civil liberties were added such benefits as the right to work and to bargain collectively, social equality, and equality of the sexes. Universal adult suffrage was established, with a bicameral Diet, and a cabinet responsible to the House of Representatives. The Constitution also incorporated the American principles of separation of church and state and judicial review of acts of the legislature. Particularly arresting was Article 9, which declared that "the Japanese people forever renounce war as a sovereign right of the nation" and that "land, sea, and air forces, as well as other war potential, will never be maintained." Its highly utopian flavor made the new Constitution one of the most remarkable documents of its kind ever issued. If its principles could have been carried into active and complete realization, they would have made Japan a more advanced democratic nation than the United States.

While introducing political changes the Occupation authorities projected a far-reaching reform program. In conformity with the policy of demilitarization, an extensive purge was conducted to remove from office and from teaching positions all persons suspected of ultranationalist proclivities. A direct attack was launched against the Zaibatsu groups with the passage of an Antimonopoly Law and the creation of a Fair Trade Commission. Pursuant to the liberal economic provisions of the new Constitution, labor organizations were encouraged. Between 1945 and 1950 membership in labor unions increased from 5,000 to more than 6,000,000 and the government enacted a comprehensive labor welfare code. Perhaps most significant among the reforms was that which dealt with the long-neglected problem of land ownership. An agrarian law of 1946, providing for government purchase of tracts from absentee landlords and for the sale of these tracts to tenant farmers at moderate prices, led to a sweeping transformation of agricultural land ownership.

The character of the Occupation and its accompanying reforms were clearly stamped with the complex personality of General MacArthur. Filled with a strong sense of mission that sometimes made him arrogant, he was nevertheless capable of sound judgment, and he strove vigorously and sincerely to promote what he believed to be Japan's long-range best interests. He successfully opposed demands to abolish the imperial office, realizing its value both as a symbolic link to the past and as a vehicle for legitimatizing institutional reforms. Honored as a military hero in America, MacArthur came to be looked upon almost as a demigod in Japan. His policies, however, were sometimes impractical and even contradictory. He insisted on the disestablishment of Shinto as a state religion to further the objective of complete religious freedom, yet he entertained hopes of converting the Japanese to Christianity. The purge directed against militarists and ultranationalists caught some liberals whose only fault seemed to be their adherence to ideals boldly announced in the new Constitution. Labor was prodded into organizing and collective bargaining, but strikes were restricted by the Occupation government. MacArthur took particular pride in his campaign to promote free enterprise by breaking up the huge Zaibatsu combinations. The ultimate results of this trust-busting program could hardly have been foreseen and were considerably different from what MacArthur intended. The efficient organizational structures that Mitsui and Mitsubishi had developed were, with their dissolution, replaced by a rigid bureaucracy created by the Occupation to enforce competition and control foreign trade. Clumsily and inflexibly managed, it temporarily disrupted the economy and hampered recovery. But the precedent of a centralized bureaucracy, remaining as a legacy of the Occupation,

Destruction of Japanese Naval Weapons. Miniature submarines at the naval base at Kure are being destroyed. In its new constitution, Japan renounced the right to make war.

eventually proved useful in speeding Japan's economic growth. The Japanese government, which before the war had exercised relatively weak control over the private sector, at the end of the Occupation stepped into SCAP's role as chief economic planner and director. Although the great trusts were not formally reconstituted, Japan acquired a centrally guided rather than a laissez-faire economy. Beginning in 1948, the economic restraints imposed by SCAP were gradually relaxed. Occupation policy, reflecting the pressures of global power politics, shifted from reform to retrenchment and recovery. The program of decentralizing industry halted with the realization that if Japan's industrial strength were preserved it could be an asset to the West in the Cold War with the Communist powers.

The Peace of 1951 and end of the Occupation

A peace treaty between the United States and Japan was negotiated at San Francisco in September 1951, and ratified the following April. It was also signed by forty-eight other countries, not including the Soviet Union, however, which remained technically in a state of war with Japan until 1956. The peace settlement, although it ended the Occupation and restored formal independence to Japan, was very drastic territorially. Depriving the nation of all its empire, the treaty reduced Japan to the same area it had held at the time of Commodore Perry's visit in 1853, although its population was now three times as great. The peace treaty, supplemented by a security treaty, acknowledged Japan's right to arm for "self-defense" and authorized the stationing of foreign troops (meaning American) in Japan for the defense of the country.

Political trends in postwar Japan: The Liberal Democratic party

Encouraged by a democratic constitution, numerous political parties sprang into being, but the persisting tradition of loyalty to personalities, kinship groups, or local interests made it difficult to establish them on a nationwide basis with broad popular support. In 1955 two major organizations, successors respectively of prewar Seiyukai and Minseito, merged to form the Liberal Democratic party, which has held a predominant position ever since. In spite of its name the party is conservative, and its continual success reflects the conservative bias of the majority of voters. Deriving support from the business community, old-line bureaucrats, rural constituents—which are overrepresented in the Diet—and civil service officials, it has operated as a coalition of factions without a clear program or well-organized and active membership. In power for two and a half decades, the party became in effect the Japanese Establishment, nourishing the country's expanding economy and maintaining its ties with the United States. Revelation that officials had accepted bribes from Lockheed Corporation shook the party in 1974. The prime minister, Kakuei Tanaka, was forced to resign and later was tried and imprisoned. Bickering and rivalry among factions reached such a point in 1980 that an opposition coalition led by the Socialists won a vote of no confidence in the ministry. Parliament was dissolved for the second time within eight months, but in the election of June 1980 the Liberal Democratic party was returned to power with a comfortable majority. Unpopular government policies, scandals in high places, and even economic recessions have not sufficed to dislodge the LDP, largely because unprecedented material prosperity came about under a succession of conservative administrations.

The principal political opposition has come from the Socialists, who in 1955 won a third of the seats in the lower house of Parliament but were unable to repeat this performance. Groups challenging the dominant party have diverged widely in aims, and opposition parties have been plagued by factional disputes. A small Japanese Communist party, aligned neither with Moscow nor Peking, minimizes radical ideology and attempts to woo the electorate with such innocuous slogans as "Cover drainage ditches" and "Build more day nurseries." At the extreme right the Clean Government party, political arm of a militant Buddhist sect, has appealed primarily to middle- and lower-income groups.

To what extent political democracy has taken root in Japan is a matter for debate. The Constitution, organs of government, judicial and electoral processes clearly meet democratic standards. The press is free and of high caliber. At the same time, Japanese political habits and psychology carry overtones of an earlier tradition. The tenacity of local loyalties and personality cults—a preference for government "by men" rather than "by law"—has prevented the rise of national parties with clearly defined policies, or even the development of a national political consciousness. Without presenting a distinctive platform on which to stand or fall the LDP has been able to keep the reins of office by balancing the claims of competing groups. Minorities and opposition parties, in spite of their poor showing at the polls, are not without political input. Their pressure is sometimes reflected in initiatives of the ruling party, which respects the Japanese fondness for reaching a consensus acceptable to all rather than a victory for one contestant.

The economic difficulties confronting Japan immediately after its surrender seemed practically insurmountable. Before the close of hostilities almost one-third of the homes in Japan's urban areas were destroyed by air attacks, and the direct economic loss caused by the war was staggering. Japan was shorn of its empire, industrial production had fallen 80 percent below the 1937 level, foreign trade stood at zero, and the country depended upon imports even for foodstuffs. Viewed against this dismal background, Japan's economic recovery and advance have been spectacular. By 1953 the index of production was 50 percent above the level of the mid-1930s, and it continued upward, with textiles, metal goods, and machinery leading the way. During the 1950s economic productivity doubled; in the next decade it overtook that of England, France, and West Germany to become the third largest in the world. By the late 1970s Japan's gross national product was more than half that of the United States. A remarkable aspect of this economic expansion was that Japan both competed successfully in long-established industries and also pioneered in new fields. It became the world's largest shipbuilder, exported steel, light and heavy machinery, and gained a commanding position in such areas as chemicals, synthetics, optics, electronics, and computer technology. The Japanese outpaced most Western nations in the development of mass transit facilities, especially railways, famous in recent years for their "bullet trains." By the 1980 experiments were under way with magnetically levitated "floating trains," reportedly capable of speeds in excess of 300 miles an hour. Although the farm population declined to about 18 percent of the total, through the application of scientific methods Japan was able to increase agricultural output by 50 percent.

Explanation of Japan's rise to prosperity

Several factors explain Japan's seemingly miraculous rise from a condition of prostration to one of dizzying prosperity. First, in spite of devastating losses from the war, the Japanese retained their technical proficiency, labor force, and traditions of hard work. A determination to recover lost ground and to overtake and surpass the West became a national obsession, eliciting self-sacrifice and mitigating disputes between management and underpaid labor. Employees of large corporations served them with a loyalty like that of the old feudal samurai to his lord. Statistics reporting the growth of the GNP were scanned with the avidity devoted in more leisurely societies to the sports pages. Postwar Japan achieved an extremely high ratio of savings to earnings, in some years amounting to 30 percent. A second factor helping to stimulate recovery was American financial aid, not only during the Occupation but especially by the purchase of goods and services for the Korean conflict. A third factor was the initiative of the government in stimulating and guiding the growth of an essen-

The Mitsubishi Shipyards. A Greek tanker is under construction.

Electronics Industry of Japan. Mass-production lines of television sets at the Matsushita Electrical Industrial Company plant in Ibaragi. Better than 90 percent of Japanese families own television sets. The Japanese electronics industry has also become a major factor in the American market for such products.

tially private-enterprise economy. The government encouraged capital investment by incentive tax and loan policies, operated an Economic Planning Agency to compile data and predict market trends, and through a Ministry of International Trade and Industry took the lead in directing industrial development. The Japanese economic system, combining governmental guidance with private ownership and initiative, has been called the "most successful economic model in the world in recent years."[1] Probably the most important asset of all was—paradoxically—the defeat and elimination of Japan's military establishment, which had systematically drained the country's resources. During a crucial period Japan enjoyed the distinction of being the only great industrial nation operating on a peace economy instead of a war economy. This situation is unlikely to continue indefinitely. Japan's strength in conventional weapons is already greater than it was at the peak of World War II and the country has moved up to seventh rank in military spending. Still, the Defense Agency has never consumed more than 1 percent of the GNP or more than 8 percent of the national budget. In 1969 the government allotted over three times as much to social security, education, and the promotion of science as to defense.

[1] E. O. Reischauer, *The Japanese*, p. 194.

Japanese society has been profoundly affected by the tremendous expansion of the nation's economy. A continual rise in the standard of living—the highest in Asia and approaching that of Western Europe—is illustrated by successive changes reported in the traditional Japanese conception of the "three sacred treasures" desired by every household. The mirror, jewel, and sword of ancient times gave way to the electric refrigerator, washing machine, and television set. By 1970, 90 percent of the families possessed these items, and they aspired to a color TV, "room cooler," and motor car; or even to the luxury of central heating, an electric cooking range, and a vacation cottage. Rising inflation and a decline in the rate of industrial growth that accompanied the world recession of 1974–1976 forced a lowering of expectations and a reassessment of goals. Far from solving all of Japan's problems, prosperity augmented some of them. A staggering rate of population increase, which brought the total to 115 million by 1978, has apparently been successfully halted, as it has in China. But half the inhabitants are concentrated on 2 percent of the land, the bulk of them in an urban belt stretching from Tokyo to Osaka. Tokyo, with nearly 9 million people, became the largest city in the world—until it yielded this dubious honor to Shanghai. Tokyo is still one of the dirtiest, noisiest, and most congested of cities. With population density in urban areas three times as great as in the United States, Japan faces a major problem of air and water pollution. While industrial progress has created large fortunes, it has done little to raise wages in the small shops and home factories that still employ a majority of the working force. Although Japan's GNP is the third largest in the world, the nation ranks only sixteenth in per capita income. Social services have lagged behind the need for better roads, sewers, environmental protection, and housing. Most residents of Tokyo live in tiny two-room apartments. One precarious element in Japan's situation is its dependence on external markets. Japan is the world's largest importer of oil, coal, iron ore, lead, copper, zinc, lumber, wood, cotton, and many other raw materials. It must also import about half of its food, including almost all feed grains, although it has become self-sufficient in rice. The Japanese depend on foreign fuels for 85 percent of their energy supply, 60 percent of which is provided by Persian Gulf oil. The development of nuclear power to the point where, by 1976, Japan ranked fourth in nuclear-produced kilowatts of electricity, has encountered popular resistance because of the hazards involved in this technology. In exploiting solar energy Japan has forged ahead, equipping more than 2 million houses with solar water heaters, in comparison with some 30,000 in the United States.

Japanese society, like politics and the economy, is a blend of innovation and tradition. In income distribution and in providing opportunities for advancement it has become more equalitarian than most societies. The old feudal class structure has disappeared along with

Pollution in Industrial Japan. Kawasaki is a heavily industrialized city in the Tokyo-Yokohama Industrial Zone. The works of numerous heavy and chemical industry companies are located here.

Innovation blended with tradition

titles of nobility, and pedigrees are no longer important. But to a considerable extent society is still hierarchical, with status dependent not upon birth but upon identification with a group, rank in an organization, or, especially, educational credentials. Japan is one of the most literate and most educated nations in the world, its people benefiting from superior instructional standards in the lower and middle schools. Higher education is expensive and deficient in breadth and flexibility, but a degree from a prestigious institution, especially Tokyo University, is normally a stepping stone to a leadership career in business or politics. The persistence of paternalistic and patriarchal traditions tends to inhibit the development of individuality, while at the same time offering the individual a degree of security lacking in less closely organized societies. For example, although labor is much more fully unionized than in the United States, strikes are rarer. Employees of large firms—comparatively well paid, assured of gradual advancement, often kept on the payroll when no longer needed, or trained for other jobs to keep pace with technological change—develop a sense of identity with and loyalty to the corporate entity. The preservation of social harmony is valued above the attainment of abstract justice, and litigation is infrequent. Japan has only one-fifteenth as many lawyers per capita as the United States. There are unfortunate exceptions to the laudable ideal of equality of opportunity and merit as a determinant of status. About 2 percent of the population, known as *burakumin* or "hamlet people" and possibly a carryover from feudal times, are treated as outcasts. Although physically indistinguishable from other

*Japan's economic
ascendancy in Southeast
Asia*

Japanese and equal before the law, they are generally socially ostracized. Another exception to the homogeneity of Japanese society is the failure to assimilate a resident Korean minority of some 600,000.

The position of women in Japan, reflecting the persistence of an antiquated feudal mentality in spite of constitutional and legal changes, constitutes the most glaring failure in the implementation of the democratic ideal. Women have not been accepted in significant numbers in positions of leadership, and they are still exploited economically and in family relationships. In 1972, although 57 percent of all factory workers were women, their average wage was less than half that of male workers. Regarded as temporary employees and forced to retire at an early age, women are not permitted to share in the benefits extended to labor by management. While the claim of one critic that Japanese women "are virtually as fully oppressed as they have been since the victory of the warrior culture in the Kamakura period of the twelfth century" is an exaggeration, it is doubtless true that they "continue as unrecognized and undervalued servants of Japan's prosperity."[2]

Since World War II Japan's foreign policy has been conditioned by two main factors: a struggle for economic recovery and ascendancy, and a close relationship with the United States. Striving to dispel the hostility and distrust remaining as a legacy from its imperialist era, Japan made generous reparations settlements with the small states of Southeast Asia that its armies had overrun, and contributed substantially to various development programs. When the Asian Development Bank was inaugurated in 1966, a Japanese became the first president of this regional organization. Japan's foreign aid, although extensive, has been criticized for being geared more to its own economic needs than to those of the recipient countries. Most of it has been in the form of loans, under terms profitable to Japanese investors and traders. Japan's successful penetration of the market in Indonesia, Malaysia, Singapore, the Philippines, and Thailand aroused resentment throughout Southeast Asia. The image of the "ugly American" gave way to one inspired by Japanese businessmen, bankers, and technicians, disparagingly referred to as "honorary whites" or "Yellow Yankees." But it is doubtful that Japan, through economic superiority, will dominate Southeast Asia completely, partly because the Japanese are sensitive to accusations of neocolonialism and, more importantly, because the Southeast Asian market is not adequate to fulfill their needs. To reap full benefit from their specialized and advanced technology they must have access to high-income areas, such as Australia, western Europe, and North America. In 1965 Japan's share of the Asian market was only 17 percent. It will undoubtedly grow larger, especially as Chinese-Japanese trade

---

[2]Joan Mellen, *The Waves at Genji's Door: Japan through the Cinema*, p. 27.

increases. Meanwhile the Japanese are seeking other areas for investment and are already active in Latin America.

Japan found it more difficult to reach an understanding with the Soviet Union than with any other of her former enemies. An agreement signed by the two countries in October 1956 restored diplomatic relations and paved the way for Japan's entrance into the United Nations, but it was not a formal treaty of peace. There have been frequent disputes—over Japanese prisoners of war never accounted for by Russia, fishing rights, and Japanese claims in the Kuril Islands, all of which are held by Russia. Russian attempts, beginning in the early 1970s, to enlist Japan's help in developing Siberian reserves of oil and gas have not met with much success.

The American presence continued to be felt in Japan by virtue of the Security Treaty of 1951, which pledged the two countries to mutual consultation and allowed the United States to retain military bases in Japan. Successive Japanese administrations followed Washington's lead in international diplomacy so dutifully that some critics accused the foreign ministry of being "the Asian Department of the United States State Department." Popular resentment provoked riotous demonstrations against renewal of the Security Treaty in 1960 and again in 1970, and escalation of the war in Indochina further intensified anti-American feeling. Friction between Japan and the United States, never severe enough to invalidate the relationship, was alleviated by the return to Japanese sovereignty, in 1968 and 1972 respectively, of the Bonin and the Ryukyu Islands, which had been heavily fortified and used as bomber bases in the Korean and Vietnam wars. The terms of the transfer agreement called for the removal of nuclear weapons but left the United States the right to continue to use the bases.

Relations with the Soviet Union

Japanese-American relations

Automobile Assembly Line, Toyota Motor Company. In 1980 the Japanese automobile industry became the largest in the world.

Changes in the
relationship

Significant changes in the semipartnership between the United States and Japan resulted from the latter's growing economic strength, which stimulated dissatisfaction with a condition of dependence. The balance of trade between the two countries shifted in Japan's favor, by 1976 yielding an annual surplus of $5 billion and continuing upward. Moreover, as the islanders gained pre-eminence in specialized and sophisticated technologies, the United States in its trade with them played a "colonial" role, providing grains, lumber, cotton, and other raw materials in exchange for steel, machinery, cameras, watches, electronic components for radio and television, and innumerable other manufactures ranging from pianos to barber chairs. American automobile sales in Japan matched only a small fraction of Japanese car sales in the United States. A continual trade deficit, bringing the prospect of falling profits and rising unemployment, worried United States manufacturers. The president of Zenith Radio Corporation warned that the American consumer-electronics industry faced a threat "every bit as real as the threat of extinction faced by the coyotes, the bald eagles, the seals, the alligators, and the rattlesnakes." While Japanese exports were aided by government subsidies, the main reasons for their success were the innovative initiative of management and the high productivity of Japanese labor.

The "Nixon shock"

President Nixon's announcement in the summer of 1971 of his intention to visit Peking the following year surprised and angered the Japanese. Washington had pressured them into close ties with the Nationalist regime in Taiwan and had stressed the necessity of joint action in dealing with mainland China, yet had not consulted with nor informed them in advance of the United States' dramatic reversal of policy. Beyond suffering a temporary loss of face, the Japanese now felt impelled to mend their own diplomatic fences. In September 1972 Prime Minister Tanaka made his pilgrimage to a summit meeting in Peking, offered an apology to the Chinese people for Japan's past misconduct, and—in advance of the United States—established full diplomatic relations between Japan and the People's Republic of China. The Chou-Tanaka joint statement issued in Peking was a masterpiece of diplomatic finesse and graceful ambiguity which laid a basis for "peace and friendship" without a formal peace treaty and with important issues left unresolved. Japan recognized that Taiwan "ought to" belong to China, withdrew its ambassador from Taipei, but replaced its embassy there with unofficial liaison offices which effectively served the same purposes. (The United States adopted a similar procedure half a dozen years later.)

The "oil shock" and its
consequences

Japan's foreign relations have inevitably been affected by the recurring crises of the 1970s. Closely following the "Nixon shock" was the "oil shock" of 1974, the quadrupling of oil prices by OPEC. It struck no nation more severely than Japan, totally dependent on outside sources for this essential commodity. The recession following the oil crisis slowed the economic growth rate, brought the threat of unemployment—negligible heretofore—and caused the Japanese to re-examine national priorities and to question whether the "miracle of Japan" was reality or illusion. A factor hampering economic recovery was, ironically, the strength of the yen in comparison with the dollar and other depreciating Western currencies. The yen's high valuation made goods produced in Japan expensive (although products were exported at lower than the domestic prices), and the Japanese found they were being undersold by such Asian competitors as South Korea, Taiwan, and Hong Kong. Many small firms were forced out of business; in 1977 more than 18,000 bankruptcies were reported in Japan. To alleviate the situation the government promised to spend more on public works and, to help reduce huge trade surpluses with the United States and western Europe, sought to expand the market for exports and investments in less developed areas. In February 1978 Japan signed a $20-billion eight-year trade agreement with China, followed six months later by a formal peace treaty with the People's Republic.

In seeking new economic opportunities the Japanese have also been mindful of political and strategic factors, realizing that a major conflict in the Far East would place them in grave jeopardy. The nation that for centuries remained in almost complete isolation is today one of the least isolated, dependent for its survival upon reciprocal relations with many other countries. The Japanese have stepped warily around the Peking-Moscow confrontation, and they sense the danger, uncomfortably close, of eruption in a bitterly divided Korea—especially since neither of the two divisions exhibits friendly feelings toward Japan. Paralleling an active economic role in Southeast Asia, Japan has attempted to strengthen diplomatic ties there. In 1977 Prime Minister Fukuda strongly endorsed ASEAN (Association of Southeast Asian Nations, comprising the Philippines, Indonesia, Singapore, Malaysia, and Thailand) and announced a program of $1 billion to support regional projects. Premier Zenko Suzuki, for his first trip abroad after taking office in the fall of 1980, chose a tour of ASEAN capitals rather then the customary courtesy visit to Washington, D.C. Russian attempts either to woo Japan into partnership or to keep the nation isolated have failed. While cultivating relations both with China and with non-Communist Asian countries, Japan has remained within the United States defense system. Even the opposition parties in Japan no longer denounce the Security Treaty of 1951. There is pressure from the United States and from elements within Japan to convert the Defense Agency into a force with offensive capability. In 1978 the Japanese foreign minister asserted that defensive *nuclear* weapons were not prohibited by Article 9 of the Constitution. However, a drive to rearm Japan or take it down the nuclear road would meet with resistance because of the strong antimilitarist sentiment of a majority of the Japanese people.

SELECTED READINGS (*See also Readings for Chapters 23 and 32*)

• *Items so designated are available in paperback editions.*

CHINA

• Barnett, A. Doak, *China and the Major Powers in East Asia,* Washington, D.C., 1977. A careful study of recent international relations.

Bianco, Lucien, *Origins of the Chinese Revolution, 1915–1949,* tr. Muriel Bell, Stanford, 1971. A brilliant interpretive summary.

Brugger, Bill, *Contemporary China,* New York, 1977. An impressive historical interpretation of the period 1942–1973.

• Ch'en, Jerome, *Mao and the Chinese Revolution,* New York, 1965.

• Clubb, O. E., *Twentieth-Century China,* 3d ed., New York, 1978. One of the best surveys of recent Chinese history.

Davies, J. P., Jr., *Dragon by the Tail: American, British, Japanese, and Russian Encounters with China and One Another,* New York, 1972. An American diplomat's jolting account of bungling and intrigue.

De Crespigny, R. R. C., *China This Century,* New York, 1975. A concise introduction.

Dulles, F. R., *American Policy toward Communist China—the Historical Record: 1949–1969,* New York, 1972.

Fisher, Lois, *A Peking Diary: A Personal Account of Modern China,* New York, 1979. Intimate glimpses of lives of the common people.

• Floyd, David, *Mao against Khrushchev: A Short History of the Sino-Soviet Conflict,* New York, 1964. A readable account.

Gittings, John, *The World and China, 1922–1972,* New York, 1974. Informative for Sino-Soviet relations.

• Griffith, W. E., *The Sino-Soviet Rift,* Cambridge, Mass., 1964. An analysis with pertinent documents.

• Hinton, H. C., *China's Turbulent Quest: An Analysis of China's Foreign Relations since 1949,* Bloomington, Ind., 1972. Accurate; coldly objective.

Hsiung, J. C., *Ideology and Practice: The Evolution of Chinese Communism,* New York, 1970. Valuable for an understanding of the Cultural Revolution.

• Isaacs, H. R., *The Tragedy of the Chinese Revolution,* Stanford, 1964.

• Larkin, B. D., *China and Africa, 1949–1970: The Foreign Policy of the People's Republic of China,* Berkeley, 1973.

• Milton, David, and Nancy Milton, *The Wind Will Not Subside: Years in Revolutionary China—1964–1969.* New York, 1976. Vivid account of the Cultural Revolution.

Selden, Mark, *The Yenan Way in Revolutionary China,* Cambridge, Mass., 1971. Scholarly treatment of the "Border Region," 1935–1947.

• Shabad, Theodore, *China's Changing Map: National and Regional Development, 1949–71,* rev. ed., New York, 1972. A valuable reference work.

Sharmon, Lyon, *Sun Yat-sen: His Life and Its Meaning,* New York, 1934. A critical biography.

• Snow, Edgar, *Red Star over China,* New York, 1938. A classic account of the Communists' early years of struggle.

- Terrill, Ross, *800,000,000: The Real China*, New York, 1972. A vivid and discriminating account by an Australian journalist-scholar.
- Topping, Seymour, *Journey between Two Chinas*, New York, 1972. An able narrative of the Communist Revolution.
- Tuchman, Barbara, *Stilwell and the American Experience in China, 1911– 1945*, New York, 1972.
- Waller, D. J., *The Government and Politics of Communist China*, Garden City, N.Y., 1971. Concise and informative.
- Wang Gungwu, *China and the World since 1949; The Impact of Independence, Modernity, and Revolution*, New York, 1977. An able, brief survey.

  Wilbur, C. M., *Sun Yat-sen: Frustrated Patriot*, New York, 1976. Provides fresh insights.

  Wilson, Dick, *The Long March: The Epic of Chinese Communist Survival*, New York, 1971.

  ———, ed., *Mao Tse-tung in the Scales of History*, New York, 1977. Ten essays of high quality.

  Zupnick, Elliot, *China's Economic Development: The Interplay of Scarcity and Ideology*, Ann Arbor, 1976. A penetrating study.

JAPAN

  Allen, G. C., *Japan's Economic Expansion*, New York, 1965.

  Axelbank, Albert, *Black Star over Japan: Rising Forces of Militarism*, New York, 1972. An alarming prognosis.
- Benedict, Ruth, *The Chrysanthemum and the Sword*, New York, 1967. A classic analysis of prewar Japanese society.

  Blaker, Michael, *Japanese International Negotiating Style*, New York, 1977. A study of diplomacy between 1895 and Pearl Harbor.

  Brzezinski, Z. K., *The Fragile Blossom: Crisis and Change in Japan*, New York, 1972. An analysis of Japan's economic, political, and strategic position.

  Buck, Pearl, *The People of Japan*, New York, 1966. A personal account.
- Burks, A. W., *The Government of Japan*, 2d ed., New York, 1964.

  Butow, R. J. C., *Japan's Decision to Surrender*, Stanford, 1954.

  ———, *Tojo and the Coming of the War*, Princeton, 1961.

  Emmerson, J. K., *Arms, Yen and Power: The Japanese Dilemma*, New York, 1971. Balanced, informative, optimistic.
- Ishida Takeshi, *Japanese Society*, New York, 1971.

  Kawai Kazuo, *Japan's American Interlude*, Chicago, 1960.
- Maki, J. M., *Government and Politics in Japan: The Road to Democracy*, New York, 1962.
- Mellen, Joan, *The Waves at Genji's Door: Japan through the Cinema*, New York, 1976. Provides a feminist critique of Japanese character and society.

  Minear, R. H., *Victors' Justice: The Tokyo War Crimes Trial*, Princeton, 1972. Challenges the moral and legal validity of the trials.

  Morris, Ivan, *Nationalism and the Right Wing in Japan: A Study of Post-War Trends*, London, 1960. A clear and forceful study.
- Nakane Chie, *Japanese Society*, Berkeley, 1972. A social anthropologist's analysis.

Packard, G. R., *Protest in Tokyo: The Security Treaty Crisis of 1960*, Princeton, 1966.

• Reischauer, E. O., *The Japanese*, Cambridge, Mass., 1977. A highly informative survey by an eminent scholar.

———, *The United States and Japan*, 3d ed., New York, 1965.

Thayer, N. B., *How the Conservatives Rule Japan*, Princeton, 1969.

Tsuneishi, W. M., *Japanese Political Style: An Introduction to the Government and Politics of Modern Japan*, New York, 1966. An excellent brief study.

• Van Alstyne, Richard W., *The United States and East Asia*, New York, 1973.

Vogel, E. F., *Japan As Number One: Lessons for America*, Cambridge, Mass., 1979.

Yanaga Chitoshi, *Big Business in Japanese Politics*, New Haven, 1968.

SOURCE MATERIALS

• Brandt, C., B. F. Schwartz, and J. K. Fairbank, *A Documentary History of Chinese Communism*, London, 1952.

• Chai, Winberg, ed., *The Essential Works of Chinese Communism*, New York, 1969.

Chiang Kai-shek, *China's Destiny*, New York, 1947.

• de Bary, W. T., ed., *Sources of Chinese Tradition*, Chaps. XXVII, XXVIII, XXIX, New York, 1960.

• ———, ed., *Sources of Japanese Tradition*, Chaps. XXVI, XXVII, XXVIII, XXIX, New York, 1958.

Grew, Ambassador Joseph C., *Ten Years in Japan*, New York, 1944.

• Lin, N. T., tr., *In Quest: Poems of Chou En-lai*, Cambridge, Mass., 1979.

• Minear, R. H., ed., *Through Japanese Eyes*, 2 vols., New York, 1974. Selections from the period of the Pacific War to the 1970s.

• Schram, Stuart, ed., *Chairman Mao Talks to the People: Talks and Letters, 1956–1971*, New York, 1975.

• Starr, J. B., *Continuing the Revolution: The Political Thought of Mao*, Princeton, 1979.

Chapter 40

NEW POWER RELATIONSHIPS

Africa, all I ask from you is the courage to know: to look about you and see what is happening in this old and tired world; to realize the extent and depth of its rebirth and the promise which glows on your hills.

—W. E. B. Du Bois, *Autobiography*

Put any economist in the capital of an underdeveloped country and give him a few assistants, and he will in no time produce a plan.

—Gunnar Myrdal, *Against the Stream*

W orld War II left the political world of Europe, Asia, and the United States in a state of disorder. As victory approached, wartime allies began to mistrust each other and to protect themselves against those whom they now perceived as prospective rivals. In addition, the war spawned nationalist revolts throughout the world. Many of these struggles were attempts by colonies to gain independence. Although these wars were often no more than local, they threatened to lead to major conflict and, because of the increasing proliferation of nuclear weapons, to general holocaust. This threat, if it did not reduce tensions, may in fact have operated to prevent nations from pursuing their interests to the point of no return.

Tensions in the postwar world

1. SOVIET-AMERICAN WORLD RIVALRY

As a result of the Second World War, world power relationships were drastically altered. Germany, Italy, and Japan had been defeated so overwhelmingly that they seemed for a time destined to play a subordinate role in world affairs. Officially, the list of great powers included five states—the Soviet Union, the United States, Great Britain, France, and the Republic of China. These were the Big Five that, as the war ended, seemed fated to rule the world. China was soon over-

Changing power relationships

whelmed by a communist revolution, however, while Britain and France became increasingly dependent upon the United States. As a consequence, the world of nations, during the ten years after 1945, took on a bipolar character, with the United States and the Soviet Union contesting for supremacy and striving to draw the remaining states into their orbits.

From the standpoint of economic power, the United States had far outdistanced the rest of the nations. Since 1939 Americans had doubled their national income and quadrupled their savings. Though they constituted only 7 percent of the world's population, they enjoyed over 30 percent of the world's estimated income. For the first time in its history the United States was in a position to be the arbiter of the destinies of at least half the earth. Japan was virtually its colony; the U.S. controlled both the Atlantic and Pacific Oceans, policed the Mediterranean, and shaped the development of international policy in western Europe. Until 1949, America had a monopoly of death-dealing atomic weapons. When the Soviet Union cracked this monopoly U.S. policy-makers remained convinced that their assumption of superior strength was still valid. All that was now necessary was to add new and more deadly weapons, thereby making sure that no rival could successfully challenge the United States.

Soviet Russia emerged from World War II as the second strongest power on earth. Though its navy was small, its land army and possibly its air force by 1948 were the largest in the world. Soviet population was climbing rapidly toward 200 million and this in spite of the loss of 7 million soldiers and about 8 million civilians during the war. In mineral wealth Russia's position compared favorably with that of the richest countries. After 1946 it claimed a large percentage of the world supply of petroleum. On the other hand, there can be no doubt that its industrial machine had been badly crippled by the war. No fewer than 1700 Russian cities and towns had been totally destroyed and about 40,000 miles of railway and 31,000 factories. Stalin declared in 1946 that it would probably require at least six years to repair the damage and rebuild the devastated areas.

It seems reasonable to suppose that much of the hostility displayed by the USSR in its dealings with other nations during the years after 1945 was attributable in some measure to the losses sustained during the war. Resentful of the fact that they had been compelled to make such sacrifices, the Soviets became obsessed with security as a goal that must be attained regardless of the cost to their neighbors. Fearful that poverty and hardship might make their own people rebellious, Russia's rulers encouraged their people to think that their country was in imminent danger of attack by capitalist powers. Following the end of the war, the Russians were determined to maintain the influence their military advance had secured for them in eastern Europe. Building on the agreements reached at Yalta, the Soviet

Union remained as an occupying force throughout that area, working meanwhile to establish "people's republics" sympathetic to the Soviet regime. By 1948, governments which owed allegiance to Moscow were established in Poland, Hungary, Rumania, Bulgaria, and Czechoslovakia. Albania and Yugoslavia, liberated by their own anti-Nazi forces, were not directly linked to Russia as satellites, although the governments of those two countries were also communist. The nations of eastern Europe did not succumb without a struggle. Greece, which the Russians wished to include within their sphere of influence, was torn by civil war until 1949, when with Western aid its monarchy was restored. Perhaps the most direct challenge to the Yalta guarantee of free, democratic elections occured in Czechoslovakia, where in 1948 the Soviets crushed the coalition government of liberal leaders Eduard Beneš and Jan Masaryk.

The United States countered these aggressive moves with massive programs of economic and military aid to western Europe. In 1947, President Truman proclaimed the so-called Truman Doctrine, which provided assistance programs to prevent further communist infiltration into the governments of Greece and Turkey. The following year, the Marshall Plan, named for Secretary of State George Marshall who first proposed it, provided funds for the reconstruction of western European industry. The plan was notable in two respects: first, it represented an attempt by the United States to restore the strength of its most serious economic competitors, and of its former enemy Germany, under the notion that an economically independent Europe would be less likely to fall prey to Soviet domination. Second, it relied upon a willingness on the part of the western European nations to coordinate their economic efforts, substituting, at least to some degree, cooperation for competition.

The Marshall Plan

At the same time, the U.S. moved to shore up the military defenses of the West. In April 1949, a group of representatives of North Atlantic states together with Canada and the United States signed an agreement providing for the establishment of the North Atlantic Treaty Organization (NATO). Subsequently Greece, Turkey, and West Germany were added as members. The treaty declared that an armed attack against any one of the signatory parties would be regarded as an attack against all, and that they would combine their armed strength to whatever extent necessary to repel the aggressor. It was decided also that the joint military command, or NATO army established in 1950, should be increased from thirty to fifty divisions in 1953, and that West Germany should be rearmed and invited to contribute twelve of the divisions. It was thereby hoped that NATO would be ready for an emergency that might arise as a consequence of the expansionist policies of Soviet Russia.

NATO

The Russians reacted with understandable alarm to the apparent determination of the United States to strengthen western Europe eco-

Crises in Berlin. Left: The Berlin Airlift, 1948. For fifteen months the United States, Britain, and France airlifted over two million tons of supplies into West Berlin, around which the Russians had imposed a land blockade. Right: The Berlin Wall, 1961. Thirteen years after the blockade, the East German government constructed a wall between East and West Berlin to stop the flow of escapees to the West.

nomically and militarily. They were particularly concerned when U.S. money began to flow into those areas of western Germany occupied by British, French, and U.S. forces. In 1946, the joint administration of Germany by the four powers collapsed. Russia remained in control of its satellite, which eventually became the nominally independent German Democratic Republic (East Germany), while the Western powers continued to support the industrial recovery of that area under their control—in its turn to emerge as the Federal Republic of Germany (West Germany). A crisis arose in 1948 when, in retaliation for the reunification of the western zones of control under one authority, the Russians closed down road and rail access from the west to Berlin. Berlin, though within the territory of East Germany, was administered by all four powers. The Western powers countered with an airlift of food and other necessary supplies which prevented the collapse of the city into Soviet hands. After almost a year the Russians lifted the blockade. For many years to come, however, Berlin was to remain one of the hottest spots in the ongoing "Cold War," as it came to be called, between Russia and the West.

> The most serious armed clash of the immediate postwar period was the Korean war of 1950–1953. At the end of World War II it had been agreed that Korea, under Japanese rule since 1910, was to become an independent and united country. The United States and the Soviet Union left occupying forces there until 1949, however, the Americans

The Berlin Blockade

The Korean war

south of the thirty-eighth parallel, the Russians to the north of it. During this period of occupation, the Soviets refused to cooperate with the United Nations–sponsored plan to hold free elections for the entire country. Instead, they established in the north a people's republic similar to those they had erected in eastern Europe. In June 1950, troops from this republic crossed the thirty-eighth parallel and invaded the south. Taking advantage of a temporary Russian boycott of the United Nations, the United States was able to avoid a Soviet veto of its plan to counter this invasion by sending a contingent of troops to oppose it. The troops, though nominally under United Nations command, were largely American, directed and supplied by the United States. Initial military gains by this force were countered in November by the invasion into Korea of troops from the newly established People's Republic of China, sent into the peninsula after General Douglas las MacArthur had, without authorization, advanced to the Chinese border. A stalemate ensued, President Truman and his advisers being as unwilling to widen the conflict into China as they were to abandon their South Korean allies. After two years of military and diplomatic deadlock, a peace settlement was concluded, recognizing the existence of both North and South Korea.

The Korean conflict, unprecedented in its savagery, revealed the disastrous effects of letting superpower rivalry erupt into open conflict. By the second year of the war, half of South Korea's population had been driven from their homes. After military targets were exhausted without bringing the enemy to its knees, American bombing planes systematically destroyed mines, factories, power plants, and irrigation dams. Casualties of military personnel and civilians numbered 6 million; one third of South Korea's surviving population was left destitute. The war adversely affected relationships between the United States and the nations of the Far East. While Japan had welcomed American intervention as a sign of its determination to halt the spread of communism, other countries had looked on America's role with suspicion. The United States claimed to be acting in accordance with United Nations principles. Powers such as India, Burma, and Indonesia, however, saw the war as a neocolonialist intrusion by America on behalf of its client state, South Korea. China's determination to understand the war in this light contributed greatly to the deep hostility that characterized Sino-American relations during the next twenty years.

Effects of the Korean war

The tensions between the United States and Russia eased somewhat during the late 1950s and 1960s. America, it is true, continued to adhere to a policy of Soviet "containment," seeking as allies those most willing to oppose by military force, if necessary, the spread of international communism. And Russia was never afraid to risk Western military reaction when suppressing revolts within the countries of its satellite allies. Yet the period has not incorrectly been labeled one of

The "thaw"

Nikita Khrushchev

Continued tensions

"thaw." A change in direction was signaled by the death of Stalin in 1953 and the accession to power after a brief interregnum of Nikita Khrushchev (1894–1971) in 1955. Khrushchev created the impression that the Soviet Union was prepared to pursue a new diplomatic line: for example, he denounced Stalinist tyranny and continued the program of destalinization begun after Stalin's death. In addition, he and his colleagues announced their approval of the doctrine of "more than one road to socialism." In accordance with this new attitude, the Russians concluded peace with Austria and withdrew their occupying troops. In 1955 they agreed to a "conference at the summit" with the chiefs of government of Great Britain, France, the United States, and the USSR as the participants.

This change in policy was undoubtedly prompted in part by discontent within the country. The Russian people had no desire for another war, and were weary of the restrictions and rigidities imposed by the Stalin regime. They believed that the time had come for less emphasis on expanding the production of heavy industry and armaments and more on providing the amenities of life. This switch in emphasis would mean a lessening of the Soviet role as overlord of the socialist world. Khrushchev was disposed to sympathize with the demands of the Russian people. The new policy, however, soon ran into trouble. The first sign of change was the Soviet suppression of revolts in Poland and Hungary in 1956. The Poles escaped serious repressions when they promised to remain within the Soviet orbit in return for permission to make various modifications in their socialist system. The Hungarians, however, were repressed with bloody violence when they attempted not merely to change the economic system but to break all ties with the Soviet Union.

At the beginning of another "summit" conference in Paris in May 1960 with President Dwight D. Eisenhower (1890–1969), Premier Khrushchev erupted violently when he learned that the Russians had shot down an American high-altitude reconaissance plane far over Soviet territory, whose mission was to discover the location of bases and other military installations. Though at first Washington officials denied these flights, they later admitted them and sought to justify them as necessary for the military security of the United States. The summit conference terminated immediately, with nothing but a poisoned atmosphere to mark its effects, despite the subsequent suspension of these flights. Yet Khrushchev was not ready to completely abandon his policy of conciliation. Later in 1960 he enunciated his principle of "peaceful coexistence." Though he did not renounce the ultimate triumph of communism, insisting that "we will bury you," he refused to admit that this triumph must be accomplished by force of arms.

With respect to Germany, Soviet leaders remained unyielding. They nurtured the fear that Germany might launch a new war, aided and abetted by its capitalist allies. For this reason they staunchly op-

Revolt in Hungary. By 1956 discontent with Soviet domination manifested itself in several of the satellite states. Violent revolt broke out in Poland and Hungary. Left: The photograph indicates the extent of the violence in Budapest. Right: A group of Hungarian freedom fighters.

posed unification of the country and insisted upon recognizing East Germany as one of their satellites. In 1961 the East German government built a high wall separating the two sectors of Berlin, in order to cut off the escape of thousands of East Germans to West Berlin and thence to western Germany. Many did make their escape, but the wall remained as a symbol of Soviet determination to prevent the formation of a united Germany. Khrushchev eventually fell prey to political rivals and was deposed in 1964, reduced to the level of a "non-person." The reins of power passed into the hands of a joint dictatorship of Aleksei Kosygin as premier and Leonid Brezhnev as secretary of the Communist party. The government did not return to Stalinist policy, but some of the new trends moved noticeably in that direction. A cardinal example was the occupation of Czechoslovakia in 1968. The Soviet dictators accused the Czechs of flirtation with West Germany to such an extent as to threaten the Soviet system and weaken its ties over eastern Europe. In particular, they resented the economic and social privileges allowed by the Czech government to its own citizens. Accordingly, they sent in armored troops and puppet rulers to take over the country. They followed this action by issuance of the Brezhnev Doctrine, which asserted the right of Moscow to interfere in the affairs of any satellite that strayed from the path of Soviet leadership.

The Berlin Wall

During the 1970s, the Soviets showed, by their intervention in the affairs of newly emerging nations of the so-called Third World—Africa, Asia, and Latin America—that they remained vitally interested in extending their sphere of influence wherever they could. At the same time, they continued to adhere to a policy which allowed for a further easing of tensions, a policy pursued with some enthusiasm, as well, by American diplomats. Henry Kissinger, secretary of state under Presidents Richard Nixon and Gerald Ford in the 1970s, proclaimed détente with the Russians as his goal, and devoted much time to

Arms limitation

The Occupation of Czechoslovakia. In 1968 the liberalized regime of Alexander Dubček was suppressed by the Soviets. The violent response by the citizens was put down by military force.

negotiations aimed at defusing potentially explosive areas of conflict between the two nations. Both countries were particularly concerned to curb the spread of nuclear weapons and to limit, if possible, the apparently endless expansion of their own arsenals. The Strategic Arms Limitation Treaty (SALT) talks, in which the Russians and Americans engaged during the 1970s, were an indication of mutual willingness to recognize and tackle a problem of awesome dimensions, even if their initial attempts to solve that problem resulted in at least temporary stalemate.

The European Common Market

Meanwhile, developments in Europe assisted in altering the balance of power and hence the nature of the international rivalry between the United States and Russia. European economic recovery led in 1958 to the establishment of a Common Market, or tariff union. By the mid-1970s, most of the major western European nations, including Britain, France, and West Germany, were members. Although the market was by no means the equivalent of a United States of Europe, its formation and continuing operation declared the existence of a new and important power bloc which, while more generally sympathetic to U.S. than to Soviet aims, nevertheless was determined to speak with a voice of its own.

2. IMPERIAL DECLINE AND THE EMERGENCE OF THE THIRD WORLD

The Third World

Probably more significant in the long run than U.S.-Soviet rivalry in the postwar period has been the decline of the Western imperial powers and the concurrent emergence of the Third World. Many of these countries have established themselves in territories which were formerly part of European empires. Others—China and the various nations of the Middle East, for example—while nominally independent of the West before 1945, nevertheless existed under European hegemony and were forced to acquiesce to European demands. Such is the case no longer. Although most of these so-called emerging nations are poor, and although the people of the Third World are by no means a united bloc, they represent a new and increasingly independent factor in the world power equation.

Some of these countries are rich in natural resources. Nations in the Middle East, Venezuela in South America, and Nigeria in Africa, possess oil in quantities sufficient to make their every move of vital importance to the West. Other African nations, Zaire and Angola, for example, are immensely rich in many mineral resources. Population is both a liability and an asset in the Third World. The people of China, by their sheer numbers, constitute an implicit threat to the balance of power at all times. The people of India, again by their sheer numbers, and lack of food, represent a perpetual threat to the stability of their own country and hence to all Asia. Every area in the Third World is a potential "trouble spot." This is so not only because the problems of racism, poverty, hunger, and overpopulation make them particularly vulnerable to violent civil conflicts. It is so, as well, because the superpowers, the United States and Russia—and lesser powers, including European nations and China—engage each other through the medium of Third World adversaries, thus increasing the possibility of conflict by their willingness to encourage it. To protect themselves from direct confrontation with each other, these developed nations interfere in the civil wars of others, on opposite sides and with an intensity that frequently belies their declared interest in avoiding general world war.

Relations with the West

The most radical change affecting both the Third World and established power relationships was the Chinese Revolution, described in the preceding chapter. Of comparable importance was the emergence of independent states in the Indian subcontinent, revolutionary upheavals in the Middle East, and the rise of black Africa (discussed in Chapters 37 and 38, respectively). Great Britain, having surrendered India and Burma, was further constrained to give up most of the remaining portions of its empire. Over a period of years Britain liberated Ceylon, Malaysia, Mauritius, Fiji, Singapore, and Nauru, among others, together with the Caribbean colonies of Guyana, Trinidad and Tobago, Jamaica, and Antigua, and significant territories in sub-Saharan Africa as well. The years following World War II also witnessed the liquidation of Dutch and French colonial empires in Southeast Asia.

Liquidation of empires

Indonesia, known for more than two centuries as the Netherlands Indies, was the most valuable jewel of the Dutch imperial crown. Indeed, it was one of the richest countries in the world in natural resources. When Japan extended its aggressions to Southeast Asia in 1941, the empire of the Dutch was a prize conquest. But toward the

Indonesian independence

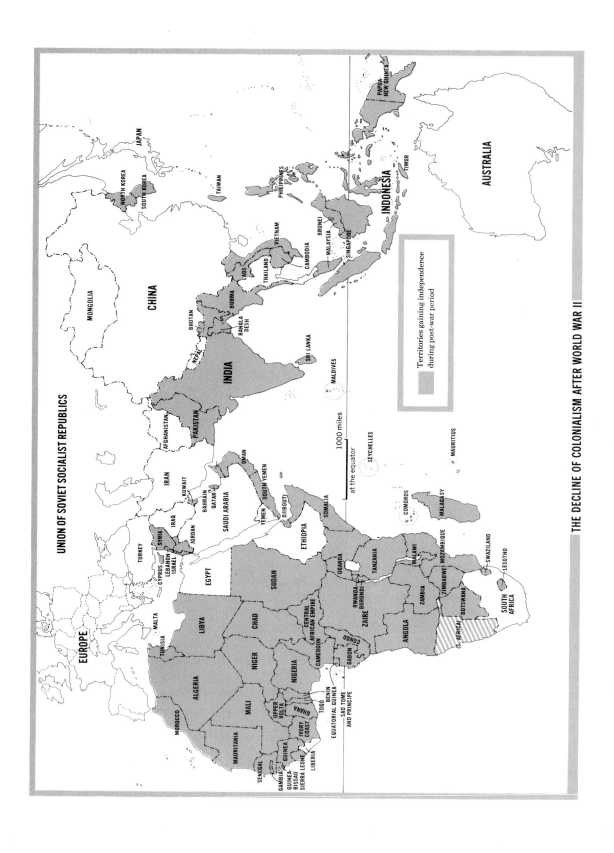

THE DECLINE OF COLONIALISM AFTER WORLD WAR II

Territories gaining independence during post-war period

end of the war, nationalists, under the leadership of Achmed Sukarno, a one-time architect and flamboyant politician, rebelled and proclaimed an independent republic. Although the Dutch attempted for four years to regain their sovereignty, the opposition of the indigenous population proved too strong. In 1949 the kingdom of the Netherlands recognized the independence of its former colony.

Developments in Indonesia

Under the colorful but erratic President Sukarno, the Republic of Indonesia assumed an aggressive role in Asian politics, but his reckless policies brought both economic disaster and internal discord. With encouragement from China, and to some extent from Sukarno, communist influence increased, and the Indonesian Communist party for a few years was the third largest in the world. An abortive coup in September 1965, attributed to the Communists, led to the imposition of a military regime which stripped Sukarno of his power. The Indonesian Communist party was shattered but at the price of a reign of terror lasting several months and a bloodbath that took the lives of at least half a million people. General Suharto, who replaced Sukarno as president, projected an ambitious program of industrial development for Indonesia, while maintaining a rigid dictatorship, stifling dissent, and incarcerating thousands of political prisoners. The nation of 130 million, fifth largest in the world, is among the poorest, with a per capita income of about $130 a year. But the sprawling republic has the potential to become highly prosperous. It has attained a favorable balance of trade, owing to the strong demand for its exports—petroleum, timber, rubber, palm oil, tin, and coffee.

Ho Chi Minh

France after World War II faced almost simultaneous revolts in two of its richest colonies, Algeria and Indochina. Indochina had been a casualty of Japanese conquests, and after the defeat of Japan in 1945 France sought to recover its lost empire in the Far East. These efforts ended in failure, however. The French were immediately confronted by a rebellion of Vietnamese nationalists under the leadership of Ho Chi Minh (1890–1969). The rebels resorted to guerrilla warfare and inflicted such costly defeats upon the French that the latter decided to abandon the struggle. An agreement was signed at Geneva in 1954 providing for the division of Vietnam into two zones, pending elections to determine the future government of the entire country. Ho Chi Minh became president of North Vietnam and established his capital at Hanoi. His followers, who came to be called Viet Cong, were numerous in both halves of the country. Had elections been held as provided by the Geneva Agreement, Ho Chi Minh would probably have been elected president of all of Vietnam. But the government of South Vietnam, backed by the United States, refused to permit elections to be held.

The war in Vietnam

From this point on, involvement by the United States in the Vietnamese civil war steadily increased. President Kennedy was convinced that the Chinese Communist juggernaut would soon roll over all of Southeast Asia. The first victims would be Vietnam, Laos, Cambodia,

Kennedy's intrusion into Vietnam

Malaysia, and Singapore. Then would come Thailand, Burma, and India. How far Kennedy would have gone in his crusade against communism had he escaped assassination in 1963 is impossible to say with certainty. Kennedy's successor, Lyndon B. Johnson (1908–1973), hoped that a relatively small force of perhaps 100,000 men would be sufficient to defeat the Viet Cong and drive them back into their own country. Little consideration was given to the fact that these forces were solidly entrenched in both states of Vietnam, and that they had been waging a bitter national struggle for upwards of eighteen years. They had succeeded in driving out the French in 1954 and were not likely to surrender to a new invader, as they conceived the Americans to be. The Viet Cong and the North Vietnam regulars, though less well-equipped, nevertheless fought the South Vietnamese and their American allies to a standstill on several occasions. During the Tet offensive of 1968 they came close to capturing Saigon, the South Vietnamese capital.

President Johnson escalates the war

Exasperated by failure to win an easy victory in South Vietnam, the American civilian and military chiefs determined upon aerial bombing. A series of incidents in 1964 provided the justification. Reports, of doubtful veracity, indicated that North Vietnamese ships had attacked American naval vessels in the Tonkin Gulf. President Johnson pronounced these incidents acts of war and immediately obtained from Congress authorization to use whatever measures necessary to repel communist aggression. Soon afterward American bombers unloaded their first cargoes upon towns and villages occupied by the North Vietnamese and the Viet Cong. Although evidence accumulated which cast doubt on the efficacy of these raids, they continued to be used. It has been estimated that the total American bomb tonnage dropped on Indochina (an area about the size of Texas) was more than three times as much as the United States dropped on enemy territory during all of World War II. In a single year (1974) the 250,000 tons of bombs dropped on tiny Cambodia exceeded the total expended on

War in Vietnam. Confronted with a new kind of warfare, the American military sought to adapt its methods to the Vietnamese situation.

Japan before Hiroshima. Still the deadly onslaught continued. The only answer of those responsible for strategy in Washington and Saigon seemed to be "Cover up the failure by escalating the war." As the struggle entered its fifth year, with no end in sight, disillusionment spread throughout the United States. Criticism of President Johnson was so harsh in 1968 that he was forced to abandon his plans to run for a second term.

Johnson's successor, Richard M. Nixon, was elected on the strength of promises to end the war. But this turned out to be a shadowy promise. While ground troops were being withdrawn from Vietnam, in May 1970, the United States invaded Cambodia and a few months later the kingdom of Laos. In April 1972, the North Vietnamese, with massive aid from Russia and China, launched a powerful counteroffensive with the apparent objective of conquering South Vietnam and driving all foreign armies out of the country. A number of South Vietnamese strongholds were captured and the offensive seemed more dangerous than the famous Tet offensive of 1968. Nixon countered with increased bombing of North Vietnam's factories and railroads and by mining its harbors, including savage raids while negotiations were under way in December 1972. A cease-fire, early in 1973, did no more than postpone the inevitable. Two years later, South Vietnam fell to the Viet Cong and the North Vietnamese. The massive intervention had proved a ghastly failure.

A focal point in a global power struggle, Indochina remained the most distressed area in all of Southeast Asia. The Vietnam War foreshadowed the possibility of the total annihilation of a country by the technology of modern warfare. In South Vietnam alone, besides those killed and wounded, at least 8 million people were turned into homeless refugees. Crops had been destroyed and farmlands ravaged. Exposure to the highly toxic defoliant, Agent Orange—sprayed on forests over a nine-year period—may have inflicted permanent genetic damage upon human survivors. One casualty of the Indochina conflict was the downfall of Prince Norodom Sihanouk's government in Cambodia, which in the midst of conflict had managed to remain neutral. Under pressure from both sides, Sihanouk succeeded in holding communist influence to a minimum, until he was ousted by a military coup in 1970 and replaced by Marshal Lon Nol. Although supported by the United States, Lon Nol was so corrupt and incompetent that he reduced his country to a shambles and soon lost three-fourths of it to the Communists.

*Prince Norodom Sihanouk of
Cambodia*

The aftermath of the Indochina war bore little resemblance to what either United States planners or their revolutionary adversaries had intended. Expulsion of the foreign invaders led not to peace, but to desperate internal struggles and renewed warfare. In Cambodia the Communist Khmer Rouge, which had overthrown Lon Nol's regime, proclaimed the new state of Kampuchea in January 1976 and instituted a reign of terror that came close to a policy of genocide. The paranoid leader Pol Pot, in his determination to create an agrarian society more radically equalitarian than that of China, liquidated bourgeoisie and intellectuals and forced entire city populations to move to the country. Khmer Rouge zealots abolished currency, private property, and private households, and were responsible for the death of some 2 million Cambodians. The Communist rulers of the Socialist Republic of Vietnam (SRV), whose forces had borne the brunt of the fighting, appeared more conciliatory than the fanatics of Kampuchea and placed a high priority on rebuilding Vietnam's economy. The task of reconstruction was staggering, with industry destroyed, per capita annual income only $150 and declining, and foreign aid not readily forthcoming.

Regional antagonisms and realignments

The conflicts in Indochina of the late 1970s and beyond, although aggravated by great power rivalry, stemmed basically from the resurgence of centuries-old ethnic and national rivalries that had been temporarily suppressed by the common effort against French and American imperialism. Both Thailand and Vietnam aspired to dominance in the area, forcing the smaller states of Laos and Cambodia to serve as pawns or buffers between them. A Communist regime installed in Laos in 1975 was held closely aligned with Vietnam, but antagonisms rankled between Vietnamese and Cambodians, and Pol Pot, with only a shaky hold over his own Kampuchea, staged military incursions into Vietnam. Relations between Vietnam and China had never been cordial, even while they were nominally allied. The Chinese viewed Vietnamese with the same disdain the Vietnamese felt toward Cambodians, and the Vietnamese remembered their long struggle to win independence from imperial China. When Peking terminated its aid program with Hanoi, the SRV was forced to look for support elsewhere. Hoping to balance aid from the socialist countries with contributions from the United States and its allies, the Hanoi government participated in a United States—North Vietnam Joint Economic Commission. Although Secretary of State Kissinger broke off these negotiations in July 1973, the Vietnamese did not abandon hope of winning American diplomatic recognition and financial assistance until 1978, when Washington's Indochina policy—reflecting National Security Adviser Brzezinski's determination to play the "China card"—shifted toward closer alignment with Peking. Rebuffed by the United States, the Vietnamese yielded to Russian pressure to sign a Treaty of Friendship and Cooperation with the Soviet Union in March 1978.

Pol Pot of Kampuchea

Vietnam's wars with Kampuchea and China

War between Vietnam and Kampuchea was preceded by Khmer Rouge raids into Vietnam and punitive strikes by Vietnamese troops deep into Cambodia. Unable to induce Pol Pot to accept a demilitarized zone, Hanoi opened a full-scale assault in December 1978 and toppled the Khmer Rouge government the following month. The war threatened to destroy what little was left of Cambodia. After the fall of Phnom Penh, the capital, fighting continued between the new

Vietnamese-backed regime and various guerrilla groups, including a sizable remnant of Pol Pot's Khmer Rouge. Thousands of sick, wounded, and starving refugees swarmed to the Thai border. International relief agencies, attempting to avert famine, were frustrated by the dictates of rival political authorities. The war put a heavy strain on Vietnam's stunted economy. Finally, Vietnam's Cambodian adventure provoked an attack by the People's Republic of China. In line with its socialization program, Hanoi had in 1978 decreed the nationalization of small businesses and banks, most of which in the vicinity of Saigon (Ho Chi Minh City) were owned by resident Chinese. Before the border was closed, 170,000 had returned to China. Although the SRV's treatment of "bourgeois tradesmen" was precisely that which the Chinese Communists had meted out to the bourgeoisie in their own country, the procedure intensified hostile feelings between the two socialist states. The Chinese felt it necessary to support Pol Pot—in spite of his unsavory reputation—because his was the only regime in Indochina aligned with Peking and because its destruction would remove a check on Vietnam's expansionist ambitions. The Chinese invasion of Vietnam, which began on February 17, 1979, and lasted only seventeen days, destroyed bridges, utilities, mining operations, and thousands of homes, without producing any discernible advantage for either side to offset the heavy losses. Peking claimed its intent was to "teach" Vietnam "a lesson." Actually, the brief but costly encounter failed to change the status quo in the peninsula. The Vietnamese continued to occupy the greater part of Cambodia and, utilizing emergency supplies donated by private relief agencies, began to revive the economy. Because Hanoi refused to withdraw its troops as long as China was helping the Khmer Rouge, the United States and its allies continued to support the Khmer Rouge's dubious claim to represent Kampuchea in the United Nations General Assembly. A majority of the Cambodians, while displaying

The Flight from Cambodia. Thousands of Cambodian refugees fled the fighting between the Pol Pot regime and the Vietnamese army. Here civilians, wearing traditional Khmer head scarves, are streaming across the border into Thailand. On this day alone (April 27, 1979) some 12,000 sought refuge in Thailand, where the facilities for caring for them were woefully inadequate.

little affection for the Vietnamese invaders, apparently preferred their continued occupation of the country to the return of the hated Pol Pot.

The nations of the Third World differ widely in degree of development and in potential, ranging from the fabulously wealthy Persian Gulf oil emirates to the semitribal peasant communities of Africa. The most impoverished areas are sometimes referred to as the "Fourth World." The overall disparity between the new or developing nations—constituting a majority of the world's population—and the minority of advanced industrial societies is startling. A recent report of the U.N. Food and Agricultural Organization disclosed that a billion people—one-fourth of the earth's inhabitants—live in "absolute poverty and destitution," and the situation is worsening. This presents a problem for the countries enjoying high levels of consumption as well as for those suffering deprivation. As ideologies fade and superpower rivalry reaches a stalemate, the most critical confrontation may prove to be between the industrially advanced "have" nations and the dispossessed—a confrontation sometimes phrased as "North" versus "South." Prosperous nations of the "North" are by no means indifferent to the Third World. They have supplied billions of dollars in "aid," but much of this has gone to feed military establishments or has been in the form of loans designed to benefit the donor's economy rather than the recipient's. Contrary to a widely shared notion, wealthy nations have on the whole been niggardly rather than generous. In 1975 the foreign aid contributed by western European nations averaged .36 percent of their GNP. The figure for the United States was .27 percent. The Soviet Union—professed friend and benefactor of the Third World—did worse, giving proportionately one-tenth as much as the United States. Underdeveloped nations could help improve their condition by forgoing excessive purchases of armaments. Unfortunately, they have followed the opposite course, yielding to the enticements of the arms-exporting states. Third World countries—some of which cannot feed or house their own people—doubled their expenditures on armaments between 1960 and 1975.

Many of the countries born of revolutions following World War II were at first inclined to throw in their lot with the Communist half of the postwar world. This was partly because their revolutions had been against Western capitalist governments and partly because they were anxious to achieve rapid economic growth and believed this could be done only through centralized planning and controls, which might require the curtailment of individual freedom of choice. Third World countries, however, soon showed that they were determined to remain independent and preferred not to attach themselves to either of the global power blocs, pursuing generally a policy of nonalignment.

The artificiality of the divisions between the several "worlds" is illustrated by the situation in Korea, where an imaginary line—the thirty-eighth parallel (plus real fortifications)—separates the two competing spheres of communism and capitalism. Both Koreas actually display characteristics common to the Third World. The Republic of Korea, with its capital at Seoul, and the Democratic People's Republic of Korea in the north, with Pyongyang as its capital, not only survived as separate political entities but showed remarkable recuperative ability. Both capitals were rebuilt and industrial complexes restored and expanded. In each case the price of economic progress has been submission to the dictates of a police state, as repressive in South Korea as in the northern Communist republic. Hostility between the two divisions of the peninsula has forced each to maintain an army of more than half a million troops and has repeatedly threatened to ignite another Far Eastern conflagration. However, even in 1979–1980, when South Korea was shaken by internal upheaval and the threat of civil war, there was no overt move on the part of North Korea to seize the opportunity provided by confusion in Seoul to attack its southern neighbor. It is doubtful that either of the two republics will resort to war unless prodded into it by one or both of the superpowers. On the contrary, there are occasional signs that, if left alone, they may eventually effect a peaceful reunification of the peninsula.

Progress in the two Koreas

The United States, resolved to keep South Korea within its alliance system, supplied military and economic aid—amounting to nearly $200 billion—in spite of flagrant violation of human rights by the Seoul government. In the mid-1970s it was revealed that agents of the Korean C.I.A., operating extensively in the United States, had engaged in wholesale bribery of congressmen to ensure continued support. South Korea's president, General Park Chung Hee, after seven years of absolute rule, was assassinated in October 1979 by the head of the Korean C.I.A. The hope that Park's removal might open the door to democratic progress—or that Washington might use the occasion to apply pressure for reform—was not fulfilled. General Chun Doo-hwan, who seized power in a coup in December, proved himself an apt pupil of the slain dictator. Widespread demonstrations demanding a return to constitutional government reached a climax in May 1980, when 100,000 students marched on Seoul and other cities and popular uprisings spread throughout an entire province. Chun crushed the revolt with 10,000 armored troops, reinvoked martial law, and jailed all resisters. In August he made himself president and soon afterward appointed a rubber-stamp assembly to legalize the muzzling of every political leader disapproved by Chun. Most prominent among the many persons arrested and tried for the May uprising was Kim Dae-jung, battle-scarred veteran of a long campaign for democratic government. Although he had been in prison at the time of the riots, Kim was charged with sedition and sentenced to death. The sentence was commuted to life imprisonment after vehement protests from abroad and a threat from Japan to cut off economic aid. In February 1980 the newly inaugurated American president, Ronald

*Upheaval and continued
dictatorship in South
Korea*

Chun Doo-hwan, President of South Korea

Reagan, gave Chun a warm reception in Washington, promised to retain U.S. troops at full strength in Korea, and declared, "We share your commitment to freedom."

Of the several attempts to promote solidarity among nations of the Third World—beginning with the Asian-African Conference of twenty-nine states held at Bandung, Indonesia, in 1955—the most promising to date is the Association of Southeast Asian Nations (ASEAN), established in 1967 by Indonesia, Singapore, Malaysia, Thailand, and the Philippines. Not a military alliance, the organization sought at the outset to win recognition of Southeast Asia as a "zone of peace, freedom, and neutrality." It aims to develop regional interdependence among a significant group of Third World states and has the potential to make their collective weight felt in international affairs. An ASEAN summit meeting in 1976 produced a Treaty of Amity and Concord, providing for mutual economic assistance and trade. ASEAN undertakes to strengthen ties among states scattered over a wide geographical area and differing in culture and in degree of economic development. Each has internal problems; the government of each is anti-Communist but repressive. Indonesia and Thailand are under military rule, while the Philippines and Singapore are civilian dictatorships. Thailand, nominally a monarchy, has experienced frequent coups. The ASEAN countries have high potential for economic development, and they have sustained impressive growth rates during the past two decades. Indonesia, though presently poor, ranks first in size, population, and natural resources. The island of Singapore, tiny by comparison, is a thriving port and financial center. Although the military regimes of Indonesia and Thailand have depended upon United States support and the Philippines are the site of important American bases, the ASEAN countries may be useful as a bridge between opposing camps. Vietnam's hostilities with Cambodia and China forced Hanoi to improve relations with staunchly anti-Communist Thailand and to revise its stance toward ASEAN, which it had previously denounced as an American "scheme of aggression and intervention." In 1978 the Vietnamese prime minister toured all the ASEAN capitals and pronounced ASEAN "a genuine regional organization for economic cooperation." Rebuffed by Thailand and Singapore, Vietnam's overtures were viewed more sympathetically by Malaysia and Indonesia, both of which had had experiences that made them distrustful of China. If ASEAN could succeed in forging a link between Communist-oriented Indochina and anti-Marxist Indonesia, it could prove to be an effective counterbalance to the superpowers of East and West.

3. THE LIMITS OF POWER

The period embraced by the two world wars brought not only nationalist revolutions but also fundamental changes in power relationships.

The postwar emergence of two "superpowers" marked the climax of an evolutionary process which seemed to leave the world at the mercy of two rival colossi, commanding tremendous material and human resources and, temporarily, a monopoly of nuclear weapons. This concentration of power, with its accompanying pressure upon weaker states, eventually reached the point of diminishing returns and began to frustrate the national objectives of the superpowers themselves. The reasons for this paradox are several. First, both Russia and the United States, in seeking military superiority, neglected the needs of their own societies. Fifty years after the Revolution of 1917 the Soviet Union had not succeeded in overtaking a single country—with the possible exception of Italy—in per capita income. In this category the U.S.S.R. ranked twentieth in a list of 130 countries. Agriculture was too inefficient to free the Soviets from the need to import foodstuffs, and they required foreign capital to implement plans for developing the oil and gas deposits of Siberia. At the same time the United States, boasting the world's largest GNP and displaying record-breaking affluence, was becoming a poor society in terms of the quality of life. In the mid-1970s the United States ranked thirteenth in the number of teachers per school-age population; seventeenth (just below Poland) in the ratio of physicians to population; seventeenth (tied with East Germany) in the infant mortality rate; and twentieth in life expectancy. An industrial slump triggered by the oil crisis of 1974 curtailed vital services, including police and fire protection, and threatened major American cities with bankruptcy. By 1980 a huge foreign trade deficit, runaway inflation, and rising unemployment underlined serious weaknesses in the economy and sapped public confidence in the government's ability to cope with them. The United States and the Soviet Union, superpowers militarily, were like two exceedingly dangerous but partially crippled giants.

Limiting factors in the supremacy of the superpowers

A second factor limiting the usefulness of massive power was the difficulty of enforcing compliance from allies and client states. The Soviet Union, besides suffering a major blow when Communist China embarked on an independent course, has met with formidable resistance in its east European satellites. In 1980, Polish workers—over a period of months and at the risk of Soviet military intervention—defied both their own Communist rulers and the Kremlin. Through a series of strikes that almost paralyzed the economy, they forced the party bosses to grant major concessions, including recognition of an independent union (Solidarity), labor's access to the media, and, in February 1981, the dismissal of four provincial officials accused of corruption. In July 1981 the impact of Solidarity's demands on the Communist Party was dramatically manifested at an extraordinary congress of the Polish Communist Party where the 1,955 delegates (90% of whom were attending their first congress), utilizing the secret ballot for the first time, completely reshaped the Party's central committee and politburo. The United States, while retaining and

The unreliability of alliances

Proliferation of armaments

Confrontations and pull-backs

shoring up NATO, had only limited success in building alliance systems elsewhere, in spite of great expenditure of time and money.

A third negative factor was the proliferation of weapons among nations rich and poor and, ominously, a shattering of the dream of an elite "nuclear club." It became evident that sooner or later midget states, or even private gangs of terrorists, could procure atomic weapons for purposes of blackmailing or destroying an enemy. Finally, the "balance of terror" created by the superpowers was, in effect, a continuing crisis that made peace impossible. The nuclear giants, armed with the power to destroy the world, could not police it; they could not effectively restrain even their own dependents. They were impotent to prevent conflict from erupting or to extinguish it when it came, because armed intervention by a nuclear power carries the risk of triggering Doomsday. This fact has not escaped the notice of small states embroiled in regional feuding, especially when these states are equipped with conventional weapons conveniently supplied by one or both of the superpowers.

The limitations upon power as an instrument for achieving political solutions was illustrated during the Korean War of 1950–1953. The United States government refused to permit General MacArthur to invade China or to employ nuclear weapons, as he had requested, for fear that such moves might lead irrevocably to a world war. This

Defiance in Poland. Thousands of striking workers take part in religious services in the Lenin Shipyards in Gdansk on August 24, 1980. This was the scene of the first in a series of strikes that paralyzed an already troubled economic and political system and challenged Soviet domination of Polish governmental policy.

General Douglas MacArthur Returns from Korea. MacArthur, who had recently been relieved of his command for disobeying President Truman's orders, was given a hero's welcome in New York on April 20, 1951. This effusive approval of MacArthur's behavior reflected the frustration felt by many Americans at the inability of the United States government to bring the Korean conflict to a swift and victorious conclusion.

policy puzzled and angered many Americans, accustomed to the concepts of all-out war and unconditional surrender. Especially galling to them was the fact that President Harry Truman saw fit to fire General MacArthur, hero of the Pacific theater in World War II and now commander of the United Nations forces, because MacArthur refused to fight a limited war. In 1962, the United States and the Soviet Union were again forced to ask themselves how much they were willing to risk in order to protect their own strategic interests. During the early 1960s, President John F. Kennedy and his advisers grew increasingly concerned about the activities of Premier Fidel Castro of Cuba. In October 1962 Kennedy ordered a naval blockade of the island to prevent delivery of missiles and other war matériel the Russians had promised to supply. The Soviet government, alarmed by the threat of war, agreed to remove the bombers and missiles already on Cuban soil. The incident posed an extremely difficult question for the two superpowers. How could one nation convince another of its determination to brook no further interference with its plans, if its adversary could be fairly certain that because of the fear of nuclear war the threat was no more than a bluff?

The unfinished lessons of Vietnam

Its unhappy adventure in Indochina provided the United States with the most searing demonstration of the futility of a policy based solely on force. Although the American commander, General William Westmoreland, claimed a victory in Vietnam, it would be hard to conceive a more decisive reversal than the United States had experienced. After fifteen years of struggle, a sickening toll of lives, and the expenditure of $150 billion, the result was the triumph of communism and the overthrow of every American-sponsored government in Indochina except Thailand, which had remained neutral. In retrospect it seems obvious that American objectives could have been better served at far less cost. Following the withdrawal of American trooops the states of Southeast Asia did not "fall like dominoes," but the Indochinese Communist regimes—temporarily forced into union against foreign intervention—fell upon one another in a regional power struggle. A senior U.S. diplomat who had been associated with the Vietnam commitment, observed aptly that the United States was better off than if it had won the war. The lessons of Indochina, not yet fully assimilated, are probably not yet finished. Before attacking Cambodia in the fall of 1978, the Vietnamese Communists allied themselves by treaty with the Soviet Union, hoping thereby to discourage China from interfering. The alliance did not keep China from invading Vietnam, but, by the same token, neither did China's alliance with Kampuchea deter the Vietnamese from attacking that pitiable country.

The U.S.S.R. in Afghanistan

The U.S.S.R., as if to prove that it had learned nothing from the experience of the French and the Americans in Vietnam, decided to compel obedience from Afghanistan, a Middle Eastern country bordering on Russia, where a pro-Soviet regime had been installed in April 1978. Weary of the stubborn resistance offered by the Muslim population of Afghanistan, the Soviets attacked in strength in December 1979 and installed a compliant puppet as prime minister in Kabul. While Russian troops policed the cities, Afghan tribesmen inflamed the countryside with guerrilla attacks from their mountain strongholds, foreshadowing a long and ruinous civil war.

The dissolution of alliance systems: the demise of SEATO

Recent decades have recorded the weakening or dissolution of alliance systems originally designed to bolster the shaky bipolar balance of power or to give one side an advantage over the other. Nations of the Third World, weak and dependent as they are, have resisted interference in their domestic affairs as well as attempts to absorb them into power blocs. Communist China hoped in vain to manipulate Indonesia through that country's large Communist party. The U.S.S.R., frustrated in Egypt and Iraq, struggled laboriously to gain footholds in the new African states. While accepting a Soviet alliance, born of desperation, in 1978, the Vietnamese rejected Russia's request for naval bases in their territory. In the Western Hemisphere, the United States is no longer able to dictate to the Organization of American States. After pouring billions of dollars into the Shah's Iran to make it a Middle East bastion, Washington's influence collapsed to zero with the revolution of 1979, and it could only watch helplessly as American nationals, seized as hostages by militant revolutionaries, were imprisoned for fourteen months. For a couple of decades United States strategists hoped to retain leverage with an alliance they had organized for Southeast Asia in 1954. The Southeast Asia Defense Treaty (SEATO) was designed as a counterpart to NATO, in an overall program for containing communism. The organization was never popular nor effective. Only three of its eight members were Asian states (Thailand, Pakistan, and the Philippines); by 1967 France had virtually withdrawn from the alliance, and Pakistan left in 1972. In June 1977 what remained of SEATO was quietly laid to rest with a brief ceremony in Bangkok. The Southeast Asian states, disinclined to revive the Cold War, looked toward ASEAN as an association more suitable to promoting their common interests.

SELECTED READINGS

- *Items so designated are available in paperback editions.*
- Brzezinski, Z. K., *The Soviet Bloc: Unity and Conflict,* rev. ed., Cambridge, Mass., 1967.

  Cady, J. F., *Southeast Asia: Its Historical Development,* New York, 1964.

  Chaliand, Gérard, *Revolution in the Third World: Myths and Prospects,* New York, 1977. Gloomy but insightful.
- Degler, Carl N., *Affluence and Anxiety: The United States Since 1945,* Glenview, Ill., 1968.
- Dehio, Ludwig, *Germany and World Politics in the Twentieth Century,* London, 1959. A series of essays assessing Germany's twentieth-century drive for European hegemony.

  Ehrmann, Henry W., *Politics in France,* Boston, 1968. French politics since 1958.
- Falk, Richard, *A Study of Future Worlds,* New York, 1975.

  Fall, Bernard B., *The Two Vietnams: A Political and Military Analysis,* rev. ed., New York, 1967.
- Fanon, Frantz, *The Wretched of the Earth,* New York, 1968. The extraordinary and brilliant delineation of the oppression of Third World peoples.

  Fitzgerald, Frances, *Fire in the Lake: The Vietnamese and the Americans in Vietnam,* Boston, 1972. A detailed and moving account.

  Henderson, W. O., *The Genesis of the Common Market,* Chicago, 1963.

  Hoffman, Stanley, et al., *In Search of France,* Cambridge, Mass., 1963. Essays providing perceptive analyses of postwar French politics and society.

  Knapp, Wilfrid, *Unity and Nationalism in Europe Since 1945,* Elmsford, N.Y., 1969.

  Kolko, Gabriel, *The Politics of War: The World and United States Foreign Policy, 1943–45,* New York, 1969. Argues that the blame for the Cold War rests with the Western allies.

• Moore, Barrington, *The Social Origins of Dictatorship and Democracy: Lord and Peasant in the Making of the Modern World,* Boston, 1966.

Mozingo, David, *China's Policy toward Indonesia, 1949–1967,* Ithaca, 1976.

Myrdal, Gunnar, *Against the Stream: Critical Essays on Economics,* New York, 1972. Offers pertinent comments on problems of the Third World.

———, *The Challenge of World Poverty: A World Anti-Poverty Program in Outline,* New York, 1970.

Nogueira, Franco, *The Third World,* London, 1968.

Reischauer, Edwin O., *Beyond Vietnam: The United States and Asia,* New York, 1968.

Seabury, Paul, *The Rise and Decline of the Cold War,* New York, 1967.

Shawcross, William, *Sideshow: Kissinger, Nixon and the Destruction of Cambodia,* New York, 1979.

• Williams, Lea E., *Southeast Asia: A History,* New York, 1976. From the fifteenth century to the present.

• Worsley, Peter, *The Third World,* 2d ed., Chicago, 1970.

• Wylie, Laurence, *Village in the Vaucluse,* rev. ed., Cambridge, Mass., 1974. Analyzes the social structure of French rural life in 1950. An afterword reveals the changes wrought by the intrusion of modern life in the ensuing twenty years.

SOURCE MATERIALS

Adenauer, Konrad, *Memoirs, 1945–53,* Chicago, 1966. Adenauer served as chancellor of the Federal Republic of Germany from 1949 to 1963 and sought both American support and the reunification of dismembered Germany.

Barnes, Thomas G., and Gerald D. Feldman, comps., *Breakdown and Rebirth: 1914 to the Present,* Boston, 1972. An excellent documentary collection of contemporary history, primarily European.

• Caputo, Philip, *A Rumor of War,* New York, 1977. The best memoir of the American experience in the Vietnam war.

De Gaulle, Charles, *Memoirs of Hope: Renewal and Endeavor,* New York, 1971.

Kennan, George F., *Memoirs, 1925–1950,* New York, 1967. Kennan, a career diplomat, was America's leading expert on Russia and instrumental in the formation of the containment policy.

Chapter 41

PROBLEMS OF WORLD CIVILIZATION

This conjunction of an immense military establishment and a large arms industry is new in American experience. The total influence—economic, political, even spiritual—is felt in every city, every statehouse, every office of the federal government. . . . We must guard against the acquisition of unwarranted influence, whether sought or unsought, by the military-industrial complex. The potential for the disastrous rise of misplaced power exists and will persist.

—Dwight D. Eisenhower, "Farewell Address"

The writing of a final chapter in a text book of this sort is, for the authors, a difficult task. Not only are they called upon to attempt an instant analysis of their own society and time; they are expected as well to discern in present events patterns that will continue to be of some consequence five to ten years hence. In other words, they are called upon to pick historical winners, to decide not what *has* mattered, which is difficult enough, but what *will* matter. Historians, whose job it is to acknowledge the way in which human idiosyncrasies make prediction a tricky business, are particularly loath to single out this movement or that trend and to pronounce it "significant" in terms of the future. We shall therefore merely content ourselves with a discussion of some of the most serious problems confronting society in the 1970s, calling attention at the outset to the fact that these problems are rooted in many of the historical developments—industrialization, urbanization, and international competition, for example—that we have traced in the preceding chapters.

The present as history

I. THE GROWTH OF CENTRALIZED GOVERNMENT AND ITS CONSEQUENCES

The responsibilities central governments assumed, and the power they arrogated to themselves to discharge those responsibilities, increased significantly around the world after World War II. In almost all countries, successive administrations either intitiated or expanded social welfare programs, insuring that entire populations would receive protection from the depredations of unemployment, sickness, and old age. Building upon the examples set by Germany and Britain before World War I, Western nations instituted increasingly comprehensive national programs for health and social security. Socialist and Third World countries likewise moved, in some cases with remarkable speed, to alleviate the problems and disabilities of people who for generations had been denied the chance of a healthy and secure existence.

This movement to expand social welfare systems resulted in an increased tendency on the part of governments to manage and control their citizenry. Programs of social insurance were designed to benefit and hence to regulate the lives of all classes of men and women, not just the destitute. New agencies, staffed by armies of newly recruited bureaucrats, imposed rules while they dispensed assistance to a clientele that grew to include the entire citizenry. Many of those responsible for the institution of these programs were motivated by a genuine desire to provide a decent life to all citizens, regardless of economic class. An equally powerful incentive, however, was the conviction of governments that without a strong and generally satisfied population a country was doomed to recurring unrest, that social insecurity would contribute to rapid national decline into domestic inefficiency and international ineffectiveness.

Concern to improve or at any rate to stabilize a nation's international position, within a world in which power relationships were constantly shifting, contributed further to the growth of centralized government. New nations wanted to attain some new measure of international power. Older nations wanted to retain whatever measure had been theirs. In either case, governments recognized the importance of a stable economy and a strong military defense. Few countries, old or new, managed to attain those twin goals in the 1970s to the extent they deemed necessary. Inflation in particular proved an intractable obstacle to their achievement. Nevertheless as nations strained to assert themselves, their governments tightened their hold on the economy, working to do so with the forces of both management and labor, while investing enormous sums in the most sophisticated and up-to-date armaments of war. The result of these activities was a further growth of the power and control of government.

What have been the consequences of such growth? Some observers have argued that the general worldwide increase in the authority of central governments is a symptom of a decline in the importance of political and economic ideology. Whether a nation declares itself to be a capitalist democracy (as does the United States), a socialist commonwealth (as does the Soviet Union) or something in between (as do many of the nations of western Europe), all appear to some degree to have blunted ideological differences as they have attempted to rationalize—or nationalize—their industries, manage their economies, provide for the well-being of their citizens, and arm themselves against the possibilities of future war. Fewer socialists now advocate collective ownership of the means of production; they have become instead exponents of the welfare state. Defenders of capitalism still exist in theory but few would recognize it if they saw it in full swing. Capitalist economies are no longer free enterprise systems but "mixed" economies, involving government controls, managed currencies, and forced distribution of profits. Small-time capitalists are permitted to enjoy their gains only until they turn them over to the government to finance its wars, armaments, and social welfare programs.

*Political reaction to
centralization*

To suggest that there has been some ideological blurring in the movement toward more generally accepted goals does not mean, however, that men and women do not continue to call themselves capitalists or socialists, or that those terms have lost their meaning. Nor should it imply that there is not continuing and heated debate about both ends and means. During the mid-1970s a reaction of some magnitude occurred in several Western countries against the notion that governments should manage the lives of their citizens to the extent they were. Social reform, critics said, has cost too much, and has not really achieved what it was supposed to. There is still poverty and misery. Admit that they will always exist, these people argued, and moderate your goals accordingly; in the process, put an end to big government. This viewpoint was occasionally translated into political victory. The socialist government of Sweden, in power for decades, was succeeded by a conservative one. Margaret Thatcher, arch-conservative leader of Britain's Tory party, became the first woman prime minister of that country in 1979, as well as the first woman head of state of a Western nation, on a platform which blamed her country's economic decline in the 1970s on the fact that the government had overextended itself. In the United States there was a relatively successful campaign by citizens to curb government activity by limiting taxation.

*Critics of bureaucratic
centralization*

This debate has been carried on not only in the political arena but in the writings of thoughtful and angry critics of modern society. Two of the most powerful voices raised against the growth of worldwide governmental expansion and authoritarianism were those of Alexsandr Solzhenitsyn and Herbert Marcuse. Solzhenitsyn, an exiled Russian novelist, attacked the brutal methods employed by the Soviet Union in its rapid climb to world power. His *Gulag Archipelago*, published in 1973, is a fictionalized account of the fate of those whose

Margaret Thatcher

Alexsandr Solzhenitsyn

President Nixon Resigns. Here Nixon bids his last farewell to the White House in the wake of his resignation.

willingness to stand in the way of Soviet "progress" sentenced them to life in Siberian labor camps. Marcuse, an American, charged that authoritarianism was just as much a fact of life under capitalism as under communism. He argued that industrial capitalism had produced a "one-dimensional" society, in which the interests of individual citizens had been ruthlessly subordinated to those of the powerful corporate interests which were the true governors of the world.

Marcuse urged the adoption of revolutionary measures to accomplish the overthrow of authoritarian capitalist imperialism. Those unwilling to follow him to that extreme nevertheless concurred in his denunciation of the manner in which big government and big business together appeared to be draining power from individual citizens. Indeed, as devoted a capitalist as Dwight D. Eisenhower, general in the U.S. Army during the Second World War and president of the United States in the 1950s, warned in his farewell presidential address of the growing might of what he called "the military-industrial complex." In those countries calling themselves democracies, democracy seemed to many to have less and less meaning, as people appeared to enjoy little control over their government and hence over their lives. Concerns of this sort received apparent confirmation in the late 1960s and early 1970s, when the United States was at war in Vietnam. Evidence subsequently published showed that the democratically elected Congress was misled by President Lyndon Johnson and his advisors into believing that hostile North Vietnamese attacks on American ships had compelled U.S. intervention, whereas the attacks had instead been "manufactured" to allow the government to pursue its own aggressive policies. Concern about the arrogance of governmental power reached its peak in the United States during the Watergate investigations leading to the resignation of President Richard Nixon in 1974, when it was learned that Nixon had authorized domestic spying in the name of national security but without proper regard for the constitutional rights of American citizens. Following that dramatic episode came revelations about the role played in secret by the U.S. Central Intelligence Agency in subverting leftist Third World governments, along with the intervention of giant multinational corporations and the C.I.A. together in assisting to overthrow a democratically elected socialist government in Chile. Knowledge of these events brought home the extent to which centralized authority in supposedly democratic governments had removed itself from popular control and accountability.

2. COMMITMENT: THE GROWTH OF BLACK CONSCIOUSNESS

Partly in response to revelations of this sort, partly as a result of long-standing grievances and dissatisfactions, groups that had hitherto lived as subordinates in society, kept powerless and in large part silenced, raised their voices in the 1960s and 1970s, demanding not only to be heard but to have their demands met. At the very time when democracies were being charged with ignoring the wishes of their constituents, blacks, youth, and women, in particular, began to assert their right to equality.

The growth of insurgency among American blacks has to some extent paralleled the rise of black nations in Africa and the Caribbean. Through most of the years from the Civil War to 1900, black people were condemned, in the North as well as the South, to a subordinate role within a predominantly white culture. The emancipation of slaves, and the Thirteenth and Fourteenth Amendments to the Constitution brought little change in a quality of existence which was centuries-old and which was underwritten by the racist attitudes and practices of most whites. These attitudes and practices were realized in substandard education, lack of jobs, poor housing, inequality under the law, lynching of both black men and women, and other conditions of life with which black people were faced. Any changes in this reality might have been indefinitely postponed had it not been for the spread of black political consciousness and the rise of a number of black leaders, both male and female, during the course of the twentieth century. Black political consciousness and black leaders were not unknown before the turn of the century: Harriet Tubman, Sojourner Truth, Frederick Douglass, Nat Turner, and others, were eloquent and powerful spokespeople and activists. But with the twentieth century came a massive emigration of blacks from the South to the North. Although the North shared most of the attitudes of the South, there were more opportunities for blacks in the industrial cities than in the primarily agrarian South. Many thousands of black people emigrated to the North during the years of the First World War, when the lack of white labor created a need for their services; it should also be mentioned that over 400,000 blacks were made to serve in the war even though, in most parts of the United States, they were essentially disenfranchised citizens. During the postwar depression, however, black workers were the first to suffer and to lose their jobs. But the emigration brought a changed political consciousness for black people; more voted, for example.

In 1910 the National Association for the Advancement of Colored People was founded and contributed to this political progress and the growing awareness among black people that they were an oppressed group and that this should be changed. The work of the NAACP was supplemented in 1911 with the founding of the National League on Urban Conditions Among Negroes (later known as the National Urban League). The work of black leaders of this time—for example, Ida Wells-Barnett (1862–1931), A. Philip Randolph (1889–1979), W. E. B. Du Bois (1868–1963), Mary Mcleod Bethune (1875–1955)—who were visible and vocal opponents of lynching, promoters

W. E. B. Du Bois

Marcus Garvey

The Black Muslims

Martin Luther King, Jr.

of educational opportunities for blacks, and labor union organizers, kept this movement toward equality and against oppression a vital force in American history, which would culminate in the civil rights movement of the 1960s.

The year 1919 saw the rise to prominence of another important black leader, Marcus Garvey (1887–1940), a native of Jamaica. Garvey's political base was Harlem in New York City, a major black ghetto. Garvey emphasized the African origins of black Americans and taught his followers to refer to themselves as "black" rather than "Negro." He claimed his people were the descendents of the "greatest and proudest race who ever peopled the earth," and generated a movement of black emigration from America to Africa. Garvey encouraged and influenced an important black literary movement, the so-called Harlem Renaissance of the 1920s. Several of its leaders derived inspiration from him, notably Langston Hughes and Countee Cullen.

Garvey's philosophy also extended indirectly to the Black Muslim movement, through his influence on the father of its most vigorous proselytizer, Malcom X (1925–1965). Malcolm X was converted in prison by his brother to the religion of Islam. After his release he became a spokesman for Elijah Muhammad, founder of the movement. Most of his followers were people of the same background who had flocked to Garvey's standard—recent migrants from the South who now lived in poverty in the black ghettos of northern cities. Malcolm X attempted to overcome their feeling of helplessness by giving them a new religion to take the place of the white man's Christianity and by restoring black pride. This new religion was Islam, which Malcolm X described as the true faith of Africans. Though he and his followers were firm believers, they were not fanatics. They did not renounce worldliness as a life of sin. They urged blacks to pool their resources and establish black-owned businesses. This would lead to economic independence and a heightened sense of self. The Muslims taught their adherents to avoid aggression and to fight only when attacked. Their charismatic minister broke with the Black Muslims in 1964. In February 1965 he was assassinated as he started to speak at a rally in Harlem.

In the meantime black consciousness was being expressed through other forms. One was the Congress of Racial Equality (CORE), founded by James Farmer in 1942. His announced aim was to translate "love of God and man" into specific crusades against injustice. By 1960 CORE had combined its efforts with those of other political organizations seeking to end discrimination against blacks. It helped in promoting "freedom rides" for civil rights into the South and boycotts against racist shopkeepers. After 1955 Farmer often collaborated with Martin Luther King, Jr. (1929–1968), a young Baptist minister. Like Farmer, King also embraced the Gandhian philosophy of nonviolence. For more than ten years he was widely regarded—and feared—as the most effective defender of black rights. His career was brought to a tragic end by an assassin's bullet as he stood on the balcony of a motel in Memphis in 1968.

Important successors to King, Farmer, and in a sense the Black Muslims, were the Black Panthers. Their movement began during the civil rights confrontations of the 1950s and 1960s in Alabama and Mississippi. From there it rapidly spread northward and about 1968 established its headquarters in Oakland, California. Its leaders—such men as Huey Newton, Bobby Seale, and Eldridge Cleaver—adopted for their party the name of Black Panthers. They saw in the panther an animal slow to take the initiative of aggression but fierce in retaliation when attacked by its enemies. The Panthers differed from other black activists in a number of ways. First of all, they were frankly revolutionary and not nonviolent. They believed that only by seizing power could they redress society's wrongs against black people. Second, the Black Panthers, unlike some of their forerunners, did not advocate a return to Africa, but sought an end to racism in America. The Black Panthers also professed a kind of internationalism similar to that of other revolutionaries.

The Black Panthers

Black movements in the 1970s to some degree retreated from militant commitment. Even the Black Panthers declared their willingness to work within the existing system for reform. Civil rights laws enacted under the Johnson administration in the 1960s have brought U.S. blacks some measure of equality with regard to voting rights—and, to a much lesser degree, school desegregation. In other areas, such as housing and job opportunities, blacks continue to suffer disadvantage and discrimination, as a result of white racism, which underwrites the belief that blacks should be satisfied with the gains they have made, and the general recalcitrance of administrations following Lyndon Johnson's domestically innovative one. These problems are not confined to the United States. In Great Britain, for example, where there has been a large immigration of blacks from former colonies, extreme discrimination in jobs and housing menaces the chances for early or satisfactory integration. Because the momentum for reform has slowed, black leaders are less able than in the 1960s to chart their movement's direction. Meanwhile black people derive continued strength not only from the conviction that the battle for equality is both justified and still to be won, but from the example of African and Caribbean nations emerging into independent statehood.

Blacks in the 1970s

3. COMMITMENT: YOUTH AND WOMEN

The years from 1964 through 1972 were marked by a protest and upheaval by the younger generation more rampant than the world had witnessed in many decades. They were committed, as were blacks, to

Vietnam Protest, 1971. Veterans of the U.S. Armed Forces march on the capitol to protest continued U.S. involvement in the war in Vietnam.

The youth rebellion

the assertion of their right to be heard. In the United States this rebellion was fueled by the war in Vietnam. Young men, drafted to fight in a war they despised, rebelled against the idea that it was their "duty" to serve. Together, young men and women proclaimed instead their duty to question anew the presuppositions that had led the U.S. into its unhappy military predicament. Science antagonized them because of its association with war-making. Knowledge that was not "relevant" to the world's problems was questioned with regard to its worth. Young leaders urged their peers to leave their college books and address the problems of the "real" world: overpopulation, industrial pollution, mistreatment of blacks and other minorities. It was this rebellion that exposed the inhumanity of the American adventure in Southeast Asia. Long before adult liberals spoke out against the bombing raids and body-counts of that war, students in colleges and universities stormed the institutions of the Establishment in angry protest. Although they did not stop the war, they helped to bring about President Johnson's retirement in 1968. Their *compères* in France, who rioted in May 1968, contributed to the defeat of President Charles de Gaulle.

Radicalism in the 1970s

Political radicalism no longer shapes the mind of the West's youth as it did in the late 1960s, a fact explained in large part by the end of hostilities in Vietnam. Radicalism's much-distorted reflection, however, appears in the activities of terrorist gangs such as that which in 1978 abducted and eventually killed the moderate Italian political leader Aldo Moro. Hoping their extremist tactics would help divide Italy and somehow produce a revolution, the gang's leaders discovered instead that they had conducted a sterile exercise in terror for its own sake.

Not all young rebels in the 1960s and 1970s committed themselves to a life of radical political activism. Some turned for spiritual or psychological comfort to fundamentalist religious movements. Some declared their disgust with the world by "dropping out," living in communities of their own design apart from society. Others devoted themselves to a counterculture reflected in the intensely personal music and lyrics of young popular musicians, in the custom of drug-taking, and in the freedom to live with each other without marriage. Social rebellion of this sort infected various countries to various degrees. It was primarily a movement of urban middle-class youths. Though in some cases their rejection of older values was the result of deeply held and enduring convictions, in many others their declaration of independence was short-lived, amounting to little more than the customary behavior of uncertain and impatient adolescents.

Youthful counterculture

Women, like blacks and young people, began to assert themselves during the 1960s and 1970s. As was the case with the youth rebellion, the women's movement began in the United States and was first directed from within the middle class. Some women in western European countries joined in the struggle for equal rights; by the mid-seventies the movement had spread worldwide, including the Third World nations, and was no longer limited to the middle class. Many of the early activists within the movement had been part of the youth rebellion during its most intense phase in the sixties. Their activism, in part, stemmed from a realization that even in a radical political atmosphere, women were relegated to second place. Women's position within society had changed radically since the nineteenth century. The assumption that the middle-class woman's place was in the home had been challenged by the ever-increasing demand for women workers and by the need experienced by more and more women to hold a job—either for financial reasons or because housework was for a growing

The women's movement

Students of the University of Paris During the Uprisings of 1968

Margaret Sanger, a Leader in the Movement to Awaken the World to the Necessity of Birth Control

number an unfulfilling occupation. The increased availability and social acceptance of birth-control devices meant that women were having fewer children, and that they could begin to exercise more control over the pattern of their lives.

Yet society seemed loath to acknowledge the implication of these changes: that women are equal to men. Women were paid less than men for similar work. Women with qualifications no different from men were turned down because of their gender when they applied for jobs. Women with excellent employment records were forced to rely on their husbands to establish credit. Political action helped alleviate some of these inequities in the late 1960s and the 1970s. The U.S. government instituted programs of "affirmative action" which mandated the hiring of qualified women as well as members of racial minority groups. The campaign for equality did not meet with universal approval, however. A particularly volatile subject was a woman's right to an abortion. Feminists argued that women must enjoy the freedom to plan for their future unencumbered by the responsibilities of motherhood if they choose, and that their bodies are theirs to govern. Their opponents, which included members of the so-called right-to-life movement, countered with the argument that abortion encouraged sexual irresponsibility; some declared that abortion is the equivalent of murder. By the end of the seventies the campaigners for women's equality, though still battling in the United States for passage of a constitutional Equal Rights Amendment, had a good many successes to their credit. Unlike the youth rebellion, which had run its course by that time, the women's movement, like that of black people, was based not on the disaffections of only one generation, but on a history of discrimination experienced by great numbers and recognized as unjust by a sizable proportion of majority opinion.

Abortion as a central issue

4. LITERATURE AND ART AS REFLECTIONS OF CONTEMPORARY PROBLEMS

Postwar authors

Not surprisingly, the work of many of the West's leading writers reflect the difficulties and commitments we have been surveying. During the immediate postwar years novelists concerned themselves with the horrors of war and of the totalitarian systems which had spawned the conflict of the 1940s. The Americans James Jones and Norman Mailer, in *From Here to Eternity* and *The Naked and the Dead,* portrayed the coarseness and cruelty of military life with ruthless realism. The German Günter Grass's first and probably most important novel, *The Tin Drum,* depicted the vicious and politically diseased life of Nazi Germany in the 1930s. In France, Jean-Paul Sartre, as a result of his own and his country's wartime experiences, recommitted himself in his novels, plays, and other writings to a life of active political involvement as a Marxist. Whereas he had previously defined hell in terms of individual hostilities, he now defined it in terms of class inequality. Unlike Sartre, his compatriot Albert Camus (1913–1960) was unable to construct a secular faith from his own perceptions of the world and its apparent absurdities. Though idealist enough to participate in the French resistance movement against the German occupation in World War II, and though proclaiming the virtues of rebellion, Camus remained tortured in novels such as *The Fall, The Plague,* and *The Rebel* by the problem of humanity's responsibility for its own miserable dilemma and by the limitations placed upon the ability of men and women to help each other.

The theme of individual alienation and helplessness, a reflection of the problems arising from the growth of state power, was one which writers addressed themselves to with increasing frequency in the 1960s and 1970s. The Russian Boris Pasternak, in his novel *Dr. Zhivago,* indicted the Soviet campaign to shape all its citizens to the same mold. Although both Pasternak and his compatriot Solzhenitsyn were awarded the Nobel Prize for literature, the former in 1958 and the latter in 1970, their works were condemned by the Soviet government and Solzhenitsyn was sent into exile. Western novelists dealt with the threat to individuality as well, building upon a prewar tradition most forcefully expressed in the writings of the Austrian Franz Kafka (1883–1924). Kafka's novels present a vision of humans in a hostile universe, hopelessly striving to come to terms with a remote and unknown power. It is not so much a dream as it is a nightmare composed of weird, fantastic details brought together in a terrifying pattern. His best-known work, *The Castle,* is at once a satire on bureaucracy and a philosophical representation of the isolation of the individual in the universe. The American novelist Saul Bellow (1915–   ) was concerned with many of these same themes, though Bellow spoke with a far gentler, if less compelling, voice than Kafka. He chose the modern city as the milieu for his fiction. His heroes in novels such as *The Adventures of Augie March, Henderson the Rain King,* and *Mr. Sammler's Planet* were all men trapped in a world turned upside down, condemned to seek personal understanding—indeed to maintain their sanity—in an environment at worst savage, at best absurd.

Alienation and helplessness

Simone de Beauvoir

Women authors wrote not only of the general loneliness of the human condition, but of the particular plight of women trapped in a world not of their own making. The Frenchwoman Simone de Beauvoir (1908–   ) in *The Second Sex,* a germinal study of the female condition, denounced the male middle class for turning not only workers but also its own women into objects for its own ends. American writers like Adrienne Rich, Tillie Olsen, and the philosopher Mary Daly helped define the politics and culture of the women's movement.

Women writers

The specific issues that drove men and women to committed action

James Baldwin

Black women authors

The absurd and fantastic

in the mid-1960s compelled writers to take sides as well. Günter Grass, in *Local Anaesthetic,* published in 1970, wrote of student unrest and political involvement. The movement for black equality encouraged a tradition in America that had burgeoned in the wake of the depression and World War II. One initiator of this tradition was Richard Wright (1908–1960), who grew up amid the rural poverty and violent racism of Mississippi. As a youth Wright drifted to Chicago and became a resident of and spokesman for the black ghetto. In his novel, *Native Son,* and his autobiography, *Black Boy,* he portrayed with scathing realism the oppression of working-class blacks. Despite the pretensions of the New Deal, he found that the burdens of that group had not been appreciably lightened. One of the most effective articulators of black aspiration and disenchantment in the 1960s was James Baldwin, the son of a Harlem clergyman. Living under the dual stigmas of his blackness and his homosexuality, Baldwin remained a self-exile in Paris for ten years following the Second World War. He returned to the United States to warn, in his most powerful book, *The Fire Next Time,* that unless whites awoke soon to the extent and pervasiveness of their racism, American society would be consumed by its own animosities.

Not only black men, but black women also wrote of the oppression and struggle of their race. Zora Neale Hurston (c. 1901–1960) was a novelist, anthropologist, and folklorist. In both her novels and anthropological studies Hurston wrote eloquently of the history of black people, their language and traditions. Her major novel, *Their Eyes Were Watching God* (1937), is about the strength of one black woman and her belief in her own strength and in herself. The poet Audre Lorde and the novelist Toni Morrison are two black women writers who also deal in detail and with an assured sense of history with the experience of black people, particularly with the black female experience. One of the most sensitive of contemporary black women writers was Lorraine Hansberry (1930–1965). A poet and dramatist, Hansberry won distinction in her tragically brief lifetime for her play *A Raisin in the Sun,* specifically the story of one black family in Chicago but actually the story of many black families existing under racism. Her dramatic talent was displayed even more clearly in *To Be Young, Gifted, and Black,* produced four years after her death. Hansberry wrote with defiance and anger, and sometimes in bitterness, when the beauty she saw in life was dimmed by bigotry and extinguished by repression.

Some authors, although they agreed with indictments of contemporary civilization, believed the human condition too hopeless to warrant direct attack. These writers expressed their despair by escaping into the absurd and fantastic. In the plays of Samuel Beckett (1906–   ), an Irishman who wrote in French, and of the Englishman Harold Pinter (1930–   ), nothing happens. Characters speak in the banalities that have become the hallmark of modern times. Words which are meaningless when spoken by human beings nevertheless take on a logic of their own; yet they explain nothing. Other authors, less willing, perhaps, to attempt to make a statement out of nothingness, have invaded the realms of hallucination, science fiction, and fantasy. The novels of the Americans William Burroughs and Kurt Vonnegut convey their readers from interior fantasizing to outer space. Significantly one of the most popular books among the youth of the sixties and seventies was *The Lord of the Rings,* a pseudosaga set in the fantasy world of "Middle Earth," written before the Second World War by the Englishman J. R. R. Tolkien.

Filmmakers, in the decades after the Second World War, made films which mirrored the problems and concerns of society, with a depth and artistic integrity seldom attempted or achieved previously. The Swede Ingmar Bergman, the Frenchmen Jean-Luc Godard and François Truffaut, the Italians Frederico Fellini and Michelangelo Antonioni, to name but a few of the most gifted directors, dealt in their films with the same themes that marked the literature of the period: loneliness, war, oppression, and corruption. One important factor facilitating the achievement of artistic quality was the general willingness on the part of censors—state or industry sponsored—to reflect public taste by permitting filmmakers great license in the handling of themes such as racism, violence, and sexuality. While there is no question that this relaxation led to exploitation, it cleared the way for extraordinarily powerful film statements, such as the American Arthur Penn's *Bonnie and Clyde* (1967) and the Italian Bernardo Bertolucci's *Last Tango in Paris* (1972), shocking declarations about humanity made possible by explicit depictions of violence and sex. Film, while gaining a general maturity it had heretofore lacked, did not desert its role as entertainment. The international popularity of the British rock-and-roll group, the Beatles, was translated, for example, into equally successful films, charming, slapstick escapism which nevertheless proclaimed the emancipation of youth from the confining formalities and conventions of their elders.

Film

Unlike writers or filmmakers, the majority of postwar artists did not use their work as a vehicle to express either ideological commitment or a concern for the human situation. Following trends established by the impressionists and cubists, they spoke neither about the world or to the world, but instead to each other and to the extremely small coterie of initiates who understood their artistic language. Foremost among the postwar schools of art was abstract expressionism, whose chief exponents were the painters Jackson Pollack (1912–1956), William deKooning (1904–   ), and Franz Kline (1910–1962). Their interests lay in further experimentation with the relationships between color, texture, and surface, to the total exclusion of "meaning" or "message" in the traditional sense. Jasper

Fine arts

Mahoning by Franz Kline. A work representative of the abstract expressionists' desire to explore the varieties of light, texture, and surface.

See color plates following page 1088

Johns's painting of the American flag insisted that the viewer see it not as *a* painting—that is, something to be interpreted—but instead as painting, the treatment of canvas with paint. Robert Rauschenberg, in revolt against the abstract expressionists, exhibited blank white panels, insisting that by so doing he was pressing art to the ultimate question of a choice of medium. Painters fought the notion that their work in some way expressed disgust with an empty civilization. "My paintings are based on the fact that only what can be seen is there," declared the American Frank Stella, who painted stripes on irregularly shaped canvases. "Pop" art, a phenomenon of the late sixties which took as its subject everyday objects such as soup cans and comic-strip heroes, was likewise, according to its practitioners, not a protest against the banality of industrialism but another experiment in abstractions.

Rothko

Even the remote and yet extraordinarily compelling abstractions of Mark Rothko (1903–1970), glowing or somber rectangles of color imposed upon other rectangles, were said by the artist himself to represent "nothing but content—no associations, only sensation." Only with the coming, in the 1970s, of the so-called hyper-realists, artists such as the American Duane Hanson, who recreates his invariably depressing human subjects in plastic down to the last eyelash, can we perhaps say that some artists are making a statement not only about technique but about what they perceive as the vacuity of life.

5. THE CRISIS OF ECOLOGY AND POPULATION

Pessimism about the human condition derived not only from concern for the problems of the present that we have been considering. It stemmed as well from a fear about the future, the future of the earth's human beings, of the earth itself, and of what is termed its ecology. The word "ecology" is often used primarily to refer to human beings and their environment, but it is much broader than that. Ecologists think of humans as a link in a vast chain of life which extends all the way back through mammals, amphibians, invertebrates, and the simplest microorganisms, which may be either plants or animals. In popular usage ecology may be synonymous with pollution problems. Again this is an oversimplification. The causes and prevention of pollution make up important elements in the study of ecology, but they are not the whole subject. Equally important is the use of our environment in ways that will safeguard the heritage of fertile soil, pure air, fresh water, and forests for those who come after us.

The meaning of ecology

Ecological violations consist not merely of poisoning the atmosphere and contaminating oceans, rivers, and lakes by dumping wastes into them, but of any assault upon them that makes them less valuable for human survival. The excessive construction of dams, for example, causes the silting of rivers and the accumulating of nitrates at a faster rate than the surrounding soil can absorb. The use of insecticides, especially those containing DDT, may result in upsetting the balance of nature. An example in the recent history of Malaysia illustrates such an occurrence. The Malaysian government resorted to extensive spraying of remote areas with DDT in the hope of stamping out malaria-carrying mosquitoes. The DDT killed the mosquitoes but also poisoned the flourishing cockroaches. The cockroaches in turn were eaten by the villages cats. The cats died of the DDT poison. The net result was a multiplication of rats formerly kept from a population explosion by their natural enemies, the cats. So badly disturbed was the balance of nature that a fresh supply of cats had to be airlifted from other regions. Other assaults upon the balance of nature have been even more serious. The Aswan High Dam of Egypt, undoubtedly valuable for increasing the water supply of that country, has at the same time cut down the flow of algal nutrients to the Mediterranean, with damaging effects on the fishing industry of various countries. From the ecological standpoint the rapid development of industry in modern times is almost an unmitigated disaster. For thousands of years the human race introduced into the environment no more waste substances than could easily be absorbed by the environment. But modern technology has introduced into nature a variety of wastes never abundant before. Among them are carbon monoxide, sulfur dioxide, and nitrogen oxides. And this is to say nothing of the discharge into nature of pesticides, the great host of synthetic products that are not biologically degradable, and the fruits of nuclear weapons testing.

*Other assaults upon
nature*

The ecological problem is caused not simply by the dumping of harmful and nondegradable products. It is also the result of wastage of land as our most valuable natural resource. In many parts of the world

Industrial Pollution. This photo shows steel mills in Westfalenhuette, West Germany. While polluting gases and particular matter are released into the air, industrial wastes, both thermal and chemical, are released into nearby waters.

Diminishing land resources

rivers run brown because they are filled with earth washed from the fields bordering them. In some of the largest American cities two-thirds to three-quarters of the land area is paved with streets and parking lots. Meanwhile, the nation's crop land is shrinking at an alarming rate. Ecologists say that much of this land will probably have to be abandoned.

Ecology and the population explosion

A close link exists between the problems of ecology and the population explosion. Indeed, if population control had remained a reality, the problems of ecology might well have passed unnoticed for many years. For example, New York City on the eve of the Civil War had a total population of 700,000. The area was not essentially smaller than what it is now. Yet the inhabitants of the five boroughs constituting the city have multiplied ten times over. This increase has been accompanied by physical transformations that have facilitated crowded living by masses of people. Oil lamps were replaced by gaslight and then by electricity, horse-drawn wagons and carriages by trolley cars, automobiles, subways, and buses. While some of these inventions eliminated a few forms of pollution, the general effect was to multiply sources of contamination and abuse of the natural environment. The example of New York City can be duplicated in many other overcrowded areas, not only in America but especially in Asia. Calcutta now has a population of 7 million, compared with 3 million in 1961. Tokyo has grown from 9 million to over 11.5 million in little more than fifteen years.

As the population increases, human beings create more and more problems and the damage done by each person escalates rapidly. Conditions in Los Angeles illustrate the danger. Despite excellent laws, the city makes little progress in carrying them out. Increases in the number of smog-producers nullify every victory the smog-control experts succeed in gaining. The worst offenders in vitiating ecological progress are the big industrial powers. They combine exhaustion of natural resources with contamination of the environment by industrial poisons, and consume hundreds of times more natural products than do most of the inhabitants of the Third World. The oil shortages of the 1970s, produced by the uncertain political state of the Middle East, forced the West—and particularly the United States—to become aware of its wasteful ways. Whether those shortages will also compel the West to expend its resources less extravagantly remains to be seen.

Most nations of the contemporary world are in danger of being overwhelmed by a population explosion. Its major cause has been what the experts call the demographic revolution. By this is meant an overturning of the ancient balance between births and deaths, which formerly kept the population on a stationary or slowly rising level. This balance is a biological condition common to nearly all species. For thousands of years humankind was no exception. It is estimated, for example, that the total population of the earth at the beginning of the Christian era was about 250 million. More than sixteen centuries passed before another quarter-billion had been added to the total. Not until 1860 did the population of the globe approximate 1 billion. From then on the increase was vastly more rapid. The sixth half-billion, added about 1960, required scarcely more than ten years.

What have been the causes of this radical imbalance known as the demographic revolution? Fundamentally, what has happened has been the achievement of a twentieth-century deathrate alongside a medieval

Effects of population explosion

The demographic revolution

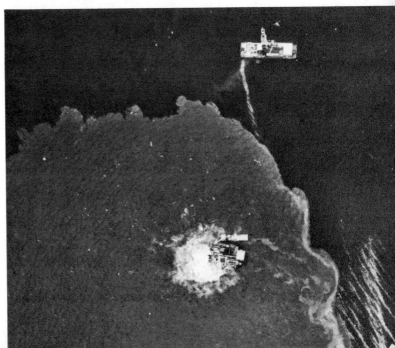

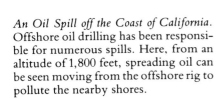

An Oil Spill off the Coast of California. Offshore oil drilling has been responsible for numerous spills. Here, from an altitude of 1,800 feet, spreading oil can be seen moving from the offshore rig to pollute the nearby shores.

birthrate. Infant mortality rates have markedly declined. Deaths of mothers in childbirth have also diminished. The great plagues, such as cholera, typhus, and tuberculosis, take a much smaller toll than they did in earlier centuries. Wars and famines still number their victims by the millions, yet such factors are insufficient to counteract an uncurbed rate of reproduction. Though the practice of contraception has been approved by the governments of such nations as India, China, and Japan, only in the last decade have the effects been worthy of notice. In some countries poverty, religion, and ignorance have made the widespread use of contraceptives difficult. Leaders in Third World countries charge that attempts by Western powers to encourage them to limit population growth, either by contraceptive devices or by sterilization, is a not-so-subtle form of genocide.

The demographic revolution has not affected all countries uniformly. Its incidence has been most conspicuous in the underdeveloped nations of Central and South America, Africa, and Asia. Whereas the population of the world as a whole will double, at present rates. of increase, in thirty-five years, that of Central and South America will multiply twofold in only twenty-six years. An outstanding example is that of Brazil. In 1900 its population was estimated to be 17 million. By 1975 this total had grown to 98 million, more than a fivefold increase. Mexico and Venezuela have two of the highest birthrates in the world. The population of Asia (excluding the USSR and Japan) grew from 813 million in 1900 to approximately 2 billion in 1975. By way of summary, at mid-century, the population of the underdeveloped portions of the globe was more than twice that of the developed portions. Their total land areas were about equal.

6. ACHIEVEMENTS AND LIMITATIONS OF SCIENCE AND TECHNOLOGY

The magnitude of the world's problems has encouraged doubt and pessimism among some of its most creative thinkers. Yet the majority of those charged with the responsibility of finding solutions to the problems—primarily politicians and civil servants—remain cautiously optimistic. For solutions they have continued to turn, paradoxically, to those agencies responsible, in many cases, for the creation of the problems: science and technology. Scientists and technicians invented and perfected the internal combustion engine and the chemical DDT. Now other scientists and technicians are seeking ways to combat their deleterious effects. Scientific research has been responsible for the medical advances which have helped to produce worldwide population increase. No one would argue, of course, that the research should not have taken place, or that the continuing battle against disease is not one of humanity's most worthwhile engagements. Most would agree, however, that science must move as quickly as possible to come up with a safe and simple method of controlling birth, as it continues to fight to prolong life.

The achievements of science in the field of health during the past half-century have been truly remarkable. Two discoveries of great importance have enabled scientists to understand more clearly the ways in which the human body receives and transmits disease. The discovery of viruses was the result of experimentation conducted chiefly by the American biochemist Wendell Stanley in the 1930s. Viruses are microscopic organisms which show signs of life—including the ability to reproduce—only when existing inside living cells. They are the cause of many human diseases, including measles, poliomyelitis (infantile paralysis), and rabies. Not until the nature of viruses was understood could scientists begin to develop means of treating and preventing the virus-produced illnesses in human beings. A second most important discovery that has increased our understanding of human life occurred in 1953, when the Englishman F. H. C. Crick and the American James D. Watson further unlocked the mysteries of genetic inheritance that had been explored by Gregor Mendel at the end of the nineteenth century. Crick and Watson successfully analyzed deoxyribonucleic acid, or DNA, the chemical molecular structure that occurs in the nuclei of gene cells. They discovered that DNA is composed of smaller molecules of four different kinds, linked together in spiral chains. The arrangement of these molecules in each cell forms a

The discovery of viruses;
DNA

The Decoding of DNA. Left: F. H. C. Crick and James D. Watson discuss their efforts to analyze the molecular structure of DNA. Right: A model of the molecular structure of DNA. The dual spiral chains are called a double helix.

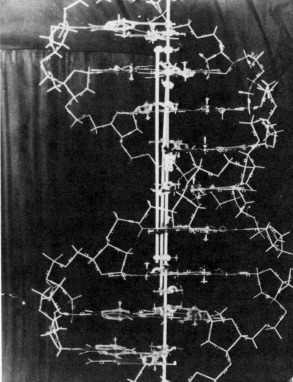

distinct chemical message which determines the character of the genes and therefore of the human organism of which they are a part. The knowledge gained through analysis of DNA has enabled scientists and doctors to understand the causes of hereditary disease and also, by altering a patient's body chemistry, to prevent it. Despite the great benefits that have resulted from this recent discovery, scientists and others have warned that an understanding of the workings of DNA could lead to dangerous tampering with the genetic processes, as, for example, in attempts to produce artificially a breed of more "perfect" human beings.

Medical advances: sulfa drugs, antibiotics, tranquilizers

Experimentation based upon a fuller understanding of the causes of disease has led to the discovery of new medicines to treat it. In 1935 a German named Gerhard Domagk discovered the first of the sulfa drugs, which he called sulfanilamide. Soon others were added to the list. Each was found to be marvelously effective in curing or checking such diseases as rheumatic fever, gonorrhea, scarlet fever, and meningitis. About 1930, the Englishman Sir Alexander Fleming described the first of the antibiotics, which came to be known as penicillin. Antibiotics are chemical agents produced by living organisms and possessing the power to check or kill bacteria. Many have their origin in molds, fungi, algae, and in simple organisms living in the soil. Penicillin was eventually found to be a drug that could produce spectacular results in the treatment of pneumonia, syphilis, peritonitis, tetanus, and numerous other maladies hitherto frequently fatal. Scientists used knowledge obtained through the analysis of DNA to strengthen the cultures used to develop penicillin. In the 1940s the second most famous of the antibiotics—streptomycin—was discovered by the American Dr. Selman W. Waksman. Streptomycin seems to hold its greatest promise in the treatment of tuberculosis, though it has been used for numerous other infections that do not yield to penicillin. Another category of so-called miracle drugs is tranquilizers. Introduced in 1955, they came to be used frequently in the treatment of mental disorders such as manic-depression and have achieved success in making violent patients more tractable. Although these drugs do not themselves effect cures, they help make patients more accessible to other forms of therapy and enable them in many instances to lead relatively normal lives outside institutions in which they would otherwise be incarcerated. That tranquilizers have been misused by men and women indiscriminately as a dangerously simple method of achieving a desired state of mind is no more than further confirmation of the fact that science continues to create new problems as it solves old ones.

Dr. Jonas Salk in His Laboratory

As important as the discovery of new drugs to treat disease has been the development of new means of preventing it. Sir Edward Jenner discovered the first successful vaccine, used to prevent smallpox, in 1796. But not until the 1950s were vaccines found that could protect from diseases such as mumps, measles, and cholera. One of the most exciting breakthroughs occurred with the development of an innoculation against poliomyelitis by the American Dr. Jonas Salk, in 1953. Still to be discovered are effective agents for the successful treatment of two of the world's most deadly killers, heart disease and cancer. The technique of transplanting a heart from a recently dead human being to a live but ailing heart patient, first perfected by the South African, Dr. Christiaan Barnard, has proved of limited usefulness. More effective have been operations substituting plastic valves for defective arteries leading to the heart, and the insertion of electrical devices—"pacemakers"—to steady or stimulate heartbeat. Testing has produced a definite link between cancer and cigarette smoking, as well as industrial and urban pollution—another example of the way in which technology generates difficulties as it resolves others. Doctors continue to experiment with cancer treatment by X-ray and chemical therapy. But despite the dedication of researchers and the expenditure of large sums to assist their work, a cure eludes them.

Vaccines, heart disease, and cancer

Few would today oppose continued campaigns by scientists intent upon eradicating disease. Governments have found it increasingly difficult, however, to justify the spending of vast sums of public money on programs designed to facilitate the exploration of outer space. From their inception, these "experiments" have resembled international competitions between the United States and the Soviet Union as much as they have scientific and technological investigations. On October 4, 1957, the government of the Soviet Union rocketed the first artificial satellite into space at a speed of about 18,000 miles an hour. Though it weighed nearly 200 pounds, it was propelled upward higher than 500 miles. This Russian achievement gave the English language a new word—Sputnik, the Russian for satellite or fellow traveler. A month later the Soviet scientists surpassed their first success by sending a new and much larger Sputnik to an altitude of approximately 1,000 miles. These Sputniks were the forerunners of others of greater significance. In April 1961, the Russians succeeded in sending the first man into orbit around the earth. Meanwhile, scientists and military specialists in the United States had been competing to match the Soviets' achievements. After a number of successes with animals and "uninhabited" capsules, and the suborbital journey of a manned capsule, they succeeded, on February 20, 1962, in launching the first American manned spaceship into orbit around the earth. The successful astronaut was Lieutenant-Colonel John H. Glenn, Jr., who circled the globe three times at a top speed of over 17,000 miles per hour. In 1966 a United States Navy officer left the cabin of his spacecraft and walked in space for forty-four minutes, hundreds of miles above the earth. His feat was surpassed in July 1969, when Neil Armstrong, a civilian astronaut, left his lunar landing module and became the first man on the moon's surface. All over the world these successful voyages and those that followed were hailed as events of capital importance. They did promise an extension of our knowledge of outer space and could doubtless prepare the way for exploration of the

Space exploration

The First Lunar Landing. Astronaut Edwin E. Aldrin, Jr., is photographed walking near the lunar module of Apollo 11. Astronaut Neil Armstrong, who took the picture, and part of the lunar module are reflected in Aldrin's face plate.

moon and eventually of distant planets. But by the mid-1970s, both the United States and the Soviet Union had drastically cut back their space programs in response to demands on their economies from other quarters. Plans for a space "shuttle" and laboratory, plus continuing experiments of a minor nature, kept the programs alive. But their value was being questioned, in view of the billions required to keep them operational.

Nuclear science: Einstein's discoveries

Undoubtedly it was in the area of nuclear science that the largest and most disturbing questions arose as to the capabilities, limitations, and implications of science and technology. Most of the eventual twentieth-century developments in this area were based upon the pioneering work of the physicist Albert Einstein (1879–1955). In 1905 Einstein began to challenge not merely the older conceptions of matter but practically the entire structure of traditional physics. The doctrine for which he is most noted is his principle of relativity. During the greater part of the nineteenth century, physicists had assumed that space and motion were absolute. Space was supposed to be filled with an intangible substance known as *ether,* which provided the medium for the undulations of light. But experiments performed by English and American physicists near the end of the century virtually exploded the ether hypothesis. Einstein then set to work to reconstruct the scheme of the universe in accordance with a different pattern. He maintained that space and motion, instead of being absolute, are relative to each other. Objects have not merely three dimensions but four. To the familiar length, breadth, and thickness, Einstein added a new dimension of *time* and represented all four as fused in a synthesis which he called the *space-time continuum.* In this way he sought to explain the idea that mass is dependent upon motion. Bodies traveling at high velocity have proportions of extension and mass different from what they would have at rest. Included also in the Einstein physics is the conception of a finite universe—that is, finite in space. The region of matter does not extend into infinity, but the universe has limits. While these are by no means definite boundaries, there is at least a region beyond which nothing exists. Space curves back upon itself so as to make of the universe a gigantic sphere within which are contained galaxies, solar systems, stars, and planets.

The Einstein theories had a major influence in precipitating other revolutionary developments in physics. By 1960 it had been discovered that the conception of the subatomic world as a miniature solar system was much too simple. The atom was found to contain not only positively charged protons and negatively charged electrons, but *positrons,* or positively charged electrons; *neutrons,* which carry no electric charges; and *mesons,* which may be either negative or positive. Mesons, it was discovered, exist not only within the atom (for about two millionths of a second) but are major components of the cosmic rays that are constantly bombarding the earth from somewhere in outer space.

Albert Einstein

Several of the developments in physics outlined above helped to make possible one of the most spectacular achievements in the history of science, the splitting of the atom to release the energy contained within it. Ever since it became known that the atom is composed primarily of electrical energy, physicists had dreamed of unlocking this source of tremendous power and making it available for man. As early as 1905 Einstein became convinced of the equivalence of mass and energy and worked out a formula for the conversion of one into the other, which he expressed as follows: $E = mc^2$. E represents the energy in ergs, m the mass in grams, and c the velocity of light in centimeters per second. In other words, the amount of energy locked within the atom is equal to the mass multiplied by the square of the velocity of light. But no practical application of this formula was possible until after the discovery of the neutron by the Englishman Sir James Chadwick in 1932. Since the neutron carries no charge of electricity, it is an ideal weapon for bombarding the atom. It is neither repulsed by the positively charged protons nor absorbed by the negatively charged electrons. Moreover, in the process of bombardment it produces more neutrons, which hit other atoms and cause them in turn to split and create neutrons. In this way the original reaction is repeated in an almost unending series.

In 1939 two German physicists, Otto Hahn and Fritz Strassman, succeeded in splitting atoms of uranium by bombarding them with neutrons. The initial reaction produced a chain of reactions, in much the same way that a fire burning at the edge of a piece of paper raises

Releasing the energy within the atom

The development of the atomic bomb

the temperature of adjoining portions of the paper high enough to cause them to ignite. Scientists in Germany, Great Britain, and the United States were spurred on by governments anxious to make use of these discoveries for military purposes during the Second World War. The first use made of the knowledge of atomic fission was in the preparation of an atomic bomb. The devastating weapon was the achievement of scientists working for the War Department of the United States. Some were physicists who had been exiled by Nazi or Fascist oppression. (Einstein himself, a native of Germany and a Jew, had left that country in the 1930s for the United States.)

The hydrogen bomb

Even more disturbing than the results of the bombs dropped on Japan at the end of World War II were the first tests of a hydrogen bomb by the United States Atomic Energy Commission in November 1952. The tests were conducted at Eniwetok Atoll in the South Pacific; an entire island disappeared after burning brightly for several hours. The hydrogen bomb, or H-bomb, is based upon fusion of hydrogen atoms, a process which requires the enormous heat generated by the splitting of uranium atoms to start the reaction. The fusion results in the creation of a new element, helium, which actually weighs less than the sum of the hydrogen atoms. The "free" energy left over provides the tremendous explosive power of the H-bomb. The force of hydrogen bombs is measured in *megatons,* each of which represents 1,000,000 tons of TNT. Thus a 5-megaton H-bomb would equal 250 times the power of the A-bombs dropped on Hiroshima and Nagasaki.

Clearly the scientists had, at the behest of their government, unleashed a weapon of devastating proportions upon the world. By the 1970s, not only the United States, but the Soviet Union, China, Brit-

An H-Bomb Mushrooms. The cloud spreads into a huge mushroom following a 1952 explosion of a hydrogen bomb in the Marshall Islands of the Pacific. The photo was taken 50 miles from the detonation site at about 12,000 feet. The cloud rose to 40,000 feet two minutes after the explosion. Ten minutes later the cloud stem had pushed about 25 miles. The mushroom portion went up to 10 miles and spread 100 miles.

Calder Hall. Built in 1956 in England, this was the world's first large-scale atomic power station. The two towers on the left are for cooling. Since this time such power plants have proliferated around the world. However, the near-catastrophic accident at the Three Mile Island Power Station close to Harrisburg, Pennsylvania, in March 1979 has spurred opponents to press even harder for a reexamination of the use of nuclear power.

ain, France, India, Israel, and other nations either possessed atomic weapons or were in the process of developing the technology to do so. Science was once and for all proved to be something other than "pure," that is, without practical and political implications. The application of its discoveries had become a burdensome fact of life for humanity the world over.

The proliferation of nuclear weapons

Governments experimented with schemes to harness nuclear energy for peaceful purposes. Some progress has been made in the development of atomic power as an alternative source of domestic and industrial fuel. But the dangers of radiation as a by-product suggest that this scheme may prove of limited value. During the late 1970s, when the West's supplies of oil were threatened, heated debate continued between advocates of further construction of atomic power plants and those who argued in favor of other energy forms—among them solar—as safer and cheaper alternatives. Meanwhile, technologists working for private industry made use of discoveries in atomic physics to pioneer the field of electronics. Electronics derives from that branch of physics which deals with the behavior and effects of electrons, or negative constituents within the atom. Electronic devices have multiplied in staggering profusion since World War II. Among them are devices to measure the trajectory of missiles, to give warnings of approaching missiles or aircraft, to make possible "blind" landings of airplanes, to store and release electrical signals, to amplify and regulate the transmission of light and sound images, and to provide the power for photoelectric cells that open doors and operate various automatic machines. The spacecraft industry, which has made possible the exploration of outer space, is closely dependent upon electronics.

The uses of atomic energy; electronics

The Age of Television. Left: The first working television pickup camera, 1929. Right: The Telstar communications satellite. Weighing only 170 pounds, and measuring 34 inches in diameter, it is powered by 3,600 solar cells. It circles the earth at a speed of 1,600 miles per hour, at a height of from 500 to 3,000 nautical miles.

Automation

The use of electronic devices for radio reception led to initial progress in automation. Automation should not be confused with mechanization, though it may be considered the logical extreme of that process. More correctly conceived, automation means a close integration of four elements: (1) a processing system; (2) a mechanical handling system; (3) sensing equipment; and (4) a control system. Though all of these elements are necessary, the last two are the most significant. Sensing equipment performs a function similar to that of the human senses. It observes and measures what is happening and sends the information thus gained to the control unit. It employs such devices as photoelectric cells, infra-red cells, high-frequency devices, and devices making use of X-rays, isotopes, and resonance. It operates without fatigue and much faster and more accurately than do the human senses. Moreover, its observations can be made in places unsafe for, or inaccessible to, human beings. A control system receives information from a sensing element, compares this information with that required by the "program,'" and then makes the necessary adjustments. This series of operations is continuous, so that a desired state is constantly maintained without any human intervention, except for that initially involved in "programming." This revolution has been greatly extended by the invention of lasers. A laser is a device for amplifying the focus and intensity of light. High-energy atoms are stimulated by light to amplify a beam of light. Lasers have demonstrated their value recently in medicine. They have been used effectively in arresting hemorrhaging in the retina in eye afflictions. Through automation, expensive and complicated machines are constantly taking the place of much human labor. Data processing machines and electronic computers are employed to control switching operations in railroad yards, to operate assembly lines, to operate machines that control other machines, and even to maintain blood pressure during critical operations in hospitals.

Electronic inventions have proved no more an unmixed blessing than have the other discoveries and developments of scientists and technicians. One obvious problem generated by devices that can do the work of humans is that they put humans out of work. Technological unemployment has become an important problem for the modern world. Though new industries absorbed many workers, others were bound to be displaced by automation. While the demand for skilled labor remained high, the so-called entry jobs performed by the unskilled were fast disappearing. They were being eliminated not by computers so much as by fork-lift trucks and motorized conveyors and sweepers. Mechanization of agriculture also eliminated thousands of jobs for unskilled and uneducated workers.

Technological Unemployement

Science and technology provide no panaceas for the problems of the world. If those problems are to be solved, men and women, not machines, will have to do the work. They will be better equipped to do so if they possess some sense of their own past. The lesson of history is not that it repeats itself. The lesson is, rather, that the present can be clearly perceived, and the future intelligently planned for, only when those responsible for the world's destiny understand the workings of human nature. And for knowledge of that extraordinarily complicated and fascinating mechanism, there is no better source than history.

SELECTED READINGS

• *Items so designated are available in paperback editions.*
• Banfield, Edward C., *The Unheavenly City: The Nature and Future of Our Urban Crisis,* rev. ed., Boston, 1974.
• Bell, Daniel, *The End of Ideology: On the Exhaustion of Political Ideas in the Fifties,* Glencoe, Ill., 1960.
  Beynon, Huw, *Working for Ford,* London, 1973. A recent analysis of England's industrial and labor problems. Stimulating and perceptive.
  Collins, Doreen, *The European Economic Community, 1958–72,* London, 1975. A thorough analysis of the Common Market, emphasizing the social policies that have emerged in Europe since 1958.
• Erlich, Paul, *The Population Bomb,* New York, 1968.
• Galbraith, John Kenneth, *The New Industrial State,* Boston, 1967. A penetrating analysis of the changes in capitalism wrought by advanced technology.
• Harrington, Michael, *The Other America: Poverty in the United States,* New York, 1962.
• Heilbroner, Robert, *The Future as History,* New York, 1960.

• ———, *An Inquiry into the Human Prospect,* New York, 1975, 1980.

Infeld, Leopold, *Albert Einstein: His Work and Its Influence on Our World,* New York, 1950. A general introduction.

Lerner, M., *The Age of Overkill,* New York, 1962.

• McKenzie, A. E. E., *The Major Achievements of Science,* New York, 1960.

• Marcuse, Herbert, *Counterrevolution and Revolt,* Boston, 1972.

• Popper, Karl, *The Open Society and Its Enemies,* rev. ed., London, 1962. A vigorous comparison of the totalitarian and democratic philosophies by a libertarian.

Rosenberg, Harold, *The Anxious Object: Art Today and Its Significance,* New York, 1964.

• Shonfield, Andrew, *Modern Capitalism: The Changing Balance of Public and Private Power,* New York, 1965.

• Toffler, Alan, *Future Shock,* New York, 1971. An extended essay on the consequences of rapid change in modern industrial society.

Von Laue, T. H., *The Global City: Freedom, Power and Necessity in the Age of World Revolutions,* Philadelphia, 1969.

SOURCE MATERIALS

Bowges, Hervé, comp., *The Student Revolts: The Activists Speak,* London, 1968. Interviews with participants of the student riots of May 1968 which shook France and almost toppled the government.

• Jackson, George, *Soledad Brother: The Prison Letters of George Jackson,* New York, 1970.

• Rich, Adrienne, *On Lies, Secrets, and Silence,* New York, 1979. Essays by a leading feminist thinker.

Snow, C. P., *The Two Cultures and a Second Look: An Expanded Version of the Two Cultures and the Scientific Revolution,* Cambridge, 1965. Argues that in the modern world the great divergence between science and the humanities has been a disastrous process.

• Solzhenitsyn, Alexsandr, *The Gulag Archipelago, 1918–1956,* New York, 1974–75. An account of prison camps during the Stalinist era by the exiled Russian novelist.

RULERS OF PRINCIPAL STATES SINCE 700 A.D.

The Carolingian Dynasty

Pepin, Mayor of the Palace, 714
Charles Martel, Mayor of the Palace, 715–741
Pepin I, Mayor of the Palace, 741; King, 751–768
Charlemagne, King, 768–814; Emperor, 800–814
Louis the Pious, Emperor, 814–840

MIDDLE KINGDOMS

Lothair, Emperor, 840–855
Louis (Italy), Emperor, 855–875
Charles (Provence), King, 855–863
Lothair II (Lorraine), King, 855–869

WEST FRANCIA

Charles the Bald, King, 840–877; Emperor, 875
Louis II, King, 877–879
Louis III, King, 879–882
Carloman, King, 879–884

EAST FRANCIA

Ludwig, King, 840–876
Carloman, King, 876–880
Ludwig, King, 876–882
Charles the Fat, Emperor, 876–887

Holy Roman Emperors

SAXON DYNASTY

Otto I, 962–973
Otto II, 973–983
Otto III, 983–1002
Henry II, 1002–1024

FRANCONIAN DYNASTY

Conrad II, 1024–1039
Henry III, 1039–1056
Henry IV, 1056–1106
Henry V, 1106–1125
Lothair II (of Saxony), King, 1125–1133; Emperor,
1133–1137

HOHENSTAUFEN DYNASTY

Conrad III, 1138–1152
Frederick I (Barbarossa), 1152–1190
Henry VI, 1190–1197
Philip of Swabia, 1198–1208 } Rivals
Otto IV (Welf), 1198–1215
Frederick II, 1220–1250
Conrad IV, 1250–1254

INTERREGNUM, 1254–1273

EMPERORS FROM VARIOUS DYNASTIES
Rudolf I (Hapsburg), 1273–1291

Adolf (Nassau), 1292–1298
Albert I (Hapsburg), 1298–1308
Henry VII (Luxemburg), 1308–1313
Ludwig IV (Wittelsbach), 1314–1347
Charles IV (Luxemburg), 1347–1378
Wenceslas (Luxemburg), 1378–1400
Rupert (Wittelsbach), 1400–1410
Sigismund (Luxemburg), 1410–1437

HAPSBURG DYNASTY

Albert II, 1438–1439
Frederick III, 1440–1493
Maximilian I, 1493–1519
Charles V, 1519–1556
Ferdinand I, 1556–1564
Maximilan II, 1564–1576
Rudolf II, 1576–1612
Matthias, 1612–1619
Ferdinand II, 1619–1637
Ferdinand III, 1637–1657
Leopold I, 1658–1705
Joseph I, 1705–1711
Charles VI, 1711–1740
Charles VII (not a Hapsburg), 1742–1745
Francis I, 1745–1765
Joseph II, 1765–1790
Leopold II, 1790–1792
Francis II, 1792–1806

Rulers of France from Hugh Capet

CAPETIAN KINGS

Hugh Capet, 987–996
Robert II, 996–1031
Henry I, 1031–1060
Philip I, 1060–1108
Louis VI, 1108–1137
Louis VII, 1137–1180
Philip II (Augustus), 1180–1223
Louis VIII, 1223–1226
Louis IX, 1226–1270
Philip III, 1270–1285
Philip IV, 1285–1314
Louis X, 1314–1316
Philip V, 1316–1322
Charles IV, 1322–1328

HOUSE OF VALOIS

Philip VI, 1328–1350
John, 1350–1364
Charles V, 1364–1380
Charles VI, 1380–1422
Charles VII, 1422–1461
Louis XI, 1461–1483
Charles VIII, 1483–1498
Louis XII, 1498–1515
Francis I, 1515–1547

Henry II, 1547–1559
Francis II, 1559–1560
Charles IX, 1560–1574
Henry III, 1574–1589

BOURBON DYNASTY

Henry IV, 1589–1610
Louis XIII, 1610–1643
Louis XIV, 1643–1715
Louis XV, 1715–1774
Louis XVI, 1774–1792

AFTER 1792

First Republic, 1792–1799
Napoleon Bonaparte, First Consul, 1799–1804
Napoleon I, Emperor, 1804–1814
Louis XVIII (Bourbon dynasty), 1814–1824
Charles X (Bourbon dynasty), 1824–1830
Louis Philippe, 1830–1848
Second Republic, 1848–1852
Napoleon III, Emperor, 1852–1870
Third Republic, 1870–1940
Pétain regime, 1940–1944
Provisional government, 1944–1946
Fourth Republic, 1946–1958
Fifth Republic, 1958–

Rulers of England

ANGLO-SAXON KINGS

Egbert, 802–839
Ethelwulf, 839–858
Ethelbald, 858–860
Ethelbert, 860–866
Ethelred, 866–871
Alfred the Great, 871–900
Edward the Elder, 900–924
Ethelstan, 924–940
Edmund I, 940–946
Edred, 946–955
Edwy, 955–959
Edgar, 959–975

Edward the Martyr, 975–978
Ethelred the Unready, 978–1016
Canute, 1016–1035 (Danish Nationality)
Harold I, 1035–1040
Hardicanute, 1040–1042
Edward the Confessor, 1042–1066
Harold II, 1066

ANGLO-NORMAN KINGS

William I (the Conqueror), 1066–1087
William II, 1087–1100
Henry I, 1100–1135
Stephen, 1135–1154

Angevin Kings

Henry II, 1154–1189
Richard I, 1189–1199
John, 1199–1216
Henry III, 1216–1272
Edward I, 1272–1307
Edward II, 1307–1327
Edward III, 1327–1377
Richard II, 1377–1399

House of Lancaster

Henry IV, 1399–1413
Henry V, 1413–1422
Henry VI, 1422–1461

House of York

Edward IV, 1461–1483
Edward V, 1483
Richard III, 1483–1485

Tudor Sovereigns

Henry VII, 1485–1509
Henry VIII, 1509–1547
Edward VI, 1547–1553
Mary, 1553–1558
Elizabeth I, 1558–1603

Stuart Kings

James I, 1603–1625
Charles I, 1625–1649

Commonwealth and Protectorate, 1649–1659

Later Stuart Monarchs

Charles II, 1660–1685
James II, 1685–1688
William III and Mary II, 1689–1694
William III alone, 1694–1702
Anne, 1702–1714

House of Hanover

George I, 1714–1727
George II, 1727–1760
George III, 1760–1820
George IV, 1820–1830
William IV, 1830–1837
Victoria, 1837–1901

House of Saxe-Coburg-Gotha

Edward VII, 1901–1910
George V, 1910–1917

House of Windsor

George V, 1917–1936
Edward VIII, 1936
George VI, 1936–1952
Elizabeth II, 1952–

Prominent Popes

Silvester I, 314–335
Leo I, 440–461
Gelasius I, 492–496
Gregory I, 590–604
Nicholas I, 858–867
Silvester II, 999–1003
Leo IX, 1049–1054
Nicholas II, 1058–1061
Gregory VII, 1073–1085
Urban II, 1088–1099
Paschal II, 1099–1118
Alexander III, 1159–1181

Innocent III, 1198–1216
Gregory IX, 1227–1241
Boniface VIII, 1294–1303
John XXII, 1316–1334
Nicholas V, 1447–1455
Pius II, 1458–1464
Alexander VI, 1492–1503
Julius II, 1503–1513
Leo X, 1513–1521
Adrian VI, 1522–1523
Clement VII, 1523–1534
Paul III, 1534–1549

Paul IV, 1555–1559
Gregory XIII, 1572–1585
Gregory XVI, 1831–1846
Pius IX, 1846–1878
Leo XIII, 1878–1903
Pius X, 1903–1914
Benedict XV, 1914–1922

Pius XI, 1922–1939
Pius XII, 1939–1958
John XXIII, 1958–1963
Paul VI, 1963–1978
John Paul I, 1978
John Paul II, 1978–

Rulers of Austria and Austria-Hungary

*Maximilian I (Archduke), 1493–1519
*Charles I (Charles V in the Holy Roman Empire), 1519–1556
*Ferdinand I, 1556–1564
*Maximilian II, 1564–1576
*Rudolph II, 1576–1612
*Matthias, 1612–1619
*Ferdinand II, 1619–1637
*Ferdinand III, 1637–1657
*Leopold I, 1658–1705
*Joseph I, 1705–1711
*Charles VI, 1711–1740
Maria Theresa, 1740–1780

*Joseph II, 1780–1790
*Leopold II, 1790–1792
*Francis II, 1792–1835 (Emperor of Austria as Francis I after 1804)
Ferdinand I, 1835–1848
Francis Joseph, 1848–1916 (after 1867 Emperor of Austria and King of Hungary)
Charles I, 1916–1918 (Emperor of Austria and King of Hungary)
Republic of Austria, 1918–1938 (dictatorship after 1934)
Republic restored, under Allied occupation, 1945–1956
Free Republic, 1956–

*Also bore title of Holy Roman Emperor.

Rulers of Prussia and Germany

*Frederick I, 1701–1713
*Frederick William I, 1713–1740
*Frederick II (the Great), 1740–1786
*Frederick William II, 1786–1797
*Frederick William III, 1797–1840
*Frederick William IV, 1840–1861
*William I, 1861–1888 (German Emperor after 1871)

Frederick III, 1888
William II, 1888–1918
Weimar Republic, 1918–1933
Third Reich (Nazi Dictatorship), 1933–1945
Allied occupation, 1945–1952
Division into Federal Republic of Germany in west and German Democratic Republic in east, 1949–

*Kings of Prussia.

Rulers of Russia

Ivan III, 1462–1505
Basil III, 1505–1533
Ivan IV, 1533–1584
Theodore I, 1584–1598
Boris Godunov, 1598–1605

Theodore II, 1605
Basil IV, 1606–1610
Michael, 1613–1645
Alexius, 1645–1676
Theodore III, 1676–1682

Ivan V and Peter I, 1682–1689
Peter I (the Great), 1689–1725
Catherine I, 1725–1727
Peter II, 1727–1730
Anna, 1730–1740
Ivan VI, 1740–1741
Elizabeth, 1741–1762
Peter III, 1762

Catherine II (the Great), 1762–1796
Paul, 1796–1801
Alexander I, 1801–1825
Nicholas I, 1825–1855
Alexander II, 1855–1881
Alexander III, 1881–1894
Nicholas II, 1894–1917
Soviet Republic, 1917–

Rulers of Italy

Victor Emmanuel II, 1861–1878
Humbert I, 1878–1900
Victor Emmanuel III, 1900–1946
Fascist Dictatorship, 1922–1943
   (maintained in northern Italy until 1945)

Humbert II, May 9–June 13, 1946
Republic, 1946–

Rulers of Spain

Ferdinand { and Isabella, 1479–1504
and Philip I, 1504–1506
and Charles I, 1506–1516
Charles I (Holy Roman Emperor Charles V),
  1516–1556
Philip II, 1556–1598
Philip III, 1598–1621
Philip IV, 1621–1665
Charles II, 1665–1700
Philip V, 1700–1746
Ferdinand VI, 1746–1759
Charles III, 1759–1788
Charles IV, 1788–1808

Ferdinand VII, 1808
Joseph Bonaparte, 1808–1813
Ferdinand VII (restored), 1814–1833
Isabella II, 1833–1868
Republic, 1868–1870
Amadeo, 1870–1873
Republic, 1873–1874
Alfonso XII, 1874–1885
Alfonso XIII, 1886–1931
Republic, 1931–1939
Fascist Dictatorship, 1939-1975
Juan Carlos I, 1975-

Principal Rulers of India

Chandragupta (Maurya Dynasty), c. 332–298 B.C.
Asoka (Maurya Dynasty), c. 273–232 B.C.
Vikramaditya (Gupta Dynasty), 375–413 A.D.
Harsha (Vardhana Dynasty), 606–648
Babur (Mogul Dynasty), 1526–1530
Akbar (Mogul Dynasty), 1556–1605
Jahangir (Mogul Dynasty), 1605–1627
Shah Jahan (Mogul Dynasty), 1627–1658

Aurangzeb (Mogul Dynasty), 1658–1707
Regime of British East India Company, 1757–1858
British *raj*, 1858–1947
Division into self-governing dominions of India
  and Pakistan, 1947
Republic of India, 1950–
Republic of Pakistan, 1956–
Republic of Bangladesh, 1971–

Dynasties of China

Hsia, c. 2205–1766 B.C. (?)
Shang (Yin), c. 1766 (?)–1100 B.C.
Chou, c. 1100–256 B.C.
Ch'in, 221–207 B.C.
Han (Former), 206 B.C.–8 A.D.
Interregnum (Wang Mang, usurper), 8–23 A.D.
Han (Later), 25–220
Wei, 220–265
Tsin (Chin), 265–420
Southern Dynasties: Sung (Liu Sung), Ch'i, Liang, Ch'eñ, 420–589

Northern Dynasties: Northern Wei, Western Wei, Eastern Wei, Northern Ch'i, Northern Chou, 386–581
Sui, 589–618
T'ang, 618–907
Five Dynasties: Later Liang, Later T'ang, Later Tsin, Later Han, Later Chou, 907–960
Sung, 960–1279
Yüän (Mongol), 1279–1368
Ming, 1368–1644
Ch'ing (Manchu) Dynasty, 1644–1912

Periods of Chinese Rule

Chinese Republic, 1912–1949

Communist Regime, 1949–

Periods of Japanese Rule

Legendary Period, c. 660 B.C.–530 A.D.
Foundation Period, 530–709 A.D.
Taika (Great Reform) Period, 645–654
Nara Period, 710–793
Heian Period, 794–1192
Kamakura Period, 1192–1333
Namboku-cho ("Northern and Southern Dynasties") Period, 1336–1392

Muromachi (Ashikaga) Period, 1392–1568
Sengoku ("Country at War") Period, c. 1500–1600
Sengoku Period, c. 1500–1600
Edo (Tokugawa) Period, 1603–1867
Meiji Period (Mutsuhito), 1868–1912
Taisho Period (Yoshihito), 1912–1926
Showa Period (Hirohito), 1926–

Rulers of Principal African States

Ewuare the Great, Oba of Benin, 1440–1473
Muhammad Runfa, King of Kano, 1463–1499
Afonso I, King of Kongo, 1506–1543
Ibrahim Maje, King of Katsina, 1549–1567
Idris Alooma, Mai of Bornu, 1569–ca. 1619
Osei Tutu, King of Asante, ca. 1670–1717
Agaja, King of Dahomey, 1708–1740
Sayyid Said, ruler of Zanzibar and Muscat, 1804–1856
Shaka, King of the Zulu, 1818–1828
Moshesh, King of Basutoland, 1824–1868
Menelik, King of Shoa, 1865–1889; Emperor of Ethiopia, 1889–1913
Haile Selassie, Emperor of Ethiopia, 1930–1974
H. F. Verwoerd, Prime Minister of South Africa, 1958–1966

Gamal Abdul Nasser, President of Egypt, 1956–1970
Leopold Sedar Senghor, President of Senegal, 1960–
Felix Houphouet-Boigny, President of the Ivory Coast, 1960–
Kwame Nkrumah, President of Ghana, 1960–1966
Julius K. Nyerere, President of Tanzania, 1962–
Jomo Kenyatta, President of Kenya, 1964–1978
Sese Seko Mobutu, President of Zaire, 1965–
Houari Boumedienne, head of Algeria, 1965–1978
Anwar el Sadat, President of Egypt, 1970–
Agostinho Neto, President of Angola, 1975–1979
Olusegun Obasanjo, head of Nigeria, 1975–1979
P. W. Botha, Prime Minister of South Africa, 1978–
Robert Mugabe, Prime Minister of Zimbabwe, 1980–

Index

Guide to Pronunciation

The sounds represented by the diacritical marks used in this Index are illustrated by the following common words:

āle   ēve   īce   ōld   ūse   b$\overline{oo}$t

ăt   ĕnd   ĭ11   ŏf   ŭs   f$\overline{oo}$t

fătality   ēvent   ôbey   ūnite

câre   fôrm   ûrn

ärm

ȧsk

Vowels that have no diacritical marks are to be pronounced "neutral," for example: Aegean = ē-je′an, Basel = bäz′el, Basil = bă′zil, common = kŏm′on, Alcaeus = ăl-sē′us. The combinations ou and oi are pronounced as in "out" and "oil."

Abbasid caliphate, 377–78, 389
Abbasid Empire, 378
Abdul Hamid II (äb′dŭl hä-mēd′), 998
Abdul ibn Saud, king of Saudi Arabia, 1258
Abdullah, Sheikn Muhammad, 1230
Abelard, Peter, 463, 468–69
Aborigines, 335, 341
abortion, 61, 1366
Abraham, 72, 76
absolutism, 43, 73, 100, 207, 361, 377, 421, 430, 608, 609, 633, 775, 836, 866, 1262
  see also names of countries
  Age of (c. 1500–1789), 661–94
  in Central Europe, 679–81
  in England, 661, 662–74
  in France and Spain, 661, 674–79
  political theory of, 690–92
  in Russia, 679, 681–85
  significance of, 692–93
  warfare, 679, 685–89
abstract expressionism, 1369–70
Abu-Bakr (á-bōō′ băk′ēr), Caliph, 373–74
Academus, grove of, 192
Achaean (á-kē′an) League, 213
Achilles (á-kĭl′ēz), 195
Acre, city of, 452
Actium, naval battle of (31 B.C.), 247
Act of Settlement, 672
Act of Supremacy, 625
Addis Ababa, 1050
Addresses to the German Nation (Fichte), 889, 892, 897
Adoration of the Magi (Dürer), 582
Adrianople, Battle of (378), 289
Adrian VI, Pope, 626
Adriatic Sea, 1006
Advancement of Learning, The (Bacon), 696
Adventures of Augie March, The (Bellow), 1367
adversity theory, 18
advertising industry, 1112
Aegean Sea, 76, 105, 175, 176, 207, 215
Aelius Aristides, 229
Aeneid (Virgil), 252

Aeschylus (ĕs′kĭ-lŭs), 196, 197, 198, 200, 205
Aesop, 309, 474
Aetolian (ē-tō′lĭ-àn) League, 213
affirmative action programs, 1366
Afghanistan, 114, 134, 305, 316, 323, 520, 524, 728, 729, 1209, 1213, 1265
  Russian invasion of (1979), 1239, 1247, 1354
Africa, 17, 51, 301, 352, 370, 380, 386, 519, 636, 637, 657, 814, 927, 942, 1135, 1273–82
  see also names of countries
  agriculture, 344, 546
  Bantu migrations, 343–44
  early modern era (1500–1800), 753–64
  emergency of civilizations (sub-Saharan), 544–53
  European contacts, 728, 754, 761–63
  European imperialism in, 943, 944, 945, 946, 947, 1040–50
  free black colonies, 1041
  first industrial city south of the Sahara, 45
  influences on art, 975
  Iron Age, 343–44
  Islamic trade routes, 384
  militarism, 1281–82
  missionaries in, 629, 1043, 1047, 1048
  nationalism, 1270, 1271, 1273–74, 1278
  Neolithic period, 12–13, 344
  oil industry, 1277, 1282
  population explosion, 343, 1374
  royal authority beliefs, 754–55, 759
  slave trade, 345, 347, 558, 756, 757, 758, 759, 762–63, 1040–41, 1042, 1043, 1044, 1046
African National Congress, 1270, 1271
Afrikaans language, 1048, 1271, 1273
Against the Thievish, Murderous Hordes of Peasants (Luther), 617
Agamemnon, 103
Agent Orange, 1345
Agincourt, Battle of (1415), 504
Agni (god), 118
Agnosticism, 965

Agra, India, 732
Agrarian Reform Institute (El Salvador), 1182
Agriculture, 6, 41, 46, 53, 57, 326, 329, 332, 344, 362, 1101, 1147, 1207, 1229, 1254, 1257, 1383
  collectivization, 1087, 1088
  development of, 12–13, 14
  early Middle Ages, 402
  ecology crisis, 1370–72
  effects of the Commercial Revolution on, 651–55
  industrialism and, 834–35
  open-field system, 408
  revolution, 400–6
  specializations, 487
  three-field system, 653
Ahmose, Pharaoh, 28
Ahriman (ä′rĭ-màn), 70
Ahura-Mazda (ä′hōō-rà-mäz′dà), 70, 73, 117
Ainu people, 332
airplane industry, 931
air pollution, 1371
Ajanta, Buddhist caves at, 311, 314
Aja states, 758
Akan forest, 758
Akan people, 550, 758
Akbar (ŭk′bàr), the Great Mogol, 728–31, 733, 734, 735
Akkadians, 50, 52
Alaric (ăl′à-rĭk), king of the Visigoths, 289
Alba, Victor, 1141
Albania, 1006
  communism, 1335
Alberta, 1191, 1194, 1195
Alberti, Leon Battista, 567–68
Albigensian Crusade, 453, 459
Albigensian heresy, 445, 453, 459
Alcaeus (ăl-sē′us), 196
Alcestis (Euripides), 196
alchemy, 382, 385, 599
Alcibiades (ăl′sĭ-bĭ′a-dēz), 190
Alcuin, 390
Alexander VI, Pope, 567, 569
Alexander I, tsar of Russia, 809, 862–63,